AMERICA ON WHEELS

California
and Nevada

MACMILLAN • USA

Frommer's America on Wheels: California & Nevada
Regional Editor: Risa R Weinreb
Inspections Coordinator: Laura Van Zee
Deputy Editor: Alan David

Contributors: Pat Alexander, Lisa Alpine, Marguerite Cook, Connie Emerson, Laura Kath Fraser, Gerry Furth, Catherine Gibbs, Alexander S Gray, Arline Inge, Erin Kelly, Kathleen Landis, Barbara Long, Margie Nelson, Suzanne Osborne, Jean Pierce, Francine Proctor, Peg Rahn, Eric Seyfarth, David Stratton, Peter F Tittl, Terri Vandercook, Jonathan Volzke, Sharon Young, Bobbi Zane

Frommer's America on Wheels Staff
Project Director: Gretchen Henderson
Senior Editor: Christopher Hollander
Database Editor: Melissa Klurman
Assistant Editor: Marian Cole
Editorial Assistant: Tracy McNamara

Design by Michele Laseau

Macmillan Travel
A Simon & Schuster Macmillan Company
1633 Broadway
New York, NY 10019

Find us online at **http://www.mgr.com/travel** or on America Online at keyword **Frommer's**.

MACMILLAN is a registered trademark of Macmillan, Inc.

Manufactured in the United States of America

ISSN: 1079-3577
ISBN: 0-02-861109-8

SPECIAL SALES
Bulk purchases (10+ copies) of Frommer's and selected Macmillan travel guides are available to corporations, organizations, mail-order catalogs, institutions, and charities at special discounts, and can be customized to suit individual needs. For more information write to Special Sales, Macmillan General Reference, 1633 Broadway, New York, NY 10019.

Contents

Introduction

America on Wheels introduces a brand-new lodgings rating system—one that factors in the latest trends in travel preferences, technologies, and amenities and is based on thorough inspections by experienced travel professionals. We rate establishments from one to five flags, plus a unique rating we call Ultra, a special award reserved for only a handful of outstanding properties in each category. Our restaurant selections represent the ethnic diversity of today's dining scene and are categorized with symbols according to their special features, ambience, and services available. In addition, the series provides in-depth sightseeing information, including driving tours and best-of-the-state highlights.

State Introductions

Coverage of each state in the *America on Wheels* series begins with background information that will help familiarize you with your destination. Included is a summary of the state's history and an overview of its geography, followed by practical tips that we hope you will find useful in planning your trip—what kind of weather to expect, what to pack, sources of information within the state, driving rules and regulations, and other essentials.

The "Best of the State" section provides you with a rundown of the top sights and attractions and the most popular festivals and special events around the state. It also includes information on spectator sports and an A-to-Z list of recreational activities available to you.

Driving Tours

The scenic driving tours included guide you along some of the most popular sightseeing routes. Every tour is keyed to a map and includes mileage information and precise directions, refreshment stops, and, for longer tours, recommended places to stay.

The Listings

The city-by-city listings of lodgings, dining establishments, and attractions together make up the bulk of the book. Cities are organized alphabetically within each state. You will find a brief description or "profile" for most cities, including a source to contact for additional information. Any listings will follow.

TYPES OF LODGINGS

Here's how we define the lodging categories used in *America on Wheels*.

Hotel

A hotel usually has three or more floors with elevators. It may or may not have parking, but if it does, entry to the guest rooms is likely to be through the lobby rather than directly from the parking lot. A range of lodgings is available (such as standard rooms, deluxe rooms, and suites), and a range of services is available (such as bellhops, room service, and a concierge). Many hotels have a restaurant or coffee shop open for breakfast, lunch, and dinner; they may have a cocktail lounge/bar. Recreational facilities may be available (such as a swimming pool, fitness center, and tennis courts).

Motel

A motel usually has one to three floors, and many of the guest rooms have doors facing the parking lot or outdoor corridors. A motel may only have a small, serviceable lobby and usually offers only limited services; the nearest restaurant may be down the street. A motel is most likely to be located alongside a highway or in a resort area.

Inn

An inn is a small-scale hotel or lodge, usually in an older building that may or may not have been designed for lodgings, and it is often located in scenic surroundings. An inn should have a warm, welcoming atmosphere, with a more homelike quality to its furnishings and facilities. The guest rooms may be individually decorated in a style appropriate to the inn's age and location, and the rooms may or may not have telephones, televisions, or private bathrooms. An inn usually has a lounge or sitting room for guests (with parlor games and perhaps a television) and a small dining room that may or may not be open to the public. Breakfast, however, is almost always served.

Lodge
A lodge is essentially a small hotel in a rural, remote, or mountainous location. The atmosphere, service, and furniture may be more casual than you'd find in a regular hotel, and there may not be televisions or telephones in every guest room. The facilities usually include a coffee shop or restaurant, bar or cocktail lounge, games room, and indoor or outdoor swimming pool or hot tub. In ski areas, the lounge usually has a fireplace and facilities for storing ski gear.

Resort
A resort usually has more extensive facilities and recreational activities than a hotel, and offers three meals a day. The atmosphere is generally more informal than at comparable hotels.

How the Lodgings Are Rated
Every hotel, motel, resort, inn, and lodge rated in this series has been subjected to a thorough hands-on inspection by our team of accomplished travel professionals. We ask the kinds of questions that readers would ask if they could inspect the rooms in advance for themselves (How good is the sound-proofing? How firm is the bed? What condition are the room furnishings in?). Then all of the inspection reports are reviewed by regional editors who are experts on their territories. The top-rated properties are then rechecked by a special consultant who has been reviewing and critiquing luxury hotels around the world for almost 25 years. *Establishments are not charged to be included in our series.*

Our ratings are based on *average* guest rooms—not lavish suites or concierge floors—so they're not artificially high. Therefore, in some cases a hotel rated four flags may indeed have individual rooms or suites that might fall into the five-flag category; conversely, a four-flag hotel may have a few rooms in its lowest price range that might otherwise warrant three flags.

The detailed ratings vary by category of lodgings—for example, the criteria imposed on a hotel are more rigorous than those for a motel—and some features that are considered essential in, for example, a four-flag city hotel are relaxed for a resort that offers alternative attractions, sporting facilities, and/or beautiful and spacious grounds. Likewise, amenities such as telephones and televisions—essential in hotels and motels—are not required in inns, whose guests are often seeking peace and quiet. Instead, the criteria take into account such features as individually decorated rooms and complimentary afternoon tea.

There are, of course, several basic attributes that apply to all lodgings across the board: the cleanliness and maintenance of the building as a whole; the housekeeping in individual rooms; safety, both indoors and out; the quality and practicality of the furnishings; the quality and availability of the amenities; the caliber of the facilities; the extent and/or condition of the grounds; the ambience and cleanliness in the dining rooms; and the caliber and professionalism of the service in relation to the rates and types of lodging. Since the *America on Wheels* rating system is highly rigorous, just because a property has garnered only one flag does not mean it is inadequate or substandard.

WHAT THE INDIVIDUAL RATINGS MEAN
One Flag
These properties have met or surpassed the minimum requirements of cleanliness, safety, convenience, and amenities. The staff may be limited, but guests can generally expect a friendly, hospitable greeting. Rooms will have basic amenities, such as air conditioning or heating where appropriate, telephones, and televisions. The bathrooms may have only showers rather than tubs, and just one towel for each guest, but showers and towels must be clean. The one-flag properties are by no means places to avoid, since they can represent exceptional value.

Two Flags
In addition to having all of the basic attributes of one-flag lodgings, these properties will have some extra amenities, such as bellhops to help with the luggage, ice buckets in each room, and better-quality furnishings. Some extra services may include availability of cribs and irons, and wake-up service.

Three Flags
These properties have all the basics noted above but also offer a more generous complement of ameni-

ties, such as firmer beds, larger desks, more drawer space, extra blankets and pillows, cable or satellite TV, alarm clock/radios, room service (although hours may be limited), and dry cleaning and/or laundry services.

≣≣≣ Four Flags

This is the realm of luxury, with refinements in amenities, furnishings, and service—such as larger rooms, more dependable soundproofing, two telephones per room, in-room movies, in-room safes, thick towels, hair dryers, twice-daily maid service, turndown service, concierge service, and 24-hour room service.

≣≣≣≣ Five Flags

These properties have everything the four-flag properties have, plus a more personal level of service and more sumptuous amenities, among them bathrobes, superior linens, and blackout drapes for lightproofing. Facilities normally include a business center and fitness center. Generally speaking, guests pay handsomely to stay in these properties.

◊ Ultra

This crème-de-la-crème rating is reserved for those rare hotels and resorts, possibly also motels and inns, that are truly outstanding in every or almost every department—places with a "grand hotel" presence, an almost flawless level of service, and a standard of dining equal to that of the finest restaurants.

UNRATED

In the few cases where an inspector was not able to make a detailed inspection, the property is listed as unrated. Also, in some cases where a property was in the process of changing owners or managers, or if the property was undergoing the kind of major renovations that made formal evaluation impossible, then, again, it is listed as unrated.

TYPES OF DINING

Restaurant

A restaurant serves complete meals and almost always offers seating.

Refreshment Stop

A refreshment stop serves drinks and/or snacks only (such as an ice cream parlor, bakery, or coffee bar) and may or may not have seating available.

HOW THE RESTAURANTS WERE EVALUATED

All of the restaurants reviewed in this series have

been through the kind of thorough inspection described above for lodgings. Our inspectors have evaluated everything from freshness of ingredients to noise level and spacing of tables.

Unique to the *America on Wheels* series are the easy-to-read symbols that identify a restaurant's special features, its ambience, and special services. (See the inside front cover for the key to all symbols.) With them you can determine at a glance whether a place is a local favorite, offers exceptional value, or is "worth a splurge."

HOW TO READ THE LISTINGS

LODGINGS

Introductory Information

The rating is followed by the establishment's name, address, neighborhood (if applicable), telephone number(s), and fax number (if there is one). Where appropriate, location information is provided. In the resort listings, the acreage of the property is indicated. Also included are our inspector's comments, which provide some description and discuss any outstanding features or special information about the establishment. You can also find out whether an inn is unsuitable for children, and if so, up to what age.

Rooms

Specifies the number and type of accommodations available. If a hotel has an "executive level," this will be noted here. (This level, sometimes called a "concierge floor," is a special area of a hotel. Usually priced higher than standard rooms, accommodations at this level are often larger and have additional amenities and services such as daily newspaper delivery and nightly turndown service. Guests staying in these rooms often have access to a private lounge where complimentary breakfasts or snacks may be served.) Check-in/check-out times will also appear in this section, followed by information on the establishment's smoking policy ("No smoking" for properties that are entirely nonsmoking, and "Nonsmoking rms avail" for those that permit smoking in some areas but have rooms available for nonsmokers). This information may be followed by comments, if the inspector noted anything in particular about the guest rooms, such as their size, decor, furnishings, or window views.

Amenities

If the following amenities are available in the majority of the guest rooms, they are indicated by symbols (see inside front cover for key) or included in a list: telephone, alarm clock, coffeemaker, hair dryer, air conditioning, TV (including cable or satellite hook-up, free or pay movies), refrigerator, dataport (for fax/modem communication), VCR, CD/tape player, voice mail, in-room safe, and bathrobes. If some or all rooms have minibars, terraces, fireplaces, or whirlpools, that will be indicated here. Because travelers usually expect air conditioning, telephones, and televisions in their guest rooms, we specifically note when those amenities are not available. If any additional amenities are available in the majority of the guest rooms, or if amenities are outstanding in any way, the inspector's comments will provide some elaboration at the end of this section.

Services

If the following services are available, they are indicated by symbols (see inside front cover for key) or included in a list: room service (24-hour or limited), concierge, valet parking, airport transportation, dry cleaning/laundry, cribs available, pets allowed (call ahead before bringing your pet; an establishment that accepts pets may nevertheless place restrictions on the types or size of pets allowed, or may require a deposit and/or charge a fee), twice-daily maid service, car-rental desk, social director, masseur, children's program, babysitting (that is, the establishment can put you in touch with local babysitters and/or agencies), and afternoon tea and/or wine or sherry served. If the establishment offers any special services, or if the inspector has commented on the quality of services offered, that information will appear at the end of this section. Please note that there may be a fee for some services.

Facilities

If the following facilities are on the premises, they are indicated by symbols (see inside front cover for key) or included in a list: pool(s), bike rentals, boat rentals (may include canoes, kayaks, sailboats, powerboats, jet-skis, paddleboats), fishing, golf course (with number of holes), horseback riding, jogging path/parcourse (fitness trail), unlighted tennis courts (number available), lighted tennis courts (number available), waterskiing, windsurfing, fitness center, meeting facilities (and number of people this space can accommodate), business center, restaurant(s), bar(s), beach(es), lifeguard (for beach, not pool), basketball, volleyball, board surfing, games room, lawn games, racquetball, snorkeling, squash, spa, sauna, steam room, whirlpool, beauty salon,

day-care center, playground, washer/dryer, and guest lounge (for inns only). If cross-country and downhill skiing facilities are located within 10 miles of the property, then that is indicated by symbols here as well. Our "Accessible for People With Disabilities" symbol appears where establishments claim to have guest rooms with such accessibility. If an establishment has additional facilities that are worth noting, or if the inspector has commented about the facilities, that information appears at the end of this section.

Rates

If the establishment's rates vary throughout the year, then the rates given are for the peak season. The rates listed are EP (no meals included), unless otherwise noted. We'll tell you if there is a charge for an extra person to stay in a room; if children stay free, and if so, up to what age; if there are minimum stay requirements; and if AP (three meals) and/or MAP (breakfast and dinner) rates are also available. The parking rates (if the establishment has parking) are followed by any comments the inspector has provided about rates.

If the establishment has a seasonal closing, this information will be stated. A list of credit cards accepted ends the listing.

DINING

Introductory Information

If a restaurant is a local favorite, an exceptional value (one with a high quality-to-price ratio for the area), or "worth a splurge" (more expensive by area standards, but well worth it), the appropriate symbol will appear at the beginning of the listing (see inside front cover for key to symbols). Then the establishment's name, address, neighborhood (if applicable), and telephone number are listed, followed by location information when appropriate. The type of cuisine appears in boldface type and is followed by our inspectors' comments on everything from decor and ambience to menu highlights.

The "FYI" Heading

"For your information," this section tells you the reservations policy ("recommended," "accepted," or "not accepted"), and whether there is live entertainment, a children's menu, or a dress code (jacket required or other policy). If the restaurant does not have a full bar, you can find out what the liquor policy is ("beer and wine only," "beer only," "wine only," "BYO," or "no liquor license"). This is also where you can check to see if there's a no-smoking policy for the entire restaurant (please note that smoking policies are in flux throughout the country; if smoking—or avoiding smokers—is important to you, it's a good idea to call ahead to verify the policy). If the restaurant is part of a group or chain, address and phone information will be provided for additional locations in the area. This section does not appear in Refreshment Stop listings.

Hours of Operation
Under the "Open" heading, "Peak" indicates that the hours listed are for high season only (dates in parentheses); otherwise, the hours listed apply year-round. If an establishment has a seasonal closing, that information will follow. It's a good idea to call ahead to confirm the hours of operation, especially in the off-season.

Prices
Prices given are for dinner main courses (unless otherwise noted). If a prix-fixe dinner is offered throughout dinner hours, that price is listed here, too. This section ends with a list of credit cards accepted. Refreshment Stop listings do not include prices.

Symbols
The symbols that fall at the end of many restaurant listings can help you find restaurants with the features that are important to you. If a restaurant has romantic ambience, historic ambience, outdoor dining, a fireplace, a view, delivery service, early-bird specials, valet parking, or is family-oriented, open 24 hours, or accessible to people with disabilities (meaning it has a level entrance or an access ramp, a doorway at least 36 inches wide, and restrooms that are on the same floor as the dining room, with doorways at least 36 inches wide and properly outfitted stalls), then these symbols will appear (see inside front cover for key to symbols).

ATTRACTIONS

Introductory Information
The name, street address, neighborhood (if located in a major city), and telephone number are followed by a brief rundown of the attraction's high points and key attributes so you can quickly determine if it's worth a full day of exploration or just a brief detour.

Hours of Operation & Admission
Service information includes hours of operation ("Peak" indicates that the hours listed are for high season only) and the cost of admission. The cost is

ABBREVIATIONS

A/C	air conditioning
AE	American Express (charge card)
AP	American Plan (rates include breakfast, lunch, and dinner)
avail	available
BB	Bed-and-Breakfast Plan (rates include full breakfast)
bkfst	breakfast
BYO	bring your own (beer or wine)
CC	credit cards
CI	check-in time
CO	check-out time
CP	Continental Plan (rates include continental breakfast)
ctr	center
D	double (indicates room rate for two people in one room (one or two beds))
DC	Diners Club (credit card)
DISC	Discover (credit card)
EC	EuroCard (credit card)
effic	efficiency (unit with cooking facilities)
ER	En Route (credit card)
info	information
int'l	international
JCB	Japanese Credit Bureau (credit card)
ltd	limited
MAP	Modified American Plan (rates include breakfast and dinner)
MC	MasterCard (credit card)
Mem Day	Memorial Day
mi	mile(s)
min	minimum
MM	mile marker
refrig	refrigerator
rms	rooms
S	single (indicates room rate for one person)
satel	satellite
stes	suites (rooms with separate living and sleeping areas)
svce	service
tel	telephone
V	Visa (credit card)
w/	with
wknds	weekends

indicated by one to four dollar signs (see inside front cover for key to symbols). It's a good idea to call ahead to confirm the hours.

SPECIAL INFORMATION

DISABLED TRAVELER INFORMATION

The Americans with Disabilities Act (ADA) of 1990 required that all public facilities and commercial establishments be made accessible to disabled persons by January 26, 1992. Any property opened after that date must be built in accordance with the ADA Accessible Guidelines. Note, however, that not all establishments have completed their renovations to conform with the law; be sure to call ahead to determine if your specific needs can be met.

TAXES

State and city taxes vary widely and are not included in the prices in this book. Always ask about the taxes when you are making your reservations. State sales tax is given under "Essentials" in the introduction to each state.

A DISCLAIMER

Readers are advised that prices fluctuate in the course of time, and travel information changes under the impact of the varied and volatile factors that affect the travel industry. The publisher cannot be held responsible for the experiences of readers while traveling. Readers are invited to send ideas, comments, and suggestions for future editions to: *America on Wheels,* Macmillan Travel, 1633 Broadway, New York, NY 10019-6785.

TOLL-FREE NUMBERS/WORLD WIDE WEB SITES

The following toll-free telephone numbers and URLs for World Wide Web sites were accurate at press time; *America on Wheels* cannot be held responsible for any number or address that has changed. The "TDD" numbers are answered by a telecommunications service for the deaf and hard-of-hearing. Be sure to dial "1" before each number.

LODGINGS

Best Western International, Inc
800/528-1234 North America
800/528-2222 TDD

Budgetel Inns
800/4-BUDGET Continental USA and Canada

Budget Host
800/BUD-HOST Continental USA

Clarion Hotels
800/CLARION Continental USA and Canada
800/228-3323 TDD
http://www.hotelchoice.com/cgi-bin/res/
webres?clarion.html

Comfort Inns
800/228-5150 Continental USA and Canada
800/228-3323 TDD
http://www.hotelchoice.com/cgi-bin/res/
webres?comfort.html

Courtyard by Marriott
800/321-2211 Continental USA and Canada
800/228-7014 TDD
http://www.marriott.com/lodging/courtyar.html

Days Inn
800/325-2525 Continental USA and Canada
800/325-3297 TDD
http://www.daysinn.com/daysinn.html

DoubleTree Hotels
800/222-TREE Continental USA and Canada
800/528-9898 TDD

Drury Inn
800/325-8300 Continental USA and Canada
800/325-0583 TDD

Econo Lodges
800/55-ECONO Continental USA and Canada
800/228-3323 TDD
http://www.hotelchoice.com/cgi-bin/res/
webres?econo.html

Embassy Suites
800/362-2779 Continental USA and Canada
800/458-4708 TDD
http://www.embassy-suites.com

Exel Inns of America
800/356-8013 Continental USA and Canada

Fairfield Inn by Marriott
800/228-2800 Continental USA and Canada
800/228-7014 TDD
http://www.marriott.com/lodging/fairf.html

Fairmont Hotels
800/527-4727 Continental USA

Forte Hotels
800/225-5843 Continental USA and Canada

Four Seasons Hotels
800/332-3442 Continental USA
800/268-6282 Canada

Friendship Inns
800/453-4511 Continental USA
800/228-3323 TDD
http://www.hotelchoice.com/cgi-bin/res/
webres?friendship.html

Guest Quarters Suites
800/424-2900 Continental USA

Hampton Inn
800/HAMPTON Continental USA and Canada
800/451-HTDD TDD
http://www.hampton-inn.com

Hilton Hotels Corporation
800/HILTONS Continental USA and Canada
800/368-1133 TDD
http://www.hilton.com

Holiday Inn
800/HOLIDAY Continental USA and Canada
800/238-5544 TDD
http://www.holiday-inn.com

Howard Johnson
800/654-2000 Continental USA and Canada
800/654-8442 TDD
http://www.hojo.com/hojo.html

Hyatt Hotels and Resorts
800/228-9000 Continental USA and Canada
800/228-9548 TDD
http://www.hyatt.com

Inns of America
800/826-0778 Continental USA and Canada

Intercontinental Hotels
800/327-0200 Continental USA and Canada

ITT Sheraton
800/325-3535 Continental USA and Canada
800/325-1717 TDD

La Quinta Motor Inns, Inc
800/531-5900 Continental USA and Canada
800/426-3101 TDD

Loews Hotels
800/223-0888 Continental USA and Canada
http://www.loewshotels.com

Marriott Hotels
800/228-9290 Continental USA and Canada
800/228-7014 TDD
http://www.marriott.com/MainPage.html

Master Hosts Inns
800/251-1962 Continental USA and Canada

Meridien
800/543-4300 Continental USA and Canada

Omni Hotels
800/843-6664 Continental USA and Canada

Park Inns International
800/437-PARK Continental USA and Canada
http://www.p-inns.com/parkinn.html

Quality Inns
800/228-5151 Continental USA and Canada
800/228-3323 TDD
http://www.hotelchoice.com/cgi-bin/res/
webres?quality.html

Radisson Hotels International
800/333-3333 Continental USA and Canada

Ramada
800/2-RAMADA Continental USA and Canada
http://www.ramada.com/ramada.html

Red Carpet Inns
800/251-1962 Continental USA and Canada

Red Lion Hotels and Inns
800/547-8010 Continental USA and Canada

Red Roof Inns
800/843-7663 Continental USA and Canada
800/843-9999 TDD
http://www.redroof.com

Renaissance Hotels International
800/HOTELS-1 Continental USA and Canada
800/833-4747 TDD

Residence Inn by Marriott
800/331-3131 Continental USA and Canada
800/228-7014 TDD
http://www.marriott.com/lodging/resinn.html

Resinter
800/221-4542 Continental USA and Canada

Ritz-Carlton
800/241-3333 Continental USA and Canada

Rodeway Inns
800/228-2000 Continental USA and Canada
800/228-3323 TDD
http://www.hotelchoice.com/cgi-bin/res/
webres?rodeway.html

Scottish Inns
800/251-1962 Continental USA and Canada

Shilo Inns
800/222-2244 Continental USA and Canada

Signature Inns
800/822-5252 Continental USA and Canada

Super 8 Motels
800/800-8000 Continental USA and Canada
800/533-6634 TDD
http://www.super8motels.com/super8.html

Susse Chalet Motor Lodges & Inns
800/258-1980 Continental USA and Canada

Travelodge
800/255-3050 Continental USA and Canada

Vagabond Hotels Inc
800/522-1555 Continental USA and Canada

Westin Hotels and Resorts
800/228-3000 Continental USA and Canada
800/254-5440 TDD
http://www.westin.com

Wyndham Hotels and Resorts
800/822-4200 Continental USA and Canada

CAR RENTAL AGENCIES

Advantage Rent-A-Car
800/777-5500 Continental USA and Canada

Airways Rent A Car
800/952-9200 Continental USA

Alamo Rent A Car
800/327-9633 Continental USA and Canada
http://www.goalamo.com

Allstate Car Rental
800/634-6186 Continental USA and Canada

Avis
800/331-1212 Continental USA
800/TRY-AVIS Canada
800/331-2323 TDD
http://www.avis.com

Budget Rent A Car
800/527-0700 Continental USA and Canada
800/826-5510 TDD

Dollar Rent A Car
800/800-4000 Continental USA and Canada

Enterprise Rent-A-Car
800/325-8007 Continental USA and Canada

Hertz
800/654-3131 Continental USA and Canada
800/654-2280 TDD

National Car Rental
800/CAR-RENT Continental USA and Canada
800/328-6323 TDD
http://www.nationalcar.com

Payless Car Rental
800/PAYLESS Continental USA and Canada

Rent-A-Wreck
800/535-1391 Continental USA

Sears Rent A Car
800/527-0770 Continental USA and Canada

Thrifty Rent-A-Car
800/367-2277 Continental USA and Canada
800/358-5856 TDD

U-Save Auto Rental of America
800/272-USAV Continental USA and Canada

Value Rent-A-Car
800/327-2501 Continental USA and Canada
http://www.go-value.com

AIRLINES

American Airlines
800/433-7300 Continental USA and Western Canada
800/543-1586 TDD
http://www.americanair.com/aahome/aahome.html

Canadian Airlines International
800/426-7000 Continental USA and Canada
http://www.cdair.ca

Continental Airlines
800/525-0280 Continental USA
800/343-9195 TDD
http://www.flycontinental.com

Delta Air Lines
800/221-1212 Continental USA
800/831-4488 TDD
http://www.delta-air.com

Northwest Airlines
800/225-2525 Continental USA and Canada
http://www.nwa.com

Southwest Airlines
800/435-9792 Continental USA and Canada
http://iflyswa.com

Trans World Airlines
800/221-2000 Continental USA
http://www2.twa.com/TWA/Airlines/home/
home.html

United Airlines
800/241-6522 Continental USA and Canada
http://www.ual.com

USAir
800/428-4322 Continental USA and Canada
http://www.usair.com

TRAIN

Amtrak
800/USA-RAIL Continental USA
http://amtrak.com

BUS

Greyhound
800/231-2222 Continental USA
http://greyhound.com

THE TOP-RATED LODGINGS

ULTRA
Hotel Bel-Air, Los Angeles, CA
Lodge at Pebble Beach, Pebble Beach, CA
Regent Beverly Wilshire, Beverly Hills, CA

5 FLAGS
The Beverly Hills Hotel and Bungalows, Beverly Hills, CA
Mandarin Oriental, San Francisco, CA
The Peninsula Beverly Hills, Beverly Hills, CA
Post Ranch Inn, Big Sur, CA
The Ritz-Carlton Laguna Niguel, Dana Point, CA
The Ritz-Carlton San Francisco, San Francisco, CA

4 FLAGS

Albion River Inn, Albion, CA
ANA Hotel, San Francisco, CA
Anaheim Hilton & Towers, Anaheim, CA
Anaheim Marriott Hotel, Anaheim, CA
Auberge du Soleil, Rutherford, CA
Beverly Hilton, Beverly Hills, CA
Blue Lantern Inn, Dana Point, CA
Beverly Prescott Hotel, Los Angeles, CA
Bodega Bay Lodge, Bodega Bay, CA
Campton Place Hotel, San Francisco, CA
Casa Madrona Hotel, Sausalito, CA
Century Plaza Hotel & Tower, Los Angeles, CA
Chateau du Sureau, Oakhurst, CA
Claremont Resort, Spa & Tennis Club,
Berkeley, CA
The Cliffs at Shell Beach, Shell Beach, CA
The Clift, San Francisco, CA
Country Side Suites, Ontario, CA
Disneyland Hotel, Anaheim,CA
DoubleTree Hotel at Plaza las Fuentes,
Pasadena, CA
Ducey's on the Lake,
Bass Lake, CA
El Encanto Hotel & Garden Villas,
Santa Barbara, CA
Fairmont Hotel, San Jose, CA
Fountaingrove Inn, Santa Rosa, CA
Four Seasons Biltmore, Santa Barbara, CA

Four Seasons Hotel at Beverly Hills,
Los Angeles, CA
Four Seasons Hotel, Newport Beach, CA
Furnace Creek Inn Resort,
Death Valley National Park, CA
The Gingerbread Mansion, Ferndale, CA
Givenchy Hotel & Spa, Palm Springs, CA
Grand Hyatt San Francisco on Union Square,
San Francisco, CA
Green Gables Inn, Pacific Grove, CA
Harbor House, Elk, CA
Harrah's Casino Hotel Lake Tahoe,
Stateline, NV
Harveys Resort Hotel/Casino, Stateline, NV
Hotel Carter and Carter House, Eureka, CA
Hotel De Anza, San Jose, CA
Hotel del Coronado, Coronado, CA
Hotel Inter-Continental Los Angeles
at California Plaza, Los Angeles, CA
Hotel Monaco, San Francisco, CA
Hotel Nikko San Francisco, San Francisco, CA
Hotel Sofitel, Redwood City, CA
Huntington Hotel, San Francisco, CA
Hyatt Grand Champions, Indian Wells, CA
Hyatt Regency La Jolla, La Jolla, CA
Hyatt Regency Sacramento, Sacramento, CA
Hyatt Regency San Diego, San Diego, CA
Hyatt Regency Suites Palm Springs,
Palm Springs, CA

Hyatt Sainte Claire, San Jose, CA
The Inn Above Tide, Sausalito, CA
Inn at Depot Hill, Capitola-by-the-Sea, CA
The Inn at Saratoga, Saratoga, CA
Inn at Rancho Santa Fe, Rancho Santa Fe, CA
Inn at Spanish Bay, Pebble Beach, CA
Inn at the Opera, San Francisco, CA
Janet Kay's, Big Bear Lake, CA
The Kenwood Inn, Kenwood, CA
L'Auberge Del Mar, Del Mar, CA
La Costa Resort and Spa, Carlsbad, CA
La Maida House, North Hollywood, CA
La Quinta Resort & Club, La Quinta, CA
La Valencia Hotel, La Jolla, CA
Lafayette Park Hotel, Lafayette, CA
Le Meridien San Diego at Coronado,
Coronado, CA
Loews Coronado Bay Resort, Coronado, CA
The Lost Whale Inn B & B, Trinidad, CA
Madrona Manor, Healdsburg, CA
Mark Hopkins Inter-Continental San Francisco,
San Francisco, CA
Marriott's Desert Springs Resort & Spa,
Palm Desert, CA
Meadowood Resort Hotel, St Helena, CA
Mill Valley Inn, Mill Valley, CA
New Otani Hotel and Garden, Los Angeles, CA
Newport Beach Marriott Hotel & Tennis Club,
Newport Beach, CA
Ojai Valley Inn, Ojai, CA
Old Monterey Inn, Monterey, CA
The Pan Pacific Hotel San Francisco,
San Francisco, CA
Park Hyatt Los Angeles at Century City,
Los Angeles, CA
Park Hyatt San Francisco, San Francisco, CA
Pelican Cove Inn, Carlsbad, CA
Prescott Hotel, San Francisco, CA
Quail Lodge Resort & Golf Club,
Carmel Valley, CA
Radisson Miyako Hotel, San Francisco, CA
Rancho Valencia Resort, Rancho Santa Fe, CA
Renaissance Esmeralda Resort, Indian Wells, CA

Renaissance Stanford Court Hotel,
San Francisco, CA
Resort at Squaw Creek, Olympic Valley, CA
Ritz-Carlton Huntington Hotel, Pasadena, CA
Ritz-Carlton Marina del Rey, Marina del Rey, CA
Ritz-Carlton Rancho Mirage,
Rancho Mirage, CA
San Ysidro Ranch, Montecito, CA
Santa Clara Marriott, Santa Clara, CA
Seal Beach Inn & Gardens, Seal Beach, CA
Seal Cove Inn, Moss Beach, CA
Seven Gables Inn, Pacific Grove, CA
Sheraton Anaheim Hotel, Anaheim, CA
Sheraton Gateway Hotel Los Angeles Airport,
Los Angeles, CA
Sheraton Grande Torrey Pines, La Jolla, CA
Sheraton Grande, Los Angeles, CA
Sheraton Miramar Hotel, Santa Monica, CA
Sheraton Universal, Universal City, CA
The Sherman House, San Francisco, CA
Shutters on the Beach, Santa Monica, CA
Simpson House Inn, Santa Barbara, CA
Sonoma Mission Inn & Spa, Sonoma, CA
Stanford Inn by the Sea–Big River Lodge,
Mendocino, CA
Stanford Park Hotel, Menlo Park, CA
Sunset Marquis Hotel & Villas,
West Hollywood, CA
Surf and Sand Hotel, Laguna Beach, CA
Timberhill Ranch, Cazadero, CA
Universal City Hilton, Universal City, CA
Ventana, Big Sur, CA
Westgate Hotel, San Diego, CA
Westin Hotel, Millbrae, CA
Westin Mission Hills Resort, Rancho Mirage, CA
Westin South Coast Plaza, Costa Mesa, CA
Westwood Marquis Hotels and Garden,
Los Angeles, CA
Whale Watch Inn, Gualala, CA
Wyndham Bel Age, West Hollywood, CA
Wyndham Checkers Hotel Los Angeles,
Los Angeles, CA

CALIFORNIA

A World in One State

The "promised land" is how generations have viewed California. Its great natural beauty, enviable climate, promise of boundless wealth, and carefree, can-do mentality have lured millions west in pursuit of the American dream, if only for a few

days' or weeks' vacation. Few return home disappointed, though many people are surprised to find that there's far more to California than they thought there was.

The state is large enough and diverse enough that half the vacationers in California are Californians seeing a California other than their own. The state's dozen separate regions are as distinct from each other as the nations of Europe—with equally distinctive scenery.

Within the state's borders are the Lower 48's lowest point—Death Valley—and its highest point—Mount Whitney, which anchors America's longest mountain chain, wherein you'll find the nation's tallest waterfall (Yosemite Falls). California's native giant sequoia is the world's largest tree; its coast redwood is the tallest. The state even has the world's oldest living thing—the bristlecone pine tree, which lives more than 5,000 years at a chilly altitude of 11,000 feet. In California, snowcapped mountains loom over parched deserts. Lava landscapes border lush valleys. Even the 1,245-mile coastline baffles with its changing moods: While the southern quarter has golden beaches of Hollywood lore, farther north, breakers crash ashore and tear at windswept headlands.

California is also a convergence of climatic extremes, a fact that takes many visitors to San Francisco by surprise (they're the ones shivering in shorts in summer, when the cool fogs roll in). In winter you can sunbathe in San Diego while skiers are making the most of fresh snow in the mountains.

The state, with the largest population in the United States, is an economic powerhouse; if cast adrift, it would have the world's seventh largest economy. It leads the nation, for example, in the bounty of its agricultural products. And high-tech Sili-

Frommer's

#1

con Valley is aptly named: The birthplace of micro-computers still leads the way into the future. Californians like to flaunt their wealth—not ostentatiously, but in a casual, cosmopolitan lifestyle that makes the most of the pleasures the state has to offer. California is a haven for boaters, surfers, hikers, bikers, horseback riders, and other lovers of sport and the great outdoors. And Californians have parlayed their love of the good life into a sophisticated style—even a "state of mind"—that is reflected in everything from fashion and architecture to California nouvelle cuisine.

Even the people revel in being different, whether it's a matter of personal idiosyncracy or ethnic and cultural diversity. The cities, too, have their own character. San Francisco, for example, compact and stylish, bounded by water and bristling with hills, is not cut from the same cloth as Los Angeles, which sprawls nondescriptly, its parts connected by a network of freeways. Add to these facets the fact that despite its glitzy, up-to-date image, the state also has a historic dimension—everything from prehistoric fossils to movie-star footprints is preserved here, from the Wells Fargo Overland Stage to the *Queen Mary*. The state may not have everything, but one thing is sure. When you've seen one California, you haven't seen them all.

> ## Fun Facts
> • One of every seven Americans lives in California.
> • The grizzly bear, the official state animal, is actually extinct in California.
> • The 275-foot-tall General Sherman giant sequoia tree in Sequoia National Park adds enough wood growth annually to make a 60-foot-tall tree of average proportions.
> • At any given time, there are more cars on southern California's highways than in any other area of the country.
> • San Francisco's cable cars are the country's only moving National Landmark.

A Brief History

The New Frontier California's recorded history began when the Portuguese-born sailor Juan Rodríguez Cabrillo landed at San Diego on September 24, 1542, and planted the flag of Spain. No "white" face was seen again until 1579, when Francis Drake stopped for repairs near Point Reyes and claimed "Nova Albion" for Queen Elizabeth I of England. It was the Spanish legacy that was to endure, however, and fittingly, in 1602, after landing at what he christened Monterey, Sebastian Vizcaino gave many other bays and promontories along the coast the Spanish names we still use today.

Mission Accomplished The area languished for another 140 years before King Charles of Spain decided to press his claim. In 1742, he ordered the construction of a chain of Franciscan missions, ostensibly for the purpose of converting the Native Americans to Catholicism. The 21 missions, which stretch from San Diego to Sonoma, were completed in 1823 and connected by a dirt road—El Camino Real—that closely parallels today's US 101.

Many missions brutally exploited Native American labor and grew into vast, wealthy estates. Perhaps 500,000 Indians lived widely scattered throughout the region when the Spanish arrived; within two centuries they were almost extinct, decimated by European diseases, the whip, and the musket ball.

Remarkably, in all this time no European sailors had come upon San Francisco Bay—it was a Spanish expedition seeking an overland route to Monterey that first saw the magnificent natural harbor, in 1769. That same year, Gaspar de Portola founded San Diego, the first permanent settlement in California and one of four military *presidios* built to deter the intrusion of rival colonial powers. Small towns, or *pueblos,* followed: San Jose in 1777; Los Angeles in 1781.

The Russians Are Coming Although the region was neglected by colonial Spain for the first half of the 19th century, colonists were arriving from other quarters. In 1812, Russian fur trappers had descended from Alaska and established Fort Ross, north of San Francisco. French trappers, too, made incursions, as did the English, emboldened in their weakened claims on North America by the Vancouver-based Hudson Bay Company.

In 1821, when Mexico gained independence from Spain, California declared its allegiance to Mexico. The region quickly fell under the influence of a few *Californios,* Mexican ranchers who grew immensely rich rearing cattle on vast land grants. When Mexico secularized the missions in 1834, the *rancheros* seized these lands, too, and established near-feudal fiefdoms over the Indians.

Up With the Stars 'n' Stripes The Mexicans forbid US citizens from settling in California. The early 1800s, however, saw many Americans arrive, some after a three-month journey by sea, others after having blazed overland trails in wagon trains. The US government fostered the migration, inspired by the expansionist doctrine of Manifest Destiny—a belief that the United States was almost duty-bound to acquire the West.

The United States attempted to purchase California from Mexico in 1846, prompting a band of zealous American settlers to hoist the Bear Flag standard in Sonoma and to declare California an independent republic. The standard, carrying the words "California Republic," is today the official state flag. The outbreak of the Mexican-American War ended the republic 23 days later when Commodore John Sloat raised the US standard in Monterey. America's acquisition of California was ratified on February 2, 1848.

Gold!   Only nine days before that, a more momentous event had occurred. On January 24, James Marshall, a sawmill foreman, had found flakes of gold on the banks of the South Fork of the American River. The leaked word led to a flood of would-be millionaires, and California became truly an El Dorado in December, when President Polk exhibited 230 ounces of gold to Congress. The news reverberated around the world, sparking the California Gold Rush. Within three years, California's population soared from fewer than 10,000 people to more than 100,000. San Francisco Bay was choked by sailing vessels that dropped anchor and were promptly abandoned by gold-hungry crews. Lands lay idle as farmers and laborers took to the Sierra foothills.

Prices soared and many farmers and merchants —and even a few miners—grew fabulously rich on the trade that transformed inland river ports such as Sacramento and Stockton into major cities. Many of the new arrivals even brought a degree of culture to the frontier: Operatic and literary societies sprouted alongside gambling halls and bordellos.

Money means might; the gold boom hastened statehood in 1850, and lit the development fuse. The wineries of the Napa and Sonoma Valleys, for example, were established in the late 1850s. And many towns in northern California are still wedded to the logging industry that grew up to supply lumber to the mines.

Boom & Bust   Within 15 years the gold boom was over. While Civil War battles raged to the east, Californians busied themselves completing the transcontinental railroad, finished in 1869 with the help of large numbers of Irish and Chinese laborers. Mexican laborers helped turn the northern Central Valley into a breadbasket. And industries began to flourish in the cities.

By 1874, when the State Capitol building—a copy of the one in Washington, DC—was completed in Sacramento, California had come of age as a self-reliant, dynamic entity.

Coming on Strong   Southern California had lagged behind until now: Its population was no more than 10,000 in 1875, the year the Santa Fe railroad reached Los Angeles. Settlers taking advantage of $1 fares from Kansas City soon became the first wave in a migratory trend that has barely faltered. The railroad opened southern California to trade. Oranges were planted and quickly took to the sunshine and fertile soil, launching San Diego and Los Angeles to prominence as shipping ports.

The oil discovered beneath Los Angeles in 1892 helped to fuel the automobile and, later, the aeronautical industries, which grew rapidly after the turn of the century. When the motion picture industry moved here in the first decade of the 20th century (after William Selig filmed *The Count of Monte Cristo* in Los Angeles in 1907), the glamorous lifestyle of the movie stars and the all-year pleasant climate that served as their backdrop boosted southern California's popularity even further. In response, a whole generation packed its bags, said goodbye to the snow storms and dust bowls, and headed west in search of the good life of the Golden State.

A Closer Look
GEOGRAPHY

California is the third-largest state (only Alaska and Texas are bigger). Pushed up against the **Pacific Ocean,** its coast extends north in a series of sweeping beaches, bays, and soaring headlands for over 1,200 miles from Mexico to the Oregon border. A series of mountain chains—the forested **Coast Ranges**—lie just inland, paralleling almost the entire coastline. Most of the state's population lives on the relatively narrow strip of land between these mountains and the ocean—a questionable location, since it is subject to the ever-present jerks and upheavals of a thousand seismic fault lines.

At the southwestern corner of the state sits **San**

Diego. This pretty naval town with a vital Mexican community has Spanish roots dating back to 1769, when a mission, which still stands, was built. From here, you can make a pilgrimage north along El Camino Real, the mission trail stretching from San Diego to Sonoma. Los Angeles, the nation's second-largest city, dominates southern California beneath its pall of smog. Much of the city sprawls across miles of flat, uneventful terrain, marked by monotonous housing developments and unending strip malls and crisscrossed by an amazing number of freeways. Of course, Los Angeles is also a magnetic and fashionable city that is home to the world's most important film industry, world-class restaurants, high-class shopping, beaches, and a variety of attractions.

The **Central Coast** displays California's natural drama at its best. North of the seaside resort of Santa Barbara, CA 1 dips and careens along Big Sur, with the sea a thousand feet below. Inland, grapes and other fruits and vegetables grow sheltered from seasonal fogs. Here you'll find **Monterey,** with its venerable fishing wharfs and superb aquarium; and **Carmel,** with historic charm and art galleries.

San Francisco anchors the Bay Area and combines the best qualities of the world's great cities. "The City" can boast of its Chinatown, Golden Gate Park, sky-high financial district, Union Square for shopping, Alcatraz, and gabled, bay-windowed Victorian houses that survived the 1906 quake. It even has the nation's only moving National Landmark—its historic cable cars —museums galore, and more restaurants per capita than any other city on Earth. Across the Bay, **Berkeley** is famed for its university and zany living; **Oakland** has a fabulous museum and an inner-city tidal lake that is the world's largest and was also America's first nature reserve.

Cross the Golden Gate Bridge and you'll be surrounded by the extraordinary calm of California's romantic **North Coast.** Inland, beyond the artist colony/resort of Sausalito, are the Napa and Sonoma Valleys—wine regions par excellence. Along the coast are Point Reyes National Seashore, Bodega Bay, delicately beautiful beaches, and rugged promontories that lead the way to **Mendocino,** one of several New England–style villages where writers and artists rub shoulders with fishermen, ranchers, and lumberjacks. Farther north, Eureka and Ferndale are repositories of Victorian grandeur, and pockets of coast redwood spiral above the fogbound landscape.

Northeast California is a rugged, less-traveled region unfamiliar to most Californians. Two active volcanoes—snow-capped Mount Lassen (10,457 feet) and Mount Shasta (14,162 feet)—reign over a wilderness favored by hardy backpackers. Here, real cowboys still travel to the biggest rodeo in the West, and Native Americans still net leaping salmon. Lakes and hot springs provide for relaxation. Naturalist John Muir exhorted: "Climb the mountains and get their good tidings." The Pacific Crest Trail, which passes through here and ultimately reaches the Mexican border, lets you do just that.

To the south, flanking the Nevada border, are the mighty **Sierra Nevada** with, to their east, the White Mountains separated by a thin depression called the Owens Valley. The Sierras—a massive block of granite that continues to rise three inches a year—run 400 miles north-to-south and soar to over 14,000 feet at Sequoia, Kings Canyon, and Yosemite National Parks. They are sheathed in the remnants of glaciers that gouged massive valleys, with resplendent waterfalls that cascade from their flanks.

Gold Country, in the Sierra Nevada foothills, rings with the echoes of the Gold Rush era. When gold was discovered in 1848, 100,000 adventurers rushed in to pan the rivers and tear down the

---

DRIVING DISTANCES

Los Angeles

96 mi SW of Santa Barbara
103 mi W of Palm Springs
120 mi NW of San Diego
265 mi SW of Las Vegas, NV
332 mi SE of Monterey
379 mi SE of San Francisco
383 mi SE of Sacramento
659 mi SE of Eureka

San Francisco

87 mi SW of Sacramento
115 mi NW of Monterey
227 mi SW of Reno, NV
278 mi SE of Eureka
321 mi NW of Santa Barbara
379 mi NW of Los Angeles
548 mi NW of San Diego
577 mi NW of Las Vegas, NV

Sacramento

87 mi NE of San Francisco
134 mi SW of Reno, NV
185 mi NE of Monterey
304 mi SW of Eureka
383 mi NW of Los Angeles
391 mi NE of Santa Barbara
484 mi NW of Palm Springs
557 mi NW of Las Vegas, NV

hillsides. The only gold you're likely to see today is on the autumn leaves, but the region is liberally sprinkled with quaint bed-and-breakfast inns, historic mining museums, and many of the original settlements, such as Placerville, Sutter Creek, Sonora, and colorful Nevada City.

Between the Sierra Nevada and the Coast Ranges is the **Central Valley,** a 400-mile long, 100-mile wide stretch of some of the richest soil on Earth. **Sacramento,** the state capital, anchors the valley, which extends down the center of California. Farther south, towns such as Fresno are booming from cotton, rice, grapes, and other agricultural products of the valley.

Southeast California is the state's dry corner, sizzling hot in summer, when temperatures in **Death Valley** can top 130°F. Death Valley's 3,000 square miles encompass wind-blown sand, dry salt flats, and sere mountains. Joshua Tree National Monument and Anza-Borrego Desert State Park embody a different aspect—a living desert, palette-bright in spring. Lush **Palm Springs** boasts the largest desert palm oasis in the world. Golf courses and upscale resorts complete the picture.

AVG MONTHLY TEMPS (°F) & RAINFALL (IN)		
	Los Angeles	San Francisco
Jan	64/2.8	56/4.0
Feb	64/3.0	60/3.6
Mar	66/1.5	64/2.6
Apr	69/1.0	67/1.7
May	72/0.2	70/0.6
June	75/0.1	72/0.2
July	80/0.0	74/0.0
Aug	78/0.0	74/0.0
Sept	80/0.2	77/0.2
Oct	77/0.4	71/0.6
Nov	74/1.5	64/2.0
Dec	68/2.5	58/3.7

CLIMATE

The common perception that California has a Mediterranean climate characterized by sun and warmth, with rain mainly in winter, holds true for much, but not all, of the state. Climatic extremes based on elevation and distance from the ocean are dramatic.

San Diego, in the south, is generally warm and dry year-round; Los Angeles' pleasingly warm (and occasionally rainy) winters tempt sun-lovers to the beach, as do summers, which are hot and often humid. The great desert areas east of Los Angeles invite exploration November through April, when days are dry and warm but not searing as they are in summer, when 120° temperatures discourage probing.

San Francisco's maritime climate is temperate: cool to mild in winter, though never freezing, and rarely topping 70°F in summer, when fogs often roll in to keep things cool. Indeed, San Francisco can be chilly in summer (other Bay Area cities escape the fog and are correspondingly warmer). The Central Coast shares San Francisco's climate, though warming farther south. North along the coast, the fogs and rain increase and winds can be forceful.

Farther inland, the mercury soars in summer and many folks leave town for the milder temperatures of the mountains. In winter, snow settles over the Sierras and Shasta-Cascades, drawing skiers to the downhill slopes. Winter storms often lash the mountains.

Annual rainfall varies from 80 inches in Del Norte County in the state's northwestern corner to as low as 3 inches in Imperial County in the southeastern corner.

WHAT TO PACK

Where and when you go dictates what to pack. If traveling widely throughout the state, pack with varying climates in mind, though there's no need to overload.

Cool, cotton clothes will suffice for most of the year, though adequately warm clothing for San Francisco, the North Coast, and nights in the mountains may be required even in summer (San Francisco is often much cooler than first-time visitors expect).

Californians tend to dress casually, though upscale restaurants may have a dress code. San Francisco is more elegant by both day and night.

Pack sturdy footwear for exploring state and national parks. Bring sunscreen, too, especially if heading to the deserts or mountains (even in winter) or beaches. Don't forget your sunglasses!

TOURIST INFORMATION

For a free state map and *Discover the Californias* visitors guide listing attractions, events, and accommodations, call toll free 800/862-2543. Additional information on the state can be obtained from the **California Division of Tourism,** 801 K St, Suite 1600, Sacramento, CA 95814 (tel 916/322-2881). The Division also maintains a Web page (http://gocalif.ca.gov) with general information about the state.

Almost every town and region has its own visitors

bureau or chamber of commerce, listed in the *Discover the Californias* guide. For information on northern California, contact the **San Francisco Convention and Visitors Bureau,** 201 3rd St, Suite 900, San Francisco, CA 94133 (tel 415/974-6900); or the **Redwood Empire Association,** 2801 Leavenworth Ave, San Francisco, CA 94103 (tel 415/543-8334). For southern California, contact the **Greater Los Angeles Visitors and Convention Bureau,** 633 W 5th St, Suite 6000, Los Angeles, CA 90071 (tel 213/624-7300); or the **San Diego Convention and Visitors Bureau,** 11 Horton Plaza, San Diego, CA 92101 (tel 619/236-1212).

For camping reservations and information on state parks, contact the **Department of Parks and Recreation,** Box 2390, Sacramento, CA 95811 (tel 916/653-6995).

DRIVING RULES AND REGULATIONS

Minimum age for drivers is 16 with driver's training, 18 without. Unless otherwise noted, the speed limit on California highways is 55 mph, although on many sections motorists drive well in excess of the limit. The California Highway Patrol is extremely efficient and uses aircraft to help enforce speed limits. Use of seat belts is mandatory for all passengers, and children under 4 years or under 40 pounds must be secured in an approved child safety seat. Motorcyclists must wear a helmet. Auto insurance is also mandatory; the car's registration and proof of insurance must be carried in the car. Right turns are allowed after stops at a red light.

Drunk driving laws are restrictive and strictly enforced. Note that it is illegal to carry an open container of alcohol in your car. A zero tolerance law is in effect—anyone under 21 with a measurable amount of alcohol loses his or her driver's license for a year.

If heading into the Sierras or Shasta-Cascades for a winter ski trip, top up on antifreeze and carry snow chains for your tires; chains are mandatory in certain areas.

RENTING A CAR

All of the major car rental firms have offices throughout the state. Minimum age requirements range from 19 to 25. Collision damage waiver (CDW) protection is sold separately (check with your credit card or insurance company to see if you are already covered). Many local companies also offer car rentals at lower rates.

- **Alamo** (tel toll free 800/327-9633)
- **Avis** (tel 800/331-1212)
- **Budget** (tel 800/527-0700)
- **Dollar** (tel 800/421-6868)
- **General** (tel 800/327-7607)
- **Hertz** (tel 800/654-3131)
- **National** (tel 800/328-4567)
- **Thrifty** (tel 800/367-2277)

ESSENTIALS

Area Code: California has 14 area codes. **Southern California:** The area code for Los Angeles is 213; for the Pasadena area, 818; for Buena Park and Long Beach, 562; for Beverly Hills, Santa Monica, and environs, 310; for Orange County, 714; for the Riverside region, 909; for San Diego and the deserts, 619; for Bakersfield, Santa Barbara, and the south-central coast, 805. **Central California:** for Fresno, the south Central Valley, and Yosemite, the area code is 209; for San Jose, Monterey, and the north-central coast, 408. **Northern California:** for San Francisco, the area code is 415; for Oakland and the East Bay, 510; for Napa Valley and the North Coast, 707; for Sacramento, the north Central Valley, Lake Tahoe, and Shasta-Cascade, 916.

Emergencies: Call 911 from anywhere in the state to summon emergency police, fire, or ambulance services.

Liquor Laws: Alcoholic beverages may be purchased by anyone 21 years or older, with proof of age. Licensing hours are 6am to 2am.

Road Info: For road conditions in northern California, call 916/445-7623; in southern California, call 213/628-7623.

Smoking: California is aggressively anti-smoking, though local ordinances vary widely. Smoking is not allowed on public transportation or in public buildings. Many restaurants maintain a small smoking section, though even many bars are nonsmoking. Many car rental companies have smoke-free cars and hotels offer smoke-free rooms.

Taxes: California's base statewide sales tax is 7.25%. Most cities and counties impose an additional tax of 0.25 to 1.25%.

Time Zone: California is in the Pacific time zone (GMT minus eight hours), three hours behind New York.

Best of the State

WHAT TO SEE AND DO

National Parks California boasts 17 national parks, including national monuments, historic sites, and recreational areas totaling 4.1 million acres. In addition, 18 state forests offer recreation such as backpacking, trailbiking, and downhill skiing, as well as picnic areas and marinas. **Yosemite** is the crowning glory of California's extensive park system. Rounded granite domes, spectacular waterfalls, alpine meadows, groves of giant sequoias—all accessed by miles of hiking trails that crisscross the valley and mountainous backcountry. Yet you don't need to hike if you don't want to—it's all visible from the car window.

Two parks side by side and administered as one, **Sequoia/Kings Canyon** challenges Yosemite with more of the same high-mountain splendor. Jewel-like lakes, high-country wilderness, and the state's largest concentration of giant sequoias, including the General Sherman Tree, the largest of *all* living things, are topped off by the Palisades Glacier, North America's most southerly.

The sere, wind-scoured landscapes of **Death Valley National Monument** feature salt lake beds and sand dunes nestled at 282 feet below sea level in the hollow of purple-tinged mountains. Visitors to **Point Reyes National Seashore** can view the widely varied, but always dramatically wild, coastal landscapes, as well as explore the historic Point Reyes lighthouse, a Miwok Indian village replica, and miles of trails. And in **Redwoods National Park,** visitors can drive through a redwood tree and see the thousands of other soaring redwoods that loom over a matrix of parks preserving 113,200 acres of these 350-foot-tall giants.

State Parks If you thought deserts were stark, visit **Anza-Borrego Desert State Park** in spring, when the cactus and wildflowers bloom. Hiking and

biking trails lead through 1,000 square miles of spectacular beauty. **Humboldt Redwoods State Park** is a driver's delight. Scenic CA 254 winds 33 miles along the Avenue of the Giants, and there are also hiking and riding trails leading through the 51,000-acre park. **Julian Pfeiffer Burns State Park** may be a small package, but it delivers Big Sur's spectacular coastal scenery of plunging cliffs and crashing breakers backed by mountains sheltering majestic redwoods. And for a change of pace there's **Marshall Gold Discovery Site,** at Coloma in the Gold Country, a re-created Gold Rush town at the site where it all began. The museum tells the tale.

Natural Wonders Tallest, oldest, deepest, highest—the state is full of natural wonders, many of them enshrined in national or state parks. For one there's **Yosemite Valley,** a seven-mile-long, glacier-carved nave with granite walls rising almost a mile straight up, giant sequoias, and plunging waterfalls, including Yosemite Falls—the fifth-highest and, possibly, the most beautiful in the world. **Lake Tahoe,** the largest alpine lake in North America (12 miles wide and 22 miles long), plummets to depths of 1,645 feet. Hiking, biking, boating, and winter skiing make this a year-round favorite. **Mono Lake,** 5 miles south of Lee Vining, hosts the state's largest nesting colony of California gulls. Exotic tufa flowers formed by mineral deposits rise up eerily from the briny waters of this shrimp-filled lake. Off the beaten track and overlooked by tourists, the deep **underground caverns** of the Sierra foothills feature fabulous crystalline formations and lakes you can paddle across. The largest are Moaning Cavern and California Caverns, near the towns of San Andreas and Angels Camp.

Family Favorites Some people say California itself is a theme park. Families are offered a multitude of attractions—most concentrated in southern California. **Disneyland** bills itself as the "Happiest Place on Earth," and 12 million visitors a year seem to think so. Mickey and Minnie and other Disney characters can show you around seven theme lands where family fun blends with fantasy and some genuinely scary rides. The newest attraction is Mickey's Toontown. **Universal Studios,** America's third-largest manmade attraction, hosts 5 million visitors a year. Simulated earthquakes, the Wild West with gunfights and nose-diving stunt men, *Jaws* lunging menacingly, the *ET* adventure into another world, and dozens of other attractions give Disneyland a run for its money. **Knott's Berry Farm** offers 150 landscaped acres of family entertainment, including rides and specialty shops. San Diego's **Sea World** is the world's largest marine park, where you can feed the dolphins, stingrays, walruses, seals, and sea lions and watch killer whales perform. And then there's **Marine World Africa/USA** in Vallejo, northern California's answer to the San Diego Zoo and Sea World. Kids and parents and more than 2,000 animals enjoy the oceanarium and wildlife park.

Beaches A whole lifestyle has evolved around southern California's beaches—the inspiration of legend and song. Swimmers should respect warnings posted by lifeguards. Farther north, where the beaches are for wading and strolling, leave the ocean to surfers.

The beach at **Oceanside,** north of San Diego, offers shallow water for swimming and waves that lure surfers for the annual World Body Surfing Championships. **Huntington Beach** is the self-proclaimed "Surfing Capital of the World." Sunbathe, play volleyball, and when the sun goes down light a barbecue in a beachside fire-ring. In **Venice** the beach is outshone by its boardwalk: a stage for bikini-clad in-line skaters, jugglers, and muscular beefcakes showing their bodies beautiful. **Stinson Beach,** north of San Francisco, is two golden miles long, perfect for strolling, and popular with surf fishers.

Historic Buildings Contrary to popular opinion, California does have a past, and important and intriguing buildings illustrate it. Some of the best include **Hearst San Simeon,** better known as Hearst Castle, which fulfilled tycoon William Randolph Hearst's neoclassic dream. The sprawling mansion contains more than 100 rooms filled with priceless art and antiques. **Carmel Mission,** dating from 1770, represents a unique style of early Spanish architecture, while **Scotty's Castle,** a mansion built in the 1920s by desert rat "Death Valley Scotty" (Walter Scott), shows off its Spanish-Moorish style.

Architecture At one time or another, the Japanese, Spanish, Chinese, English, and many others have settled in California, so take your pick of architectural styles. **Chinatown,** San Francisco, whisks you to the Orient with its 24 square blocks of red-and-green pagoda roofs festooned with dragons, while **Eureka** boasts more gingerbread Victorian houses than anywhere in America; the gothic Carson Mansion lords over them all. **Solvang** has been called cute and kitschy, but everyone agrees it has charm. It was founded by Danes who erected their half-timbered houses and even a windmill in hommage to the style they'd left behind.

Gardens If you tire of the wilds, nature's beauty can be found growing at parks and gardens around the state. **Golden Gate Park,** in San Francisco, showcases over 1,000 acres of meadows, lakes, and flowers, including the Japanese Tea Garden, Strybing Arboretum, and the Conservatory of Flowers, the oldest botanical garden west of the Mississippi. **Mendocino Coast Botanical Gardens** has almost 50 acres of colorful flowers and shrubs accessible by nature trails, while the **Los Angeles State and County Arboretum,** in Arcadia, features 130 acres of showy plants from around the globe.

Wildlife California boasts an amazing array of plant and animal life and offers an abundance of places to view the variety. At the **San Diego Zoo,** one of the world's finest zoos, you'll find aardvarks, zebras, and everything in between; happily, birds and beasts live in replicated natural environments, sort of a "home away from home." The **Monterey Bay Aquarium,** on historic Cannery Row, has over 6,500 creatures in various aquariums, including a three-story, 335,000-gallon tank that provides an unmatched look at local sea life.

The largest marine preserve in North America, the **National Marine Sanctuary** extends along California's coast from just north of the Golden Gate Bridge south past Big Sur to San Simeon in Monterey County. Humpback whales and sea otters are commonly seen, and blue whales, one of the largest creatures on earth, have even made a reappearance. The **Tule Elk State Reserve,** near Stockdale, protects this endangered native species, which was once as common throughout the Central Valley as bison were on the central plains. And **Año Nuevo State Park,** 20 miles north of Santa Cruz, protects a rookery of elephant seals. Don't get too close—the ill-tempered bulls can weigh 2,000 pounds.

EVENTS AND FESTIVALS

LOS ANGELES AND SOUTHERN CALIFORNIA

- **Tournament of Roses Parade,** Pasadena. Colorful festival of flowers, music, and equestrian splendor. New Year's Day. For tickets, contact Pasadena Tournament of Roses, 391 S Orange

Grove Blvd, Pasadena, CA 91184 (tel 818/449-ROSE).

- **Rose Bowl,** Pasadena. One of the country's most prestigious college football showdowns. New Year's Day. Call 818/449-ROSE for tickets.
- **Los Angeles Marathon,** Los Angeles. Mid-March. Call 310/444-5544 for information.
- **Renaissance Pleasure Faire,** San Bernadino. A re-created Elizabethan marketplace with over 2,000 costumed performers and living history displays. April–June. Call 800-52-FAIRE.
- **Festival of Arts and Pageant of the Masters,** Laguna Beach. Arts and crafts fair and a pageant re-creating great works of art with live models and music. Mid-July through August. Call 714/494-1145.
- **Parade of Lights,** Long Beach. A parade of boats illuminates the Long Beach harbor. December. Call 310/562-4093.

CENTRAL CALIFORNIA

- **Whale Watch,** Big Sur. Guided whale-watching as gray whales migrate to and from their Mexican breeding grounds. Saturdays throughout January. Call 408/667-2315.
- **Annual Dixieland Festival,** Monterey. Mid-March. Call 408/443-5260.
- **Big Sur Marathon,** Big Sur. A 26-mile marathon run on scenic CA 1 along the Big Sur coast. April. Call 408/625-6226.
- **Calaveras County Fair and Jumping Frog Jubilee,** Angels Camp. World-famous jumping frog competition, plus professional rodeo, music, dancing. Mid-May. Call the 39th District Agricultural Association at 209/736-2561.
- **Gilroy Garlic Festival,** Gilroy. Late July. Call 408/842-1625.
- **San Luis Obispo Mozart Festival,** San Luis Obispo. Orchestra, chamber, solo, choral, and opera performances. Late July. Call 805/781-3008 for information and tickets.
- **Monterey Jazz Festival,** Monterey. Jazz greats gather for the oldest jazz festival in the United States. September. Call 408/373-3366.
- **Annual Clam Festival,** Pismo Beach. Lively family festival with clam dig. Mid-October. Call 805/773-3113.
- **Butterfly Parade,** Pacific Grove. Costumed schoolchildren welcome returning monarch butterflies. October. Call 408/646-6520.
- **Monterey Grand Prix,** Monterey. One of the oldest continuously held race events in the United States. September 8, 9, 10. Contact SCRAMP, PO Box 2078, Monterey, CA 98940 (tel 408/648-5111).

SAN FRANCISCO AND NORTHERN CALIFORNIA

- **Chinese New Year Festival and Parade,** San Francisco. Annual celebration of the Chinese lunar New Year, with colorful parade and Miss Chinatown USA pageant. Early February. Call 415/982-3000.
- **Snowfest,** Tahoe City. The largest winter festival in the West, including fireworks, ski races, polar bear swim, and torchlight ski parade. Mid-March. Call 916/583-7625.
- **San Francisco International Film Festival,** San Francisco. Acclaimed as the most eclectic and adventurous film festival in the United States. April–May. Call 415/931-3456.
- **Carnaval,** San Francisco. Salsa, samba, and reggae. Late May. Call 415/826-1401.
- **Lesbian/Gay Freedom Day Parade and Celebration,** San Francisco. Late June. Call 415/864-FREE.
- **Western States 100-Mile Run,** Foresthill. 100-mile run in 24 hours begins in Squaw Valley and ends in Auburn. June. Contact Western States Foundation, 701 High St, Auburn, CA 95603 (tel 916/823-7282).
- **California State Fair,** Sacramento. One of the largest agricultural fairs in the country, with carnival exhibitions, horse racing, and top-name entertainment. Late August. Call 916/541-5458.
- **Sausalito Art Festival,** Sausalito. One of the West's finest outdoor art exhibitions. Early September. Call 415/332-0505.
- **Russian River Blues Festival,** Guerneville. American and international blues and jazz greats play beneath the redwoods. Early September. Call 707/869-3940.
- **Fleet Week,** San Francisco. Gathering of ships ranging from aircraft carriers to sailing vessels. Mid-October. Call 415/395-3923.

SPECTATOR SPORTS

Auto Racing In northern California, auto-racing fans gather at **Sears Point** (tel 707/938-8448), in the heart of wine country, from February through September. Farther south, the Sports Car Racing Association of Monterery Peninsula sponsors a wide roster of events, including motorcycle races, at

Laguna Seca (tel 408/373-1811), off CA 68, near Monterey. In southern California, the choices are **Riverside International Raceway**; San Diego's **Del Mar** racetrack; or **Long Beach,** whose streets echo with the roar of Formula One cars during the Toyota Grand Prix, held in April (tel 310/981-2600).

Baseball   Take your pick of no less than five major league teams. The **San Francisco Giants** of the National League and the **Oakland Athletics** of the American League, the Bay Area's contingent, play at 3COM Park (tel 415/467-8000) and the Oakland Coliseum (tel 510/638-0500), respectively. Dodger Stadium (tel 213/224-1400) hosts the **Los Angeles Dodgers,** the Giants' archrivals, while in Orange County the **California Angels,** the A's divisional rival, swing their bats at Anaheim Stadium (tel 714/634-2000). Farther south, the **San Diego Padres,** the third National League team in California, play at Jack Murphy Stadium (tel 619/283-4494).

Basketball   Californians are enthusiastic basketball fans during the National Basketball Association season, November through May. Undisputed best of the state, at least in past years, have been the **Los Angeles Lakers,** who play at the Great Western Forum (tel 310/673-1300). If you can't get tickets, try the **LA Clippers,** who appear at the Sports Arena (tel 213/748-8000). In northern California, the **Golden State Warriors** keep the fans on their toes at Oakland's Coliseum Arena (tel 510/639-7700).

College Football   California has produced some of America's finest college football teams, whose clashes culminate in the **Rose Bowl,** held each New Year's Day between the champions of the West and Midwest divisions, and in the battle between Stanford University and the Bears of UC Berkeley. A lottery is held for the Rose Bowl—send a postcard (postmarked between September 15 and October 15) to Rose Bowl Ticket Drawing, PO Box 7122, Pasadena, CA 91109 (tel 818/577-3100).

Pro Football   Three professional football teams take to the gridiron September through late December. The **San Francisco 49ers** kick off their games at 3COM Park (tel 415/468-2249) while the **Oakland Raiders** play at the Oakland–Alameda County Coliseum; call the Oakland Football Marketing Association (tel 510/615-1888) for Raiders ticket info. Farther south, the **San Diego Chargers** take

to the gridiron at Jack Murphy Stadium (tel 619/280-2111).

Hockey   California is home to three NHL teams, which play regular season games from October to April. For game information contact the **Los Angeles Kings** at the Great Western Forum (tel 310/673-6003), the **San Jose Sharks** at the San Jose Arena (tel 408/287-9200), and the **Anaheim Mighty Ducks** at Arrowhead Pond (tel 714/704-2700).

Horse Racing   There are several horse racing venues within the compass of both Los Angeles and San Francisco. Southern Californians go to **Hollywood Park Racetrack** in Inglewood (tel 310/419-1500), home of the $1 million Hollywood Gold Cup Race, where thoroughbred races are held April to June and November to December. **Santa Anita Park** in Arcadia (tel 818/574-7223) also offers thoroughbred racing, with a season stretching from October to April. In northern California, **Golden Gate Fields** (tel 510/526-3020) has thoroughbred racing January to June, and **Bay Meadows** in San Mateo (tel 415/574-RACE) has a schedule of both thoroughbred and quarterhorse races September to January.

ACTIVITIES A TO Z

Bicycling   California is tailor-made for bicycle touring. The state is laced with bicycle lanes and off-road trails, and many locally based tour companies specialize in group bicycle tours designed for everyone from beginners to competitive cyclers. Popular routes include the Pacific coast, the redwood forests, Napa Valley, and Gold Country. CALTRANS, the state highway department, publishes a *Bikecentennial Tour Guide* that includes detailed route maps, typical weather conditions, grades, and safety tips. Contact CALTRANS, 6002 Folsom Blvd, Sacramento, CA 95819.

Among operators of organized tours, **Backroads** of Berkeley (tel 510/527-1555) offers a wide range of weekend and week-long guided trips with overnights in deluxe country inns and/or campgrounds. The **American Youth Hostels** also offers organized bicycle tours for all age groups. Their programs cover a wide span of regions and are generally less expensive than trips run by commercial tour companies. Contact AYH, Central California Council, PO Box 59024, San Jose, CA 95159 (tel 408/741-9555). Mammoth Mountain, on the Sierra Nevada's eastern slope, and the Tahoe region offer miles of ski runs "groomed" in summer for mountain biking. For information on guided bike tours, contact **Mammoth Mountain Bike Park** at 619/934-0606. Sports shops around Lake Tahoe and Mammoth rent mountain bikes for around $30 a day.

Camping California's vast state park system has more than 17,500 campsites; most are open year-round. Many have walk-in environmental campsites. Reservations are recommended for summer, holidays, and weekends, and can be made up to eight weeks in advance by contacting MISTIX, PO Box 85705, San Diego, CA 92138 (tel 800/444-7275). The California Travel Parks Association can provide an *RV & Camping Guide* listing locations and facilities of private campgrounds; write to ESG Mail Service, PO Box 5648, Auburn, CA 95604 (tel 916/885-1624).

Climbing The Sierra Nevada have countless near-vertical granite rock faces, of which Yosemite's Half Dome and El Capitan are best known. Several top-quality climbing schools, including the Yosemite Mountaineering School (tel 209/372-1244), teach beginners the rudiments of rock climbing.

Fishing This is the state's most popular participatory sport. A fishing license is required of all persons 16 or over for both ocean and inland waters (some public piers allow ocean fishing without a license). For information contact the California Department of Fish and Game, License and Revenue Branch, 3211 S St, Sacramento, CA 95816 (tel 916/227-2244). Public fishing piers are legion along the coast, and rock cod, salmon, and albacore are all prized catches. Rivers throughout the state—especially those in Trinity and Shasta counties—prove happy hunting grounds, particularly when the salmon and steelhead head upstream. Lakes such as Clear Lake and Lake Almanor are stocked with a wide variety of species. Guided sportfishing trips are offered from most major coastal ports.

Golf Hundreds of public and private golf courses throughout the state cater to golfers. San Diego, with 82 courses, is billed as "Golfland USA." Likewise, Palm Springs enjoys its moniker as "Winter Golf Capital of the World," with 85 courses and 1,435 holes. Although the Monterey Peninsula has "only" 17 courses, it claims to be *the* "Golf Capital of the World"—Pebble Beach Golf Course leads the way, with rippling ocean-side fairways that challenge the world's finest players (alas, green fees here are

$200 per person). Local telephone directories provide listings of golf courses.

Hiking Hiking opportunities abound in the state and national parks. The trails system is well developed and maintained. Trail maps for individual parks are available at the ranger stations upon entry. Hardy backpackers may wish to hike the magnificent **John Muir Trail,** which follows the crest of the Sierra Nevada for 212 miles from the summit of Mt Whitney to Yosemite National Park. The **Sierra Club** offers dozens of guided backpacking trips in the Sierra Nevada, as well as in Anza-Borrego Desert State Park and the Mojave Desert. Contact the Outings Department, Sierra Club, 85 2nd St, 2nd floor, San Francisco, CA 94105 (tel 415/977-5630).

Pack Trips These offer a premier way to explore the Sierra Nevada and the remote, starkly beautiful northeastern corner of California. On some, mules or llamas carry your gear (you hike unhindered); on others, you ride horseback. For information on the Eastern Sierra High Packers Association and a list of members, contact the Bishop Chamber of Commerce, 690 N Main St, Bishop, CA 93514 (tel 619/873-8405). The Rock Creek Pack Station, PO Box 248, Bishop, CA 93514 (tel 619/935-4493), welcomes participants on mustang-tracking trips into the Inyo National Forest.

Sailing Sailing clubs and yacht charter companies line the coast from San Diego to San Francisco Bay, and both San Diego and San Francisco enjoy conditions—and settings—that are the envy of sailors worldwide. The **Olympic Circle Sailing Club** (tel 510/843-4200) in Berkeley, and the **California Sailing Academy** (tel 310/821-3433) in Marina del Rey are both recommended for certification courses and yacht rentals. Boaters also have access to more than 420 recreational lakes.

Skiing With 15 alpine and 9 cross-country areas, Lake Tahoe offers the greatest concentration of skiing in North America; it blossomed on the world scene in 1960 when the Winter Olympics were held at Squaw Valley. Resorts here cover 19 mountains, with 400 runs. For information, contact Lake Tahoe Chamber of Commerce, PO Box 884, Tahoe City, CA 96145 (tel 916/581-6900). Ski season normally runs November through May. Most popular downhill areas are:

• **Squaw Valley,** 6 miles northwest of the town of

Tahoe City, on CA 89, with 4,000 acres of slopes and 32 lifts, including a 150-passenger cable car.

- **Alpine Meadows,** 6 miles west of the town of Tahoe City, on CA 89, with over 100 runs, and 13 lifts.
- **Heavenly,** 2 miles southeast of the town of South Lake Tahoe, with more than 85 runs and 23 lifts.
- **Kirkwood,** 30 miles S of the town of South Lake Tahoe, off CA 88 with over 70 runs, 11 lifts, and an extensive Nordic ski center.
- **Northstar,** 12 miles northeast of the town of Tahoe City, off CA 267, with 55 runs and 11 lifts.

Farther south, **Mammoth Lakes** (tel 619/934-2571) is equally popular and boasts miles of outstanding runs. Here, too, an expansive web of cross-country trails lure Nordic skiers into the wilderness. Cross-country skiers are also drawn to **Mount Shasta Ski Park** (tel 916/926-8600) and **Lassen Ski Park** (tel 916/529-1512) in northern California; and to Yosemite National Park, at the **Tamarack Cross-Country Ski Center** (tel 619/934-2442) and **Yosemite Cross-Country Ski School** (tel 209/372-1244).

Tennis One look at a roll-call of Grand Slam champions can prove that California produces its share of tennis stars. The state's idyllic climate makes tennis one of its most popular sports. Virtually every hotel worth its salt has courts, and public courts are found all over the state. Almost every city has a parks and recreation department, which you'll find listed under "Government" in local telephone directories. The following can provide information: Northern California Tennis Association (tel 510/748-7373) and Southern California Tennis Association (tel 310/208-3838).

Whale Watching The annual December-through-April migration of the beloved California gray whale can be viewed from promontories all along the coast. Good spots are **Whale Point** in La Jolla, **Cabrillo National Monument** at Point Loma, **Chimney Rock** at Point Reyes National Seashore, **Mendocino Headlands State Park,** and **Trinidad Head** in Humboldt County. For an eyeball-to-eyeball encounter take a guided cruise. Dolphin Charters, 1007 Leneve Place, El Cerrito, CA 94530 (tel 510/527-9622) offers half-day and longer whale-watching cruises from San Francisco Bay. In southern California, contact Pacific Sea-Fari Tours, 2803 Emerson St, San Diego, CA 92106 (tel 619/222-1414).

White-Water Rafting The Sierra foothills and Trinity Alps of northern California are drained by effervescent rivers that offer superb white-water rafting. The Kern River, deep in Sequoia National Park, is closest to southern California. The American, Tuolumne, Merced, and Stanislaus Rivers all plunge from the Sierras and tumble through historic Gold Country. Farther north, the Klamath is popular, and wilder runs are available on the Burnt Gorge of the Trinity River. Echo: The Wilderness Company, 6529 Telegraph Ave, Oakland, CA 94609 (tel 510/652-1600) and Whitewater Voyages, PO Box 20400, El Sobrante, CA 94820 (tel 510/222-5994) provide brochures describing professionally guided raft trips throughout the state.

Driving the State

THE NORTH COAST

Start	Bodega Bay
Finish	Leggett
Distance	155 miles
Time	3–4 days
Highlights	Stunning coastal vistas, a 19th-century fort, New England–style villages, a scenic train ride, redwood forests for hiking, and small, quiet beaches

This tour follows California's North Coast, a rugged region of plunging shorelines and pounding surf that reaches nearly 400 miles north from San Francisco to the Oregon border. You'll be following CA 1 (the State Coast Highway), a sinuous, thin line of two-lane asphalt just north of the Golden Gate Bridge. CA 1 takes you away from big-city skyscrapers as it hugs steep cliffs and wraps around hairpin turns, rarely moving from the sight, sound, and smell of the Pacific Ocean. The further north you drive, the more rugged the scenery. Starting your tour from Bodega Bay, you'll encounter an ever-changing landscape of windswept headlands, long, lonesome stretches of sand, and windswept moors. In places, the recently uplifted Coast Range Mountains come close to shore. Groves of tall redwoods, reaching heights in excess of 300 feet, lie tucked in the cool, fern-choked riverbottoms. Much of the coast is preserved in state parks and beaches perfect for fishing, hiking, horseback riding, collecting shells, and picnicking. Swimming, however, is not recommended, due to dangerous riptides, treacherous undertows, and offshore eddies.

Along the way, you'll drive through villages packed with well-preserved Victorian homes, many of them resurrected as cozy bed-and-breakfasts, often on the very edge of the cliffs. You'll find numerous art galleries, gift shops, and seafood restaurants. Sometimes the highway descends to cross at the rivermouths where giant sand bars form warm gathering places for crowds of seals. Great blue herons, coots, ducks, and egrets also wade in the rivermouth waters and lagoons. From November through April, gray whales make their annual 6,000-mile migrations between Alaska and Baja California; they come close to the North Coast shore, where they are easily spotted from high vantage points. There are few boat tours, however, because the cold and stormy waters discourage them.

Yellow road signs warn of road hazards—cows or deer, which are commonly seen grazing the margins.

Keep your speed down, for logging trucks, too, careen around the blind curves north of Fort Bragg. A dozen or so gas stations are spaced well-apart in the 100 miles between Jenner and Fort Bragg.

Allow four days for dawdling. Summer is high season; mid-week travel is best, as inns are often fully booked well in advance on weekends. Spring and autumn are best. Note that some inns and restaurants close in off-season, and many do not accept credit cards. For additional information on accommodations, restaurants, and attractions in the region covered by this tour, look under specific cities in the listings portion of this book.

CA 1 is reached from San Francisco across the Golden Gate Bridge by traveling north on US 101 to the Mill Valley (CA 1) exit. The road climbs over the coastal mountains and drops to Stinson Beach; follow CA 1 north past the shores of pencil-thin Tomales Bay to Bodega Bay. An alternate route follows US 101 to San Rafael. Take the 4th St (Sir Francis Drake Hwy) exit and continue west to CA 1 at Point Reyes Station; turn right. Alternately, continue north on US 101 to Santa Rosa; take CA 12 (Bodega Hwy) west via Sebastopol to CA 1. Begin at the **Bodega Bay Area Visitors Center** (tel 707/875-3422) at 850 CA 1, where you can pick up maps and brochures.

1. **Bodega Bay** is a relaxed fishing village that was named by Spanish explorer Juan Fransisco de la Bodega, who anchored the *Sonora* here in 1775. The Russians established a sea otter hunting base here in 1808 but left in 1841. They were replaced by Yankees who built a steam-operated sawmill in 1843. Today the community is a popular weekend vacation spot for San Franciscans; trendy bed-and-breakfast inns and boutiques are multiplying while the local fishing fleet—the largest between San Francisco and Eureka—dwindles. The broad bay itself supports gulls, egrets, herons, pelicans, and other bird species. California gray whales also come close to shore in winter. Catch the town's tranquil mood at **The Tides,** at Lucas Wharf, a dockside tackle shop that doubles as fish market, bar, and restaurant. It's a great place to enjoy breakfast as fishing boats unload their catches of salmon or Dungeness crab.

   Drive north 1 mile on CA 1 to East Shore Rd and

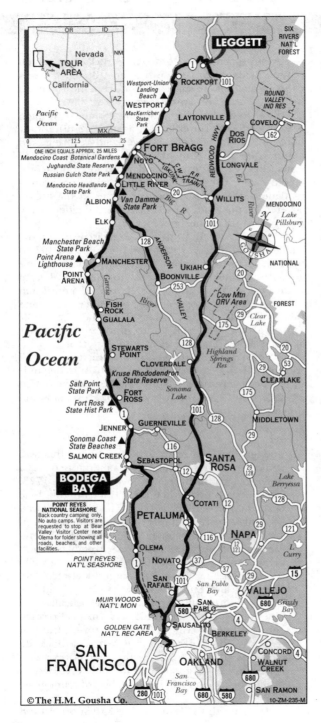

2. **Sonoma Coast state beaches** (tel 707/875-3483), which protect 13 miles of coast north of Bodega Bay. Craggy headlands separate tiny coves (many renowned for their tidepools) and wide beaches backed by sweeping dunes. Bodega Head, to the south, is a popular whale-watching spot. Footpaths lead from the Head to Bodega Dunes, while trails lead down to the many other beaches from CA 1; the beaches and their access points are clearly signposted. Shell Beach is favored by beachcombers seeking a treasure chest of shells. Surf anglers favor Portuguese Beach. Goat Rock, to the north, at the mouth of the Russian River, is popular with seals. The park headquarters and information center is on Salmon Creek Beach.

Follow CA 1 north as it turns briefly inland and crosses the Russian River to the junction with CA 116. Guerneville is 13 miles to the right. Turn left and proceed on CA 1 heading west towards the Pacific and Jenner, which perches on the steep bluff on the north bank of the Russian River. As you continue north on CA 1, several pull-offs provide superb views south to Goat Rock and the Sonoma Coast beaches. After 12 miles you reach:

3. **Fort Ross State Historic Park** (tel 707/847-3286). The Russian-American Company founded Fort Ross in 1812 as imperial Russia's furthermost permanent protective outpost against the Spanish. The Russians hunted the local sea otter population to near extinction before departing in 1852. The weathered redwood stockade with octagonal turrets, officers' quarters, barracks, and a Russian Orthodox chapel have been meticulously reconstructed to look as they did when occupied. The commandant's house is the original. The visitor center in this 1,160-acre park features fascinating displays about Native American, Russian, and Yankee logging communities, as well as historic artifacts.

Continue north on CA 1. After 2.3 miles you will pass the Benjamin Bufano *Peace* sculpture that looms over Timber Cove. Proceed north 3 miles through cypress forest until you reach:

4. **Salt Point State Park** (tel 707/847-3221), with 6 miles of rugged coastline and neighboring inland mountains. Miles of trails tempt hikers and horseback riders for forays through forests of stunted pines, cypress, and mature redwoods that attain only a few feet in height. Dozens of snug coves hidden along the shore feature *tafoni*, strange formations sculpted from the soft sandstone cliffs by wind and wave. Several old Pomo Indian village sites are scattered throughout the 6,000-acre park.

As you head north 4 miles on CA 1 you will pass

turn left. After less than ½ mile, turn right onto Bay Flat Rd and follow it about 3½ miles to Bodega Head, from where you have a spectacular view of:

several beaches before turning right to follow the hard-packed dirt road uphill for ½ mile to:

5. **Kruse Rhododendron State Reserve** (tel 707/847-3221), where you can experience the contrast between the intimate (rhododendrons) and the spectacular (redwoods) on a loop trail that leads through 317 acres of coastal vegetation. Clusters of pink and cream-colored rhododendrons blaze gloriously April through June; they grow more than 15 feet tall. Ferns, violets, orchids, and other plants linger year-round.

Back on CA 1, head north 5 miles to Stewarts Point. Proceed through Sea Ranch, a residential community of 1,200 or so houses that stretch for 7 miles along the coast. You will have ample access to Sea Ranch's many beaches, indicated by signs reading "Coastal Access." Ten miles north of Stewarts Point you reach:

Take a Break

Picture windows overlook the California coast and the sea at the artfully rustic **River's End**, CA 1, Jenner (tel 707/865-2484); the eclectic menu features Indonesian *bahmi goreng*, Indian curries, beef Wellington, and seafood and steaks.

---

6. **Gualala Regional Park,** a coastal reserve enveloping redwoods and secluded beaches. A trail leads to Del Mar Landing, a perfect spot for watching seals, which bask on the rocks offshore. The waters are popular with abalone divers, and fishermen cast for silver salmon and steelhead trout.

As you continue north on CA 1 you will cross the Gualala River into Mendocino County, and after 1 mile enter:

7. **Gualala,** which nestles atop the northern coastal bluffs overlooking the pretty rivermouth of the Gualala River. Once a logging settlement and now a budding art center, sleepy Gualala (pronounced wah-LA-la; from the Pomos Indians' *wala'li* or "meeting place of the waters") comes alive each August when it hosts the Arts in the Redwoods Festival, with local artists' displays. Many artists also show their works year-round at the Gallery.

Exit Gualala heading north on CA 1 and proceed 13 miles to Iversen Lane, on your left. Follow Iversen for 1.2 miles to Arena Cove Wharf, a large public pier. Back on CA 1, continue north 100 yards into:

8. **Point Arena,** a peaceful hamlet with venerable timber-framed facades facing the street. In the 1870s, the now-shrunken town was the busiest port between San Francisco and Eureka. Today the seasonal sea urchin harvest to serve Japanese tastebuds is revitalizing Point Arena. A restored 1927 vauderville theater (The Arena) still functions as concert hall, movie house, and playhouse.

Two miles north of Point Arena on CA 1 you will pass an interesting cemetery on the left, immediately beyond which is Lighthouse Rd. Turn left and follow the paved but bumpy road about 2 miles through windswept meadows to:

9. **Point Arena Lighthouse** (tel 707/882-2777). This historic 115-feet-tall lighthouse was built in 1908 of steel-reinforced concrete. Climb to the top for the fabulous view and superb whale-watching; gray whales often pause in the cove near the lighthouse during their annual migrations. Then, tour the adjacent maritime museum in the Fog Signal Building.

Continue north through pastureland along CA 1. After almost 2½ miles you will reach Stoneboro Rd on your left. Stoneboro and Kinney Rd, about 1½ miles further north in the tiny village of Manchester, both lead to:

10. **Manchester State Beach** (tel 707/937-5804) a 5-mile-long sandy strip, windswept and strewn with driftwood, and backed by tall dunes with heaps of wildflowers. The **Arena Rock Underwater Preserve,** 2 miles offshore, is a favorite of divers. The San Andreas fault, which runs along the North Coast for many miles, threatens this area. Winter steelhead run in the Garcia River, whose bottomlands are a favored winter habitat for whistling swans that migrate from the Arctic Circle.

As you continue north on CA 1 via the lovely clifftop village of Irish Beach, you may stop after 4 miles at a vista point to enjoy the sweeping coastal views. After 5 miles, the road makes a 2-mile-long snaking descent and ascent of the Elk River valley to the quaint village of Elk. Proceed north 7 miles to the junction of CA 128. CA 1 continues to the left, westward to Fort Bragg. To the right, CA 128 leads 20 miles to the:

11. **Anderson Valley,** a thriving farming and apple-growing region well worth the short detour. At its center is **Boonville,** where friendly locals may "harp Boont" for you. The local dialect called Bootling dates back to isolated pioneer days and can be sampled, along with robust local ales, at the **Buckhorn Saloon** brew pub (tel 707/895-BEER).

Return to CA 1. Back at the junction with CA 128, follow CA 1 west, heading toward the Pacific. Continue 3 miles via the hamlet of Albion. After another 4 miles you will pass through the former-lumber-port-turned-hostelry-hub of Little River, on the northern edge of which on the right is the entry to:

12. **Van Damme State Park** (tel 707/937-5804), which has a tiny beach safe for swimming (one of the few along the North Coast) and alluring forests. A visitor center and museum made of handsplit timbers provide exhibits on the area's natural history. The Bog Trail leads to a marsh of foul-smelling skunk-cabbage. An additional 10 miles of trails (including a wheelchair-accessible trail) penetrate the 5-mile-long, 2,160-acre preserve, following the Little River from its mouth through a ravine of ferns and redwoods to a bonsai-like pygmy forest. Rhododendrons also grow in profusion.

Take a Break

For superb service and a romantic ambience, dine at **Little River Inn,** 7751 N CA 1 (tel 707/937-5942), where California nouvelle finds its way into such tasty entrees as spring rack of lamb, herb roasted chicken, fresh margarita swordfish, and grilled polenta with porcini mushroom sauce.

Back on CA 1 continue north almost 2½ miles and cross the bridge over the Big River to Main St. Turn left and enter the town of:

13. **Mendocino,** an impressive showcase of Cape Cod–style architecture that is included in its entirety on the National Register of Historic Places. It often stars as a New England stand-in for films and television shows. Mendocino's name was bestowed as early as 1542 by a Spanish expedition in honor of Antonio de Mendoza, Viceroy of New Spain. In 1852, Yankee loggers established a sawmill on the beach and built their handsome redwood homes and prim churches on the bluffs overlooking the rivermouth. In the 1960s, Mendocino was discovered by hippies and artists, lured by the town's irrepressible beauty and the opening of the **Mendocino Art Center,** at 45200 Little Lake Rd (tel 707/937-5818), which displays the work of local and national artists. Ranchers, artists, loggers, and marijuana farmers still make up the core of the populace.

Mendocino is small enough to be easily explored on a two-hour walking tour, yet deserves a two-day stay. Your tour should begin at **Ford House** (tel 707/937-5804), on the south side of Main St, an immaculately restored 1854 structure that is Mendocino's oldest existing residence; it now functions as the **Visitor Information Bureau.** Across the road is the **Kelley House Museum,** 45007 Albion St (tel 707/937-5791), in a pretty 1861 gingerbread-trim home that is furnished with Victoriana and local memorabilia. Also on Main St is the landmark Gothic-style **Presbyterian Church,** built in 1868. **Blair House,** at the junction of Ford and Little Lake Sts, was the setting for the television series *Murder, She Wrote.* Note the old Masonic Temple—now the **Savings Bank of Mendocino**—topped by an allegorical statue of Father Time and The Maiden carved from a single redwood. Another local curiosity is the **Kwan Ti Temple,** on Albion St between Kasten and Osborne Sts (by appointment only; tel 707/937-4506).

When you're sated with architectural delights, there are countless antique stores, art galleries, and chic restaurants to enthrall you. Feeling romantic? Then take a horse-drawn carriage ride offered by **Mendocino Carriage Company** (tel 800/399-1454), May to December.

A trail from the corner of Hesser and Main Sts leads to the meadow-topped:

14. **Mendocino Headlands State Park** (tel 707/937-5804), immediately north and west of town. The 347-acre park provides tidepools, wave tunnels, and tiny coves for exploring; two beaches for bronzing and bathing; and clifftop trails. The headlands form vantage points for mid-winter whale-watching. Sea otters can often be seen amid the kelp beds.

Back on Coast CA 1, continue north 3½ miles to Point Cabrillo Dr and turn left to enter:

15. **Russian Gulch State Park** (tel 707/937-5804), combining a canyon thick with redwoods and rhododendrons, a sweeping bay with sandy beach and well-protected tidepools, and coastal headlands splashed with wildflowers. Hiking and cycling trails braid the park. Separate trails lead up the canyon to Russian Gulch Falls.

Continue north on CA 1 for a little over 1 mile to:

16. **Jughandle State Reserve** (tel 707/937-5804), where cliffs offer the 2.5-mile "Ecological Staircase" nature trail that leads from sea level through five terraces uplifted from the sea approximately 100,000 years apart. Each of the terraces is covered with a unique vegetation: The lowermost, youngest step has been colonized by salt-resistant wildflowers; fir, pine, spruce, and hemlock dominate the second terrace; the uppermost features a rare example of Mendocino pygmy forest of gnarled, stunted cypress trees and pine. At the south end of the 769-acre park is **Casper Headlands State**

Beach, which protects a ½-mile of sand bordered by seasonal wildflowers.

Proceed 2½ miles north on CA 1, and on your left you will pass the entrance to:

17. **Mendocino Coast Botanical Garden** (tel 707/964-4352), fronted by a nursery. Two miles of trails lead through 47 acres of splashy shrubs and wildflowers. A self-guided tour leads through native plant communities and coastal pine forest complemented by rhododendrons, azaleas, and fuschias planted by human hand.

Continue north along CA 1 for 2 miles to N Harbor Dr, on your right. Follow N Harbor Dr as it snakes down into the Noyo River canyon and the wharfs of:

18. **Noyo,** a tiny fishing port sheltered in the river mouth at the southern end of Fort Bragg. The fishing fleet that harbors here supplies local restaurants with fresh seafood daily. Noyo is a good place for whale-watching and fishing forays.

Take a Break

At 780 N Harbor Dr is the unpretentious **Wharf Restaurant** (tel 707/964-4283), which combines harborside views with reasonably priced steaks, salads, and seafood specialties—grilled halibut and salmon, crabs, and shellfish stews—fresh from the wharfs.

Back on CA 1, continue north ½ mile past the:

19. **Georgia-Pacific Sawmill,** the world's largest redwood sawmill, stretching 9.6 miles from just north of the Noyo River. More than 3½ million redwood and Douglas fir seedlings are raised annually in a miniature forest at the **Georgia Pacific Tree Nursery** (tel 707/964-5651), on Main St (CA 1). A nature trail leads through the nursery, which is open to the public.

As you drive past the lumber yards, you will enter:

20. **Fort Bragg,** the largest town on the North Coast between San Francisco and Eureka. The robust, no-nonsense logging community retains a strong Finnish and Portuguese heritage. A large Native American population also remains. Fort Bragg began as a fort, built in 1857 to oversee the Mendocino Indian Reservation, and is named for Confederate hero General Braxton Bragg; it was abandoned in 1867 when the reservation was moved. Stop by the **Guest House Museum,** Main St, (tel 707/961-2825), next to the Laurel Street Train Depot, for a

history of logging. It's housed in a 1892 Victorian home built for the Union Lumber Company's founder. The town also has a thriving artists' community.

You should park your car next to the Guest House Museum and Skunk Depot at the foot of Laurel St and take a journey on the:

21. **California Western Railroad's** *Skunk* **Train** (tel 707/964-6371), which offers a cliff-hanging ride up Noyo River Gulch and over the rugged coastal mountains to Willits. Disembark midway at Northspur for a snack before returning to Fort Bragg, or continue to Willits. The scenic excursion follows a 40-mile route, crisscrossing the river on wooden trestles as it ascends from 80-feet elevation to 1,365 feet at Willits. In sleepy Willits, call in at the **Mendocino County Museum,** 400 E Commercial St (tel 707/459-2736), where Native American basketry and pioneer-period artifacts are displayed, along with contemporary and traditional art. *Skunk* schedules vary between a choice of four venerable engines, including the "Ole No 45" Baldwin Steam Engine.

Exit Fort Bragg continuing north on CA 1 with an old trestle railway bridge on the left. On the left, after 3 miles, is the entrance to:

22. **MacKerricher State Park** (tel 707/937-5804), 1,600 acres and 10 miles of dark sand beach favored by hikers, bikers, and fishermen. Harbor seals gather at Seal Rock. The park's headland, Laguna Point, is a favored spot, too, for viewing migrating whales November through April. Lake Cleone is a fancied rest spot for migratory waterfowl.

Back on CA 1, you will cut temporarily inland through forests encroached upon by massive sand dunes that come right up to the road. After 9 miles, a vista point on the left allows you to savor views along 10 Mile Dunes beach. Another 3 miles brings you to:

23. **Westport,** the last village on the coast. This remote and pretty New England–style coastal mill "town" is popular with abalone divers and for surf fishing. From here, you can have intoxicating views north towards the Lost Coast.

One mile north of Westport on CA 1, you will pass the first of several turn-offs on your left for:

24. **Westport-Union Landing State Beach** (tel 707/937-5804), a slender 41-acre park that attracts tidepoolers, surf fishermen, and abalone divers.

As you continue north on CA 1 you will pass a sign on the right that reads NARROW WINDING ROAD FOR NEXT 22 MILES. WATCH FOR BICYCLES. Five miles north of Westport, CA 1 suddenly swings inland and follows a tortuous route through the mountains to Leggett, where a sign announces END HIGHWAY 1. Drive carefully. The narrow road snakes steeply, and giant logging trucks thunder downhill through the gloomy forest en route to the Georgia-Pacific coast sawmill. About 21 miles after leaving the coast, you reach Leggett Drive-Thru Tree Rd on your right. Turn right and follow the road ½ mile through the homespun hamlet of Leggett to:

25. **Drive-Thru Tree Park** (tel 707/925-6363), a privately-owned 200-acre virgin redwood grove dominated by the renowned Chandelier Drive-Thru Tree (315 feet tall, with a 21-foot base).

Return to CA 1, turn right and proceed to the junction with US 101 (the Redwood Hwy). Turn right to return to San Francisco on US 101. Turn left for the great redwood parks and Oregon.

Driving the State

Start	Monterey
Finish	Santa Barbara
Distance	Approximately 275 miles
Time	2–3 days
Highlights	Phenomenal scenery, seaside towns, redwood forests, Spanish missions, factory outlets, America's most outrageous castle

One minute, you're driving at sea level; less than a mile later, the road skedaddles up to 1,000 feet and your eardrums are popping. Welcome to one of the most famous roadways in the world—California's Highway 1, also known as the Cabrillo Highway (and referred to in this tour as CA 1). The road skims the California coast from Mendocino to south of Los Angeles, but during this tour, you'll explore its most celebrated stretch, running from the Monterey Peninsula to Santa Barbara. Located 120 miles south of San Francisco and 330 miles north of Los Angeles, the Monterey Peninsula forms the southernmost nub of Monterey Bay and encompasses four distinct communities: Monterey, Pacific Grove, Pebble Beach, and Carmel-by-the-Sea. It's easy to travel from one town to the next, since only 3 miles separate Carmel from Monterey.

Because the peninsula offers so many attractions, you'll probably want to stay overnight in the area. The top address is **The Lodge at Pebble Beach,** on 17 Mile Dr (tel 408/624-3811 or toll free 800/654-9300), where most rooms have fireplaces and an ocean view. If you're looking for the quintessential B&B, head for **Seven Gables Inn** (tel 408/372-4341), overlooking Lover's Point in Pacific Grove. A good choice for bargain hunters is the **Best Western Inn–Town House Lodge** in Carmel—homely, but right near the center of town.

For additional information on accommodations, restaurants, and attractions in the region covered by the tour, look under specific cities in the listings portion of this book.

To reach the peninsula from San Francisco, take I-280 south to San Jose, then pick up US 101 S. At Prunedale, take CA 156 W, which merges into CA 1, and proceed south to:

1. **Monterey.** Try to spend a day exploring this town before embarking on the rest of your journey. Monterey owes its prominence to its immense bay, measuring almost 60 miles long and 13 miles wide. First settled in 1770, Monterey served as the capital of Alta (Upper) California originally for the Spanish and later for the Mexicans. Step back into the past along Monterey's "Path of History," a self-guided walking tour past about a dozen well-preserved 18th- and 19th-century adobe structures. You can visit some of the buildings, including the Spanish colonial–style **Larkin House,** 510 Calle Principal, and **Colton Hall,** 522 Pacific St between Madison and Jefferson Sts, where California's first constitution was written in 1849. You can obtain a free walking-tour map from **Monterey State Historic Park,** Cooper-Molera Adobe, Polk and Alvarado Sts (tel 408/649-7118).

Next head for the waterfront and **Fisherman's Wharf.** Although the pier is lined with T-shirt and souvenir shops, it still retains a seafaring spirit, amplified by the gulls' squawks and briny aromas from the boiling crab pots. Pick up a "walkaway" shrimp or crab cocktail from a food stall, or enjoy a seafood dinner at **Abalonetti** or **Domenico's.**

From the 1920s to the 1940s, Monterey was the sardine-packing capital of the world. John Steinbeck vividly captured this raucous era of factory workers, fishermen, and hustlers in his novel *Cannery Row.* Today, **Cannery Row,** on Monterey Bay between David and Drake Aves, has been reborn, with souvenir shops and restaurants occupying former bars and bordellos. The biggest attraction here is the **Monterey Bay Aquarium,** 886 Cannery Row (tel 408/648-4888), located in the former Hovden sardine cannery. The star exhibit is the three-story kelp forest aquarium, where leopard sharks and schools of silver sardines cruise. Visitors can also watch the captivating sea otters, aquatic clowns who float on their backs and whack open clams with small stones.

From Cannery Row, drive southwest (inland) on David Ave, then turn right on Lighthouse Ave. Proceed through the town of **Pacific Grove,** which was founded at the turn of the century as a strict Methodist summer community; several of the ornate Victorian houses have been converted into bed-and-breakfast inns. Turn left at:

2. **17 Mile Drive.** At the Pacific Grove Gate entrance to this scenic drive, you must pay a toll of $6.50 per car. Set your odometer to "zero"; mileages given in the following section are calculated from the entrance gate. The route runs through privately owned, 5,000-acre Del Monte Forest and Pebble Beach, twining its way past wave-lashed seacoast

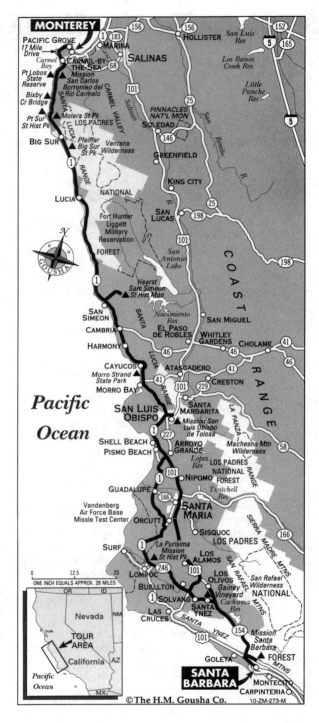

Bluff Walking Trail (mile 2.2) offers a good opportunity to stretch your legs and observe the scenery. At mile 3.4, you'll come to **Bird and Seal Rocks,** offshore outcrops where sea lions and harbor seals ("downstairs") and thousands of cormorants and sea gulls ("upstairs") share their rocky roost in cacophonous harmony; you can gaze at the scene through fuzzy-quality telescopes for 25 cents. The symbol of the Monterey Peninsula, the famous **Lone Cypress** stands grandly on a nearly barren rock facing the sea (mile 6). Experts estimate the tree is between 200 and 300 years old.

The next section of roadway is flanked by some spectacular homes—minicastles, really, in styles ranging from Mediterranean to Norman to Cape Cod. Zip code 93953 for Pebble Beach vanquishes Beverly Hills in terms of exclusivity. A prime ocean-front estate recently sold for $12 million; vacant lots can run $1 million to $6 million. At mile 8, you'll pass the elegant **Lodge at Pebble Beach,** known for its top-ranked Pebble Beach Golf Links. Since 1919, this beautiful course designed by Jack Neville and Douglas Grant has been home to some of golf's most prestigious tournaments, including the annual AT&T Pebble Beach National ProAm, plus several US Open Championships.

While 17 Mile Drive swings back north and inland through Del Monte Forest, the driving tour bears south into Carmel-by-the-Sea. Exit 17 Mile Drive through Carmel Gate onto North San Antonio. Turn right (west) onto Ocean Ave. Continue to:

3. **Carmel Beach,** a mile-long sweep of sand edged by Monterey pines and steep sand dunes. Sunsets here are usually marvelous, with vistas stretching from Point Lobos to Pebble Beach. Drive back east on Ocean Ave to explore the town of Carmel itself, which centers on Ocean Ave between Monte Verde and Mission Sts. Park where you can—traffic is a jungle, especially on summer weekends. Your best bet might be the free parking lot at Vista Lobos Park (on 3rd Ave and Junipero St).

Carmel can best be described by what it lacks. The community has no neon signs, courthouse, or jail, and few sidewalks. Instead of street addresses, houses are identified by locale (such as "on Lincoln between 7th and 8th) or melodic names, such as "Merry Oaks" or "Sea Nymph." The town has an abundance of art galleries and gourmet restaurants that give it the panache of the south of France.

Shopping and browsing are preferred pastimes here. Art lovers will want to check out galleries such as **Simic,** San Carlos St between 5th and 6th Aves, and **Hanson,** Ocean Ave and San Carlos St. **Weston Gallery,** 6th Ave between Dolores and Lincoln Sts, displays works by major 19th- and 20th-century

and through pine groves shrouded in mist. Much of the vegetation you see is unique to this region, and some plant species are endangered. The **Coastal**

photographers. For antiques, top stores include **Luciano Antiques,** San Carlos St between 5th and 6th Aves, and **Great Things Antiques,** Ocean Ave between Lincoln and Dolores Sts.

Other favorite shops include **Walter White Gallery,** San Carlos St between 5th and 6th Aves, for art glass; **Ladyfingers,** Dolores St between Ocean and 7th Aves, for designer jewelry; **Pierre Deux,** Ocean Ave at Monte Verde St, with Country French furnishings; and **Conway of Asia,** Dolores St between Ocean and 7th Aves, displaying fantastic Asian art objects, from bronze Buddhas to gilded sword hilts.

Reclaim your car and go east on Ocean Ave, then south (right) on Junipero St, which turns into Rio Rd. Drive to:

4. **Carmel Mission,** 3080 Rio Rd at Lausen Dr (tel 408/624-3600), officially known as the Basilica of Mission San Carlos Borromeo del Rio Carmelo. Built in 1793 of local sandstone, this lovely structure has a star window over the rough-hewn

---

Take a Break

At **Casanova,** 5th Ave between San Carlos and Mission Sts (tel 408/625-0501), you can sit at a table in the garden courtyard while enjoying excellent Northern Italian and French country cuisine. **The Grill,** Ocean Ave between Dolores and Lincoln Sts (tel 408/624-2569), is garnering local raves for its modern, art-filled interior and creative cuisine, such as oak-grilled salmon with okra and sweet-potato tempura.

---

doorway and two uneven towers, one of them capped by a Moorish dome. In addition, the mission is known for its attractive gardens and fountains. It is most closely associated with Father Junipero Serra, the Franciscan friar who oversaw the establishment of 21 different California missions; he is buried at the foot of the church altar.

Leaving the mission, turn right (east) on Rio Rd, and continue about ½ mile to CA 1. Turn right (south). In just over 2 miles, you come to:

5. **Point Lobos State Reserve** (tel 408/624-4909), which Robert Louis Stevenson called "the most beautiful meeting of land and sea on earth." At this preserve just south of Carmel Bay, you can hike past stands of cypress twisted by the ocean winds and stroll along hidden coves and lagoons, perhaps spying some sea otters floating in the kelp beds. Park rangers often lead guided nature walks. This is a wonderful spot for a picnic.

Retrace your route back to CA 1 and turn south. The roadway sidewinds the cliffs, with nothing between you and the blue Pacific but a sheer 1,000-foot drop. There are plenty of scenic overlooks, so you can pull over to photograph the views. About 11 miles after Point Lobos, you'll come to a CA 1 landmark:

6. **Bixby Creek Bridge,** which looks as if it were spun by a drunken spider. Measuring 260 feet high and 700 feet long, it was the highest single-arch bridge in the world when constructed in 1932.

Roughly 9 miles after the bridge, your next stop is:

7. **Point Sur Lighthouse** (tel 408/625-4419), a State Historic Park and the only intact 19th-century lighthouse open to the public in California. The beacon stands 361 feet above the surf at what was once a notorious ships' graveyard. Threehour tours of the area are offered Wednesday, Saturday, and Sunday, weather permitting.

The landscape changes dramatically in about 9 miles, heading inland from sun-bleached coastal grasslands to cool green redwoods and oaks. You are now entering famous:

8. **Big Sur,** one of the last American frontiers, a place where the highway first came through in the 1930s, and phone service began in the 1950s. Residents still have to drive 30 miles to Carmel to pick up their dry cleaning or a new oil filter for the pickup. The name comes from the Spanish, who referred to the entire unexplored region south of their settlement in Monterey as El Sur Grande. Vistas offer contrasts: jagged cliffs and smooth white beaches, towering redwoods and scruffy chaparral. For years, the region has been a haven for avant-garde

---

Take a Break

Time your drive so you can ogle the views from one of Big Sur's clifftop restaurants, all 2 to 3 miles south of Molera State Park. Under chef David Daniels, major gourmet American food is happening at **Ventana** (tel 408/667-2331), where you can dine on a deck beneath trees, under white umbrellas, or in a ridgetop pergola woven with vines. Perched at the very brink of the cliffs, **Sierra Mar at Post Ranch Inn** (tel 408/667-2200) offers views heretofore known only by seagulls, and excellent contemporary Californian cuisine. Or slip into a 1960s hippie time warp at **Nepenthe** (tel 408/667-2345), serving basic burgers, sandwiches, chicken, and fish in a casual atmosphere.

writers such as Henry Miller and Jack Kerouac. You can hike through the forests at **Pfeiffer Big Sur State Park** (tel 408/667-2315), where the Waterfall Trail climbs through a redwood canyon to 40-foot falls. **Andrew Molera State Park** (tel 408/667-2315) covers 9,000 acres and has a variety of hiking trails along the river, cliffs, and beach.

Once again, head south on CA 1, which continues its scenic crescendos with the unusual boulder formations at **Pacific Valley** (23 miles south of Nepenthe) and the vista point at **Willow Creek** in **Los Padres National Forest** (34 miles south of Nepenthe), commanding spectacular views of sentinel-like rocks and pounding surf. About 60 miles south of Nepenthe, the road suddenly levels off into undulating green cow country. About 70 years ago, everything you can see around you—about 50 miles of prime coastline—belonged to William Randolph Hearst. Your next stop is his most outrageous and most lasting achievement:

9. **Hearst Castle (San Simeon).** Some 130 rooms; art treasures ranging from tapestries by Rubens to a wine bucket made from 30 pounds of pure silver; a dining room lined with a 13th-century Italian choir stall. This is the larger-than-life world of La Cuesta Encantada—the Enchanted Hill—the estate built by tycoon William Randolph Hearst. In 1935, Hearst, the newspaper publisher who perfected yellow journalism and the Hollywood producer who made movies like *Young Mr Lincoln,* was worth $220 million—the equivalent of $2 billion today. Working with architect Julia Morgan, he spent $3 million and almost 30 years crafting this extravagant Mediterranean revival mansion, which in fact was never completed. Hearst heirs donated the castle to the state of California in 1958, and the California Park Service now runs several different tours of the grounds.

On the tour, you experience the castle as guests would have, sauntering past the magnificent white Carrera marble Neptune Pool, walking through a guest "cottage" with its plaster ceiling leafed in 22-karat gold, and entering the castle itself, known as La Casa Grande. In its heyday, guests included luminaries from the world of politics (Winston Churchill, Calvin Coolidge); royalty (the Duke and Duchess of Windsor); and Hollywood (Cary Grant, Vivien Leigh, Rudolph Valentino).

Because of the tremendous popularity of Hearst Castle, it is absolutely essential that you purchase your tickets in advance. To make reservations, call toll free 800/444-4445.

Leaving Hearst Castle, turn left (south) on CA 1. From here to Santa Barbara, you'll be driving along both good roads and highways, with none of the vertiginous curves found between Carmel and Hearst Castle. Continue another 5 miles to:

10. **Morro Strand State Park.** At this 2-mile-long beach, you might see surfers shredding the waves against the backdrop of Morro Rock, a 576-foot outcrop attached to the mainland by a skinny sand isthmus. Unfortunately, the vistas are marred by a trio of smoke stacks from Pacific Gas & Electric. Swimming is usually safe at Morro Strand, although no lifeguards are on duty.

Continue south on CA 1. On the outskirts of San Luis Obispo, CA 1 joins up with US 101, a main north-south route through California. You can continue south on US 101, or, if you are interested in California missions, continue straight on CA 1, which becomes Santa Rosa St in town. Go right on Monterey St, which dead-ends at:

11. **Mission San Luis Obispo de Tolosa,** 782 Monterey (tel 805/543-6850), with its shady plaza and thick walls. Founded in 1772, it has three bells hanging from an opening above the entrance and was one of the first buildings in California to have a red clay-tile roof—now a fixture of West Coast architecture. In addition to early photos, artifacts on view include a re-creation of a friar's bedroom.

If you've visited the mission, retrace your route and pick up US 101 south. In a little over 8 miles, you'll reach Pismo Beach, where you should continue south on US 101 to Buellton; then take CA 246 west 15 miles to Purisima Rd. After 2 miles, you'll arrive at:

12. **La Purisima Mission State Historic Park,** 2295 Purisima Rd (tel 805/733-3713). Dating to 1787, the enclave is the most completely restored of California's 21 missions. It's one of the best places to get a sense of early mission life, with re-created workshops including a soap factory and tannery, and real cattle, sheep, and horses grazing in the corrals.

Leaving the mission, turn east (left) on CA 246. Continue approximately 18 miles to:

13. **Solvang.** Founded in 1911 by Danish-American educators, most of the town features old-world architecture. The result is Scandinavia as it might have been rendered by Walt Disney, with half-timbered and thatched storefronts, cobblestone walks, and a few windmills. There is a good selection of shops selling such Danish treats as *ableskivers,* a round pancake drizzled with jam and powdered sugar, and *medisterpole,* a locally made sausage. But the main draw here is the factory outlets for brands like Izod, Dansk, and Oneida.

A slice of old-time California lies just up the road in the rolling hills of Santa Ynez Valley. Resume your route east on CA 246. At the last light leaving Solvang, turn left on Alamo Pintado Rd. Continue about 5 miles, then turn right at the only stop sign for miles onto an unmarked road. A hundred yards later, turn left at the next stop sign onto Grand Ave. Drive about ½ mile and you're in:

14. **Los Olivos,** formerly a stagecoach stop at a narrow-gauge railroad. This quintessential small town—all two blocks of it—has one- and two-story wood-frame buildings, and a flagpole plunked in the middle of the main street, Grand Ave. Men ride fine Arabian horses through the center of town, and kids wander barefoot into the grocery store.

There are also some fine shops for browsing. **Gallery Liz Montana** (2890 Grand Ave) carries some intriguing western art. **Los Olivos Tasting Room & Wine Shop** (2905 Grand Ave) offers samples of mostly Santa Barbara County wines, from vintners who do not have their own tasting rooms. **Donlee Gallery** (2920 Grand Ave) features paintings and sculpture, and **White Oak Gallery** (2920 Grand Ave) has paintings and hand-crafted furniture.

From Los Olivos, retrace your route back on Grand Ave and Alamo Pintado Rd. Turn left (east) on CA 246. If you've got more wine-tasting on your mind, stop at:

15. **The Gainey Vineyard,** 3950 E CA 246, Santa Ynez (tel 805/688-0558), part of 1,800-acre Gainey Ranch in the Santa Ynez Valley. The Spanish-style winery opened in 1984 and soon achieved a reputation for its premium varietals, including cabernet sauvignon, pinot noir, and chardonnay. In addition to winery tours and tastings, there's a vineyard garden with picnic tables.

Leaving Gainey, turn right (east) on CA 246. Proceed ½ mile to CA 154 and turn right (south). Designated a California Scenic Highway, CA 154 lives up to its appellation as you leave Santa Ynez, curving through a lovely valley backed by the crumpled green face of the Santa Ynez Mountains. Shortly, on the left, you'll pass Lake Cachuma, a shimmering blue mirror washing into the receding lines of ridges. Watch for the Vista Point on your left.

About 30 miles from Los Olivos, CA 154 shimmies its way down through narrow mountain passes to Santa Barbara. Turn left on State St, then left on Constance and left on Los Olivos to:

16. **Mission Santa Barbara,** 2201 Laguna St (tel 805/ 682-4713). Established in 1786 and called the

---

Take a Break

About 8 miles after you merge onto CA 154 from CA 246, look for the Stagecoach Rd exit on your right. Turn right and head for a drink at **Cold Spring Tavern,** 5995 Stagecoach Rd (tel 805/ 967-0066), a 126-year-old former stagecoach stop. There's great live music Wednesday through Sunday nights, featuring anything from country-and-western to jazz.

"Queen of the Missions," it commands a beautiful view of the Pacific, with twin bell towers set against a backdrop of eucalyptus-clad foothills. Its unusual design blends classical and colonial styles: The padres adapted a design from a Roman temple. Today, the former living quarters house an excellent museum tracing mission history.

After leaving the mission, turn right on Los Olivos, then left on State St to downtown Santa Barbara. Snuggled between the Santa Ynez Mountains and the Pacific about 90 miles north of Los Angeles, the city's setting equals that of any village along the Côte d'Azur. Santa Barbara has always appealed to major power brokers from business (the Armours and Firestones), movies and television (Michael Douglas, Jonathan Winters, Jane Seymour), and politics (Ronald Reagan established his "White House West" here).

Santa Barbara's finest accommodations match the scenic setting. Queen of the city is the **Four Seasons Biltmore** (tel 805/969-2261 or toll free 800/332-3442), built Spanish-style with tranquil courtyards and located right across from the beach. Located in the Santa Ynez foothills, the individual cottages at **San Ysidro Ranch** (tel 805/969-5046 or toll free 800/868-6788) offer hideaway seclusion on 540 acres. **Harbor View Inn** (tel 805/963-0780 or toll free 800/755-0222) is located directly across from Stearns Wharf and the Pacific Ocean.

With the improvement of US 101 so that it no longer slices downtown Santa Barbara in half, State St is booming with recently opened shops and restaurants. State St ends at the oceanfront and:

17. **Stearns Wharf,** which extends a half-mile over the Pacific. The wharf, which was owned by actor Jimmy Cagney and his brother in the 1940s, offers a picture-postcard California view—sailboats heeling with the wind, sunbathers strolling along the shore, and a chorus line of swaying palm trees along the esplanade.

Driving the State

Start	Carneros Alambic Distillery, Napa
Finish	Silverado Trail
Distance	Approximately 65 miles
Time	5–8 hours
Highlights	Wining and dining at America's best wineries and restaurants, a museum dedicated to Robert Louis Stevenson, a geyser, a petrified forest, shopping

Flanked by the Mayacamas and Vacaville mountain ranges, the peaceful, green Napa Valley, America's foremost wine-growing region, is dotted with wood-frame houses, stone wineries, and ordered rows of vineyards. The region stretches about 30 miles from Carneros to Calistoga. In between, road signs identify towns whose names grace many a wine label: Oakville, Yountville, Rutherford, St Helena. This tour loops through the valley, stopping at several wineries renowned for not only their wines but their settings and architecture. You'll also have time to explore the historic towns of St Helena and Calistoga, and lunch or dine at one of the valley's superb restaurants.

Should you want to stay overnight in Napa Valley, you have many excellent choices. With individual villas snuggled in an olive grove in the Rutherford foothills, luxurious **Auberge du Soleil** (tel 707/963-1211 or toll free 800/348-5406) feels like an inn in Provence. **Vintage Inn** (tel 707/944-1112 or toll free 800/351-1133) offers a lot of charm for the price, with two-story units surrounded by lovely manicured grounds.

For additional information on accommodations, restaurants, and attractions in the region covered by the tour, look under specific cities in the listings portion of this book.

Napa Valley is located 45 miles north of San Francisco, about an hour's drive from the city. Take the Golden Gate Bridge from San Francisco, which puts you on US 101 N. Drive approximately 20 miles and exit at CA 37/Napa-Vallejo, which goes east. Continue 7.7 miles and turn left (north) on CA 121. After a little more than 6½ miles, CA 121 veers off sharply to the right (east) just before a red blinking traffic light—stay on CA 121, which in a few miles runs together with CA 12. About 5 miles from the traffic light, you reach the **Napa-Sonoma county line,** where Napa Valley suddenly makes a grand appearance, laid out like an intricate tapestry of trellised greenery. Continue on CA 12/121. About 3 miles from the county line, turn right (south) on Cuttings Wharf Rd. Proceed 1 mile to:

1. **Carneros Alambic Distillery,** 1250 Cuttings Wharf Rd (tel 707/253-9055), the first alambic brandy distillery in the United States. Depending on the time of year you visit, you might be able to sample ugni blanc or French colombard grapes in the field, or watch the stills in action. Although there's no sampling, you do get to sniff and identify the different spirits that go into the final blend. You'll enjoy a look at the stills, copper pots that look like giant Aladdin's lamps, and a visit to the barrel room.

Retrace your route to CA 12/121 and turn right (east), rejoining the main tour route. At the intersection of CA 12/121 and CA 29, turn left (north) on CA 29, the main north/south route through Napa Valley, also called St Helena Hwy between Yountville and St Helena. In 3 miles, you'll see **Napa Factory Stores,** name-brand outlets that just recently opened.

Many prominent vineyards are located directly on CA 29. But to get a real sense of Napa, explore some of the side roads, such as the byway suggested for the next stop. From the intersection of CA 12/121 with CA 29, proceed north to the first stoplight and the Redwood Rd/Trancas intersection. Turn left on Redwood Rd. Drive 4.3 miles; watch for the marked turnoff on the left for:

2. **The Hess Collection,** 4411 Redwood Rd (tel 707/255-1144), set in two historic stone buildings built in 1903 on the slopes of Mount Veeder. This elegant Napa winery has tastings ($2.50 per person), video screenings about wine making, and spacious galleries displaying paintings and sculptures by contemporary American and European artists, including Morris Louis, Robert Motherwell, Frank Stella, and Francis Bacon. Both the winery and the art collection are owned by Donald Hess, Swiss-American scion of a beer and beverage fortune.

Return to CA 29 and turn left (north). The landscape remains busily suburban for about 5½ miles until you reach the small town of Yountville, named after the area's first permanent settler and grape planter, George Yount, who arrived in 1831. Take the Yountville–Veterans Home exit, turn left (west). After crossing the railroad tracks, turn right into:

3. **Domaine Chandon,** California Dr (tel 707/944-2280). Lakes, fountains, and spreading oak trees enhance the grounds at this stone-faced winery

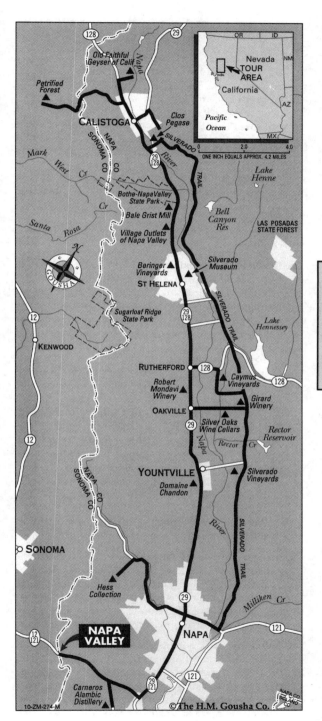

Valley, in 1973. Domaine Chandon's product is called sparkling wine, not champagne—the name champagne is properly limited to wines produced in the designated region of France. Domaine Chandon wines are produced by the classic French *méthode champenoise* and undergo two fermentations: the first in open tanks, the second in the bottle. On the tour given here, you'll find out how both white and red grapes go into champagne, and walk through the huge tank room where each 14,100-gallon steel container holds enough liquid to supply you with the equivalent of a bottle of wine a day for 200 years. At the end of the one-hour tour, you can sample the winery's five different *cuvées* (blends) for $3 to $5 a glass, or eat at the fine restaurant.

Take a Break

The best restaurant in the valley is also the loveliest—**The French Laundry,** 6640 Washington St, Yountville (tel 707/944-2380), set in an enchanting stone cottage. Opened in 1994, the restaurant under chef/owner Thomas Keller is deftly turning out contemporary French-influenced cuisine that rivals France's finest.

Return to CA 29 and go north. You are now driving through one of Napa's most illustrious wine growing regions, encompassing the towns of Oakville, Rutherford, and St Helena. This is the district of the "Rutherford Bench," a gravelly soil said to impart a unique flavor to wines produced here. The next stop in Oakville visits the operations of the grower and vintner regarded as the leading force in California wine making today, the:

4. **Robert Mondavi Winery,** 7801 St Helena Hwy in Oakville (tel 707/226-1335). Housed in serene, Spanish-style buildings, this winery, founded in 1966, is today run by Robert Mondavi along with his two sons and a daughter. They provide the most comprehensive winery-tour program in Napa Valley. The basic one-hour complimentary tour and tasting (no reservations required) covers grape growing, wine making, and the sensory appreciation of wine. Other sessions (reservations required) delve more deeply into viticulture and wine making, wine and food pairings, and "essence" tasting. The winery is also a setting for art shows, literary presentations, concerts, and the annual Summer Music Festival.

Leaving Mondavi, turn left (north) on CA 29. This area has scenic back roads such as the follow-

built into the hillside. Founded in 1743 by Claude Moet, Moet-Hennessy was the first respected French wine producer to begin operations in Napa

ing circular route, which winds past some of the valley's top small vineyards. Turn right on CA 128 (also called Rutherford Cross Rd) and almost immediately you are surrounded by vineyards. The road crosses the Napa River, which flows through the valley. Turn right on Conn Creek Rd; at the intersection is **Caymus Vineyards** (tel 707/963-4204), a good choice for wine tasting ($2). Continue south on Conn Creek Rd and turn left on Skellenger Lane to the Silverado Trail, where you turn right. Just before Oakville Cross Rd is **Girard Winery** (tel 707/944-8577) on your right. Girard produces some notable wines, including cabernet sauvignon, chardonnay, and a Benton Lane pinot noir (from Oregon); tastings are complimentary. Turn right (west) on Oakville Cross Rd, where you'll pass **Silver Oaks Wine Cellars** (tel 707/944-8808) on the left, with some wonderful cabernets from both Napa and Alexander Valleys. Tastings cost $5. You'll also see one of the boldest examples of the different architectural styles that have flourished in the valley: the pink Moorish towers of **Groth,** 750 Oakville Crossroad (open for tours and tastings by appointment only; tel 707/944-0290). Tastings cost $3 and are refundable against wine purchases. Continue back to CA 29, having completed the scenic loop.

Continue about 5 miles north on CA 29 to:

5. St Helena. This enclave is Napa Valley's answer to Carmel, with many splendid 19th-century stone and brick buildings renovated into boutiques and galleries. Park your car and stroll down Main St (CA 29). Interesting stores include **Reeds,** 1302 Main St, for women's clothing and accessories, and **Napa Valley Olive Oil Manufacturing,** 835 Charter Oak Ave, which has produced California regular and extra-virgin olive oil for 70 years. Nearby, Dansk and Gorham factory outlets are located at 801 Main St.

Literary buffs should visit the **Silverado Museum,** 1492 Library Lane (tel 707/963-3757). The small museum packs in an enormous variety of Robert Louis Stevenson's manuscripts and personal belongings; when the writer was broke and unable to afford $10 a week for room and board in Calistoga, he stayed in an abandoned bunkhouse at the Old Silverado Mine on Mount St Helena. The book he wrote about his experiences, *The Silverado Squatters,* provides a fascinating glimpse of late 1800s Napa Valley life and of Stevenson's prescience in praising early valley wines: "The smack of Californian earth shall linger on the palate of your grandson."

Once again, point your wheels "up valley," to the north. The landscape starts to change here as the valley narrows and becomes more lush. Tem-

> ## Take a Break
>
> At **Tra Vigne** (1050 Charter Oak Ave, St Helena (tel 707/963-4444), chef/part owner Michael Chiarello's Italian dishes showcase fresh-garnered produce in dishes like ripe figs grilled in a band of prosciutto, and tender raviolis stuffed with sweet crab and whipped potatoes, napped in a saffron-butter sauce.

peratures will also be considerably warmer than in Carneros or Napa—often 10°F hotter—since the coolness and fog of San Francisco Bay do not penetrate this far north.

Less than ½ mile north of the town of St Helena, you'll come to:

6. Beringer Vineyards, 2000 Main St (tel 707/963-7115). Built in 1883, the turreted mansion on the grounds, called Rhine House, is a copy of the Beringer family's ancestral home in Germany, complete with inlaid wood floors, handcrafted wainscoting, and stained-glass windows. Today, the mansion serves as a hospitality center and tasting room for visitors to the award-winning winery, which produces such classics as the Beringer Private Reserve cabernet sauvignons. Complimentary tours are held every half hour.

Just north of Beringer, the **Culinary Institute of America** (tel 707/967-1010) has taken over the century-old Greystone building as its West Coast campus. Back east, the school is considered the most important training ground for new chefs in the country. In addition to classrooms, kitchens, and bakeshops, the structure houses a public restaurant where students hone their skills.

About 1½ miles north of the Culinary Institute, you'll arrive at:

7. Village Outlets of Napa Valley, 3111 North St Helena Hwy. This small, select factory outlet is beautified by olive trees in the parking lot. It includes boutiques for Joan & David, Brooks Brothers, London Fog, and Donna Karan.

Continue north on CA 29 for almost 1 mile to:

8. Bale Grist Mill, a former flour mill founded by an early Napa Valley pioneer, Dr Edward Bale. Today, the mill is a state historic park; fully restored, it has the largest working water wheel in America. You can enjoy several cool and shady walking trails here, plus picnic areas at **Bothe-Napa Valley State Park** (tel 707/942-4575), just to the north.

Drive about 3½ miles north on CA 29 to Dunaweal Lane and turn right (east). Go east ½ mile on Dunaweal Lane to:

9. **Clos Pegase,** 1060 Dunaweal Lane, Calistoga (tel 707/942-4981). With larger-than-life portals and columns, this monumental, neoclassical structure reflects architect Michael Graves's goal to build "a temple to wine." In the early 1980s, owner Jan Shrem worked with legendary winemaker Andre Tchelistcheff (the Russian émigré who first brought fine French wine-making techniques to the valley) to create the elegant wines produced here. Tastings ($3) showcase the best of the winery's varietals; the merlots are especially round and juicy. Guided tours are held daily.

Return to CA 29 and turn right (north). In 2 miles, CA 29 veers off to the right and becomes known as Lincoln Ave as it enters downtown:

10. **Calistoga.** The town was founded in the mid–19th century as a health spa, thanks to its mineral-rich underground hot springs. The main promoter behind the town was flamboyant newspaperman Sam Brannan, who had scooped reports about the discovery at Sutter's Fort that sparked the California Gold Rush. He dubbed the burg Calistoga, "The Saratoga of California," linking its waters to the most famous spa resort back east.

Lincoln Ave, the town's principal thoroughfare, is lined by a mix of turn-of-the-century stone, stucco, and brick-front buildings. Compared with the groomed gentrification of St Helena, Calistoga has a slower pace and a small-town sweetness. There are a few interesting stores to browse. **Donlee Fine Arts,** 1316 Lincoln Ave, has a fine selection of paintings and sculpture, especially western art. For book lovers, **The Calistoga Bookstore,** 1343 Lincoln Ave, carries a wide range of titles, including works on Napa Valley. Located just south of town on CA 29 is the **Calistoga Pottery,** 1001 Foothill Blvd. Owner Jeff Manfredi crafts some appealing mugs, plates, and vinegar pots, among other pieces.

Next, in contrast to the ancient art of wine making, turn your attention to a natural wonder. From Calistoga, go north 1.2 miles on CA 128 and turn right on Tubbs Lane. Drive ½ mile to:

11. **Old Faithful Geyser,** 1299 Tubbs Lane (tel 707/942-6463). Like its namesake in Yellowstone National Park, this geyser is one of the few in the world to erupt on a regular schedule—every 40 minutes or so. Starting with a few wisps of steam, the geyser suddenly blows 350° water some 60 to 100 feet in the air.

At the small front counter, you may meet Olga Kolbek, the retired university professor who has owned the geyser since 1973. After logging eruptions for several years, she noticed that the geyser acts erratically before major earthquakes, stretching intervals between performances. Scientists have verified her observations, and researchers are now tracking the geyser's behavior to help predict earthquakes. Call ahead to get some idea what time eruptions are expected that day.

Return south on CA 128 towards Calistoga. At Petrified Forest Rd, you can turn right to:

12. **The Petrified Forest** (tel 707/942-6667). The same volcanic activity that fuels Old Faithful Geyser caused a huge eruption of lava and ash some 3 million years ago, burying a redwood forest. Over the years, wood cells in the fallen trees were replaced with crystallized silica until the trees turned completely to stone. You can walk a trail past petrified wood specimens, many of which were already 2,000 years old when they were covered over.

From Calistoga town, continue northeast on Lincoln Ave/CA 29 to the **Silverado Trail,** and turn right (south). During the 19th-century, the route was used to carry cinnabar from mines at Mount St Helena to the river docks in Napa. Aside from its wineries (prestigious names such as Stag's Leap, Clos du Val, and more), the Silverado Trail is almost totally noncommercial and far less trafficked than CA 29. If you'd like to sample more wines, try **Silverado Vineyards,** 6121 Silverado Trail, Napa (tel 707/944-1770), owned by the family of the late Walt Disney. Wines are good and very reasonably priced, and there's no charge to taste current releases; sampling of reserves and library wines runs from $2 to $5 per glass.

At Trancas Street in Napa (the only traffic light), turn right (west) to CA 29.

Driving the State

SONOMA COUNTY

Start	Sonoma Valley Visitors Association
Finish	Twin Hill Ranch, Sebastopol
Distance	Approximately 95 miles
Time	5–8 hours
Highlights	Sonoma town and its Mission, wine tasting, Jack London's former ranch, quaint towns, farm stands, and the Russian River Valley

While outsiders often group Sonoma together with Napa as "California Wine Country," the two adjoining countries north of San Francisco are as different as chardonnay and cabernet sauvignon. In practically every way, Sonoma is more laid-back than its counterpart to the east. Sonoma landscapes are gentler, with green-velvet hills manicured by contented Holsteins. Fog tendrils linger among redwood groves, and rivers meander gently from mountains to the sea. The whole Sonoma lifestyle seems more rural, a sweet throwback to vintage Americana. This driving tour concentrates on the southern portion of the county.

Sonoma's 1,600 square miles take in about 120 wineries and 10 different appellations (wine growing regions), each with unique soil conditions and microclimates. But in contrast to Napa, where wine is the "raisin d'être," Sonoma remains more agrarianly diversified. On 100-acre farms and in tiny backyard plots, over 170 specialty food growers produce edibles so impeccable that their specialties are airlifted to such elite restaurants as Spago in Los Angeles and Paul Prudhomme's in New Orleans.

The Sonoma County line is roughly 25 miles (a 45-minute drive) from San Francisco. From the city, take the Golden Gate Bridge, which puts you on US 101 N. Drive approximately 20 miles and exit at CA 37/Napa-Vallejo, which goes east. Continue 7.7 miles and turn left (north) on CA 121, where the tour begins. As you drive north on CA 121, you'll soon see vineyards. This is the Carneros region, the southernmost wine-growing appellation in Sonoma. Fog and wind from San Pablo Bay cool this region, making it ideal for growing chardonnay and pinot noir. In about 5 miles, you'll come to:

1. **Sonoma Valley Visitors Association**, 25200 Arnold Dr (CA 121), Sonoma (tel 707/996-1090), the perfect place to pick up brochures and maps about area attractions and obtain information about the area. The office is located at the same turn-off as Viansa Winery.

Approximately 2 miles later, CA 121 veers off sharply to the right (east) just before a red blinking traffic light—stay on CA 121. In less than a mile, turn left on CA 12, towards Sonoma town. Drive approximately ¼ mile to:

2. **Hardin Gardens**, 22660 Broadway (tel 707/935-7466). Owned by Dennis and Maria Hardin, this is the best little farm stand in southern Sonoma. On their 3 acres, the Hardins grow impeccable produce: sweet cucumbers, glossy purple eggplants, ripe, red tomatoes. Open June–October.

Leaving the farm, resume your northerly route on CA 12 as you drive through the southernmost nub of Sonoma Valley, a crescent-shaped dale measuring 17 miles long and 7 miles wide. Its environs take in 35 wineries and 6,000 acres of vineyards, as well as one of the most historic towns in California:

3. **Sonoma.** The community quickly captivates visitors with its lovely green plaza, laid out in 1835 and now a National Historic Landmark. If City Hall looks familiar, that's because it doubled for the Tuscany County Courthouse on the TV series *Falcon Crest*. The **Sonoma Valley Visitors Center** (tel 707/996-1090) is located here at 453 1st St E.

Several Spanish and Mexican colonial–era structures remain along the Plaza on Spain St, including the **Mission San Francisco Solano de Sonoma,** 114 E Spain St (tel 707/938-9560), known more commonly as the Sonoma Mission. Founded in 1823, the adobe church is the last and northernmost of the 21 California missions built by the Franciscan friars. Although extensively restored, the mission still conveys the simplicity and isolation of life at the end of the Camino Real with its austere padre's quarters and courtyard shaded by olive trees. Also stop at the **Barracks** (1st St E and E Spain St), erected in 1836 to house Mexican army troops; exhibits here chronicle early 19th-century California history.

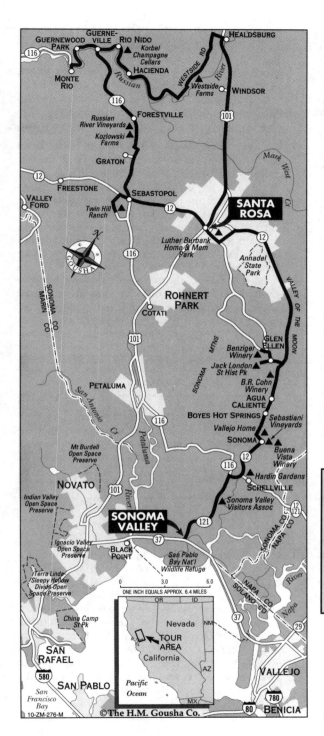

Legends, 483 1st St W, for crafts and jewelry; Zambezi Trading Co, 107 W Napa St, with a wonderful selection of African furnishings and artifacts; and Vine Arts Gallery, 107 E Napa St, with wine country paintings and prints by Claudia Wagner. The Wine Exchange, 452 1st St E, carries many West Coast labels and offers beer and wine tastings. Just a few blocks from the Plaza, cheese lovers should head for the Vella Cheese Company, 315 2nd St E, run by the Vella family for over 60 years.

Two historic wineries are located just short drives from the center of town. The California wine industry literally began at Buena Vista, 18000 Old Winery Rd (tel 707/938-1266), founded in 1857 by Colonel Agoston Haraszthy, a Hungarian count. In the early 1860s, California's governor commissioned Haraszthy to go to Europe and bring back hundreds of the best grape varieties, which became the foundation stock for California's wine industry. On the self-guided winery tour, you can peruse delightful old photos, visit the tasting room, and view the cellars, which were chipped out of limestone cliffs by Chinese laborers with pick-axes.

Sonoma's first vineyards were planted by Mission friars in 1825. Those same lands now produce grapes for Sebastiani Vineyards, 389 4th St E (tel 707/938-5532), established at the turn of the century by Samuele Sebastiani. A complete tour explains the wine-making process and showcases the winery's beautiful collection of hand-carved casks.

Take a Break

For innovative and delicious cuisine, try the East Side Oyster Bar & Grill, 133 E Napa St, Sonoma (tel 707/939-1266), under owner/chef Charles Saunders. Packed with "multicultural" ingredients, the dishes taste as good as they sound. A typical dish: clam linguine soused with garlic, smoked chile peppers, chorizo sausage, oregano, and a splash of tequila.

Because there is so much to see and do in Sonoma town, you can easily spend your entire day here. But should you want to explore the county further, resume your drive by heading west from the Plaza on W Spain St. Drive 2 blocks from the Plaza, then turn right into the:

4. Vallejo Home, W Spain St near 3rd St E (tel 707/938-9559), built by General Mariano Guadalupe Vallejo, the Mexican commandante who supported the American takeover of the territory. He

The century-old adobe and stone buildings surrounding Sonoma Plaza now house fashionable shops and restaurants. Interesting stores include

served as a state senator and mayor of Sonoma after California became a US state in 1850, and was also California's first commercial wine maker. In contrast to the adobe-and-red-tile style of Sonoma, the house Vallejo chose for himself reflects a New England Gothic style architecture. Most of the furniture in the house, including a rosewood concert grand piano, belonged to the Vallejo family.

Leaving the Vallejo home, turn right (west) on W Spain St, continue several blocks, then turn right (north) on CA 12, also called Sonoma Hwy. The names of towns you'll pass—Boyes Hot Springs, Agua Caliente—clue you in that this is thermal territory. About 1½ miles from where you turned onto CA 12, you'll pass one of California's finest resort spas, the **Sonoma Mission Inn,** CA 12 and Boyes Blvd (tel 707/938-9000). Spa facilities are superb, and recently the resort began filling its pools and whirlpools with water from natural hot springs, which had been dormant for many years.

This is also one of Sonoma's premier wine-growing regions. One of the best wineries in the area open to the public is:

5. **BR Cohn,** 15140 Sonoma Hwy (tel 707/938-4064), set in an gnarled olive grove nearly a century old (the former dairy now serves as the aging room). The winery is owned by the former manager of the rock group the Doobie Brothers. Nearby hot springs create a "banana belt" warm climate, enabling the winery to produce some especially good cabernets. During the summer, Shakespeare plays are performed in the outdoor amphitheater.

A little over 1 mile from BR Cohn, turn left on Arnold Dr, which heads into the petitely picturesque town of Glen Ellen. Go straight onto London Ranch Rd and continue 1 mile to:

6. **Jack London State Historic Park,** 2400 London Ranch Rd (tel 707/938-5216). "When I first came here, tired of cities and people, I settled down on 130 acres of the most beautiful land to be found in California," Jack London wrote, speaking about the tract that he named Beauty Ranch. Today the former ranch is part of this park, where you can visit **The House of Happy Walls,** filled with London memorabilia, from rejection slips to the old-fashioned dictaphone and typewriter on which the writer created such American classics as *The Call of the Wild* and *The Sea Wolf.* Another exhibit features a silent newsreel showing a vibrant London on his farm, driving a team of Shire horses and balancing an armful of squirming piglets. Six days after the footage was shot, London committed suicide.

The 800 acres included in the park today are laced with excellent trails where you can hike or horseback-ride through woods of oaks and madrona (call 707/996-8566 for information about horseback riding). And, if you've brought lunch, picnic tables are available.

Leaving Jack London State Historic Park, retrace your route back to CA 12. Just down from the park on London Ranch Rd, you can also stop at:

7. **Benziger Family Winery,** 1883 London Ranch Rd (tel 707/935-3000). Although the winery is a major operation, you'll be struck by the low-key facilities, set in a series of white, wood-frame buildings modeled after the 1868 ranch house that is the property's centerpiece. In addition to free tours and tastings, the winery has an excellent "wine discovery center," a walk-through vineyard where exhibits explain rootstocks, grafting and trellising techniques, and different varietals.

Back at CA 12, resume your route north. Soon you'll pass some of Sonoma's best-known vineyards, many of which offer complimentary tastings, including **Chateau St Jean,** 8555 Sonoma Hwy, Kenwood (tel 707/833-4134); **St Francis,** 8450 Sonoma Hwy, Kenwood (tel 707/833-4666); and **Kenwood,** 9592 Sonoma Hwy, Kenwood (tel 707/833-5891).

Take a Break

In Sonoma Valley, the dining highlight is **Kenwood,** 9900 CA 12, Kenwood (tel 707/833-6326), a small restaurant serving French country fare, with only 15 tables inside, plus seating on the terrace surrounded by vineyards.

CA 12 continues to the northwest and then melds into:

8. **Santa Rosa,** the urban hub of Sonoma and the county seat. Among the car dealerships and fast food joints, you'll locate some special places, if you want to stop. Visit the **Luther Burbank Home and Gardens,** Santa Rosa Ave at Sonoma Ave (tel 707/524-5445) where the famous horticulturist worked from 1875 to 1926. Another famous Santa Rosa resident is cartoonist Charles Schulz. You can buy Charlie Brown, Lucy, and Linus paraphernalia at **Snoopy's Gallery and Gift Shop** at the Redwood Empire Ice Arena, 1667 W Steele Lane (tel 707/546-3385).

In Santa Rosa, CA 12 makes a sharp left onto Farmers Lane, then resumes its westerly route—keep following the signs for CA 12. At the junction with US 101, take US 101 north (towards Eureka) approximately 12 miles to the Central Healdsburg exit. Go straight ½ mile to the town of:

9. **Healdsburg.** Located in the heart of Russian River country, the tiny burg enchants visitors with its tree-shaded plaza surrounded by lively shops and restaurants. Browse through the excellent selection of boutiques. **Irish Cottage,** 112 Matheson St, carries fine antiques, while **Innpressions Gallery,** 110 Matheson St, features paintings and handmade jewelry, and **Robinson & Co,** 108 Matheson St, offers neat kitchen wares. **RS Basso,** 115 Plaza, has decorative objects for the home, and **Options,** 126 Plaza, displays international crafts.

From the plaza, take Healdsburg Ave to Mill St and turn right. Mill St soon becomes Westside Rd—one of the most beautiful drives in Sonoma. The road passes through acres of vineyards along the banks of the Russian River, which stretches 70 miles from Ukiah to its juncture with the Pacific Ocean at Jenner. There are several small swimming beaches along its winding route, including **Memorial Beach** in Healdsburg, **Monte Rio Beach** in Monte Rio, and **Johnson's Beach** in Guerneville.

Cool redwood scenery and an interesting history come together here. The area draws its name from Russian fur traders who settled along the coast during the 1800s, moving from their territory in Alaska. Interestingly, the Russians are credited with planting the first grapevines in northern California, importing them from Peru as early as 1817. Heavy rainfall in winter and frequent fog on summer mornings make the region suited to the pinot noir and chardonnay grapes used in sparkling wines.

Drive 7 miles to:

10. **Westside Farms,** 7097 Westside Rd (tel 707/431-1432). If you've ever pondered changing your life, chat with Ron and Pam Kaiser, who own Westside Farms, set right on the Russian River. In the late 1980s, the Kaisers quit their fast-paced careers in investment banking to become farmers and wine growers. In addition to 40 acres of pinot noir and chardonnay, they plant over 20 acres of produce.

Take a Break

A "must" for visitors is **the Downtown Bakery & Creamery,** 308-A Center St, Healdsburg (tel 707/431-2719), partly owned by Lindsey Shere, pastry chef at the celebrated Chez Panisse restaurant in Berkeley. You'll quickly be seduced by the thick milkshakes and the delectable baked goods.

The fruits (and vegetables) of their labors are on sale at their old-time farm stand (open May to December), displaying basket after basket of just-harvested produce.

After 5 miles, Westside Rd ends at River Rd; turn right (west). Continue on River Rd 2½ miles to:

11. **Korbel Champagne Cellars,** 13250 River Rd, Guerneville (tel 707/887-2294). The brick and red-wood timber winery was built in 1886 by the three Korbel brothers, Czech immigrants. On the tour, you can learn all about champagne-making, viewing production from the press to the corking machines. Tours and tastings are free. Outdoors, don't miss the lovely gardens, with over 250 varieties of antique roses in bloom during the summer.

Leaving Korbel, turn right (west) back onto River Rd. After about 3 miles, you'll come to:

12. **Guerneville.** This former logging town is now a hippie community, where you'll encounter plenty of tie-dye T-shirts and posters about meditation therapy; it's also a popular gay getaway.

At junction of River Rd with CA 116, proceed southeast on CA 116, almost immediately crossing the Russian River. In 6 miles, you'll reach:

13. **Russian River Vineyards,** 5700 Gravenstein Hwy N, Forestville (tel 707/887-1575). This small, family-owned winery has earned top reviews with its organically grown grapes, especially for the Rossi Ranch zinfandel, intensely flavored with grapes harvested from dry-farmed vines planted in 1910. In addition to the winery, the property also has a good Greek restaurant, **Topolos**.

Resume your route southeast on CA 116 and drive for ¼ mile to:

14. **Kozlowski Farms,** 5566 Gravenstein Hwy (CA 116), Forestville (tel 707/887-1587). Over 40 years ago, the Kozlowski family decided to plant a few raspberry bushes among their apple orchards. Soon, Mrs. Kozlowski was wondering what to do with all those berries, so she made a pot of raspberry jam, gluing paper labels on a few jars to sell. The product of her home kitchen became the precursor for the 67 items produced by Kozlowski Farms. The shop sparkles like a Tiffany showcase, with rows of jewel-tone preserves, all made on the premises.

Continue along CA 116 to **Sebastopol.** Turn right (west) on Bodega Ave and go about 1 mile before turning left immediately after the cemetery onto Pleasant Hill Rd. Proceed approximately 1½ miles to:

15. **Twin Hill Ranch,** 1689 Pleasant Hill Rd (tel 707/823-2815), farmed by Darrel Hurst and his family

for over 50 years. You can choose from 40 varieties of flavorful apples, plus luscious homemade pies.

Return down Pleasant Hill Rd and turn right (east) on Bodega Ave, which becomes CA 12.

Continue about 8 miles to US 101 S; it is about a 45-mile drive from the Golden Gate Bridge and San Francisco.

HIGHWAY 49 AND GOLD COUNTRY

Start	Nevada City
Finish	Jamestown
Distance	230 miles, including sidetrips
Time	3–4 days
Highlights	Columbia State Historical Park, Railtown 1897, gold rush-era mine towns, natural caverns, white-water rafting

California State Highway 49—the Golden Chain Highway—slices a nearly 300-mile route through Gold Country, linking the main towns and villages created in the Sierra foothills by the Gold Rush of 1848-59. The region, about 150 miles east of San Francisco, is awash in history, and following this former stagecoach and supply route is tantamount to a historic adventure. This tour covers sights between Nevada City, in the north, and Jamestown, in the south.

Beginning in the spring of 1848, the cry of "Gold!" brought tens of thousands of settlers to the western foothills of the Sierras. The peak mining years lasted a decade, during which over $600 million in gold was plucked from the hills. The flood of wanna-be-millionaires ended with the last of the gold, and left behind were some 500 towns; more than half disappeared as quickly as the miners, who migrated to San Francisco and other cities. Today, many communities in the region pride themselves on their well-preserved Gold Rush–era buildings, with main streets straight out of old western movies. The rustic mining towns have antique shops, pioneer cemeteries, and general stores, while ubiquitous museums tell the history of Gold Country. Peaceful backroads lead to boutique wineries in sheltered valleys.

The gently sloping terrain is cut through by fast-flowing rivers—the American, Stanislaus, Mokelumne, and Tuolumne—that offer white-water thrills for kayakers, canoers, and rafters. Active visitors can also take advantage of rock climbing, caving, and hiking. The region is full of natural splendors: rolling whalebacked foothills and dramatic canyons; woodlands of blue oak, incense cedar, and ponderosa pine dominating the hills; poplar, alder, and willow lining the riverbanks; and groves of giant sequoia sequestered in cooler hollows. With luck, you may sight black bears, raccoons, skunks, and deer, which are abundant throughout the foothills. Be wary, however, of poison oak, which is also common.

CA 49 can be reached from San Francisco or Sacramento by traveling east on I-80 to exit 14, at Auburn. Alternately, take I-580 to I-205 to I-5 to Manteca to CA 120, which meets CA 49 at Chinese Camp, near Jamestown. A longer but prettier route follows CA 24 from Oakland to I-680 to CA 4, a two-lane road that snakes through farmland to CA 49 at Angels camp. From the Lake Tahoe area, head north on CA 89 to I-80 and west to CA 20 to Nevada City. Located at the junction of CA 49 and CA 20 is the heart of:

1. **Nevada City,** a pretty town where at one point during the Gold Rush, 10,000 miners were working every foot of ground within a radius of 3 miles. Later, Nevada City became the inland retreat of wealthy San Francisco families, whose carefully preserved Victorian houses still hug the hillsides. The town is a happy blend of Old West and art deco, exemplified by the Nevada County Courthouse. Take a carriage ride through the narrow, historic streets, or opt for a self-guided walking tour. The **Chamber of Commerce** (tel 916/265-2692), in the old Assay Office at 132 Main St, has free guides and maps. The slender 1861 Firehouse Number 1 (214 Main St) is festooned with gingerbread trim and houses the **Nevada County Historical Society Museum** (tel 916/265-5468), with its collection of gold rush relics. Dominating the gas-lamp-lit town center is the handsome, three-story, green-and-white 1856 **National Hotel,** 211 Broad St (tel 916/265-4551). The **Miners Foundry and Cultural Center,** in the old foundry building at 325 Spring St (tel 916/265-5804), is a showplace of Victorian arts and crafts. Linger overnight to take in a performance of the **Nevada Theater,** 401 Broad St (tel 916/265-8587); built in 1865, it hosted Mark Twain's first-ever lecture. Friday and Saturday afternoon, tours are offered at the **Nevada City Brewing Company,** 75 Bost Ave (tel 916/265-2446). **The Nevada City Winery,** 321 Spring St (tel 916/265-9463), also offers tastings and tours.

   At the junction of Broad and Union Sts is the ramp onto CA 49. Go south 3.3 miles to E Main St and turn left into:

2. **Grass Valley,** the former hard-rock capital of the Northern Mines that yielded $14 million in the first year of the Gold Rush. Today it lures tourists with its balconied Victorian-era buildings and gas lamps along Main and Mill Sts; its Cornish heritage (many Cornish hard-rock miners once settled here); and

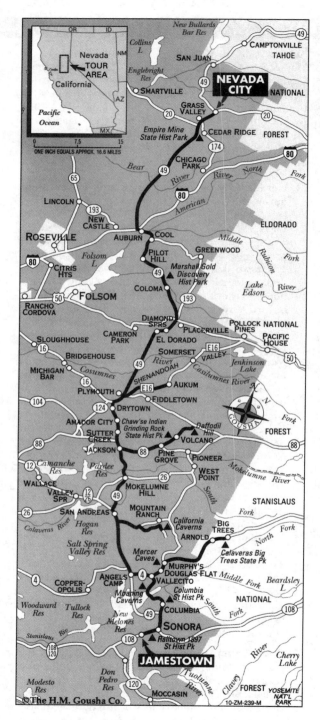

Take a Break

Follow the locals to **Moore's Cafe,** 216 Broad St (tel 916/265-9440), a hole-in-the-wall diner serving down-to-earth breakfast. Omelettes run the gamut from plain to bacon and avocado, and zesty green chile and cheese. Filling meals at '50s prices.

making her way across America to settle in Grass Valley in 1852. Lola passed her skills on to a young local lass, Lotta Crabtree, who captivated the miners and the rest of America and eventually amassed a fortune. The **Lola Montez Home,** a replica of the original, at 248 Mill St (tel 916/273-4667), is now the local tourist office. The **Grass Valley Museum,** corner of Church and Chapel Sts (tel 916/272-8188), boasts historical displays and a collection of 10,000 antiquarian books in the town's former (1865) schoolhouse.

Exit North Star and turn left on McCourtney Rd. Turn right on CA 20 (Empire St), cross over CA 49, and head east uphill 1½ miles to:

3. **Empire Mine State Historic Park,** 10791 E Empire St (tel 916/273-8522), where you can tour what once was the deepest, richest, and largest hard-rock gold mine in California. Its owner, William Bourne, became one of the wealthiest men in California. A shaft leads more than a mile down to 367 miles of underground mines. A model of the tunnel complex can be viewed near the park entrance. Some 10 miles of hiking trails lead past mining relics, old shafts, and forest. Bourn's baronial cottage, replete with original furnishings, overlooks the site amid imposing formal gardens.

Return via E Empire St to CA 49 and continue south. The route narrows down to a single lane; you will have plenty of opportunity to pass slower vehicles using passing lanes spaced at regular intervals. After 2 miles, a sign advises you to "Turn on headlights for the next 14 miles." Proceed south to Lincoln Way. Turn right and enter historic:

4. **Auburn,** whose five-square-block, perfectly preserved "old town" is steeped in Gold Rush flavor. A walk along Lincoln Way, and Commercial, Court, and Sacramento Sts takes you back into the past; the **Chamber of Commerce,** 601 Lincoln Way (tel 916/885-5616), has a walking tour brochure. Begin at the base of Washington St and the massive statue of Claude Chana making his historic find of gold in Auburn Creek in 1848. Nearby is the 1893 **Hook and Ladder Company Firehouse,** still home to California's first motorized fire engine. The **post office** at the corner of Lincoln and Sacramento Sts

the colorful saga of Irish-born Lola Montez, paramour of European royals and notables, who scandalized Europe with her racy "spider dance" before

is the oldest continuously used post office in California, opened in 1851. The stately, neoclassical structure clinging to the hill above Old Town is the 1894 **Placer County Courthouse,** featuring an impressive dome. Downtown Auburn, centered on Lincoln Way, is a piece of homey 1950s Americana. At 1273 High St, a log-and-stone building (a 1940s WPA project) houses the **Placer County Museum** (tel 916/889-4156), home to a walk-through mining tunnel and historical items telling the tale of Placer County.

Exit Auburn along Lincoln Way, which merges with CA 49 (High St). Continue south as CA 49 scales the flanks of the American River ravine. After 16 miles enter **Coloma** and the:

5. **Marshall Gold Discovery Site,** 310 Back St (tel 916/622-3470), site of the discovery that changed the history of the West. The 240-acre historic park contains a functioning full-size replica of John Sutter's sawmill where, in 1848, overseer James Marshall found flecks of gold on the banks of the American River. Within a year, 10,000 miners

Take a Break

For a taste of the Gold Country's Chinese connection, try **Shanghai Restaurant,** 289 Washington St (tel 916/823-2613), which dishes out standard but flavorful Cantonese fare at budget prices.

poured in. Sutter lost most of his land with the invasion and died impoverished in 1880. Marshall was tricked out of his claim, and died in poverty in 1879. He lies buried on the hillside, where his massive effigy (reached via One Way Rd) overlooks the site of his momentous find. A nature trail begins here and is particularly pleasing in fall when the leaves turn gold. Demonstrations of panning for gold are given at Sutter's Mill each afternoon. Most of Coloma lies within the Historic Park, and includes a working smithy, Chinese stores, a theater, and a pioneer cemetery. In summer, Columa is also a mecca for whitewater enthusiasts who push off here to run the American River's south fork.

Continue 7 miles south through pine and oak forest to the junction with I-50. Cross, staying on CA 49, and enter:

6. **Placerville,** where you can take a sidewalk stroll that brings you back to the '50s—of this century and last. Placerville was formerly known as Hangtown, named for the "necktie party" by which three desperadoes met their demise in 1849. A dummy

strung up outside the **Hangman's Tree Bar,** 905 Main St (tel 707/622-3878), reminds tourists to

Take a Break

When locals hanker for "hangtown fry" they head for the **Miner's Cafe,** 480 Main St, Placerville (tel 916/622-6018). The hometown creation is an omelette stuffed with oysters and bacon.

behave. Many of California's richest men grew wealthy in Placerville catering to the mining stampede. Mark Hopkins, who rose to become a railroad magnate, began his steam-powered ascent selling groceries on Main St, where Leland Stanford (later founder of Stanford University) also had a store; and John Studebaker launched his success with wheeled vehicles by building wheelbarrows. You can see one of his barrows at the **El Dorado County Historical Museum,** 100 Pacerville Dr (tel 916/621-5865), 2 miles west of town, which also displays Native American baskets and arts, mining equipment, plus an old stagecoach and steam locomotive. Northwest of town is the **Gold Bug Mine,** Bedford Ave (tel 916/642-5232), America's only city-owned gold mine and one of the few where the public can descend narrow, well-lit, but chilly mine tunnels (bring a jacket).

Turn left onto CA 49 (Pacific St) at the base of Main St (a Shell gas station is on your right) and continue south, noticing the cottonwoods as the two-lane road winds through rolling foothills then dips into oak woodland as you ascend a steep-sided canyon to Plymouth. Turn left on Plymouth-Shenandoah Rd (County Rd E-16) and proceed east 7 miles through the:

7. **Shenandoah Valley,** where wine grapes were first planted during the Gold Rush, when the valley was named for the Virginians who settled here. The original California wine region dwindled to just one winery before a recent blossoming revived the Amador County region. Tours and tastings are offered by most of the 18 wineries clustered throughout the valley. The **Sobon Estate,** 14430 Shenadoah Rd (tel 209/245-6555), was founded in 1856. California's fourth oldest winery (formerly D'Agostini Winery) is now a state historic landmark, with a free museum in a fieldstone building displaying early agricultural and winemaking techniques. For a map listing wineries, contact the **Amador County Chamber of Commerce,** 125 Peek St, Ste B, in Jackson (tel 209/223-0350).

Back on CA 49, continue south 6 miles through Amador City, whose buildings cluster around a sharp bend in the road; it's California's smallest incorporated city—just 1 block long. Proceed 2 miles south to:

8. **Sutter Creek,** a real charmer with its high sidewalks and balconied facades along spiffed-up Main St, full of false-front brick-and-timber art galleries, gift stores, and dusty antique stores. At the end of Eureka St, on the creek east of Main St, is the 1873 **Knights Foundry** (tel 209/267-5543), the only existing water-powered foundry in the United States.

Take a Break

In the heart of Sutter Creek is the fancifully named **Ron and Nancy's Palace Restaurant & Saloon,** 76 Main St (tel 209/267-1355). Classic Italian favorites like linguine with clam sauce, veal scaloppine, and chicken marsala are served amid historic surroundings highlighted by lace tablecloths and period furnishings.

Continue south on CA 49 for 4 miles to the Jackson Fire Station and turn left onto Main St in:

9. **Jackson,** the region's largest town (pop. 3,800). The **Amador County Museum,** 225 Church St (tel 209/223-6386), parlays Jackson's mining history with working scale models and a stamp mill with piston-like crushers that pulverized rock. The museum's mementos also commemorate the Chinese who worked as indentured laborers in the area. **Kennedy Tailing Wheels Park,** on Jackson Gate Rd, preserves two soaring 58-foot wheels that once lifted mine waste to an impounding dam. A walk along the well-worn wooden sidewalks of crooked Main St leads past brick buildings with iron doors and shutters to guard against fire. Jackson's renowned bordellos and gambling halls didn't close until the late 1950s, and even today there are card parlors on Main St.

Continue south on CA 49 ½ mile to CA 88. A Chevron gas station and the Chamber of Commerce will be on the right, at the junction. Turn left and follow the snaking road east to Pine Grove. After 10 miles, turn left on Pine Grove–Volcano Rd and continue north 1½ miles to:

10. **Chaw'se Indian Grinding Rock State Historic Park,** 14881 Pine Grove–Volcano Rd (tel 209/296-7488), a 136-acre preserve of grassy meadows, black oaks, and pine that was once home to the Miwok tribe. Gold miners brutally chased out and decimated the largely peaceable Native American populations who inhabited the Sierra foothills. The

Chaw'se Regional Indian Museum profiles their vibrant culture and features a reconstructed native village replete with bark tepees, a granary, roundhouse (or *hun'ge*), and a Miwok ball field.

Continue north on Pine Grove–Volcano Rd to the Y-junction with Pioneer-Volcano Rd (be wary of merging traffic). Proceed into:

11. **Volcano,** a remote hamlet nestled in a deep, crater-like setting. Little remains to remind visitors that Volcano was once sinfully sybaritic, or that in its gold rush heyday it boasted the state's first observatory, lending library, literary and debating societies, and community theater. Performances by Volcano Pioneers Community Theater Group at the **Cobblestone Theater** (tel 209/296-4696), a former assay office on Main St, are a far cry from Volcano's once bawdy nightlife.

Take a Break

The place to eat hereabouts is the **St George Hotel,** 16104 Pine Grove–Volcano Rd (tel 209/296-4458), an 1864 structure on the National Register of Historic Places, with maple vines clambering up the outside walls. Inexpensive American fare, including a special Sunday chicken lunch, are served in the genteel dining room.

In Volcano, Pioneer-Volcano Rd swings right and becomes Ram's Horn Grade. In springtime, follow Ram's Horn north 3 miles to the junction of Shake Ridge Rd and:

12. **Daffodil Hill,** where the McLaughlin family has been planting daffodils—over 300,000 at current count—for over 140 years. Mid-March to mid-April, the forested hillside explodes in a stunning floral display.

Return via Volcano and Pine Grove to Jackson. Turn left on CA 49 and proceed south on the meandering road for 16 miles to:

13. **Mokelumne Hill,** another once-bawdy town where gold claims were limited to 16 square feet because the local hills were so rich. Fires ravaged Mokelumne in 1854, 1864, and 1874, but the now sleepy village still has several venerable Victorian structures.

Back on CA 49, the road straightens out for most of the 7 miles south to the T-junction with CA 12. Turn left and continue on CA 49 1 mile to:

14. **San Andreas,** named for the mission church that served the Mexicans who founded the town in 1848. The charming classical revival buildings date

from 1858, after a fire destroyed the town; the Queen Anne homes sprang up during the 1893–1905 boom, when San Andreas thrived as a copper-producing town. The handsome brick **County Courthouse,** 30 N Main St, has been immaculately restored and now houses the **Calaveras County Museum** (tel 209/754-6513), which provides a pamphlet that describes a self-guided historic walking tour of the town. The museum pays deference to the Miwok Indians. It also features re-creations of a miner's cabin and general store. The gentleman bandit Black Bart (alias Charles Bolton) was tried and sentenced here in 1883; he robbed gold from 28 Wells Fargo stagecoaches between 1875 and 1883.

Continue south on CA 49 and turn left after 1 mile onto Mountain Ranch Rd (opposite the law offices of Airola & Airola). After 8 miles, turn right onto Michel Rd to Cave City Rd. Turn left and continue as the road descends to:

15. **California Caverns** (tel 209/736-2708), within whose bowels noted 19th-century naturalist John Muir recorded "chamber after chamber more and more magnificent, all a-glitter like a glacier cave with icicle-like stalactites and stalagmites combining in forms of indescribable beauty." The caverns first opened to the public in 1850 and a small resort town, Cave City, grew around the small inconspicuous entrance, which gives no hint of the grandeur of the many crystal chambers within. The one-hour "Trail of Lights" tour gives no indication, either, of the size of the caverns, which have not yet been fully explored. Adventurous souls can take a Wild Expedition tour to reach underground lakes.

Return to CA 49 and continue south 11 miles to:

16. **Angels Camp,** whose name is derived from commercial, not spiritual, reasons—Henry Angel was the first storekeeper. The town began life in 1849 as a gold rush boomtown and later became a hardrock gold mining capital. Mark Twain worked the diggings briefly from 1864 to 1865 and heard the tale that inspired his first successful short story, "The Celebrated Jumping Frog of Calaveras County." The annual Jumping Frog Jubilee—in which frogs compete over three measured hops for a $1,500 purse for the winner's owner—is held the 3rd weekend in May in the Frogtown fairgrounds south of town. A short hop west of town is the **Angels Camp Museum,** 753 S Main St (tel 209/736-2963), displaying gold rush artifacts and horse-drawn wagons.

Turn left onto CA 4 (Vallecito Rd) at the south end of town, head east 10 miles, and take the "Business District" turn-off to the left into historic:

17. **Murphys,** an attractive one-street former gold rush town shaded by cottonwoods, sycamores, and elms, and known to locals as "Queen of the Sierras." Murphys is named for two Irish brothers who founded the town in 1848. On Main St, the iron-shuttered **Old Timers Museum** (tel 209/728-3679) houses such curiosities as a smithy that still clangs out showers of sparks. The **Black Bart Playhouse** (tel 209/728-3675) has weekend performances in April and November. Black Bart, Ulysses S Grant, Mark Twain, and William Randholph Hearst were among the famous lodgers at the 1856 **Murphys Hotel.** The hostelry once had a reputation for Wild West violence. Its atmospheric bar has many tales to tell—the bullet holes in the doors are real—and is *the* place to enjoy a cool beer from the Murphy

---

Take a Break

The historic **Murphys Hotel Restaurant,** Main St (tel 209/728-3444), serves liver and onions and other steadfast meat-based American fare, alongside pastas, cioppino, pork dijonnaise, and seafood fettuccine.

Creek Brewing Company.

Opposite the Murphys Hotel is the narrow entrance to Sheep Ranch Rd. Turn right and follow the bumpy road uphill 1 mile to:

18. **Mercer Caverns,** 1665 Sheep Ranch Rd (tel 209/728-2101), exhibiting an enormous variety of bizarre and exotic limestone formations within its 10 subterranean caverns. Miwok Indians used to bury their dead inside the chilly caves, which Mother Nature maintains at a steady 55°F.

Back in Murphys, return to CA 4 and continue east, following the snaking road uphill for 14 miles through stately pine to:

19. **Calaveras Big Tree State Park** (tel 209/795-2334), at an elevation of between 4,000 and 5,000 feet, and well worth the detour. The park protects two magnificent groves of giant sequoias, which grow only on the western slopes of the Sierra Nevada. The North Grove offers an easy mile-long loop trail; the larger South Grove, 9 miles south, is easily seen on the Big Trees Creek self-guided loop. A longer Lava Bluffs Trail leads to ancient lava formations. There are also deep canyons for exploring, riverside beaches for picnicking, guided hikes, fishing, and winter snow-shoeing and cross-country skiing.

Return via Murphys on CA 4 to Parrotts Ferry Rd (County Rd E-18). Turn left and proceed south 1½ miles to:

20. **Moaning Caverns,** 5350 Moaning Cave Rd (209/736-2708), where a 100-foot spiral staircase leads down to the floor of a natural limestone cavern, the deepest in the state and large enough to hold the Statue of Liberty. Native Americans held the caves in awe because of the moans that emanated from the entrance. Alas, the staircase altered the acoustics, and the caves no longer moan. The oldest human remains ever found in America were discovered here, preserved in the mineral deposits (they date back more than 13,000 years).

    Continue on Parrotts Ferry Rd as it winds south through the ravine of the Stanislaus River to:

21. **Columbia State Historic Park** (tel 209/532-4301), where you recall a time when the "Gem of the Southern Mines" was the state's second-largest city. Gone are the bordellos and 159 gambling halls where dirty, bearded miners rubbed shoulders with bankers and ladies of the night. But the whole 12-square-block "downtown" has been restored as an outdoor living-history museum where shop clerks wear period costumes, a blacksmith forges tools, and a saloon with swing doors still serves sarsaparilla. You can also take a bumpy, 15-minute ride in an authentic stagecoach.

    "Talking buttons" on building exteriors provide taped information for a self-guided tour. Highlights include California's oldest barbershop (dating back to 1865), an early dentist's office, and the **Livery Stable,** at Fulton St and Broadway, with displays of old-time wagons. Engine Co No 1 firehouse, on State St, houses the restored, fancifully decorated *Papeete* fire pumper acquired in 1859. The **Columbia Gazette & Printing Museum,** housed in a replica of the original 1855 building, has exhibits on printing and newspaper life in early California. The **Miwok Heritage Museum,** 11175

Take a Break

Crisp linens, high-back chairs, and period decor add to the pleasure of eating at the **City Hotel Dining Room,** Main St (tel 209/532-1479). The moderately priced French cuisine is delicious—typical treats include angel-hair pasta, roast leg of lamb, and duck breast with black fig and apple-raisin sauce.

Damin Rd (tel 209/984-4244), displays artifacts in a cedar bark lodge. "Mellerdramers" by the Columbia Actors' Repertory are still offered at the **Fallon House Theatre** (tel 209/532-4644) in the restored **Fallon Hotel** on Washington St. Finally, don't leave town before visiting the **Nelson Candy Kitchen,** on Main St, to purchase hand-dipped chocolates made using gold rush–era recipes. The town is open daily 9am–5pm.

    Continue south on Parrott's Ferry Rd until reaching the T-junction with CA 49. Turn left and proceed 2 miles to:

22. **Sonora,** founded by Mexican miners who were soon driven out by greedy gringo miners. Sonora's Big Bonanza was the richest pocket mine in the Mother Lode, and the town was known as "Queen of the Southern Mines." The town continues to prosper thanks to its impressive, well-preserved Victorian homes and a tranquility that attracts tourists and retirees, young and old. Washington St, the main street, has 19th-century mansions as well as the 1859 **St James Episcopal Church.** Old West paintings and local history exhibits are on display at the **Tuolumne County Museum & History Center,** 158 W Bradford Ave (tel 209/532-1317), housed in the town's 1857 jail. The **Tuolumne County Courthouse,** on W Yaney St, is an intriguing amalgam of marble, green sandstone, and yellow brick; it has a copper door and a Byzantine clock tower.

    Turn right at the Bank of America in downtown Sonora to continue on CA 49, which after 2 miles merges with CA 108. Turn left at the T-junction and continue 1½ miles south to 5th Ave. Turn left and after ½ mile enter:

23. **Railtown 1897 State Historic Park** (tel 209/984-3953), which preserves the locomotives and carriages of the Sierra Railway Company in the old Sierra Railway Depot. Trains began operating from Jamestown in 1897, hauling passengers and freight through the Mother Lode. The 23-acre, open-air museum includes the West's only operating steam roundhouse. During summer weekends, board the 80-year-old steam-powered *Mother Lode Cannon* for excursions through the Sierra foothills.

    Return along 5th Ave to Willow St. Turn left and follow Willow to Main St, in the heart of downtown:

24. **Jamestown,** which, beloved by Hollywood, has starred in such films and TV shows as *High Noon, Lassie, The Lone Ranger, Butch Cassidy and the Sundance Kid,* and *Little House on the Prairie.* The ¼-mile-long Main St features shops, galleries, and Gold Rush buildings turned into cozy bed-and-breakfast inns. Kids can pan for fake gold in the horse trough outside the livery stable at 18170 Main St; adults can sign up with **Gold Prospecting Expeditions** (tel 209/984-4653) and go panning for the real thing.

    The end of Main St merges with CA 49 announcing the end of your tour.

Driving the State

Start	Santa Monica
Finish	Tijuana
Distance	Approximately 190 miles
Time	2–3 days
Highlights	Little beach towns, sophisticated seaside resorts, sea life parks and museums, historic buildings, yacht marinas, trend-setting restaurants and luxurious hotels

Take a Break

On the corner of Main and Marine Sts is **Schatzi on Main** (tel 310/399-4800), an appealing, casual restaurant owned by Arnold Schwarzenegger and Maria Shriver, with an imaginative menu of light entrees. "The Terminator" himself often stops by.

This meandering route winds through some of southern California's most well-known towns and cities, with the Pacific Ocean serving as a backdrop. Although the area certainly has its share of museums, nature is the main highlight of this scenic drive, which focuses on seaside communities with wide sandy beaches, where you'll find tanned, buffed bodies engaged in volleyball games and wet-suited surfers poised to catch that perfect wave. In certain places, restrictions of nature or development take the tour a mile or more away from the surging surf, but it always manages to wander back toward the ocean.

For additional information on accommodations, restaurants, and attractions in the region covered by the tour, look under specific cities in the listings portion of this book.

Santa Monica may be reached from the Los Angeles area by traveling west on US 10 (the Santa Monica Fwy) to the Main St exit. If at any time on this trip you zigzag off the prescribed route, it's easy to find your way back if you remember that as you go south the ocean will always be on your right.

1. **Santa Monica** is worth a stop even before you begin your drive. As you exit US 10 onto Main St, turn right and proceed 1 block to Colorado Ave, then turn left and the famed **Santa Monica Pier** is directly in front of you. At the pier, you can take a look at the beautifully restored carousel with its 46 galloping horses. Some come here to fish or for the bumper cars, shooting gallery, and arcade games. Back on Main St, proceed south and turn right on Beach St, continuing 2 blocks to Ocean Ave, a palm-lined thoroughfare along the beach.

   At Hollister Ave, Ocean Ave changes its name to Barnard, which curves to the right, bringing you back to Main St.

   From Schatzi on Main, continue south on Main St 1 block to:

2. **Venice,** a funky beach town with ramshackle buildings (many being restored) supported by grandiose Doric columns. These are remnants of a turn-of-the-century city with canals, meant to mimic its Italian namesake. Today Venice is a web of little one-way streets, hardly more than alleys. From Main St, turn right on Windward Ave, find a place to park, and you'll be set for a stroll on the **Venice Boardwalk** with **Muscle Beach** and its sidewalk musicians, bikini-clad rollerbladers, and bodybuilders.

   Leave the Venice area on any small street heading away from the ocean, turn right on to Pacific Ave, and you're headed for:

3. **Marina del Rey,** the world's largest manmade small craft harbor. Turn left onto Washington St, proceed 3 blocks, then go right on Via Marina one short block, then left on Admiralty Way. This takes you through the heart of the marina area, full of trendy restaurants, ritzy hotels, and gorgeous yachts.

   For a stop, turn right on Mindanao Way 1 block to:

4. **Burton W Chace County Park,** a pleasant grassy area for boat watching. Backtrack to Admiralty Way, turn right 1 block, and you'll find that Admiralty dead-ends into Fiji Way.

   Turn left onto Fiji Way and proceed ½ block to Lincoln Blvd. Follow Lincoln for ½ mile to Jefferson Blvd, turn right onto Jefferson, then angle left onto Culver Blvd and you'll be in Playa del Rey, yet another funky little beach town. At Vista del Mar, angle left 2 blocks through town to parallel Dockweiler State Beach. Within 3 miles you'll come to:

5. **Manhattan Beach,** where Vista del Mar changes names to Highland Ave, which soon becomes Manhattan Beach Blvd. Narrow streets near the ocean provide limited parking, and if you're here on a

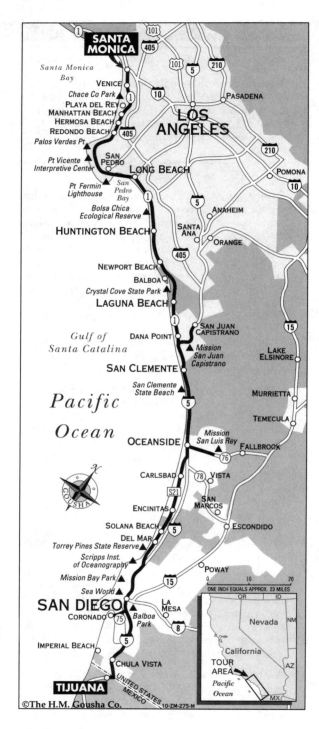

sunny summer weekend, count on creeping along at about 5 miles an hour. Look to the right as you cross Manhattan Beach Blvd to see the **Manhattan**

Beach Pier, where you can stroll and catch the breezes.

Take Manhattan Beach Blvd a mile or so until it becomes Hermosa Ave, and you're in Hermosa Beach, following a wide boulevard with typical beach houses. Crossing Herondo St, Hermosa Ave becomes Harbor Dr, and you're now in:

6. **Redondo Beach,** where, at the corner of Harbor Dr and Marina Way, the Southern California Edison building is decorated with a marvelous whale mural. On the right, luxury yachts snuggle into King Harbor, an upscale private marina. Within blocks Harbor Dr almost turns back on itself, and becomes Pacific Ave for 1 short block. At Catalina Ave, turn right and follow Catalina to Torrance Ave. You can park in the area and explore the shops and restaurants on the **Redondo Pier.** For dramatic views of wave-washed beaches and the ocean, angle left off of Torrance onto Esplanade. This cliffside road winds past beautiful upscale homes, leads into Paseo de la Playa, then connects with Palos Verdes Blvd S, taking you out onto the:

7. **Palos Verdes Peninsula,** one of Southern California's loveliest residential areas, strikingly different from the crowded little beach towns you've just inched through. The Peninsula affords sweeping ocean vistas and estate-like homes with red Spanish-tile roofs.

Palos Verdes Blvd becomes Palos Verdes Dr, which takes you for about 4 miles along the bluffs. On the right, just past Hawthorne Blvd you come to the:

8. **Point Vicente Interpretive Center,** where you can park in the lot to enjoy coastline views, and look at exhibits on the area's geology and videos on Pacific Gray whales. Behind the center, a little trail lined with cypress and palos verdes trees has scattered picnic tables where you can scan the sea for a glimpse of the area's famous sea mammals. Whale-watching season extends from December 1 to April 30.

Return to Palos Verdes Dr. About 2 miles south of Point Vicente you come to:

9. **Wayfarer's Chapel,** designed by Lloyd Wright, son of Frank Lloyd Wright. The chapel is dramatically constructed of stone and glass, with the same plants flourishing inside that grow beyond the transparent walls.

Back on Palos Verdes Dr, through an area called Portuguese Bend, signs warn of "earth movement." The roller-coaster road verifies that the terrain is subject to occasional landslides triggered by the infamous earthquake faults in most of Southern California.

Continue south on Palos Verdes Dr 1½ miles where the road splits, and veer right on 25th St. Proceed 1 mile to Western Ave, turn right onto Western, then left onto Paseo Del Mar within 1 mile. This brings you to:

10. **Point Fermin Lighthouse and the Cabrillo Marine Museum** in San Pedro. This 1800s clapboard structure topped with a beacon is now a great place for whale-watching. The **Cabrillo Marine Museum,** 3720 Stephen White Dr, has a shark tank and three dozen huge aquariums housing denizens of the deep.

Leaving the Marine Museum, turn right onto Pacific Ave, and you'll have the opportunity to turn right onto any number of small side streets that will take you to:

11. **The Los Angeles Harbor,** the busiest commercial port on the West Coast. Before getting on the bridge, you can detour to any close-to-the water streets to take a look at the container ships, tankers, and luxury liners. As you explore, at the bottom of 6th St, you'll come to:

12. **Ports O'Call Village,** a little enclave of boutiques and restaurants that looks like an 1800s port town.

This can be a confusing area, so your best bet is to watch for signs for the Vincent Thomas Bridge, and green signs that indicate CA 47 and Terminal Island, which take you directly onto the:

13. **Vincent Thomas Bridge,** a graceful 6,060-foot-long suspension structure 185 feet above the shipping channel and built in 1963. There is no toll as you proceed toward Long Beach. Once you've crossed the bridge, you can start looking for signs that say:

14. *Queen Mary,* **Long Beach Harbor** (tel 310/435-3511), which direct you to the famous liner that became permanently moored here at Pier J in 1964. The elegant *Queen* is a fascinating remnant of the golden age of cruising when well-to-do families often traveled with maids. Take a guided tour to see how the ship looked during World War II when it became a troop transport. The liner is now a first-class hotel.

Leave the Queen Mary the way you entered, cross the Queensway Bridge, and you'll be on Shoreline Dr entering:

15. **Long Beach,** once a rowdy navy town with a slightly unsavory image. As you drive along Ocean Ave you'll find that it's now a pleasant place with landmark historic buildings amicably co-existing with sleek skyscrapers and modern edifices. As you follow along Ocean Ave, take the time to admire the whale mural by the famous artist Weiland on the

Convention Center's walls. **Bluff Park,** along Ocean Blvd, has benches for views of passing ships. Four-mile-long **Belmont Shore** is the city's most attractive beach area with boutiques, bookstores, and restaurants.

Within about 3 miles you'll come to:

16. **Naples,** a canal-crossed section in south Long Beach, best seen via **Gondola Getaway,** 5437 E Ocean Blvd. Gondoliers in stripe shirts serenade you while they pole authentic Italian gondolas past expensive homes.

Leaving Gondola Getaway, backtrack about 6 blocks on Ocean Blvd to Livingston, and bear right onto Livingston. Within about 2 miles, turn right (south) onto CA 1 (Pacific Coast Hwy). You'll stay on CA 1 past the marshy Bolsa Chica Ecological Reserve on the right. You'll have sight of an unbroken expanse of silvery sand for about 8 miles, until you come to:

17. **Huntington Beach,** one of the largest beach towns in the area, and Huntington State Beach, famed for its reliable waves and considered by many to be the surfing capital of the world.

If you're ready for a meal, continue on to the Huntington Beach Pier.

Back on CA 1, head south and in 5 minutes you'll be in:

18. **Newport Beach,** a series of manmade islands and attractive neighborhoods. As you enter town you can stop at **Balboa Marina** to hop aboard the *Isla Mujeres* for a close-up look at gorgeous waterside homes.

Follow the signs on CA 1 to **Balboa Island,** the most famous of the little islands that dot a large small-craft harbor. You'll see small, expensive cottages with private boats moored at their front doors. Take the three-car ferry to the **Balboa Peninsula** and the "Fun Zone," a carnival-like strip along the bay with a ferris wheel and arcade games. It surrounds the landmark Victorian **Pavilion** (tel 714/675-9444), built in 1906 as a bathhouse and now the terminal for Catalina Island Passenger Service boats, harbor cruises, and whale-watching trips.

Back on CA 1 heading south, follow **Crystal Cove State Park** on your right for about 8 miles to:

19. **Laguna Beach,** a renowned art colony. Get off traffic-clogged CA 1 as soon as possible, park your car, and then explore the community's wonderful galleries and shops, such as **Pottery Shack,** 1212 S Coast Hwy (CA 1), an open-air market with gourmet foods and tableware for sale, and **Fahrenheit 451,** 540 S Coast Hwy, an intellectually stimulating bookstore with unusual titles. (Note that in Laguna

Beach, CA 1 is called "Coast Highway" on signs). At **Heisler Park,** take a pleasant stroll among fragrant roses along bluffs overlooking the ocean.

Take a Break

If you blink, you might pass **242 Cafe,** 242 N Coast Hwy (tel 714/494-2444), a cozy place right on the highway, which looks more like a deli than a restaurant. There's often a line of locals waiting to get in to sample the offerings on the health-conscious menu of salads, sandwiches, and pastries.

Exceptional hotels and inns make this area an ideal first-night stop. By continuing on CA 1 a couple of miles south to Ritz-Carlton Dr, then turning right, you can follow signs to the luxurious:

20. **Ritz-Carlton Laguna Niguel,** 33533 Ritz-Carlton Dr (tel 714/240-2000), which is actually in the town of Dana Point. This hotel exudes elegance, although it's perfectly all right to check in wearing shorts and T-shirts. Like a classic Mediterranean villa, it sits on a 150-foot bluff with a 180-degree view of the sea. If you wander down the hill to the hotel's lovely beach, a tram will be waiting so you don't have to endure the uphill climb. Even if you're not staying here, time your visit for afternoon tea, a civilized custom executed to perfection at this famous hostelry.

    Leave the Ritz-Carlton and head back to CA 1 going south where within 2 miles you'll come to:

21. **Dana Point,** named for author Richard Henry Dana, who visited the area in 1835 and wrote the novel *Two Years Before the Mast.* The town recalls his trip with a full-size replica of his schooner, *The Pilgrim,* at anchor in Dana Cove. **Dana Island** has picnic tables, walking paths, shops, and fishing at Dana Wharf.

    Get back on CA 1 and continue south about 3 miles to Del Obispo St. Turn left, proceed about 4 miles, turn left on Camino Capistrano St and within 2 blocks you'll reach:

22. **Mission San Juan Capistrano** (tel 714/248-2049), in the town the swallows flock back to each March. Although the 1812 earthquake destroyed much of this magnificent mission, its restoration is in progress. Its Serra Chapel (1777) and exhibits representing 18th-century mission life are part of a self-guided tour.

    Backtrack to CA 1 which becomes Camino Real, and continue south about 5 miles to:

23. **San Clemente,** famous as Richard Nixon's Western White House, although the town today bears little trace of the controversial president. You can take a look at **Casa Romantica,** the first home built in the area, overlooking the **San Clemente Pier.** At **San Clemente State Beach,** for $6 per car, you can drive to a pleasant wooded area, opening onto the sand, for a picnic and a swim.

    In San Clemente, CA 1 and Camino Real pretty much disappear, and your only option is to join up with US 5 (San Diego Fwy) for the first freeway driving on this trip. The yellow "fleeing family" signs you see note the state's illegal immigrant situation, warning motorists that Mexican nationals who may have come this far by vehicle, may now jump out and run through traffic as they try to evade Immigration and Naturalization officers at the checkpoint ahead.

    The two huge mounds on the right along the ocean are part of the San Onofre Nuclear Power Plant. About 5 miles down the freeway, exit on Mission Ave (CA 76) and turn left (inland) about 4½ miles to:

24. **Mission San Luis Rey de Francia** (tel 916/757-3651), one of the best-preserved missions established by Father Serra along the coast. There's a shady picnic area and a small museum.

    Retrace your steps on Mission Ave, cross over US 5 and where Mission dead-ends into the beach you'll find yourself at Oceanside Pier, where the waves will be dotted with surfers if the surf's up.

    Backtrack to Mission Ave, and turn right (south) onto Hill St (S21) to:

25. **Carlsbad,** where S21 becomes a wide four-lane road next to a great beach for swimming. Snack stands are conveniently available. Follow S21 about 5 miles south to:

26. **Encinitas,** where the golden Middle-Eastern-looking domes you see on the right belong to the **Self Realization Fellowship.** This monastic retreat belonging to an East Indian religious sect was built in the 1920s. Continue south on S21 another mile or so to:

27. **San Elijo Lagoon,** which provides a safe, marshy habitat for dozens of species of migrating birds, some of which you can glimpse from on-site walking trails.

    Follow S21 along the ocean to:

28. **Solana Beach,** with numerous restaurants and fuel stations. At the seaside end of Lomas Santa Fe Dr, **Fletcher Cove** shelters a good, accessible swimming beach beneath towering cliffs.

    Continue south on S21 about 2 miles to:

29. **Del Mar** and its famous race track, which you can see on the left from S21. The track was a hangout for the cream of Hollywood glitterati during the 1930s. Today Del Mar has luxury hotels, upscale boutiques, and a delightful beach. You can park your car at the old Del Mar train station (where surfers with boards are regular passengers) and take a walk along breezy ocean bluffs.

Back on S21, within 4 miles you'll find you're in the middle of:

30. **Torrey Pines State Reserve,** which protects the world's rarest pine, the gnarled, knotted Torrey Pine. You may want to allow a morning or afternoon to explore the trails in this wild, lovely place with stunning ocean views.

From here on into **San Diego** you can follow any of the roads marked "Scenic Drive," and enjoy what you see. As you leave the reserve, S21 veers to the left, and North Torrey Pines Rd angles to the right. Follow North Torrey Pines Rd for about a mile until you come to La Jolla Shores Dr (not La Jolla Village Dr) on the right. Follow La Jolla Shores Dr and in about a mile signs will direct you to the:

31. **Stephen Birch Aquarium-Museum** (tel 619/534-3474), part of the Scripps Institution of Oceanography. Mammoth wall-size aquariums house such favorites as the giant octopus and toothy moray eels. Outside, a man-made tidepool hides spiny sea urchins, starfish, anemones, and sea cucumbers. You can take a simulated submersible ride in the DSV Deep Diver to see strange creatures of the ocean's abysses.

Continue on La Jolla Shores Dr which connects back up with Torrey Pines Rd within about a mile and a half. Follow Torrey Pines Rd to Prospect Place and turn right about 6 blocks to:

32. **La Jolla Village,** a special shopping-dining area of La Jolla. Park wherever you can as walking is the only way to see this charming little area successfully. Stop at **John Cole's Book Shop** with its rare, out-of-print collection and current titles. Everyone spends time at **The Cove,** popular since pirates used it to hide their stash. The small, sandy crescent is ringed with cliffs that continue under water, forming the nooks and crannies of the **San Diego–La Jolla Underwater Park,** a favorite of snorkelers and scuba divers. The grassy park above The Cove is a scenic spot for picnics.

When you're ready to leave, inch through the traffic on Prospect Place for less than a mile where it connects with La Jolla Blvd. Continue through Pacific Beach where you turn left on Garnet Ave and proceed about 8 blocks to Ingraham St. Go right onto Ingraham and within minutes you'll be in:

33. **Mission Bay Park,** San Diego's great aquatic playground. Once an odoriferous tidal basin, it now has almost 30 miles of beaches and quiet lagoons that attract swimmers, windsurfers, water skiers, cyclists, and other sports-minded sorts. Explore at your leisure, being sure not to miss:

34. **Sea World,** 1720 S Shores Rd (tel 619/226-3901), accessible by following signs directing you from Ingraham St. It is home to the world-famous killer whale, Shamu, and baby Shamu, whose aquatic antics are broadcast onto a giant screen in Shamu Stadium. Bottlenose dolphins, pilot whales, otters, and others perform in regularly scheduled shows. The aquariums and animal exhibits are always open for between-show visits.

Leave Sea World via Mission Bay Dr, cross the San Diego River and you see freeway entrance signs for US 8 E. Stay on US 8 E for just over a mile, then proceed to US 5 S. In about 2½ miles, exit at Front St/2nd Ave, continue straight onto 2nd Ave, turn right on 4th St, and continue 7 blocks to:

35. **Horton Plaza** (tel 619/238-1596), a mega-shopping center with classy boutiques and four major department stores. It is part of a recently-renewed downtown San Diego, and features entertainment and cultural exhibits. Adjacent is the **Gaslamp Quarter,** bounded by Broadway and Waterfront, and 4th and 5th Sts. This historic area encompasses 16 blocks of 19th-century buildings, now restored to house offices, restaurants, and shops.

You can leave downtown via 5th St (it's one-way in the direction you want to go), and proceed to Broadway where you'll turn left onto 12th Ave which becomes Park Blvd, taking you directly to:

36. **Balboa Park** (tel 619/235-1100), San Diego's crown jewel, with one of the greatest collections of galleries and museums in the state. The **San Diego Museum of Art,** 1450 El Prado (tel 619/232-7931), has French Impressionist paintings, Italian Renaissance art, and Asian works among its permanent collections. American and European paintings are represented at the **Timken Gallery,** 1500 El Prado (tel 619/239-5548). **Reuben H Fleet Space Theater and Science Center,** 1875 El Prado (tel 619/238-1233), has an Omnimax film theater, a Laserium, and a science center with hands-on learning exhibits. Half a dozen other museums make Balboa Park definitely worth a day's visit. Also within Balboa Park is the:

37. **San Diego Zoo,** 2920 Zoo Dr (tel 619/234-3153), considered one of the finest zoos in the world. San

Diego's climate makes it possible to keep an enormous variety of animals—including rare and exotic species—outdoors all year long; they're housed in barless enclosures resembling their natural habitats.

The San Diego area is a wonderful spot for an overnight stop because it has so much to offer. Hotels range from sleek high-rises and luxury resorts to historic dowagers to small budget inns.

To reach an area of very special hotels and resorts, backtrack to US 5 S, and follow signs to CA 75 and:

38. **Coronado,** a peninsula reached via a graceful bridge across San Diego Bay. On its southern end, Coronado is attached to the mainland by a narrow strip of sand called the Silver Strand, an exclusive enclave since the late 1800s. The elegant Victorian **Hotel Del Coronado,** 1500 Orange Ave (tel 619/522-8000), built in 1888, has tall cupolas, turrets, and gingerbread trim.

Leaving the hotel, turn left onto Orange Ave, which becomes Silver Strand Blvd in less than a mile, and continue past the US Naval Amphibious Base, a total of about 7 miles to:

39. **Loews Coronado Bay Resort,** 4000 Coronado Bay Rd (tel 619/424-4000), a sleek, new recreational accommodation that offers posh, casual elegance and views of Pacific sunsets on one side and the sparkling lights of San Diego on the other. It has its own 80-slip yacht marina.

If you can bear to leave, exit the resort onto Silver Strand Blvd (CA 75), turn left, and within 10 minutes you'll hook up with US 5 (San Diego Fwy). Follow it for another 10 minutes and you're at the Mexican border.

40. **Tijuana** is far from the drowsy, dusty little border town it once was, when all you could do was buy trinkets and liquor, and bargain for leather goods and ladies of the evening. The town has cleaned up its act and now has first-class hotels, restaurants, and attractions. It's best to park your car on the American side and walk across the border, avoiding the necessity to buy Mexican auto insurance. Within walking distance is **Mexitlan,** with scale models of Mexican sculptures, temples, monuments, and other architectural works. You'll also see handiwork of some of Mexico's master craftsmen. You'll need a taxi to get over to the **Tijuana Cultural Center, Paseo de los Héroes,** unmistakable on the city's low-rise skyline because of the globular shape of its Omnimax film theater. Fast-paced jai alai is played nightly in the **Caliente Fronton Palacio,** 1578 Avenida Revolucion at Calle 7. Traditional bullfights are held in two local rings each Sunday from May to September.

An alternative to driving to Tijuana is the Tijuana Trolley, a light-rail system with frequent daily runs from downtown San Diego to the border.

You can be back in the Los Angeles area within 2½ hours if you pick your times carefully, avoiding a drive between 7 and 9:30am and between 3:30 and 7pm. Just hop back on US 5 and head north.

California Listings

Albion

See also Elk, Little River, Mendocino

One of the original North Coast mill towns, but its formerly bustling lumber and fishing operations have been replaced by tourism as travelers have been attracted to the coastal hills that overlook the Albion River and the ocean.

INN 🏨

≣≣≣≣ Albion River Inn
3790 CA 1, PO Box 100, 95410; tel 707/937-1919 or toll free 800/479-7944. 10 acres. Perched on bluffs above the Mendocino coast, with sweeping lawns bordered by flowers. Llama ranch across the street. **Rooms:** 16 rms; 4 cottages/villas. CI 3pm/CO noon. No smoking. All rooms overlook Albion Cove and have classy decor, huge bathrooms, stone fireplaces, and fabulous wooden furniture. **Amenities:** 🛎 ⌚ 🖥 Bathrobes. No A/C or TV. Some units w/terraces, all w/fireplaces, some w/whirlpools. Complimentary wine and binoculars in room. **Services:** ✗ ↵ Masseur, babysitting. **Facilities:** ⅙ 1 restaurant (bkfst and dinner only; see "Restaurants" below), 1 bar (w/entertainment). Great restaurant. Rates include an elaborate, ample breakfast. Good walking trails to beaches and bluffs. **Rates (BB):** $160 S or D; $165–$250 cottage/villa. Extra person $20. Children under age 6 stay free. Min stay wknds. Parking: Outdoor, free. MC, V.

RESTAURANT 🍴

Albion River Inn
3790 CA 1; tel 707/937-1919. 7 mi S of Mendocino. **Californian/Southwestern.** Offers one of the best ocean views on the Pacific coast and overlooks a manicured, flower-fringed lawn that leads to Albion Cove. Work of famous photographers is displayed on walls. Menu includes local fish, Pacific Rim bouillabaisse, roasted garlic, caesar salad, breast of Muscovy duck, pasta. The steamed mussel appetizer alone is worth the trip. Bar offers over 250 wines and 24 scotch whiskies. Excellent service. **FYI:** Reservations recommended. Piano. Beer and wine only. **Open:** Daily 5–10pm. **Prices:** Main courses $11–$19. AE, MC, V. 🛋 ⛰ ⅙

Anaheim

Perhaps the West's epicenter of family entertainment, Anaheim is adjacent to Knott's Berry Farm and Movieland Wax Museum and is home of the granddaddy of all theme parks, Disneyland. Once a planned agricultural community of German immigrants, the city is now the model of Southern California suburban sprawl. **Information:** Anaheim Area Convention & Visitors Bureau, 800 W Katella Ave, Anaheim 92802 (tel 714/999-8999).

HOTELS 🏨

UNRATED Anaheim Conestoga Hotel
1240 S Walnut St, 92802; tel 714/535-0300 or toll free 800/824-5459; fax 714/491-8953. Harbor Blvd exit off I-5. With a turn-of-the-century Victorian/Gold Rush theme, this hotel has a charm that's absent from other area lodgings. Currently very run-down, but the new owners are doing a major renovation. **Rooms:** 254 rms and stes. CI 3pm/CO 11am. Nonsmoking rms avail. Accommodations are small and some furnishings show wear. The best rooms are on the top floors. **Amenities:** 🛎 ⌚ 🖥 A/C, cable TV. **Services:** ✗ 🚐 △ ↵ Car-rental desk, babysitting. Shuttle to Disneyland. **Facilities:** 🏊 🈯 2 restaurants, 2 bars (1 w/entertainment), games rm, whirlpool, washer/dryer. Use of 8 lighted tennis courts next door for a fee. **Rates:** Peak (May 24–Sept 5) $79–$119 S or D; $175–$255 ste. Extra person $10. Children under age 18 stay free. Lower rates off-season. Parking: Outdoor, free. AE, CB, DC, DISC, JCB, MC, V.

≣≣≣≣ Anaheim Hilton & Towers
777 Convention Way, 92802; tel 714/750-4321 or toll free 800/445-8667, 800/233-6904 in the US, 800/433-9923 in Canada; fax 714/740-4737. Harbor Blvd S exit off I-5. This business-oriented hotel is one of the better members of the Hilton chain, with well-kept rooms, attentive service, and an abundance of facilities. The largest hotel in the Disneyland/Convention Center area, it bustles with activity most of the time. The three-story atrium lobby features a dramatic marble fountain and reflection pool. **Rooms:** 1,576 rms and stes. Executive level. CI 3pm/CO noon. Nonsmoking rms avail. Redecorated in 1996, rooms sport a bright, airy, and casual

California-resort look. **Amenities:** 🛅 🅰 🖪 🍽 A/C, cable TV w/movies, dataport, voice mail. Some units w/terraces. Coffeemakers in some rooms. **Services:** ✕ 🛏 VP 🚗 🛍 ⤴ 🛎 Car-rental desk, social director, masseur, children's program, babysitting. Shuttle to Disneyland, multilingual staff, retail shopping area with boutiques, art gallery, duty-free shop, foreign-currency exchange, and automatic-teller machine. **Facilities:** 🎣 🏌 ⌷6000⌷ 🖥 ♿ 4 restaurants (see "Restaurants" below), 4 bars (1 w/entertainment), basketball, games rm, sauna, steam rm, whirlpool, beauty salon. Golf putting green and practice center, basketball court, and state-of-the-art sports and fitness center. **Rates:** $195–$275 S; $220–$300 D; $600–$1075 ste. Extra person $25. Children under age 18 stay free. Parking: Indoor, $6/day. AE, CB, DC, DISC, EC, JCB, MC, V.

≣≣≣≣ Anaheim Marriott Hotel
700 W Convention Way, 92802; tel 714/750-8000 or toll free 800/228-9290; fax 714/750-9100. Katella Ave exit off I-5. Outstanding service and attention to detail make this one of the best hotels in the Marriott chain and a first choice for businesspeople attending functions at the adjacent Anaheim Convention Center. Recently renovated, public areas center around a beautifully landscaped indoor/outdoor swimming pool surrounded by a patio for warm-weather dining. **Rooms:** 1,033 rms and stes. Executive level. CI 4pm/CO noon. Nonsmoking rms avail. Rooms on higher floors have nice views in good weather. **Amenities:** 🛅 🅰 🍽 A/C, cable TV w/movies, dataport, voice mail, in-rm safe. Some units w/minibars, some w/terraces. Coffeemakers, refrigerators, and microwaves available on request. **Services:** ✕ 🛏 VP 🚗 🛍 ⤴ 🛎 Twice-daily maid svce, car-rental desk, children's program, babysitting. **Facilities:** 🎣 🏌 ⌷3200⌷ ♿ 3 restaurants (see "Restaurants" below), 2 bars, sauna, whirlpool. Business center offers teleconferencing. **Rates:** $165 S; $185 D; $225–$1100 ste. Extra person $15. Children under age 18 stay free. Parking: Indoor/outdoor, $8/day. AE, CB, DC, DISC, ER, JCB, MC, V.

≣ Anaheim Plaza Hotel
1700 S Harbor Blvd, 92802; tel 714/772-5900 or toll free 800/228-1357; fax 714/772-8386. Harbor Blvd exit off I-5. A 30-year-old property that could use some cleaning up and landscaping. **Rooms:** 300 rms and stes. CI 3pm/CO noon. Nonsmoking rms avail. Renovations made rooms only average. Very nice large counter in the bathroom. **Amenities:** 🛅 🅰 🖪 A/C, cable TV. Some units w/terraces. **Services:** ✕ 🚗 🛍 ⤴ Car-rental desk, babysitting. Complimentary shuttle to Disneyland. **Facilities:** 🎣 ⌷450⌷ ♿ 1 restaurant (bkfst and dinner only), 1 bar, games rm, whirlpool, washer/dryer. Meeting rooms overlook the very large pool. **Rates:** Peak (June–Aug) $69–$109 S; $79–$119 D; $275 ste. Extra person $10. Children under age 17 stay free. Lower rates off-season. Parking: Outdoor, free. AE, CB, DC, DISC, JCB, MC, V.

≣≣≣ Crown Sterling Suites
3100 E Frontera, 92806; tel 714/632-1221 or toll free 800/433-4600; fax 714/632-9963. Glassell exit off CA 91, S to Frontera. A bit off the beaten path, this lovely all-suite hotel is decorated like the old South, with a pretty atrium, koi pond, and bridges. **Rooms:** 222 stes. CI 3pm/CO noon. Nonsmoking rms avail. All suites have a sofa sleeper in the living room. **Amenities:** 🛅 🅰 🖪 A/C, cable TV w/movies, refrig, voice mail. All units w/minibars, all w/terraces. Suites have two TVs, microwave, and iron with ironing board. **Services:** ✕ 🚗 🛍 ⤴ 🛎 Car-rental desk, babysitting. Free shuttle to Disneyland and Knott's Berry Farm. **Facilities:** 🎣 ⌷350⌷ ♿ 2 restaurants, 2 bars (w/entertainment), sauna, steam rm, whirlpool, washer/dryer. New indoor pool. **Rates (BB):** Peak (June–Aug) $129 ste. Extra person $10. Children under age 12 stay free. Lower rates off-season. Parking: Outdoor, free. AE, CB, DC, DISC, MC, V.

≣≣≣ Disneyland Pacific Hotel
1717 S West St, 92802; tel 714/999-0990 or toll free 800/821-8976, 800/821-8976, 800/321-8976 in CA; fax 714/776-5763. Ball Rd exit off I-5; turn right on Ball, left on West St. Located adjacent to the Disneyland Hotel, this one-time business-oriented property is now part of the Disneyland Resort complex. Guests have access to all facilities at the Disneyland Hotel, as well as transportation to the theme park. **Rooms:** 502 rms and stes. Executive level. CI 3pm/CO 11am. Nonsmoking rms avail. Fairly large rooms have distinctive art deco furnishings; those on the third floor have access to a roof garden. **Amenities:** 🛅 🅰 🍽 A/C, cable TV w/movies, dataport, voice mail. **Services:** ✕ 🛏 VP 🚗 🛍 ⤴ Car-rental desk, social director, babysitting. Electric cart to Disneyland Hotel. Great kids' club is in a large room with lots of activities plus an outside play area. **Facilities:** 🎣 ⌷1740⌷ 🖥 ♿ 2 restaurants, 1 bar, games rm, whirlpool. Nice pool area with shuffleboard, table tennis, large whirlpool, snack bar. Grassy area with gazebo available for weddings. Japanese restaurant with sushi bar. **Rates:** Peak (June 15–Sept 15) $140–$210 S or D; $325–$1000 ste. Extra person $15. Children under age 18 stay free. Lower rates off-season. Parking: Indoor/outdoor, $10/day. Guests may charge all theme park expenses to hotel room. AE, CB, DC, ER, JCB, MC, V.

≣≣ Holiday Inn Maingate
1850 S Harbor Blvd, 92802; tel 714/750-2801 or toll free 800/624-6855; fax 714/971-4754. Harbor Blvd exit off I-5; 3 blocks W of freeway. Conveniently located two-building hotel. **Rooms:** 313 rms and stes. CI 3pm/CO noon. Nonsmoking rms avail. Average, with old-fashioned furniture. Small bathrooms with no counter space. **Amenities:** 🛅 🅰 🖪 A/C, cable TV w/movies. **Services:** ✕ 🛏 🚗 🛍 ⤴ Car-rental desk, babysitting. Complimentary shuttle service to Knott's Berry Farm and Disneyland. **Facilities:** 🎣 ⌷400⌷ ♿ 1 restaurant, 1 bar (w/entertainment), games rm, washer/dryer. Children's pool. Children under 12 eat free at the

hotel restaurant. **Rates:** $89 S; $99 D; $175–$250 ste. Children under age 19 stay free. Parking: Outdoor, free. AE, CB, DC, DISC, JCB, MC, V.

≡≡≡ Howard Johnson Hotel
1380 S Harbor Blvd, 92802; tel 714/776-6120 or toll free 800/422-4228; fax 714/533-3578. Harbor Blvd exit off I-5. This hotel has much to recommend it: a good location across the street from Disneyland; the design of eminent architect, William Periera; beautifully landscaped and well-kept gardens with colorful flowers and mature trees; and an accommodating staff. **Rooms:** 320 rms and stes. CI 3pm/CO noon. Nonsmoking rms avail. Rooms are located in four two-story buildings and in two taller structures. Ground-level rooms have spacious patios; most others have balconies. Although Tower rooms have Disneyland views, they can also be subject to freeway noise. Accommodations are very bright; some have walk-in closets. Bathrooms feature decorator tile and extra vanities with sinks; some have small TVs. **Amenities:** 🛎 🗞 📺 A/C, cable TV w/movies, refrig. Some units w/terraces. **Services:** ✕ ☞ 🚐 🖄 🛏 Car-rental desk, babysitting. Shuttle to Disneyland. Tour desk in lobby. **Facilities:** 🛋 🏊40 🔥 Games rm, whirlpool, washer/dryer. **Rates:** $64–$94 S or D; $129–$139 ste. Extra person $7. Children under age 18 stay free. Parking: Outdoor, free. AE, DC, DISC, JCB, MC, V.

≡≡≡ Hyatt Regency Alicante
100 Plaza Alicante, Garden Grove, PO Box 4669, Anaheim, 92803; tel 714/750-1234 or toll free 800/972-2929; fax 714/971-1721. 1 mi S of Disneyland. This dramatic-looking hotel, with its 14-story-high, fully landscaped lobby, is located some distance from the heart of the Disneyland complex. The entrance is distinguished by a palm-lined drive and an impressive fountain. **Rooms:** 396 rms and stes. Executive level. CI 3pm/CO noon. Nonsmoking rms avail. Accommodations are somewhat larger and better furnished than other business-oriented hotels in the area; most offer views of mountains or the atrium. **Amenities:** 🛎 🗞 📺 🍴 A/C, cable TV w/movies. Some units w/terraces. Some rooms have dataports and refrigerators; in-room safes are available. **Services:** ✕ ☞ 🅥🅟 🚐 🖄 🛏 Children's program, babysitting. **Facilities:** 🛋 🏊2 🎱150 🖵 🔥 2 restaurants, 2 bars, games rm, whirlpool. The roof garden pool facility is very attractive; it's wind protected, landscaped with mature potted plants and flowers, and furnished with deck chairs and umbrella tables. **Rates:** $139 S; $164 D; $225–$295 ste. Extra person $25. Children under age 18 stay free. Min stay special events. Parking: Outdoor, $5/day. AE, CB, DC, DISC, JCB, MC, V.

≡≡ Peacock Suites
1745 S Haster St, 92802; tel 714/535-8255 or toll free 800/522-6401; fax 714/535-8914. Katella exit off I-5. Attractive, new suites. **Rooms:** 140 stes. CI 3pm/CO 11am. No smoking. **Amenities:** 🛎 📺 🍴 A/C, cable TV w/movies, refrig, VCR, in-rm safe. Some units w/whirlpools. Microwave. **Services:** ☞ 🚐 🖄 🛏 Babysitting. Shuttle to Disneyland. **Facilities:** 🛋

🎱 🔥 Games rm, whirlpool, washer/dryer. **Rates:** Peak (June–Sept) $69 ste. Children under age 16 stay free. Lower rates off-season. Parking: Indoor/outdoor, free. AE, CB, DC, DISC, MC, V.

≡≡ Quality Hotel & Conference Center
616 Convention Way, 92802; tel 714/750-3131 or toll free 800/231-6215; fax 714/750-9027. Harbor Blvd exit off I-5; drive south; turn left on Convention Way. This is the hotel of choice for budget-minded travelers attending events at the Convention Center; it's within walking distance of both the center and Disneyland. **Rooms:** 284 rms. CI 3pm/CO noon. No smoking. Rooms are attractively decorated with blond wood furnishings and pink floral spreads and drapes. Parlor rooms, accommodating up to five persons, offer one of the best values in the area. **Amenities:** 🛎 🗞 📺 A/C, cable TV w/movies, refrig, dataport. Studio suites have refrigerators, microwaves, sofa beds. Parlor rooms have refrigerators, microwaves, and dishes. **Services:** ✕ ☞ 🚐 🖄 🛏 🍽 Car-rental desk, babysitting. Free shuttle bus to Disneyland. **Facilities:** 🛋 🎱600 🔥 2 restaurants, 1 bar (w/entertainment), games rm, beauty salon, washer/dryer. Pool has new bar and snack cabana. **Rates:** $89–$109 S or D. Extra person $15. Children under age 18 stay free. Min stay peak. Parking: Outdoor, $6/day. AE, CB, DC, DISC, ER, JCB, MC, V.

≡≡≡ Residence Inn by Marriott
1700 S Clementine St, 92802; tel 714/533-3555 or toll free 800/331-3131; fax 714/535-7626. Katella Ave exit off I-5. Apartment-style accommodations within walking distance of Disneyland. **Rooms:** 200 effic. CI 4pm/CO noon. Nonsmoking rms avail. **Amenities:** 🛎 🗞 📺 A/C, cable TV, refrig. Some units w/terraces, some w/fireplaces, some w/whirlpools. **Services:** ✕ 🖄 🛏 🍽 Car-rental desk, babysitting. Hospitality hour. Shuttle to Disneyland and Convention Center. Local restaurants will deliver. **Facilities:** 🛋 🔲 🏊40 🔥 Whirlpool, playground, washer/dryer. Basketball and volleyball areas. **Rates (CP):** Peak (June 15–Aug 25) $195–$235 effic. Extra person $10. Children under age 12 stay free. Lower rates off-season. Parking: Outdoor, free. AE, CB, DC, DISC, EC, ER, JCB, MC, V.

≡≡≡≡ Sheraton Anaheim Hotel
1015 W Ball Rd, 92802; tel 714/778-1700 or toll free 800/325-3535; fax 714/533-7801. Ball Rd exit off I-5 S; Harbor exit off I-5 N. One of the nicest hotels in the Disneyland area, the Sheraton resembles a medieval castle on the outside. The dungeon look that once characterized it has been replaced by bright and airy public areas and rooms with Mediterranean sea and sky colors. Extensive gardens and colorful plants are everywhere. There are two koi ponds, one in the bar and another in the Japanese garden. A friendly multilingual staff caters to visitors from Asia and Europe. **Rooms:** 490 rms and stes. Executive level. CI 3pm/CO noon. Nonsmoking rms avail. Featuring traditional furnishings, the tastefully decorated rooms are the largest in the area. Those on the ground-floor interior offer direct access to the gardens and pool.

Accommodations for guests with disabilities are state-of-the-art, with roll-in showers, laser alarms for the hearing impaired, and emergency evacuation speakers. **Amenities:** 🛏 🔆 A/C, cable TV w/movies, dataport, voice mail, in-rm safe. Refrigerators and coffeemakers on request. **Services:** ✗ 🕿 🚗 🖾 ⌁ Social director, babysitting. Environmentally-conscious guests can request staff not to change bed linen daily. **Facilities:** 🔩 🛳 🏊 ⬚ 🔆 2 restaurants, 1 bar, games rm, whirlpool, washer/dryer. The California Deli is a great alternative to restaurant dining. Snacks, heat-it-yourself breakfast food, frozen entrees, sweets, and beverages are always available. **Rates:** Peak (Apr–Oct) $130 S; $145 D; $200–$300 ste. Extra person $15. Children under age 18 stay free. Lower rates off-season. Parking: Outdoor, free. AE, CB, DC, DISC, EC, ER, JCB, MC, V.

MOTELS

▬▬ Anaheim Desert Palm Inn & Suites

631 W Katella Ave, 92802; tel 714/535-1133 or toll free 800/635-5423; fax 714/491-7409. Harbor Blvd exit off I-5; west on Katella. **Rooms:** 103 rms and stes. CI 2pm/CO 11am. Nonsmoking rms avail. **Amenities:** 🛏 A/C, cable TV w/movies, refrig, VCR. Some units w/terraces, some w/whirlpools. Microwave. **Services:** 🚗 🖾 ⌁ Car-rental desk, babysitting. Shuttle to Disneyland. Continental breakfast. **Facilities:** 🔩 🛳 🔆 Games rm, sauna, whirlpool, washer/dryer. **Rates (CP):** Peak (June–Sept 15) $59–$69 S; $69–$79 D; $89–$99 ste. Extra person $4. Children under age 18 stay free. Min stay special events. Lower rates off-season. Parking: Indoor/outdoor, free. AE, CB, DC, DISC, ER, JCB, MC, V.

▬ Anaheim Inn Best Western

1630 S Harbor Blvd, 92802; tel 714/774-1050 or toll free 800/854-8175; fax 714/776-6305. This very basic motel, located across the street from Disneyland, is a bit confusing to find; its two long narrow buildings fill one side of a complex containing a Denny's restaurant and a Days Inn. Despite appearances, parking isn't shared. **Rooms:** 88 rms. CI 3pm/CO noon. Nonsmoking rms avail. Rooms are simple, but adequate for budget travelers; most have two double beds. Sound insulation is insufficient to filter out noise from busy street. **Amenities:** 🛏 🗐 A/C, cable TV w/movies, refrig. **Services:** 🚗 🖾 ⌁ Babysitting. **Facilities:** 🔩 🔆 Whirlpool, washer/dryer. **Rates:** $55–$95 S or D. Children under age 18 stay free. Parking: Outdoor, free. Special packages available. AE, DC, DISC, MC, V.

▬▬▬ Anaheim International Inn & Suites

2060 S Harbor Blvd, 92802; tel 714/971-9393 or toll free 800/251-2345; fax 714/971-2706. Harbor Blvd exit off I-5. Motel-style property, clean and well maintained. **Rooms:** 119 rms and stes. CI 3pm/CO 11am. Nonsmoking rms avail. In good condition. **Amenities:** 🛏 🔆 🗐 A/C, cable TV w/movies, refrig, in-rm safe. Some units w/minibars. Microwave. **Services:** 🚗 🖾 ⌁ Car-rental desk, babysitting. Complimen-

tary shuttle service to Disneyland. **Facilities:** 🔩 🔆 Games rm, whirlpool, washer/dryer. **Rates (CP):** Peak (June–Aug) $49–$69 S; $59–$78 D; $125–$160 ste; $78–$98 effic. Children under age 18 stay free. Lower rates off-season. Parking: Outdoor, free. AE, CB, DC, DISC, MC, V.

▬▬ Anaheim Ramada Inn

1331 E Katella Ave, 92805; tel 714/978-8088 or toll free 800/228-0586; fax 714/937-5622. Exit I-5 at Katella; go E. Recently renovated older motel near Anaheim Stadium, the Pond, and Disneyland. A waterfall marks the nicely landscaped entry. The attractively decorated lobby has two large aquariums. Friendly, helpful staff. **Rooms:** 232 rms and stes. CI 3pm/CO noon. Nonsmoking rms avail. **Amenities:** 🛏 🔆 🗐 A/C, TV w/movies, voice mail, in-rm safe. **Services:** ✗ 🚗 🖾 ⌁ Free shuttle to Disneyland, Knott's Berry Farm, and Anaheim Convention Center. Security a bit questionable, with doors that open onto the street. **Facilities:** 🔩 🛳 🔆 1 restaurant, 1 bar (w/entertainment), games rm, sauna, whirlpool, washer/dryer. Large swimming pool in garden setting with ample deck space and many tables and chairs. **Rates:** Peak (June 15–Sept 15) $65 S or D; $90 ste. Extra person $10. Children under age 12 stay free. Lower rates off-season. Parking: Outdoor, free. AE, DC, DISC, MC, V.

▬ Anaheim Stadium Travelodge

1700 E Katella Ave, 92805; tel 714/634-1920 or toll free 800/634-1920; fax 714/634-0366. Katella exit off I-5. Clean but dreary motel on a busy street. Close to Anaheim Stadium, the Pond, Disneyland. Renovation underway, but this property is definitely marginal. **Rooms:** 72 rms. CI 3pm/CO 11am. Nonsmoking rms avail. Average in size, with dark furniture in disrepair. **Amenities:** 🛏 A/C, satel TV w/movies. **Services:** 🖾 ⌁ Continental breakfast served in summer. **Facilities:** 🔩 🔆 Whirlpool, washer/dryer. **Rates:** Peak (June–Sept) $49 S; $54 D. Children under age 17 stay free. Lower rates off-season. Parking: Outdoor, free. Security deposit for phone and room key. AE, DC, DISC, MC, V.

▬▬ Best Western Anaheim Stardust Inn

1057 W Ball Rd, 92802; tel 714/774-7600 or toll free 800/222-3639; fax 714/535-6953. Ball Rd exit off I-5. Located close to the freeway, this well-kept motel caters to families and visitors from Japan and China. **Rooms:** 97 rms. CI 3pm/CO 11am. Nonsmoking rms avail. Furnishings are spotless. Some bathrooms have sunken Roman tubs. **Amenities:** 🛏 🔆 A/C, cable TV, refrig, dataport. Some units w/terraces. Microwaves in all rooms. **Services:** ✗ 🚗 🖾 ⌁ 🍴 Babysitting. Japanese, Mandarin, Taiwanese, Spanish spoken. **Facilities:** 🔩 🔆 1 restaurant, sauna, whirlpool, washer/dryer. Orient Express restaurant on premises. **Rates (CP):** Peak (June 15–Aug 25) $48–$85 S or D. Children under age 18 stay free. Lower rates off-season. Parking: Outdoor, free. Extra charge for hot breakfast. AE, CB, DC, DISC, JCB, MC, V.

≣≣ Best Western Stovall's Inn

1110 W Katella Ave, 92802; tel 714/778-1880 or toll free 800/854-8175; fax 714/778-5805. Harbor Blvd exit off I-5, S to Katella, turn right. This well-kept motel has long been popular with families and tour groups visiting Disneyland. **Rooms:** 290 rms and stes. CI 3pm/CO noon. Nonsmoking rms avail. Old-fashioned motel-style rooms are simply furnished, but well maintained. **Amenities:** ☎ 🎮 A/C, cable TV w/movies. Nintendo available. **Services:** 🚐 🏊 ☕ Car-rental desk, babysitting. Staff is pleasant and helpful. **Facilities:** 🏊 ⑫ 1 bar, whirlpool, washer/dryer. Both pools are better than average, set in an unusual topiary garden. One pool is heated. **Rates:** Peak (Mar–Apr/June–Aug) $65–$85 S or D; $120–$145 ste. Children under age 18 stay free. Min stay special events. Lower rates off-season. Parking: Outdoor, free. Rates permit up to five people in a room. AE, CB, DC, DISC, ER, JCB, MC, V.

≣ Brookhurst Plaza Inn

711 S Brookhurst St, 92804; tel 714/999-1220 or toll free 800/909-1220; fax 714/758-1047. Brookhurst exit off I-5. Located a bit far from major attractions. **Rooms:** 91 rms and stes. CI 2pm/CO 11am. Nonsmoking rms avail. **Amenities:** ☎ 🍷 A/C, cable TV, refrig. Some units w/whirlpools. **Services:** 🚐 🏊 ☕ Car-rental desk, babysitting. Shuttle available to Knott's Berry Farm. **Facilities:** 🏊 🚭 & 1 bar, sauna, whirlpool, washer/dryer. Restaurant and lounge have recently been remodeled. **Rates (CP):** Peak (June–Aug) $68–$80 S or D; $68–$120 ste. Children under age 11 stay free. Lower rates off-season. Parking: Outdoor, free. AE, DC, DISC, MC, V.

≣≣ Candy Cane Inn

1747 S Harbor Blvd, 92802; tel 714/774-5284 or toll free 800/345-7057; fax 714/772-5462. Harbor Blvd exit off I-5; go south. Really a motel, this is located within walking distance of the Magic Kingdom and close to a dozen more attractions. **Rooms:** 172 rms. CI 3pm/CO 11am. Nonsmoking rms avail. Decorated in bright floral motifs with comfortable furnishings, including queen-size beds and a separate dressing and vanity area. **Amenities:** ☎ 🍷 A/C, cable TV w/movies. **Services:** 🚐 🏊 ☕ Complimentary breakfast in courtyard. Shuttle to Disneyland. 24-hour switchboard for business travelers. **Facilities:** 🏊 & Whirlpool, washer/dryer. **Rates (CP):** Peak (Dec 21–Jan 1/Mar 18–Apr 9/June 16–Sept 5) $85–$95 S or D. Children under age 17 stay free. Lower rates off-season. Parking: Outdoor, free. AE, DC, DISC, MC, V.

≣≣ Cavalier Inn & Suites

11811 Harbor Blvd, 92802; tel 714/750-1000 or toll free 800/821-2768; fax 714/971-3539. Harbor Blvd S exit off I-5 S. A very clean small property, enhanced by plants and flowers. **Rooms:** 100 rms and stes. CI 3pm/CO 11am. Nonsmoking rms avail. Nice furniture for a motel. Some rooms are being upgraded with new mattresses and furnishings. **Amenities:** ☎ 🍷 A/C, cable TV w/movies, refrig.

Microwave. **Services:** ☕ 🏊 Car-rental desk, babysitting. Complimentary shuttle to Disneyland. **Facilities:** 🏊 & Whirlpool, washer/dryer. Very nice pool and hot tub area. **Rates (CP):** Peak (Jun–Aug) $79 S or D; $99 ste. Children under age 16 stay free. Min stay peak. Lower rates off-season. Parking: Outdoor, free. AE, DC, DISC, MC, V.

≣ Comfort Inn Maingate

2200 S Harbor Blvd, 92802; tel 714/750-5211 or toll free 800/479-5210; fax 714/750-2226. Harbor Blvd exit off I-5 S. This is a small, family-oriented motel, located on a busy street several blocks south of Disneyland in a somewhat rundown neighborhood. Not particularly well maintained. **Rooms:** 66 rms. CI 3pm/CO 11am. Nonsmoking rms avail. Rooms need sprucing up. **Amenities:** ☎ 🎮 A/C, TV w/movies. Some rooms have refrigerators. **Services:** 🚐 ☕ Coffee available all day in lobby. Shuttle to Disneyland. $5 fee for crib. **Facilities:** 🏊 & Whirlpool, washer/dryer. **Rates (CP):** Peak (June–Aug) $57–$66 S or D. Extra person $5. Children under age 18 stay free. Lower rates off-season. Parking: Outdoor, free. AE, DC, DISC, JCB, MC, V.

≣ Days Inn Suites

1111 S Harbor Blvd, 92805; tel 714/533-8830 or toll free 800/654-7503; fax 714/758-0573. Harbor Blvd N off I-5. This former dumpy motel has been partially upgraded. Although there's an attractive lobby with pretty, contemporary furnishings, the exterior needs work. **Rooms:** 81 rms and stes. CI 3pm/CO 11am. Nonsmoking rms avail. Rooms have been cleaned up and furnished Spartanly with new pieces. **Amenities:** ☎ A/C, cable TV. Microwaves. **Services:** 🏊 ☕ Free shuttle to Disneyland. Fax and copying available at front desk. **Facilities:** 🏊 & Whirlpool. **Rates:** Peak (June–Sept 15) $49–$79 S or D; $125 ste. Children under age 12 stay free. Lower rates off-season. Parking: Outdoor, free. AE, DC, DISC, MC, V.

≣ Travelodge Maingate

1717 S Harbor Blvd, 92802; tel 714/635-6550 or toll free 800/826-1616; fax 714/635-1502. Harbor Blvd exit off I-5; go south. A sprawling, very basic motel consisting of two older properties combined, it's located on the southeast edge of Disneyland's parking lot. **Rooms:** 254 rms. CI 3pm/CO noon. Nonsmoking rms avail. Furnishings in some rooms show wear; some bathrooms need fresh paint. **Amenities:** ☎ 🎮 A/C, cable TV. **Services:** 🚐 🏊 ☕ Car-rental desk, babysitting. Front desk will help arrange tours and shopping shuttles. **Facilities:** 🏊 Whirlpool, washer/dryer. A Disney store fills most of the lobby. **Rates:** Peak (June 15–Sept 5) $50 S; $55–$70 D. Children under age 18 stay free. Lower rates off-season. Senior, corporate, and military discounts. AE, DC, DISC, ER, JCB, MC, V.

RESORT

≣≣≣≣ Disneyland Hotel

1150 W Cerritos Ave, 92802; tel 714/778-6600; fax 714/956-6582. 60 acres. This hotel is in every way a lodging, dining, and entertainment extension of the Happiest Place on Earth, with the Disney signature everywhere—from the bronze statues of Mickey and Minnie that greet arriving guests, to the original art found throughout the complex. Beautifully landscaped grounds have mature trees, continuously blooming flower gardens, meandering streams, koi ponds, a marina, beach area, and waterfalls. **Rooms:** 1,136 rms and stes. Executive level. CI 3pm/CO 11am. Nonsmoking rms avail. Rooms are attractively furnished, decorated with Disney touches; most have views of the grounds or the park across the street. **Amenities:** 🛏 🔌 📺 A/C, cable TV w/movies, dataport, voice mail, in-rm safe. All units w/minibars. Some rooms have wet bars, refrigerators, and daybeds; most have balconies. Disney movies available on TV. **Services:** ✕ ⊷ VP 🚐 🖨 ↺ Car-rental desk, social director, babysitting. Interpreter available. Sports and theater ticket services. Airport bus terminal on premises, limousine service, tram, and monorail to Disneyland. **Facilities:** 🛝 △ 🏋 ⛳ 7700 💻 ♿ 6 restaurants (see "Restaurants" below), 4 bars (3 w/entertainment), volleyball, games rm, whirlpool. Many Disney shops. Remote-controlled boats and cars, pedal boats. Entertainment includes a strolling quintet, two nightclubs, and a nightly display of Fantasy Waters. **Rates:** Peak (June 15–Sept 15) $155–$250 S or D; $325 ste. Extra person $15. Children under age 18 stay free. Lower rates off-season. Parking: Indoor/outdoor, $15/day. AE, CB, DC, ER, JCB, MC, V.

RESTAURANTS 🍴

Blue Bayou
In Disneyland, 1313 Harbor Blvd; tel 714/781-4547. **Cajun/Creole.** Located in New Orleans Square, this is Disneyland's award-winning, fine dining restaurant. The setting is right out of a bayou at twilight, as diners watch the boats of Pirates of the Caribbean glide by, and hear the shouts of passengers as the boats hit the first waterfall. Fare here is cajun, with dishes like jambalaya, grilled Creole chicken, and the ever-popular Monte Cristo sandwiches and Caribbean crab cakes. Reservations must be made at the restaurant on the day of the park visit. **FYI:** Reservations accepted. Children's menu. No liquor license. **Open:** Peak (June–Sept) Sun–Fri 11am–9pm, Sat 11am–10pm. **Prices:** Main courses $10–$16. AE, DC, MC, V. 📺 ♿

★ The Catch
1929 S State College Blvd; tel 714/634-1829. Near Anaheim Stadium. **Seafood.** A longtime favorite among sports fans attending events at nearby Anaheim Stadium. The menu includes fresh, well-prepared swordfish, blackened red snapper, and seafood brochette, as well as a few steaks, some chicken, and pasta. Service is good without being obtrusive. **FYI:** Reservations recommended. Children's menu. **Open:** Lunch Mon–Fri 11:30am–2:30pm; dinner Mon–Thurs 5–9:30pm, Fri–Sat 5–10pm, Sun 5–9pm. **Prices:** Main courses $11–$22. AE, CB, DC, DISC, MC, V. VP ♿

Goofy's Kitchen
In Disneyland Hotel, 1150 W Cerritos Ave; tel 714/778-6600. **American.** Minnie Mouse passes out kisses and Goofy gives hugs in this restaurant designed to appeal to kids, big and small. Better-than-average food is served buffet style: for youngsters, there's a special pint-size buffet stocked with mini hot dogs, spaghetti, and macaroni; meanwhile, adults can cruise a fresh salad bar and pick from a number of hot entrees, such as carved meat. Milk is the beverage of choice here. Not open for lunch on weekdays off season. **FYI:** Reservations accepted. Children's menu. **Open:** Peak (June–Aug/Nov 15–Jan 2) breakfast daily 7:30–11:30am; lunch daily noon–2:30pm; dinner daily 5–9pm. **Prices:** Prix fixe $8–$18. AE, CB, DC, ER, MC, V. 📺 ♿

Hastings Grill
In Anaheim Hilton & Towers, 777 Convention Way; tel 714/740-4422. S Harbor Blvd exit off I-5. **Californian.** Elegant decor features polished teak, mahogany, and lots of etched glass. Modern California cuisine with Pacific Rim influences includes steaks, seafood, and poultry imaginatively prepared. **FYI:** Reservations recommended. Dress code. **Open:** Lunch Mon–Fri 11:30am–2pm; dinner Mon–Sat 6–10:30pm. **Prices:** Main courses $15–$26. AE, CB, DC, DISC, ER, MC, V. ♿

♥ JW's
In the Anaheim Marriott Hotel, 700 W Convention Way; tel 714/750-0900. Harbor Blvd exit off I-5. **Eclectic.** This is one of the most romantic restaurants in Orange County. Each dining space is very private, tucked into one of many small rooms. Decor includes original art, library shelves filled with books, and candlelight. Chef John McLaughlin designs a completely new menu every three months, featuring an eclectic selection of hors d'oeuvres and entrees based on Asian, Italian, and contemporary cuisines. Menu usually offers game, seafood, and vegetarian items. **FYI:** Reservations recommended. Harp. Jacket required. **Open:** Mon–Sat 6–10pm. **Prices:** Main courses $19–$28. AE, CB, DC, DISC, ER, MC, V. ♥ VP ♿

Mr Stox
1105 E Katella Ave; tel 714/634-2994. Katella Ave exit off I-5; located near Anaheim Stadium. **Californian.** Charming decor, with excellent choice of seafood, meat, and game. Bake own breads and desserts. Good wine cellar. **FYI:** Reservations recommended. Piano. Children's menu. Dress code. **Open:** Lunch Mon–Fri 11:30am–2:30pm; dinner Mon–Sun 5:30–10pm. **Prices:** Main courses $13–$28. AE, CB, DC, DISC, MC, V. ♥ VP

Pavia
In Anaheim Hilton & Towers, 777 Convention Way; tel 714/740-4419. Harbor Blvd exit off I-5. **Italian.** This very appealing and elegant dining room feels like a bit of Italy, with a setting framed by marble columns and murals of Venice's Grand Canal and the Piazza San Marco. Menu features a selection of northern Italian items, including pasta, seafood,

veal, and lamb. Operating hours may vary, so call ahead. **FYI:** Reservations recommended. Piano. **Open:** Tues–Sun 6–11pm. **Prices:** Main courses $14–$25. AE, CB, DC, DISC, ER, MC, V. ● ⓥⓟ &

Peppers Restaurant
12361 Chapman Ave, Garden Grove (Disneyland); tel 714/740-1333. Harbor Blvd exit off I-5; 5 blocks S on Harbor, right on Chapman. **Mexican.** Typical LA cantina/restaurant, bright and busy. There are two greenhouse dining rooms, plus an outdoor dining area. Menu features tacos, burritos, fajitas, enchiladas, and a selection of steaks and seafood. Bar decorated with a surfing motif. Complimentary bus service to local hotels. **FYI:** Reservations recommended. Dancing/rock. Children's menu. Dress code. **Open:** Lunch daily 11:30am–3pm; dinner Sun–Thurs 3–10pm, Fri–Sat 3–11pm; brunch Sun 9am–3pm. **Prices:** Main courses $7–$16. AE, DC, MC, V. &

★ **Thee White House**
887 S Anaheim Blvd; tel 714/772-1381. Ball Rd exit off I-5. **Italian.** A restaurant in a large 1909 house, with decorations of the period. Northern Italian specialties include pan-seared ahi with pinot grigio sauce, medallions of pork with pink peppercorn-Cointreau sauce, and grilled swordfish with citrus beurre blanc. Alfresco dining when weather permits. Complimentary limo service from local hotels and businesses. **FYI:** Reservations recommended. Children's menu. Dress code. **Open:** Lunch daily 11:30am–2pm; dinner daily 5–10pm. **Prices:** Main courses $16–$25. AE, DC, MC, V. ● ⬤ ⓥⓟ &

ATTRACTIONS 🖾

DISNEYLAND ATTRACTIONS

Disneyland
Conceived by Walt Disney as a theme park that adults could enjoy along with their kids, Disneyland debuted in 1955. Located at 1313 Harbor Blvd (tel 714/999-4565), the park is divided into eight sections, each with rides, shows, and attractions that coincide with that area's particular theme. These areas are:

Main Street, USA, recalling the aura of American small town life around the turn of the century. A steam-powered train that circles the entire park departs from the Main Street Depot, and amid the penny arcades and novelty shops are the Audio-Animatronic show, "Great Moments with Mr Lincoln," and an old-time cinema featuring "The Walt Disney Story."

Adventureland is inspired by exotic regions of Asia, Africa, and the South Pacific. Audio-Animatronic flowers, birds, and talking tiki statues present a musical comedy in the Enchanted Tiki Room. On the Jungle Cruise, riders encounter wild animals and hostile natives. Also here are Pirates of the Caribbean, a hydroflume ride down a plunging waterfall and through pirate caves; and Splash Mountain, one of the largest towering log-flume attractions in the world.

Frontierland, depicting the pioneer spirit of America's westward expansion, includes Tom Sawyer's Island, Gold Rush–era entertainment at the Golden Horseshoe Jamboree, and a ride aboard a runaway mine train on the Big Thunder Mountain Railroad.

Fantasyland has rides based on famous children's books, including Disney movie favorites like Pinocchio, Snow White, and Dumbo. Featured attractions here are It's a Small World, and the Matterhorn Bobsleds, a fog-shrouded rollercoaster trip through chilling caverns and cloud banks.

Tomorrowland envisions the world of the future. Two of the most popular rides in Disneyland are here: Space Mountain, an indoor rollercoaster ride through the void of interstellar space; and Star Tours, a flight simulator–based excursion to the Moon of Endor.

New Orleans Square, set in the roisterous atmosphere of colonial New Orleans, features the eerie Haunted Mansion and the extremely popular Audio-Animatronic escapades of the Pirates of the Caribbean.

Critter Country is the Old South, but populated by the likes of Audio-Animatronic bears, who perform at the Country Bear Playhouse. Also here is the log flume ride, Splash Mountain, based on a scene from the classic Disney film *Song of the South.*

Mickey's Toontown is a brightly colored, out-of-scale animated cartoon town brought to life, where guests can visit the home of Mickey Mouse. Also featured are Chip 'n Dale's Tree Slide and Acorn Crawl, and Roger Rabbit's Car Toon Spin. **Open:** Mid-Sept–May, Mon–Fri 10am–6pm, Sat–Sun 9am–midnight; June–mid-Sept plus Thanksgiving, Christmas, and Easter, daily 8am–1am. $$$$

ANOTHER ATTRACTION

Anaheim Stadium
2000 Gene Autry Way; tel 714/254-3120. Behind-the-scenes guided tours of "the Big A" (home of the LA Rams and California Angels) visit the players' locker rooms, press areas, private suites, and other working areas of the stadium (all subject to availability). **Open:** Daily, phone for schedule. $

Aptos

HOTEL 🖾

≝≝≝ **Seacliff Inn Best Western**
7500 Old Dominion Court, 95003; tel 408/688-7300 or toll free 800/528-1234, 800/367-2003 in CA; fax 408/685-3003. Seacliff Blvd exit off CA 1. This property is very nice and well kept. Beautifully tended grounds. **Rooms:** 140 rms and stes. CI 2pm/CO 11am. No smoking. In size and decor, superior to the average hotel/motel accommodations.

Amenities: ⌂ ⌂ ▤ A/C, cable TV w/movies, VCR, in-rm safe. Some units w/minibars, some w/terraces, some w/fireplaces, some w/whirlpools. **Services:** X ⬌ 🚐 🖾 ⤵ Babysitting. **Facilities:** 🛖 500 ⛾ 1 restaurant, 1 bar (w/entertainment). **Rates:** Peak (May 24–Oct 26) $79–$165 S; $89–$165 D; $129–$215 ste. Extra person $10. Min stay peak. Lower rates off-season. Parking: Outdoor, free. Lovers' Getaway package ($149–$229) includes two-room luxury suite, whirlpool, satin sheets, champagne, fruit, and late check-out. AE, DISC, MC, V.

Arcadia

Nestled against the looming San Gabriel Mountains, Arcadia was founded by Elias Jackson "Lucky" Baldwin, who turned his love of horses into popular Santa Anita Park. **Information:** Arcadia Chamber of Commerce, 388 W Huntington Dr, Arcadia 91007 (tel 818/445-1400).

HOTELS 🏨

≣≣≣ Embassy Suites Hotel
211 E Huntington Dr, 91006; tel 818/445-8525 or toll free 800/EMBASSY; fax 818/445-8548. Huntington Dr exit off I-210. Lovely atrium and courtyard entrance. Near Santa Anita Racetrack, and a short ride from the Rose Bowl. Good for families. **Rooms:** 194 stes. CI 1pm/CO 1pm. Nonsmoking rms avail. **Amenities:** ⌂ ⌂ ▤ ▯ A/C, cable TV w/movies, refrig. All units w/minibars, some w/terraces. 2 TVs. **Services:** X 🚐 🖾 ⤵ ⧖ Car-rental desk, babysitting. Complimentary happy hour. Meeting planning services. **Facilities:** 🛖 1100 ⛾ 1 restaurant (lunch and dinner only), 2 bars (1 w/entertainment), sauna, steam rm, whirlpool, washer/dryer. **Rates (MAP):** $119–$149 ste. Extra person $10. Children under age 12 stay free. Parking: Outdoor, free. Senior discounts. AE, CB, DC, DISC, MC, V.

≣≣≣ Residence Inn by Marriott
321 E Huntington Dr, 91105; tel 818/446-6500 or toll free 800/331-3131; fax 818/446-5824. Huntington Dr exit off I-210. Like a home away from home; lovely gardens. **Rooms:** 120 effic. CI 3pm/CO noon. Nonsmoking rms avail. **Amenities:** ⌂ ⌂ ▤ ▯ A/C, cable TV w/movies, refrig, VCR. Some units w/terraces, some w/fireplaces. Rooms have full kitchens. **Services:** X 🚐 🖾 ⤵ ⧖ Children's program, babysitting. **Facilities:** 🛖 🎣1 30 ⛾ Whirlpool, day-care ctr, playground, washer/dryer. Use of barbecue. Sport court for baseball, volleyball, or tennis. **Rates:** $129–$169 effic. Children under age 18 stay free. Parking: Outdoor, free. Honeymoon packages. AE, CB, DC, DISC, MC, V.

INN

≣≣≣ Hampton Inn
311 E Huntington Dr, 91106; tel 818/574-5600 or toll free 800/HAMPTON; fax 818/446-2748. Nice hotel 5 minutes

from Santa Anita Racetrack. Good value. **Rooms:** 131 rms. CI 3pm/CO noon. Nonsmoking rms avail. Pleasant, clean accommodations. **Amenities:** ⌂ ⌂ ▤ ▯ A/C, satel TV w/movies, dataport. Free local telephone calls. **Services:** 🖾 ⤵ ⧖ Babysitting. Free coffee in lobby 24 hours. **Facilities:** 🛖 25 ⛾ Complimentary passes to local gym. **Rates (CP):** Children under age 18 stay free. Min stay special events. Higher rates for special events/hols. Parking: Outdoor, free. AE, CB, DC, DISC, JCB, MC, V.

RESTAURANTS 🍴

♥★ Chez Sateau
850 S Baldwin Ave; tel 818/446-8806. Baldwin Ave exit off I-210. **French.** Chef/owner Ryo Sato was on the US Culinary Olympic Team and has a very loyal following. His menu features roast sea bass, grilled swordfish, festival of lobster, roast duck with mango chutney, marinated pork tenderloin, and grilled filet mignon. **FYI:** Reservations recommended. Guitar. Jacket required. **Open:** Lunch Tues–Fri 11:30am–2:30pm; dinner Tues–Thurs 5:30–9pm, Fri–Sat 5:30–10pm, Sun 5:30–9pm; brunch Sun 10:30am–2:30pm. **Prices:** Main courses $15–$23. AE, CB, DC, DISC, MC, V. ♥ 🍷 🖼 🚗 ◩ VP ⛾

Coco's
1150 W Colorado Blvd; tel 818/446-5551. Michillinda exit off I-210. **American.** This neighborhood restaurant, popular with families and seniors, is decorated in aqua and peach in a southwestern motif and offers fresh fish, steaks, and barbecued ribs. **FYI:** Reservations not accepted. Children's menu. Dress code. Beer and wine only. **Open:** Sun–Thurs 6:30am–11pm, Fri–Sat 6:30am–midnight. **Prices:** Main courses $6–$13. AE, CB, DC, DISC, ER, MC, V. 🖼 ⛾

ATTRACTION 🏛

Santa Anita Park
285 W Huntington Dr; tel 818/574-RACE. Thoroughbred racing facility offers pari-mutuel betting; grandstand and clubhouse seating. Dining facilities; children's playground. Free behind-the-scenes guided tours weekend mornings. **Open:** Racing early Oct–early Nov and late Dec–late Apr Wed–Sun; phone for schedule. $$$

Arcata

HOTEL 🏨

≣≣ Hotel Arcata
708 9th St, 95521; tel 707/826-0217 or toll free 800/344-1221; fax 707/826-1737. 7 mi N of Eureka on CA 101. Historic 1915 hotel located on the main plaza in a busy college town. The original woodwork is still intact. **Rooms:** 32 rms and stes. CI 3pm/CO 11am. Nonsmoking rms avail. Accommodations have old radiators and claw-foot bathtubs. **Amenities:** ⌂ ⌂ ▤ Cable TV w/movies. No A/C. **Services:** X

🚐 🛎 🦽 Social director, masseur. **Facilities:** 🏊90 ♿ 1 restaurant (lunch and dinner only), 1 bar (w/entertainment), beauty salon. Very good Japanese restaurant. Free passes to full-service health club. **Rates (CP):** Peak (May–Oct) $65–$120 S; $75–$130 D; $85–$140 ste. Extra person $10. Children under age 2 stay free. Lower rates off-season. Parking: Outdoor, free. AE, CB, DC, DISC, JCB, MC, V.

Auburn

Auburn's carefully maintained Old Town remains a 19th-century living showcase. Evidence of the boom years still exists in the historic Gold Rush architecture, and many of the buildings have been converted to shops. **Information:** Auburn Area Chamber of Commerce, 601 Lincoln Way, Auburn 95603 (tel 916/885-5616).

MOTELS 🏨

🏨🏨 Auburn Inn
1875 Auburn Ravine Rd, 95603; tel 916/885-1800 or toll free 800/272-1444; fax 916/888-6424. Off I-80. Clean, moderately priced highway motel with interior corridors and neatly landscaped pool area. **Rooms:** 81 rms. CI 4pm/CO noon. Nonsmoking rms avail. Quiet. **Amenities:** 🛁 ☎ A/C, cable TV w/movies. 1 unit w/terrace. **Services:** 🦽 🛎 Coffee 24 hours. **Facilities:** 🏊 🏋120 ♿ Whirlpool, washer/dryer. Kitchen adjacent to conference room allows catering for small groups. **Rates:** $54–$120 S or D. Extra person $6. Children under age 12 stay free. Parking: Outdoor, free. AE, CB, DC, DISC, MC, V.

🏨🏨 Best Western Golden Key Motel
13450 Lincoln Way, 95603; tel 916/885-8611 or toll free 800/201-0121; fax 916/885-0319. Lincoln Way exit off I-80. Good bet for a comfortable stay, with tidy landscaped grounds, and fine furniture. **Rooms:** 68 rms. CI 2pm/CO noon. Nonsmoking rms avail. Upholstered chairs, desk, country pine furniture—a step up from most motels. Ask for room on back tier to avoid highway noise. **Amenities:** 🛁 ☎ 📺 A/C, cable TV, dataport. **Services:** ✕ 🛎 🦽 Complimentary sweet rolls and coffee in morning; 24-hour staff; fax services; hearing-assist devices. **Facilities:** 🏊 🏋15 ♿ Whirlpool, washer/dryer. Pool heated all year and covered for off-season use. **Rates (CP):** Peak (Apr–Labor Day) $52–$62 S; $58–$68 D. Extra person $6. Children under age 13 stay free. Lower rates off-season. Parking: Outdoor, free. AE, CB, DC, DISC, EC, MC, V.

RESTAURANT 🍴

★ Latitudes
130 Maple St; tel 916/885-9535. Maple or Nevada exit off I-80. **International.** A light and airy country garden setting across the street from the old courthouse. Patio dining available. Unusual dishes include African peanut stew, cur-

ried tofu, and poulet fromage; at lunch, there are spinach-chicken crêpes and tempeh burgers. Different regional cuisines and wines featured each month. Vegetarian dishes and microbrewery beers are available. **FYI:** Reservations recommended. Beer and wine only. **Open:** Lunch Mon–Fri 11am–2:30pm; dinner Wed–Sun 5–9pm, Fri–Sat 5–10pm; brunch Sun 10am–3pm. **Prices:** Main courses $9–$17. AE, MC, V. 🍴 🏖 🏔

Avalon

Named after the legendary Elysium of King Arthur, Avalon has become a legend in its own right. Twenty-six miles across the sea on the island of Catalina, and a world away from Los Angeles, the small city wraps around picturesque Avalon Bay. **Information:** Catalina Island Visitors Bureau, #1 Green Pier, PO Box 217, Avalon 90704 (tel 310/510-1520).

HOTELS 🏨

🏨🏨🏨 Catalina Canyon Hotel
888 Country Club Dr, PO Box 736, 90704; tel 310/510-0325 or toll free 800/253-9361; fax 310/510-0900. Located in a canyon above Avalon, with beautiful grounds and a lovely swimming pool. Recently under new management. **Rooms:** 83 rms, stes, and effic. CI 3pm/CO 11am. Nonsmoking rms avail. Large, somewhat sparse rooms. **Amenities:** 🛁 ☎ A/C, cable TV. All units w/terraces, 1 w/whirlpool. **Services:** ✕ 🛎 🚐 🛎 Masseur, babysitting. **Facilities:** 🏊 🏋180 ♿ 1 restaurant, 1 bar, sauna, whirlpool, washer/dryer. Only heated pool on island. Golf and tennis nearby. **Rates (CP):** Peak (May 15–Oct 15) $135 S; $145 D; $250–$350 ste; $250–$350 effic. Extra person $20. Children under age 18 stay free. Min stay peak and wknds. Lower rates off-season. AE, CB, DC, DISC, JCB, MC, V.

🏨 Glenmore Plaza Hotel
120 Sumner Ave, PO Box 155, 90704; tel 310/510-0017 or toll free 800/748-5660, 800/422-8254 in CA; fax 310/510-2833. A bit off the beaten path, in an old Victorian house. Not the best value in town. **Rooms:** 46 rms, stes, and effic. CI 1pm/CO 10:30am. Nonsmoking rms avail. Rooms are small and decorated with wicker furniture. **Amenities:** ☎ Cable TV. No A/C or phone. Some units w/terraces, some w/whirlpools. **Services:** 🛎 Babysitting. **Facilities:** 🏋30 **Rates (CP):** Peak (June–Oct) $125–$175 S or D; $200–$400 ste; $140–$400 effic. Children under age 21 stay free. Min stay peak and wknds. Lower rates off-season. AE, DISC, MC, V.

🏨🏨 Hotel Mac Rae
409 Crescent Ave, PO Box 1517, 90704; tel 310/510-0246 or toll free 800/698-2266; fax 310/510-9632. On the promenade, just steps from the beach; a real California feeling with Mediterranean decor. **Rooms:** 24 rms. CI 2pm/CO 11am. Nonsmoking rms avail. Rooms are small; some have views of the harbor. **Amenities:** ☎ Cable TV, VCR. No A/C or phone.

All rooms have TVs with built-in VCRs; good selection of movies (complimentary) in lobby. **Services:** ☎ ➰ Babysitting. Free use of beach towels and chairs. **Rates (CP):** Peak (July–Sept) $110–$170 S or D. Children under age 21 stay free. Min stay wknds. Lower rates off-season. MC, V.

🗏🗏🗏 Hotel Metropole
205 Crescent Ave, PO Box 1900, 90704; tel 310/510-1884 or toll free 800/541-8528, 800/300-8528 in CA; fax 310/510-2534. One of the nicest hotels on the island, located in the Metropole Marketplace. Relaxing and lovely. **Rooms:** 48 rms, stes, and effic. CI 3pm/CO 11am. No smoking. Rooms are large and tastefully decorated; smoking is allowed only on balconies. **Amenities:** 🗏 A/C, cable TV w/movies, refrig, dataport, bathrobes. All units w/minibars, some w/terraces, some w/fireplaces, some w/whirlpools. HBO, Movie Channel. **Services:** X ⬚ ➰ Twice-daily maid svce, social director, masseur, babysitting. Staff is very helpful and courteous. Free use of beach towels. **Facilities:** 🗏 ⛓ 2 restaurants, 1 bar (w/entertainment), games rm, whirlpool, beauty salon, washer/dryer. **Rates (CP):** Peak (May–Oct) $109–$199 S or D; $249–$295 ste; $595 effic. Children under age 21 stay free. Min stay wknds. Lower rates off-season. AE, MC, V.

🗏🗏 Hotel St Lauren
231 Beacon St, PO Box 497, 90704; tel 310/510-2299 or toll free 800/400-0744; fax 310/510-1369. Great old-style hotel with incredible views, built in the late 1980s to re-create the Victorian era. Lovely rooftop patio. Good value. **Rooms:** 42 rms and stes. CI 2pm/CO 11am. Nonsmoking rms avail. Rooms are spacious and tastefully decorated in dark woods, with ceiling fans and Victorian armchairs. **Amenities:** 🗏 A/C, cable TV. Some units w/terraces, some w/whirlpools. **Services:** ➰ **Facilities:** 🗏 ⛓ **Rates (CP):** Peak (May–Sept) $125–$225 S or D; $235–$275 ste. Extra person $20. Children under age 12 stay free. Min stay wknds. Lower rates off-season. AE, MC, V.

🗏🗏 Hotel Villa Portofino
111 Crescent Ave, 90704; tel 310/510-0555 or toll free 800/34-OCEAN; fax 310/510-0839. With its inviting facade, this hotel looks like a California garden apartment building. **Rooms:** 34 rms and stes. CI 1pm/CO 11am. Light, airy rooms. **Amenities:** 🗏 A/C, cable TV. No phone. Some units w/terraces, some w/fireplaces. **Services:** ➰ Masseur, babysitting. **Facilities:** 🗏 1 restaurant (dinner only), 1 bar. **Rates (CP):** Peak (June 15–Oct 1) $90–$275 S or D; $240–$295 ste. Children under age 21 stay free. Min stay wknds and special events. Lower rates off-season. Roll-away bed, $10. AE, CB, DC, DISC, MC, V.

🗏🗏🗏 Hotel Vista Del Mar
417 Crescent Ave, PO Box 1979, 90704; tel 310/510-1452; fax 310/510-2917. One of the most pleasant hotels on the island, on the main promenade across from the beach. The lobby is airy and inviting with palm trees, orchids, wicker rocking chairs, and fountains. **Rooms:** 15 rms and stes. CI

2pm/CO 11am. No smoking. Rooms, decorated in soothing pastel colors, are extremely spacious with great views. Smoking allowed only on balconies. **Amenities:** 🗏 🗏 🗏 A/C, cable TV w/movies, refrig, VCR, bathrobes. Some units w/terraces, some w/fireplaces, some w/whirlpools. Showtime, Movie Channel. **Services:** X ➰ Free use of beach towels. **Facilities:** 🗏 1 beach (ocean), lifeguard. Near fishing, golf, boat rentals, and snorkeling. **Rates (CP):** Peak (May–Oct) $95–$275 S or D; $225–$275 ste. Extra person $10–$15. Min stay wknds and special events. Lower rates off-season. Parking: Outdoor, free. Reservations recommended 1–2 months in advance in summer. AE, DISC, MC, V.

🗏🗏 Zane Grey Pueblo Hotel
Off Chimes Tower Rd, PO Box 216, 90704; tel 310/510-0966 or toll free 800/378-3256. Rustic, pueblo-style hotel decorated with Native American art and earth tones. Like being in a cabin in the hills overlooking Avalon Bay. The living room offers a grand piano, fireplace, and TV. **Rooms:** 18 rms and stes. CI 11am/CO 10am. Nonsmoking rms avail. Rooms are named after Zane Grey's books. All are furnished differently; some have decorative fireplaces. **Amenities:** No A/C, phone, or TV. Some units w/terraces, 1 w/fireplace. **Services:** 🗏 **Facilities:** 🗏 **Rates (CP):** Peak (June–Sept) $75–$125 S or D; $140 ste. Extra person $35. Min stay peak and wknds. Lower rates off-season. AE, CB, DC, DISC, MC, V.

INN

🗏🗏 Catalina Island Inn
125 Metropole, PO Box 467, 90704; tel 310/510-1623; fax 310/510-7218. Lovely Victorian-style hotel, one block from the beach. Same owner-managers for 18 years. **Rooms:** 36 rms and stes. CI 1pm/CO 11am. Nonsmoking rms avail. Top-floor rooms are the best, with high ceilings and 1920s decor. Many accommodations have ocean views. **Amenities:** 🗏 Cable TV. No A/C. Some units w/terraces. **Services:** ➰ Masseur, babysitting. **Facilities:** Washer/dryer. **Rates (CP):** Peak (June–Oct) $99–$179 S or D; $189 ste. Children under age 21 stay free. Min stay peak and wknds. Lower rates off-season. Higher rates for special events/hols. AE, DISC, JCB, MC, V.

RESTAURANTS 🍽

★ The Busy Bee
306 Crescent Ave; tel 310/510-1983. **American/Burgers.** A very beachy place, with a patio bar on stilts over the water. Very popular on nice days for large salads, deli-style sandwiches, health-food sandwiches, salads, buffalo burgers, pork chops, and prime steaks. Closed in bad weather. Open for dinner in summer only. **FYI:** Reservations not accepted. Children's menu. **Open:** Peak (Apr–Oct) lunch Mon 11am–2pm, Tues 10am–2pm, Wed–Fri 11am–2pm, Sat–Sun 9am–3:30pm; dinner daily 5–11pm. **Prices:** Main courses $9–$17. AE, DISC, MC, V. 🖴 🖾

The Channel House
In the Hotel Metropole, 205 Crescent Ave; tel 310/510-1617. **International.** With bamboo and one wall of mirrors, it evokes the feeling of a country club. Inside are wicker chairs and plants hanging from the rafters. An outdoor patio with harbor views is available. Pepper steak flambé, duck à l'orange with Grand Marnier, and fresh fish daily. The calamari steak and the caesar salad are highly recommended. **FYI:** Reservations accepted. Piano. Children's menu. **Open:** Peak (July–Sept) daily 5–10pm. Closed Jan–Feb. **Prices:** Main courses $15–$25. AE, DC, DISC, MC, V.

El Galleon
411 Crescent Ave; tel 310/510-1188. **Pub/Seafood.** Located on the waterfront, this place is popular with tourists. It features pirate-ship decor, complete with portholes, heavy wrought-iron chandeliers, and wooden captain's chairs. Outdoor dining offered. Menu features English-style fish fritters, mahimahi, and Maine or local lobster. **FYI:** Reservations accepted. Guitar/karaoke/singer. **Open:** Lunch daily 11am–3pm; dinner Mon–Sun 5–11pm. **Prices:** Main courses $14–$21. AE, DISC, MC, V.

Sand Trap
Avalon Canyon Rd; tel 310/510-1349. **Mexican.** Good value and an inviting Mexican ambience. Outdoor dining available on a large brick patio. Dishes include fish tacos, fresh guacamole, several types of burritos, and a myriad of breakfast omelettes. Just a short walk out of town next to the golf course. **FYI:** Reservations recommended. Children's menu. Beer and wine only. **Open:** Peak (May–Oct) daily 7:30am–3:30pm. **Prices:** Lunch main courses $7–$9. No CC.

ATTRACTIONS

Avalon Casino Building
Crescent Ave; tel toll free 800/428-2566. The most famous structure on Catalina Island is also one of the oldest. The casino was the first resort building erected to attract vacationers from the mainland. Built in 1929, the massive circular rotunda, topped by a red tile roof, appears on posters and postcards in shops all around town. The casino is best known for its beautiful art deco ballroom that once hosted top big bands like the Tommy Dorsey and the Glen Miller orchestras. You can see the inside of the building by attending a ballroom event or a film (the Casino is Avalon's primary movie theater). Otherwise, admission is by guided tour only, operated daily by the Santa Catalina Island Company (tel 310/510-2500 or toll free 800/4-AVALON).

Catalina Island Museum
Crescent Ave; tel 310/510-2414. Located on the ground floor of the Avalon Casino, the museum features exhibits on island history and archeology, as well as an excellent relief map that details the island's interior. **Open:** Daily 10:30am–4pm. $

Wrigley Memorial and Botanical Garden
Tel 310/510-2288. The Wrigley Memorial honors William Wrigley, Jr, and his contributions to the development of Catalina Island. It was built from 1933 to 1934, and as many Catalina materials as possible were used in its construction. The red roof tiles and the colorful, handmade glazed tile used for finishing came from the Catalina Pottery plant, which operated from 1927 to 1937.

In 1969 the garden was expanded and revitalized. Special emphasis is given to plants that are native to one or more California islands, but grow nowhere else. Eight of these are found only on Catalina Island itself. **Open:** Daily 8am–5pm. $

Avalon Pleasure Pier
Crescent Ave and Catalina St. Jutting out into Crescent Cove, the wood plank pier affords excellent views of the town and surrounding mountains. Food stands and bait-and-tackle shops line the pier.

Bakersfield

The southern anchor of the Central Valley and one of the richest agricultural zones in the world, Bakersfield has become one of the major urban centers in California, though it still remains true to its roots. With the sound of country music, the countless outlets for country cooking, and the oil derricks, you could easily mistake it for Texas or Oklahoma. **Information:** Greater Bakersfield Convention & Visitors Bureau, 1033 Truxtun Ave, Bakersfield 93301 (tel 805/325-5051 or toll free 800/325-6001).

HOTELS

Best Western Hill House
700 Truxtun Ave, 93301 (Downtown); tel 805/327-4064 or toll free 800/528-1234; fax 805/327-1247. The best hotel in central downtown Bakersfield, located across from the Convention Center. Pleasant building with white columns and worn brick facade. **Rooms:** 97 rms. CI 3pm/CO noon. Nonsmoking rms avail. Clean and simple. **Amenities:** A/C, cable TV. Some units w/terraces. **Services:** **Facilities:** 2 restaurants (lunch and dinner only), 1 bar. **Rates (CP):** $60–$70 S or D. Extra person $5. Children under age 12 stay free. Parking: Outdoor, free. AE, CB, DC, DISC, MC, V.

Courtyard by Marriott
3601 Marriott Dr, 93308 (Downtown); tel 805/324-6660 or toll free 800/321-2211; fax 805/324-1185. Fastidiously clean property, reliable and quiet despite location. Filled mostly with business travelers on weekdays, and leisure travelers on weekends. **Rooms:** 146 rms and stes. CI 3pm/CO 1pm. Nonsmoking rms avail. Rooms for travelers with disabilities connect to other rooms. Entire wings are nonsmoking. **Amenities:** A/C, cable TV w/movies. All units w/terraces. **Services:** **Facilities:** 1

restaurant (bkfst and dinner only), 1 bar, games rm, whirlpool, washer/dryer. **Rates:** $74 S; $84 D; $95–$105 ste. Children under age 18 stay free. Parking: Outdoor, free. AE, DC, DISC, MC, V.

≣≣≣ Four Points Hotel by ITT Sheraton

5101 California Ave, 93309; tel 805/325-9700 or toll free 800/500-5399; fax 805/323-3508. ¾ mi W of California Ave exit off CA 99. Exceptionally quiet, upscale property catering to business travelers. Spacious, comfortable lobby. **Rooms:** 197 rms and stes. Executive level. CI 3pm/CO 1pm. Nonsmoking rms avail. **Amenities:** 🛏 🔥 📺 A/C, cable TV w/movies, voice mail. Some units w/terraces. **Services:** ✗ 🍽 📐 📬 🥤 Social director, babysitting. **Facilities:** 🏊 🏋 🚗200 💻 🛗 1 restaurant (*see* "Restaurants" below), 1 bar, spa, whirlpool. Beautiful pool area in central courtyard shaded by trellises and plants. Free use of nearby Family Fitness Center. **Rates (CP):** Peak (Spring–Fall) $99 S; $109 D; $125 ste. Extra person $10. Children under age 18 stay free. Lower rates off-season. Parking: Outdoor, free. AE, CB, DC, DISC, MC, V.

≣≣≣ Holiday Inn Select Convention Center

801 Truxtun Ave, 93301 (Downtown); tel 805/323-1900 or toll free 800/HOLIDAY; fax 805/323-2844. A beautiful, new, nine-story hotel adjacent to the Convention Center; opened in June 1995. **Rooms:** 259 rms and stes. Executive level. CI 3pm/CO noon. Nonsmoking rms avail. Each floor has one room for travelers with disabilities. **Amenities:** 🛏 🔥 📺 🍴 A/C, cable TV w/movies, dataport, voice mail. 1 unit w/whirlpool. Irons and ironing boards in all rooms. **Services:** ✗ 🍽 📐 📬 Car-rental desk. **Facilities:** 🏊 🏋 🚗1700 💻 🛗 1 restaurant, 1 bar (w/entertainment), games rm, sauna, steam rm, whirlpool. **Rates:** Peak (June–Aug/Oct) $95 S; $105 D; $250–$400 ste. Extra person $10. Children under age 18 stay free. Min stay special events. Lower rates off-season. Parking: Outdoor, free. AE, CB, DC, DISC, JCB, MC, V.

≣≣ Radisson Suites Inn

828 Real Rd, 93309; tel 805/322-9988 or toll free 800/333-3333; fax 805/322-3668. CA Ave exit off CA 99. Near busy highway, but rooms are quiet. **Rooms:** 80 rms and effic. CI 3pm/CO noon. Nonsmoking rms avail. Accommodations can be small, but are clean and bright. **Amenities:** 🛏 🔥 📺 🍴 A/C, cable TV w/movies, refrig. Some units w/whirlpools. Wet bar. **Services:** 📐 📬 Babysitting. **Facilities:** 🏊 🏋 🛗 Whirlpool, washer/dryer. Breakfast served in a room off the lobby that resembles a cafeteria. **Rates (CP):** $79 S; $89 D; $119 effic. Extra person $5. Children under age 16 stay free. Parking: Outdoor, free. AE, CB, DC, DISC, JCB, MC, V.

≣≣≣ Red Lion Hotel

3100 Camino del Rio Court, 93308; tel 805/323-7111 or toll free 800/547-8010; fax 805/323-0331. CA 58 E exit off CA 99. The most elegant hotel in Bakersfield; as quiet as a library, despite busy freeway nearby. **Rooms:** 262 rms and stes. CI 3pm/CO 1pm. Nonsmoking rms avail. Light sleepers

should ask for a room on the quieter side of the hotel. Only 1 room (with 2 beds) for guests with disabilities. **Amenities:** 🛏 🔥 📺 A/C, cable TV w/movies, voice mail. All units w/terraces, some w/whirlpools. **Services:** ✗ 🍽 🚗 📐 📬 🥤 **Facilities:** 🏊 🚗500 🛗 2 restaurants (*see* "Restaurants" below), 1 bar (w/entertainment), whirlpool. Guests can use Family Fitness Center across the street. **Rates:** $109–$149 S or D; $200–$400 ste. Children under age 12 stay free. Parking: Outdoor, free. AE, CB, DC, DISC, JCB, MC, V.

≣≣≣ Residence Inn by Marriott

4241 Chester Lane, 93309; tel 805/321-9800 or toll free 800/331-3131; fax 805/321-0721. 1 block W of California Ave exit off CA 99. Very homey and comfortable. **Rooms:** 114 effic. CI 3pm/CO 1pm. Nonsmoking rms avail. All rooms have full kitchens and breakfast bars equipped with utensils. Special smoke alarm in suite for guests with disabilities. **Amenities:** 🛏 🔥 📺 A/C, satel TV, refrig, voice mail. Some units w/fireplaces. **Services:** ✗ 🚗 📐 📬 🥤 Social director, babysitting. Social hour in lounge Mon–Fri 5–7pm. Videos available in lobby. **Facilities:** 🏊 🏋 🚗30 🛗 Whirlpool, playground, washer/dryer. **Rates (BB):** $85 effic. Children under age 18 stay free. Min stay special events. Parking: Outdoor, free. AE, CB, DC, DISC, MC, V.

MOTELS

≣≣ California Inn

1030 Wible Rd, 93304; tel 805/834-3377 or toll free 800/707-8000; fax 805/834-4439. Ming Ave exit off CA 99. Newer property; a good budget choice. **Rooms:** 61 rms. CI noon/CO noon. Nonsmoking rms avail. Simple but clean rooms. **Amenities:** 🛏 📺 A/C, cable TV. 1 unit w/terrace. **Services:** 📬 🥤 **Facilities:** 🏊 🛗 Sauna, whirlpool. **Rates (CP):** $36 S; $39 D. Extra person $2. Children under age 14 stay free. Parking: Outdoor, free. AE, DC, MC, V.

≣≣ La Quinta Motor Inn

3232 Riverside Dr, 93308 (Downtown); tel 805/325-7400 or toll free 800/531-5900; fax 805/324-6032. Clean, newish property with a comfortable lobby and a convenient location. Good value. **Rooms:** 129 rms and stes. Executive level. CI open/CO noon. Nonsmoking rms avail. Smallish rooms, newly painted; fine for a short stay. **Amenities:** 🛏 🔥 A/C, satel TV w/movies. **Services:** 🚗 📐 📬 🥤 **Facilities:** 🏊 🚗35 🛗 Washer/dryer. **Rates (CP):** $54–$61 S; $62–$69 D; $67–$75 ste. Children under age 18 stay free. Parking: Outdoor, free. AE, DC, DISC, MC, V.

≣≣ Ramada Inn

3535 Rosedale Hwy, 93308 (Downtown); tel 805/327-0681 or toll free 800/228-2828; fax 805/324-1648. Rosedale exit off CA 99. Convenient to freeways. Looks deluxe because of recent upgrading, but basically a standard chain hotel. **Rooms:** 197 rms. CI 4pm/CO noon. Nonsmoking rms avail. **Amenities:** 🛏 🔥 A/C, cable TV. Some units w/terraces. **Services:** ✗ 🚗 📐 📬 **Facilities:** 🏊 🚗400 🛗 1 restaurant, 1 bar (w/entertainment), whirlpool, washer/dryer. **Rates:** $72 S; $77 D. Extra person $6. Children under age 18 stay free. Parking: Outdoor, free. AE, DISC, MC, V.

≣ ≣ Skyway Inn

1305 Skyway Dr, 93308 (Oildale); tel 805/399-9321; fax 805/399-2615. Airport Dr exit off CA 99. Convenient location for air travelers. Inexpensive and clean. **Rooms:** 63 rms. CI open/CO noon. Nonsmoking rms avail. Rooms are light, airy, and unique, each with a name and theme, such as "Modern Romance" or "Ocean View." Adorned with bric-a-brac and creative lighting in an attempt to add personality to otherwise ordinary rooms. **Amenities:** 📱 🛢 📺 A/C, cable TV w/movies. **Services:** ✕ 🖼 ⟲ Car-rental desk, babysitting. **Facilities:** 🍴 1 restaurant (see "Restaurants" below), 1 bar, whirlpool. **Rates:** $45 S; $51 D. Extra person $6. Children under age 12 stay free. Parking: Outdoor, free. AE, CB, DC, DISC, MC, V.

RESTAURANTS 🍴

Anton's Airport Bar & Grill

In the Skyway Inn, 1229 Skyway Dr (Oildale); tel 805/399-3300. Airport Dr exit off CA 99. **Californian.** Quiet and elegant with comfortable booths and plush chairs, as well as large windows facing airport runways. Menu features pasta, lobster, and seafood. Good bets are the orange-sesame shrimp, or the salmon "hurricane" (a jumbo sea scallop and salmon rolled in sesame seeds, then sautéed with fresh basil, orange, and ginger). **FYI:** Reservations recommended. Piano. Dress code. **Open:** Breakfast daily 5:30–11am; lunch daily 11am–4pm; dinner Mon–Sat 4–10pm, Sun 5:30–9pm; brunch Sun 10am–2pm. **Prices:** Main courses $7–$18. AE, CB, DC, MC, V. ❦

❦ The Bistro

In Four Points Hotel by ITT Sheraton, 5105 California Ave; tel 805/323-3905. Stockdale Hwy exit off CA 99. **Californian/Continental.** Southwestern Indian artifacts displays, plush booths, wooden shutters on windows. Cuisine is a mixture of ethnic and California dishes— pastas, seafood, salads, and poultry, prepared imaginatively. Selection of cognacs. **FYI:** Reservations recommended. Guitar. Dress code. **Open:** Breakfast Mon–Fri 6:30–10am, Sat 7:30–11am; lunch Mon–Fri 11am–2pm, Sat 11:30am–2pm; dinner daily 6–10pm; brunch Sun 10am–2pm. **Prices:** Main courses $14–$24. AE, CB, DC, DISC, ER, MC, V. ❦ ❦

Cafe Med

In Northridge Plaza, 5600 Auburn St; tel 805/873-8106. Fairfax exit off Calif 178. **Mediterranean/Middle Eastern.** Small storefront restaurant with cramped elegance. Bright, tasteful, clean. Eclectic menu features Italian, Greek, Spanish, French, Egyptian, and Moroccan foods. Also at: 5486 California Ave, Bakersfield (805/327-3544). **FYI:** Reservations recommended. Dancing. Beer and wine only. **Open:** Sun–Thurs 11am–9pm, Fri–Sat 11am–10pm. **Prices:** Main courses $8–$18. AE, CB, DC, DISC, MC, V. ❦

❦ Frugatti's Wood-Fired Pizza

In Fountain Plaza Shopping Center, 600 Coffee Rd; tel 805/836-2000. 2 mi W of downtown At Truxtun Ave. **Italian.** Eclectic mix of old produce labels, nostalgic soda signs, old lights, and old pictures. Brick wood-burning oven in center of the room for making pizzas and baking pastas. Low-fat and vegetarian choices. Great cheesecakes. **FYI:** Reservations not accepted. Children's menu. Beer and wine only. **Open:** Lunch daily 11am–2pm; dinner Sun–Thurs 4:30–10pm, Fri–Sat 4:30–11pm. **Prices:** Main courses $5–$11. AE, DC, DISC, MC, V. 🎬 ❦

❦ ❋ Mama Tosca's Ristorante Italiano

In Laurelglen Plaza, 6631 Ming Ave; tel 805/831-1242. 3 mi W from Ming Ave exit off CA 99 Ashe Rd. **Italian.** A small room with white stucco walls and green carpeting. Among the Italian specialties, osso buco is popular. Steaks and seafood also available. Marinated carrots with garlic and olive oil come with the bread. **FYI:** Reservations recommended. Blues/jazz. Dress code. **Open:** Lunch Mon–Fri 11:30am–2pm; dinner Mon–Sat 5:30–10pm. **Prices:** Main courses $12–$34. AE, CB, DC, DISC, MC, V. ❦ ❦

Misty's

In the Red Lion Hotel, 3100 Camino del Rio Court; tel 805/323-7111. Rosedale Hwy exit off CA 99. **Californian/Continental.** A high-beamed ceiling gives the impression of a ski lodge, but the decor is subdued and elegant. Booths are plush and inviting. Menu highlights pastas, such as tortellini with Dungeness crab and Gorgonzola cheese. **FYI:** Reservations recommended. Country music. Children's menu. Dress code. **Open:** Lunch Mon–Fri 11:30am–1:30pm; dinner Mon–Sun 5:30–9:30pm; brunch Sun 9am–2pm. **Prices:** Main courses $12–$21. AE, CB, DC, DISC, MC, V. ❦ ❦

The Noriega Hotel

525 Sumner St; tel 805/322-8419. **Basque.** This Basque bar-restaurant is difficult to find, but worth the effort. Specialties include pickled tongue, oxtail soup, lamb stew, and spare ribs. Everything is served family-style at a fixed price that includes wine and dessert. More food than you can eat. **FYI:** Reservations accepted. **Open:** Breakfast Tues–Sun 7–9am; lunch Tues–Sun noon–3pm; dinner Tues–Sun 7pm–close. **Prices:** Prix fixe $15. No CC. ■

❋ Uricchio's Trattoria

1400 17th St (Downtown); tel 805/326-8870. E Chester Ave, N of Truxtun. **Italian.** This small Italian place is owned and operated by the same family who ran the Beverly Hills restaurant for years. Almost all entrees are priced under $10; dinner for two, including wine and dessert, comes to about $30. Try the chicken with pearl onions, artichoke hearts, mushrooms, and red wine sauce. A great dessert is the tiramisù with a chocolate brownie base. The bar is open when meals are not being served. **FYI:** Reservations recommended. **Open:** Lunch Mon–Fri 11am–2pm; dinner Mon–Thurs 5–9pm, Fri–Sat 5–10pm. **Prices:** Main courses $6–$15. AE, CB, DC, DISC, MC, V. ❦

ATTRACTIONS

Kern County Museum
3801 Chester Ave; tel 805/861-2132. More than 50 buildings depicting the natural and human history of Kern County are spread over 14 shaded acres. Structures include an 1868 log cabin, general store, schoolhouse, church, oil rig, and 1891 Queen Anne–style house. The main museum building houses a variety of permanent and changing exhibitions. **Open:** Mon–Fri 8am–5pm, Sat 10am–5pm, Sun noon–5pm. $$$

Tule Elk State Reserve
8653 Station Rd, Buttonwillow; tel 805/765-5004. Located 20 miles west of Bakersfield via Stockdale Hwy. From the mid-1800s, Tule elk, native to California, gradually lost their habitat to agricultural development. By 1895, only 28 animals survived. The elk have been given protection on this 956-acre reserve. Viewing platform, binoculars available for rent; exhibits of local wildlife at headquarters. **Open:** Daily 8am–sunset. $$

Barstow

Founded as a railroad line intersection, the city is now at the center of a newer set of crossroads: I-15 and I-40, which form the borders of the ruggedly beautiful and mountainous 1.4 million-acre Mojave National Preserve. **Information:** Barstow Area Chamber of Commerce, 222 E Main St #216, PO Box 698, Barstow 92312 (tel 619/256-8617).

MOTELS

≣≣ Holiday Inn Express
1861 West Main St, 92311; tel 619/256-1300 or toll free 800/HOLIDAY; fax 619/256-6807. E Main St exit off I-15; ¾ mi W. Built in 1992, the property still feels brand new. **Rooms:** 148 rms and stes. CI 3pm/CO noon. Nonsmoking rms avail. **Amenities:** 🔒 ⚬ A/C, cable TV. 1 unit w/terrace. **Services:** ✕ ⊠ ⌐ ⬩ Children's program in summer. Pets allowed at an additional charge. **Facilities:** ⌐ ⌐225⌐ ⬩ 1 restaurant, 1 bar, whirlpool. **Rates:** $75 S or D; $85–$95 ste. Extra person $6. Children under age 18 stay free. Parking: Outdoor, free. Discount for government employees. AE, CB, DC, DISC, JCB, MC, V.

≣≣ Quality Inn
1520 E Main St, 92311; tel 619/256-6891 or toll free 800/221-2222. E Main St exit off I-15; ¼ mi W. Nice lobby and interior courtyard. **Rooms:** 100 rms. CI 2pm/CO noon. Nonsmoking rms avail. **Amenities:** 🔒 A/C, cable TV. Only some rooms have TV remotes. Refrigerators are $6 per night. **Services:** ✕ ⊠ ⌐ ⬩ **Facilities:** ⌐ ⌐100⌐ ⬩ 1 restaurant, 1 bar. **Rates:** $49 S; $55 D. Extra person $6. Children under age 18 stay free. Parking: Outdoor, free. AE, DC, DISC, MC, V.

ATTRACTIONS

California Desert Information Center
831 Barstow Rd; tel 619/256-8313. The center provides regional visitor services, including current local road information, campground and recreation area information, and California campfire permits. Exhibits include desert plants and animals, an outdoor desert plant exhibit, a pond containing desert fish, and a bookstore. **Open:** Daily 9am–5pm. **Free**

Rainbow Basin Natural Area
Tel 619/256-8313. Located 8 miles north of Barstow via Fort Irwin Rd, Rainbow Basin is a visual treat. Millions of years worth of sediment have piled up to form a basin with an amazing array of colors. There are three hiking trails of moderate difficulty through the area. Unimproved camping facilities are available at Owl Creek Campground; visitors should bring water. Best time to visit is late fall–early spring. **Open:** Daily 24 hours. **Free**

Calico Early Man Archaeological Site
Tel 619/256-3591. Located 15 miles northeast of Barstow via I-15; take the Mineola exit and follow signs north 2½ miles along graded dirt roads. Begun in 1964, this site has been classified as a stone tool workshop, quarry, and campsite used by early nomadic hunter-gatherers about 200,000 years ago. It is the oldest evidence of human activity in the Americas. The Calico project was the only New World project undertaken by the archeologist/paleontologist Dr Louis S B Leakey, who was director of the project until his death in 1972.

On guided tours through two of the master pits, chipped-stone tools fashioned by the earliest Americans are still visible in the walls and floors. A small museum displays examples of recovered artifacts. For further information contact the Bureau of Land Management, Barstow Resource Area, 150 Coolwater Lane, Barstow, CA 92311. **Open:** Tours: Wed 1:30 and 3:30pm, Thurs–Sat 9:30am–4pm. **Free**

Afton Canyon
Located 40 miles east of Barstow via I-15. Afton Canyon, the "Grand Canyon of the Mojave," was created about 19,000 years ago when Lake Manix drained. The canyon walls tower 300 feet above the Mojave River, their multicolored stratigraphy and varied textures providing a unique scenic experience. Hiking is possible along the river and through numerous side canyons, but trails are unmarked and rough, and a flashlight is essential when exploring some of the side canyons. Afton Canyon Campground ($6/night) provides restrooms, grills, picnic tables, water, and shade ramadas (camping limit is 14 days). More information can be provided by the California Desert Information Center (see above). **Open:** Daily sunrise–sunset. **Free**

Calico Ghost Town
Ghost Town Rd, Yermo; tel 619/254-2122. In its heyday, the town of Calico boasted 22 saloons, a population of about 4,000, and the richest silver strike in California history. The Silver King Mine was found by two prospectors in 1881. Soon

thereafter, hundreds of miners arrived and the new town was founded. In a little over a decade, $86 million in silver ore and $9 million in borax had been removed from the area. When silver prices declined in 1896, most of the miners moved on to more lucrative diggings.

In 1950 the site was purchased by the Knott family and completely restored. Mine tour; railroad excursion; bunkhouse; cabins; playhouse. Camping area nearby. **Open:** Daily 8am–dusk; shops and attractions 9am–5pm. **$$**

Beaumont

MOTEL 🛄

≣ Best Western El Rancho Motel
550 Beaumont Ave, 92223; tel 909/845-2176; fax 909/845-7559. Beaumont Ave exit off I-10. Contemporary, basic motel lacking character and landscaping. Restaurant is located nearby. **Rooms:** 52 rms and stes. CI 2pm/CO noon. Nonsmoking rms avail. **Amenities:** 🛅 A/C, cable TV. **Services:** 🛆 **Facilities:** 🛆 Pool area needs work. **Rates:** $36–$40 S; $39–$43 D; $55–$61 ste. Extra person $3. Parking: Outdoor, free. AE, CB, DC, DISC, MC, V.

Berkeley

See also Oakland

Still the icon of progressive politics and left-wing activism, Berkeley was born with the formation of the University of California in the 1870s. While the campus still forms the heart of the community, the city is also an enclave of first-rate restaurants, pricey shopping districts, and expensive hillside homes. **Information:** Berkeley Convention & Visitors Bureau, 1834 University Ave, 1st Floor, Berkeley 94703-1516 (tel 510/549-7040 or toll free 800/847-4823).

HOTELS 🛄

≣≣≣ Berkeley Marina Marriott
200 Marina Blvd, 94710 (Berkeley Marina); tel 510/548-7920 or toll free 800/243-0625; fax 510/548-7944. University Ave exit off I-80. Very well kept, with new furnishings. Located a bit out of the way, but still convenient to town and the Bay Bridge. **Rooms:** 375 rms and stes. Executive level. CI 3pm/CO noon. Nonsmoking rms avail. Many rooms face the marina with views of San Francisco or the bay. **Amenities:** 🛅 A/C, cable TV w/movies, dataport, voice mail. All units w/terraces, 1 w/whirlpool. Iron and ironing board in rooms. **Services:** ✕ 🛒 🚗 🛆 🛆 Twice-daily maid svce, babysitting. Business services available. Hotel can arrange for windsurfing, waterskiing, or sailing excursions. **Facilities:** 🛆 🛆 🛒 🛆 1 restaurant, 1 bar (w/entertainment), volleyball, spa, sauna, steam rm, whirlpool, day-care ctr, washer/dryer. Pool with fitness center is for adults only.

Rates: $94–$170 S or D; $250–$700 ste. Children under age 18 stay free. Min stay special events. Parking: Outdoor, free. AE, CB, DC, DISC, MC, V.

≣ The French Hotel
1538 Shattuck Ave, 94709 (North Berkeley); tel 510/548-9930; fax 510/649-0982. Excellent location in an upscale Berkeley neighborhood near shops and fine restaurants. **Rooms:** 18 rms. CI 3pm/CO 11am. Nonsmoking rms avail. Decidedly basic, with wire-basket drawers, wire closet racks. **Amenities:** 🛅 🛆 TV. No A/C. Some units w/terraces. **Services:** 🍴 🛆 **Facilities:** 1 restaurant (bkfst only). Popular ground-level cafe is pleasant if noisy, with some sidewalk tables in the French tradition. **Rates:** $68–$125 S or D. Children under age 18 stay free. Parking: Indoor/outdoor, free. AE, CB, DC, DISC, JCB, MC, V.

≣≣≣ Gramma's Rose Garden Inn
2740 Telegraph Ave, 94705; tel 510/549-2145; fax 510/549-1085. Charming, with three cottages and two Victorian houses clustered around a landscaped courtyard. **Rooms:** 40 rms, stes, and effic. CI noon/CO 2pm. No smoking. Decor in keeping with turn-of-the-century theme. Some cottages have leaded-glass windows. **Amenities:** 🛅 🛆 🛆 Cable TV w/movies, dataport. No A/C. Some units w/terraces, some w/fireplaces. **Services:** ✕ 🚗 🛆 🛆 🛆 Twice-daily maid svce. Complimentary wine and cheese 5–8pm daily. **Facilities:** 🛆 1 restaurant (dinner only), 1 bar. **Rates (BB):** $89 S; $99 D; $125–$145 ste; $145 effic. Extra person $10. Children under age 2 stay free. Parking: Outdoor, free. Some lower rates Sun–Thurs. AE, CB, DC, DISC, MC, V.

≣≣ Holiday Inn Bay Bridge
1800 Powell St, Emeryville, 94608; tel 510/658-9300 or toll free 800/HOLIDAY; fax 510/547-8166. Off I-80. Closest hotel to San Francisco–Oakland Bay Bridge. Good freeway access to East Bay events. **Rooms:** 280 rms and stes. Executive level. CI 3pm/CO noon. Nonsmoking rms avail. Comfortable, clean, standard Holiday Inn style. Some rooms have bay and San Francisco views. **Amenities:** 🛅 🛆 A/C, cable TV w/movies. **Services:** ✕ 🛒 🛆 🛆 **Facilities:** 🛒 🛆 🛆 🛆 1 restaurant, 1 bar, spa, whirlpool. Recently renovated fitness center and health spa. **Rates:** $119 S; $129 D; $300–$350 ste. Extra person $10. Children under age 18 stay free. Min stay special events. Parking: Outdoor, free. AE, CB, DC, DISC, JCB, MC, V.

≣≣≣ Hotel Durant
2600 Durant Ave, 94704; tel 510/845-8981 or toll free 800/238-7268; fax 510/486-8336. Best location in Berkeley, close to Telegraph Ave and the University of California. **Rooms:** 140 rms and stes. CI 2pm/CO noon. Nonsmoking rms avail. Tastefully decorated in a traditional homey style. **Amenities:** 🛅 🛆 Cable TV w/movies. No A/C. **Services:** ✕ 🛆 🚗 🛆 🛆 **Facilities:** 🛆 🛆 2 restaurants, 1 bar. Guests may purchase discounted day passes for university sports facilities, such as a pool and tennis and racquetball courts. **Rates (CP):** $91–

$101 S; $101–$111 D; $186–$282 ste. Extra person $15. Children under age 12 stay free. Min stay peak. Parking: Outdoor, $5/day. AE, CB, DC, DISC, JCB, MC, V.

Hotel Shattuck

2086 Allston Way, at Shattuck Ave, 94704 (Downtown); tel 510/845-7300 or toll free 800/237-5359, 800/742-8825 in CA; fax 510/644-2088. In downtown Berkeley, yet within walking distance of the University of California. Older building nicely updated. Outside street noise fairly bad during the day. **Rooms:** 175 rms and stes. CI 3pm/CO noon. Nonsmoking rms avail. Older, traditional style, but neat and clean. **Amenities:** TV w/movies. No A/C. 1 unit w/fireplace. **Services:** **Facilities:** Washer/dryer. **Rates (CP):** Peak (May, June, Aug, Nov) $90 S; $100 D; $100–$110 ste. Extra person $15. Children under age 12 stay free. Lower rates off-season. AE, DC, DISC, MC, V.

Ramada Inn

920 University Ave, 94710; tel 510/849-1121 or toll free 800/954-7575; fax 510/845-4397. University exit off I-80. Spacious lobby, recently redecorated. **Rooms:** 110 rms. CI 2pm/CO noon. Nonsmoking rms avail. **Amenities:** A/C, TV w/movies. Some units w/terraces. **Services:** Car-rental desk. **Facilities:** 2 restaurants, 1 bar (w/entertainment). Nice pool, a rarity in Berkeley. Restaurant has giant-screen TV. **Rates:** Peak (May–Sept) $69 S; $79 D. Extra person $10. Children under age 12 stay free. Lower rates off-season. Parking: Outdoor, free. Group rates for 10 or more. AE, DC, DISC, MC, V.

RESORT

Claremont Resort, Spa & Tennis Club

41 Tunnel Rd, 94705 (Berkeley Hills); tel 510/843-3000 or toll free 800/551-7266; fax 510/848-6208. Claremont Ave exit off CA 24 E. 22 acres. Built in 1915, this grand old hotel—complete with gables, turrets, and dormers—is reputed to be the largest wooden structure in California. Lovingly updated without losing any of its historic charm, the Claremont is located in the wooded Berkeley foothills with views of the San Francisco Bay and skyline. Contemporary Pacific Northwest art from the owners' private collection is displayed throughout the hotel. **Rooms:** 279 rms and stes. CI 3pm/CO noon. Nonsmoking rms avail. Accommodations are beautifully decorated in English manor style, with framed botanical prints and chinoiserie or floral chintz bedspreads. (The rather homely linoleum floors in the bathrooms are a bit of a disappointment, however.) All rooms feature either bay or hillside views. Turret suites, with rounded walls, offer sensational San Francisco views. **Amenities:** A/C, cable TV w/movies, voice mail, in-rm safe. 1 unit w/terrace, 1 w/whirlpool. Irons and ironing boards in closets. **Services:** Car-rental desk, masseur, babysitting. The $6 million spa is one of the largest and finest in Northern California, offering a full range of massages, facials, hydrotherapy treatments, and more. **Facilities:** 3 restaurants, 2 bars (1 w/entertainment), spa, sauna, steam rm, whirlpool, beauty salon. Fitness center features first-rate exercise bikes, step machines, treadmills, Cybex equipment, and free weights, along with aerobics classes and personal training sessions; there's also a tennis pro shop. Two gorgeous Olympic-size pools are heated all year. **Rates:** $165–$190 S or D; $225–$700 ste. Extra person $20. Children under age 12 stay free. Min stay special events. Parking: Outdoor, $8/day. "Weekend Getaway" packages avail. AE, CB, DC, DISC, EC, ER, JCB, MC, V.

RESTAURANTS

Chez Panisse

1517 Shattuck Ave; tel 510/548-5525. At Cedar St. **Californian.** The birthplace of California cuisine, this warm and cozy spot, owned by acclaimed chef Alice Waters, offers perfectly prepared and wonderfully fresh dishes, using only the finest ingredients. The ambience is quiet and a bit formal, but not stuffy. Fixed-price menu changes daily and may include grilled quail, salmon, and eggplant ravioli. Make reservations one month in advance. **FYI:** Reservations recommended. Dress code. Beer and wine only. **Open:** Mon–Sat 6–9:15pm. **Prices:** Prix fixe $35–$65. AE, DC, DISC, MC, V.

Chez Panisse Cafe

1517 Shattuck Ave; tel 510/548-5525. At Cedar St. **Californian.** Upstairs from the original Chez Panisse, this offers a perfect opportunity to try renowned chef Alice Waters's innovative California cuisine at a much lower price than the more formal restaurant downstairs. Especially nice for lunch (reservations recommended for Sunday lunch). **FYI:** Reservations not accepted. Children's menu. Beer and wine only. **Open:** Lunch Mon–Sat 11:30am–3pm; dinner Mon–Sat 5–10:30pm. **Prices:** Main courses $14–$18; prix fixe $20. AE, DC, DISC, MC, V.

Ginger Island

1820 4th St; tel 510/644-0444. At Hearse St. **Asian.** Open, airy, and cozy, this sophisticated restaurant specializes in highly stylized cuisine inspired by the cooking of Thailand and China. Ginger is used throughout the menu on specialties like tea-smoked duck, red-curry noodles, fresh sea scallops, and hamburger with Asian salsa. **FYI:** Reservations recommended. **Open:** Lunch Mon–Sat 11:30am–2:30pm; dinner Sun–Thurs 5–10pm, Fri–Sat 5–11pm; brunch Sun 10:30am–3:30pm. **Prices:** Main courses $9–$16. AE, DC, MC, V.

Lalime's

1329 Gilman St; tel 510/527-9838. **Mediterranean.** This split-level dining room is decorated with modern touches and is a perfect setting to enjoy the highly stylized cooking. Dishes inspired by the south of France and northern Italy. Frequently changing menu; extensive wine list. **FYI:** Reservations recommended. Beer and wine only. **Open:** Mon–Thurs 5:30–9:30pm, Fri–Sat 5:30–10pm, Sun 5–9pm. **Prices:** Main courses $11–$18; prix fixe $17–$30. MC, V.

Larry Blake's

2367 Telegraph Ave; tel 510/848-0886. **American.** Three floors of eating, drinking, and dancing: Upstairs is a cocktail lounge. On the ground floor, sandwiches, salads, steaks, stir fry, and burritos are served. In the basement is a blues bar complete with dance floor—big names in blues often play here. **FYI:** Reservations accepted. Blues. **Open:** Daily 11am–2am. **Prices:** Main courses $6–$10. AE, DC, DISC, MC, V.

Nakapan

1921 Martin Luther King Jr Way; tel 510/548-3050. 1½ mi W of University Ave exit off I-880/80. **Thai.** Tucked away from the main street, this is one of the best-kept secrets in town. The hardwood floors and open-beamed ceiling create a warm and cozy ambience in which to enjoy the wide variety of curries and other Thai specialties. Daily specials typically include seafood. **FYI:** Reservations accepted. Beer and wine only. **Open:** Lunch Mon–Fri 11:30am–3pm; dinner daily 5–10pm. **Prices:** Main courses $7–$10. AE, MC, V.

Petrouchka

2930 College Ave; tel 510/848-7860. **Russian.** Russian cuisine is generally considered to be extremely robust, with its more-than-generous quantities of butter, cream, sour cream, and richly-stewed meats. Here, however, entrees are light and thoughtfully prepared. The menu changes regularly and features sophisticated vegetarian dishes. **FYI:** Reservations recommended. Beer and wine only. **Open:** Lunch Mon–Fri 11:30am–2pm, Sat–Sun 11:30am–5pm; dinner daily 5–10pm. **Prices:** Main courses $9–$13. DISC, MC, V.

Santa Fe Bar & Grill

1310 University Ave; tel 510/841-4740. **Southwestern.** A popular restaurant in a remodeled Santa Fe Railway station. The mission-revival building has a whitewashed exterior and interior done in earth tones, with a tiled-floor entryway. The chef prepares grilled and smoked meat (over a wood-burning rotisserie), as well as seafood and pasta dishes. A pianist specializes in popular tunes of the 1930s and 1940s. **FYI:** Reservations recommended. Jazz. Dress code. **Open:** Lunch Mon–Fri 11:30am–3:30pm; dinner daily 5–10pm. **Prices:** Main courses $14–$18. AE, CB, DC, MC, V. &

★ Triple Rock Brewery and Ale House

1920 Shattuck Ave; tel 510/843-2739. **Pub.** This bustling North Berkeley hangout serves fresh soups and hot sandwiches, but the real attraction is the handcrafted beers and ales brewed just behind giant glass walls in the taproom cum restaurant. **FYI:** Reservations not accepted. Beer and wine only. **Open:** Sun–Wed 11:30am–midnight, Thurs–Sat 11:30am–1am. **Prices:** Main courses $4–$6. MC, V. &

Venezia Caffe & Ristorante

1799 University Ave; tel 510/849-4681. University Ave exit off I-880/80. **Italian.** Attractively designed to resemble an Italian piazza, featuring a fountain in the center and wrought-iron balconies hanging from the walls. Serves up classic Italian food with an emphasis on the freshest Califor-

nia produce. Diners can watch the chef at work through a large picture window. **FYI:** Reservations accepted. Children's menu. Beer and wine only. **Open:** Lunch Mon–Fri 11:30am–2:30pm; dinner Mon–Thurs 5:30–10pm, Fri–Sat 5–10pm, Sun 5–9:30pm. **Prices:** Main courses $10–$14. AE, DC, MC, V. &

ATTRACTIONS 📷

UNIVERSITY OF CALIFORNIA

University of California Visitor Center

2200 University Ave; tel 510/642-5215. Tours of the Berkeley campus, the oldest of the nine University of California campuses, begin at the Visitor Center and are offered during the school year on Monday, Wednesday, and Friday, at 10am and 1pm, with some pre-scheduled tours on Saturday (call ahead for details). Included on the tour is the campus's signature feature, a 307-foot **Campanile,** officially known as the Jane K Sather Memorial Tower. The granite tower houses a clock with four faces measuring 17 feet in diameter along with a 61-bell carillon that is played several times daily. **Open:** Mon–Sat 10am–3:30pm, Sun 10am–1:45pm. **Free**

Phoebe A Hearst Museum of Anthropology

103 Kroeber Hall; tel 510/643-7648. Contains permanent and changing exhibitions dealing with all aspects of human culture. **Open:** Wed and Fri 10am–4:30pm, Thurs 10am–9pm, Sat–Sun 10am–4:30pm. **$**

University Art Museum and Pacific Film Archive

2626 Bancroft Way; tel 510/642-0808 (galleries) or 642-1124 (film). Founded in the 1960s as UC–Berkeley's principal visual arts center, the UAM/PFA has become one of the largest university art museums in the United States. Its collections emphasize 20th-century painting, sculpture, photography, and conceptual art, and it has significant holdings in Asian art. The Pacific Film Archive maintains a collection of 7,000 film titles, with strengths in Soviet, American avant-garde, and Japanese cinema. A complimentary program of guided tours, lectures, and special events is offered; 650 films and videos are screened each year. **Open:** Wed and Fri–Sun 11am–5pm, Thurs 11am–9pm. **$$$**

University of California Botanical Garden

Centennial Dr; tel 510/642-3343. Established in 1890, the Botanical Garden was moved to this site in Strawberry Canyon in the 1920s. More than 10,000 species of plants are spread over 33 acres, all arranged by region; one-third of the area is devoted to plants native to California. Some of the other 19 areas include the 5-acre **Mather Redwood Grove,** a re-created coastal redwood forest; the **Southern African region,** with lilies, iceplants, and aloes; and the **Mesoamerican region,** featuring a large Mexican handflower tree.

Shuttle buses run from the campus at half-hour intervals on weekdays only. Free guided tours are offered on weekends only (contact the Visitor Center for more information). **Open:** Daily 9am–4:45pm. **Free**

OTHER ATTRACTIONS

Judah L Magnes Museum (Jewish Museum of the West)

2911 Russell St; tel 510/549-6950. Permanent collection of over 10,000 Jewish ceremonial objects, folk, and fine art, including works by Marc Chagall, Max Liebermann, and many others from around the world. Changing exhibits feature shows of Jewish history and art. Also Western Jewish History Center, with the world's largest archive of records of Jews in the 13 Western states; Blumenthal Library with rare books, manuscripts, and photographs. Museum shop. **Open:** Sun–Thurs 10am–4pm. **Free**

Tilden Regional Park

Tel 510/635-0135. Accessible via Cañon Dr, Shasta Rd, or South Park Dr, all off Grizzly Peak Blvd. Tilden is one of the three oldest parks in the East Bay District. The park includes Lake Anza, with a sandy beach for swimming (generally May–Oct; fee charged); the Brazil Building, with interiors from the Brazilian exhibit at the 1939 World's Fair; a splendid antique carousel with hand-carved animals and a calliope; and the Little Train, a scaled-down steam train offering rides along a scenic ridge. An 18-hole golf course with clubhouse and pro shop; hiking and bridle trails; pony rides.

Within the park is the **Tilden Nature Study Area,** offering nature study programs in a 70-acre setting that includes a wide variety of plant and animal life; Little Farm and Environmental Education Center; 10 miles of hiking trails; several ponds; and a creek. **Open:** Daily 8am–10pm. **Free**

Beverly Hills

The very ideal of luxury, conspicuous consumption, and exclusivity, Beverly Hills continues to live up to its reputation. The famed Rodeo Drive is a shopper's mecca, not to be upstaged by any other street in the world. Window shopping and stargazing are free, however. **Information:** Beverly Hills Visitors Bureau, 239 S Beverly Dr, Beverly Hills 90212 (tel 310/271-8174 or toll free 800/345-2210).

HOTELS 🏨

🏨🏨🏨🏨🏨 Beverly Hills Hotel & Bungalows

9641 Sunset Blvd, 90210; tel 310/276-2251 or toll free 800/283-8885; fax 310/887-2887. At the junction of Sunset Blvd and Rodeo Dr. 12 acres. This classic hotel was built in the days when Beverly Hills was still a collection of bean fields. A one-time hangout of stars and starlets, as well as royalty (Howard Hughes, Maryilyn Monroe, and Yves Montand stayed here, among others), it has managed to retain the romantic aura of the original "Pink Palace" while adding up-

to-the-minute amenities after a $100-million renovation. The curvaceous, colorful decor, which retains the hotel's trademark banana leaf wallpaper, may be overdone for some guests, but walking into this lobby puts others in the mood for fun rather than business. **Rooms:** 194 rms, stes, and effic; 21 cottages/villas. CI 3pm/CO noon. Nonsmoking rms avail. The original room count has been reduced over 20% by eliminating cubbyhole singles to create spacious lodgings, most of them with space for real sitting areas (sofa, two armchairs, coffee table) and oversize, marble-and-granite bathrooms. Cottages, some with whirlpools or wood-burning fireplaces, nestle among 12 acres of hibiscus, incense cedar, and Montezuma cypress trees. All rooms and cottages with state-of-the-art soundproofing, door chimes, screened windows, and Ralph Lauren linens. **Amenities:** 🛏 🔥 🗑 A/C, cable TV w/movies, dataport, VCR, CD/tape player, voice mail, in-rm safe, bathrobes. All units w/minibars, some w/terraces, some w/fireplaces, some w/whirlpools. Every room comes with fax and three-line phones with speaker. Bathrooms come with color TVs, gilt faucets, and striped hat boxes overflowing with toiletries and doodads. Some rooms have electronicly operated drapes. Minibars in custom-made Biedermeier cabinets. **Services:** 🍽 ☛ 📁 🛄 🔧 🐕 Twicedaily maid svce, car-rental desk, masseur, babysitting. Many of the old-timers have been rehired and their pride has brushed off on the newcomers—you don't have to be a star to be greeted cordially. Round-the-clock concierge; room service perfumes. Afternoon chilled towels and sorbet for poolside sun-worshippers; afternoon tea in the lounge acccompanied by a piano decorated with gold leaf. There is a library of CDs and cassettes. **Facilities:** 🗂 🏊 2 🛳 🎱 🎳 1000 🖥 👣 4 restaurants (*see* "Restaurants" below), 2 bars (1 w/entertainment), spa, whirlpool, beauty salon. The most famous swimming pool in LA (for guests only) and poolside cafe; poolside cabanas equipped with fax and phone. The distinctive 1920s-style Fountain Coffee Shop has a curved, 20-stool counter. **Rates:** $275–$335 S or D; $625–$3,000 ste; $350–$3,500 effic; $350–$3,500 cottage/villa. Extra person $25. Children under age 12 stay free. Parking: Indoor/outdoor, $15/day. Expensive, of course, but the rates compare favorably with nearby rivals—which don't have fax machines, stereo, VCR, and TV in every room. AE, DC, JCB, MC, V.

🏨🏨🏨🏨 Beverly Hilton

9876 Wilshire Blvd, 90210; tel 310/274-7777 or toll free 800/445-8667; fax 310/285-1313. The 1950s certainly weren't one of architecture's finest decades, but the sterile modern design of the facade encloses a warm and welcoming hotel, owned by performer/producer Merv Griffin. Griffin is very involved in the running of the property, and he oversaw the recent multimillion-dollar renovation of the lobby area, restaurants, and rooms. **Rooms:** 581 rms, stes, and effic. CI 3pm/CO noon. Nonsmoking rms avail. All the tower accommodations were completely redecorated in 1996 and look lovely, with cherry wood cabinetry and fine fabrics in shades of pale apple green and cinnamon. Preferred views overlook the pool or Beverly Hills. Celebrities often book into the garden lanai rooms overlooking the pool. Superb accommodations for guests with disabilities. **Amenities:** 🎛️🦺📺 📶A/C, cable TV w/movies, refrig, dataport, voice mail, bathrobes. All units w/minibars, some w/terraces. Irons and ironing boards in all rooms. **Services:** 🍴 🔑 VP 🚐 🧺 🧷 🛎️ Car-rental desk, social director, masseur, babysitting. **Facilities:** 🎣 🛶 🏊1200 💻 ♿ 3 restaurants, 2 bars (1 w/entertainment), spa, beauty salon. The renovated pool area looks jaunty, with red and white striped awnings, limestone deck, cascades of bougainvillea, and a new, state-of-the-art sound system. Most major airline booking offices on premises. On-site Budget car rental can supply everything from a Ford Fiesta to a Lamborghini. Ballroom hosts many major film industry events, including the Golden Globe Awards; peek into the opulent marble bathrooms. **Rates:** $230–$260 S or D; $500–$700 ste; $750–$900 effic. Extra person $25. Children under age 21 stay free. Parking: Indoor, $14/day. AE, CB, DC, DISC, EC, ER, JCB, MC, V.

The Peninsula Beverly Hills
9882 Little Santa Monica Blvd, 90212; tel 310/551-2888 or toll free 800/462-7899; fax 310/788-2319. Shoehorned into a tiny spot just a corner too far from the shops, but the curved driveway with fountains and flowers makes an appropriately posh entrance. Superior rooms, elegant service. **Rooms:** 195 rms, stes, and effic; 16 cottages/villas. CI 2pm/CO noon. Nonsmoking rms avail. Meticulous appointments. French doors open inward from wrought iron balustrade to form a pseudo-balcony. Ultra-luxurious suites in "garden villas" (two-story town houses in a courtyard with planters) are elegant and quiet but don't get much daylight. **Amenities:** 🎛️🦺📶A/C, cable TV w/movies, dataport, VCR, voice mail, in-rm safe, bathrobes. All units w/minibars, some w/terraces, some w/fireplaces, some w/whirlpools. Bedside panel summons maid and valet and activates "Do Not Disturb" sign. Reading pillows. **Services:** 🍴 🔑 VP 🧺 🧷 🛎️ Twice-daily maid svce, car-rental desk, masseur, babysitting. Tea and cookies on arrival. Courtesy Rolls-Royce for trips to Century City and Rodeo Drive. 24-hour concierge. The hotel comes close to the style of service offered by its pacesetter namesake in Hong Kong—white-gloved page boys open doors, and valets are made available for each floor around the clock. **Facilities:** 🎣 🛶 🏊200 💻 ♿ 2 restaurants (see "Restaurants" below), 1 bar (w/entertainment), spa, sauna, steam rm, whirlpool. 60-foot lap pool (attended 6am—10pm), 12 poolside cabanas with phones and faxes. Fitness center (6 am—10pm) offers personal trainers. Business center services include personalized stationery and resumes. Outstanding dining room, mansion-like sitting room for afternoon tea, clubby wood-paneled bar. **Rates:** $315–$350 S; $345–$380 D; $500–$750 ste; $800–$3000 cottage/villa. Extra person $35. Children under age 18 stay free. Min stay special events. Parking: Indoor, $17/day. AE, CB, DC, DISC, JCB, MC, V.

Regent Beverly Wilshire
9500 Wilshire Blvd, 90212; tel 310/275-5200 or toll free 800/545-4000; fax 510/274-2851. This old-time favorite in a prime location is looking better than ever under Regent ownership. It is perhaps the only hotel in LA that comes close in appearance and style to its grand European peers. The elegance of the marble and wood-paneled lobby can at times be marred by batches of tourists taking each other's picture in the place where Julia Roberts and Richard Gere cavorted in *Pretty Woman*. **Rooms:** 290 rms and stes. CI 3pm/CO noon. Nonsmoking rms avail. Spacious and stylish, yet very efficient. **Amenities:** 🎛️🦺📶A/C, dataport, voice mail, in-rm safe, bathrobes. All units w/minibars, some w/terraces, 1 w/fireplace, 1 w/whirlpool. Extra-large shower stalls with twin adjustable shower heads; 60-channel TV, plus 8-inch TV in bathroom; VCRs on request, free of charge; bathroom scale. "Welcome" snack—strawberries, crème fraîche, and brown sugar. Special "pet amenity" kit. **Services:** 🍴 🔑 VP 🧺 🧷 🛎️ Twice-daily maid svce, car-rental desk, masseur, babysitting. Overnight laundry service. **Facilities:** 🎣 🛶 🏊1000 💻 ♿ 3 restaurants (see "Restaurants" below), 2 bars (w/entertainment), spa, sauna, steam rm, whirlpool, beauty salon. Elegant art deco dining room, perky streetside cafe, sumptuous lounge for light snacks and afternoon tea. Rooftop pool (open 24 hours) with cabanas. Fitness center with personal trainers. Spacious, well-equipped business center (including laptop, cellular phone, and fax machine rentals). **Rates:** $255–$380 S; $275–$400 D; $450–$4000 ste. Extra person $30. Children under age 12 stay free. Parking: Indoor, $17/day. A few dollars less than its cousin, the Four Seasons, but offers more. AE, CB, DC, DISC, EC, JCB, MC, V.

Summit Hotel Rodeo Drive
360 N Rodeo Dr, 90210; tel 310/273-0300 or toll free 800/356-7575; fax 310/859-8730. Boutique hotel catering to Europeans and corporate travelers. Not particularly posh. Close to Beverly Hills shops. **Rooms:** 86 rms and stes. Executive level. CI 2pm/CO noon. Nonsmoking rms avail. Rooms are small but passable, some with king-size beds. **Amenities:** 🎛️🦺📺 📶A/C, cable TV w/movies. Some units w/minibars, some w/terraces. **Services:** ✕ 🔑 VP 🚐 🧺 🧷 Twice-daily maid svce, car-rental desk, babysitting. **Facilities:** 🏊14 💻 1 restaurant, 1 bar, washer/dryer. Indoor/outdoor restaurant in front of the hotel. **Rates (CP):** Peak (Late May–late Aug) $150–$225 S or D. Extra person $20. Children under age 17 stay free. Lower rates off-season. AP and MAP rates avail. Parking: Indoor/outdoor, $9/day. AE, CB, DC, DISC, JCB, MC, V.

RESTAURANTS 🍴

The Belvedere
In the Peninsula Beverly Hills, 9882 Little Santa Monica Blvd; tel 310/788-2306. At Wilshire Blvd. **Californian.** Overlooking a blooming garden, this opulently appointed restaurant was designed like a lush summer villa. Chef Bill Bracken's

contemporary dishes with subtle ethnic influences include house-smoked salmon on potato cakes with marinated onions, breaded rare ahi tuna with mango and mizuna salad, and an exotic California fruit plate. Outrageous desserts, served on gold-painted Japanese glassware, include white chocolate peanut-butter crunch, and hot chocolate and sorbet. **FYI:** Reservations recommended. Children's menu. Dress code. **Open:** Breakfast daily 6:30–11am; lunch Mon–Sat 11:30am–2pm; dinner daily 6:30–10:30pm; brunch Sun 11:30am–2:30pm. **Prices:** Main courses $19–$28. AE, CB, DC, DISC, MC, V. ♥ VP &

Bombay Palace

8690 Wilshire Blvd; tel 310/659-9944. **Indian.** Nestled behind arched, 16-foot windows, this candlelit restaurant honoring the city of Bombay is filled with art objects and miniature Indian paintings. Around the upper walls are 200 individually illuminated wall pockets filled with gold-plated Indian gods. Large variety of regional favorites from the tandoor ovens, as well as vegetarian dishes, including homemade cottage cheese stewed in tomato gravy and sautéed okra fingers. **FYI:** Reservations recommended. **Open:** Lunch Mon–Fri 11:30am–2:30pm; dinner daily 5:30–11pm; brunch Sat–Sun noon–3pm. **Prices:** Main courses $15–$20; prix fixe $20–$25. AE, CB, DC, MC, V. ░ 🚗 VP &

Chez Hélène

267 S Beverly Dr; tel 310/276-1558. Between Wilshire and Olympic Blvds at corner of Gregory Way. **French/Canadian.** Housed in a charming cottage with patio that provides outdoor dining in the middle of busy Beverly Hills, this is the only French-Canadian restaurant in LA. Uncomplicated preparations by chef-owner Mimi Hebert include chilled cucumber soup and poached chicken with Dijon mustard and béchamel. Homemade pies and tortes, plus specialties like a prize-winning torte tatin and flourless chocolate cake for dessert. **FYI:** Reservations recommended. Beer and wine only. **Open:** Lunch Mon–Sat 11:30am–2pm; dinner daily 5:30–10pm. **Prices:** Main courses $13–$24. AE, DISC, MC, V. ♥ ≜ 🖼 ░ VP &

⑤ Club Room

In Neiman Marcus, 9700 Wilshire Blvd; tel 310/550-5900. Corner of Wilshire Blvd and Roxbury 4th level. **Eclectic.** Stellar food together with extraordinary service make this a "find" for lunch. Views of nearby Beverly Hills homes and fine paintings of floral subjects. Specialties include crabmeat cakes with sweet-corn puree, lobster salad, and signature popovers; for dessert, toasted pecan ball and cappuccino ice cream pie. Afternoon tea is elegantly served. **FYI:** Reservations recommended. **Open:** Lunch Mon–Sat 11:30am–3:30pm. **Prices:** Lunch main courses $8–$25. AE. ░ VP &

♣ The Dining Room

In the Regent Beverly Wilshire, 9500 Wilshire Blvd; tel 310/275-5200. At Rodeo Dr. **Eclectic.** Renovated and refined, filled with Biedermeier and Regency furnishings, silk cur-

tains, and oil paintings. Specialties include hand-carved smoked Scottish salmon, oven-roasted Maine lobster and cauliflower-fennel puree, and Russian caviars. Lavish Sunday brunch (prix fixe at $38) may include butterflied fillet of beef or grilled swordfish. **FYI:** Reservations recommended. Piano. Children's menu. Jacket required. **Open:** Breakfast Mon–Fri 7–10:30am, Sat 8–10:30am; lunch Mon–Sat 11:30am–3pm; dinner Mon–Sat 6–10pm, Sun 5–9pm; brunch Sun 10:30am–3pm. **Prices:** Main courses $24–$37. AE, CB, DC, DISC, MC, V. ♥ VP &

Ed Debevic's

134 N La Cienega Blvd; tel 310/659-1952. La Cienega Blvd exit off I-10. **Burgers/American.** Friendly, frenzied, spacious 1950s-themed restaurant. Comfort food includes meatloaf, freshly baked bread, chili, and burgers. The world's smallest hot fudge sundae is only 69¢. **FYI:** Reservations not accepted. **Open:** Sun–Thurs 11:30am–10pm, Fri–Sat 11:30am–midnight. **Prices:** Main courses $4–$7. AE, CB, DC, DISC, MC, V. ░ VP &

The Grill on the Alley

9560 Dayton Way; tel 310/276-0615. **American Grill.** A handsome turn-of-the-century–style grill featuring a massive mahogany bar, wooden booths, and a black-and-white tiled floor. The front door is located in an alleyway off Wilshire. Specialties are charcoal-broiled swordfish and calf's liver with bacon and onions. **FYI:** Reservations recommended. Dress code. **Open:** Mon–Sat 11:30am–11pm, Sun 5–9pm. **Prices:** Main courses $15–$28. AE, DC, MC, V. ■ VP &

Il Pastaio

400 N Canon Dr; tel 310/205-5444. **Italian.** Recently opened, this tiny, casual restaurant is decorated with burnished wood, floor-to-ceiling windows, and artwork. Menu includes several variations of carpaccio (venison, swordfish, ahi tuna), pasta, and risotto. Try the tagliolini with Sicilian-style pesto or risotto with saffron and parmesan cheese. **FYI:** Reservations not accepted. **Open:** Daily 11:30am–11pm. **Prices:** Main courses $8–$13. AE, DC, DISC, MC, V. VP

★ Kate Mantilini

9101 Wilshire Blvd; tel 310/278-3699. **American.** Dedicated to a hard-boiled female fight promoter, this restaurant features dramatic, stylish, concrete and glass architecture and serves generous portions to both celebrities and insomniacs all day and late into the night. The upscale diner-style menu includes rotisserie chicken, white chili, meatloaf, and garlic spinach. **FYI:** Reservations accepted. **Open:** Mon–Thurs 7:30am–1am, Fri 7:30am–3am, Sat noon–3am, Sun 10am–midnight. **Prices:** Main courses $9–$32. AE, MC, V. ░ VP &

⑤ ★ Lawry's The Prime Rib

100 N La Cienega Blvd; tel 310/652-2827. **American.** Founded in 1938 as a mecca for lovers of aged prime rib. Today it also attracts diners who seek a good value. The cavernous main dining room has a dignified air and is filled with oil portraits and a fresco of Versailles. Service is

ceremonial, yet friendly. The menu has expanded in recent years to include fish and lobster dishes. Among the favorites of regulars are creamed spinach, huge baked potatoes, and pecan praline torte. **FYI:** Reservations recommended. Dress code. **Open:** Mon–Thurs 5–10pm, Fri 5–11pm, Sat 4:30–11pm, Sun 4–10pm. **Prices:** Main courses $19–$25. AE, DC, DISC, MC, V. 💿 📷 VP &

★ The Mandarin
430 N Camden Dr; tel 310/859-0638. **Chinese.** The mother of all Chinese restaurants in Los Angeles, the Mandarin offers both Szechuan and Mandarin fare. The restaurant is decorated with lacquered woods and bamboo, with long windows overlooking a plant-filled brick walkway. Specialties include Peking duck, curried vegetable fried rice, and glazed walnuts on fried spinach leaves. **FYI:** Reservations recommended. **Open:** Mon–Thurs 11:30am–10pm, Fri 11:30am–10:30pm, Sat 5–10:30pm, Sun 5–10pm. **Prices:** Main courses $9–$35. AE, DC, MC, V. 📷 🚗 VP

★ Maple Drive
In Maple Plaza Office Building, 345 N Maple Dr; tel 310/274-9800. 2 blocks N of Burton Way. **Regional American.** A spacious, multilevel, wood-and-concrete structure, with wraparound windows looking out to the tree-lined neighborhood. A creation of owner Tony Bill and chef Leonard Schwarz, it's a favorite with art and entertainment luminaries who come for original, American-style comfort food with international touches, such as its signature dish, meatloaf with spinach and mashed potatoes. Other treats include leg of lamb and charred tuna with Japanese vinaigrette. **FYI:** Reservations recommended. Jazz. **Open:** Lunch Mon–Fri 11:30am–2:30pm; dinner Mon–Thurs 6–10pm, Fri–Sat 6–11pm. **Prices:** Main courses $17–$29. AE, MC, V. 🏛 VP &

Matsuhisa
129 N La Cienega Blvd; tel 310/659-9639. **Japanese.** Owner/chef Nobu Matsuhisa is the most popular and well-known sushi chef in Los Angeles. Sample the tempura and sushi bar, or opt for an entree such as squid "pasta" with garlic sauce, halibut cheek with pepper sauce, or baked black cod and tiger shrimp in pepper sauce. **FYI:** Reservations recommended. **Open:** Lunch Mon–Fri 11:45am–1:45pm; dinner daily 5:45–10:15pm. **Prices:** Main courses $12–$40; prix fixe $25–$30. AE, CB, MC, V. VP &

McCormick & Schmick's
In Two Rodeo, 206 N Rodeo Dr; tel 310/859-0434. **Seafood.** Completely gutted and redesigned two-story space located in the Two Rodeo complex on some of the most expensive real estate in the world. Luxurious and comfortable, with dark wood and beveled glass and an open kitchen. Daily seafood specials may include cedar-planked salmon, rare oysters, or Pacific halibut. **FYI:** Reservations accepted. **Open:** Daily 11:30am–11:30pm. **Prices:** Main courses $15–$30. AE, DISC, MC, V. 💿 📷 VP &

♦ Mr Chow's
433 N Camden Dr; tel 310/278-9911. **Chinese.** Portraits of Michael Chow by Keith Haring and Andy Warhol dominate the room, which is often packed with celebrities. Specialties include Mr Chow's classic noodles; other choices include marinated gambler's duck, chicken satay, gambei (mushrooms, chicken, seaweed, and walnuts), squab rolled in lettuce, and sweet-and-sour soup. A bargain for lunch. **FYI:** Reservations recommended. **Open:** Lunch daily noon–2:30pm; dinner daily 6–11:30pm. **Prices:** Main courses $10–$25. AE, DC, MC, V. 💿 VP &

♦ Polo Grill
In the Beverly Hills Hotel & Bungalows, 9641 Sunset Blvd; tel 310/276-2251. **Eclectic.** Chef Frank Cramme combines German and various Asian influences in his creative cuisine served in a formal, art deco dining room facing a garden. Menu dishes include tuna carpaccio with beluga caviar; ginger broth with scallops; grilled blue prawns; and grilled côte de boeuf with truffled potato pancakes. There is also a chef's tasting menu which presents changing seafood, fish, poultry, beef, and game dishes. **FYI:** Reservations recommended. Piano. Jacket required. **Open:** Daily 6–10:30pm. **Prices:** Main courses $18–$26; prix fixe $55. AE, DC, MC, V. 💿 🍷 VP &

♦ The Polo Lounge
In the Beverly Hills Hotel & Bungalows, 9641 Sunset Blvd; tel 310/276-2251. **Eclectic.** This landmark restaurant/lounge, where scores of movie deals have been spawned and famous love affairs have been conducted, is back in action once more. Breakfast, lunch, and dinner are available indoors in the Lounge and Loggia, or outdoors on the Patio beneath an 86-year-old Brazilian pepper tree. The dinner menu is filled with inventive—and usually pricey—appetizers (tea-smoked duck breast, cracked-pepper scallops), pastas (white truffle ravioli, angel-hair pomodoro), and entrees (wok-seared pepper ahi, rack of lamb with ginger ragout, mesquite-grilled veal chops). The lunch menu offers a greater selection of moderately priced options: Dutch apple pancakes, parsley gnocchi, and the popular Polo Club sandwich are all less than $15 each. Early reservations are essential for the traditional Sunday brunch with a choice of 5 cocktails, 15 appetizers, 12 entrees, and a sumptuous array of desserts, all accompanied by a strolling mariachi band. Outstanding selection of wines begins at $25 a bottle. **FYI:** Reservations recommended. Piano. Children's menu. Dress code. **Open:** Daily 7am–1am. **Prices:** Main courses $19–$26. AE, CB, DC, DISC, ER, MC, V. 💿 🏛 VP &

★ RJ's The Rib Joint
252 N Beverly Dr; tel 310/274-7427. **Regional American.** A rollicking, old-fashioned, country-style, cavernous party center in the heart of the Beverly Hills shopping district. Created by Bob Morris of Gladstone fame, the restaurant is known for generously portioned baby back ribs, firehouse chili, hickory-smoked baked potatoes, and the Rib Joint Sampler with

armadillo eggs (actually a nest of mild jalapeños stuffed with cream cheese, then fried). **FYI:** Reservations recommended. Children's menu. **Open:** Fri–Sat 11:30am–11pm, Sun 10:30am–10pm, Mon–Thurs 11:30am–10pm. **Prices:** Main courses $6–$22. AE, DISC, MC, V. 🖼 VP

Ruth's Chris Steak House

224 S Beverly Dr; tel 310/859-8744. **American/Steak.** Upscale yet low-key, with an open kitchen and elevated leather booths. The restaurant's trademark is consistently excellent fare, especially the aged, corn-fed beef, broiled at very high temperatures to seal in the flavor. Seven potato preparations to choose from. **FYI:** Reservations recommended. **Open:** Sun 5–9:30pm, Mon–Thurs 5–10pm, Fri–Sat 5–10:30pm. **Prices:** Main courses $17–$45. AE, CB, DC, DISC, MC, V. VP ⚬

ATTRACTION 🖼

The Museum of Television & Radio

465 North Beverly Dr; tel 310/786-1000. Beverly Hills is the new West Coast home of this museum, which presents a program of exhibitions, series, and gallery exhibits. Currently, you can enjoy *Stand–Up Comedians on Television*—a major exhibition on comedy that pays homage to the nation's great stand–up comedy entertainers. Children can enjoy *An International Children's Television Festival*—a six month screening series of children's programming from around the world. And, *Trekkies* will enjoy *Star Trek: The Tradition Continues*—a gallery of the costumes, makeup, and facial appliances from *Star Trek: The Next Generation, Deep Space Nine* and *Voyager*.

Big Bear City

See Big Bear Lake

Big Bear Lake

This is a vacation and outdoor sports spot for the flatlanders of Southern California, offering skiing, hiking, boating, and woodsy resorts. **Information:** Big Bear Chamber of Commerce, 630 Bartlett Rd, PO Box 2860, Big Bear Lake 92315 (tel 909/866-4608).

HOTEL 🖼

≣≣≣ Forest Shores Inn

40670 Lakeview Dr, PO Box 946, 92315; tel 909/866-6551. ¼ mi W of downtown just off CA 18. Located on the lakeshore, a complex of three-story condo units. Guests can rent a ground-floor fully-equipped studio apartment, one of the two-bedroom apartments on the top two floors, or an entire unit. **Rooms:** 23 effic. CI 3pm/CO noon. No smoking. **Amenities:** 🖼 ⚬ 🖼 Cable TV, refrig, VCR. No A/C. All units w/terraces, all w/fireplaces. **Facilities:** 🖼 🖼 🖼 Games rm, sauna, whirlpool. **Rates:** Peak (June–Sept/Nov–Apr) $120

effic. Children under age 18 stay free. Min stay wknds. Lower rates off-season. Parking: Indoor/outdoor, free. AE, DC, DISC, MC, V.

MOTELS

≣≣ Frontier Lodge & Motel

40472 Big Bear Blvd, PO Box 687, 92315; tel 909/866-5888 or toll free 800/451-6401, 800/457-6401 in CA; fax 909/866-4372. ¼ mi W of Big Bear Lake Village on CA 18. An interesting mix of cabins and motel rooms. Some need renovation. **Rooms:** 44 rms; 26 cottages/villas. CI 2pm/CO 11am. Quality varies widely. Cabin 30 is splendid with two bedrooms, whirlpool, and stone fireplace. **Amenities:** 🖼 Cable TV. No A/C. Some units w/terraces, some w/fireplaces, some w/whirlpools. **Services:** 🖼 VCR and movie rentals. **Facilities:** 🖼 🖼 🖼 1 beach (lake shore), basketball, volleyball. Ping-Pong, boat slips. Pool open summer only. **Rates (CP):** Peak (Dec–Apr/July–Sept) $65–$100 S or D; $65–$200 cottage/villa. Min stay wknds and special events. Lower rates off-season. Parking: Outdoor, free. AE, CB, DC, DISC, MC, V.

≣≣ Goldmine Lodge

42268 Moonridge Rd, PO Box 198, 92315; tel 909/866-8786 or toll free 800/487-3168; fax 909/866-1592. Just off CA 18, 1½ mi E of Big Bear Lake Village. Nestled in a grove of large pine trees, this property is rustic but comfortable. **Rooms:** 11 rms, stes, and effic. CI 2pm/CO 11am. **Amenities:** 🖼 ⚬ 🖼 Cable TV w/movies, refrig. No A/C. Some units w/fireplaces. **Services:** 🖼 **Facilities:** 🖼 🖼 Whirlpool, playground. Nice picnic and barbecue area. **Rates (CP):** Peak (Nov–Apr) $69–$99 S or D; $99–$149 ste; $99–$149 effic. Extra person $10. Children under age 12 stay free. Min stay special events. Lower rates off-season. Parking: Outdoor, free. AE, DC, DISC, MC, V.

≣≣ Grey Squirrel Resort

39372 Big Bear Blvd, PO Box 5404, 92315; tel 909/866-4335; fax 909/866-6271. Nicely furnished cabins with fully equipped kitchens. **Rooms:** 18 rms and stes; 15 cottages/villas. CI 2pm/CO 11am. Nonsmoking rms avail. The quality of cabins varies considerably. "Doe" is one of the most charming, with an upscale country motif and in-room whirlpool. **Amenities:** 🖼 ⚬ 🖼 Cable TV, refrig, VCR. No A/C. Some units w/terraces, some w/fireplaces, 1 w/whirlpool. **Services:** 🖼 🖼 Pets are $5 per night. **Facilities:** 🖼 🖼 🖼 Basketball, volleyball, lawn games, whirlpool, washer/dryer. Barbecue grills. Pool is enclosed in fall and winter. **Rates:** Peak (June–Sept/Nov–Apr) $75–$95 S or D; $125 ste; $75–$95 cottage/villa. Min stay wknds. Lower rates off-season. Parking: Outdoor, free. AE, DISC, MC, V.

≣≣≣ Sleepy Forest Cottages

426 Eureka Dr, 92315; tel 909/866-7567 or toll free 800/544-7454. 1 mi E of Big Bear Lake Village. Very nice cottages decorated in an upscale country motif and set amid tree-shaded grounds. **Rooms:** 16 cottages/villas. CI 1pm/CO

11am. Nonsmoking rms avail. Great family units, with two TVs and a master bedroom with whirlpool. **Amenities:** 📺 ⏰ 🔌 Cable TV, refrig. No A/C. Some units w/terraces, all w/fireplaces, some w/whirlpools. **Services:** 🗝 🍴 Babysitting. **Facilities:** 🏊 🍽 🚐 **Rates (CP):** $119–$199 cottage/villa. Extra person $10. Children under age 18 stay free. Min stay wknds. Parking: Outdoor, free. AE, CB, DC, DISC, MC, V.

≣≣ Wishing Well Motel

540 Pine Knot Blvd, PO Box 577, 92315; tel 909/866-3505 or toll free 800/541-3505; fax 909/866-6821. ½ block from CA 18. Right in the village, among lovely pine trees. Charming, homey operation. **Rooms:** 15 rms. CI 1pm/CO 11am. Nonsmoking rms avail. **Amenities:** 📺 Cable TV. No A/C. **Services:** 🍴 🛎 Babysitting. **Facilities:** 🏊 🍽 **Rates (CP):** Peak (July–Sept/Nov–Apr) $39–$79 S; $49–$89 D. Children under age 18 stay free. Min stay special events. Lower rates off-season. Parking: Outdoor, free. AE, CB, DC, MC, V.

INN

≣≣≣≣ Janet Kay's

695 Paine Rd, PO Box 3874, 92315; tel 909/866-6800 or toll free 800/243-7031. 1 block S of CA 18. Beautiful colonial-style bed-and-breakfast. **Rooms:** 19 rms and stes (2 w/shared bath). CI 3pm/CO noon. No smoking. Rooms are large, luxuriously appointed, and all unique in their decor. **Amenities:** 📺 Cable TV, VCR. No A/C. Some units w/terraces, some w/fireplaces, some w/whirlpools. **Services:** 🍴 Babysitting, afternoon tea and wine/sherry served. Full breakfast. **Facilities:** 🏊 🍽 🎱 Guest lounge. **Rates (BB):** Peak (Nov–Apr) $79 S or D w/shared bath, $89–$175 S or D w/private bath; $159 ste. Children under age 18 stay free. Min stay special events. Lower rates off-season. Parking: Outdoor, free. Ski packages avail. AE, DISC, MC, V.

RESTAURANTS 🍴

Blue Whale Lakeside

350 Alden Rd; tel 909/866-5514. N of CA 18; 2 blocks E of Pine Knot Blvd. **Seafood/Steak.** Nautical decor, and great views of Big Bear Lake from every table. Fresh fish and lobsters are delivered three times each week. Broiled and roasted meats and poultry are imaginatively prepared. The Tail of the Whale lounge becomes an oyster bar on weekend summer afternoons. **FYI:** Reservations recommended. Guitar/piano. Children's menu. **Open:** Lunch Fri–Sun noon–3pm; dinner daily 4–10pm; brunch Sun 9am–2pm. **Prices:** Main courses $13–$40. AE, DISC, MC, V. 🏔

♣ The Iron Squirrel

646 Pine Knot Blvd, Big Bear Lake Village; tel 909/866-9121. 1 block S of CA 18. **French.** A restaurant that transports you to the French countryside. The dining room has tapestry-covered booths, French antiques, and gentle lighting. Cuisine is traditional French with a contemporary lightness; duck in orange and Grand Marnier sauce is a house

favorite. **FYI:** Reservations recommended. Children's menu. **Open:** Lunch Tues–Sun 11:30am–2pm; dinner daily 5:30–9pm. **Prices:** Main courses $14–$22. AE, MC, V. 🔲

$ Landings–The Cafe

In the airport terminal, 829 W Big Bear Blvd, Big Bear City; tel 909/585-3762. **Californian.** A fine restaurant at a tiny airport. The larger dining room faces the runway but is not too close. Good for breakfast, lunch, and dinner, with dishes like pecan pancakes and cedar-planked salmon. The now-famous special is Dom Perignon champagne and two peanut butter sandwiches for $99.99. **FYI:** Reservations recommended. Children's menu. Beer and wine only. **Open:** Peak (July–Sept) Mon 11am–9pm, Wed–Fri 11am–9pm, Sat–Sun 8am–9pm. **Prices:** Main courses $8–$22. DISC, MC, V. ♿

ATTRACTION 🏛

Alpine Slide and Recreation Area

Tel 909/866-4626. Located in Big Bear Lake Village, about ¼ mile W on CA 18. This amusement park features an Alpine sled–type ride that operates year-round (call ahead in winter), plus a water slide in the summer and a snow hill with inner tube rentals in winter. Also miniature golf, horseback riding, and go-carts. **Open:** Peak (mid-June–mid-Sept) daily 10am–6pm. Reduced hours off-season. $$$$

Big Sur

High above the Pacific Ocean, CA 1 snakes through the little communities of Big Sur in one of the most scenic drives in America. Protected coastal redwood forests cling to the headlands for dizzying views, and small artist colonies offer funky roadside attractions.

HOTEL 🏨

≣≣≣≣ Ventana

CA 1, 93920; tel 408/667-2331 or toll free 800/628-6500; fax 408/667-2419. 28 mi S of Carmel. Located among redwoods and bay trees on a ridge 1,200 feet above the Pacific, Ventana's low cedar buildings harmonize with the golden Santa Lucia foothills. **Rooms:** 59 rms, stes, and effic; 3 cottages/villas. CI 4:30pm/CO 1pm. Nonsmoking rms avail. Rooms have the feel of a sumptuous wilderness lodge, with rough-hewn plank walls and tiled floors. Even standard rooms have ocean views and lattice-shaded balconies. **Amenities:** 📺 ⏰ 🔌 🍷 Cable TV w/movies, refrig, VCR, in-rm safe, bathrobes. No A/C. All units w/minibars, all w/terraces, some w/fireplaces, some w/whirlpools. Almost every room has a fireplace, with logs already stacked. **Services:** ✕ 🆚 🍴 Twice-daily maid svce, masseur, babysitting. Continental breakfast, with fresh-squeezed juice, granola, yogurt, and more. Complimentary wine and cheese each afternoon. Video rentals available from front desk. **Facilities:** 🏋 🏊 🎾 🚐 ♿ 1 restaurant (see "Restaurants" below), 1 bar. Japanese-style bathhouse has hot tubs and saunas tactfully divided into areas for men, women, and couples. **Rates (CP):** Peak (June–Oct) $195–$525 S or D; $350–$970 ste; $525–$970 effic; $295–$550 cottage/villa. Extra person $50. Min stay wknds and special events. Lower rates off-season. Parking: Outdoor, free. AE, CB, DISC, MC, V.

MOTEL

≡≡ Big Sur River Inn

CA 1 at Pheweber Creek, 93920; tel 408/667-2700 or toll free 800/548-3610; fax 408/667-2743. Nestled in the Big Sur woods along the river, the inn dates to 1888, when the Pfeiffer family settled the property. **Rooms:** 20 rms and stes. CI 4pm/CO 12:30pm. Nonsmoking rms avail. Five suites have decks overlooking the river. **Amenities:** ▨ No A/C, phone, or TV. Some units w/terraces. **Services:** ⟳ Masseur, babysitting. **Facilities:** ⎗ ⎘ 1 restaurant (*see* "Restaurants" below), 1 bar (w/entertainment). Restaurant and grocery store on premises—guests get 10% discount. **Rates:** Peak (May–Sept) $70–$80 S; $80–$90 D; $110–$160 ste. Min stay peak and wknds. Lower rates off-season. Parking: Outdoor, free. Winter special rates (Nov–Apr): Queen room, dinner, and breakfast for two at $99/night; weekends, $115/night. AE, DISC, MC, V.

INN

≡≡≡≡ Post Ranch Inn

CA 1, PO Box 219, 93920; tel 408/667-2200 or toll free 800/527-2200; fax 408/667-2824. Opened in 1992, amid the seaside cliffs of Big Sur. Redwood villas are built into the hillsides (deer sometimes graze on the roofs) or among the trees. Ambience is very modern, very romantic, yet rustic. **Rooms:** 31 cottages/villas. CI 4pm/CO 1pm. No smoking. Coast House villas occupy round "towers," with a curvilinear sofa in front of the fireplace. Top-of-the-line Ocean Houses, with cliff-edge perches and private slate terraces, book up fast. **Amenities:** ▨ ⊘ ▨ ⎖ Refrig, dataport, VCR, CD/tape player, in-rm safe, bathrobes. No A/C or TV. All units w/minibars, all w/terraces, all w/fireplaces, all w/whirlpools. All accommodations have spa tables for in-room treatments. **Services:** ✕ �VP⎕ ⟳ Twice-daily maid svce, masseur, babysitting. Guided nature hikes, pioneer history walks, wine tastings, astronomy sessions. Many different massages and treatments are offered, and there's a tarot reader on staff. **Facilities:** ⎗ ▨ ⎖⎘ ⎗ 1 restaurant (*see* "Restaurants" below), 1 bar, spa. Small fitness center; yoga and aerobics classes are held by the stunning lap-length pool. **Rates (CP):** $285–$900 cottage/villa. Extra person $50. Min stay wknds and special events. Parking: Outdoor, free. Midweek, midwinter package includes two nights' accommodations and two massages for $595 per couple. AE, MC, V.

LODGE

≡≡ Big Sur Lodge

Pfeiffer Big Sur State Park, PO Box 190, 93920; tel 408/667-3100 or toll free 800/424-4787; fax 408/667-3110. Pfeiffer Big Sur State Park exit off CA 1. A reasonably priced alternative to camping. There's tourist hubbub around the lobby and restaurant, but rooms are set beyond a stand of redwoods. Grounds are extremely well kept, and you'll often see deer nibbling on the grass. **Rooms:** 61 rms, stes, and effic. CI 4pm/CO 11am. Nonsmoking rms avail. Standard motel-quality rooms clustered in one-story buildings with two to six units in each, surrounded by broad green lawns. **Amenities:** No A/C, phone, or TV. All units w/terraces, some w/fireplaces. **Services:** Masseur, babysitting. **Facilities:** ⎗ ⎘ 1 restaurant. The pool is especially attractive, set off by a wrought-iron fence. Restaurant serves beer and wine. **Rates:** Peak (June–Labor Day) $115–$165 S or D; $143 ste; $104 effic. Children under age 18 stay free. Min stay wknds. Lower rates off-season. Parking: Outdoor, free. You must pay for your room before you stay. Rates include admission to Pfeiffer Big Sur State Park. AE, MC, V.

RESTAURANTS ⎟⎟⎟

✦ Big Sur River Inn Restaurant

CA 1 at Pheneger Creek; tel 408/667-2700. **Regional American.** Views of the river and forest, weekend entertainment, and 1930s nostalgia make this a local favorite. Specialties include burgers, and grilled portobello mushrooms on polenta, served with crispy spinach and grilled eggplant. Late night snacks are served in front of the fireplace Apr–Oct. **FYI:** Reservations recommended. Jazz/drummers. **Open:** Peak (Apr–Oct) daily 8am–10pm. **Prices:** Main courses $14–$25. AE, MC, V. ⊛ ⛴ ⛰ ▦

✦ Nepenthe

CA 1; tel 408/667-2345. 30 mi S of Carmel. **Californian.** A 1960s counterculture holdout, complete with piped-in sitar music. Climb the zigzagging stairway to dine on decks with Pacific views. Burgers and sandwiches for lunch; fish, steaks, or chicken for dinner. **FYI:** Reservations accepted. **Open:** Lunch daily 11:30am–4:30pm; dinner daily 5–10pm. **Prices:** Main courses $10–$24. AE, MC, V. ⊛ ⛴ ⛰ ▦ ⚇

⚑ Sierra Mar

In Post Ranch Inn, CA 1, PO Box 219; tel 408/667-2200. 28 mi S of Carmel. **Californian.** Floor-to-ceiling windows at the cliff's edge provide great ocean views (if you get there before sunset). The decor is minimalist, with slate floors and wooden chairs that are chic rather than comfortable. The four-course prix fixe menu changes daily (and is always full of surprises—for example, grilled escolar with soft polenta, or braised Sonoma rabbit with pumpkin spaetzle), but can also be ordered course by course. The comprehensive wine list is the sort you would expect in San Francisco, rather than a small, out-of-the-way inn. Reserve your table well in advance. **FYI:**

Reservations recommended. **Open:** Breakfast daily 8:30–10:30am; dinner daily 5:30–10pm. **Prices:** Main courses $25–$35; prix fixe $55. AE, MC, V. 💙 VP ⌖

♥ ★ Ventana
CA 1; tel 408/667-2331. 28 mi S of Carmel; Look for Ventana sign on east side of road. **Californian.** Poised 1,000 feet above the Pacific, the restaurant offers panoramic views of 50 miles of seacoast, as well as wonderful food. Meals are served both on the broad wooden deck and in the skylit dining room, which has an unusual floor made from six-inch blocks of wood. Menu emphasizes fresh local produce. **FYI:** Reservations recommended. **Open:** Lunch Mon–Fri noon–3pm, Sat–Sun 11am–3pm; dinner daily 6–9:30pm. Closed Dec 1–14. **Prices:** Main courses $19–$28; prix fixe $39–$49. AE, CB, DC, DISC, MC, V. 💙 🏊 ⛰ ⌖

ATTRACTIONS 📷
Bixby Bridge
CA 1 (Cabrillo Hwy). Perhaps the most photographed structure on the Big Sur coast, this vertigo-inducing bridge, towering nearly 260 feet above Bixby Creek Canyon, was said to be the longest concrete arch span in the world when it was constructed in 1932. Several observation alcoves are located at regular intervals along the bridge. **Free**

Andrew Molera State Park
CA 1 (Cabrillo Hwy); tel 408/667-2315. Enter the park via a short driveway off CA 1 that leads to the parking lot; the park is ¼-mile walk from there. Here you will find a beach and walk-in campground as well as equestrian trails and hiking and nature trails. Hikes include the Bluffs Trail, an easy 2-mile trail that winds along the ocean to the bluff; the Headlands Trail, a 1-mile hike that leads to the headlands above the mouth of Big Sur River as it flows into the ocean; and the Bobcat Trail, about 2 miles long, which passes through the redwoods along the Big Sur River. **Open:** Daily sunrise–sunset. **$$$**

Julia Pfeiffer Burns State Park
CA 1 (Cabrillo Hwy); tel 408/667-2315. This 1,800-acre wooded day-use park offers several trails, including one geared to novice hikers (⅓-mile long) that ends with a view of McWay Falls, which drop 50 feet into the ocean. Picnic area. **Open:** Daily sunrise–sunset. **$$$**

Pfeiffer–Big Sur State Park
Sycamore Canyon Rd off CA 1 (Cabrillo Hwy); tel 408/667-2315. The Big Sur River runs through the center of this thickly wooded 810-acre park. An information booth at the park entrance can provide detailed maps of the well-tended nature trails that crisscross through the redwoods. Nature center has displays on the natural and cultural history of the area. Popular hikes include an easy ½-mile trek to Pfeiffer Falls; the ¼-mile-long Oak Grove Trail, which takes off from the Pfeiffer Falls trailhead; and the Valley View Trail, which begins at the falls and climbs 400 feet in a distance of a ½-

mile—the trail ends in a high point that provides a view of the entire Big Sur Valley and Point Sur. **Open:** Daily sunrise–sunset. **$$$**

Bishop

Bishop is an agricultural community in the rich Owens Valley, and the gateway to Mammoth Lakes and Mammoth Mountain. **Information:** Bishop Chamber of Commerce, 690 N Main St, Bishop 93514 (tel 619/873-8405).

MOTELS 🏨
≣≣ Best Western Bishop Holiday Spa Lodge
1025 North Main St, 93514; tel 619/873-3543 or toll free 800/576-3543; fax 619/872-4777. On US 395. Clean, pleasant property with beautiful landscaping. **Rooms:** 89 rms and stes. CI 3pm/CO 11am. Deluxe rooms are much nicer than standard ones, which are small and old. **Amenities:** 📺 ❄ 🍴 A/C, cable TV w/movies, refrig. 1 unit w/fireplace. Microwave. VCR for rent. **Services:** 🔔 **Facilities:** 🏊 ⌖ Whirlpool. **Rates (CP):** Peak (May–Oct) $56–$66 S; $66–$80 D; $89 ste. Extra person $10. Children under age 18 stay free. Lower rates off-season. Parking: Outdoor, free. AE, CB, DC, DISC, MC, V.

≣≣ Creekside Inn Best Western
725 N Main St, 93514; tel 619/872-3044 or toll free 800/273-3550; fax 619/872-1300. Attractive brick facade and beautiful new landscaping. Handsome lobby with fireplace. **Rooms:** 89 rms and effic. CI 1pm/CO 1pm. Nonsmoking rms avail. Nice colonial furniture. **Amenities:** 📺 ❄ A/C, cable TV. **Services:** 🚗 🔔 **Facilities:** 🏊 ⌖ Whirlpool. Room for cleaning fish. Creekside pool. **Rates (CP):** Peak (May–Oct) $89–$129 D; $129 effic. Extra person $12. Children under age 12 stay free. Lower rates off-season. Parking: Outdoor, free. AE, CB, DC, DISC, MC, V.

≣ Days Inn
724 W Line St, 93514; tel 619/872-1095 or toll free 800/325-2525; fax 619/872-1095. 25 mi S of Mammoth Lakes. 2 blocks off US 395. New property in an attractive southwestern style. **Rooms:** 34 rms and stes. CI 2pm/CO 11am. Nonsmoking rms avail. Clean, simple, well-appointed rooms. **Amenities:** 📺 ❄ A/C, cable TV, refrig. 1 unit w/whirlpool. Ceiling fan; microwave. VCRs for rent. **Services:** 🔔 **Facilities:** ⌖ Whirlpool. **Rates:** Peak (Apr–Oct) $59–$69 S; $69–$79 D; $80 ste. Extra person $6. Children under age 12 stay free. Lower rates off-season. Parking: Outdoor, free. AE, CB, DC, DISC, ER, JCB, MC, V.

ATTRACTIONS 📷
Paiute Shoshone Indian Cultural Center
2300 W Line St (CA 168); tel 619/873-4478. More than 1,000 years ago, the Owens Valley, bordered by the Sierra Nevada Mountains to the west and the White and Inyo ranges

on the east, was the territory of the Shoshone and the Paiute. Hunters and gatherers, these people lived in harmony with nature; all of their needs—food, clothing, housing, medicine, arts, and entertainment—were satisfied by the land. Museum exhibits display food preparation methods, basketry, artwork, and other "life ways" of the Paiute and Shoshone people. **Open:** Mon–Fri 9am–5pm, Sat–Sun 10am–4pm. **Free**

Laws Railroad Museum and Historical Site

Silver Canyon Rd; tel 619/873-5950. The legacy of the last narrow-gauge railroad west of the Rockies is preserved at this site. Visitors can see the original 1883 Laws Depot, Laws Post Office, and Agent's House, as well as the locomotive, string of cars, and exhibits of railroad memorabilia. Museum buildings house fascinating collections from Owens Valley pioneer days. Reception center with gifts, books, and souvenirs. **Open:** Daily 10am–4pm, weather permitting. **Free**

Ancient Bristlecone Pine Forest

CA 168; tel 619/873-2500. The oldest known continuously growing organism in the world is a 4,700-year-old bristlecone pine named **Methuselah** in the Schulman Grove of the Ancient Bristlecone Pine Forest. Sculpted over centuries by wind, blowing ice, and sand, bristlecones develop unique and exquisite shapes of golden-hued wood. The visitor center offers interpretive talks, self-guided trails, displays, books and maps, and a picnic area (no drinking water available). **Open:** Mem Day–Columbus Day, daily 24 hours. **Free**

Blue Jay

See Lake Arrowhead

Bodega Bay

The community was a Russian fur-trading center in the late 1800s, as well as the setting for Alfred Hitchcock's film *The Birds.* Now the big draw is birdwatching, rugged bay views, and down-home, reasonably priced seafood. **Information:** Bodega Bay Area Chamber of Commerce, 850 CA 1, PO Box 146, Bodega Bay 94923 (tel 707/875-3422).

HOTEL 🏨

≣≣≣ Inn at the Tides

800 CA 1, PO Box 640, 94923; tel 707/875-2751 or toll free 800/541-7788; fax 707/875-3023. 6 acres. Attractive hotel overlooking Bodega Bay; located near several state beaches and a golf course. **Rooms:** 86 rms. CI 3pm/CO noon. Nonsmoking rms avail. Spacious rooms with views of bay and highway, but some smelled a bit smoky. **Amenities:** 🛏 🍷 📺 ❄ Cable TV, refrig, dataport, bathrobes. No A/C. Some units w/terraces, some w/fireplaces. **Services:** ✕ 🔑 Masseur. Firewood supplied. Daily newspaper delivered to room. **Facilities:** 🏊 🏌 50 占 2 restaurants, 1 bar, sauna, whirlpool,

washer/dryer. Large pool area is glassed in to protect from wind. **Rates (CP):** Peak (June–Nov 15) $109–$199 S or D. Extra person $20. Children under age 12 stay free. Min stay special events. Lower rates off-season. Parking: Outdoor, free. Golf packages avail. AE, JCB, MC, V.

LODGE

≣≣≣≣ Bodega Bay Lodge

103 CA 1, 94923; tel 707/875-3525 or toll free 800/368-2468. 4 acres. A quiet, peaceful place ¼ mile from the beach, with beautiful grounds and expansive views of the bay, ocean, and protected wetlands. Lobby has fish tanks with local marine life. **Rooms:** 78 rms and stes. CI 3pm/CO 11:30am. Nonsmoking rms avail. Rooms are very cozy, clean, and comfortable and have views of the bay and marshlands. **Amenities:** 🛏 🍷 📺 ❄ Cable TV w/movies, dataport, bathrobes. No A/C. All units w/minibars, all w/terraces, all w/fireplaces, some w/whirlpools. **Services:** ✕ 🚗 🔑 Masseur, babysitting. Complimentary afternoon wine in lobby. Gourmet picnic lunch for excursions available. **Facilities:** 🏊 🏌 125 占 1 restaurant, 1 bar, sauna, whirlpool, washer/dryer. Fine California cuisine restaurant serves seafood, pastas, steaks—some of the best food on this part of the coast. An 18-hole golf course is next door. One mile to public beach. **Rates:** Peak (Mar–Dec) $120–$195 S or D; $190–$215 ste. Extra person $10. Children under age 18 stay free. Min stay wknds. Lower rates off-season. Parking: Outdoor, free. Golf packages avail. Rates $20 less Sun–Thurs. AE, CB, DC, DISC, MC, V.

RESTAURANTS 🍽

The Duck Club

In Bodega Bay Lodge, 103 CA 1; tel 707/875-3525. **Californian/Seafood.** This is an ideal shore restaurant, with a light, airy, and elegant setting and good food. Three big windows overlook the tidal flats, dunes, and ocean just beyond Bodega's harbor. The menu, strong on seafood, features Dungeness crab cakes with tomato chutney, and the chef's seafood sampler. Other good bets are the crisp-roasted Liberty duck and the hot Sonoma apple cobbler. Eleven Sonoma County wines offered by the glass. **FYI:** Reservations recommended. Children's menu. Beer and wine only. **Open:** Breakfast daily 8–10am; dinner daily 6–9pm. **Prices:** Main courses $16–$20. AE, DC, DISC, MC, V. 📷 占

Lucas Wharf

595 CA 1; tel 707/875-3522. **Seafood.** Popular seafood spot in Bodega, right on a working fishing wharf. It serves good local seafood: calamari, steamed mussels and clams, salmon, crab Louis; also tasty appetizers, chowder, burgers, barbecued oysters, and fish and chips. Wide selection of microbrewed beers and Sonoma County wines. **FYI:** Reservations not accepted. Children's menu. **Open:** Peak (May–Oct) Sun–Thurs 11am–9:30pm, Fri–Sat 11am–10pm. **Prices:** Main courses $11–$16. DISC, MC, V. 📷 📷 占

Boonville

RESTAURANT 🍴

⭐ The Boonville Hotel
CA 128 at Lambert Lane; tel 707/895-2210. **Californian.** A charming restaurant set in a historic hotel surrounded by beautiful gardens. The atmosphere is fresh and clean, refined yet casual. The menu changes daily; typical offerings include delicious pizza, ahi tuna with mango-and-lime salsa, superb caesar salad, and lamb chops. Local wines and beers served. **FYI:** Reservations recommended. Beer and wine only. **Open:** Wed–Sun 6–9pm. Closed Jan. **Prices:** Main courses $11–$20. AE, MC, V. 🚗 ♿

Borrego Springs

Surrounded entirely by the Anza-Borrego Desert State Park, a beautiful preserve for Colorado Desert plants and animals as well as a great camping spot, Borrego Springs is popular among the retired and desert-resort sets. The park's excellent visitor center in town is a noteworthy attraction. **Information:** Borrego Springs Chamber of Commerce, 622 Palm Canyon Dr, PO Box 66, Borrego Springs 92004 (tel 619/767-5555).

MOTEL 🏨

☰☰ Palm Canyon Resort
221 Palm Canyon Dr, PO Box 956, 92004; tel 619/767-5341 or toll free 800/242-0044. It looks like a movie set from an old Hollywood Western, with two-story, wood-frame buildings and wooden boardwalks. Despite the rustic theme, everything is new and in tip-top shape. **Rooms:** 60 rms and stes. CI 4pm/CO noon. Nonsmoking rms avail. Large accommodations feature very good quality, English-style furnishings and lace curtains. Bathrooms offer a separate vanity area with two sinks and plenty of counter space. **Amenities:** 🛁 📺 ❄ A/C, cable TV. Some units w/terraces, 1 w/whirlpool. VCRs available for rent. **Services:** ✗ 🚐 🛎 Twice-daily maid svce, masseur, babysitting. **Facilities:** 🏋 [150] ♿ 1 restaurant (see "Restaurants" below), 1 bar, basketball, lawn games, whirlpool, washer/dryer. Good-size pool and spa in courtyard. Guests can play tennis at a club across the street. RV park on premises. **Rates:** Peak (Nov–May) $75–$110 S or D; $115–$150 ste. Extra person $10. Children under age 12 stay free. Min stay peak and wknds. Lower rates off-season. Parking: Outdoor, free. AE, CB, DC, DISC, MC, V.

RESORT

☰☰☰ La Casa del Zorro
3845 Yaqui Pass Rd, PO Box 127, 92004; tel 619/767-5323 or toll free 800/824-1884; fax 619/767-4782. 42 acres. "Slow—Adults At Play," reads the yellow sign at the resort's entrance. Designed like a small Spanish Colonial town, with low, stucco buildings capped by red-tile roofs. Not showy or fancy, but very, very comfortable. Excellent art adorns the walls of the main building, especially the stagecoach scenes by Marjorie Reed. **Rooms:** 58 rms, stes, and effic; 19 cottages/villas. CI 4pm/CO noon. Nonsmoking rms avail. Accommodations are in either low buildings or in one-to-four-bedroom casitas. Although simple, rooms are very attractively decorated with Early California–style furnishings and Western prints. Deluxe suites offer separate living, sleeping, and dressing areas, with plenty of counter space in the tile baths. **Amenities:** 🛁 ♨ 📺 ❄ A/C, cable TV w/movies, bathrobes. All units w/minibars, all w/terraces, some w/fireplaces, some w/whirlpools. **Services:** ✗ 🚐 🚗 🛎 🔔 Social director, masseur, babysitting. Most of the staff are long-time local residents, and they go out of their way to be friendly and helpful. $50 deposit for pets. During high-occupancy periods, they run a children's program. **Facilities:** 🏊 🚲 🏌6 🎾 [200] ♿ 1 restaurant, 2 bars (1 w/entertainment), volleyball, lawn games, whirlpool, beauty salon, playground. Very attractive main pool, with a stone deck. Both the boutique and the pro shop are very well stocked with quality merchandise, including books about the region. **Rates:** Peak (Oct 16–May 1) $90–$220 S or D; $135–$340 ste; $160–$505 effic; $160–$505 cottage/villa. Extra person $10. Children under age 12 stay free. Min stay wknds. Lower rates off-season. Parking: Outdoor, free. AE, CB, DC, DISC, MC, V.

RESTAURANT 🍴

Pablito's of the Desert
In Palm Canyon Resort, 221 Palm Canyon Dr; tel 619/767-5753. **Mexican.** A friendly place built to resemble an Old West stagecoach stop. In addition to a wide range of enchiladas and chimichangas, the menu also offers more elaborate selections, such as shrimp in a piquant garlic sauce. Excellent, hearty Mexican breakfasts too, such as chilaquiles or eggs scrambled with nopales (cactus). **FYI:** Reservations accepted. Children's menu. **Open:** Breakfast daily 7am–noon; lunch daily 11am–2pm; dinner daily 5–9pm. **Prices:** Main courses $6–$16. DISC, MC, V. 🚗 🏞 🍽 ♿

ATTRACTION 🎭

Anza-Borrego Desert State Park
Tel 619/767-4205 (Visitor Center) or 767-5311 (Park). The nation's largest state park, Anza-Borrego encompasses over 600,000 acres of desert wilderness just 40 miles east of Temecula. The best time to visit is mid-March through early April when wildflowers and cactus bloom throughout the park. The Visitor Center, located just west of Borrego Springs, can provide maps, books, and cards, and screens an audiovisual presentation on the changing faces of the desert. Self-guided hikes of the Borrego Palm Canyon lead to an oasis of fan palms with a spring and waterfall. **Open:** Peak (Oct–May) daily 9am–5pm. Reduced hours off-season. **$$**

Brea

See also Fullerton

HOTEL

⧠⧠⧠ Embassy Suites

900 E Birch St, 92621; tel 714/990-6000 or toll free 800/EMBASSY; fax 714/990-1653. 10 mi NE of Disneyland. Imperial Hwy exit off CA 57. All-suite hotel decorated in an Egyptian motif. Well-suited for business travelers and families; located between the Brea Civic Center and the Brea Mall. **Rooms:** 229 stes. Executive level. CI 3pm/CO 1pm. Nonsmoking rms avail. All suites have queen-size beds and are beautifully decorated. **Amenities:** 🕪 A/C, cable TV w/movies, refrig, voice mail. All units w/terraces. Iron and ironing board in each room. **Services:** ✕ ⧠ Complimentary breakfast and afternoon snacks. Free shuttle to Disneyland and Knott's Berry Farm. **Facilities:** 1 restaurant (lunch and dinner only), 1 bar, spa, sauna, whirlpool, washer/dryer. Gift shop. **Rates (BB):** $119–$189 ste. Extra person $10. Children under age 12 stay free. AP rates avail. Parking: Indoor, free. AE, CB, DC, DISC, JCB, MC, V.

Buena Park

See also Cerritos

A Santa Fe Railroad site since the 1920s (and thus one of Orange County's industrial transportation hubs), Buena Park's biggest attraction is Knott's Berry Farm, the oldest theme park in the nation. **Information:** Buena Park Chamber of Commerce, 6280 Manchester Blvd #102, Buena Park 90621 (tel 714/521-0261).

HOTELS

⧠⧠⧠ Buena Park Hotel

7675 Crescent Ave, 90620; tel 714/995-1111 or toll free 800/422-4444 in the US, 800/325-8734 in Canada; fax 714/828-8590. Beach Blvd exit off CA 91. A great location—guests can walk to Knott's Berry Farm or take a shuttle to Disneyland, just 10 minutes away. **Rooms:** 350 rms and stes. Executive level. CI 3pm/CO noon. Nonsmoking rms avail. Rooms are large. **Amenities:** 🕪 A/C, satel TV w/movies. 1 unit w/terrace, 1 w/whirlpool. **Services:** ✕ ⧠ Car-rental desk, babysitting. **Facilities:** 2 restaurants, 1 bar (w/entertainment), games rm, whirlpool, washer/dryer. **Rates:** Peak (June–Aug) $79 S; $89 D; $89–$125 ste. Children under age 18 stay free. Lower rates off-season. Parking: Outdoor, free. AE, CB, DC, DISC, MC, V.

⧠⧠⧠ Embassy Suites

7762 Beach Blvd, 90620; tel 714/739-5600 or toll free 800/362-2779; fax 714/521-9650. Beach Blvd exit off CA 91.

This all-suite property has a nice courtyard and open lobby. **Rooms:** 202 stes. CI 3pm/CO noon. Nonsmoking rms avail. **Amenities:** 🕪 A/C, cable TV w/movies, refrig, voice mail. All units w/minibars, some w/terraces. Microwaves. **Services:** ✕ ⧠ Babysitting. Complimentary breakfast buffet and morning newspaper. **Facilities:** 1 restaurant, 1 bar, games rm, whirlpool, washer/dryer. Gas barbecue grills. **Rates (BB):** Peak (June–Aug) $129–$179 ste. Extra person $15. Children under age 13 stay free. Lower rates off-season. Parking: Outdoor, free. AE, CB, DC, DISC, JCB, MC, V.

⧠⧠⧠ Holiday Inn Buena Park

7000 Beach Blvd, 90620; tel 714/522-7000; fax 714/522-3230. Beach Blvd exit off CA 91. Close to the freeway, but well soundproofed. **Rooms:** 246 rms and stes. Executive level. CI 3pm/CO noon. Nonsmoking rms avail. Nicely decorated with a fresh, contemporary look. **Amenities:** 🕪 A/C, cable TV w/movies. **Services:** ✕ ⧠ **Facilities:** 1 restaurant, 1 bar (w/entertainment), games rm, whirlpool, washer/dryer. **Rates:** Peak (June–Aug) $89–$109 S; $109–$129 D; $150–$175 ste. Extra person $10. Children under age 18 stay free. Lower rates off-season. Parking: Outdoor, free. AE, CB, DC, DISC, JCB, MC, V.

MOTELS

⧠⧠ Colony Inn

7800 Crescent Ave, 90620; tel 714/527-2201; fax 714/826-3826. Beach Blvd exit off CA 91. New management, newly renovated. Close to Disneyland; right across from Knott's Berry Farm. **Rooms:** 130 rms. CI 2pm/CO 11am. Nonsmoking rms avail. Rooms are a bit small. **Amenities:** 🕪 A/C, cable TV. **Services:** ⧠ Babysitting. **Facilities:** Steam rm, washer/dryer. **Rates:** Peak (June–Aug) $90 S; $98 D. Children under age 18 stay free. Lower rates off-season. Parking: Outdoor, free. AE, DC, DISC, MC, V.

⧠⧠⧠ Courtyard by Marriott

7621 Beach Blvd, 90620; tel 714/670-6600 or toll free 800/321-2211; fax 714/670-0360. Beach Blvd exit off CA 91. Very attractively landscaped oasis of tranquillity amid the bustle of Beach Blvd. Popular with business travelers, it also offers good vales for weekend tourists. **Rooms:** 145 rms and stes. CI 3pm/CO noon. Nonsmoking rms avail. **Amenities:** 🕪 A/C, cable TV w/movies, dataport, voice mail. Some units w/terraces. Rooms on the second floor have balconies; those surrounding the pool have patios. **Services:** ✕ ⧠ Babysitting. Efficient and gracious staff. Evening hors d'oeuvres served in the lobby. **Facilities:** 1 restaurant (bkfst and dinner only), 1 bar, whirlpool, washer/dryer. Colorful flower gardens; gazebo. **Rates:** Peak (Apr 15–Aug) $74 S or D; $94–$99 ste. Children under age 18 stay free. Lower rates off-season. Parking: Outdoor, free. Rates include up to five persons per room. AE, CB, DC, DISC, ER, MC, V.

≣≣≣ Fairfield Inn by Marriott

7032 Orangethorpe Ave, 90621; tel 714/523-1488 or toll free 800/228-2800; fax 714/523-1488. Beach Blvd exit off CA 91. This very well-kept motel, although located some distance from Orange County tourist attractions, is popular with families. Also caters to long-haul truckers doing business nearby. **Rooms:** 134 rms. CI 3pm/CO noon. No smoking. Rooms are basic, but great for the price. **Amenities:** 🛏 🗑 A/C, cable TV w/movies, dataport. Some rooms have coffee-makers, microwaves, refrigerators, irons, and ironing boards. **Services:** 🚗 ⬛ ⬗ Coffee and tea available all day in lobby. **Facilities:** 🛝 ⬛ ⬗ Guest privileges at nearby health club for a nominal fee. **Rates (CP):** Peak (June 15–Sept) $48 S or D. Children under age 18 stay free. Lower rates off-season. Parking: Outdoor, free. AE, DC, DISC, MC, V.

≣≣ Inn at Buena Park

7828 Orangethorpe Ave, 90620; tel 714/670-7200 or toll free 800/727-7205; fax 714/522-3319. Beach Blvd exit off CA 91. Clean and functional motel fine for quick stops. **Rooms:** 172 rms. CI 2pm/CO noon. Nonsmoking rms avail. Bare-bones rooms with little decoration. Bathrooms are cramped, and the counterspace is barely adequate for one person. No closet or armoire for clothing. **Amenities:** 🛏 🗑 A/C, cable TV w/movies. **Services:** 🚗 ⬛ Free shuttle to Knott's Berry Farm and Disneyland. Passes to local health club for a nominal fee. Staff not very helpful. **Facilities:** 🛝 ⬛ ⬗ Whirlpool, washer/dryer. Pool heated. **Rates (CP):** $84 S; $89 D. Children under age 18 stay free. Parking: Outdoor, free. Rate include up to four people per room. AE, DISC, MC, V.

RESTAURANT

Marie Callender Restaurant

5960 Orangethorpe Ave; tel 714/522-0170. Off CA 91. **American.** Homey restaurant known for its extensive salad bar and homemade soups. Part of a chain that began as a pie shop, it's a great place for family dining. **FYI:** Reservations accepted. Children's menu. **Open:** Mon–Thurs 11am–10pm, Fri–Sat 11am–11pm, Sun 9am–10pm. **Prices:** Main courses $8–$12. AE, DISC, MC, V. 🍽 ⬗

ATTRACTIONS

Knott's Berry Farm

8039 Beach Blvd; tel 714/827-1776 or 220-5200 (recorded info). Knott's Berry Farm grew out of the enormous popularity of the roadside stand operated by Walter and Cordelia Knott during the Great Depression. The Knotts sold pies, preserves, and homemade chicken dinners from their 10-acre farm, and lines became so long that they decided to create an Old West Ghost Town to amuse waiting customers. The famous Chicken Dinner Restaurant now serves more than a million meals a year, and the park maintains the Old West motif throughout five themed adventure areas, each with rides, shows, and other attractions:

Old West Ghost Town, the original attraction, is a collection of authentic buildings that have been relocated from actual western ghost towns and refurbished; **Fiesta Village** has a south-of-the-border theme and features a rollercoaster that runs backward; **Roaring '20s** contains the Sky Tower, a thrilling parachute ride; **Wild Water Wilderness** features a whitewater ride called Bigfoot Rapids; and **Camp Snoopy** is a six-acre play area where members of the Peanuts gang greet guests and pose for pictures. **Open:** Peak (Mem Day–Labor Day) Mon–Thurs 9am–11pm, Fri–Sun 9am–midnight. Reduced hours off-season. Opening times vary; call for lastest information. $$$$

Movieland Wax Museum

7711 Beach Blvd (CA 39); tel 714/522-1155. Memorable motion picture scenes are painstakingly re-created here in wax. Tableaux depicting stars and famous films include Humphrey Bogart and Katherine Hepburn in *The African Queen*, Laurel and Hardy in *The Perfect Day*, plus more contemporary productions such as *Superman* and *Star Trek*. New personalities are added yearly. **Open:** Daily 9am–7pm. $$$$

Burbank

HOTELS

≣≣≣ Burbank Airport Hilton & Convention Center

2500 Hollywood Way, 91505; tel 818/843-6000 or toll free 800/468-3576; fax 818/842-9720. Twin high-rise towers offer an excellent location for business and pleasure travelers. Across the street from Burbank Airport, but quiet. Five miles to Universal Studios. **Rooms:** 486 rms and stes. CI 3pm/CO noon. Nonsmoking rms avail. **Amenities:** 🛏 🗑 🖥 ☎ A/C, satel TV w/movies, dataport, voice mail. **Services:** 🍽 🚗 ⬛ ⬗ ⬗ Twice-daily maid svce, car-rental desk, babysitting. Free 24-hour airport shuttle. **Facilities:** 🛝 🏋 2000 ⬛ ⬗ 1 restaurant, 1 bar (w/entertainment), sauna, whirlpool, washer/dryer. Two outdoor heated pools served by separate, private elevators. Extensive convention facilities with 43 meeting rooms. **Rates:** $109–$179 S; $119–$189 D; $129–$499 ste. Extra person $10. Children under age 18 stay free. Min stay special events. Parking: Outdoor, $4/day. AE, CB, DC, DISC, EC, MC, V.

≣≣≣ Ramada Inn Burbank Airport

2900 N San Fernando Blvd, 91504; tel 818/843-5955 or toll free 800/228-2828; fax 818/845-9030. Very nice hotel for the neighborhood; located close to the studios. Great pool area and attractive garden. **Rooms:** 144 rms and stes. CI 2pm/CO noon. Nonsmoking rms avail. Large rooms with little or no freeway or airport noise. **Amenities:** 🛏 🗑 A/C, cable TV w/movies, refrig. Some units w/whirlpools. **Services:** ✗ 🚗 ⬛ ⬗ ⬗ Car-rental desk. **Facilities:** 🛝 300 ⬗ 1 restaurant (bkfst and dinner only), 1 bar, games rm.

Rates: Peak (June 15–Sept 1) $72–$92 S; $82–$102 D; $99–$130 ste. Extra person $10. Children under age 18 stay free. Lower rates off-season. Parking: Outdoor, free. AE, CB, DC, DISC, JCB, MC, V.

ATTRACTION

Warner Brothers Studios

Olive Ave at Hollywood Way; tel 818/954-1744. Warner Brothers offers a studio tour that is probably the most comprehensive and intimate around. Called the VIP Tour, it takes only 12 people per group, who look in on actual facilities to watch real actors and technicians at work, whether it is a music score being recorded, a show being edited, or a scene being shot. Because actual production is involved, tours change day to day, and there is no set itinerary. Reservations are recommended; children under 10 are not admitted. **Open:** Mon–Fri 9, 10, and 11am and 1, 2, and 3pm. **$$$$**

Burlingame

See San Francisco Int'l Airport

Calabasas

RESTAURANT

Saddlepeak Lodge

419 Cold Canyon Rd (Malibu Canyon); tel 818/222-3888. **Regional American.** Located in the heart of spectacular Malibu Canyon, this elegantly refurbished lodge (once a bordello) presents a handsome, rustic set of dining rooms. Chef Josie La Balch (formerly of Remi) prepares excellent and unusual fare, such as game hen, calf's sweetbreads, buffalo tenderloin, and Texas black boar chops. They're especially known for their three-course Sunday brunch. **FYI:** Reservations recommended. Dress code. **Open:** Dinner Wed–Fri 6–9:30pm, Sat–Sun 5–9:30pm; brunch Sun 11am–2pm. **Prices:** Main courses $20–$28. AE, MC, V.

Calexico

MOTEL

UNRATED Hollie's Fiesta Motel

801 Imperial Ave, 92231; tel 619/357-3271; fax 619/357-7975. Off CA 98. Only minutes from Mexico; popular with business travelers. **Rooms:** 60 rms, stes, and effic. CI open/CO noon. Nonsmoking rms avail. **Amenities:** A/C, cable TV. Some units w/terraces. Some rooms have refrigerators. **Services:** X **Facilities:** 1 restaurant, 1 bar

(w/entertainment). **Rates:** $41 S; $47 D; $58 ste; $79 effic. Extra person $6. Children under age 12 stay free. Parking: Indoor/outdoor, free. AE, CB, DC, DISC, MC, V.

Calistoga

Founded in the picturesque Napa Valley in 1859, the name is a cross between California and Saratoga. Its mineral waters have been famous for over a century, and the local wines are prized by connoisseurs. **Information:** Calistoga Chamber of Commerce, 1458 Lincoln #4, Calistoga 94515 (tel 707/942-6333).

MOTELS

Comfort Inn

1865 Lincoln Ave, 94515; tel 707/942-9400 or toll free 800/221-2222; fax 707/942-5262. E on Lincoln off CA 128. Reasonably attractive, comfortable motel, well located for exploring Calistoga and the rest of the Napa Valley. **Rooms:** 55 rms. CI 3pm/CO 11am. Nonsmoking rms avail. **Amenities:** A/C, cable TV, refrig. Some units w/terraces. **Services:** Babysitting. **Facilities:** 1 restaurant, spa, sauna, steam rm, whirlpool. **Rates:** Peak (Apr–Nov) $45–$120 S; $50–$130 D. Extra person $7. Children under age 18 stay free. Lower rates off-season. Parking: Outdoor, free. Spa packages include room, spa visit, and dinner for two. AE, CB, DC, DISC, ER, JCB, MC, V.

Dr Wilkinson's Hot Springs

1507 Lincoln Ave, 94515; tel 707/942-4102. E on Lincoln off CA 128. 3 acres. Family-owned and -operated motel with a full-service spa. **Rooms:** 43 rms; 4 cottages/villas. CI 3pm/CO 11am. Nonsmoking rms avail. Average motel-style rooms. **Amenities:** A/C, cable TV, refrig. **Services:** Masseur, babysitting. **Facilities:** Spa, steam rm, whirlpool. Separate spa facilities for men and women. Volcanic-ash mud baths, as well as mineral pools and baths. Facial salon. Exercise class offered once a week. **Rates:** Peak (July–Aug) $74–$99 S; $79–$109 D; $79–$109 cottage/villa. Extra person $12. Children under age 7 stay free. Min stay wknds. Lower rates off-season. Parking: Outdoor, free. Special spa and salon packages available. AE, DC, DISC, MC, V.

INN

Silver Rose Inn

351 Rosedale Rd, 94515; tel 707/942-9581 or toll free 800/995-9381. E of Silverado Trail. 20 acres. Family-owned and -operated inn located on a knoll, surrounded by terraced rock-and-rose gardens. Gathering room has huge stone fireplace and vaulted ceiling. Pure mineral water is piped throughout the inn. **Rooms:** 20 rms. CI 3pm/CO noon. No smoking. Spacious, individually decorated rooms have either mountain or vineyard views. **Amenities:** A/C, bathrobes. No TV. Some units w/terraces, some w/fireplaces, some

w/whirlpools. **Services:** ✗ 🛁 Masseur, wine/sherry served. Breakfast offered in dining room, guest room, or on the terrace. Massages available in guest rooms. **Facilities:** 🔥 ⛳ 🏊 Spa, whirlpool, guest lounge. New 11-room section, set in vineyards, features a wine bottle–shaped swimming pool. Very private spa is for guests only. Excellent hiking trails nearby. **Rates (CP):** $125–$210 S or D. Extra person $50. Min stay wknds and special events. Parking: Outdoor, free. AE, DISC, JCB, MC, V.

RESTAURANTS 🍽

★ All Seasons Cafe & Wine Shop
1400 Lincoln Ave; tel 707/942-9111. E off CA 128. **New American.** Located on the ground floor of the old Mayflower Hotel (built in 1912), the cafe has a comfortable, old-fashioned interior with ceiling fans, a checkerboard floor, and marble-topped tables. Atmosphere is casual and personal. Food is California-American with various ethnic influences. Menu offers imaginative pizzas and pastas based on seasonal ingredients. **FYI:** Reservations recommended. Beer and wine only. **Open:** Lunch Thurs–Tues 11am–3pm; dinner Thurs–Tues 5:30–10pm. **Prices:** Main courses $12–$18. MC, V. ♥ 🍴 ♿

♣ Catahoula
In Mount View Hotel, 1457 Lincoln Ave; tel 707/942-2275. Between Washington St and Fairway. **Regional American.** Launched in 1994, this restaurant quickly became a mega-hit. The decor is a pastiche of objects rescued from salvage yards and marinas. The wonderful food is spiced with accents from noted chef Jan Birnbaum's southern heritage. Top choices include griddled hominy cakes or whole roasted fish from the brick oven. In addition to the dining room, there's also a lively saloon. **FYI:** Reservations recommended. **Open:** Peak (June–Oct) lunch Wed–Fri noon–2:30pm, Sat–Sun noon–3:30pm, Mon noon–2:30pm; dinner Wed–Fri 5:30–10pm, Sat–Sun 5:30–10:30pm, Mon 5:30–10pm. Closed Jan. **Prices:** Main courses $11–$24. MC, V. ♿

ATTRACTIONS 📷

Petrified Forest
4100 Petrified Forest Rd; tel 707/942-6667. Volcanic ash blanketed this area after the eruption of Mount St Helena three million years ago. As a result, visitors today can find redwoods that have turned to rock through the slow infiltration of silicas and other minerals. There are also petrified seashells, clams, and other marine life—indicating that water covered this area even before the redwood forest. **Open:** Peak (Mem Day–Labor Day) daily 10am–5:30pm. Reduced hours off-season. **$**

Calistoga Depot
1458 Lincoln Ave; tel 707/942-5556. The tiny town's former railroad station now houses a variety of shops, a restaurant, and the Calistoga Chamber of Commerce. Alongside the building are six restored passenger cars dating from 1916 to the early 1920s, each of which houses enticing shops.

Old Faithful Geyser of California
1299 Tubbs Lane; tel 707/942-6463. Situated between CA 29 and CA 128; follow signs from downtown Calistoga. One of three Old Faithful geysers in the world, this one normally erupts at intervals of about 40 minutes. The display lasts about three minutes, and you'll learn a lot about the origins of geothermal steam. There are picnic facilities and a gift and snack shop. **Open:** Peak (Mem Day–Labor Day) daily 9am–6pm. Reduced hours off-season. **$$**

Camarillo

Tucked into the rolling coastal hills of Ventura County, Camarillo is a quiet residential community just outside Los Angeles's sphere of influence. The surrounding farmland yields citrus fruits and flowers. **Information:** Camarillo Chamber of Commerce, 632 Las Posas Rd, Camarillo 93010 (tel 805/484-4383).

HOTELS 🏨

≣≣ Camarillo Courtyard by Marriott
4994 Verdugo Way, 93012; tel 805/388-1020 or toll free 800/321-2211; fax 805/987-6274. Pleasant Valley Rd exit off US 101. Excellent location within a shopping center, with restaurants surrounding it. Although adjacent to the freeway, this property, which caters to a corporate clientele, is quiet and peaceful. The light, attractive lobby is filled with plants. **Rooms:** 130 rms and stes. CI 3pm/CO 1pm. Nonsmoking rms avail. All suites face a sunny, nicely landscaped courtyard. **Amenities:** 🛏 ♨ 🖭 A/C, cable TV w/movies, dataport. Some units w/terraces. Cable TV service offers 45 movie channels. Suites have refrigerators, wet bars, and two TVs. **Services:** 🛁 🚗 Car-rental desk. Complimentary morning newspaper delivered to room. 24-hour fax and copy services. 24-hour complimentary coffee, tea, and iced tea in lobby. **Facilities:** 🔥 ⛳ 🏊 ♿ 1 restaurant (bkfst only), 1 bar, whirlpool, washer/dryer. **Rates:** $59–$74 S or D; $86–$99 ste. Children under age 12 stay free. Parking: Outdoor, free. Lower rates on weekends. AE, CB, DC, DISC, MC, V.

≣≣ Country Inn at Camarillo
1405 Del Norte Rd, 93010; tel 805/983-7171 or toll free 800/44-RELAX; fax 805/988-1838. Central Ave exit off US 101, left on Del Norte Rd. Visible from freeway but still hard to find on access road. Very quiet. **Rooms:** 100 rms and stes. CI 3pm/CO noon. Nonsmoking rms avail. **Amenities:** 🛏 ♨ 🖭 A/C, cable TV, refrig, VCR. Some units w/fireplaces, some w/whirlpools. Microwave. **Services:** 🛁 🚗 Complimentary breakfast and two-hour evening cocktail party. **Facilities:** 🔥

&. Whirlpool, washer/dryer. **Rates (BB):** $110–$125 S; $120–$135 D; $155–$165 ste. Extra person $10. Children under age 12 stay free. Parking: Outdoor, free. AE, MC, V.

≣≣ Del Norte Inn

4444 Central Ave, 93010; tel 805/485-3999 or toll free 800/44-RELAX; fax 805/485-1820. Central Ave exit off US 101. Recently renovated, with basic but acceptable rooms. **Rooms:** 111 rms and stes. CI 3pm/CO noon. Nonsmoking rms avail. **Amenities:** ⌂ ⌂ ⌐ A/C, cable TV, refrig, VCR. Some units w/fireplaces. **Services:** ⌂ ⌐ **Facilities:** ⌂ &. Whirlpool, washer/dryer. **Rates (CP):** $79 S; $89 D; $120 ste; $89–$99 effic. Extra person $10. Children under age 12 stay free. Min stay. Parking: Outdoor, free. AE, DC, DISC, MC, V.

RESTAURANT ⍟

★ Giovanni's

In Mission Oaks Shopping Center, 5227 Mission Oaks Blvd; tel 805/484-4376. Pleasant Valley exit off US 101. **Italian.** One of the best Italian restaurants in the area. Decor is simple, and tables are spaced far enough apart to ensure privacy. Homemade pasta specialties are featured; fruit-flavored gelati is prepared daily. Monthly fixed-price wine dinners. Banquet rooms for private parties. **FYI:** Reservations recommended. Children's menu. **Open:** Lunch Tues–Fri 11:30am–2:30pm; dinner Tues–Sun 5–10pm. **Prices:** Main courses $12–$23; prix fixe $35. AE, MC, V. ♥ ✉ &.

Cambria

Originally called Slabtown, Cambria was renamed by the image-conscious early settlers. The artist colony on the sea has a newer section of town with seaside hotels, as well as a historic district with delightful architecture, inns, and eateries. **Information:** Cambria Chamber of Commerce, 767 Main St, Cambria 93428 (tel 805/927-3624).

MOTELS ⌂

≣≣≣ Best Western Fireside Inn

6700 Moonstone Beach Dr, 93428; tel 805/927-8661 or toll free 800/528-1234; fax 805/927-8584. Off CA 1. A serene property across from Moonstone Beach. **Rooms:** 46 rms. CI 3pm/CO 11am. Nonsmoking rms avail. Decor changes from building to building. Some rooms have been nicely redone with blond wood furniture and rose-patterned wallpaper. Room 131 offers an ocean view, four-poster bed, armoire, and loveseat. **Amenities:** ⌂ ⌂ ⍟ ⌐ Cable TV w/movies, refrig. No A/C. Some units w/terraces, some w/fireplaces, some w/whirlpools. **Services:** ⌂ ⌐ Twice-daily maid svce, masseur. Fax and copying services available. Expanded continental breakfast in fireside breakfast room includes delicious scones, muffins, and sweet rolls. **Facilities:** ⌂ ⌂ &. 1 beach (ocean), whirlpool. **Rates (CP):** Peak (June–Aug) $89–$149 S

or D. Extra person $10. Children under age 12 stay free. Min stay wknds. Lower rates off-season. Parking: Outdoor, free. AE, CB, DC, MC, V.

≣≣≣ Blue Dolphin Inn

6470 Moonstone Beach Dr, 93428; tel 805/927-3300. Off CA 1. A thoroughly and thoughtfully decorated modern property that looks like a cross between a little bed-and-breakfast and a country inn. Romantic and feminine. **Rooms:** 18 rms. CI 3pm/CO 11am. No smoking. Rooms decorated with print wallpaper, pine desks, and iron and brass bedsteads. Suites with ocean view have double-canopied beds. **Amenities:** ⌂ ⌂ ⍟ Cable TV w/movies, refrig, VCR. No A/C. Some units w/terraces, all w/fireplaces, some w/whirlpools. Rooms offer a selection of books, plus complimentary mineral water in refrigerator. Tote bags and shoe polishers in bathrooms. **Services:** ⌐ ⌐ Masseur. Videos for rent. Afternoon tea and cookies. **Facilities:** Tea room. **Rates (CP):** Peak (Apr–Oct) $95–$195 S or D. Extra person $5. Lower rates off-season. Parking: Outdoor, free. AE, CB, DISC, MC, V.

≣≣≣ Cambria Landing on Moonstone Beach

6530 Moonstone Beach Dr, 93428; tel 805/927-1619. Moonstone Beach Dr exit off CA 1. The inside is much nicer than the exterior. **Rooms:** 21 rms. CI 3pm/CO 11am. Nonsmoking rms avail. Spacious ocean-view rooms. Nice prints accent the walls, and beds are either cherry-wood sleigh style or early American oak. **Amenities:** ⌂ ⍟ A/C, cable TV w/movies. Some units w/terraces, all w/fireplaces. Champagne or wine in room upon arrival. Gas fireplaces. **Services:** Front desk open until 10pm. Continental breakfast in bed, with homemade coffee cake. **Facilities:** ⌂ 1 beach (ocean), whirlpool. **Rates (BB):** Peak (July–Sept) $79–$179 S or D. Children under age 5 stay free. Min stay special events. Lower rates off-season. Parking: Outdoor, free. DISC, MC, V.

≣≣≣ Fog Catcher Inn

6400 Moonstone Beach Dr, 93428; tel 805/927-1400 or toll free 800/425-4121. 6 mi S of Hearst Castle. Newer but quaint property; looks like something from an English village. **Rooms:** 60 rms, stes, and effic. CI 3pm/CO 11am. Nonsmoking rms avail. Country decor. Many rooms have ocean views. **Amenities:** ⌂ ⍟ ⍟ Cable TV, refrig. No A/C. All units w/minibars, 1 w/terrace, all w/fireplaces. Microwave. **Services:** ⌐ Complimentary full breakfast. **Facilities:** ⌂ &. Whirlpool. **Rates (BB):** Peak (Mem Day–Labor Day) $105–$175 S or D; $135 ste; $215 effic. Extra person $5. Children under age 2 stay free. Min stay peak and special events. Lower rates off-season. Parking: Outdoor, free. AE, CB, DC, DISC, MC, V.

≣≣ Mariners Inn

6180 Moonstone Beach Dr, 93428; tel 805/927-4624; fax 805/927-3425. Moonstone Beach Dr exit off CA 1. Old-style motel; acceptable if not romantic. **Rooms:** 26 rms. CI 3pm/CO 11am. Nonsmoking rms avail. **Amenities:** ⌂ Cable TV w/movies. No A/C. Some units w/minibars, some w/fireplaces. **Services:** ⤸ 🐾 **Facilities:** ♿ 1 beach (ocean), whirl-pool. **Rates (CP):** Peak (July–Aug) $69–$109 S; $79–$109 D. Extra person $10. Children under age 12 stay free. Lower rates off-season. Parking: Outdoor, free. Lower than for other nearby lodging. AE, DISC, MC, V.

≋≋≋ Sand Pebbles Inn
6252 Moonstone Beach Dr, 93428; tel 805/927-5600. Off CA 1. A newer property decorated like a bed-and-breakfast, it shares ownership with the Blue Dolphin Inn down the street. Spotless, but management could be friendlier. **Rooms:** 23 rms. CI 3pm/CO 11am. No smoking. Rooms are decorated with personal touches: original art, books, fresh flowers. **Amenities:** 📺 ⬧ 🍷 Cable TV w/movies, VCR. No A/C. Some units w/terraces, all w/fireplaces, some w/whirlpools. **Services:** 🔑 ⤸ Masseur. Afternoon coffee, tea, and refreshments. Hearst Castle reservations can be made here. **Facilities:** Tea room. **Rates (CP):** Peak (Apr–Oct) $95–$210 S or D. Extra person $5. Lower rates off-season. Parking: Outdoor, free. AE, CB, DISC, MC, V.

≋≋≋ Sea Otter Inn
6656 Moonstone Beach Dr, 93428; tel 805/927-5888. Moonstone Beach Dr exit off CA 1. Across from the beach, a gray wooden Victorian-style low-rise trimmed with pink and maroon. Clean and thoughtfully appointed. **Rooms:** 25 rms and stes. CI 3pm/CO 11am. Nicely decorated rooms with bleached pine furniture. Some have four-poster beds and patchwork quilts; some ocean views. **Amenities:** 📺 ⬧ 🎵 Cable TV, refrig, VCR. No A/C. All units w/fireplaces, some w/whirlpools. Gas fireplaces. **Services:** ⤸ **Facilities:** 🏊 ♿ Whirlpool. Well-landscaped pool and hot-tub area. **Rates (CP):** Peak (Mem Day–Labor Day) $80–$110 S or D; $110–$120 ste. Extra person $5. Children under age 8 stay free. Min stay wknds. Lower rates off-season. Parking: Outdoor, free. AE, CB, DC, DISC, MC, V.

LODGE

≋≋≋ Cambria Pines Lodge
2905 Burton Dr, 93428; tel 805/927-4200 or toll free 800/445-6868; fax 805/927-4016. Burton Dr exit off CA 1. This 25-acre wooded property, which boasts a resident peacock, is ideal for group functions and family reunions. The alpine-style lodge features a river-stone fireplace and antler chandelier. **Rooms:** 100 rms and stes; 25 cottages/villas. CI 3pm/CO 11am. Nonsmoking rms avail. Accommodations range from funky cabins to large, tastefully appointed suites with original artwork. Standard rooms could use more drawer space. Suites offer additional sofa beds and queen-size Murphy beds. **Amenities:** 📺 🎵 Cable TV w/movies. No A/C. Some units w/terraces, some w/fireplaces. Some suites have refrigerators and two fireplaces. **Services:** ⤸ 🐾 Masseur. VCRs and tapes available for rent. Newspaper rack and video games adjacent to lobby. **Facilities:** 🏊 🎾 🏐 🐾 ♿ 1 restaurant (dinner only), 1 bar (w/entertainment), volleyball, sauna, whirlpool, beauty salon. Indoor, junior Olympic–size

pool and whirlpool area need renovation. Gazebo and bandstand. **Rates (BB):** Peak (Mem Day–Labor Day) $65–$115 S or D; $95 ste; $65 cottage/villa. Extra person $5. Children under age 3 stay free. Min stay peak and special events. Lower rates off-season. Parking: Outdoor, free. Special packages for Hearst Castle 8 miles to the north. AE, DC, DISC, MC, V.

RESTAURANTS 🍴

★ The Brambles Dinner House
4005 Burton Dr; tel 805/927-4716. **Seafood/Steak.** This English-style cottage has several rooms decorated with antiques. The menu is traditional: prime rib with Yorkshire pudding, rack of lamb, chicken Cordon Bleu, steak, lobster tail, crab legs, and other seafood. **FYI:** Reservations recommended. Children's menu. Dress code. **Open:** Dinner Mon–Fri 4–9:30pm, Sat 4–10pm; brunch Sun 9:30am–2pm. **Prices:** Prix fixe $11–$20. AE, CB, DC, DISC, MC, V. ■ 📠 📺 ♿

The Hamlet Restaurant at Moonstone Gardens
CA 1; tel 805/927-3535. Exotic Garden Dr exit off CA 1. **Californian.** Lovely two-story wood and glass building offers casual dining with exquisite coastal views. Seasonal whale watching from upstairs bar. Menu features poached salmon, calamari, red snapper, filet mignon, and daily pasta specials. In addition to the extensive wine list, there's a wine-tasting bar and wine shop. You can also stroll through three-acre Moonstone Gardens with its fine collection of succulents and kitchen herbs. Outdoor patio. **FYI:** Reservations accepted. Piano/singer. **Open:** Peak (June–Oct) lunch daily 11:30am–4pm; dinner Fri–Sat 4–10pm, Sun–Thurs 4–9pm. Closed Dec 18–Dec 25. **Prices:** Main courses $11–$23. MC, V. ♥ 🛥 📠 ♿

Moonstone Beach Bar & Grill
6550 Moonstone Beach Dr; tel 805/927-3859. **New American/Seafood.** Casual indoor and outdoor dining with ocean views. Menu items include seafood pastas, many fish specials, grilled meats, and chicken. **FYI:** Reservations not accepted. Children's menu. **Open:** Breakfast Mon–Sat 7–11am; lunch Mon–Sat noon–3pm; dinner daily 5:30–9pm; brunch Sun 10am–3pm. **Prices:** Main courses $12–$25. MC, V. 🛥 📠

★ Mustache Pete's Italian-American Eatery
In the Corner Store, 4090 Burton Dr; tel 805/927-8589. Main St exit off CA 1. **Italian.** Something for everyone here, with an antiques-filled dining room and outdoor patio, a heated sidewalk cafe, and a lively sports bar with big-screen TV. Menu choices include pizza, pasta, cioppino, veal, chicken, and seafood dishes like rock cod and rack-grilled shrimp. They also offer 15 beers on tap, an espresso bar, and a Sunday champagne brunch. **FYI:** Reservations accepted. **Open:** Lunch Mon–Sat 11am–4pm, Sun 1–4pm; dinner Mon–Fri 4–10pm; brunch Sun 10am–1pm. **Prices:** Main courses $10–$22. AE, CB, DC, MC, V. 🛥 ♿

Campbell

Once the center of fruit orchards for the Santa Clara Valley, Campbell is now a bedroom community of houses and apartments. **Information:** Campbell Chamber of Commerce, 1628 W Campbell Ave, Campbell 95008 (tel 408/378-6252).

HOTELS

Campbell Inn

675 E Campbell Ave, 95008; tel 408/374-4300 or toll free 800/582-4449; fax 408/379-0695. Hamilton Ave exit off CA 17 S. Centrally located. Sports-minded guests like this property. **Rooms:** 95 rms and stes. CI 2pm/CO noon. Nonsmoking rms avail. **Amenities:** A/C, cable TV w/movies, refrig, VCR, CD/tape player. Some units w/terraces, some w/fireplaces, some w/whirlpools. **Services:** Car-rental desk. Free movies for VCR. Complimentary shuttle transports guests up to 10 miles. **Facilities:** Spa, whirlpool. **Rates (CP):** $115–$125 S or D; $160–$190 ste. Extra person $10. Children under age 12 stay free. Parking: Outdoor, free. AE, DC, DISC, MC, V.

Pruneyard Inn

1995 S Bascom Ave, 95008; tel 408/559-4300 or toll free 800/822-4200 in the US, 800/631-4200 in Canada; fax 408/559-9919. 5 mi SW of San Jose. Hamilton Ave exit off Hwy 17 S. Next to a shopping center, a pleasant surprise, with large, cheery rooms. **Rooms:** 118 rms, stes, and effic. Executive level. CI 2pm/CO noon. Nonsmoking rms avail. **Amenities:** A/C, cable TV w/movies, dataport, VCR. All units w/minibars, some w/terraces, some w/fireplaces, some w/whirlpools. European-style breakfast with cheese, ham, turkey, croissants, and fruits. Coffee available 24 hours. **Services:** Complimentary shuttle within a 10-mile radius. **Facilities:** Whirlpool. Free passes to several nearby athletic clubs. **Rates (CP):** $125–$145 S; $135–$155 D; $195 ste; $135–$145 effic. Extra person $10. Children under age 11 stay free. Min stay special events. Parking: Outdoor, free. For an additional $10, you can upgrade to a room with fireplace or spa tub. AE, DC, DISC, MC, V.

Residence Inn by Marriott

2761 S Bascom Ave, 95008; tel 408/559-1551 or toll free 800/331-3131; fax 408/371-9808. Camden Ave exit off CA 17; left on Bascom Ave. Like living in a condo complex; popular with corporate clients and leisure travelers who stay for long periods. **Rooms:** 80 stes. CI 3pm/CO noon. Nonsmoking rms avail. Up to three people can stay in a studio suite; up to five in a penthouse suite. **Amenities:** A/C, cable TV w/movies, refrig. Some units w/terraces, some w/fireplaces. All have full kitchen. **Services:** Complimentary breakfast, newspapers, and evening beverages and hors d'oeuvres; full barbecue Thursdays in summer. **Facilities:** Whirlpool, washer/dryer. **Rates (BB):** $116–$144 ste. Parking: Outdoor, free. Rates fluctuate according to availability. Lower rates for longer stays, and for stays reserved further in advance. AE, DC, DISC, JCB, MC, V.

Capitola-by-the-Sea

INN

Inn at Depot Hill

250 Monterey Ave, 95010; tel 408/462-3376 or toll free 800/572-2632; fax 408/462-3697. Off CA 1. An exquisite inn in a vintage 1901 railroad terminal, combining turn-of-the-century flair with modern comforts. Serene garden courtyard features a lily pond with goldfish. Unsuitable for children under 18. **Rooms:** 8 rms and stes. CI 3pm/CO 11:30am. No smoking. Each room is unique. Delft Room has featherbed swathed in linen and lace, and private patio with whirlpool. Capitola Beach Room is done in modulations of beige. Opulent marble bathrooms. **Amenities:** Cable TV w/movies, refrig, dataport, VCR, CD/tape player, in-rm safe, bathrobes. No A/C. All units w/terraces, all w/fireplaces, some w/whirlpools. **Services:** Twice-daily maid svce, afternoon tea and wine/sherry served. Breakfast can be served in guest rooms, the dining room, or gardens. Extensive library of videotapes and cassettes available. **Facilities:** Guest lounge. The courtyard is popular for weddings. **Rates (BB):** Peak (July–Sept) $165–$195 S or D; $195–$250 ste. Lower rates off-season. Parking: Outdoor, free. AE, MC, V.

Carlsbad

The presence of mineral water with reputed healing powers similar to that found in Karlsbad, Bohemia, gave this growing suburb of San Diego its name. Known for its sparkling beaches and great surfing, Carlsbad has also recently undergone a downtown revitalization. **Information:** Carlsbad Chamber of Commerce, 5411 Avenida Encinas #100, PO Box 1605, Carlsbad 92018 (tel 619/931-8400).

MOTELS

Best Western Beach Terrace Inn

2775 Ocean St, 92008; tel 619/729-5951 or toll free 800/433-5415; fax 619/729-1078. Carlsbad Village Dr exit off I-5. One of few motels in the area located right on the beach; no frills but great location. **Rooms:** 49 rms, stes, and effic. Executive level. CI 2pm/CO 11am. Nonsmoking rms avail. Many rooms have excellent ocean views. **Amenities:** A/C, cable TV w/movies, refrig, VCR, in-rm safe, bathrobes. Some units w/terraces, some w/fireplaces, 1 w/whirlpool. **Services:** Telephone services for the deaf and hard of hearing. **Facilities:** 1 beach (ocean), whirlpool, washer/dryer. Even meeting rooms have ocean vistas. **Rates (CP):** Peak (June 16–Sept 15) $99–$168 S or D; $270 ste; $99 effic. Extra person $10. Min stay special events. Lower rates off-season. Parking: Outdoor, free. AE, CB, DC, DISC, EC, ER, JCB, MC, V.

≣≣≣ Tamarack Beach Resort
3200 Carlsbad Blvd, 92008; tel 619/729-3500 or toll free 800/334-2199; fax 619/434-5942. 30 mi N of San Diego. Tamarack exit off I-5. Across the road from a beautiful white-sand beach, and close to the shops and restaurants at Carlsbad Village. **Rooms:** 77 rms, stes, and effic. CI 3pm/CO noon. Tasteful, modern decor. Rooms that face west have great ocean views. **Amenities:** 🛱 💆 📱 🗐 A/C, cable TV w/movies, refrig, VCR. Some units w/terraces. VCRs are built into entertainment centers. **Services:** 🖳 🍴 Children's program. Free film library. **Facilities:** 🔗 🐎 🏊 🛌 🕹 1 restaurant, games rm, whirlpool. Barbecue grills, pool tables, video games, table tennis. **Rates:** Peak (May 15–Sept 15) $130 S; $140 D; $180–$260 ste; $180–$260 effic. Extra person $10. Children under age 12 stay free. Min stay special events. Lower rates off-season. Parking: Indoor, free. AE, MC, V.

INN

≣≣≣ Pelican Cove Inn
320 Walnut Ave, 92008; tel 619/434-5995. A gem located close to the beach and Carlsbad Village. Guests immediately feel at home at this peaceful, romantic, cozy bed-and-breakfast. Unsuitable for children under 5. **Rooms:** 8 rms. CI 3pm/CO 11am. No smoking. Exceptional rooms, well decorated with antique and contemporary furnishings. **Amenities:** 🛱 💆 Cable TV. No A/C. Some units w/terraces, all w/fireplaces, some w/whirlpools. **Services:** ✕ Masseur, afternoon tea served. Management will help with touring needs, and for an extra charge will prepare a picnic basket. **Facilities:** 🕹 Guest lounge. Romantic garden area for breakfast or a chat before dinner. **Rates (BB):** $85–$175 S or D. Extra person $15. Children under age 5 stay free. Min stay wknds. Parking: Outdoor, free. AE, MC, V.

RESORTS

≣≣≣ Carlsbad Inn Beach Resort
3075 Carlsbad Blvd, 92008; tel 619/434-7020 or toll free 800/235-3939; fax 619/729-4853. 35 mi N of San Diego. Carlsbad Village W exit off I-5; left on Carlsbad Blvd. 4 acres. Overlooking the ocean, convenient to shops and restaurants, this European-style inn has all the modern comforts amid well-kept grounds. **Rooms:** 55 rms, stes, and effic. Executive level. CI 4pm/CO 11am. Nonsmoking rms avail. **Amenities:** 🛱 💆 A/C, cable TV w/movies, refrig, VCR. All units w/terraces, some w/fireplaces, some w/whirlpools. **Services:** 🅥🅟 🖳 🍴 Free walking tours of historic Carlsbad. **Facilities:** 🔗 🐎 🛌 🕹 🏊 2 restaurants, 1 bar, 1 beach (ocean), lifeguard, board surfing, games rm, sauna, washer/dryer.

Guests have access to hotel's beach cabana and surfboards and boogie boards. **Rates:** $140–$160 S or D; $168–$198 ste; $195–$250 effic. Extra person $15. Children under age 12 stay free. Parking: Indoor/outdoor, free. AE, DC, DISC, JCB, MC, V.

≣≣≣≣ La Costa Resort and Spa
Costa del Mar Rd, 92009; tel 619/438-9111 or toll free 800/854-5000; fax 619/931-7585. 30 mi N of San Diego. La Costa exit off I-5. 450 acres. One of the finest spa resorts in the country, this place has something for everyone, from children to seniors. Attention to detail is apparent throughout the property. **Rooms:** 475 rms and stes; 5 cottages/villas. CI 4pm/CO noon. Nonsmoking rms avail. Rooms are elegantly appointed. Deluxe rooms overlooking the golf course; one- and two-bedroom suites and three- and four-bedroom executive homes available. **Amenities:** 🛱 💆 🗐 A/C, cable TV w/movies, dataport, in-rm safe, bathrobes. All units w/minibars, some w/terraces, some w/fireplaces. **Services:** ✕ 🖙 🅥🅟 🚐 🖳 🍴 🍽 Car-rental desk, masseur, children's program, babysitting. Excellent staff. Nutrition programs and spa cuisine. **Facilities:** 🔗 🚴 ▶36 🏌 🎾14 ⛳ 🛌 🏊 💻 🕹 4 restaurants, 1 bar (w/entertainment), basketball, volleyball, spa, sauna, steam rm, whirlpool, beauty salon, day-care ctr, playground. **Rates:** $225–$400 S or D; $500–$2,100 ste; $300–$1,575 cottage/villa. Extra person $35. Children under age 18 stay free. MAP rates avail. Parking: Outdoor, $10/day. Golf, tennis, and spa packages. AE, DC, DISC, JCB, MC, V.

≣≣ Olympic Resort Hotel & Spa
6111 El Camino Real, 92009; tel 619/438-8330 or toll free 800/522-8330; fax 619/431-0838. Palomar Airport Rd exit off I-5; east to El Camino Real. 11 acres. Close to the small Palomar Airport, this is a good deal for the active traveler. **Rooms:** 78 rms and stes. CI 3pm/CO noon. Nonsmoking rms avail. Below average rooms. **Amenities:** 🛱 💆 🗐 A/C, cable TV w/movies, dataport. All units w/terraces. **Services:** 🖳 🍴 Masseur, babysitting. Spa services such as facials and herbal wraps. **Facilities:** 🔗 🏌 ⛳ 🛌 🏊 🕹 1 restaurant, 1 bar, spa, sauna, steam rm, whirlpool, beauty salon, day-care ctr. Good-size meeting and banquet rooms; 4 putting greens, 53 driving stations; lap pool in addition to the main pool. **Rates:** $75 S; $85 D; $135 ste. Extra person $10. Children under age 12 stay free. Parking: Outdoor, free. AE, DC, DISC, MC, V.

RESTAURANTS 🍽

Branci's Caldo Pomodoro
2907 State St; tel 619/720-9998. Carlsbad Village Dr exit off I-5. **Italian.** A quaint corner cafe with lots of natural light, brick floors, and an outdoor patio. Known for superb sauces over pasta, particularly the chicken caldo pomodoro made with a spicy marinara sauce, and the fresh clams and mussels sautéed in a spicy red sauce. **FYI:** Reservations accepted.

Children's menu. Beer and wine only. **Open:** Sun–Thurs 11am–10pm, Fri–Sat 11am–10:30pm. **Prices:** Main courses $8–$12. AE, CB, DC, DISC, MC, V. 🛥 ✅ ♿

Neimans

2978 Carlsbad Blvd; tel 619/729-4131. Carlsbad Village Dr exit off I-5. **Californian.** A town landmark in a turn-of-the-century Victorian mansion. In addition to the casual bar area with hardwood floors and wooden stools, there's a more formal rotunda for dining, with large picture windows. Known for Cajun chicken with pasta, prime rib, fresh sourdough bread, and Snickers pie for dessert. **FYI:** Reservations not accepted. Dress code. **Open:** Peak (Mem Day–Oct) lunch Mon–Sat 11:30am–5pm; dinner Mon–Sun 5–10pm; brunch Sun 9:30am–2pm. **Prices:** Main courses $7–$25. AE, DC, DISC, MC, V. 🍴 🍽 ✅ ♿

⑤ Tip Top Meats

6118 Paseo del Norte; tel 619/438-2620. Palomar Airport Rd exit off I-5; E to Paseo del Norte. **Deli.** A European deli with a western flair. The specialty is meats in massive portions, including prime rib roast with mashed potatoes, sausages of all kinds, sauerbraten, country-style pork ribs, steaks, and meatloaf. **FYI:** Reservations not accepted. Beer and wine only. **Open:** Daily 7am–8pm. **Prices:** Main courses $3–$6. MC, V. 🛥 🍽 ♿

Carmel-by-the-Sea

See also Carmel Valley, Monterey, Pacific Grove, Pebble Beach

Originally an artists' colony (which included Upton Sinclair, Sinclair Lewis, and Jack London among its members), Carmel still draws celebrities from all fields. The shops and restaurants are decidedly upscale, but the undeveloped beaches are some of the loveliest in the state. **Information:** Carmel Business Association, PO Box 4444, Carmel 93921 (tel 408/624-2522).

HOTELS 🛏

🗏🗏🗏 Best Western Carmel Bay View Inn

Junipero St, between 5th and 6th Aves, PO Box 3715, 93921; tel 408/624-1831 or toll free 800/343-1831; fax 408/625-2336. Ocean Ave exit off CA 1. Well maintained, with lovely flower borders everywhere. **Rooms:** 58 rms and stes. CI 2pm/CO 11am. Nonsmoking rms avail. Clean, cozy, and comfortable. Each individually decorated. **Amenities:** 🛏 🗄 📺 Cable TV. No A/C. Some units w/terraces, some w/fireplaces. **Services:** 🛁 Masseur, babysitting. **Facilities:** 🚣 ♿ **Rates (CP):** Peak (July–Sept) $110–$180 S or D; $180 ste. Extra person $10. Children under age 12 stay free. Min stay peak, wknds, and special events. Lower rates off-season. Parking: Indoor/outdoor, free. AE, MC, V.

🗏🗏 Carmel Mission Inn Best Western

3665 Rio Rd, 93922; tel 408/624-1841 or toll free 800/348-9090; fax 408/624-8684. E of CA 1. Located near the Barnyard and the Crossroads Shopping Center, this property has a little too much asphalt despite lots of flowers. Very well maintained. **Rooms:** 165 rms and stes. CI 4pm/CO noon. Nonsmoking rms avail. Rooms are clean, spacious, and pleasant. **Amenities:** 🛏 🗄 Cable TV, refrig. No A/C. Some units w/minibars, some w/terraces. **Services:** ✗ 🖼 🛁 🗨 Masseur, babysitting. **Facilities:** 🚣 💺 ♿ 1 restaurant (bkfst and dinner only), 1 bar, whirlpool. **Rates:** Peak (June–Oct) $129–$169 S or D; $359 ste. Extra person $10. Children under age 15 stay free. Min stay wknds and special events. Lower rates off-season. Parking: Outdoor, free. AE, CB, DC, DISC, MC, V.

🗏🗏🗏 Dolphin Inn

San Carlos St and 4th Ave, PO Box 1900, 93921; tel 408/624-5356 or toll free 800/433-4732; fax 408/624-2967. N on San Carlos off Ocean Ave. Grounds are full of flowers. **Rooms:** 27 rms, stes, and effic. CI 3pm/CO noon. Nonsmoking rms avail. **Amenities:** 🛏 🗄 📻 🗨 Cable TV w/movies, refrig, dataport, VCR, bathrobes. No A/C. Some units w/terraces, some w/fireplaces, 1 w/whirlpool. **Services:** 🖼 🛁 Masseur. **Facilities:** 🚣 **Rates (CP):** Peak (July–Oct) $79–$149 S or D; $149–$199 ste; $149–$199 effic. Extra person $15. Children under age 12 stay free. Min stay wknds. Lower rates off-season. AE, DISC, MC, V.

🗏🗏🗏 Highlands Inn

Carmel Highlands, PO Box 1700, 93921; tel 408/624-3801 or toll free 800/682-4811; fax 408/626-1574. 4 mi S of Carmel on CA 1. 17 acres. Just a stone's throw from Carmel proper, Carmel Highlands counterpoints cliffs and wind-bowed Monterey cypresses with the Pacific Ocean. The inn feels like a sophisticated mountain lodge, with two-story, cedar-shingled villas and lovely grounds. **Rooms:** 140 rms and stes. CI 4pm/CO noon. Nonsmoking rms avail. Light earth tones and contemporary furnishings complement the seaside locale. Some rooms have views of the water. Ongoing renovations. **Amenities:** 🛏 🗄 📻 🗨 Cable TV w/movies, refrig, VCR, bathrobes. No A/C. Some units w/minibars, all w/terraces, some w/fireplaces, some w/whirlpools. **Services:** ✗ 🖛 🅥🅟 🖼 🛁 Twice-daily maid svce, masseur, babysitting. Very service-oriented, especially helpful for guests with disabilities. **Facilities:** 🚣 💺 ♿ 2 restaurants (see "Restaurants" below), 1 bar (w/entertainment), beauty salon. Attractive kidney-shaped pool surrounded by decks and ferns. **Rates:** Peak (July–Oct) $175–$200 S; $225–$325 D; $275–$375 ste. Extra person $25. Children under age 16 stay free. Min stay wknds and special events. Lower rates off-season. Parking: Indoor/outdoor, free. AE, DC, DISC, ER, MC, V.

🗏🗏🗏 Horizon Inn

Junipero St and 3rd Ave, PO Box 1693, 93921; tel 408/624-5327 or toll free 800/350-7723; fax 408/626-8253. Ocean Ave exit off CA 1. Lovely hotel with lots of flower-filled gardens and excellent views of the bay. **Rooms:** 26 rms, stes, and effic. CI 3pm/CO noon. Nonsmoking rms avail. Rooms are large, well maintained, and comfortably furnished. **Amenities:** 🛏 📺 ☎ Cable TV, refrig. No A/C. Some units w/terraces, some w/fireplaces, some w/whirlpools. **Services:** 🍽 **Facilities:** 🏊 & **Rates (CP):** Peak (May–Oct) $79–$149 S or D; $109–$149 ste; $79–$149 effic. Extra person $15. Children under age 12 stay free. Min stay wknds. Lower rates off-season. Parking: Outdoor, free. AE, DISC, MC, V.

≣≣≣ La Playa Hotel
Camino Real at 8th St, PO Box 900, 93921; tel 408/624-6476 or toll free 800/582-8900; fax 408/624-7966. A Mediterranean-style resort with brick patios and a red-tile roof, located close to town and Carmel Beach. The lobby creates a grand first impression, with Mexican-tile floors, antiques, and a fireplace flanked by two statues from Hearst Castle. **Rooms:** 80 rms, stes, and effic; 5 cottages/villas. Executive level. CI 3pm/CO noon. Nonsmoking rms avail. In keeping with the architecture, rooms have Mediterranean-style furnishings (curlicued chairs, low chests); many pieces are carved with the hotel's mermaid logo. Accommodations face the ocean, gardens, patio, or Carmel residences. **Amenities:** 🛏 ⚘ ☎ Cable TV, refrig. No A/C. All units w/minibars, some w/terraces, some w/fireplaces, 1 w/whirlpool. **Services:** ✕ 🛎 VP 🖨 🍽 Twice-daily maid svce, masseur, babysitting. Concierge can assist with restaurant reservations, golf or tennis times, and sightseeing excursions. **Facilities:** 🏊 🏊 & 1 restaurant (see "Restaurants" below), 1 bar. Award-winning formal gardens. **Rates:** $116–$215 S; $139–$159 D; $215–$495 ste; $300–$495 effic; $215–$495 cottage/villa. Extra person $15. Children under age 12 stay free. Min stay wknds. AE, DC, DISC, MC, V.

≣≣ Mission Ranch
26270 Dolores, 93923; tel 408/624-6436 or toll free 800/538-8221; fax 408/626-4163. Rio Rd exit off CA 1, head west. Turn left on Lasuen (after Carmel Mission). 22 acres. Clint Eastwood not only has a restaurant in town, but also owns this 1857 farmhouse, once home to the Marin family. Cottages and bunkhouses are scattered around this large property, in a setting of cypress and eucalyptus trees near the sea. **Rooms:** 31 rms. CI 3pm/CO 11am. No smoking. Six rooms in the farmhouse, surrounding a Victorian parlor. The Bunkhouse is a restored cottage with living, dining, and bedrooms. Best values are the Main rooms. Meadow View rooms offer ocean views. **Amenities:** 🛏 ⚘ 📺 Cable TV, bathrobes. No A/C. Some units w/terraces, some w/fireplaces, some w/whirlpools. **Services:** 🍽 Twice-daily maid svce, masseur, babysitting. Continental breakfast in the clubhouse. **Facilities:** 🏌6 🎾 🏊45 & 1 restaurant (dinner only), 1 bar (w/entertainment). Two party barns for special events for up to 50 people. Pro shop. **Rates (CP):** $100–$230 S or D. Extra person $15. Min stay wknds and special events. Parking: Outdoor, free. AE, MC, V.

≣≣≣ Pine Inn
Monte Verde St and Ocean Ave, PO Box 250, Carmel, 93921; tel 408/624-3851 or toll free 800/228-3851; fax 408/622-9095. Located downtown in a building over a century old, the inn has been completely refurbished. It is flanked by brick paths laden with beautiful potted flowers. Reasonable rates. **Rooms:** 47 rms and stes. CI 4pm/CO 1pm. Nonsmoking rms avail. Suite 64 is plush with dark green carpet, antique furniture, and oriental motif. **Amenities:** 🛏 Cable TV. No A/C. 1 unit w/fireplace. **Services:** ✕ 🖨 🍽 **Facilities:** 🍴60 1 restaurant (see "Restaurants" below), 1 bar. Bakery. **Rates:** $85–$100 S; $100–$130 D; $205 ste. Extra person $10. Children under age 2 stay free. Min stay wknds and special events. Parking: Outdoor, free. AE, CB, DC, DISC, JCB, MC, V.

≣≣≣ Sundial Lodge
Monte Verde at 7th St, PO Box J, 93921; tel 408/624-8578; fax 408/626-1018. Pleasant 100-year-old garden apartments converted into a hotel, with lots of flowers and ocean views. Not recommended for children; children under age 5 not permitted. **Rooms:** 19 rms. CI 2pm/CO 11:30am. No smoking. Extensive remodeling has created beautiful, individually decorated rooms in styles ranging from Victorian to French country. Three accommodations offer ocean views. **Amenities:** 🛏 ⚘ A/C, cable TV, refrig. **Services:** Masseur. **Rates (CP):** $114–$190 S or D. Extra person $15. Min stay wknds and special events. AE, MC, V.

MOTELS
≣≣≣ Adobe Inn Carmel
Dolores St and 8th Ave, PO Box 4115, 93921; tel 408/624-3933 or toll free 800/388-3933; fax 408/624-8636. Comparatively reasonable rates make this one of the best places to stay in Carmel. Very attractive grounds with lots of flowers. **Rooms:** 20 rms and stes. CI 3pm/CO noon. Nonsmoking rms avail. Rooms are attractive and spacious. Some have views. **Amenities:** 🛏 ⚘ 📺 ☎ Cable TV, refrig. No A/C. Some units w/terraces, all w/fireplaces. **Services:** ✕ 🖨 Masseur, babysitting. Continental breakfast delivered to room. Staff is extremely professional. **Facilities:** 🏊 & 1 restaurant (see "Restaurants" below), 1 bar, sauna. **Rates (CP):** Peak (June–Oct) $99–$200 S or D; $226–$266 ste. Extra person $20. Children under age 13 stay free. Min stay peak, wknds, and special events. Lower rates off-season. Parking: Indoor, free. AE, MC, V.

≣≣ Candlelight Inn
San Carlos St between 4th and 5th Aves, PO Box 1900, 93921; tel 408/624-6451 or toll free 800/433-4732; fax 408/624-2967. Charming, with a shingled roof, brick chimneys, and wood-trimmed exterior. **Rooms:** 20 rms and effic. CI 3pm/CO noon. Nonsmoking rms avail. Decorated in country French style. **Amenities:** 🛏 📺 Cable TV. No A/C. Some units w/fireplaces. Many accommodations have kitchens. **Services:** 🍽 **Facilities:** 🏊 **Rates (CP):** $99–$154 S or D;

$114–$154 effic. Extra person $15. Children under age 12 stay free. Min stay wknds. Parking: Outdoor, free. AE, DISC, MC, V.

Carmel Resort Inn
Carpenter and 2nd, 93921; tel 408/624-3113 or toll free 800/454-3700; fax 408/624-5456. Cottages and bungalows interspersed with fountains, flowers, tables, and umbrellas. **Rooms:** 26 rms, stes, and effic; 5 cottages/villas. CI 2pm/CO 11am. Nonsmoking rms avail. **Amenities:** Cable TV, refrig. No A/C. Some units w/terraces, some w/fireplaces. Microwaves, popcorn poppers in all rooms. **Services:** Babysitting. **Facilities:** Sauna, whirlpool. Barbecue pit. Oriental gardens with waterfalls. **Rates (CP):** Peak (May–Oct) $70–$149 S or D; $125–$159 ste; $155–$189 effic; $125–$159 cottage/villa. Lower rates off-season. Parking: Outdoor, free. AE, DC, DISC, MC, V.

Carmel's Best Western Town House Lodge
San Carlos St and 5th Ave, PO Box 3574, 93921; tel 408/624-1261. Located close to shops, galleries, and restaurants. Nice interior. **Rooms:** 28 rms. CI 2pm/CO 11am. Nonsmoking rms avail. Decorated in earth tones, the rooms are large, clean, and airy. **Amenities:** Cable TV. No A/C. **Facilities:** Rates: Peak (Apr–Oct) $89–$95 S or D. Extra person $6. Min stay peak and wknds. Lower rates off-season. Parking: Outdoor, free. AE, CB, DC, DISC, MC, V.

Carmel Wayfarer Inn
4th Ave and Mission St, PO Box 1896, 93921; tel 408/624-2711 or toll free 800/533-2711. Colorful Carmel stone steps lead up to this 1910 building. It's nicer outside than inside, but still functional. **Rooms:** 15 rms and stes. CI 3pm/CO noon. No smoking. Rooms have aging decor, but are clean. **Amenities:** Cable TV, refrig, VCR. No A/C. Some units w/terraces, some w/fireplaces. **Services:** Babysitting. **Rates (CP):** Peak (July–Sept) $70–$142 S or D; $138 ste. Extra person $16. Lower rates off-season. Parking: Outdoor, free. AE, CB, DC, DISC, MC, V.

Hofsas House
San Carlos and 4th, PO Box 1195, 93921; tel 408/624-2745 or toll free 800/421-4000, 800/252-0211 in CA. Looks like a Scandinavian cottage, with lots of flowers and some ocean views. **Rooms:** 38 rms, stes, and effic. CI 3pm/CO noon. Nonsmoking rms avail. Individually decorated rooms are spacious and comfortable with lots of bright colors. **Amenities:** Cable TV, refrig. No A/C. Some units w/terraces, some w/fireplaces. **Services:** Babysitting. Continental breakfast brought to your room. **Facilities:** Sauna. **Rates (CP):** Peak (July–Sept) $80–$130 S or D; $120–$150 effic; $120–$180 cottage/villa. Lower rates off-season. Parking: Outdoor, free. AE, MC, V.

Tickle Pink Inn at Carmel Highlands
155 Highland Dr, 93923; tel 408/624-1244 or toll free 800/635-4774; fax 408/626-9516. Surrounded by overgrown foliage, this property is hidden away in the lovely Carmel Highlands above the ocean. **Rooms:** 35 rms, stes, and effic; 1 cottage/villa. CI 3pm/CO noon. Nonsmoking rms avail. Soft colors, such as sea-foam green and pink, decorate each room. Standard rooms are average but roomy. **Amenities:** Cable TV, refrig, VCR, bathrobes. No A/C. Some units w/terraces, some w/fireplaces, some w/whirlpools. **Services:** Wine and cheese in the afternoon. **Facilities:** Rates (CP): $189–$209 S or D; $249–$289 ste; $249–$269 cottage/villa. Extra person $25. Min stay wknds and special events. Parking: Outdoor, free. AE, MC, V.

Wayside Inn
7th and Mission, 93921; tel 408/624-5336 or toll free 800/433-4732; fax 408/624-2967. Small, but very cozy and quiet. Carmel rustic decor with lots of pine. Close to everything. **Rooms:** 22 rms and stes. CI 3pm/CO noon. Nonsmoking rms avail. Clean and comfortable. **Amenities:** Cable TV, refrig. No A/C. Some units w/terraces, some w/fireplaces. **Services:** Continental breakfast and morning newspaper delivered to your door. **Rates (CP):** $89–$154 S or D; $114–$199 ste; $114–$154 effic. Extra person $15. Children under age 12 stay free. Min stay wknds. Parking: Outdoor, free. AE, DISC, MC, V.

INNS

Carriage House Inn
Junipero St, 93921; tel 408/625-2585 or toll free 800/433-4732; fax 408/626-6974. Looks like a large wood-shingled apartment complex outside, but becomes like a charming home away from home once you enter. **Rooms:** 13 rms and stes. CI 3pm/CO noon. Nonsmoking rms avail. Rooms are lush and homey, with king-size beds, down comforters, and sunken tubs. All bathrooms recently remodeled. **Amenities:** Cable TV w/movies, refrig, VCR, in-rm safe, bathrobes. No A/C. All units w/minibars, all w/fireplaces, some w/whirlpools. Breakfast served in the lounge or in your room. **Services:** Twice-daily maid svce, babysitting, wine/sherry served. **Facilities:** Guest lounge. **Rates (CP):** Peak (July–Oct) $139–$259 S or D; $189–$259 ste. Extra person $15. Min stay wknds and special events. Lower rates off-season. Parking: Outdoor, free. AE, DISC, MC, V.

Cobblestone Inn
Junipero between 7th and 8th, PO Box 3185, 93921; tel 408/625-5222; fax 408/625-0478. Located in a quiet neighborhood, this stone-covered inn is managed by a family that owns several others in northern California. Guest rooms wrap around a slate courtyard and gardens, while French doors lead to a lobby with a stone fireplace. Small, but not without charm. **Rooms:** 24 rms and stes. CI 2pm/CO noon. No smoking. Individually decorated in tasteful English decor, with a stone fireplace, sitting chair, and queen or king bed. The Honeymoon Suite is the nicest accommodation. **Amenities:** Cable TV, refrig, bathrobes. No A/C. All units w/fireplaces. **Services:** Masseur, babysitting, after-

noon tea and wine/sherry served. Breakfast served in bed or on the stone patio. Very knowledgeable, professional staff. **Facilities:** Guest lounge. **Rates (BB):** $95–$125 S or D; $145–$175 ste. Extra person $15. Children under age 2 stay free. AE, MC, V.

☰☰☰ Cypress Inn

Lincoln at 7th, PO Box Y, 93921; tel 408/624-3871 or toll free 800/443-7443 in CA; fax 408/624-8216. A warm, comfortable place with lovely gardens; resembles a striking Moorish Mediterranean palace with a red tile roof. Very tasteful, with attention to aesthetic details. **Rooms:** 34 rms and stes. CI 3pm/CO noon. Nonsmoking rms avail. Rooms are elegantly furnished and comfortable. **Amenities:** 🛏 🕯 Cable TV, refrig. No A/C. Some units w/minibars, some w/terraces, some w/fireplaces, 1 w/whirlpool. **Services:** ⊶ 🅰 🕭 Twice-daily maid svce, masseur, babysitting, afternoon tea and wine/sherry served. Breakfast in sunny breakfast room; complimentary fruit basket, daily newspaper. **Facilities:** ⟦20⟧ ♿ 1 bar, guest lounge. **Rates (CP):** Peak (May–Sept) $78–$98 S or D; $132–$245 ste. Extra person $15. Children under age 5 stay free. Min stay peak and special events. Lower rates off-season. Higher rates for special events/hols. Parking: Outdoor, free. AE, MC, V.

☰☰ Green Lantern Inn

7th and Casanova, PO Box 1114, 93921; tel 408/624-4392; fax 408/624-9591. This large, turn-of-the-century gabled house occupies a spacious corner location. Surrounded by flowers, plants, statuettes, and little walkways. **Rooms:** 19 rms and stes. CI 2pm/CO 11am. No smoking. Each room is different and very unusual; all are within earshot of the ocean. **Amenities:** 🛏 Cable TV. No A/C. 1 unit w/minibar, some w/terraces, some w/fireplaces. **Services:** 🕭 Afternoon tea and wine/sherry served. Innkeeper will help book reservations for restaurants and attractions. **Facilities:** ⟦30⟧ Guest lounge. **Rates (CP):** Peak (May–Oct) $110–$120 S or D; $165–$210 ste. Extra person $10. Children under age 18 stay free. Min stay wknds and special events. Lower rates off-season. Higher rates for special events/hols. AE, CB, DC, DISC, MC, V.

☰☰ Svendsgaard's

San Carlos St at 4th Ave, PO Box 1900, 93921; tel 408/624-1511 or toll free 800/433-4732; fax 408/624-2969. This well-maintained two-story inn has extensive gardens flanking a courtyard and swimming pool. **Rooms:** 34 rms and stes. CI 3pm/CO noon. No smoking. All are tastefully decorated. **Amenities:** 🛏 🕯 📺 Cable TV, refrig. No A/C. Some units w/fireplaces. Coffee in each room. Many have kitchenettes. **Services:** 🅰 🕭 Babysitting. Excellent staff. **Facilities:** 🏊 Guest lounge. **Rates (CP):** Peak (May–Oct) $79–$149 S or D; $139–$189 ste. Extra person $15. Children under age 12 stay free. Min stay wknds and special events. Lower rates off-season. Parking: Outdoor, free. AE, DISC, MC, V.

☰☰ Village Inn

Ocean Ave and Junipero St, PO Box 5275, 93921; tel 408/624-3864 or toll free 800/346-3864; fax 408/626-6763. Winner of the 1995 Carmel Flower Fair. The gardens are lovely, but a large asphalt parking lot and steady traffic detract from the inn's charm. **Rooms:** 34 rms, stes, and effic. CI 2pm/CO 11am. Nonsmoking rms avail. **Amenities:** 🛏 🕯 Cable TV, refrig. No A/C. Some units w/fireplaces. **Services:** 🕭 Twice-daily maid svce, babysitting. **Rates (CP):** Peak (June–Oct) $69–$108 S or D; $89–$159 ste; $159–$189 effic. Extra person $10. Children under age 2 stay free. Min stay special events. Lower rates off-season. Higher rates for special events/hols. Parking: Outdoor, free. AE, MC, V.

RESTAURANTS 🍴

Adobe Inn Bully III

Dolores St; tel 408/625-1750. At 8th Ave. **Pub.** Carmel's answer to an authentic English pub, with a cozy fireplace and a friendly staff. Serves classic British fare, like bangers and mash, and shepherd's pie. Two large-screen TVs, and a private room that accommodates 30. **FYI:** Reservations recommended. **Open:** Lunch daily 11:30am–5pm; dinner daily 5:30–9:30pm. **Prices:** Main courses $13–$25. AE, MC, V. 🍴 📺 ♿

♥ Anton & Michel

Mission St; tel 408/624-2406. Between Ocean and 7th Aves. **Continental.** Lovely ambience, with a flower-filled courtyard and one of the prettiest bars in Carmel. This local favorite serves rack of lamb, chicken Jerusalem, and several varieties of seafood. Bar menu features an excellent caesar salad prepared tableside. Wine list has over 450 offerings. **FYI:** Reservations recommended. Dress code. **Open:** Lunch daily 11:30am–3pm; dinner daily 5:30–9:30pm. Closed 1 week in Jan. **Prices:** Main courses $20–$37. AE, MC, V. ♥

♥ Casanova

5th Ave; tel 408/625-0501. Between San Carlos and Mission Sts. **French/Italian.** One of the most romantic restaurants around; winner of numerous awards for ambience and cuisine. Decor gives the feel of a fine European home. Specialties include rabbit in a wild mushroom broth, fresh swordfish, and suckling pig. **FYI:** Reservations recommended. Beer and wine only. **Open:** Breakfast daily 8–11:30am; lunch daily noon–3pm; dinner daily 5–10pm; brunch Sun 9:30am–3pm. **Prices:** Main courses $18–$32. MC, V. ♥ ♿

★ Chez Felix Restaurant Français

Monte Verde & 7th St; tel 408/624-4707. **French.** Intimate European-style restaurant is a favorite of locals. Try the chicken with five different types of mushrooms. **FYI:** Reservations recommended. Beer and wine only. **Open:** Mon–Sat 6–9pm. Closed Jan 1–21. **Prices:** Main courses $10–$20. AE, MC, V. ♥

✹ Clam Box
Mission St; tel 408/624-8597. Between 5th and 6th Aves. **Seafood.** Cozy and intimate, and comfortable without being fancy, it's popular with locals. In addition to the restaurant, there's seating on an outdoor glass-roofed patio. A separate lounge has paintings of sports figures. The menu emphasizes fresh fish, such as a baked salmon Breval, with mushrooms, tomatoes, shrimp, and white wine sauce, topped with parmesan. There are also casseroles, a daily pasta, great steaks, and many seafood appetizers. **FYI:** Reservations accepted. Children's menu. **Open:** Daily 4:30–9pm. **Prices:** Main courses $9–$48. AE, MC, V. ▼ ⛆

The General Store & Forge in the Forest
Junipero and 5th Aves; tel 408/624-2233. **New American.** Casual indoor and outdoor dining make the General Store popular with tourists and locals alike. Patio features a cozy fireplace. Choose from a wide variety of appetizers, soups, salads, burgers, pasta, pizzas, and grilled specialties including steaks, fish, chicken, or pork chops. The Forge in the Forest offers more formal dining. **FYI:** Reservations accepted. **Open:** Lunch daily 11:30am–3pm; dinner daily 5–10pm; brunch Sun 11:30am–3pm. **Prices:** Main courses $9–$18. MC, V. 🍰 🖼 🖼 ⛆

The Grill
Ocean Ave; tel 408/624-2569. Between Delores St and Lincoln Ave. **New American/Asian.** Decorated with Eyvind Earle paintings and exotic bromeliads, this new restaurant is run by the owners of the highly regarded Anton & Michel. Menu includes rack of lamb in herb mustard with tarragon, duck ravioli, and changing daily specials. **FYI:** Reservations recommended. Beer and wine only. **Open:** Lunch daily 11:30am–4:30pm; dinner daily 5–10pm. **Prices:** Main courses $15–$20. AE, MC, V. ⛆

The Hog's Breath Inn
San Carlos St; tel 408/625-1044. Between 5th and 6th Aves. **American.** Everyone who comes here hopes to spy co-owner Clint Eastwood, former mayor of Carmel. The rustic setting features a boar's head, bed warmers on the walls, and movie posters for Clint's films. Specials include the High Plains prime rib with vegetables, the Dirty Harry burger with cheese, and the Sudden Impact, broiled Polish sausage with jack cheese and jalapeños. **FYI:** Reservations not accepted. **Open:** Lunch daily 11:30am–3pm; dinner daily 5–10pm; brunch Sun 11am–3pm. **Prices:** Main courses $10–$20. AE, DC, MC, V. 🍰 🖼 ⛆

⑤ Il Fornaio
In the Pine Inn, Monte Verde and Ocean Ave; tel 408/622-5100. **Italian.** An oak-wood fire cooks chicken, rabbit, and duck specialties on a slowly turning rotisserie; another favorite is the grilled 22-oz Black Angus porterhouse steak. A good bet for pasta lovers is the paglia e fieno con gamberetti—spinach and egg linguine with rock shrimp, tomato, garlic, and parsley. A very popular drink is the "Negroni" (Bombay gin, Campari, and sweet vermouth).

Breads and pastries are available in the adjoining bakery. **FYI:** Reservations recommended. Children's menu. **Open:** Mon–Fri 7am–10:30pm, Sat–Sun 8am–11pm. **Prices:** Main courses $8–$15. AE, DC, MC, V. 🖼 ⛆

⑤ ✹ La Bohême
Dolores St; tel 408/624-7500. At 7th St. **European Country.** Romantic European atmosphere. All dinners are prix-fixe, and only one menu (which changes daily) is served each night. Vegetarian meal also available. **FYI:** Reservations not accepted. Beer and wine only. **Open:** Daily 5:30–10pm. Closed Dec 4–25. **Prices:** Prix fixe $22. MC, V. ♥

L'escargot
Mission St; tel 408/624-4914. Between 4th and 5th Aves. **French.** A romantic country-French–style restaurant with an antique plate collection. Specialties include rack of lamb, chicken in cream sauce with mushrooms, and truffles, as well as veal, steak, and duck dishes. A private dining room accommodates groups of up to 20. **FYI:** Reservations recommended. Piano/Classical. **Open:** Mon–Sat 5:30–9:30pm. Closed 2 weeks after Thanksgiving. **Prices:** Main courses $16–$24. AE, CB, DC, MC, V. ♥

Mondo's Trattoria
Dolores St; tel 408/624-8977. Between Ocean and 7th Aves. **Italian.** Charmingly decorated with Italian accents, this attractive, cozy restaurant has won lots of local awards. The menu features roast chicken with herbs served with polenta and vegetables, as well as fish and many pasta dishes. **FYI:** Reservations recommended. Beer and wine only. **Open:** Lunch daily 11:30am–3pm; dinner daily 5:30–10pm. **Prices:** Main courses $8–$17. AE, DISC, MC, V. ♥

♣ Pacific's Edge
In the Highlands Inn, CA 1; tel 408/624-0471. **Regional American.** The best ocean views from the Monterey Peninsula are visible from almost every table in this spacious, romantic room. This is the place to splurge on a romantic sunset dinner, or enjoy cocktails in the lounge. Award-winning chef Cal Stamenov turns out delights such as pancetta-wrapped salmon and a wide assortment of vegetable dishes starring produce from the Central Valley. **FYI:** Reservations recommended. Piano. Children's menu. Jacket required. **Open:** Lunch Mon–Sat 11:30am–2pm; dinner Sun–Thurs 6–10pm, Fri–Sat 6–10:30pm; brunch Sun 10am–2pm. **Prices:** Main courses $21–$29; prix fixe $45. AE, DC, DISC, MC, V. ♥ 🖼 📖 ⛆

Patisserie Boissiere
In Carmel Plaza, Mission St; tel 408/624-5008. Between Ocean and 7th Aves. **French.** Refined but not fancy, with lovely art. A bakery on the premises makes the place smell wonderful, both at small glass tables and outside on the little terrace. A specialty is half a duck, oven-roasted and served with apricot-orange brandy sauce. **FYI:** Reservations recommended. Beer and wine only. **Open:** Breakfast Mon–Fri 9–

11:30am, Sat–Sun 9:30–11:30am; lunch daily 11:30am–4:30pm; dinner Wed–Sun 5:30–9pm. **Prices:** Main courses $8.95–$12.95. AE, MC, V.

Piatti
Junipero and 5th (Downtown); tel 408/625-1766. **Italian.** Light and airy Tuscan ambience draws locals who come to eat and discreetly peek at visiting celebrities. Specialties include thick pork chops with porcini mushroom sauce; lasagne with layers of spinach pasta, grilled zucchini, sun-dried tomatoes, pesto, and assorted Italian cheeses; and a risotto selection which changes twice daily. **FYI:** Reservations recommended. **Open:** Daily 11:30am–10pm. **Prices:** Main courses $9–$25. AE, MC, V.

♥ Rafaello
Mission St; tel 408/624-1541. Between Ocean and 7th Aves. **Italian.** Rafaello and "Mama" have pleased the palates of locals and visitors for 31 years. This restaurant is at once intimate, beautiful, and formal (however, jackets for gentlemen are no longer required). Exquisite cooking and experienced service. Entrees include veal scaloppine Toscana with wine sauce, mushrooms, and tomatoes; lamb dishes; chicken cacciatore; and homemade pastas and desserts. The wine list features more than 500 choices. **FYI:** Reservations recommended. Dress code. Beer and wine only. **Open:** Daily 6–10pm. **Prices:** Main courses $17–$22. AE, MC, V. ♥

★ Rio Grill
In the Crossroads Center, 101 Crossroads Blvd; tel 408/625-5436. **Californian/Southwestern.** Consistently rated by locals as the best restaurant in town. Decorated in a colorful southwestern motif, with butcher paper and crayons on each table and tasteful artwork lining the walls. Specialties include fire-roasted artichoke, smoked baby back ribs, smoked chicken, and oak-grilled fresh fish. **FYI:** Reservations recommended. **Open:** Sun–Thurs 11:30am–10pm, Fri–Sat 11:30am–11pm. **Prices:** Main courses $9–$19. AE, DISC, MC, V.

Sans Souci
Lincoln St; tel 408/624-6220. Between 5th and 6th Aves. **French.** This restaurant composed of three rooms offers genteel and elegant service without being the least bit stuffy. Menu features abalone, chateaubriand for two, and rack of lamb with bread crumbs, served with Dijon mustard and garlic-thyme sauce. **FYI:** Reservations recommended. **Open:** Daily 5:30–10pm. **Prices:** Main courses $19–$28. AE, MC, V.

Ⓢ Silver Jones
3690 The Barnyard; tel 408/624-5200. **Eclectic.** A casual and inviting setting, with sculpture by local artist Nick Lulitch and year-round outdoor dining. One specialty is Greek lamb fillet, cooked in red wine with eggplant and olives and served with spinach polenta. **FYI:** Reservations accepted. Children's menu. **Open:** Lunch Mon–Sat 11:30am–3pm; dinner Sun–

Thurs 5:30–9pm, Fri–Sat 5:30–9:30pm; brunch Sun 11am–3pm. **Prices:** Main courses $8–$17. AE, DC, DISC, MC, V.

Terrace Grill
In La Playa Hotel, Camino Real at 8th St; tel 408/624-4010. **Regional American.** Among the house specialties are grilled quail salad with feta cheese, Calamata olives, and red onions; mushroom and Roquefort ravioli; and lobster tamales. The fine antique bar offers an excellent light menu and extensive wine list. A special "martini menu" boasts 13 varieties, well prepared by popular mixologists who have been here for decades. A happy-hour theme buffet (Mon–Fri) is a local favorite. Outdoor seating offers ocean views. **FYI:** Reservations recommended. **Open:** Breakfast daily 7–10am; lunch Mon–Sat 11am–4pm; dinner daily 5:30–10pm; brunch Sun 8am–2pm. **Prices:** Main courses $10–$18. AE, DC, MC, V.

Tuck Box English Room
Dolores St; tel 408/624-6365. At 7th Ave. **British.** Cozy and charmingly decorated. Simple fare is prepared well in this often-crowded English tea room. Specials include scones and homemade jams. **FYI:** Reservations not accepted. No liquor license. **Open:** Breakfast Wed–Sun 8–11:30am; lunch Wed–Sun noon–3:30pm. Closed Dec 25–Jan 15. **Prices:** Lunch main courses $5–$10. No CC.

ATTRACTIONS

Carmel Mission
Tel 408/624-3600. Located on Basilica Rio Rd at Lasuen Dr. The burial ground of Father Junípero Serra and the second-oldest of the 21 Spanish missions the Franciscan missionary founded. Built in 1771 on a scenic site overlooking the Carmel River, it remains one of the largest and most interesting of California's missions. The present stone church, with its gracefully curving walls and Moorish bell tower, was begun in 1793. Its walls are covered with a lime plaster made of burnt seashells. The old mission kitchen, the first library in California, the high altar, and the flower gardens are all worth visiting. More than 3,000 Native Americans are buried in the adjacent cemetery. **Open:** Mon–Sat 9:30am–4:30pm, Sun 10:30am–4:30pm. **$**

Point Lobos State Reserve
Tel 408/624-4909. 3 mi S of town on CA 1. Situated on cliffs that provide breathtaking ocean vistas, the 550-acre reserve is home to sea lions, harbor seals, sea otters, and thousands of seabirds; in season, whales can be viewed, too. Trails follow the shoreline and lead to hidden coves. **Open:** Daily 9am–5pm. **Free**

Carmel Valley

See also Carmel-by-the-Sea, Monterey, Pacific Grove, Pebble Beach

Well-heeled and secluded, Carmel Valley is inland from Carmel-by-the-Sea, and features a drier, warmer climate than its coastal neighbors. **Information:** Carmel Valley Chamber of Commerce, 71 W Carmel Valley Rd #206, PO Box 288, Carmel Valley 93924 (tel 408/659-4000).

HOTEL

Country Garden Inns
102 W Carmel Valley Rd, PO Box 504, 93924; tel 408/659-5361 or toll free 800/367-3336; fax 408/659-2392. CA 68 W exit off US 101, left on Los Laureles Grade, left on Carmel Valley Rd. Located in lovely, sunny Carmel Valley, surrounded by hilly, tree-covered countryside and beautiful gardens. **Rooms:** 46 rms, stes, and effic. CI 2pm/CO noon. No smoking. Country French decor; tasteful and very individual with lots of wicker. **Amenities:** Cable TV. No A/C. All units w/terraces, some w/fireplaces. **Services:** Babysitting. **Facilities:** Rates (BB): Peak (May–Oct) $121–$132 S; $131–$142 D; $186 ste; $164 effic. Extra person $20. Children under age 3 stay free. Min stay special events. Lower rates off-season. Parking: Outdoor, free. AE, MC, V.

LODGE

Los Laureles Lodge
313 W Carmel Valley Rd, PO Box 2310, 93924; tel 408/659-2233 or toll free 800/553-4404; fax 408/659-0481. 10½ mi E off CA 1 on Carmel Valley Rd. Once a ranch property, this historic wooden building nestled in the hills has been an inn since 1890. The lodge feels very removed, although some traffic noise invades from Carmel Valley Rd. Reasonably priced. **Rooms:** 31 rms, stes, and effic; 3 cottages/villas. CI 3pm/CO noon. No smoking. Rooms 12–30 are charmingly renovated former stables, built in the 1930s. Fresh flowers in rooms. **Amenities:** Cable TV, refrig. No A/C. Some units w/terraces, some w/whirlpools. **Services:** Babysitting. Friendly staff can arrange varied sports activities for guests. Daily sunset cocktail hour; evening entertainment Fri–Sat. **Facilities:** 1 restaurant (see "Restaurants" below), 1 bar (w/entertainment), whirlpool. A popular venue for weddings. **Rates:** Peak (Apr–Oct) $70–$100 S or D; $150–$250 ste; $450 effic; $450 cottage/villa. Extra person $20. Children under age 17 stay free. Min stay peak and wknds. Lower rates off-season. Parking: Outdoor, free. AE, MC, V.

RESORTS

Carmel Valley Ranch Resort
1 Old Ranch Rd, 93923; tel 408/625-9500 or toll free 800/4-CARMEL; fax 408/624-2858. Off CA 1. 1,700 acres. Located in a serene valley that's often sunny when the coast is fogged in. The grounds and the rooms have undergone a $6.5 million renovation. **Rooms:** 100 stes. CI 4pm/CO noon. Nonsmoking rms avail. Spacious (800 to 1,200 square-foot) accommodations in low gray buildings surrounded by oaks. Carpets and upholsteries look noticeably fatigued. Deluxe rooms are nicer than standard ones, which seem dark. **Amenities:** Cable TV w/movies, refrig, dataport, in-rm safe, bathrobes. No A/C. All units w/minibars, all w/terraces, all w/fireplaces, some w/whirlpools. Some rooms feature private hot tubs. **Services:** Twice-daily maid svce, car-rental desk, masseur, children's program, babysitting. A host greets guests at the front entrance and personally escorts them to their rooms. **Facilities:** 3 restaurants, 2 bars (1 w/entertainment), sauna, whirlpool. Pete Dye–designed championship golf course. Pool is splendid, banked with colorful planters and flower beds. Otherwise, the grounds could use more spit and polish. **Rates:** Peak (July–Nov) $195–$465 ste. Extra person $20. Children under age 16 stay free. Min stay wknds and special events. Lower rates off-season. AP and MAP rates avail. Parking: Outdoor, free. Golf, tennis, romance, and adventure packages avail. AE, MC, V.

Quail Lodge Resort & Golf Club
8205 Valley Greens Dr, 93923; tel 408/624-1581 or toll free 800/538-9516; fax 408/624-3726. 5 mi E of Carmel-by-the-Sea. Carmel Valley Rd exit off US 1, then 3½ miles east. 825 acres. A longtime favorite and an alternative to the million-aire-priced golf resorts in nearby Pebble Beach. Serene, hilly setting, tucked into the corner of an 800-acre preserve, with ponds, well-tended gardens and walkways shaded by trumpet vine. **Rooms:** 100 rms and stes; 1 cottage/villa. Executive level. CI 4pm/CO 11am. Nonsmoking rms avail. One- and two-story motel-like wings, fashioned from pine in contemporary rustic style, with patios or balconies. Bathrooms have separate dressing areas. Doorside parking for most rooms. Extensive redecorating has made property more luxurious. Rooms 171 through 185 are too close to main road traffic. **Amenities:** Cable TV w/movies, refrig, bathrobes. No A/C. All units w/minibars, all w/terraces, some w/fireplaces, some w/whirlpools. Executive Villas with fireplaces and hardwood hot tubs in walled patios. Complimentary half-bottle of California wine in rooms. Krups coffeemakers and six types of tea; minibars come with enough glasses for entertaining. **Services:** Twice-daily maid svce, masseur, babysitting. Complimentary afternoon tea and cookies in the lounge library. Fleet of minivans and Mercedes sedans for airport transfers (by reservation, for a fee). VCRs and 100 cassettes for rent. Friendly, polite, country-club–like service. **Facilities:** 2 restaurants (see "Restaurants" below), 2 bars (1 w/entertainment), lawn games, spa, whirlpool. Lots of nature trails, biking, and jogging paths. Ideal venue for golfers: challenging, rarely crowded course; moderate green fees; optional carts; starting times eight minutes apart. **Rates:** Peak (Mar–Nov) $180–

$275 S or D; $255–$320 ste; $590–$985 cottage/villa. Extra person $25. Children under age 12 stay free. Min stay special events. Lower rates off-season. Parking: Outdoor, free. AE, MC, V.

RESTAURANTS 🍴

♣ The Covey
In Quail Lodge Resort & Golf Club, 8205 Valley Greens Dr; tel 408/624-1581. 5 mi E of Carmel From US 1, take Carmel Valley Rd exit, then drive 3½ miles east. **Continental.** Comfortable atmosphere and commendable cuisine. The decor is contemporary rustic, with dark pine walls, roof beams, and large windows overlooking a pond. Tables are on two levels. Specialties include rack of lamb, beluga caviar, Santa Barbara abalone with lemon butter, vacherin au chocolat. Outstanding wine list. **FYI:** Reservations recommended. Jazz/piano. Jacket required. **Open:** Sun–Thurs 6:30–10pm, Fri–Sat 6–10pm. **Prices:** Main courses $19–$60. AE, DC, MC, V. ♥ ⛰ ♿

The Vanderbilt House
In Los Laureles Lodge, 313 W Carmel Valley Rd; tel 408/659-2233. **Regional American.** The historic main house has been transformed into a restaurant with several intimate dining rooms, each decorated in a rustic 1940s motif. Some tables overlook the pool. A specialty is tenderloin of wild pig, flambéed in brandy, served with candied bananas and port wine sauce. Poolside food and beverages available May–Oct. **FYI:** Reservations recommended. Jazz/piano. **Open:** Breakfast daily 7–11am; lunch daily 11:30am–2:30pm; dinner daily 5:30–10:30pm. Closed Nov 1–Apr 1. **Prices:** Main courses $8–$22; prix fixe $14. AE, MC, V. ♥ ■

Will's Fargo Restaurant in the Village
W Carmel Valley Rd; tel 408/659-2774. At El Caminito Chambers Lane. **Seafood/Steak.** Sometimes noisy steak house built of brick and Carmel stone and filled with antiques. Meals include a relish tray, soup, and salad. Steaks can be cut to size. **FYI:** Reservations recommended. **Open:** Mon–Sat 5:30–10pm, Sun 5–9pm. **Prices:** Main courses $14–$22. AE, MC, V. 🎫

Catalina Island

See Avalon

Cathedral City

Cathedral City is a growing community with a new downtown area, similar in character to its Coachella Valley neighbor, Palm Desert. **Information:** Cathedral City Chamber of Commerce, 68845 Perez Rd #6, Cathedral City 92234 (tel 619/328-1213).

MOTEL 🏨

≣≣ Days Inn Suites
69-151 E Palm Canyon Dr, 92234; tel 619/324-5939 or toll free 800/325-2525; fax 619/324-3034. Located just minutes from Restaurant Row in Rancho Mirage. **Rooms:** 97 rms. CI 3pm/CO noon. Nonsmoking rms avail. Ideal for families; the one- and two-bedroom suites have kitchens. **Amenities:** 📺 🅰 A/C, cable TV w/movies, refrig. 1 unit w/terrace. **Services:** 🚗 ➡ 🍴 **Facilities:** 🏋 56 ♿ Whirlpool. **Rates (CP):** Peak (Jan 11–May) $85–$165 S; $95–$175 D. Extra person $10. Children under age 16 stay free. Lower rates off-season. Parking: Outdoor, free. AE, CB, DC, DISC, JCB, MC, V.

RESORT

≣≣≣ DoubleTree Resort
67-967 Vista Chino, PO Box 1644, 92263; tel 619/322-7000 or toll free 800/637-0577; fax 619/322-6853. Exit Gene Autry Trail off I-10. 400 acres. This resort offers spectacular views of the surrounding mountains. **Rooms:** 289 rms and stes; 60 cottages/villas. CI 3pm/CO noon. Nonsmoking rms avail. Spacious rooms. **Amenities:** 📺 🅰 🍴 A/C, cable TV w/movies, refrig, voice mail, in-rm safe. All units w/terraces, some w/fireplaces. A box of DoubleTree chocolate chip cookies is given to guests upon arrival. **Services:** ✕ 🅥🅟 🚗 ➡ 🍴 Babysitting. Pets up to 20 lbs allowed. **Facilities:** 🏋 ⛳27 🏊5 🏊5 🎾 1400 ♿ 1 restaurant, 2 bars (1 w/entertainment), volleyball, games rm, spa, sauna, whirlpool, beauty salon. Access to health club at Desert Princess Country Club. **Rates:** Peak (Jan 8–Apr 28) $250–$290 S or D; $340 ste; $260–$340 cottage/villa. Extra person $20. Children under age 18 stay free. Min stay special events. Lower rates off-season. AP and MAP rates avail. Parking: Outdoor, free. AE, CB, DC, DISC, ER, MC, V.

RESTAURANT 🍴

The Red Bird Diner
In Mission Plaza-Lucky Center, 35-955 Date Palm Dr; tel 619/324-7707. Date Palm Dr exit off I-10. **American.** Transports you back to the 1950s, complete with old-fashioned jukebox, soda fountain, and murals depicting Jimmy Dean and Elvis. Lipstick-red vinyl banquettes and chrome-backed chairs complete this time-capsule. Milkshakes, giant hamburgers, banana splits. **FYI:** Reservations accepted. Children's menu. Beer and wine only. **Open:** Daily 7am–8:30pm. Closed Aug 15–31. **Prices:** Main courses $7–$13. AE, CB, DC, DISC, ER, MC, V. 🎫

Cazadero

LODGE 🏨

≣≣≣≣ Timberhill Ranch

35755 Hauser Bridge Rd, 95421; tel 707/847-3258; fax 707/847-3258. Meyers Grade Rd exit off CA 1. 80 acres. A narrow country road twines through redwood groves to this country retreat hidden away on 80 acres. It's a paradise for couples who want to get away from it all, located near some spectacular hiking trails to the Pacific. Fifty percent of guests are returnees. **Rooms:** 15 cottages/villas. CI 4pm/CO noon. No smoking. Decorated country style, with patchwork quilts and armoires. Sitting on the large deck, you'll be astounded by the utter silence of the woodlands. **Amenities:** Refrig, bathrobes. No A/C, phone, or TV. All units w/terraces, all w/fireplaces. At these prices, you would expect more than a bathroom with a prefab plastic shower (no tub). **Services:** X ⟟ Masseur. Personalized service. Rates include continental breakfast and a six-course dinner for two at the well-regarded restaurant. Dinners are served on exquisite china, with cut-crystal and sterling silver. **Facilities:** 🛠 ⟦50⟧ 🕭 1 restaurant (lunch and dinner only), spa, sauna, steam rm, whirlpool. TV in main lodge. The resident menagerie includes miniature horses, pot-bellied goats, llamas, ducks pond, and dogs. Clay tennis courts. **Rates (MAP):** $250–$350 cottage/villa. Min stay wknds and special events. Parking: Outdoor, free. AE, MC, V.

Cerritos

See also Buena Park

HOTEL 🏨

≣≣≣ Sheraton Cerritos Towne Center

12725 Center Court Dr, 90703; tel 562/809-1500 or toll free 800/325-3535; fax 562/403-2080. Bloomfield exit off CA 91. A very nice new hotel, conveniently located midway between Los Angeles and Orange County Airports. Most guests are business travelers, but the hotel also makes a nice place for couples to hide out for the weekend. Attractive lobby with marble and brass decor. **Rooms:** 203 rms and stes. Executive level. CI 3pm/CO noon. Nonsmoking rms avail. Nicely appointed rooms are larger than normal. **Amenities:** 🛠 🗘 🖭 ⦿ A/C, cable TV w/movies, refrig, dataport, voice mail. Some units w/minibars. **Services:** X ⟟ ⟦VP⟧ 🐾 🖾 ⟿ ⟁ Babysitting. **Facilities:** 🛠 ⟦⟧ ⟦400⟧ ⬛ 🕭 1 restaurant, 1 bar, whirlpool. **Rates:** $160–$175 S or D; $400 ste. Extra person $15. Children under age 18 stay free. Parking: Outdoor, free. Rates often lower on weekends. AE, CB, DC, DISC, ER, MC, V.

Channel Islands National Park

The islands are the meeting point of two distinct marine ecosystems: The cold waters of Northern California and the warmer currents of Southern California swirl together here, creating an awesome array of marine life. On land, the relative isolation from mainland influences has allowed distinct species, like the island fox and the night lizard, to develop and survive here. The islands are also the most important seabird nesting area in California, and home to the biggest seal and sea lion breeding colony in the United States.

The park encompasses the five northernmost islands of the eight-island chain of the Channel Islands: Santa Barbara, Anacapa, Santa Cruz, Santa Rosa, and San Migual. Tiny Santa Barbara Islands sits very much by itself, about 46 miles off the Southern California coast. The other four are clustered in a 40-mile long chain that begins with tiny Anacapa; it continues with Santa Cruz, then Santa Rosa, and ends with wild and windy San Miguel. The park also protects the ocean one mile offshore from each island, thereby prohibiting oil drilling, shipping, and other industrial uses.

There are no park fees, but to reach the islands visitors need to fly or take a boat, both of which are expensive options. Camping is free and permitted on all park-owned islands, but is limited to 30 people per island per night. For more information contact the **Channel Islands National Park Headquarters and Visitors Center,** 1901 Spinnaker Dr, Ventura, CA 93001 (tel 805/664-8262).

Chico

Perched on the forested flanks of the Sierra, the city is within close range of the mountains. Lively Cal State Chico forms much of the character of the town, which is home to an array of bookstores, cafes, and restaurants. **Information:** Chico Chamber of Commerce, 500 Main St, PO Box 3038, Chico 95927 (tel 916/891-5556).

HOTELS 🏨

≣≣ Best Western Heritage Inn

25 Heritage Lane, 95926; tel 916/894-8600 or toll free 800/446-4291; fax 916/894-8600 ext 142. Cohasset Rd exit off CA 99 N. Nicely run establishment. **Rooms:** 101 rms. CI noon/CO 11am. Nonsmoking rms avail. **Amenities:** 🛠 🗘 ⦿ A/C, cable TV, refrig. **Services:** 🖾 ⟿ **Facilities:** 🛠 ⟦135⟧ Whirlpool. **Rates (CP):** $53–$67 S; $54–$75 D. Extra person $5. Children under age 12 stay free. Parking: Outdoor, free. Various discounts avail. AE, CB, DC, DISC, JCB, MC, V.

≣≣≣ Holiday Inn

685 Manzanita Court, 95926; tel 916/345-2491 or toll free 800/HOLIDAY; fax 916/893-3040. Cohassett Rd exit off CA 99. A full-service hotel. **Rooms:** 172 rms and stes. CI

4pm/CO noon. Nonsmoking rms avail. **Amenities:** 🛅 Ⓠ A/C, satel TV w/movies. **Services:** 🚗 🖼 🛍 🍴 **Facilities:** 🎿 🏌️
🏊 ⛳ 1 restaurant, 1 bar (w/entertainment), whirlpool, washer/dryer. Good facilities for business meetings. **Rates:** Peak (Sept–May) $76–$86 S; $86–$96 D; $156–$176 ste. Extra person $6. Children under age 12 stay free. Lower rates off-season. Parking: Outdoor, free. AE, CB, DC, DISC, MC, V.

⊨⊨⊨ Oxford Suites Resort

2035 Business Lane, 95928; tel 916/899-9090 or toll free 800/870-SUITE; fax 916/899-9476. 20th St E exit off CA 99; ¼ mi to Business Lane; turn right. Superb lodging at a reasonable price for business or pleasure travelers. **Rooms:** 183 stes. CI 2pm/CO 1pm. Nonsmoking rms avail. Options range from simple rooms to grand suites. **Amenities:** 🛅 Ⓠ A/C, cable TV w/movies, refrig, VCR. Suites have microwaves. **Services:** 🚗 🖼 🛍 🍴 Complimentary full breakfast and evening reception with drinks and hors d'oeuvres. Fax and copying services available. **Facilities:** 🎿 🛍 ⛳ Whirlpool, washer/dryer. **Rates (BB):** $66–$122 ste. Extra person $6. Children under age 10 stay free. Parking: Outdoor, free. Discounts for qualified business travelers and government-agency personnel. Add 10% for pets. AE, DC, DISC, MC, V.

RESTAURANT 🍴

Ⓢ ✹ Sierra Nevada Brewing Co Taproom & Restaurant

1075 E 20th St; tel 916/345-2739. **Pub.** This highly acclaimed microbrewery is nirvana for the aficionado of finely crafted beer, ale, porter, and stout. It has a joyfully boisterous pub with good food. The pub fare at lunch focuses on a selection of sandwiches, while the dinner menu includes pasta, seafood, steaks, and chicken dishes. Enormous, gleaming copper brewing vessels are visible from the copper-covered bar. Families with small kids will feel comfortable here. **FYI:** Reservations not accepted. Children's menu. Beer and wine only. **Open:** Lunch Tues–Sat 11am–3pm; dinner Tues–Sat 5–9pm; brunch Sun 10am–2pm. **Prices:** Main courses $8–$20. MC, V. ⛳

ATTRACTIONS 🏛

Chico Museum

141 Salem St; tel 916/891-4336. A museum of regional history, the Chico Museum features permanent and changing exhibits housed in the 1904 Carnegie Library. A special children's interactive learning exhibit with gold-panning, photography, and a variety of science presentations will be featured in 1997. **Open:** Wed–Sun noon–4pm. **Free**

Bidwell Mansion State Historic Park

525 Esplanade; tel 916/895-6144. This 26-room mansion was the home of Gen John Bidwell, Chico founding father and US presidential candidate in 1892. Guests who were once entertained in the house included such notables as President and Mrs Rutherford B Hayes, Gen William T Sherman, Susan B Anthony, and naturalist John Muir. Acquired by the State of California in 1964, the mansion has been restored and furnished in period style. **Open:** Mon–Fri noon–5pm, Sat–Sun 10am–5pm. **$**

Chiriaco Summit

ATTRACTION 🏛

General Patton Memorial Museum

2 Chiriaco Rd; tel 619/227-3483. Established to honor the flamboyant, colorful, and controversial general, this museum is on a site selected and developed by Patton in 1942 as a desert training center to prepare troops for US involvement in North Africa. Known as Camp Young, the area once covered 18,000 square miles, making it the largest military installation and maneuver area in the world.

Exhibits display memorabilia from General Patton's life and career as well as displays on southern California water development and regional geology and plant and animal life of the desert and mountains. **Open:** Daily 9am–5pm. **$$**

Chula Vista

Adjacent to the southern reaches of San Diego Bay, Chula Vista serves as a commercial and residential link between the Mexican border town of Tijuana and San Diego. **Information:** Chula Vista Chamber of Commerce, 233 4th Ave, Chula Vista 91910 (tel 619/420-6602).

MOTELS 🏨

⊨ Good Nite Inn

225 Bay Blvd, 91910; tel 619/425-8200 or toll free 800/453-3297; fax 619/426-7411. 8 mi S of San Diego. E St exit off I-5. Exterior needs some attention and landscaping. Across from Ecology Center and close to trolley. **Rooms:** 118 rms. CI 2pm/CO noon. Nonsmoking rms avail. Rooms are nice with new wallpaper. **Amenities:** 🛅 A/C, satel TV w/movies, in-rm safe. **Services:** 🖼 🛍 Small charge for local phone calls. Photocopy and fax services available. **Facilities:** 🎿 ⛳ 1 restaurant, washer/dryer. Restaurant adjacent. **Rates:** Peak (July–Aug) $41 S; $54 D. Children under age 18 stay free. Lower rates off-season. Parking: Outdoor, free. No personal checks; $20 telephone deposit required. AE, CB, DC, DISC, MC, V.

⊨⊨⊨ La Quinta Motor Inn

150 Bonita Rd, 91910; tel 619/691-1211 or toll free 800/531-5900; fax 619/427-0135. E St/Bonita Rd exit off I-805. Newly renovated, with a clean and nicely decorated lobby. Restaurant next door. **Rooms:** 141 rms. CI 3pm/CO noon. Nonsmoking rms avail. Rooms are attractive; king rooms have recliners. **Amenities:** 🛅 Ⓠ A/C, satel TV w/movies. Free toiletries available in lobby. **Services:** 🖼 🛍 🍴 Fax available;

24-hour coffee service in lobby. Arrangements can be made for group check-in and checkout. **Facilities:** 🛗 ⚂ ♿ Spa. Free use of nearby health club. **Rates (CP):** $65–$70 S; $73–$120 D. Extra person $6. Children under age 18 stay free. Parking: Outdoor, free. Special commercial rates and AARP rates. AE, DC, DISC, MC, V.

⊨⊨ Vagabond Inn
230 Broadway, 91910; tel 619/422-8305 or toll free 800/522-1555; fax 619/425-3645. E St exit off I-5. Nice grounds but inconsistent maintenance in the pool area. Parking is handy and plentiful. **Rooms:** 91 rms and effic. CI 2pm/CO noon. Nonsmoking rms avail. Rooms are pleasantly coordinated and clean, but bathrooms need updating. Family suites and kitchenettes are convenient for groups. **Amenities:** 🛏 🗄 A/C, cable TV w/movies. **Services:** 🖨 ⊐ ⇔ Babysitting. **Facilities:** ⚁ ♿ Playground. Pools and playground are to undergo renovation. **Rates (CP):** Peak (May 16–Sept 15) $42–$50 S or D; $55 effic. Extra person $5. Children under age 16 stay free. Lower rates off-season. Parking: Outdoor, free. AE, DC, DISC, MC, V.

RESTAURANT 🍽
Jakes–South Bay
In Chula Vista Marina, 570 Marina Pkwy; tel 619/476-0400. 8 mi S of San Diego; J St exit off I-5. **Seafood.** Nautical-themed restaurant decorated with polished wood, brass, and historical photos of San Diego, with large windows overlooking the marina. Specialties of the house include cioppino, shrimp scampi, and pasta. **FYI:** Reservations recommended. Children's menu. **Open:** Lunch Mon–Fri 11:15am–2:30pm; dinner Mon–Sat 5–10pm, Sun 4:30–9:30pm; brunch Sun 10am–2:30pm. **Prices:** Main courses $11–$26. AE, DC, DISC, MC, V. 🏞 💟 ♿

ATTRACTION 🖼
Chula Vista Nature Center
1000 Gunpowder Point Dr; tel 619/422-2473. Located within the Sweetwater Marsh National Wildlife Refuge. Visitors must take a shuttle bus from the parking area, just off I-5 at the E St exit. The nature center offers a rare view into the natural history and ecology of California wetlands. A variety of exhibits provide an experiential tour through the different ecological zones of the marsh. A number of wildlife specimens from the refuge are on display, including leopard sharks and burrowing owls. Several 1½-mile interpretive trails. Observation tower and deck (binoculars available for rent). Special programs; bookstore and gift shop. **Open:** Peak (Mem Day–Labor Day) daily 10am–5pm. Reduced hours off-season. $$

Citrus Heights

RESTAURANTS 🍽
Aric's Java Cafe
In Green Faire Village, 8097 Greenback Lane; tel 916/726-5282. Off I-80 at Fair Oaks Blvd. **Cafe.** A high ceiling and lots of windows give this neighborhood coffeehouse an open, airy feeling. In addition to a comprehensive selection of specialty coffees, it offers exceptional baked goods and desserts (like blackout cake and New York–style cheesecake). Light lunch fare also available. **FYI:** Reservations not accepted. No liquor license. **Open:** Mon–Thurs 6am–11pm, Fri 6am–midnight, Sat 7am–midnight, Sun 7am–11pm. **Prices:** Lunch main courses $2–$5. No CC. ♿

Que Pasta
In The Almond Orchard, 11773 Fair Oaks Blvd, Fair Oaks; tel 916/967-4668. Madison Ave exit off I-80. **Italian.** A classy, but cozy, neighborhood eatery offering a menu combining Italian, French, and Spanish cuisines. Specialties are veal saltimbocca, chicken marsala, chicken piccata, and creative pastas. For dessert, the apricot-mousse cake is recommended. Sometimes-slow service makes this a better bet for a relaxed dinner than for a quick lunch. **FYI:** Reservations accepted. Children's menu. **Open:** Tues–Thurs 11am–10pm, Fri 11am–11pm, Sat 5–11pm, Sun 5–9pm. **Prices:** Main courses $11–$34. AE, MC, V. ♿

Claremont

Home to six private colleges, Claremont—situated at the foot of the San Gabriel Mountains—is a tidy collection of quiet tree-lined streets and shaded boulevards, giving it a feel that is more New England than Southern California. **Information:** Claremont Chamber of Commerce, 205 Yale Ave, Claremont 91711 (tel 909/624-1681).

HOTEL 🏨
⊨⊨⊨ The Claremont Inn
555 W Foothill Blvd, 91711; tel 909/626-2411 or toll free 800/854-5733; fax 909/624-0756. Indian Hill Blvd exit off I-10; N 1¾ mi to CA 66. This well-established complex of hotel, restaurants, theater, and shops is undergoing a total renovation and upgrade. **Rooms:** 266 rms, stes, and effic. CI 3pm/CO noon. Nonsmoking rms avail. Attractive black-and-white tile floors in renovated bathrooms. **Amenities:** 🛏 🗄 A/C, cable TV w/movies. All units w/terraces. **Services:** ✕ 🖨 🖨 ⊐ Car-rental desk. Friday and Saturday night murder-mystery dinners. **Facilities:** ⚁ 🍽 ⚂ ♿ 1 restaurant, 1 bar (w/entertainment), whirlpool. **Rates:** $59–$69 S or D; $85–$110 ste; $110 effic. Extra person $10. Children under age 16 stay free. Parking: Outdoor, free. AE, CB, DC, DISC, MC, V.

MOTEL

≣≣ Ramada Inn & Tennis Club

840 S Indian Hill Blvd, 91711; tel 909/621-4831 or toll free 800/322-6559; fax 909/621-0411. S Indian Hill Blvd exit off I-10. Average motel with first-class tennis facilities and a Japanese restaurant. **Rooms:** 125 rms. CI 3pm/CO noon. Nonsmoking rms avail. Simply decorated rooms. **Amenities:** 🛏 🕎 A/C, cable TV w/movies, refrig. **Services:** ✗ 🚐 🖊 🛎 **Facilities:** 🏋 🏊⁸ 🛥⁶⁰ 👪 1 restaurant, sauna, washer/dryer. Tennis Academy on premises offers classes from beginner to advanced. **Rates (CP):** $45–$50 S; $60–$65 D. Children under age 12 stay free. Parking: Outdoor, free. AE, CB, DC, DISC, JCB, MC, V.

ATTRACTION 🎏

Rancho Santa Ana Botanic Garden

1500 N College Ave; tel 909/625-8767. This 86-acre garden at the base of the San Gabriel Mountains displays a rich collection of California's diverse native plants. The 2½-acre California Cultivar Garden exhibits cultivated plant varieties selected or hybridized from native plants, with cedar pavilions and interpretive panels discussing the origin of cultivated varieties. Gift shop. **Open:** Daily 8am–5pm. **Free**

Clearlake

The spring-fed, volcanic lake is one of the state's largest. Located between the two Northern California arteries, I-5 and US 101, the quiet town is surrounded by rugged hills and dense national forest. **Information:** Clearlake Chamber of Commerce, 14335 Lakeshore Dr, PO Box 629, Clearlake 95422 (tel 707/994-3600).

MOTELS 🎏

≣≣ Best Western El Grande Inn

15135 Lakeshore Dr, PO Box 4598, 95422; tel 707/994-2000 or toll free 800/528-1234; fax 707/994-2042. 3 mi NW of jct CA 53/CA 29 via 40th Ave. Dramatic 45-foot-tall atrium lobby with fountain is very inviting. **Rooms:** 67 rms and stes. CI 3pm/CO 11am. Nonsmoking rms avail. **Amenities:** 🛏 🕎 🖊 A/C, cable TV w/movies, refrig. Some units w/minibars. **Services:** 🖊 🛎 **Facilities:** 🏋 🛥¹⁵⁰ 👪 1 restaurant, 1 bar, steam rm, whirlpool. Coffee shop open 24 hours. **Rates:** Peak (Apr–Oct 15) $67 S; $74 D; $79 ste. Extra person $7. Children under age 11 stay free. Min stay peak and wknds. Lower rates off-season. Parking: Outdoor, free. AE, CB, DC, DISC, MC, V.

≣≣ Days Inn

13865 Lakeshore Dr, 95422; tel 707/994-8982 or toll free 800/300-8982; fax 707/994-0613. 4 mi NW of jct CA 53/CA 29 via 40th Ave. Built in 1992. Sparkling clean. Stark exterior but attractive rooms. **Rooms:** 20 rms and stes. CI noon/CO 11am. Nonsmoking rms avail. **Amenities:** 🛏 🕎 🖊 A/C, cable

TV. **Services:** 🖊 🛎 **Facilities:** 🏋 🛥 👪 1 beach (lake shore), washer/dryer. **Rates:** Peak (June–Sept) $50–$75 S; $55–$75 D; $80–$120 ste. Extra person $10. Children under age 5 stay free. Min stay peak and wknds. Lower rates off-season. Parking: Outdoor, free. AE, DISC, MC, V.

RESORT

≣≣ Konocti Harbor Resort & Spa

8727 Soda Bay Rd, Kelseyville, 95451; tel 707/279-4281 or toll free 800/862-4930; fax 707/279-9205. CA 29 N from Lower Lake or S from Kelseyville to Soda Bay Rd; 5 mi to resort. 100 acres. Many resort features, including full spa and golf courses nearby. Popular entertainers perform here on weekends. **Rooms:** 208 rms, stes, and effic; 42 cottages/villas. CI 4pm/CO 11am. Nonsmoking rms avail. **Amenities:** 🛏 A/C, cable TV, refrig. Some units w/terraces. **Services:** 🛎 Social director, masseur, children's program, babysitting. **Facilities:** 🏋 🛥 🏊⁸ 🎾 🛥⁷⁰⁰ 🖥 👪 2 restaurants, 5 bars (4 w/entertainment), games rm, spa, sauna, steam rm, whirlpool, beauty salon, playground, washer/dryer. Private heliport. **Rates:** Peak (May–Oct) $69–$95 S; $79–$95 D; $185–$360 ste; $150 effic. Extra person $10. Children under age 12 stay free. Min stay peak. Lower rates off-season. Parking: Outdoor, free. Discounts for senior citizens, government employees, and other groups. AE, CB, DC, MC, V.

Coalinga

HOTEL 🎏

≣≣≣ Harris Ranch Inn

Rte 777, 93210; tel 209/935-0717 or toll free 800/942-2333; fax 209/935-2844. Just E of jct I-5/CA 198 at Hanford-Lemoore exit. A beautiful early California–style property just off the highway. Rooms surround huge courtyard and large pool. Lush grounds are perfectly maintained. **Rooms:** 123 rms and stes. Executive level. CI 3pm/CO noon. Nonsmoking rms avail. Top-quality furnishings and decor include cotton duvets and bedskirts. All linens and mattresses replaced every 1½ years. **Amenities:** 🛏 🕎 🖊 🕎 A/C, cable TV w/movies, refrig. All units w/minibars, some w/terraces, 1 w/fireplace, 1 w/whirlpool. All rooms have TVs in armoires and generous seating. Suites offer additional sofa beds. **Services:** ✗ 🛎 🖊 Twice-daily maid svce. **Facilities:** 🏋 🎾 🛥²²⁰ 👪 2 restaurants (see "Restaurants" below), 1 bar, whirlpool, washer/dryer. Private air strip, two restaurants, and a bar where smoking is allowed. Country store sells Harris Ranch beef, baked goods, California gourmet foods, and specialty items, including leather goods from Harris Ranch hides. **Rates:** Peak (Apr–Nov 1) $86–$108 S; $89–$111 D; $98–$225 ste. Extra person $8. Children under age 12 stay free. Lower rates off-season. Parking: Outdoor, free. Special packages like Winemaker Weekends and Valentine's Day. Senior discount. AE, CB, DC, DISC, MC, V.

RESTAURANT 🍴

★ Fountain Court Grill
In Harris Ranch Inn, I-5 at CA 198; tel 209/935-0717. Hanford-Lemoore exit. **Regional American.** There are four distinctively decorated dining rooms, one featuring the fountain that gives the restaurant its name. Menu features weekly "Farm Report" specials, highlighting locally grown produce; 98% of ingredients come from the Central Valley. Fresh herbs from on-site garden flavor many dishes. The flavor of the steaks is excellent, but they are cut a bit thin, so perfectly cooked medium-rare is a real stretch for the kitchen. **FYI:** Reservations recommended. Children's menu. **Open:** Daily 5:30–10pm. **Prices:** Main courses $10–$30. AE, CB, DC, DISC, MC, V. 🍷 ⅋

Concord

See also Pleasant Hills, Walnut Creek

Once a sleepy bedroom community for commuters to San Francisco and the East Bay, Concord is now a fast-growing city in the heart of Contra Costa County. **Information:** Concord Convention & Visitors Bureau, 2151 Salvio St #N, Concord 94520 (tel 510/685-1184).

HOTELS 🏨

Concord Hilton
1970 Diamond Blvd, 94520; tel 510/827-2000 or toll free 800/826-2644; fax 510/827-2113. Willow Pass Rd exit off I-680. Attractive hotel with rather luxurious interiors. **Rooms:** 330 rms and stes. CI 3pm/CO noon. Nonsmoking rms avail. Rooms are slightly larger than average and tastefully decorated. **Amenities:** 🔋 ⚲ 📺 ⅋ A/C, cable TV w/movies, dataport, voice mail. Some units w/whirlpools. **Services:** ✕ 🚐 🛎 ⅋ Twice-daily maid svce. Free shuttle to shopping and rapid-transit station. **Facilities:** 🛗 🏋 🖫 ⅋ 1 restaurant, 2 bars (1 w/entertainment), whirlpool. **Rates:** $147 S; $157 D; $325–$450 ste. Extra person $10. Children under age 18 stay free. Parking: Outdoor, free. AE, CB, DC, DISC, MC, V.

Sheraton Hotel & Conference Center
45 John Glenn Dr, 94520; tel 510/825-7700 or toll free 800/325-3535; fax 510/825-9567. Concord Ave exit off I-680; left onto Diamond Rd; right onto Concord. Low-rise hotel built around a large, landscaped central atrium with skylights. There is even a koi pond. Private airport across the street. **Rooms:** 323 rms and stes. Executive level. CI 3pm/CO noon. Nonsmoking rms avail. **Amenities:** 🔋 ⚲ 📺 ⅋ A/C, cable TV w/movies, dataport, voice mail. 1 unit w/terrace. **Services:** ✕ 🚐 🛎 ⅋ **Facilities:** 🛗 🏋 🖫 💻 ⅋ 1 restaurant, 1 bar (w/entertainment), whirlpool. Pool is small for number of guests. Indoor putting green. 18-hole golf course adjacent to property. **Rates:** Peak (May–Sept) $130 S; $140 D; $165–

$400 ste. Extra person $10. Children under age 21 stay free. Lower rates off-season. Parking: Outdoor, free. AE, CB, DC, DISC, JCB, MC, V.

Corona

Located at the foot of the Santa Ana Mountains and the Cleveland National Forest, Corona is the gateway to recreation in Riverside, Orange, and San Diego Counties. **Information:** Corona Chamber of Commerce, 904 E Sixth St, Corona 91719 (tel 909/737-3350).

MOTELS 🏨

Best Western Kings Inn
1084 Pomona Rd, 91720; tel 909/734-4241 or toll free 800/892-5464; fax 909/279-5371. Lincoln Ave exit off CA 91. Quiet, nicely kept property with easy highway access. Close to Glen Ivy Hot Springs Spa. **Rooms:** 88 rms. CI 2pm/CO noon. Nonsmoking rms avail. Although located near highway, rooms are quiet. **Amenities:** 🔋 ⚲ ⅋ A/C, cable TV w/movies, in-rm safe. Some rooms have VCRs and refrigerators. **Services:** 🛎 ⅋ **Facilities:** 🛗 🖫 Whirlpool. **Rates (CP):** $52–$69 S; $59–$69 D. Extra person $10. Children under age 12 stay free. Parking: Outdoor, free. AE, CB, DC, DISC, JCB, MC, V.

Corona Travelodge
1701 W 6th St, 91720; tel 909/735-5500 or toll free 800/578-7878. Off CA 91. Not fancy, but nicely kept. **Rooms:** 46 rms. CI 11am/CO 11am. Nonsmoking rms avail. Extremely large rooms. **Amenities:** 🔋 ⚲ A/C, cable TV. 1 unit w/whirlpool. **Services:** ⅋ 🛎 **Facilities:** 🛗 **Rates:** $34–$37 S; $38 D. Extra person $5. Children under age 17 stay free. Parking: Outdoor, free. AE, CB, DC, DISC, JCB, MC, V.

Country Side Inn
2260 Griffin Way, 91719; tel 909/734-2140 or toll free 800/448-8810. McKinley exit off Calif 91; 1 block N. This well-maintained property is part of a southern California chain. **Rooms:** 100 rms. CI 3pm/CO noon. Nonsmoking rms avail. Rooms boast cherry-wood poster beds. **Amenities:** 🔋 ⚲ A/C, cable TV, refrig. **Services:** 🖐 🛎 ⅋ Complimentary full breakfast buffet, evening refreshments, morning newspaper, and fresh fruit in the lobby. **Facilities:** 🛗 🖫 ⅋ Whirlpool. Free passes to a local health club. **Rates (BB):** Peak (Jan–Oct) $65 S; $75 D. Extra person $10. Children under age 12 stay free. Lower rates off-season. Parking: Outdoor, free. AE, CB, DC, DISC, MC, V.

Corona del Mar

A small but upscale seaside community, the Crown of the Sea sits on the southern edge of Newport Beach and its bustling small-boat harbor. The Corona del Mar State Beach is an excellent spot for ocean swimming and snorkeling.

Information: Corona del Mar Chamber of Commerce, 2843 E Coast Hwy, PO Box 72, Corona del Mar 92625 (tel 714/673-4050).

RESTAURANT 🍽

ⓢ Mayur

2931 East Coast Hwy; tel 714/675-6622. **Indian.** Considered one of the best places in the area for Indian food. Mayur means "peacock," and the interior colors here reflect this. Cuisine features chicken cooked in a clay oven, and fresh vegetables in spicy curries. Many vegetarian dishes. **FYI:** Reservations recommended. Beer and wine only. **Open:** Lunch Mon–Fri 11:30am–2:30pm; dinner Mon–Sun 5:30–10:30pm; brunch Sun 11:30am–2:30pm. **Prices:** Main courses $9–$26; prix fixe $25–$45. AE, DC, MC, V. ♥ &

ATTRACTION 📷

Sherman Library and Gardens

2647 E Pacific Coast Hwy; tel 714/673-2261. Begun in 1966, the Sherman Library and Gardens now occupy a full city block along the Pacific Coast Hwy (CA 1). They are named after Moses H Sherman (1853–1932), educator and California pioneer. The library provides a historical research center devoted to the study of the Pacific Southwest. It contains 15,000 books and pamphlets, large collections of maps and photographs, and about 2,000 papers and documents.

The botanical collections range from rare cacti and succulents of desert regions to exotic vegetation of tropical climates. In effect, the gardens are a museum of living plants, displayed in an attractive setting of fountains, sculpture, and well-tended shrubs and lawns. The Discovery Garden is designed especially (but not exclusively) for the visually impaired, with an emphasis on plants whose essential appeal is to the sense of touch or smell. **Open:** Daily 10:30am–4pm. $

Coronado

An island connected to San Diego by a toll bridge, the quiet neighborhoods of Coronado seem worlds away from the surrounding metropolitan area. The island's centerpiece is the legendary, Victorian-style Hotel del Coronado. **Information:** Coronado Chamber of Commerce, 1009 C Ave, Coronado 92118 (619/435-9260).

HOTELS 🏨

≡ ≡ El Cordova Hotel

1351 Orange Ave, 92118; tel 619/435-4131 or toll free 800/229-2032; fax 619/435-0632. 4 mi SW of San Diego. Coronado Bridge exit off I-5; left on Orange Ave. A historic country mansion built in 1902 and converted to a hotel in the 1930s. Rooms are approached by stairways from the central courtyard. **Rooms:** 40 rms and effic. CI 2pm/CO noon.

Nonsmoking rms avail. Furnishings are color-coordinated and in fair condition. **Amenities:** 📺 ⓐ Cable TV w/movies. No A/C. Some units w/terraces. **Services:** ⚐ Babysitting. Secretarial service. Security desk open until 11pm. **Facilities:** ⚐ 🚲 💻 1 restaurant (lunch and dinner only), 1 bar, beauty salon, washer/dryer. Florist, travel agency, deli, gift shop, sport shop. Charcoal grills available for use by guests. **Rates:** Peak (June 16–Sept 15) $95 S or D; $105–$145 effic. Extra person $10. Children under age 16 stay free. Min stay wknds. Lower rates off-season. AE, DC, DISC, MC, V.

≡ ≡ ≡ ≡ Le Meridien San Diego at Coronado

2000 2nd St, 92118; tel 619/435-3000 or toll free 800/543-4300; fax 619/435-3032. Coronado Bay Br exit off I-5, right on Glorieta Blvd. 16 acres. The French Riviera on San Diego Bay, with potted palms in the lobby, plus koi ponds, waterfalls, and an aviary in the courtyard. The sounds of rushing water and cooing birds create a tranquil mood. Major faux pas is the soiled, worn-out carpeting in corridors. **Rooms:** 272 rms and stes; 28 cottages/villas. CI 3pm/CO noon. Nonsmoking rms avail. All accommodations measure over 500 square feet and reflect plenty of style, especially the large blue-and-white tiled bathrooms with marble counters and huge mirrors. **Amenities:** 📺 ⓐ 🍴 A/C, cable TV w/movies, dataport, bathrobes. All units w/minibars, all w/terraces, some w/whirlpools. Standard rooms offer deep soaking tubs, while executive suites and villas feature whirlpools. All have European-style shower heads and outdated hairdryers. **Services:** 🍽 🔑 📼 🐾 📠 ⚐ Car-rental desk, social director, masseur, babysitting. **Facilities:** ⚐ 🚲 ⛳ 🎾 ⊞ 💻 ⓐ & 2 restaurants (see "Restaurants" below), 1 bar, games rm, spa, sauna, steam rm, whirlpool, beauty salon. Edged by palm trees, the large, free-form main pool enjoys great views. The spa is associated with Clarins Institut de Beauté, which offers a range of services from massages and herbal body wraps to personal fitness training. **Rates:** Peak (June 14–Sept 14) $195–$255 S or D; $525 ste; $395–$795 cottage/villa. Extra person $15. Children under age 12 stay free. Lower rates off-season. Parking: Indoor/outdoor, $7/day. AE, DC, DISC, ER, JCB, MC, V.

MOTEL

≡ ≡ ≡ Glorietta Bay Inn

1630 Glorietta Blvd, 92118; tel 619/435-3101 or toll free 800/283-9383; fax 619/435-6182. Coronado Bridge exit off I-5. Formerly the Spreckels Mansion (built circa 1908), this Edwardian-style hotel is a historic landmark. Just two blocks from the beach. Close to shops, restaurants, golf, jogging trails, and surfing area. **Rooms:** 98 rms, stes, and effic. CI 4pm/CO noon. Nonsmoking rms avail. Rooms are nicely appointed. **Amenities:** 📺 ⓐ ⊞ 🍴 A/C, cable TV w/movies, refrig. Some units w/terraces, 1 w/whirlpool. Phone equipment for deaf or hard of hearing. **Services:** 🔑 📠 ⚐ Babysitting. **Facilities:** ⚐ ⊞ & Spa, whirlpool, washer/dryer. **Rates:** Peak (June–Oct) $99–$125 S; $109–$135 D;

$139–$179 ste; $109–$135 effic. Extra person $10. Children under age 4 stay free. Min stay special events. Lower rates off-season. Parking: Outdoor, free. AE, CB, DC, DISC, JCB, MC, V.

RESORTS

≡≡≡≡ Hotel del Coronado

1500 Orange Ave, 92118; tel 619/522-8000 or toll free 800/ HOTEL-DEL; fax 619/522-8262. Coronado Bay Bridge exit off I-5. 33 acres. An extravagant, red-turreted seaside palace, opened in 1888, that shimmers with Gilded Age romance. Here, the duke of Windsor met his duchess, and Marilyn Monroe frolicked in *Some Like It Hot*. A National Historic Landmark. **Rooms:** 692 rms and stes; 2 cottages/villas. CI 3pm/CO noon. Nonsmoking rms avail. Rooms in the vintage main building offer old-time charm, with high ceilings, creaky floors, and period fixtures. (The resident ghost—a young lady of tragic past—is said to haunt room 3312.) The newer Ocean Tower accommodations are bland but up to date, and air-conditioned. **Amenities:** 🛏 ⚱ ☎ Cable TV w/movies, in-rm safe, bathrobes. Some units w/terraces. Some units have A/C. **Services:** ⏋ ⚟ VP 🚗 ⊿ ⊙ Car-rental desk, social director, masseur, children's program, babysitting. Summer activities for kids include day camps, tennis programs, supervised evening programs, and more. **Facilities:** 🏗 🚲 ⚠ 🔍 ✦ ⚘ ♨ 🎱 📺 □ ⚐ 3 restaurants (*see* "Restaurants" below), 2 bars (1 w/entertainment), 1 beach (ocean), lifeguard, volleyball, board surfing, games rm, lawn games, racquetball, spa, sauna, steam rm, whirlpool, beauty salon. The history gallery showcases old photos of the hotel's construction and visiting celebrities. The Galleria features stores selling everything from fudge to precious jewels. **Rates:** $169–$329 S or D; $499–$649 ste; $309–$389 cottage/villa. Extra person $25. Children under age 18 stay free. Parking: Outdoor, $10–$14/day. AE, CB, DC, DISC, JCB, MC, V.

≡≡≡≡ Loews Coronado Bay Resort

4000 Coronado Bay Rd, 92118; tel 619/424-4000 or toll free 800/81-LOEWS; fax 619/424-4400. Off Silver Strand Blvd. Set on a private peninsula, this hotel is beachy and business-like at the same time. Views range from downtown San Diego to the Mexican border. Open, airy lobby is embellished with a grand double stairway of polished brass. Beautiful Silver Strand State Beach is a short stroll away. **Rooms:** 438 rms and stes; 12 cottages/villas. CI 3pm/CO noon. Nonsmoking rms avail. Rooms are nicely if not lavishly decorated with floral-print bedspreads. Large bathrooms with deep "steeping" tubs. **Amenities:** 🛏 ⚱ ⊟ ☎ A/C, cable TV w/movies, dataport, voice mail, in-rm safe, bathrobes. All units w/mini-bars, all w/terraces. **Services:** ⏋ ⚟ VP 🚗 ⊿ ⊙ ⏏ Car-rental desk, social director, masseur, children's program, babysitting. Year-round Commodore Kids Club program includes arts and crafts projects, nature hikes, beach games, plus evening events. **Facilities:** 🏗 🚲 ⚠ 🔍 🎾 🎱 ♨ ⚘ 🎱 1700 □ ⚐ 3 restaurants (*see* "Restaurants" below), 4 bars (1

w/entertainment), volleyball, board surfing, games rm, lawn games, snorkeling, spa, sauna, whirlpool, beauty salon, day-care ctr, washer/dryer. For sailing enthusiasts, there's an 80-slip marina, sailboat instruction and rental, powerboats, and lots more. **Rates:** Peak (May–Sept) $195–$245 S or D; $375–$800 ste; $1,100–$1,500 cottage/villa. Extra person $20. Children under age 12 stay free. Min stay special events. Lower rates off-season. AP and MAP rates avail. Parking: Indoor/outdoor, $12/day. AE, DC, DISC, MC, V.

RESTAURANTS 🍴

Azzura Point

In Loews Coronado Bay Resort, 4000 Coronado Bay Rd; tel 619/424-4000. 8 mi SW of San Diego Coronado Bay Br exit off I-5. **Californian/Asian.** Palladian windows set in white walls, teal and ivory stenciled flooring, and rattan chairs create a lovely foreground for the bay views here. California seafood dishes predominate; also available are seared sea scallops with pasta, Chinese smoked lobster, and a changing wine list. **FYI:** Reservations recommended. **Open:** Sun–Thurs 6–10pm, Fri–Sat 6–11pm. **Prices:** Main courses $18–$25. AE, CB, DC, DISC, ER, MC, V. 🏞 VP ⚐

The Brigantine

1333 Orange Ave; tel 619/435-4166. 4 mi SW of San Diego Coronado Bay Br exit off I-5. **Seafood.** Polished wood and brass coordinate nicely with the nautical motif. The specialty is fresh seafood, as well as corn-fed beef and free-range chicken. The wine list is extensive. **FYI:** Reservations accepted. **Open:** Lunch Mon–Fri 11:30am–2:30pm; dinner Sun–Thurs 5–10:30pm, Fri–Sat 5–11:30pm. **Prices:** Main courses $14–$29. AE, DC, MC, V. 🔲 ⚐

Chart House

1701 Strand Way; tel 619/435-0155. 4 mi SW of San Diego Coronado Bay Br exit off I-5 Across from Hotel del Coronado. **American.** Built in 1887, this restaurant was first a boat house for the Hotel del Coronado. Decor is nautical Victorian, with tiffany lamps in the dining room and leaded glass in the back bar. Fresh fish, including sea bass and mahi mahi, predominates, but prime rib and mud pie are also popular. **FYI:** Reservations recommended. Children's menu. Additional locations: 525 Harbor Dr, San Diego (tel 233-7391); 2588 S Hwy 101, Cardiff-By-The-Sea (tel 436-4044). **Open:** Daily 5–10:30pm. **Prices:** Main courses $15–$37. AE, CB, DC, DISC, MC, V. 🏞 ⚐

Crown-Coronet Room

In Hotel Del Coronado, 1500 Orange Ave; tel 619/522-8496. 4 mi SW of San Diego Coronado Bay Br exit off I-5. **Californian/French.** A Victorian setting, with a soaring ceiling, damask fabric walls above wainscoting, and tapestry chairs. The chandeliers were designed by *Wizard of Oz* author Frank Baum. Sunday brunch is a tradition here; at other meals, seafood is a good choice. **FYI:** Reservations recommended. Piano. **Open:** Breakfast daily 7–11am; lunch daily

11:30am–3pm; dinner daily 5–9:30pm; brunch Sun 9am–2pm. **Prices:** Main courses $12–$25; prix fixe $17.50–$25. AE, CB, DC, DISC, MC, V. ▪ ♥ VP &

Mandarin Cafe
In Coronado Plaza, 1330 Orange Ave; tel 619/435-2771. 4 mi SW of San Diego Coronado Bay Br exit off I-5; just north of Hotel del Coronado. **Chinese.** Offers a wide range of Mandarin and Szechuan cuisine in a charming setting with skylights, windows looking out to a garden, and some ocean views. **FYI:** Reservations recommended. Beer and wine only. **Open:** Mon–Thurs 11am–10pm, Fri–Sat 11am–11pm, Sun 1–10pm. **Prices:** Main courses $7–$13. AE, MC, V. &

Marius
In Le Meridien San Diego at Coronado, 2000 2nd St; tel 619/435-3000. Calif 75/San Diego–Coronado Bay Br exit off I-5; go over bridge; right onto Glorieta Blvd. **French.** Elegant but not stuffy, adorned with crystal sconces, mirrors, and oil paintings. The Provençale cuisine features such entrees as duck breast encrusted with rosemary in a lavender-honey sauce, or lobster galettes. Prix-fixe dinners are offered in three, four, or five courses. **FYI:** Reservations recommended. **Open:** Tues–Sat 6–10pm. Closed Jan 1–10. **Prices:** Main courses $39–$50. AE, DC, DISC, ER, MC, V. ♥ VP &

McP's Irish Pub
1107 Orange Ave; tel 619/435-5280. 4 mi SW of San Diego Coronado Bay Br exit off I-5. **American/Irish.** A classic pub with green accents and lots of wood. The patio with 20 tables is a good place to people-watch. Specialties include corned beef with cabbage and Mulligan stew. **FYI:** Reservations recommended. Children's menu. **Open:** Peak (June–Sept) Mon–Fri 11am–9pm, Sat–Sun 9am–9pm. **Prices:** Main courses $5–$18. AE, DC, DISC, MC, V. ⛴ &

Primavera Ristorante
932 Orange Ave; tel 619/435-0454. 4 mi SW of San Diego Coronado Bay Br exit off I-5 to Orange Ave and turn left. **Italian.** An elegant dining room and bar decorated in muted mauve tones, with cream linens and polished wood. The upstairs room has an adjoining patio for private parties. Entrees include veal chops, osso buco, and fresh fish. For dessert, homemade tiramisù. **FYI:** Reservations recommended. **Open:** Lunch Mon–Fri 11am–2:30pm; dinner Mon–Fri 5–10:30pm, Sat–Sun 5–10:30pm. **Prices:** Main courses $13–$20. AE, CB, DC, DISC, MC, V. &

Corte Madera

MOTEL 🏨

≡≡≡ Corte Madera Inn–Best Western
1815 Redwood Hwy, 94925; tel 415/924-1502 or toll free 800/777-9670; fax 415/924-5419. From US 101 S: Madera Blvd exit. From US 101 N: Mt Tamalpais/Paradise Dr exit; left over freeway, right on Madera Blvd. A typical motel

exterior surrounded by beautifully landscaped grounds with rolling lawns which belie its location right off the freeway. Large lobby has a massive stone fireplace and complimentary coffee bar. **Rooms:** 110 rms, stes, and effic. CI 3pm/CO noon. Nonsmoking rms avail. Some rooms have showers only, no tub. Solarium rooms have large skylights, while deluxe courtyard accommodations are larger and have wet bars. Live plants in many rooms. **Amenities:** 🛁 🕹 A/C, satel TV w/movies, refrig, dataport, voice mail. All units w/terraces, some w/fireplaces, some w/whirlpools. **Services:** 🔑 🚐 ⛱ 🍴 Car-rental desk, babysitting. Complimentary van service to local shops, restaurants, and to airport bus. "Dining passport" allows guests to eat at selected fine, local restaurants and charge meals to their rooms. **Facilities:** 🏋 🏓 🏊150 & 1 restaurant, 2 bars, games rm, whirlpool, playground, washer/dryer. Spectacular junior olympic–size pool with lap lanes, heated all year. Compact but complete workout room with Lifecycles, rowing machine, and more. **Rates (CP):** Peak (May–Oct) $92–$118 S or D; $135–$150 ste; $135–$150 effic. Extra person $10. Children under age 18 stay free. Min stay special events. Lower rates off-season. Parking: Outdoor, free. AE, CB, DC, DISC, JCB, MC, V.

Costa Mesa

Inland from Huntington Beach and Newport Beach, Costa Mesa has the distinction of being home to one of the world's largest malls. Orange Coast College and Southern California College are in town. **Information:** Costa Mesa Chamber of Commerce, 1835 Newport Blvd, E-270, Costa Mesa 92627 (tel 714/574-8780).

HOTELS 🏨

≡ Best Western Newport Mesa Inn
2642 Newport Blvd, 92627; tel 800/554-2378 or toll free 800/554-2378; fax 714/642-1220. Fair Del Mar exit off CA 55. Clean and efficient. In a good, if slightly noisy, location. **Rooms:** 98 rms and stes. CI 2pm/CO noon. Nonsmoking rms avail. Basic but adequate. **Amenities:** 🛁 🕹 A/C, cable TV. Some units w/whirlpools. **Services:** 🚐 ⛱ 🍴 ⚬ Children's program, babysitting. **Facilities:** 🏋 🏓 🏊45 & Sauna, whirlpool, washer/dryer. **Rates:** Peak (June–Aug) $59–$99 S; $69–$109 D. Extra person $6. Children under age 12 stay free. Lower rates off-season. Parking: Indoor/outdoor, free. AE, CB, DC, DISC, JCB, MC, V.

≡≡≡ Costa Mesa Marriott Suites
500 Anton Blvd, 92626; tel 714/957-1100 or toll free 800/228-9290; fax 714/966-8495. Bristol N exit off I-405; right on Anton. Excellent hotel close to airports, business parks, and shopping center. Especially attractive for the business traveler. **Rooms:** 253 stes. CI 4pm/CO noon. Nonsmoking rms avail. Large, spacious, and airy. **Amenities:** 🛁 🕹 📺 📞 A/C, cable TV w/movies, refrig, voice mail. Some units w/terraces. **Services:** ✕ 🔑 🚐 ⛱ 🍴 ⚬ Car-rental desk,

babysitting. **Facilities:** ⚙ 🚴 🎿 🛶 🔲 ♿ 1 restaurant, 1 bar, whirlpool, washer/dryer. **Rates:** $89–$139 ste. Extra person $10. Children under age 17 stay free. Parking: Indoor/outdoor, free. AE, DC, DISC, MC, V.

≣≣≣ Country Side Inn & Suites

325 Bristol St, 92626; tel 714/549-0300 or toll free 800/322-9992; fax 714/662-0828. Bristol St S exit off I-405 S; at Red Hill. Quiet area, yet close to business parks, major shopping centers, and Orange County Airport. **Rooms:** 300 rms and stes. Executive level. CI 3pm/CO noon. Nonsmoking rms avail. Undergoing renovation, including fresh paint and new carpets. **Amenities:** 🛁 🔥 A/C, cable TV w/movies, refrig, VCR, voice mail. Some units w/fireplaces, some w/whirlpools. **Services:** ✕ 🖴 VP 🚐 🛄 ⫯ Babysitting. **Facilities:** ⚙ 🛶 🔲 🖥 ♿ 1 restaurant, 1 bar, steam rm, whirlpool, washer/dryer. **Rates (BB):** $138–$300 S; $148–$310 D; $148–$300 ste. Children under age 12 stay free. AP and MAP rates avail. Parking: Outdoor, free. AE, CB, DC, DISC, EC, ER, JCB, MC, V.

≣≣ Holiday Inn Costa Mesa/Orange County Airport

3131 Bristol St, 92626; tel 714/557-3000 or toll free 800/221-7220; fax 714/957-8185. Bristol S exit off I-405. Clean, efficient hotel adjacent to the airport. **Rooms:** 197 rms and stes. CI 3pm/CO noon. Nonsmoking rms avail. Comfortable and clean. **Amenities:** 🛁 🔥 A/C, cable TV w/movies, dataport, voice mail. All units w/terraces. **Services:** ✕ 🖴 🚐 🛄 ⫯ Children's program, babysitting. On Mon–Fri drink specials and complimentary hors d'oeuvres and popcorn are available for guests in the Bristol Bar & Grill. **Facilities:** ⚙ 🛶 🔲 ♿ 1 restaurant, 1 bar, sauna. **Rates (CP):** Peak (June–Aug) $60–$90 S or D; $175 ste. Children under age 18 stay free. Lower rates off-season. Parking: Outdoor, free. AE, CB, DC, DISC, ER, JCB, MC, V.

≣≣≣≣ Westin South Coast Plaza

686 Anton Blvd, 92626; tel 714/540-2500 or toll free 800/228-3000; fax 714/662-6695. Bristol St exit off I-405; go right on Anton Blvd. Located in the middle of a business park next to South Coast Plaza mall. A sleekly sophisticated beige marble lobby opens onto a center courtyard with a huge waterfall. Recently refurbished. **Rooms:** 390 rms and stes. Executive level. CI 3pm/CO 1pm. Nonsmoking rms avail. Rooms are large—almost 300 square feet—and decorated in a medley of beiges. All have oversize work desks. **Amenities:** 🛁 🔥 🖵 🍽 A/C, cable TV w/movies, dataport, voice mail. All units w/minibars. Fax machines in 15th-floor rooms. **Services:** 🍴 🖴 VP 🚐 🛄 ⫯ 🍷 Car-rental desk, masseur, babysitting. Complimentary evening hors d'oeuvres served in the lobby lounge. Transportation available to Disneyland and Newport Beach. **Facilities:** ⚙ 🏊2 🛶 🔲 ♿ 1 restaurant, 1 bar (w/entertainment), basketball, volleyball, beauty salon. In addition to the workout facilities on the pool deck (with cardio machines and free weights), guests have privileges ($20) at a nearby health club. **Rates:** $189–$209 S or D;

$275–$920 ste. Extra person $20. Children under age 18 stay free. Parking: Indoor, $6/day. AE, CB, DC, DISC, JCB, MC, V.

MOTELS

≣ Comfort Inn

2430 Newport Blvd, 92626; tel 714/631-7840 or toll free 800/221-2222; fax 714/548-3720. Del Mar exit off CA 55. A better-than-expected property in a run-down area of Costa Mesa, 10 minutes from beach. Clean and adequate, with cheap rates. **Rooms:** 58 rms. CI noon/CO 11am. Nonsmoking rms avail. Carpets thoroughly cleaned recently. Many rooms have new beds and spreads. **Amenities:** 🛁 A/C, TV w/movies. **Services:** ⫯ 🍷 **Facilities:** ⚙ ♿ Whirlpool. Spartan, fenced pool area with a lot of concrete. **Rates (CP):** Peak (Apr–Labor Day) $49–$59 S or D. Children under age 18 stay free. Lower rates off-season. Parking: Outdoor, free. AE, DC, DISC, JCB, MC, V.

≣ La Quinta Inn

1515 S Coast Dr, 92626; tel 714/957-5841 or toll free 800/531-5900; fax 714/432-7159. Harbor Blvd exit off I-405. Understaffed motel in a commercial/industrial area right off the freeway. The lobby is small and rundown. **Rooms:** 160 rms. CI 1pm/CO noon. Nonsmoking rms avail. Clean, light, and airy. **Amenities:** 🛁 🔥 A/C, cable TV, dataport. **Services:** 🚐 🛄 ⫯ 🍷 **Facilities:** ⚙ 🔲25 ♿ **Rates (CP):** $50–$68 S or D. Extra person $8. Children under age 18 stay free. Parking: Outdoor, free. AE, CB, DC, DISC, MC, V.

≣≣ Newport Beach Days Inn

2100 Newport Blvd, 92627; tel 714/642-2670; fax 714/642-2677. 22nd St/Victoria exit off CA 55 S, left onto Bay, left onto Newport. A family-oriented property in a noisy location. Convenient to freeways. **Rooms:** 31 rms and stes. CI 11am/CO 11am. Nonsmoking rms avail. **Amenities:** 🛁 🔥 🍷 A/C, cable TV, refrig. All units w/minibars, some w/terraces. **Services:** ⫯ Children's program. **Facilities:** ⚙ Washer/dryer. **Rates:** Peak (May–Sept) $46–$52 S; $50–$56 D; $54–$64 ste. Extra person $4. Children under age 18 stay free. Lower rates off-season. Parking: Outdoor, free. AE, CB, DC, DISC, MC, V.

RESTAURANTS 🍽

Bangkok IV

In Crystal Court, 3333 Bear St; tel 714/540-7661. Bristol St exit off I-405. **Thai.** Simple, black-and-white decor, accented with single pink anthuriums at the tables. Thai menu emphasizes fresh ingredients, lots of spices, and attractive arrangements. Customers can choose degree of hotness in dishes from a scale of one to ten. **FYI:** Reservations recommended. Beer and wine only. **Open:** Mon–Sat 11am–10pm, Sun 11am–9pm. **Prices:** Main courses $9–$18. AE, CB, DC, DISC, MC, V. ▰▰ VP ♿

✦ Diva
In Plaza Tower, 600 Anton Blvd, Ste 100; tel 714/754-0600. Bristol St N exit off I-405 S. **New American/Californian.** Great for business entertaining. Yellow walls, magenta and gold drapes, plus purple light fixtures create a New York bistro–style atmosphere. Imaginative dishes include grilled radicchio with goat cheese and crispy prosciutto, and herb and mustard-crusted lamb. **FYI:** Reservations recommended. Jazz. **Open:** Lunch Mon–Fri 11:30am–3pm; dinner Sun–Mon 4:30–9pm, Tues–Wed 5–10pm, Thurs 5–11pm, Fri–Sat 5pm–midnight. **Prices:** Main courses $9–$20. AE, DC, MC, V. ⓥ ⅋

The Golden Truffle
1767 Newport Blvd; tel 714/645-9858. CA 55 S off I-405, right at 17th St. **Caribbean/French.** Colorful flower boxes invite diners into this restaurant in the heart of Costa Mesa. Menu ranges from spa-type dishes to more traditional offerings; among the specialties are roasted gypsy chicken, macaroni and cheese with truffles, and New York steak with chianti. Daily specials feature fresh fish. Location makes this a good takeoff spot for an after-dinner stroll. **FYI:** Reservations recommended. Beer and wine only. **Open:** Lunch Tues–Sat 11:30am–2:30pm; dinner Tues–Sat 5:30–10pm. Closed Dec 24–Jan 3. **Prices:** Main courses $7–$32; prix fixe $45. AE, DC, MC, V. ❤ ⅋

Il Fornaio
650 Anton; tel 714/668-0880. Bristol St N exit off I-405. **Italian.** Italian-style bistro with tile floors and dark wood accents. Wide variety of Italian specialties includes antipasti, pizza, and pasta, as well as chicken, veal, fish, beef, and pork dishes. Wood-burning rotisserie chicken is a specialty, as is the Parmesan ciabatta, an Italian bread served with all meals. **FYI:** Reservations recommended. Children's menu. Additional location: 18051 Von Karmann, Irvine (tel 261-1444). **Open:** Sun–Mon 11:30am–9pm, Tues–Thurs 11:30am–10pm, Fri–Sat 11:30am–11pm. **Prices:** Main courses $8–$17. AE, DC, MC, V. ❤ ⓥ ⅋

Crescent City

The northernmost coastal town in California, Crescent City caters to motorists visiting nearby Jedediah Smith and Del Norte Coast State Parks. **Information:** Crescent City–Del Norte County Visitors Center, 1001 Front St, Crescent City 95531 (tel 707/464-3174).

MOTEL ▥

▤ Curly Redwood Lodge
701 Redwood Hwy S, 95531; tel 707/464-2137; fax 707/464-1655. US 101 to S end of Crescent City. Built from a single redwood tree; the wood exhibits an extremely rare curly grain. Across the highway from 6-mile-long beach and harbor. **Rooms:** 36 rms. CI noon/CO 11am. Nonsmoking rms avail. **Amenities:** ▥ ⅋ Cable TV. No A/C. **Services:** ◁ Outgoing telephone calls anytime, but incoming calls can be received only until 11pm. **Facilities:** ⅋ **Rates:** Peak (June–Oct) $60 S; $65 D. Extra person $5. Children under age 5 stay free. Lower rates off-season. Parking: Outdoor, free. AE, DISC, MC, V.

ATTRACTIONS ▣

Battery Point Lighthouse
At Battery Point, foot of A St; tel 707/464-3089. Accessible only at low tide, this is one of the tallest lighthouses in the United States. Completed in 1892, it was considered the worst duty in the Lighthouse Station Service (later the US Coast Guard); between 1892 and 1937, there were 37 resignations and 26 transfer requests made from the lighthouse. During a storm in 1952, waves broke windows in the lantern room, 146 feet above sea level. The lighthouse was automated in 1953, and abandoned in 1975.

Now maintained as a museum, the lighthouse contains the restored keeper's room, an 1856 Lighthouse Service banjo clock, and items from the *Emidio,* the first commercial vessel torpedoed off the Pacific coast in World War II. **Open:** Apr–Sept, Wed–Sun 10am–4pm (tides permitting). $

Del Norte County Historical Society Museum
577 H St; tel 707/464-3922. Local history exhibits contained in the former county jail building include the First Order Fresnel Lens From the Abandoned St George Reef Lighthouse (18 feet tall and weighing 5,000 pounds), as well as Native American and pioneer artifacts and displays. **Open:** Peak (May–Sept) Mon–Sat 10am–4pm. Reduced hours off-season. $

Undersea World
304 US 101S; tel 707/464-3522. Featured here is a 500,000-gallon tank containing a reef exhibit and a variety of undersea creatures; large shark exhibit; sea lion shows; tide pool. **Open:** Peak (May–Sept) daily 8am–8pm. Reduced hours off-season. $$$

Lake Earl State Park
Old Mill Rd; tel 707/464/9533 or 445-6547. Located just north of town, Lake Earl is surrounded by 5,000 acres of wetlands, wooded hillsides, grassy meadows, sand dunes, and beaches. Numerous species of birds, including the Peregrine falcon and the rare Canada Aleutian goose, may be seen in the forests and wetlands. Coyotes, deer, and raccoons may be observed along the trails, while sea lions and harbor seals can be found along the coast. Spring and early summer bring spectacular displays of blooming wildflowers.

About 20 miles of hiking and bridle trails wind through a variety of landscapes. Fishing for salmon and steelhead is good in the Smith River; Cutthroat trout can be found in Lake Earl; and bass and crappie abound in Dead Lake.

Two primitive camping areas are available in the park. One is a horse camp with corrals (also available to hikers); the other includes six secluded walk-in sites near the parking lot.

(**Note:** Potable water is *not* provided at these sites.) Camping fees are collected at Jedediah Smith and Del Norte campgrounds (see below). **Open:** Daily sunrise–sunset. **Free**

Del Norte Coast Redwoods State Park

4241 Kings Valley Rd; tel 707/464-9533 or 458-3310. Located 7 miles south of town via US 101, this park is in the heart of California's rain forest, with an average annual rainfall of 100 inches. Nine hiking trails of varying difficulty traverse the park, leading through fields of wildflowers and stands of redwoods covering the slopes leading up from the rocky coastline.

Mill Creek Campground, situated in a lush, second-growth forest, contains 145 campsites, most able to accommodate trailers and RVs. A logging company occupied the site in the 1920s and 1930s; remnants of the operation can be seen along some of the trails. **Open:** Daily sunrise–sunset. **$$**

Jedediah Smith Redwoods State Park

1375 Elk Valley Rd; tel 707/464-9533 or 445-6547. Named for famous mountain man Jedediah Strong Smith, this 10,000-acre park is reached by US 199 off of US 101. It consists mainly of old-growth coast redwood forest, and is bisected by the Smith River, one of the cleanest in the nation. Fishing, canoeing, and other water sports are popular in summer, and there are trails suited to hiking, cycling, and horseback riding.

There are more than 100 campsites, many along the river. Reservations are recommended Mem Day–Labor Day. There is a beautiful riverside picnic area as well. **Open:** Daily 24 hours. **$$**

Culver City

See Los Angeles Int'l Airport

Cupertino

Cupertino, which rests up against the Santa Cruz Mountains to the west, is home to high-tech industry (including Macintosh computers) and De Anza College. **Information:** Cupertino Chamber of Commerce, 20455 Silverado Ave, Cupertino 95014 (tel 408/252-7054).

HOTELS 🏨

≣≣≣ Courtyard by Marriott

10605 N Wolfe Rd, 95014; tel 408/252-9100 or toll free 800/321-2211; fax 408/252-0632. 10 mi N of San Jose. Wolfe Rd N exit off I-280; left at Pruneridge Rd; left to Courtyard. Located near major Silicon Valley companies; a popular hotel for businesspeople. **Rooms:** 149 rms and stes. Executive level. CI 3pm/CO 1pm. Nonsmoking rms avail. **Amenities:** 🛏 🕭 A/C, satel TV w/movies. Some units w/terraces. Hot water dispenser in room for tea and coffee.

Services: 🖎 🖵 Free hors d'oeuvres Mon–Thurs. "Courtyard Club" guests receive free weekday newspapers, local calls, and domestic faxes. **Facilities:** 🛏 🏋 🗔 👍 1 restaurant (bkfst only), 1 bar, whirlpool, washer/dryer. Exercise room with Nautilus equipment in separate building. **Rates:** $111 S or D; $123 ste. Parking: Outdoor, free. Lower weekend rates. AE, CB, DC, DISC, MC, V.

≣≣≣ Cupertino Inn

10889 N DeAnza Blvd, 95014; tel 408/996-7700 or toll free 800/222-4828; fax 408/257-0578. 6 mi N of San Jose. Cupertino/Sunny Ave exit off I-280 N; go right, make U-turn. Located near major Silicon Valley companies; a good choice for bargain weekends. Although right next to I-280, it somehow seems to be in its own world, thanks to a pleasant courtyard. Lobby has floor-to-ceiling windows, a big-screen TV, and attractive, comfortable furniture. **Rooms:** 125 rms and stes. CI 4pm/CO noon. Nonsmoking rms avail. **Amenities:** 🛏 🕭 🗔 🍴 A/C, satel TV, dataport, VCR, voice mail. All units w/minibars, some w/fireplaces, some w/whirlpools. **Services:** 🍽 🚗 🖎 🖵 Twice-daily maid svce. Portable bar serves complimentary drinks and hors d'oeuvres from 5pm. **Facilities:** 🛏 🗔 🖥 👍 1 bar, whirlpool. **Rates (BB):** $120 S; $135 D; $131–$146 ste. Extra person $15. Children under age 16 stay free. Parking: Outdoor, free. Weekend discounts. AE, DC, DISC, JCB, MC, V.

RESTAURANT 🍽

$ ✹ Armadillo Willy's

10235 S De Anza Blvd; tel 408/252-7427. CA 9 exit off I-280. **Barbecue/Burgers.** Popular eatery known for its barbecued ribs. Chili, Cajun hot links, and charbroiled chicken served. Country-western music plays in background. **FYI:** Reservations not accepted. Beer and wine only. **Open:** Mon–Sat 11am–10pm, Sun noon–9pm. **Prices:** Main courses $5–$15. AE, MC, V. 🚢 🚐 👍

Dana Point

See also Laguna Beach

In the 1830s Dana Point was immortalized by Richard Henry Dana in *Two Years Before the Mast,* which chronicled everyday life and labor along the desolate seaside cliffs. Nowadays the city is a modern complex of shops, restaurants, hotels, and a man-made marina. **Information:** Dana Point Chamber of Commerce, 24681 La Plaza #120, PO Box 12, Dana Point 92629 (tel 714/496-1555).

HOTEL 🏨

≣≣≣ Dana Point Hilton All-Suite Inn

34402 Pacific Coast Hwy, 92629; tel 714/661-1100 or toll free 800/634-4586; fax 714/489-0628. Great location across the street from the beach. Convenient access to marina, shopping center, and beach parks. **Rooms:** 197 stes. Executive level. CI 4pm/CO noon. Nonsmoking rms avail. Spacious rooms with views of the ocean. **Amenities:** 🔒 🐾 A/C, cable TV w/movies, refrig, VCR. All units w/minibars, all w/terraces, some w/fireplaces, some w/whirlpools. **Services:** ✗ ☛ 🆅🅿 ⛱ 🎵 Social director, masseur, children's program. **Facilities:** 🏋 🚲 🏐 🏊⌜125⌝ 💻 ♿ 1 restaurant, 2 bars (1 w/entertainment), board surfing, games rm, sauna, whirlpool. **Rates (CP):** Peak (June 16–Sept 15) $85–$400 ste. Extra person $15. Children under age 18 stay free. Min stay special events. Lower rates off-season. Parking: Indoor, $3/day. AE, CB, DC, DISC, MC, V.

INN

≣≣≣≣ Blue Lantern Inn

34343 St of the Blue Lantern, 92629; tel 714/661-1304 or toll free 800/950-1236; fax 714/496-1483. From I-5 N, take the Beach Cities exit. From I-5 S, take the Pacific Coast Hwy exit. With ocean views from its promontory perch, this contemporary Victorian–style mansion combines the personal services of an inn with all the amenities and spaciousness of a hotel. Beaches are a five-minute drive away. **Rooms:** 29 rms. CI 2pm/CO noon. No smoking. Rooms are large and done in English, French Country, or wicker decor. Some rooms have separate sitting areas. Spacious tiled bathrooms feature excellent mirrors and lighting. **Amenities:** 🔒 🐾 🖥 A/C, cable TV, bathrobes. All units w/minibars, some w/terraces, all w/fireplaces, all w/whirlpools. Tubs come with rubber duckies for company. **Services:** ✗ 🚐 ⛱ 🎵 Twice-daily maid svce, car-rental desk, masseur, babysitting, afternoon tea served. The teddy bears displayed around the inn are "adoptable" (ie, for sale). Fruit and iced tea are always available for guests, along with complimentary newspapers. Picnic lunches can be arranged. **Facilities:** 🏐 ⌜50⌝ ♿ Games rm. **Rates (BB):** $135–$350 S or D. Extra person $15. Parking: Outdoor, free. AE, DC, MC, V.

RESORTS

≣≣≣ Marriott's Laguna Cliffs Resort

25135 Park Lantern, 92629; tel 714/661-5000 or toll free 800/533-9748; fax 714/661-5358. Pacific Coast Hwy N exit off I-5. 42 acres. Lovely, picturesque property with stunning ocean views beyond well-maintained lawns. Perched on a precipice, within walking distance of the harbor, beach, and shops. Spacious and colorful, with red roof and white clapboard. **Rooms:** 346 rms and stes. CI 3pm/CO noon. Nonsmoking rms avail. New, clean, and spacious, rooms are nicely decorated in neutrals and sea green. Some accommodations have full ocean views. Well-designed marble bathrooms offer abundant counter space, plus an extra ledge running alongside the bathtub. **Amenities:** 🔒 🐾 🖥 A/C, cable TV w/movies, dataport, voice mail. All units w/minibars, some w/terraces. Irons and ironing boards in all rooms. Bathroom hairdryers and vanity mirrors are very outmoded. **Services:** ✗ 🆅🅿 🚐 ⛱ 🎵 Car-rental desk, masseur, babysitting. Very service-orient-

ed staff. **Facilities:** 🏋 🚲 ▣3 🏐 ⌜600⌝ 💻 ♿ 1 restaurant, 1 bar (w/entertainment), volleyball, lawn games, sauna, steam rm, whirlpool, playground. Large but utilitarian workout room with Cybex equipment and new cardio machines; health club services include personal training and tennis lessons. Two miles from Monarch Links Golf Course; one-quarter mile to beach. **Rates:** $159–$229 S or D; $350–$1,200 ste. Extra person $20. Children under age 12 stay free. Min stay special events. Parking: Indoor/outdoor, free. AE, CB, DC, DISC, EC, JCB, MC, V.

≣≣≣≣≣ The Ritz-Carlton Laguna Niguel

1 Ritz-Carlton Dr, 92629 (Monarch Beach); tel 714/240-2000 or toll free 800/241-3333; fax 714/240-1061. 17 mi S of Newport Beach. 18 acres. Old World meets Pacific Rim at this majestic setting on a 150-foot-high bluff above a 2-mile-long beach. Glorious gardens, terraces, and fountained patios outdoors; silk-lined lobby, limestone fireplace, vaulted ceilings, and more than a 1,000 potted plants indoors. But some guests may find the palatial airs out of keeping with the location. **Rooms:** 393 rms and stes. Executive level. CI 4pm/CO noon. Nonsmoking rms avail. Above-average dimensions. Italian marble bathrooms with double vanities. Sumptuous furnishings and fabrics, though in some cases rooms are overfurnished to the point of being cramped. **Amenities:** 🔒 🐾 🍴 A/C, cable TV w/movies, dataport, in-rm safe, bathrobes. All units w/minibars, all w/terraces, some w/fireplaces, some w/whirlpools. **Services:** 🍽 ☛ 🆅🅿 ⛱ 🎵 🎵 Twice-daily maid svce, car-rental desk, masseur, children's program, babysitting. Regular shuttle to and from beach and golf course. Room service on Rosenthal china. Two staffers for every room; generally alert response to requests (and the maids still take time to insert a bookmark at the appropriate place in *TV Guide*). **Facilities:** 🏋 🚲 ⛳ ▸18 🏊 ⛱4 🏐 ⌜800⌝ 💻 ♿ 4 restaurants (*see* "Restaurants" below), 4 bars (2 w/entertainment), 1 beach (ocean), lifeguard, volleyball, board surfing, lawn games, spa, sauna, steam rm, whirlpool, beauty salon. 24-hour business center. First-rate sports facilities; public (not private) golf course designed by Robert Trent Jones II. Smart fitness center with unisex steam rooms. Ritz-Carlton Club in penthouse. Ravishing arched lounge for sunset watching; clubby library lounge for afternoon tea and nightcaps. **Rates:** Peak (May 24–Sept 1) $275–$550 S or D; $600–$3000 ste. Children under age 18 stay free. Min stay special events. Lower rates off-season. Parking: Indoor/outdoor, $17/day. Lower rates for rooms facing courtyards, not coastline. AE, CB, DC, DISC, ER, JCB, MC, V.

RESTAURANT 🍴

The Dining Room

In the Ritz-Carlton Laguna Niguel, 1 Ritz-Carlton Dr (Monarch Beach); tel 714/240-2000. 2 mi N of Dana Point Take Crown Valley Pkwy exit from San Diego Fwy west to Pacific Coast Hwy. **Continental/Mediterranean.** Serious dining and knowledgeable waiters, with dishes that generally live up to their lofty titles. The gracious setting features French provincial chandeliers and European genre paintings. Specialties include seared ahi tuna, pyramid of salmon with truffles and golden tomato emulsion, breast of Petaluma chicken with couscous and curry sauce, and orange chocolate fondant with blood orange sauce. Excellent wine list. **FYI:** Reservations recommended. Children's menu. Dress code. **Open:** Tues–Sat 6–10pm. **Prices:** Main courses $27–$38; prix fixe $65. AE, CB, DC, DISC, ER, MC, V. ⊗ VP ￼

Davis

HOTEL ￼

￼ Ramada Inn Davis

110 F St, 95616; tel 916/753-3600 or toll free 800/753-0035; fax 916/758-8623. Richards Blvd exit off I-80. Only hotel in university town. Pleasant town atmosphere, safe neighborhood. **Rooms:** 135 rms and stes. CI 3pm/CO noon. Nonsmoking rms avail. Rather basic. **Amenities:** ￼ ￼ A/C, cable TV w/movies. Some units w/terraces, 1 w/whirlpool. VCR and refrigerator available for rent. **Services:** ￼ ￼ Car-rental desk. Group check-in available. **Facilities:** ￼ ￼ ￼ 1 restaurant, 1 bar. Pool heated Apr–Nov. Use of Davis Athletic Club. **Rates:** Peak (Mar–Oct) $70–$95 S or D; $90–$130 ste. Extra person $10. Children under age 12 stay free. Min stay special events. Lower rates off-season. MAP rates avail. Parking: Outdoor, free. Business rate includes voucher for free complete breakfast at adjacent restaurant. AE, CB, DC, DISC, MC, V.

Death Valley National Park

Long the unchallenged domain of the Panamint tribe, an offshoot of the Shoshone, Death Valley is one of the most enthralling natural wonders in the United States. From atop the rocky platform symbolically named **Dante's View,** at the edge of a dizzying sheer drop of 5,120 feet, sprawls in blinding clarity the vast expanse of the salt flats and the lowest point on the continent, 282 feet below sea level. On the other side of the **Devil's Golf Course** and its weird salt formations, the eternal snows of Mount Whitney rise in contrast with sun-blasted rocks and sand dunes. Near Scotty's Castle is **Ubehebe Crater.** It is known as an explosion crater; hot magma rose from the depths of the earth to meet the ground water, the resultant steam blasted out a crater and scattered cinders. **Mosaic Canyon,** located near Stovepipe Wells, displays mosaics of water-polished white, gray, and black rock. Nature has cemented the canyon's stream gravel into mosaics large and small.

The 2-billion-year-old valley, once the bed of an Ice Age sea, is home to a surprising array of animal life. More than 30 species of mammal, including coyote, porcupine, and kangaroo rat, survive here, along with dozens of insects, reptile species, and birds, most notably vultures and crows. Certain kinds of small fish can be found nowhere on earth except in the scanty waters of Salt Creek or the palm groves of Furnace Creek.

A national monument since 1933, the region was upgraded in 1994 to national park status and expanded to 3.3 million acres, making it the largest national park outside Alaska. Death Valley was named when a group of pioneers died of thirst and exhaustion while attempting to cross it on Christmas Day, 1849. (When visiting Death Valley, it is extremely important to carry plenty of water—an untrained person could die of dehydration in three hours in this climate.)

Two excellent highways run north–south and east–west through the park. Only the main roads are patrolled regularly; it can be very dangerous to venture off of them in summer. The **visitor center** at Furnace Creek provides information and directions, and presents an orientation film (tel 619/786-2331). Following are some highlights of the monument.

Scotty's Castle, 52 miles NW of Furnace Creek on Calif 190 and Grapevine Rd. Wealthy Chicago businessman Albert Johnson and his friend, Walter Scotty, a professional cowboy from the Buffalo Bill troupe, built this sumptuously decorated and improbable castle in the Hollywood Hispano-Moorish style between 1922 and 1931. Guided tours daily, on the hour.

Artists Drive, 11 miles S of Furnace Creek. A narrow, one-way road amid splendid gorges and multicolored landscapes. A treat for color photographers.

Devil's Golf Course, 8 miles S of Furnace Creek. A vast salt flat studded with 20-inch-high salt rocks that lives up to its name.

Golden Canyon, 4 miles S of Furnace Creek. This half-mile path cuts through splendid rock formations of gold, bright red, ochre, and bronze. A photographer's dream.

HOTEL ￼

￼ Furnace Creek Inn Resort

CA 190, PO Box 187, Death Valley, 92328; tel 619/786-2345; fax 619/786-2307. 140 mi W of Las Vegas. Beautiful Spanish-Moorish hotel built of stone and adobe, with arched entries, abundant Spanish tile and beamed ceilings. Surrounded by flower gardens, palm trees, and a stream that feeds three koi ponds. Horseback riding stables and golf located nearby. **Rooms:** 67 rms and stes. CI 4pm/CO noon. Nonsmoking rms avail. Elegantly appointed, with adobe walls and overstuffed furniture. **Amenities:** ￼ ￼ A/C, cable TV w/movies, refrig. Some units w/terraces, some w/fireplaces. **Services:** VP ￼ ￼ ￼ Twice-daily maid svce. **Facilities:** ￼ ￼ ￼ 2 restaurants, 2 bars (1 w/entertainment), games rm. Tranquil sitting room off lobby has clubby atmosphere with couches, a grand piano, bookshelves, and floral arrangements. Inn dining room has formal atmosphere with views of Death Valley. L'Ottimos Italian Restaurant has an extensive wine list. **Rates (MAP):** $285 S; $335 D; $425 ste. Extra person $14. Children under age 18 stay free. Parking: Outdoor, free. AE, DC, DISC, MC, V.

MOTELS

▤▤ Furnace Creek Ranch Resort

CA 190, PO Box 187, Death Valley, 92328; tel 619/786-2345; fax 619/786-2514. 140 mi W of Las Vegas. Weathered buildings, corrals, stables, and western artifacts form the backdrop for this rambling ranch, set in a lush oasis. **Rooms:** 196 rms. CI 4pm/CO noon. Nonsmoking rms avail. Older rooms in duplex cabins have wood paneling, brown carpeting, wooden tables, and chairs. The more modern "deluxe" and "park view" rooms in motel have comfortable furnishings, patios, and balconies. **Amenities:** 🛏 A/C, cable TV w/movies, refrig. Some units w/terraces. **Services:** 🚐 🗘 **Facilities:** 🔁 ▶₁₈ 🛬 🏊 3 restaurants, 3 bars (1 w/entertainment), washer/dryer. Steak house serves up huge portions of mostly American fare. Saloon has western atmosphere, with Stetsons and spurs on the walls. **Rates:** $98–$120 S or D. Extra person $14. Children under age 18 stay free. Parking: Outdoor, free. AE, DC, DISC, MC, V.

▤▤ Stove Pipe Wells Village

CA 190, Death Valley, 92328; tel 619/786-2387; fax 619/786-2389. 23 miles from Furnace Creek. Lobby overlooks pool and is decorated with wooden tables and chairs, and a handmade Indian rug. The wall-sized map of Death Valley is handy for travelers. **Rooms:** 83 rms. CI 3:30pm/CO 11am. Nonsmoking rms avail. Older, motel-style rooms have a rustic feel, with brown carpeting and bedspreads, and wooden armchairs. Western landscapes adorn the walls. **Amenities:** A/C, refrig. No phone or TV. **Services:** 🗘 🖘 **Facilities:** 🔁 🛌₅₅ 🛬 1 restaurant, 1 bar. Bar is a western-style saloon. **Rates:** $53–$76 S or D. Extra person $10. Children under age 12 stay free. Parking: Outdoor, free. AE, DISC, MC, V.

Del Mar

Flanked by the Torrey Pines State Reserve, with its strain of pine trees found in only two places in the world, this seaside town is known for the Del Mar Race Track and the late-June Southern California State Exposition. **Information:** Greater Del Mar Chamber of Commerce, 1104 Camino Del Mar, Del Mar 92014 (tel 619/755-4844).

HOTELS 📠

▤▤ Del Mar Hilton

15575 Jimmy Durante Blvd, 92014; tel 619/792-5200 or toll free 800/345-6565; fax 619/792-0353. Via de la Valle exit off I-5; go west. Located across from the Del Mar Race Track and a mile from the beach, this is an elegant hotel in every respect. Grounds and restrooms are sparkling clean. **Rooms:** 245 rms and stes. Executive level. CI 4pm/CO noon. Nonsmoking rms avail. **Amenities:** 🛏 🗘 🗇 A/C, cable TV w/movies, dataport. All units w/minibars, some w/terraces. **Services:** ✕ 🖚 🆅🅿 🏊 🗘 🖘 Car-rental desk, masseur, babysitting. **Facilities:** 🔁 🛌₆₀₀ 🛬 2 restaurants, 2 bars (1 w/entertainment), whirlpool. Next door is a 59-tee driving range and tennis courts, all lighted, as well as a miniature golf course and arcade. **Rates:** Peak (July–Sept) $115–$135 S; $130–$150 D; $225–$500 ste. Extra person $15. Children under age 18 stay free. Min stay special events. Lower rates off-season. Parking: Outdoor, free. AE, CB, DC, DISC, ER, JCB, MC, V.

▤▤▤▤ L'Auberge Del Mar

1540 Camino del Mar, 92014; tel 619/259-1515 or toll free 800/553-1336; fax 619/755-4940. Del Mar Heights Rd exit off I-5; go west, then right on Camino del Mar. This hotel has a jewel of a setting, located on a hill just above a popular swimming and surfing beach. Also convenient to shops and restaurants downtown. Architecture features a shingled roof with gables. Everything looks lovely after a complete refurbishment. **Rooms:** 123 rms and stes. CI 4pm/CO noon. Nonsmoking rms avail. Rooms are large; top-floor rooms have high ceilings. **Amenities:** 🛏 🗘 🗐 🗇 A/C, cable TV w/movies, dataport, voice mail, bathrobes. All units w/minibars, some w/terraces, some w/fireplaces, 1 w/whirlpool. **Services:** ✕ 🖚 🆅🅿 🚐 🏊 🗘 Car-rental desk, social director, masseur, children's program, babysitting. **Facilities:** 🔁 🚲 🛤 🛬 ╘╕₂₀₀ 🛬 1 restaurant, 1 bar, volleyball, board surfing, spa, sauna, steam rm, whirlpool, beauty salon. The Jimmy Durante pub is a popular hangout after the races at nearby Del Mar Racetrack. Exercise bikes, stair machines, and free weights are available at the outdoor sports pavilion; personal trainer available by appointment. **Rates:** Peak (June–Sept) $259–$319 S; $279–$339 D; $500–$950 ste. Extra person $10. Children under age 18 stay free. Min stay wknds. Lower rates off-season. AP and MAP rates avail. Parking: Indoor/outdoor, $5–$8/day. AE, CB, DC, DISC, EC, ER, MC, V.

INNS

▤▤ Del Mar Inn

720 Camino del Mar, 92014; tel 619/755-9765 or toll free 800/451-4515; fax 619/792-8196. 1½ acres. A Charming, cozy inn located near the ocean and Del Mar Village. An exceptional flower garden and grounds add the elegance of old England. **Rooms:** 80 rms and effic. CI 2pm/CO 2pm. Nonsmoking rms avail. **Amenities:** 🛏 A/C, TV w/movies. Some units w/terraces. **Services:** ✕ 🚐 🏊 🗘 Babysitting, afternoon tea served. **Facilities:** 🔁 🛌₆₀ 🛬 Whirlpool, washer/dryer, guest lounge. **Rates (CP):** Peak (June 15–Labor Day) $105–$135 S or D; $130–$155 effic. Extra person $4.

Children under age 16 stay free. Lower rates off-season. Higher rates for special events/hols. Parking: Outdoor, free. AE, CB, DC, DISC, JCB, MC, V.

≣≣≣ Rock Haus Bed & Breakfast Inn
410 15th St, 92014; tel 619/481-3764. Within walking distance of the beach, Del Mar Village, and shops and restaurants; a famous romantic retreat. Unsuitable for children under 13. **Rooms:** 10 rms (6 w/shared bath). CI 2pm/CO 11am. No smoking. Each room is different. Some have ocean views, and the Huntsman room has a fireplace. **Amenities:** 🛋 ⚱ No A/C or TV. 1 unit w/fireplace. **Facilities:** 🏛 Guest lounge. Breakfast area with stunning view of ocean can be set up for business meetings. **Rates (CP):** $90–$100 S or D w/shared bath, $120–$150 S or D w/private bath. Min stay special events. Higher rates for special events/hols. Parking: Outdoor, free. MC, V.

RESTAURANTS 🍽

Cilantros
3702 Via de la Valle; tel 619/259-8777. 22 mi N of San Diego Via de la Valle exit off I-5. **Southwestern.** Southwestern decor, with whitewashed tables, wrought-iron accents, etched stone pillars, and cactus centerpieces. Choices include spit-roasted chicken, shark fajitas, and tapas bar. **FYI:** Reservations recommended. Children's menu. **Open:** Mon–Thurs 11am–11pm, Fri–Sat 11am–midnight, Sun 11am–10:30pm. **Prices:** Main courses $5–$20. AE, CB, DC, MC, V. 📼 🅅🄿 ⚱

Il Fornaio Cucina Italiana
In Del Mar Plaza, 1555 Camino Del Mar; tel 619/755-8876. 20 mi N of San Diego Del Mar Heights Rd exit off I-5. **Italian.** With a spectacular ocean view, frescoed walls, and a heated patio where you can watch the sunset, this lovely Italian restaurant has a sophisticated feel. Food choices include grilled eggplant with goat cheese and sun-dried tomatoes; pasta stuffed with lobster, ricotta cheese, leeks, and lemon cream; and for dessert, ricotta cheesecake. **FYI:** Reservations accepted. Children's menu. **Open:** Mon–Sat 11:30am–11pm, Sun 10am–10pm. **Prices:** Main courses $8–$19. AE, CB, DC, MC, V. 🛥 🏔 🅅🄿 ⚱

Pacifica Del Mar
In Del Mar Plaza, 1555 Camino Del Mar; tel 619/792-0476. 20 mi N of San Diego Del Mar Heights Rd exit off I-5. **Californian/Pacific Rim.** Newly refurbished bar just off the stylish dining room has become a gathering place for Del Mar locals. Cozy restaurant features an aquarium in the main salon, a glass-enclosed patio with heaters, and a lovely ocean view. Menu includes corn chowder with chicken, wok-seared duck salad, and sashimi ahi tempura. **FYI:** Reservations recommended. Dress code. **Open:** Lunch daily 11am–4pm; dinner daily 4–10:30pm; brunch Sun 9am–2pm. **Prices:** Main courses $14–$20. AE, DC, DISC, MC, V. 🛥 🏔 📼 🅅🄿 ⚱

Spices Thai Cafe
In Piazza Carmel, 3810 Carmel Valley Rd; tel 619/259-0891. 19 mi N of San Diego Carmel Valley Rd exit off I-5. **Thai.** A modest restaurant located in a shopping center, with quite pleasant ambience. Decorated with pink walls and black lacquer furniture; a nice bar lines one side of the room. Menu highlights include eggplant with chile sauce; spicy duck with ginger, chile, and black bean sauce; and pineapple curry. Many vegetarian dishes available. **FYI:** Reservations accepted. Beer and wine only. **Open:** Daily 11am–10pm. **Prices:** Main courses $7–$15. AE, DISC, MC, V. ⚱

Desert Hot Springs

A desert hideaway for the Hollywood elite since the 1930s (most notably at the Two Bunch Palms retreat), Desert Hot Springs has evolved into a larger community, part of the expanding Palm Springs area. **Information:** Desert Hot Springs Chamber of Commerce, 11711 West Dr, PO Box 848, Desert Hot Springs 92240 (tel 619/329-6403 or toll free 800/346-3347).

HOTELS 🏨

≣ Desert Hot Springs Spa Hotel
10-805 Palm Dr, 92240; tel 619/329-6495 or toll free 800/808-7727, 800/843-6053 in CA; fax 619/329-6915. Palm Dr exit off I-10. The San Jacinto and San Gorgonio peaks provide a dramatic backdrop for the spa's seven mineral pools. **Rooms:** 50 rms and stes. CI 3pm/CO 11am. Some rooms and corridors are in need of renovation. **Amenities:** 🛋 A/C, cable TV. All units w/terraces. **Services:** ✕ ⤸ Masseur. **Facilities:** 🏛 1 restaurant, 1 bar, lawn games, spa, sauna, whirlpool, beauty salon. **Rates:** Peak (Dec 24–May) $79–$99 S or D; $119 ste. Extra person $10. Children under age 12 stay free. Min stay wknds. Lower rates off-season. Parking: Outdoor, free. AE, CB, DISC, MC, V.

≣≣≣ Mirage Springs Hotel Casino & Spa
10-625 Palm Dr, 92240; tel 619/251-3399 or toll free 800/MIRAGE-1; fax 619/251-0460. Palm Dr exit off I-10. Located at the top of Palm Drive, overlooking Palm Springs and the Coachella Valley, this contemporary-style hotel, casino, and spa is the newest addition to Desert Hot Springs. **Rooms:** 113 rms and stes. CI 3pm/CO noon. Nonsmoking rms avail. Accommodations are decorated in the soft hues of the desert; panoramic views and private patios are featured. **Amenities:** 🛋 ⚱ A/C, cable TV, refrig. All units w/terraces. **Services:** ⤸ Masseur, babysitting. **Facilities:** 🏛 🏊 ⚱ 2 restaurants, 1 bar (w/entertainment), spa, sauna, whirlpool. Seven mineral pools, a large swimming pool, spa facilities, and a California-style casino. **Rates:** Peak (Oct–May) $89–$119 S or D; $159–$179 ste. Extra person $15. Children under age 16 stay free. Lower rates off-season. Parking: Outdoor, free. AE, DC, DISC, MC, V.

RESORT

≣≣≣ Two Bunch Palms Resort & Spa

67-425 Two Bunch Palms Trail, 92240; tel 619/329-8791 or toll free 800/472-4334; fax 619/329-1317. Palm Dr exit off I-10. 50 acres. This posh yet intimate spa resort, renowned for its mineral waters, is truly an oasis in the desert. Widely considered one of the world's best spas. **Rooms:** 40 rms, stes, and effic; 5 cottages/villas. CI 3pm/CO noon. Nonsmoking rms avail. One- and two-bedroom villas are decorated with antiques and contemporary touches. **Amenities:** 📞 🔊 ☕ A/C, cable TV, VCR. Some units w/terraces, 1 w/fireplace, some w/whirlpools. Many cottages have wet bars. Welcome basket includes bottles of juices and water, fruit, crackers, etc. **Services:** Masseur. Excellent staff. **Facilities:** 🔊 🚲 📺 ⛳ 🔟 ♿ 1 restaurant (lunch and dinner only), spa, sauna, whirlpool. Mud-bath complex, hot mineral pool, two lakes. **Rates (CP):** $120–$232 S or D; $252–$570 ste; $220–$480 effic; $375–$570 cottage/villa. Children under age 18 stay free. Min stay. Parking: Outdoor, free. Closed Aug. AE, MC, V.

ATTRACTION 🏛

Cabot's Old Indian Pueblo Museum

67616 E Desert View; tel 619/329-7610. A designated California Point of Historic Interest, this 35-room mansion serves as a showcase of Native American culture. Guided tours take in exhibits of Native American history, art, and artifacts, including a 43-foot Indian head carved out of redwood. **Open:** Sept–June, Wed–Sun 10am–4pm; July–Aug phone for hours. **$**

Devils Postpile National Monument

For lodgings, see Mammoth Lakes

This 800-acre monument was created in 1911 to preserve the Devils Postpile and the spectacular Rainbow Falls, which are located about two miles downstream. The picturesque river valley is at 7,600 feet on the western slopes of the Sierra Nevada. An outstanding example of columnar-jointed basalt, Devils Postpile was formed approximately 100,000 years ago by basalt lava erupting from volcanic vents in the earth. As a glacier moved down the Middle Fork of the San Joaquin River about 10,000 years ago, it quarried away one side of the postpile, exposing a 60-foot wall of clearly defined columns; many fallen columns lay in fragments on the talus slope below. A hike to the top of the postpile reveals that the columns have from three to seven sides, their polished tops showing parallel striations where rocks, frozen to the glacial ice, scraped across them. The formation is a half-mile hike from the ranger station.

At **Rainbow Falls** the Middle Fork of the San Joaquin River drops 101 feet over a dark cliff of volcanic lava. The name was inspired by the rainbows that appear at the base of the falls in the afternoon light. Not far from the postpile are the **Soda Springs,** created by gases driven up from areas deep below the surface combining with ground water. The springs consist of cold, highly carbonated, mineralized water. Iron in the water oxidizes upon exposure to the air and stains the surrounding gravel a reddish brown.

The 211-mile **John Muir Trail,** linking Yosemite National Park with Sequoia and Kings Canyon National Parks, passes through Devils Postpile National Monument, with access at Rainbow Falls Trailhead and the ranger station. Hiking is also available along the Rainbow Falls, King Creek, and Pacific Crest trails, and on several short loop trails within the monument.

Camping is usually available at a 21-site area near the ranger station from July to mid-October (fee charged). Day-use visitors are *not* allowed to drive into the monument between 7:30am and 5:30pm. During these hours, park at Mammoth Lakes Ski Area and take the shuttle bus to the ranger station (fee charged). Fishing is permitted for persons age 16 and over with a California fishing license. Hunting is prohibited. For further information, write to the Superintendent, Devils Postpile National Monument, PO Box 501, Mammoth Lakes, CA 93546.

Diamond Bar

See Pomona

Disneyland

See Anaheim

Dunsmuir

Dunsmuir is one of a series of small towns along I-5, the main artery of northern California. Located near the Pacific Crest National Scenic Trail, the town is the gateway to Castle Crags State Park. **Information:** Dunsmuir Chamber of Commerce, PO Box 17, Dunsmuir 96025 (tel 916/235-2177).

MOTEL 🏨

≣≣≣ Railroad Park Resort–Caboose Motel

100 Railroad Park Rd, 96025; tel 916/235-4440 or toll free 800/974-RAIL; fax 916/235-4470. Railroad Park Rd exit off I-5; 1 mi S of Dunsmuir. A unique concept: a motel housed in superbly restored cabooses and a boxcar from famous American railroads, on tracks surrounded by spectacular Castle Crags State Park. **Rooms:** 23 rms; 4 cottages/villas. CI noon/CO 11am. Nonsmoking rms avail. **Amenities:** 📞 🔊 📺 A/C,

satel TV w/movies, refrig. Some units w/terraces. **Services:** Wonderful staff. **Facilities:** 1 restaurant (dinner only), 1 bar (w/entertainment), whirlpool, washer/dryer. Boxcar with lift for travelers with disabilities. **Rates:** Peak (May–Sept) $60–$80 S; $65–$85 D. Extra person $5. Lower rates off-season. Parking: Outdoor, free. AE, DISC, MC, V.

RESORT

≋≋ Cave Springs
4727 Dunsmuir Ave, 96025; tel 916/235-2721. Dunsmuir-Siskiyou exit off I-5; go west. 15 acres. Affable hosts Louie and Belinda Dewey work hard to ensure that a good time is had by all at this low-key resort, with its forested grounds and 20-inch trout just waiting to be caught in the restored Sacramento River that borders the property. **Rooms:** 10 rms, stes, and effic; 15 cottages/villas. CI 2pm/CO 11am. Nonsmoking rms avail. Intriguing mix of motel rooms, suites, cabins, and stationary mobile homes. Space to park RV. **Amenities:** A/C, cable TV w/movies, refrig, VCR. All units w/terraces. The one-bedroom cabins each have a two-burner stove. The two-bedroom cabins each have a three-burner stove with oven. **Services:** Daily maid service is not included in the cabin rates, but fresh linen is furnished. **Facilities:** Whirlpool, playground, washer/dryer. **Rates:** Peak (May–Sept/Nov–Apr) $39–$46 S; $46–$54 D; $55–$85 ste; $35–$55 effic; $35–$55 cottage/villa. Extra person $3. Children under age 2 stay free. Min stay special events. Lower rates off-season. Parking: Outdoor, free. Cabins and mobile homes can be rented by the week. Cabin rates discounted 25% September 21–June 9. AE, DISC, MC, V.

El Cajon

On the foothilled, eastern fringes of the San Diego area, El Cajon is the jumping-off point for Cuyamaca Rancho State Park, a little-known gem of the state park system. **Information:** El Cajon Chamber of Commerce, 109 Rea Ave, El Cajon 92020 (tel 619/440-6161).

MOTELS

≋≋≋ Best Western Continental Inn
650 N Mollison Ave, 92021; tel 619/442-0601 or toll free 800/88-BEST-1; fax 619/442-0152. Mollison Ave exit off I-8. Very clean, with brand-new three-story building. **Rooms:** 97 rms, stes, and effic. CI 2pm/CO 11am. Nonsmoking rms avail. Nicely decorated in blue and beige. **Amenities:** A/C, cable TV, refrig. Some units w/minibars, some w/terraces, some w/whirlpools. Some rooms have wet bars. **Services:** Coffee in lobby. Staff will arrange for airport shuttle. **Facilities:** Whirlpool, washer/dryer. **Rates (CP):** Peak (June 15–Sept 12) $61 S; $75 D; $90 ste; $75 effic.

Extra person $5. Children under age 12 stay free. Lower rates off-season. Parking: Outdoor, free. AE, CB, DC, DISC, MC, V.

≋ Super 8 Motel
588 N Mollison Ave, 92021; tel 619/579-1144 or toll free 800/800-8000; fax 619/579-1787. Mollison Ave exit off I-8. S on Mollison ½ block. The lobby (behind a fast-food restaurant) can be difficult to locate, but the staff is welcoming. **Rooms:** 40 rms. CI 11am/CO 11am. Nonsmoking rms avail. Rooms are adequate but need improved security. **Amenities:** A/C, cable TV w/movies, refrig. **Services:** **Facilities:** Whirlpool. **Rates (CP):** Peak (June–Nov) $35 S; $35–$42 D. Extra person $3. Children under age 12 stay free. Lower rates off-season. Parking: Outdoor, free. AE, DC, DISC, MC, V.

RESORT

≋≋≋ Singing Hills Country Club & Lodge
3007 Dehesa Rd, 92019; tel 619/442-3425 or toll free 800/457-5568; fax 619/442-9574. Exit 2nd Ave off I-8. 720 acres. Peaceful resort with beautiful rustic grounds. **Rooms:** 102 rms and stes. CI 4pm/CO 1:30pm. Nonsmoking rms avail. Rooms are nicely coordinated thanks to ongoing renovation. **Amenities:** A/C, satel TV, refrig. All units w/terraces. Some rooms have coffeemakers and hair dryers. **Services:** Use of fax machine available. VCR rentals. **Facilities:** 1 restaurant, 1 bar (w/entertainment), whirlpool, washer/dryer. Golf and tennis and pros available for lessons. **Rates:** $85–$93 S or D; $102–$135 ste. Extra person $10. Children under age 18 stay free. Parking: Outdoor, free. AE, DISC, MC, V.

El Centro

The desert was made to bloom with the help of massive irrigation in the fields surrounding El Centro. Now El Centro is the agricultural hub of Imperial Valley, and the region is one of the most productive in the nation. **Information:** El Centro Chamber of Commerce, 1100 Main St, PO Box 3006, El Centro 92244-3006 (tel 619/352-3681).

HOTELS

≋≋ Ramada Inn
1455 Ocotillo Dr, 92243; tel 619/352-5152 or toll free 800/272-6232; fax 619/337-1567. Imperial Ave exit off I-8; 1 mi N to Ocotillo Dr. Popular with business travelers. **Rooms:** 147 rms and stes. CI 3pm/CO noon. Nonsmoking rms avail. **Amenities:** A/C, satel TV w/movies, refrig, dataport. **Services:** **Facilities:** 1 restaurant, 1 bar, washer/dryer. **Rates:** Peak (Jan–May) $51–$67 S; $54–$73 D; $177 ste. Extra person $6. Children under age 17 stay free. Lower rates off-season. Parking: Outdoor, free. AE, CB, DC, DISC, JCB, MC, V.

≣≣ Vacation Inn
2000 Cottonwood Circle, 92243; tel 619/352-9523 or toll free 800/328-6289; fax 619/353-7620. Imperial Ave exit off I-8. Everything for the corporate and leisure traveler. **Rooms:** 189 rms, stes, and effic. Executive level. CI open/CO noon. Nonsmoking rms avail. Kitchenettes available. **Amenities:** 🛗 🍸 A/C, cable TV, refrig, dataport. **Services:** ✕ 🛏 🥂 **Facilities:** 🔥 🛗 🚻 1 restaurant, 1 bar, whirlpool, washer/dryer. RV park on-site. **Rates:** $49 S; $51–$54 D; $75 ste; $59–$64 effic. Extra person $5. Children under age 17 stay free. Parking: Outdoor, free. AE, CB, DC, DISC, MC, V.

MOTEL

≣≣ Travelodge El Dorado Motel
1464 Adams Ave, 92243 (Downtown); tel 619/352-7333 or toll free 800/874-5532. Imperial Ave exit off I-8; 1 mi N to Adams Ave. Small but friendly motel with lots of extras. **Rooms:** 73 rms. CI noon/CO noon. Nonsmoking rms avail. **Amenities:** 🛗 A/C, cable TV w/movies, refrig. Refrigerators available at no extra charge. Many rooms have VCRs and free HBO. **Services:** 🚗 🥂 Free local phone calls; free videos. **Facilities:** 🔥 Large parking lot for trucks and RVs. **Rates (CP):** $36–$36 S; $45–$45 D. Extra person $4. Children under age 12 stay free. Parking: Outdoor, free. AE, CB, DC, DISC, MC, V.

El Granada

See Half Moon Bay

Elk

See also Albion, Little River, Mendocina

The tiny town perched on a remote stretch of coast was originally called Greenwood, due to its location on Greenwood Cove. Lumber built the community, and all-redwood historic buildings dot the town.

INNS 🏨

≣≣≣ Greenwood Pier Inn
5928 CA 1, PO Box 36, 95432; tel 707/877-9997. Artist-owners have created a slightly funky inn, perched on the cliffs overlooking the Mendocino coast. Stunning views of bay and rocks from lobby and guestrooms. **Rooms:** 9 rms; 3 cottages/villas. CI 2pm/CO noon. No smoking. Rooms are cozy and individually furnished, with decks overlooking ocean. **Amenities:** 📻 🍸 Refrig, bathrobes. No A/C, phone, or TV. Some units w/terraces, some w/fireplaces, some w/whirlpools. **Services:** ✕ 🛏 🥂 Babysitting. Homebaked breakfast goods are delivered to rooms in morning. **Facilities:** 1 restaurant (see "Restaurants" below), whirlpool, guest lounge. Hot tub on edge of cliff overlooking ocean. Beautiful beach within walking distance. New cafe/restaurant. During week, dinners can be delivered to rooms. **Rates (CP):** Peak (May–Nov) $110–$165 S or D; $210–$225 cottage/villa. Extra person $12. Min stay wknds. Lower rates off-season. Parking: Outdoor, free. AE, MC, V.

≣≣≣≣ Harbor House
5600 S CA 1, PO Box 369, 95432; tel 707/877-3203. A romantic hideaway for couples. Built in 1916 entirely of redwood, from the vaulted ceilings to the hand-rubbed paneling. The grand parlor has lovely ocean views. Beautiful flower gardens; winding path leads down to ocean. Unsuitable for children under 18. **Rooms:** 6 rms; 4 cottages/villas. CI 2pm/CO noon. No smoking. Spacious, with ocean views, antique furnishings, clawfoot tubs, and fireplaces. Velvet love seats give accommodations a romantic touch. **Amenities:** No A/C, phone, or TV. Some units w/terraces, all w/fireplaces. Cottages have private decks. **Services:** Masseur, afternoon tea served. Meals created from local products are excellent. **Facilities:** 🚻 1 restaurant (bkfst and dinner only), 1 beach (ocean), lawn games, guest lounge. Private beach not suited for swimming. Dining room has beautiful view of bay. **Rates (MAP):** Peak (Apr–Dec) $139–$229 S; $175–$265 D; $175–$225 cottage/villa. Extra person $50. Min stay wknds. Lower rates off-season. MAP rates avail. Parking: Outdoor, free. Include full breakfast and a four-course dinner (one seating at 7 pm). No CC.

RESTAURANT 🍴

Greenwood Pier Cafe
In Greenwood Pier Inn, 5928 CA 1; tel 707/877-9997. **Californian.** Artfully decorated cafe in a gardenlike setting offers a variety of snacks, as well as full-scale entrees such as pan-seared salmon with lemon aioli, or grilled steak with sun-dried tomato butter. Fabulous wine selection and an espresso bar. **FYI:** Reservations accepted. Beer and wine only. **Open:** Breakfast daily 8–10am; lunch daily noon–3pm; dinner Thurs–Mon 5:30–9pm. **Prices:** Main courses $10–$16. AE, MC, V. 🚻

El Portal

See Yosemite National Park

El Segundo

See Los Angeles Int'l Airport

Emeryville

See Berkeley

Encino

RESTAURANT

⑤ ✱ Tempo
16610 Ventura Blvd; tel 818/905-5855. **Middle Eastern.** The area's premier non-kosher Israeli restaurant began as a falafel stand run by a family of new immigrants, and has not lost its friendliness or heart. Now expanded into two storefronts with a patio, the restaurant features Israeli-style mezze (appetizer) platters, plus a variety of Middle Eastern and Mediterranean salads and kabobs, and dishes such as moussaka and baked lamb shank. They draw crowds for the Sabbath-lighting ceremony on Friday. **FYI:** Reservations recommended. Guitar/piano/singer. Children's menu. **Open:** Mon–Sat 11am–11pm, Sun 11am–10pm. **Prices:** Main courses $9–$18. AE, MC, V. ▦ VP ♿

Escondido

The quiet hamlet of Escondido (fittingly from the Spanish word for *hidden*) is a bit of a cultural curiosity: it is the home of the Lawrence Welk Village, complete with a museum that documents the entertainer's life, as well as the San Diego Wild Animal Park, where humans are enclosed and animals are allowed to roam free. **Information:** San Diego North County Convention & Visitors Bureau, 720 N Broadway, Escondido 92025 (tel 619/745-4741).

MOTEL

≡≡ Escondido West Travelodge
1290 W Valley Pkwy, 92029; tel 619/489-1010 or toll free 800/541-6012; fax 619/489-7847. Valley Rd exit off I-15. Pleasantly decorated motel affords easy access to the freeway. Some maintenance problems. **Rooms:** 88 rms. CI 2pm/CO noon. Nonsmoking rms avail. Average-size rooms have a bit too much freeway noise. **Amenities:** ☎ ⚏ ▣ A/C, cable TV w/movies. Some units w/terraces, some w/whirlpools. **Services:** ⬒ ↵ Car-rental desk. Room service from nearby restaurants. **Facilities:** ⟨ ⌷50⌷ ♿ Whirlpool. **Rates:** $53 S; $57–$61 D. Extra person $5. Children under age 18 stay free. Parking: Outdoor, free. AE, DC, DISC, MC, V.

RESORT

≡≡≡ Welk Resort Center & the Greens Executive Conference Center
8860 Lawrence Welk Dr, 92026; tel 619/749-3000 or toll free 800/932-9355; fax 619/749-9537. Deer Springs Rd exit off I-15. 1,000 acres. Attractive accommodations in a quiet country setting nine miles north of the city. Facilities are immaculate and grounds are carefully manicured. **Rooms:** 132 rms and stes. CI 2pm/CO noon. Nonsmoking rms avail. Rooms have pleasant decor with floral bedspreads and light wood furnishings. Most have balconies overlooking the golf course. **Amenities:** ☎ ⚏ ▣ A/C, cable TV w/movies, refrig. All units w/terraces. **Services:** ⬒⎯ ⬒ ↵ ⬤ Car-rental desk, social director, masseur, babysitting. **Facilities:** ⟨ ⚲ ▶ 36 ▨ ⌷250⌷ ⬚ ♿ 3 restaurants, 1 bar (w/entertainment), volleyball, whirlpool, beauty salon. Eateries include main dining room, pizza restaurant, yogurt shop, snack shop, deli. Welk Theatre offers live entertainment. **Rates:** $110 S or D; $160–$220 ste. Extra person $10. Children under age 12 stay free. AP and MAP rates avail. Parking: Outdoor, free. AE, CB, DC, DISC, MC, V.

RESTAURANTS

Marie Callender Restaurant
515 W 13th St; tel 619/741-3636. Center City Pkwy exit off I-15. **American.** A great place for families. Famous for pies, also serves traditional American fare—roast turkey, hamburgers, and chicken pot pie—and has a huge salad bar. **FYI:** Reservations not accepted. Children's menu. **Open:** Mon–Thurs 11am–10pm, Fri–Sat 11am–11pm, Sun 10am–10pm. **Prices:** Main courses $7–$13. AE, DISC, MC, V. ▦ ♥ ♿

✱ 150 Grand Cafe
150 West Grand Ave; tel 619/738-6868. **Californian.** Bright, airy decor and great food entice diners to linger. Owners Cyril and Vicki Lucas and their engaging staff have created a winner. Menu items include grilled filet mignon, forest mushroom pizza, sautéed salmon, and roast game hen. **FYI:** Reservations recommended. **Open:** Lunch Mon–Sat 11:30am–2:30pm; dinner Sun–Thurs 4:30–9pm, Fri–Sat 4:30–9:30pm; brunch Sun 10:30am–2pm. **Prices:** Main courses $15–$18. AE, DC, MC, V. ⚓ ♿

ATTRACTIONS

San Diego Wild Animal Park
15500 San Pasqual Valley Rd; tel 619/747-8702. The park is home to more than 3,000 animals, many of them endangered species, which roam freely over 2,200 acres. Concealed barriers separate the animals into five biogeographical areas that simulate the natural environments found in regions of Africa and Asia.

Nairobi Village is a 17-acre area that contains many single-species exhibits, including kangaroos, tigers, cheetahs, lemurs, and gorillas; the Petting Karal, with young sheep, antelopes, and goats; and the 1¾-mile Kilimanjaro Hiking Trail, with larger animal exhibits and several gardens along the way. Also here are animal shows that feature elephants, free-flying birds, and exotic species.

The rest of the park is accessible only via the **Wgasa Bush Line,** a 5-mile, open-air monorail "safari" (included in price of admission). During the 50-minute ride, guides provide narration as the train travels around the perimeter of each of the African and Asian habitats and the Kilimanjaro Trail. Trains leave every 20–30 minutes; informative videos are presented to those waiting to board.

Most visitor facilities, including shops, food concessions, and a children's playground, are located in Nairobi Village. Wheelchair and stroller rentals are available. Inquire in advance about annual events, special programs, and behind-the-scenes tours. **Open:** June–Aug, daily 9am–5pm. Reduced hours off-season. **$$$$**

Escondido Historical Society History Museum
321 N Broadway; tel 619/743-8207. This museum is housed in five turn-of-the-century buildings that are known collectively as the "Escondido Heritage Walk." Museum offices are in an 1894 library building; the remaining buildings are furnished with period antiques and reproductions to represent how they were used 100 years ago. The other buildings are: an 1890 Victorian house; a 1900 barn; an 1888 Santa Fe Railroad Depot; a re-created blacksmith shop (where local residents can sign up for blacksmithing classes); and an authentic 1920 Santa Fe Railroad car. **Open:** Thurs–Sat 1–4pm. Closed for rain. **Free**

Mount Palomar Observatory
Tel 619/742-2119 (recorded info). Located about 35 miles northeast, on County Road S-6. A department of the California Institute of Technology, Palomar Observatory has a 200-inch Hale telescope, the second-largest in the United States, with a visitor gallery in its dome. Exhibits display the workings of the observatory as well as photographs taken by the telescopes. **Open:** Visitors gallery open daily 9am–4pm. **Free**

Essex

ATTRACTION 🏛
Providence Mountains State Recreation Area
I-40; tel 805/942-0662. This 6,000-acre recreation area is best known for Mitchell Caverns Natural Preserve. Two of the Mitchell Caverns are open to the public; both feature classic examples of stalactites, stalagmites, and other, less common types of limestone formations. Guided cavern tours are given fall–spring and last approximately 90 minutes. Hiking trails; campsites available for tents and RVs. **Open:** Park, daily. Cavern tours: mid-Sept–mid-June, Mon–Fri 1:30pm, Sat–Sun 10am, 1:30, and 3pm. **$$**

Eureka

The largest coastal city north of San Francisco, Eureka came of age as a gritty lumber and industrial town, and the community retains much of that character. Following a period of decline, the Old Town section has been spruced up and is now a showcase for Victorian homes and shops. **Information:** Eureka/Humboldt County Convention & Visitors Bureau, 1034 2nd St, Eureka 95501 (tel 707/443-5097).

HOTEL 🏨
≡≡≡ Eureka Inn
518-7th St, 95501 (Downtown); tel 707/442-6441 or toll free 800/862-4906; fax 707/442-1683. US 101 N or S to 7th St; E 2 blocks. A National Historic Landmark built in 1922 in the Tudor style. Huge lobby with potted plants and a view of the lovely swimming pool. **Rooms:** 105 rms and stes. CI 4pm/CO noon. Nonsmoking rms avail. **Amenities:** 🛁 🍴 Cable TV, dataport, voice mail. No A/C. 1 unit w/fireplace, 1 w/whirlpool. **Services:** ✕ 📺 🐕 🛎 ⇩ ⇪ Babysitting. **Facilities:** 🏋 🏊 🍴 2 restaurants (see "Restaurants" below), 2 bars (w/entertainment), sauna, whirlpool. Free use of nearby health club. **Rates:** Peak (May–Oct) $110–$225 S or D; $165–$225 ste. Extra person $10. Children under age 16 stay free. Lower rates off-season. Parking: Outdoor, free. AE, DC, DISC, MC, V.

MOTELS
≡≡ Best Western Thunderbird Inn
232 W 5th St, 95501; tel 707/443-2234 or toll free 800/521-6996; fax 707/443-3489. At US 101, 4 blocks S of downtown. A very agreeable place for business and vacation travelers, with a fireplace in lobby. **Rooms:** 115 rms and stes. CI 2pm/CO noon. Nonsmoking rms avail. **Amenities:** 🛁 🍴 A/C, cable TV, refrig, dataport. 1 unit w/whirlpool. **Services:** ✕ 🛎 ⇩ Car-rental desk, babysitting. Linens changed daily on request. Room service from adjacent coffee shop noon–10pm. VCRs for rent. **Facilities:** 🏋 🏊 🍴 1 restaurant, whirlpool. Guest passes to nearby health club. **Rates:** Peak (July–Sept) $81 S; $86 D; $140 ste. Extra person $5. Children under age 18 stay free. Lower rates off-season. Parking: Outdoor, free. AE, CB, DC, DISC, MC, V.

≡ Carson House Inn
1209 4th St, 95501; tel 707/443-1601 or toll free 800/772-1622; fax 707/444-8365. Centrally located near old town and Eureka's attractions. Family-run. **Rooms:** 63 rms and stes. CI open/CO noon. Nonsmoking rms avail. **Amenities:** 🛁 🍴 Cable TV w/movies, refrig, bathrobes. No A/C. Some units w/whirlpools. **Services:** 🛎 ⇩ ⇪ Car-rental desk, babysitting. **Facilities:** 🏋 🏊 🍴 Sauna, whirlpool. Conference facilities in nearby Campton House, owned by same family. **Rates (CP):** $65–$120 S or D; $95–$150 ste. Extra person $15. Children under age 12 stay free. Min stay special events. Parking: Outdoor, free. AE, DC, DISC, MC, V.

≡ Eureka Super 8 Motel
1304 4th St, 95501 (Downtown); tel 707/443-3193 or toll free 800/235-3232. On US 101 S. Comfortable place convenient to downtown. **Rooms:** 50 rms and effic. CI open/CO 11am. Nonsmoking rms avail. **Amenities:** 🛁 🍴 Cable TV. No A/C. **Facilities:** 🏋 🏊 🍴 Sauna, whirlpool. **Rates (CP):** Peak

(June–Sept) $69–$72 S or D; $96–$110 effic. Extra person $8. Lower rates off-season. Parking: Outdoor, free. DC, DISC, MC, V.

≣≣ **Red Lion Inn**

1929 4th St, 95501; tel 707/445-0844 or toll free 800/547-8010; fax 707/445-2752. US 101 to V St. Well run, newly modernized, regularly upgraded. **Rooms:** 178 rms and stes. CI 3pm/CO noon. Nonsmoking rms avail. **Amenities:** 🛏 🗏 🍽 A/C, cable TV w/movies, dataport. Some units w/terraces. **Services:** ✗ 🚐 🖼 ↩ 🏊 **Facilities:** 🏋 ⊠ 🚶 1 restaurant, 1 bar (w/entertainment), whirlpool. **Rates:** $118–$125 S or D; $130–$150 ste. Extra person $10. Children under age 17 stay free. Parking: Outdoor, free. Frequent guest program. Weekend packages available with two weeks' notice. AE, DC, DISC, MC, V.

INN

≣≣≣≣ **Hotel Carter and Carter House**

301 L St, 95501 (Old Town); tel 707/444-8062 or toll free 800/404-1390; fax 707/444-8067. 1 acre. Perfectly proportioned, seamless blend of old-world refinement and California informality. The decor combines fine European antique furnishings with contemporary American art. Very restful. **Rooms:** 33 rms and stes. CI 3pm/CO 11am. No smoking. Guest rooms are beautifully appointed and very comfortable. Choose between the Inn (23 rooms and suites), the Cottage (3 rooms), or the Original House (7 rooms and suites). **Amenities:** 🛏 🗏 🍽 Cable TV w/movies, refrig, dataport, VCR, CD/tape player, bathrobes. No A/C. All units w/minibars, some w/fireplaces, some w/whirlpools. **Services:** ✗ 🗝 🚐 🖼 ↩ Twice-daily maid svce, car-rental desk, masseur, babysitting, afternoon tea and wine/sherry served. Included is an exquisite breakfast, late afternoon hors d'oeuvres with wine, and late evening tea with cookies and cordials. **Facilities:** ⊠ 🚶 1 restaurant (bkfst and dinner only; *see* "Restaurants" below), guest lounge. Gift shop and wine store features 1,200 American and European wines; owner (aka "The Wine Guy") is extremely knowledgeable. CD and video library. **Rates (BB):** $65–$195 S or D; $185–$275 ste. Extra person $25. Children under age 2 stay free. AP and MAP rates avail. Parking: Outdoor, free. AE, CB, DC, DISC, JCB, MC, V.

RESTAURANTS 🍴

Cafe Marina and Woodley's Bar

Startare Dr; tel 707/443-2233. CA 255 W exit off US 101. **Seafood.** Popular, informal seafood restaurant with fine outdoor dining deck overlooking the marina. Grilled, broiled, or fried fish and shellfish, plus burgers and steaks. **FYI:** Reservations not accepted. Children's menu. **Open:** Daily 7am–10pm. **Prices:** Main courses $9–$17. AE, DC, DISC, MC, V. 🛥 🖼 🚶

★ Cafe Waterfront

102 F St; tel 707/443-9190. **Seafood.** Best seafood in town, in a lively setting with a view of sailboats. Entree choices include grilled oysters, sautéed scallops, clam fritters, and snapper. Good beers on tap; two bed-and-breakfast suites upstairs. **FYI:** Reservations accepted. Jazz. **Open:** Daily 9am–9pm. **Prices:** Main courses $8–$15. MC, V. 🖼

★ Lost Coast Brewery

617 4th St (Downtown); tel 707/445-4480. Between G and H Sts. **Burgers/Pub.** America's first microbewery to be run by two women. Set in a restored 1892 frame building, the award-winning pub offers eight Eureka-crafted beers on tap, plus the usual pub-grub (onion rings, deep-fried mushrooms, oyster shooters, burgers, and fish-and-chips). Tofu burgers are also available. **FYI:** Reservations accepted. Piano. Beer and wine only. **Open:** Daily 11am–1am. **Prices:** Main courses $5–$10. MC, V. 🚶

🍷★ Restaurant 301

In Hotel Carter, 301 L St (Old Town); tel 707/444-8062. L St exit off US 101. **New American.** Elegantly presented, creative cuisine from well-known resident chef Jean-Louis Hamiche. The wine list includes more than 1,000 selections (some quite rare). A well-priced five-course prix fixe menu with appropriate wines is an option. Exquisitely sauced entrees might be baked Dungeness crab, grilled salmon, or Mark's chicken cacciatore, followed by inspired versions of popular desserts such as bread pudding and crème brûlée. A tour is offered of the chef's immense kitchen garden, and a wine shop on the premises stocks the entire wine menu. **FYI:** Reservations recommended. Jazz. **Open:** Breakfast daily 7:30–10am; dinner daily 6–9:30pm. **Prices:** Main courses $12–$20; prix fixe $28–$38. AE, DC, DISC, MC, V. 🚶

The Rib Room

In the Eureka Inn, 518 7th St; tel 707/442-6441. 2 blocks E of 7th St exit off US 101. **American.** Enhanced by nice lighting, a fireplace, and fresh flowers, this meat-eaters haven has a regal dark wood interior and burgundy-colored leather booths. Features grilled or roasted meats, poultry and seasonal game, plus grilled or poached fish, all finely cooked and presented. Good bets are the grilled medallions of chicken Helena or roast rack of garlic-rosemary lamb. Traditional tableside preparations of caesar salads and cherries jubilee. The award-winning wine list highlights California selections with over 160 cabernets. The new "Monday Club" offers members cigars, cognacs, and single-malt whiskeys with a private bartender and hors d'oeuvres. **FYI:** Reservations recommended. Jazz. **Open:** Daily 5–10pm. **Prices:** Main courses $12–$20. AE, DC, DISC, MC, V. 🅥🅟 🚶

Samurai Japanese Cuisine

621 5th St (Downtown); tel 707/442-6802. Between G and H Sts. **Japanese.** The clean, basic decor acts as a good backdrop for the sushi and other dishes prepared from very fresh fish.

Usual favorites include tempura, sukiyaki, and teriyaki. Sushi bar. **FYI:** Reservations accepted. Beer and wine only. **Open:** Tues–Sat 5–9pm. **Prices:** Main courses $10–$15. MC, V. &

ATTRACTIONS

Clarke Memorial Museum
240 E St; tel 707/443-1947. The main attraction of this museum is its world-class collection of Native American basketry and artifacts, including works of the Hoopa, Wiyot, Yurok, and Karuk people. Humboldt County history is also covered, with collections of pioneer artifacts, 19th- and 20th-century firearms, oil paintings, Victorian furnishings and decorative arts, and examples of early commercial enterprise. **Open:** Tues–Sat noon–4pm. **Free**

Sequoia Park Zoo
3414 W St; tel 707/442-6552 or 441-4203. This small zoo is surrounded by a 46-acre redwood grove. Among the numerous animal exhibits are a children's playground, picnic areas, and a duck pond. **Open:** Peak (Mem Day–Labor Day) Tues–Sun 10am–7pm. Reduced hours off-season. **Free**

Blue Ox Millworks
At foot of X St; tel 707/444-3437 or toll free 800/248-4259. A working full-production millworks, this facility is also a living museum. It uses machinery from 1852 to 1940 to produce custom and reproduction materials for construction and restoration projects across the country. Visitors are welcome to tour the shop, via elevated walkways and platforms, to see how intricate items of wood, plaster, and metal were fabricated during the Victorian era; workers on hand answer questions about the machinery or their current projects. Also part of the facility are a small sawmill and a blacksmith shop; displays of old-time logging machinery; and a re-created logging "skid" camp. Tours take about 1 hour; casual dress and low-heeled shoes advised. **Open:** Mon–Sat 9am–5pm, Sun 11am–4pm. Closed some hols. $$

Fairfield

ATTRACTION

Anheuser-Busch Fairfield Brewery
3101 Busch Dr; tel 707/429-7595. Guided, 1-hour tours offer a live demonstration of the brewing process and relate the history of one of the world's largest producers of beer. Children are welcome on tour, but not allowed on production floor. **Open:** Tues–Sat 9am–4pm. Closed some hols. **Free**

Fair Oaks

See Citrus Heights

Fallbrook
Located on coastal hills to the west of forested mountains, Fallbrook is tucked behind the huge Camp Pendleton Marine Corps Base. **Information:** Fallbrook Chamber of Commerce, 233-A E Mission Rd, Fallbrook 92028 (tel 619/728-5845).

MOTELS

Fallbrook Travelodge
1608 S Mission Rd, 92028; tel 619/723-1127 or toll free 800/578-7878; fax 619/723-2917. Pala Rd/CA 76 exit off I-15; take Pala Rd W 5 mi to Mission Rd and turn N. Located on a main street, with some traffic noise during the day. **Rooms:** 36 rms, stes, and effic. CI 2pm/CO 11am. Nonsmoking rms avail. Rooms have large bathrooms but require improved maintenance. Efficiencies have two-burner stoves and small refrigerators. **Amenities:** A/C, cable TV w/movies. Some units w/terraces. **Services:** Car-rental desk. Free coffee in lobby. **Facilities:** & Whirlpool. **Rates:** $50–$55 S or D; $75–$100 ste; $60–$75 effic. Extra person $5. Children under age 18 stay free. Parking: Outdoor, free. AE, DC, DISC, MC, V.

La Estanica Inn
3135 S Old Hwy 395, 92028; tel 619/723-2888. CA 76/Pala Rd exit off I-15. Looks like a Mexican hacienda, with cream-colored stucco walls and a red tile roof, against the backdrop of the unspoiled countryside. The entire property is clean, attractive, and well maintained. **Rooms:** 41 rms, stes, and effic. CI 1:30pm/CO noon. Nonsmoking rms avail. Decor is southwestern-style. Some rooms have spa baths, two sinks, and large showers. **Amenities:** A/C, cable TV, in-rm safe. Some units w/terraces, some w/whirlpools. **Services:** Car-rental desk, babysitting. **Facilities:** 1 restaurant (lunch and dinner only), 1 bar, whirlpool, washer/dryer. Very attractive restaurant. Nearby are golf courses, hot-air ballooning, and wineries. **Rates:** $68–$78 S or D; $90–$139 ste; $50–$60 effic. Extra person $10. Children under age 12 stay free. Parking: Indoor/outdoor, free. Parking: Outdoor, free. Rates often lower than published. AE, CB, DC, MC, V.

RESORT

Pala Mesa Resort
2001 Old Hwy 395, 92054; tel 619/728-5881 or toll free 800/722-4700; fax 619/723-8292. CA 76/Pala Rd exit off I-15. 205 acres. This "golfer's heaven" is a lovely place with well-kept grounds and plenty of activities for the entire family. Good value. **Rooms:** 135 rms and stes; 2 cottages/villas. CI 4pm/CO noon. Nonsmoking rms avail. Rooms are spacious. Attractive decor features marble-countered bathrooms and upholstered easy chairs. **Amenities:** A/C, cable TV, dataport. All units w/minibars, some w/terraces. **Services:** Twice-daily maid svce, car-rental desk, social director, masseur, babysitting. Very hospitable staff.

Room-service menu also served poolside. Will arrange tours to wineries and other area attractions. **Facilities:** 🔲 ▶18 🔲 🔲 🔲 🔲 ⚡ 3 restaurants (*see* "Restaurants" below), 1 bar (w/entertainment), basketball, volleyball, lawn games, racquetball, whirlpool. Driving range, putting green, and pro shop. Golf and tennis lessons available. **Rates:** $110 S or D; $135 ste; $250 cottage/villa. MAP rates avail. Parking: Outdoor, free. AE, DC, MC, V.

RESTAURANTS 🍴

Alexander's
In Pala Mesa Resort, 2001 Old Hwy 395; tel 619/728-5881. CA 76 exit off I-15. **Californian.** Alexander's offers indoor and outdoor dining with a golf-course view. Dining room is very attractive, spacious and gracious, with a country-club feel. Large tables are topped with white tablecloths and fresh flowers. Emphasis is on fresh local produce, especially avocado and citrus. **FYI:** Reservations recommended. Guitar. **Open:** Breakfast daily 6–11am; lunch daily 11:30am–2pm; dinner Sun–Thurs 5–9pm, Fri–Sat 5–10pm; brunch Sun 10:30am–2pm. **Prices:** Main courses $16–$23. AE, MC, V. 🔲 ⚡

Garden Center Cafe
1625 S Mission Rd; tel 619/728-4147. Pala Rd/CA 76 exit off I-15, take Pala Rd W 5 mi. **Californian.** This building formerly housed a garden nursery, which explains the inspiration for the decor. It's charming: flowers galore, floral-print chairs, impressionist-style paintings, ceiling fans, and floor-to-ceiling windows. The house specialty is southwest chicken salad. Raspberry muffins, cinnamon rolls, scones, and desserts are all made on the premises. **FYI:** Reservations not accepted. Beer and wine only. **Open:** Mon–Fri 7:30am–2:30pm, Sat 7:30am–2:30pm, Sun 8am–2pm. **Prices:** Lunch main courses $6–$7. MC, V. 🔲 ⚡

Ferndale

INN 🔲

📧📧📧 **The Gingerbread Mansion**
400 Berding St, 95536 (Downtown); tel 707/786-4000 or toll free 800/952-4136; fax 707/786-4381. 5 mi W of CA 101. Largely unchanged since the late-19th century, the historic landmark village of Ferndale has many fine Victorian mansions. Unsuitable for children under 12. **Rooms:** 10 rms and stes. CI 3pm/CO 11am. No smoking. Elegant accommodations are romantically appointed with fireplaces and claw-foot tubs. The Empire Suite is one of the most opulent hotel rooms on the north coast, with fireplaces and marble floors, gorgeous wallpaper, and Ionic columns. **Amenities:** 🔲 🔲 Refrig, bathrobes. No A/C, phone, or TV. Some units w/terraces, some w/fireplaces, some w/whirlpools. Some rooms have TVs. **Services:** ✗ 🔲 🔲 Twice-daily maid svce, afternoon tea and wine/sherry served. Full high tea served in

four parlors every afternoon. **Facilities:** 🔲 Guest lounge. Perfectly manicured English gardens. Complimentary use of bicycles. **Rates (BB):** Peak (Apr–Dec) $120–$290 S; $140–$350 D; $150–$350 ste. Extra person $40. Min stay special events. Lower rates off-season. Parking: Outdoor, free. AE, MC, V.

Fern Valley
See Idyllwild

Fish Camp
See Yosemite National Park

Folsom
See also Rancho Cordova

HOTEL 🔲

📧📧 **Radisson Inn at Lake Natoma**
702 Gold Lake Dr, 95630; tel 916/351-1500 or toll free 800/333-3333; fax 916/351-1511. 20 mi E of Sacramento. Folsom Blvd exit off US 50; follow signs to Old Folsom. Quiet property adjacent to American River Parkway, in park surroundings. Although newish, hotel is aging prematurely. People working the front desk can be curt. **Rooms:** 131 rms and stes. CI 3pm/CO noon. Nonsmoking rms avail. Furnishings showing wear; cracks in sink. **Amenities:** 🔲 🔲 🔲 A/C, voice mail. Some units w/fireplaces, some w/whirlpools. **Services:** ✗ 🔲 🔲 🔲 Masseur, babysitting. **Facilities:** 🔲 🔲 🔲 🔲 ⚡ 1 restaurant, 1 bar, basketball, volleyball, sauna. Small pool amid lovely grounds; nine-hole putting green. Cafe/bar has outdoor tables. **Rates:** Peak (Sept–June) $115 S; $125 D; $210–$220 ste. Extra person $10. Children under age 16 stay free. Lower rates off-season. Parking: Outdoor, free. "Romance" package for $179 includes room, breakfast in bed, massage for two, champagne on arrival, cheese and fruit platter, and late checkout. AE, CB, DC, DISC, ER, MC, V.

Forestville
See Guerneville

Fort Bragg
This community hugs the coast in the shadow of the massive Georgia Pacific Corporation lumber mills, and the logging giant is the town's economic lifeline. The harbor is host to the

World's Largest Salmon Barbecue held in July. **Information:** Fort Bragg–Mendocino Coast Chamber of Commerce, 332 N Main St, PO Box 1141, Fort Bragg 95437 (tel 707/ 961-6300).

MOTEL 🏨

☰ Vista Manor Lodge/Best Western

1100 N Main St, 95437; tel 707/964-4776 or toll free 800/ 821-9498. Located across from a white-sand beach, reachable via an access tunnel. Extensive grounds not landscaped. **Rooms:** 52 rms and stes; 2 cottages/villas. CI 3pm/CO 11am. Nonsmoking rms avail. Bare and basic. **Amenities:** 📺 Cable TV. No A/C. Some units w/terraces, some w/fireplaces. **Services:** Free morning coffee and doughnuts. **Facilities:** 🚣 1 beach (ocean), volleyball, lawn games. Large indoor swimming pool right off the lobby. Volleyball net. **Rates:** Peak (May 24–Sept 20) $40–$95 S; $45–$100 D; $65–$125 ste; $100–$200 cottage/villa. Extra person $5. Lower rates off-season. Parking: Outdoor, free. AE, DC, DISC, MC, V.

INNS

☰☰ The Grey Whale Inn

615 N Main, 95437; tel 707/964-0640 or toll free 800/ 382-7244; fax 707/964-4408. 1 acre. Stately 1915 hospital building, well decorated but too close to highway traffic. Unsuitable for children under 6. **Rooms:** 14 rms. CI noon/ CO noon. No smoking. Huge rooms. Albion Terrace is cozy, with lovely antiques. Unique Navarro Ridge is very big. **Amenities:** 📺 ☕ 📹 Cable TV, refrig. No A/C. Some units w/terraces, some w/fireplaces, 1 w/whirlpool. **Services:** Breakfast menu changes daily. **Facilities:** � Guest lounge w/TV. Pool table room, gardens. **Rates (BB):** Peak (Apr–Nov) $60–$140 S; $80–$160 D. Extra person $20. Min stay wknds. Lower rates off-season. Parking: Outdoor, free. Winter rates: 20% off first night, 50% off second night AE, DISC, MC, V.

☰☰☰ Noyo River Lodge

500 Casa Del Noyo, 95437; tel 707/964-8045 or toll free 800/628-1126. A large breakfast and lounging deck overlooking harbor and river affords a picturesque view of fishing boats and sea lions. Wonderful gardens surround the inn. **Rooms:** 16 rms and stes. CI 3pm/CO 11am. No smoking. Suites in main building have sitting areas with harbor views, fabulous antiques, and spacious dimensions. **Amenities:** ☕ 📹 Cable TV. No A/C or phone. Some units w/terraces, some w/fireplaces. **Services:** Afternoon tea and wine/sherry served. Coffee and fruit always available in lobby. Nice breakfasts. **Facilities:** Ꮕ Breakfast room has a fireplace and view of the harbor. **Rates (BB):** Peak (Mar–Nov) $90–$125 S or D; $140 ste. Extra person $15. Min stay wknds. Lower rates off-season. Parking: Outdoor, free. 50% off second night's stay, Sun–Thurs. AE, MC, V.

RESTAURANTS 🍴

The Cliff House

1011 S Main St; tel 707/961-0255. **Californian/Seafood.** Pleasant dining room with floor-to-ceiling windows; all tables enjoy view of the Noyo River and the harbor. The creative menu offers seafood appetizers, smoked duck pasta, chicken in béarnaise sauce, and daily specials. **FYI:** Reservations accepted. Children's menu. **Open:** Daily 4–9pm. **Prices:** Main courses $10–$19. AE, DISC, MC, V. 🍱 Ꮕ

Country Gardens Restaurant and Grill

In Mendocino Botanical Gardens, 18220 N CA 1; tel 707/ 964-7474. 1 mi S of downtown Fort Bragg. **Californian/ Mediterranean.** Simple floral decor. An outdoor deck has umbrella-topped tables in a garden setting. There are many vegetarian specialties, along with fresh grilled fish sandwiches, mushroom crêpe torte, and Chinese chicken salad at lunch. Heartier dinner fare includes grilled steak, kebabs, and shrimp and scallion fritters. **FYI:** Reservations accepted. Beer and wine only. **Open:** Lunch Tues–Sat 11:30am– 2:30pm; dinner Tues–Sat 5:30–9:30pm; brunch Sun 10am– 3pm. **Prices:** Main courses $10–$18. MC, V. 🍱 Ꮕ

North Coast Brewing Company

444 Main St; tel 707/964-2739. **Pub/American.** American-style pub featuring a taproom and high ceilings. Besides freshly brewed beer, the menu offers grilled fish, cajun popcorn shrimp, pasta, clam chowder, burgers, and barbecued pork. The salmon is house-smoked and the fish and chips are the best on the coast. Brewery tours given Tues–Fri at 3:30pm and Sat at 1:30pm. **FYI:** Reservations not accepted. Jazz. Beer and wine only. **Open:** Tues–Fri 4–11pm, Sat 2–11pm, Sun noon–5pm. **Prices:** Main courses $6–$17. MC, V. Ꮕ

$ Viraporn's Thai Cafe

Chestnut at Main (Downtown); tel 707/964-7931. ¼ block off CA 1. **Thai.** This Thai diner, in a tiny location, is very popular for lunch and dinner. The Thai owner is also the chef and dishes up traditional favorites such as chicken satay, squid salad, shrimp curry, pad Thai, and ginger fish. **FYI:** Reservations not accepted. Beer and wine only. **Open:** Lunch Mon–Fri 11:30am–2pm; dinner Mon–Tues 5–9pm, Thurs– Sun 5–9pm. **Prices:** Main courses $6–$10. No CC.

ATTRACTIONS 🏛

MacKerricher State Park

CA 1; tel 707/937-5804. 3 mi N of town. This 1,700-acre park offers trails for biking, hiking, and horseback riding, as well as 142 campsites. The eight-mile-long "Haul Road," an old logging road, offers fine ocean vistas all the way to Ten Mile River. Harbor seals make their home at the park's Laguna Point. Ricochet Ridge Ranch, on CA 1 at the park entrance, offers trail rides along the beach and in the park. **Open:** Daily sunrise–sundown. **Free**

Mendocino Coast Botanical Gardens
18220 N CA 1; tel 707/964-4352. Several thousand varieties of native and cultivated plants grow here, making it a garden for all seasons. Major collections in the 47-acre gardens include hybrid and species rhododendrons, species fuchsias, heathers, perennials, succulents, ivies, dwarf conifers, heritage roses, and camellias. Pods of migrating gray whales can be seen passing by in December and March. Picnickers welcome. **Open:** Peak (Mar–Oct) daily 9am–5pm. Reduced hours off-season. **$$**

Skunk Train (California Western Railroad)
Fort Bragg Depot; tel 707/964-6371. These trains, which can be boarded at the foot of Laurel Ave, travel 40 miles inland along the Redwood Highway (US 101) to Willits. The serpentine route traverses 31 bridges and trestles and two deep tunnels, encompassing scenery from forest to fields of wildflowers, grazing cattle, and apple orchards. The nickname "skunk" came from the trains' original gasoline engines. Today the journey is made by deisel-powered trains and motorcars.

The round trip takes six–seven hours, with time to lunch in Willits before the return leg of the journey. Half-day trips are offered on weekends throughout the year, and daily from mid-June–early Sept. Call for schedule and fare information. **Open:** Round-trip, daily; phone for schedule. **$$$$**

Georgia–Pacific Corporation Tree Nursery
275 N Main St; tel 707/964-5651. Located at the junction of CA 1 and Walnut St. Visitors are welcome to stop in for a free look at some three million small trees and seedlings. Visitor center, self-guided nature trail, picnic area. **Open:** Mon–Fri 8am–4pm. **Free**

Foster City

Jutting into the bay on the tip of Brewer Island, Foster City borders the San Francisco Bay National Wildlife Refuge. **Information:** Foster City Chamber of Commerce, 1125 E Hillsdale Blvd #114, Foster City 94404 (tel 415/573-7600).

HOTELS 🏨

≣≣≣ Courtyard by Marriott
550 Shell Blvd, 94404; tel 415/377-0600 or toll free 800/321-2211; fax 415/377-1983. Foster City Blvd exit off CA 92. Pleasant lounge and lobby with European-style furnishings and a fireplace. A courtyard garden is visible through many windows. Very good values. **Rooms:** 147 rms and stes. CI 3pm/CO 1pm. Nonsmoking rms avail. Rooms have good desks for conducting business. **Amenities:** 🛁 🖥 A/C, cable TV w/movies. Some units w/minibars, all w/terraces. **Services:** ✗ 🚗 🗽 🖐 Babysitting. Breakfast bar and business services. **Facilities:** 🛗 ⛳ 🏊 👤 1 restaurant (bkfst and dinner only), whirlpool, washer/dryer. Beautiful indoor pool with a partial glass ceiling in a spacious setting with nice

views. **Rates:** Peak (May–Oct) $110 S; $120 D; $125–$135 ste. Extra person $10. Children under age 3 stay free. Lower rates off-season. Parking: Outdoor, free. AE, CB, DC, DISC, MC, V.

≣≣≣ Holiday Inn Foster City
1221 Chess Dr, 94404; tel 415/570-5700 or toll free 800/477-5700; fax 415/570-0540. Foster City Blvd exit off CA 92. Atrium-style hotel. **Rooms:** 238 rms and stes. Executive level. CI 2pm/CO noon. Nonsmoking rms avail. Rooms facing atrium are darker and may be noisier. **Amenities:** 🛁 🖥 🖐 A/C, cable TV w/movies. Some units w/minibars, some w/terraces. **Services:** ✗ 🗝 🚗 🗽 🖐 🦺 Twice-daily maid svce, car-rental desk, children's program, babysitting. **Facilities:** 🛗 ⛳ 🏊 👤 2 restaurants, 2 bars, sauna, whirlpool, washer/dryer. **Rates (CP):** $89 S or D; $225 ste. Extra person $10. Children under age 18 stay free. Parking: Indoor/outdoor, free. AE, CB, DC, DISC, MC, V.

Fountain Valley

HOTEL 🏨

≣≣≣ Courtyard by Marriott
9950 Slater Ave, 92708; tel 714/968-5775 or toll free 800/321-2211; fax 714/968-0112. Brookhurst exit off I-405; go north; left at first light onto Slater; hotel on left. Geared toward the leisure traveler. Attractive pool area. **Rooms:** 150 rms and stes. CI 3pm/CO noon. Nonsmoking rms avail. Clean and adequate. **Amenities:** 🛁 🖥 A/C, cable TV w/movies. Some units w/terraces. All rooms have hot-water dispensers and irons. **Services:** 🗽 🖐 **Facilities:** 🛗 ⛳ 🏊 👤 1 restaurant (bkfst only), 1 bar, whirlpool, washer/dryer. **Rates:** $69 S or D; $89 ste. Children under age 21 stay free. Parking: Outdoor, free. Breakfast plan avail. AE, DC, DISC, MC, V.

Fremont

Named after California pioneer John Fremont, the city at various times has been a Spanish mission trade center, a Gold Rush supply stop, a resort featuring artesian spring water, and a Hollywood filming location. Today, Central Park and adjacent Lake Elizabeth are popular urban recreation areas. **Information:** Fremont Chamber of Commerce, 2201 Walnut Ave #110, Fremont 94538 (tel 510/795-2244).

HOTELS 🏨

≣≣ Best Western Thunderbird Inn
5400 Mowry Ave, 94538; tel 510/792-4300 or toll free 800/541-4909; fax 510/792-2643. Mowry E exit off I-880. Although close to the freeway, this lowrise property has a rural ambience because of its setting on landscaped, tree-studded acres. A good value. **Rooms:** 122 rms and stes. CI 2pm/CO

noon. Nonsmoking rms avail. Recent redecoration. **Amenities:** 🔌 🛁 A/C, cable TV w/movies. Some units w/terraces. Refrigerators and hair dryers available upon request. VCR rental available. **Services:** 🏖 🍽 🐾 Children's program, babysitting. Use of computer, fax, and copy machine at front desk. **Facilities:** 🎱 [50] 🚴 1 restaurant, 1 bar (w/entertainment), lawn games, sauna, whirlpool. Volleyball court. Complimentary use of nearby fitness center. **Rates (CP):** $78 S; $88 D; $125 ste. Extra person $5. Children under age 15 stay free. Parking: Outdoor, free. AE, DC, DISC, MC, V.

🎗🎗 Courtyard by Marriott
47000 Lakeview Blvd, 94538 (Bayside Business Park); tel 510/656-1800 or toll free 800/321-2211; fax 510/656-2441. Warren Ave W exit off I-880 S; Gateway Blvd exit off I-880 N. Located in a business park and oriented to the business traveler. **Rooms:** 146 rms and stes. CI 3pm/CO 1pm. Nonsmoking rms avail. **Amenities:** 🔌 🛁 A/C, cable TV w/movies. Some units w/terraces. Suites have refrigerators. **Services:** ✗ 🏖 🍽 **Facilities:** 🎱 🏓 [45] 🚴 1 restaurant, 1 bar, whirlpool, washer/dryer. Large, well-designed indoor pool and whirlpool. More extensive Club Sport gym charges $4 daily fee to guests and is located within walking distance. **Rates:** $110 S or D; $125 ste. Extra person $10. Children under age 18 stay free. Parking: Outdoor, free. AE, DC, DISC, MC, V.

🎗🎗🎗 Residence Inn by Marriott
5400 Farwell Place, 94536; tel 510/794-5900 or toll free 800/331-3131; fax 510/793-6587. Mowry E exit off I-880. An attractive townhouselike complex close to restaurants, shopping, and the freeway. **Rooms:** 80 stes. CI 3pm/CO noon. Nonsmoking rms avail. All suites have full kitchens seating from two people in the studio to four in the other guest rooms. **Amenities:** 🔌 🛁 📺 A/C, cable TV w/movies, refrig. All units w/fireplaces. Each room contains an iron and ironing board. Games are available from front desk. **Services:** ✗ 🚐 🏖 🍽 🐾 Complimentary social hour Monday-Thursday. **Facilities:** 🎱 [40] 🚴 Whirlpool, washer/dryer. Sport court for volleyball and paddle tennis. **Rates (CP):** $149–$169 ste. Children under age 18 stay free. Parking: Outdoor, free. AE, CB, DC, DISC, MC, V.

ATTRACTIONS 🏛

Mission San Jose Chapel and Museum
43300 Mission Blvd; tel 510/657-1797. Mission San Jose was founded June 11, 1797, the 14th of the 21 Spanish Missions in California. The adobe church is a 1985 replica of the 1809 original; its interior was extensively decorated by following detailed descriptions made during an 1830s decorating project. A small museum containing mission-era artifacts and exhibits on the Ohlone Indians and the restoration is located in a portion of the padres' original living quarters. **Open:** Daily 10am–5pm. $

San Francisco Bay National Wildlife Refuge
1 Marshlands Rd; tel 510/792-0222. Created in 1972, this 23,000-acre refuge preserves a variety of natural habitats,

protecting a vast array of plant and animal life. In the course of a year, more than 250 species of birds visit San Francisco Bay, which provides food, nesting sites, and resting space for migratory birds on the Pacific flyway.

The visitors center is located a half mile south of the Dumbarton Bridge (eastern side), off Thornton Rd (follow signs). Here visitors will find indoor exhibits and a self-guided trail introducing the bay environment and local wildlife. Schedules of naturalist programs and other events can be found here. Books, posters, and other items are for sale.

Miles of trails crisscross the refuge and offer opportunities to glimpse rabbits, ground squirrels, gopher snakes, and other small animals. Boating is permitted in some areas (canoes or kayaks recommended). Some fishing and hunting is permitted (phone ahead for specifics). Camping is not permitted in the refuge, but sites are available at several nearby parks and beaches. **Open:** Visitors center Tues–Sun 10am–5pm. Environmental Education Center, Sat–Sun 10am–5pm. **Free**

Central Park
40000 Paseo Padre Pkwy; tel 510/791-4340. This 450-acre park was created around 83-acre Lake Elizabeth in the 1960s. Located at the south end of the park is a swim lagoon with 2½ acres of swimming area surrounded by a 2½-acre beach (swimming fee charged). Throughout the park are numerous recreational opportunities, including several playgrounds, play fields, drop-in picnic areas, snack bars, fishing areas, boat launching facilities and rentals, a fitness course, 18 tennis courts, and a driving range. **Open:** Daily dawn–10pm. **Free**

Coyote Hills Regional Park
8000 Patterson Ranch Rd; tel 510/795-9385. A 1,000-acre wetlands preserve and wildlife sanctuary, this park contains four Native American shell mounds that span a period of 2,200 years. The largest site has been set up for group programs by park naturalists. The Visitors Center contains exhibits and has naturalists on hand to answer questions and distribute information.

Hiking, bridle, and bicycle trails lead through all of the major habitat areas and along the Coyote Hills. A variety of naturalist programs are offered to the public (usually on weekends). **Open:** Park, daily 8am–sundown; Visitors Center, Tues–Sun and hols 9:30am–5pm. $

Fresno

See also Selma

Located in the heart of the San Joaquin Valley, Fresno is both an agricultural center and a busy commercial city. Several museums celebrate the history of the area, while Roeding Park is a great urban escape, and the Tower District caters to artist types and college students with coffeehouses, book-stores, and galleries. **Information:** Fresno Convention & Visitors Bureau, 808 M St, Fresno 93721 (tel 209/233-0836).

HOTELS 🏨

🏳🏳🏳 Fresno Hilton Hotel

1055 Van Ness, 93721 (Downtown); tel 209/485-9000 or toll free 800/445-8667 in the US, 800/221-2424 in Canada; fax 209/485-3210. Ventura St exit E off CA 99. Nine-story, downtown hotel conveniently located near government and financial offices, public transportation, and freeways. Popular convention site. Favored by businesswomen because of good security. Rooms and public areas completely remodeled. **Rooms:** 192 rms and stes. Executive level. CI 3pm/CO noon. Nonsmoking rms avail. King accommodations feature recliner or sofa. Twenty-six rooms are handicapped accessible. **Amenities:** 🛁 🍸 📺 A/C, cable TV w/movies. Some units w/terraces. Irons and ironing boards in every room on 7th floor. Many rooms have dataports. Refrigerators, VCRs, and microwaves available on request. **Services:** ✕ 🖃 🚗 🖂 🎷 🐕 Car-rental desk. **Facilities:** 🛗 🏋️ [2400] 🖥️ ⚕️ 2 restaurants, 1 bar, whirlpool, washer/dryer. Skyroom on 9th floor offers banquet facilities and view of the city. Lovely ballroom. Security-patrolled underground parking. **Rates:** $59–$119 S or D; $149–$359 ste. Children under age 18 stay free. Parking: Indoor, free. Special corporate rates and services, senior rate, and Hilton promotional rates. AE, CB, DC, DISC, MC, V.

🏳🏳🏳 Holiday Inn Airport

5090 E Clinton Ave, 93727 (Fresno Airport); tel 209/252-3611 or toll free 800/HOLIDAY; fax 209/456-8243. This spacious facility arranged around a 15,000-square-foot atrium was completely refurbished in 1995. All rooms facing atrium on ground level have sliding glass doors. **Rooms:** 210 rms. CI 3pm/CO noon. Nonsmoking rms avail. 65 rooms surrounding atrium have both king-size beds and sofa beds. **Amenities:** 🛁 🍸 A/C, satel TV w/movies, dataport. Some units w/terraces. Refrigerators available. **Services:** ✕ 🚗 🖂 🎷 Babysitting. **Facilities:** 🛗 🏋️ [400] ⚕️ 1 restaurant, 1 bar (w/entertainment), whirlpool, washer/dryer. King Tut's Wah Wah Hut lounge popular for dancing. Complimentary pass and transportation provided to nearby family fitness center. **Rates:** $79–$94 S or D. Extra person $8. Children under age 18 stay free. Parking: Outdoor, free. Special weekend romance package features chocolates, champagne, and breakfast. AE, DC, DISC, JCB, MC, V.

🏳🏳🏳 Hotel Inn Centre Plaza

2233 Ventura Ave, 93721 (Downtown); tel 209/268-1000 or toll free 800/HOLIDAY; fax 209/486-6625. Exit off CA 99. Part of the downtown Fresno Convention Center complex. Elegant, ten-year-old highrise has attractive atrium lobby with waterfall. Renovation just completed. **Rooms:** 320 rms and stes. CI 3pm/CO noon. Nonsmoking rms avail. Comfortable and spacious. **Amenities:** 🛁 🍸 A/C, cable TV w/movies.

Some units w/minibars. **Services:** ✕ 🚗 🖂 🎷 🐕 Twice-daily maid svce, babysitting. **Facilities:** 🛗 🏋️ [1400] ⚕️ 2 restaurants, 2 bars, sauna, whirlpool, beauty salon. **Rates:** $89 S; $99 D; $109 ste. Extra person $8. Children under age 19 stay free. Min stay special events. Parking: Indoor/outdoor, free. AE, CB, DC, DISC, MC, V.

🏳🏳🏳 Piccadilly Inn Airport

5115 E McKinley Ave, 93727 (Fresno Airport); tel 209/251-6000 or toll free 800/HOTEL-US, 800/HOTEL-CA in CA; fax 209/251-6956. Comfortable hotel, located across from the Fresno Air Terminal. **Rooms:** 185 rms and stes. Executive level. CI 3pm/CO 1pm. Nonsmoking rms avail. **Amenities:** 🛁 🍸 📺 🍷 A/C, satel TV w/movies. Some units w/terraces. Some rooms have refrigerators. **Services:** ✕ 🚗 🖂 🎷 Car-rental desk. **Facilities:** 🛗 🏋️ [300] 🖥️ ⚕️ 2 restaurants, 1 bar (w/entertainment), whirlpool, washer/dryer. The Steak and Anchor Restaurant and Lounge, which serves award-winning ribs, rates highly with Fresno residents. **Rates:** $94 S; $104 D; $185–$240 ste. Extra person $10. Children under age 18 stay free. AP rates avail. Parking: Outdoor, free. Weekend discounts available. AE, CB, DC, DISC, EC, ER, JCB, MC, V.

🏳🏳🏳 Piccadilly Inn University

4961 N Cedar Ave, 93726; tel 209/224-4200 or toll free 800/HOTEL-US, 800/HOTEL-CA in CA; fax 209/227-2382. Shaw Ave exit off CA 99 or CA 41. Excellent full-service hotel close to university, restaurants, shopping, and mountain-access routes. Beautifully decorated and maintained property; popular for meetings. **Rooms:** 190 rms and stes. CI 3pm/CO 1pm. Nonsmoking rms avail. Six "green" rooms offer air purification systems, as well as hypoallergenic soaps. Six luxurious suites, each decorated differently, feature exquisite furnishings, robes, fully stocked refrigerators, and wet bars. Standard rooms beautifully decorated with floral spreads and drapes, valances, and dark wood furniture. **Amenities:** 🛁 🍸 📺 🍷 A/C, cable TV w/movies, dataport, voice mail. Some units w/minibars, some w/whirlpools. Irons and small ironing boards in every room. Complimentary cookies. Some rooms have refrigerators and turndown service. **Services:** ✕ 🚗 🖂 🎷 **Facilities:** 🛗 🏋️ [800] ⚕️ 1 bar, whirlpool, washer/dryer. Well-equipped exercise room (accessible via room key) open 24 hours. **Rates (BB):** $94–$104 S or D; $195–$235 ste. Extra person $10. Children under age 18 stay free. Parking: Outdoor, free. Special Parliament Club rates and services for frequent travelers. Honeymoon special includes champagne, truffles, robes, and one night free on anniversary date. Special lower promotional rates Nov–Jan. AE, DC, DISC, MC, V.

🏳🏳🏳 Ramada Inn

324 E Shaw, 93710; tel 209/224-4040 or toll free 800/241-0756; fax 209/222-4017. CA 41 N exit off CA 99 N; Shaw Ave exit off CA 99 S. This centrally located hotel is a pleasant place to hang your hat. Within walking distance of Fashion Fair shopping mall. **Rooms:** 167 rms, stes, and effic.

Executive level. CI 3pm/CO noon. Nonsmoking rms avail. Nicely appointed, spacious rooms. **Amenities:** A/C, cable TV w/movies. Some units w/minibars, some w/terraces. Four "green suites" available for those with allergies, with special filtration systems and biodegradable soaps. **Services:** Car-rental desk, babysitting. **Facilities:** 1 restaurant, 1 bar, whirlpool. Sports bar. **Rates:** $69–$75 S; $75–$81 D; $120–$200 ste; $180–$200 effic. Extra person $6. Children under age 18 stay free. Parking: Outdoor, free. AE, CB, DC, DISC, EC, ER, JCB, MC, V.

Sheraton Four Points Hotel
3737 N Blackstone Ave, 93726; tel 209/226-2200 or toll free 800/742-1911; fax 209/222-7147. Ashlan exit off CA 99. Exceptionally lovely, well-maintained grounds include beautiful swimming pool and extensive landscaping with trees, shrubs, flowers, and lawn. Well-decorated public areas and rooms with top-quality furnishings and carpeting. **Rooms:** 204 rms and stes. Executive level. CI 3pm/CO 1pm. Nonsmoking rms avail. Excellent wood furniture throughout; TV and refrigerator in armoire. King rooms have leather recliner and sofa. Lovely upholstery and spreads. Rooms facing pool area offer sliding glass doors and patio. **Amenities:** A/C, satel TV w/movies, refrig, dataport, voice mail. Some units w/terraces. The bathroom hairdryer is ancient. **Services:** **Facilities:** 1 restaurant, 1 bar (w/entertainment), whirlpool, washer/dryer. Exercise room; reduced-rate pass to nearby full-service gym available. **Rates:** $85–$100 S or D; $175 ste. Extra person $5. Children under age 17 stay free. Parking: Outdoor, free. Corporate rates available. AE, CB, DC, DISC, JCB, MC, V.

MOTELS

Best Western Village Inn
3110 N Blackstone Ave, 93703; tel 209/226-2110 or toll free 800/722-8878; fax 209/226-0539. Ashlan Ave exit off CA 99, E to Blackstone Ave. New furnishings and a paint job have freshened the look of this conveniently located older motel, close to a mall and fast-food restaurants. **Rooms:** 153 rms. CI 3pm/CO noon. Nonsmoking rms avail. **Amenities:** A/C, cable TV w/movies. **Services:** **Facilities:** Whirlpool. **Rates (CP):** $55 S; $63 D. Extra person $3. Children under age 12 stay free. Parking: Outdoor, free. AE, CB, DC, DISC, MC, V.

Best Western Water Tree Inn
4141 N Blackstone Ave, 93726; tel 209/222-4445 or toll free 800/762-9071; fax 209/226-4589. Ashlan Ave exit off CA 99. Tastefully decorated and spotless rooms and public areas make this 30-year-old motel a favorite with corporate clients. Conveniently located near business, shopping, and dining areas. **Rooms:** 136 rms and stes. CI noon/CO noon. Nonsmoking rms avail. Larger than average rooms feature new teal and rose carpeting. Well-appointed bathrooms. Parson's tables offer large work surfaces. **Amenities:** A/C,

satel TV w/movies, refrig, dataport. Some units w/terraces. **Services:** Car-rental desk. **Facilities:** 1 restaurant (lunch and dinner only), 1 bar. **Rates:** $56–$60 S; $60–$64 D; $80 ste. Extra person $4. Children under age 12 stay free. Parking: Outdoor, free. VIP Club for frequent clients give preferred rates and express check-out. Other group and corporate rates available. AE, CB, DC, DISC, JCB, MC, V.

Chateau Inn by Piccadilly Inn
5113 E McKinley Ave, 93727 (Airport); tel 209/456-1418 or toll free 800/445-2428; fax 209/456-1418 ext 200. Clinton Ave exit off CA 99S; Clovis Ave exit off CA 99 N. Clean, pleasant, small motel adjacent to airport. **Rooms:** 78 rms. Executive level. CI 3pm/CO 1pm. Nonsmoking rms avail. Colorful spreads and bedskirts and good quality furniture. Four rooms for guests with disabilities. **Amenities:** A/C, cable TV w/movies, VCR. Rooms in deluxe building have refrigerators. **Services:** Complimentary movies available from large selection in lobby. **Facilities:** Guests have access to spa, exercise facilities, laundry, and gift shop in neighboring Picadilly Inn, where guests also get a 20% discount on breakfast. **Rates:** $58–$64 S or D. Extra person $6. Children under age 18 stay free. Parking: Outdoor, free. Special weekend rates. AE, DC, DISC, JCB, MC, V.

Courtyard by Marriott
1551 N Peach Ave, 93727 (Fresno Airport); tel 209/251-5200 or toll free 800/321-2211; fax 209/454-0552. Clinton exit off CA 99 N, Clovis Ave exit off CA 99 S. Recently renovated with new carpeting, furniture, and accessories. **Rooms:** 116 rms. CI 4pm/CO noon. Nonsmoking rms avail. Lovely and inviting. **Amenities:** A/C, cable TV w/movies. **Services:** Car-rental desk, babysitting. **Facilities:** 1 restaurant (bkfst only), 1 bar, washer/dryer. **Rates:** $49–$74 S; $59–$84 D. Extra person $10. Children under age 18 stay free. Parking: Outdoor, free. Special rates on weekends. AE, DC, DISC, MC, V.

Days Inn
4061 N Blackstone Ave, 93726; tel 209/222-5641; fax 209/225-0144. Ashlan exit off CA 99; E to Blackstone, turn right. An older motel, newly renovated. **Rooms:** 111 rms and stes. CI 3pm/CO noon. Nonsmoking rms avail. Clean and spacious. **Amenities:** A/C, cable TV w/movies. **Services:** **Facilities:** George's Shish Kabob, a popular local restaurant and nightclub, is adjacent to the motel. **Rates (CP):** $42–$52 S; $47–$57 D. Extra person $6. Children under age 18 stay free. Parking: Outdoor, free. AE, DISC, MC, V.

Holiday Inn Express
6051 N Thesta, 93710; tel 209/435-6593 or toll free 800/435-9746; fax 209/435-8694. Bullard exit off CA 41. This property, opened in spring of 1994, is located near the Fresno Surgery Center in the northwest area of the city. **Rooms:** 55 rms. CI 3pm/CO 11am. Nonsmoking rms avail. Comfortable and nicely decorated. **Amenities:** A/C,

cable TV. **Services:** 🖨 📞 **Facilities:** ঙ় **Rates (CP):** $69–$85 S or D. Extra person $10. Children under age 19 stay free. Min stay special events. Parking: Outdoor, free. AE, CB, DC, DISC, MC, V.

≣≣ La Quinta Inn
2926 Tulare Ave, 93721 (Downtown); tel 209/442-1110 or toll free 800/531-5900; fax 209/237-0415. Off CA 41. Attractive downtown motel with beautiful, spacious lobby. Convenient to freeways. **Rooms:** 130 rms. CI 3pm/CO noon. Nonsmoking rms avail. King rooms feature recliners. **Amenities:** 📺 🛁 A/C, satel TV w/movies, dataport. Toiletries and necessities free at front desk. **Services:** ✕ 🖨 📞 🕊 Babysitting. Discounts on meals at adjacent restaurants. Free local calls. Coffee and tea offered in lobby 24 hours a day. **Facilities:** 🗄 🏊 ঙ় Guests can use nearby YMCA for $5 per day. **Rates (CP):** $47–$65 S or D. Extra person $7. Children under age 18 stay free. Parking: Outdoor, free. AE, DC, DISC, MC, V.

RESTAURANTS 🍴

Applebee's Neighborhood Grill & Bar
In Fig Garden Village Shopping Center, 5126 N Palm Ave; tel 209/244-6904. **New American.** A lively bar and grill with a neighborhood atmosphere and a diverse menu. Oak tables and upholstered booths are surrounded by memorabilia from local celebrities and sports figures. The menu includes Santa Fe chicken salad, ribs, and daily specials. Irish coffee and other specialty drinks are available from the bar. **FYI:** Reservations not accepted. Children's menu. **Open:** Mon–Thurs 11am–midnight, Fri–Sat 11am–1am, Sun 11am–10pm. **Prices:** Main courses $7–$9. AE, DISC, MC, V. 🅿️ ঙ়

Bobby Salazar's Mexican Restaurant & Cantina
2839 N Blackstone; tel 209/227-1686. **Mexican.** Simple decor, fun atmosphere. This family-run operation offers a large menu of Mexican specialties, including Bobby Salazar's fancy burrito, baked short ribs, chili rellenos, and fajitas. **FYI:** Reservations not accepted. Children's menu. Additional locations: 7044 N Cedar Ave (tel 323-7409); 434 Clovis Ave, Clovis (tel 298-7898). **Open:** Mon–Thurs 11am–9:30pm, Fri–Sat 11am–10pm, Sun 10am–9:30pm. **Prices:** Main courses $5–$11. AE, DC, DISC, MC, V. ঙ়

★ Butterfield Brewing Company
777 E Olive Ave (Tower District); tel 209/264-5521. Olive Ave exit off CA 99. **New American.** A fun hangout with views of the brewery vats from the dining area and bar. Home of award-winning, handcrafted Butterfield Brewery beers. Eclectic menu offers hearty salads, burgers, pasta, chili, appetizers, smoked meats, and fresh fish. Specialties include stuffed chicken wings. **FYI:** Reservations recommended. Blues/jazz. Children's menu. Dress code. Beer and wine only. **Open:** Mon–Thurs 11am–10pm, Fri–Sat 11am–11pm, Sun 11am–9pm. **Prices:** Main courses $6–$13. AE, MC, V. ঙ়

♥ Harland's
In Fig Garden Village, 722 W Shaw Ave; tel 209/225-7100. **Californian.** A whimsical mural, stunning flower arrangements, cobalt blue and green color accents, and a gorgeous curved bar welcome the sophisticated patrons at this upscale establishment. Creative combinations of meat, seafood, and produce (often organic) grace the daily-changing menu. Special dietary requests are handled with ease. Fine wine list. **FYI:** Reservations recommended. Piano. Dress code. **Open:** Mon–Thurs 11:30am–9pm, Fri 11:30am–10pm, Sat 6–10pm. **Prices:** Main courses $14–$24. AE, MC, V. ঙ়

ATTRACTIONS 🏛

Fresno Metropolitan Museum of Art, History, and Science
1555 Van Ness Ave; tel 209/441-1444. Featured at this museum are traveling exhibits ranging from art exhibitions to the history of auto racing, along with a permanent collection that includes the Salzer Collection of American and European still-life paintings. Also here are the Rotary Playland Science Gallery, the Bio-Met-Rics Laboratory, and an exhibit on the life of Fresno native William Saroyan, the Pulitzer prize–winning author. **Open:** Tues–Sun 11am–5pm. **$$**

Kearney Mansion Museum
7160 W Kearney Blvd; tel 209/441-0862. Guided tours are offered of the residence of pioneer land-developer M Theo Kearney. Known as the "Raisin King of California," Kearney had the house built in the center of his 5,000-acre Fruit Vale Estate. Today the museum is located within the historic 225-acre Kearney Park and contains 50% of the mansion's original furnishings, including European wallpapers and art nouveau light fixtures; a thorough restoration project has duplicated much of the remainder. The adjoining servants' quarters now house the ranch kitchen and museum gift shop. **Open:** Fri–Sun 1–4pm. **$$**

Meux Home
1007 R St; tel 209/233-8007. This elegant Victorian home was one of the most elaborate residences in Fresno. It was built in 1889 for Dr Thomas R Meux, a former Confederate surgeon and pioneer Fresno physician, and is the last remaining example of the Victorian houses of Fresno's early years. The house remained in the Meux family until 1973, when it was puchased by the City of Fresno and faithfully restored to its original charm.

The large, roofed porch features several beautifully turned posts and is accented with gingerbread details. The exterior walls of the house are covered with a variety of textures including clapboards, fishscale shingles, and ornamental floral-like relief decoration. Inside, one of the most interesting features is the octagonal master bedroom, with its steep, turreted roof. **Open:** Fri–Sun noon–3:30pm. **$**

Chaffee Zoological Gardens
894 W Belmont Ave; tel 209/498-2671. Located between Olive and Belmont Sts, at the south end of Roeding Park, this

18-acre zoo features a tropical rain forest exhibit, a reptile house, an elephant breeding center, and a petting zoo. An Australian aviary is open. **Open:** Peak (Mar–Oct) daily, 9am–5pm. Reduced hours off-season. **$$**

Fullerton

See Brea

Situated in the inland reaches of Orange County, this manufacturing city founded in 1887 is home to Fullerton College and California State University at Fullerton. **Information:** Fullerton Chamber of Commerce, 219 E Commonwealth Ave, PO Box 529, Fullerton 92632 (tel 714/871-3100).

HOTELS

Chase Suite Hotel
2932 E Nutwood Ave, 92631; tel 714/579-7400 or toll free 800/79-SUITE; fax 714/528-7945. Nutwood exit off CA 57. Clientele consists of business travelers and weekend romantics alike. **Rooms:** 96 rms, stes, and effic. CI 3pm/CO noon. Nonsmoking rms avail. Sitting areas, wet bars, and two-person whirlpools. (One room has a heart-shaped whirlpool.) No closets, but a large armoire contains hanging space for clothing. **Amenities:** A/C, cable TV, refrig, dataport. Some units w/terraces, some w/whirlpools. **Services:** Babysitting. Two nearby restaurants provide room service. **Facilities:** Washer/dryer. Free use of nearby health club. **Rates (CP):** $99–$109 S or D; $129–$199 ste; $149–$199 effic. Extra person $10. Children under age 12 stay free. Parking: Indoor/outdoor, free. AE, DC, DISC, JCB, MC, V.

Fullerton Marriott
2701 E Nutwood Ave, 92631; tel 714/738-7800 or toll free 800/228-9290; fax 714/738-0288. On campus of CA State University Fullerton. Nutwood exit off CA 57. Attractive, well-maintained property caters to business travelers, sports teams, and visitors to nearby university. **Rooms:** 225 rms and stes. Executive level. CI 4pm/CO noon. Nonsmoking rms avail. Small rooms are nicely appointed—comfortable for one person. **Amenities:** A/C, cable TV w/movies, dataport, voice mail. Some units w/terraces. Iron and ironing board in closet. **Services:** Twice-daily maid svce, social director. **Facilities:** 1 restaurant, 1 bar, sauna, whirlpool. **Rates:** $64–$128 S or D; $250 ste. Children under age 18 stay free. Parking: Indoor/outdoor, free. AE, DC, DISC, JCB, MC, V.

MOTEL

Holiday Inn
222 W Houston Ave, 92632; tel 714/992-1700 or toll free 800/553-3441; fax 714/992-4843. Harbor Blvd exit off CA 91. Classic Holiday Inn style of early 1970s, remodeled in 1991. Interior is pleasant, exterior average, landscaping minimal. **Rooms:** 289 rms and stes. Executive level. CI 3pm/CO noon. Nonsmoking rms avail. Clean, bright rooms. Furniture is nice but plain. Lots of beige. **Amenities:** A/C, cable TV w/movies, in-rm safe. Some units w/terraces. **Services:** Twice-daily maid svce, babysitting. **Facilities:** 1 restaurant, 1 bar, games rm, washer/dryer. Children's pool. Pool area could be cleaner. **Rates:** Peak (Apr–Oct) $90–$110 S; $100–$120 D; $125 ste. Extra person $5. Children under age 16 stay free. Lower rates off-season. Parking: Outdoor, free. AE, CB, DC, DISC, ER, JCB, MC, V.

RESTAURANTS

Aurora
1341 S Euclid St; tel 714/738-0272. Off CA 91; 2 blocks N of exit. **Continental/Italian.** Chef/owner Leo Holczer, with his old-world Swiss charm, makes diners feel right at home. Lots of flowers and paintings in the restaurant. Award-winning cuisine features many game specialties; more than 800 different wines are offered. **FYI:** Reservations recommended. Dress code. **Open:** Lunch Mon–Fri 11am–2pm; dinner Mon–Sat 5–9pm. **Prices:** Main courses $10–$27. AE, CB, DC, DISC, ER, MC, V.

The Cellar
In Villa del Sol, 305 N Harbor Blvd (Old Fullerton); tel 714/525-5682. Harbor Blvd exit off I-5; 4 mi N on Harbor. **French.** Located in a cellar, down a steep flight of stairs, this intimate, elegant restaurant offers classical French entrees such as Dover sole meunière, and grilled venison medallions with raspberry-wine sauce and caramelized apples. Staff is exceptionally knowledgeable about food and wine. Dessert soufflés are a specialty. The prix fixe early bird dinner is an excellent value at $28.75. Access for people with disabilities is via an elevator (notify when making reservations). **FYI:** Reservations recommended. Jacket required. **Open:** Tues–Sat 5:30–10pm. **Prices:** Main courses $18–$25. AE, DC, MC, V.

The Olde Ship
709 N Harbor Blvd; tel 714/871-7447. **British.** This British-owned and -operated pub is popular with Orange County's English expatriates, who come for pub grub such as bangers and mash, steak-and-kidney pie, and trifle. The extensive beer list includes many British brews. English accents predominate at the cozy and convivial bar. **FYI:** Reservations accepted. **Open:** Mon–Sat 11am–10pm. **Prices:** Main courses $6–$9. AE, DISC, MC, V.

ATTRACTIONS

Fullerton Arboretum
Tel 714/773-3579. Located on the campus of California State University, Fullerton; entrance via Associated Rd. These 26 acres at the northeast corner of the campus were opened to the public in 1979. Some of the themed areas include the Botanical Collection; Palm Garden; Subtropical

Fruit Grove; Conifer Area; Historic Area; and the Carnivorous Plant Bog. Guided tours are usually available (additional fee charged).

Also on the grounds is the **Heritage House,** built in 1894 and moved to its present site in 1972. Restored to its original appearance, the house is accessible by guided tour on weekends 11:30am–1:30pm (closed Jan and Aug). **Open:** Daily 8am–4:45pm. **$**

Muckenthaler Cultural Center
1201 W Malvern Ave; tel 714/738-6595. The historic Muckenthaler home, surrounded by 8½ acres of manicured grounds, is now a cultural center offering art exhibitions, children's art activities, performing arts, lectures, films, and workshops; dinner theater performances in summer. **Open:** Tues–Sat 10am–4pm, Sun noon–5pm. **$**

Children's Museum at La Habra
301 S Euclid St, La Habra; tel 310/905-9793 or 905-9693. Located 5 mi N of Fullerton. Housed in a restored 1923 railroad station, this museum puts children in touch with exhibits dealing with science, history, art, the humanities, and everyday life. Changing exhibits, special events, and programs. **Open:** Mon–Sat 10am–5pm, Sun 1–5pm. **$$**

Garberville

The North Coast is so rugged that two-lane CA 1 must swing inland through much of mountainous and forested Humbolt County. The small community of Garberville is located in the heart of wild Humboldt. The town swells in size in June for the Garberville Rodeo and again in August for the Reggae on the River festival, which attracts top talent from Jamaica and America. **Information:** Garberville–Redway Area Chamber of Commerce, 773 Redwood Dr #E, PO Box 445, Garberville 95542 (tel 707/923-2613).

HOTEL 🏨

≣≣≣ Benbow Inn
445 Lake Benbow Dr, 95542; tel 707/923-2124 or toll free 800/355-3301. Benbow exit off US 101. Charming National Historic Landmark inn located on the Eel River built in 1926 in a Tudor style. **Rooms:** 55 rms and stes. CI 2pm/CO noon. No smoking. Many rooms have been beautifully renovated. **Amenities:** 🔞 ⚖ 🎽 A/C, refrig. No TV. Some units w/terraces, some w/fireplaces, 1 w/whirlpool. Some rooms have cable TV and VCR; all have sherry decanters, glassware, special teas, and signature roasted coffees. **Services:** 🚗 🔜 Twice-daily maid svce, babysitting. Complimentary tea and scones served in the lobby 3–4pm, mulled wine from 4–5pm in chilly weather. **Facilities:** ♻ ⚠ 🔲 🔃 1 restaurant (see "Restaurants" below), 1 bar (w/entertainment), 1 beach (lake shore), games rm, lawn games. Well-kept mini-beach on river shore (no lifeguard). Beautiful garden terrace for dining in good weather. Nine-hole golf course (fee) within walking

distance. **Rates:** $115–$170 S or D; $215–$295 ste. Extra person $20. Children under age 12 stay free. Min stay wknds. Parking: Outdoor, free. Closed Jan 2–Apr 15. AE, DISC, MC, V.

MOTELS

≣≣ Best Western Humboldt House Inn
701 Redwood Dr, 95542 (Downtown); tel 707/923-2771 or toll free 800/528-1234; fax 707/923-4259. Garberville exit off US 101. A well-run place where the staff strives to please. **Rooms:** 76 rms, stes, and effic. CI 3pm/CO 11am. Nonsmoking rms avail. **Amenities:** 🔞 ⚖ A/C, cable TV, refrig. Some units w/terraces. **Services:** 🔜 🔜 Babysitting. Pets allowed in smoking rooms only. **Facilities:** 🔲 🔃 ⚖ Whirlpool, washer/dryer. **Rates (CP):** Peak (June–Oct 18) $76 S; $78 D; $80–$120 ste; $80–$95 effic. Extra person $7. Children under age 2 stay free. Lower rates off-season. Parking: Outdoor, free. MC, V.

≣ Sherwood Forest Motel
814 Redwood Dr, 95542 (Downtown); tel 707/923-2721 or toll free 800/544-5756; fax 707/923-3677. Garberville exit off US 101. Beautiful landscaping and warm hospitality lift the spirits of weary travelers. **Rooms:** 32 rms and effic. CI 2pm/CO 11am. Nonsmoking rms avail. **Amenities:** 🔞 ⚖ 🎽 🍽 A/C, cable TV, refrig. Microwaves in most rooms. **Services:** 🔜 🔜 **Facilities:** 🔲 ⚖ Whirlpool, washer/dryer. **Rates:** Peak (Apr–Oct) $50–$52 S; $54–$66 D; $69–$81 effic. Extra person $5. Lower rates off-season. Parking: Outdoor, free. AE, DC, DISC, MC, V.

RESTAURANT 🍴

Benbow Inn Dining Room
445 Lake Benbow Dr; tel 707/923-2124. Benbow exit off US 101. **New American.** Hearty meat, fish, and vegetarian dishes are prepared in imaginative contemporary style. Extensive selection of California wines, including many available by the glass. **FYI:** Reservations recommended. Children's menu. **Open:** Breakfast Mon–Sat 8–11am; lunch Mon–Sat noon–1:30pm; dinner daily 6–9pm; brunch Sun 8am–1:30pm. Closed Jan 2–Apr 15. **Prices:** Main courses $13–$22. AE, DISC, MC, V. ■

ATTRACTIONS 📷

Avenue of the Giants
Phillipsville; tel 707/923-2265. Located 6 miles north of Garberville on US 101. This scenic 33-mile roadway, which roughly parallels US 101, was left intact for sightseers when the freeway was built. The "giants" are majestic coast redwoods (Sequoia sempervirens). Over 500,000 acres of them make up the most outstanding display in the redwood belt, where more than 90% of the world's redwoods grow, and which roughly extends between Garberville and the Oregon state line. Their rough-barked columns climb 100 feet or

more without a branch—some predate Christianity and are taller than a football field is long. The oldest dated coast redwood is over 2,200 years old.

The drive can be made either north or south, and will take about 1½ hours. Auto tour signs along the roadway indicate stopping points. A driving tour brochure can be picked up at the Phillipsville exit off CA 101 (northbound) or the Jordan Creek exit off CA 101 (southbound). Headquarters for Humboldt Redwoods State Park (see below) is on the Avenue at Burlington, 2 miles south of Weott.

Humboldt Redwoods State Park

Weott; tel 707/946-2409. Located 15 miles north of Garberville via US 101. The 3rd-largest California state park, Humboldt Redwoods covers over 50,000 acres. Approximately 17,000 of these acres consist of old growth redwood forests, which are generally defined as containing trees over 200 years old. Both US 101 and the Avenue of the Giants (see above) run through the park, paralleling the south fork of the Eel River.

The **visitors center** has several displays that interpret the redwood environment. Slide shows and videos highlight the natural history of the region; naturalist programs are offered as well. The park has facilities for swimming, fishing, hiking, and camping. **Open:** Daily 24 hours. $$

Garden Grove

See Anaheim

Geyserville

INN

Hope-Bosworth House & Hope-Merrill House

21238/21253 Geyserville Ave, PO Box 42, 95441; tel 707/857-3356 or toll free 800/825-4BED; fax 707/857-4673. 6 mi N of Healdsburg of US 101. 2 acres. Located in a wine-growing town and surrounded by vineyards, this Queen Anne Victorian house has been perfectly restored to its past grandeur. Owner Rosalie Hope enjoys cooking in her immense kitchen. **Rooms:** 12 rms and stes. CI 4pm/CO 11am. No smoking. Cozy accommodations are packed with antiques. **Amenities:** No A/C, phone, or TV. Some units w/fireplaces, some w/whirlpools. Luxurious beds boast down quilts. **Services:** Afternoon tea served. **Facilities:** Guest lounge. Pool set in vineyard. **Rates (BB):** $95–$125 S or D; $140 ste. Extra person $20. Children under age 2 stay free. Min stay peak and wknds. Parking: Outdoor, free. Four-night Pick-n-Press package includes picking and crushing grapes at inn's own vineyard, winemaker dinner, and a bottling and labeling party. AE, MC, V.

Giant Forest

See Sequoia and Kings Canyon National Parks

Glendale

It sits between Los Angeles and the San Fernando Valley in the foothills of the San Gabriel Mountains, but Glendale maintains its own character. The city was founded on part of a ranch that had been the first Spanish land grant in California. Morbidly fascinating, kitschy Forest Lawn cemetery is here. **Information:** Glendale Chamber of Commerce, 200 S Louise St, PO Box 112, Glendale 91209 (tel 818/240-7870).

HOTELS

Best Western Golden Key Motor Hotel

123 W Colorado St, 91204; tel 818/247-0111 or toll free 800/528-1234; fax 818/545-9393. Basic, decent motel. **Rooms:** 55 rms. CI noon/CO noon. Nonsmoking rms avail. **Amenities:** A/C, satel TV w/movies, refrig, VCR, bathrobes. Bottled water included with each room. Microwave. **Services:** Car-rental desk, babysitting. Continental breakfast looked sparse. **Facilities:** Whirlpool. **Rates (CP):** $92–$97 S; $97–$102 D. Extra person $5. Children under age 12 stay free. Parking: Outdoor, free. AE, CB, DC, DISC, MC, V.

Red Lion Hotel Glendale

100 W Glenoaks Blvd, 91202; tel 818/956-5466 or toll free 800/547-8010; fax 818/956-5490. Gorgeous hotel with futuristic deco design. Great views of city from 19th floor. **Rooms:** 348 rms and stes. Executive level. CI 3pm/CO noon. Nonsmoking rms avail. Lovely pastel decor, very quiet; comfortable for family or business travelers. **Amenities:** A/C, cable TV w/movies, bathrobes. All units w/minibars. **Services:** Twice-daily maid svce, car-rental desk, babysitting. **Facilities:** 2 restaurants, 3 bars (2 w/entertainment), games rm, sauna, whirlpool, washer/dryer. Orange and magnolia trees soften pool area. Pool has lift for guests with disabilities. Superb fitness room with stacks of towels, drink machine with juice and mineral water. **Rates:** $148–$173 S; $163–$188 D; $250 ste. Extra person $10. Children under age 18 stay free. Parking: Indoor, $5–$8/day. AE, CB, DC, DISC, EC, JCB, MC, V.

RESTAURANT

Cinnabar

933 S Brand Blvd; tel 818/551-1155. **Californian/Asian.** Restaurant is the ground floor of historic Bekins Warehouse building. Old safe next to 1950s jukebox, cane and bamboo chairs, pillars, ornate bar with Japanese lanterns, a high ceiling. Light California-style cuisine offers lemongrass bouillabaisse, yellowtail mille-feuille, and air-dried duck with

grapefruit sauce. **FYI:** Reservations recommended. **Open:** Lunch Tues–Fri 11:30am–2pm; dinner Tues–Thurs 6–9:30pm, Fri–Sat 6–10:30pm, Sun 5:30–9pm. Closed 2 weeks in September. **Prices:** Main courses $8–$19; prix fixe $20. CB, DC, DISC, MC, V. ♥ ▆ ♿

ATTRACTION

Forest Lawn Memorial Park

1712 S Glendale Ave; tel 213/254-3131. There are five Forest Lawns in LA, but this is the one you've heard about. Among those entombed here are Jean Harlow, Clark Gable, Carole Lombard, and WC Fields. The Memorial Court of Honor reserves crypts for those whose service to humanity has been outstanding; Gutzon Borglum, creator of Mount Rushmore, and composer Rudolph Friml rest here. The cemetery's biggest draws are two paintings, *The Crucifixion* and *The Resurrection*, part of a narrated show presented daily every hour from 10am to 4pm. There are also three churches and the **Forest Lawn Museum,** with 13th-century stained-glass cathedral windows from the William Randolph Hearst collection, and reproductions of famous artworks, including Michelangelo's *Sotterraneo* and *David.* **Open:** Daily 9am–6pm. **Free**

Glen Ellen

Cradled within Sonoma Valley, near many top wineries, the town celebrates the memory of its most famous resident, writer Jack London, with a museum, gravesite, and what remains of his charred dream home.

INN

▆▆▆ Gaige House Inn

13540 Arnold Dr, 95442; tel 707/935-0237 or toll free 800/935-0237; fax 707/935-6411. 3 acres. One of the most attractive inns in the county, in a Queen Anne Victorian house decorated with lavish antiques and artwork. Peaceful setting. Unsuitable for children under 16. **Rooms:** 9 rms. CI 3pm/CO 11am. No smoking. Some rooms have 4-poster beds. **Amenities:** ☎ ♨ No A/C or TV. Some units w/fireplaces. **Facilities:** ♿ Guest lounge w/TV. Beautiful pool and grounds with hammocks and picnic tables. **Rates (BB):** Peak (Apr–Oct) $125–$245 S or D. Extra person $25. Min stay wknds. Lower rates off-season. Parking: Outdoor, free. AE, DISC, MC, V.

RESTAURANTS

Garden Court Cafe & Bakery

13875 Sonoma Hwy 12; tel 707/935-1565. 7 mi N of Sonoma. **Cafe.** A fine lunch spot. This sunny place is set in a lovely part of the Sonoma wine country, amid tall oaks and grassy knolls. Kitchen serves up fresh homemade breads and heart-shaped biscuits, plus sandwiches, soups, and salads.

FYI: Reservations not accepted. Beer and wine only. **Open:** Wed–Sun 7am–2pm. **Prices:** Lunch main courses $6–$8. DISC, MC, V. ⛴

Glen Ellen Inn

13670 Arnold Dr (Valley of the Moon); tel 707/996-6409. **Californian.** At this small, gourmet haven, owner/chefs Chris and Karen Bertrand present a creative menu along with a world-class wine list. Menu changes seasonally, but might include salmon coated in black pepper with ginger lemon sauce, or roast pork loin rolled in sun-dried tomatoes with mozzarella cheese. For dessert, there's chocolate truffle cake with raspberry sauce. **FYI:** Reservations accepted. Beer and wine only. **Open:** Lunch Tues–Sun 11:30am–2:30pm; dinner Tues–Sun 5:30–9:30pm. **Prices:** Main courses $11–$17. MC, V.

ATTRACTIONS

Benziger Winery

1883 London Ranch Road; tel toll free 800/989-8890. This family-owned winery produces a wide variety of wines: zinfandel, pinot noir, chardonnay, cabernet sauvignon, fumé blanc, and merlot. Tours and tastings offered. **Free**

Jack London State Historic Park

2400 London Ranch Rd; tel 707/938-5216. 8 miles north of Sonoma via CA 12. The 800-acre park includes the "House of Happy Walls," built in 1919 by London's wife, Charmian, which now houses a considerable collection of objects and memorabilia from the author's life. London's cottage has recently been restored and is open to visitors on weekends. Trails lead up to the site of Wolf House, the Londons' mansion, which burned down in 1913, and to their gravesite; maps available. On weekends, a free golf cart service is offered to the elderly and visitors with disabilities who may have trouble negotiating the trails. **Open:** Park: Peak (early Apr–Labor Day) 9:30am–7pm. Reduced hours off-season. Museum: daily 10am–5pm. **$$**

Sonoma Cattle Company

Glen Ellen; tel 707/996-8566. Located in Jack London State Historic Park (see above), this operation offers guided tours on horseback over various trails (the same ones that Jack London once followed), which wind through redwood stands, eucalyptus groves, and vineyards. Some trails ascend to the top of Mount Sonoma for a magnificent view of the countryside. **Open:** Daily, by appointment only. **$$$$**

Gold Country

See Auburn, Grass Valley, Jackson, Nevada City, Placerville, Sutter Creek

Goleta
See Santa Barbara

Grant Grove
See Sequoia and Kings Canyon National Parks

Grass Valley

Grass Valley was a legendary Gold Rush boom town that never went bust, as other industries and industrious residents have kept the place lively. Located in a beautiful setting high in the Sierra Nevada, Grass Valley is one of the best Gold Country destinations. **Information:** Grass Valley–Nevada County Chamber of Commerce, 248 Mill St, Grass Valley 95945 (tel 916/273-4667).

HOTEL

≣≣ Holbrooke Hotel
212 W Main St, 95945; tel 916/273-1353 or toll free 800/933-7077; fax 916/273-0434. CA 174 exit off CA 49. This landmark inn has modern conveniences and creature comforts. Non-smokers may be put off by the smell of smoke from the first-floor lounge, which opens onto public spaces. **Rooms:** 28 rms and stes. CI 3pm/CO 11am. Nonsmoking rms avail. Each room is unique, with high-quality, comfortable furnishings. Some have verandas overlooking Main Street. **Amenities:** A/C. No TV. Some units w/terraces, some w/fireplaces. **Services:** Some business services available. Complimentary continental breakfast, except Sunday when brunch is sold in the dining room. **Facilities:** 1 restaurant (lunch and dinner only), 1 bar. Reading room. Checkers in the lobby. **Rates (CP):** Peak (Apr–Dec) $66–$106 S or D; $120–$145 ste. Extra person $15. Lower rates off-season. Parking: Outdoor, free. AE, CB, DC, DISC, MC, V.

RESTAURANTS

Main Street Cafe and Bar
213 W Main St; tel 916/477-6000. CA 174 exit off CA 49/20. **Regional American.** Located in Grass Valley's first post office building, this pleasantly quiet eatery offers a decor of exposed brick walls, historic photos, and white tablecloths. Cajun specialties include Louisiana seafood linguine, and pasta with andouille sausage. Small patio. **FYI:** Reservations recommended. Blues/country music/folk. **Open:** Lunch Mon–Sat 11:30am–3pm; dinner Sun–Thurs 5–9pm, Fri–Sat 5–10pm; brunch. **Prices:** Main courses $10–$19. AE, MC, V.

Tofanelli's
302 W Main St; tel 916/272-1468. CA 174 exit off CA 49. **International.** This popular bistro-style restaurant serves international dishes featuring fish, chicken, and vegetables in a 19th-century setting, with tin ceiling and brick walls. **FYI:** Reservations accepted. Children's menu. Beer and wine only. **Open:** Peak (June–Oct) Mon–Fri 7am–8:30pm, Sat–Sun 9am–2pm, Sat–Sun 5–8:30pm. **Prices:** Main courses $7–$13. AE, MC, V.

ATTRACTION

Empire Mine State Historic Park
10791 E Empire St; tel 916/273-8522. This is the site of the oldest and richest hardrock gold mine in California. From its discovery in 1850 until its closure in 1956, an estimated 5.8 million ounces of gold were extracted from its 367 miles of underground passages. The 784-acre property was purchased by the State of California in 1975, and a gradual restoration program has transformed the mine into an educational and recreational resource.

Hiking trails are accesible year-round, as are the formal gardens surrounding the residence of the wealthy Bourn family, who owned the mine from 1879–1929. From March–November, guided tours of the mine, the lovely stone "cottage" of the mine owner, and a scale model of the system of mineshafts are made available to visitors. Call ahead for detailed tour information. **Open:** Schedule varies; phone ahead. $

Gualala
See also Sea Ranch

Located on the southern flank of Mendocino county where the Gualala River meets the sea, Gualala is a one-street town where far-flung locals meet each other to shop and socialize.

INNS

≣≣≣ Breakers Inn
CA 1, PO Box 389, 95445; tel 707/884-3200 or toll free 800/BREAKER; fax 707/884-3400. 2 acres. Overlooking the Gualala River and Pacific Beaches, most accommodations have decks that offer stupendous 180-degree views. Known for having lowest rates on coast for ocean-view rooms. Especially good value weekdays and off-season. **Rooms:** 27 rms. CI 3pm/CO noon. Nonsmoking rms avail. Honeymoon rooms are extra large. **Amenities:** Cable TV, refrig, VCR. No A/C. All units w/terraces, all w/fireplaces, all w/whirlpools. Complimentary wine and chocolate on arrival. **Services:** Masseur, afternoon tea and wine/sherry served. Room service from restaurant next door. **Facilities:** 1 bar (w/entertainment), guest lounge. **Rates (CP):** Peak (Mar–Dec) $85–$225 S or D. Extra person $10. Lower rates off-season. Parking: Outdoor, free. AE, DISC, MC, V.

≡≡ St Orres

36601 S CA 1, PO Box 523, 95445; tel 707/884-3303. 50 acres. Set on a wooded hillside overlooking the ocean. Main building features Russian-style architecture, with copper onion domes and wisteria-covered terraces. Charming lobby, restaurant, and bar. Unsuitable for children under 5. **Rooms:** 8 rms (all w/shared bath); 11 cottages/villas. CI 3pm/CO noon. No smoking. Cottages have kitchens and are a bit bare. Decks have views of ocean and meadows. **Amenities:** 🛁 📺 📞 Refrig. No A/C, phone, or TV. Some units w/terraces, some w/fireplaces. **Services:** ✗ Masseur. Breakfast with homemade breads, hot entrees, and fresh fruit. **Facilities:** 1 restaurant (dinner only; *see* "Restaurants" below), 1 bar, sauna, whirlpool, guest lounge. Good hiking trails on property. Excellent massage available. **Rates (BB):** $65–$75 S or D w/shared bath; $85–$270 cottage/villa. Extra person $15. Children under age 5 stay free. Min stay wknds. Parking: Outdoor, free. MC, V.

≡≡≡ Seacliff

39140 CA 1, PO Box 1317, 95445; tel 707/884-1213 or toll free 800/400-5053; fax 707/884-1731. 2 acres. Very peaceful and offers ocean views. Lobby is outfitted with a fireplace and telescope for watching wildlife. Unsuitable for children under 18. **Rooms:** 16 rms. CI 3pm/CO 11am. Nonsmoking rms avail. Rooms on bluff overlook Gaulala River and beach and have balconies facing the ocean. Upstairs rooms have vaulted ceilings. **Amenities:** 🛁 📺 Cable TV, refrig, bathrobes. No A/C or phone. All units w/terraces, all w/fireplaces, all w/whirlpools. Complimentary champagne or cider in refrigerator; champagne glasses. Binoculars for watching seals, pelicans, and whales. **Facilities:** 👍 Guest lounge. **Rates:** Peak (Apr–Dec) $100–$180 S or D. Min stay special events. Lower rates off-season. Parking: Outdoor, free. Rates lower Sunday–Thursday. MC, V.

≡≡≡≡ Whale Watch Inn

35100 CA 1, 95445; tel 707/884-3667 or toll free 800/WHALE-42. 2½ acres. A romantic retreat with a private staircase down to Mendocino's most beautiful beach. Many activities nearby. Unsuitable for children under 18. **Rooms:** 18 rms, stes, and effic. CI 3pm/CO 11am. No smoking. Rooms have gorgeous views and are beautifully furnished. One has an upstairs fireplace and sitting room. **Amenities:** No A/C, phone, or TV. All units w/terraces, all w/fireplaces, some w/whirlpools. The whirlpools are huge and have great views. **Services:** 🛎 Twice-daily maid svce, masseur, babysitting. Full, fancy breakfast can be served in room. Wine and cheese on Saturday night. **Facilities:** 👍 1 beach (ocean), guest lounge. Separate lounge area with fireplace, library, kitchen, and telescope. **Rates (BB):** $170–$255 S or D; $210 ste; $210 effic. Extra person $20. Children under age 1 stay free. Min stay wknds. Parking: Outdoor, free. AE, MC, V.

RESTAURANT 🍴

St Orres

36601 CA 1; tel 707/884-3303. **Californian.** A romantic dining room in a Russian-style copper-domed building. With copper place settings and long-stemmed flowers on the tables. The prix-fixe dinner includes three courses, with entrees such as wild boar or quail, local turkey, plus vegetarian selections such as grilled vegetable tart. Menu changes regularly. Sunday brunch Mar–Nov. **FYI:** Reservations recommended. Beer and wine only. **Open:** Sun–Fri 6–9pm, Sat 5:15–9:45pm. **Prices:** Prix fixe $30. No CC.

Guerneville

INN 🏨

≡≡≡ Ridenhour Ranch House Inn

12850 River Rd, 95446; tel 707/887-1033; fax 707/869-2967. 12 mi W of US 101. 2¼ acres. Situated alongside the Russian River, next door to Korbel Champagne Cellars, this inn is surrounded by ancient redwoods, oaks, and fruit orchards. Ranch house was constructed in 1906 with heart redwood. Reasonable rates. **Rooms:** 6 rms and stes; 2 cottages/villas. CI 3pm/CO 11am. No smoking. Accommodations are named after trees and plants on property. **Amenities:** Bathrobes. No A/C, phone, or TV. Some units w/terraces, 1 w/fireplace. **Services:** 🚐 🐕 Masseur, babysitting, afternoon tea and wine/sherry served. Austrian owner/chef provides fine breakfast, including jams and applesauce made from homegrown fruit. Wine bar specializes in wines from region. Five-course dinner available Saturday night on request—$30. **Facilities:** 🏊 👍 1 restaurant (bkfst and dinner only), lawn games, whirlpool, guest lounge w/TV. Lounge has Steinway piano for guests to play. **Rates (BB):** Peak (Mar–Nov) $95–$130 S or D; $120 ste; $130 cottage/villa. Extra person $15. Min stay wknds. Lower rates off-season. Parking: Outdoor, free. AE, MC, V.

RESTAURANT 🍴

Topolos

In Russian River Vineyards, 5700 Gravenstein Hwy N (CA 116), Forestville; tel 707/887-1562. 1 mi S of Forestville. **Continental/Greek.** The only family-owned and -operated winery/restaurant combination in California. Best for a summery outdoor lunch (the inside dining room is decidedly ordinary). Many Greek specialties on the menu, such as spanakopita (spinach and cheese in filo pastry). Many herbs and vegetables come from the family gardens. The tasting room of this winery is known for its zinfandels. **FYI:** Reservations recommended. Guitar. Beer and wine only. **Open:** Peak (June–Sept) lunch daily 11:30am–2:30pm; dinner daily 5:30–9:30pm; brunch Sun 11:30am–2:30pm. **Prices:** Main courses $9–$20. AE, CB, DC, DISC, MC, V. 🍴

ATTRACTION

Korbel Champagne Cellars

13250 River Rd; tel 707/887-2294. Tours of this brick-and-redwood winery, built in 1886, explain the champagne-making process brought to the United States by the three Korbel brothers from Czechoslovakia. Free tastings are included in the winery tour; garden tours are offered in summer. **Open:** Peak (May–Sept) daily 9am–5:30pm. Reduced hours off-season. **Free**

Half Moon Bay

See also Moss Beach, Princeton-by-the-Sea

Although the San Francisco metropolis is just on the other side of the coastal hills, the big city seems a world away in this small Pacific town with its quiet beaches and coves. Half Moon Bay fills up in late October for the Art and Pumpkin Festival. **Information:** Half Moon Bay Coastside Chamber of Commerce, 520 Kelly Ave, Half Moon Bay 94019 (tel 415/726-8380 or 726-5202).

HOTEL

Half Moon Bay Lodge

2400 S Cabrillo Hwy, 94019; tel 415/726-9000 or toll free 800/368-2468; fax 415/726-7951. CA 1 exit off CA 92. Very clean, neat, and attractive throughout. Several beaches within 5 miles. Good value. **Rooms:** 80 rms. CI 3:30pm/CO 11:30am. Nonsmoking rms avail. Large rooms with queen- or king-size beds. Suites are spacious and well appointed. Many rooms overlook the golf course. **Amenities:** A/C Cable TV w/movies. No A/C. All units w/terraces, some w/fireplaces, 1 w/whirlpool. **Services:** Babysitting. Staff can arrange limos to airport and car rentals. **Facilities:** 18 70 Whirlpool. Two restaurants adjacent to lodge, one moderate and one upscale. Glass-walled poolside gazebo with large whirlpool spa. Beach horseback riding. Hiking on beach trails. **Rates:** $145–$185 S or D. Extra person $10. Children under age 12 stay free. Min stay special events. Parking: Outdoor, free. AE, DC, DISC, MC, V.

MOTELS

Harbor View Inn

51 Ave Alhambra, El Granada, 94018; tel 415/726-2329. CA 1 exit off CA 92. Go N 4 mi. Not fancy, but clean. Small lobby. **Rooms:** 17 rms. CI 1pm/CO 11am. Nonsmoking rms avail. Plain, but clean. **Amenities:** Cable TV. No A/C. **Services:** Morning coffee in lobby, which is small and cluttered. **Facilities:** **Rates (CP):** $75–$85 S or D. Children under age 18 stay free. Parking: Outdoor, free. AE, MC, V.

Holiday Inn Express

230 Cabrillo Hwy (CA 1), 94019; tel 415/726-3400 or toll free 800/HOLIDAY; fax 415/726-1256. ¼ mi S of Half Moon Bay, exit CA 1 off CA 92. Smaller than typical Holiday Inn. Clean and basic, with no facilities or restaurant. **Rooms:** 52 rms. CI 3pm/CO noon. Nonsmoking rms avail. **Amenities:** A/C, cable TV w/movies. Some units w/terraces. VCRs may be rented at front desk. **Services:** **Facilities:** **Rates (CP):** Peak (June–Oct) $75–$95 S or D; $120–$150 ste; $120–$150 effic. Extra person $12. Children under age 16 stay free. Lower rates off-season. Parking: Outdoor, free. AE, CB, DC, DISC, JCB, MC, V.

Ramada Limited

3020 CA 1, 94019; tel 415/726-9700 or toll free 800/2-RAMADA; fax 415/726-5269. CA 4 exit off CA 92. 2 mi N on CA 1. Property is clean, pleasant, and very basic. **Rooms:** 20 rms. CI 2pm/CO 11am. Nonsmoking rms avail. Small and very plain. **Amenities:** A/C, cable TV w/movies. Microwave and refrigerator in five rooms. **Services:** $10 charge for pets. **Facilities:** **Rates:** Peak (Apr–Oct) $75–$125 S or D. Children under age 5 stay free. Lower rates off-season. Parking: Outdoor, free. Rates fluctuate depending on length of stay. AE, MC, V.

RESTAURANTS

★ Papa George's Restaurant and Saloon

2320 Cabrillo Hwy; tel 415/726-9417. CA 1 exit off CA 92. **Italian.** Popular with locals and guests from nearby hotels. Country decor with solid tables and chairs and fresh flowers. Colorful pub. Menu features pasta filled with ricotta and Parmesan cheese; roast duck with Italian sausage and fresh herbs; and rack of lamb. **FYI:** Reservations recommended. Blues/jazz/singer. **Open:** Peak (spring–fall) lunch Tues–Sat 11:30am–2:30pm; dinner Tues–Sat 5–9pm; brunch Sun 9am–4pm. **Prices:** Main courses $9–$15. AE, DISC, MC, V.

★ Pasta Moon

315 Main St; tel 415/726-5125. Off CA 92. **Italian.** Recently expanded, this restaurant offers a wide selection of pastas, sandwiches, and entree salads, such as grilled fillet of fresh salmon with spinach, shaved fennel, oranges, and citrus-basil vinaigrette. **FYI:** Reservations accepted. Wine only. Additional location: 425 Marina Blvd, Oyster Point Marina, San Francisco (tel 876-7090). **Open:** Lunch Sat–Sun noon–3pm, Mon–Fri 11:30am–2:30pm; dinner Mon–Thurs 5:30–9pm, Fri 5:30–10pm, Sat–Sun 5:30–9:30pm. **Prices:** Main courses $9–$17. AE, DISC, MC, V.

Hanford

Just off CA 99 (which links the rural towns of the Central Valley), Hanford was a Southern Pacific railroad stopover between Los Angeles and San Francisco. The town has preserved its ornate courthouse and jail (now a restaurant), and the Chinese laborers' district called China Alley, complete with a Taoist temple. **Information:** Hanford Visitor Agency, 200 Santa Fee Ave #D, Hanford 93230 (tel 209/582-5024 or toll free 800/722-1114).

MOTEL

≣≣ Best Western Hanford Inn
755 Cadillac Lane, 93230; tel 209/583-7300 or toll free 800/528-1234; fax 209/582-8455. 11th St exit off CA 198. An upcoming restoration is needed. **Rooms:** 40 rms and stes. CI 1pm/CO 11am. Nonsmoking rms avail. Mini-suites are a good buy. **Amenities:** A/C, cable TV w/movies. **Services:** Facilities: Washer/dryer. **Rates:** $42–$55 S; $48–$59 D; $48 ste. Extra person $6. Children under age 12 stay free. Parking: Outdoor, free. AE, CB, DC, DISC, MC, V.

INN

≣≣ Irwin St Inn
522 N Irwin St, 93230 (Downtown); tel 209/583-8000; fax 209/583-8793. A B&B inn made up of 4 late–19th-century Victorian homes moved here and restored in the 1970s. **Rooms:** 31 rms and stes. CI 2pm/CO 11am. Nonsmoking rms avail. Each room is large and distinctively decorated. **Amenities:** A/C, cable TV. All units w/terraces. **Services:** Babysitting. Continental breakfast with homemade "morning glory" muffins. **Facilities:** 1 restaurant. Charming restaurant with patio serves breakfast, lunch, and dinner. **Rates (CP):** $70–$90 D; $100–$111 ste. Children under age 12 stay free. Parking: Outdoor, free. AE, CB, DC, DISC, MC, V.

Hawthorne

See Los Angeles Int'l Airport

Hayward

The anchor of the South Bay, Hayward has long been a mix of Bay-related industry and residential neighborhoods. The community is also home to California State University at Hayward. **Information:** Hayward Chamber of Commerce, 22320 Foothill Blvd #600, Hayward 94541 (tel 510/537-2424).

HOTEL

≣≣ Executive Inn Hayward Airport
20777 Hesperian Blvd, 94541 (Oakland Int'l Airport); tel 510/732-6300 or toll free 800/553-5083; fax 510/783-2265. A St W exit off I-880, to Hesperian Blvd. Very pleasant, fairly new hotel adjacent to private airport. Walking distance to good restaurants, golf course, and tennis courts. **Rooms:** 146 rms and stes. CI 1pm/CO noon. Nonsmoking rms avail. Deluxe king rooms are large, with sofa and coffee table. Bathrooms have separate tub and toilet/sink area. **Amenities:**

A/C, cable TV w/movies. Some units w/terraces. King rooms have wet bars, refrigerators. VCRs for rent; videos are free. **Services:** Car-rental desk. Complimentary wine and cheese Tuesday and Wednesday 5–7pm. Free shuttle to rapid transit station. **Facilities:** Whirlpool, washer/dryer. **Rates (CP):** $72–$77 S; $72–$82 D. Extra person $4. Children under age 12 stay free. Parking: Outdoor, free. AE, CB, DC, DISC, MC, V.

RESTAURANT

Rue de Main
22622 Main St; tel 510/537-0812. Between B and C Sts. **French.** Located in a historic building. The dining room is painted with murals depicting Parisian street scenes. Standard French menu features such staples as escargots, onion soup, and many dishes with wine- or cream-based sauces. **FYI:** Reservations recommended. Beer and wine only. **Open:** Lunch Tues–Fri 11:30am–2:15pm; dinner Tues–Sat 5:30–10pm. Closed June 23–30. **Prices:** Main courses $15–$34. AE, MC, V.

ATTRACTIONS

Hayward Area Historical Society Museum
22701 Main St; tel 510/581-0223. Housed in a 1927 brick post office building, the museum features permanent displays of a 1923 fire engine, a 1860s fire pumper, a re-created 1930s post office, and maps and photographs of local history. Changing exhibits; gift shop. **Open:** Mon–Fri 11am–4pm, Sat noon–4pm. **$**

McConaghy House
18701 Hesperian Blvd; tel 510/581-0223. Guided tours are offered of this 12-room Victorian farmhouse, which is furnished in the style of 1886, the year of its construction. Also on the tour are the carriage house, containing farm equipment, and the tank house. The house sports Victorian Christmas decorations during the holiday season. Gift shop with Victorian-style gifts. **Open:** Thurs–Sun 1–4pm. **$**

Healdsburg

Healdsburg was founded in the 1860s after failed miners took up residence on a large rancho. The town is now home to several wineries; several more can be found in the surrounding Alexander Valley. **Information:** Healdsburg Area Chamber of Commerce, 217 Healdsburg Ave, Healdsburg 95448 (tel 707/433-6935).

HOTEL

≣≣ Best Western Dry Creek Inn
198 Dry Creek Rd, 95448; tel 707/433-0300 or toll free 800/222-5784. At US 101. Close to area attractions. **Rooms:** 102 rms. CI 3pm/CO noon. Nonsmoking rms avail. Rooms are clean but lackluster. **Amenities:** A/C, cable TV

w/movies, refrig. **Services:** 🛏 🍽 Complimentary bottle of wine. **Facilities:** 🔧 🏊 ♿ Washer/dryer. **Rates (CP):** Peak (June–Oct) $55–$89 S or D. Extra person $10. Children under age 18 stay free. Min stay special events. Lower rates off-season. Parking: Outdoor, free. Low mid-week rates and special packages. AE, CB, DC, DISC, JCB, MC, V.

INNS

≡≡≡ Camellia Inn
211 North St, 95448 (2 blocks off Plaza); tel 707/433-8182 or toll free 800/727-8182. Located in a historic district, this 1869 Italianate Victorian is within walking distance of the central plaza and great restaurants. Very reasonable rates for fine quality. **Rooms:** 9 rms and stes. CI 4pm/CO 11am. No smoking. Accommodations are well appointed, with antiques and four-poster or canopy beds, marble fireplaces, and whirlpools. Many rooms have private entrances. **Amenities:** Bathrobes. No A/C, phone, or TV. Some units w/fireplaces, some w/whirlpools. **Services:** 🛏 Masseur, babysitting, afternoon tea served. Staff will help with winery tours and restaurant reservations. **Facilities:** 🔧 🍽 ♿ Guest lounge w/TV. Lovely manicured gardens. **Rates (BB):** $70–$135 S or D; $115 ste. Extra person $20. Children under age 20 stay free. Min stay wknds. Parking: Outdoor, free. AE, MC, V.

≡≡≡ Healdsburg Inn on the Plaza
116 Matheson St, PO Box 1196, 95448; tel 707/433-6991 or toll free 800/431-8663. Cute, historic, bed-and-breakfast-style inn right on the plaza, with an art gallery in the lobby. Unsuitable for children under 5. **Rooms:** 10 rms. CI 3pm/CO 11am. No smoking. Each room is unique; most have antique clawfoot tubs and iron beds. All rooms are located upstairs; no elevators. **Amenities:** 📺 🍷 A/C, cable TV w/movies, dataport, VCR. Some units w/terraces, some w/fireplaces, 1 w/whirlpool. **Services:** 🖼 🛏 Masseur, afternoon tea and wine/sherry served. Complimentary coffee, tea, and cookies in lounge 24 hours. Free use of videos. Complimentary champagne brunch on weekends. **Facilities:** 🍽 Guest lounge w/TV. Nice breakfast room; dine indoors or in garden. **Rates (BB):** Peak (Apr–Dec) $145–$195 S or D. Extra person $35. Children under age 5 stay free. Lower rates off-season. Parking: Outdoor, free. MC, V.

≡≡≡≡ Madrona Manor
1001 Westside Rd, PO Box 818, 95448; tel 707/433-4231 or toll free 800/258-4003; fax 707/433-0703. 8 acres. You can't ask for more romantic lodgings than this splendid 1881 Victorian that's included on the National Register of Historic Places. Camellias, palms, and oak trees grace the grounds, and everything is spread out enough that guests enjoy a feeling of privacy. The property could use more spit and polish however, with some siding and terracing in need of fresh paint. **Rooms:** 20 rms and stes; 1 cottage/villa. CI 3pm/CO 11am. Accommodations are offered in both the Mansion and Carriage House. With its high ceilings and wide corridors, the Mansion is gorgeous. Furnished with antiques,

room #203 features French doors, a painted-tile fireplace, and claw-foot tub. In the Carriage House, decor is a bland contemporary modern, enlivened by some artifacts from Nepal—a legacy of the owners' travels. Room 400 has a step-up marble-edged whirlpool. Children under the age of 18 are permitted in the Carriage House only. **Amenities:** 📺 🍷 🔔 Bathrobes. No A/C or TV. Some units w/terraces, some w/fireplaces, 1 w/whirlpool. Some rooms are air conditioned. **Services:** 🛏 🍽 Twice-daily maid svce, masseur, babysitting. For breakfast, there's a European-style buffet, featuring imported meats and cheeses, as well as fruits, cereal, pastries, and hot dishes such as quiche. **Facilities:** 🔧 🍽 1 restaurant (dinner only; *see* "Restaurants" below), guest lounge. **Rates (CP):** $140–$180 S or D; $240 ste; $210 cottage/villa. Extra person $30. Children under age 6 stay free. Min stay wknds. Parking: Outdoor, free. April through October, reserve three months in advance for weekend stays. AE, CB, DC, DISC, MC, V.

RESTAURANTS 🍴

★ Bistro Ralph
109 Plaza St; tel 707/433-1380. 17 mi N of Santa Rosa. **Californian.** A culinary gem right on the main plaza. Modern restaurant with bentwood chairs, fine linen, and a huge vase of sunflowers at the entrance. Menu highlights organic ingredients from local farmers: dishes include lamb stew niçoise, Szechuan calamari, and sautéed tuna. Local wines. **FYI:** Reservations recommended. Beer and wine only. **Open:** Lunch Mon–Fri 11:30am–2:30pm; dinner daily 5:30–9:30pm. **Prices:** Main courses $13–$16. MC, V. ♿

Madrona Manor
1001 Westside Rd; tel 707/433-4231. Central Healdsburg exit off US 101; follow Healdsburg Ave to Mill St and turn left; Mill turns into Westside Rd after you cross US 101. **Californian/French.** Exquisite Victorian retreat in wine country, with romantic ambience and outdoor dining overlooking the gardens. Fine cuisine uses exclusively fresh ingredients; four-course prix-fixe dinner includes wine. All breads, pastries, ice cream, pasta, and cured meats are prepared on site. **FYI:** Reservations recommended. Dress code. Beer and wine only. **Open:** Peak (Mar–Oct) breakfast daily 8–9:45am; dinner daily 6–9pm; brunch Sun 11am–2pm. **Prices:** Main courses $22–$30; prix fixe $40–$50. AE, MC, V. ♥ 🍴 🛏 🖼 🏞 ♿

Plaza Street Market
113 Plaza St; tel 707/431-2800. Central Healdsburg exit off US 101. **Cafe/Deli.** Lovely restaurant in a beautifully restored 1883 building, with nice wood bar and marble tables. Pleasant indoor and outdoor dining areas face the plaza. Wide variety of sandwiches includes roast turkey breast, smoked chicken, and roasted eggplant. **FYI:** Reservations not accepted. Beer and wine only. **Open:** Mon–Sat 7am–5pm, Sun 9am–4pm. **Prices:** Main courses $7. MC, V. ♿

★ Ravenous

In Raven Theater, 117 North St; tel 707/431-1770. 1 block N of Plaza. **Californian.** Located next to an art film theater, this cozy restaurant welcomes diners with jazz music and warm terra-cotta walls. Since they don't take reservations, there's a wait most nights—but it's definitely worth it for the creative fare such as grilled flank steak with sweet peppers and roasted potatoes, or spaghetti with clams, prawns, and mahimahi. **FYI:** Reservations not accepted. Beer and wine only. **Open:** Lunch Wed–Sun 11:30am–3:30pm; dinner Wed–Thurs 5–9pm, Fri–Sat 5–9:30pm, Sun 5–9pm. **Prices:** Main courses $11–$14. No CC.

Southside Saloon & Dining Hall

106 Matheson St; tel 707/433-4466. On Plaza. **Californian.** Decorated with historical photos and art tapestries, this lively restaurant offers a tempting array of dishes from chef Charles Saunders, also proprietor of the award-winning East Side Oyster Bar & Grill in Sonoma. Oysters are a specialty here, too, served raw, in oyster shooters, and also atop a wonderful "Hangtown Fry" salad, where they're fried, then perched on a stack of greens with bacon and thin-sliced veggies. Entrees also include baby back ribs with slaw, grilled prawns in curry, and garlic-rosemary roasted chicken. The long list of libations features hand-squeezed juices, good beers, and California wines. **FYI:** Reservations accepted. Cabaret. Children's menu. **Open:** Lunch daily 11:30am–2:30pm; dinner Sun–Thurs 5:30–9pm, Fri–Sat 5:30–10pm. **Prices:** Main courses $10–$18. AE, MC, V. &

REFRESHMENT STOP 🥤

Downtown Bakery and Creamery

308A Center St; tel 707/431-2719. 20 mi N of Santa Rosa Central Healdsburg exit off US 101. **Cafe.** Large, open bakery right on the plaza, owned by Lindsey Shere, also pastry chef at Chez Panisse. Specializes in peach-polenta cherry tarts, chocolate macaroons, tiramisù, flaky croissants, and gooey cinnamon rolls. They make their own ice cream and sorbets, too. **Open:** Mon–Fri 6am–5:30pm, Sat–Sun 7am–5:30pm. Closed Jan 1–7. No CC.

ATTRACTION 🏛

Simi Winery

16275 Healdsburg Ave; tel 707/433-6981. In 1876, brothers Guiseppe and Pietro Simi emigrated to northern California, establishing their own cellars in 1890. These cellars housed the entire winemaking operation for 100 years and are now part of the guided tours of the facility, offered at 11am, 1pm, and 3pm. A fee is charged for tasting of premium wines. **Open:** Daily 10am–4:30pm. **Free**

Hemet

Situated at the foot of the San Jacinto Mountains, Hemet is an agricultural and retirement community that comes alive every late April with the Ramona Pageant, an outdoor dramatization of Helen Hunt Jackson's 1884 novel that features a cast of more than 350. **Information:** Hemet Chamber of Commerce, 395 E Latham Ave, Hemet 92543 (tel 909/658-3211).

MOTELS 🏨

≣≣ The Hemet Inn

800 W Florida Ave, 92543; tel 909/929-6366 or toll free 800/909-6366; fax 909/925-3016. CA 79 exit off I-10. Flowering trees provide a nice welcome to this Spanish-style motel. **Rooms:** 65 rms. CI noon/CO noon. Nonsmoking rms avail. Rooms refurbished in 1996. King and queen beds available. **Amenities:** 🛜 A/C, cable TV w/movies. **Services:** ⟑ **Facilities:** 🛢 ⊡75 & Whirlpool, washer/dryer. **Rates (CP):** Peak (Jan–May) $40–$45 S or D. Extra person $6. Children under age 17 stay free. Lower rates off-season. Parking: Outdoor, free. AE, CB, DC, DISC, MC, V.

≣ Hemet Travelodge

1201 W Florida Ave, 92543; tel 909/766-1902 or toll free 800/578-7878; fax 909/766-7739. Spanish-style architecture with modern, clean interior. **Rooms:** 46 rms. CI noon/CO noon. Nonsmoking rms avail. Rooms have choice of king-size or queen-size beds. **Amenities:** 🛜 ⊚ A/C, cable TV w/movies, refrig. **Services:** ⊠ ⟑ ⊲⟑ Babysitting. **Facilities:** 🛢 ⊡25 & Whirlpool, washer/dryer. **Rates (CP):** Peak (Oct–May) $45–$50 S or D. Extra person $5. Min stay special events. Lower rates off-season. Parking: Outdoor, free. AE, DC, DISC, MC, V.

≣ Ramada Inn

3885 W Florida Ave, 92545; tel 909/929-8900 or toll free 800/272-6232, 800/858-8594 in the US, 800/858-8574 in Canada; fax 909/925-3716. CA 79 exit off I-10. Conveniently located just minutes from shopping and restaurants. **Rooms:** 99 rms, stes, and effic. CI noon/CO noon. Nonsmoking rms avail. **Amenities:** 🛜 ⊚ A/C, satel TV w/movies. Some units w/terraces, 1 w/whirlpool. **Services:** ⊠ ⟑ ⊲⟑ **Facilities:** 🛢 ⊡175 & Whirlpool, washer/dryer. Two restaurants next door. **Rates (CP):** Peak (Jan–Apr) $50–$62 S or D; $50–$70 ste; $55–$80 effic. Extra person $8. Children under age 18 stay free. Lower rates off-season. Parking: Outdoor, free. AE, CB, DC, DISC, ER, JCB, MC, V.

RESTAURANT 🍴

★ Alejandro's

3909 W Florida Ave; tel 909/766-1192. **Mexican.** Features white adobe walls hand-painted with festive scenes, high ceilings dotted with elaborate chandeliers, and a thatched-roof cantina. Menu offers enchiladas and burritos and mesquite-grilled meats and seafood, all served by a friendly staff. **FYI:** Reservations accepted. **Open:** Lunch daily 11am–3pm; dinner daily 3–10pm. **Prices:** Main courses $6–$11. MC, V. 🍴 &

ATTRACTION 🏛

Ramona Bowl
27400 Ramona Bowl Rd; tel 909/658-3111. Amphitheater built into the side of a mountain. Seating close to 7,000 people, it is the home of the annual Ramona Pageant held every spring. *Ramona*, based on Helen Hunt Jackson's 1884 love story of old California, has been staged since 1923 and is one of the nation's oldest outdoor dramas. Call in advance for detailed information. **$$$$**

Hollywood

See also North Hollywood, West Hollywood

Located on the slopes of the Santa Monica Mountains, Hollywood was consolidated with the city of Los Angeles in 1910. The first film studio set up shop here in 1911, and within a few years Hollywood became the glamour and glitter capital of the world. A slow decline set in during the 1950s, as many of the movie studios moved to surrounding areas and suburbs. But all is not lost, and reminders of the Golden Age are everywhere: the Hollyhock House, Paramount Studios, Hollywood Memorial Park Cemetery, Capital Records Tower, Mann's Chinese Theater, the Walk of Fame, to name only a few. **Information:** Hollywood Chamber of Commerce, 7018 Hollywood Blvd, Hollywood 90028 (tel 213/469-8311).

HOTELS 🏨

≣≣≣ Chateau Marmont Hotel and Bungalows
8221 Sunset Blvd, 90046; tel 213/656-1010 or toll free 800/CHATEAU; fax 213/655-5311. This hotel, set on a hill above Sunset Blvd, is favored by the European and Hollywood entertainment crowd because of its privacy. The original 1929 structure was an apartment building. Howard Hughes lived here, John Belushi died here. **Rooms:** 50 rms, stes, and effic; 13 cottages/villas. CI 2pm/CO noon. Nonsmoking rms avail. Accommodations are all newly refurbished, although pieces look skimpy in some. Bathrooms are decidedly retro, with original tiling and no counter space; many rooms have kitchens with prehistoric appliances. Every layout is different. The more popular rooms overlook Sunset Blvd, but courtyard rooms are more serene. But the neatest places to stay are the cottages and bungalows, which look like fairytale dwellings, with rough stucco facades and brick walkways. **Amenities:** 📺 🛁 ▣ 🍷 Cable TV w/movies, refrig, dataport, VCR, CD/tape player, voice mail, in-rm safe, bathrobes. No A/C. All units w/minibars, some w/terraces, some w/fireplaces. Some rooms are air-conditioned. **Services:** 🍽 📠 VP 🚗 △ 🛎 ⟳ Twice-daily maid svce, car-rental desk, masseur, babysitting. **Facilities:** 🏋 🏌 200 1 restaurant, 1 bar (w/entertainment). The grassy courtyard is surrounded by an arched loggia, where guests can enjoy cocktails seated in wicker chairs. Surrounded by lots of trees, the oval pool stays open 24 hours, heated to 85°F. The fitness center, located in

the "attic" of one of the towers, combines hefty open beams with state-of-the-art equipment, including a great stereo system. **Rates:** $190 S or D; $290–$390 ste; $240–$1400 effic; $260–$800 cottage/villa. Extra person $30. Children under age 18 stay free. Min stay special events. Parking: Indoor, $13/day. AE, DC, EC, MC, V.

≣≣≣ Holiday Inn Hollywood
1755 N Highland Ave, Los Angeles, 90028; tel 213/462-7181 or toll free 800/HOLIDAY; fax 213/466-9072. A 23-story modern, well-kept property within easy walking distance of Hollywood Hall of Fame, Mann's Chinese Theatre, Wax Museum, and Hollywood Bowl Amphitheater. Very courteous, helpful staff. Popular with tour groups. **Rooms:** 470 rms and stes. Executive level. CI 3pm/CO noon. Nonsmoking rms avail. Spacious, standard accommodations have panoramic city or Hollywood hillside views. **Amenities:** 📺 🛁 ▣ 🍷 A/C, satel TV w/movies, dataport, voice mail, in-rm safe. **Services:** ✕ 📠 🚗 △ ⟳ ⟳ Twice-daily maid svce, car-rental desk, babysitting. Tour desk and ticket office in lobby. **Facilities:** 🏋 🏌 180 ♿ 2 restaurants, 1 bar (w/entertainment), games rm, washer/dryer. Deli/snack shop on premises. $5 guest passes to adjacent Hollywood Fitness Center. **Rates:** $130–$160 S or D; $145–$250 ste. Extra person $10. Children under age 18 stay free. Min stay special events. Parking: Indoor/outdoor, $7/day. AE, CB, DC, DISC, JCB, MC, V.

RESTAURANTS 🍽

Dav Maghreb
7651 Sunset Blvd; tel 213/876-7651. Between Fairfax and La Brea Aves. **Moroccan.** Spacious restaurant with elaborate, authentic appointments. Low seating on couches or pillows around tables. Belly dancing show takes place while you eat. Menu includes specialties such as roast squab with rice, almonds, and raisins; traditional roast lamb flavored with cumin and served with lentils; and Morocco's most famous dish, b'stilla (pastry filled with chicken, almonds, eggs and spices). **FYI:** Reservations recommended. Children's menu. **Open:** Tues–Sat 6–11pm, Sun 5:30–10:30pm. **Prices:** Prix fixe $29. CB, DC, MC, V. ⦿ 🍷 👪 VP

★ Hamptons
1342 N Highland Ave; tel 213/469-1090. **Regional American/Burgers.** A very friendly, freewheeling show-biz hangout popular with writers, actors, and production crews. It's known for its wide array of huge burgers. In addition to the basics of cheese and bacon, more unusual adornments include creamy peanut butter or salsa and sour cream. They also offer a highly eclectic American menu that features an extensive salad bar as well as grilled fish and chicken dishes. **FYI:** Reservations accepted. Children's menu. Beer and wine only. **Open:** Mon 11am–3pm, Tues–Thurs 11am–9pm, Fri–Sun 11am–10pm. **Prices:** Main courses $5–$10. AE, DC, MC, V. 🍴 🖼 👪 🚗 ♿

ATTRACTIONS

Hollywood Sign
Hollywood Blvd. These 50-foot-high, white, sheet-metal letters have become a world-famous symbol of this movie industry town. Erected in 1923 to promote real estate development, the sign originally spelled out "HOLLYWOODLAND." Laws prohibit climbing up to the base.

Walk of Fame
Hollywood Blvd and Vine St; tel 213/469-8311. Nearly 2,000 stars are honored on the world's most famous sidewalk. Bronze medallions set into the center of each star pay tribute to famous personalities of all entertainment media. Some of the most popular include Marilyn Monroe, 6744 Hollywood Blvd; James Dean, 1719 Vine St; John Lennon, 1750 Vine St; and Elvis Presley, 6777 Hollywood Blvd. A new star is added to the walk of fame each month, and the public is invited to attend. For dates and times, call the Hollywood Chamber of Commerce's "Event Info Line," 213/469-8311.

Mann's Chinese Theatre
6925 Hollywood Blvd; tel 213/461-3331. One of Hollywood's greatest landmarks (famous for its entry court, where movie stars' signatures and hand- and footprints are set in concrete), Grauman's Chinese Theatre was opened in 1927 by Sid Grauman, the impresario credited with originating the idea of the spectacular Hollywood "premiere." Opulent both inside and out, the theater combines authentic and simulated Chinese decor; two of the theater's columns actually come from a Ming Dynasty temple. Movie tickets cost about what they do at any other movie house. **Open:** Call for showtimes. **$$$**

Hollywood Memorial Park Cemetery
6000 Santa Monica Blvd; tel 213/469-1181. Dedicated movie buffs may visit the graves of such stars as Peter Lorre; Douglas Fairbanks, Sr; Tyrone Power; Norma Talmadge; and Cecil B DeMille. Almost every day a mysterious lady in black pays homage at the crypt of Rudolph Valentino. **Open:** Daily 8am–5pm. **Free**

Hollywood Wax Museum
6767 Hollywood Blvd; tel 213/462-8860. Dozens of lifelike figures of famous movie stars are featured here, including characters from films such as *Hook* and *Home Alone*. The Chamber of Horrors includes the coffin used in the filming of *The Raven*, as well as a scene from Vincent Price's old hit, *The House of Wax*. Exhibits usually change every few months. **Open:** Sun–Thurs 10am–midnight, Fri–Sat 10am–2am. **$$$**

Holtville

See also El Centro

RESORT

≡≡ Barbara Worth Country Club
2050 Country Club Dr, 92250; tel 619/356-2806 or toll free 800/356-3806; fax 619/356-4653. 12 mi E of El Centro. 100 acres. Good for business travelers and golfers. **Rooms:** 103 rms, stes, and effic. CI 3pm/CO noon. Nonsmoking rms avail. Most rooms have view of golf course. Some have ceiling fans. **Amenities:** A/C, cable TV, refrig, voice mail. Some units w/terraces, some w/whirlpools. **Services:** Restaurant has Friday-night fresh seafood buffet. Champagne brunch buffet offered on Sundays. **Facilities:** 18 1 restaurant, 1 bar, whirlpool, washer/dryer. **Rates:** $48 S; $54 D; $129 ste; $130 effic. Extra person $6. Children under age 13 stay free. Parking: Outdoor, free. AE, CB, DC, DISC, MC, V.

Hopland

Hopland gets its name from the brewery hops that used to be farmed in the region. The hops are no longer grown, but the brewing tradition is kept alive by the Hopland Brewery, which serves excellent handcrafted beers under the Mendocino Brewing Company name. The town has made a successful transition to the tourism industry, with shops, eateries, an inn, as well as wineries outside of town.

INN

≡≡≡ Thatcher Inn
13401 S US 101, 95449; tel 707/744-1890 or toll free 800/266-1891; fax 707/744-1219. Located in the middle of downtown Hopland. The inn was built in 1890 as a stagecoach stop; it is now a designated historic landmark. **Rooms:** 20 rms. CI 3pm/CO noon. No smoking. Decorated in Victorian-style, with brass beds. **Amenities:** No A/C or TV. **Services:** Babysitting. **Facilities:** 1 restaurant, 1 bar, guest lounge. Great, old-fashioned library with fireplace is available for guests' use. The bar is fabulous, with a malachite counter, oak, and mirrors on the walls. There is also a nice garden, a patio, and a restaurant open on weekends. **Rates (CP):** Peak (May–Sept) $95–$140 S; $105–$155 D; $135–$155 ste. Extra person $25. Children under age 10 stay free. Lower rates off-season. Parking: Outdoor, free. Weekday escape package includes room, champagne, dinner, and breakfast for two for $125. Closed Jan 1–15. AE, MC, V.

RESTAURANT

★ The Hopland Brewery

13351 US 101 S; tel 707/744-1015. 14 mi N of Cloverdale. **Pub.** Beloved for its Red Tail ale, this microbrewery is also a restaurant, with a beer garden popular with locals. Fifty cents buys a 4-ounce sampler of one of the brews. The menu includes a variety of appetizers, Red Tail beans, hamburgers, bratwurst with German potato salad, and similar pub-style food. Bands perform on weekends. **FYI:** Reservations not accepted. Blues/jazz/rock. Beer and wine only. **Open:** Sun–Thurs 11am–10pm, Fri 11am–midnight, Sat 11am–2am. **Prices:** Main courses $5–$8. MC, V. 🍴 &

Huntington Beach

Once a sleepy seaside town populated by laid-back surfers, Huntington Beach has come of age and grown into one of the largest cities in Orange County. But the beach culture still holds sway, particularly in September for the annual surfing competition. **Information:** Huntington Beach Chamber of Commerce, 2100 Main St #200, Huntington Beach 92648 (tel 714/536-8888).

HOTELS

≡≡ Comfort Suites

16301 Beach Blvd, 92647; tel 714/841-1812 or toll free 800/221-2222; fax 714/841-0214. Beach Blvd exit off I-405 S. Good choice for business travelers and families; close to a shopping center. **Rooms:** 100 stes. CI noon/CO 11am. Nonsmoking rms avail. Rooms are comfortable with chairs and couches. Suites are particularly nice, and have sofa beds. **Amenities:** 🛁 📶 A/C, cable TV w/movies, refrig. Some units w/terraces, some w/whirlpools. **Services:** 🛎 Twice-daily maid svce. 24-hour coffee service. **Facilities:** 🏋 🛗 & Whirlpool, washer/dryer. **Rates (CP):** $49–$89 S; $54–$99 D. Extra person $5. Children under age 18 stay free. Parking: Outdoor, free. AE, CB, DC, DISC, JCB, MC, V.

≡≡ Holiday Inn Huntington Beach

7667 Center Ave, 92547; tel 714/891-0123 or toll free 800/HOLIDAY; fax 714/895-4591. ½ mi S of Huntington Beach. Beach Blvd exit off I-405; follow Beach Blvd toward Huntington Beach; right on Center Ave. This eight-story, modern-looking place offers a good location just off the San Diego Freeway and close to beach and shopping areas. Not many frills, but not many failings either—a good deal. **Rooms:** 224 rms and stes. Executive level. CI 2pm/CO noon. Nonsmoking rms avail. Rooms are basic and a bit small. The best suites boast two separate living areas. **Amenities:** 🛁 📶 A/C, satel TV w/movies. **Services:** ✕ 🚗 📠 🛎 Babysitting. Coffee and doughnuts in the lobby. **Facilities:** 🏋 🛗 300 & 1 restaurant, 1 bar, whirlpool, washer/dryer. **Rates:** $89 S or D; $99–$180

ste. Children under age 21 stay free. AP and MAP rates avail. Parking: Indoor/outdoor, free. AE, CB, DC, DISC, EC, JCB, MC, V.

≡≡≡ Waterfront Hilton Beach Resort

21100 Pacific Coast Hwy, 92648 (Downtown); tel 714/960-7873 or toll free 800/HILTONS; fax 714/960-3791. Beach Blvd exit off I-405. Very well situated hotel, just across from an 8½-mile beach—southern California's longest. **Rooms:** 300 rms and stes. Executive level. CI 4pm/CO noon. Nonsmoking rms avail. Tastefully appointed, each with an ocean view. **Amenities:** 🛁 📶 🍴 A/C, cable TV w/movies, refrig. All units w/minibars, all w/terraces, some w/whirlpools. **Services:** ✕ 🚗 VP 🚗 📠 🛎 Twice-daily maid svce, car-rental desk, social director, children's program, babysitting. Multilingual staff. **Facilities:** 🏋 🚴 ⛵ 🛗 4500 💻 & 2 restaurants (see "Restaurants" below), 2 bars (1 w/entertainment), 1 beach (ocean), lifeguard, board surfing, spa, whirlpool, day-care ctr, washer/dryer. 14,000 square feet of meeting facilities; 21 meeting rooms available. **Rates:** $135–$245 S or D; $275–$800 ste. Children under age 18 stay free. Parking: Indoor/outdoor, free. AE, CB, DC, DISC, JCB, MC, V.

MOTEL

≡ Best Western Regency Inn

19360 Beach Blvd, 92648; tel 714/962-4244 or toll free 800/528-1234; fax 714/963-4724. No-frills hotel located near the beach and close to town; needs some maintenance. Renovation should be completed. **Rooms:** 63 rms, stes, and effic. CI 2pm/CO noon. No smoking. Rooms are clean but furniture is old. Not much privacy in ground-floor rooms. **Amenities:** 🛁 📶 A/C, TV w/movies. 1 unit w/fireplace. **Services:** 🛎 Car-rental desk, babysitting. Movie rentals. **Facilities:** 🏋 30 & Lifeguard, whirlpool, washer/dryer. **Rates:** Peak (mid May–Oct) $69–$99 S; $79–$99 D; $129 ste; $79 effic. Extra person $10. Children under age 12 stay free. Lower rates off-season. Parking: Outdoor, free. AE, DISC, MC, V.

RESTAURANTS

♣ Baci

18748 Beach Blvd; tel 714/965-1194. Beach Blvd exit off I-405 Restaurant is between Alice and Garfield Sts. **Italian.** Feels like you've stepped into Venice, with Italian paintings, soft lights, and lots of old-world charm. The cozy atmosphere and attentive service create a nice place to dine on Northern Italian dishes of veal osso buco, penne with beef and red wine, and risotto with fresh seafood. **FYI:** Reservations recommended. Guitar. **Open:** Daily 5–10pm. **Prices:** Main courses $8–$19. AE, CB, DC, DISC, MC, V. 💟 VP &

Palm Court

In the Waterfront Hilton Beach Resort, 21100 Pacific Coast Hwy; tel 714/960-7873. Beach Blvd exit off I-405. **New American.** Small restaurant with a garden atmosphere, frequented by guests of the hotel. Filled with plants and birds of paradise, decorated in soothing pastel colors. Serves brunch, salads, as well as chicken, beef, and other entrees. House specialty is Maine lobster at $45. **FYI:** Reservations recommended. Piano. Children's menu. **Open:** Breakfast Mon–Sat 6:30–11:30am, Sun 6:30–11am; lunch daily 11am–3pm; dinner Mon–Thurs 5–10pm, Sat–Sun 5–11pm; brunch Sun 10am–3pm. **Prices:** Main courses $14–$45; prix fixe $39. AE, CB, DC, DISC, MC, V. 🍷 🍴 🏔 🏕 VP ♿

ATTRACTIONS 📷

Huntington Beach International Surfing Museum
411 Olive St; tel 714/960-3483. Featured here are permanent and changing exhibits relating to surfing and surfers. Also here is the Nalu Art Gallery, featurng examples of surf-related artwork. **Open:** Peak (Mem Day–Labor Day) daily noon–5pm. Reduced hours off-season. **$**

Huntington State Beach
Pacific Coast Hwy (CA 1); tel 714/536-1455. Popular with visitors as well as locals, this 2-mile beach area lies between Brookhurst Ave and Beach Blvd. A bike trail connects to Bolsa Chica State Beach (see below). **Open:** Daily 6am–10pm. **Free**

Bolsa Chica State Beach
Pacific Coast Highway (CA 1); tel 714/536-1455. This 4-mile stretch, roughly between Goldenwest and Warner Aves, is one of southern California's most popular. A bike trail runs to Huntington State Beach (see above). **Open:** Daily 6am–10pm. **Free**

Idyllwild

The San Jacinto Mountains form the alpine setting of Idyllwild, a hub for rock climbing, hiking, and camping. Although Palm Springs and the 10,000-foot mountains of Idyllwild are linked by a tram, the two regions seem a world apart. **Information:** Idyllwild Chamber of Commerce, 54274 N Circle Dr, PO Box 304, Idyllwild 92549 (tel 909/659-3259).

MOTEL 📷

Woodland Park Manor
55350 S Circle Dr, Fern Valley, 92549; tel 909/659-2657. CA 243 exit off I-10. 5 acres. Set amid Ponderosa and Jeffrey pines, cedars, and oak trees. Floor-to-ceiling windows showcase the forest; property could use some updating. **Rooms:** 11 cottages/villas. CI 2pm/CO 11am. Nonsmoking rms avail. Rustic. **Amenities:** Cable TV, refrig. No A/C or phone. All units w/terraces, all w/fireplaces. **Services:** 🛎 **Facilities:** 🏊 ♿ Lawn games, playground. Picnic tables, Ping-Pong, horseshoes in wooded park. Heated pool open in summer. **Rates:** $69–$94 cottage/villa. Children under age 18 stay free. Min stay wknds. Parking: Outdoor, free. MC, V.

INN

Quiet Creek Inn
26345 Delano Dr, PO Box 240, 92549; tel 909/659-6110 or toll free 800/450-6110; fax 909/659-4287. CA 243 exit off I-10. 6½ acres. Nestled in a heavily forested area of the San Jacinto Mountains; modern versions of the old log cabin. The ambience throughout is warm and comfortable. Unsuitable for children under 18. **Rooms:** 12 cottages/villas. CI 2pm/CO 11am. Nonsmoking rms avail. Cedar cabins (five duplexes) blend with their surroundings; decks overlook Strawberry Creek. **Amenities:** 📺 Cable TV, refrig. No A/C or phone. All units w/terraces, all w/fireplaces. **Services:** 🛎 **Facilities:** 🎮 Lawn games, guest lounge w/TV. Stone barbecue area for guests to use. Lounge chairs and picnic tables are tucked away in creekside locations. **Rates:** $71–$150 cottage/villa. Min stay wknds and special events. Parking: Outdoor, free. AE, JCB, MC, V.

RESTAURANT 🍴

Gastrognome Restaurant
54381 Ridgeview Dr; tel 909/659-5055. CA 243 exit off I-10. **Eclectic.** A stone fireplace, antiques, and stained-glass windows create a charming atmosphere. In addition to regular offerings of meat and seafood, specials may include fiery chicken on pasta, New Zealand rack of lamb, or shrimp cilantro-pesto pasta. **FYI:** Reservations accepted. Children's menu. Dress code. **Open:** Lunch Fri–Sun 11:30am–2:30pm; dinner Sun–Sat 5–9pm. **Prices:** Main courses $11–$34. CB, DC, DISC, ER, MC, V. 🍴 🎵 💟 ♿

ATTRACTION 📷

Mount San Jacinto State Park
Tel 909/659-2607. This 13,500-acre park consists mostly of wilderness, and contains three mountain peaks over 10,000 feet in elevation. Visitors can hike in from the park's west side or ride the Palm Springs Aerial Tramway (see PALM SPRINGS) up the mountain. Wilderness permits are required for hikers and backpackers. **Open:** Peak (Mem Day–Labor Day) 8am–5pm, Sat–Sun 8am–10pm. Reduced hours off-season. **$$**

Indian Wells

Indian Wells is one of several resort-and-country-club desert communities that have sprung up around Palm Springs.

RESORTS 📷

Hyatt Grand Champions
44-600 Indian Wells Lane, 92210; tel 619/341-1000 or toll free 800/233-1234; fax 619/568-2236. Washington exit off I-10, to CA 111. 34 acres. Set on 34 acres of manicured fairways and gardens, with the San Jacinto Mountains as a backdrop. This is one of the region's major sports venues, host to the Evert and *Newsweek* Champions tennis tourna-

ments and previous site of events on the Senior PGA Tour. **Rooms:** 316 rms and stes; 20 cottages/villas. Executive level. CI 4pm/CO 1pm. Nonsmoking rms avail. Units in the main building are large split-level parlor suites, with a bedroom and a sunken sitting room with sofa and work desk. Handsome with gray-and-cognac marble, the spacious bathrooms have separate tubs and glass-enclosed showers. One- and two-bedroom garden villas (President Clinton stayed in one when he came to town) have garden courtyards, individual whirlpools, wood-burning fireplaces, and oversize marble baths. **Amenities:** 🕾 🖏 🖃 ⬠ A/C, cable TV w/movies, refrig, voice mail. Some units w/fireplaces. Iron and ironing board in all rooms. **Services:** 🍽 🗝 VP 🚍 ⎙ ⏚ Car-rental desk, masseur, children's program, babysitting. **Facilities:** 🏌 🚴 ▶36 🎾 ●4 🏊 ⛳ 🎱 1000 ⬚ & 3 restaurants, 3 bars (1 w/entertainment), basketball, volleyball, lawn games, spa, sauna, steam rm, whirlpool, beauty salon, playground. Third-largest tennis stadium in the country (10,500 seats), as well as hard, clay, and grass courts. Two 18-hole championship golf courses designed by Ted Robinson. Onsite Aveda Salon offers hair, nail, and complete skin treatments. **Rates:** Peak (Jan–May) $270–$310 S or D; $395 ste; $760–$970 cottage/villa. Extra person $25. Children under age 18 stay free. Min stay special events. Lower rates off-season. Parking: Indoor/outdoor, $8/day. AE, CB, DC, DISC, JCB, MC, V.

≣≣≣ Indian Wells Resort Hotel

76-661 CA 111, 92210; tel 619/345-6466 or toll free 800/248-3220; fax 619/772-5083. Washington exit off I-10. 15 acres. Located on 15 acres in the heart of Indian Wells, this contemporary-style resort offers panoramic views of the Santa Rosa Mountains. **Rooms:** 152 rms, stes, and effic. CI 3pm/CO noon. Nonsmoking rms avail. Accommodations are decorated with washed-ash furnishings and bedspreads with colorful mosaics of peach, burnt orange, green, and lavender. **Amenities:** 🕾 🖏 A/C, cable TV w/movies, voice mail. All units w/minibars, all w/terraces, 1 w/fireplace, 1 w/whirlpool. **Services:** ✗ 🗝 VP 🚍 ⎙ ⏚ Babysitting. **Facilities:** 🏌 🚴 ●2 🎱 330 & 1 restaurant, 1 bar (w/entertainment), whirlpool. Guests have golf privileges at the Indian Wells Country Club. **Rates:** Peak (Jan 12–Apr 20) $189–$249 S or D; $269–$309 ste; $269–$309 effic. Extra person $15. Children under age 18 stay free. Min stay special events. Lower rates off-season. Parking: Outdoor, free. AE, DC, DISC, JCB, MC, V.

≣≣≣≣ Renaissance Esmeralda Resort

44-400 Indian Wells Lane, 92210; tel 619/773-4444 or toll free 800/552-4386; fax 619/346-9308. Washington exit off I-10 to CA 111. 14 acres. Although this art deco–inspired hotel looks stark on the outside, the seven-story atrium lobby is quite stunning, with twin curving stairways and crystal chandeliers. The golf course winds around the property. **Rooms:** 560 rms and stes. CI 3pm/CO noon. Nonsmoking rms avail. Very large rooms, with comfortable seating areas. Sliding plantation shutters screen the balconies, some of which have sweeping golf-course views. Bathrooms have marble counters, small TVs, and separate WCs; clever "two-sided" closets allow access to clothes from both the bedroom and bathroom. **Amenities:** 🕾 🖏 ⬠ A/C, cable TV w/movies, dataport, voice mail, bathrobes. All units w/minibars, all w/terraces, some w/fireplaces, some w/whirlpools. Iron and ironing board in room. **Services:** 🍽 🗝 VP 🚍 ⎙ ⏚ Twice-daily maid svce, car-rental desk, social director, masseur, children's program, babysitting. Complimentary newspaper, along with coffee or tea, served with morning wake-up call. **Facilities:** 🏌 🚴 ▶36 🎾 ●5 🏊 🎱 1800 ⬚ & 3 restaurants (*see* "Restaurants" below), 2 bars (1 w/entertainment), basketball, volleyball, games rm, lawn games, spa, sauna, steam rm, whirlpool. One of the "shores" of the large, freeform main pool is a small sandy beach. Spectacular rose garden. **Rates:** Peak (Jan–May) $290–$390 S or D; $500–$2000 ste. Extra person $15. Children under age 12 stay free. Min stay special events. Lower rates off-season. Parking: Indoor/outdoor, $10/day. AE, CB, DC, DISC, EC, ER, JCB, MC, V.

RESTAURANTS 🍽

Le St Germain

74-895 CA 111; tel 619/773-6511. Monterey exit off I-10. **French/Mediterranean.** Formerly one of Los Angeles's most renowned restaurants, this new incarnation captures the feeling of Paris's Left Bank. The French-Mediterranean menu offers such choices as grilled rack of lamb with herb crust, seared whitefish on spinach with Pommery mustard sauce, and grilled filet mignon with roasted shallots and merlot sauce. **FYI:** Reservations recommended. Piano. Dress code. **Open:** Daily 5–11pm. **Prices:** Main courses $20–$29. AE, CB, DC, DISC, ER, MC, V. �> VP &

Sirocco

In the Renaissance Esmeralda Resort, 44-400 Indian Wells Lane; tel 619/773-4444. Washington exit off I-10. **Mediterranean.** Crisp linen and gleaming silver help create an elegant setting for this intimate restaurant. Specializing in Mediterranean cuisine, it serves a selection of different tapas each day, as well as such classic Mediterranean meals as bouillabaisse of fish and shellfish; and a paella of chicken, spicy sausage, and shellfish. Boasts climate-controlled exhibition wine cellars. **FYI:** Reservations recommended. Dress code. **Open:** Lunch Mon–Sat 11:30am–2:30pm; dinner daily 6–10pm. Closed July–Aug. **Prices:** Main courses $11–$25. AE, CB, DC, DISC, MC, V. 🏔 VP &

Vicky's

45-100 Club Dr; tel 619/345-9770. Washington exit off I-10. **Southwestern.** Set in a large adobe-style building with high ceilings, Mexican accents, and original artwork by Norman Laiberte, the restaurant has three separate dining rooms and a piano bar. The menu is simple: large portions of lamb, shrimp, chicken, New York steak or filet, veal, rib steak, halibut, or salmon. Each entree is served with baked potato or Saratoga chips, salad, and a vegetable. **FYI:** Reservations not accepted. Dress code. **Open:** Daily 5–10:30pm. Closed mid-June–mid-Sept. **Prices:** Main courses $11–$20. DC, MC, V. &

Indio

Known as the date capital of the nation, Indio serves not only as the distribution point for the heavily irrigated fruit-growing areas of the surrounding desert but also as a center for winter A-circuit horse shows and high-goal polo matches. The town showcases its talents during a mid-February National Date Festival. **Information:** Indio Chamber of Commerce, 82-503 CA 111, PO Box TTT, Indio 92201 (tel 619/347-0676).

MOTELS

Best Western Date Tree Motor Hotel
81-909 Indio Blvd, 92201; tel 619/347-3421 or toll free 800/292-5599; fax 619/347-3421. Landscaped citrus and cactus gardens surround this contemporary hotel with its Olympic-size pool. **Rooms:** 117 rms, stes, and effic. CI 1pm/CO noon. Nonsmoking rms avail. **Amenities:** A/C, cable TV, refrig. All units w/terraces, 1 w/whirlpool. **Services:** Babysitting. **Facilities:** Games rm, lawn games, whirlpool, playground, washer/dryer. **Rates (CP):** Peak (Jan–Apr) $59–$130 S or D; $89–$150 ste; $89–$150 effic. Extra person $5. Children under age 18 stay free. Min stay wknds. Lower rates off-season. Parking: Outdoor, free. AE, CB, DC, DISC, EC, ER, JCB, MC, V.

Comfort Inn
43-505 Monroe St, 92201; tel 619/347-4044 or toll free 800/221-2222; fax 619/347-1287. Monroe exit off I-10, turn left. Just minutes away from the business district and shopping area, and situated close to the Indio Date Festival grounds. **Rooms:** 63 rms. CI 1pm/CO 11am. Nonsmoking rms avail. **Amenities:** A/C, cable TV w/movies, refrig. **Services:** **Facilities:** Whirlpool. **Rates (CP):** Peak (Jan–Mar) $54–$94 S or D. Extra person $6. Children under age 18 stay free. Lower rates off-season. Parking: Outdoor, free. AE, CB, DC, DISC, JCB, MC, V.

RESTAURANT

Devane's
80-755 CA 111; tel 619/342-5009. Washington exit off I-10. **Italian.** Small California mission-style building with adobe walls, brick floors, and huge planters. Italian cuisine is the specialty, including such dishes as chicken marsala, veal piccata, pastas, and pizzas. **FYI:** Reservations accepted. Dress code. **Open:** Peak (Jan–Apr) lunch Tues–Fri 11am–3pm; dinner Tues–Sun 4–9:30pm. Closed July–Sept. **Prices:** Main courses $10–$15. AE, DC, DISC, MC, V.

ATTRACTION

Coachella Valley Museum and Cultural Center
82616 Miles Ave; tel 619/342-6651. Housed in the former home and medical office of Dr Harry Smiley, this museum features Native American artifacts, memorabilia of early Coachella Valley pioneers, and changing art exhibits. **Open:** Peak (Oct–May) Wed–Sat 10am–4pm, Sun 1–4pm. Reduced hours off-season. $

Inglewood
See Los Angeles Int'l Airport

Irvine
The Irvine Ranch, a former Spanish land grant, has become the site of the quintessential Orange County planned community—open space, residential areas, shopping, and some commerce. The fast-growing city is the seat of the University of California, Irvine. **Information:** Irvine Chamber of Commerce, 17755 Sky Park E #101, Irvine 92714 (tel 714/660-9112).

HOTELS

Atrium Hotel at Orange County Airport
18700 MacArthur Blvd, 92715 (John Wayne Airport); tel 714/833-2770 or toll free 800/854-3012; fax 714/757-1228. 1 mi off exit from I-405. Nicely landscaped grounds. Quiet location makes this ideal for the business traveler. **Rooms:** 209 rms and stes. CI 3pm/CO noon. Nonsmoking rms avail. Light and cheerful. **Amenities:** A/C, cable TV, dataport, voice mail. All units w/terraces, 1 w/whirlpool. **Services:** Car-rental desk. **Facilities:** 2 restaurants, 2 bars (1 w/entertainment), games rm, beauty salon, washer/dryer. **Rates:** $112–$122 S; $129–$159 ste. Children under age 21 stay free. Parking: Outdoor, free. AE, CB, DC, DISC, MC, V.

Courtyard by Marriott
2701 Main St, 92714 (John Wayne Airport); tel 714/757-1200 or toll free 800/321-2211; fax 714/757-1596. Jamboree exit off I-405; take Jamboree Blvd to Main St; property on corner. Clean and well kept. Convenient location near business parks, shopping centers, and airport. **Rooms:** 153 rms and stes. CI 3pm/CO 1pm. Nonsmoking rms avail. Very well maintained. **Amenities:** A/C, cable TV w/movies, voice mail. All units w/terraces. **Services:** Babysitting. Friendly, efficient staff. **Facilities:** 1 restaurant, 1 bar, whirlpool, washer/dryer. Attractive gazebo and pool in central courtyard. **Rates:** $94–$99 S or D; $109–$115 ste. Extra person $10. Children under age 18 stay free. Parking: Indoor/outdoor, free. AE, CB, DC, DISC, MC, V.

≣≣≣ Embassy Suites
2120 Main St, 92714 (John Wayne Airport); tel 714/553-8332 or toll free 800/362-2779; fax 714/261-5301. McArthur exit off I-405 S. Close to airport, shopping center, and business parks; suitable for business travelers. Clean. **Rooms:** 293 stes. CI 3pm/CO 1pm. Nonsmoking rms avail. Separate living area good for conducting business meetings. All upholsteries and carpeting are new. **Amenities:** 🛅 ⚬ 🖵 📶 A/C, cable TV w/movies, refrig, dataport, voice mail. **Services:** ✕ ☞ 🚗 🖎 🗗 Babysitting. **Facilities:** 🛁 🛏150 ᕗ 1 restaurant (lunch and dinner only), 1 bar, sauna, whirlpool. **Rates (BB):** $104–$139 ste. Extra person $10. Children under age 12 stay free. Parking: Indoor/outdoor, free. Good value. AE, CB, DC, DISC, EC, ER, JCB, MC, V.

≣≣≣ Hyatt Regency Irvine
17900 Jamboree Blvd, 92714 (John Wayne Airport); tel 714/975-1234 or toll free 800/233-1234; fax 714/863-0531. Jamboree exit off I-405 S. Light and airy atrium-style property. Located in a business park near freeway, airport, and shopping centers. The well-manicured grounds make this the nicest hotel in the area. **Rooms:** 536 rms and stes. Executive level. CI 3pm/CO noon. Nonsmoking rms avail. Comfortable and newly upgraded. Decorated in creamy colors with pastel accents. **Amenities:** 🛅 ⚬ 📶 A/C, cable TV w/movies, bathrobes. Some units w/terraces, some w/whirlpools. **Services:** ✕ ☞ 📶 🚗 🖎 🗗 ⟳ Twice-daily maid svce, car-rental desk, social director, masseur, children's program, babysitting. Shuttle to South Coast Plaza. **Facilities:** 🛁 🚲 🖼 📱 🛏 🛏2100 🖳 ᕗ 2 restaurants, 3 bars (1 w/entertainment), games rm, spa, sauna, steam rm, whirlpool. **Rates:** $169–$194 S; $189–$214 D; $450–$3,000 ste. Extra person $25. Children under age 18 stay free. Parking: Outdoor, free. AE, CB, DC, DISC, JCB, MC, V.

≣≣≣≣ Irvine Marriott at John Wayne Airport
18000 Von Karman Ave, 92715; tel 714/553-0100 or toll free 800/228-9290; fax 714/261-7059. Jamboree exit off I-405 S; right on Michaelson to Von Karman; right into Voll Center Complex. Impressive marble lobby and a uniformed staff set a nice tone. Located in the heart of a business park. **Rooms:** 491 rms and stes. Executive level. CI 4pm/CO noon. Nonsmoking rms avail. Tastefully decorated with rich green carpeting and dark wood dressers. **Amenities:** 🛅 ⚬ A/C, cable TV w/movies, dataport, voice mail. Some units w/terraces. **Services:** ✕ ☞ 📶 🚗 🖎 🗗 ⟳ Car-rental desk, masseur, babysitting. Efficient, polite staff. **Facilities:** 🛁 🚲 📱 🛏 🛏1500 🖳 ᕗ 3 restaurants, 2 bars (1 w/entertainment), games rm, sauna, whirlpool, washer/dryer. **Rates:** $160 S or D; $350–$600 ste. Children under age 18 stay free. Parking: Outdoor, free. AE, CB, DC, DISC, JCB, MC, V.

≣≣≣ La Quinta Motor Inn
14972 Sand Canyon Ave, 92718 (Old Town Complex); tel 714/551-0909 or toll free 800/531-5900; fax 714/551-2945. Sand Canyon exit off I-5. Unique property in a historic landmark, a former grainery. **Rooms:** 148 rms. Executive level. CI 3pm/CO noon. Nonsmoking rms avail. Each room is individually decorated. **Amenities:** 🛅 ⚬ A/C, cable TV w/movies. **Services:** 🚗 🖎 🗗 ⟳ **Facilities:** 🛁 🛏 🛏72 3 restaurants, 2 bars (1 w/entertainment), whirlpool, beauty salon, washer/dryer. **Rates (CP):** $62–$77 S; $70–$85 D. Extra person $5. Children under age 18 stay free. Parking: Outdoor, free. AE, CB, DC, DISC, MC, V.

≣≣ Orange County Airport Hilton
18800 MacArthur Blvd, 92715 (John Wayne Airport); tel 714/833-9999 or toll free 800/445-8667; fax 714/833-3317. MacArthur exit off I-405; turn left at Douglas; then make 2nd left. Older hotel near the airport; site is quite noisy. **Rooms:** 289 rms and stes. Executive level. CI 3pm/CO noon. Nonsmoking rms avail. Rooms are designed for the business traveler, with large desks and good lighting. **Amenities:** 🛅 ⚬ 📶 A/C, satel TV w/movies, dataport, voice mail. Some units w/minibars, all w/terraces. Rooms are fully stocked for entertaining. **Services:** ✕ 📶 🚗 🖎 🗗 Car-rental desk, babysitting. Free shuttle to John Wayne Airport. **Facilities:** 🛁 🛏1300 🖳 ᕗ 1 restaurant, 2 bars, whirlpool. Piano bar in lobby, Mon–Thurs, 4–10pm **Rates (BB):** $145 S; $145 D; $250–$800 ste. Parking: Outdoor, free. Corporate rates available. AE, CB, DC, DISC, EC, JCB, MC, V.

RESTAURANTS 🍴

Bistro 201
In TransAmerica Building, 18201 Von Karman Ave; tel 714/631-1551. ½ mi S of John Wayne Airport MacArthur Blvd exit off I-405. **International.** Decor features rich colors, white tablecloths, and elegant banquettes; a beautiful bamboo grove is visible from windows. Menu offers an eclectic mix, from carpaccio with arugula, Parmesan, capers, and horseradish vinaigrette, to grilled shrimp on a bed of polenta with roasted peppers and basil pesto. Desserts include hot Belgian chocolate soufflé and hot apple tart with caramel sauce. **FYI:** Reservations recommended. Jazz/piano. **Open:** Lunch Mon–Fri 11:30am–3:30pm; dinner Mon–Sat 5:30–10:30pm. **Prices:** Main courses $10–$20. AE, DC, MC, V. ♥ 🍴 📶 ᕗ

♣ Chanteclair
18912 MacArthur Blvd; tel 714/752-8001. Within ¼ mile of John Wayne Airport. **French.** This restaurant is designed like a country château, with several different dining rooms with fireplaces—very intimate and unusual. The rooms reflect different themes, from pure romance to a French-style study. The menu features changing specialties like frogs' legs, fresh tuna, and smoked mackerel with cabbage and Riesling sauce. **FYI:** Reservations recommended. Dress code. **Open:** Lunch Mon–Fri 11:30am–2:30pm; dinner Mon–Sat 6–10pm. **Prices:** Main courses $18–$37. AE, CB, DC, DISC, MC, V. ♥ 🖼 📶

★ Prego
18420 Von Karman Ave; tel 714/553-1333. Jamboree exit off I-405. **Italian.** A bistro-style restaurant with an extremely

attractive and well-trained staff. Glass partitions provide some privacy, yet allow a clear view of the entire restaurant. Lovely flowers accentuate the well-designed space. **FYI:** Reservations recommended. **Open:** Mon–Fri 11:30am–10:30pm, Sat 5–11pm, Sun 5–10pm. **Prices:** Main courses $8–$14. AE, CB, DC, MC, V. ♥ ⚏ VP ₠

ATTRACTION 📷

Wild Rivers Waterpark

8770 Irvine Center Dr; tel 714/768-WILD. Spread over 20 acres, this park offers water rides in three main themed sections: Wild Rivers Mountain, with more than 20 thrilling water rides; Thunder Cove, featuring two giant wave pools; and Explorer's Island, with child-size water rides, wading and jacuzzi pools. Also several sun decks, sand beaches, arcade, shops, and food concessions. **Open:** Peak (late-June–Labor Day) daily 10am–8pm. Reduced hours off-season. **$$$$**

Jackson

Jackson has enough colorful gold rush history to fill volumes of Wild West novels. The Amador County Museum and self-guided walking and bicycle tours offer modern perspectives on the past. **Information:** Amador County Chamber of Commerce, 125 Peek St, PO Box 596, Jackson 95642 (tel 209/223-0350).

MOTELS 🏨

≡≡ Best Western Amador Inn

200 S CA 49, 95642; tel 209/223-0211 or toll free 800/543-5221; fax 209/223-4836. Clean, new buildings have basic amenities with few frills. Convenient to Old Jackson. Lots of parking. **Rooms:** 118 rms and effic. CI 3pm/CO noon. Nonsmoking rms avail. Rooms in rear are quieter than those in front. **Amenities:** 🛋 🖥 A/C, cable TV w/movies, voice mail. Some units w/fireplaces. **Services:** 🚗 🖼 🍴 **Facilities:** 🏊 300 ₠ 1 restaurant, 1 bar. Meeting facilities are in adjacent restaurant. **Rates:** $49–$69 S; $59–$89 D; $60–$100 effic. Extra person $10. Children under age 12 stay free. Parking: Outdoor, free. AE, CB, DC, DISC, JCB, MC, V.

≡ El Campo Casa Resort Motel

12548 Kennedy Flat Rd, 95642; tel 209/223-0100. Exit off CA 88. Large garden and pool. Hillside views. Great for families. **Rooms:** 15 rms. CI 3pm/CO noon. Nonsmoking rms avail. Tile dates from the 1940s or 1950s. Small showers only. Rooms seen are a bit cramped with two queen-size beds. **Amenities:** 🛋 🖥 A/C, TV. **Services:** 🍴 🐕 Babysitting. **Facilities:** 🏊 Playground. Swimming pool has an extra-shallow section for young children. Kids toys, sports equipment: tetherball, horseshoes, badminton. Barbecue pits for guest use. **Rates:** Peak (May–Oct) $43–$75 S or D. Extra person $5. Children under age 12 stay free. Lower rates off-season. Parking: Outdoor, free. AE, MC, V.

≡≡ Jackson Holiday Lodge

850 N CA 49, 95642; tel 209/223-0486; fax 209/223-2905. Older property. Furnishings are simple, clean, and comfortable. Lobby recently renovated. Rooms are quieter than at many roadside motels. **Rooms:** 28 rms and stes; 8 cottages/villas. CI 3pm/CO 11am. Nonsmoking rms avail. Basic. Some roomy cottages with their own patios—great for families. **Amenities:** 🛋 🖥 🍴 A/C, cable TV. Some units w/terraces. **Services:** 🚗 🐕 🛎 Personal requests honored when possible. Can cater to small groups. **Facilities:** 🏊 Pool open May–October. **Rates (CP):** $40–$50 S; $46–$55 D; $70–$75 ste; $70–$75 cottage/villa. Extra person $5. Children under age 5 stay free. Parking: Outdoor, free. AE, CB, DC, DISC, MC, V.

INN

≡≡≡ National Hotel

2 Water St, 95642 (Historic Downtown); tel 209/223-0500. Historic brick and timber hotel retains the ambience of the Gold Rush days. **Rooms:** 30 rms (5 w/shared bath). CI 2pm/CO 1pm. Charming rooms, furnished with period antiques, are undergoing renovation; all will be air-conditioned. **Amenities:** No A/C, phone, or TV. Some units w/terraces, some w/fireplaces. Bar/restaurant is rather dour, but springs to life on weekends with honky-tonk and other entertainment. The saloon is the 1862 original. **Facilities:** 1 restaurant (dinner only), 1 bar (w/entertainment), games rm. **Rates:** $20–$50 D w/shared bath, $45–$75 D w/private bath. Extra person $25. Parking: Outdoor, free. Rates include a $10 credit toward dinner or two, $5 credits toward champagne brunch/breakfast. AE, MC, V.

ATTRACTION 📷

Amador County Museum

225 Church St; tel 209/223-6386. Housed in an 1859 building, this museum includes exhibits on the history of the region, especially the Gold Rush. Large-scale working models of the Kennedy Mine make up the museum's featured exhibit. **Open:** Wed–Fri 10am–4pm, Sat–Sun 11am–3pm. **Free**

Jamestown

Known less formally by the locals as Jimtown, this Sierra foothills community has preserved Main Street so well that it has been used as a set in countless movies.

MOTEL

≣≣ Sonora Country Inn
18755 Chanbroullian Lane, 95327; tel 209/984-0315 or toll free 800/847-2211; fax 209/984-4849. 1 mi W of Sonora. Small, adequate roadside hotel near skiing and Gold Country. **Rooms:** 61 rms and stes. CI noon/CO noon. Nonsmoking rms avail. **Amenities:** 🛋 A/C, cable TV, refrig. Some units w/terraces. **Services:** 🍽 🛎 Complimentary continental breakfast delivered to room. Pets allowed with prior approval. **Facilities:** 🏋 & Pool heated April–November. **Rates (CP):** Peak (Apr–Oct) $49–$54 S; $58–$69 D; $78–$95 ste. Extra person $5. Children under age 12 stay free. Min stay special events. Lower rates off-season. Parking: Outdoor, free. AE, CB, DC, DISC, MC, V.

RESTAURANTS

Bella Union Dining Saloon
18242 Main St; tel 209/984-2421. **Californian/Continental.** This 1888 tin shop has been lovingly converted into a historic treasure, complete with 20-foot high copper ceilings and old brick walls. The turn-of-the-century Victorian bar was brought from San Francisco. Specialties include fresh fish, homemade pasta, and a variety of meats. All soup stocks, sauces, and condiments made fresh. Large selection of imported beers. **FYI:** Reservations recommended. Children's menu. **Open:** Lunch Wed–Sun 11:30am–2:30pm; dinner Tues–Sun 5–10pm. **Prices:** Main courses $12–$29; prix fixe $22–$29. AE, MC, V. 🍴 🛋 &

⑤ Country Kitchen Gourmet Café & Gifts
18231 Main St; tel 209/984-3326. **American.** Country-kitchen eatery offering traditional American meals. Try the chicken pot pie, baked breads, pies, or candy. **FYI:** Reservations not accepted. Children's menu. No liquor license. **Open:** Lunch daily 11:30am–5pm. **Prices:** Main courses $3–$6. AE, MC, V. 🍴 &

Kamm's Chinese Restaurant
18208 Main St; tel 209/984-3105. **Chinese.** A pleasant dining room decorated like a fine tearoom with floral wall coverings; popular with both tourists and locals. Family-run for more than 30 years, they offer a large selection of Chinese specialties, including Kung Pao chicken and shrimp. **FYI:** Reservations recommended. Beer and wine only. **Open:** Lunch Mon–Fri 11:30am–2pm; dinner Mon–Fri 4–9pm, Sat 4–9:30pm. **Prices:** Main courses $6–$11. MC, V. &

Michelangelo Ristorante Italiano
18128 Main St; tel 209/984-4830. **Italian.** Located in a historic building, with marble tabletops, oak floors, and black vinyl booths. Pasta, plus fresh-made pizza with a variety of toppings. **FYI:** Reservations accepted. Children's menu. **Open:** Dinner Wed–Mon 5–10pm. **Prices:** Main courses $7–$16. DISC, MC, V.

★ The Smoke Cafe
18191 Main St; tel 209/984-3733. **Mexican.** Festive southwestern atmosphere and well-prepared food. Tamales, mole poblano and black beans, vegetarian items. Bar offers 15 varieties of tequila. **FYI:** Reservations accepted. Children's menu. **Open:** Peak (May–Labor Day) Tues–Sat 5–10pm, Sun 4–10pm. Closed Dec 15–31. **Prices:** Main courses $7–$11. MC, V. &

Jenner

The Russian River meets the Pacific at the tiny town of Jenner. From here, CA 1 spirals north along the Pacific.

INN

≣≣≣ Murphy's Jenner Inn
10400 CA 1, PO Box 69, 95450; tel 707/865-2377 or toll free 800/732-2377; fax 707/865-0829. Perched near the mouth of the Russian River. Some cabins are right at the water's edge, with spectacular sunset views. Unsuitable for children under 12. **Rooms:** 9 rms, stes, and effic; 4 cottages/ villas. CI 3pm/CO noon. No smoking. Each cabin is individually decorated; many have kitchens. **Amenities:** 📺 Refrig. No A/C, phone, or TV. All units w/terraces, some w/fireplaces, some w/whirlpools. **Services:** Masseur, afternoon tea and wine/sherry served. Breakfast and afternoon tea served in nice parlor. Staff will make reservations for area attractions, including kayaking, harbor cruises, fishing, etc. **Facilities:** 🍽 & 1 restaurant, 1 bar, guest lounge. Boat launch across street. **Rates (CP):** $85–$125 S or D; $140–$175 ste; $130–$175 effic; $130–$195 cottage/villa. Extra person $15. Min stay wknds. Parking: Outdoor, free. Discount of 15% on weekdays November–April. AE, MC, V.

LODGE

≣≣≣ Salt Point Lodge
23255 CA 1, 95450; tel 707/847-3234. Picturesque gardens and large but peculiar sculptures surround this property, three miles from Salt Point State Park. **Rooms:** 16 rms. CI 2pm/CO 11am. Nonsmoking rms avail. Rooms are quiet. Ask for an ocean view. **Amenities:** 📺 Satel TV, refrig, VCR. No A/C or phone. Some units w/terraces, some w/fireplaces. **Services:** 🍽 Masseur, babysitting. **Facilities:** & 1 restaurant, 1 bar, sauna, whirlpool, playground. **Rates:** Peak (Apr–Nov) $49–$150 S or D. Extra person $10. Children under age 12 stay free. Min stay wknds. Lower rates off-season. Parking: Outdoor, free. AE, MC, V.

RESTAURANT

River's End
In River's End Resort, US 1; tel 707/865-2484. **Eclectic.** Located at the mouth of the Russian River, overlooking Goat Rock Beach and the Pacific. A great place to watch the sunset from the solarium dining area, or to spy whales through a

telescope provided on the deck. Inside, the room is gracious, with wood paneling and salmon-hued tablecloths set with candles. Specialties are coconut-fried shrimp with orange-rum sauce, lobster and beef brochette, medallions of venison with crayfish sauce, and rack of lamb stuffed with oysters. Wine list highlights Sonoma County vintages. **FYI:** Reservations recommended. **Open:** Peak (June–Sept) Mon–Sun 11am–9:30pm. Closed Dec 2–Feb 14. **Prices:** Main courses $13–$27; prix fixe $23–$27. MC, V. ♿

ATTRACTIONS 📷

Fort Ross State Historic Park
19005 Coast Hwy; tel 707/847-3286. A reconstruction of the fort that was established here in 1812 by the Russians, this served as a base for seal and otter hunting (the fort was abandoned in 1842). At the visitors center are displays of the silver samovars and elaborate table services that the Russians used. Visitors can park their cars and walk down to the dramatically situated, fenced compound, which includes the first Russian Orthodox Church built on the North American continent outside Alaska. The park offers beach trails and picnicking facilities on its more than 1,000 acres. **Open:** Daily 10am–4:30pm. **$$**

Kruse Rhododendron Reserve
Tel 707/847-3221. 3 mi N of Salt Point State Park via CA 1; turn right on Kruse Ranch Rd. This reserve contains 317 acres of redwood, Douglas fir, tan oak, and, of course, rhododendron, some of which have grown to a height of 30 feet. There are five miles of hiking trails through the forest, and picturesque bridges over streams in fern-filled canyons. **Open:** Sunrise–sundown. **Free**

Salt Point State Park
Tel 707/847-3221. 20 mi N of town on CA 1. The park offers some 4,300 acres containing 30 campsites, 14 miles of hiking rails, a pygmy forest, unique rock formations, and old Pomo village sites. Its rugged northern coastline varies dramatically, from protected sandy beach coves such as Stump Beach on the northern end of the park to the sharp bluffs and sheer sandstone cliffs that plunge straight down to the sea at Salt Point and Gerstle Cove. The park includes one of the first underwater parks to be established in the state; except for areas posted as natural preserves, it is open for fishing. **Open:** Sunrise–sundown. **Free**

Joshua Tree National Park

For lodging and dining, see Palm Springs, Twentynine Palms, Yucca Valley

The 793,000-acre national park, newly established with the passage of the California Desert Protection Act of 1994, takes its name from a large yucca belonging to the agave

family that in this region grows to between 20 and 30 feet tall. These "trees" were named by early Mormon settlers, who thought the unusual forms looked like Joshua beckoning them farther west. The park connects the Mojave and Colorado Deserts. The Mojave, to the west, is high desert, with an average elevation of 3,000 feet. The eastern low desert is drier and more barren. Five oases scattered around this arid region attract golden eagles, tarantulas, sidewinders, jackrabbits, coyotes, and rattlesnakes.

Over 3,500 established rock climbs make this one of the world's most popular climbing areas. Most visitors, however, come to camp and hike over dozens of marked trails. Most of the western part of the park is relatively flat, so trails are not particularly strenuous. Hikers should carry an ample supply of water at all times, as desert hiking leads quickly to dehydration. Water is available at the visitor centers, Black Rock Canyon campground, and at the Indian Cove Ranger Station.

There are two main entrances to Joshua Tree; the most popular approach is via Twentynine Palms, 45 miles northwest of Palm Springs. At this north entrance the **Oasis Visitor Center** offers trail maps, safety information, and advice on visiting the park (open daily 8am–4:30pm; closed Dec 25). The Cottonwood Visitor Center is at the southern entrance to the park, near I-10, 55 miles east of Palm Springs (open daily 8am–4:30pm; closed Dec 25). Call toll free 800/365-2267 (park code #5674) for campsite reservations and general information.

Julian

Once a mining town, this quaint, mountainous region is now a burgeoning artists' enclave. Julian provides a gateway to the Anza-Borrego Desert. **Information:** Julian Chamber of Commerce, 2133 Main St, PO Box 413, Julian 92036 (tel 619/765-1857).

INNS 🏨

≣≣≣ Julian Hotel
2032 Main St, 92036; tel 619/765-0201. Wonderful hotel built in 1897. Victorian decor shows much attention to detail, and there's usually a nice breeze on the veranda. **Rooms:** 15 rms (12 w/shared bath); 2 cottages/villas. CI 2pm/CO noon. Each room is individually decorated. Some have clawfoot tubs. **Amenities:** No A/C, phone, or TV. 1 unit w/terrace, 1 w/fireplace. **Services:** 🛎 Babysitting, afternoon tea served. **Facilities:** 🎲 Games rm, guest lounge. **Rates (BB):** $68–$135 S or D. Min stay wknds. Only 2 people to a room. Discounts on 2nd rooms are often available midweek. JCB, MC.

≣≣ Julian Lodge
4th and C Sts, PO Box 1930, 92036; tel 619/765-1420 or toll free 800/542-1420. A cross between a country inn and a motel. Nice rooms and friendly hosts in a charming rural

area. **Rooms:** 23 rms. CI 3pm/CO noon. **Amenities:** A/C, cable TV. No phone. Some units w/terraces. **Services:** Breakfast, newspapers, coffee in lobby. **Facilities:** 40 & Piano in lobby. **Rates (CP):** $69–$92 S or D. Extra person $10. Children under age 1 stay free. Parking: Outdoor, free. DC, JCB, MC.

RESTAURANTS

Julian Cafe
2112 Main St; tel 619/765-2712. CA 79 exit off I-8. **American.** An Old West theme restaurant in a building constructed in 1872. The cheerful staff serves apple-walnut pancakes, tortilla soup, meatloaf, and apple pie. **FYI:** Reservations not accepted. No liquor license. **Open:** Sat–Sun 7am–8:30pm, Mon–Tues 8am–7:30pm, Thurs–Fri 8am–7:30pm, Wed 8am–5pm. **Prices:** Main courses $8–$13. MC, V.

Julian Grille
2224 Main St; tel 619/765-0173. CA 79 exit off I-8. **American.** Housed in a country Edwardian cottage that was a private residence in the early 1900s. The menu includes prime rib, chicken Jerusalem, sweet Georgia peach chicken, steaks, and seafood. **FYI:** Reservations recommended. Children's menu. Beer and wine only. **Open:** Lunch daily 11am–3pm; dinner Tues–Sun 5–9pm. **Prices:** Main courses $12–$20. AE, MC, V.

Romano's Dodge House
2718 B St; tel 619/765-1003. CA 79 exit off I-8. **Italian.** A good family restaurant, with standard Italian red-and-white decor. Serving pizza, frittatas, braciole (Sicilian rolled and stuffed meat), and homemade breads. **FYI:** Reservations recommended. Beer and wine only. **Open:** Sun–Mon 11am–9pm, Thurs 11am–9pm, Fri–Sat 11am–10pm. **Prices:** Main courses $9–$15. No CC.

ATTRACTION

Eagle Mining Company
C St; tel 619/765-0036. The town of Julian was created in the boom that resulted from the discovery of gold in this area in 1870. The Eagle Mining Company was one of 18 mining operations that produced as much as $13 million worth of gold in their day. Shut down during World War II, the mine was reopened as an attraction in 1967. Guided one-hour tours through mineshafts bored into the mountain a century ago offer a glimpse into the process of hardrock mining and what life was like for miners of the era. Gold panning demonstration; small museum. **Open:** Daily 10am–3pm. $$$

Kelseyville

See Clearlake

Kenwood

Part of the small but sophisticated Valley of the Moon wine-growing region, Kenwood is a wine enthusiast's treat.

INN

The Kenwood Inn
10400 Sonoma Hwy, 95452 (Valley of the Moon); tel 707/833-1293 or toll free 800/353-6966; fax 707/833-1247. 2 acres. Set amidst vineyards, it resembles a Mediterranean-style village. Unsuitable for children under 16. **Rooms:** 12 rms and stes. CI 3pm/CO 11am. No smoking. Decorated in rich brocades and cream-colored fabrics, the spacious rooms have balconies overlooking the swimming pool. **Amenities:** Bathrobes. No A/C or TV. All units w/terraces, all w/fireplaces. Complimentary biscotti and bottle of local wine in rooms. **Services:** Twice-daily maid svce, masseur, afternoon tea and wine/sherry served. The full breakfast includes choices such as focaccia with prosciutto and eggs with pesto sauce. **Facilities:** Lawn games, spa, steam rm, whirlpool, guest lounge. First-rate spa facilities, with trained therapists available for body wraps, facials, sea-salt rubs, waxing, and eight different types of massages. **Rates (BB):** Peak (Apr–Nov) $165–$265 S or D; $245–$315 ste. Lower rates off-season. Parking: Outdoor, free. Spa packages available. AE, MC, V.

RESTAURANTS

Caffe Citti
9049 Sonoma Hwy; tel 707/833-2690. **Italian.** This deli/trattoria with counter service emphasizes hearty Italian fare. Although there's not much decor, a fireplace glows warmly in the winter. You can take out food or eat in the restaurant, selecting from dishes such as a whole herb-roasted chicken, pastas (10 sauces to choose from), well-seasoned salads, or sandwiches on focaccia. Expect generous portions and excellent quality. There's outdoor dining in summer, and Italian wines are available by the glass. **FYI:** Reservations not accepted. Children's menu. Beer and wine only. **Open:** Daily 11am–9pm. **Prices:** Main courses $6–$10. MC, V.

Kenwood
9900 CA 12; tel 707/833-6326. **Californian/French.** Surrounded by pastures and vineyards, this is a tranquil spot for a wine-country meal. Decor is simple, with rattan chairs, wood floors, and contemporary art. There's also a lovely slate patio, with tables sheltered under green umbrellas. The same menu runs all day—from hamburgers to bouillabaisse to a daily pasta special, such as gnocchi with pheasant. Good selection of Sonoma wines by the glass. **FYI:** Reservations recommended. **Open:** Tues–Sun 11:30am–9pm. **Prices:** Main courses $13–$25. MC, V.

ATTRACTIONS

Château St Jean

8555 Sonoma Hwy (CA 12); tel 707/833-4134. Located at the foot of Sugarloaf Ridge on what was once a private 250-acre country estate built in 1920. A self-guided tour allows observation of the winemaking process. Visitors can sample St Jean's wines, such as Chardonnay, Cabernet sauvignon, Fume blanc, Merlot, Johannisberg Riesling, and Gewürztraminer, at no charge in the tasting room. Picnic grounds. **Open:** Daily 10am–4:30pm. **Free**

Kunde Winery

10155 Sonoma Hwy; tel 707/833-5501. Located between Sonoma and Santa Rosa in the heart of the Sonoma Valley, the winery has been owned and operated by the Kunde family since the turn of the century. The vineyards feature 22 varietals planted on 750 acres. Tours of aging caves available on weekends. Huge visitor center features a full production area and bottling line. Tastings and sales. **Open:** Daily 11am–5pm. **Free**

Kernville

Kernville sits between the Upper Kern River to the north and Isabella Lake to the south. The river offers serious whitewater rafting in the mountainous areas of the Sequoia National Forest, while the lake is better for boating and water skiing. **Information:** Kernville Chamber of Commerce, 11447 Kernville Rd, PO Box 397, Kernville 93238 (tel 619/376-2629).

MOTELS

Kern Lodge Motel

67 Valley View, PO Box 66, 93238; tel 619/376-2223. This charmingly rustic property has wood-paneled walls and a picnic area with barbecue pits. Porch connects the rooms. Humble, but clean. **Rooms:** 15 rms and effic. CI 2pm/CO 11am. Nonsmoking rms avail. **Amenities:** 🛆 🖭 A/C, cable TV, refrig. All units w/terraces. All units have microwaves. **Services:** 🖎 Babysitting. Pet fee $10. **Facilities:** 🛆 Large picnic area with barbecues available. RV parking slated to be available soon. **Rates:** Peak (Mar–Oct) $50–$80 S or D; $60–$70 effic. Min stay wknds. Lower rates off-season. Parking: Outdoor, free. Rates are reduced on weekdays. AE, CB, DC, DISC, MC, V.

Whispering Pines Lodge Bed & Breakfast

13745 Sierra Way, 93238; tel 619/376-3733; fax 619/376-3735. Refurbished cottage-style motel in lovely, rustic country area right on the river. **Rooms:** 17 rms, stes, and effic. CI 3pm/CO 11am. No smoking. Accommodations have gorgeous hardwood floors and ceilings. Most rooms have kitchens. **Amenities:** 🛆 🖭 A/C, cable TV w/movies, refrig, VCR. Some units w/terraces, some w/fireplaces, some w/whirlpools. Gourmet coffee in every room. **Facilities:** 🛆 🖎

🛆 **Rates (BB):** $89–$119 S or D; $129–$149 ste; $109–$119 effic. Extra person $10. Min stay wknds and special events. Parking: Outdoor, free. AE, CB, DC, DISC, JCB, MC, V.

RESTAURANT

Ewing's on the Kern

125 Buena Vista; tel 619/376-2411. **Steak/Pasta.** An incredible view of the Kern River and the cliffs surrounding it enhance the rustic country theme. Get there before dusk and you can watch the sun dip beyond the bluffs. Steaks, seafood, chicken, and pastas come in large portions. Ribs are tender and slow-roasted over hickory. **FYI:** Reservations recommended. Country music. Children's menu. Jacket required. **Open:** Peak (Mem Day–Labor Day) dinner Sun–Mon 4–8pm, Wed–Thurs 4–8pm, Fri–Sat 4–9pm; brunch Sun 11am–3pm. **Prices:** Main courses $8–$20. AE, CB, DC, DISC, MC, V. 🖼 🖎🛆

King City

Farming roots run deep in this Salinas Valley town. Nearby, founding Father Junípero Serra broke ground on the Mission San Antonio De Pauda on July 14, 1771. The mission is one of the largest and best restored from the Spanish period. It holds its fiesta on the second weekend of June. **Information:** King City & Southern Monterey County Chamber of Commerce and Agriculture, 203 Broadway, King City 93930 (tel 408/385-3814).

HOTEL

Keefer's Inn

615 Canal, 93930; tel 408/385-4843; fax 408/385-1254. E off Canal exit off US 101. Functional as a travel stop on a long trip. **Rooms:** 47 rms. CI 2pm/CO 11am. Nonsmoking rms avail. **Amenities:** 🛆 A/C, cable TV. **Services:** 🖎 🖎 Babysitting. **Facilities:** 🛆 🛆 1 restaurant, 1 bar, whirlpool. **Rates (CP):** Peak (Apr–Oct) $45 S; $51 D. Extra person $5. Children under age 16 stay free. Min stay special events. Lower rates off-season. Parking: Outdoor, free. AE, DC, DISC, MC, V.

MOTEL

Courtesy Inn

4 Broadway, 93930; tel 408/385-4646 or toll free 800/350-5616; fax 408/385-6024. Broadway W exit off US 101. Located right off the freeway. Clean and well maintained. Fine as a travel-stop motel. **Rooms:** 64 rms and stes. CI noon/CO noon. Nonsmoking rms avail. **Amenities:** 🛆 🖭 A/C, cable TV, refrig. Microwaves. **Services:** ✕ 🖎 🖎 🖎 **Facilities:** 🛆 🔳 🛆 1 restaurant, whirlpool, washer/dryer. Barbecue facilities. **Rates (CP):** Peak (May–Sept) $65–$115 S

or D; $68 ste. Extra person $6. Children under age 14 stay free. Lower rates off-season. Parking: Outdoor, free. AE, CB, DC, DISC, MC, V.

ATTRACTIONS 🏛

Monterey County Agricultural and Rural Life Museum

Tel 408/385-8020. Located within San Lorenzo Regional Park (see below). The story of Monterey County's agricultural heritage, from mission times to today's advanced agricultural technology, is explored at this museum. The main exhibit barn is filled with artifacts and equipment, and antique farm machinery—some unique to this region—is scattered throughout the site. There is also a working blacksmith shop. A 19th-century schoolhouse, farmhouse, and train depot have been brought to the site and restored; all are open for tours on weekends.

The main exhibit barn also features a Monterey County tourist information center. **Open:** Main exhibit barn, daily 10am–5pm; outbuildings Apr–Oct, Sat–Sun noon–4pm or by appointment. **Free**

San Lorenzo County Park

1160 Broadway; tel 408/385-5964. Located just outside King City, via Broadway exit from US 101. Nestled along the Salinas River, surrounded by the picturesque Salinas Valley, this county park includes the Monterey County Agricultural and Rural Life Museum (see above). The park's day-use amenities include picnic areas, ball fields, and a children's playground. Tent and trailer camp sites. **Open:** Daily sunrise–sunset. $$$$

Kings Canyon National Park

See Sequoia and Kings Canyon National Parks

Lafayette

See also Concord, Pleasant Hill, Walnut Creek

HOTEL 🏨

▤ ▤ ▤ ▤ Lafayette Park Hotel

3287 Mount Diablo Blvd, 94549; tel 510/283-3700 or toll free 800/368-2468 ext 6; fax 510/284-1621. Pleasant Hills exit off CA 24. Styled after a French Norman château, with lush courtyards and fountains. The lobby, housed in a three-story rotunda, is accented by sculptures, Chinese vases, and a baby grand piano. Jogging trails are nearby. **Rooms:** 139 rms and stes. CI 3pm/CO noon. Nonsmoking rms avail. Over-size rooms (ranging from 375 to 540 square feet) are attractively decorated with cherry-wood furnishings and floral bedspreads. Nice touches include framed prints, polished granite

bathroom counters, and a baker's rack stocked with books and plants. Fourth-floor accommodations offer vaulted ceilings; many also have high arched windows. **Amenities:** 🛁 🌂 A/C, cable TV w/movies, dataport, voice mail, bathrobes. No phone. All units w/minibars, some w/terraces, some w/fireplaces. All rooms have wet bars, plus irons and ironing boards. **Services:** 🍽 VP 🚗 ⛱ 🔔 Twice-daily maid svce, car-rental desk, masseur, babysitting. Complimentary afternoon wine. Fresh-baked cookies with coffee and tea in the lobby weekday mornings. **Facilities:** 🏋 🏊 300 💻 🛝 1 restaurant, 1 bar, sauna, whirlpool. Beautiful 50-foot pool is heated year-round, but you do hear freeway noise. Small but well-equipped workout room. Guests also have privileges at tennis club one mile away. **Rates:** $170–$190 S or D; $200–$370 ste. Extra person $15. Children under age 12 stay free. Parking: Indoor/outdoor, $6/day. AE, CB, DC, DISC, MC, V.

Laguna Beach

See also Dana Point

Laguna Beach has been renowned as an artists' colony through the decades, and art can be found everywhere: in galleries, restaurants, street corners, front porches, even car dashboards. The highlight of the annual homage to the arts that takes place from July through August is the wholly unique Pageant of the Masters, in which live models and elaborate backgrounds are used to re-create famous paintings. **Information:** Laguna Beach Chamber of Commerce, 357 Glenneyre Ave, Laguna Beach 92652 (tel 714/494-1018).

HOTELS 🏨

▤ ▤ Capri Laguna Inn on the Beach

1441 S Coast Hwy, 02651; tel 714/494-6533 or toll free 800/225-4551; fax 714/497-6962. Off CA 1. Great location right on the main beach. You can walk down a staircase to the ocean and hear the pounding waves from your room. **Rooms:** 37 rms and effic. CI 3pm/CO noon. No smoking. Some rooms have kitchenettes. Decor is rather plain, but acceptable. Honeymoon suite is available. **Amenities:** 📺 🛁 Cable TV, refrig, CD/tape player. No A/C. All units w/terraces, some w/fireplaces. **Services:** 🔔 Twice-daily maid svce. **Facilities:** 🏋 🏊 25 1 beach (ocean), lifeguard, sauna. Outside picnic area with gas grill. Conveniently located within walking distance of restaurants. **Rates (CP):** Peak (July–Sept) $140–$225 D; $140–$225 effic. Extra person $10. Children under age 12 stay free. Lower rates off-season. Parking: Outdoor, free. Prices are fair when you consider the location. AE, CB, DC, DISC, MC, V.

≣≣ **Hotel Laguna Beach Club & Conference Center**

425 S Coast Hwy, 92651; tel 714/494-1151 or toll free 800/524-2927; fax 714/497-2163. Historic 1930s hotel, still comfortable and charming, set in a Spanish-style building. Located near shops and restaurants, it's right in the heart of town, with its own beach. **Rooms:** 64 rms. Executive level. CI 3pm/CO noon. Nonsmoking rms avail. Small and oldish, but most rooms have ocean views. Although hotel is located on the highway in the busiest part of town, the rooms are quiet. However, bathrooms are antiquated. **Amenities:** 🛁 🧴 🗄 TV w/movies. No A/C. **Services:** ✕ 🖙 ⅦⅤ 🛆 🕭 Masseur. Boat rentals can be arranged. **Facilities:** 🔟 1 restaurant, 1 bar (w/entertainment), 1 beach (ocean), beauty salon. Rose garden and a gazebo for weddings. **Rates (CP):** Peak (June–Sept) $95–$200 S or D. Children under age 15 stay free. Min stay peak. Lower rates off-season. Parking: Outdoor, free. AE, CB, DC, DISC, JCB, MC, V.

≣≣ **Inn at Laguna Beach**

211 N Pacific Coast Hwy, 92651; tel 714/497-9722 or toll free 800/544-4479; fax 714/497-9972. Laguna Canyon Rd exit off I-405. Great location on a cliff overlooking the ocean and the beach; close to shops, galleries, restaurants, and the Laguna scene. **Rooms:** 70 rms. CI 4pm/CO noon. Nonsmoking rms avail. Some accommodations overlook the highway, but traffic noise is muffled. Other rooms have an ocean view and balcony away from the street. **Amenities:** 🛁 🧴 🗄 A/C, cable TV w/movies, refrig, VCR, bathrobes. All units w/minibars, some w/terraces. Some rooms have microwaves. The only hotel on the beach with air conditioning. **Services:** 🛆🕭 Masseur, babysitting. **Facilities:** 🔟 🔢 🔽 1 beach (ocean), lifeguard, sauna, whirlpool. **Rates:** Peak (July 1–Sept 4) $139–$349 S or D. Extra person $20. Children under age 16 stay free. Min stay peak and wknds. Lower rates off-season. Parking: Indoor, free. AE, DC, DISC, MC, V.

≣≣≣ **Surf and Sand Hotel**

1555 S Coast Hwy, 92651; tel 714/497-4477 or toll free 800/524-8621; fax 714/494-2897. 20 mi S of John Wayne Airport; CA 133 exit off I-40S. Lovely and romantic, this Mediterranean-style hotel is located right on the beach—so close, waves practically lap the three buildings at high tide. **Rooms:** 157 rms and stes. CI 3pm/CO noon. Nonsmoking rms avail. White, plantation shutters slide back to reveal spectacular ocean views. Balconies are very private. Tower rooms tend to be the largest. **Amenities:** 🛁 🧴 🗄 Cable TV w/movies, dataport, in-rm safe, bathrobes. No A/C. All units w/minibars, all w/terraces, some w/fireplaces, some w/whirlpools. Repeat guests receive Godiva chocolates and a split of champagne. Children get Animal Crackers and a balloon upon check-in. **Services:** ✕ 🖙 ⅦⅤ 🕭 🛆 🕭 Twice-daily maid svce, masseur, babysitting. Complimentary morning coffee and newspapers in the lobby. Special events for kids during the summer, such as beach games and movie nights. **Facilities:** 🔟 🔢 🔽 2 restaurants (see "Restaurants" below), 2 bars (1 w/entertainment), lifeguard, spa, beauty salon. Seaview swimming pool has a glass-screened sundeck. Guest privileges at local health club for an additional fee. **Rates:** Peak (May 23–Oct) $215–$325 S or D; $500–$750 ste. Extra person $15. Children under age 17 stay free. Min stay wknds. Lower rates off-season. Parking: Indoor, $9/day. AE, CB, DC, DISC, MC, V.

≣≣≣ **Vacation Village**

647 S Coast Hwy, PO Box 66, 92652; tel 714/494-8566 or toll free 800/843-6895; fax 714/494-1386. Unique hotel in a prime location on the beach, with several buildings and something for everyone; rooms, suites, condos, and a private house used for weddings. Good choice for families. **Rooms:** 130 rms, stes, and effic. CI 3pm/CO 11am. Nonsmoking rms avail. Many rooms and suites have kitchenettes. Rooms are clean and comfortable. Bathrooms are tiny but immaculate. Ocean-view rooms are worth the extra cost. **Amenities:** 🛁 🧴 🗄 🗄 A/C, cable TV. All units w/terraces. **Services:** 🕭 Babysitting. **Facilities:** 🔟 🔽 1 restaurant, 1 beach (ocean), lifeguard, whirlpool. **Rates:** Peak (June–Sept) $80–$145 S or D; $95 ste; $95 effic. Extra person $10. Children under age 12 stay free. Min stay peak. Lower rates off-season. Parking: Outdoor, free. AE, CB, DC, DISC, MC, V.

MOTELS

≣≣ **Best Western Laguna Reef Inn**

30806 S Coast Hwy, 92651; tel 714/499-2227 or toll free 800/922-9905; fax 714/499-5575. On CA 1. Clean, no-nonsense hotel right across from the beach, surrounded by palm trees and flower gardens. A good value. **Rooms:** 43 rms. CI 2pm/CO noon. Nonsmoking rms avail. **Amenities:** 🛁 🧴 A/C, cable TV, refrig. **Services:** 🚗 Twice-daily maid svce. **Facilities:** 🔟 1 beach (ocean), lifeguard, sauna, whirlpool. **Rates (CP):** Peak (July–Aug) $89–$99 S or D. Extra person $10. Lower rates off-season. Parking: Outdoor, free. AE, CB, DC, DISC, MC, V.

≣≣ **Quality Inn Laguna Beach**

1404 N Coast Hwy, 92651; tel 714/494-6464 or toll free 800/221-2222; fax 714/494-9776. N from Laguna Beach exit off CA 1. Beach is across the street and down the hill. The hotel is one mile from downtown Laguna Beach; out of the congested area, but still convenient for business travelers. **Rooms:** 22 rms and stes. CI 3pm/CO 11am. Good-size rooms feature pink-and-green decor with light wood furniture and large bathrooms. **Amenities:** 🛁 🗄 A/C, cable TV, refrig. Some units w/terraces, some w/whirlpools. **Services:** 🕭 Twice-daily maid svce. **Facilities:** 🔟 🔢 🔽 Washer/dryer. **Rates (CP):** Peak (June–Sept) $79–$94 S or D; $148 ste. Extra person $10. Children under age 17 stay free. Min stay peak and wknds. Lower rates off-season. Parking: Indoor, free. AE, CB, DC, DISC, MC, V.

INN

Eiler's Inn
741 S Pacific Coast Hwy, 92651; tel 714/494-3004; fax 714/497-2215. Cozy inn, with a fountain and flowers in its romantic brick courtyard. Located half a block from the ocean. Unsuitable for children under 18. **Rooms:** 12 rms and stes. CI 2pm/CO noon. Smallish, individually decorated rooms have appealing touches such as Victorian dressers and lace portieres and a guest register. Bathrooms, however, are of 1950s vintage and are completely lacking in charm; all have showers, no tubs. **Amenities:** No A/C, phone, or TV. 1 unit w/fireplace. One suite has a refrigerator and a microwave. **Services:** Masseur, wine/sherry served. Breakfast served in the fireplace room or the courtyard. **Facilities:** Guest lounge w/TV. Sundeck faces toward the Pacific. Small guest parlor with TV and board games. Parking is limited—there are not enough reserved spots for all rooms. **Rates (CP):** Peak (Mem Day–Labor Day) $120–$145 S or D; $175 ste. Min stay peak. Lower rates off-season. Parking: Outdoor, free. AE, DISC, MC, V.

RESORTS

Aliso Creek Inn
31106 S Coast Hwy, 92677; tel 714/499-2271 or toll free 800/223-3309; fax 714/499-4601. 83 acres. Big resort nestled in a canyon across the Pacific Coast Highway from the beach—like being in the mountains, with the ocean just a short walk away. Although just off the highway, it feels light years away. **Rooms:** 62 rms and stes. CI 3pm/CO noon. Nonsmoking rms avail. Most units are duplexes with a sitting room and kitchen on the first floor, bedroom upstairs. Most have walk-in closets. **Amenities:** Cable TV w/movies, refrig, CD/tape player. No A/C. All units w/terraces. **Services:** Sun-deck dining. **Facilities:** 1 restaurant, 1 bar (w/entertainment), whirlpool, washer/dryer. Putting green, driving range, shuffleboard. Bar with wide-screen TV. Ben Brown's, a famous Laguna Beach restaurant, is on the premises. **Rates:** Peak (July–Aug) $125–$130 S or D; $142–$205 ste. Children under age 12 stay free. Lower rates off-season. Parking: Outdoor, free. AE, DC, MC, V.

Laguna Riviera Beach Resort & Spa
825 S Coast Hwy, 92651; tel 714/494-1196 or toll free 800/999-2089; fax 714/494-8421. Right on the beach. The hallways are like big decks, and there are lots of palm trees, even on the sun deck in the center of the building. Good for families and a good deal. **Rooms:** 41 rms, stes, and effic. CI 3pm/CO noon. Nonsmoking rms avail. Average in size, rooms have green-and-pink flowered bedspreads. Renovation is ongoing. Some rooms have kitchenettes, some have big balconies. **Amenities:** Cable TV w/movies, refrig. No A/C. Some units w/terraces, some w/fireplaces, some w/whirlpools. Microwave. **Services:** Afternoon tea. VCR with classic movies in the lobby. **Facilities:** 1 beach (ocean),

lifeguard, games rm, sauna, whirlpool. Indoor pool surrounded by glass and a removable roof. Parking spaces are very tight. **Rates (CP):** Peak (June 14–Sept 14) $74–$108 S or D; $69–$173 ste; $74–$108 effic. Extra person $10. Children under age 6 stay free. Min stay peak and special events. Lower rates off-season. Parking: Outdoor, free. AE, CB, DC, DISC, JCB, MC, V.

RESTAURANTS

Cafe Zoolu
860 Glenneyre St; tel 714/494-6825. **Californian.** A former antique shop, this cafe has black straw chairs, two tiny fireplaces, and a tiled floor. Varied sophisticated menu features Hawaiian and Chinese dishes as well as old-fashioned meatloaf with mashed potatoes. **FYI:** Reservations recommended. Beer and wine only. **Open:** Peak (June–Aug) Tues–Sun 5–10pm. **Prices:** Main courses $10–$20. AE, CB, DC, DISC, MC, V.

Five Feet
328 Glenneyre St; tel 714/497-4955. 1 block E of the Pacific Coast Hwy. **Asian/Eclectic.** A popular place tucked away under a big tree off the main street. Decor is high-tech Asian, with black and gray chairs, beamed ceilings, open duct-work, and flowers on each table. An eclectic menu offers fresh fish from all over the world prepared in many unusual ways, from Dover sole steamed with sake, black beans, ginger, and chili, to halibut topped with a lichee-ginger salsa. Meat dishes range from New York steak to Australian kangaroo. Highest quality, fresh ingredients used, and most recipes succeed brilliantly. **FYI:** Reservations recommended. Beer and wine only. **Open:** Sun–Thurs 5–10pm, Fri–Sat 5–11pm. **Prices:** Main courses $15–$28. AE, CB, DC, DISC, MC, V.

Sorrento Grille
370 Glenneyre St; tel 714/494-8686. Forest Ave exit off Pacific Coast Hwy (CA 1); N to Glenneyre. **American/Eclectic.** A bistrolike, noisy, but fun place to dine downtown, it's decorated with terra-cotta tiles, cowboy hats, and Mexican ponchos. Menu features mesquite-grilled entrees and organic produce. Sea bass, ahi, osso buco, and grilled artichokes are favorites. There is a martini bar in addition to the full bar. **FYI:** Reservations recommended. Dress code. **Open:** Peak (June–Sept) dinner Sun–Thurs 5:30–10pm, Fri–Sat 5:30–11pm. **Prices:** Main courses $10–$22. AE, DC, MC, V.

Splashes
In Surf & Sand Hotel, 1555 S Coast Hwy; tel 714/497-4477. 12 mi S of John Wayne Airport. **Mediterranean.** Just a few steps from the beach, with simple yet elegant decor. Dine inside by the fireplace, or on the patio, listening to the calming sounds of the ocean. Dishes include salmon, swordfish, Moroccan chicken, osso buco, and other fresh house specialties. **FYI:** Reservations recommended. Children's menu. **Open:** Breakfast daily 7–11am; lunch daily 11:30am–

4:30pm; dinner Sun–Thurs 5–10pm, Fri–Sat 5–11pm; brunch Sun 10am–4:30pm. **Prices:** Main courses $15–$20. AE, CB, DC, DISC, ER, MC, V. ♥ ⛵ ▣ ⛰ ⛲ 🆅🅿 ♿

♥ The Towers Restaurant
In Surf & Sand Hotel, 1555 S Coast Hwy; tel 714/497-4477. **French/Italian.** As romantic as they come. Art deco motif in a room furnished with soft chairs in beige and green. The bar has a fireplace and a piano player, and picture windows offer spectacular ocean panoramas. Popular dishes include roasted rack of lamb with Dijon crust and garlic pureed potatoes, Maine lobster with pinot noir sauce, tarragon linguini, and crème brûlée for dessert. **FYI:** Reservations recommended. Piano. Dress code. **Open:** Daily 5:30–10pm. **Prices:** Main courses $18–$32. AE, CB, DC, DISC, MC, V. ♥ ▣ ⛰ 🆅🅿 ♿

★ 242 Cafe
242 N Coast Hwy; tel 714/494-2444. **Health/Spa.** If you blink, you might pass this cozy place right on the highway, which looks more like a deli than a restaurant. Very popular, there's often a line of locals waiting to get in to sample the offerings on the health-conscious menu of salads, sandwiches, and pastries. **FYI:** Reservations recommended. Beer and wine only. **Open:** Mon–Fri 11am–10pm, Sat–Sun 8:30am–11pm. **Prices:** Main courses $7–$13. MC, V. ⛲

★ Zinc Cafe and Market
350 Ocean Ave; tel 714/494-6302. **Californian/Vegetarian.** Good for people-watching, a pleasant artsy place with simple decor. Serves popular breakfasts. Innovative vegetarian dishes include black-bean chili, mini-pizza, and roasted eggplant. Tasty desserts. **FYI:** Reservations not accepted. Beer and wine only. Additional location: 132 S Cedros Ave, Solano Beach (tel 619/793-5436). **Open:** Mon–Sat 7am–5:30pm, Sun 7am–5pm. **Prices:** Lunch main courses $5–$7. No CC. ⛰

ATTRACTION 🏛
Laguna Art Museum
307 Cliff Dr; tel 714/494-6531. Ten galleries house exhibitions focusing on American art, with particular emphasis on the art and artists of California. The permanent collection is notable for its collection of Southern California works created between the two World Wars, for early 20th-century photography, and for contemporary art. Lectures, symposia, special events. **Open:** Tues–Sun 11am–5pm. $$

La Jolla
A city of art boutiques and fine dining by the sea, La Jolla boasts secluded beaches and serene coves nestled below the green coastal hills. The community works hard to maintain a separate identity from San Diego just to the south. **Information:** La Jolla Town Council, 1055 Wall St #110, PO Box 1101, La Jolla 92038 (tel 619/454-1444).

HOTELS 🏨

≡≡ Best Western Inn by the Sea
7830 Fay Ave, 92037 (La Jolla Village); tel 619/459-4461 or toll free 800/462-9732; fax 619/456-2578. Ardath Rd exit off I-5 N; La Jolla Village Dr W exit off I-5 S. Well-located property. Adjacent coffee shop. **Rooms:** 133 rms and stes. CI 2pm/CO noon. Nonsmoking rms avail. Pleasant rooms with very attractive decor. All have sliding glass doors that open onto balconies. **Amenities:** 🕾 ⚡ A/C, cable TV w/movies. All units w/terraces, 1 w/fireplace. **Services:** ✕ ⌷ ⤸ Car-rental desk, babysitting. **Facilities:** 🏊 🏋 ▣ ♿ 1 restaurant, whirlpool, washer/dryer. **Rates (CP):** Peak (June–Sept) $99–$155 S or D; $275–$325 ste. Children under age 12 stay free. Min stay special events. Lower rates off-season. Parking: Indoor/outdoor, free. AE, CB, DC, DISC, JCB, MC, V.

≡≡≡ Colonial Inn
910 Prospect St, 92037 (La Jolla Village); tel 619/454-2181 or toll free 800/832-5525, 800/826-1278 in CA; fax 619/454-5679. Ardath Rd exit off I-5 N; La Jolla Village Dr W exit off I-5 S. Take Torrey Pines Rd to Prospect St and turn right. A 1913 inn with a charming old-world atmosphere, one block from the ocean and the park. **Rooms:** 75 rms and stes. CI 3pm/CO noon. Nonsmoking rms avail. Very nice furnishings and fabrics. Every room has a ceiling fan. Some lack air conditioning but have windows that open. **Amenities:** 🕾 ⚡ 🍴 Cable TV. No A/C. Some units w/terraces. **Services:** ✕ 🆅🅿 ⌷ ⤸ Car-rental desk, masseur, babysitting. Afternoon tea in lobby. Turndown service on request. Pianist plays in lobby lounge some afternoons and evenings. Complimentary shoeshine. **Facilities:** 🏊 ▣ ♿ 1 restaurant (see "Restaurants" below), 1 bar (w/entertainment), whirlpool. **Rates:** Peak (June–Sept) $150–$200 S or D. Extra person $10. Children under age 18 stay free. Lower rates off-season. AE, DC, DISC, MC, V.

≡≡≡ Embassy Suites San Diego La Jolla
4550 La Jolla Village Dr, 92122 (Golden Triangle); tel 619/453-0400 or toll free 800/362-2779; fax 619/453-4226. La Jolla Village Dr exit off I-5. Very user-friendly hotel. A 12-story atrium is filled with plants, ponds, and waterfalls. Convenient to University Towne Center and Golden Triangle businesses. **Rooms:** 335 stes. CI 4pm/CO noon. Nonsmoking rms avail. Sofa-sleeper in living room, microwave, wet bar. **Amenities:** 🕾 ⚡ 📺 🍴 A/C, cable TV w/movies, refrig, voice mail. Some units w/whirlpools. Two TVs in every room. Complimentary evening cocktails. **Services:** ✕ ▥ ⌷ ⤸ Twice-daily maid svce, car-rental desk, babysitting. **Facilities:** 🏊 🏋 ▣ 💻 ♿ 1 restaurant (lunch and dinner only), 1 bar (w/entertainment), games rm, sauna, whirlpool, washer/dryer. Restaurant has outdoor seating. Avis car rental on premises. **Rates (BB):** Peak (July–Aug) $149–$189 ste. Extra person $10. Children under age 12 stay free. Min stay special events. Lower rates off-season. Parking: Indoor/outdoor, free. AE, CB, DC, DISC, JCB, MC, V.

≋≋≋ Empress Hotel of La Jolla

7766 Fay Ave, 92037 (La Jolla Village); tel 619/454-3001 or toll free 800/525-6552; fax 619/454-6387. Ardath Rd exit off I-5 N; La Jolla Village Dr W exit off I-5 S. Take Torrey Pines Rd to Girard, turn right, then left on Kline St. A small, European-style hotel with a convenient village location. **Rooms:** 73 rms, stes, and effic. Executive level. CI 3pm/CO noon. Nonsmoking rms avail. Rooms are spacious with high-quality furnishings, marble bathrooms, large mirrors, and soothing decor. **Amenities:** 🛎 🕹 🖥 📞 A/C, cable TV, refrig, bathrobes. Some units w/whirlpools. **Services:** ✕ VP 🛄 ↻ Car-rental desk, social director, masseur, babysitting. Shoe polishers on every floor. Room service for lunch and dinner. **Facilities:** 🍽 ⌷65 🕹 1 restaurant (lunch and dinner only), 1 bar, sauna, whirlpool. Restaurant on premises is considered one of the best in La Jolla. **Rates (CP):** Peak (June 14–Sept 20) $95–$100 S or D; $140–$300 ste; $300 effic. Extra person $25. Children under age 18 stay free. Min stay special events. Lower rates off-season. AP and MAP rates avail. Good-value packages during low season. AE, CB, DC, DISC, MC, V.

≋≋≋ Hyatt Regency La Jolla

3777 La Jolla Village Dr, 92122; tel 619/552-1234 or toll free 800/233-1234; fax 619/552-6066. La Jolla Village Dr exit off I-5. Epic-proportioned elegance, from the massive pillared entrance to the lobby's highly polished brown Italian marble floors. A few Greco-Roman torsos and art deco couches are thrown in for good measure by noted architect Michael Graves. **Rooms:** 400 rms and stes. Executive level. CI 3pm/CO noon. Nonsmoking rms avail. The signature cherrywood grid pattern from the lobby shows up on the room furnishings, including the armoire, desk, and nightstand. Very nice bathrooms are tiled in a gray and white, to contrast with a brown marble sink. **Amenities:** 🛎 🕹 📞 A/C, cable TV w/movies, dataport, bathrobes. All units w/minibars, some w/whirlpools. Irons and ironing boards in all rooms. **Services:** 🍽 ☎ VP 🚐 🛄 ↻ Car-rental desk, masseur, babysitting. **Facilities:** 🕹 🚲 🖥2 🍽 ⌷1400 🕹 5 restaurants, 2 bars, racquetball, sauna, steam rm, whirlpool. Large pool flanked by Herculean columns. Access to the very exclusive Sporting Club next door, with weight machines, aerobics classes, and spa treatments. Hotel is convenient to other facilities in the Aventine complex, with 5 restaurants including the well-regarded Cafe Japengo (see "Restaurants" below). **Rates:** $128–$214 S or D; $229–$750 ste. Extra person $25. Children under age 18 stay free. Min stay special events. Parking: Indoor, $7/day. AE, CB, DC, DISC, MC, V.

≋≋ La Jolla Beach & Tennis Club

2000 Spindrift Dr, 92037 (La Jolla Shores); tel 619/454-7126 or toll free 800/624-2582; fax 619/456-3805. Ardath Rd exit off I-5 N; La Jolla Village Dr exit off I-5 S. 14 acres. One of the few true beachfront hotels in southern California, formerly an exclusive private club. **Rooms:** 90 rms and effic. CI 4pm/CO noon. Nonsmoking rms avail.

Amenities: 🛎 🕹 🖥 Cable TV, refrig. No A/C. Some units w/terraces. **Services:** 🛄 ↻ Social director, masseur, babysitting. Children's program in summer only. **Facilities:** 🕹 🏖 🏄4 🕹8 ⌷160 2 restaurants, 2 bars (1 w/entertainment), 1 beach (ocean), board surfing, lawn games, playground, washer/dryer. Wedding facilities. **Rates:** Peak (June 16–Sept 8) $135–$175 S or D; $160–$409 ste; $155–$225 effic. Extra person $15. Min stay special events. Lower rates off-season. Parking: Outdoor, free. AE, CB, DC, DISC, EC, ER, JCB, MC, V.

≋≋≋≋ La Valencia Hotel

1132 Prospect St, 92037 (La Jolla Village); tel 619/454-0771 or toll free 800/451-0772; fax 619/456-3921. Ardath Rd exit off I-5 N; La Jolla Village Dr W exit off I-5 S. La Jolla's best accommodations, in a landmark Spanish-colonial hotel with tiled roof and elegant appointments, and fantastic views of the ocean. **Rooms:** 97 rms, stes, and effic; 8 cottages/villas. CI 3pm/CO noon. Nonsmoking rms avail. Elegant rooms have beautiful furnishings, small but lovely marble bathrooms, and excellent ocean views. Two-bedroom bungalows are spacious and good for families. **Amenities:** 🛎 🕹 🖥 📞 A/C, cable TV w/movies, dataport, voice mail, in-rm safe, bathrobes. All units w/minibars, some w/terraces, some w/whirlpools. Fresh fruit basket on arrival. **Services:** 🍽 ☎ VP 🛄 ↻ 🔔 Twice-daily maid svce, car-rental desk, masseur, babysitting. Complimentary daily newspaper and shoeshine. **Facilities:** 🕹 🚲 🕹 3 restaurants (see "Restaurants" below), 2 bars (1 w/entertainment), sauna, steam rm, whirlpool. Wonderful lounge with ocean view. **Rates:** $160–$350 S or D; $375–$625 ste; $160 effic; $625 cottage/villa. Extra person $15. Children under age 12 stay free. Min stay special events. Parking: Indoor, AE, CB, DC, DISC, MC, V.

≋≋ Prospect Park Inn

1110 Prospect St, 92037 (La Jolla Village); tel 619/454-0133 or toll free 800/433-1609; fax 619/454-2056. Ardath Rd exit off I-5 N; La Jolla Village Dr W exit off I-5 S. A 1947 boarding house for women converted to a charming boutique hotel. Near beach, park, shops, and restaurants. No elevator. **Rooms:** 23 rms, stes, and effic. CI 3pm/CO 11am. No smoking. Rooms are modern, clean, and attractive. Cove suite is large with lovely ocean view. **Amenities:** 🛎 🕹 🖥 📞 A/C, cable TV. Some units w/terraces. Bottled water provided in every room. **Services:** 🛄 ↻ Car-rental desk, babysitting. Library area offers fruit, cookies, and beverages in the afternoon. Breakfast served in rooms or on sundeck with great ocean view. Beach towels and chairs provided free. Guests may use adjacent indoor parking structure at no charge. **Rates (CP):** $85–$140 S; $95–$150 D; $200–$300 ste; $115–$150 effic. Extra person $10. Min stay wknds. AE, CB, DC, DISC, ER, JCB, MC, V.

≋≋ Radisson Hotel La Jolla

3299 Holiday Court, 92037 (Golden Triangle); tel 619/453-5500 or toll free 800/333-3333; fax 619/453-5550. La Jolla Village Dr exit off I-5. Lowrise hotel with good proximity to freeway, Golden Triangle businesses, and University of California–San Diego. Bar and dining area are popular with UCSD staff and faculty. **Rooms:** 200 rms and stes. CI 3pm/ CO noon. Nonsmoking rms avail. Bright, contemporary decor. **Amenities:** �🅰🖭 🍴A/C, cable TV, VCR. Some units w/terraces. **Services:** 🍴 🚐 🖼 🍽 Car-rental desk. **Facilities:** 🖼 🚐 🛃 2 restaurants, 1 bar (w/entertainment), whirlpool. Shuffleboard. **Rates:** Peak (June–Sept) $89–$149 S; $99–$149 D; $150 ste. Extra person $10. Children under age 17 stay free. Min stay special events. Lower rates off-season. Parking: Outdoor, free. AE, DISC, MC, V.

🏨🏨🏨 San Diego Marriott La Jolla

4240 La Jolla Village Dr, 92037 (Golden Triangle); tel 619/ 587-1414 or toll free 800/228-9290; fax 619/546-8518. La Jolla Village Dr exit off I-5. A 15-story hotel located in a business park, part of the Golden Triangle. Connected by an elevated walkway to University Towne Center. **Rooms:** 360 rms and stes. Executive level. CI 4pm/CO noon. Nonsmoking rms avail. **Amenities:** 🚪 🅰 A/C, cable TV w/movies, voice mail. All units w/minibars, all w/terraces. Iron and ironing board in every room. **Services:** 🍴 🔑 🆅🅿 🛃 🍽 ⬩ Car-rental desk, babysitting. Hertz car rental and American Airlines have offices on the premises. **Facilities:** 🖼🛶🖼🅻 2 restaurants, 2 bars, games rm, sauna, whirlpool. Indoor and outdoor pools. **Rates:** Peak (July–Apr) $170–$209 S or D; $360 ste. Children under age 18 stay free. Min stay special events. Lower rates off-season. Parking: Indoor/outdoor, $7–$10/day. AE, DC, DISC, JCB, MC, V.

🏨🏨🏨 Sea Lodge

8110 Camino del Oro, 92037 (La Jolla Shores); tel 619/ 459-8271 or toll free 800/237-5211; fax 619/456-9346. Ardath Rd exit off I-5 N, La Jolla Village Dr exit off I-5 S. 2 acres. Ideal location along the boardwalk on the beach. **Rooms:** 128 rms, stes, and effic. CI 4pm/CO noon. Nonsmoking rms avail. **Amenities:** 🚪🅰🖭 🍴 A/C, cable TV, refrig, dataport, bathrobes. All units w/terraces. **Services:** 🍴 🛃 🍽 Car-rental desk, babysitting. **Facilities:** 🖼 🛶 🖼 🅻 1 restaurant, 1 bar, 1 beach (ocean), lifeguard, lawn games, sauna, whirlpool, washer/dryer. **Rates:** Peak (July–Aug) $135–$175 S or D; $160–$295 ste; $160–$295 effic. Extra person $15. Children under age 12 stay free. Min stay peak and wknds. Lower rates off-season. Parking: Indoor, free. AE, DC, DISC, MC, V.

🏨🏨 Summer House Inn

7955 La Jolla Shores Dr, 92037 (La Jolla Shores); tel 619/ 459-0261 or toll free 800/666-0261; fax 619/459-7649. Ardath Rd exit off I-5 N; La Jolla Village Dr W exit off I-5 S. Located just four blocks from the beach at a busy intersection. A bit noisy, but rooms on highest floors are acceptably quiet. **Rooms:** 90 rms, stes, and effic. CI 3pm/CO noon. Nonsmoking rms avail. Rooms are in need of renovation. **Amenities:** 🚪🅰🍴A/C, cable TV, refrig, voice mail. All units w/terraces, some w/whirlpools. **Services:** 🍴 🚐 🛃 🍽 Car-rental desk, masseur. Complimentary continental breakfast.

Facilities: 🖼 🖾 🅻 1 restaurant (*see* "Restaurants" below), 1 bar (w/entertainment), sauna, whirlpool, beauty salon, washer/dryer. **Rates (CP):** Peak (June–Aug) $240–$270 S or D; $240–$420 ste; $240–$420 effic. Extra person $8. Children under age 13 stay free. Min stay peak and wknds. Lower rates off-season. Parking: Outdoor, free. AE, DC, DISC, MC, V.

MOTELS

🏨🏨 Andrea Villa Inn

2402 Torrey Pines Rd, 92037 (La Jolla Shores); tel 619/ 459-3311 or toll free 800/LA-JOLLA; fax 619/459-1320. La Jolla Village Dr W exit off I-55; Ardath Rd exit off I-5 N. Located five blocks from the beach on a busy thoroughfare, but set back from the street so it's quiet in most rooms. **Rooms:** 49 rms and effic. CI 3pm/CO noon. Nonsmoking rms avail. Rooms are spacious and attractively decorated, with large closets. Half have full kitchens. **Amenities:** 🚪 A/C, cable TV. 1 unit w/terrace. **Services:** 🛃 🍽 **Facilities:** 🖼 🖾 Whirlpool, washer/dryer. Attractive pool area. Homey breakfast room. **Rates (CP):** Peak (June–Sept) $85 S or D; $90 effic. Children under age 17 stay free. Min stay special events. Lower rates off-season. Parking: Outdoor, free. Higher rates on weekends. AE, DC, DISC, MC, V.

🏨🏨 La Jolla Cove Suites

1155 Coast Blvd, PO Box 1067, 92038 (La Jolla Village); tel 619/459-2621 or toll free 800/248-2683; fax 619/454-3522. Ardath Rd exit off I-5 N; La Jolla Village Dr W exit off I-5 S. Take Torrey Pines Rd to Prospect St, turn right. Right across from the La Jolla Cove, with a nice beach and a marine sanctuary popular with divers. Good choice for families. **Rooms:** 116 rms, stes, and effic. CI 3pm/CO 11am. Decor is somewhat dated, with old, worn furniture and carpets, but rooms are very spacious and have enormous closets. **Amenities:** 🚪🅰 Cable TV w/movies, refrig. No A/C. All units w/terraces. **Services:** 🚐 🛃 🍽 Car-rental desk, babysitting. Staff is unusually friendly and helpful. Continental breakfast available in the solarium. **Facilities:** 🖼 🖾 🅻 Sauna, whirlpool, washer/dryer. Good laundry facilities, nice putting green (putters and balls are provided for free), and lovely pool area. **Rates:** Peak (Mem Day–Labor Day) $95–$130 S or D; $165–$285 ste; $95–$125 effic. Extra person $15. Children under age 18 stay free. Min stay special events. Lower rates off-season. Parking: Indoor/outdoor, free. AE, CB, DC, DISC, MC, V.

🏨 La Jolla Travelodge

1141 Siverado St, 92037 (La Jolla Village); tel 619/454-0791 or toll free 800/578-7878; fax 619/459-8534. La Jolla Village Dr W exit off I-5 S; Ardath Rd exit off I-5 N. Located three blocks from the beach in La Jolla Village. **Rooms:** 30 rms and effic. CI 2pm/CO noon. Nonsmoking rms avail. Rooms are clean and simple. **Amenities:** 🚪🅰🖭 🍴A/C, cable TV. **Services:** 🍽 Free newspapers. **Rates:** Peak (July–Aug)

$79–$159 S or D. Extra person $5. Children under age 17 stay free. Min stay special events. Lower rates off-season. Parking: Outdoor, free. AE, DC, DISC, MC, V.

Residence Inn by Marriott

8901 Gilman Dr, 92037; tel 619/587-1770 or toll free 800/ 331-3131; fax 619/552-0387. Gilman Dr exit off I-15. Feels like a condominium complex. Homey ambience. **Rooms:** 87 stes. CI 4pm/CO noon. Nonsmoking rms avail. Suites have complete kitchens and living rooms; two-bedroom, two-bath suites available. **Amenities:** 🗄 🖧 🖥 A/C, cable TV, refrig. All units w/terraces, some w/fireplaces. Some units have VCRs. **Services:** ✗ 🖳 🖧 🖧 Car-rental desk, children's program, babysitting. Complimentary fresh fruit and coffee served all day. **Facilities:** 🖧 🖭 🖧 Basketball, volleyball, whirlpool, washer/dryer. Five whirlpools. Use of gas barbecues. Free use of local YMCA. **Rates (CP):** $139–$299 ste. Extra person $10. Min stay special events. Parking: Outdoor, free. AE, CB, DC, DISC, JCB, MC, V.

Scripps Inn

555 Coast Blvd S, 92037 (La Jolla Village); tel 619/454-3391. Ardath Rd exit off I-5 N; La Jolla Village Dr W exit off I-5 S. Charming older motel across the street from a beautiful park and the beach. Small, friendly place to stay. **Rooms:** 13 rms and stes. CI 3pm/CO noon. Quaint furnishings. Five rooms have cooking facilities. **Amenities:** 🗄 🖥 🖧 Cable TV, refrig, in-rm safe. No A/C. Some units w/fireplaces. Shared ocean-view terrace. **Services:** 🖧 🖧 Complimentary continental breakfast is offered in the tiny lobby; guests may take it to their rooms or to the terrace. **Rates (CP):** Peak (June–Sept) $110–$155 D; $140–$180 ste. Extra person $10. Children under age 12 stay free. Min stay wknds. Lower rates off-season. Parking: Outdoor, free. AE, DISC, MC, V.

INN

Bed & Breakfast Inn at La Jolla

7753 Draper Ave, 92037 (La Jolla Village); tel 619/ 456-2066; fax 619/454-9055. Historic property built in 1913, then expanded and converted to an inn in 1985. Great location, across from the recreation center and Museum of Contemporary Art. Unsuitable for children under 12. **Rooms:** 16 rms and stes (1 w/shared bath). CI 2:30pm/CO 11:30am. No smoking. Beautiful decor and fresh flowers in each uniquely decorated room. **Amenities:** 🖧 A/C, bathrobes. No phone or TV. 1 unit w/terrace, some w/fireplaces. You can request a telephone. **Services:** Wine/sherry served. Complimentary breakfast delivered to room or served in the dining room or garden. **Facilities:** 🖧 Guest lounge w/TV. **Rates (CP):** $85 S or D w/shared bath, $100–$180 S or D w/private bath; $225 ste. Extra person $25. Min stay wknds. Parking: Indoor/outdoor, free. AE, MC, V.

RESORT

Sheraton Grande Torrey Pines

10950 N Torrey Pines Rd, 92037; tel 619/558-1500 or toll free 800/762-6160; fax 619/450-4584. Genesee Ave exit off I-5. A modern, angular hotel with a country-club feel, perched on bluffs above the Pacific. Adjoins Torrey Pines Golf Course. Newly refurbished lobby is austere, verging on the plain. **Rooms:** 394 rms and stes. Executive level. CI 3pm/ CO noon. Nonsmoking rms avail. Very spacious. All accommodations have views of the pool, golf course, or ocean. Mirrored windows provide privacy. **Amenities:** 🗄 🖧 🖥 A/C, cable TV w/movies, refrig, dataport, voice mail, in-rm safe, bathrobes. All units w/minibars, all w/terraces, 1 w/whirlpool. Valet stand, shoehorn, bathroom scale, and iron and ironing board in each room. **Services:** ✗ 🖳 🖫 🖧 🖧 🖧 Twice-daily maid svce, car-rental desk, social director, masseur, babysitting. All rooms are served by a butler, who delivers morning coffee or tea, presses clothes, etc. Complimentary limo service available within the area; free hors d'oeuvres and entertainment nightly. **Facilities:** 🖧 🖧 🖾 🖳 🖭 🖧 1 restaurant, 2 bars (w/entertainment), lawn games, sauna, steam rm, whirlpool. Lovely pool area flanked by a balustrade, cypresses, and palms. In addition to the on-premises health club, guests can use the premier facility next door, with weight room, aerobics classes, running track, and basketball courts. **Rates:** $220–$285 S or D; $425–$2,500 ste. Extra person $20. Children under age 17 stay free. Parking: Indoor/outdoor, $7–$11/day. AE, CB, DC, DISC, EC, ER, JCB, MC, V.

RESTAURANTS 🍴

Alfonso's of La Jolla

1251 Prospect St (La Jolla Village); tel 619/454-2232. 12 mi NW of San Diego Ardath Rd exit off I-5. **Mexican.** A colorful, homey place with brick walls and two fireplaces. Menu lists carne asada burritos, charbroiled steaks in ranchero sauce, large quesadillas, tostadas, tacos, and seafood dishes. **FYI:** Reservations not accepted. **Open:** Mon–Thurs 11am–11pm, Fri–Sat 11am–midnight, Sun 11am–10pm. **Prices:** Main courses $10–$17. AE, DC, DISC, MC, V. 🖳 🖳

Bully's

5755 La Jolla Blvd (Bird Rock); tel 619/459-2768. 11 mi NW of San Diego Grand/Garnet exit off I-5 Take either Grand Ave or Garnet Ave W to Mission Blvd and turn north; turn left onto La Jolla Blvd. **American/Steak.** A San Diego watering hole with a dark, publike atmosphere. People come here for the huge portions of prime rib, chicken breast, burgers, and the like. **FYI:** Reservations not accepted. Children's menu. Additional locations: 2401 Camino del Rio S, San Diego (tel 291-2665); 1404 Camino del Mar, Del Mar (tel 755-1660). **Open:** Lunch Mon–Fri 11am–4:30pm, Sat–Sun 10am–4:30pm; dinner daily 4:30pm–midnight. **Prices:** Main courses $6–$39. AE, CB, DC, MC, V. 🖳 🖧

Cafe Japengo

In the Aventine, 8960 University Center Lane; tel 619/450-3355. La Jolla Village Dr exit off I-5. **Pacific Rim.** The interior designer describes the ultramodern decor as "East meets West," and that sums up the menu as well. In addition to a number of Pacific Rim specialties (10-ingredient fried rice and crisp whole New Zealand snapper Japonaise are two favorites), there's a full sushi bar. **FYI:** Reservations accepted. **Open:** Lunch Mon–Fri 11:30am–2:30pm; dinner Mon–Thurs 5–11pm, Fri–Sat 5–11pm. **Prices:** Main courses $19–$25. AE, DC, DISC, MC, V. [VP] &

♥ Cindy Black's

5721 La Jolla Blvd; tel 619/456-6299. Garnet Ave exit off I-5. **French.** A very luxurious setting and a menu to match. Modern art is on display, amid antiques and lovely orchids and roses. Dishes include roasted eggplant soup with tomato-basil relish, pan-broiled Alaskan halibut, and Maryland soft-shell crabs in season. **FYI:** Reservations recommended. **Open:** Lunch Fri 11:30am–2pm; dinner Mon–Sat 5:30–10pm, Sun 5–8pm. **Prices:** Main courses $10–$30. AE, DC, DISC, MC, V. ● ◖

$ ✱ D'lish Gourmet

7514 Girard Ave (La Jolla Village); tel 619/459-8118. Ardath Rd exit off I-5. **Italian/Pizza.** This is a popular place with locals. A lovely restaurant with black-and-white marble floor, black metal chairs with green leather seats, and an art deco ambiance. Wonderful food includes wood-fired pizza, pasta, and Greek grilled chicken. Really amazing value. **FYI:** Reservations accepted. Beer and wine only. **Open:** Sun–Thurs 11:30am–10pm, Fri–Sat 11:30am–11pm. **Prices:** Main courses $7–$15. AE, DISC, MC, V. &

Elario's

In the Summer House Inn, 7955 La Jolla Shores Dr (La Jolla Shores); tel 619/459-0541. Ardath Rd exit off I-5. **Continental.** A wonderful view, elegant decor, and intimate booths all add up to a romantic dining experience. The menu offers contemporary continental fare such as veal loin medallions with wild mushrooms, seared sea bass with pan-fried potatoes and applewood-smoked bacon, and five-pepper filet mignon with garlic mashed potatoes and peppery cognac cream. **FYI:** Reservations recommended. Jazz. Dress code. **Open:** Breakfast Mon–Sat 7–11am, Sun 7–9am; lunch daily 11:30am–2pm; dinner daily 5:30–10pm; brunch Sun 10am–2pm. **Prices:** Main courses $13–$30. AE, DC, DISC, MC, V. ● ▲ &

♥ George's at the Cove

1250 Prospect St (La Jolla Village); tel 619/454-4244. Ardath Rd exit off I-5. **Eclectic.** There are three settings to choose from here: a deck with white furnishings and a good view; an upstairs nautical room with ceiling fans; and a downstairs area with wicker furniture and light wood walls. Typical dishes outside are grilled chicken breast, fresh fish, pastas, salads, and some Mexican options; inside, offerings include sea scallops, grilled prawns, and beef tenderloin. **FYI:** Reser-

vations recommended. **Open:** Lunch daily 11:30am–2:30pm; dinner Fri–Sat 5:30–11pm, Sun–Thurs 5:30–10pm. **Prices:** Main courses $15–$27; prix fixe $35. AE, CB, DC, DISC, MC, V. ▲ [VP]

✱ La Jolla Brewing Co

7536 Fay Ave; tel 619/456-BREW. **New American.** An ultracasual spot that turns out beers named for local surfing spots. Brews can be sampled at 75¢ apiece. The food is good: menu includes oyster "shooters," fish or shrimp tacos, and mahi-mahi sandwiches. **FYI:** Reservations not accepted. Children's menu. Beer and wine only. **Open:** Sun–Thurs 11:30am–11:30pm, Fri–Sat 11:30am–1am. **Prices:** Main courses $6–$9. AE, DC, DISC, MC, V. &

Mandarin House

6765 La Jolla Blvd (Wind n' Sea); tel 619/454-2555. Ardath Rd exit off I-5. **Chinese.** Most popular Chinese restaurant in San Diego, and winner of many awards. Pretty decor features silk plants, green booths, and peach cloth napkins. Menu specialties include Peking duck, pungent chicken, Mandarin noodles, and cashew chicken. **FYI:** Reservations accepted. **Open:** Mon–Thurs 11am–10pm, Fri–Sat 11am–11pm, Sun 2–10pm. **Prices:** Main courses $7–$14; prix fixe $17–$24. AE, DISC, MC, V.

Pannikin Coffee & Tea

7467 Girard Ave (La Jolla Village); tel 619/454-5453. **Cafe.** This cafe serves what may be the best cup of coffee in town. Set in an old home with a patio and little study nooks. Besides an extensive list of teas and coffees, the changing menu includes soups, salads, curries, pastries, fruits, and desserts. **FYI:** Reservations not accepted. No liquor license. Additional location: 3145 Rosecrans St, Point Loma (tel 224-2891). **Open:** Mon–Thurs 6–9pm, Fri 6–11pm, Sat–Sun 7–11pm. **Prices:** Main courses $4–$7. AE, DISC, MC, V.

Pannikin's Brockton Villa Restaurant

1235 Coast Blvd (La Jolla Village); tel 619/454-7393. Ardath Rd exit off I-5. **Californian.** Located in a restored, charming, 100-year-old beach cottage. The view of La Jolla Cove is stunning. Among the most popular dishes on the menu are the Greek steamers (three eggs steam-scrambled, then tossed with feta, tomato, and basil), and the turkey meatloaf sandwich on toasted sourdough with tomato chutney. **FYI:** Reservations recommended. Beer and wine only. **Open:** Peak (June–Sept) daily 8am–9pm. **Prices:** Main courses $8–$14. AE, DISC, MC, V. ▮ ▲ ▲

Piatti

2182 Avenida de la Playa (La Jolla Shores); tel 619/454-1589. Ardath Rd exit off I-5. **Italian.** A roomy place with tiled floors and pastel walls painted with larger-than life vegetables and herbs. There is also patio dining. Various pastas, wood-oven pizzas, and seafood dishes are specialties. Italian wines. **FYI:** Reservations recommended. **Open:** Mon–Thurs 11:30am–10pm, Fri–Sat 11am–11pm, Sun 11am–10pm. **Prices:** Main courses $8–$17. AE, MC, V. ▲ &

Putnam's Restaurant & Bar
In the Colonial Inn, 910 Prospect St (La Jolla Village); tel 619/454-2181. Ardath Rd exit off I-5. **New American/Californian.** Set in the old Putnam's Drug Store, a slice of La Jolla history. Old-world decor, with polished terrazzo floors, crisp white tablecloths, and fresh flowers, is very appealing. Menu changes seasonally, but could include barbecued chicken, roast duckling, grilled salmon, and roast rack of lamb. **FYI:** Reservations recommended. Piano. Children's menu. Dress code. **Open:** Breakfast Mon–Sat 7–10:30am; lunch Mon–Sat 11am–2:30pm; dinner Sun–Thurs 5–10pm, Fri–Sat 5–11pm. **Prices:** Main courses $11–$20; prix fixe $18–$22. AE, CB, DC, MC, V. 🍴 📷 💟 VP

Sammy's California Woodfired Pizza
702 Pearl St (La Jolla Village); tel 619/456-5222. Ardath Rd exit off I-5. **Californian/Pizza.** Healthy California cuisine at an upscale pizzeria with tiled floors, wood furnishings, and abundant plants. In addition to exotic pizzas, menu includes pastas and many salads. **FYI:** Reservations not accepted. Children's menu. Beer and wine only. **Open:** Peak (Mem Day–Labor Day) daily 11:30am–11pm. **Prices:** Main courses $8–$10. AE, MC, V. 📷 ⅙

⑤ Samson's
In La Jolla Village Square, 8861 Villa La Jolla Dr; tel 619/455-1461. La Jolla Village Dr exit off I-5. **Deli/Jewish.** A lively place, completely renovated in 1994 to evoke the feel of a New York–style deli. One room has walls lined with movie posters; another is decorated with a mural of customers eating at a deli. Menu features corned beef on rye, chicken in a pot, and other classics. Each table is topped with a wooden barrel filled with dill pickles. **FYI:** Reservations accepted. Accordian. Children's menu. Beer and wine only. **Open:** Mon–Thurs 7am–11pm, Fri–Sat 7am–midnight, Sun 7am–10pm. **Prices:** Main courses $6–$10. AE, DC, DISC, MC, V. 📷 💟 ⅙

♣ The Sky Room Restaurant
In La Valencia Hotel, 1132 Prospect St (La Jolla Village); tel 619/454-0771. Ardath Rd exit off I-5. **Californian/Mediterranean.** Intimate (only 12 tables) penthouse room with stunning ocean views from every table. Furnished with wing chairs, fine china, and elegant accoutrements. Known for dishes such as California sea bass with roasted scallops, grilled lobster, free-range chicken, and rack of lamb. **FYI:** Reservations recommended. Jacket required. **Open:** Mon–Sat 6–9pm. **Prices:** Main courses $21–$28; prix fixe $52. AE, CB, DC, DISC, MC, V. 💟 🍴 VP ⅙

♣ Top O' the Cove
1216 Prospect St (La Jolla Village); tel 619/454-7779. Ardath Rd exit off I-5. **Continental.** Award-winning restaurant set in a vintage 1893 bungalow. Downstairs, decor is understated and a patio offers garden dining; cuisine includes French classics such as filet mignon in burgundy-wine sauce, or roast rack of lamb. Upstairs are views of La Jolla, and a menu featuring fish and pastas, such as grilled rainbow trout and fusilli with artichoke hearts. **FYI:** Reservations recommended. Piano. **Open:** Lunch daily 11:30am–3:30pm; dinner daily 5:30–10:30pm. **Prices:** Main courses $25–$29. AE, CB, DC, MC, V. 💟 🏔 VP ⅙

The Whaling Bar
In La Valencia Hotel, 1132 Prospect St (La Jolla Village); tel 619/454-0771. Ardath Rd exit off I-5. **Californian/Mediterranean.** Located in a historic 1926 hotel, a restaurant with the look of an elegant club—with brass lamps and black leather upholstery, and whaling memorabilia at the bar. Specials include paella valenciana with sausage; marinated filet mignon; and local lobster salad. **FYI:** Reservations recommended. Dress code. **Open:** Lunch daily 11:30am–5pm; dinner Fri–Sat 6–11pm, Sun–Thurs 6–10pm. **Prices:** Main courses $13–$25. AE, CB, DC, DISC, MC, V. 🍴 VP

ATTRACTIONS 🏛

Torrey Pines State Reserve
San Diego; tel 619/755-2063. 1 mi S of Del Mar on N Torrey Pines Rd. Perched on sandstone cliffs, this setting offers hiking trails with wonderful ocean views, plus a chance to see the rare torrey pine. **Open:** Daily 9am–sundown. $$

Stephen Birch Aquarium-Museum
2300 Expedition Way; tel 619/534-FISH. A part of the Scripps Institution of Oceanography, University of California, San Diego. Situated on a hillside overlooking the Pacific Ocean, this complex is divided into three exhibit areas. The north wing contains the aquarium, which has more than 30 tanks housing over 3,000 fish. A kelp forest two stories tall is maintained in a giant tank that can be studied from a specially designed viewing gallery. The south wing contains the Scripps Hall of Oceanography, which features the nation's largest oceanographic exhibition, "Exploring the Blue Planet." Interpretive exhibits here illustrate the history of oceanography, Scripps research, man's relationship with the sea, and include interactive displays on weather, climate, and earthquakes. A simulated submarine ride takes visitors to the ocean floor. Connecting the two wings is the Tidepool Plaza, which features an artificial tidal pool where visitors can get a close-up look at the population of sea urchins, sea stars, sea cucumbers, and many other specimens. **Open:** Daily 9am–5pm. $$$

Lake Arrowhead

Residents of Lake Arrowhead take their zoning laws seriously, and this vigilance has helped them to preserve much of the original character of their mountain town. The best vantage point to see the shoreline is aboard the *Arrowhead Queen*, a 60-passenger paddlewheeler that plies the lake. **Information:** Lake Arrowhead Community Chamber of Commerce, 28200 CA 189, Bldg J, PO Box 219, Lake Arrowhead 92352 (tel 909/337-3715).

MOTEL

Arrowhead Tree Top Lodge

CA 173 at Rainbow Dr, PO Box 186, 92352; tel 909/
337-2311 or toll free 800/358-TREE. Nestled in the pines a
few minutes walk from Lake Arrowhead and Lake Arrowhead
Village. This place draws many repeat guests. **Rooms:** 20 rms,
stes, and effic. CI 2pm/CO 11am. Nonsmoking rms avail.
Very simple decor. **Amenities:** Cable TV, refrig. No A/C or
phone. Some units w/terraces, some w/fireplaces. **Services:**
Babysitting. **Facilities:** Nice picnic area with
barbecue. Nature trail and access to fishing. **Rates:** Peak
(June 15–Jan) $68–$140 S or D; $97–$135 ste; $84–$129
effic. Children under age 18 stay free. Min stay peak. Lower
rates off-season. Parking: Outdoor, free. AE, CB, DC, DISC,
JCB, MC, V.

RESORT

Lake Arrowhead Resort

Lake Arrowhead Village, PO Box 1699, 92352; tel 909/
336-1511 or toll free 800/800-6792; fax 909/336-1378. This
year-round mountain lake resort is great for families as well
as for off-site corporate meetings. **Rooms:** 175 rms, stes, and
effic; 86 cottages/villas. CI 4pm/CO noon. Nonsmoking rms
avail. **Amenities:** A/C, cable TV w/movies, refrig. All
units w/minibars, some w/terraces, some w/fireplaces, some
w/whirlpools. **Services:** Social director,
masseur, children's program, babysitting. **Facilities:**
2 restaurants (see "Restaurants"
below), 2 bars (1 w/entertainment), 1 beach (lake shore),
games rm, lawn games, racquetball, spa, sauna, steam rm,
whirlpool, beauty salon, day-care ctr, playground. **Rates:**
Peak (June 13–Oct) $125–$225 S or D; $285–$395 ste;
$255–$285 effic; $255–$305 cottage/villa. Extra person
$15. Children under age 18 stay free. Lower rates off-season.
Parking: Outdoor, free. AE, CB, DC, DISC, MC, V.

RESTAURANTS

The Royal Oak

27187 CA 189, Box 373, Blue Jay; tel 909/337-6018. 1½ mi
SW of Lake Arrowhead Village. **Continental.** The ambience
melds English Tudor style with a country-club atmosphere.
Cuisine is rich and hearty, featuring steaks, chops, seafood,
and pasta. **FYI:** Reservations recommended. Piano. Children's menu. Dress code. **Open:** Lunch Tues–Sat 11:30am–
2:30pm; dinner Sun–Thurs 5–9pm, Fri–Sat 5–11pm. **Prices:**
Prix fixe $13–$55. AE, MC, V.

Seasons

In Lake Arrowhead Resort, 27984 CA 189; tel 909/
336-1511. **New American.** The decor is grand and luxurious,
featuring tapestry-covered banquettes and Louis XV–style
chairs covered in blue velour. Large windows offer expansive
lakeside views from nearly every seat. Dine on chicken in
chardonnay cream, pecan-rolled halibut, filet mignon in

peppercorn sauce, and medallions of venison. Well-chosen
wine list. **FYI:** Reservations recommended. Dress code.
Open: Dinner Wed–Sun 6–10pm; brunch Sun 10am–2pm.
Prices: Main courses $12–$23. AE, DISC, MC, V.

ATTRACTION

Arrowhead Queen

Big Bear Lake; tel 909/336-6992. Located on the waterfront
in Lake Arrowhead Village. Narrated, 50-minute cruises
depart on the hour to explore the scenic beauty and rich
history of the lake and surrounding area. **Open:** Daily 10am–
6pm. $$$

Lake Tahoe Area

In California, see Olympic Valley, South Lake Tahoe, Tahoe
City, Tahoe Vista, Truckee; in Nevada, see Carson City,
Incline Village, Stateline

Lancaster

See also Palmdale

Once a remote, high-desert town primarily known for Ed-
ward's Air Force Base, Lancaster is now a bedroom commu-
nity for commuters making the long haul to Los Angeles. In
the spring, many from LA reverse the commute to see the
spectacular blooming display at the nearby California Poppy
State Reserve. **Information:** Antelope Valley Board of Trade,
44812 Elm Ave, Lancaster 93534 (tel 805/942-9581).

HOTEL

Best Western Antelope Valley Inn

44055 N Sierra Hwy, 93534; tel 805/948-4651 or toll free
800/528-1234; fax 805/948-4651. Ave K exit off US 14.
Southwest-themed property has striking pink adobe facade.
Large shade trees keep things cool, even in summer. **Rooms:**
148 rms and stes. CI 1pm/CO 1pm. Nonsmoking rms avail.
Amenities: A/C, satel TV w/movies, refrig. **Services:**
Babysitting. **Facilities:** 2 restaurants
(see "Restaurants" below), 1 bar (w/entertainment), whirl-
pool, beauty salon, playground. Japanese garden in court-
yard. **Rates:** $59–$69 S; $66–$76 D; $95–$120 ste. Extra
person $7. Children under age 12 stay free. Parking: Out-
door, free. AE, CB, DC, DISC, MC, V.

RESTAURANTS

Casa de Miguel

44245 N Sierra Hwy; tel 805/948-0793. Ave K exit off CA
14. **Mexican.** Underwent extensive remodeling in 1994.
Elevated loft-like dining room is used for banquets. Offers a
wide variety of Mexican fare. Try camarones Miguel wrapped
in bacon with rice, or chile verde made with pork. **FYI:**

Reservations recommended. Singer. Children's menu. **Open:** Mon–Thurs 11am–10pm, Fri–Sat 11am–11pm, Sun 10am–10pm. **Prices:** Main courses $8–$15. AE, MC, V.

The Desert Rose Bar & Grill
In Best Western Antelope Valley Inn, 44055 N Sierra Hwy; tel 805/948-4651. Ave K exit off CA 14, between J and K Aves. **Southwestern.** A southwestern theme restaurant, complete with a stage and dance floor with live entertainment. Specialties include prime rib, steaks, chicken, and seafood, including trout and catfish. Friday all-you-can-eat buffet. **FYI:** Reservations accepted. Country music/dancing. Children's menu. **Open:** Dinner Mon–Sat 5–10pm. **Prices:** Main courses $7–$18. AE, CB, DC, DISC, MC, V.

★ Downtown Bistro & Cafe
858 W Lancaster Blvd; tel 805/948-2253. Ave K exit off CA 14. **Californian/French.** A high-ceilinged restaurant with tapestry booths and banquettes, original artwork, and teak floors. The menu includes Italian, French, Thai, and hearty country cuisine. Desserts are excellent; don't miss the pear and walnut salad. **FYI:** Reservations recommended. Children's menu. **Open:** Breakfast Tues–Fri 7:30–11am, Sat–Sun 8:30–11am; lunch Tues–Sun 11am–2:30pm; dinner Tues–Thurs 5–8:30pm, Fri–Sat 5–9:30pm, Sun 5–8:30pm; brunch Sat–Sun 8:30am–2:30pm. **Prices:** Main courses $10–$18. AE, DISC, MC, V.

ATTRACTION

NASA Dryden Flight Research Center
Rosamond Blvd exit off CA 14, Edwards; tel 805/258-3449. Located at Edwards Air Force Base. NASA's primary institution for flight research, Dryden has been involved in modern flight testing from the days of the *X-1*, the first aircraft to break the sound barrier, to the early developmental research on the space shuttle. Two guided, 90-minute tours begin with a film, after which guests are escorted through a hangar where aircraft can be viewed. The walking portion of the tour is within a controlled-access area. Advance reservations are required. **Open:** Visitors center, Mon–Fri 7:45am–3:45pm; tours Mon–Fri 10:15am and 1:15pm. Closed some hols and shuttle landing days. **Free**

La Quinta

Perhaps the most secluded enclave of the Palm Springs area, La Quinta has some of the highest rated golf courses in the world. Currently, La Quinta has a golf course for every 1,289 permanent residents. **Information:** La Quinta Chamber of Commerce, 51-351 Avenida Bermudas, PO Box 255, La Quinta 92253 (tel 619/564-3199).

RESORT

≡≡≡≡ La Quinta Resort & Club
49-499 Eisenhower Dr, PO Box 69, 92253; tel 619/564-4111 or toll free 800/598-3828; fax 619/564-5758. Washington exit off I-10; right on Eisenhower Dr. 45 acres. Nestled against the Santa Rosa Mountains, this 70-year-old resort resembles a fantasy Spanish Colonial village, with red-roofed, white stucco villas and a central plaza, which offers shops and restaurants. It has long been a favorite hideout of the Hollywood elite: Bette Davis and Greta Garbo stayed here; Ginger Rogers got married here. Guests can walk the grounds, plucking ripe citrus fruits from the trees. **Rooms:** 640 rms and stes. CI 4pm/CO noon. Nonsmoking rms avail. Clustered in one- and two-story villas named after various saints, the casitas have Spanish-style decor; many also have fireplaces. Layouts vary: "Starlight" rooms offer very large decks, and the original 1926 accommodations feature thick adobe walls. Bathrooms are large and exceedingly well laid out. **Amenities:** A/C, cable TV w/movies, dataport, voice mail, bathrobes. All units w/minibars, all w/terraces, some w/fireplaces. Iron and ironing board in all rooms. **Services:** Twice-daily maid svce, car-rental desk, social director, masseur, children's program, babysitting. Turn-down gifts left on pillows each night are geared to local culture and traditions, such as tiny Cahuilla dolls, said to ward off worries. **Facilities:** 5 restaurants (see "Restaurants" below), 1 bar (w/entertainment), lawn games, whirlpool, beauty salon. Since there are 25 pools and 38 whirlpools, the property never seems crowded. Fifty gardeners primp roses and bougainvillea into perfection. Meeting facilities include a 17,000-square-foot ballroom. Golf courses include the PGA WEST TPC Stadium Golf layout, the Jack Nicklaus Tournament course, and the Mountain Course. Tennis facilities include 6 grass, 3 clay, and 21 hard courts. **Rates:** Peak (Nov–Apr) $220–$365 S or D; $315–$2,600 ste. Extra person $25. Children under age 18 stay free. Lower rates off-season. Parking: Indoor/outdoor, free. AE, CB, DC, DISC, ER, JCB, MC, V.

RESTAURANTS

Beachside Cafe
78-477 CA 111; tel 619/564-4577. Washington exit off I-10. **American.** Unique cafe decorated with colorful surfboards and other beach paraphernalia. Favorite dishes include barbecued ribs, fish and chips, and prime rib. **FYI:** Reservations not accepted. Beer and wine only. **Open:** Daily 7am–9pm. **Prices:** Main courses $9–$14. CB, DC, DISC, MC, V.

Cunard's
78-045 Calle Cadiz; tel 619/564-4443. **Eclectic.** A country estate turned into a restaurant. Five distinct dining areas offer views of gardens and rock fountains. The eclectic menu includes rack of lamb with herbs, and charred chiles with four

cheeses. **FYI:** Reservations recommended. Piano/singer. Dress code. **Open:** Dinner daily 5–10pm. Closed June–Sept. **Prices:** Main courses $16–$28. AE, DC, DISC, MC, V. ♥ ▲ VP

La Quinta Cliffhouse
78-250 CA 111; tel 619/360-5991. Washington exit off I-10. **Regional American.** Dramatically perched halfway up a small mountain. Large picture windows look out on the surrounding mountains; dining terraces are carved into granite outcroppings. Menu favorites include aged filet mignon, marinated rack of lamb, and fresh fish. **FYI:** Reservations recommended. Guitar. Children's menu. Dress code. **Open:** Peak (Jan–Apr) Mon–Thurs 5–9:30pm, Fri–Sat 5–10pm, Sun 10am–2pm. **Prices:** Main courses $13–$20. AE, DC, MC, V. 🛥 ▲ ♥ VP &

Montañas
In La Quinta Resort & Club, 49-499 Eisenhower Dr; tel 619/564-4111. Washington exit off I-10. **Mediterranean.** Set in what was the original dining room at this posh resort back in 1926. Casual and charming, with works of art from local artists displayed in this Spanish-style hacienda. The robust cuisine features such items as roast maple chicken and paella. **FYI:** Reservations recommended. Piano. Jacket required. **Open:** Peak (Sept–May) dinner daily 6–10pm; brunch Sun 10am–2pm. Closed June–Sept. **Prices:** Main courses $18–$30. AE, CB, DC, DISC, MC, V. ▆ VP &

Larkspur

The small residential community of Larkspur is the gateway to Marin County from the Richmond–San Rafael toll bridge. A small harbor opens into the sheltered waters of San Francisco Bay. The region's great scenic beauty and fine beaches attract legions of visitors. **Information:** Larkspur Chamber of Commerce, PO Box 315, Larkspur 94977 (tel 415/927-4360).

HOTEL 🏨

≡≡≡ Courtyard by Marriott
2500 Larkspur Landing Circle, 94939; tel 415/925-1800 or toll free 800/321-2211; fax 415/925-1107. Exit off US 101; bear east towards Richmond Bridge, turn left at 1st light onto Larkspur Landing Circle. Extensive landscaping surrounds New England–style, wood-trimmed buildings. Lobby has attractive sitting areas with fireplace and bar. Conveniently located near shopping center and ferry to San Francisco. **Rooms:** 146 rms and stes. CI 4pm/CO noon. Nonsmoking rms avail. Standard rooms are compact but nicely laid out, with all the comforts. All sofas convert into beds—good for families. **Amenities:** 📺 ♨ A/C, dataport, voice mail. Some units w/terraces. **Services:** ✗ 🚗 ☒ 🛎 Car-rental desk, masseur, babysitting. **Facilities:** 🛋 🍽 🏊 & 1 restaurant (bkfst only), 1 bar, whirlpool, washer/dryer. The courtyard

gardens are lovely, with a nice gazebo for reading and relaxing. **Rates:** Peak (March–Nov 1) $109 S or D; $145 ste. Children under age 18 stay free. Lower rates off-season. Parking: Outdoor, free. AE, CB, DC, DISC, MC, V.

RESTAURANTS 🍴

Bolero
125 E Sir Francis Drake Blvd (Larkspur Landing); tel 415/925-9391. **Spanish.** Spanish restaurant is dramatically set in an old, towering brick kiln. Exposed brick walls, lots of candles, and cozy tables enhance the already romantic ambience. The tapas, sherries, entrees, and fine wines would please a Spanish native. Tapas might include paper-thin prosciutto, garlicky mussels, or well-aged Manchego cheese. Several versions of paella, rabbit stew, and grilled sirloin are a few of the entrees. Live flamenco dancing and music Fri and Sat. **FYI:** Reservations recommended. **Open:** Lunch daily 11:30am–3pm; dinner Sun–Fri 5:30–10pm, Sat 5:30–11pm. **Prices:** Main courses $10–$18. AE, DC, DISC, MC, V. ♥ VP &

♣ Lark Creek Inn
234 Magnolia Ave (Downtown); tel 415/924-7766. 10 mi N of San Francisco Tamalpais Dr/Paradise Dr exit off US 101; West on Tamalpais Dr 1 mi, right on Corte Madera Ave, ½ mi. **New American.** Groves of redwoods, a meandering stream, and a yellow-painted Victorian house create a fairytale setting. Chef Bradley Ogden's philosophy of "Keep it simple; use only the freshest ingredients" shines through. Depending on what's in season, entrees might include grilled quail with tomatillo salsa, or pan-seared local halibut on summer bean and beet salad. **FYI:** Reservations recommended. Children's menu. **Open:** Lunch Mon–Fri 11:30am–2pm; dinner Mon–Thurs 5:30–9:30pm, Fri–Sat 5–10pm, Sun 5–9pm; brunch Sun 10am–2pm. **Prices:** Main courses $14–$23. AE, DC, MC, V. ♥ 🛥 &

★ Left Bank
507 Magnolia Ave (Downtown); tel 415/927-3331. **French.** This highly successful restaurant creates a St-Germain-des-Pres ambience with its simple decor of oak floors and alabaster chandeliers. Authentic brasserie fare, from the real cornichons that accompany the rillettes to main courses such as steak with crispy fried potatoes, or whole roasted fish. Wonderful desserts include fresh-fruit tarts. **FYI:** Reservations recommended. Children's menu. **Open:** Tues–Thurs 11:30am–11pm, Fri–Sat 11:30am–midnight, Sun–Mon 11:30am–10pm. **Prices:** Main courses $9–$21. AE, MC, V. ▲ VP &

Lassen Volcanic National Park

For lodgings, see Red Bluff, Redding

Located 44 miles east of Redding via CA 44, this 165-square-mile national park reveals a history of violent volcanic activity. Lassen Peak (10,457 feet) is one of only two active volcanoes in the continental United States (the other is Mount St Helens in Washington), although it has been dormant since 1921. Today, peaceful coniferous forests, alpine meadows, and mountain lakes coexist with cinder cones, lava flows, boiling mud pots, and thermal springs. The summit affords a superb panoramic view of the surrounding area; access is via a 2- to 3-hour walk along a marked trail. There is also a scenic 30-mile drive between the park's southern entrance and Manzanita Lake (Lassen Park Rd).

Although the park is open year-round, heavy snowslides prevent access to Lassen Park Rd and certain areas of the park from late October to early June. There are seven fully equipped campgrounds (late May–late Sept). The visitor center on Manzanita Lake (northwest park entrance) is open in summer. For further information, contact the Superintendent, Lassen Volcanic National Park, PO Box 100, Mineral, CA 96063 (tel 916/595-4444).

Lava Beds National Monument

For lodging and dining, see Mount Shasta

Lava Beds National Park

The aboveground terrain of Lava Beds National Monument is desolate and windy, with high plateaus, spiky buttes, and rolling hills covered with lava cinders, coyote bush, and tortured-looking junipers. Miles of land just like it cover most of this corner of California. The difference here is the Swiss cheese-like underground, the result of lava whose outer edges cooled while the core kept flowing, forming underground tunnels like a giant pipeline system.

More than 200 lava tube caves lace the earth at Lava Beds. In the winter of 1872, a small band of Modec Indians held off a siege by a large army of US cavalrymen for nearly six months by using the lava tube tunnels as hideouts. On June 1, 1873, weakened by starvation and exhausted, the Modocs surrendered.

Today, the caves are open to the public to explore on their own or with park rangers. All visitors need to explore the caves is a good flashlight or head lamp, sturdy walking shoes, and a sense of adventure. Many of the tunnels are entered by ladders or stairs, others by holes in the side of a hill.

One-way **Cave Loop Road** just southwest of the visitiors center is the starting point for many of the best cave hikes. About 15 lava tubes have been marked and made accessible. Two are ice caves, where the air temperature remains below freezing all year and ice crystals form on the walls. The easiest cave to explore is the **Mushpot Cave,** located almost adjacent to the visitors center and outfitted with lights and a smooth walkway.

For more information, contact Lava Beds National Monument, Box 867, Tulelake, CA 96134 (tel 916/667-2282).

Lee Vining

A recreation center for the Eastern Sierra, Lee Vining is located on the shores of Mono Lake and is the gateway to Tioga Pass and Yosemite National Park. A small visitors center offers information on the history and delicate ecology of the ancient lake. **Information:** Mono Lake Community Visitor Center, US 395, PO Box 29, Lee Vining 93541 (tel 619/647-6386).

MOTEL 🏨

🛏 **Best Western Lake View Lodge**
30 Main St, PO Box 345, 93541; tel 619/647-6543 or toll free 800/528-1234. 2 mi N of jct CA 120/US 395. The only decent hotel in town. Located 28 miles from the ghost town Bodie, 3 miles from Mono Lake. **Rooms:** 47 rms and stes. CI 4pm/CO 11am. Nonsmoking rms avail. Small but clean. **Amenities:** 🛏 📺 A/C, cable TV w/movies. **Services:** 🕹 🐕 **Facilities:** 🔥 **Rates:** Peak (June–Oct 1) $72–$94 S or D; $72 ste. Lower rates off-season. Parking: Outdoor, free. AE, CB, DC, DISC, MC, V.

ATTRACTION 📷

Mono Lake
Tel 619/647-6595. Located 15 miles east of Yosemite National Park, just east of the town of Lee Vining, Mono Lake is one of the oldest lakes in the Western Hemisphere. An immense inland sea, it covers an area of just over 100 square miles with waters 250 percent more saline than sea water. Lowering of the lake due to diversion of its tributaries has exposed formations of calcium carbonate, which stick out above the waterline. Stratified limestone formations, called tufa, surround the lake. More than a million waterfowl, gulls, and shorebirds populate the surrounding area from April to October.

Mono Basin National Forest Scenic Area Visitor Center, situated on a bluff overlooking the lake, presents an interpretive film on the lake and offers exhibits and interpretive programs led by Forest Service rangers and staff. **Mono Lake Tufa State Reserve,** south on US 395, then east on CA 120, is the site of several major tufa outcroppings. Interpretive signs along the South Tufa trail explain the origin and formation of tufa. **Mono Lake County Park** offers an idyllic picnicking spot along a small stream shaded by cottonwoods, and a boardwalk trail through delicate tufa formations that leads to the lakeshore. **Open:** Daily 24 hours. **Free**

Little River

See also Elk, Mendocino

Located a few miles south of Mendocino on a very remote stretch of coast, Little River takes its name from the nearby waterway that wends to the ocean. The small town is a showcase of New England architecture, which was popular with its mid-19th-century settlers.

HOTELS

Heritage House
5200 N CA 1, 95456; tel 707/937-5885 or toll free 800/235-5885; fax 707/937-0318. Located on 37 acres amid gardens, pine forests, and rhododendron dells, overlooking the Mendocino coast. This place has a museumlike quality, with original fixtures and a history display. **Rooms:** 70 rms and stes. CI 2pm/CO noon. Nonsmoking rms avail. Cozy rooms are not luxurious. Each has its own landscaped garden area; most have bay or ocean views. Stay on ocean side of building. Vista 3 and Carousel 4 and 5 are very special rooms. **Amenities:** No A/C, phone, or TV. Some units w/minibars, some w/terraces, some w/fireplaces, some w/whirlpools. Complimentary wine in some rooms. **Services:** Masseur, babysitting. **Facilities:** 1 restaurant, 1 bar (w/entertainment), 1 beach (ocean). Restaurant has French country feel, and a dining terrace. **Rates (MAP):** Peak (Apr–Oct) $180–$360 S or D; $320–$430 ste. Extra person $70. Children under age 6 stay free. Min stay wknds and special events. Lower rates off-season. Parking: Outdoor, free. Closed Jan. AE, DC, DISC, JCB, MC, V.

Little River Inn
7751 CA 1, PO Box B, 95456; tel 707/937-5942; fax 707/937-3944. 250 acres. This charming inn, built in the 1850s and run by the same family for four generations, is nestled among the trees next to Van Damme State Park. **Rooms:** 61 rms and stes; 3 cottages/villas. CI 3pm/CO noon. Nonsmoking rms avail. Rooms are clean, cheerful, and have breathtaking views. Ask for the Van Damme units, which are new, private, have whirlpools, and are nearest the ocean. **Amenities:** Cable TV, refrig, VCR, bathrobes. No A/C. Some units w/terraces, some w/fireplaces, some w/whirlpools. **Services:** Masseur, babysitting. Free videos. **Facilities:** 1 restaurant (bkfst and dinner only; see "Restaurants" below), 1 bar. **Rates:** Peak (Apr–Nov) $85–$155 S or D; $165–$225 ste; $165–$225 cottage/villa. Extra person $10. Children under age 13 stay free. Min stay wknds. Lower rates off-season. Parking: Outdoor, free. MC, V.

Stevenswood Lodge
8211 Shoreline, PO Box 170, 95460; tel 707/937-2810 or toll free 800/421-2810; fax 707/937-1237. ⅓ mi N of Van Dam State Park. 6 acres. Like staying in an art gallery in the woods. This peaceful, contemporary hotel on the inland side of the highway is filled with modern paintings and sculptures in the lobby, halls, and garden. Lounge area with fireplace opens to garden. **Rooms:** 10 rms and stes. CI 3pm/CO noon. No smoking. Modern rooms overlook wooded grounds. **Amenities:** Cable TV, bathrobes. No A/C. All units w/minibars, all w/fireplaces. Down comforters. **Services:** Masseur, babysitting. Complimentary hors d'oeuvres, wine, and full gourmet breakfast. **Facilities:** Small business meeting area with fax machines. **Rates (BB):** Peak (Mar–Nov) $95–$125 S or D; $120–$195 ste. Extra person $20–$25. Children under age 2 stay free. Min stay wknds. Lower rates off-season. Parking: Outdoor, free. AE, DISC, MC, V.

INN

Glendeven
8221 N CA 1, 95456; tel 707/937-0083 or toll free 800/822-4536; fax 707/937-6108. 2½ acres. Beautiful, soothing garden setting, with an extensive art gallery on the premises. **Rooms:** 10 rms and stes. CI 3pm/CO 11am. No smoking. Rooms are spacious and decorated in early American motif, with quilts, pine furniture, four-poster beds, rag rugs. Some have French doors opening into the gardens. **Amenities:** No A/C, phone, or TV. Some units w/terraces, some w/fireplaces. **Services:** Masseur, afternoon tea and wine/sherry served. Coffee, tea, and homemade chocolate-chip cookies are available in the lounge. Expanded continental breakfast is delivered to your room. **Facilities:** Guest lounge. Baby grand piano for guests to play in lounge. **Rates (CP):** Peak (Aug) $80–$140 S; $100–$160 D; $150–$200 ste. Extra person $20. Children under age 2 stay free. Min stay wknds. Lower rates off-season. Parking: Outdoor, free. AE, MC, V.

RESTAURANT

Little River Inn Restaurant
7751 N CA 1; tel 707/937-5942. **Californian/Seafood.** Opened in 1939 and run by the same family for four generations. Airy and pleasant, with large windows framing a garden montage of flowers and ferns. Try Ole's hotcakes for breakfast. Dinner specialties include pepper steak, lemon prawns, grilled polenta with porcini mushroom sauce, spring rack of lamb. All entrees come with appetizers and salad. **FYI:** Reservations recommended. Guitar. Children's menu. **Open:** Breakfast Mon–Fri 7:30–10:30am, Sat 7:30–11am; dinner daily 6–9pm; brunch Sun 7:30am–1pm. **Prices:** Main courses $17–$20. MC, V.

Lodi

Situated in the northern reaches of the Central Valley in San Joaquin County, Lodi has become a wine center of late, with at least a dozen respectable wineries in the area. The March Spring Wine Show is dedicated to the fruit of the local vintners. **Information:** Lodi District Chamber of Commerce, 1330 S Ham Lane #102, PO Box 386, Lodi 95241 (tel 209/367-7840 or toll free 800/304-LODI).

MOTEL

Best Western Royal Host Inn

710 S Cherokee Lane, 95240; tel 209/369-8484 or toll free 800/720-LODI; fax 209/369-0654. Turner exit off CA 99. Little ambience, but suitable for an overnight stopover. **Rooms:** 48 rms and stes. CI 2pm/CO 11am. Nonsmoking rms avail. Slightly worn, but clean. **Amenities:** A/C, cable TV w/movies. **Services:** Fax service available through office. **Facilities:** **Rates:** Peak (Mar–Nov) $43–$46 S; $49–$59 D. Extra person $8. Children under age 12 stay free. Lower rates off-season. Parking: Outdoor, free. AE, CB, DC, DISC, MC, V.

Lompoc

Lompoc boasts that it is the flower-growing capital of the world, a believable claim when one sees the surrounding rolling hills explode in color from May to September. **Information:** Lompoc Valley Chamber of Commerce, 111 S I St, PO Box 626, Lompoc 93438-0626 (tel 805/736-4567).

HOTEL

Embassy Suites

1117 North H St, 93436; tel 805/735-8311 or toll free 800/433-3182, 800/433-3182, 800/433-0680 in CA; fax 805/735-8459. Lovely lobby decorated with lots of brick, Spanish tiles, plants, and charming murals. Grounds feature a beautifully landscaped waterfall and pond. Top choice for accommodations in Lompoc. **Rooms:** 156 stes. CI 3pm/CO noon. Nonsmoking rms avail. Suites are decorated in French country style. Ladies' executive rooms have more feminine decor with lots of flowers and ruffles. **Amenities:** A/C, satel TV w/movies, dataport, voice mail. **Services:** Social director, masseur, babysitting. Complimentary evening cocktails. **Facilities:** 1 bar (w/entertainment), spa, whirlpool, washer/dryer. Well-maintained pool and spa. Free use of nearby health spa. Bar, for hotel guests only, offers Saturday evening entertainment. **Rates (BB):** $85–$95 ste. Extra person $10. Children under age 12 stay free. Min stay special events. Parking: Outdoor, free. AE, CB, DC, DISC, EC, ER, JCB, MC, V.

MOTEL

Tally Ho Motor Inn

1020 E Ocean Ave, 93436; tel 805/735-6444 or toll free 800/332-6444; fax 805/735-5558. CA 246 N exit off US 1. Attractive lobby decorated in hunter green. Near La Purisima Mission. Popular with visitors to Solvang who don't want to pay tourist-town rates. **Rooms:** 53 rms, stes, and effic. CI 3:30pm/CO 11am. Nonsmoking rms avail. Clean, acceptable rooms in pleasing shades of mauve and green. **Amenities:** A/C, cable TV, refrig. All units w/terraces. Microwaves in some rooms. VCR and videos available. TDD for hard-of-hearing guests. **Services:** Free use of nearby health club. **Facilities:** Sauna, whirlpool, washer/dryer. **Rates (CP):** $40 S; $45 D; $55 ste; $40 effic. Children under age 18 stay free. Parking: Outdoor, free. AE, DISC, MC, V.

ATTRACTIONS

Lompoc Museum

200 South H St; tel 805/736-3888. This museum, housed in a former Carnegie library, focuses on the archeology and history of the Lompoc Valley and Santa Barbara County. The Clarence Ruth Gallery contains ethnographic and archaeological pieces from across the world; the Lompoc Valley Historical Society Gallery has exhibits on the Mission Period, Rancho Period, early Lompoc, and local industries; Gallery III features temporary exhibits and the museum's theater. **Open:** Tues–Fri 1–5pm, Sat–Sun 1–4pm. **Free**

La Purisima Mission State Historic Park

2295 Purisima Rd; tel 805/733-3713. Of the 21 Franciscan missions in California, three are preserved within the state park system. Of these, La Purisima is considered to be the most authentically restored. All major buildings have been rebuilt and furnished as they were around 1820, the grounds have been planted with plants typical of that time, livestock of the correct genetic type have been acquired, and the original aqueduct system is being maintained.

The first mission was destroyed by earthquake in 1812. It was rebuilt the following year, but as the missions gradually came under civil control, the site was abandoned. Beginning in 1934, a combined federal, state, and county effort undertook a complete restoration of La Purisima. It was turned over to the state park system in 1941.

More than 30 rooms are completely restored and furnished, including the church, weaving room, and mission kitchen. Crafts demonstrations, living history programs, and guided tours are offered. There are 12 miles of walking trails on the 900-acre site. **Open:** Daily 9am–5pm. **$$**

Long Beach

See also San Pedro, Seal Beach

Long Beach boomed in the 1930s when offshore oil and gas were discovered, and the downtown area retains authentic art deco touches from that era. Some sections of town suffered from industrial decline, but revitalization efforts have restored downtown Long Beach to much of its former glory. **Information:** Long Beach Area Convention & Visitors Bureau, One World Trade Center #300, Long Beach 90831-0300 (tel 562/436-3645).

HOTELS

Best Western Golden Sails Hotel

6285 E Pacific Coast Hwy, 90803; tel 562/596-1631 or toll free 800/762-5333; fax 562/594-0623. W of 7th St exit off I-405. Fairly typical Best Western. **Rooms:** 172 rms. Executive level. CI 1pm/CO noon. Nonsmoking rms avail. Rooms are tasteful, clean, and comfortable. **Amenities:** A/C, cable TV w/movies, refrig. Some units w/terraces, some w/whirlpools. **Services:** Social director, babysitting. **Facilities:** 1 restaurant, 1 bar (w/entertainment), whirlpool, washer/dryer. Reggae music in lounge on weekends. **Rates (BB):** $109-$130 S or D. Children under age 18 stay free. MAP rates avail. Parking: Outdoor, free. AE, CB, DC, DISC, MC, V.

Long Beach Marriott

4700 Airport Plaza Dr, 90815 (Long Beach Airport); tel 562/425-5210 or toll free 800/228-9290; fax 562/425-2744. Lakewood Blvd exit off I-405. Spacious, well-maintained property. Waterfall in pool area. **Rooms:** 311 rms and stes. Executive level. CI 3pm/CO noon. Nonsmoking rms avail. Some rooms are noisy. **Amenities:** A/C, cable TV w/movies, CD/tape player. **Services:** Car-rental desk, social director, babysitting. **Facilities:** 2 restaurants, 2 bars (1 w/entertainment), spa, sauna, whirlpool. **Rates (BB):** $79-$119 S or D; $250 ste. Children under age 18 stay free. Parking: Outdoor, free. AE, DC, DISC, JCB, MC, V.

UNRATED Renaissance Long Beach Hotel

111 E Ocean Blvd, 90802; tel 562/437-5900 or toll free 800/HOTELS1; fax 562/499-2509. Broadway exit off I-710; follow Broadway to Pine, turn right. This 12-story hotel is in the heart of the Long Beach financial district, and within walking distance of shops and restaurants. Beaches and freeways are nearby. **Rooms:** 374 rms, stes, and effic. Executive level. CI 3pm/CO noon. Nonsmoking rms avail. Large, with views of either the city or the ocean. **Amenities:** A/C, cable TV w/movies. All units w/minibars, some w/terraces, some w/whirlpools. **Services:** Twice-daily maid svce, car-rental desk, babysitting. Courtesy shuttle to Long Beach, including the Queen Mary. **Facilities:** 1 restaurant, 1 bar (w/entertainment), spa,

sauna, steam rm. **Rates:** Peak (Dec-May) $104-$156 S or D; $400-$800 ste. Extra person $15. Children under age 18 stay free. Lower rates off-season. Parking: Indoor, $6-$8/day. Special honeymoon packages. AE, CB, DC, DISC, JCB, MC, V.

UNRATED Seaport Marina Hotel

6400 E Pacific Coast Hwy, 90803; tel 562/434-8451 or toll free 800/434-8451; fax 562/598-6028. 7th St exit off I-405, W to Pacific Coast Hwy. Recently renovated. By a marina and surrounded by palm trees and extensive, well-kept grounds. **Rooms:** 203 rms. Executive level. CI 3pm/CO 1pm. Nonsmoking rms avail. Some rooms have nice views of marina. **Amenities:** A/C, TV. Some units w/minibars, all w/terraces. **Services:** **Facilities:** 1 restaurant, 1 bar (w/entertainment), spa, whirlpool, washer/dryer. **Rates:** Peak (July-Sept) $99 S or D. Extra person $10. Children under age 12 stay free. Lower rates off-season. Parking: Outdoor, free. AE, CB, DC, DISC, MC, V.

Sheraton Long Beach

333 E Ocean Blvd, 90802; tel 562/436-3000 or toll free 800/325-3525; fax 562/499-2096. Broadway exit off I-710 S; right on Elm, right on Ocean. The lobby, airy and filled with greenery, has large windows and skylights; a nice change from similar large hotels. **Rooms:** 460 rms and stes. CI 3pm/CO noon. Nonsmoking rms avail. **Amenities:** A/C, cable TV w/movies, in-rm safe. All units w/minibars, some w/whirlpools. **Services:** Twice-daily maid svce, babysitting. **Facilities:** 2 restaurants, 2 bars (w/entertainment), spa, sauna, whirlpool. The largest ballroom in Long Beach is on the premises. **Rates:** $175 S or D; $285 ste. Extra person $20. Children under age 16 stay free. Parking: Indoor, $5-$8/day. AE, CB, DC, DISC, EC, ER, JCB, MC, V.

MOTEL

Vagabond Inn Long Beach

185 Atlantic Ave, 90802; tel 562/435-7621 or toll free 800/522-1555; fax 562/436-7510. Atlantic S exit off I-405. A two-story structure surrounding a pool, this motel is plain, but decent. Management has attempted to beautify the grounds with plantings. **Rooms:** 48 rms and effic. CI 1pm/CO noon. Nonsmoking rms avail. A bit dated and dingy. **Amenities:** A/C, cable TV. Some units w/terraces. **Services:** Continental breakfast includes cereal, yogurt, muffins, danishes and coffee. **Facilities:** **Rates (CP):** Peak (May-Aug) $50 S; $55 D; $50 effic. Extra person $5. Children under age 12 stay free. Min stay special events. Lower rates off-season. Parking: Outdoor, free. AE, CB, DC, DISC, MC, V.

RESTAURANTS

★ 555 East American Steak House

555 E Ocean Blvd; tel 562/437-0626. **American.** Very 1940s-New York, with dark wood, black-and-white flooring,

brass accents, mirrors, and black-and-white photographs. Specialties are prime steaks, fresh seafood, and pastas. **FYI:** Reservations recommended. Children's menu. **Open:** Lunch Mon–Fri 11:30am–3pm; dinner Sun–Mon 5:30–9pm, Tues–Thurs 5:30–10pm, Fri–Sat 5:30–11pm. **Prices:** Main courses $12–$27. AE, DC, DISC, MC, V. 🍴🏛️🖼️ VP ♿

♣ L'Opera Ristorante
101 Pine Ave; tel 562/491-0066. Broadway exit off I-710 W; turn right on Pine Ave. **Italian.** This former bank is now an elegant restaurant, with pale-yellow walls offset by faux marble pillars and dark wood accents. Appropriate for people looking for a relaxing, traditional ambience. The large menu has pastas and antipasti; grilled veal lion and osso buco are both popular. The one-time bank vault serves as a wine cellar. **FYI:** Reservations recommended. **Open:** Lunch Mon–Fri 11:30am–5pm; dinner Mon–Thurs 5–11pm, Fri–Sat 5pm–midnight, Sun 5–10pm. **Prices:** Main courses $8–$22. AE, DC, DISC, MC, V. 🖼️ VP ♿

♣ Mums
144 Pine Ave; tel 562/437-7700. Broadway exit off I-710 W; turn right on Pine Ave. **Californian.** Golden wood tones, pillars, palms, exotic flowers, and interesting lighting make this a place for a special occasion. Fresh seafood, pasta, pizza, and unusual choices like Thai chicken linguini and blackened halibut are offered. **FYI:** Reservations recommended. Blues. **Open:** Sun–Mon 11am–10pm, Tues–Wed 11am–11pm, Thurs 11am–midnight, Fri–Sat 11am–1:30am. **Prices:** Main courses $11–$20. AE, DC, MC, V. 🍷🏛️ VP ♿

ATTRACTIONS 🏛️

Queen Mary Seaport
Pier J; tel 562/435-3511. Last of the great super liners, the legendary *Queen Mary* was the largest and most luxurious ocean liner ever built. Catering to the rich and famous of Europe and America, the ship accommodated 2,000 passengers on its maiden voyage to New York City in May, 1936. When it was converted for use as a troop carrier during World War II, the repainted ship became known as the "Gray Ghost" for its ability to avoid German U-boats. It carried a total of 800,000 troops during six years of military service and was returned to passenger service in 1947. When the *Queen Mary* was turned over to the city of Long Beach in 1967, it had completed 1,001 crossings of the Atlantic.

Today the ship is a major tourist attraction. Guided and self-guided tours are available that explore various areas of the ship, including the bridge, officers' quarters, engine room, staterooms, and the first-class lounge. Part of the ship contains a 365-room hotel, with rooms that were originally first-class staterooms.

There are numerous restaurants, lounges, and shops aboard the *Queen Mary*. Surrounding the ship is the **Queen's Marketplace,** a 55-acre site featuring still more shops and restaurants, along with strolling musicians and street performers. **Open:** Peak (mid-June–Labor Day) Sun–Thurs 10am–6pm, Fri–Sat 10am. Reduced hours off-season. **$$$**

Long Beach Museum of Art
2300 E Ocean Blvd; tel 310/439-2119. Situated on a bluff overlooking the Pacific ocean, this museum contains a permanent collection spanning 100 years of American and European art, including an internationally renowned collection of video art; also rotating multimedia exhibitions of modern and contemporary art. Sculpture garden; outdoor cafe. Museum shop. **Open:** Wed–Thurs and Sat–Sun 10am–5pm, Fri 10am–8pm. **$**

Rancho Los Alamitos Historic Ranch and Gardens
6400 Bixby Rd; tel 310/570-1755. The current 7½-acre site is all that remains of what was once a vast land grant that originally comprised 300,000 acres. Rancho Los Alamitos now consists of a 17-room ranch house (circa 1800), four acres of graceful gardens, and six early-20th-century agricultural outbuildings. Guided tours of the site illustrate ranch life in the 18th and 19th centuries. Special programs throughout the year. **Open:** Wed–Sun 1–5pm. **Free**

Los Altos

See also Mountain View

RESTAURANT 🍴

★ Chef Chu's
1067 N San Antonio Rd; tel 415/948-2696. San Antonio Rd S exit off US 101. **Chinese.** Large floral paintings, etched-glass dividers, and mirrors enhance the simple but tasteful decor. Over 50 beef, lamb, poultry, seafood, pork, and vegetable dishes. Specialties include tangerine beef, candied pecans with prawns, velvet chicken. **FYI:** Reservations recommended. **Open:** Lunch daily 11:30am–4pm; dinner Sun–Thurs 4–9:30pm, Fri–Sat 4–10pm. **Prices:** Main courses $8–$15; prix fixe $14. AE, DC, MC, V. 🖼️🚗 ♿

Los Angeles

See also Beverly Hills, Burbank, Culver City, Glendale, Hollywood, Malibu, Marina del Rey, North Hollywood, Pasadena, Redondo Beach, Santa Monica, Studio City, West Hollywood; for airport lodgings, see Los Angeles Int'l Airport

Freeways. Surfers. Movie stars. A sign that spells out H-O-L-L-Y-W-O-O-D. It seems fitting that Los Angeles presents itself in montage images. Not only is LA linked, twin-like, with the movie industry—the city itself isn't so much a place as it is places, some 140 different cities stretched together like a patchwork quilt. With a population of 14.5 million, Greater Los Angeles is the second largest metropolitan area in the country. Los Angeles County itself is huge, encompassing over 4,000 square miles and stretching from the San Gabriel

Mountains to the Pacific Ocean. Its lowest point lies some nine feet below sea level; its tallest, Mount Baldy, towers 10,080 feet above it. Most of all, Los Angeles is the World City, with a mix of languages, culture, architecture, cuisine, arts, politics, and lifestyles unmatched anywhere else on the globe.

PUBLIC TRANSPORTATION

The **Los Angeles County Metropolitan Transit Authority (MTA)** operates the city's trains and buses. Basic bus fare is $1.35 for all local lines, with transfers costing 25¢. The **Downtown Area Short Hop (DASH)** shuttle system operates buses throughout downtown and the west side. It costs 25¢. The **Metro Blue Line**, an underused aboveground rail system, connects downtown with Long Beach. Trains operate daily 6am–9pm; fare is $1.35. The **Metro Red Line** operates in the downtown area; fare is 25¢. The **Metro Green Line** runs for 20 miles along the center of the new I-105 Glenn Anderson (Century) Freeway and connects Norwalk in eastern Los Angeles County to Los Angeles Int'l Airport (LAX). For information on all Metro lines call the MTA at 213/626-4455.

HOTELS 🏨

≣≣ Best Western Mayfair Hotel

1256 W 7th St, 90017; tel 213/484-9789 or toll free 800/821-8682; fax 213/484-2769. Built in 1927 and last renovated in 1984, it's located just outside of LA's central business district in the downtown redevelopment area. A frequent backdrop for Hollywood movies, it features a lovely lobby with high ceilings, and neoclassical pillars. Hosts mostly business travelers and tour groups. **Rooms:** 300 rms and stes. CI 3pm/CO noon. Nonsmoking rms avail. Rooms are basic and not as nice as the lobby. **Amenities:** 🛏 A/C, cable TV w/movies, voice mail. Nintendo in rooms. **Services:** ✗ ⬛ ⬦ Car-rental desk. Free coffee, newspapers, and happy hour. Free shuttle to downtown and Dodger Stadium. **Facilities:** ⬛ ⬛ ⬦ 1 restaurant, 1 bar (w/entertainment). Lounge features karaoke. **Rates:** $75–$80 S or D; $125–$150 ste. Extra person $10. Children under age 18 stay free. Parking: Indoor, free. AE, CB, DC, DISC, JCB, MC, V.

≣≣ Best Western Mid Wilshire Plaza Hotel

603 S New Hampshire Ave, 90005; tel 213/385-4444 or toll free 800/528-1234; fax 213/380-5413. Small midtown hotel. Tiny lobby is right off parking area, so security is good at night. **Rooms:** 90 rms and stes. CI noon/CO noon. Nonsmoking rms avail. Plain but comfortable. **Amenities:** 🛏 A/C, cable TV, refrig. **Services:** ⬛ ⬛ ⬦ Car-rental desk. **Facilities:** ⬛ Sauna, whirlpool, washer/dryer. **Rates (CP):** Peak (July–Aug) $59–$65 S; $65–$72 D. Extra person $3. Children under age 12 stay free. Lower rates off-season. Parking: Indoor, free. AE, DC, DISC, MC, V.

≣≣≣ Beverly Hills Plaza Hotel

10300 Wilshire Blvd, 90024; tel 310/275-5575 or toll free 800/800-1234; fax 310/278-3325. A very modern setting east of the towers of Wilshire Blvd, near Westwood and Beverly Hills shopping, this property has an inviting environment. **Rooms:** 116 stes and effic. CI 1pm/CO noon. Nonsmoking rms avail. Well-soundproofed rooms are nice and tidy, with contemporary furniture. **Amenities:** 🛏 ⬦ ⬦ A/C, cable TV w/movies, refrig, VCR, in-rm safe. All units w/minibars, some w/terraces. **Services:** ✗ ⬛ ⬛ ⬛ ⬦ ⬦ Twice-daily maid svce, car-rental desk, social director, masseur, babysitting. Good service. **Facilities:** ⬛ ⬛ ⬛ ⬦ 1 restaurant, 1 bar, games rm, whirlpool, washer/dryer. Tiny bar and restaurant. **Rates:** $135–$175 ste; $165–$285 effic. AP and MAP rates avail. Parking: Indoor/outdoor, $8/day. AE, DC, MC, V.

≣≣≣≣ Beverly Prescott Hotel

1224 S Beverwil Dr, PO Box 3065, 90212; tel 310/277-2800 or toll free 800/421-3212; fax 310/203-9537. Rising 12 stories on a hilltop, the hotel offers great views of Beverly Hills, Century City, and Hollywood (you can see the Hollywood sign from some of the upper-story, northside rooms). Opened by hotel impresario Bill Kimpton in 1993, it boasts up-to-the-minute stylish decor—interior designers come here just to ooh and aah at the furnishings, which include one-of-a-kind hand-painted pieces. Although located in a nondescript residential neighborhood several long blocks away from points of interest and the business district, it allows easy access to both Beverly Hills and downtown. **Rooms:** 139 rms and stes. CI 3pm/CO noon. Nonsmoking rms avail. Sophisticated design boldly pairs stripes and florals in shimmering Southern California hues of salmon, ochre, magenta, and gold. Only downfall is the minimalist drawer space. Bathrooms feature excellent lighting, large marble counters, and a separate vanity area; some have step-up whirlpools big enough to accommodate four people. **Amenities:** 🛏 ⬦ ⬦ A/C, cable TV w/movies, dataport, voice mail, in-rm safe, bathrobes. All units w/minibars, all w/terraces, some w/whirlpools. All rooms have fax machines, plus irons and ironing boards. **Services:** ⬛ ⬛ ⬛ ⬛ ⬛ ⬦ Twice-daily maid svce, social director, masseur, babysitting. Complimentary morning tea, afternoon wine and cheese served in the lobby living room, which has a fireplace. **Facilities:** ⬛ ⬛ ⬛ ⬛ ⬦ 1 restaurant, 1 bar. Small fitness room, with stairmaster, cycle, and weight machines; guests also have privileges at a nearby gym. **Rates:** $190–$275 S or D; $250–$700 ste. Extra person $25. Children under age 18 stay free. Parking: Indoor, $14/day. AE, DC, DISC, MC, V.

≣≣≣ Carlyle Inn

1119 S Robertson Blvd, 90035; tel 310/275-4445 or toll free 800/322-7595; fax 310/859-0496. A real find, this charming, modern, European-style hotel is right near Beverly Hills. Rooms are reached by outdoor corridors overlooking a lovely patio. **Rooms:** 32 rms. CI noon/CO 1pm. Nonsmoking rms avail. **Amenities:** 🛏 ⬦ ⬦ ⬦ A/C, cable TV, VCR, bathrobes. All units w/minibars, all w/terraces. Movies are available for rent. **Services:** ✗ ⬛ ⬛ ⬛ ⬦ Afternoon tea, and apples at front desk. Complimentary shopping shuttle to nearby Beverly Hills. **Facilities:** 🛎 ♿ 1 restaurant (bkfst and dinner only), whirlpool. **Rates (BB):** $110 S; $120 D. Extra person $10. Children under age 10 stay free. Parking: Indoor, $8/day. AE, DC, DISC, MC, V.

≡≡≡≡ Century Plaza Hotel & Tower

2025 Ave of the Stars, 90067 (Century City); tel 310/277-2000 or toll free 800/228-3000; fax 310/551-3355. Big city, big hotel glamour, with a curvilinear facade and sweeping marble lobby with three airline offices. There are actually two hotels; the 322-room tower, and the 750-room main hotel. **Rooms:** 1,072 rms and stes. Executive level. CI 3pm/CO 1pm. Nonsmoking rms avail. Tower rooms have a sophisticated beige-and-black color scheme, with marble baths. In the main building, west-facing garden rooms are larger. Tiled bathrooms here look a tad outdated. **Amenities:** 📺 ⚗ ☕ A/C, dataport, voice mail, in-rm safe. All units w/minibars, all w/terraces. Tower rooms have fax/modem compatible phones and upgraded toiletries. **Services:** 🍴 🔑 VP 🚐 🗋 ↩ ↺ Twice-daily maid svce, car-rental desk, children's program, babysitting. In tower rooms: complimentary shoeshine, evening turn-down, and ice service. **Facilities:** 📶 🛎 [2000] 🖥 ♿ 2 restaurants, 2 bars (1 w/entertainment), spa, sauna, steam rm, whirlpool, beauty salon. Both the main building and the Tower have their own health club and swimming pool. The reflecting pool area is popular for weddings. **Rates:** $215–$265 S; $240–$290 D; $250–$3,000 ste. Extra person $25. Children under age 18 stay free. Parking: Indoor, $18/day. AE, CB, DC, DISC, EC, ER, JCB, MC, V.

≡≡≡≡ Four Seasons Hotel at Beverly Hills

300 Doheny Dr, 90048; tel 310/273-2222 or toll free 800/332-3442 in the US, 800/268-6282 in Canada; fax 310/859-3824. The exterior of the 16-story structure looks like every other neighborhood condo, but the interior reflects the marbled gleam and refined appointments of a grand manor house. The lobby and living room lead to a small backyard garden with jasmine and magnolia trees. **Rooms:** 285 rms and stes. CI 3pm/CO 1pm. Nonsmoking rms avail. Spacious and efficient but uninspired. Specially equipped Executive Suite available for early arrivals/late departures. **Amenities:** 📺 ⚗ ☕ A/C, satel TV w/movies, dataport, voice mail, bathrobes. All units w/minibars, all w/terraces, some w/fireplaces. Complimentary fax machines and VCRs available upon request. **Services:** 🍴 🔑 VP 🚐 🗋 ↩ ↺ Twice-daily maid svce, car-rental desk, masseur, children's program, babysitting. Courtesy limos to Rodeo Drive and Century City shops. Car care. Airline ticketing computer. Overnight laundry/dry cleaning; 24-hour seamstresses. Snap-to-it staffers are polite and responsive. **Facilities:** 📶 🛎 [500] ♿ 2 restaurants (see "Restaurants" below), 1 bar (w/entertainment), whirlpool. 2nd-floor pool and sundeck with indoor/outdoor fitness room and refreshment terrace. Despite its top-echelon business clientele, the hotel coddles kids, providing special menus, coloring books, teddy bears, and video games. **Rates:** $295–$365 S; $325–$395 D; $460–$3,500 ste. Extra person $25. Children under age 12 stay free. Parking: Indoor, $18/day. Rates determined by room size and floor. AE, CB, DC, EC, JCB, MC, V.

≡≡≡ Holiday Inn City Center

1020 S Figueroa St, 90015 (Downtown); tel 213/748-1291 or toll free 800/HOLIDAY; fax 213/748-6028. Adjacent to the LA Convention Center, it's a favorite hotel for conventioneers and business travelers. Built in 1960, it was fully renovated in 1990, and all carpets, linens, and drapes were replaced in 1996. Friendly staff. **Rooms:** 195 rms. Executive level. CI 3pm/CO noon. Nonsmoking rms avail. Rooms are neat, clean, and quite large. **Amenities:** 📺 ⚗ A/C, cable TV, dataport, voice mail. **Services:** ✕ 🗋 ↩ ↺ Twice-daily maid svce, car-rental desk. **Facilities:** 📶 🛎 [250] ♿ 1 restaurant, 1 bar, sauna, washer/dryer. Attractive rooftop pool and adjoining patio bar overlooking city, as well as a sun deck. **Rates:** $140–$160 S; $150–$170 D. Extra person $10. Children under age 18 stay free. Min stay special events. Parking: Indoor/outdoor, $8/day. AE, CB, DC, DISC, EC, ER, JCB, MC, V.

≡≡≡ Holiday Inn Los Angeles Downtown

750 Garland Ave, 90017; tel 213/628-5242 or toll free 800/628-5240; fax 213/628-1201. Well-kept and comfortable lodging for the business traveler. Located on a hill on the outskirts of downtown Los Angeles. **Rooms:** 205 rms. CI 1pm/CO noon. Nonsmoking rms avail. **Amenities:** 📺 ⚗ 📺 ☕ A/C, cable TV w/movies. **Services:** ✕ 🔑 🚐 🗋 ↩ ↺ Complimentary hors d'oeuvres during cocktail hour. Van service to LA tourist spots for small fee. **Facilities:** 📶 [100] 🖥 ♿ 1 restaurant, 1 bar, washer/dryer. Restaurant offers superb buffet lunch at reasonable price. **Rates:** $119 S or D. Extra person $10. Children under age 17 stay free. AP and MAP rates avail. Parking: Indoor/outdoor, free. AE, DC, DISC, JCB, MC, V.

⚜ Hotel Bel-Air

701 Stone Canyon Rd, 90077; tel 310/472-1211 or toll free 800/648-4097; fax 310/476-5890. 11 acres. Not so much a hotel as a botanical garden, with a lake for swans and romantic little bungalows for guests, all tucked away in one of the city's most exclusive communities. Built in the 1920s in Mediterranean/mission style with red tile roofs, arcades, and fountained courtyards lined with beautiful and unusual flowers. **Rooms:** 92 rms, stes, and effic. CI 3pm/CO 1pm. Each room styled individually; most have terra-cotta tiled floors. **Amenities:** 📺 ⚗ ☕ A/C, dataport, VCR, in-rm safe, bathrobes. All units w/minibars, some w/terraces, some w/fireplaces, some w/whirlpools. Some rooms with secluded, flower-perfumed patio. Umbrella in closet; battery-powered emergency lighting; earthquake survival kit. **Services:** 🍴 🔑 VP 🗋 ↩ ↺ Twice-daily maid svce, car-rental desk, babysitting. Despite the three-to-one staff-to-guest ratio and extra touches like setting and lighting guests' fires, the service is

sometimes uneven; however, the sheer seductiveness of the place makes service shortcomings seem less important than they would be elsewhere. **Facilities:** ⟦icons⟧ 1 restaurant (*see* "Restaurants" below), 1 bar (w/entertainment), beauty salon. Swank dining room, ravishing dining terrace with bougainvillea vines overhead and heated floor underfoot. **Rates:** $285–$435 S or D; $495–$2,500 ste. Children under age 18 stay free. Parking: Outdoor, $13/day. AE, CB, DC, EC, ER, JCB, MC, V.

≣≣≣ Hotel Del Capri
10587 Wilshire Blvd, 90024; tel 310/474-3511 or toll free 800/444-6835; fax 310/470-9999. Small, older hotel. Despite the busy street, rooms are quiet. **Rooms:** 81 rms and stes. CI 3pm/CO noon. Nonsmoking rms avail. **Amenities:** ⟦icons⟧ A/C, cable TV, refrig. Some units w/whirlpools. Adjustable beds. **Services:** ✗ ⟦icons⟧ Twice-daily maid svce, car-rental desk. Multilingual staff speaks Italian, French, and German. **Facilities:** ⟦icons⟧ Washer/dryer. **Rates (CP):** $85–$100 S; $110–$140 D; $140 ste. Extra person $10. Parking: Indoor/outdoor, free. AE, CB, DC, DISC, EC, ER, JCB, MC, V.

≣≣≣≣ Hotel Inter-Continental Los Angeles at California Plaza
251 S Olive St, 90012 (Downtown); tel 213/617-3300 or toll free 800/442-5251; fax 213/617-3399. Marble lobby reflects understated elegance, with two grand stairways and works by many of the same artists on exhibit at the nearby Museum of Contemporary Art. Located next to the prestigious California Plaza Business Center. **Rooms:** 433 rms and stes. Executive level. CI 3pm/CO 1pm. Nonsmoking rms avail. Even standard accommodations are large, with plenty of room to move around. The nicest views take in the Water Court with its "performing" fountains. Most bathrooms feature a separate tub and glass-enclosed shower. **Amenities:** ⟦icons⟧ A/C, cable TV w/movies, dataport, voice mail, bathrobes. All units w/minibars, some w/whirlpools. Nintendo in all rooms. **Services:** ⟦icons⟧ Car-rental desk, masseur, babysitting. **Facilities:** ⟦icons⟧ 1 restaurant, 1 bar (w/entertainment), sauna. Business center rents out both Macs and PCs. Bright and airy fitness center features exercise bikes, step machines, treadmills, and free weights; the men's locker facility has a steam room. **Rates:** $190–$240 S or D; $375–$1,300 ste. Extra person $30. Children under age 12 stay free. Min stay special events. Parking: Indoor, $18/day. AE, CB, DC, DISC, EC, JCB, MC, V.

≣ Hotel Stillwell
838 S Grand Ave, 90017 (Downtown); tel 213/627-1151 or toll free 800/553-4774; fax 213/622-8940. Old low-budget hotel in the heart of downtown. **Rooms:** 250 rms. CI 11am/CO 11am. Nonsmoking rms avail. Adequate rooms with walk-in closets. **Amenities:** ⟦icons⟧ A/C, cable TV w/movies. **Services:** ✗ ⟦icons⟧ Car-rental desk, social director, masseur, children's program. Free shuttle to convention center. **Facilities:**

⟦icons⟧ 2 restaurants, 1 bar, washer/dryer. **Rates (CP):** $39 S; $49 D. Children under age 5 stay free. MAP rates avail. Parking: Outdoor, $3/day. AE, CB, DC, MC, V.

≣≣≣ Hyatt Regency Los Angeles
711 S Hope St, 90017 (Downtown); tel 213/683-1234 or toll free 800/233-1234; fax 213/612-3179. A shining gem of a hotel with a big, beautiful lobby; located at the Broadway Plaza shopping mall. **Rooms:** 485 rms and stes. Executive level. CI 3pm/CO noon. Nonsmoking rms avail. Large rooms, with attractive furnishings. **Amenities:** ⟦icons⟧ A/C, cable TV w/movies, dataport, voice mail. Some units w/minibars, some w/whirlpools. Irons and ironing board in every room. **Services:** ✗ ⟦icons⟧ Car-rental desk, masseur, babysitting. Shoe shine service. **Facilities:** ⟦icons⟧ 2 restaurants, 2 bars (w/entertainment), whirlpool, beauty salon. Rooftop Polaris Room has wonderful city views. **Rates:** $155–$180 S; $180–$205 D; $225–$700 ste. Extra person $25. Children under age 18 stay free. Min stay special events. Parking: Indoor, $15/day. AE, CB, DC, DISC, EC, ER, JCB, MC, V.

≣ InnTowne Hotel
925 S Figueroa St, 90015 (Downtown); tel 213/628-2222 or toll free 800/457-8520; fax 213/687-0566. Scruffy but clean motel downtown. **Rooms:** 170 rms and stes. CI noon/CO noon. Nonsmoking rms avail. **Amenities:** ⟦icons⟧ A/C, cable TV w/movies, VCR. **Services:** ✗ ⟦icons⟧ Car-rental desk. **Facilities:** ⟦icons⟧ 1 restaurant, 1 bar. **Rates:** $84 S; $95 D; $125 ste. Extra person $12. Children under age 12 stay free. Min stay. Parking: Indoor/outdoor, free. AE, DC, DISC, MC, V.

≣≣ Kawada Hotel
200 S Hill St, 90012 (Downtown); tel 213/621-4455 or toll free 800/752-9232; fax 213/687-4455. Bunker Hill historic re-hab district. Four-story modern hotel caters primarily to Asian business travelers and tour groups. **Rooms:** 116 rms and stes. CI 3pm/CO noon. Nonsmoking rms avail. Very small but smartly furnished rooms. Some units have wet bars and microwaves. **Amenities:** ⟦icons⟧ A/C, cable TV w/movies, refrig, VCR. **Services:** ✗ ⟦icons⟧ Babysitting. Daily newspapers in lobby. Staff speaks Japanese, Tagalog, French, and Spanish, as well as English. Free shuttle van service within surrounding business district. **Facilities:** ⟦icons⟧ 1 restaurant, 1 bar (w/entertainment), washer/dryer. **Rates:** $79–$129 S or D. Extra person $10. Children under age 18 stay free. Min stay special events. Parking: Outdoor, $6/day. AE, CB, DC, DISC, EC, ER, JCB, MC, V.

≣≣ Metro Plaza Hotel
711 N Main St, 90012 (Chinatown); tel 213/680-0200 or toll free 800/223-2223; fax 213/620-0200. Downtown. Four-story hotel built and opened in 1991, located across the street from Union Station (Amtrak and Metro Line). Easy walking distance to Chinatown and Olvera Street Historic District. Reasonable rates. **Rooms:** 80 rms and stes. CI noon/CO noon. Nonsmoking rms avail. Rooms are small and spare, but

imported Chinese furniture adds flair. **Amenities:** 🔒 A/C, cable TV w/movies, refrig, in-rm safe. Some units w/terraces, some w/whirlpools. **Services:** VP 🛏 🍽 Car-rental desk, babysitting. **Facilities:** 🅿40 & Free indoor parking is a major plus in this downtown area. **Rates:** $59–$69 S; $75 D; $109–$139 ste. Extra person $6. Children under age 12 stay free. Parking: Indoor, free. AE, CB, DC, DISC, JCB, MC, V.

≣≣≣ Miyako Inn
328 E 1st St, 90012 (Little Tokyo); tel 213/617-2000 or toll free 800/228-6596; fax 213/617-2700. Handy for Japanese visitors, this hotel is in the heart of Little Tokyo and has convenient underground parking nearby. **Rooms:** 174 rms. Executive level. CI 2pm/CO noon. Nonsmoking rms avail. Plain but with imported Asian bedspreads. **Amenities:** 🔒 🗘 A/C, cable TV w/movies, in-rm safe. All units w/minibars. **Services:** ✗ VP 🚗 🛏 🍽 Car-rental desk, masseur. Complimentary Japanese newspaper. Japanese spoken. **Facilities:** 🅿100 1 restaurant, 1 bar (w/entertainment), spa, sauna, steam rm, whirlpool, washer/dryer. Gift shop. **Rates:** $92–$102 S; $102–$112 D. Extra person $15. Children under age 12 stay free. Parking: Indoor, $6.60/day. AE, CB, DC, JCB, MC, V.

≣≣≣ New Otani Hotel and Garden
120 S Los Angeles St, 90012 (Little Tokyo); tel 213/629-1200 or toll free 800/421-8795; fax 213/622-0980. Although just a few blocks from downtown, this hotel is a soothing oasis, with a Japanese garden and furnishings reflecting subdued elegance. Neighborhood a bit scruffy, however. **Rooms:** 434 rms and stes. CI 2pm/CO noon. Nonsmoking rms avail. Western-style rooms have contemporary decor in soft pastels. There are also Japanese suites, with a Western-style parlor and tatami bedroom; the bath offers a deep soaking tub. **Amenities:** 🔒 🗘 🗔 A/C, cable TV w/movies, in-rm safe. All units w/minibars, some w/terraces, some w/whirlpools. Teapots in rooms. **Services:** ✗ 🖙 VP 🚗 🛏 🍽 Car-rental desk, social director, masseur, babysitting. Japanese-American cultural programs are offered fall through spring, featuring activities such as calligraphy, kimono-tying, and tea ceremonies. **Facilities:** 🍴 🅿600 🖥 & 3 restaurants (*see* "Restaurants" below), 3 bars, sauna, whirlpool. On-premises shops include an art gallery, which sells works ranging from Art Nouveau to abstract. The hotel is also located next to Weller Court shopping mall, which include a Hermes boutique. Azalea Restaurant is a big favorite with high-powered lawyers trying cases at the Civic Center. **Rates:** $95–$160 S; $95–$185 D; $475–$1800 ste. Extra person $10. Children under age 12 stay free. Parking: Indoor, $13–$18/day. "Japanese Experience" package ($599 per couple) includes Japanese suite accommodations, shiatsu massage, sake and hors d'oeuvres, breakfast and dinner for two at a hotel restaurant, and a live bonsai tree. AE, CB, DC, DISC, JCB, MC, V.

≣≣≣ Omni Los Angeles Hotel & Centre
930 Wilshire Blvd, 90017 (Downtown); tel 213/688-7777 or toll free 800/445-8667; fax 213/612-3977. Big, commercial hotel with good downtown location. **Rooms:** 900 rms and stes. Executive level. CI 3pm/CO noon. Nonsmoking rms avail. **Amenities:** 🔒 🗘 A/C, cable TV w/movies, voice mail. **Services:** ✗ 🖙 VP 🚗 🛏 🍽 🛎 Twice-daily maid svce, car-rental desk, babysitting. **Facilities:** 🍴 🖙 🅿900 🖥 & 3 restaurants, 1 bar, sauna, steam rm, whirlpool, beauty salon. Many shops located on first level. **Rates:** $169–$199 S or D; $279–$579 ste. Children under age 18 stay free. MAP rates avail. Parking: Indoor, $16.50/day. AE, CB, DC, DISC, JCB, MC, V.

≣≣≣≣ Park Hyatt Los Angeles at Century City
2151 Ave of the Stars, 90067; tel 310/277-2777 or toll free 800/233-1234; fax 310/785-9240. This hotel shows plenty of panache, especially in the lobby with champagne marble floors, skylight ceiling, crystal chandeliers, and chinoiserie accents. **Rooms:** 367 rms and stes. CI 3pm/CO noon. Nonsmoking rms avail. Decorated with light furnishings and rich-colored fabrics. Executive rooms have separate living and sleeping areas. **Amenities:** 🔒 🗘 🖐 A/C, dataport, voice mail, bathrobes. All units w/minibars, all w/terraces, 1 w/fireplace. Toiletries are nicely arranged on a little étagère by the sink. The 27-inch TV provides video messages and checkout. **Services:** 🍽 🖙 VP 🚗 🛏 🍽 Twice-daily maid svce, car-rental desk, babysitting. Complimentary shoeshine and newspaper, plus free limo service within Century City and to Rodeo Drive. **Facilities:** 🍴 🖙 🅿300 🖥 & 1 restaurant, 1 bar (w/entertainment), spa, sauna, whirlpool. Although the outdoor pool figured in a scene from *Lethal Weapon 2*, the deck is largely ordinary. **Rates:** $205 S; $230 D; $280–$550 ste. Extra person $25. Children under age 18 stay free. Parking: Indoor, $15/day. AE, CB, DC, DISC, EC, ER, JCB, MC, V.

≣≣≣ Radisson Wilshire Plaza
3515 Wilshire Blvd, 90010; tel 213/381-7411 or toll free 800/333-3333; fax 213/386-7379. Elegantly furnished, with a beautiful beige marble floor in lobby. An excellent location, in a mid-Wilshire neighborhood, with a Metro stop outside. **Rooms:** 391 rms and stes. Executive level. CI 3pm/CO noon. Nonsmoking rms avail. **Amenities:** 🔒 🗘 🗔 A/C, cable TV w/movies, voice mail. All units w/minibars. **Services:** ✗ 🖙 VP 🚗 🛏 🍽 🛎 Twice-daily maid svce, car-rental desk, social director, masseur, children's program, babysitting. **Facilities:** 🍴 🖙 🅿400 🖥 & 2 restaurants, 2 bars (1 w/entertainment), beauty salon. **Rates:** $99–$109 S; $109–$129 D; $250–$500 ste. Extra person $10. Children under age 12 stay free. Parking: Indoor, $5.50–$7.70/day. AE, CB, DC, DISC, MC, V.

≣≣≣ The Regal Biltmore Hotel
506 S Grand Ave, 90071 (Downtown); tel 213/624-1011 or toll free 800/245-8673; fax 213/612-1545. Across from Pershing Square. The Biltmore has one of LA's most grand, historic lobbies, with lion's-head fountain, parquet floors, and hand-painted ceilings. Furnishings, however, look worn. **Rooms:** 683 rms and stes. Executive level. CI 3pm/CO noon.

Nonsmoking rms avail. Club and executive suites are attractively done in updated deco style with marble baths. But standard rooms are strictly ordinary, with tired upholstery and small but functional bathrooms. **Amenities:** 🛏 ☖ A/C, satel TV w/movies, voice mail. Some units w/minibars, 1 w/fireplace. **Services:** 🍽 ☎ VP 🚐 🖼 🛎 Car-rental desk, masseur, babysitting. **Facilities:** 🏋 🏊 1000 🖥 ♿ 4 restaurants, 3 bars, spa, sauna, steam rm, whirlpool, beauty salon. Opulent, art deco indoor swimming pool is inlaid with mosaics. Exclusive health club has outstanding equipment. Its 16 plush banquet and meeting rooms include the Biltmore Bowl, site of the first Academy Awards presentation. **Rates:** $195–$285 S; $225–$285 D; $350–$2000 ste. Extra person $30. Children under age 18 stay free. Parking: Indoor, $20/day. AE, CB, DC, DISC, EC, JCB, MC, V.

☰☰☰ Sheraton Grande

333 S Figueroa St, 90012 (Downtown); tel 213/617-1133 or toll free 800/LA-GRAND; fax 213/613-0291. Glamorous skylit lobby with marble floors, fine furnishings, and a sunken bar featuring live piano music in the evenings. **Rooms:** 469 rms and stes. CI 3pm/CO noon. Nonsmoking rms avail. Very attractive, well-outfitted rooms all have separate sitting areas and large desks; mattresses and bedspreads are new. Request a city view. **Amenities:** 🛏 ☖ ☎ A/C, cable TV w/movies, dataport, voice mail, in-rm safe, bathrobes. All units w/minibars, 1 w/fireplace, 1 w/whirlpool. Enhanced by nice touches such as clothes racks, small sofas, and live plants. **Services:** 🍽 ☎ VP 🚐 🖼 🛎 Twice-daily maid svce, car-rental desk, masseur, babysitting. Free coffee, tea, and newspapers delivered to your room. Free shoeshines and pressing of clothes. **Facilities:** 🏋 1000 🖥 ♿ 3 restaurants, 2 bars. The big surprise in this downtown location is the lushly landscaped pool area, where palm trees contrast with adjoining office skyscrapers. You do get freeway noise, however. Very nice gift shop, stocked with LA memorabilia. Complimentary passes to nearby YMCA for fitness facilities. **Rates:** $179 S or D; $250–$425 ste. Children under age 18 stay free. Parking: Indoor, $17/day. AE, CB, DC, DISC, EC, ER, JCB, MC, V.

☰☰☰ Westin Bonaventure Hotel and Suites

404 S Figueroa St, 90071 (Downtown); tel 213/624-1000 or toll free 800/228-3000; fax 213/612-4797. Enormous convention hotel with a huge lobby, outdoor atrium elevators, and numerous areas to drink, dine, and relax. With its mirrored exterior and cylindrical shape, it's been nicknamed "the LA espresso machine." **Rooms:** 1,368 rms and stes. CI 3pm/CO 1pm. Nonsmoking rms avail. Rooms have contemporary furnishings. Newly refurbished. **Amenities:** 🛏 ☖ ☎ A/C, cable TV w/movies, voice mail, in-rm safe. **Services:** 🍽 ☎ VP 🚐 🖼 🛎 Car-rental desk, children's program, babysitting. **Facilities:** 🏋 2000 🖥 ♿ 2 restaurants, 3 bars, beauty salon. **Rates:** $157 S; $175 D; $195–$2,500 ste. Extra person $25. Children under age 12 stay free. Parking: Indoor, $16.50/day. AE, CB, DC, DISC, JCB, MC, V.

☰☰☰☰ Westwood Marquis Hotel and Gardens

930 Hilgard Ave, 90024 (Westwood Village); tel 310/208-8765 or toll free 800/421-2317; fax 310/824-0355. Located on a quiet residential avenue a few blocks from Westwood and the campus of UCLA, but only 7 minutes from the freeway. The two midrise, office-like towers have greenery-swathed facades; the lobby is swank and seems to belong to a different hotel. The gardens of the name refer to a flowery backyard oasis with pool, private cabanas, and patio restaurant. **Rooms:** 258 stes. Executive level. CI 3pm/CO 1pm. Nonsmoking rms avail. Spacious, efficient suites (one, two, or three bedrooms), measuring 550 square feet and up—ideal for longer stays. Recently upgraded and beautified. **Amenities:** 🛏 ☖ ☎ A/C, dataport, voice mail, bathrobes. All units w/minibars. Two TVs. Some rooms have VCRs and stereos. **Services:** 🍽 ☎ VP 🚐 🖼 🛎 🕑 Twice-daily maid svce, car-rental desk, babysitting. **Facilities:** 🏋 🏊 200 🖥 ♿ 3 restaurants, 1 bar (w/entertainment). 2 popular restaurants: The Dynasty, serving continental cuisine, and the Garden Terrace, particularly popular for breakfast and weekend brunch. **Rates:** $235–$650 ste. Children under age 18 stay free. Parking: Indoor, $14/day. AE, CB, DC, DISC, EC, ER, JCB, MC, V.

☰☰☰☰ Wyndham Checkers Hotel Los Angeles

535 S Grand Ave, 90071 (Downtown); tel 213/624-0000 or toll free 800/WYNDHAM; fax 213/626-9906. Between 5th and 6th. An oasis amid the skyscrapers of downtown LA. Small, personalized hotel offers a soothing blond-on-blond color scheme, plus a tranquil library. **Rooms:** 188 rms and stes. CI 3pm/CO noon. Nonsmoking rms avail. Beige room decor mingles Louis XV–style furnishings with serene contemporary pieces. Large bathrooms feature coral and white marble, plus big mirrors. **Amenities:** 🛏 ☖ ☐ ☎ A/C, dataport, voice mail, bathrobes. All units w/minibars, some w/terraces. VCRs, CD/tape players, fax machines delivered on request. Lots of pampering in the bathrooms, with luxurious toiletries, bathroom scales, and even a bathtub thermometer. **Services:** 🍽 ☎ VP 🚐 🖼 🛎 🕑 Twice-daily maid svce, car-rental desk, masseur, babysitting. Continental breakfast served by the pool. Complimentary limousine service to central downtown area on weekday mornings. Complimentary shoeshine. **Facilities:** 🏋 🏊 80 🖥 ♿ 1 restaurant, 1 bar, spa, sauna, steam rm, whirlpool. Beautiful rooftop lap pool. **Rates:** $239–$259 S or D; $450–$1,000 ste. Extra person $20. Children under age 18 stay free. Min stay special events. Parking: Indoor, $10–$18/day. AE, CB, DC, DISC, EC, ER, JCB, MC, V.

RESTAURANTS 🍴

★ The Apple Pan

10801 W Pico Blvd, West Los Angeles; tel 310/475-3585. **Burgers.** A little white shack with Formica counter and stools—and a favorite of locals for 47 years. The limited menu includes steak-burgers, their famous hickory burger, home-made sandwiches, and all sorts of pies baked every morning. **FYI:** Reservations not accepted. No liquor license. **Open:** Tues–Thurs 11am–midnight, Fri–Sat 11am–1am. **Prices:** Main courses $3–$5. No CC. 🔳 📠

★ Arnie Morton's of Chicago

435 S La Cienega Blvd; tel 310/246-1501. **Steak.** This clubby steak house lets you choose your own steak as a cart of meat is rolled past your table. Prime aged beef is expertly prepared, as is Maine lobster. Excellent for business entertaining. **FYI:** Reservations recommended. **Open:** Daily 5–11pm. **Prices:** Main courses $20–$30. AE, CB, DC, DISC, MC, V. 📠 VP &

A Thousand Cranes

In New Otani Hotel and Garden, 120 S Los Angeles St; tel 213/253-9255. **Japanese.** This serene, Japanese-style dining room overlooks absolutely stunning Japanese gardens with fountains and rock ponds—especially beautiful in spring when the azaleas are in bloom. All the food is absolutely top notch, with a sushi bar and a tempura bar, as well as private tatami rooms. On Sundays, there's a lavish Japanese brunch, where delicacies include tuna roll, sashimi, tempura, beef teriyaki, grilled fish, and more; $21 per person. **FYI:** Reservations recommended. Dress code. **Open:** Breakfast daily 7–10am; lunch Mon–Fri 11:30am–2pm; dinner daily 6–9:30pm; brunch Sun 11am–2pm. **Prices:** Main courses $6–$30; prix fixe $22–$32. AE, CB, DC, DISC, MC, V. VP &

Authentic Cafe

7605 Beverly Blvd; tel 213/939-4626. **Eclectic.** Small, storefront restaurant with southwestern decor and cactus plants on each table. Informal service and good, interesting dishes, including Yucatan marinated chicken breast, Szechaun dumplings, and Argentinean skirt steak. **FYI:** Reservations not accepted. No liquor license. **Open:** Sun 10am–10pm, Mon–Thurs 11:30am–10pm, Fri 11:30am–11pm, Sat 10am–11pm. **Prices:** Main courses $8–$14. MC, V. ❤ 📠 &

★ Caffe Latte

6254 Wilshire Blvd; tel 213/936-5213. **Regional American.** Tom Kaplan's storefront-cafe spin-off of Hugo's has the same generously portioned menu with lower prices, a more mellow crowd, plus a coffee roaster and a market for tea and coffee on the premises. Specials include cappuccino pancakes, breakfast classics like Pasta Mama (scrambled with eggs, garlic, and cheese), and an array of sausage dishes. Unusual southwestern-style vegetarian entrees and health-oriented standards like blackened turkey loaf round out the menu. **FYI:** Reservations not accepted. Beer and wine only. **Open:** Mon–Thurs 7am–9pm, Fri 7am–10pm, Sat–Sun 8am–3pm. **Prices:** Main courses $7–$12. AE, MC, V. &

★ Caffe Luna

7463 Melrose Ave; tel 213/655-8647. **New American/Italian.** Hip, funky Italian-American cafe spilling out onto the busy street, with an intimate garden patio nestled in the trees out back and a new retail shop/coffeehouse next door called Luna C. Owned and operated by congenial Frenchwoman

Corrine Lorain and daughter Stephanie, it's crowded from early morning until well past midnight all week. The menu offers wood-burning oven pizzas, regional pastas, panini, homemade desserts, and baked goods. **FYI:** Reservations accepted. Beer and wine only. **Open:** Sun–Thurs 9am–3am, Fri–Sat 9am–5am. **Prices:** Main courses $7–$10. AE, CB, DC, DISC, MC, V. 🚢 📠 🚙 VP &

Campanile

624 S La Brea Ave; tel 213/938-1447. **Italian/Mediterranean.** One of the most popular places in Los Angeles, with a setting reminiscent of an Italian garden. It's always busy and noisy and is a local favorite of those in the entertainment business. The food is excellent and may feature crispy duck, grilled prime rib, and rack of lamb. Fresh breads and desserts made on the premises. **FYI:** Reservations recommended. **Open:** Breakfast Mon–Fri 8–11am, Sat–Sun 8am–1:30pm; lunch Mon–Fri 11:30am–2pm; dinner Mon–Thurs 6–10pm, Fri–Sat 5:30–11pm. **Prices:** Main courses $18–$28. AE, DC, DISC, MC, V. VP &

Cantor's Fairfax Restaurant Delicatessen & Bakery

419 N Fairfax Ave (Fairfax District); tel 213/651-2030. **Deli.** A large, somewhat shabby delicatessen, but a Los Angeles institution nonetheless. Known for its excellent bakery goods and Jewish delicacies of corned beef, pastrami, chicken in a pot, and matzo ball soup. Best for lunch, when the neighborhood is lively. **FYI:** Reservations accepted. Jazz/rock. Beer and wine only. **Open:** Daily 24 hrs. **Prices:** Main courses $8–$13. MC, V. 📠 🈳 &

★ Cava Restaurant and Tapas Bar

In Beverly Plaza Hotel, 8384 W 3rd; tel 213/658-8898. 2 blocks E of Beverly Center. **Spanish.** Consistently excellent cuisine served in two dining rooms and on an inviting outdoor patio. Tapas include fried eggplant stuffed with Spanish ham and Manchego cheese. Among entrees, the paella is a seafood delight. **FYI:** Reservations accepted. Blues/comedy/reggae. **Open:** Daily 6:30am–midnight. **Prices:** Main courses $8–$16. AE, DC, DISC, MC, V. 🚢 📠 🚙 VP &

Chaya Brasserie

8741 Alden Dr; tel 310/859-8833. **Italian/Asian.** Exposed pipes and stands of bamboo create an indoor-outdoor Asian fantasy with a hip Los Angeles feel. Mingle with celebrity agents from nearby Beverly Hills as you feast on Asian- and Italian-inspired cuisine, including salmon, chicken, fresh seaweed salad, and saffron risotto. **FYI:** Reservations recommended. **Open:** Lunch Mon–Fri 11:30am–2:30pm; dinner Mon–Thurs 6–10:30pm, Fri–Sat 6–11pm, Sun 6–10pm. **Prices:** Main courses $7–$27. AE, DC, MC, V. VP &

♣ Citrus

6703 Melrose Ave; tel 213/857-0034. **Californian/French.** Chef Michel Richard is regarded as one of the best chefs in Los Angeles, offering superb cuisine at this now famous restaurant. Specialties include salmon terrine, peppered tuna with dijon sauce, and caramelized apple tarts. A large outdoor patio offers fine dining outdoors under Japanese umbrellas. Award-winning wine list. **FYI:** Reservations recommended. **Open:** Lunch Mon–Fri noon–2:30pm; dinner Mon–Thurs 6:30–10:30pm, Fri 6:30–11pm, Sat 6–11pm. **Prices:** Main courses $22–$29; prix fixe $45–$60. AE, DC, MC, V. ❤ 🚲 VP ♿

★ **Delphi Greek Cuisine**

1383 Westwood Blvd; tel 310/478-2900. **Greek.** Inexpensive gourmet Greek food makes this small cafe a favorite for both Greeks and locals. Consummate and spirited old-world service is shown off with flaming dishes such as saganaki. Entrees include chicken Athenian (stuffed with feta cheese and fresh spinach) and moussaka. Owner and former Metropolitan Opera singer Estelle Prineas sings at the annual Easter dinner and presents cultural entertainment during holidays; if the mood is right, she'll also read your coffee grinds. **FYI:** Reservations recommended. Beer and wine only. **Open:** Lunch Mon–Fri 11:30am–3pm; dinner Mon–Fri 5–10:30pm, Sat 5–11pm. **Prices:** Main courses $9–$22. CB, DC, DISC, MC, V. 👥 🚐 ♿

★ **Dive!**

10250 Santa Monica Blvd (Century City); tel 310/788-DIVE. Santa Monica Blvd exit off I-405. **Eclectic.** Theme park–style restaurant worthy of co-owners Steven Spielberg and Jeffrey Katzenberg. Monster screens at either end of the "sub" display periscope sightings, and costumed servers communicate with walkie-talkies. Specialties include a vegetarian submarine sandwich with grilled portobello mushrooms, roasted red peppers, and Romano cheese. Desserts include slabs of S'mores and lemon bars with swirls of white chocolate mousse. **FYI:** Reservations not accepted. Children's menu. **Open:** Sun–Thurs 11:30am–10pm, Fri–Sat 11:30am–11pm. **Prices:** Main courses $7–$15. AE, DISC, MC, V. 🚐 👥 VP ♿

★ **Engine Co 28**

644 S Figueroa St; tel 213/624-6996. **American.** Located in a memorabilia-filled, landmark firehouse, the restaurant has become a prime gathering place for attorneys and power politicos. The impressive bar features over 500 fine beers, bourbons, and single-malt scotches, as well as wines. They specialize in straightforward foods, such as firehouse oysters, whiskey-fennel sausages, and meatloaf. **FYI:** Reservations recommended. Dress code. **Open:** Mon–Fri 11:15am–9pm, Sat–Sun 5–9pm. **Prices:** Main courses $10–$20. AE, MC, V. 🍴 ♿

Farmer's Market

Fairfax and 3rd Aves; tel 213/933-9211. **Food Court.** The granddaddy of the modern food court, and a Los Angeles landmark. An indoor-outdoor complex of over 100 food stalls, offering everything from a corned beef sandwich to Mexican food to Italian pasta. Excellent pastries and a fresh produce market. **FYI:** Reservations not accepted. Beer and wine only. **Open:** Mon–Sat 9am–7pm, Sun 10am–6pm. **Prices:** Main courses $4–$10. No CC. 🍴 🚐 ♿

🍸 **Four Oaks Restaurant**

2181 N Beverly Glen Blvd; tel 310/470-2265. **Californian/ French.** Formerly a railway station and a brothel, this century-old country inn surrounded by oak trees is minutes from Beverly Hills. The menu offers house smoked salmon, potato and caramelized onion tart with capers, plum barbequed swordfish, beef tenderloin, and desserts like crème brûlée. Sunday brunch is popular. **FYI:** Reservations recommended. Guitar. **Open:** Lunch Tues–Sun 11:30am–2pm; dinner daily 6–10pm; brunch–Sun 10:30am–2pm. **Prices:** Main courses $21–$28. AE, MC, V. ❤ 🍴 🚐 🔲 👥 VP

🍸★ **Gardens**

In the Four Seasons Hotel, 300 S Doheny Dr; tel 310/ 273-2222. **International.** Surrounded by marble, magnificent flower arrangements, and lush garden patio areas, the spacious, individual dining rooms in this distinctive hotel offer a variety of experiences, including a Japanese breakfast and private Garden Court room with prix fixe menu. Copious Sunday buffet brunch is the best buy in town, offering many varieties of fish, seafood, sushi, meats, unusual salads, made-to-order omelettes, waffles and traditional American breakfasts, breads, cheeses, pastries, and desserts. Of note are the seared duck or scallop salads; spaghetti squash soufflé; and a vast array of smoked fish. **FYI:** Reservations recommended. Singer. Children's menu. **Open:** Breakfast daily 6–11:30am; lunch daily 11:30am–2:30pm; dinner daily 6am–10pm. **Prices:** Main courses $26–$35; prix fixe $75. AE, CB, DC, DISC, MC, V. ❤ 🚐 👥 VP ♿

Horikawa

111 S San Pedro St (Little Tokyo); tel 213/680-9355. **Japanese.** Good choice for a business lunch. Japanese-style elegance, with shoji screens, damask fabrics, and soft background music. Offerings include sushi, shrimp tempura, lobster, sukiyaki, and filet mignon. There's a sushi bar and a teppan room for cooking at your table. **FYI:** Reservations recommended. **Open:** Lunch Mon–Fri 11:30am–2pm; dinner Mon–Fri 6–10pm, Sat 5–10pm. **Prices:** Main courses $18–$30; prix fixe $25. AE, CB, DC, MC, V. ❤ VP ♿

The Ivy

113 N Robertson Blvd; tel 310/274-8303. **Regional American.** Casual decor and beautiful flowers; reminiscent of a country farmhouse. Frequented by Hollywood celebrities. Crab cakes, caesar salad, prime rib, and meat loaf, as well as great desserts. **FYI:** Reservations recommended. Additional location: 1541 Ocean Ave, Santa Monica (tel 393-3113). **Open:** Mon–Sat 11:30am–11pm, Sun 11am–10pm. **Prices:** Main courses $11–$23. AE, DC, MC, V. 🚐 VP ♿

Langer's

704 S Alvarado St; tel 213/483-8050. **Deli.** This large, typical New York–style deli in a somewhat run-down neighborhood

is an old favorite with regulars, who come from all over LA. Phone ahead and a waiter will deliver your order to your car. Lean pastrami sandwich, chopped liver, stuffed cabbage, gefilte fish, chicken in a pot. **FYI:** Reservations accepted. Beer and wine only. **Open:** Mon–Sat 8am–4pm. **Prices:** Main courses $4–$14. MC, V. ▆ 🎦 ⚅

★ LA Trattoria

8022 W 3rd St; tel 213/658-7607. **Italian.** Clean, minimalist lines, rustic Neapolitan dishes, and chef-owner Peppe Miele's sense of humor make this the place where LA's Italian chefs (and tourists) dine. On the upstairs garden terrace, diners enjoy a changing variety of pizzas, grilled sandwiches, and carpaccio, including a version made with lamb and truffle oil. Risotto with porcini mushrooms in herb sauce and penne pasta with vodka in a light pink sauce are other specialties. **FYI:** Reservations recommended. Beer and wine only. **Open:** Tues–Thurs 5:30–10:30pm, Fri 5:30–11:30pm, Sat 5:30–11pm, Sun 5:30–10pm. **Prices:** Main courses $12–$22. AE, DC, MC, V. ▨ 🎦 VP ⚅

★ Le Chardonnay

8284 Melrose Ave; tel 213/655-8880. **French.** A romantic spot that evokes a Belle Epoque Paris bistro, with dark wood, etched glass, and lots of brass. The open rotisserie produces dishes such as roasted chicken and Peking duck; other specialties include Maine lobster bisque, grilled turkey sausage, and warm, crispy sweetbreads. **FYI:** Reservations recommended. Jacket required. **Open:** Lunch Tues–Fri noon–2pm; dinner Tues–Sat 6–10pm. **Prices:** Main courses $16–$28. AE, CB, DC, DISC, MC, V. ❤ VP ⚅

♣ Le Dôme

8720 Sunset Blvd; tel 310/659-6919. **Continental/French.** Nationally famous and celebrity driven, Le Dome remains a congenial, impeccably staffed Sunset Boulevard retreat and power lunch meeting place. The dramatic, dome-ceilinged bar opens onto several softly lit rooms, a front garden room, and a new, enclosed glass patio. The menu features entrees such as cassoulet Toulousain, loup de mer (sea bass), pig knuckles with sauerkraut, and fatless rotisserie chicken. Surprisingly low-priced lunch menu. **FYI:** Reservations recommended. **Open:** Mon–Fri noon–11:45pm, Sat 6:30–11:45pm. **Prices:** Main courses $15–$25. AE, CB, DC, MC, V. ❤ ♠ VP ⚅

Little Joe's

900 N Broadway (Chinatown); tel 213/489-4900. **Italian/American.** One of the oldest restaurants in Los Angeles, with historic photos lining the wood-paneled walls. Six dining rooms, including a sports bar with giant television. Northern Italian and American cuisine includes veal saltimbocca, homemade ravioli, steaks, chops, and prime rib. **FYI:** Reservations recommended. **Open:** Mon–Fri 11am–9pm, Sat 3–9pm. **Prices:** Main courses $8–$19; prix fixe $12–$25. AE, CB, DC, DISC, MC, V. ▆ 🎦 VP ⚅

★ Locanda Veneta

8638 W 3rd St; tel 310/274-1893. Between Robertson and San Vincente Blvds. **Italian.** An intimate, low-key dining room with a high-profile celebrity following. Open kitchen track lighting. The chef has transformed classically hearty Venetian fare into lighter versions. Ravioli filled with lobster in saffron sauce, roasted baby rack of lamb grilled with garlic, mustard and goat cheese, and a vanilla cream custard with caramel sauce have become trademarks. **FYI:** Reservations recommended. **Open:** Lunch Mon–Fri 11:30am–2:30pm; dinner Mon–Thurs 5:30–10:30pm, Fri–Sat 5:30–11pm. **Prices:** Main courses $9–$21. AE, CB, DC, DISC, MC, V. ♠ 🎦 🚗 VP ⚅

♣ L'Orangerie Restaurant

903 N La Cienega Blvd (Restaurant Row); tel 310/652-9770. **French.** A romantic spot with old-world charm, designed by noted French architect Valerian S Rybar. Dine on the new front garden terrace among potted orange topiary trees, or in one of the three dramatic rooms inside. Fresh Santa Barbara–grown produce, Sonoma County chicken and lamb, fresh fish, Maine lobster. **FYI:** Reservations recommended. Piano. Jacket required. **Open:** Tues–Sun 6:30–11pm. **Prices:** Main courses $26–$35. AE, CB, DC, DISC, MC, V. ❤ ♠ VP

♣ Lunaria

10351 Santa Monica Blvd (Century City); tel 310/282-8870. At Beverly Glen Blvd. **French.** Summery Mediterranean restaurant, created by legendary owner Bernard Jacoupy, with original impressionist paintings and playfully hand-painted dinner plates. Chef Jean Pierre Bosc's California-French Provençal cuisine uses spectacular sauces and reductions for healthy dishes, like gazpacho and tomato-and-seabass tart. Also on the menu are special steak dishes and a duck confit with cabbage, caramelized apple, and peppercorn sauce. **FYI:** Reservations recommended. Jazz/piano. Dress code. **Open:** Lunch Mon–Fri 11:30am–2:30pm; dinner Tues–Thurs 6:30–10:30pm, Fri–Sat 6pm–midnight. **Prices:** Main courses $10–$22; prix fixe $20. AE, CB, DC, DISC, MC, V. ❤ ▼ VP ⚅

Ⓢ Mandarette

8386 Beverly Blvd; tel 213/655-6115. **Chinese.** High ceilings and minimalist, modern decor with subtle lighting. This restaurant introduced the concept of an Asian menu to Los Angeles. Helpful staff presents light, inexpensive gourmet versions of regional dishes, such as Phan rice with smoked chicken or roast duck, eggplant with pork, and green beans with ginger and sesame oil. **FYI:** Reservations recommended. Beer and wine only. **Open:** Peak (June–Sept) Mon–Thurs 11am–10:30pm, Fri 11am–11:30pm, Sat noon–11:30pm, Sun 3–10:30pm. **Prices:** Main courses $6–$15. AE, DC, MC, V. 🎦 🚗

The Milky Way

9108 W Pico Blvd; tel 310/859-0004. **Kosher.** A friendly, cozy place with soothing classical music on tape and Steven Spielberg's poster collection down the back hall. The tiny firecracker hostess, Spielberg's mom Leah Adler, schmoozes with everyone. Kosher specialties (dairy and fish but no meat) include Santa Fe and Pizza de Lox pizzas, salmon roulades, and cabbage rolls. Family-recipe cheesecake for dessert. **FYI:** Reservations recommended. Beer and wine only. **Open:** Lunch Sun–Thurs 11:30am–2:30pm, Fri 11:30am–2pm; dinner Sun–Thurs 5:30–8:30pm. **Prices:** Main courses $8–$15. AE, MC, V. ♿

♟ Modada Restaurant
8115 Melrose Ave; tel 213/653-4612. **New American/Eclectic.** At Modada, or "more than Dadaism," San Marvin's eclectic menu is enhanced by a candlelit dining room encased in copper, wrought-iron, and bold textiles. Divided into Air, Land, and Sea categories, the whimsical menu features fresh (often homegrown) ingredients in surprising combinations, such as Dali Lobster, Lamb in 3-D, and Erotic Chicken (the latter stuffed with forest mushrooms and topped with a rose-petal sauce). This current hot spot draws a celebrity crowd. **FYI:** Reservations recommended. **Open:** Mon–Sat 6–11pm. **Prices:** Main courses $14–$26. AE, DC, MC, V. VP ♿

Mortons
8764 Melrose Ave; tel 310/276-5205. **New American.** This is Hard Rock Cafe creator Peter Morton's room for adults. The airy barn of a building is filled with oversized plants, paintings, and power producers. Mortons has more room for non-celebrities since the move across the street, although Monday night is still big-star dinner time. Spicy tuna tartare; endive salad; grilled swordfish with tomato and papaya chutney; roasted rack of lamb. **FYI:** Reservations recommended. **Open:** Lunch Mon–Fri noon–2:30pm; dinner Mon–Sat 6–11:30pm. **Prices:** Main courses $17–$27. AE, DC, MC, V. VP ♿

★ Nicola
In Sanwa Bank Building, 601 S Figueroa; tel 213/485-0927. **New American.** The decor melds futuristic design with lots of comforting wood and a glass-enclosed patio. Long a city favorite from its Silverlake days. Proprietor/chef Larry Nicola not only welcomes diners, but also loves to prepare individual meals in the open kitchen. Fresh, hearty cuisine, with dishes such as grilled duck breast over risotto-leek cakes, or grilled chicken-apple sausage on braised red cabbage. For dessert, they're known for warm apple-rhubarb crisp and chocolate-espresso semifreddo. **FYI:** Reservations recommended. Dress code. **Open:** Lunch Mon–Fri 11:30am–2pm; dinner Tues–Sat 5–9pm. **Prices:** Main courses $12–$17. AE, CB, DC, DISC, MC, V. ⛴ VP ♿

Ⓢ Nyala
1076 S Fairfax Ave; tel 213/936-5918. **Ethiopian.** Stylish with light wood and African art, Nyala, named for a gazelle-like animal, is considered the best Ethiopian eatery in this enclave. Owners Michael and Elizabeth themselves embody Ethiopian beauty and warmth. Traditional meat and poultry stews and vegetarian dishes are prepared for hours and are

rolled into a spongy pancake and eaten by hand. There's also an Italian menu. Coffee ceremony on request. **FYI:** Reservations accepted. **Open:** Sun–Thurs 11:30am–11pm, Fri–Sat 11:30am–midnight. **Prices:** Main courses $10–$15. AE, MC, V. ♿

The Original Pantry
877 S Figuero St (Downtown); tel 213/972-9279. **American.** A landmark of early Los Angeles, with dark wood paneling and a scruffy Formica counter. Huge portions of meatloaf, steak, corned beef and cabbage, and short ribs. **FYI:** Reservations not accepted. No liquor license. **Open:** Daily 24 hrs. **Prices:** Main courses $9–$11. No CC. ▤ |24| ♿

Pacific Dining Car
1310 W 6th St; tel 213/483-6000. **Steak/American.** Landmark restaurant since 1921, with a dated but elegant atmosphere reminiscent of an old railroad dining car. Specialties include steaks, chops, and lobster. **FYI:** Reservations recommended. Additional location: 2700 Wilshire Blvd, Santa Monica (tel 310/453-4000). **Open:** Daily 24 hrs. **Prices:** Main courses $20–$35. AE, CB, DC, MC, V. |24| VP ♿

♟ Patina
5955 Melrose Ave; tel 213/467-1108. **Californian/French.** Features three intimate dining rooms, decorated with understated elegance. Considered one of the best restaurants in the city. Try the Santa Barbara shrimp and the peppered tournedos of tuna with Chinese greens and ponzu sauce. **FYI:** Reservations recommended. **Open:** Lunch Tues–Fri 11:30am–2:30pm; dinner Sun–Thurs 6–9:30pm, Fri 6–10:30pm, Sat 5:30–10:30pm. **Prices:** Main courses $22–$25; prix fixe $49–$55. AE, MC, V. VP ♿

Philippe the Original
1001 N Alameda St; tel 213/628-3781. **Pub/American.** The oldest restaurant in Los Angeles, this landmark still offers coffee at 10¢ a cup. The decor is downright grungy, with sawdust on the floor, long Formica tables, and brown walls. But the food is great and well worth a trip downtown. Known for their french dip sandwich, they also have other sandwiches and potato salad, coleslaw, soups, and pies. **FYI:** Reservations not accepted. Beer and wine only. **Open:** Daily 6am–10pm. **Prices:** Main courses $4–$6. No CC. ▤ ♿

♟ The Restaurant
In Hotel Bel-Air, 701 Stone Canyon Rd; tel 310/472-1211. 1½ mi W of Beverly Hills Sunset Blvd exit off I-405. **Californian/Continental.** Set in a private park bordering Bel-Air estates. There's a leafy but heated patio for outdoor dining. Menu features cuisines of the Americas, the Mediterranean, and California—a medley of unusual, seasonal ingredients. The daily menu may include roasted duck breast with creamy citrus polenta or pistachio-crusted striped bass with wild rice, wilted spinach, pancetta, and basil in Dijon sauce. **FYI:** Reservations recommended. Jacket required. **Open:** Breakfast Mon–Sat 7–10:30am; lunch daily noon–2:30pm;

dinner daily 6:30–10:30pm; brunch Sun 11am–2:30pm. **Prices:** Main courses $22–$26. AE, CB, DC, ER, MC, V. ♥ 🆅🅿 &

♣ Rex Il Ristorante
617 S Olive St (Downtown); tel 213/627-2300. **Italian.** A split-level, art deco–style restaurant reminiscent of a 1930s ocean liner, located in a landmark downtown building. It features elegant, formal service, a piano, and dancing on a black marble floor. Chicken cacciatore, fettuccine, split-pea soup, tiramisù. **FYI:** Reservations recommended. Piano. Jacket required. **Open:** Lunch Thurs–Fri noon–2pm; dinner Mon–Sat 6–10pm. **Prices:** Main courses $18–$32. AE, CB, DC, MC, V. ♥ 🏛 🆅🅿 &

Ⓢ Sonora Cafe
180 S La Brea at 2nd St; tel 213/857-1800. **Southwestern.** Southwestern cuisine with intriguing European and Asian touches, served amid stucco walls adorned with southwestern art. Specialties include blue-corn chile rellenos, duck tamales with guajillo chile sauce, and crab and wild Oregon mushroom enchilada with smoked chipotle cream sauce. **FYI:** Reservations recommended. Dress code. **Open:** Lunch Mon–Fri 11:30am–4:30pm; dinner Mon–Thurs 5:30–10pm, Fri–Sat 5:30–11pm, Sun 5–9pm. **Prices:** Main courses $11–$23. AE, CB, DC, MC, V. 🍴 🏔 🆅🅿 &

★ The Terrace Il Ristorante
In Century Plaza Hotel, 2025 Avenue of the Stars; tel 310/277-2000. **Italian/Northern Italian.** This centrally located restaurant adjoins Century City and features manicured gardens and a striking, panoramic view to the west. The cuisine is contemporary northern and central Italian; specialities include grilled shrimp on saffron risotto; pan-seared salmon on wilted greens with mashed potatoes and pesto sauce; and thinly sliced New York steak with pear-tomato sauce on crispy potato strings. Nightly performances of light opera, classic arias, and Broadway stage favorites. Lavish Sunday brunch with spectacular ice sculptures by Kazu Ogino and pastry artwork by Thomas Henzi. **FYI:** Reservations recommended. Children's menu. Jacket required. **Open:** Lunch Mon–Sat 11:30am–2:30pm; dinner daily 4:30–10pm; brunch Sun 10am–2:30pm. **Prices:** Main courses $14–$24; prix fixe $23. AE, CB, DC, DISC, MC, V. ♥ 🍴 🏔 🎮 💟 🆅🅿 &

Tokyo Kaikan
225 S San Pedro St (Little Tokyo); tel 213/489-1333. **Japanese.** The tropical atmosphere is reminiscent of a country inn, with several intimate dining rooms separated by bamboo and reed walls. Very busy lunch spot in downtown location, with sushi bar, shabu-shabu bar, and cocktail lounge. **FYI:** Reservations recommended. **Open:** Lunch Mon–Fri 11:30am–2pm; dinner Mon–Fri 6–10:30pm, Sat 5–10:30pm. **Prices:** Main courses $7–$40. AE, CB, DC, MC, V. 🆅🅿 &

Tommy Tang
7313 Melrose Ave; tel 213/937-5733. **Thai/Sushi Bar.** Tommy Tang's breezy, animated, celebrity-filled restaurant helped to make Melrose Ave internationally known. Sophisticated white walls, high ceilings, and a Spanish patio planted with trees and ivy. Progressive Thai cuisine features Tommy Duck, with honey-ginger sauce, Thai black bean soup, wild mushroom risotto with basil, and spicy mint noodles. Sushi bar. **FYI:** Reservations recommended. Beer and wine only. **Open:** Mon–Thurs 11:30am–10:30pm, Fri–Sat 11:30am–midnight, Sun 1–10pm. **Prices:** Main courses $7–$14. AE, DC, MC, V. 🍴 🎮 🚗 🆅🅿 &

★ Vida
1930 Hillhurst Ave (Silverlake); tel 213/660-4446. **Eclectic.** Stacked "postmodern" dishes are the specialty at this favorite for the entertainment industry near Hollywood. A wood decor dominates the several dining rooms; musicians and girls in short black dresses hang out at the bar. Look for familiar ingredients prepared with a unique take, including dishes such as Ty Cobb salad (with crispy duck and spinach), or Okra Winfrey creole gumbo. **FYI:** Reservations recommended. **Open:** Sun–Thurs 6–11pm, Fri–Sat 6–11:30pm. **Prices:** Main courses $8–$28. AE, CB, DC, DISC, MC, V. 🆅🅿 &

Water Grill
544 S Grand Ave (Downtown); tel 213/891-0900. **Seafood.** Upscale dining room is a good choice for business lunches and dinner, offering lobster, several salmon choices, and a wide variety of other seafood. **FYI:** Reservations recommended. **Open:** Lunch Mon–Fri 11:30am–5pm; dinner Mon–Tues 5–9pm, Wed–Sat 5–10pm, Sun 4:30–9pm. **Prices:** Main courses $15–$25. AE, CB, DC, DISC, MC, V. 🆅🅿 &

ATTRACTIONS 🧳
MUSEUMS

Los Angeles County Museum of Art
5905 Wilshire Blvd; tel 213/857-6111. The complex consists of five modern buildings, all built around a central plaza. The Ahmanson Building houses the permanent collection. Galleries for prints, drawings, and photographs are in the adjacent Hammer Building. The Robert O Anderson Building features mainly 20th-century painting and sculpture, and also houses major special loan exhibitions. The Leo S Bing Center has a 600-seat theater and a 116-seat auditorium. The Pavilion for Japanese Art houses the internationally known Shin'enkan collection of Edo Period (1615–1865), and there are two sculpture gardens. Free guided tours daily (phone 213/857-6108 for details). Free admission second Wed of every month. **Open:** Wed–Thurs 10am–5pm, Fri 10am–9pm, Sat–Sun 11am–6pm. $$$

Natural History Museum of Los Angeles County
900 Exposition Blvd (Exposition Park); tel 213/744-3466 or 744-3414. The largest natural history museum in the West,

this facility houses a seemingly endless array of exhibits chronicling the history of the Earth and its environment from 600 million years ago to the present day. Permanent exhibits include a walk-through vault containing priceless gems, a Children's Discovery Center, insect zoo, and a state-of-the-art Bird Hall. Free guided tours daily at 1pm. **Open:** Tues–Sun 10am–5pm. **$$**

Los Angeles Children's Museum
310 N Main St; tel 213/687-8800. An interactive, fun environment where children learn by doing, the museum is geared toward kids ages 2–10. Areas for exploration include an art studio, a city street scene, TV and recording studios, a water exhibit, and giant foam-filled, Velcro-edged building blocks in Sticky City. In addition, there are all kinds of special activities and workshops, and a theater for children where live performances or special productions are scheduled every weekend. **Open:** Peak (Mem Day–Labor Day) Tues–Fri 11:30am–5pm, Sat–Sun 10am–5pm. Reduced hours off-season. **$$**

Southwest Museum
234 Museum Dr; tel 213/221-2164 or 221-2163. Founded in 1907, this is Los Angeles's oldest museum. It contains one of the finest collections of Native American art and artifacts in the United States, complete with a Cheyenne summer tepee, rare paintings, weapons, moccasins, and other artifacts. Major exhibit spaces are dedicated to the art and culture of Native American groups of the Northwest Coast, the Plains, California, and the Southwest. Three exhibit halls house rotating and traveling exhibits, and an entire wing is devoted to a changing display of more than 400 examples of native North American basketry from the museum's 11,000-piece collection. Guided tours are available on weekends. **Open:** Tues–Sun 11am–5pm. **$$**

Charles F Lummis Home (*El Alisal*)
200 E Avenue 43; tel 213/222-0546. Charles F Lummis, founder of the Southwest Museum, built this rugged two-story building himself, using rocks from a nearby arroyo and telegraph poles purchased from the Santa Fe Railroad. Called El Alisal (meaning "place of the sycamores"), Lummis's home became a cultural center for many famous people in the literary, theatrical, political, and arts worlds during the early 1900s.

The house is now occupied by the Historical Society of Southern California, which offers guided tours of the house and 2-acre waterwise garden. **Open:** Fri–Sun noon–4pm. **Free**

Autry Museum of Western Heritage
4700 Western Heritage Way (Griffith Park); tel 213/667-2000. Fronted by a life-size bronze sculpture of Autry and his horse, Champion, this museum houses one of the most comprehensive collections of Western nostalgia in the world. More than 16,000 artifacts and art pieces, including Gene Autry's personal treasures, illustrate the American West, as well as the romanticism with which it was viewed by artists, authors, and the entertainment industry. Many exhibits were designed by Walt Disney Imagineering. Also included are the *Los Angeles Times* Children's Discovery Gallery, with interactive exhibits, and the Spirit of Community Gallery, which emphasizes the ethnic diversity of the West, including Mormons, Chinese, Germans, and others. **Open:** Tues–Sun 10am–5pm. **$$$**

Wells Fargo History Museum
333 S Grand Ave; tel 213/253-7166. This museum highlights the history of Wells Fargo and its impact on California and the American West. Among the artifacts and exhibits are a 19th-century Concord stagecoach; the Challenge Nugget—a 2-pound lump of 76% pure gold; audiovisual room with films; and mining entrepreneur and Wells Fargo agent Sam Dorsey's gold collection. **Open:** Mon–Fri 9am–5pm. **Free**

OTHER ATTRACTIONS

Descanso Gardens
1418 Descanso Dr, La Cañada; tel 818/952-4402 or 952-4400 (recorded info). Purchased by Los Angeles County in 1953, Descanso Gardens is famous for the world's largest camelia garden (there are 600 different varieties). The 4-acre rose garden includes some varieties dating back 2,000 years. Each season features different plants. A Japanese-style tea house (open Tuesday–Sunday 11am–4pm) is surrounded by pools, waterfalls, and a rock garden. Free guided walking tours are offered every Sunday at 1pm; guided tram tours (additional fee charged) run Tuesday–Friday at 1, 2, and 3pm, and Saturday–Sunday at 11am. **Open:** Daily 9am–4:30pm. **$**

Griffith Park
Tel 213/665-5188. Accessible via I-5 (Griffith Park or Zoo Dr exits). Home of the Los Angeles Zoo and the Griffith Observatory (see both below), the park's facilities include golf courses, a bird sanctuary, tennis courts, a huge swimming pool, picnic areas, an old-fashioned merry-go-round, and large expanses of wilderness. **Free**

Griffith Observatory
2800 E Observatory Rd (Griffith Park); tel 213/663-8171 (Sky Report) or 664-1181. Located on the south slope of Mount Hollywood, this observatory's 12-inch telescope is one of the largest in California available for use by the public. Before nightfall, guests can enjoy the exhibits in the observatory's Hall of Science or see a planetarium or laser show (phone for schedule; children under 5 admitted only on weekends to the 1:30pm show). **Open:** Peak (Mem Day–Labor Day) daily 12:30–9:45pm. Reduced hours off-season. **$$$**

Los Angeles Zoo
5333 Zoo Dr (Griffith Park); tel 213/666-4090. A zoo with a "cast of thousands," including more than 1,200 mammals, birds, and reptiles. The research facility houses more than 50 endangered species. There is an aviary, aquatic section,

reptile house, children's zoo, animal nursery, and outdoor theater for animal performances. The Safari Shuttle transports visitors around the park for a small fee. **Open:** Daily 10am–5pm. **$$$**

PROFESSIONAL SPORTS

Dodger Stadium
1000 Elysian Park Ave; tel 213/224-1500. The LA **Dodgers** major league baseball team plays home games here during the mid-April to early October season. **$$$$**

Great Western Forum
3900 W Manchester Ave (Inglewood); tel 213/419-3100. The Forum is the home of the NBA's Los Angeles **Lakers** and the Los Angeles **Kings** of the NHL. Both teams' seasons run from about October to June. **$$$$**

Los Angeles Memorial Coliseum
3911 S Figueroa St (Exposition Park); tel 213/747-7111. The Coliseum hosts college football games featuring USC, from September to December. **$$$$**

Sports Arena at Exposition Park
3911 S Figueroa St (Exposition Park); tel 213/748-8000. Part of the same complex as the Coliseum, the Sports Arena is home court for the Los Angeles **Clippers,** also of the NBA. **$$$$**

Los Angeles Int'l Airport

HOTELS 🏨

🛏🛏🛏 Cockatoo Inn
4334 W Imperial Hwy, Hawthorne, 90250; tel 310/679-2291 or toll free 800/458-2800; fax 310/679-4390. Beautiful red-brick and half-timbered complex with garden patios and formal lobby. **Rooms:** 213 rms, stes, and effic. CI 1pm/CO noon. Nonsmoking rms avail. **Amenities:** 🛏 A/C, TV, refrig. Some units w/terraces, some w/fireplaces, 1 w/whirlpool. **Services:** ✕ 🚐 🛎 Car-rental desk, babysitting. Free shuttle to shopping centers. **Facilities:** 🛗 450 🚻 1 restaurant, 1 bar (w/entertainment), whirlpool. **Rates:** $54 S; $64 D; $98–$225 ste; $64–$74 effic. Extra person $13. Children under age 17 stay free. Parking: Indoor/outdoor, free. AE, CB, DC, DISC, EC, ER, JCB, MC, V.

🛏🛏🛏 Continental Plaza, Los Angeles Airport
9750 Airport Blvd, Los Angeles, 90045; tel 310/645-4600 or toll free 800/LAX-HOTEL; fax 310/645-7486. High-rise hotel near the airport is very comfortable and well maintained. **Rooms:** 570 rms and stes. CI 3pm/CO noon. Nonsmoking rms avail. **Amenities:** 🛏 A/C, voice mail, bathrobes. Some units w/minibars, some w/terraces. **Services:** ✕ 🛎 VP 🚐 🛎 Twice-daily maid svce, car-rental desk, babysitting. **Facilities:** 🛗 500 🚻 1 restaurant, 2 bars (1 w/entertainment), beauty salon, washer/dryer. **Rates:** $85 S;

$92 D; $125 ste. Children under age 18 stay free. Parking: Indoor/outdoor, $6/day. Rates will rise after renovation. AE, CB, DC, DISC, EC, ER, JCB, MC, V.

🛏🛏🛏 Embassy Suites LAX/Century Blvd
9801 Airport Blvd, Los Angeles, 90045; tel 310/215-1000 or toll free 800/EMBASSY; fax 310/215-1952. Typical Embassy Suites atrium design, with glass elevator. Very impressive and upbeat. **Rooms:** 215 stes. CI 1/CO 1pm. Nonsmoking rms avail. Two-room suites, nicely furnished with sofa bed in living room. **Amenities:** 🛏 A/C, cable TV w/movies, refrig, VCR, voice mail. All units w/terraces. Wet bar, microwave. Nintendo available. **Services:** ✕ 🛎 🚐 Car-rental desk, babysitting. Complimentary cocktails and children's drinks, full cooked-to-order breakfast. **Facilities:** 🛗 370 🚻 1 restaurant, 1 bar, sauna, steam rm, whirlpool, day-care ctr, washer/dryer. **Rates:** $109 ste. Extra person $15. Children under age 18 stay free. AP rates avail. Parking: Indoor, $7.70/day. DC, DISC, MC, V.

🛏🛏🛏 Embassy Suites LAX South
1440 E Imperial Ave, El Segundo, 90245; tel 310/640-3600 or toll free 800/433-4600; fax 310/322-0954. With its palm trees and pond with koi fish, ducks, and turtles, this Mediterranean-style hotel built around an atrium feels like a tropical world away from LAX. Scenes from *The Net* with Sandra Bullock were filmed in the West Courtyard, which is also popular for weddings. **Rooms:** 350 stes. CI 1pm/CO 11am. Nonsmoking rms avail. All accommodations are two-room suites. Because the living room is situated along the atrium corridor, it tends to be dark and exposed to view through the hallway windows. Although bathrooms are small, they feature marble counters. From the small balcony in many rooms, you can watch planes taking off from LAX. **Amenities:** 🛏 A/C, cable TV w/movies, refrig, dataport, voice mail. All units w/terraces. Wet bar, microwave, 2 vanity sinks, 2 phone lines. **Services:** 🛎 🚐 Car-rental desk, social director. The general manager often sits at a desk in the lobby, to help with guests' requests. Coffee is available in the lobby 24 hours, along with a computer terminal that displays airline schedules. Free shuttle service to area restaurants and the Manhattan Beach beach. **Facilities:** 🛗 650 🚻 1 restaurant, 1 bar, whirlpool. Attractive indoor pool surrounded by plants and a flagstone terrace. Workout room very poorly equipped. **Rates (CP):** $89–$129 ste. Extra person $10. Children under age 18 stay free. Parking: Indoor, free. Stay & Fly packages available. AE, CB, DC, DISC, MC, V.

🛏🛏 Hampton Inn
10300 La Cienega Blvd, Inglewood, 90304; tel 310/337-1000 or toll free 800/HAMPTON; fax 310/645-6925. Small airport hotel, well kept but with minimal decor. Lobby is OK but not inviting. **Rooms:** 148 rms. CI 1pm/CO noon. Nonsmoking rms avail. **Amenities:** 🛏 A/C. **Services:** 🚐 🛎 Car-rental desk. No charge for local calls. **Facilities:**

⌨ 🖵 67 ⅖ **Rates (CP):** $65–$75 S; $75–$85 D. Extra person $10. Children under age 18 stay free. Parking: Outdoor, free. AE, CB, DC, DISC, EC, ER, JCB, MC, V.

≡≡≡ Holiday Inn Crowne Plaza
5985 W Century Blvd, Los Angeles, 90045; tel 310/642-7500 or toll free 800/255-7606; fax 310/417-3608. **Rooms:** 615 rms and stes. Executive level. CI 3pm/CO noon. Nonsmoking rms avail. **Amenities:** 🛏 👓 🎛 ⌨ A/C, dataport, voice mail, bathrobes. Some units w/minibars. **Services:** 🍽 🗝 VP 🚗 ⚡ ⌨ Twice-daily maid svce, car-rental desk, babysitting. Complimentary newspaper. Free shuttle to beach and shopping. **Facilities:** 🏋 ⌨ 800 ⌸ ⅖ 2 restaurants, 1 bar, sauna, steam rm, whirlpool, washer/dryer. **Rates:** $154 S or D; $350–$450 ste. Extra person $10. Children under age 12 stay free. Parking: Indoor, $8/day. AE, CB, DC, DISC, EC, ER, JCB, MC, V.

≡≡≡ Holiday Inn LAX Airport
9901 La Cienega Blvd, Los Angeles, 90045; tel 310/649-5151 or toll free 800/624-0025; fax 310/670-3619. Immaculate hotel near the airport with a small, well-kept lobby. **Rooms:** 403 rms. Executive level. CI 3pm/CO noon. Nonsmoking rms avail. **Amenities:** 🛏 👓 🎛 A/C, cable TV w/movies. **Services:** ✗ 🗝 🚗 ⌨ ⚡ Car-rental desk, babysitting. **Facilities:** 🏋 ⌨ 350 ⅖ 1 restaurant, 1 bar, spa, washer/dryer. **Rates:** $119–$149 S; $129–$159 D. Extra person $10. Children under age 12 stay free. MAP rates avail. Parking: Indoor/outdoor, $7/day. AE, CB, DC, DISC, JCB, MC, V.

≡≡≡ Los Angeles Airport Marriott
5855 W Century Blvd, Los Angeles, 90045; tel 310/641-5700 or toll free 800/228-9290; fax 310/337-5358. Well-kept, very adequate business hotel. **Rooms:** 1,012 rms and stes. Executive level. CI 3pm/CO 1pm. Nonsmoking rms avail. **Amenities:** 🛏 👓 A/C, cable TV w/movies, voice mail. Some units w/terraces. **Services:** 🍽 🗝 VP 🚗 ⌨ ⚡ ⌨ Car-rental desk, babysitting. Complimentary coffee in lobby in morning, punch in afternoon. ITT language service. Courteous, multilingual staff. **Facilities:** 🏋 ⌨ 1200 ⌸ ⅖ 4 restaurants, 2 bars (1 w/entertainment), games rm, spa, sauna, steam rm, whirlpool, beauty salon, washer/dryer. Large, serpentine pool and big lounge area. **Rates:** $85–$139 S or D; $159 ste. Children under age 18 stay free. Parking: Indoor/outdoor, $9/day. AE, CB, DC, DISC, JCB, MC, V.

≡≡≡ Los Angeles Renaissance Hotel
9620 Airport Blvd, Los Angeles, 90045; tel 310/337-2800 or toll free 800/647-6437; fax 310/216-6681. Tasteful and impressive, the lobby has a marble foyer and two bronze lions standing guard over the stairway to the elevators. A $14 million art collection is displayed throughout the hotel. Furnishings were refurbished in 1996. **Rooms:** 505 rms and stes. Executive level. CI 3pm/CO noon. Nonsmoking rms avail. Even standard rooms are large, and offer quality touches such as marble-topped desks and nightstands, plus attractive, two-tone wood furnishings. Excellent

soundproofing. **Amenities:** 🛏 👓 🎛 ⌨ A/C, cable TV w/movies, dataport, voice mail, in-rm safe. All units w/minibars. **Services:** 🍽 🗝 VP 🚗 ⌨ ⚡ ⌨ Car-rental desk, masseur, babysitting. **Facilities:** 🏋 ⌨ 800 ⌸ ⅖ 2 restaurants, 2 bars (1 w/entertainment), sauna, whirlpool. Nice, airy workout room facing the pool; Lifecycles can also be brought to guests' rooms. Piano music in the lobby bar 5–7pm. **Rates:** $130–$190 S or D; $190–$210 ste. Extra person $10. Children under age 18 stay free. Parking: Indoor, $8–$10/day. Park & Fly package for $99 includes one night's accommodations and five nights' free parking. AE, CB, DC, DISC, MC, V.

≡≡≡ Ramada Park International Airport
6333 Bristol Pkwy, Culver City, 90230; tel 310/670-3200 or toll free 800/321-5575; fax 310/641-8925. Small business hotel near airport. Features expansive, marble-floored lobby and numerous comfortable sitting areas. **Rooms:** 260 rms and stes. Executive level. CI 1pm/CO noon. Nonsmoking rms avail. **Amenities:** 🛏 👓 🎛 ⌨ A/C, refrig, voice mail. **Services:** 🍽 🗝 🚗 ⌨ ⚡ Twice-daily maid svce, car-rental desk, babysitting. **Facilities:** 🏋 ⌨ 300 ⅖ 1 restaurant, 1 bar (w/entertainment), whirlpool, washer/dryer. **Rates:** $79–$99 S; $79–$109 D; $250 ste. Extra person $10. Children under age 18 stay free. Parking: Outdoor, free. AE, CB, DC, DISC, EC, ER, JCB, MC, V.

≡≡≡ Red Lion Hotel
6161 Centinela Ave, Culver City, 90230; tel 310/649-1776 or toll free 800/547-8010; fax 310/547-8010. Well-kept commercial airport hotel with large, impressive lobby. **Rooms:** 368 rms, stes, and effic. Executive level. CI 3pm/CO noon. Nonsmoking rms avail. **Amenities:** 🛏 👓 ⌨ A/C, cable TV w/movies, refrig. 1 unit w/whirlpool. **Services:** ✗ 🗝 🚗 ⌨ ⚡ Car-rental desk, social director, masseur, children's program. Free shopping shuttle to nearby mall. **Facilities:** 🏋 ⌨ 600 ⌸ ⅖ 2 restaurants, 1 bar (w/entertainment), whirlpool, washer/dryer. **Rates (CP):** $106 S or D; $350 ste; $325 effic. Children under age 18 stay free. Parking: Indoor/outdoor, free. AE, CB, DC, DISC, MC, V.

≡≡≡≡ Sheraton Gateway Hotel Los Angeles Airport
6101 W Century Blvd, Los Angeles, 90045; tel 310/642-1111 or toll free 800/325-3535; fax 310/410-1267. Decorated with hefty wrought-iron chandeliers and potted palms, the enormous marble lobby hums with big-city bustle. Completely renovated in 1995, the hotel is very well maintained. **Rooms:** 804 rms and stes. Executive level. CI 3pm/CO noon. Nonsmoking rms avail. These are rooms you can really live in, large and with lots of drawer space and two comfy armchairs. Everything is new, including light wood furnishings and blue and beige bedspreads. Excellent security—guest floors accessible by elevator only by using room key card. **Amenities:** 🛏 👓 🎛 ⌨ A/C, cable TV w/movies, dataport, voice mail. All units w/minibars. Nintendo in all rooms, along with big-screen 27" TVs. Iron and ironing

board in all rooms. **Services:** 🖳 ⏻ VP 🚗 ☒ ⤶ Twice-daily maid svce, car-rental desk, social director, masseur, babysitting. Free 800# and calling-card calls. **Facilities:** ⟨⟩ 🛁 1000 🖳 ⚤ 2 restaurants, 2 bars (1 w/entertainment), whirlpool. American Airlines desk on premises. Overlooking the pool, the fitness center is open 24 hours and has Universal gym equipment. The casual Brasserie restaurant hosts an extensive lunchtime buffet with a carvery; Landry's fine dining restaurant also has a sushi bar. **Rates:** $82–$155 S or D; $300–$1,000 ste. Extra person $20. Children under age 18 stay free. Parking: Outdoor, $8–$12/day. Park & Fly packages available. AE, CB, DC, DISC, ER, JCB, MC, V.

≣≣ Travelodge at LAX

5547 W Century Blvd, Los Angeles, 90045; tel 310/649-4000 or toll free 800/421-3939; fax 310/649-0311. The hotel lobby is nondescript, but there's a surprisingly beautiful tropical garden surrounding the pool area. **Rooms:** 147 rms. CI open/CO noon. No smoking. **Amenities:** 🛏 ⚬ 🖭 A/C, cable TV w/movies, VCR. Some units w/terraces. **Services:** ✕ ⏻ 🚗 ☒ ⤶ ⤻ Car-rental desk, babysitting. **Facilities:** ⟨⟩ 30 🖳 1 restaurant, 1 bar, washer/dryer. Denny's restaurant attached. **Rates:** Peak (June 15–Aug) $69 S; $74 D. Extra person $8. Children under age 18 stay free. Lower rates off-season. Parking: Outdoor, free. ER, JCB, MC, V.

≣≣≣ Wyndham Garden Hotel

5990 Green Valley Circle, Culver City, 90230; tel 310/641-7740 or toll free 800/WYNDHAM; fax 310/645-7045. Sepulveda exit off I-405. Small lobby and average rooms. **Rooms:** 199 rms. CI 3pm/CO noon. Nonsmoking rms avail. **Amenities:** 🛏 ⚬ 🖭 ✆ A/C, dataport, voice mail, bathrobes. **Services:** ✕ 🚗 ☒ ⤶ Twice-daily maid svce. **Facilities:** ⟨⟩ 🛁 244 ⚤ 1 restaurant, 1 bar. **Rates (BB):** $79 S; $89 D. Extra person $10. Children under age 18 stay free. Parking: Outdoor, free. AE, CB, DC, DISC, EC, ER, JCB, MC, V.

≣≣≣ Wyndham Hotel at Los Angeles Airport

6225 W Century Blvd, Los Angeles, 90045; tel 310/670-9000 or toll free 800/233-1234; fax 310/670-8110. Large lobby with neoclassical decor, library, and several sitting areas. Completely renovated in 1996. **Rooms:** 594 rms and stes. Executive level. CI 3pm/CO noon. Nonsmoking rms avail. Bright, attractive, newly decorated rooms. **Amenities:** 🛏 ⚬ 🖭 ✆ A/C, dataport, voice mail, bathrobes. **Services:** ✕ ⏻ VP 🚗 ☒ ⤶ ⤻ Car-rental desk, babysitting. Airport shuttle with handicapped access. **Facilities:** ⟨⟩ 🛁 1500 🖳 ⚤ 2 restaurants, 2 bars (1 w/entertainment), spa, steam rm, whirlpool. **Rates:** $109–$149 S; $129–$169 D; $295–$495 ste. Extra person $20. Children under age 18 stay free. Parking: Indoor/outdoor, $9/day. AE, CB, DC, DISC, EC, ER, JCB, MC, V.

MOTEL

≣≣≣ Motel 6

5101 Century Blvd, Inglewood, 90304; tel 310/419-1234; fax 310/677-7871. Recently renovated by new owners, motel

is surprisingly good. **Rooms:** 255 rms. CI noon/CO noon. Nonsmoking rms avail. Remarkably well-furnished rooms. **Amenities:** 🛏 A/C, cable TV w/movies. **Services:** 🚗 ⤶ **Facilities:** ⟨⟩ 50 1 restaurant, 1 bar. Pool is situated next to the highway. **Rates:** $44–$46 S; $50–$52 D. Extra person $6. Children under age 18 stay free. Parking: Outdoor, free. AE, CB, DC, DISC, MC, V.

Los Gatos

This well-heeled community on the fringes of San Jose has a sophisticated downtown area of upscale shops and quiet hillside neighborhoods. **Information:** Los Gatos Chamber of Commerce, 322 Los Gatos Saratoga Rd, PO Box 1820, Los Gatos 95030 (tel 408/354-9300).

HOTELS 🏨

≣≣≣ La Hacienda Inn Hotel

18840 Saratoga-Los Gatos Rd, 95030; tel 408/354-9230 or toll free 800/235-4570; fax 408/354-7590. A lovely oasis near the Santa Cruz Mountains. Lots of rustic charm. **Rooms:** 21 rms and stes. CI 2pm/CO noon. Cathedral ceilings, redwood walls, skylights, and custom furnishings. **Amenities:** 🛏 ⚬ ✆ A/C, TV, refrig. All units w/terraces, some w/fireplaces. **Services:** ✕ ☒ ⤶ Babysitting. **Facilities:** ⟨⟩ 18 1 restaurant (lunch and dinner only), 1 bar (w/entertainment), whirlpool, washer/dryer. **Rates (CP):** $80–$100 S; $85–$105 D; $85–$125 ste. Extra person $10. Children under age 6 stay free. Parking: Outdoor, free. AE, CB, DC, DISC, JCB, MC, V.

≣ Los Gatos Lodge

50 Los Gatos-Saratoga Rd, 95032; tel 408/354-3300 or toll free 800/322-8811; fax 408/354-5451. E Los Gatos exit off CA 17. Grounds are spacious and appealing, but the hotel itself needs some renovation. **Rooms:** 120 rms, stes, and effic. CI 3pm/CO noon. Nonsmoking rms avail. **Amenities:** 🛏 🖭 A/C, TV. All units w/terraces, 1 w/fireplace. **Services:** ✕ 🚗 ☒ ⤶ ⤻ Masseur, babysitting. **Facilities:** ⟨⟩ 200 ⚤ 1 restaurant, 1 bar (w/entertainment), lawn games, whirlpool, washer/dryer. **Rates:** Peak (June–Aug) $65–$85 S or D; $80 ste; $100 effic. Lower rates off-season. Parking: Outdoor, free. AE, CB, DC, DISC, MC, V.

≣≣≣ Toll House Hotel

140 S Santa Cruz Ave, 95030; tel 408/395-7070 or toll free 800/238-6111, 800/821-5518 in CA; fax 408/395-3730. CA 9 exit off CA 17. After a $2 million renovation by its new ownership, this hotel has been restored to its original glory. There's plenty of old-world charm, with teak-paneled elevators and a cozy sitting area in the lobby enhanced by European decor, fresh flowers, and a fireplace. **Rooms:** 97 rms and stes. CI 3pm/CO noon. Nonsmoking rms avail. Tasteful, spacious accommodations; second-floor rooms open onto large terrace overlooking the courtyard.

Amenities: 🕙 ⚸ ▣ ⓠ A/C, cable TV w/movies, dataport. Some units w/terraces, some w/whirlpools. **Services:** ✕ 🚗 ⬛ ♪ Friendly, helpful staff. **Facilities:** 🛏 📷 🖥 ♿ 1 restaurant (dinner only), 1 bar, washer/dryer. Large central courtyard is pleasant place to relax. **Rates (CP):** $94–$102 S; $102–$110 D; $185 ste. Extra person $10. Children under age 16 stay free. Parking: Indoor/outdoor, free. AE, CB, DC, DISC, JCB, MC, V.

LODGE

≣≣≣ Lodge at Villa Felice
15350 S Winchester Blvd, 95030; tel 408/395-6710 or toll free 800/662-9229; fax 408/354-1826. 6 mi SW of San Jose. Lark Ave exit off CA 17; right on Lark, left on Winchester. Overlooking beautiful Lake Vasona and the Santa Cruz Mountains, this hotel offers fresh air and tranquility in the midst of the bustling Silicon Valley. **Rooms:** 33 rms, stes, and effic. CI 3pm/CO noon. Nonsmoking rms avail. Some rooms have steam saunas. **Amenities:** 🕙 ⚸ A/C, cable TV, refrig, dataport. All units w/terraces, some w/fireplaces, some w/whirlpools. **Services:** ✕ ⬛ ♪ **Facilities:** 🛏 📷 ♿ 1 restaurant (lunch and dinner only), 1 bar (w/entertainment), whirlpool. **Rates (CP):** $98–$119 S or D; $138–$184 ste; $220 effic. Children under age 18 stay free. Parking: Outdoor, free. AE, DC, MC, V.

ATTRACTIONS 🏛

Forbes Mill Regional Museum
75 Church St; tel 408/395-7375. Forbes Mill was an actual flour mill, completed in 1854, and was the first business in Los Gatos. Today it is preserved as a historical landmark. A large photograph on the west interior wall shows the mill site as it appeared in the 1880s. **Open:** Wed–Sun 1–4pm. $

Tait Avenue Art and Natural History Museum
4 Tait Ave; tel 408/395-7375. Art on display here includes exhibits by painters, sculptors, designers, photographers, and other talented regional artists. Natural history exhibits include specimens of wildlife, flora and fauna, and gems and minerals of the Los Gatos area and from around the world. Also permanent and changing displays of regional history. **Open:** Wed–Sun 1–4pm. $

Los Olivos

The wine-growing heart of the Santa Ynez Valley, Los Olivos is a quiet, uncrowded community amid gently rolling hills above Santa Barbara.

HOTEL 🏨

≣≣≣ Los Olivos Grand Hotel
2860 Grand Ave, PO Box 526, 93441; tel 805/688-7788 or toll free 800/446-2455; fax 805/688-1942. CA 154 exit off US 101; 2 mi to Grand Ave, turn right. Situated in the middle

of wine country and horse farms, this small hotel trimmed with a turret, dormers, and clapboard siding looks venerably old, but was built in 1984. Guests wishing more privacy can stay in the annex across the street. **Rooms:** 21 rms and stes. CI 2pm/CO noon. No smoking. Extremely welcoming and spacious, with brass faucets, European armoires, eyelet sheets, down comforters. All rooms have a separate sitting area. Tasteful furnishings are somewhat dull. Second-story accommodations have high vaulted ceilings. **Amenities:** 🕙 ⚸ ⓠ A/C, cable TV, refrig. All units w/fireplaces, some w/whirlpools. Complimentary bottle of wine on request. VCRs available on request. **Services:** ✕ 🖙 ⬛ ♪ Twice-daily maid svce, masseur. Complimentary hot and cold hors d'oeuvres every afternoon served with different regional wines. **Facilities:** 🛏 📷 ♿ 1 restaurant (lunch and dinner only), 1 bar, whirlpool. Pretty gardens, including a wisteria arbor and gazebo that's popular for weddings. Pool located in the west wing annex. **Rates (CP):** $160–$255 S or D; $300–$325 ste. Children under age 18 stay free. Min stay wknds. Parking: Outdoor, free. Rates drop about 20% during the week. AE, DC, DISC, MC, V.

RESTAURANT 🍴

★ Side Street Cafe
2375 Alamo Pintado; tel 805/688-8455. **Californian/Coffeehouse.** A bohemian cafe with entertainment ranging from folk singers to string quartets and even political debates. A tea garden out back has tables under the locust trees. Fresh, tasty soups, specials, and coffees change daily; offerings might include pesto pasta or tomato salad with goat cheese. Great desserts. **FYI:** Reservations recommended. Blues/cabaret/guitar/jazz/piano. Beer and wine only. **Open:** Sun–Thurs 9am–9pm, Fri–Sat 9am–11pm. **Prices:** Main courses $7–$12. MC, V. 🍺 ♿

Madera

Just northwest of Fresno, the Central Valley agricultural outpost of Madera straddles both CA 99 and the Southern Pacific and Santa Fe rail lines. **Information:** Madera District Chamber of Commerce, 131 W Yosemite Ave, Madera 93637 (tel 209/673-3563).

HOTEL 🏨

≣≣ Best Western Madera Valley Inn
317 North G St, 93637; tel 209/673-5164 or toll free 800/528-1234; fax 209/661-8426. 4th St exit off CA 99 N; Central Madera exit off CA 99 S. Quiet, pleasant. **Rooms:** 95 rms and stes. CI 11am/CO noon. Nonsmoking rms avail. **Amenities:** 🕙 ⚸ ▣ A/C, satel TV w/movies. 1 unit w/terrace. **Services:** ✕ 🚗 ⬛ ♪ 🐾 Car-rental desk. **Facilities:** 📷 1 restaurant, 1 bar. Free use of nearby athletic club. **Rates:** $56 S; $60 D; $85 ste. Extra person $4. Children under age 12 stay free. Parking: Outdoor, free. AE, CB, DC, DISC, MC, V.

RESTAURANT 🍴

★ Lucca's
325 N Gateway Dr; tel 209/674-6744. Gateway Dr exit off CA 99 N or S. **Italian.** The place to go for lunch or dinner in Madera, owned by the Del Bianco family since they opened it in 1935. Serves old-style hearty Italian cuisine. Famous for its handmade ravioli with special meat sauce; a full range of beef, chicken, lamb, and seafood dishes are also available. Entrees can be ordered à la carte, or, for about $3 more, you get a full dinner, with soup, salad, and a serving of spaghetti or ravioli. **FYI:** Reservations accepted. Karaoke. Children's menu. **Open:** Lunch Tues–Sat 11:30am–3pm; dinner Tues–Sat 3–9:30pm, Sun 4–9:30pm. **Prices:** Main courses $9–$23. MC, V. 🔲 ♿

Malibu

See also Pacific Palisades

Perhaps the most legendary Southern California beach town, Malibu does a remarkable job of living up to its image. The beaches are wide (but can be crowded in the summer) with gently rolling breakers, the homes are spectacular, and the attitude is decidedly laid-back. **Information:** Malibu Chamber of Commerce, 23805 Stuart Ranch Rd #100, Malibu 90265 (tel 310/456-9025).

HOTEL 🏨

📧📧📧 Malibu Beach Inn
22878 Pacific Coast Hwy, 90265; tel 310/456-6444 or toll free 800/4MALIBU; fax 310/456-1499. This pink, Spanish mission–style hotel with fountains and wrought-iron trim is located right on Carbon Beach, one of Malibu's most exclusive strands. Great for a romantic weekend at the shore. **Rooms:** 47 rms and stes. CI 3pm/CO noon. Nonsmoking rms avail. All you see is ocean from most rooms. Accommodations are simply decorated with tile floors and rattan furnishings; most have gas fireplaces. All soft goods were replaced in 1996. **Amenities:** 🔔 🕐 🖵 🍴 A/C, cable TV, refrig, dataport, VCR, in-rm safe. All units w/minibars, all w/terraces, some w/fireplaces, some w/whirlpools. **Services:** 🍽️ 🚗 🔺 🛎️ Twice-daily maid svce, car-rental desk, masseur, babysitting. Friendly staff. Room service from neighboring Alice's Restaurant. (*see* "Restaurants" below). **Facilities:** 🔲 ♿ 1 beach (ocean). Use of fitness center across the street ($20 fee). **Rates (CP):** Peak (June–Sept) $135–$225 S or D; $235–$250 ste. Extra person $15. Min stay wknds. Lower rates off-season. Parking: Indoor/outdoor, free. Book two to three weeks in advance for summer weekends. AE, CB, DC, DISC, MC, V.

MOTELS

📧📧 Casa Malibu
22752 Pacific Coast Hwy, 90265; tel 310/456-2219 or toll free 800/831-0858; fax 310/456-5418. Located right on the beach, this friendly, family-run motel is comfortable and casual, decorated with pretty furnishings and tropical plants. Spacious deck with great ocean views. **Rooms:** 21 rms, stes, and effic. CI 1pm/CO noon. Nonsmoking rms avail. **Amenities:** 🔔 🕐 🖵 Cable TV, refrig. No A/C. Some units w/terraces, some w/fireplaces. **Services:** ✗ 🔺 🛎️ Babysitting. **Facilities:** 1 beach (ocean). **Rates:** Peak (June–Sept) $99–$169 S or D; $169–$199 ste; $109–$165 effic. Extra person $10. Min stay special events. Lower rates off-season. Parking: Indoor, free. AE, DISC, MC, V.

📧📧 Malibu Country Inn
6506 Westward Beach Rd, 90265; tel 310/457-9622 or toll free 800/FUN-N-SURF; fax 310/457-1349. Old California stucco building covered with vines and flowers, set on a hillside overlooking the ocean near Zuma Beach. **Rooms:** 16 rms, stes, and effic. CI 3pm/CO noon. Nonsmoking rms avail. Rooms are pretty and furnished with rattan. **Amenities:** 🔔 🖵 Cable TV, refrig. No A/C. All units w/terraces, 1 w/fireplace. Flowers and basket of snacks in rooms. **Services:** ✗ 🛎️ 🚗 Babysitting. **Facilities:** 🔲 📺 1 restaurant (bkfst and lunch only). Pretty restaurant at one end of the garden serves poolside breakfast. **Rates:** Peak (June–Sept) $95–$140 S or D; $120–$180 ste; $135–$195 effic; $120–$180 cottage/villa. Extra person $10. Children under age 18 stay free. Lower rates off-season. Parking: Outdoor, free. Corporate rates available. AE, CB, DC, DISC, MC, V.

RESTAURANTS 🍴

Alice's Restaurant
23000 Pacific Coast Hwy; tel 213/456-6646. **Californian/Seafood.** In a blue-and-white building on Malibu Pier, this old California beach shack–style restaurant with a funky interior is always crowded. Features barbecued Chilean sea bass, grilled ahi tuna with fresh fruit salsa, broiled mahimahi with soy ginger glaze, grilled chicken adobo. **FYI:** Reservations recommended. **Open:** Daily 11am–10pm. **Prices:** Main courses $13–$19. MC, V. ♥ 🍷 🏞️ 🅥🅟

★ Beau Rivage
26025 Pacific Coast Hwy; tel 310/456-5733. **Mediterranean.** The labor of love of attentive proprietors Daniel and Luciana Forge, who spent 40 years in the restaurant business before transforming a building on their four-acre Malibu property into a vine-covered country inn, reminiscent of the south of France. Six dining areas include an intimate, awesomely-stocked wine cellar, a glass hall overlooking the ocean, and a garden patio. High, beamed ceilings and a fireplace in the main room make it warm in winter. Menu features French and Italian seafood, meat and game dishes, pastas, and a fine array of desserts. Specialties are rack of lamb Cypriot with

onions and mushrooms; and filet of wild boar with chestnuts. **FYI:** Reservations recommended. Guitar/piano/singer. **Open:** Dinner Mon–Sun 5–10pm; brunch Sun 11am–4pm. **Prices:** Main courses $12–$26. AE, CB, DC, DISC, MC, V. ♥ ⬛⬛⬛⬛⬛⬛

♥ **Granita**
In Malibu Colony Plaza, 23725 W Malibu Rd; tel 310/456-0488. **Californian/Mediterranean.** A romantic experience with Wolfgang Puck's innovative cooking. Fantasy "underwater" setting—a grotto in pink, aqua, pastel yellow, and greens, with tropical fish tanks sunk into the walls. Features crisp potato pancake with smoked salmon, Mediterranean soup with half lobster and couscous, blood-orange granita with brandy-snap tuille. **FYI:** Reservations recommended. **Open:** Lunch Wed–Fri 11:30am–2pm, Sat 11am–2pm; dinner Mon–Fri 6–10:30pm, Sat–Sun 5:30–10:30pm; brunch Sun 11am–2pm. **Prices:** Main courses $20–$27; prix fixe $35. CB, DC, DISC, MC, V. ♥ ⬛⬛⬛

Sand Castle
28128 W Pacific Coast Hwy; tel 310/457-2503. At Paradise Cove, 3 mi S of Zuma Beach. **American.** A traditional fish house set in a small cove right on the beach and overlooking the Pacific Ocean. Dine on lobster, steaks, bouillabaisse, and daily fish specials. **FYI:** Reservations recommended. Children's menu. **Open:** Daily 6am–9:30pm. **Prices:** Main courses $10–$35. AE, CB, DC, MC, V. ♥ ⬛⬛⬛

ATTRACTIONS 🏛

J Paul Getty Museum
17985 Pacific Coast Hwy; tel 310/458-2003. A reconstruction of a Roman villa, this magnificent museum is particularly strong in Greek and Roman antiquities and pre-20th-century western European paintings and decorative arts; also medieval and Renaissance manuscripts, drawings, and sculpture, and late 19th- and early 20th-century European and American photography. Two educational interactive videodiscs allow visitors to guide themselves through the rich and complex worlds of Greek vases and illuminated manuscripts with the touch of a finger. *Important:* Parking is free, but visitors are required to phone for a parking reservation 7 to 10 days in advance; walk-in visitors are not permitted. Collection scheduled to change in June 1997. **Open:** Tues–Sun 10am–5pm. **Free**

Adamson House and Malibu Lagoon Museum
23200 Pacific Coast Hwy; tel 310/456-8432. This restored 1929 Moorish-Spanish Colonial Revival residence incorporates lavish use of the exquisite ceramic tile produced by Malibu Potteries between 1926 and 1932. In addition, the house features hand-carved teakwood doors, hand-painted murals, hand-wrought filigree ironwork, and lead-framed bottled glass windows. The pool and bathhouse, extensively decorated with Malibu tile, several fountains, and winding flagstone pathways, are additional highlights.

The adjoining museum contains artifacts, rare photographs, maps, documents, and other items relating to the history of Malibu. Gift shop. **Open:** Wed–Sat 11am–3pm. **$**

Mammoth Lakes

In the summer, hikers are drawn to the beautiful high-country lakes for camping and fishing, and in the winter, the crowd switches to skiing at Mammoth Mountain. **Information:** Mammoth Lake Visitors Bureau, PO Box 48, Mammoth Lake 93546 (tel 619/934-2712 or toll free 800/367-6572).

MOTELS 🏨

≣≣ Quality Inn
CA 203, PO Box 3507, 93546; tel 619/934-5114 or toll free 800/626-1900; fax 619/934-5165. CA 203/Main St exit off US 395. New property. Nicely appointed but with minimal public space. **Rooms:** 61 rms and stes. CI open/CO 11am. Nonsmoking rms avail. Spacious and clean with very attractive furniture. **Amenities:** 🛁 📺 Cable TV. No A/C. Some units w/minibars, some w/whirlpools. **Services:** ⬛ **Facilities:** ⬛ ⬛ ⬛ Whirlpool. **Rates:** Peak (Nov 25–Mem Day) $79–$95 S or D; $115–$130 ste. Extra person $12. Children under age 18 stay free. Min stay wknds. Lower rates off-season. Parking: Indoor, free. AE, MC, V.

≣≣ Shilo Inn
2963 Main St, PO Box 2179, 93546; tel 619/934-4500 or toll free 800/222-2244 in the US, 800/228-4489 in Canada; fax 619/934-7594. CA 203/Main St exit off US 395. New property, nicest in Mammoth Lakes. **Rooms:** 70 rms. CI 4pm/CO noon. Nonsmoking rms avail. All rooms are mini-suites, with attractive contemporary furniture. **Amenities:** 🛁 ⬛ ⬛ A/C, cable TV w/movies, refrig. All units w/minibars. Microwave in room. **Services:** ⬛ ⬛ **Facilities:** ⬛ ⬛ ⬛ ⬛ ⬛ Spa, sauna, steam rm, whirlpool, washer/dryer. Indoor pool. **Rates (CP):** Peak (Nov 15–Apr 16) $95–$130 S or D. Extra person $12. Children under age 12 stay free. Min stay special events. Lower rates off-season. Parking: Indoor, free. AE, CB, DC, DISC, MC, V.

≣≣ Sierra Nevada Inn
164 Old Mammoth Rd, PO Box 918, 93546; tel 619/934-2515 or toll free 800/824-5132; fax 619/934-7319. CA 203/Main St exit off US 395; left on Old Mammoth Rd. Big, cozy lobby with a ski-lodge atmosphere; decor is out of date. **Rooms:** 156 rms and stes. CI 3pm/CO 11am. Nonsmoking rms avail. "Suites" are actually connecting rooms. Family rooms with kitchen are rather cold. **Amenities:** 🛁 Cable TV, refrig. No A/C. Some units w/fireplaces. **Services:** ⬛ ⬛ Special services for groups. **Facilities:** ⬛ ⬛ ⬛ ⬛ 1 restaurant (bkfst and dinner only), 1 bar (w/entertainment), whirlpool, washer/dryer. Pool is small, but whirlpool is large enough for 35 people. **Rates:** Peak (Nov 15–Apr 15) $52–

$219 S or D; $109–$154 ste; $84–$109 effic. Extra person $6–$10. Children under age 12 stay free. Min stay special events. Lower rates off-season. Parking: Outdoor, free. AE, DC, DISC, MC, V.

LODGE

≡≡ Mammoth Mountain Inn
1 Minaret Rd, PO Box 353, 93546; tel 619/934-2581 or toll free 800/228-4947; fax 619/934-0701. CA 203/Main St exit off US 395. High-ceilinged lobby with nice carpeting. Good location for winter and summer sports. **Rooms:** 213 effic. CI 4pm/CO 11am. Nonsmoking rms avail. Rooms range from small and simple to huge suites that sleep 13. Some are attractive, some look like dorm rooms. **Amenities:** Cable TV w/movies, refrig. No A/C. Some units w/terraces. **Services:** ✗ Car-rental desk, social director, children's program, babysitting. Outdoor adventure-tour service planned. **Facilities:** 3 restaurants, 3 bars (1 w/entertainment), games rm, whirlpool, day-care ctr, playground, washer/dryer. Next to ski slope; guests can ski to lift. In summer, near biking, hiking, rock climbing. Flower shop, sport/gift shop on premises. **Rates:** Peak (Nov–Mar) $110–$210 S or D; $185–$425 effic. Lower rates off-season. Parking: Indoor/outdoor, free. AE, MC, V.

ATTRACTION

Mammoth Lakes Recreation Area
A 200,000-acre district of Inyo National Forest located off CA 203, the Mammoth Lakes Recreation Area offers fishing, hiking, boating, snowmobiling, and skiing. It includes many historic and archeological points of interest, and rangers lead interpretive tours in the summer. The visitors center (tel 619/924-5500) conducts evening programs throughout the year.

Dominated by the 11,053-foot peak of Mammoth Mountain, the area is especially centered around **Mammoth Mountain Ski Area** (tel 619/934-2571 or toll free 800/832-7320), with more than 3,500 skiable acres (200 acres with snowmaking facilities), 31 ski lifts, ski instruction, and rentals. Also cross-country trails; sledding and tobogganing; 3 day lodges; day-care facilities; shops, restaurants, and lounges. A scenic gondola ride to the summit operates year-round.

In the summer, **Mammoth Mountain Bike Park** (tel 619/934-0606) offers a variety of trails suited to all levels of expertise. Rentals and equipment shops. Self-guided trail maps available; guided tours. Hiking, picnicking. **Open:** Daily 24 hours. **Free**

Marina del Rey

See also Venice

One of the world's largest man–made marinas, Marina Del Rey is lined with private boats, some of which are the size of houses. This popular residential community is worth a detour for the excellent restaurants alone. **Information:** Marina del Rey Area Visitors & Convention Bureau, 4371 Glencoe #B14, Marina del Rey 90292 (tel 310/821-0555).

HOTELS

≡≡ The Marina Beach Marriott
4100 Admiralty Way, 90292; tel 310/301-3000; fax 310/301-6890. Spacious, charming hotel. **Rooms:** 372 rms and stes. Executive level. CI 3pm/CO noon. Nonsmoking rms avail. Rooms have simple, modern furnishings, and are scheduled to be redecorated. **Amenities:** A/C, cable TV w/movies, refrig, in-rm safe. All units w/terraces, 1 w/whirlpool. **Services:** ✗ VP babysitting. **Facilities:** 1 restaurant, 1 bar (w/entertainment). Free use of nearby health club; on-site fitness center. **Rates:** $125–$180 S or D; $175 ste. Children under age 18 stay free. Parking: Indoor, $8–$10/day. AE, DC, DISC, MC, V.

≡≡ Marina del Rey Hotel
13534 Bali Way, 90292; tel 310/301-1000 or toll free 800/882-4000, 800/862-7462 in CA; fax 310/301-8167. 5 mi N of Los Angeles Int'l Airport. Marina Fwy exit off I-405; left onto Lincoln Blvd; right onto Bali Way. The best hotel location in the area, overlooking the boat marina. The lobby is small and modern, and the hotel was renovated in 1996. **Rooms:** 160 rms and stes. CI 3pm/CO noon. Nonsmoking rms avail. Travertine marble bathrooms have separate dressing area. **Amenities:** A/C, refrig, dataport, voice mail. Some units w/terraces. **Services:** ✗ Car-rental desk. **Facilities:** 1 restaurant, 1 bar (w/entertainment). Free admission at nearby health clubs. Tennis also close by. New waterfront conference center. **Rates:** $110 S; $120 D. Extra person $20. Children under age 12 stay free. Parking: Outdoor, free. AE, CB, DC, DISC, EC, ER, JCB, MC, V.

≡≡ Marina International Hotel & Bungalows
4200 Admiralty Way, 90292; tel 310/301-2000 or toll free 800/529-2525; fax 310/301-6687. Charming wood-shingled buildings with patios and decks are arranged among well-tended gardens. Just across the highway from marina and several restaurants. Lobby is pretty and inviting. **Rooms:** 135 rms; 25 cottages/villas. CI 3pm/CO noon. Nonsmoking rms avail. Bright and airy rooms, tastefully decorated in pastels, with views of the marina or the gardens. **Amenities:** A/C, satel TV w/movies, voice mail. All units w/terraces. **Services:** ✗ Car-rental desk, babysitting. Complimentary newspapers in lobby; passes to nearby fitness center. **Facilities:** 1 restaurant, 1 bar, whirlpool, washer/dryer. **Rates:** $110–$280 S; $130–$280 D; $180–$280 cottage/villa. Extra person $20. Children under age 12 stay free. Parking: Indoor, free. AE, CB, DC, DISC, EC, ER, JCB, MC, V.

≣≣≣ Ritz-Carlton Marina del Rey
4375 Admiralty Way, 90292; tel 310/823-1700 or toll free 800/241-3333; fax 310/823-2403. I-90 W exit off I-405; continue on I-90, then exit on Mindanao. A waterside setting on the marina promenade, 15 minutes from the LA airport. Crystal chandeliers and oriental-style carpets create a clubby feel. **Rooms:** 306 rms and stes. Executive level. CI 3pm/CO noon. Nonsmoking rms avail. All rooms have marina vistas, English-style furnishings, and dark wooden armoires accented by Wedgwood and cream fabrics. Gray and white marble baths feature excellent counter space. **Amenities:** 🛎 🕭 🕯 A/C, refrig, dataport, voice mail, in-rm safe, bathrobes. All units w/minibars, all w/terraces. **Services:** ⦿ ⊶ VP 🚗 ⊠ 🛁 Twice-daily maid svce, car-rental desk, masseur, babysitting. Service can be slow. Complimentary shoeshine available. **Facilities:** 🗗 ▦ ⚓ 🖳 600 ⬛ & 3 restaurants, 1 bar, spa, sauna, steam rm, whirlpool, day-care ctr. Promenade is part of the 21-mile coastal path from Malibu to Manhattan Beach—a scenic (and flat) bike ride. Tennis pro on staff. **Rates:** $230–$345 S; $250–$365 D; $375–$550 ste. Children under age 18 stay free. Parking: Indoor/outdoor, $15/day. AE, CB, DC, DISC, EC, ER, JCB, MC, V.

RESTAURANTS 🍽️

★ Aunt Kizzy's Back Porch
In the Villa Marina Shopping Center, 4325 Glencove Ave; tel 310/578-1005. **Southern.** Large, barn-like building with a long cafeteria counter with country decor. One of the few southern-style restaurants in Los Angeles, it offers fried chicken, barbecued beef, and catfish, with buffet service at lunch and table service at dinner. **FYI:** Reservations not accepted. No liquor license. **Open:** Sun–Thurs 11am–10pm, Fri–Sat 11am–11pm. **Prices:** Main courses $8–$14. AE. 🍴 &

♥ ★ Cafe Del Rey
4451 Admiralty Way (at Bali Way); tel 310/823-6395. **Californian/Pacific Rim.** The crisply contemporary, sophisticated interior offers a dramatic view of the marina. Chef Katsuo Nagasawa provides cosmopolitan fare with many fish and seafood choices. The mood is LA casual at its friendliest and healthiest—this was the first local restaurant to go entirely "no smoking." Signature dishes include blue-crab cakes with mache, fried leeks, and pink grapefruit sauce; and spicy wild-boar sausage pizza with portobello mushrooms, shallots, jalapeños, and mozzarella di bufala. **FYI:** Reservations recommended. Piano. **Open:** Lunch Mon–Sat 11:30am–2:30pm; dinner Mon–Sat 5:30–10:30pm, Sun 5–10pm; brunch Sun 10:30am–2:30pm. **Prices:** Main courses $12–$28. AE, CB, DC, DISC, MC, V. ♥ ⛴ 🖼 🏔 VP &

Marshall
See Point Reyes Station

Mendocino
See also Albion, Elk, Little River

Mendocino is perched high above a point at the confluence of the Big River and the sea. Its 19th-century, weather-worn wooden buildings and shops sell locally produced art. Performing artists are showcased for two weeks in July during the Mendocino Music Festival.

HOTEL 🏨

≣≣≣ Mendocino Hotel and Garden Suites
45080 Main St, PO Box 587, 95460; tel 707/937-0511 or toll free 800/548-0513; fax 707/937-0513. Exit 128 W off US 101. An 1878 hotel decorated with Victorian-era antiques. There's a fun red Victorian plush bar on the ground floor, and loads of historic photos and memorabilia. **Rooms:** 26 rms and stes; 25 cottages/villas. CI 4pm/CO noon. Nonsmoking rms avail. Rooms in the main building are small and share baths. Those in the garden are nicer, with fine upholstery and private baths. **Amenities:** 🛎 Cable TV, bathrobes. No A/C. Some units w/terraces, some w/fireplaces. **Services:** ✗ 🛁 Masseur. **Facilities:** 30 & 2 restaurants, 1 bar (w/entertainment). Beach across street. **Rates:** Peak (Apr–Oct) $80–$225 S or D; $190–$225 ste; $190–$225 cottage/villa. Extra person $20. Children under age 12 stay free. Min stay wknds and special events. Lower rates off-season. Parking: Outdoor, free. AE, MC, V.

INNS

≣≣≣ Agate Cove Inn
11201 N Lansing St, PO Box 1150, 95460; tel 707/937-0551 or toll free 800/527-3111. 3 acres. A country decor with flowers and quilts—very cute, yet classy at the same time. Lovely seaside setting with beautiful gardens and the sound of waves. **Rooms:** 2 rms; 8 cottages/villas. CI 2pm/CO 11am. No smoking. All cottages are surrounded by gardens; those near the beach are quieter. Ask for Sunshine cottage, which is pretty and has a wood-burning fireplace. **Amenities:** 🕭 Cable TV w/movies, VCR. No A/C or phone. Some units w/terraces, all w/fireplaces. All rooms come with sherry decanters and spring water coolers. **Services:** Masseur. Breakfast in the lounge might include fresh-baked bread and eggs Benedict. **Facilities:** Guest lounge. Breakfast room has great ocean view. **Rates (BB):** Peak (July–Oct) $89–$170 S or D; $129–$250 cottage/villa. Extra person $25. Min stay wknds. Lower rates off-season. Parking: Outdoor, free. Midweek discounts. Add $10 for credit card charges. AE, MC, V.

≣≣≣ Joshua Grindle Inn
44800 Little Lake Rd, PO Box 647, 95460; tel 707/937-4143 or toll free 800/GRINDLE. At CA 1. 2 acres. This historic bed-and-breakfast was built in 1879 as the home of banker Joshua Grindle. The innkeepers also own an antique store and have furnished the rooms with period antiques. Main

house offers vista views of town and coast. Beautiful grounds and gardens. Unsuitable for children under 18. **Rooms:** 10 rms. CI 1pm/CO 11am. No smoking. Each room has a unique theme. **Amenities:** No A/C, phone, or TV. Some units w/fireplaces, 1 w/whirlpool. **Services:** Afternoon tea and wine/sherry served. Sherry and fruit in lounge throughout the day and evening. **Facilities:** Lawn games, guest lounge. **Rates (BB):** Peak (July–Oct) $95–$175 S or D. Extra person $30. Min stay wknds. Lower rates off-season. Parking: Outdoor, free. AE, MC, V.

≣≣ MacCallum House Inn
45020 Albion St, PO Box 206, 95460; tel 707/937-0289 or toll free 800/609-0492. Off CA 1. A bed-and-breakfast in a historic home built in 1882. Each guest room individually decorated with antiques owned by original Mendocino settlers. **Rooms:** 21 rms and effic (12 w/shared bath). CI 4pm/CO noon. No smoking. Rooms in main building share bath. Upstairs barn guest room has big stone fireplace and vista views over town to ocean. Other rooms located in refurbished water tower, greenhouse, and other buildings. Accommodations are a bit musty. **Amenities:** No A/C, phone, or TV. Some units w/terraces, some w/fireplaces. **Services:** Masseur. **Facilities:** 1 restaurant (dinner only), 1 bar, guest lounge. **Rates:** Peak (May–Dec) $90–$100 S or D w/shared bath, $105–$210 S or D w/private bath; $160 effic. Extra person $15. Min stay wknds. Lower rates off-season. Parking: Outdoor, free. MC, V.

≣≣≣ Whitegate Inn
499 Howard St, PO Box 150, 95460 (Downtown); tel 707/937-4892 or toll free 800/531-7282; fax 707/937-1131. Welcoming innkeeper, lots of antiques, fine meals, and a short distance from the center of the village. **Rooms:** 9 rms; 1 cottage/villa. CI 3pm/CO 11am. No smoking. **Amenities:** Cable TV, bathrobes. No A/C or phone. Some units w/terraces, some w/fireplaces. **Services:** Masseur, babysitting, afternoon tea and wine/sherry served. Lavish, full breakfast served with lovely table settings. Complimentary home-baked cookies, fruit, and honor bar for snacks and wine. Wed and Sat at 2:30pm a full English afternoon tea is open to the public. Fax service available. **Facilities:** Guest lounge. Fireplace in lounge. Pretty gazebo in garden. **Rates (BB):** Peak (July–Oct) $109–$189 S or D; $179 cottage/villa. Extra person $20. Children under age 5 stay free. Min stay wknds. Lower rates off-season. Parking: Outdoor, free. AE, DISC, MC, V.

LODGE

≣≣≣≣ Stanford Inn by the Sea—Big River Lodge
44850 Comptche-Ukiah Rd, PO Box 487, 95460; tel 707/937-5615 or toll free 800/331-8884; fax 707/937-0305. On CA 1. 10 acres. Beautiful grounds, with an indoor swimming pool in a tropical garden setting, extensive flower and organic vegetable gardens, a duck pond, and a llama breeding farm. The ivy-covered lodge is warm and cozy, and filled many antique furnishings. **Rooms:** 29 rms and stes; 4 cottages/villas. CI 4pm/CO noon. No smoking. Many of the rooms have four-poster beds, artwork from local artists, flower-lined decks overlooking the gardens, down comforters. **Amenities:** Cable TV w/movies, refrig, dataport, VCR, CD/tape player, bathrobes. No A/C. All units w/minibars, all w/terraces, all w/fireplaces. Complimentary wine and chocolate truffles in rooms. 500 videos available for rent. **Services:** Masseur, babysitting. **Facilities:** 1 restaurant (bkfst and dinner only), sauna, whirlpool. The beach and state park are within walking distance. Gift shop in lobby. Vegetarian restaurant. **Rates (BB):** $175–$225 S or D; $175–$485 ste; $200–$485 cottage/villa. Extra person $20. Children under age 2 stay free. Min stay peak and wknds. Parking: Indoor/outdoor, free. AE, CB, DC, DISC, ER, JCB, MC, V.

RESTAURANTS

♀ Cafe Beaujolais
961 Ukiah St; tel 707/937-5614. 10 mi S of Fort Bragg. **Californian/French.** In a charming old house surrounded by beautiful flower gardens, this is an especially nice spot for a hearty meal. The cafe has its own bakery and vegetable gardens. Menu changes daily, and may list asparagus and mussel soup with saffron, Thai crab cakes, or homemade tangerine ice. Weekends are often booked weeks or months in advance. Prix fixe country French menu for $20 available Tues–Thurs. **FYI:** Reservations recommended. Beer and wine only. **Open:** Daily 5:45–9pm. Closed Dec 1–26. **Prices:** Main courses $14–$22. No CC.

Mendocino Cafe
10451 Lansing St; tel 707/937-2422. **Eclectic.** Casual, comfortable dining room, with outdoor tables. Menu is Californian with an Asian twist, featuring hot Thai shrimp, chicken Oaxaca, and many light and healthy dishes. Kitchen will accommodate special dietary needs. **FYI:** Reservations not accepted. Children's menu. Beer and wine only. **Open:** Lunch Mon–Fri 11am–4pm, Sat–Sun 10am–4pm; dinner daily 5–9pm. **Prices:** Main courses $11–$15. MC, V.

ATTRACTIONS

Mendocino Headlands State Park
Tel 707/937-5804. Three miles of trails wind through the park, giving visitors panoramic views of sea arches and hidden grottoes. The headlands are home to many unique species of birds, including black oystercatchers. Behind the Mendocino Presbyterian Church on Main St is a trail leading to stairs that take visitors down to the beach. **Open:** Daily sunrise–sundown. **Free**

Kelley House Museum
45007 Albion St; tel 707/937-5791. Built in 1861 as the residence of William Henry Kelley and family, this house now contains an extensive library and archives of Mendocino area

history. Displays include an outstanding collection of 19th-century photographs of historic Mendocino buildings as well as family portraits. **Open:** Museum: June–Sept, daily 1–4pm; Oct–May, Fri–Mon 1–4pm. Library: Tues–Fri 9am–4pm. $

Russian Gulch State Park

Tel 707/937-5804. Located 2 miles north of town on the west side of CA 1. The rocky headlands and small, sandy beaches of this park are popular access points for ocean fishing and diving. There are several scenic hiking trails, some also designated for biking and horseback riding. One trail leads to a small but majestic waterfall, and weaves through coastal forests in moderate terrain. A picnic area lies on the headlands portion of the park near a scenic "blowhole," where visitors may enjoy views of misty ocean spray and magnificent sunsets.

The park contains a few fully developed campsites that can accommodate tents, trailers, or motor homes. A little-known horse camp with primitive facilities is located along the boundary of Jackson State Forest. Camping reservations highly recommended in summer; contact MISTIX (tel toll free 800/444-7275). **Open:** Daily 24 hours; may be closed in winter.

Montgomery Woods State Reserve

Tel 707/937-5804 (District Office). Remote and beautiful, this reserve is near the hot springs resort of Orrs Springs, on Comptche Rd. These 1,140 acres in the heart of the Coast Range offer picnicking and a 2-mile nature trail through small but impressive old-growth stands of redwoods. **Open:** Daily sunrise–sundown. **Free**

Menlo Park

Situated between south San Francisco Bay and the Santa Cruz Mountains, Menlo Park is sophisticated suburbia. The Allied Arts Guild may be one of the best places in the state to shop for ceramics, woodworks, and weavings. **Information:** Menlo Park Chamber of Commerce, 1100 Merrill St, Menlo Park 94025 (tel 415/325-2818).

HOTEL 🏨

≡≡≡≡ Stanford Park Hotel

100 El Camino Real, 94025; tel 415/322-1234 or toll free 800/368-2468; fax 415/322-0975. Embarcadero Rd W exit off US 101. Right on El Camino. With cedar shingles, copper-clad gables, and arched dormers, hotel resembles an over-size California cottage. English-accented lobby features a large brick fireplace. **Rooms:** 162 rms and stes. CI 2pm/CO noon. Nonsmoking rms avail. Good-size rooms feel comfortable and homey. All offer duvet comforters and oversize pillows. Bathrooms feature two sinks and red granite counters. Courtyard rooms are quietest. **Amenities:** 🗑 🗄 🍷 A/C, cable TV w/movies, refrig, dataport, voice mail. All units w/minibars, some w/terraces, some w/fireplaces. **Services:** 🔟 🆅🅿 🖾 ⤴

Twice-daily maid svce, babysitting. Complimentary morning coffee or tea in the lobby; fresh-baked cookies and coffee in the evening. Free shuttle within the Menlo Park/Palo Alto area. **Facilities:** 🗄 🛎 ⏏️130 ⅙ 1 restaurant, 1 bar, sauna, whirlpool. Surrounded by hedges and brick walls, the pool is absolutely lovely, except for the traffic drone. Small workout room with Lifecycle, Lifestep, and treadmill. Piano bar three nights a week. **Rates:** $190–$210 S; $205–$225 D; $230–$315 ste. Extra person $15. Children under age 15 stay free. Parking: Outdoor, free. AE, DC, DISC, JCB, MC, V.

RESTAURANTS 🍴

Dal Baffo

878 Santa Cruz Ave; tel 415/325-1588. Marsh Rd W exit off US 101. **Eclectic.** Dal Baffo (house of the moustache) brings Europe to Santa Cruz. Small dining alcoves, private dining room. Walls are upholstered in Laura Ashley fabrics and watercolors adorn the walls. The Italian dishes are recommended. Extra special is the veal-filled cannelloni with Italian herbs and mozzarella. **FYI:** Reservations recommended. **Open:** Lunch Mon–Fri 11:30am–2pm; dinner Mon–Thurs 5–10pm, Fri–Sat 5–10:30pm. **Prices:** Main courses $9–$24. AE, CB, DC, DISC, ER, MC, V. 💟 ⅙

Flea St Café

3607 Alameda de las Pulgas; tel 415/854-1226. Sand Hill Rd exit off CA 280. **Californian.** Chef/owner Jesse Cool is dedicated to organic, chemical-free food. All soup stocks are made from scratch, and salads use locally grown organic lettuces and greens. Many items are available as vegetarian entrees with tofu substitutions. Menu choices not extensive, but carefully chosen and creative. Recommended are the lamb with rosemary–Pinot noir sauce, and grilled duck with mango chutney. Pastry, biscuits, and breads are all made on-site. **FYI:** Reservations recommended. Beer and wine only. **Open:** Lunch Tues–Fri 11:30am–2pm; dinner Tues–Sun 5:30–9:30pm; brunch Sun 9am–2pm. **Prices:** Main courses $14–$21. AE, MC, V. ⚓

Late for the Train

150 Middlefield Rd; tel 415/321-6124. Willow Rd exit off US 101. **American.** Previously located near the commuter-train stop, this cottage-like restaurant with indoor greenery and rich wood surfaces serves gourmet breakfasts until 2:30pm. You'll find challah French toast, blintzes, whole-grain pancakes, and many omelette choices. Organic foods are featured on the seasonally adjusted menu, which offers dishes such as hot-fish salad with mild curry sauce, tabbouleh, smoked chicken with greens, and veggie burritos. Bottles of wines priced $5 above cost. **FYI:** Reservations accepted. Children's menu. Beer and wine only. **Open:** Breakfast Mon–Fri 7am–2:30pm; lunch daily 11am–2:30pm; dinner Tues–Sat 5–9:30pm; brunch Sat–Sun 8am–2:30pm. **Prices:** Main courses $12–$16. AE, MC, V. ⚓ 🍽 ⅙

ATTRACTION 🏛

Allied Arts Guild

75 Arbor Rd; tel 415/325-3259. Located on a small parcel of what was once the vast Rancho de las Pulgas, a land grant from the King of Spain, the Allied Arts Guild is now the site of a European-style crafts guild. Visitors can shop or browse through distinctive shops and studios amid a setting of Spanish colonial architecture and beautiful gardens. Dining at the Allied Arts Guild Restaurant (reservation required). **Open:** Mon–Sat 10am–5pm. Closed some hols. **Free**

Merced

Merced, the western gateway to Yosemite National Park and a center for tourism and farm trade, lies in a thriving cotton, fruit, and dairy region. **Information:** Merced Conference & Visitors Bureau, 690 W 16 St, Merced 95340 (tel 209/384-3333 or toll free 800/446-5353).

MOTELS 🏨

〓〓 Best Western Pine Cone Inn

1213 V St, 95340; tel 209/723-3711 or toll free 800/735-3711; fax 209/722-8551. A 30-year-old motel close to area attractions and restaurants. **Rooms:** 98 rms. Executive level. CI 2pm/CO noon. Nonsmoking rms avail. Ask for one of the more recently decorated rooms away from CA 99. **Amenities:** 🛏 📺 A/C, satel TV w/movies. **Services:** ✗ 🛄 🗘 🗘 **Facilities:** 🖼 ⌊25⌋ ⴷ 1 restaurant, 1 bar (w/entertainment). **Rates:** Peak (May–Aug) $52–$56 S; $57–$61 D. Extra person $5. Children under age 12 stay free. Lower rates off-season. Parking: Outdoor, free. Guests are given a 10% discount at the restaurant. AE, CB, DC, DISC, MC, V.

〓〓 Holiday Inn Express

730 Motel Dr, 95340; tel 209/383-0333 or toll free 800/337-0333; fax 209/383-0643. CA 140 E exit of CA 99. This well-maintained property, just off a major freeway, won Holiday Inn's Excellence Award as one of the top 10 inns in 1995. A favorite of business travelers. **Rooms:** 65 rms and stes. Executive level. CI 2pm/CO noon. Nonsmoking rms avail. Clean, comfortable rooms, well furnished but small. **Amenities:** 🛏 🛆 A/C, cable TV w/movies, dataport. **Services:** 🛄 🗘 🗘 Babysitting. Free local calls. **Facilities:** 🖼 🖥 ⴷ Sauna, whirlpool. Guests enjoy free use of Merced Sports Club, a full-service facility located five miles from motel. **Rates (CP):** Peak (May–Oct) $75 S or D; $105 ste. Extra person $6. Children under age 12 stay free. Lower rates off-season. Parking: Outdoor, free. AE, CB, DC, MC, V.

〓〓 Ramada Inn Merced

2000 E Childs Ave, 95340; tel 209/723-3121 or toll free 800/272-6232; fax 209/723-0127. Off CA 99. Comfortable facility with easy freeway access. **Rooms:** 110 rms and stes. Executive level. CI 2pm/CO noon. Nonsmoking rms avail. Spacious, with plenty of extra seating. **Amenities:** 🛏 🛆 📺

A/C, satel TV w/movies, refrig. Microwaves in many rooms. **Services:** ✗ 🚗 🛄 🗘 Babysitting. **Facilities:** 🖼 ⌊95⌋ ⴷ 1 restaurant, 1 bar. Free use of nearby health club. **Rates (BB):** Peak (May–Labor Day) $69 S; $71 D; $79 ste. Extra person $5. Children under age 18 stay free. Lower rates off-season. MAP rates avail. Parking: Outdoor, free. AE, CB, DC, DISC, EC, ER, JCB, MC, V.

ATTRACTION 🏛

Yosemite Wildlife Museum

2040 Yosemite Pkwy (CA 140); tel 209/383-1052. A variety of mounted birds and animals is displayed in natural dioramas depicting their natural habitat, providing up-close views not possible in the wild. **Open:** Mon–Sat 10am–5pm. $

Millbrae

See San Francisco Int'l Airport

Mill Valley

One of the most exclusive communities in the Bay Area, Mill Valley is tucked amid redwoods at the foot of Mount Tamalpais. While the downtown shops are decidedly high-end, the square has a small-town feel. **Information:** Mill Valley Chamber of Commerce, 85 Throckmorton Ave, PO Box 5123, Mill Valley 94942 (tel 415/388-9700).

HOTEL 🏨

〓〓 Holiday Inn Express

160 Shoreline Hwy, 94941; tel 415/332-5700 or toll free 800/258-3894; fax 415/331-1859. Stinson Beach exit off US 101. Centrally located between Sausalito and Mill Valley on the road to Stinson Beach. Good restaurant next door. **Rooms:** 100 rms and stes. CI 3pm/CO noon. Nonsmoking rms avail. Clean, comfortable, simple. Executive King rooms are slightly nicer. **Amenities:** 🛏 🛆 📺 🗘 A/C, refrig, dataport. Some units w/terraces. **Services:** 🛄 🗘 Masseur, babysitting. **Facilities:** 🖼 🚲 ⌊100⌋ ⴷ Free passes to nearby 24-hour health club. **Rates (CP):** Peak (May–Oct) $90–$105 S or D; $180–$270 ste. Extra person $10. Children under age 18 stay free. Min stay special events. Lower rates off-season. Parking: Outdoor, free. AE, DC, DISC, JCB, MC, V.

INN 🏨

〓〓〓〓 Mill Valley Inn

165 Throckmorton Ave, 94941; tel 415/389-6608 or toll free 800/595-2100; fax 415/389-5051. Old-world charm and contemporary whimsy come together in this stylish Mediterranean-style hotel. A block from downtown, and next to redwood-shaded Cascade Canyon Creek. Highly recommended. **Rooms:** 18 rms; 2 cottages/villas. CI 4pm/CO 11am. No smoking. Everything is top-of-the-line, from the Portuguese

linens to the cast-stone door frames. Many handcrafted furnishings. **Amenities:** 🛏 ⬚ 🍸 A/C, cable TV, dataport, bathrobes. All units w/terraces, some w/fireplaces. Many rooms have French windows opening onto small balconies; cabins and upper-story rooms feature fireplaces. Extra large bathtubs. **Services:** ✕ 🚗 🖼 🍹 Car-rental desk, masseur. Continental breakfast and afternoon tea served daily in the open-air espresso bar. Limited room service (pizzas and salads) by excellent Piazza D'Angelo restaurant nearby. **Facilities:** ♿ **Rates (CP):** $155 cottage/villa. Extra person $15. Children under age 4 stay free. Min stay wknds. Parking: Indoor, free. Spa packages available in association with several health centers in town. AE, DC, DISC, MC, V.

RESTAURANTS 🍽

★ Avenue Grill
44 E Blithedale Ave; tel 415/388-6003. **New American/Grill.** Lively and loud—an upscale diner, with chrome bar stools and an open-to-view kitchen. Great food comes in large portions, from steak with chipotle butter, garlic mashed potatoes, and broccoli to grilled Indonesian glazed chicken with vegetable-fried basmati rice. **FYI:** Reservations recommended. **Open:** Sun–Thurs 5:30–10pm, Fri–Sat 5:30–11pm. **Prices:** Main courses $9–$15. AE, MC, V. ♿

Buckeye Roadhouse
15 Shoreline Hwy; tel 415/331-2600. **Regional American.** An original, slick wayside tavern, with red-leather banquettes, a high-beamed ceiling, and a big stone fireplace. Prices are reasonable and portions huge. Selections from the grill include ahi tuna, and a skirt steak enlivened by roasted shallots and garlic-mashed potatoes. **FYI:** Reservations recommended. Children's menu. **Open:** Mon–Thurs 11:30am–10:30pm, Fri–Sat 11:30am–11pm, Sun 10:30am–10pm. **Prices:** Main courses $15–$25. CB, DC, DISC, MC, V. 🍴 🖼 VP ♿

Frantoio
152 Shoreline Hwy; tel 415/289-5777. Take Mill Valley, Stinson Beach exit W off US 101. **Italian.** The name is Italian for "olive crusher"—appropriate for this new restaurant, which actually has its own olive press. When the press is in action, you can watch the process through huge windows; the oil is served at the table with delicious olive bread. Salads are ultra-fresh; entrees might include pasta with red wine sausage or osso buco. For dessert, the homemade gelati are the specialties. Extensive Californian and Italian wine list, with a choice of 25 labels by the glass. **FYI:** Reservations recommended. **Open:** Lunch Mon–Sun 11:30am–3pm; dinner Sun–Thurs 5–10pm, Fri–Sat 5–11pm. **Prices:** Main courses $7–$15. AE, DISC, MC, V. VP ♿

★ Piazza D'Angelo
22 Miller Ave; tel 415/388-2000. **Italian.** A slice of Italy in an airy trattoria that's always packed. It's a favorite with members of the Italian diplomatic community. Dishes include unusual recipes such as potato and porcini gnocchi, or lamb

noisette with green peppercorns and balsamic vinegar. Ten good wines offered by the glass. **FYI:** Reservations recommended. **Open:** Mon–Thurs 11:30am–11pm, Fri–Sat 10:30am–11:30pm, Sun 10:30am–11pm. **Prices:** Main courses $10–$17. AE, DC, MC, V. VP ♿

ATTRACTIONS 📷

Mount Tamalpais State Park
801 Panoramic Hwy; tel 415/388-2070. A favorite retreat of San Franciscans, this park is located 6 miles west of Mill Valley on Panoramic Hwy. The 2,571-foot summit of "Mount Tam" is accessible to cars; bicyclists tackle the slope via the various fire roads up the mountain. The park's numerous trails make it very popular with hikers. Although primarily a day-use park, it offers campsites and several rustic cabins perched on a bluff overlooking the Pacific Ocean. Muir Woods National Monument (see below) is at the foot of the mountain, south of the park. **Open:** Daily; hours vary. **$$**

Muir Woods National Monument
CA 1; tel 415/388-2595 or 388-2596. Named in honor of naturalist John Muir, this 550-acre monument, covered with redwoods, is located at the south foot of Mount Tamalpais. The area is maintained much as it was before the arrival of white settlers in the mid-1800s. Picnicking, camping, fishing, and hunting are *not* permitted in the monument. There are 6 miles of trails, including a 1½-mile trail for the disabled. **Open:** Daily 8am–sundown. **Free**

Milpitas

Tucked into the hills adjacent to the Ventana Wilderness and Fort Hunter Liggett Military Reservation, Milpitas is a growing suburb of San Jose. **Information:** Milpitas Chamber of Commerce, 75 S Milpitas Blvd #205, Milpitas 95035 (tel 408/262-2613).

HOTELS 🏨

▰▰▰ Beverly Heritage Hotel
1820 Barber Lane, 95035; tel 408/943-9080 or toll free 800/443-4455; fax 408/432-8617. Montague W exit off I-880. Very attractive hotel with the ambience of an English club. The lobby is embellished with antique furniture, silver pots, potted palms, and classical music. Lovely gardens. Located in fairly quiet area. **Rooms:** 196 rms and stes. Executive level. CI 3pm/CO noon. Nonsmoking rms avail. Suites, which have skylights in living area instead of windows, are a bit odd. Nice furniture with quality upholstery. Bathrooms are in need of upgrading. Lots of seating in king room, with full-size sofa and bench at foot of bed. **Amenities:** 🛏 ⬚ 🍸 A/C, cable TV w/movies. Some units w/minibars, some w/whirlpools. **Services:** ✕ 🔑 🚗 🖼 🍹 Twice-daily maid svce, babysitting. **Facilities:** 🏋 🚴 🏊 🛎 💯 ♿ 2 restaurants, 1 bar (w/entertainment), whirlpool. New bar decorated

in English club–style. Lovely restaurant with outdoor seating. Greenhouse. **Rates (CP):** $175 S; $185 D; $190–$200 ste. Extra person $10. Parking: Outdoor, free. AE, DC, DISC, MC, V.

≣≣≣ Embassy Suites

901 Calaveras Blvd, 95035; tel 408/942-0400 or toll free 800/433-4600; fax 408/262-8604. Calaveras exit off I-680 W. Lobby has a tropical feel, with wicker furniture, terracotta tile floors, and green and peach carpets. Nine-story enclosed atrium has restaurant, waterfalls, and a rock garden. **Rooms:** 266 stes. CI 3pm/CO 1pm. Nonsmoking rms avail. All suites face the atrium, with good soundproofing, sealed windows, and kitchens. **Amenities:** 🛅 ⚱ 🖭 A/C, cable TV w/movies, refrig, voice mail. All units w/terraces. Wet bars; 2-line telephones. **Services:** ✕ 🚗 🖂 ⌂ Babysitting. **Facilities:** 🗗 🛏 400 🛁 1 restaurant, 1 bar, sauna, steam rm, whirlpool, washer/dryer. **Rates (BB):** $149–$169 ste. Extra person $10. Children under age 12 stay free. Parking: Outdoor, free. AE, DC, DISC, JCB, MC, V.

≣≣≣ Holiday Inn San Jose North

777 Bellew Dr, 95035; tel 408/321-9500 or toll free 800/524-2929; fax 408/321-9599. McCarthy Ave exit off CA 237; E on McCarthy. Built in 1986, but still fresh-looking. A nicely run small hotel. Quiet, surrounded by farmland. **Rooms:** 305 rms and stes. Executive level. CI 3pm/CO noon. Nonsmoking rms avail. Pleasant color scheme with coordinated upholstery, linens, and carpeting. **Amenities:** 🛅 ⚱ A/C, satel TV w/movies. **Services:** ✕ 🚗 🖂 ⌂ **Facilities:** 🗗 🛏 430 🛁 1 restaurant, 1 bar (w/entertainment), sauna, whirlpool, washer/dryer. Pool with view of hillsides and farmland. **Rates:** $150 S; $160 D; $180 ste. Extra person $10. Children under age 12 stay free. Parking: Outdoor, free. AE, CB, DC, DISC, JCB, MC, V.

≣≣≣ Sheraton San Jose Hotel

1801 Barber Lane, 95035; tel 408/943-0600 or toll free 800/943-0660; fax 408/943-0484. Montague Expwy exit off I-880; right on McCarthy; right on Barber Lane. Attractive hotel with a lobby overlooking the gardens, pool area, and rock quarry waterfall. **Rooms:** 229 rms and stes. Executive level. CI 3pm/CO noon. Nonsmoking rms avail. Some rooms have views of and access to garden area. **Amenities:** 🛅⚱🖭 A/C, cable TV w/movies, dataport, voice mail. Some units w/terraces. **Services:** ✕ 🕿 🚗 🖂 ⌂ Cocktail party on Wednesday nights. **Facilities:** 🗗 🛏 200 🖥 🛁 2 restaurants, 1 bar (w/entertainment), whirlpool. Spacious pool area with palms, shrubbery, and waterfall. Guests have access to South Bay Athletic Club for $5 per day. **Rates:** $160 S; $170 D; $180 ste. Extra person $15. Children under age 17 stay free. Parking: Indoor/outdoor, free. AE, CB, DC, DISC, EC, ER, JCB, MC, V.

Mission Viejo

HOTEL 🏨

≣ Fairfield Inn by Marriott

26328 Oso Pkwy, 92691; tel 714/582-7100 or toll free 800/950-1099; fax 714/582-3287. W of Oso Pkwy exit off I-5. Site is adjacent to freeway and quite noisy. **Rooms:** 147 rms. CI 3pm/CO noon. Nonsmoking rms avail. Clean and adequate. **Amenities:** 🛅 ⚱ A/C, cable TV w/movies. **Services:** 🚗 🖂 ⌂ **Facilities:** 🗗 40 🛁 **Rates:** $53–$60 S; $60 D. Extra person $5. Children under age 18 stay free. Parking: Outdoor, free. AE, DC, DISC, MC, V.

Modesto

Modesto received its 15 minutes of fame as the inspiration for the film *American Graffiti*, and the cruising tradition continues in mid-June every year with the Graffiti USA festival, in which all things '50s and car-related are celebrated. **Information:** Modesto Convention & Visitors Bureau, 1114 J St, PO Box 844, Modesto 95353 (tel 209/577-5757).

HOTELS 🏨

≣≣≣ Holiday Inn Modesto

1612 Sisk Rd, 95350; tel 209/521-1612 or toll free 800/334-2030; fax 209/527-7666. Briggsmore exit off CA 99, E to Sisk Rd, then left. This well-maintained property boasts many features, most notably the Holidome, an indoor recreation center. A great place for families. **Rooms:** 186 rms and stes. CI 3pm/CO noon. Nonsmoking rms avail. Nicely furnished. Because of noise from CA 99, ask for an interior room by the swimming pool. **Amenities:** 🛅 ⚱ 🖭 A/C, TV. **Services:** ✕ 🖂 ⌂ **Facilities:** 🗗 🛏 200 🛁 1 restaurant, 1 bar, games rm, sauna, whirlpool, washer/dryer. Table tennis, billards, putting green. **Rates:** $7485–$89 S; $8495–$99 D; $155 ste. Extra person $10. Children under age 18 stay free. Parking: Outdoor, free. AE, CB, DC, DISC, JCB, MC, V.

≣≣≣ Red Lion Hotel

1150 9th St, 95354; tel 209/526-6000 or toll free 800/547-8010; fax 209/526-6096. Off CA 99. A gorgeous hotel that is part of the city's convention center complex. Elegant lobby with marble floors, oak furnishings, and huge chandeliers. **Rooms:** 258 rms and stes. CI 3pm/CO 11am. Nonsmoking rms avail. Oversized rooms; city views. **Amenities:** 🛅 ⚱ 🖭 A/C, TV w/movies, dataport. Some units w/terraces, some w/whirlpools. Irons and ironing boards in all rooms. **Services:** ✕ 🕿 VP 🚗 🖂 ⌂ 🕮 Social director. **Facilities:** 🗗 🛏 3000 🖥 🛁 2 restaurants, 2 bars (1 w/entertainment), spa, sauna, steam rm, whirlpool, beauty salon. Lap pool; Club Max, a smartly styled nightclub with regular entertainment. **Rates:** $125–$150 S; $140–$165 D; $200–$500 ste. Extra person $15. Children under age 18 stay free. MAP rates avail. Parking: Indoor/outdoor, free. Frequent guest plan. AE, DC, DISC, MC, V.

MOTELS

≣≣≣ Best Western Mallard's Inn
1720 Sisk Rd, 95350; tel 209/577-3825 or toll free 800/528-1234; fax 209/577-1717. Briggsmore exit off CA 99; E to Sisk Rd; turn left. Tastefully decorated motel, with traditional decor of dark wood and brick, accented by artwork focusing on mallard ducks. **Rooms:** 126 rms. Executive level. CI 3pm/CO noon. Nonsmoking rms avail. Rooms are clean and pretty. Honeymoon suite available. Ask for a room away from CA 99. **Amenities:** 🛏 🛁 🖭 A/C, cable TV w/movies. Some units w/whirlpools. **Services:** ✕ 🚗 🛍 🍴 **Facilities:** 🐟 🏊 🛁 1 restaurant (bkfst and dinner only), whirlpool. Guest may use nearby fitness center for $5. Vintage Faire shopping mall is 1½ miles away. **Rates:** $79–$195 S or D. Extra person $5. Children under age 16 stay free. Parking: Outdoor, free. AE, DC, DISC, MC, V.

≣≣ Days Inn
1312 McHenry Ave, 95350; tel 209/527-1010 or toll free 800/843-6633; fax 209/527-2033. Briggsmore exit off CA 99. Recently renovated. **Rooms:** 103 rms. CI 2pm/CO noon. Nonsmoking rms avail. Rooms are spacious and nicely appointed, and most overlook the pool. Accommodations for corporate travelers are separate from family travelers. **Amenities:** 🛁 A/C, cable TV. No phone. Some units w/terraces. **Services:** 🛍 🍴 **Facilities:** 🐟 🛁 1 restaurant (lunch and dinner only), 1 bar, whirlpool, washer/dryer. Mexican restaurant on premises. Guests can use a nearby fitness center for $5. **Rates (CP):** $60–$65 S or D. Extra person $6. Children under age 12 stay free. Parking: Outdoor, free. AE, CB, DC, MC, V.

≣≣≣ Holiday Inn Express
4100 Salida Blvd, 95358; tel 209/543-9000 or toll free 800/768-3500; fax 209/543-9500. Pelandale exit off CA 99; W to Salida Blvd. New hotel with nice appointments and many of the features of much more expensive hotels. Easy access to CA 99, but some freeway noise in rooms. **Rooms:** 65 rms. CI 2pm/CO 11am. Nonsmoking rms avail. **Amenities:** 🛏 🛁 🖭 🍴 A/C, cable TV w/movies, refrig. **Services:** 🛍 🍴 Free local phone calls. **Facilities:** 🐟 🏋 🛁 Sauna, steam rm, whirlpool, washer/dryer. **Rates (CP):** $69–$75 S or D. Extra person $5. Children under age 12 stay free. Parking: Outdoor, free. AE, CB, DC, DISC, EC, JCB, MC, V.

≣≣ Ramada Inn Modesto
2001 W Orangeburg Ave, 95350; tel 209/521-9000 or toll free 800/228-2828; fax 209/521-6034. Briggsmore exit off CA 99. Spanish-style motel with easy freeway access; located two miles from Vintage Faire Shopping Mall. **Rooms:** 113 rms and stes. CI 3pm/CO noon. Nonsmoking rms avail. **Amenities:** 🛏 🛁 🖭 A/C, cable TV w/movies, refrig. Some units w/minibars. **Services:** 🛍 Car-rental desk. **Facilities:** 🐟

🛁 Whirlpool, washer/dryer. Cozy lounge area with fireplace and TV. Free privileges at nearby fitness center. **Rates (CP):** $64–$70 S; $74–$79 D; $95–$105 ste. Extra person $10. Parking: Outdoor, free. AE, CB, DC, DISC, MC, V.

≣ Vagabond Inn
1525 McHenry Ave, 95350; tel 209/521-6340 or toll free 800/522-1555; fax 209/575-2015. Briggsmore exit off CA 99. Exterior and landscaping need renovation. **Rooms:** 99 rms and stes. CI 2pm/CO noon. Nonsmoking rms avail. Basic and slightly worn. New mattresses, carpeting, and more planned by new owner, Imperial Hotels. **Amenities:** 🛏 🛁 🖭 A/C, cable TV w/movies. **Services:** 🛍 🍴 📶 Free local calls, free ironing. Complimentary incoming faxes and weekday newspapers. **Facilities:** 🐟 🛁 **Rates (CP):** $53 S; $56–$63 D; $60 ste. Extra person $5. Children under age 18 stay free. Parking: Outdoor, free. 10th night free; corporate and senior discounts. AE, DC, DISC, MC, V.

RESTAURANT 🍽

Mallard's
In McHenry Village, 1700 McHenry Ave; tel 209/522-3825. E of Briggsmore Ave exit off CA 99. **Californian.** A modern-day hunting lodge decorated with ducks, books, and rifles. Comfortable, warm, and intimate. Mesquite wood is used in grilling poultry, meat, and seafood. A selection of pasta dishes is also offered. **FYI:** Reservations recommended. Children's menu. **Open:** Mon–Thurs 11am–9pm, Fri–Sat 11am–10pm, Sun 10am–9pm. **Prices:** Main courses $7–$18. AE, CB, DC, DISC, MC, V. 🖤 🛁

ATTRACTIONS 🏛

McHenry Museum
1402 I St; tel 209/577-5366. Located one block southwest of the McHenry Mansion (see below), this museum deals with the history and development of the Modesto area. Exhibits include complete re-creations of a doctor's office and a general store; gold mining and firefighting equipment; and a collection of guns and cattle brands from Stanislaus County. Changing exhibit gallery with monthly presentations of pioneer artifacts or other historical subjects. Slide shows, movies; special events. **Open:** Tues–Sun noon–4pm. **Free**

McHenry Mansion
15th and I Sts; tel 209/577-5341. Built in 1883 by Robert McHenry, this Victorian Italianate-style residence has a truncated hip roof with six chimneys and an octagonal cupola capped by an iron cresting and a weather vane. The interior features period decor typically found in Modesto homes of the era. **Open:** Tues–Thurs and Sun 1–4pm, Fri noon–3pm. **Free**

Hershey Chocolate USA, Western Plant
120 S Sierra Ave, Oakdale; tel 209/848-8126. 10 mi N of Modesto. Thirty-minute guided tours of this facility examine

the chocolate-making process from cocoa bean to candy bar. The visitors center has exhibits and displays on the history of the company and of chocolate manufacture. Tours begin at the visitors center and are conducted from 8:30am–3pm. **Open:** Mon–Fri 8:30am–5pm. **Free**

Mojave National Preserve

For lodgings, see Baker, Barstow

To most Americans, the East Mojave is that vast, bleak, interminable stretch of desert to be crossed as quickly as possible while driving I-15 from Los Angeles to Las Vegas. Few realize that I-15 is the northern boundary of what desert rats have long considered the crown jewel of the California desert. Its 1.5 million acres include the world's largest Joshua tree forest; wild burros and grazing cattle; spectacular canyons and volcanic formations; lava flows; nationally honored scenic back roads and footpaths to historic mining sites; tabletop mesas, and a dozen mountain ranges. One of the preserve's most spectacular sights is the **Kelso Dunes,** the most extensive dune field in the West. The 45-square-mile formation of magnificently sculpted sand is famous for its "booming": visitors' footsteps cause mini-avalanches and the dunes make "sha-booming" sounds. Another preserve highlight is **Cima Dome,** a 75-square-mile chunk of uplifted volcanic rock; it has been called the most symmetrical natural dome in the United States. One of the most scenic drives is the **Wildhorse Canyon Road,** an 11-mile, horseshoe-shaped road which crosses wide-open country dotted with cholla, dramatic volcanic slopes, and flat-top mesas. Just west of the preserve is **Afton Canyon,** often called the "Grand Canyon of the Mojave."

The 140-mile-long **Mojave Road** offers extensive mountain biking opportunities. The major campgrounds are the Mid Hills Campground, Hole-in-the-Wall Campground, and Afton Canyon Campground. Accommodations can be found in the nearby towns of Baker and Barstow. For more information contact the California Desert Information Center (tel 619/256-8313).

Montecito

See Santa Barbara

Monterey

See also Carmel-by-the-Sea, Carmel Valley, Pacific Grove, Pebble Beach

Once a rowdy town of sailors and fishermen centered around legendary Cannery Row (chronicled in detail by John Steinbeck), Monterey is now a magnet for tourism, with restaurants, shops, and attractions lining its waterfront. **Information:** Monterey Peninsula Convention & Visitors Bureau, 380 Alvarado St, PO Box 1770, Monterey 93942 (tel 408/649-1770).

HOTELS 🏨

≣ Bay Park Hotel
1425 Munras Ave, 93940; tel 408/649-1020 or toll free 800/338-3564; fax 408/373-4258. Off CA 1 near Del Monte Shopping Center. Located next to a service station, functional, and fine for a pit stop. **Rooms:** 80 rms. CI 2pm/CO noon. Nonsmoking rms avail. **Amenities:** 🛏 ⚙ 📺 TV. No A/C. Some units w/terraces. **Services:** ✕ ⤴ ⬤ **Facilities:** 🔥 🏊 ⚿ 1 restaurant, 1 bar (w/entertainment), whirlpool. **Rates:** Peak (June–Sept) $59–$145 S or D. Extra person $10. Children under age 18 stay free. Min stay special events. Lower rates off-season. AP rates avail. Parking: Indoor/outdoor, free. AE, CB, DC, DISC, MC, V.

≣≣ Best Western Monterey Inn
825 Abrego St, 93940; tel 408/373-5345 or toll free 800/528-1234; fax 408/373-3246. CA 156 W exit off CA 1. Conveniently located, close to downtown and restaurants. **Rooms:** 80 rms. CI 2pm/CO 11am. Nonsmoking rms avail. Very clean and nice. **Amenities:** 🛏 ⚙ 📺 Cable TV, refrig. No A/C. Some units w/terraces, some w/fireplaces. **Services:** ⤴ **Facilities:** 🔥 🏊 ⚿ Whirlpool. Small lending library. **Rates (CP):** Peak (June–Oct) $93–$108 S; $108–$128 D. Extra person $10. Min stay peak and special events. Lower rates off-season. Parking: Indoor/outdoor, free. AE, DISC, MC, V.

≣≣≣ Best Western Victorian Inn
487 Foam St, 93940; tel 408/373-8000 or toll free 800/232-4141; fax 408/373-4815. Fisherman's Wharf exit off CA 1; exit between Hoffman and McClellan. Wonderful gardens make this one of the prettiest properties in the area. The lobby features oriental rugs, Victorian-style sofas, and a fireplace. **Rooms:** 68 rms. CI 4pm/CO noon. Nonsmoking rms avail. Beautifully decorated, furnished in natural fabrics. **Amenities:** 🛏 ⚙ 📺 Cable TV, refrig, VCR, bathrobes. No A/C. All units w/minibars, some w/terraces, all w/fireplaces. **Services:** 📠 ⤴ ⬤ Babysitting. Wine and cheese from 4–6pm. **Facilities:** 🏊 ⚿ Whirlpool. **Rates (CP):** Peak (June–Oct) $99–$289 S or D. Extra person $10. Children under age 13 stay free. Min stay peak and special events. Lower rates off-season. Parking: Indoor, free. AE, CB, DC, DISC, ER, JCB, MC, V.

≣≣ **Casa Munras Garden Hotel**
700 Munras Ave, PO Box 1351, 93942; tel 408/375-2411 or toll free 800/222-2558, 800/222-2446 in CA; fax 408/375-1365. Monterey/Muras Ave exit off CA 1. This 1824 inn is an enduring symbol of hospitality. The location is deceptive; inside, the grounds are nice and well maintained, with lovely gardens around the pool. Popular with bus tours. **Rooms:** 131 rms and stes. CI 3pm/CO noon. Nonsmoking rms avail. **Amenities:** 🛅 ⚗ Cable TV. No A/C. Some units w/terraces, some w/fireplaces. **Services:** 🖼 ⌛ Babysitting. **Facilities:** 🛅 🏊 ⚓ 1 restaurant, 1 bar (w/entertainment). Library. **Rates:** Peak (July–Sept) $75–$115 S; $85–$125 D; $175–$225 ste. Extra person $15. Children under age 12 stay free. Min stay peak and special events. Lower rates off-season. AP and MAP rates avail. Parking: Outdoor, free. AE, CB, DC, JCB, MC, V.

≣≣≣ **DoubleTree Hotel at Fisherman's Wharf**
2 Portola Plaza, 93940 (Downtown); tel 408/649-4511 or toll free 800/222-TREE; fax 408/649-4115. Del Monte exit off CA 1. A well-maintained property with a pleasant atrium-style lobby in the heart of downtown Monterey. **Rooms:** 373 rms and stes. CI 3pm/CO noon. Nonsmoking rms avail. Nicely furnished rooms; some have views of the water. **Amenities:** 🛅 ⚗ Cable TV w/movies. No A/C. Some units w/terraces. **Services:** ✗ 🖼 VP 🖼 ⌛ Car-rental desk, babysitting. **Facilities:** 🛅 🚲 ⚓ 🖼 🖼 🖼 ⚓ 1 restaurant, 2 bars (1 w/entertainment), lawn games, whirlpool. Brasstree Lounge offers live entertainment several nights a week. Nintendo machines. **Rates:** Peak (July–Oct) $159–$225 S or D; $225 ste. Extra person $20. Children under age 18 stay free. Min stay wknds and special events. Lower rates off-season. Parking: Indoor/outdoor, $9–$11/day. AE, DC, DISC, MC, V.

≣≣≣ **Holiday Inn Resort**
1000 Aguajito Rd, 93940; tel 408/373-6141 or toll free 800/234-5697; fax 408/655-8608. Pleasant property located in Monterey's "sun belt"—usually sunny in summer, while surrounding areas are covered with fog. Gardeners take great pride in the landscaping. **Rooms:** 204 rms and stes. Executive level. CI 4pm/CO 1pm. Nonsmoking rms avail. Accommodations have upgraded carpeting, drapes, and wallpaper. **Amenities:** 🛅 ⚗ 🖼 Cable TV w/movies, dataport, voice mail, in-rm safe. No A/C. All units w/terraces. **Services:** ✗ 🖼 ⌛ Car-rental desk. **Facilities:** 🛅 ⚓2 🖼 ⚓ 1 restaurant, 1 bar, lawn games, sauna, whirlpool. **Rates:** Peak (Apr–Oct) $105–$160 S or D; $175–$220 ste. Extra person $15. Children under age 18 stay free. Min stay peak, wknds, and special events. Lower rates off-season. Parking: Indoor, free. Parking: Outdoor, free. AE, MC, V.

≣≣ **Hotel Pacific**
300 Pacific St, 93940; tel 408/373-5700 or toll free 800/554-5542; fax 408/373-6921. Designed like an adobe enclave and secluded from the bustle of downtown. Very attractive lobby, decorated in a southwestern motif, as is the rest of the hotel. Minimal grounds. Located near the Monterey Confer-

ence Center. **Rooms:** 105 stes. CI 4pm/CO noon. Nonsmoking rms avail. Decorated in light tones of taupe in a southwestern style. **Amenities:** 🛅 ⚗ 🖼 🖼 Cable TV, refrig, voice mail. No A/C. All units w/terraces, all w/fireplaces. **Services:** ✗ 🖼 🖼 ⌛ Afternoon tea. **Facilities:** 🖼 ⚓ Whirlpool. **Rates (CP):** Peak (May–Oct) $169–$309 ste. Extra person $10. Children under age 12 stay free. Min stay wknds and special events. Lower rates off-season. Parking: Indoor/outdoor, free. AE, CB, DC, DISC, JCB, MC, V.

≣≣≣ **Monterey Bay Inn**
242 Cannery Row, 93940; tel 408/373-6242 or toll free 800/424-6242; fax 408/373-7603. Del Monte exit off CA 1. One of the best places on Cannery Row. **Rooms:** 47 rms. CI 4pm/CO noon. Nonsmoking rms avail. Spectacular ocean views. Rooms are tastefully decorated with wicker furniture and upholstery in sunset hues. **Amenities:** 🛅 ⚗ 🖼 Cable TV w/movies, refrig, VCR, bathrobes. No A/C. All units w/minibars, all w/terraces. **Services:** ✗ 🖼 ⌛ Staff will arrange kayak rentals. **Facilities:** 🖼 🖼 ⚓ 1 beach (bay), spa, sauna, whirlpool. **Rates (CP):** Peak (June–Nov) $119–$329 S or D. Extra person $10. Children under age 12 stay free. Min stay peak and special events. Lower rates off-season. Parking: Indoor, free. Honeymoon and aquarium packages. AE, CB, DC, DISC, ER, JCB, MC, V.

≣≣≣ **Monterey Marriott**
350 Calle Principal, 93940 (Downtown); tel 408/649-4234 or toll free 800/228-9290; fax 408/375-4313. Del Monte/Pacific Grove exit off CA 1 S; Aguajito exit off CA 1 N. A clean, well-maintained hotel close to Monterey's many attractions. Ideal for meetings and conferences; adjacent to the Monterey Conference Center. **Rooms:** 341 rms and stes. CI 3pm/CO noon. Nonsmoking rms avail. **Amenities:** 🛅 ⚗ 🖼 A/C, cable TV w/movies, refrig, CD/tape player, voice mail. Some units w/terraces. **Services:** ✗ 🖼 VP 🖼 ⌛ 🖼 Masseur, babysitting. **Facilities:** 🖼 🖼 🖼 ⚓ 3 restaurants, 2 bars, whirlpool, beauty salon. **Rates:** Peak (Apr–Oct) $189–$229 S or D; $250–$600 ste. Extra person $15. Children under age 18 stay free. Min stay special events. Lower rates off-season. Parking: Indoor/outdoor, $10/day. AE, CB, DC, DISC, ER, JCB, MC, V.

≣≣≣ **Monterey Plaza Hotel**
400 Cannery Row, 93940; tel 408/646-1700 or toll free 800/631-1339, 800/334-3999 in CA; fax 408/646-0285. Luxury hotel on Cannery Row has many rooms with lovely views of Monterey Bay. **Rooms:** 285 rms and stes. CI 4pm/CO noon. Nonsmoking rms avail. Rooms are large and comfortable. **Amenities:** 🛅 ⚗ 🖼 🖼 Cable TV w/movies, refrig, dataport, voice mail, bathrobes. No A/C. All units w/minibars, some w/terraces. **Services:** ✗ 🖼 VP 🖼 ⌛ Masseur, babysitting. **Facilities:** 🖼 🖼 ⚓ 1 restaurant, 1 bar (w/entertainment), 1 beach (ocean). **Rates:** Peak (June–Nov) $140–$270 S or D; $275–$705 ste. Extra person $20. Children under age 12

stay free. Min stay wknds and special events. Lower rates off-season. Parking: Indoor, $10/day. AE, CB, DC, DISC, ER, MC, V.

☰☰☰ Spindrift Inn

652 Cannery Row, 93940; tel 408/646-8900 or toll free 800/841-1879; fax 408/646-4532. This romantic beachfront inn has oriental carpets, tiled floors, distinctive antiques, and original art. The lobby, with its fireplace, conveys a lovely ambience. **Rooms:** 41 rms. CI 4pm/CO noon. Comfortable and clean; however, some are vulnerable to street noise. **Amenities:** 🛅 ⬛ ⌇ Cable TV w/movies, refrig, VCR, bathrobes. No A/C. Some units w/minibars, some w/terraces, all w/fireplaces. **Services:** ⓋⓅ ⬜ ⌒ Twice-daily maid svce. Afternoon wine and cheese. Continental breakfast can be delivered to guest rooms. **Facilities:** 🔲 ⅃ 1 bar, 1 beach (bay). **Rates (CP):** Peak (June–Oct) $189–$389 S or D. Extra person $10. Min stay peak and special events. Lower rates off-season. Parking: Indoor, $6/day. AE, CB, DC, DISC, JCB, MC, V.

MOTELS

☰☰☰ Best Western De Anza Inn

2141 N Fremont St, 93940; tel 408/646-8300 or toll free 800/858-8775; fax 408/646-8130. CA 218 exit off CA 1. Designed by a well-known architect, this is the best bet in this part of town. Quiet and secluded. **Rooms:** 43 rms and stes. CI 3pm/CO 11am. Nonsmoking rms avail. **Amenities:** 🛅 ⚓ ⬛ Cable TV w/movies, refrig, dataport. No A/C. **Services:** ⬜ ⌒ Babysitting. **Facilities:** 🔲 ⏲ ⅃ Whirlpool. **Rates (CP):** Peak (July–Sept) $55 S or D; $99–$200 ste. Extra person $8. Children under age 12 stay free. Min stay peak, wknds, and special events. Lower rates off-season. Parking: Outdoor, free. AE, CB, DC, DISC, MC, V.

☰☰ Best Western Park Crest Motel

1100 Munras Ave, 93940; tel 408/372-4576 or toll free 800/528-1236; fax 408/372-2317. CA 156 W exit off CA 1. Conveniently located near the heart of Monterey. Set amid flowers, pines, and palm trees. **Rooms:** 53 rms and stes. CI 2pm/CO 11am. No smoking. Nonsmoking rms avail. **Amenities:** 🛅 ⚓ Cable TV w/movies, VCR. No A/C. **Services:** ⌒ **Facilities:** 🔲 Whirlpool. **Rates (CP):** Peak (June–Oct) $75–$130 S; $95–$159 D; $109–$179 ste. Extra person $10. Children under age 12 stay free. Min stay wknds and special events. Lower rates off-season. Parking: Outdoor, free. AE, CB, DC, DISC, JCB, MC, V.

☰☰☰ Mariposa Inn

1386 Munras Ave, 93940; tel 408/649-1414 or toll free 800/824-2295; fax 408/649-5308. Munras Ave exit off CA 1. Excellent location across from the Del Monte shopping center; set back off the street for quiet and privacy. **Rooms:** 51 rms and stes. CI 3pm/CO noon. Nonsmoking rms avail. Tastefully decorated rooms. **Amenities:** 🛅 ⚓ ⬛ Cable TV, refrig. No A/C. Some units w/terraces, some w/fireplaces, some w/whirlpools. **Services:** ⌒ Babysitting. **Facilities:** 🔲 ⅃

Whirlpool. Golf at nearby Rancho Canada or Laguna Seca golf clubs. **Rates (CP):** Peak (June 12–Sept 7) $88–$98 S; $98–$118 D; $110–$125 ste. Extra person $10. Children under age 18 stay free. Min stay special events. Lower rates off-season. Parking: Outdoor, free. Golf and aquarium packages. AE, CB, DC, DISC, MC, V.

☰ Motel 6

2124 N Fremont St, 93940; tel 408/646-8585; fax 408/372-7429. Casa verde exit off CA 1 S; Seaside/Fremont St exit off CA 1 N. Basic economy hotel. Located close to the Monterey County Fairgrounds, it's almost always filled to capacity. Clean, convenient, safe. **Rooms:** 52 rms. CI 2pm/CO noon. Nonsmoking rms avail. **Amenities:** 🛅 Cable TV w/movies. No A/C. **Services:** ⬜ ⌒ ⟳ Friendly managers provide guests with information about Monterey Peninsula attractions. **Facilities:** 🔲 ⅃ **Rates:** Peak (Jan–Sept) $39–$50 S or D. Children under age 17 stay free. Lower rates off-season. Parking: Outdoor, free. AE, CB, DISC, MC, V.

☰☰ Sand Dollar Inn

755 Abrego St, 93940; tel 408/372-7551 or toll free 800/982-1986; fax 408/372-0916. CA 68 W exit off CA 1. In the heart of the city, close to downtown and restaurants. **Rooms:** 63 rms and stes. CI 3pm/CO noon. Nonsmoking rms avail. Rooms are tasteful and clean. **Amenities:** 🛅 ⚓ ⬛ Cable TV w/movies, refrig. No A/C. Some units w/terraces, some w/fireplaces. **Services:** ⬜ ⌒ Babysitting. **Facilities:** 🔲 ⅃ 1 restaurant, 1 bar (w/entertainment), whirlpool, washer/dryer. **Rates:** Peak (June–Oct) $64–$74 S; $74–$84 D; $94 ste. Extra person $5. Children under age 13 stay free. Min stay special events. Lower rates off-season. Parking: Outdoor, free. AE, MC, V.

☰ Way Station

1200 Olmsted Rd, 93940; tel 408/372-2945; fax 408/375-6267. Off CA 68. The brown-shake buildings are not attractive, but the location is convenient to the airport. **Rooms:** 46 rms. CI 3pm/CO 11am. Nonsmoking rms avail. Large and clean, done in shades of brown and tan. **Amenities:** 🛅 ⚓ Cable TV. No A/C. Some units w/terraces, some w/fireplaces. **Facilities:** 1 restaurant. **Rates (CP):** $69–$129 S; $79–$129 D. Extra person $10. Children under age 12 stay free. Min stay wknds and special events. Parking: Outdoor, free. AE, CB, DC, DISC, EC, ER, JCB, MC, V.

INN

☰☰☰☰ Old Monterey Inn

500 Martin St, 93940; tel 408/375-8284 or toll free 800/350-2344; fax 408/375-6730. Mariras exit off CA 1. Built in 1929, this Tudor-style half-timbered manse is set on 1¼ acres of parklike grounds with over 100 venerable trees. Throughout the house there are antiques and family heirlooms, as well as live orchids. **Rooms:** 9 rms and stes; 1 cottage/villa. CI 3pm/CO noon. No smoking. Each has its own personality. The Ashford Suite has a fireplace and a private sitting room. The Library has a private sun deck. **Amenities:** ⚓ ⌇ Bath-

robes. No A/C, phone, or TV. Some units w/terraces, 1 w/fireplace, 1 w/whirlpool. **Services:** Twice-daily maid svce, masseur, afternoon tea and wine/sherry served. Full breakfast, in your room, the dining room, or the garden, might include a soufflé or berry-pear pancakes, plus fresh-baked scones and crumpets with homemade jam. Fruit and sherry available in the lounge round the clock. The owners will also lend you beach blankets and picnic baskets. **Facilities:** Gardens are lovingly tended. Brick and stone paths wind to the rose garden, or to hammocks strung between the pines. **Rates (BB):** $170–$240 S or D; $240 ste; $240 cottage/villa. Extra person $50. Min stay wknds and special events. MC, V.

RESORT

≡≡≡ Hyatt Regency Monterey

1 Old Golf Course Rd, 93940; tel 408/372-1234 or toll free 800/824-2196; fax 408/375-9428. 26 acres. Adjacent to the Del Monte Golf Course. Well-maintained hotel. **Rooms:** 583 rms and stes. Executive level. CI 3pm/CO noon. Nonsmoking rms avail. Large, comfortable, but typical, in shades of green and beige with modern furniture. All rooms have live plants. **Amenities:** 🛎 ⚲ 🗇 Dataport, voice mail. No A/C. Some units w/minibars, some w/terraces, some w/fireplaces. **Services:** ✕ 🔑 🚗 🛍 🗃 👟 Masseur, children's program, babysitting. **Facilities:** 🔧 🚴 ▶18 🎿 🛶4 🥎 🏓 1000 💻 ♿ 2 restaurants, 1 bar, lawn games, whirlpool, beauty salon, playground. **Rates:** Peak (Aug–Oct) $185–$200 S; $200 D; $275–$1,200 ste. Extra person $25. Children under age 18 stay free. Min stay special events. Lower rates off-season. MAP rates avail. Parking: Indoor/outdoor, free. AE, DISC, MC, V.

RESTAURANTS 🍴

Abalonetti Seafood Trattoria

57 Fisherman's Wharf; tel 408/373-1851. **Seafood.** Dining room features bay views, marble-topped tables, and hardwood floors. Menu offers a variety of fresh fish dishes, including local calamari. "Marty's Special" has been a favorite entree for 40 years—it consists of fried calamari and eggplant in marinara sauce. There's also a wood-burning pizza oven. **FYI:** Reservations recommended. Children's menu. **Open:** Peak (July–Aug) daily 11am–9pm. Closed Dec 7–14. **Prices:** Main courses $11–$41. AE, CB, DC, DISC, MC, V. 🖼 ♿

The Clock Garden Restaurant

565 Abrego St; tel 408/375-6100. **Regional American.** This is a nice place for a leisurely meal: a bright, airy space with high beamed ceilings, a glassed atrium, and clocks galore. There's also a charming patio. Specialties include barbecue ribs, veal, prime ribs and fresh seafood. **FYI:** Reservations recommended. Jazz. Children's menu. **Open:** Peak (June–Sept) lunch Mon–Sat 11am–3:30pm; dinner Mon–Sat 5–10pm; brunch Sun 10am–3pm. **Prices:** Main courses $9–$17. AE, DISC, MC, V. 🛥 🖼 💟

Cove Restaurant

46 Fisherman's Wharf; tel 408/373-6969. **Regional American/Seafood.** A good place for early risers to enjoy breakfast. Very casual restaurant with captain's chairs, vinyl tablecloths, and a view of the bay. The fish and chips is made with Monterey rock cod. Seafood entrees, steaks, pasta. **FYI:** Reservations recommended. **Open:** Breakfast daily 6:30–11:30am; lunch daily 11:30am–4:30pm; dinner daily 4:30–9:30pm. **Prices:** Main courses $7–$16. MC, V. 🖼

✸ Domenico's

50 Fisherman's Wharf; tel 408/372-3655. **Italian/Seafood.** Although the bar is noisy, the restaurant is quiet and tastefully decorated in blue and white, a color scheme that befits its harbor location. Much attention is paid to the presentation of such dishes as pasta Capri with tomatoes, shallots, olives, and baby shrimp; and angel-hair pasta with prawns. **FYI:** Reservations recommended. Children's menu. **Open:** Lunch daily 11am–3pm; dinner daily 4–10pm. **Prices:** Main courses $13–$40. AE, CB, DC, DISC, MC, V. 🖼

✸ The Duck Club

400 Cannery Row; tel 408/646-1706. **Continental.** An elegant atmosphere and beautiful ocean views create a unique ambience. Among the specialties is Steinbeck duck, prepared in a wood-burning oven and topped with Valencia orange sauce. **FYI:** Reservations recommended. Jazz/piano. **Open:** Breakfast daily 6:30–10:30am; lunch daily 11:30am–2pm; dinner daily 5:30–10pm. **Prices:** Main courses $14–$20. AE, CB, DC, DISC, ER, MC, V. ❤

The Fish Hopper and Old Fisherman's Grotto

700 Cannery Row; tel 408/372-8543. **Seafood.** Jutting pier-like out over the water, this new addition to Cannery Row boasts a beautiful 180-degree panoramic view. Owned by the Shake family (whose fishing boats literally provide the catch of the day), this onetime sardine cannery has been decorated by celebrated local artist Robert Lynn Nelson. The oyster bar features jumbo prawns and cracked crab. Landlubbers can order steaks. **FYI:** Reservations accepted. Children's menu. **Open:** Peak (Mar–Oct) lunch daily 11am–4pm; dinner daily 5–10pm. **Prices:** Main courses $13–$25; prix fixe $20–$29. AE, MC, V. ❤ 🖼 🎀 💟 ♿

♣ Fresh Cream

99 Pacific St (Monterey Harbor); tel 408/375-9798. **French.** Intimate, elegant, yet unpretentious restaurant offers a lovely view in addition to fine food. Starters include lobster ravioli napped with butter, and black and gold caviar. A featured entree is veal with wild mushrooms, roasted shallots, and white-wine butter sauce. For dessert, the flourless dark chocolate torte with vanilla-bean ice cream on a raspberry coulis is recommended. **FYI:** Reservations recommended. **Open:** Daily 6–10pm. **Prices:** Main courses $21–$30. AE, CB, DC, DISC, MC, V. ❤

Monterey Joe's Ristorante
2149 N Fremont; tel 408/655-3355. **Italian.** Monterey Joe's is worth a drive across town, with a charming ambience, fine food, and an excellent wine list with nearly 100 choices. Lots of fresh fish, pasta, hearty soups, and pizza are offered. **FYI:** Reservations accepted. Children's menu. **Open:** Mon–Thurs 11am–10pm, Fri 11am–11pm, Sat 4–11pm, Sun 10am–10pm. **Prices:** Main courses $8–$17. AE, DISC, MC, V. ⅁

Montrio
414 Calle Principal; tel 408/648-8880. **Regional American/French.** Brick, plaster, and concrete walls are accented by copper and iron at this attractive restaurant with a Mediterranean decor, the latest venture by the owners of the popular Rio Grill. Daily menu specialties include fish and pastas, as well as rotisserie items such as duck. **FYI:** Reservations recommended. Children's menu. **Open:** Lunch Mon–Sat 11:30am–3pm; dinner Mon–Thurs 5:30–10pm, Fri–Sat 5:30–11pm, Sun 5–10pm. **Prices:** Main courses $14–$20. AE, DISC, MC, V. ♥ ⅁

♥ Sardine Factory
701 Wave St; tel 408/373-3775. **Continental/Seafood.** Located in the former sardine processing district near Cannery Row. Plush, tasteful dining room is decorated with vintage photos of the cannery era, along with the works of local artists. Hallmarks of the menu are cioppino and fresh abalone bisque. Wine list with over 900 offerings. **FYI:** Reservations recommended. Children's menu. **Open:** Mon–Thurs 5–10:30pm, Fri–Sat 5–11pm, Sun 2–10pm. Closed Christmas week. **Prices:** Main courses $12–$40. AE, DISC, MC, V. ♥ ▪ ♥ VP

★ The Whaler Steakhouse & Fresh Seafood Grill
635 Cass St; tel 408/373-1933. **Seafood/Steak.** A local favorite for 30 years. Dimly lit steak-house atmosphere with leather chairs. Features slow-roasted prime rib, steaks, and fresh seafood. **FYI:** Reservations recommended. Children's menu. **Open:** Lunch Tues–Fri 11:30am–2:30pm; dinner Tues–Thurs 5–9pm, Fri–Sat 5–10pm. **Prices:** Main courses $11–$20; prix fixe $12–$14. AE, MC, V.

★ Whaling Station Inn
763 Wave St (Cannery Row); tel 408/373-3778. Between Prescott and Irving Aves. **New American.** Dark wood, Leroy Neiman lithographs, and almost century-old French posters add charm to this old-fashioned dinner house. Specials include pasta, steaks, and seafood. **FYI:** Reservations recommended. Children's menu. **Open:** Daily 5pm–close. **Prices:** Main courses $15–$28; prix fixe $28. AE, DC, MC, V. ♥ ▲ VP ⅁

Wharfside Restaurant and Lounge
60 Fisherman's Wharf; tel 408/375-3956. **Seafood.** Very casual restaurant overlooking Monterey Bay and marina. Decor's nothing special, but menu offers an array of fresh fish dishes, including award-winning clam chowder, cioppino, and bouillabaisse. Among various pasta dishes, homemade ravioli is a specialty. Desserts made fresh daily. **FYI:** Reservations accepted. Children's menu. **Open:** Daily 11am–10pm. Closed Christmas week. **Prices:** Main courses $8–$40. AE, DISC, MC, V. ▲ ▪ ♥ ⅁

ATTRACTIONS

Cannery Row
On Monterey Bay between David and Drake Aves; tel 408/649-6690. Author John Steinbeck immortalized Cannery Row in his 1945 book of the same name. But by 1948, overfishing, changing currents, and pollution contributed to the disappearance of silver sardines from the waters off Monterey. The fishermen left, the canneries closed, and the Row fell into disrepair. But curious tourists, drawn by the author's *Cannery Row* and its sequel, *Sweet Thursday*, continued to visit the areas they had read about.

It didn't take long for entrepreneurs to take notice of the Row's location and international fame. The seaside strip's canneries and warehouses were renovated and converted; they now hold harbor restaurants, local artists' galleries, touristy hotels, and visitor-oriented gift shops. Many of the larger buildings have become self-contained mini-malls, containing myriad shops and eateries.

Fisherman's Wharf
Pacific St. Lined with gift shops, boating and fishing operations, and fish markets, the wharf remains perpetually busy year-round. But its primary attraction is its array of seafood restaurants, where hungry tourists can get anything from a simple cup of shrimp to a full sit-down meal. For details, phone 408/373-0600.

Maritime Museum of Monterey
5 Custom House Plaza; tel 408/373-2469. Seven exhibit areas are housed in this facility located on the waterfront across from Fisherman's Wharf. Serving as a beacon for the museum is a two-story Fresnel lens, taken from the Lighthouse at Point Sur; it is illuminated and rotates on its original mechanism, just as it did at Point Sur in the 1890s. Other highlights include a 6-foot-long model of John Drake Sloat's ship, *Savannah;* rare, handcrafted sextants, chronometers, and other antique navigational instruments; a re-created sea captain's quarters; and comprehensive exhibits from the era of the Spanish conquistadores to Monterey's heyday as the sardine capital of the world in the 1930s and 40s. A 20-minute film chronicles Monterey's relationship with the sea.

Guided tours; research library with 4,000 volumes; gift shop. **Open:** Daily 10am–5pm; extended summer hours. Closed some hols. $$

Monterey Bay Aquarium
886 Cannery Row; tel 408/648-4888. Opened in 1984, the Monterey Bay Aquarium quickly gained fame as one of the best exhibit aquariums in the world, and it is one of the largest as well. The facility sits on the border of one of the largest underwater canyons on earth—wider and deeper than even the Grand Canyon.

The museum's main exhibit is the Outer Bay, a million-gallon indoor ocean that showcases the outer reaches of Monterey Bay. With more water than all current aquarium exhibits combined, it is home to open ocean sharks like blues and soupfins, ocean sunfish that can grow to be 10 feet tall and weigh 1½ tons, green sea turtles, barracuda, pelagic stingrays, and schools of yellowfin tuna and other fast-swimming open ocean fish. Another attraction is a three-story, 335,000-gallon tank, which contains a towering kelp forest and hundreds of specimens of undersea life. Other "wet" exhibits re-create coastal streams, tidal pools, and other habitats found in Monterey Bay. A petting pool allows visitors to handle specimens such as bat rays and sea stars. Visitors also watch a live video feed continuously transmitted from a deep-sea research submarine below the surface of Monterey Bay. **Open:** Peak (June–Aug) daily 9:30am–6pm. Reduced hours off-season. **$$$$**

Dennis the Menace Playground
Pearl St, in the park at El Estero; tel 408/646-3866. Built in 1956 with the assistance of Hank Ketcham, creator of the Dennis the Menace comic strip, the park has undergone three renovations, the latest in 1988. Unique playground pieces include the Old No 1285 steam engine for climbing, a Dennis the Menace Sculpture and Climbing Structure, the Giant Swing Ride, and the Maze. A bronze statue of Dennis himself watches over the children at play. **Open:** Peak (June–Dec) 10am–dusk. Reduced hours off-season. **Free**

MONTEREY HISTORIC AREA

Monterey State Historic Park
A 7-acre site preserving Monterey's cultural heritage, the park contains several old buildings, which are preserved as historical monuments. Collectively, these structures are part of the Path of History, which includes building clustered around Fisherman's Wharf and the adjacent city. Many of the path's best buildings are featured below; those without formal addresses have been listed with street references. Building hours and fees vary and are subject to change; call for the latest information (tel 408/649-7118) or visit the Orientation Center at 20 Custom House Plaza. Walking tours of the park begin at the center, and a Monterey history film is shown free of charge every 20 minutes. **Open:** Daily 10am–5pm. **$$**

Casa de Oro
Scott and Oliver Sts. Originally built as a warehouse, barracks, and hospital for American seamen who were left at the port under consular care, this two-story adobe structure is called Casa de Oro (House of Gold) because miners supposedly stored their treasures in an iron safe here during the Gold Rush days. In 1849 the building was sold to Joseph Boston and Company and operated as a general store.

Today, Casa del Oro is once again a general store. It is preserved as it was in the 19th century.

Casa Soberanes
336 Pacific St. Often called the "House with the Blue Gate," this colonial-era adobe structure was built in the 1840s by the warden of the Custom House for his bride. The well-maintained interior is decorated with early New England furnishings and modern Mexican folk art.

Monterey Custom House
1 Custom House Plaza. Dating from about 1827, the Custom House, located just across from what is now the entrance to Fisherman's Wharf, is the oldest government building in California, the place where customs duties were collected when the area was under Mexican rule. The facility became obsolete in 1867, when San Francisco took over as California's primary port.

Larkin House
510 Calle Principal. Built in 1835, this balconied two-story adobe house was the home of Thomas Oliver Larkin, the US consul to Mexico from 1843 to 1846. The house doubled as the consular office and is furnished with many fine antiques, including some original pieces. Next door is a house used by William Tecumseh Sherman, which now contains a museum depicting the roles of the two men in California history.

Pacific House
10 Custom House Plaza. Built in 1847 for Thomas O Larkin, Pacific House was first used to house army offices and to store military supplies. Horses were corralled behind the building, which was also a popular spot for Sunday bull and bear fights. In later years, Pacific House has contained several small stores, a tavern, a courtroom, a newspaper office, a church—and a ballroom where a temperance society called the Dashaways held dances.

The first floor now houses a museum of California history. The second floor has an extensive collection of Native American artifacts, as well as a few Mexican-Indian and Inuit pieces.

Stevenson House
530 Houston St. The original portion of this two-story home dates to the 1830s, when it was the home of the first administrator of customs of Alta California. The owners made some additions and rented spare bedrooms to boarders, one of whom was Robert Louis Stevenson, who occupied a second-floor room during the autumn of 1879. While here, he wrote *The Old Pacific Capital,* an account of Monterey in the 1870s.

The building has been restored to its period look, and several rooms are devoted to Stevenson memorabilia.

Morro Bay

The center of attention is the protected water of Morro Bay, which is surrounded by a state park. Quiet and unassuming, the area offers excellent birdwatching and boating. **Information:** Morro Bay Chamber of Commerce, 895 Napa Ave #A-1, Morro Bay 93442 (tel 805/772-4467).

MOTELS

≡≡≡ Bay View Lodge
225 Harbor St, 93442; tel 805/772-2771 or toll free 800/742-8439 in CA. Morro Bay Blvd exit off CA 1. Older-style, well-kept motel one block from the waterfront. **Rooms:** 22 rms. CI 1:30pm/CO 11am. Nonsmoking rms avail. Rooms are nicely furnished in Queen Anne style, with ceiling fans and pretty quilts and pillows. **Amenities:** ☎ 🕏 🖭 Cable TV w/movies, refrig, VCR. No A/C. Some units w/fireplaces. **Services:** ⌑ **Facilities:** Whirlpool, washer/dryer. Sundeck. **Rates (CP):** Peak (June–Sept) $68–$74 S or D. Extra person $8. Min stay peak and special events. Lower rates off-season. Parking: Outdoor, free. AE, MC, V.

≡≡≡ Best Western San Marcos Motor Inn
250 Pacific St, 93442; tel 805/772-2248 or toll free 800/772-7969; fax 805/772-6844. Morro Bay Blvd exit off CA 1; left on Morro Ave. Lobby has a cheerful fireplace. A three-story atrium in a separate building leads to rooms. **Rooms:** 32 rms. CI 5pm/CO noon. Nonsmoking rms avail. **Amenities:** ☎ 🕏 🖭 Cable TV w/movies, refrig, dataport, voice mail. No A/C. All units w/terraces. Microwaves available. **Services:** ⌑ Evening wine, cheese, and apple cider; continental breakfast in lobby. Fax and copy services available. **Facilities:** Whirlpool. **Rates (CP):** Peak (May–Oct) $64–$101 S or D. Extra person $5. Min stay wknds. Lower rates off-season. Parking: Outdoor, free. AE, CB, DC, DISC, JCB, MC, V.

≡≡≡ Blue Sail Inn
851 Market Ave, 93442; tel 805/772-7132 or toll free 800/336-0707; fax 805/772-8406. Morro Bay Blvd exit off CA 1. Attractive, clean property on a bluff overlooking the bay, with great views and easy walking access to the waterfront. **Rooms:** 48 rms. CI 3pm/CO 11am. Nonsmoking rms avail. **Amenities:** ☎ 🕏 🖭 Cable TV w/movies, refrig. No A/C. Some units w/terraces, some w/fireplaces. **Services:** ⌑ **Facilities:** 🕏 Whirlpool. Outstanding hot tub/Jacuzzis in Cal-Japanese–style room. An ocean beach is a mile away. **Rates:** $65–$90 S or D. Children under age 18 stay free. Parking: Indoor/outdoor, free. AE, CB, DC, DISC, MC, V.

≡≡ The Breakers
780 Market Ave, PO Box 110, 93443; tel 805/772-7317 or toll free 800/932-8899; fax 805/772-4771. At Morro Bay Blvd. 1960s-style motel; dated but convenient to embarcadero/waterfront. **Rooms:** 25 rms. CI 2pm/CO noon. Nonsmoking rms avail. Great views from third floor accommodations. Although interiors are dated, rooms are clean. **Amenities:** ☎ 🕏 🖭 Cable TV w/movies, refrig. No A/C. Some units w/terraces, some w/fireplaces. Upstairs units have air conditioning, while most rooms have ceiling fans. **Services:** ⌑ **Facilities:** 🖼 Whirlpool. Pool area landscaping is surprisingly attractive, featuring a Japanese rock garden, wooden bench-

es, topiary, and lanterns. **Rates:** Peak (May–Sept) $70–$96 S or D. Extra person $10. Lower rates off-season. Parking: Outdoor, free. AE, CB, DISC, MC, V.

≡≡≡ El Morro Lodge
1206 Main St, 93442; tel 805/772-5633 or toll free 800/527-6782; fax 805/772-1404. Main St exit off CA 1. A fun place, appointed with antiques in lobby and rooms. Good value. **Rooms:** 27 rms. CI 2pm/CO 11am. Rooms have French provincial decor—an antique feel, but not stuffy. El Mirador Suite is very romantic. **Amenities:** ☎ 🕏 🖭 🖵 Cable TV w/movies, refrig, VCR. No A/C. Some units w/terraces, some w/fireplaces, some w/whirlpools. **Services:** ⌑ **Facilities:** 🕏 Whirlpool, washer/dryer. **Rates (CP):** Peak (June–Sept) $45–$90 S; $50–$90 D. Extra person $8. Children under age 18 stay free. Min stay wknds. Lower rates off-season. Parking: Outdoor, free. AE, CB, DC, DISC, MC, V.

≡≡≡ Embarcadero Inn
456 Embarcadero, 93442; tel 805/772-2700 or toll free 800/292-ROCK; fax 805/772-2700. Main St exit off CA 1; at Harbor. Clean, contemporary inn with nautical brass theme. **Rooms:** 32 rms and stes. CI 3pm/CO 11am. Nonsmoking rms avail. Security is good for a motel; access to elevators by room key only. Attractive rooms, all with lovely bay views, are decorated with photos of local fisherman and divers. Spiffy, sparkling clean bathrooms feature brass hardware. **Amenities:** ☎ 🕏 🖭 Cable TV, refrig, VCR. No A/C. Some units w/terraces, some w/fireplaces. **Services:** ⌑ Masseur. Free videos. Monopoly and other games available. **Facilities:** 🕏 Whirlpool, washer/dryer. Cozy, clean spa area features two hot tubs with refreshing views of a eucalyptus grove—especially nice at sunset. **Rates (CP):** $85–$125 S or D; $130–$180 ste. Extra person $10. Children under age 12 stay free. Parking: Indoor/outdoor, free. AE, CB, DC, DISC, MC, V.

≡≡≡ La Serena Inn
990 Morro Ave, 93443; tel 805/772-5665 or toll free 800/248-1511; fax 805/772-5665. Main St exit off CA 1 S; Morro Bay Blvd exit off CA 1 N. Well kept. **Rooms:** 37 rms and stes. CI 1pm/CO 11am. Nonsmoking rms avail. Rooms are clean and nicely furnished, decorated with light pastels in southwestern style. Some have ocean views and balconies. **Amenities:** ☎ 🕏 A/C, cable TV w/movies, refrig. Some units w/terraces, some w/fireplaces. **Services:** ⌑ Fax service available. **Facilities:** 🔟 🕏 Sauna. Outside deck, outside showers, deck chairs with views. **Rates (CP):** Peak (June–Sept) $71–$88 S or D; $110–$160 ste. Extra person $5. Children under age 9 stay free. Min stay special events. Lower rates off-season. Parking: Indoor/outdoor, free. AE, CB, DC, DISC, MC, V.

≡≡ Sundown Motel
640 Main St, 93442; tel 805/772-7381 or toll free 800/696-6928. Morro Bay Blvd exit off CA 1. Small, bright, airy, clean motel. **Rooms:** 17 rms. CI noon/CO 11am. Nonsmoking rms avail. Quiet, with pleasant art. **Amenities:** ☎ 🖭 Cable

TV w/movies. No A/C. Magic Fingers massage bed. **Services:** ⟡ **Rates:** Peak (June–Sept) $42–$78 S or D. Extra person $5. Children under age 12 stay free. Min stay special events. Lower rates off-season. Parking: Outdoor, free. AE, DISC, MC, V.

≋ The Villager

1098 Main St, 93442; tel 805/772-1235 or toll free 800/444-0782. Morro Bay Blvd exit off CA 1. Basic motel. Priced a bit high for what it delivers. **Rooms:** 22 rms. CI noon/CO 11am. Nonsmoking rms avail. Carpets recently replaced in first-floor rooms. Some rooms have king-size beds. **Amenities:** 🛏 📺 ⟡ Cable TV w/movies. No A/C. Some units w/fireplaces. **Services:** ⟡ **Facilities:** Whirlpool. **Rates:** Peak (June 10–Sept 10) $75–$95 S or D. Extra person $5. Lower rates off-season. Parking: Outdoor, free. AE, DC, DISC, MC, V.

RESORT

≋≋≋ The Inn at Morro Bay

60 State Park Rd, 93442; tel 805/772-5651 or toll free 800/321-9566; fax 805/772-4779. 5 acres. The only lodging on the water in Morro Bay, this appealing property overlooks a marina and is adjacent to a state park. Gazing out the windows may bring sightings of blue heron or sea lions at play in the bay. The dining rooms offer spectacular views. **Rooms:** 96 rms. CI 4pm/CO noon. Nonsmoking rms avail. Rooms, furnished in country French style, are accented with lovely wallpaper and fabrics. **Amenities:** 🛏 ♨ ⟡ Cable TV w/movies, refrig. No A/C. Some units w/terraces, some w/fireplaces, 1 w/whirlpool. Special amenities include soaps from Saks Fifth Avenue. **Services:** ✗ 📠 🚗 🖨 ⟡ Twice-daily maid svce, babysitting. **Facilities:** 🏋 🚴 📚 🎿 🍸1 🏊150 ♿ 1 restaurant (see "Restaurants" below), 1 bar (w/entertainment). Free use of bicycles for guests. Tennis, horseback riding, canoeing, and kayaking are nearby. Adjoining 18-hole public golf course. **Rates:** Peak (Apr–Oct) $95–$140 S; $95–$145 D. Extra person $15. Children under age 18 stay free. Min stay special events. Lower rates off-season. Parking: Outdoor, free. AE, DC, DISC, MC, V.

RESTAURANTS 🍴

Dom's Original Breakers Cafe

801 Market St; tel 805/772-4415. Morro Bay Blvd exit off CA 1. **Seafood/Steak.** This perennial local favorite, located in the same spot since 1942, is in a white clapboard building overlooking Morro Bay. The dining room is nicely decorated in a nautical motif, with gleaming mahogany tables, impressive clippership models, and photos of the Rock and local fishermen. Menu choices include a wide variety of fish, shellfish, and meat dishes. For breakfast, popular selections include oyster omelets and buckwheat pancakes. Cozy bar and new wraparound deck. **FYI:** Reservations recommended.

Children's menu. **Open:** Breakfast daily 7am–2pm; lunch daily 11am–4pm; dinner daily 4–10pm. **Prices:** Main courses $12–$32. AE, MC, V. 🍴 🏔 🎴 ♿

♣ The Inn at Morro Bay Dining Room

60 State Park Rd; tel 805/772-5651. Morro Bay Blvd exit off CA 1. **New American.** A casual spot with outdoor deck for lunch. Fabulous views of Morro Rock. Excellent menu offers crispy crab risotto, soft-shell crab, and vegetarian filet. **FYI:** Reservations recommended. Cabaret/jazz. **Open:** Breakfast Mon–Sat 7–11am, Sun 7–10am; lunch Mon–Sat 11:30am–2pm; dinner daily 5–9pm; brunch Sun 10am–2pm. **Prices:** Main courses $15–$28. AE, CB, DC, DISC, MC, V. 🍷 🍽 🏔 ❤

ATTRACTIONS 🏛

Morro Bay State Park

State Park Rd; tel 805/772-7434. Among the various activities offered here are fishing, boating, camping, golfing on an 18-hole public course, and birdwatching. There is also a natural history museum located within the park (see below), perched on the cliffs overlooking the bay. **Open:** Daily dawn–dusk. **$$$$**

Morro Bay State Park Museum of Natural History

State Park Rd; tel 805/772-2694. Located on White Point in Morro Bay State Park (see above), this museum contains exhibits covering various topics, including regional geology, flora and fauna, and the Chumash Indians. The Art Gallery shows original works portraying the many aspects of nature along the central coast; exhibits change periodically. The Discovery Center offers hands-on exploration of a variety of natural science subjects. **Open:** Daily 10am–5pm. **$**

Moss Beach

See also Half Moon Bay, Princeton-by-the-Sea

INN 🏨

≋≋≋≋ Seal Cove Inn

221 Cypress Ave, 94038; tel 415/728-4114; fax 415/728-4116. 2 acres. Set on a ridge above Fitzgerald Marine Reserve, this European-style inn peeks out at the Pacific through towering cypress trees and past colorful wildflower gardens. Opened in 1991, it was built from scratch by Rick Herbert and his wife Karen Brown, a writer known for her country-inn travel series. **Rooms:** 10 rms. CI 3pm/CO 11am. No smoking. Upstairs rooms feature vaulted ceilings; downstairs accommodations have doors opening to the garden. Furnishings include country antiques and reproductions, original watercolors, and grandfather clocks. However, soft goods are showing signs of wear, and drawer and bathroom counter space are minimal. Children permitted in downstairs rooms only. **Amenities:** 🛏 ♨ ⟡ TV w/movies, refrig, VCR. No A/C. All units w/minibars, all w/terraces, all w/fireplaces,

some w/whirlpools. Nice touches include heated towel racks in bathrooms. Complimentary soft drinks, bottled water, and wine in rooms. **Services:** 🚐 🛏 Twice-daily maid svce, masseur, afternoon tea and wine/sherry served. Breakfast might include Grand Marnier french toast or caramel-raspberry pancakes; guests can also enjoy a continental breakfast in their rooms. Extensive free video library, and the popcorn is "on the house" too. **Facilities:** 🏊 ⌗15 ⅙ Guest lounge. 2 beaches within easy walking distance. **Rates (BB):** $165–$250 S or D. Extra person $25. Parking: Outdoor, free. Reserve up to four weeks in advance for summer weekends. AE, DISC, MC, V.

Mountain View

See also Los Altos

This industrial and manufacturing town got its name from the Santa Cruz Mountains just to the west; to the east is Moffett Field, a naval air station. **Information:** Mountain View Chamber of Commerce, 580 Castro St, Mountain View 94041 (tel 415/968-8378).

HOTEL 🏨

≣≣≣ Residence Inn by Marriott

1854 El Camino Real W, 94040; tel 415/940-1300 or toll free 800/331-3131; fax 415/969-4997. Geared toward long-term stays by corporate clients or relocating families. **Rooms:** 112 effic. CI 3pm/CO noon. Nonsmoking rms avail. Apartments, two to eight per building. Good soundproofing. All have separate entrance and full-size kitchen. Tub and toilet separate from sink area. **Amenities:** 📺 ☕ 🖭 A/C, satel TV w/movies, refrig. Some units w/terraces, some w/fireplaces. **Services:** 🛏 🔧 🐾 Babysitting. Continental breakfast and buffet in area off lobby; evening appetizers; Thursday barbecues May–Sept. **Facilities:** 🏸 ▨ 🍴 ⌗40 Volleyball, whirlpool, washer/dryer. Meeting room with audiovisual capabilities. Gazebos in garden area between buildings. **Rates (CP):** Peak (May–Sept) $159–$184 effic. Children under age 18 stay free. Lower rates off-season. Parking: Outdoor, free. Corporate rates available. AE, CB, DC, DISC, EC, JCB, MC, V.

MOTELS

≣≣≣ Best Western Inn

93 El Camino Real W, 94040; tel 415/967-6957 or toll free 800/445-7774; fax 415/967-4834. Rengstorff Ave exit off US 101; turn left on El Camino Real. Undergoing complete renovation of rooms in main building; lobby recently expanded and upgraded. **Rooms:** 58 rms, stes, and effic. Executive level. CI 1pm/CO 11am. Nonsmoking rms avail. Second building has larger rooms updated with new carpeting and kitchenette. Smaller rooms have all new furnishings, seating area. **Amenities:** 📺 ☕ 🖭 🕾 A/C, satel TV w/movies, refrig,

dataport, VCR, voice mail. Some units w/whirlpools. All rooms have trouser presses, microwaves. **Services:** 🛏 🔧 Children's program, babysitting. **Facilities:** 🏋 🍴 ⅙ 1 restaurant, 1 bar, washer/dryer. Full fitness center has new equipment. **Rates (CP):** Peak (May–Sept) $90 S or D; $130 ste; $100 effic. Children under age 12 stay free. Lower rates off-season. Parking: Indoor/outdoor, free. AE, CB, DC, DISC, EC, MC, V.

≣≣ Mountain View Inn

2300 W El Camino Real, 94040; tel 415/962-9912 or toll free 800/785-0005; fax 415/962-9011. Rengstorff Ave exit off US 101. Attractive Cal-Mex-style building has teal-trimmed stucco exterior, wood-paneled Spanish-style doors, terra-cotta tile roof. **Rooms:** 71 rms, stes, and effic. CI 2pm/CO 11am. Nonsmoking rms avail. Satisfactory rooms. **Amenities:** 📺 ☕ 🖭 🕾 A/C, cable TV w/movies, refrig, VCR. Some units w/whirlpools. **Services:** 🛏 🔧 Lackluster service. **Facilities:** 🏋 🍴 ⌗30 ⅙ Sauna, steam rm, whirlpool, washer/dryer. **Rates (CP):** $89–$200 S or D; $125–$200 ste; $125–$200 effic. Extra person $10. Children under age 12 stay free. Parking: Outdoor, free. AE, DC, DISC, MC, V.

RESTAURANT 🍴

Chez TJ

938 Villa St; tel 415/964-7466. Moffett Blvd exit off US 101. **French.** Like going to a friend's house for dinner, if your friend happens to be a gourmet chef. This inviting restaurant welcomes diners with old-fashioned verandas, magnolia trees, and a restful dove-gray exterior. Inside are four dining areas in southwestern style. Entrees include duck with acorn-maple custard and Hawaiian ono with wasabi aioli. **FYI:** Reservations recommended. Beer and wine only. **Open:** Dinner Tues–Sat 5:30–9pm. **Prices:** AE, CB, DC, DISC, ER, MC. ♥

ATTRACTION 🏛

NASA Ames Research Center

Moffett Field; tel 415/604-6497. Located at Moffett Field, off US 101, the Ames Research Center is engaged in a variety of research tasks relating to space flight and exploration. The facility includes the world's most sophisticated wind tunnel complex and the most advanced supercomputing system.

Guided tours are conducted on weekdays and last two hours (two-week advance reservation required). Tour stops vary depending on research activities, but possible highlights include the world's largest wind tunnel, research aircraft, and flight simulation facilities. Gift shop. **Open:** Visitors center, Mon–Fri 8am–4:30pm. Tours by reservation only. **Free**

Mount Shasta

The white volcanic dome of Mount Shasta (14,162 ft) looms over the surrounding forest and lava lands of Northern California. Native American legend holds that the mountain has been granted spiritual powers, and it continues to be the site of truth-seeking pilgrimages. The resort town of Mount Shasta sits at the foot of the mountain. **Information:** Mount Shasta Chamber of Commerce, 300 Pine St, PO Box 273, Mount Shasta 96067 (tel 916/926-6212).

MOTELS 🏨

≣≣ Mountain Air Lodge & Ski House
1121 S Mount Shasta Blvd, 96067; tel 916/926-3411. Lake St exit off I-5; E to Mt Shasta Blvd. Spectacularly large lobby looks like a combination ski lodge and lumber mill. Huge old trees shade property. **Rooms:** 38 rms, stes, and effic; 1 cottage/villa. CI 2pm/CO 11am. Nonsmoking rms avail. **Amenities:** 🛏 A/C, cable TV w/movies. **Services:** 🛎 ⟰ **Facilities:** Whirlpool. **Rates:** Peak (June–Oct/Dec–Mar) $42–$49 S; $47–$57 D; $68–$85 ste; $65–$85 effic; $85–$130 cottage/villa. Extra person $5. Lower rates off-season. Parking: Outdoor, free. AE, CB, DC, DISC, MC, V.

≣ Mount Shasta Swiss Holiday Lodge
2400 S Mount Shasta Blvd, PO Box 335, 96067; tel 916/926-3446. McCloud/CA 89 exit off I-5. No-frills lodging, close to skiing with a great view of the mountains. **Rooms:** 21 rms and stes. CI 2pm/CO 11am. Nonsmoking rms avail. **Amenities:** 🛏 A/C, cable TV w/movies. **Services:** 🛎 **Facilities:** 🛁 🏊 Whirlpool. **Rates:** Peak (Dec 16–Jan 1/May 25–Nov 1) $41–$43 S; $45–$47 D. Extra person $4. Lower rates off-season. Parking: Outdoor, free. Special rates for seniors, business travelers. AE, DC, DISC, MC, V.

≣≣ Sis-Q-Inn Motel
1825 Shastina Dr, Weed, 96094; tel 916/938-4194; fax 916/938-2569. South Weed exit off I-5. Spectacular views of Mount Shasta from many rooms. Many repeat customers. **Rooms:** 22 rms and stes. CI 1pm/CO 11am. Nonsmoking rms avail. **Amenities:** 🛏 🧊 A/C, cable TV. **Services:** 🛎 ⟰ **Facilities:** Whirlpool. **Rates (CP):** $42–$46 S; $45–$50 D. Extra person $5. Parking: Outdoor, free. AE, CB, DC, DISC, MC, V.

INN

≣≣≣ Strawberry Valley Inn
1142 S Mt Shasta Blvd, 96067; tel 916/926-2052. An obvious first choice for the discerning traveler. Inn has a great deal of charm without being cloying. **Rooms:** 27 rms and stes. CI 3pm/CO 11am. Nonsmoking rms avail. Rooms are beautifully designed, restored, and furnished. **Amenities:** 🛏 🧊 📼 Cable TV. No A/C. 1 unit w/fireplace. **Services:** 🛎 Wine/sherry served. **Rates (CP):** Peak (June–Oct) $55–$60 S or D; $69 ste. Extra person $6. Children under age 10 stay free. Lower rates off-season. Parking: Indoor/outdoor, free. AE, DISC, MC, V.

RESTAURANT 🍽

★ Lily's
1013 S Mt Shasta Blvd; tel 916/926-3372. Lake St exit off I-5. **New American.** This superb, informal restaurant, housed in a pretty garden cottage, serves the best food in Mount Shasta. The seasonal menu emphasizes California cuisine, with a touch of Mexico and the Pacific Rim. Rack of lamb is a specialty. A nice wine list, with a good selection by the glass. **FYI:** Reservations accepted. Children's menu. Beer and wine only. **Open:** Peak (June–Oct) breakfast Mon–Fri 7–11am; lunch Mon–Fri 11am–3pm; dinner Mon–Fri 5–9:30pm, Sat–Sun 4–9:30pm; brunch Sat–Sun 7am–2pm. **Prices:** Main courses $10–$16. MC, V. &

Muir Beach

Just south of the more popular Stinson Beach, Muir Beach is small but beautiful, located within the Golden Gate National Recreation Area.

INN 🏨

≣≣≣ The Pelican Inn
10 Pacific Way (CA 1), 94965; tel 415/383-6000. 2 acres. The next best thing to a ticket on British Airways. Although the inn was built in 1979, it looks like the real thing, complete with half-timbered architecture, portraits of Anne Boleyn, timeworn antiques, and a purported ghost. Romantic! **Rooms:** 7 rms. CI 2pm/CO noon. Rooms might feature oriental rugs or antique 4-poster beds. Fresh flowers add color. **Amenities:** No A/C, phone, or TV. Some units w/terraces. **Services:** 🛎 Wine/sherry served. **Facilities:** 🔲 1 restaurant (see "Restaurants" below), 1 bar, guest lounge. Cozy sitting room with sofa, brick fireplace, and piano. Very good, very British restaurant and pub downstairs. Muir Beach is a short stroll away. **Rates (BB):** $143–$165 S or D. Extra person $25. Parking: Outdoor, free. Weekend reservations are at a premium—you have to book at least six months in advance. MC, V.

RESTAURANT 🍽

The Pelican Inn
10 Pacific Way (CA 1); tel 415/383-6000. Stinson Beach exit off US 101. **British.** A restaurant with an authentic British ambience, set in a Tudor-style inn with leaded windows, wooden beams, and a roaring hearth. You can eat in the dining room at long, darkwood tables, on the patio, or in the comfy pub. In addition to Anglo classics such as fish 'n' chips or cottage pie, daily specials might include roast duck, beef Wellington, or wild game. The pub offers good brews on tap, plus a good selection of sherries and California wines by the glass. **FYI:** Reservations accepted. Children's menu. Beer and

wine only. **Open:** Lunch Tues–Fri 11:30am–3pm, Sat–Sun 11:30am–3:30pm; dinner Tues–Fri 6–9:30pm, Sat–Sun 5:30–9:30pm. **Prices:** Main courses $9–$18. MC, V. 🍴 🛗

Murphys

A remote Gold Country town in Calaveras County, Murphys is home to the nearby Mercer Canyons, an underground wonder of limestone and crystal formations.

HOTEL 🏨

📊📊📊 Murphys Historic Hotel and Lodge

457 Main St, 95247; tel 209/728-3444 or toll free 800/ 532-7684; fax 209/728-1590. Extremely well-kept historic property dating to 1856. Visitors included Ulysses S Grant, Mark Twain, and highwayman Black Bart. The hotel has a noted restaurant plus a historic saloon popular with locals and tourists alike. **Rooms:** 29 rms and stes. CI 3pm/CO 11am. Nonsmoking rms avail. Original building maintains rooms with antiques and period decor; a modern unit on the ground floor offers motel-type rooms of high standard. **Amenities:** 🛁 A/C, cable TV. TVs and phones available only in modern units. All rooms air-conditioned except for "Historic Hotel" rooms. **Services:** 🍽 **Facilities:** 🏊 1 restaurant (see "Restaurants" below), 1 bar. **Rates (CP):** $70–$80 S or D; $75 ste. Extra person $6. Children under age 12 stay free. Min stay special events. Parking: Outdoor, free. A bargain. AE, CB, DC, DISC, MC, V.

RESTAURANT 🍽

Ⓢ Murphys Restaurant

In Murphys Historic Hotel and Lodge, 457 Main St; tel 209/ 728-3444. **Continental/American.** Decorated with 19th-century furnishings, a burgundy carpet, and pink floral wallpaper. Lunch features five salads, various burgers, '49er chili, and prime-rib sandwiches; dinner choices include pastas, basil-garlic roasted chicken, rack of lamb, prime rib, and liver with caramelized onions. French nouvelle cuisine influences. **FYI:** Reservations recommended. **Open:** Breakfast daily 6:30–11:30am; lunch daily 11:30am–3pm; dinner daily 5–9:30pm. **Prices:** Main courses $9–$19. AE, CB, DC, DISC, MC, V. 🍴 📷

ATTRACTIONS 📷

Calaveras Big Trees State Park

Arnold; tel 209/795-2334. 12 mi N of town on CA 4. Home to some of the world's largest sequoias. Some of the redwoods attain a height of 300 feet and a diameter of 32 feet; their weight can reach 6,000 tons. The park has two groves with self-guiding trails. The **North Grove** offers a one-mile trail, and its "Three Senses Trail" is designed to help visitors touch, smell, and hear the wonders of nature. The larger **South Grove,** nine miles south of the park's entrance, features a trail through rolling mountain terrain.

There is swimming at Beaver Creek and the Stanislaus River, there are 129 campsites. During the winter, park staff conducts cross-country ski and snowshoe hikes for groups with a minimum of 10 people. The visitors center has exhibits on the trees and free brochures, as well as detailed interpretive guides to the major trails. **Open:** Daily sunrise–sundown. **$$**

Mercer Caverns

Tel 209/728-2101. The caverns contain a variety of formations—stalactites, stalagmites, columns, curtains, flowstone, and more. Tours take 45 minutes. **Open:** Peak (Labor Day–Mem Day) daily 9am–5pm. **$$**

Napa

Napa Valley is home to a number of wineries in close proximity, many of which offer tastings and tours. Located at the southern edge of the valley, Napa is the thriving commercial center for this renowned wine–growing region. **Information:** Napa Valley Conference & Visitors Bureau, 1310 Napa Town Center, Napa 94559 (tel 707/226-7459).

HOTELS 🏨

📊📊📊 Inn at Napa Valley Crown Sterling Suites

1075 California Blvd, 94559; tel 707/253-9540 or toll free 800/433-4600; fax 707/253-9202. 1st St exit off CA 29; go east; left on California Blvd. A property with a restful, inviting atmosphere and a very attractive courtyard. Excellent for business or family travelers. **Rooms:** 205 stes. CI 3pm/ CO noon. Nonsmoking rms avail. All rooms have kitchenette, sofa bed, and table and chairs. **Amenities:** 🛁 🍷 A/C, cable TV w/movies, refrig, voice mail. 1 unit w/fireplace. **Services:** ✕ 🔑 🛗 🍽 Babysitting. **Facilities:** 🏊 🚲 220 🖥 ⚓ 1 restaurant, 1 bar (w/entertainment), lawn games, sauna, steam rm, whirlpool. **Rates (BB):** Peak (Apr–Oct) $157–$187 ste. Extra person $10. Children under age 13 stay free. Min stay peak. Lower rates off-season. Parking: Outdoor, free. AE, DC, DISC, ER, JCB, MC, V.

📊📊📊 Napa Valley Marriott

3425 Solano Ave, 94558; tel 707/253-7433 or toll free 800/ 228-9290; fax 707/258-1320. Trancas exit off CA 29. At gateway to Napa Valley, an excellent location for touring. **Rooms:** 191 rms and stes. CI 4pm/CO noon. Nonsmoking rms avail. Rooms, renovated within past year, are well-appointed, clean, and comfortable, with good security. **Amenities:** 🛁 🍷 A/C, cable TV w/movies, voice mail. Some units w/terraces. Irons and ironing boards in all rooms. **Services:** ✕ 🔑 🛗 🍽 Social director, masseur, babysitting. Wine tasting in lobby Fri and Sat (5:30–6:30pm). **Facilities:** 🏊 🍷 🎾 300 🖥 ⚓ 2 restaurants, 1 bar (w/entertainment), whirlpool. Attractive courtyard and pool; gift shop. **Rates:** Peak (late May–early Nov) $99–$165 S or D; $250–$350 ste. Children under age 18 stay free. Min stay peak and wknds. Lower rates off-season. Parking: Outdoor, free. Breakfast packages available. AE, CB, DC, DISC, JCB, MC, V.

MOTELS

≣≣ Best Western Inn
100 Soscol Ave, 94559; tel 707/257-1930 or toll free 800/528-1234; fax 707/255-0709. CA 121 N exit off CA 29. Comfortable motel in an unattractive location off the highway. **Rooms:** 68 rms and stes. CI 3pm/CO 11am. Nonsmoking rms avail. Spacious and pleasantly furnished. **Amenities:** 🛁 ⚗ 🖥 📶 A/C, cable TV w/movies. Some units w/minibars, some w/terraces. **Services:** 🖐 🛎 Babysitting. **Facilities:** 🔂 📵 ⅙ 1 restaurant, whirlpool. **Rates:** Peak (May–Nov 15) $75–$109 S; $89–$115 D; $149 ste. Extra person $5. Children under age 12 stay free. Min stay special events. Lower rates off-season. Parking: Outdoor, free. Hot-air balloon and Marine World/USA packages available. AE, CB, DC, DISC, ER, JCB, MC, V.

≣ Chablis Lodge
3360 Solano Ave, 94558; tel 707/257-1944 or toll free 800/443-3490; fax 707/226-6862. ½ mi N of downtown; Redwood Rd exit off CA 29. No-frills motel; clean and comfortable. **Rooms:** 34 rms and effic. CI 2pm/CO noon. Nonsmoking rms avail. **Amenities:** 🛁 ⚗ 🖥 A/C, satel TV w/movies, refrig. Some units w/whirlpools. Wet bars. **Services:** 🛎 Babysitting. **Facilities:** 🔂 ⅙ Whirlpool. **Rates (CP):** Peak (Apr 15–Nov 15) $65–$115 S or D; $65–$115 effic. Extra person $5. Children under age 16 stay free. Min stay wknds. Lower rates off-season. Parking: Outdoor, free. AE, DC, DISC, MC, V.

≣≣ The Chateau
4195 Solano Ave, 94558; tel 707/253-9300; fax 707/253-0906. Wine Country Ave exit off CA 29, left on Solano Ave. Attractive, comfortable lodgings on well-kept grounds. Convenient to Napa Valley vineyards. A good value. **Rooms:** 115 rms and stes. CI 3pm/CO noon. Nonsmoking rms avail. Clean, nicely furnished. **Amenities:** 🛁 A/C, satel TV w/movies. Some units w/minibars, 1 w/terrace. **Services:** ✕ 🛎 Babysitting. **Facilities:** 🔂 💯 ⅙ Whirlpool. **Rates (CP):** Peak (Apr–Oct) $105–$110 S or D; $155–$180 ste. Extra person $10. Children under age 13 stay free. Min stay wknds. Lower rates off-season. Parking: Outdoor, free. AE, CB, DC, DISC, JCB, MC, V.

≣ Napa Valley Travelodge
853 Coombs St, 94559 (Downtown); tel 707/226-1871 or toll free 800/578-7878; fax 707/226-1707. 1st St exit off CA 29; right on Coombs St. A satisfactory motel located in downtown Napa. **Rooms:** 45 rms. CI 3pm/CO noon. Nonsmoking rms avail. **Amenities:** 🛁 ⚗ 🖥 A/C, TV w/movies. **Services:** ✕

Facilities: 🔂 **Rates:** Peak (May–Oct) $65–$175 S or D. Extra person $10. Children under age 17 stay free. Lower rates off-season. Parking: Outdoor, free. AE, CB, DC, DISC, MC, V.

INNS

≣≣≣ Beazley House
1910 1st St, 94559; tel 707/257-1649 or toll free 800/559-1649; fax 707/257-1518. off CA 29. Built in 1902, this shingled manse opened as Napa's first B&B in 1981. Main house features French doors, lots of wood, stained-glass door and windows, as well as attractive gardens. Accommodations also in the Carriage House, nestled among greenery. **Rooms:** 11 rms and stes. CI 3:30/CO 11:30. No smoking. Individually decorated with colorful fabrics and fine antiques. Carriage House accommodations are larger, with two-person whirlpools and fireplaces. **Amenities:** ⚗ 🖥 A/C, CD/tape player, bathrobes. No phone or TV. 1 unit w/terrace, some w/fireplaces, some w/whirlpools. **Services:** ✕ Afternoon tea and wine/sherry served. Breakfast of fresh-baked breads and fruits plus other selections. **Facilities:** Games rm, guest lounge. **Rates (BB):** Peak (June–Oct) $110–$145 S or D; $175–$190 ste. Extra person $30. Min stay wknds. Lower rates off-season. Parking: Outdoor, free. Wine Train and hot-air balloon packages available. MC, V.

≣≣≣ Churchill Manor Bed and Breakfast Inn
485 Brown St, 94559; tel 707/253-7733; fax 707/253-8836. 1st St exit off CA 29; E on 2nd St, right on Coombs St, left on Oak. 1 acre. Set amidst immaculate gardens, this enormous historic home was built in 1889 with details such as double doors set with bevelled glass. Comfortable public rooms downstairs are tastefully decorated with lots of antiques. Very popular for weddings. Unsuitable for children under 18. **Rooms:** 10 rms. CI 3pm/CO 11am. No smoking. Individually decorated with high-quality furnishings such as mirrored armoires and clawfoot tubs. **Amenities:** 🛁 ⚗ A/C. No TV. Some units w/fireplaces, 1 w/whirlpool. **Services:** Afternoon tea and wine/sherry served. Cookies offered outdoors in the summer. **Facilities:** 🔂 Games rm, guest lounge w/TV. Tandem bikes available. **Rates (BB):** $75–$145 S or D. Extra person $15. Min stay wknds. Parking: Outdoor, free. Wine Train and hot-air ballooning packages available. AE, DC, DISC, MC, V.

≣≣≣ La Residence Country Inn
4066 St Helena Hwy, 94558; tel 707/253-0337; fax 707/253-0382. Between Salvador and Oak Knoll Aves. 2 acres. Impressive inn located just off the highway, but in a quiet, secluded location. Property consists of an 1870 Greek revival manse and a newer annex styled after a French barn. **Rooms:** 20 rms. CI 2pm/CO 11am. No smoking. Comfortable rooms decorated with Laura Ashley prints, quality antiques, and fine linens. **Amenities:** 🛁 ⚗ 📶 A/C, CD/tape player. No TV. Some units w/terraces, some w/fireplaces. **Services:** ✕ 🖥 🛎 Babysitting, wine/sherry served. 3-course breakfast varies daily. Complimentary wine and cheese, fruit, and hors

d'oeuvres in afternoon. **Facilities:** 🔲 ⌧ ⅕ ⅙ Whirlpool, guest lounge. **Rates (BB):** $150–$180 S or D; $150–$180 D. Extra person $20. Children under age 2 stay free. Min stay wknds and special events. Parking: Outdoor, free. AE, DC, MC, V.

RESORT

≣≣≣ Silverado Country Club & Resort

1600 Atlas Peak Rd, 94558 (Silverado); tel 707/257-0200 or toll free 800/532-0500; fax 707/257-5400. Trancas exit off CA 29, E to Atlas Peak Rd. 1,200 acres. Top golf and tennis facilities built around historic Napa estate. An 1870s mansion now houses the reception area and dining room. A grand entryway through white pillars and slate floors leads to a disappointing lobby. **Rooms:** 290 cottages/villas. CI 4pm/ CO noon. Nonsmoking rms avail. In low white buildings with shingled roofs, accommodations are actually condos and private homes. Furnishings are done in a bland contemporary style. **Amenities:** 🛗 🕭 🖭 ❑ A/C, TV, voice mail. All units w/minibars, all w/terraces, some w/fireplaces. Since accommodations are individually owned, amenities vary. Some have cable TV with remote control. **Services:** ⓘⓞ❘ ⌁ 🆅🅿 🚗 🖃 ↵ Car-rental desk, masseur, babysitting. **Facilities:** 🔲 🚲 ▶36 🏊 🍸17 🏌 ⌧1000 💻 ⅙ 3 restaurants, 3 bars (1 w/entertainment), whirlpool, washer/dryer. Home to the PGA Transamerica event, with two golf courses designed by Robert Trent Jones, Jr, as well as two putting greens and a driving range. With plexipaved courts and a pro shop, the tennis complex is northern California's largest. **Rates:** Peak (Mar 25–Nov 25) $135–$195 S or D. Extra person $15. Children under age 18 stay free. Lower rates off-season. Parking: Indoor/outdoor, free. Excellent-value golf and tennis packages available. CB, DC, DISC, JCB, MC, V.

RESTAURANTS 🍴

♥ ✹ Bistro Don Giovanni

4110 St Helena Hwy (CA 29); tel 707/224-3300. **Italian/ Mediterranean.** The name honors Mozart's opera and plays upon the names of the restaurant's owners, Donna and Giovanni Scala. Stylish and airy with original art on the walls, it draws a smartly-dressed and animated crowd. Diners can start with one of the choices from the pizza oven, such as duck-sausage pizza. Several daily pastas, including what may be the definitive linguine with clam sauce. Great desserts, too. **FYI:** Reservations recommended. **Open:** Peak (June–Sept) Sun–Thurs 11:30am–10pm, Fri–Sat 11:30am–11pm. **Prices:** Main courses $8–$16. AE, CB, DC, DISC, MC, V. 🚤 ⅙

✹ Pasta Prego

In Grapeyard Shopping Center, 3206 Jefferson St; tel 707/ 224-9011. Trancas St exit off CA 29. **Californian/Italian.** Casual, bistro-style decor with an open kitchen and a friendly atmosphere. A variety of pasta specialties are served, such as lemon-pepper spaghetti with seafood in white wine sauce, as well as grilled pork chops, chicken breast, fresh fish, and imaginative pizzas. **FYI:** Reservations accepted. Beer and

wine only. **Open:** Peak (June–Sept) lunch Mon–Fri 11:30am– 2:30pm; dinner daily 5–10pm. **Prices:** Main courses $9–$16. AE, MC, V. ⅙

Napa Valley

See Calistoga, Napa, Oakville, Rutherford, St Helena

Nevada City

During the height of the Gold Rush, Nevada City was one of the largest cities in California. Today the population is smaller, but much of the legacy of the boom years remains in the Victorian homes, antique stores, and gaslamp-lit streets. **Information:** Nevada City Chamber of Commerce, 132 Main St, Nevada City 95959 (tel 916/265-2692).

MOTEL 🏨

≣≣ Northern Queen Inn

400 Railroad Ave, 95959; tel 916/265-5824; fax 916/ 265-3720. Located in a wooded setting, it's surrounded by railroad trains and related memorabilia. Newly refurbished, it offers exceptional value. **Rooms:** 70 rms, stes, and effic; 16 cottages/villas. CI 3pm/CO noon. Nonsmoking rms avail. Clean chalets have loft and deck and full kitchen. Cottages have kitchens, and wood-burning stove. **Amenities:** 🛗 🖭 A/C, cable TV w/movies. Some units w/terraces, some w/fireplaces. Picnic area and creek. **Services:** ↵ Babysitting. **Facilities:** 🔲 ⌧100 ⅙ 1 restaurant, whirlpool. **Rates:** $55 S; $55–$58 D; $80–$90 ste; $80–$90 effic; $80–$90 cottage/ villa. Extra person $5. Children under age 6 stay free. Min stay wknds. Parking: Outdoor, free. AE, CB, DC, JCB, MC, V.

RESTAURANT 🍴

Potager

320 Broad St; tel 916/265-5697. Off CA 49/20. **Californian.** Built in 1866 as a bakery, the structure stays true to its heritage with the original wood-burning oven in the kitchen, plus exposed brickwork and timbers on the lower level. High ceilings and private dining niches heighten the decor. Fresh ingredients (including some from their own garden) go into dishes such as seasonal grilled vegetables. Other specialties are beef Wellington, homemade raviolis, wild-boar entrees, and their homemade desserts. Takeout available. **FYI:** Reservations recommended. Beer and wine only. **Open:** Dinner Tues–Thurs 6–9pm, Fri 6–9:30pm, Sat 5:30–9:30pm, Sun 5– 9pm. **Prices:** Main courses $14–$23. AE, MC, V. ♥ ▪

REFRESHMENT STOP ▽

Broad Street Books & Espresso Bar

426 Broad St; tel 916/265-4204. Broad St exit off CA 49/20. **Coffeehouse.** Friendly, clean, and artistic. Books, new and used, provide the decor in a vintage home ambience. Offer-

ings include pastries, sandwiches, and light fare, as well as gourmet teas and coffees, plus tortes, cheesecakes, and other desserts. **Open:** Peak (June–Sept) Sun–Fri 7am–8pm, Sat 7am–10pm. No CC. 🍽

ATTRACTION 📷

Nevada City Winery
321 Spring St; tel 916/265-9463. Located in the Miners' Foundry Garage, this winery stands less than two blocks from the original site of its founding in the 1870s. Reopened in 1980, this producer of varietal wines offers daily tastings and guided tours by reservation. **Open:** Daily noon–5pm. **Free**

Newport Beach

The winding bay and long peninsula make Newport Beach the quintessential Orange County beach town. Upscale and suburban in feel, the summer crowds turn the place into a center for sporty, sun-splashed fun. **Information:** Newport Harbor Area Chamber of Commerce, 1470 Jamboree Rd, Newport Beach 92660 (tel 714/729-4400).

HOTELS 🛏

≣≣≣≣ Four Seasons Hotel
690 Newport Center Dr, 92660; tel 714/759-0808 or toll free 800/332-3442; fax 714/759-0568. The best luxury hotel in Newport Beach. Contemporary rendition of a grand hotel, with an impressive stone-paved driveway and a gracious marble lobby with views to the gardens and pools. Where presidents stay when they come to town. **Rooms:** 285 rms and stes. CI 3pm/CO noon. Nonsmoking rms avail. Standard rooms are large, with an abundance of mirrors and counter space in the bathroom, plus a small TV. Executive suites provide a huge bathroom with separate dressing and vanity area done in two tones of beige marble. **Amenities:** 🛁 ⓠ ⓣ A/C, cable TV w/movies, dataport, voice mail, bathrobes. All units w/minibars, all w/terraces. **Services:** 🍽 🔑 VP 🚐 🛆 ⌐ ⌐ Twice-daily maid svce, social director, masseur, babysitting. Staff/guest ratio is 2.5 to 1. Complimentary shoeshine. **Facilities:** 🏊 🚲 🎾 ⛹ 360 ⬜ ♿ 2 restaurants (see "Restaurants" below), 1 bar (w/entertainment), spa, sauna, whirlpool. In the workout room, each treadmill, Nordic Track, Stairmaster, etc, is accompanied by its own TV. Aerobics classes are also available. Complimentary cabanas available poolside. Golf can be arranged at nearby championship course. 24-hour business center. **Rates:** $275–$295 S; $315 D; $395–$2,000 ste. Extra person $35. Children under age 18 stay free. Min stay special events. Parking: Indoor, $13/day. Golf, weekend, and honeymoon packages available. AE, DC, JCB, MC, V.

≣≣≣ Le Meridien Newport Beach
4500 MacArthur Blvd, 92660; tel 714/476-2001 or toll free 800/543-4300; fax 714/476-0153. ¼ mi S of MacArthur

Blvd exit off I-405. Although this ten-story structure resembles a modern-day pyramid, the accent is old-world French. Divided into several different seating areas, the lobby feels intimate, not overblown. **Rooms:** 435 rms and stes. Executive level. CI 3pm/CO noon. Hallway carpets, as well as rugs, bedspreads, and fabrics in the rooms are worn, but are slated for replacement. Spacious accommodations with comfortable armchairs, lots of drawers, and plenty of counter space in the bathrooms. **Amenities:** 🛁 ⓠ ⓣ A/C, TV w/movies, refrig. Some units w/minibars, some w/terraces. Hairdryers and makeup mirrors are prehistoric. Many accommodations (including all suites) are outfitted with 36-inch TVs. **Services:** 🍽 🔑 VP 🚐 🛆 ⌐ Twice-daily maid svce, car-rental desk, social director, masseur, babysitting. **Facilities:** 🏊 🚲 🎾 ⬛2 ⛹ 600 ⬜ ♿ 3 restaurants, 2 bars (1 w/entertainment), spa, sauna, whirlpool. Good-size pool area is flanked by cabanas and potted palms. Exercise room features Nautilus machines. Half-court basketball court. **Rates:** $200 S or D; $250 ste. Extra person $20. Children under age 18 stay free. Parking: Outdoor, free. AE, DC, DISC, MC, V.

≣≣≣ Little Inn on the Bay
617 Lido Park Dr, 92663 (Newport Peninsula); tel 714/673-8800 or toll free 800/438-4466; fax 714/673-8800. Newport Blvd exit off CA 1. A romantic inn where you can watch boats glide by in the picturesque harbor. Easy walk to shops and restaurants. **Rooms:** 29 rms. CI 3pm/CO noon. No smoking. Simple, straightforward rooms; no frills other than location. Bottom floors have great view through sliding glass door. **Amenities:** 🛁 ⓠ A/C, TV. **Services:** ⌐ Masseur, babysitting. Wine and cheese in evening, cookies and milk at bedtime. Complimentary newspapers. Massage available. Wine and cheese cruises on the bay can be arranged. **Facilities:** 🏊 🚲 **Rates (CP):** $100–$200 S or D. Extra person $15. Children under age 12 stay free. Parking: Outdoor, free. Worth the price. AE, MC, V.

≣≣≣≣ Newport Beach Marriott Hotel & Tennis Club
900 Newport Center Dr, 92660; tel 714/640-4000 or toll free 800/228-9290; fax 714/640-5055. Jamboree Rd N from CA 1; at Santa Barbara Dr. 23 acres. Well-located resort hotel in the center of Newport Beach, close to airport and major attractions. A two-minute walk from Fashion Island, the area's best shopping center. Grounds have a pastoral feel. **Rooms:** 570 rms and stes. Executive level. CI 4pm/CO noon. Nonsmoking rms avail. Recently redecorated rooms have white-washed oak furnishings and teal and cinnamon decor. King-bed rooms are geared to the business traveler with extra-large desk and power for computer hook-ups. **Amenities:** 🛁 ⓠ ⓣ A/C, cable TV w/movies, dataport, voice mail. State-of-the-art electronics. **Services:** ✗ 🔑 VP 🚐 🛆 ⌐ ⌐ Twice-daily maid svce, car-rental desk, masseur, babysitting. Tennis pro will arrange matches. **Facilities:** 🏊 🚲 🎾 ⬛8 ⛹ 1000 ⬜ ♿ 1 restaurant, 1 bar (w/entertainment), whirlpool, washer/dryer. Lovely pool deck with a large,

freeform pool and ocean views. On a clear day, you can glimpse Catalina Island from the 16th floor view lounge. Hertz and American Airlines desks on premises; tennis pro shop. Hotel adjoins the 18-hole golf course at Newport Beach Country Club. **Rates:** Peak (June–Sept) $119–$149 S or D; $250–$750 ste. Children under age 18 stay free. Min stay special events. Lower rates off-season. Parking: Indoor/outdoor, $7/day. AE, CB, DC, DISC, EC, ER, JCB, MC, V.

≣≣≣ Newport Beach Marriott Suites
500 Bayview Circle, 92660 (Back Bay); tel 714/854-4500 or toll free 800/228-9290; fax 714/854-3072. Tamboree Rd exit off CA 73. Set high on a hill overlooking open meadows, with beautiful grounds that give a resort feel. Located in a quiet business center, close to the airport. Good choice for business travelers. **Rooms:** 250 stes. CI 4pm/CO noon. Nonsmoking rms avail. **Amenities:** 🛏 🍴 📺 ⌨ A/C, satel TV w/movies, refrig, dataport, voice mail. All units w/terraces. **Services:** ✗ 🚗 🖼 ⌨ 🔔 Babysitting. Efficient staff. **Facilities:** 🏊 🚐 [150] ♿ 1 restaurant, 1 bar, spa, sauna, whirlpool, washer/dryer. Relatively small lobby but a beautiful garden and pool area. Cozy bar with piano. **Rates:** $109–$129 ste. Children under age 18 stay free. Parking: Outdoor, free. AE, DC, DISC, MC, V.

≣≣≣ Portofino Beach Hotel
2306 W Oceanfront, 92663; tel 714/673-7030; fax 714/723-4370. 32nd St exit off CA 55 S. Cozy hotel close to shops and restaurants. **Rooms:** 15 rms; 9 cottages/villas. CI 3pm/CO noon. Nonsmoking rms avail. Each room is nicely decorated, some with brass or canopy beds. Many have ocean views. **Amenities:** 🛏 🍴 A/C, TV. Some units w/terraces, some w/fireplaces, some w/whirlpools. **Services:** ✗ 🅥🅟 🖼 Twice-daily maid svce, car-rental desk, children's program, babysitting. Friendly, helpful staff. **Facilities:** [40] 1 restaurant (dinner only), 1 bar, 1 beach (ocean), lifeguard, washer/dryer. Elegant Italian restaurant with ocean view. **Rates (CP):** Peak (June–Oct) $100–$250 S or D. Extra person $15. Children under age 18 stay free. Lower rates off-season. Parking: Outdoor, free. AE, MC, V.

≣≣≣ Sheraton Newport Beach
4545 MacArthur Blvd, 92660; tel 714/833-0570 or toll free 800/325-3535; fax 714/833-3927. 3 mi E of Newport Beach. MacArthur Blvd exit off I-405. Conveniently located near the major business center and five minutes from the airport, with easy access to freeways. Hotel occupies two buildings; public areas are large and comfortable. **Rooms:** 335 rms and stes. Executive level. CI 3pm/CO 1pm. Nonsmoking rms avail. Rooms are clean and well kept. **Amenities:** 🛏 🍴 📺 ⌨ A/C, cable TV w/movies, dataport, voice mail, bathrobes. All units w/terraces, 1 w/whirlpool. **Services:** ✗ 🖼 🅥🅟 🚗 🖼 🔔 Social director, babysitting. Free shuttle service within five miles. Professional wedding planner on staff. **Facilities:** 🏊 📷 🚐 [700] ♿ 1 restaurant, 1 bar, sauna, whirlpool. Basket-

ball court. **Rates (CP):** $65–$159 S or D; $300 ste. Children under age 13 stay free. Parking: Outdoor, free. AE, CB, DC, DISC, EC, ER, JCB, MC, V.

INN

≣≣≣ Doryman's Inn
2102 W Oceanfront, 92633; tel 714/675-7300 or toll free 800/634-3303; fax 714/675-7300. CA 55 S exit off I-405. Long on Americana and charm; located in a historical landmark, where fishermen brought their catch for over 100 years. Romance and elegance reign supreme. Close to the beach and shops. **Rooms:** 10 rms and stes. CI 3pm/CO noon. Each room personally decorated by the owner, Victorian-era antiques. All have sunken marble tubs. Many have brass or canopy beds as well as ocean views. **Amenities:** 🛏 🍴 A/C, cable TV. Some units w/terraces, all w/fireplaces, some w/whirlpools. Microwave oven and coffee on each floor. **Services:** ✗ Masseur, babysitting, afternoon tea served. Breakfast in your room consists of fresh pastries, eggs, fresh fruit, yogurt, cheese, and coffee or tea. **Facilities:** 🚲 ⛱ ♿ 1 restaurant (see "Restaurants" below), 1 beach (ocean, bay), lifeguard. One of the city's best restaurants on premises. Bicycle, rollerblade, and skateboard rentals nearby. **Rates (CP):** $160–$180 S or D; $220–$300 ste. Parking: Outdoor, free. AE, MC, V.

RESORT

≣≣≣ Hyatt Newporter
1107 Jamboree Rd, 92660; tel 714/729-1234 or toll free 800/233-1234; fax 714/644-1552. Off CA 73. 26 acres. A beautifully landscaped and well-maintained property located close to many area attractions. Family-oriented for vacation travelers, but a good choice for business travel too. **Rooms:** 406 rms and stes; 4 cottages/villas. CI 4pm/CO noon. Nonsmoking rms avail. Rooms have a fresh look. Decorated in cool pastel colors, whitewashed furniture, and wicker. **Amenities:** 🛏 🍴 📺 ⌨ A/C, cable TV w/movies, refrig, dataport, bathrobes. All units w/terraces, some w/fireplaces. All rooms have wet bars. Scheduled to add voicemail to phones in 1996. **Services:** ✗ 🍴 🅥🅟 🚗 🖼 🔔 Twice-daily maid svce, children's program, babysitting. Jazz concerts offered in summer. **Facilities:** 🏊 🚲 🏌9 🎾 ⛱ 16 ♨ 🍴 ⛳ [1000] 🖥 ♿ 2 restaurants, 2 bars (1 w/entertainment), basketball, volleyball, whirlpool, beauty salon. **Rates:** Peak (June 31–Sept 6) $99–$125 S; $125–$150 D; $300–$450 ste; $600–$750 cottage/villa. Children under age 12 stay free. Min stay peak and wknds. Lower rates off-season. Parking: Outdoor, $2–$3/day. AE, CB, DC, DISC, MC, V.

RESTAURANTS 🍴

The Arches
3334 West Coast Hwy; tel 714/645-7077. **American.** This place looks like a men's club. Gay '90s steak-house atmosphere is enhanced by dark wood paneling and lush, spacious

leather booths. John Wayne loved the New York steak, potatoes, and salad; other house specialties include beef Wellington, abalone, Maryland crab, and rack of lamb. **FYI:** Reservations recommended. **Open:** Lunch Mon–Fri 11am–3pm; dinner daily 4:30pm–1am. **Prices:** Main courses $17–$26. AE, CB, DC, DISC, MC, V. 🖤 ⚱ VP &

Bistango
In the Atrium Building, 19100 Von Karman Ave; tel 714/752-5222. **Californian/Italian.** Delivering top value and consistently good food, this is a perfect spot for a business lunch. With high-tech European design, atrium, and marble bar, it's a favorite place in the area. Specialties are oriental chicken salad, pizza with grilled eggplant, pasta, and wood-fired chicken. **FYI:** Reservations recommended. Jazz. **Open:** Lunch Mon–Fri 11:30am–3pm; dinner Mon–Thurs 5:30–10:30pm, Fri–Sat 5:30–11:30pm. **Prices:** Main courses $10–$20; prix fixe $25. AE, CB, DC, DISC, MC, V. 🖤 VP &

♣ ✦ The Cannery
3010 Lafayette Ave; tel 714/675-5777. On Newport Peninsula Harbor. **American/Seafood.** A restaurant in a former cannery that appeals to tourists and locals alike, with patio dining overlooking the harbor. Decor is tasteful, with Victorian touches throughout, and some original machinery still in place. Menu items are primarily seafood and steak; house specialty is the Australian lobster tail. **FYI:** Reservations recommended. Karaoke/singer. Children's menu. **Open:** Peak (summer) lunch daily 11:30am–3pm; dinner Sun 4:30–10pm, Mon–Sat 5–10pm; brunch Sun 10am–2:30pm. **Prices:** Main courses $17–$33. AE, CB, DC, DISC, MC, V. 🖤 ⚱ ▲ VP

Marrakesh
1100 West Coast Hwy; tel 714/645-8384. **Moroccan.** An exotic place, with black-on-black interior in two connecting domed buildings. Dinners of six to eight courses feature Moroccan renditions of lamb, chicken, rabbit, quail, duck, and seafood. **FYI:** Reservations recommended. Children's menu. Dress code. **Open:** Sun–Thurs 5–10pm, Fri–Sat 5–11pm. **Prices:** Main courses $19–$25; prix fixe $15–$23. AE, CB, DC, DISC, MC, V. 🖤 ⚐ VP &

Pascal
In Plaza Newport, 1000 Bristol St; tel 714/752-0107. **French.** Country French decor with soft pinks and blues and lots of fresh flowers. The cuisine is classic French, featuring rabbit, rack of lamb, sea bass, free-range chicken, and lamb salad with apple dressing. Gourmet deli, Pascal Epicérie, across the way. Chef/owner also gives cooking lessons. **FYI:** Reservations recommended. **Open:** Lunch Mon–Fri 11:30am–2:30pm; dinner Mon–Thurs 6–9:30pm, Fri–Sat 6–10pm. Closed Sept 15–30. **Prices:** Main courses $17–$23; prix fixe $45. AE, DC, DISC, MC, V. 🖤 &

♣ The Pavilion
In Four Seasons Hotel, 690 Newport Center Dr; tel 714/759-0808. CA 73 off I-405 S; Jamboree Rd exit off I-405 N.

Californian/French. Classic elegance. Large windows overlook flower-filled gardens and patio, where there's outdoor dining much of the year. The menu highlights dishes such as pepper-crusted lamb with port wine, or grilled whitefish with shiitake mushrooms and gnocchi. **FYI:** Reservations recommended. **Open:** Breakfast Mon–Fri 6:30–11am, Sat–Sun 6:30am–noon; lunch Mon–Fri 11am–2pm, Sat–Sun noon–2pm; dinner daily 6–10:30pm. **Prices:** Main courses $20–$25. AE, CB, DC, DISC, MC, V. ⚱ VP &

♣ The Ritz
In Fashion Island, 880 Newport Center Dr; tel 714/720-1800. Jamboree Rd exit off I-405. **International.** One of the best restaurants in town; perfect for a special occasion. Elegantly decorated European-style dining room, where people dress up. Start with the famous carousel appetizer of house-cured gravlax, prawns, Dungeness crab, lobster, and pâté; then try the rack of lamb, pepper steak, or veal scaloppine with three types of mushrooms. **FYI:** Reservations recommended. Piano. Jacket required. **Open:** Lunch Mon–Fri 11:30am–3pm; dinner Mon–Thurs 6–10pm, Fri–Sat 5:30–11pm, Sun 5–10pm. **Prices:** Main courses $17–$29. AE, DC, MC, V. VP &

✦ Sabatino
In Cannery Village, 251 Shipyard Way Cabin D (Balboa Peninsula); tel 714/723-0645. Newport Blvd exit off CA 55. **Italian.** Tucked away in historic Cannery Village, a family-run trattoria popular with locals. Hand-painted murals of old Venice line the walls. Known for homemade Sicilian sausages, from a recipe dating back to 1864; fine fettuccine, linguine, veal saltimbocca, and lasagne also served. **FYI:** Reservations recommended. Children's menu. Beer and wine only. Additional location: 33 Fortune St, Irvine (tel 450-1450). **Open:** Mon–Sat 9am–11pm, Sun 8:30am–11pm. **Prices:** Main courses $9–$25. AE, DISC, MC, V. &

♣ ✦ Tutto Mare
In Newport Fashion Island, 545 Newport Center Dr; tel 714/640-6333. **Italian.** One of the most attractive restaurants in town, with cherry wood paneling, French windows, marble floors, and a lively bar scene. Good taste is evident in both the ambience and the food. A dozen different pastas lead the menu, with choices like tagliolini with shrimp and grilled eggplant. They also serve a great veal chop and fine fried calamari, plus vegetarian risotto. **FYI:** Reservations recommended. **Open:** Lunch Mon–Sat 11:30am–5pm, Sun 11am–5pm; dinner Mon–Sat 5–11pm, Sun 5–10pm; brunch Sun 11am–2pm. **Prices:** Main courses $9–$19. AE, DISC, MC, V. 🖤 ⚱ &

♣ 21 Ocean Front
In Doryman's Inn, 2100 W Ocean Front; tel 714/675-2566. CA 55 exit off I-405. **Californian/Seafood.** Locals consider this a place for special occasions, with its beautiful setting in a historic Victorian-style inn and a spectacular ocean view. The house special is abalone ($48.50); abalone-lovers travel far

and wide to get here. Other menu highlights include a wide variety of other fresh seafood. **FYI:** Reservations recommended. Piano. Dress code. **Open:** Daily 4pm–1am. **Prices:** Main courses $19–$49. AE, DC, DISC, MC, V. 💛 🏔 VP

What's Cooking
In Newport Hills Center Mall, 2632 San Miguel Dr; tel 714/644-1820. McHarto Blvd exit off CA 73. **Italian.** Hidden away in a small strip mall, a cozy place that is worth finding. Italian pizzas and pasta here are all made by grandma herself; you'll often find the owner behind the bar. Good food at reasonable prices. **FYI:** Reservations recommended. Guitar/singer/accordian. Additional location: 24312 Del Prado, Dana Point (tel 661-6500). **Open:** Lunch daily 11am–2:30pm; dinner Mon–Fri 5–10pm, Sat–Sun 5–10:30pm. **Prices:** Main courses $8–$16. AE, MC, V. 💛 ⅙

North Hollywood

See also Hollywood, West Hollywood

Tucked against the Santa Monica Mountains, North Hollywood's most famous draw is Universal Studios and the Universal City theme park. **Information:** Universal City–North Hollywood Chamber of Commerce, 5019 Lankershim Blvd, North Hollywood 91601 (tel 818/508-5155).

HOTEL 🏨

📑📑📑 Beverly Garland's Holiday Inn
4222 Vineland Ave, 91602 (Universal City); tel 818/980-8000 or toll free 800/BEVERLY; fax 818/766-5230. Vineland exit from US 101 and CA 134. On seven beautifully landscaped acres, just down the street from Universal Studios and City Walk. This charming property is owned by movie and TV star Beverly Garland ("My Three Sons" and "Lois and Clark"), who is actively involved in daily operations. Lobby has fun display of movie memorabilia. **Rooms:** 255 rms and stes. CI 3pm/CO noon. Nonsmoking rms avail. Cool and comfortable, with decor of soft pastels and light wood. **Amenities:** 🔒 🦺 A/C, satel TV w/movies, voice mail. All units w/terraces. **Services:** ✗ 🚐 🖼 🍴 Car-rental desk. Service is very attentive. Free shuttle service to Burbank Airport and Universal Studios/City Walk. **Facilities:** 🛗 🏊2 🏌️ 600 ⅙ 1 restaurant, 1 bar, sauna. Tennis courts have pro on duty 10 hours a day. **Rates:** $89–$139 S or D; $169–$350 ste. Extra person $10. Children under age 18 stay free. Min stay special events. Parking: Outdoor, free. AE, CB, DC, DISC, MC, V.

INN

📑📑📑📑 La Maida House
11159 La Maida St, 91601; tel 818/769-3857. 1 acre. Megan Timothy, who was raised in central Africa, turned her 1920s Italianate villa into a bed-and-breakfast. Featured in international home-and-garden magazines, the inn is an oasis of serenity in the heart of North Hollywood. Unsuitable for children under 12. **Rooms:** 11 rms, stes, and effic. CI 4pm/CO 11am. No smoking. Each room is tastefully decorated with souvenirs from the innkeeper's world travels. **Amenities:** 🔒 🦺 🖥️ 🍴 A/C, TV, voice mail, bathrobes. 1 unit w/terrace, some w/fireplaces, some w/whirlpools. Fresh cut flowers in rooms. **Services:** Turn-down service. **Facilities:** 🛗 Whirlpool. Solarium, exercise room, and breakfast patio. **Rates (CP):** $95–$165 S; $85–$165 D; $160–$210 ste; $165 effic. Children under age 5 stay free. AE, MC, V.

North Shore

ATTRACTION 🏛️

Salton Sea State Recreation Area
100-225 State Park Rd; tel 619/393-3052. Located on CA 111 at State Park Rd. Located 20 m S of Indio. One of the world's largest inland seas was accidentally created when a dike broke during the 1905 construction of the All-American Canal. The 360-square-mile basin is popular with boaters and fishermen, who come to catch such ocean transplants as corvina, gulf croaker, and sargo. Swimming and waterskiing areas. Nature trails, interpretive programs; picnicking, camping. **Open:** Daily 24 hours. $$

Oakhurst

See also Yosemite National Park

INN 🏨

📑📑📑📑 Chateau du Sureau
48688 Victoria Lane, PO Box 577, 93644; tel 209/683-6860; fax 209/683-0800. 7½ acres. A storybook castle with red-tile roof and a stone turret in a snoozy, Sierra foothills town 90 minutes from the valley floor of Yosemite. Little touches captivate the eye—a statue in a niche, the 17th-century tapestry by the stairway. Part of the Relais & Chateaux group. Unsuitable for children under 12. **Rooms:** 9 rms. CI 2pm/CO noon. No smoking. Delightful rooms decked out with superb linens, antiques, and goosedown bedding. Geranium room offers a four-poster bed and huge armoire, while Saffron room has an 1834 bedroom set of ebony inlaid with ivory. **Amenities:** 🔒 🍴 A/C, CD/tape player, bathrobes. No TV. All units w/terraces, all w/fireplaces. TV available on request. Everything is top quality. Upon arrival, guests receive a bowl of fresh fruit and Austrian cake. **Services:** 🔑 VP 🚐 🖼 Twice-daily maid svce, car-rental desk, social director, masseur, babysitting, afternoon tea and wine/sherry served. Highly personalized service is lavished on guests. Complimentary laundry and ironing. **Facilities:** 🛗 🏋️ 🏌️ 100 ⅙ 1 restaurant, 1 bar, lawn games, guest lounge w/TV. Serene pool surrounded by a white balustrade and colorful gardens. Small chapel is a perfect setting for weddings. **Rates (BB):**

$310–$410 S or D. Extra person $65. Min stay wknds and special events. Parking: Outdoor, free. Closed Jan 2–23. AE, MC, V.

RESTAURANT 🎬

⚑ Erna's Elderberry House

In Chateau du Sureau, 48688 Victoria Lane; tel 209/683-6800. 2 blocks S of Oakhurst proper. **Californian/Continental.** A touch of southern France on Yosemite's outskirts. High-backed chairs, bouquets of flowers, and pewter chargers convey elegance. Prix fixe, six-course dinners feature fresh local ingredients in dishes like rabbit ragout with quail and currant-glazed pork tenderloin. The buttery, fresh-baked breads and desserts such as poppyseed cake are excellent. **FYI:** Reservations recommended. Harp/singer. **Open:** Lunch Wed–Fri 11:30am–1pm; dinner Wed–Mon 5:30–8:30pm; brunch Sun 11am–1pm. Closed Jan 2–23. **Prices:** Prix fixe $58. AE, MC, V. ❤ �

Oakland

See also Berkeley

Situated on the eastern side of San Francisco Bay, Oakland has one of the largest ports on the West Coast and is a major railroad transportation hub. Oakland itself, however, is a study in contrasts, with its poorer sections set against the affluent hillside neighborhoods. The downtown district has been refurbished, and the waterfront Jack London Square (named after its famous native son) is a popular spot for dining and shopping. **Information:** Oakland Convention & Visitors Bureau, 1000 Broadway #200, Oakland 94607 (tel 510/839-9000).

HOTELS 🏨

☰☰ Best Western Park Plaza Hotel

150 Hegenberger Rd, 94621 (Oakland Int'l Airport); tel 510/635-5300 or toll free 800/635-5301; fax 510/635-9661. 6½ mi S of Oakland. Hegenberger Rd exit off I-880. Standard airport hotel. **Rooms:** 187 rms and stes. CI 2pm/CO noon. Nonsmoking rms avail. **Amenities:** 🕾 ₢ 🎬 ⍾ A/C, cable TV w/movies, voice mail. All units w/terraces. Irons and ironing boards in all rooms. **Services:** ✕ �car 🅰 ⌂ Free transportation to airport, BART station, and Oakland Coliseum. **Facilities:** 🛎 ⍾⍾ ⬛150 2 restaurants, 1 bar, sauna, whirlpool. Walking distance to golf course. Jogging trail across the street. **Rates:** $92 S; $102 D; $130 ste. Extra person $10. Children under age 12 stay free. Parking: Outdoor, free. AE, CB, DC, DISC, JCB, MC, V.

☰☰☰ Clarion Suites Lake Merritt Hotel

1800 Madison St, 94612 (Lake Merritt Business District); tel 510/832-2300 or toll free 800/933-HOTEL; fax 510/832-7150. A meticulously maintained 76-year-old, art deco Oakland landmark, located across the street from Lake Merritt. **Rooms:** 51 rms, stes, and effic. CI 3pm/CO 11am. Nonsmoking rms avail. Many units have lake views. Bathrooms are cramped, with free-standing sinks and no counter space. **Amenities:** 🕾 ₢ 🎬 Cable TV w/movies, refrig. No A/C. Some units w/minibars, 1 w/whirlpool. Air conditioning planned. **Services:** ✕ 🗝 VP 🚐 🅰 ⌂ 🠔 Masseur, babysitting. Staff can customize suites to fit guest's needs. **Facilities:** ⬛300 ⍾ 1 restaurant (bkfst only), 1 bar, washer/dryer. Access to off-premises fitness center and health spa at a reduced rate, plus free transportation there. **Rates (CP):** $89–$159 S; $99–$169 D; $129–$159 ste; $129–$159 effic. Extra person $10. Children under age 16 stay free. Parking: Indoor, $9/day. AE, MC, V.

☰☰ Hampton Inn

8465 Enterprise Way, 94621; tel 510/632-8900 or toll free 800/950-1191; fax 510/632-4713. Hegenberger Coliseum exit off I-880. Very neat and well-maintained property. Good location and excellent value for those transiting Oakland airport. **Rooms:** 149 rms. CI 2pm/CO noon. Nonsmoking rms avail. Closets are free-standing armoires and a bit small, but adequate for most travelers. All king rooms come with either a recliner chair or a fold-out couch. **Amenities:** 🕾 ₢ 🎬 ⍾ A/C, cable TV w/movies, dataport. A mini-fridge can be rented for $5 per day. **Services:** 🗝 🚐 🅰 ⌂ 🠔 Local and state guidebooks available for use at front desk. Free 24-hour shuttle service to Coliseum or rapid transit station. **Facilities:** 🛎 ⬛35 ⍾ Whirlpool. **Rates (CP):** $68–$72 S; $73–$77 D. Children under age 18 stay free. Parking: Outdoor, free. Park-and-fly packages available. AE, DC, DISC, MC, V.

☰☰ Holiday Inn Oakland

500 Hegenberger Rd, 94621 (Oakland Int'l Airport); tel 510/562-5311 or toll free 800/HOLIDAY; fax 510/636-1539. 6½ mi S of Oakland. Hegenberger exit off I-880; entrance on Edes Ave. Close to airport and Oakland Coliseum. Excellent security and well-lit parking lot. **Rooms:** 290 rms and stes. Executive level. CI 3pm/CO noon. Nonsmoking rms avail. **Amenities:** 🕾 ₢ A/C, cable TV w/movies. Some units w/minibars. **Services:** ✕ 🚐 🅰 ⌂ Car-rental desk. Complimentary shuttle service to rapid transit station and Oakland Coliseum. **Facilities:** 🛎 ⍾⍾ ⬛250 ⍾ 1 restaurant, 1 bar (w/entertainment), washer/dryer. **Rates:** $97 S; $107 D; $129 ste. Extra person $10. Children under age 19 stay free. Parking: Outdoor, free. AE, DC, DISC, MC, V.

☰☰☰ Oakland Airport Hilton

1 Hegenberger Rd, 94621 (Oakland Int'l Airport); tel 510/635-5000 or toll free 800/HILTONS; fax 510/729-0491. Hegenberger exit off I-880. Although this hotel ranks near the top of its rating group, the grounds need a bit of work and the service could be improved. **Rooms:** 363 rms and stes. CI 3pm/CO noon. Nonsmoking rms avail. **Amenities:** 🕾 ₢ 🎬 ⍾ A/C, cable TV w/movies, refrig, dataport, voice mail, bathrobes. Some units w/terraces. Irons and ironing boards in each room. **Services:** 🍴 🚐 🅰 ⌂ Car-rental desk, babysitting. **Facilities:** 🛎 ⍾⍾ ⬛1100 ⬛ ⍾ 2 restaurants, 1 bar

(w/entertainment), games rm. **Rates:** $126 S; $146 D; $295–$395 ste. Extra person $20. Children under age 18 stay free. Parking: Outdoor, free. Special $89 weekend rate with continental breakfast. Romance package offers champagne and breakfast at $109. AE, CB, DC, DISC, JCB, MC, V.

🇪🇪 Oakland Marriott

1001 Broadway, 94607 (City Center); tel 510/451-4000 or toll free 800/338-1338; fax 510/839-0677. 12th/11th Sts exit off I-880; left on 11th St, 4 blocks. Adjacent to the Oakland Convention Center and within walking distance of many Oakland attractions, including Chinatown, City Center, restored Old Town, and Housewives Market. Next to Bay Area Rapid Transit station. **Rooms:** 488 rms and stes. Executive level. CI 3pm/CO noon. Nonsmoking rms avail. Some rooms have a bay view. **Amenities:** 🛅 🕭 A/C, cable TV w/movies, voice mail. Some units w/minibars, 1 w/whirlpool. **Services:** ✕ 🖙 🖎 🖑 Car-rental desk, masseur, babysitting. **Facilities:** 🖼 🖳 🔟1300 🖳 🖔 1 restaurant, 1 bar (w/entertainment), spa, whirlpool. **Rates:** $109 S or D; $325–$700 ste. Extra person $20. Children under age 18 stay free. Parking: Indoor, $11/day. AE, CB, DC, DISC, MC, V.

🇪🇪 Ramada Hotel

455 Hegenberger Rd, 94621; tel 510/562-6100 or toll free 800/932-4550; fax 510/569-5681. 6½ mi S of downtown. Hegenberger exit off I-880. Property needs some improvements, especially to ground-floor bathrooms and landscaping. Close to the airport. **Rooms:** 342 rms and stes. Executive level. CI 2pm/CO noon. No smoking. **Amenities:** 🛅 A/C, satel TV w/movies. **Services:** ✕ 🖎 🖑 Twice-daily maid svce, car-rental desk. **Facilities:** 🖼 🔟2000 🖔 2 restaurants, 1 bar (w/entertainment), washer/dryer. **Rates:** $99–$109 S or D; $199 ste. Extra person $15. Children under age 18 stay free. Parking: Outdoor, free. AE, DC, DISC, MC, V.

🇪🇪🇪 Waterfront Plaza Hotel

10 Washington St, 94607 (Jack London Square); tel 510/836-3800 or toll free 800/729-3638; fax 510/832-6228. Completely renovated in 1990, the Waterfront Plaza is located right on the harbor in Jack London Square. The light and airy decor boasts a nautical theme inside and out, with jaunty blue awnings and some windows cut out like portholes. **Rooms:** 144 rms and stes. CI 3pm/CO noon. Nonsmoking rms avail. Nautical decor: white-washed pine furnishings, seafaring prints, bedspreads designed with seashell motif. Most rooms have skyline or water views. Bathrooms are rather small, at least in the standard rooms, and the carpeting is getting worn. **Amenities:** 🛅 🕭 🖳 🍵 A/C, cable TV w/movies, dataport, VCR, voice mail, in-rm safe. All units w/minibars, some w/terraces, some w/fireplaces, some w/whirlpools. **Services:** ✕ 🆅🅿 🖎 🖑 Twice-daily maid svce. Free shuttle to downtown and rapid-transit station. **Facilities:** 🖼 🖳 🔟200 🖔 1 restaurant, 1 bar (w/entertainment), sauna. Large pool (heated year-round) is located right on the estuary. Small workout room has serviceable—but not great—equipment. **Rates:** $150–$165 S or D; $175–$325

ste. Children under age 18 stay free. Parking: Outdoor, $9/day. Weekend, wedding, and romance packages avail. AE, DC, DISC, MC, V.

MOTEL

🇪🇪 Best Western Thunderbird Inn

233 Broadway, 94607 (Jack London Square); tel 510/452-4565 or toll free 800/633-5973; fax 510/452-4634. Fairly nice property once you get off the street. Good location, within walking distance of Chinatown and Jack London Square. **Rooms:** 100 rms and stes. CI 2pm/CO noon. Nonsmoking rms avail. Some rooms open onto landscaped area around pool; some are a little dark. **Amenities:** 🛅 🕭 A/C, cable TV w/movies. Some units w/terraces. **Services:** 🖎 🖑 Free coffee service in an alcove on every floor. **Facilities:** 🖼 🖳 🔟40 🖔 Sauna. **Rates (CP):** $75–$90 S or D; $150–$175 ste. Extra person $5. Children under age 12 stay free. Parking: Indoor, free. AE, DC, DISC, MC, V.

RESTAURANTS 🍽

Bay Wolf

3853 Piedmont Ave; tel 510/655-6004. At Rio Vista. **Mediterranean.** Housed in a converted Victorian house with a rustic wood exterior and polished wood interior, this homey restaurant features several intimate dining rooms and a covered terrace for outdoor dining. The California cuisine relies heavily on fresh local produce, fresh seafood, and grilled meats. Sophisticated wine list highlights local California vintages. **FYI:** Reservations recommended. Dress code. Beer and wine only. **Open:** Lunch Mon–Fri 11:30am–2pm; dinner Mon–Fri 6–9pm, Sat–Sun 5:30–9pm. **Prices:** Main courses $13–$18. MC, V.

Cafe de Bordeaux

326 7th St (Chinatown); tel 510/891-2338. **Continental/French.** Clean and tidy, though a little plain. Owned and operated by husband-and-wife team who are eager to help their customers. Specialties are continental and French dishes, such as steak au poivre vert, veal scaloppine marsala, scallop and shrimp vin blanc, prawn Provençale, and eggplant parmigiana. **FYI:** Reservations recommended. Children's menu. Dress code. Beer and wine only. **Open:** Mon–Fri 11:30am–9:30pm, Sat–Sun 2–9:30pm. **Prices:** Main courses $9–$16. MC, V. 🖔

Gulf Coast Grill and Bar

736 Washington St; tel 510/836-3663. At 8th St. **Cajun.** Portions are so enormous here, it would take a hungry lumberjack to clean most plates. The narrow restaurant is decorated with polished wood, brick, tile, and large picture windows and has a distinct New Orleans flavor. Menu specialties include Cajun-style fish, jambalaya, baked oysters, and spicy sausages. **FYI:** Reservations accepted. Dress code. Beer and wine only. **Open:** Lunch Wed–Fri 11am–2:30pm; dinner Thurs–Sun 5–10pm; brunch Sun 11am–4pm. **Prices:** Main courses $10–$18; prix fixe $9–$16. AE, DC, DISC, MC, V.

Jade Villa

800 Broadway; tel 510/839-1688. **Chinese.** Utilitarian, banquet-hall atmosphere with rows of tables and chairs. Large windows admit lots of light. Standard Chinese menu leans heavily toward seafood. A popular spot for social functions. **FYI:** Reservations recommended. Beer and wine only. **Open:** Mon–Fri 9:30am–9:30pm, Sat–Sun 9am–10pm. **Prices:** Main courses $6–$13. MC, V.

Kincaid's

In Jack London Square, 1 Franklin St; tel 510/835-8600. On the waterfront. **American.** Polished wood floors, brass fixtures, and marble accents provide a turn-of-the-century elegance, and there's a superb view of the estuary. Diners may catch a glimpse of the former presidential yacht *Potomac* cruising by. Grilled top-quality meats, plump fillets of fish, tender crab. **FYI:** Reservations accepted. Children's menu. Dress code. **Open:** Lunch Mon–Sat 11:15am–3pm; dinner Mon–Sat 5–10pm, Sun 4–9pm; brunch Sun 10:30am–3pm. **Prices:** Main courses $10–$22. AE, DC, MC, V. 🏞 💟 VP &

★ Mama's Royal Cafe

4012 Broadway; tel 510/547-7600. **American.** This popular down-home cafe boasts unique pagoda decorations left over from its days as a Chinese restaurant many years ago. With comfortable booths and a friendly staff, it serves up sandwiches, burgers, and superb breakfast fare. **FYI:** Reservations accepted. Beer and wine only. **Open:** Mon–Fri 7am–3pm, Sat–Sun 8am–3pm. **Prices:** Lunch main courses $4–$10. No CC. 🎵 &

Nan Yang Rockridge

6048 College Ave; tel 510/655-3298. **Burmese.** Bright and modern Burmese restaurant shows off a European style. Tangy salads, flavorful soups, hearty curries. House specialties are ginger salad and green papaya salad. **FYI:** Reservations accepted. Dress code. Beer and wine only. **Open:** Tues–Sat 11:30am–10pm, Sun noon–9pm. **Prices:** Main courses $8–$15; prix fixe $15–$25. MC, V.

Oakland Grill

301 Franklin St; tel 510/835-1176. 3 blocks from Jack London Square. **American.** A refined truck stop, this hole-in-the-wall is tucked into the corner of a warehouse in the railroad produce terminal. Diners can peer through picture windows at produce trucks delivering their cargoes while dining on a forklift special, a juicy sirloin steak. **FYI:** Reservations accepted. Beer and wine only. **Open:** Mon–Fri 6am–9:30pm, Sat–Sun 8am–9:30pm. **Prices:** Main courses $10–$13. AE, DC, DISC, MC, V. &

Oliveto

5655 College Ave; tel 510/547-5356. **Italian.** A Tuscan dining experience. Sunny decor, exquisitely fresh food. The chefs change the menu regularly, offering the best of seasonal vegetables, fresh fish, and grilled and roasted meats. The serving staff can ably discuss daily specials, ingredients, and cooking styles. **FYI:** Reservations recommended. Beer and wine only. **Open:** Lunch Mon–Fri 11:30am–2pm; dinner Mon–Sat 5:30–10pm, Sun 5:30–9pm; brunch Sun 9:30am–2pm. **Prices:** Main courses $15–$21. AE, DC, MC, V. &

★ Rockridge Cafe

5492 College Ave; tel 510/653-1567. **American.** A local favorite for great hamburgers. They also serve a hearty breakfast, pasta, soups, and salads. Daily specials could include meatloaf, stir-fried chicken, or lamb stew. Fresh-baked pies. **FYI:** Reservations not accepted. Beer and wine only. **Open:** Mon–Thurs 7:30am–10pm, Fri–Sat 7:30am–10:30pm, Sun 8am–10pm. **Prices:** Main courses $8–$10. MC, V. &

Thornhill Cafe

5761 Thornhill Dr (Montclair); tel 510/339-0646. Off CA 13. **French/Thai.** Chef Chai Butsangde prepares French cuisine with an Asian flavor, as well as traditional Thai fish dishes. Dishes might include poached and chilled salmon; grilled mahimahi with tamarind sauce; cassoulet of lamb, pork, sausage, and duck with white beans. **FYI:** Reservations recommended. Beer and wine only. **Open:** Tues–Fri 11:30am–10pm, Sat–Mon 5:30–10pm. **Prices:** Main courses $11–$17. AE, MC, V. &

★ Yoshi's

6030 Claremont Ave (Rockridge); tel 510/652-9200. **Japanese.** Modern Japanese decor. You can dine in the relaxing dining room, sit at the sushi bar, or listen to the live musicians (this is a great jazz venue) at this pleasant neighborhood locale. **FYI:** Reservations recommended. Jazz. **Open:** Fri–Sat 5:30–10pm, Sun–Thurs 5:30–9:30pm. **Prices:** Main courses $11–$17. AE, CB, DC, DISC, MC, V. &

Zza's

552 Grand Ave; tel 510/839-9124. At MacArthur Ave. **Italian.** Straight out of a Mediterranean village, with high ceilings and cool shade trees, offering pizza, pasta, and traditional Italian fare. A great place to bring kids, as tables are covered with butcher paper and jars of crayons to keep children amused. **FYI:** Reservations not accepted. Beer and wine only. **Open:** Sun–Tues 4:30–10pm, Wed–Thurs 11am–10pm, Fri 11am–11pm, Sat 4:30–11pm. **Prices:** Main courses $8–$11. MC, V. 🎵

ATTRACTIONS 🏛

Oakland Museum

1000 Oak St; tel 510/238-3401. Actually three museums in one, this facility has galleries dedicated to California history, culture, art, and environment and ecology. It includes works by California artists from Bierstadt to Diebenkorn; artifacts such as Pomo basketry and Country Joe McDonald's guitar; and re-creations of California habitats from the coast to the White Mountains. Also featured are rotating exhibits from the museum's various collections as well as traveling exhibits covering a wide range of topics. Guided tours available on request. Book and gift shop; cafe and snack bar. **Open:** Wed–Sat 10am–5pm, Sun noon–7pm. **$$**

Jack London Square

Broadway and Embarcadero. The square, at the foot of Broadway on the waterfront, houses a complex of boutiques and eateries. In the center is the reconstructed rustic Yukon cabin in which London lived while prospecting in the Klondike during the Gold Rush of 1897. At 56 Jack London Square, at the foot of Webster St, is the First and Last Chance Saloon, where London did some of his writing (and much of his drinking); his corner remains much as he knew it. **Open:** Most restaurants and shops Mon–Sat 10am–9pm (some restaurants stay open later).

Greek Orthodox Cathedral of the Ascension

4700 Lincoln Ave; tel 510/531-3400. This beautiful and elaborate Byzantine-style church, built in 1960, features a copper-clad dome and an elaborate mosaic of the Ascension dominating the entrance to the nave. **Open:** Mon–Fri 9am–4pm. **Free**

Children's Fairyland

1520 Lakeside Dr; tel 510/452-2259. Located on the shores of Lake Merritt in Oakland, this is the first theme park of its kind in the United States. Opened in 1950, it caters to small children with an imaginative, interactive flair. Fables, fairytales, and classsic literature are brought to life with whimsical settings and talking storybook boxes. Fiberglass figures of folklore characters adorn the fantasy architecture. Features include animals, children's rides, and professional puppet shows daily. **Open:** Daily 10am–4:30pm. **$**

Oakland Mormon Temple Visitors Center

4770 Lincoln Ave; tel 510/531-1475. Situated high in the Oakland hills, the Mormon temple offers a panoramic view from its terrace and gardens. Although the interior is not open to the public, visitors may browse the temple grounds. The Temple Visitors Center offers free guided tours that include a reproduction of Danish sculptor Bertel Thorvaldsen's *Christus* statue, special audio-visual presentations, and exhibits on Mormon faith and doctrine. Also on the grounds is the Family History Center, with resources for genealogical research. **Open:** Daily 9am–9pm. **Free**

Oakland Zoo in Knowland Park

9777 Golf Links Rd; tel 510/632-9525. This 100-acre zoo has 50 exhibits with 75 different species from around the world. A new highlight is Sun Bear Canyon, a 1-acre bear habitat with honey-dispensing trees and a waterfall that delivers live fish into a large pond. Other features include the Skyride chairlift ride, a miniature train, and a carousel. Cafe, gift shop. **Open:** Daily 10am–4pm. **$$**

Rotary Nature Center

552 Bellevue, Lakeside Park; tel 510/238-3739. Located on the shores of Lake Merritt, the center offers seasonal displays of mammals, birds, and reptiles and has exhibits that cover topics like ecology and conservation. Lectures, nature walks, films, and other special programs. **Open:** Daily 10am–5pm. **Free**

Oakland Coliseum Complex

Hegenberger Rd exit off I-880; tel 510/430-8020. From April to October, the Oakland Athletics play baseball in the Oakland Coliseum Stadium, which seats close to 50,000. The NBA's Golden State Warriors play basketball from November to April in the 15,025-seat Oakland Coliseum Arena. Tickets are available from the coliseum box office or by phone through BASS Ticketmaster (tel 510/762-2277). **$$$$**

Oakville

RESTAURANT 🍽

♥ Stars Oakville Cafe

7848 St Helena Hwy; PO Box 410; tel 707/944-8905. E side of CA 29. **French/Italian.** San Francisco super-chef Jeremiah Tower's venture in wine country. In the large dining garden, diners sit amid olive trees and a flower garden. The food is very good to excellent; selections might include golden onion tart with fresh-picked salad greens, or pan-seared salmon with fresh corn, peas, potatoes, and beets. **FYI:** Reservations recommended. Beer and wine only. **Open:** Lunch Thurs–Mon noon–3pm; dinner Thurs–Mon 5:30–9pm. **Prices:** Main courses $10–$15. AE, DC, MC, V. 🛥 ♿

REFRESHMENT STOP 🥤

Oakville Grocery

7856 St Helena Hwy; tel 707/944-8802. On CA 29. **Deli.** A deli stocked with thousands of gourmet groceries from around the world—wild-mango chutney from Sri Lanka, Jamaican jerk spices, 20 varieties of olives, and a huge wine inventory. An ideal place to pick up a picnic, offering cheeses, pasta salads, sliced smoked tuna, and special sandwiches. They also have an espresso bar and sell fine pastries. **Open:** Daily 10am–6pm. AE, MC, V.

ATTRACTION 🏛

Robert Mondavi Winery

7801 St Helena Hwy (CA 29); tel 707/259-9463. This is the ultimate high-tech Napa Valley winery, housed in a magnificent Mission-style facility. Almost every variable in the wine-making process is computer controlled. A free guided tour is followed by a tasting of selected current wines, which are sold by the glass. Reservations are recommended for the guided tour. **Open:** Daily 10am–5pm. **Free**

Oceanside

MOTEL 🖼

≣≣ Best Western Marty's Valley Inn

3240 E Mission Ave, 92054; tel 619/757-7700 or toll free 800/747-3529; fax 619/439-3311. 2½ mi E of Mission Ave exit off I-5. Comfortable accommodations appealing to business travelers, who can use the conference center on site. **Rooms:** 111 rms. CI noon/CO noon. Nonsmoking rms avail. **Amenities:** 🛏 A/C, satel TV. Some units w/terraces, 1 w/fireplace. **Services:** ⤴ **Facilities:** 🛗 🏊 👍 **Rates:** $57 S; $66 D. Extra person $4. Children under age 12 stay free. Parking: Outdoor, free. AE, DC, DISC, MC, V.

ATTRACTION 🖼

Mission San Luis Rey de Francia

4050 Mission Ave, San Luis Rey; tel 916/757-3651. Founded in 1798, the largest of California's 21 missions was the 18th to be established. For a time, the mission church was the largest structure in California. Visitors may take a self-guided tour of the small museum, whose exhibits include a large collection of 18th- and 19th-century vestments; the old Indian cemetery; and the first pepper tree planted in California (1830). **Open:** Mon–Sat 10am–4:30pm, Sun noon–4:30pm. $

Ojai

Ringed by the Santa Ynez Mountains and bordering the Los Padres National Forest, Ojai boasts several spas and tennis clubs and is also renowned as a New Age haven. Bart's Books, a local institution, has a great selection of used books, and the classical Ojai Music Festival kicks off in late May. **Information:** Ojai Valley Chamber of Commerce, 338 E Ojai Ave, PO Box 1134, Ojai 93024 (tel 805/646-8126).

MOTEL 🖼

≣≣ Best Western Casa Ojai

1302 E Ojai Ave, 93023; tel 805/646-8175 or toll free 800/255-8175; fax 805/640-8247. Ojai/CA 33 exit off US 101. A clean, well-maintained two-story motel located on the outskirts of town. There's some traffic noise from CA 150 during the daytime. **Rooms:** 45 rms and stes. CI 2pm/CO noon. Nonsmoking rms avail. Rooms are light and airy, with loveseat and chair, nice artwork, and brass reading lamps. **Amenities:** 🛏 🍴 A/C, cable TV. VCR in some rooms. **Services:** ⤴ **Facilities:** 🛗 👍 Whirlpool. Public golf course across street. **Rates (CP):** Peak (May–Sept) $91–$125 S or D; $160 ste. Extra person $5. Children under age 12 stay free. Min stay special events. Lower rates off-season. Parking: Outdoor, free. Golf package available. AE, DC, DISC, MC, V.

RESORT

≣≣≣≣ Ojai Valley Inn

Country Club Rd, 93023; tel 805/646-5511 or toll free 800/422-6524; fax 805/646-7969. Exit 33 off US 101. 14 mi inland to Country Club Dr. 220 acres. Catering to golfers and a well-heeled corporate clientele, this Ojai Valley resort's centerpiece is the restored adobe golf clubhouse, designed in 1923 by Wallace Neff. After a massive renovation, the resort reopened in 1988. **Rooms:** 207 rms and stes; 3 cottages/villas. CI 4pm/CO noon. Nonsmoking rms avail. Accommodations are spacious and nicely appointed; each has views of mountains, gardens, or the golf course. Some have large patios with cushy chaise longues. Some baths feature marble countertops. **Amenities:** 🛏 🍴 A/C, cable TV w/movies, refrig, in-rm safe, bathrobes. All units w/terraces, some w/fireplaces, some w/whirlpools. VCRs on request. Nintendo games attached to TVs. **Services:** ✗ 🔑 VP 🛎 ⤴ Twice-daily maid svce, social director, masseur, children's program, babysitting. "Camp Ojai" for kids available on weekends, all summer, and major holidays. **Facilities:** 🛗 ⛳ ▶ 18 🏊 🎿 🐴 🏊 👍 2 restaurants, 1 bar, volleyball, lawn games, spa, sauna, steam rm, whirlpool, playground. Two beautiful pools, including 60-foot lap pool. Rancho Dos Rios nearby is good for hiking, horseback riding, carriage drives; shuttle provided. Full-service spa planned for 1997. The 27,000-square-foot facility will also contain an art studio, music conservatory, walled area for nude sunbathing, and a rooftop penthouse suite. **Rates:** Peak (Mar–Nov) $195–$260 S or D; $345–$395 ste; $600–$850 cottage/villa. Extra person $25. Children under age 3 stay free. Min stay peak and wknds. Lower rates off-season. Parking: Outdoor, free. AE, CB, DC, DISC, MC, V.

RESTAURANT 🍴

The Ranch House

S Lomita and Besant Rd (Meiners Oaks); tel 805/646-2360. Tico Rd off CA 33. **Continental/Vegetarian.** Tucked away in a beautiful garden setting. Dine outdoors next to meandering streams, lush foliage, and a bamboo forest while listening to classical music. Fresh herbs grown on site are used in the seasonal menu. Seafood, homemade soups, pasta; fresh-baked breads available to take home. Award-winning wine list. **FYI:** Reservations recommended. Children's menu. Beer and wine only. **Open:** Peak (May–Sept) lunch Wed–Sat 11:30am–1:30pm; dinner Wed–Sat 6–8:30pm, Sun 1–7:30pm; brunch Sun 11am–1pm. **Prices:** Main courses $19–$24. AE, CB, DC, DISC, MC, V. ♥ 🍴 👍

Olema

See also Point Reyes Station

The home of the Point Reyes National Seashore Park headquarters, the small town of Olema on CA 1 is the gateway to Tomales Bay and the Park's dunes, lagoons, hiking trails, and estuaries.

INN

The Olema Inn
10000 Sir Francis Drake Blvd, 94950; tel 415/663-9559 or toll free 800/532-9252; fax 415/457-7657. 2 acres. This 1876 inn has been updated with modern comforts, yet still maintains vintage charm. Located next to Point Reyes National Seashore, on a moderately trafficked road. **Rooms:** 6 rms. CI 2pm/CO 11am. No smoking. Pleasantly but not lavishly decorated, with a few antiques. Lined with white and Dresden-blue tiles, bathrooms offer paltry counter space; most have tubs with handheld showers. **Amenities:** No A/C, phone, or TV. **Services:** Afternoon tea and wine/sherry served. **Facilities:** 1 restaurant (see "Restaurants" below), 1 bar (w/entertainment), guest lounge w/TV. Well-regarded restaurant. **Rates (CP):** $95–$115 S or D. Children under age 2 stay free. Min stay wknds. Parking: Outdoor, free. AE, MC, V.

RESTAURANT

The Olema Inn
10000 Sir Francis Drake Blvd; tel 415/663-9559. 40 mi NW of San Francisco Sir Francis Drake Blvd exit off US 101; 30 mi to Olema. **Californian/French.** A great place for Sunday brunch either before or after heading to nearby Point Reyes. Set in a charming wood-frame inn built in 1876, the restaurant is bright and airy, with large windows overlooking the garden and a dining terrace. Cuisine might include filet of beef with pinot noir sauce; or prawns Portuguese, accented with tomato, garlic, and fresh herbs. A classical guitarist plays during brunch. **FYI:** Reservations accepted. Guitar. Beer and wine only. **Open:** Lunch Mon–Sat noon–3pm; dinner daily 5–9pm; brunch Sun 11am–3pm. **Prices:** Main courses $13–$19. AE, MC, V.

Olympic Valley

The site of the 1960 Winter Olympics in Squaw Valley, on the shore of Lake Tahoe, the village is a year-round center for outdoor sports, including world-class skiing, ice skating, horseback riding, and hiking.

HOTEL

Olympic Village Inn
1909 Chamonix Place, PO Box 2395, 96146; tel 916/581-6000 or toll free 800/845-5243. Take right at Squaw Valley entrance, go 2 mi. Looks like a Tyrolean village of condominium suites in historic Squaw Valley. World's best athletes stayed here at the 1960 Olympic Games. **Rooms:** 90 stes and effic. CI 4pm/CO 11am. Nonsmoking rms avail. Clean, well-kept one-bedroom suites with country French decor. **Amenities:** Cable TV w/movies, refrig, VCR, bathrobes. No A/C. All units w/terraces, some w/fireplaces. **Services:** Twice-daily maid svce, social director, children's program, babysitting. **Facilities:** Volleyball, lawn games, whirlpool, playground, washer/dryer. Nice lawn and play area. Luxurious patio near pool offers a comfortable place to relax. **Rates:** Peak (June–Sept/Dec–Mar) $95–$275 ste; $95–$275 effic. Children under age 18 stay free. Min stay special events. Lower rates off-season. Parking: Outdoor, free. AE, MC, V.

LODGE

Plump Jack Squaw Valley Inn
1920 Squaw Valley Rd, PO Box 2407, 96146; tel 916/583-1576 or toll free 800/323-7666; fax 916/583-1734. Take CA 89 from I-80. A two-story wood-shingled structure within walking distance of the ski lifts. **Rooms:** 59 rms and effic. CI 4pm/CO 11am. Nonsmoking rms avail. Renovated in 1995, the rooms have an Elizabethan flair. **Amenities:** Cable TV, refrig, voice mail, bathrobes. No A/C. All units w/minibars. **Services:** Twice-daily maid svce, social director, masseur, babysitting. **Facilities:** 1 restaurant, 1 bar, whirlpool, washer/dryer. Basketball court; two-level conference center. **Rates:** $150–$170 S; $170–$210 D; $210–$250 effic. Children under age 12 stay free. Min stay special events. Parking: Outdoor, free. Closed Apr 15–Dec 1. AE, CB, DC, DISC, EC, MC, V.

RESORT

Resort at Squaw Creek
400 Squaw Creek Rd, PO Box 3333, 96146; tel 916/583-6300 or toll free 800/583-6300; fax 916/581-6632. 10 mi S of Truckee. Squaw Valley exit off I-80. 632 acres. Architecturally, it's much different than what you'd expect, with a modern granite lodge and a sleek, nine-story, black-glass tower that counterpoints the chiseled hulk of the Sierras. But the resort's alpine proclivities show from the moment you enter the lobby, which has a massive stone fireplace, a few giant boulders jutting from granite floor, and unbelievable views of the mountains through tall windows. The entire property is designed to take advantage of the outdoors, with sprawling decks and walkways. **Rooms:** 403 rms, stes, and effic. CI 4pm/CO 11am. Nonsmoking rms avail. All accommodations have stunning Sierra views. However, standard rooms are disappointing, sparsely and dully furnished; bathrooms are small with paltry counter space. Suites with mountain views are much nicer (and pricier), with Southwestern-style decor and fabrics in rich hues of forest green and brown. **Amenities:** A/C, cable TV

w/movies, dataport, voice mail, bathrobes. All units w/mini-bars, some w/fireplaces, some w/whirlpools. **Services:** [icons] Car-rental desk, social director, masseur, children's program, babysitting. Camp-style "Mountain Buddies" program for children 4 to 13 offers varied half-day ($25) and full-day ($55) sessions, with educational, artistic, and outdoor activities. **Facilities:** [icons] 5 restaurants, 3 bars (2 w/entertainment), basketball, volleyball, games rm, lawn games, spa, sauna, steam rm, whirlpool, beauty salon, day-care ctr. Championship, links-style golf course designed by Robert Trent Jones, Jr, plus a Peter Burwash International tennis facility offering clinics, lessons, and junior programs. The gorgeous, landscaped pools feature a 110-foot water slide in summer. In winter, there's an ice rink, 19 miles of groomed cross-country terrain, and horse-drawn sleigh rides; a ski lift connects the resort with the Squaw Valley trails (there's also a free shuttle). Excellent fitness center offers exercise machines, aerobics classes, and a full range of spa services. The roster of restaurants includes Cascades, a California grill overlooking the night ski run; and Glissandi, with a California-Continental menu and 330-label wine list. In addition, there's 33,000 square feet of conference facilities and an upscale shopping arcade. **Rates:** Peak (Dec–Apr/June–Sept) $290 S or D; $405–$1,800 ste; $525–$855 effic. Extra person $25. Children under age 18 stay free. Min stay wknds and special events. Lower rates off-season. Parking: Outdoor, free. AE, CB, DC, DISC, JCB, MC, V.

RESTAURANT [icon]

♣ **Graham's**
In Christy Inn Lodge, 1650 Squaw Valley Rd (Squaw Valley); tel 916/581-0454. Squaw Valley exit off CA 89; ½ mi E of ski area. **Californian/Mediterranean.** Open, airy, yet cozy, with a large stone fireplace. Big mountain-view windows add light. Romantic place for an après-ski drink and appetizer. Excellent food is a bit pricey for Tahoe, but worth a splurge. **FYI:** Reservations recommended. Children's menu. Dress code. Beer and wine only. **Open:** Daily 6–10pm. Closed Oct 15–Thanksgiving/May 1–22. **Prices:** Main courses $15–$22; prix fixe $20–$25. MC, V. [icons]

ATTRACTIONS [icon]

Squaw Valley USA
CA 89; tel 916/583-6985. This was the site of the 1960 Olympic Winter Games. Some 70% of Squaw's terrain is geared toward beginners and intermediates. There are 23 chairlifts and a 120-passenger cable car (see below). In summer, the area is opened to mountain bikers, and features many trails with varying levels of difficulty. **Open:** Mid-Nov–mid-May, daily. $$$$

Squaw Valley Cable Car
Tel 916/583-6985. Located within Squaw Valley USA (see above), the cable car takes skiers, sightseers, and other

recreational visitors 2,000 vertical feet to scenic High Camp. In addition to spectacular views of Lake Tahoe and the High Sierra, visitors can take part in a variety of activities, including ice skating, swimming, tennis, and mountain biking at the High Camp Bath and Tennis Club. **Open:** Daily 8am–4pm; summer and winter peak seasons, 8am–9pm. $$$$

Ontario

Ontario, a former agricultural center, now serves as a bedroom community for the metropolis of Los Angeles and is also the site of the LA area's second international airport. **Information:** Greater Ontario Visitor & Convention Bureau, 421 N Euclid, Ontario 91762 (tel 909/984-2450).

HOTELS [icon]

≣≣≣ **Ontario Airport DoubleTree Club Hotel**
429 N Vineyard, 91764 (Ontario Int'l Airport); tel 909/391-6411 or toll free 800/222-TREE; fax 909/391-2369. Vineyard Ave S exit off I-10. This shiny new hotel is near the airport, yet quiet. **Rooms:** 170 rms and stes. CI 3pm/CO 1pm. Nonsmoking rms avail. **Amenities:** [icons] A/C, cable TV w/movies. **Services:** [icons] Complimentary evening drinks and hors d'oeuvres. **Facilities:** [icons] 1 restaurant (bkfst and dinner only), 1 bar, whirlpool. Current periodicals in the Club Room, which is reminiscent of a private club. **Rates (BB):** $89 S or D. Extra person $10. Children under age 12 stay free. Parking: Outdoor, free. AE, DC, DISC, MC, V.

≣≣≣ **Ontario Airport Hilton**
700 N Haven Ave, 91764 (Ontario Int'l Airport); tel 909/980-0400 or toll free 800/645-1379; fax 909/941-6781. Haven Ave N exit off I-10. Splendid convention and conference hotel near the airport; a favorite of airline crews. Gorgeous lobby, with pianist playing in adjacent bar area. **Rooms:** 308 rms and stes. Executive level. CI 3pm/CO noon. Nonsmoking rms avail. **Amenities:** [icons] A/C, cable TV w/movies, refrig, voice mail, bathrobes. Some units w/terraces, some w/whirlpools. **Services:** [icons] Twice-daily maid svce, car-rental desk. Secretarial services. **Facilities:** [icons] 2 restaurants (see "Restaurants" below), 1 bar (w/entertainment), whirlpool. Helicopter pad. **Rates (CP):** $85–$125 S or D; $225–$215 ste. Children under age 18 stay free. Parking: Outdoor, free. AE, DC, DISC, MC, V.

≣≣≣ **Red Lion Hotel Ontario**
222 N Vineyard, 91764 (Ontario Int'l Airport); tel 909/983-0909 or toll free 800/547-8010; fax 909/983-8005. Vineyard Ave S exit off I-10; ¼ mi on left. Located close to the Ontario Airport, this hotel always bustles with conferences. At the entrance, the grand canopy looks like a Mexican pyramid. Lobby is enormous, and hospitality pervasive. **Rooms:** 340 rms and stes. Executive level. CI 3pm/CO 1pm. Nonsmoking rms avail. **Amenities:** [icons] A/C, cable TV

w/movies, refrig. Some units w/terraces, some w/whirlpools. **Services:** ✗ ⌧ 🚐 ⌧ ↺ ⟳ Twice-daily maid svce. **Facilities:** 🅕 📞 2000 🖳 ♿ 2 restaurants, 2 bars (1 w/entertainment), whirlpool, washer/dryer. Cappuccino cart in lobby until 10am. **Rates:** $165–$185 S; $175–$195 D; $375–$500 ste. Children under age 18 stay free. Parking: Outdoor, free. AE, CB, DC, DISC, ER, JCB, MC, V.

≡≡≡ Red Roof Inn
1818 E Holt Blvd, 91761 (Ontario Int'l Airport); tel 909/988-8466 or toll free 800/760-4000; fax 909/986-5456. Vineyard S exit off I-10; ½ mi to Holt; right 1 block. Within walking distance of Ontario Airport. **Rooms:** 107 rms. CI 3pm/CO noon. Nonsmoking rms avail. Nicely renovated rooms. **Amenities:** 🛏 A/C, cable TV. Some units w/terraces. **Services:** 🚐 ⌧ ↺ ⟳ Small pets only. **Facilities:** 🅕 110 ♿ Whirlpool. **Rates:** $40–$50 S; $51 D. Extra person $7. Children under age 18 stay free. Parking: Outdoor, free. AE, CB, DC, DISC, MC, V.

MOTELS

≡≡≡≡ Country Side Suites
204 N Vineyard Ave, 91764; tel 909/986-8550 or toll free 800/248-4661; fax 909/986-4227. Vineyard Ave S exit off I-10; 2 blocks S. The crown jewel of Country Side Inns, a southern California mini-chain, has gleaming marble, fine furnishings, French-style wallpaper, and marvelous staff. **Rooms:** 106 rms and stes. CI noon/CO noon. Nonsmoking rms avail. Large rooms. **Amenities:** 🛏 ⌑ A/C, cable TV, refrig. Some units w/whirlpools. **Services:** ✗ 🚐 ⌧ ↺ Complimentary breakfast buffet and evening refreshments. Fresh fruit always available in the lobby. VCRs and videos available for rent. Free limousine rides to airports. **Facilities:** 🅕 📞 35 ♿ 1 restaurant (lunch and dinner only), whirlpool. **Rates (BB):** Peak (Sept–Oct/Mar–Apr) $125 S or D; $135 ste. Extra person $10. Children under age 12 stay free. Lower rates off-season. Parking: Outdoor, free. Great value for the price. AE, CB, DC, DISC, MC, V.

≡ Fairfield Inn by Marriott
3201 E Centrelake Dr, 91761; tel 909/390-9855 or toll free 800/228-2800; fax 909/390-9855. Haven Ave S exit from I-10; right on Guasti Rd. This hotel, opened in 1990, provides great value for the money. Very quiet despite its highway location. **Rooms:** 117 rms. CI 3pm/CO noon. Nonsmoking rms avail. Pleasant, but small. **Amenities:** 🛏 ⌑ A/C, cable TV. **Services:** ✗ 🚐 ⌧ ↺ **Facilities:** 🅕 12 ♿ **Rates (CP):** $40–$46 S; $43–$50 D. Children under age 18 stay free. Parking: Outdoor, free. AE, DC, DISC, MC, V.

≡≡ Good Nite Inn
1801 E G St, 91764; tel 909/983-3604; fax 909/986-4724. Vineyard Ave S exit off I-10; go 1 block; turn right onto G St. Just underwent renovation under new ownership. **Rooms:** 186 rms. CI 2pm/CO 11am. Nonsmoking rms avail. **Amenities:** 🛏 ⌑ A/C, satel TV w/movies, refrig. Some units w/terraces. **Services:** ✗ 🚐 ⌧ ↺ ⟳ Car-rental desk,

babysitting. **Facilities:** 🅕 200 🖳 ♿ 1 restaurant, 1 bar (w/entertainment), washer/dryer. **Rates:** $35 S; $41 D. Extra person $6. Children under age 18 stay free. Parking: Outdoor, free. AE, DC, DISC, MC, V.

RESTAURANTS 🍴

♣ Calla
In the Ontario Airport Hilton, 700 N Haven Ave; tel 909/980-0400. Haven Ave N exit off I-10. **Continental/French.** A beautiful room, with fine fabric–covered chairs, marvelously painted walls, Erté prints, and soft lighting. Chef Girard Seys, formerly of Maxim's in Paris, presents such dishes as rack of lamb with lavender herbs, braised veal chop stuffed with wild mushrooms wrapped in phyllo dough, and broiled salmon with fresh mango and curry mousseline. **FYI:** Reservations recommended. Piano. Children's menu. Jacket required. **Open:** Lunch Tues–Fri 11:30am–2pm; dinner Mon–Sat 6–10pm. **Prices:** Main courses $19–$27. AE, CB, DC, DISC, MC, V. ♥ ♿

La Cheminée
1133 W 6th St; tel 909/983-7900. Mountain Ave exit off I-10. **Californian/French.** Diners are welcomed by comfortable sofas and chairs in front of a large stone fireplace. The dining room, decorated with stained-glass panels and velvet-covered chairs, has an atmosphere of refined intimacy. Chef John Rose offers entrees such as pheasant sautéed with white wine and shallots, and chateaubriand with béarnaise sauce. **FYI:** Reservations recommended. Band. **Open:** Lunch Mon–Fri 11:30am–2:30pm; dinner Thurs–Sat 5–9:30pm. **Prices:** Main courses $13–$26. AE, CB, DC, DISC, MC, V. ♿

★ Rosa's
425 N Vineyard Ave; tel 909/391-1971. **Italian.** Like a private villa set in the Italian countryside, this restaurant delights the eye with ceilings painted in a sky motif, faux marble columns, and mirrored doors separating several cozy dining rooms. Specialties include pasta from several regions of Italy, grilled and braised meats, seafood, and chicken. Vegetarian meals are also available. Good selection of cognacs and brandies. **FYI:** Reservations recommended. Piano/singer. Children's menu. **Open:** Lunch Mon–Fri 11:30am–4pm; dinner Mon–Fri 4–10pm, Sat 5–10pm, Sun 5–9pm. **Prices:** Main courses $10–$24. AE, CB, DC, MC, V. ♥ ♿

ATTRACTION 🏛

Museum of History and Art, Ontario
225 S Euclid Ave; tel 909/983-3198. Housed in a handsome Mediterranean Revival building built in 1937 as Ontario's second city hall, this museum features exhibits on Ontario's rich heritage of agriculture, industry, and aviation. Temporary exhibits explore topics of local, regional, or national history. Art exhibits feature work by California artists Rex Brandt and Emil Kosa, as well as local and regional talent. **Open:** Wed–Sun noon–4pm. **Free**

Orange

Orange was founded in the late 1860s as a planned community, and part of that plan can still be seen around the circular central plaza at Chapman Ave and Glassel St. **Information:** Orange County Chamber of Commerce & Industry, One City Blvd W #401, Orange 92668 (tel 714/634-2900).

HOTELS 🏨

≣≣≣ DoubleTree Hotel
100 The City Dr, 92668; tel 714/634-4500 or toll free 800/222-TREE; fax 714/978-3839. 25 mi SE of Los Angeles. State College Blvd exit off I-5; turn right, then right on Chapman Ave. A tranquil oasis with colorful gardens, a meandering stream, and a gazebo, as well as a soothing waterfall in the lobby. Friendly, good service. **Rooms:** 454 rms and stes. Executive level. CI 4pm/CO noon. Nonsmoking rms avail. Accommodations are large, quiet, and have stylish furnishings plus attractive views. Some housekeeping problems in bathrooms. **Amenities:** 🛏 🍸 A/C, satel TV w/movies, dataport, voice mail. Some units w/minibars. **Services:** ✕ 🗝 VP 🚐 🖼 🍽 Twice-daily maid svce, car-rental desk, children's program, babysitting. Shuttle service to Disneyland and convention center is accessible for guests with disabilities. **Facilities:** 🏊 🏌2 🏋 🏦 🖥 ᚷ 2 restaurants, 1 bar, basketball, whirlpool. Excellent meeting facilities. **Rates:** $99–$130 S; $99–$140 D; $250–$575 ste. Children under age 18 stay free. Parking: Outdoor, $5–$9/day. AE, CB, DC, DISC, JCB, MC, V.

≣≣≣ Hilton Suites
400 N State College Blvd, 92668; tel 714/938-1111 or toll free 800/HILTONS; fax 714/938-0930. 25 mi SE of Los Angeles. State College Blvd exit off I-5. An all-suite hotel located near the new Anaheim Arena, about a mile from Disneyland and the Anaheim Convention Center. All floors open out to a lovely atrium. **Rooms:** 230 stes. Executive level. CI 3pm/CO noon. Nonsmoking rms avail. Large, bright, and airy, with nice furniture and linens. Comfortable couches and overstuffed chairs. **Amenities:** 🛏 🍸 🍷 A/C, cable TV w/movies, refrig, VCR, voice mail, bathrobes. Some units w/terraces. Microwave. **Services:** ✕ 🗝 🚐 🖼 🍽 📺 Car-rental desk, children's program, babysitting. Free videos. Complimentary shuttle to Disneyland is accessible for persons with disabilities. Complimentary evening reception. **Facilities:** 🏊 🏋 🏦 🖥 ᚷ 1 restaurant, 1 bar, sauna, whirlpool. **Rates (BB):** Peak (June–Aug) $155–$169 ste. Extra person $15. Children under age 18 stay free. Lower rates off-season. Parking: Outdoor, free. AE, DC, DISC, MC, V.

≣≣≣ Washington Suites Hotel
720 The City Dr S, 92668; tel 714/740-2700 or toll free 800/2-SUITES; fax 714/971-1692. 25 mi SE of Los Angeles. City Drive exit off I-5; go south. Clean, well kept, and nicely designed, with spotless carpets and lots of brass. Good for families as well as corporate travelers. **Rooms:** 143 stes. CI 4pm/CO noon. Nonsmoking rms avail. Suites are very large, with upgraded furniture, clean, and well maintained. Full kitchen and separate bedroom area. Up to three rooms can interconnect. **Amenities:** 🛏 🍸 🍷 A/C, cable TV w/movies, refrig, VCR. Some units w/whirlpools. **Services:** 🚐 🖼 🍽 Car-rental desk, babysitting. Complimentary American breakfast in lounge or on patio, afternoon cocktail reception, shuttle to Disneyland and local businesses. No room service, but local restaurants deliver. **Facilities:** 🏊 🏦 🖥 ᚷ Games rm, whirlpool, beauty salon, day-care ctr, washer/dryer. Library is nice for meetings. **Rates (BB):** Peak (June–Aug) $135–$150 ste. Extra person $15. Children under age 18 stay free. Lower rates off-season. Parking: Outdoor, free. AE, CB, DC, DISC, EC, JCB, MC, V.

RESTAURANT 🍽

Cafe Francais
1736 E Meats St; tel 714/998-6051. Lincoln exit off I-55 Located across from the Orange Mall. **French.** A quaint, lovely setting. Starters include French onion soup, escargot, and stuffed mushrooms. Then move on to the veal scaloppine, broiled salmon, Pacific red snapper, and duckling in raspberry sauce. **FYI:** Reservations recommended. Children's menu. Dress code. Beer and wine only. **Open:** Lunch Tues–Fri 11:30am–2pm; dinner Tues–Sat 5:30–10pm, Sun 5–9pm. **Prices:** Main courses $13–$20. AE, MC, V. ♥

Oxnard

See also Ventura

Once a sleepy seaside agricultural community, Oxnard has grown considerably in recent years. The harbor is a major draw for boaters and serves as the shipping-off point for excursions to Channel Islands National Park (see separate heading). The town returns to its agricultural roots every May for the California Strawberry Festival. **Information:** Oxnard Chamber of Commerce, 711 S A St, PO Box 867, Oxnard 93032 (tel 805/385-8860).

HOTELS 🏨

≣≣ Casa Sirena Marina Resort
3605 Peninsula Rd, 93035; tel 805/985-6311 or toll free 800/228-6026; fax 805/985-4329. 5 mi W of downtown. Victoria Ave exit off US 101. Excellent waterfront location overlooking busy marina. Easy walk to Fisherman's Village shops and restaurants. **Rooms:** 275 rms and stes. CI 3pm/CO noon. Nonsmoking rms avail. **Amenities:** 🛏 🍷 Cable TV w/movies, refrig. No A/C. Some units w/terraces, 1 w/whirlpool. **Services:** ✕ 🚐 🖼 🍽 Masseur. **Facilities:** 🏊 🏋 🎾3 🏦 🖥 ᚷ 2 restaurants, 1 bar (w/entertainment), games rm, lawn games, snorkeling, spa, sauna, steam rm, whirlpool, beauty salon, playground. Lobster Trap restaurant very good.

Rates: Peak (May–Oct) $110–$139 S or D; $159 ste. Children under age 12 stay free. Min stay special events. Lower rates off-season. Parking: Outdoor, free. AE, DC, DISC, MC, V.

≣≣≣ Mandalay Beach Resort

2101 Mandalay Beach Rd, 93035; tel 805/984-2500 or toll free 800/582-3000; fax 805/984-8339. 6 mi W of downtown. Victoria Ave exit off US 101. Outstanding location right on the sand, close to Channel Islands Harbor. Caters to conventions as well as leisure travelers. **Rooms:** 249 stes. Executive level. CI 4pm/CO 1pm. Nonsmoking rms avail. All suites are large and feature rattan headboards, peacock chairs, and round glass tables in lieu of desks; suites also offer two gray marble baths, double sinks, and Hollywood-style lighting. **Amenities:** 🛏 👌 📺 A/C, cable TV w/movies, refrig, dataport, voice mail. All units w/terraces, some w/fireplaces, some w/whirlpools. All suites boast wet bars, microwaves, two TVs; Mandalay Suites have large balconies with chaise longues. **Services:** ✕ 🖙 🚗 🛝 🔔 Social director, masseur, children's program, babysitting. Rollerblades and boogie boards for rent. **Facilities:** 🛝 🚴 🏖 🛥 800 👌 1 restaurant (lunch and dinner only), 1 bar (w/entertainment), 1 beach (ocean), whirlpool. Outstanding pool and spa area—you can shower in a rock cave. Landscaping includes streams, waterfalls, and fountains. Three championship golf courses within 10 minutes of hotel. **Rates (BB):** Peak (July–Labor Day) $149–$350 ste. Extra person $15. Children under age 12 stay free. Min stay special events. Lower rates off-season. Parking: Indoor/outdoor, free. AE, DC, DISC, MC, V.

≣≣ Oxnard Hilton Inn

600 Esplanade Dr, 93030; tel 805/485-9666 or toll free 800/44-RELAX; fax 805/485-2061. Vineyard Ave exit off US 101. Decent location near a mall and the Financial Plaza complex. **Rooms:** 160 rms and stes. CI 3pm/CO noon. Nonsmoking rms avail. Comfortable yet unremarkable. **Amenities:** 🛏 👌 🍽 A/C, cable TV, refrig, VCR. Some units w/terraces, 1 w/whirlpool. **Services:** ✕ 🚗 🛝 🔔 **Facilities:** 🛝 📷 🏊 600 👌 1 restaurant, 1 bar (w/entertainment), whirlpool, beauty salon. **Rates:** $79–$99 S; $89–$109 D; $150 ste. Extra person $10. Children under age 12 stay free. Min stay special events. Parking: Outdoor, free. AE, CB, DC, DISC, MC, V.

≣≣≣ Radisson Suite Hotel at River Ridge

2101 W Vineyard Ave, 93030; tel 805/988-0130 or toll free 800/333-3333; fax 805/983-4470. Vineyard Ave exit off US 101. This nicely planned property consists of 32 separate buildings offering comfortable and spacious suites (some are two-story lofts). Families, corporate travelers, and long-term guests will feel at ease here. **Rooms:** 250 stes and effic. CI 3pm/CO noon. Nonsmoking rms avail. **Amenities:** 🛏 👌 📺 🍽 A/C, cable TV w/movies, refrig, dataport. All units w/terraces, some w/fireplaces, 1 w/whirlpool. **Services:** ✕ 🚗 🛝 🔔 Masseur. **Facilities:** 🛝 🏊5 🛝 750 👌 1 restaurant, 1 bar (w/entertainment), whirlpool, washer/dryer. Adjacent to 18-hole championship River Ridge Golf Course. **Rates (BB):** $95 ste; $95 effic. Extra person $10. Children under age 18 stay free. Parking: Outdoor, free. AE, CB, DC, DISC, MC, V.

ATTRACTIONS 🏛

Gull Wings Children's Museum

418 W Fourth St; tel 805/483-3005. Interactive museum with exhibits and special programs that encourage children to explore topics ranging from science to entertainment. **Open:** Wed–Fri and Sun 1–5pm, Sat 10am–5pm. $

Maritime Museum at Channel Islands Harbor

2731 S Victoria Ave; tel 805/984-6260. The region's maritime history is preserved with numerous artifacts and 36 models depicting the genealogy of sailing ships. The art collection includes works by leading American and European marine artists, dating from 1700 to the present. **Open:** Peak (June–Aug) daily 11am–5pm. Reduced hours off-season. **Free**

Pacific Grove

See also Carmel-by-the-Sea, Carmel Valley, Monterey, Pebble Beach

Situated on the tip of the peninsula northwest of Monterey, charming Pacific Grove is much quieter than its neighbor but nonetheless attracts hordes trying to escape the cold winters up north—in this case the colorful monarch butterflies that congregate in the town's pine trees. **Information:** Pacific Grove Chamber of Commerce, PO Box 167, Pacific Grove 93950 (tel 408/373-3304).

MOTELS 🏨

≣≣ Pacific Grove Motel

Lighthouse Ave at Grove Acre, 93950; tel 408/372-3218 or toll free 800/858-8997; fax 408/372-8842. Pebble Beach/Pacific Grove exit off CA 1. A clean, safe motel for the economy-minded traveler, within walking distance of downtown Pacific Grove and the ocean. Also close to the Asilomar Conference Center. Caters to scuba divers. **Rooms:** 30 rms. CI 1pm/CO 11am. No smoking. **Amenities:** 🛏 👌 📺 Cable TV, refrig. No A/C. Some units w/terraces. **Facilities:** 🛝 Whirlpool, playground. **Rates:** Peak (May–Sept) $39–$79 S; $44–$116 D. Extra person $5. Min stay wknds. Lower rates off-season. Parking: Outdoor, free. AE, DISC, MC, V.

≣≣≣ Rosedale Inn

775 Asilomar Blvd, 93950; tel 408/655-1000 or toll free 800/822-5606; fax 408/655-0691. Pebble Beach/Pacific Grove exit off CA 1. A motel with a rustic feel. Located in a woodsy section of town near the Asilomar Conference Center and Asilomar State Beach. **Rooms:** 18 stes and effic. CI 2pm/CO 11am. Nonsmoking rms avail. Nothing really special, except for silk flower arrangements, microwaves, and popcorn in all rooms. **Amenities:** 🛏 👌 📺 🍽 Cable TV w/movies,

refrig, VCR. No A/C. Some units w/terraces, all w/fireplaces, all w/whirlpools. **Services:** 🖼 ⤴ Masseur, babysitting. **Facilities:** 🔥 **Rates (CP):** Peak (June–Sept) $105–$185 ste; $175–$185 effic. Extra person $10. Children under age 12 stay free. Min stay special events. Lower rates off-season. Parking: Outdoor, free. AE, DISC, MC, V.

INNS

☰☰☰ Centrella Bed & Breakfast Inn

612 Central Ave, 93950 (Downtown); tel 408/372-3372 or toll free 800/233-3372; fax 408/372-2036. A charming inn built as a boarding house in 1889. Located downtown, near Pacific Grove Museum of Natural History and Lovers Point Park. Lovely landscaping and spacious parlor. **Rooms:** 21 rms and stes; 5 cottages/villas. CI 2pm/CO 11am. No smoking. Cottages are cozy and secluded, with fireplaces. **Amenities:** 🗂 ⚙ Cable TV. No A/C. Some units w/terraces, some w/fireplaces. **Services:** 🔌 🖼 ⤴ Masseur, babysitting, afternoon tea and wine/sherry served. Self-serve breakfast. **Facilities:** 🔥 Guest lounge w/TV. **Rates (BB):** Peak (May 16–Oct 15) $89 S; $135–$145 D; $185–$225 cottage/villa. Extra person $15. Min stay wknds. Lower rates off-season. Parking: Outdoor, free. AE, MC, V.

☰☰☰ Gosby House Inn

643 Lighthouse Ave, 93950 (Downtown); tel 408/375-1287. Off CA 1. Located in the heart of the historic district, this delightful inn, more than 100 years old, reflects the town's Victorian heritage. **Rooms:** 20 rms (2 w/shared bath); 2 cottages/villas. CI 2pm/CO noon. No smoking. **Amenities:** 🗂 ⚙ 🎏 Bathrobes. No A/C or TV. Some units w/terraces, some w/fireplaces, some w/whirlpools. Bottled water. **Services:** ✗ ⤴ Twice-daily maid svce, social director, babysitting, afternoon tea and wine/sherry served. Country breakfast; freshly baked cookies. Turn-down service with chocolates and a rose. **Facilities:** Guest lounge. **Rates (BB):** $105 S w/shared bath, $150 cottage/villa w/shared bath. Extra person $15. Children under age 2 stay free. Honeymoon and other celebratory packages available. AE, MC, V.

☰☰☰☰ Green Gables Inn

104 5th St, 93950; tel 408/375-2095; fax 408/375-5437. W on CA 68 from CA 1. A lovely Victorian home, built in 1888, offering sweeping views of Monterey Bay's crashing surf and the Santa Cruz Mountains. Teddy bears can be found peeking out of bookcases, on beds, or next to the carousel horse in the living room. **Rooms:** 11 rms and stes (4 w/shared bath). CI 2pm/CO noon. No smoking. Beautifully appointed rooms are decorated with antiques. **Amenities:** 🗂 ⚙ 🖥 🎏 Bathrobes. No A/C or TV. Some units w/terraces, some w/fireplaces. Some rooms have TVs. **Services:** Afternoon tea and wine/sherry served. Cookies, soda, fruit, coffee, and tea always available. **Facilities:** Guest lounge. Small gift shop. The central area offers many places to sit and read, enjoy a fire in the fireplace, watch the ocean, or play a tune on the player piano. **Rates (BB):** $100–$135 S or D w/shared bath, $140–

$160 S or D w/private bath; $160 ste. Extra person $15. Children under age 2 stay free. Min stay wknds and special events. Parking: Outdoor, free. AE, MC, V.

☰☰☰ Martine Inn

255 Oceanview Blvd, 93950; tel 408/373-3388 or toll free 800/852-5588; fax 408/373-3896. CA 68 W off CA 1. Built in 1889 as a summer mansion for the Parke Davis family, this, Mediterranean-style property overlooking Monterey Bay is an antique lover's nirvana. Furnishings, china, and silverware reflect the turn-of-the-century ambience. **Rooms:** 20 rms and stes. CI 2pm/CO 11am. Nonsmoking rms avail. **Amenities:** 🗂 Refrig. No A/C or TV. Some units w/fireplaces, all w/whirlpools. **Services:** Babysitting, wine/sherry served. Beverage room service available; picnics prepared on request. **Facilities:** 🔢 🔥 Guest lounge w/TV. **Rates (BB):** $125–$230 S or D; $230 ste. Extra person $36. Min stay wknds and special events. Parking: Outdoor, free. AE, DISC, MC, V.

☰☰☰ Pacific Gardens Inn

701 Asilomar Blvd, 93950; tel 408/646-9414 or toll free 800/262-1566 in CA. Pebble Beach/Pacific Grove exit off CA 1. Pleasant landscaping in a woodsy setting. Convenient to beach. **Rooms:** 28 rms, stes, and effic. CI 2pm/CO 11am. Nonsmoking rms avail. All suites have fully equipped kitchens. **Amenities:** 🗂 🔢 Cable TV, refrig. No A/C. Some units w/terraces, some w/fireplaces, some w/whirlpools. Popcorn machines in all rooms. **Services:** ⤴ Masseur, babysitting, wine/sherry served. **Facilities:** 🔢 🔥 Guest lounge. **Rates (CP):** Peak (March–Oct) $95–$105 S; $110 D; $130–$160 ste; $130–$160 effic. Lower rates off-season. Higher rates for special events/hols. Parking: Outdoor, free. AE, MC, V.

☰☰ Pacific Grove Inn

581 Pine Ave, 93950; tel 408/375-2825. This inn, a Queen Anne–style structure with Colonial Revival detailing, is a National Historic Landmark. Built in 1905 for the family of Frank Buck, a prominent businessman and civic leader involved in the development of Pacific Grove. Unsuitable for children under 10. **Rooms:** 16 rms and stes. CI 2pm/CO noon. No smoking. Nicely furnished rooms are small but pretty. **Amenities:** 🗂 ⚙ Cable TV. No A/C. Some units w/terraces, all w/fireplaces. **Services:** Babysitting. **Facilities:** Guest lounge. **Rates (BB):** Peak (July–Oct) $100–$120 S; $116–$136 D; $138–$170 ste. Extra person $15–$20. Children under age 10 stay free. Min stay peak, wknds, and special events. Lower rates off-season. Higher rates for special events/hols. Parking: Outdoor, free. AE, DC, DISC, MC.

☰☰☰ Quality Inn Pacific Grove

1111 Lighthouse Ave, 93950; tel 408/646-8885; fax 408/646-5976. Nicely maintained; three blocks from the ocean and the Pacific Grove Municipal Golf Links. **Rooms:** 50 rms, stes, and effic. CI 2pm/CO noon. Nonsmoking rms avail. **Amenities:** 🗂 ⚙ 🖥 A/C, cable TV. Some units w/terraces, some w/fireplaces. **Services:** ⤴ Babysitting, wine/sherry served. **Facilities:** 🔲 📺 ⛾ Sauna, whirlpool, guest lounge w/TV. **Rates (CP):** Peak (Mem Day–Oct) Extra person $10. Children under age 18 stay free. Min stay peak, wknds, and special events. Lower rates off-season. Higher rates for special events/hols. Parking: Outdoor, free. AE, DC, DISC, MC, V.

🎏🎏🎏🎏 Seven Gables Inn
555 Ocean View Blvd, 93950; tel 408/372-4341. Off CA 68. The ultimate Victorian B&B, set in a multigabled 1886 showplace with views of Monterey Bay and Lover's Point. Decorated with fabulous antiques, including Louis XV gilded tables. Unsuitable for children under 12. **Rooms:** 14 rms. CI 2:30/CO noon. No smoking. Each has an ocean view and unique decor. Victoria Room features a real Tiffany window as well as a pressed-tin ceiling, oak armoire, and lace-edged bed ruffle. In the Cypress Room, a sitting area in the bay window commands sweeping bay views. **Amenities:** 🛁 No A/C, phone, or TV. **Services:** Twice-daily maid svce, masseur, afternoon tea and wine/sherry served. Lavish breakfast offerings include fresh-squeezed juice, varieties of fruit, egg dishes, plus hot pastries and muffins. Staff will help guests plan sightseeing excursions, picnics, etc. **Facilities:** Guest lounge w/TV. **Rates (BB):** Peak (June–Sept) $105–$215 S or D. Min stay wknds. Lower rates off-season. Parking: Outdoor, free. MC, V.

LODGE

🎏🎏🎏 Lighthouse Lodge & Suites
1150 Lighthouse Ave, 93950; tel 408/655-2111 or toll free 800/858-1249; fax 408/655-4922. Pebble Beach/Pacific Grove exit off CA 1. The lodge and suites are in separate properties, both pleasant, in a wooded area close to the ocean and the Pacific Grove Golf Links. **Rooms:** 98 rms, stes, and effic. CI 4pm/CO 11am. Nonsmoking rms avail. Suites are more luxurious and upscale, and have kitchenettes and spa tubs. Some rooms overlook cemetery. **Amenities:** 📺 🛁 📻 Refrig, dataport. No A/C. Some units w/minibars, some w/terraces, some w/fireplaces, some w/whirlpools. **Services:** 🔑 🍴 🐾 Babysitting. Accepts pets for an additional $10. **Facilities:** 🔲 📺 ⛾ Sauna, whirlpool. **Rates (CP):** Peak (May–Oct) $89–$149 S; $129–$228 ste; $275–$375 effic. Extra person $10. Children under age 12 stay free. Min stay wknds. Lower rates off-season. Parking: Outdoor, free. AE, CB, DC, DISC, JCB, V.

RESTAURANTS 🍴

★ Bagel Bakery
1180C Forest Ave; tel 408/649-6272. **Bagels.** Fresh bagels, baked daily without any oils, fats, or preservatives. The Pacific Grove outlet of this small chain is the oldest, smallest, and funkiest. A garnish of Monterey jack cheese, sprouts, and tomato–called the "Cooperman's Delight"–is the local favorite. **FYI:** Reservations not accepted. No liquor license. Additional locations: Northridge Mall, Salinas (tel 449-1110); 969

W Alisal St, Salinas (tel 758-0280). **Open:** Mon–Sat 6:30am–5pm, Sun 8am–3pm. **Prices:** Lunch main courses $1–$4. No CC. 🍴

El Cocodrilo Rotisserie & Seafood Grill
701 Lighthouse Ave; tel 408/655-3311. At Congress St. **Caribbean.** Bright, clean, fresh, and upbeat. Rain forest decor with artifacts and pottery from the tropical Americas. Specialties: Bahamian chowder, pasta paella, grilled snapper mardi gras, coconut pecan chicken, vegetarian plate, alligator nuggets El Dorado (from Florida farms), Jamaican curry crab cakes, Jamaican bread pudding with rum sauce, mango cheesecake. Imported and domestic beers from microbreweries available. **FYI:** Reservations recommended. Children's menu. Beer and wine only. **Open:** Wed–Mon 5–10pm. **Prices:** Main courses $9–$15. MC, V. 🍴 ⛾

🍷★ Fandango
223 17th St; tel 408/372-3456. Between Lighthouse and Laurel Aves. **Mediterranean.** A local favorite that has won many awards. Rustic wood beams, stucco walls, flowers on tables, fireplace, and outside patio create a warm atmosphere. Owner Pierre Bain is a 9th-generation restaurateur whose family owned the Grand Hotel Bain in southern France for 250 years. Mediterrean country-style dishes include paella, rack of lamb, and fresh fish. **FYI:** Reservations recommended. **Open:** Lunch daily 11am–3:30pm; dinner daily 5am–9:30pm; brunch Sun 10am–2:30pm. **Prices:** Main courses $10–$17; prix fixe $20. AE, MC, V. 🍷

⑤ Fifi's Cafe & Bakery
1188 Forest Ave; tel 408/372-5325. **Californian/French.** Charming French cafe. Cafe-style decor with lace curtains and floral drapes. Specialties include roast leg of lamb, duck Seville or Grand Marnier, grilled sesame chicken salad. Superb French pastries. **FYI:** Reservations recommended. Beer and wine only. **Open:** Breakfast Mon–Fri 8–11am, Sat 8–11:45am; lunch Mon–Fri 11am–2:30pm, Sat noon–3pm; dinner Sun–Thurs 5–9pm, Fri–Sat 5–9:30pm; brunch Sun 9am–2:30pm. **Prices:** Main courses $11–$17. AE, CB, DC, DISC, MC, V. 🍷 ⛾

⑤ First Awakenings (formerly First Watch)
In the American Tin Cannery Outlet Center, 125 Ocean View Blvd; tel 408/372-1125. **American.** The two young owners of this bright and airy breakfast spot worked their way up from dishwashers, busers, and waiters. The staff is happy to accommodate diners with just about any request or special order. Diners can enjoy a complimentary coffee while waiting. Omelettes and pancakes are specialties. **FYI:** Reservations accepted. Guitar. Children's menu. No liquor license. **Open:** Daily 7am–2:30pm. **Prices:** Lunch main courses $2–$7. AE, DISC, MC, V. 🍴 🖼 🍴 ⛾

★ The Fishwife at Asilomar Beach
1996 Sunset Dr; tel 408/375-7107. Sunset Dr exit off CA 68 W. **Seafood.** Local favorite with good value. Casual atmosphere; marine-life decor. Specialties include Boston clam

chowder, Talapica fish, calamari abalone style, and sea garden salad (mixed greens with grilled fish). **FYI:** Reservations recommended. Children's menu. Beer and wine only. Additional location: 789 Trinity Ave, Seaside (tel 394-2027). **Open:** Daily 11am–9:30pm. **Prices:** Main courses $10–$12. AE, DISC, MC, V. 🖼 &

Old Bath House Restaurant
620 Ocean View Blvd; tel 408/375-5195. Pacific Grove/ Pebble Beach exit off CA 1. **Californian/Continental.** A venerable local favorite in a turn-of-the century bathhouse restored to Victorian elegance. Some tables have bay views. Specialties include local seafood, Australian lobster in puff pastry, wild boar sausage, and filet mignon. **FYI:** Reservations recommended. **Open:** Mon–Fri 5–10pm, Sat 4–10pm, Sun 3–10pm. **Prices:** Main courses $14–$30. AE, CB, DC, DISC, MC, V. 💗 🖼 ☑

★ Peppers MexiCali Cafe
170 Forest Ave; tel 408/373-6892. Between Lighthouse and Central Aves. **Californian/Mexican/Latin American.** Popular restaurant with lively atmosphere, butcher-block tables, and attractive art. Specialties include snapper Yucatan and other local fresh seafood, usually accompanied by black beans, tortillas, fresh salsas. Good selection of Monterey County and Central Coast wines. **FYI:** Reservations recommended. Beer and wine only. **Open:** Sun 4–10pm, Wed–Mon 11:30am–10pm. **Prices:** Main courses $6–$11. AE, CB, DC, DISC, MC, V.

★ Taste Cafe & Bistro
1199 Forest Ave; tel 408/655-0324. Off CA 1. **French.** Very sophisticated little cafe with a rustic look, considered one of the best local restaurants. Dishes include grilled rabbit, fresh salmon on spinach leaves with herbs and vegetables in parchment paper, and many vegetarian selections. **FYI:** Reservations recommended. Beer and wine only. **Open:** Tues–Sun 5–9pm. Closed Dec 24–Jan 1. **Prices:** Main courses $9–$16. No CC.

★ Tillie Gort's
111 Central Ave; tel 408/373-0335. Pacific Grove/Pebble Beach exit off CA 1. **Vegetarian.** A local standby for 25 years, with an eclectic clientele drawn to the 1960s ambience. Food is mostly vegetarian, and servings are large. Veggie burger, quesadilla supreme, and "Jimmy's special" (steamed vegetables on grilled potatoes, topped with cheese) are among the offerings. **FYI:** Reservations accepted. Beer and wine only. **Open:** Daily 11am–10:30pm. **Prices:** Main courses $5–$8. AE, MC, V. 🖼

The Tinnery
631 Ocean View Blvd; tel 408/646-1040. **Regional American.** Popular with tourists. Bright and airy restaurant with a panoramic view of Monterey Bay at Lover's Point. Specializing in fresh fish and steaks. **FYI:** Reservations recommended.

Singer. Children's menu. **Open:** Daily 8am–11pm. **Prices:** Main courses $8–$24. AE, CB, DC, DISC, MC, V. 🖼 🖼 ☑ &

★ Toasties Cafe
702 Lighthouse Ave; tel 408/373-7543. At Congress St. **Regional American.** Flower boxes and ruffled curtains decorate the windows, while depictions of bunnies, cows, chickens, and other critters appear throughout this cozy, country-style restaurant. It's a local favorite, especially for breakfast. Specialties include huevos rancheros, corned beef hash, blintzes, and tortellini and eggs. **FYI:** Reservations not accepted. Children's menu. Beer and wine only. **Open:** Breakfast Sun 7am–2pm, Mon–Sat 6am–3pm; lunch Mon–Sat 6am–3pm; dinner Tues–Sat 5–9pm. **Prices:** Main courses $8–$13. AE, MC, V. 🖼

Vito's Italian Restaurant
1180 Forest Ave; tel 408/375-3070. Eit off CA 1 to CA 68 W. **Italian.** Adorned with an enormous mural of the owner's home town near Palermo. Very Italian menu includes pastas, gnocchi, and tiramisù made on site. **FYI:** Reservations recommended. Beer and wine only. **Open:** Lunch daily 11:30am–2:30pm; dinner daily 5–10pm. **Prices:** Main courses $9–$15. AE, DC, DISC, MC, V. 🖼 🖼 &

REFRESHMENT STOP 🗗

★ Rocky Coast Ice Cream Company
708 Lighthouse Ave; tel 408/373-0587. **Hot dogs/Ice cream.** A folksy, friendly ice-cream parlor popular with all ages. Video and pinball games for kids. Offers 37 flavors of premium ice-cream, plus six nonfat frozen yogurt specials. Also, milkshakes, sundaes, soft drinks, candy, hot dogs, and bagel dogs. Good value. **Open:** Peak (Feb–Nov) daily 11am–10pm. Closed 1st week of Jan. No CC. 🖼

ATTRACTION 🖼

Pacific Grove Museum of Natural History
165 Forest Ave; tel 408/648-3116. Considered one of the finest natural history museums of its size, this facility is fronted by a life-size sculpture of a gray whale. Exhibits inside deal mainly with local plants and wildlife, geology, and Native American culture. The **Native Plant Garden** features a number of rare and endangered species of the Monterey Peninsula. Traveling exhibitions, including those of the Smithsonian Institution, are also featured. Gift shop. **Open:** Tues–Sun and hols 10am–5pm. **Free**

Pacific Palisades

See also Malibu

RESTAURANT 🍴

⑤ ✦ Gladstone's Fish

17300 W Pacific Coast Hwy; tel 310/454-3474. **Californian/ Seafood.** Recommended for its sheer energy and great people watching. On the huge outdoor patio drinking area that overlooks the ocean, seagulls compete with patrons seated on concrete picnic benches for the free peanuts. The portions of burgers, steak, salad, and pizzas are huge, and the seven-layer chocolate cake is legendary. **FYI:** Reservations recommended. Children's menu. **Open:** Sun–Thurs 7am–11pm, Fri–Sat 7am–midnight. **Prices:** Main courses $10–$40. AE, CB, DC, DISC, MC, V. 🛳 📱 🏞 🛎 📺 &

ATTRACTION 🏛

Will Rogers State Historic Park

1501 Will Rogers State Park Rd; tel 310/454-8212. The 31-room ranch house and grounds of the "cracker-barrel philosopher" were willed to the state in 1944. Visitors may explore the grounds, including the former Rogers stables, and even watch polo matches (usually Saturday afternoons and Sunday mornings, weather permitting). Guided tours are given of the house, which is filled with original furnishings. A film on Will Rogers is shown at the visitors center, where there is also a small gift shop. **Open:** Park, daily 8am–6pm, summer 8am–7pm. House, daily 10am–5pm. $$

Palmdale

See also Lancaster

HOTEL 🏨

🛏🛏🛏 Holiday Inn Palmdale/Lancaster

38630 5th St W, 93551; tel 805/947-8055 or toll free 800/HOLIDAY; fax 805/947-9957. Palmdale Blvd exit off CA 14. Attractive, quiet, fairly new hotel. Green marble in lobby. **Rooms:** 150 rms and stes. Executive level. CI 3pm/CO noon. Nonsmoking rms avail. Little drawer and counter space. **Amenities:** 🛎 🅰 A/C, cable TV w/movies. Some units w/terraces. **Services:** ✕ 🚗 🛆 ⌃ ⌁ Some rates include breakfast buffet. **Facilities:** 🏊 🛎 📟 🖥 & 1 restaurant, 1 bar, whirlpool. **Rates:** $75–$85 S; $85–$95 D; $135–$150 ste. Extra person $5. Children under age 12 stay free. Parking: Outdoor, free. AE, CB, DC, DISC, JCB, MC, V.

Palm Desert

South of the larger community of Palm Springs, Palm Desert is home to lush resorts and golf courses, all lavishly fed by an astounding amount of water. The Living Desert, a 1,200-acre nature park, is an excellent introduction to the flora and fauna native to the Coachella Valley. **Information:** Palm Desert Chamber of Commerce & Visitors Center, 72-990 US 111, Palm Desert 92260 (tel 619/346-6111 or toll free 800/873-2428).

HOTEL 🏨

🛏🛏🛏 Embassy Suites

74-700 US 111, 92260; tel 619/340-6600 or toll free 800/EMBASSY; fax 619/340-9519. Spanish-style architecture, lush landscaping, 20 types of cactus and elaborate fountains greet guests to this all-suite hotel. **Rooms:** 198 stes. CI 3pm/CO noon. Nonsmoking rms avail. All suites have sleeper sofas. **Amenities:** 🛎 🅰 📱 A/C, cable TV w/movies, refrig. All units w/minibars, some w/terraces. Wet bar. **Services:** ✕ 🛆 ⌁ Children's program, babysitting. Complimentary evening cocktails. **Facilities:** 🏊 🛎 🎱 🛎 📟 & 1 restaurant (lunch and dinner only), 1 bar (w/entertainment), games rm, lawn games, whirlpool, washer/dryer. **Rates (BB):** Peak (Jan 15–Apr 30) $199–$219 ste. Extra person $15. Children under age 13 stay free. Min stay wknds. Lower rates off-season. Parking: Outdoor, free. AE, DC, DISC, MC, V.

MOTELS

🛏🛏 Casa Larrea Resort Motel

73-771 Larrea St, 92260; tel 619/568-0311 or toll free 800/829-1556. Monterey Ave exit off I-10. Turquoise umbrellas and lawn furniture around the pool provide a striking contrast to the white stucco buildings. **Rooms:** 12 rms, stes, and effic. CI 2pm/CO noon. Nonsmoking rms avail. Individually decorated rooms all have private patios, landscaped with desert plants. **Amenities:** 🛎 🅰 A/C, cable TV. All units w/terraces. **Services:** ⌁ **Facilities:** 🏊 & Whirlpool. **Rates (CP):** Peak (Oct–May) $60 S or D; $98 ste; $68 effic. Extra person $10. Min stay peak, wknds, and special events. Lower rates off-season. Parking: Outdoor, free. Closed July 30–Sept 4. DISC, MC, V.

🛏🛏 Deep Canyon Inn

74-470 Abronia Trail, 92260; tel 619/346-8061 or toll free 800/253-0004; fax 619/341-9120. Designed around a pool and garden area, with large rooms and wonderful rattan furniture. Needs a bit of refurbishment. **Rooms:** 31 rms and stes. CI 3pm/CO noon. No smoking. One attractive room has French doors that lead to patio. **Amenities:** 🛎 A/C, cable TV, refrig. Some units w/terraces, 1 w/fireplace. **Services:** Babysitting. **Facilities:** 🏊 & Whirlpool. **Rates (CP):** Peak (Jan–Apr) $59–$99 S; $99–$109 D; $139–$169 ste. Children under age 12 stay free. Min stay peak. Lower rates off-season. Parking: Outdoor, free. AE, DC, DISC, MC, V.

🛏🛏 Desert Patch Inn

73-758 Shadow Mountain Dr, 92260; tel 619/346-9161 or toll free 800/350-9758; fax 619/776-9661. Monterey Ave exit off I-10 at Larkspur. Well maintained, with lovely

Mexican artifacts scattered throughout the grounds. Beautiful enclosed garden is a perfect spot for morning coffee. **Rooms:** 14 rms, stes, and effic. CI 2pm/CO noon. Nonsmoking rms avail. Comfortable. **Amenities:** 🛏 🌀 📧 A/C, cable TV, refrig. Some units w/terraces, 1 w/fireplace. **Services:** 🐬 **Facilities:** 🏋 🏊 🏌 Lawn games, whirlpool. Putting green, shuffleboard, croquet. **Rates (CP):** Peak (Oct–May) $54 S or D; $94 ste; $74 effic. Extra person $20. Min stay wknds and special events. Lower rates off-season. Parking: Outdoor, free. Closed July–Aug. AE, DISC, MC, V.

≣≣ Holiday Inn Express

74-675 CA 111, 92260; tel 619/340-4303 or toll free 800/ HOLIDAY; fax 619/340-4303 ext 377. Convenient to Coachella Valley medical facilities and local shopping, this contemporary-style hotel features a three-story atrium lobby. **Rooms:** 131 rms and stes. CI 3pm/CO noon. Nonsmoking rms avail. **Amenities:** 🛏 🌀 📧 A/C, cable TV w/movies. All units w/terraces. **Services:** 🏊 🐬 Babysitting. **Facilities:** 🏋 🏊 🏌 Games rm, lawn games, whirlpool, washer/dryer. **Rates (CP):** Peak (Feb–Mar) $119–$139 S or D; $145 ste. Extra person $10. Children under age 18 stay free. Min stay wknds. Lower rates off-season. Parking: Outdoor, free. AE, DC, DISC, MC, V.

≣≣ International Lodge of Palm Desert

74-380 El Camino, 92260; tel 619/346-6161 or toll free 800/ 874-9338; fax 619/568-0563. Monterey Ave exit off I-10, CA 111 S. An exclusive enclave of individually decorated studio condominiums. **Rooms:** 50 effic. CI 2pm/CO noon. Nonsmoking rms avail. **Amenities:** 🛏 🌀 📧 A/C, cable TV, refrig. Some units w/terraces. **Facilities:** 🏋 Whirlpool, washer/dryer. Two Olympic-size swimming pools, with lovely views of mountains. **Rates:** Peak (Jan–Apr 27) $95 effic. Extra person $10. Children under age 3 stay free. Min stay peak and wknds. Lower rates off-season. Parking: Outdoor, free. AE, DISC, MC, V.

≣≣ Vacation Inn Hotel

74-715 CA 111, 92260; tel 619/340-4441 or toll free 800/ 231-8675; fax 619/773-9413. Monterey exit off I-10. The decor is casual southwest, and the location offers easy access to shops and restaurants. **Rooms:** 130 rms. CI 3pm/CO noon. Nonsmoking rms avail. **Amenities:** 🛏 🌀 📧 A/C, cable TV, refrig, in-rm safe. All units w/terraces. **Services:** 🐬 **Facilities:** 🏋 🏊 🏌 Lawn games, whirlpool, washer/dryer. **Rates (CP):** Peak (Dec 28–Apr 15) $82–$108 S or D. Extra person $10. Children under age 18 stay free. Lower rates off-season. Parking: Outdoor, free. AE, CB, DC, DISC, ER, JCB, MC, V.

RESORTS

≣≣≣≣ Marriott's Desert Springs Resort & Spa

74-885 Country Club Dr, 92260; tel 619/341-2211 or toll free 800/321-3112; fax 619/341-1872. From I-10, take the Monterey exit and head south. Turn left at Country Club Dr and proceed for 1 mi. 400 acres. This is a showy place, with a grand driveway and a front lawn filled with palm trees and flamingos. In the eight-story, multi-leveled atrium lobby, you'll encounter tiers of fountains, squawking tropical parrots, and views to the vast lakes where Venetian-style water taxis cruise. You won't quite believe you're in the desert. **Rooms:** 884 rms and stes. CI 4pm/CO noon. Nonsmoking rms avail. Attractive but not glitzy. **Amenities:** 🛏 🌀 🍷 A/C, cable TV w/movies, dataport, voice mail, in-rm safe, bathrobes. All units w/minibars, all w/terraces. **Services:** ✗ 🔑 🚐 🏊 🐬 Twice-daily maid svce, car-rental desk, social director, masseur, children's program, babysitting. "Guest Experience" staff contacts leisure travelers by mail before their arrival in order to help them arrange tee times and restaurant reservations. Daily tours of the property are offered by the boats, which can also ferry guests to the restaurants for dinner. Lake-view rooms ($30 extra) also offer complimentary valet parking and complimentary spa passes for two. **Facilities:** 🏋 🚴 🏌36 🎾 🎣14 🏊 6 🏊 🏊4000 🎱 🏌 6 restaurants, 2 bars (w/entertainment), basketball, volleyball, lawn games, spa, sauna, steam rm, whirlpool, beauty salon. The 30,000-square-foot spa—the largest in the Valley—is a knock-out, offering a long menu of facials, massages, ayurvedic treatments, and therapeutic wraps. Fitness assessments, personal training, and nutritional consultations are also available. Aerobics, step, and aquacize classes. The Peter Burwash–managed tennis center features clay, grass, and hard-surface courts. Two Ted Robinson-designed golf courses. Sister property to Marriott's Rancho Las Palmas Resort: guests can use all facilities at both properties. **Rates:** Peak (Jan–Apr) $250–$330 S or D; $535–$2,100 ste. Children under age 18 stay free. Lower rates off-season. Parking: Indoor/outdoor, $12/day. AE, DC, DISC, ER, JCB, MC, V.

≣≣≣ Marriott's Desert Springs Villas

1091 Pinehurst Lane, 92260; tel 619/779-1207 or toll free 800/331-3112; fax 619/779-1203. Monterey Ave exit off I-10. 3 acres. Well located, with luxurious grounds, near the extensive facilities of the Marriott Desert Springs Resort & Spa, where guests can use the tennis courts, golf courses, pools, spas, etc. **Rooms:** 328 cottages/villas. CI 4pm/CO 10am. Nonsmoking rms avail. Each villa is spacious and elegantly furnished; one- and two-bedroom villas feature full kitchen, washer/dryer, formal dining room, circular whirlpool, and gas fireplace. **Amenities:** 🛏 🌀 📧 A/C, cable TV w/movies, refrig, voice mail, in-rm safe. All units w/terraces, some w/fireplaces, some w/whirlpools. **Services:** ✗ 🔑 🏊 🐬 Social director, children's program, babysitting. **Facilities:** 🏋 🏊 Sauna. **Rates:** Peak (Dec 16–June 1) $475–$550 cottage/villa. Children under age 18 stay free. Min stay special events. Lower rates off-season. Parking: Outdoor, free. AE, CB, DC, DISC, ER, JCB, MC, V.

≣≣ Shadow Mountain Resort and Racquet Club

45-750 San Luis Rey Ave, 92260; tel 619/346-6123 or toll free 800/472-3713; fax 619/346-6518. Monterey Ave exit off I-10. 24 acres. Located a short walk from the fashionable shops, galleries, and restaurants of El Paseo. **Rooms:** 101 rms, stes, and effic; 9 cottages/villas. CI 3pm/CO 11am. No smoking. **Amenities:** 🛍 ⊡ A/C, cable TV w/movies, refrig. All units w/terraces, some w/fireplaces. **Services:** △ ⊕ Children's program, babysitting. **Facilities:** ⚷ ⚵ ☜10 ⬛6 ⬛ ⟦400⟧ ⚿ 1 restaurant, 1 bar, lawn games, sauna, whirlpool, washer/dryer. Golf course nearby. **Rates:** Peak (Nov 24-27/ Dec 23-Jan 1/Feb 18-Apr 16/May 27-June 1) $85-$179 S or D; $144-$256 ste; $85-$179 effic; $198-$462 cottage/ villa. Extra person $15. Children under age 18 stay free. Min stay peak, wknds, and special events. Lower rates off-season. Parking: Indoor/outdoor, free. Closed July 10-Aug 20. AE, DC, MC, V.

RESTAURANTS 🍴

Andreino's

73-098 CA 111; tel 619/773-3365. Bob Hope Dr exit off I-10. **Italian.** With knotty pine ceilings and large stone pillars. Signature dishes include fettuccine Andreino (with cream, butter, and fresh Parmesan), and other pasta dishes. If you're very hungry, try the Godfather's dinner—tenderloin of beef, spiedini, shrimp scampi, and veal picatta. **FYI:** Reservations recommended. Dress code. **Open:** Peak (Sept-July) daily 5:30-midnight. **Prices:** Main courses $13-$26. AE, DISC, MC, V. ⟦VP⟧

Club 74

73-061 El Paseo; tel 619/568-2782. Monterey Ave exit off I-10. **French.** A magnificent entryway and carved staircase lead to dining rooms with oak paneling and landscape frescoes. Cuisine features dishes like veal medallions forestière, feuilleté au King Neptune, and poulet aux framboises. **FYI:** Reservations recommended. Piano. Dress code. **Open:** Lunch Mon-Sat 11:30am-2:30pm; dinner daily 5:30-10pm. Closed July. **Prices:** Main courses $16-$25. AE, CB, DC, DISC, MC, V. ⟦▲▲⟧

Cuistot

73-111 El Paseo; tel 619/340-1000. Monterey Ave exit off I-10. **French.** A light and airy restaurant whose soft hues complement the contemporary setting. Specialties include sautéed veal chops with wild mushrooms, roasted garlic, and thyme, and Chinese-style duck in a mango-ginger sauce. **FYI:** Reservations recommended. Dress code. **Open:** Lunch Tues-Sat 11:30am-2:30pm; dinner Tues-Sun 6-10pm. Closed Aug. **Prices:** Main courses $18-$28. AE, CB, DC, ER, MC, V.

♥ Jillian's

74-155 El Paseo; tel 619/776-8242. Monterey exit off I-10. **Eclectic.** In a white, 1946 adobe building with a patio courtyard, this restaurant offers a serenely elegant dining experience. Tables are set with white linen, fine crystal and china, and fresh flowers. High-back arm chairs upholstered in tapestry fabric, antiques, and original paintings complete the decor. The eclectic menu features entrees like grilled Atlantic salmon with curry beurre blanc and couscous, or tenderloin of Angus beef on garlic mashed potatoes with roasted-garlic

cabernet sauce. **FYI:** Reservations recommended. Piano. Dress code. **Open:** Daily 6-10pm. Closed July-Oct. **Prices:** Main courses $22-$30. AE, DC, ER, MC, V. ⟦VP⟧ ⚿

Jovanna's

74-065 CA 111; tel 619/568-1315. CA 111. **Californian/ Italian.** Cozy atmosphere where fresh flowers complement the table settings of green glass plates with white china accents. Original oil paintings line the walls. Fresh-made pasta and sauces, veal marsala, osso buco, and shrimp scampi highlight the menu. **FYI:** Reservations accepted. Guitar. Dress code. **Open:** Peak (Oct-May) daily 6-10pm. **Prices:** Main courses $14-$24. AE, DC, MC, V. ⚓ ▼

Le Paon

45-640 CA 74; tel 619/568-3651. Monterey Ave exit off I-10 to CA 74. **French.** Elegant ambience, with chandeliers, fireplaces, and upholstered Victorian chairs. French doors lead to the garden. Menu favorites include veal scalloppine, baked lobster tail, steak Diane (prepared tableside), rack of lamb, and veal calvados. **FYI:** Reservations recommended. Piano. Dress code. **Open:** Sun-Thurs 6-10pm, Fri-Sat 6-11pm. **Prices:** Main courses $17-$50. AE, CB, DC, DISC, MC, V. ⚓ ⟦▲⟧ ⟦VP⟧ ⚿

LG's Steakhouse

74-225 CA 111; tel 619/779-9799. Monterey Ave exit off I-10 to CA 111. **Steak.** Located in a neo-pueblo–style building that will be declared a National Historic Monument when it turns 50 in 1998. Prime corn-fed midwestern steaks are the specialty here, but you can also order rack of lamb, prime rib, pork chops, chicken, and fish. **FYI:** Reservations recommended. Dress code. **Open:** Sun-Thurs 5-10pm, Fri-Sat 5-10:30pm. **Prices:** Main courses $18-$46. AE, CB, DC, DISC, MC, V. ⟦VP⟧

Mayo's on El Paseo

73-990 El Paseo; tel 619/346-2284. Monterey Ave exit off I-10. **Continental.** Burgundy-and-white china contrasts with gray walls, gray-and-black carpet, and a black piano bar. Cuisine is continental with an Italian flavor. Favorites include grilled veal chops, Lake Superior white fish with hollandaise, and other bistro-style dishes. **FYI:** Reservations recommended. Piano. Dress code. **Open:** Lunch Mon-Sat 11am-2:30pm; dinner daily 5:30-10pm. **Prices:** Main courses $13-$30. AE, DC, DISC, MC, V.

★ Palomino Euro Bistro

73-101 CA 111; tel 619/773-9091. Bob Hope Dr exit off I-10. **Mediterranean.** The exhibition kitchen contributes to the fun and energy of this restaurant. The ambience is decidedly elegant with Italian marble, dark veneer, hand-blown glass, and a 40-foot carved marble bar. Dishes include Pacific Northwest King salmon and original pastas. **FYI:** Reservations recommended. Dress code. **Open:** Sun-Thurs 5-10pm, Fri-Sat 5-11pm. **Prices:** Main courses $8-$20. AE, CB, DC, DISC, MC, V. ⟦VP⟧ ⚿

Ristorante Mamma Gina

73-705 El Paseo; tel 619/568-9898. Monterey exit off I-10; right on CA 111. **Tuscan.** Double oak doors open to a setting of oak and brass, mauve carpeting, and soft lights. Extensive menu includes veal, chicken, fresh fish, and homemade pasta. **FYI:** Reservations recommended. Piano. Dress code. **Open:** Peak (Oct–May) lunch Mon–Sat 11:30am–2pm; dinner daily 5:15–10pm. **Prices:** Main courses $13–$28. AE, CB, DC, MC, V. 📺 ᕭ

Ruth's Chris Steak House

74-040 CA 111; tel 619/779-1998. Bob Hope Dr exit off I-10. **Steak.** Very sophisticated steak house, with rich, cherry-wood paneling, forest green carpeting, art deco wall sconces, and marble flooring. Specializes in corn-fed prime beef, including New York strip, rib-eye, filet mignon, and porterhouse steaks. **FYI:** Reservations recommended. Dress code. **Open:** Sun–Thurs 5–10pm, Fri–Sat 5–10:30pm. **Prices:** Main courses $17–$36. AE, CB, DC, MC, V. 📺 ᕭ

Palm Springs

See also Cathedral City, Desert Hot Springs, Indian Wells, Indio, La Quinta, Palm Desert, Rancho Mirage

The desert blooms in this exclusive resort community. A playground for the rich and famous since the 1930s, Palm Springs sits in the shadow of 10,804-foot Mount San Jacinto, and its ideal winter temperatures range from the 50s (°F) at night to the 80s during the day. **Information:** Palm Springs Chamber of Commerce, 190 W Amado Rd, Palm Springs 92262 (tel 619/325-1577).

HOTELS 🏨

≣≣≣ Courtyard by Marriott

1300 Tahquitz Canyon Way, 92262; tel 619/322-6100 or toll free 800/321-2211; fax 619/322-6091. Off CA 111 Business District. Overlooks a central courtyard with a swimming pool and gazebo. **Rooms:** 149 rms and stes. CI 4pm/CO noon. Nonsmoking rms avail. Separate areas for work and relaxing. Most overlook pool area, which can be noisy. **Amenities:** 🛁 ᕭ A/C, cable TV w/movies, dataport, voice mail. Some units w/terraces. **Services:** 🚗 🛄 🛎 Babysitting. **Facilities:** 🏋 🏓 🏊 ᕭ 1 restaurant (bkfst only), 1 bar, whirlpool, washer/dryer. **Rates:** Peak (Jan 15–May 31) $39–$149 S or D; $154 ste. Children under age 12 stay free. Min stay special events. Lower rates off-season. Parking: Outdoor, free. AE, CB, DC, DISC, MC, V.

≣≣≣≣ Givenchy Hotel & Spa

4200 East Palm Canyon Dr, 92264; tel 619/770-5000 or toll free 800/276-5000; fax 619/324-7280. From I-10 take the Gene Autry exit S approx 5 mi; at Cherokee. You can't miss the sparkling white facade of this hotel, which debuted in January 1996. The 14-acre grounds are filled with impeccably manicured Versailles-style flowers beds, while the sumptuous-

ly appointed lobby features Oriental carpets, French Provençal furnishings, and bowls of giant roses so perfect they look like a Dutch still-life. Not recommended for children. **Rooms:** 98 rms and stes. CI 1pm/CO noon. Nonsmoking rms avail. Accommodations are offered in the grand Main Pavilion or in two two-story wings almost totally covered in bougainvillea (the wings house the larger, more expensive rooms). There's also a private villa. Each of the quarters is different but luxurious, accented by touches like Italian marble floors, antique armoires, exceptional linens, and upholstery in restful tones of cream, rose, and jade green. In the Pavilion, first-floor rooms feature very large, very private patios. **Amenities:** 🛁 ᕭ 🎴 🍷 A/C, cable TV w/movies, refrig, dataport, bathrobes. Some units w/terraces, some w/whirlpools. **Services:** 🍴 🛎 📺 🚗 🛄 🛎 Twice-daily maid svce, car-rental desk, social director, masseur, babysitting. High tea is served in the Garden Room. **Facilities:** 🏋 🚴 🏋 🏓 🏊 🎾 🚂 🖥 ᕭ 3 restaurants, 1 bar (w/entertainment), spa, sauna, steam rm, whirlpool, beauty salon. The spa is drop-dead gorgeous, with separate wings for men and women. A medley of facials, body treatments, massages, and hydrotherapy sessions are offered; many regimes use "Swisscare pour Givenchy" products. In the boutique, a full range of Givenchy merchandise is showcased. Although the workout room (with exercise bikes, rowing machines, and more) is good enough, it seems like a bit of an afterthought. Personal training and yoga sessions can be arranged. Very high-tech business center offers nine TV screens monitoring different stock markets, internet hook-ups, and other services. The Cafe serves many of the *cuisine legère* specialties developed at the Givenchy Spa in France by chef Gerard Vie. **Rates:** $225–$350 S; $300–$550 D; $375–$3,000 ste. Extra person $25. Children under age 18 stay free. AP and MAP rates avail. Parking: Outdoor, free. AE, CB, DC, DISC, EC, ER, JCB, MC, V.

≣≣≣ Holiday Inn Palm Mountain Resort

155 S Belardo, 92262; tel 619/325-1301 or toll free 800/HOLIDAY; fax 619/323-8937. CA 111 Business District (Palm Canyon Dr) to Tahquitz Canyon Way. A blend of southwestern- and Mediterranean-style architecture. A good location in the heart of Palm Springs makes this a very busy hotel. **Rooms:** 122 rms and effic. CI 3pm/CO noon. Nonsmoking rms avail. **Amenities:** 🛁 ᕭ 🎴 A/C, cable TV w/movies, refrig, voice mail. All units w/terraces. **Services:** ✗ 🚗 🛄 🛎 Twice-daily maid svce, babysitting. **Facilities:** 🏋 ᕭ 2 restaurants, 1 bar, lawn games, whirlpool, washer/dryer. **Rates:** Peak (Jan–June) $109–$135 S or D; $109–$135 effic. Extra person $10. Children under age 18 stay free. Min stay special events. Lower rates off-season. Parking: Outdoor, free. AE, CB, DC, DISC, JCB, MC, V.

≣≣≣≣ Hyatt Regency Suites Palm Springs

285 N Palm Canyon Dr, 92262; tel 619/322-9000 or toll free 800/233-1234; fax 619/322-6009. CA 111 exit off I-10 E; at Amado. Situated in the heart of downtown, but surprisingly

quiet for a city property. The interiors were originally designed by Pierre Cardin, including the abstract four-story-tall sculpture in the pink-marble lobby. **Rooms:** 192 stes. Executive level. CI 3pm/CO noon. Nonsmoking rms avail. One- and two-bedroom suites have contemporary furnishings, with mountain or city views from the private balconies. **Amenities:** A/C, cable TV w/movies. All units w/minibars, all w/terraces, some w/whirlpools. Each suite features plants and jars filled with candy. **Services:** Car-rental desk, masseur, babysitting. **Facilities:** 3 restaurants, 2 bars (1 w/entertainment), whirlpool, beauty salon. Although the pool area is attractive, its Astroturf matting looks somewhat gauche. Small workout room with exercise equipment, guests may also use nearby Gold's Gym for an additional fee. Guests have preferred rates and times for golf and tennis at nearby Rancho Mirage Country Club. **Rates:** Peak (Oct–May) $205–$425 ste. Extra person $25. Children under age 18 stay free. Min stay wknds and special events. Lower rates off-season. Parking: Indoor, free. AE, CB, DC, DISC, ER, JCB, MC, V.

≣≣ Las Brisas Resort Hotel—A Best Western Hotel

222 S Indian Canyon Ave, 92262; tel 619/325-4372 or toll free 800/346-5714; fax 619/320-1371. CA 111 exit off I-10 to Ramon Rd. 2½ acres. Convenient to Palm Springs' most popular attractions; designed in a Mediterranean style. **Rooms:** 90 rms and stes. CI 3pm/CO noon. Nonsmoking rms avail. **Amenities:** A/C, cable TV, refrig. Some units w/terraces, some w/whirlpools. **Services:** Babysitting. **Facilities:** 1 bar, lawn games, whirlpool, washer/dryer. **Rates (BB):** Peak (Jan–May) $79–$159 S or D; $159–$179 ste. Extra person $10. Children under age 17 stay free. Min stay wknds and special events. Lower rates off-season. Parking: Outdoor, free. AE, CB, DC, DISC, MC, V.

≣≣ Ramada Hotel Resort

1800 E Palm Canyon Dr, 92264; tel 619/323-1711 or toll free 800/245-6907; fax 619/322-1075. Located in the Smoke Tree area of Palm Springs, this hotel is designed around a garden and pool area. **Rooms:** 255 rms and stes. CI 3pm/CO noon. Nonsmoking rms avail. **Amenities:** A/C, cable TV w/movies. All units w/terraces. **Services:** **Facilities:** 2 restaurants, 1 bar (w/entertainment), sauna, whirlpool, washer/dryer. **Rates:** Peak (Feb–May) $89–$139 S; $99–$149 D; $139–$189 ste. Extra person $15. Children under age 18 stay free. Min stay peak, wknds, and special events. Lower rates off-season. Parking: Outdoor, free. AE, CB, DC, DISC, MC, V.

≣≣≣ Spa Hotel & Casino

100 N Indian Canyon Dr, 92262; tel 619/325-1461 or toll free 800/854-1279; fax 619/325-3344. Off Tahquitz Canyon Way. Built on the site of an 1871 bathhouse of the Cabrilla Indians. The mineral-rich water flowing through the property is a constant 104°F. **Rooms:** 230 rms and stes. Executive level. CI 4pm/CO noon. Nonsmoking rms avail. **Amenities:** A/C, cable TV w/movies. All units w/minibars, some w/terraces, 1 w/whirlpool. **Services:** Twice-daily maid svce, masseur, babysitting. **Facilities:** 1 restaurant, 2 bars (1 w/entertainment), games rm, spa, sauna, steam rm, whirlpool, beauty salon. Casino. Tennis is available at the Palm Springs Hilton. **Rates:** Peak (Dec 28–June 15) $129–$194 S or D; $194–$234 ste. Extra person $25. Children under age 17 stay free. Min stay special events. Lower rates off-season. Parking: Outdoor, free. AE, CB, DC, DISC, MC, V.

≣≣≣ Sundance Villas

303 Cabrillo Rd, 92262; tel 619/325-3888 or toll free 800/455-3888; fax 619/323-3029. Two- and three-bedroom villas arranged duplex-style, with an enclosed garage, around a colorful garden and recreation area. **Rooms:** 19 cottages/villas. CI 3pm/CO 1pm. Nonsmoking rms avail. Privately owned and individually decorated villas have fully equipped kitchens (complete with a spice rack) and outdoor spas; many have private swimming pools as well. **Amenities:** A/C, cable TV w/movies, refrig, VCR. All units w/minibars, all w/whirlpools. Guests are greeted with fruit and champagne and given orange juice and pastries for the following morning. **Services:** Masseur, babysitting. Small pets permitted at the discretion of the management; deposit required. Extremely friendly, service-oriented managers. **Facilities:** Whirlpool, washer/dryer. **Rates:** Peak (mid-Dec–June 1) $295–$450 effic; $295–$450 cottage/villa. Children under age 18 stay free. Min stay wknds and special events. Lower rates off-season. Parking: Indoor, free. Weekly rates avail. AE, CB, DC, DISC, JCB, MC, V.

≣≣≣ Wyndham Palm Springs Hotel

888 Tahquitz Canyon Way, 92262; tel 619/322-6000 or toll free 800/872-4335, 800/346-7308 in CA; fax 619/322-5351. CA 111 Bus (Palm Canyon Dr) to Tahquitz Canyon Way; turn left. A 60,000-square-foot courtyard, including a 5,000-square-foot oasis-style swimming pool (the largest in town) is surrounded by a Mediterranean-style hotel. Within walking distance of the business district, and connected to the convention center. **Rooms:** 409 rms. CI 3pm/CO noon. Nonsmoking rms avail. **Amenities:** A/C, cable TV w/movies. Some units w/terraces. **Services:** Car-rental desk, masseur, babysitting. **Facilities:** 2 restaurants, 2 bars, games rm, spa, sauna, whirlpool, beauty salon. **Rates:** Peak (Jan–May) $179–$259 S or D. Extra person $15. Children under age 18 stay free. Min stay special events. Lower rates off-season. Parking: Outdoor, free. AE, CB, DC, DISC, JCB, MC, V.

MOTELS

≣≣ Best Western Inn at Palm Springs

1633 S Palm Canyon Dr, 92264; tel 619/325-9177 or toll free 800/222-4678; fax 619/325-9177. CA 111 exit off I-10. Nestled against the San Jacinto Mountains, this secluded retreat offers the only hillside sundeck and pool in Palm

Springs. **Rooms:** 72 rms and stes. CI 3pm/CO noon. Non-smoking rms avail. **Amenities:** 🔒 ◯ 🖐 A/C, cable TV w/movies, refrig, dataport, voice mail. A good selection of reading material in each room. **Services:** 🖼 🛏 🖐 Babysitting. **Facilities:** 🔓 [12] Whirlpool. **Rates (CP):** Peak (Dec 25–May 31) $69–$118 S or D; $260 ste. Extra person $10. Children under age 12 stay free. Lower rates off-season. Parking: Outdoor, free. AE, CB, DC, DISC, ER, JCB, MC, V.

🍴🍴 El Rancho Lodge

1330 E Palm Canyon Dr, 92264; tel 619/327-1339. Gene Autry Trail/Vista Chino exit off I-10. A classic California ranch-style motel with a warm and friendly atmosphere and several areas to relax after a swim. **Rooms:** 19 rms, stes, and effic. CI 3pm/CO noon. **Amenities:** 🔒 ◯ 🖳 A/C, cable TV, refrig. Some units w/terraces. **Services:** Car-rental desk, babysitting. **Facilities:** 🔓 Whirlpool, washer/dryer. **Rates (CP):** Peak (Oct–May) $64 S or D; $138 ste. Extra person $20. Min stay wknds. Lower rates off-season. Parking: Outdoor, free. AE, MC, V.

🍴🍴🍴 Four Seasons Apartment Hotel

290 San Jacinto Dr, 92262; tel 619/325-6427; fax 619/325-6427. CA 111 Bus (Palm Canyon Dr) to Baristo Rd, right on San Jacinto Dr. A small apartment hotel set against the mountains in a quiet neighborhood within walking distance of downtown Palm Springs. **Rooms:** 11 rms, stes, and effic. CI 2pm/CO noon. Nonsmoking rms avail. Individually decorated suites are large and tastefully appointed. **Amenities:** 🔒 ◯ 🖳 🖐 A/C, cable TV, refrig. Some units w/terraces, 1 w/fireplace. **Services:** 🛏 Babysitting. **Facilities:** 🔓 🖐 Whirlpool. Immaculately landscaped pool area. **Rates:** Peak (Feb–Mar) $55–$60 S or D; $80–$130 ste; $65–$160 effic. Extra person $15. Min stay wknds. Lower rates off-season. Parking: Outdoor, free. MC, V.

🍴 Hampton Inn

2000 N Palm Canyon Dr, 92262; tel 619/320-0555 or toll free 800/732-7755; fax 619/320-2261. CA 111 exit off I-10. Within minutes of Palm Springs attractions. **Rooms:** 96 rms. CI 3pm/CO noon. Nonsmoking rms avail. Contemporary-style decor. **Amenities:** 🔒 ◯ A/C, cable TV w/movies. **Services:** 🖼 🛏 Babysitting. **Facilities:** 🔓 [60] 🖐 Lawn games, whirlpool. Nine-hole putting green. **Rates (CP):** Peak (Nov–Apr) $94–$104 S or D. Extra person $5. Children under age 18 stay free. Min stay special events. Lower rates off-season. Parking: Outdoor, free. AE, CB, DC, DISC, MC, V.

🍴🍴 Quality Inn Palm Springs

1269 E Palm Canyon Dr, 92264; tel 619/323-2775 or toll free 800/472-4339; fax 619/323-4234. The parklike setting of this motel affords views of the San Jacinto and Santa Rosa mountains. **Rooms:** 144 rms and stes. CI 3pm/CO noon. Nonsmoking rms avail. **Amenities:** 🔒 ◯ 🖳 A/C, cable TV w/movies. **Services:** 🚐 🛏 **Facilities:** 🔓 [50] 🖐 Whirlpool, washer/dryer. Barbecue facilities available for groups. **Rates:**

Peak (Dec 18–May) $79–$169 S or D; $169 ste. Extra person $10. Children under age 19 stay free. Lower rates off-season. Parking: Outdoor, free. AE, DC, DISC, MC, V.

🍴🍴🍴 Shilo Inn Palm Springs

1875 N Palm Canyon Dr, 92262; tel 619/320-7676 or toll free 800/222-2244; fax 619/320-9543. 3 acres. A very well-maintained motel located just one mile from the heart of Palm Springs. **Rooms:** 124 rms and effic. CI 3pm/CO noon. Nonsmoking rms avail. **Amenities:** 🔒 ◯ 🖳 A/C, cable TV, refrig. All units w/terraces. Microwaves. **Services:** 🚐 🖼 🛏 Fresh fruit and popcorn in lobby. **Facilities:** 🔓 🖐 [60] 🖐 Sauna, steam rm, whirlpool, washer/dryer. Two courtyard swimming pools surrounded by well-manicured lawns and colorful gardens. **Rates (CP):** Peak (Jan–Mar) $59–$129 S or D; $125–$165 effic. Extra person $12. Children under age 12 stay free. Lower rates off-season. Parking: Outdoor, free. AE, CB, DC, DISC, EC, ER, JCB, MC, V.

🍴🍴 Vagabond Inn

1699 S Palm Canyon Dr, 92264; tel 619/325-7211 or toll free 800/522-1555; fax 619/322-9269. Set against the San Jacinto Mountains, this motel offers immaculate accommodations in a contemporary setting. **Rooms:** 120 rms. CI 10am/CO noon. Nonsmoking rms avail. **Amenities:** 🔒 ◯ 🖳 A/C, cable TV. **Services:** 🖼 🛏 **Facilities:** 🔓 1 restaurant (bkfst and lunch only), sauna, whirlpool. **Rates:** Peak (Feb 2–May 31) $65–$116 S or D. Extra person $6. Min stay special events. Lower rates off-season. Parking: Outdoor, free. AE, CB, DC, DISC, ER, JCB, MC, V.

INNS

🍴🍴 Casa Cody

175 S Cahuilla Rd, 92262; tel 619/320-9346 or toll free 800/231-CODY; fax 619/325-8610. A historic hotel originally conceived by a niece and nephew of Buffalo Bill Cody. Located a block off Palm Canyon Dr. Built in the Santa Fe style; not in top shape. **Rooms:** 23 rms and stes. CI 2pm/CO 11am. Nonsmoking rms avail. Room decor reflects the high desert theme of the architecture. **Amenities:** 🔒 🖳 A/C, cable TV, refrig. Some units w/terraces, some w/fireplaces. **Services:** 🛏 🖐 **Facilities:** 🔓 🖐 Whirlpool. **Rates (CP):** Peak (Dec 22–Apr 30) $69 D; $135–$185 ste; $89–$115 effic; $135 cottage/villa. Extra person $10. Min stay peak, wknds, and special events. Lower rates off-season. Parking: Outdoor, free. AE, CB, DC, DISC, MC, V.

🍴🍴🍴 Estrella Inn at Palm Springs

415 S Belardo Rd, 92262; tel 619/320-4117 or toll free 800/237-3687; fax 619/323-3303. CA 111 exit off I-100. 3 acres. A 1930s property restored and reopened in 1993 to rave reviews. Alluring tile-roofed Spanish-style inn with lush fruit trees, colorful flowers, towering palms, and a fountain courtyard. **Rooms:** 62 rms and stes; 14 cottages/villas. CI 3pm/CO noon. Nonsmoking rms avail. Oversize guest rooms, 2-bedroom suites, and individually decorated 1- and 2-bedroom bungalows. **Amenities:** 🔒 ◯ 🖳 A/C, cable TV, refrig. All

units w/terraces, some w/fireplaces, all w/whirlpools. **Services:** 🚗🖼️↵🍷 Babysitting. **Facilities:** 🎱💯♿ Lawn games, whirlpool, washer/dryer, guest lounge w/TV. Golf available at several local courses; tennis available at nearby club. **Rates (CP):** Peak (Jan–Apr) $140 S or D; $175–$200 ste; $200–$250 cottage/villa. Extra person $15. Children under age 12 stay free. Min stay peak and wknds. Lower rates off-season. Higher rates for special events/hols. Parking: Outdoor, free. AE, CB, DC, EC, MC, V.

≡≡≡ Ingleside Inn

200 W Ramon Rd, 92264; tel 619/325-0046 or toll free 800/772-6655 in the US, 800/258-7755 in Canada; fax 619/325-0710. CA 111 exit off I-10. 2½ acres. Created from a 1920s estate, this historic inn surrounded by high adobe walls is situated in the heart of Palm Springs. Unsuitable for children under 18. **Rooms:** 30 rms and stes. CI 2pm/CO noon. Nonsmoking rms avail. Each of the individually decorated rooms and mini-suites contain restored antiques; some have private steam baths and whirlpools. **Amenities:** 🛁🔥📺 A/C, cable TV, refrig. All units w/minibars, some w/terraces, some w/fireplaces. Refrigerators stocked with complimentary light snacks and cold drinks. **Services:** ✕ⓥ🚗🖼️↵ Twice-daily maid svce, masseur, babysitting. Complimentary daily newspaper and fruit basket. White limousine available for shopping expeditions. **Facilities:** 🎱💯♿ 1 restaurant (see "Restaurants" below), 1 bar (w/entertainment), lawn games, whirlpool, guest lounge. **Rates (CP):** Peak (Oct–May) $75–$285 S or D; $295–$385 ste. Extra person $20. Min stay wknds and special events. Lower rates off-season. Parking: Outdoor, free. AE, DC, DISC, MC, V.

≡≡≡ Korakia Pensione

257 S Patencio Rd, 92262; tel 619/864-6411. A pension in a 1920s Mediterranean-style villa that was once center for the literary and artistic community of old Palm Springs. Unsuitable for children under 15. **Rooms:** 12 rms, stes, and effic. CI 2pm/CO noon. Great rooms, with featherbeds and cotton sheets, antiques and handcrafted Mediterranean-style furniture. **Amenities:** 🛁 A/C, refrig. No TV. Some units w/terraces, some w/fireplaces. **Services:** Expanded continental breakfast served in guest rooms or poolside. **Facilities:** 🎱 **Rates (CP):** Peak (July) $79–$169 S or D; $159–$169 ste; $129–$169 effic. Extra person $30. Min stay peak, wknds, and special events. Lower rates off-season. Parking: Outdoor, free. Closed Aug. No CC.

≡≡≡ L'Horizon

1050 East Palm Canyon Dr (CA 111 Business), 92264; tel 619/323-1858 or toll free 800/377-7855; fax 619/327-2933. off I-10. Designed by renowned architect William Cody in 1954, this quiet oasis on 2½ acres was extensively redecorated in 1996. Well-located near restaurants and shopping. Unsuitable for children under 16. **Rooms:** 22 rms and effic. CI 3pm/CO noon. Nonsmoking rms avail. Accommodations are clustered in residential-style villas. Louvered-wood-shuttered windows offer views of gardens and San Jacinto

mountains. **Amenities:** 🛁🔥 A/C, satel TV w/movies, refrig. All units w/terraces, some w/fireplaces. Complimentary morning newspaper delivered to door. Continental breakfast can be served in room, terrace, or poolside. **Services:** 🖼️↵ Babysitting. **Facilities:** 🎱 💯 ♿ Games rm, lawn games, whirlpool, washer/dryer, guest lounge. Beautifully landscaped grounds with winding path to well-maintained pool and separate enclosed whirlpool. Lawn games. **Rates (CP):** Peak (Dec–June) $95–$115 S or D; $115–$140 effic. Children under age 18 stay free. Min stay special events. Lower rates off-season. Parking: Outdoor, free. Monthly rates available. Closed July–Sept. AE, CB, DC, DISC, MC, V.

≡≡≡ Orchid Tree Inn

261 S Belardo Rd, 92262; tel 619/325-2791 or toll free 800/733-3435; fax 619/325-3855. CA 111 exit off I-10. 3½ acres. With its tile-roofed Spanish-style bungalows, the inn evokes the charm and tranquility of Old Palm Springs. Sprawling grounds abound with colorful flowers and cacti. Unsuitable for children under 18. **Rooms:** 31 rms, stes, and effic; 9 cottages/villas. CI 2pm/CO noon. Nonsmoking rms avail. Individually decorated accommodations with unique furnishings, including ranch oak, wicker, and Craftsman pieces. **Amenities:** 🛁🔥📺 A/C, cable TV. All units w/terraces, some w/fireplaces, some w/whirlpools. **Services:** 🖼️ Babysitting. **Facilities:** 🎱💯♿ Games rm, lawn games, whirlpool, guest lounge w/TV. Golf available at several local courses; tennis available at Palm Springs Tennis Club. **Rates (CP):** Peak (Nov–May) $95–$110 S or D; $115–$290 ste; $115–$145 cottage/villa. Extra person $15. Min stay peak and special events. Lower rates off-season. Parking: Outdoor, free. AE, DISC, JCB, MC, V.

≡≡≡ Villa Royale Inn

1620 Indian Trail, 92264; tel 619/327-2314 or toll free 800/245-2314; fax 619/322-3794. 3 acres. A European-style country inn, complete with cascading bougainvillea around quaint courtyards and paths that meander past fountains and shade trees. Unsuitable for children under 16. **Rooms:** 26 rms, stes, and effic; 7 cottages/villas. CI 2pm/CO noon. Nonsmoking rms avail. Each guest cottage is individually decorated with European antiques and custom-designed fabrics. Many have private spas. **Amenities:** 🛁🔥 A/C, cable TV. Some units w/terraces, some w/fireplaces, some w/whirlpools. **Services:** ✕🖼️ Newspaper delivered to your door each morning. **Facilities:** 🎱💯♿ 1 restaurant (see "Restaurants" below), 1 bar, whirlpool, guest lounge. Outdoor lounge area with fireplace and rattan chairs. **Rates (CP):** Peak (Oct–July 5) $75–$165 D; $150–$250 ste; $130–$200 effic; $200–$250 cottage/villa. Extra person $25. Min stay wknds and special events. Lower rates off-season. Parking: Outdoor, free. AE, DC, MC, V.

RESORTS

⊨⊨⊨ The Inn at the Racquet Club

2743 N Indian Canyon Dr, PO Box 1747, 92262; tel 619/325-1281 or toll free 800/367-0946; fax 619/325-3429. 25 acres. An inn comprising cottages that were part of the original 1930s hotel, as well as condos and villas. Landscaping has improved. **Rooms:** 55 rms, stes, and effic; 26 cottages/villas. CI 3pm/CO noon. Nonsmoking rms avail. **Amenities:** 🛏 🖥 A/C, cable TV, voice mail. All units w/terraces, some w/fireplaces, 1 w/whirlpool. **Services:** 📠 🛎 🍴 🏧 Masseur, babysitting. **Facilities:** 🏊 🎾11 🏋 550 🛎 1 bar, basketball, lawn games, sauna, whirlpool. **Rates (CP):** $99–$109 S or D; $129–$395 ste; $109–$395 effic; $99–$119 cottage/villa. Extra person $15. Children under age 12 stay free. Min stay special events. Parking: Indoor/outdoor, free. Closed July–Oct. AE, CB, DC, MC, V.

⊨⊨⊨ La Mancha Private Pool Villas & Spa

444 Avenida Cabelleros, 92262; tel 619/323-1773 or toll free 800/647-7482; fax 619/323-5928. CA 111 exit off I-10. A private 20-acre villa-style resort with the atmosphere of a Mediterranean village. Except for a golf course, it has all the elements to make it a top-ranked property someday; however, some sprucing up is needed. **Rooms:** 54 cottages/villas. CI 3pm/CO noon. Nonsmoking rms avail. Each one-, two-, and three-bedroom villa is individually decorated. Some have their own private pools, spas, and tennis courts. **Amenities:** 🛏 🖥 🍴 A/C, cable TV, refrig, in-rm safe, bathrobes. All units w/terraces, some w/fireplaces, some w/whirlpools. **Services:** ✕ 🍴 📠 🛎 🏧 Car-rental desk, masseur, babysitting. Fleet of 15 Chrysler LeBaron convertibles for rent. **Facilities:** 🏊 🚲 🏋 🎾3 🍴4 🏋 200 🛎 1 restaurant, 1 bar, lawn games, sauna, whirlpool. One main swimming pool and individual pools in 30 of the villas. 9-hole putting green. **Rates:** Peak (Dec 21–Apr 15) $250–$425 cottage/villa. Children under age 12 stay free. Min stay. Lower rates off-season. Parking: Indoor/outdoor, free. AE, DC, DISC, MC, V.

⊨⊨⊨ Oasis Water Resort Villa Hotel

4190 E Palm Canyon Dr, 92264; tel 619/328-1499 or toll free 800/247-4664; fax 619/328-8659. 27 acres. Resort combines villa living with a spacious water park and a 20,000-square-foot European health club. Excellent value. **Rooms:** 81 cottages/villas. CI 4pm/CO noon. Two-bedroom, two-bath villas feature enclosed garages, private patios with barbecues, and full kitchens. **Amenities:** 🛏 🖥 A/C, cable TV, refrig. All units w/terraces, 1 w/whirlpool. **Services:** 📠 🏧 Car-rental desk, masseur, babysitting. **Facilities:** 🏊 🍴5 120 Lawn games, whirlpool, washer/dryer. Nine whirlpools. Nearby golf course. **Rates (CP):** Peak (Jan 22–May 28) $149–$189 cottage/villa. Children under age 18 stay free. Min stay wknds and special events. Lower rates off-season. Parking: Indoor, free. AE, DC, DISC, MC, V.

⊨⊨⊨ Palm Springs Hilton Resort

400 E Tahquitz Canyon Way, 92262; tel 619/320-6868 or toll free 800/522-6900 in the US, 800/527-8020 in Canada; fax 619/320-2126. CA 111 Bus (Palm Canyon Dr) to Tahquitz Canyon Way; turn left. 10 acres. A three-story contemporary building surrounding a courtyard and pool, two blocks from fashionable Palm Canyon Dr. **Rooms:** 245 rms and stes; 15 cottages/villas. CI 3pm/CO noon. Nonsmoking rms avail. A bit worn, but planned renovations will make a difference. **Amenities:** 🛏 🖥 🍴 A/C, cable TV w/movies, refrig. All units w/minibars, all w/terraces, some w/whirlpools. **Services:** ✕ 🍴 VP 📠 🛎 🏧 Car-rental desk, masseur, children's program, babysitting. **Facilities:** 🏊 🍴6 🏋 1000 🛎 1 restaurant, 2 bars, games rm, sauna, beauty salon. **Rates:** Peak (Dec 28–May) $195–$235 S or D; $350–$650 ste; $350–$600 cottage/villa. Extra person $20. Children under age 18 stay free. Lower rates off-season. Parking: Outdoor, free. AE, CB, DC, DISC, EC, ER, JCB, MC, V.

⊨⊨⊨ Palm Springs Marquis Crowne Plaza Resort & Suites

150 S Indian Canyon Dr, 92262; tel 619/322-2121 or toll free 800/223-1050 in CA; fax 619/322-4365. Off CA 111. 7 acres. Inspiring mountain range complements resort's contemporary architecture. Located in the center of Palm Springs. **Rooms:** 264 rms and stes. CI 4pm/CO noon. Nonsmoking rms avail. Elegant guest rooms and suites has a private patio or balcony offering breathtaking views of the mountains and desert. **Amenities:** 🛏 🖥 🍴 A/C, cable TV w/movies, dataport, in-rm safe. All units w/terraces, some w/fireplaces, some w/whirlpools. **Services:** ✕ 🍴 VP 📠 🛎 🏧 Car-rental desk, social director, masseur, children's program, babysitting. **Facilities:** 🏊 🍴 🏋 1500 💻 🛎 2 restaurants, 3 bars (1 w/entertainment), sauna, steam rm, whirlpool, beauty salon. Special signs for the blind included in elevators and at guest room entry doors. **Rates:** Peak (Jan 5–Apr 6) $169–$210 S or D; $199–$242 ste. Extra person $15. Children under age 16 stay free. Lower rates off-season. Parking: Indoor, $6/day. AE, CB, DC, DISC, JCB, MC, V.

⊨⊨⊨ Palm Springs Riviera Resort & Racquet Club

1600 N Indian Canyon Dr, 92262; tel 619/327-8311 or toll free 800/444-8311; fax 619/327-4323. CA 111 exit off I-10 to Vista Chino, turn left on Indian Canyon Dr. 24 acres. Located minutes from the heart of Palm Springs, this resort boasts the famous Bono Restaurant and Racquet Club. **Rooms:** 480 rms and stes. CI 3pm/CO noon. Nonsmoking rms avail. Plants in every room. **Amenities:** 🛏 🖥 A/C, cable TV w/movies, refrig. All units w/terraces, some w/whirlpools. **Services:** 🍴 🍴 VP 📠 🛎 🏧 Car-rental desk, babysitting. **Facilities:** 🏊 🚲 🎾4 🍴5 🏋 3000 🛎 1 restaurant, 1 bar (w/entertainment), lawn games, whirlpool, beauty salon. Lighted 18-hole putting green and a stadium center tennis court. **Rates:** Peak (Nov 15–Mar 31) $139–$179 S or D; $235–$800 ste. Extra person $20. Children under age 17 stay free. Lower rates off-season. Parking: Outdoor, free. Closed Aug 4–29. AE, CB, DC, DISC, EC, MC, V.

RESTAURANTS

Alfredo's Italian Gardens
285 S Palm Canyon Dr; tel 619/325-4060. **Italian.** Rich green decor adds to the garden ambience. Fettucine Alfredo, chicken piccata, shrimp scampi. Also American fare, like barbecued baby back ribs. **FYI:** Reservations recommended. Dress code. **Open:** Lunch daily 11:30am–4pm; dinner daily 4–11pm. **Prices:** Main courses $11–$19. AE, CB, DC, DISC, MC, V. &

★ Billy Reed's
1800 N Palm Canyon Dr; tel 619/325-1946. CA 111 exit off I-10. **American.** With its Victorian decor and casual atmosphere, a perfect spot for family dining, offering yankee pot roast, broiled scallops, roast chicken, prime rib, and the fresh fish of the day. Known for their giant cinnamon rolls. **FYI:** Reservations not accepted. Dancing/jazz. Children's menu. Dress code. **Open:** Daily 7am–11pm. **Prices:** Main courses $10–$12. AE, CB, DC, DISC, MC, V. &

Blue Coyote Grill
445 N Palm Canyon Dr (CA 111); tel 619/327-1196. CA 111 exit off I-10. **Mexican/Southwestern.** Mexican tiled fountains and colorful gardens add to the pleasant ambience at this hacienda-style grill. Appealing courtyard with blue umbrellas, tiled bar, patio overlooking Palm Canyon Dr. Broiled twin tenderloin medallions of beef with Spanish cream sauce; rolled boneless chicken breast with jack cheese, red-corn tortillas, and cilantro. **FYI:** Reservations accepted. Cabaret. Children's menu. Dress code. **Open:** Sun–Thurs 11am–10pm, Fri–Sat 11am–11pm. **Prices:** Main courses $8–$21. AE, DC, MC, V. &

★ Cedar Creek Inn
1555 S Palm Canyon Dr; tel 619/325-7300. Ramon Rd exit off I-10. **American.** Inviting restaurant with an outdoor patio and three separate dining areas. Specialties include salmon poached in apple juice, and chicken breast stuffed with pesto cream cheese. **FYI:** Reservations accepted. Guitar/piano. Dress code. **Open:** Daily 11am–9pm. **Prices:** Main courses $11–$25. AE, MC, V. &

Elan Brasserie
415 N Palm Canyon Dr; tel 619/323-5554. CA 111 off I-10. **French/Mediterranean.** The inside dining room boasts a wonderful aquarium, fireplace, and French doors that frame the view of the outside dining area, replete with colorful umbrellas and table linen. The menu features sautéed scallops with orange-basil sauce, grilled salmon with spinach and red wine sauce, and mussels steamed with white wine, shallots, tomato, and garlic. **FYI:** Reservations recommended.

Dress code. **Open:** Lunch daily 11am–2:30pm; dinner daily 6–11pm. **Prices:** Main courses $14–$21. AE, CB, DC, DISC, ER, MC, V. &

El Mirasol
140 E Palm Canyon Dr; tel 619/323-0721. CA 111 exit off I-10. **Mexican.** A favorite dining spot for families. Dining room is decorated with a desert landscape mural. Menu features regional cuisine of Mexico, including carne adobada, carnitas, chicken mole, and pork chile verde, as well as a favorite, spinach enchiladas. **FYI:** Reservations accepted. Children's menu. **Open:** Peak (Sept–May) lunch daily 11am–3pm; dinner daily 5–10pm. **Prices:** Main courses $7–$11. AE, ER, MC, V.

Europa Restaurant & Bar
In Villa Royale Inn, 1620 Indian Trail; tel 619/327-2314. Ramon Rd exit off I-10. **Continental.** Terra-cotta stucco walls, European antiques, and old-world art define this restaurant, reminiscent of a European country inn. Specialty dishes of continental influence—one night it's Italian, another night it's French, Spanish, or Greek. **FYI:** Reservations recommended. Dress code. **Open:** Lunch Tues–Sat 11:30am–2pm; dinner Tues–Sun 5:30–10pm; brunch Sun 11:30am–2pm. Closed June–Oct. **Prices:** Main courses $13–$28; prix fixe $22–$28. AE, DC, MC, V.

★ Flower Drum
424 S Indian Canyon Dr; tel 619/323-3020. **Chinese.** A stream representing the Yangtze River threads its way through the center of the restaurant, complete with bridge and koi pond. Specializing in food inspired by the Hunan, Szechaun, Canton, Shanghai, and Peking regions of China, including tangerine beef, Kung Pao chicken, and shrimp blossom. Each evening, a traditional Chinese dance is performed. **FYI:** Reservations accepted. Dinner theater. Dress code. **Open:** Lunch daily 11:30am–3pm; dinner daily 4–10:30pm. **Prices:** Main courses $9–$28. AE, MC, V.

Ⓢ ★ John Henry's Cafe
1785 E Tahquitz Canyon Way; tel 619/327-7667. CA 111 exit off I-10. **Eclectic.** The main dining room overlooks an outdoor patio, which has potted and bedded flowers and a three-tiered fountain. Eclectic menu includes grilled Lake Superior whitefish with lemon butter, roasted herb rack of lamb, and osso buco. **FYI:** Reservations recommended. Dress code. **Open:** Mon–Sat 5–9:30pm. Closed June–Sept. **Prices:** Main courses $9–$14. AE, MC, V. &

★ Las Casuelas Terraza
222 S Palm Canyon Dr; tel 619/325-2794. CA 111 off I-10. **Mexican.** Set in a hacienda-style building with dark wood interior and colorful Mexican accents. Specialties include carne asada, spicy pork, chicken and shrimp fajitas. **FYI:** Reservations recommended. Guitar/singer. Children's menu. Additional locations: 368 N Palm Canyon (tel 325-3213);

70-050 CA 111, Rancho Mirage (tel 328-8844). **Open:** Mon–Sat 11am–10pm, Sun 10am–10pm. **Prices:** Main courses $7–$14. AE, DC, DISC, MC, V. ♨ ♿

♣ Le Vallauris
385 W Tahquitz Canyon Way; tel 619/325-5059. CA 111 exit off I-10. **Californian/French.** Historic-landmark home decorated with tapestries and Louis XV furniture. Fireplaces dominate the main dining room, and doors open out onto a tree-lined patio. The daily menu highlights fresh and seasonal ingredients in such specialties as black ravioli with lobster bisque, roasted pork tenderloin, and Lake Superior whitefish with Dijon mustard mousseline. **FYI:** Reservations recommended. Piano. Dress code. **Open:** Lunch daily 11:30am–2:30pm; dinner daily 6–11pm; brunch Sun 11:30am–2:30pm. **Prices:** Main courses $20–$30. AE, CB, DC, DISC, ER, MC, V. ♥ ♨ ♿ ♥ VP

★ Louise's Pantry
124 S Palm Canyon Dr; tel 619/325-5124. CA 111 exit off I-10. **American.** A diner-style restaurant in the heart of Palm Springs. It serves such all-American favorites as chicken and dumplings, roast turkey, and homemade cornbread, and is known for its cream pies. **FYI:** Reservations not accepted. Children's menu. Beer and wine only. Additional location: 111 Town Center Way, Palm Desert (tel 346-1315). **Open:** Daily 7am–8:30pm. Closed July–Sept. **Prices:** Main courses $7–$10. DISC, MC, V.

Lyons English Grille
233 E Palm Canyon Dr; tel 619/327-1551. Ramon Rd exit off I-10. **British.** Reminiscent of a 19th-century British inn, with dark woods, red leather, antiques, leaded-glass windows, and copper pots. Steak-and-kidney pie, prime rib, roast duckling. **FYI:** Reservations recommended. Piano/singer. Dress code. **Open:** Peak (Oct–May) daily 4–10:30pm. Closed July–Sept. **Prices:** Main courses $14–$23. AE, DC, MC, V. ♨ ♥ VP

Melvyn's
In the Ingleside Inn, 200 W Ramon Rd; tel 619/325-2323. CA 111 exit off I-10. **Continental.** Nestled in the gardens of the Ingleside Inn, this Renaissance-style restaurant features an intimate dining room as well as an enclosed patio. Menu includes veal Ingleside, steak au poivre, and chicken topped with jumbo shrimp and avocado. **FYI:** Reservations recommended. Piano. Dress code. **Open:** Lunch Mon–Fri 11:30am–3pm; dinner daily 6–11pm; brunch Sat 11am–3pm, Sun 9am–3pm. **Prices:** Main courses $16–$33. AE, DC, DISC, MC, V. ♨ VP

★ Nate's Delicatessen and Restaurant
100 S Indian Canyon Dr; tel 619/325-3506. CA 111 off I-10. **Deli.** A collection of framed caricatures (with Yiddish subtitles) line the walls of this New York–style delicatessen, where the bill of fare includes sandwiches, potato pancakes, cheese blintzes, corned beef and cabbage, and, of course, chicken

soup. **FYI:** Reservations not accepted. Children's menu. Dress code. **Open:** Daily 8am–8pm. **Prices:** Main courses $7–$11; prix fixe $9. AE, CB, DC, DISC, ER, MC, V. ♥ ♿

Otani–A Garden Restaurant
266 Avenida Caballeros; tel 619/327-6700. CA 111 exit off I-10. **Japanese.** A 40-foot peaked roof and a traditional Japanese garden create a distinctive atmosphere. Chefs present "food theater" in four separate areas: sushi bar, teppanyaki table, tempura bar, and yakitori counter. There's also a regular dining room menu. **FYI:** Reservations recommended. Children's menu. Dress code. **Open:** Lunch Sun–Fri 11:30am–2pm; dinner daily 6–9:30pm; brunch Sun 11am–2pm. **Prices:** Main courses $11–$26. AE, DC, MC, V. ♿

Palm Springs Brewery
369 N Palm Canyon Dr; tel 619/327-BREW. CA 111 exit off I-10. **American.** Located in a renovated 1934 Spanish-style building, this brew pub and grill offers draft beer and a casual menu featuring burgers, sandwiches, and appetizers, as well as soups, salads, and entrees. **FYI:** Reservations accepted. Guitar/singer. Children's menu. Beer and wine only. **Open:** Lunch daily 11am–4pm; dinner Sun–Thurs 4–9:30pm, Fri–Sat 4–10pm. **Prices:** Main courses $7–$11. AE, CB, DC, MC, V. ♨ ♿

★ St James on the Vineyard
In The Vineyard, 265 S Palm Canyon Dr; tel 619/320-8041. Exit CA 111 off I-10. **Eclectic/International.** Sculptor and designer Ian Campbell sets the stage with his art work in the three separate dining areas; one is cozy with wildly colorful cushions, another is the wine cellar featuring 160 different wines, and the third is a hideaway with an expansive terraced patio. Proprietor James Offord created an eclectic menu featuring such dishes as scallops Cubano, Burmese bouillabaisse, tofu St James, scampi Cleopatra, halibut Tangier, and a selection of curries. **FYI:** Reservations recommended. **Open:** Daily 5:30–10pm. **Prices:** Main courses $15–$25. AE, CB, DISC, MC, V. ♨ ♿

Siamese Gourmet Restaurant
4711 E Palm Canyon Dr; tel 619/328-0057. Gene Autry Trail/Vista Chino exit off I-10. **Thai.** Cheerfully decorated with bamboo chairs and emerald green tablecloths. House specialties are chicken and beef curry, barbecued chicken, and clay-pot seafood combination. **FYI:** Reservations recommended. Dress code. Beer and wine only. **Open:** Lunch Mon–Sat 11:30am–2:30pm; dinner daily 5–10pm. **Prices:** Main courses $9–$17. AE, DC, DISC, MC, V. ♥

Sorrentino's
1032 N Palm Canyon Dr; tel 619/325-2944. Calif 111 exit off I-10. **Continental.** For nearly 30 years the Sorrentino family has owned and operated this seafood house. Dining patio features a 25-foot pond. Specialties include live Maine lobster, clams, oysters, Dungeness crab cakes, and soft-shell crab; extensive menu also includes steak, veal, chicken, and pasta dishes. **FYI:** Reservations recommended. Piano. Chil-

dren's menu. Dress code. **Open:** Peak (Sept–May) daily 5–10pm. **Prices:** Main courses $11–$24. AE, CB, DC, MC, V. VP

ATTRACTIONS

Palm Springs Desert Museum
101 Museum Dr; tel 619/325-7186. The triple focus of this museum is on art, natural science, and the performing arts. Galleries feature presentations from the museum's vast permanent collection, including classic American landscapes and Western art, as well as contemporary paintings and sculpture, with a particular focus on California. The natural science wing contains a variety of permanent exhibits, including interpretive dioramas of desert plant and animal life. The 450-seat **Annenberg Theater** hosts world-class dance, theater, and music performances. Sculpture gardens, museum store, cafe. **Open:** Sat–Thurs 10am–4pm, Fri 1–8pm. Closed some hols. Schedule may vary; call ahead. $$

Palm Springs Air Museum
745 Gene Autry Trail (CA 111); tel 619/778-6262. Dedicated to the restoration, preservation, and exhibition of America's legendary World War II fighters, bombers, and other aircraft. Many of the planes are from the private collection of Robert J Pond. Visitors can see a Grumman Wildcat, a Boeing Flying Fortress, a Lockheed Lightning, and a Curtis Mustang. Special events and guided tours. **Open:** Wed–Mon 10am–5pm. $$$

Palm Springs Aerial Tramway
1 Tramway Rd; tel 619/325-1391. The tram ascends 2½ miles up the slopes of Mount San Jacinto, traveling from the desert floor to cool alpine heights in less than 20 minutes; in winter the change is dramatic, with snow often at the summit. At the top are a cafeteria and cocktail lounge, a gift shop, a picnic area, and the starting points of numerous hiking trails, many dotted with camping areas. **Open:** Mon–Fri 10am–8pm, Sat–Sun 8am–8pm; open 1 hour later during daylight saving time. $$$$

Palo Alto

Stanford University was founded in 1891, and the well-scrubbed campus remains at the center of life in Palo Alto. A trip atop the Hoover Tower, with its panoramic views of the campus and outlying areas, and a visit to the Stanford Linear Accelerator Center, with its two-mile-long atom smasher, round out a visit to the city. Palo Alto is also an important center for electronics and advanced research industries. **Information:** Palo Alto Chamber of Commerce, 325 Forest Ave, Palo Alto 94301 (tel 415/324-3121).

HOTELS

Garden Court Hotel
520 Cowper St, 94301; tel 415/322-9000 or toll free 800/824-9028; fax 415/324-3609. University Ave W exit off US 101. A charmer with a Mediterranean look in downtown Palo Alto. **Rooms:** 62 rms and stes. CI 2pm/CO noon. Nonsmoking rms avail. **Amenities:** A/C, cable TV w/movies, refrig, VCR, in-rm safe, bathrobes. All units w/minibars, all w/terraces, some w/fireplaces, some w/whirlpools. **Services:** Twice-daily maid svce, masseur, babysitting. Complimentary overnight shoe polishing. Four choices of newspaper. Complimentary shuttle within 5-mile radius. **Facilities:** 1 restaurant, 1 bar. **Rates:** $195–$245 S or D; $265–$425 ste. Extra person $15. Children under age 12 stay free. Parking: Indoor, $9/day. AE, CB, DC, DISC, JCB, MC, V.

Holiday Inn Palo Alto-Stanford
625 El Camino Real, 94301; tel 415/328-2800 or toll free 800/HOLIDAY, 800/874-3516 in CA; fax 415/327-7362. Embarcadero Rd W exit off US 101; right on El Camino. Popular for its location near downtown Palo Alto and Stanford University, and for its resortlike ambience. **Rooms:** 343 rms and stes. CI 2pm/CO noon. Nonsmoking rms avail. **Amenities:** A/C, cable TV w/movies, dataport, voice mail. Some units w/terraces, some w/whirlpools. **Services:** Babysitting. Free hors d'oeuvres and cocktails on weeknights. **Facilities:** 1 restaurant, 1 bar, washer/dryer. **Rates:** $138–$155 S; $148–$165 D; $225 ste. Children under age 18 stay free. Parking: Outdoor, free. AE, DC, DISC, JCB, MC, V.

Hyatt Rickeys in Palo Alto
4219 El Camino Real, 94306; tel 415/493-8000 or toll free 800/233-1234; fax 415/424-0836. San Antonio Rd S exit off US 101. This 50-year-old landmark hotel is still appealing, with its extensive grounds and popular restaurant. **Rooms:** 347 rms and stes. CI 3pm/CO noon. Nonsmoking rms avail. **Amenities:** A/C, cable TV w/movies. Some units w/terraces, some w/fireplaces. **Services:** Car-rental desk, masseur, children's program, babysitting. Women may request an escort for walking the grounds at night. **Facilities:** 1 restaurant, 1 bar (w/entertainment), lawn games, sauna, beauty salon. **Rates:** $145–$170 S; $170–$195 D; $230 ste. Extra person $25. Children under age 18 stay free. AP rates avail. Parking: Outdoor, free. AE, DC, DISC, MC, V.

Stanford Terrace Inn
531 Stanford Ave, 94306; tel 415/857-0333 or toll free 800/729-0332; fax 415/857-0343. Embarcadero Rd exit off US 101; turn left on El Camino, right on Stanford. Overlooks the beautiful southern campus of Stanford University. **Rooms:** 79 rms, stes, and effic. CI 2pm/CO noon. Nonsmoking rms avail. Exceptionally large rooms and suites. All mini-suites have full kitchens including pots and pans. **Amenities:**

A/C, cable TV w/movies, refrig. Some units w/terraces. **Services:** ⊠ ⇦ Masseur, children's program, babysitting. **Facilities:** ⛾ ⌗ Washer/dryer. **Rates (CP):** $120–$200 S or D; $130–$200 ste; $175–$225 effic. Extra person $10. Children under age 13 stay free. Parking: Outdoor, free. AE, CB, DC, DISC, MC, V.

MOTEL

≣≣ Creekside Inn Best Western

3400 El Camino Real, 94306; tel 415/493-2411 or toll free 800/49-CREEK; fax 415/493-6787. Oregon Expwy exit off US 101; left on El Camino. Though located on a busy street, the motel has a pool and creek that give it a country feel. **Rooms:** 136 rms, stes, and effic. CI 3pm/CO noon. Nonsmoking rms avail. **Amenities:** ⛾ ⌁ ▣ ⦂ A/C, cable TV, refrig, dataport, voice mail. All units w/terraces. Microwave in suites. **Services:** ⊠ ⇦ Babysitting. Complimentary shuttle service within 10-mile radius. **Facilities:** ⛾ ⛲ ⌗ ⅄ 1 restaurant, 1 bar. Grocery store–deli on premises. **Rates:** $90–$110 S or D; $120–$150 ste; $120–$150 effic. Extra person $5. Parking: Indoor/outdoor, free. AE, CB, DC, DISC, EC, JCB, MC, V.

INN

≣≣≣ The Victorian on Lytton

555 Lytton Ave, 94301; tel 415/322-8555; fax 415/322-7141. A cozy bed-and-breakfast located one block from charming downtown Palo Alto. Top-quality furnishings, large rooms, and special touches throughout, from fresh flowers to rubber duckies in the tubs. Lots of antiques. **Rooms:** 10 rms and stes. CI 3pm/CO 11am. No smoking. **Amenities:** ⛾ ⌁ A/C, cable TV, dataport, VCR, voice mail, bathrobes. Some units w/terraces, 1 w/fireplace. Evening sherry and bathrobes provided on request. **Services:** ⇦ Afternoon tea and wine/sherry served. Staff is friendly and helpful, yet extremely respectful of guests' privacy. **Facilities:** ⅄ Grounds are small, but quite attractive. **Rates (BB):** $99 S; $99–$220 D; $149–$220 ste. Extra person $10. Children under age 18 stay free. Parking: Indoor, free. AE, MC, V.

RESTAURANTS ⅋

⑤ Mango Cafe

435 Hamilton Ave (Downtown); tel 415/324-9443. Embarcadero Rd exit off US 101. **Caribbean.** In Jamaica, the term "jerked" refers to spicy-hot, marinated meats cooked slowly over pimento bark or guava wood. And that's exactly what you'll find at this unassuming eatery that packs a wallop with jerked entrees such as chicken legs or curried goat over rice. Milder dishes are chicken pelau cooked with rice and pigeon peas in coconut milk and olives, or curried vegetable roti in griddled bread. You can cool down with tangy ginger beer from Kingston or a 24-ounce smoothie, and finish off with bread pudding or sweet-potato pudding for dessert. Bottled hot sauces from the islands are sold. **FYI:** Reservations

recommended. BYO. **Open:** Lunch Mon–Sat 11am–3pm; dinner Mon–Sat 6–10pm. **Prices:** Main courses $5–$10. MC, V. ⚓ ⛻ ⅄

Scott's Seafood Grill and Bar

2300 E Bayshore Rd; tel 415/856-1046. Embarcadero E exit off US 101; turn right onto E Bayshore Rd. **Seafood.** Cape Cod looks, with nautical photos, beamed ceilings, and wood wainscoting. Fireplace in lounge. Monterey Bay calamari, Boston clam chowder, petrale sole, and seafood sauté. Also, steak, chicken, pasta. **FYI:** Reservations recommended. Children's menu. **Open:** Sun–Mon 7:30am–9pm, Tues–Sat 7:30am–9:30pm. **Prices:** Main courses $12–$25. AE, CB, DC, DISC, MC, V. ⚓ ▦ ⊠ ⅄

ATTRACTION ⌂

Stanford Linear Accelerator Center

2575 Sand Hill Rd, Palto Alto; tel 415/926-2204. This facility, located three miles west of the main Stanford University campus, specializes in experimental and theoretical research in elementary particle physics. Built in the 1960s, the center's two-mile-long linear electron accleterator is used to create collisions of subatomic particles to study their effects and learn about the nature of matter. The accelerator generates electron beams with the highest energy available in the world, making it a valuable research tool for scientists from all over the world.

Public tours are conducted several times a week, by advance reservation only (phone for schedule). The two-hour tour begins with an orientation and slide presentation and concludes with a guided bus tour of the 400-acre facility. The tour is not recommended for children under age 11. **Free**

Pasadena

Pasadena is an oasis of tradition and community in ever-changing Los Angeles. The city boasts some of the most sophisticated residential areas in Southern California, and it has revised its staid image by revamping its Old Town along Colorado Boulevard to include trendy stores, cafes, and restaurants. Every New Year's Day the Tournament of Roses Parade is held here. **Information:** Pasadena Convention & Visitors Bureau, 171 S Los Robles Ave, Pasadena 91101 (tel 818/795-9311).

HOTELS ⌂

≣≣≣≣ DoubleTree Hotel at Plaza las Fuentes

191 N Los Robles Ave, 91101; tel 818/792-2727 or toll free 800/222-TREE; fax 818/792-7669. Arroyo Pkwy exit off I-110. Gardens with fountains and exquisite tile work give this hotel a Spanish feel. Lovely public rooms. Located two blocks from shopping mall and convention center; six blocks from Old Town. **Rooms:** 350 rms and stes. Executive level. CI 3pm/CO noon. Nonsmoking rms avail. Rooms aren't

large but are attractively decorated. **Amenities:** 📞 🅰 🖐 A/C, cable TV w/movies, dataport. All units w/minibars, some w/terraces, some w/whirlpools. **Services:** 🍽️ 🖭 VP 🚐 🛎️ 🍹 Twice-daily maid svce, car-rental desk, social director, masseur, babysitting. Excellent staff. **Facilities:** 🏊 🐎 [1000] ⅙ 1 restaurant, 2 bars (1 w/entertainment), spa, sauna, steam rm, whirlpool. Pool has spectacular view of the city hall dome. **Rates:** $115–$159 S or D; $800–$1,000 ste. Extra person $19. Children under age 12 stay free. Min stay special events. Parking: Indoor, $4–$9/day. AE, CB, DC, DISC, JCB, MC, V.

📕📕📕 Holiday Inn Pasadena
303 E Cordova St, 91105; tel 818/449-4000 or toll free 800/457-7940; fax 818/584-1390. Arroyo Pkwy exit off I-110. Adjacent to the convention center; great lobby filled with Chinese art. Close to Old Pasadena and across from shopping mall. **Rooms:** 318 rms and stes. CI 4pm/CO noon. No smoking. Newly decorated rooms are very large and airy; deluxe suites available. **Amenities:** 📞 🅰 🖭 🖐 A/C, cable TV w/movies, dataport. Some units w/terraces. **Services:** ✕ 🖭 🚐 🛎️ 🍹 🐕 Car-rental desk, social director. Happy hour. **Facilities:** 🏊 🐎 🛥️2 [1000] ⅙ 1 restaurant, 1 bar, washer/dryer. Ice-skating rink next door. Guest privileges at nearby health club. **Rates:** $99–$120 S; $111–$132 D; $225 ste. Extra person $12. Children under age 18 stay free. Min stay special events. Parking: Indoor, $4/day. AE, CB, DC, DISC, JCB, MC, V.

📕📕📕 Pasadena Hilton
150 S Los Robles Ave, 91101; tel 818/577-1000 or toll free 800/HILTONS; fax 818/584-3148. Lake Ave exit off I-210. Well kept and pleasant; two blocks from the convention center. **Rooms:** 296 rms and stes. Executive level. CI 3pm/CO 1pm. Nonsmoking rms avail. Rooms are nicely decorated and well maintained. **Amenities:** 📞 🅰 🖭 A/C, dataport. Some units w/minibars, some w/terraces. **Services:** ✕ VP 🚐 🛎️ 🍹 Twice-daily maid svce, car-rental desk, masseur, babysitting. **Facilities:** 🏊 🛥️ [1700] ⅙ 1 restaurant, 1 bar, whirlpool, beauty salon, washer/dryer. Meeting rooms feature great city views. Sports bar offers lots of activities and a Happy Hour. Golf and tennis at nearby country club. **Rates:** $99–$175 S; $99–$185 D; $225–$275 ste. Children under age 18 stay free. Min stay special events. Parking: Indoor, $5–$10/day. AE, CB, DC, DISC, JCB, MC, V.

📕📕📕📕 Ritz-Carlton Huntington Hotel
1401 S Oak Knoll Ave, 91106; tel 818/568-3900 or toll free 800/241-3333; fax 818/568-3700. CA 110 N to Arroyo Pkwy. 23 acres. With red-tile roof and sand-beige stucco walls, this elegant hotel fits right into its crème-de-la-crème residential neighborhood. **Rooms:** 383 rms and stes; 21 cottages/villas. Executive level. CI 3pm/CO noon. Nonsmoking rms avail. Recalls an English country house; dark furnishings plus comfortable armchair with ottoman. Marble baths are nicer in standard rooms than in suites. **Amenities:** 📞 🅰 🖐 A/C, cable TV w/movies, in-rm safe, bathrobes. All units w/minibars, some w/terraces, some w/fireplaces, 1 w/whirlpool. **Services:** 🍽️ 🖭 VP 🚐 🛎️ 🍹 Twice-daily maid svce, car-rental desk, social director, masseur, babysitting. Children's program during summer. **Facilities:** 🏊 🐎 🎾 🛥️ [400] ⅙ 2 restaurants (see "Restaurants" below), 1 bar (w/entertainment), games rm, spa, sauna, steam rm, whirlpool, beauty salon. Tennis pro on staff. **Rates:** $185–$215 S; $200 D; $350–$275 ste; $500–$2,000 cottage/villa. Children under age 18 stay free. Min stay special events. Parking: Indoor, $15/day. AE, CB, DC, DISC, JCB, MC, V.

MOTELS

📕📕 Comfort Inn
2462 E Colorado Blvd, 91107; tel 818/405-0811 or toll free 800/221-2222; fax 818/796-0966. Sierra Madre exit off I-210. Nice hotel with easy access to area attractions. **Rooms:** 50 rms. CI 1pm/CO noon. Nonsmoking rms avail. Pleasantly decorated rooms. **Amenities:** 📞 🅰 🖐 A/C, cable TV w/movies, refrig, VCR, voice mail. Microwave. **Services:** 🛎️ 🍹 Babysitting. **Facilities:** 🏊 [15] ⅙ Sauna, whirlpool. **Rates (CP):** $52–$115 S; $57–$115 D. Extra person $5. Children under age 18 stay free. Min stay special events. Parking: Outdoor, free. AE, CB, DC, DISC, ER, JCB, MC, V.

📕📕📕 Saga Motor Hotel
1633 E Colorado Blvd, 91106; tel 818/795-0431 or toll free 800/793-7242; fax 818/792-0559. Allen exit off I-210, S 3 blocks. Clean, well-cared for property with easy access to the freeway. Lobby has pleasant area in which to read, sip coffee, and gaze at the garden. **Rooms:** 69 rms and stes. CI noon/CO noon. Nonsmoking rms avail. Remodeled rooms are large and airy with a country atmosphere. **Amenities:** 📞 🅰 A/C, cable TV w/movies. 1 unit w/terrace. **Services:** 🛎️ 🍹 Children's program. **Facilities:** 🏊 [25] ⅙ **Rates (CP):** Peak (around New Years) $53–$69 S; $59–$69 D. Extra person $6. Children under age 16 stay free. Min stay special events. Lower rates off-season. Parking: Outdoor, free. Call collect for reservations. AE, CB, DC, DISC, ER, JCB, MC, V.

RESTAURANTS 🍴

⑤ Abiento
110 S Lake Ave; tel 818/449-4151. Lake St exit off I-210. **New American/Mediterranean.** This lovely, trattoria-style restaurant with ocher walls, garden plants, and lots of light is a lively place to dine, although it can be a bit noisy during happy hour. Menu specialties include the veal sausages with sweet onions, quail stuffed with risotto, and daily fresh fish specials. **FYI:** Reservations recommended. Children's menu. **Open:** Mon–Fri 11am–10pm, Sat 11am–11pm, Sun 9am–9pm. **Prices:** Main courses $8–$14. AE, DC, DISC, MC, V. ❤️ 🍽️ 🍴 ⅙

★ Bistro 45
45 S Mentor Ave; tel 818/795-2478. Lake Ave exit off I-210. **French.** A charming bistro with several intimate rooms, lovely glassware, and huge floral arrangements. The French bistro

fare includes roast leg of Colorado lamb, crispy duck, roast tenderloin of pork, and bouillabaisse. Nationally recognized wine list. **FYI:** Reservations recommended. Guitar. Dress code. **Open:** Lunch Tues–Fri 11:30am–2:30pm; dinner Tues–Thurs 6–9:30pm, Fri 6–11pm, Sat 5:30–11pm, Sun 5–9pm; brunch Sun 10:30am–2:30pm. **Prices:** Main courses $15–$22. AE, CB, DC, DISC, ER, MC, V. ♥ VP ⅋

♣ The Grill Restaurant
In Ritz-Carlton Huntington Hotel, 1401 S Oak Knoll Ave; tel 818/568-3900. CA 110 W to Arroyo Pkwy, right on California Blvd, right on Lake Ave. **Californian/French.** Dark-wood appointments and nautical art welcome guests at this eatery, one of the best in the city. Windows look onto a horseshoe-shaped garden and the lights of San Marino, while piano music enhances the romantic mood. Menu specialties include game and an excellent array of fresh fish. **FYI:** Reservations recommended. Piano/singer. Jacket required. **Open:** Daily 6–10pm. **Prices:** Main courses $24–$52. AE, CB, DC, MC, V. ♥▲ VP ⅋

McCormick & Schmick's
In Las Fuentes Plaza, 111 N Los Robles; tel 818/405-0064. Lake St exit off I-210. **American.** Warm and inviting, with lots of dark wood and stained-glass windows. Open kitchen prepares Dungeness crab cakes in jalapeño hollandaise, shellfish stew, and roasted halibut stuffed with crab, shrimp, and brie. Special happy hour menu is a good value. **FYI:** Reservations recommended. Piano. **Open:** Mon–Sat 11:30am–11pm, Sun 10:30am–10pm. **Prices:** Main courses $5–$20. AE, DC, DISC, MC, V. ♥ ≛ 🖼 🖼 ⅋

★ Mi Piace
25 E Colorado Blvd (Old Town); tel 818/795-3131. Off CA 134. **Californian/Italian.** This sleek and sophisticated restaurant boasts high ceilings, natural colors, and lots of light. Always packed—the outdoor tables are great for people watching. Menu features California and Italian-style pizzas and pastas with lots of seafood choices. **FYI:** Reservations recommended. Dress code. **Open:** Fri–Sat 11:30am–1am, Sun–Thurs 11:30am–11:30pm. **Prices:** Main courses $6–$16. AE, MC, V. VP ⅋

★ Old Town Restaurant & Bakery
In Tanner Market, 166 W Colorado Blvd (Old Pasadena); tel 818/793-2993. Off CA 134. **New American.** Besides great baked goods, Amy Pressman offers chicken chorizo and eggs, homemade griddled corn tortillas, black beans, and vegetable quiche. Big mugs of cappuccino. **FYI:** Reservations not accepted. Children's menu. Dress code. Beer and wine only. **Open:** Fri–Sat 7:30am–midnight, Sun–Thurs 7:30am–10pm. **Prices:** Main courses $5–$11. AE, MC, V. ≛ 🖼 🚗 VP ⅋

♣ Parkway Grill
510 S Arroyo Pkwy; tel 818/795-1001. Arroyo Pkwy exit off I-110. **Regional American.** Housed in a beautiful old building with exposed brick walls, high ceilings with skylights, natural wood floors, and aqua accents, this place has great

food and ambience. Adjacent to a lovely garden. Try the roasted pepper stuffed chicken and the wood-fired pizza. **FYI:** Reservations recommended. Piano. Dress code. **Open:** Lunch Mon–Fri 11:30am–2:30pm; dinner Mon–Thurs 5:30–10pm, Fri–Sat 5–11pm, Sun 5–10pm; brunch Sun 11am–2:30pm. **Prices:** Main courses $15–$25. AE, MC, V. ♥ ■ 🖼 VP

ⓢ ★ Pasadena Baking Company
29 E Colorado Blvd (Old Town); tel 818/796-9966. Off CA 134. **Cafe/Bakery.** Outfitted with gray tables, black chairs, and newspapers for patrons to read, it's known for fabulous coffee drinks. A great place for breakfast or after a movie. Featuring gigantic sandwiches and omelettes, a large selection of rustic breads, and luscious desserts. **FYI:** Reservations recommended. Dress code. Beer and wine only. **Open:** Mon–Fri 7am–11pm, Sat 8am–midnight, Sun 8am–11pm. **Prices:** Main courses $4–$10. AE, MC, V. VP ⅋

ⓢ ★ Saladang
In Kelly Paper Building, 363 S Fair Oaks (Old Pasadena); tel 818/793-8123. **Thai.** In Thailand, salas are roadside pavilions offering wayfarers respite from tropical heat and/or storms. Set in a huge warehouse with contemporary decor (including tasteful accents of purple, the Thai favorite color), this place is always packed, despite the hardly visible sign. Dishes prepared with meat, chicken, fish, or completely vegetarian. The lunch special is a good deal at $6.95. **FYI:** Reservations recommended. Dress code. Beer and wine only. **Open:** Daily 10am–10pm. **Prices:** Main courses $4–$15. AE, CB, DC, MC, V. 🖼 ⅋

♣ Shiro Restaurant
1505 Mission St; tel 818/799-4774. 3 blocks S of Fair Oaks exit off I-110. **French/Japanese.** A very special place to dine; a quiet, peaceful ambience. The decor is minimalist and sophisticated. The signature dish is whole sizzling catfish in ponzu sauce. All dishes blend French and Japanese influences. **FYI:** Reservations recommended. Beer and wine only. **Open:** Tues–Thurs 6–9pm, Fri–Sat 6–10pm, Sun 5:45–9pm. Closed three weeks in Sept. **Prices:** Main courses $15–$24. AE, MC, V. ♥

Xiomara
69 N Raymond Ave (Old Town); tel 818/796-2520. Fair Oaks exit off I-210. **French.** Subtle gray, black, and lots of mirrors give this place the feel of a sophisticated French bistro. Chef Patrick Healy is considered among the best chefs, and eating his daily specials will make you feel like you're in Paris. Try the terrine of duck with foie gras and the homemade sausages with mashed potatoes. **FYI:** Reservations recommended. Dress code. **Open:** Lunch Mon–Fri 11:30am–2:30pm; dinner daily 5:30–10:30pm. **Prices:** Main courses $17–$23; prix fixe $25. AE, DC, DISC, MC, V. VP

★ Yujean Kang
67 N Raymond Ave (Old Town); tel 818/585-0855. Fair Oaks exit off I-210. **Chinese.** Sophisticated, stylized Chinese cui-

sine. Yujean Kang is among the best Chinese chefs in the San Francisco and Los Angeles areas. The house specialty is "picture in the snow," which is chicken, smoked duck, black mushrooms, and meringue. **FYI:** Reservations recommended. Beer and wine only. **Open:** Lunch daily 11:30am–2:30pm; dinner Sun–Thurs 5–9:30pm, Fri–Sat 5–10pm. **Prices:** Main courses $11–$18. AE, CB, DC, DISC, MC, V. ♥ VP

ATTRACTIONS 🏛

Norton Simon Museum
411 W Colorado Blvd; tel 818/449-6840. One of the most important art museums in California, Norton Simon has masterpieces from the Italian, Dutch, Spanish, Flemish, and French schools; also Impressionist paintings, tapestries, and 20th-century painting and sculpture. Includes works by Matisse, Van Gogh, Rembrandt, and Picasso. There is also a superb collection of Southeast Asian and Indian sculpture. **Open:** Thurs–Sun noon–6pm. $$

Pacific Asia Museum
46 N Los Robles Ave; tel 818/449-2742. The museum preserves, presents, and promotes the art and culture of Asia and the Pacific. Chinese Imperial Palace–style building, built by collector and art deal Grace Nicholson in 1925, is listed on the National Register of Historic Places. Traditional Chinese courtyard garden is one of only three in the nation.

Rotating exhibits from the museum's premanent collection are augmented by traveling exhibits. Special programs, lectures. Bookstore and gift shop. **Open:** Wed–Sun 10am–5pm. $$

Gamble House
4 Westmoreland Place; tel 818/793-3334. The David B Gamble house, built in 1908 for David and Mary Gamble, of the Procter & Gamble Company, is the most complete and best-preserved example of the work of architects Charles Sumner Greene and Henry Mather Greene, who made a profound impact on the development of contemporary American architecture. Breaking sharply with the traditions of their time, Greene and Greene used nature as their guide rather than the dictates of popular historical styles. Extensive use of wood was inspired by the traditions of the Swiss and Japanese. Other features include wide terraces, open sleeping porches, and broad, overhanging eaves. In the true spirit of the Arts and Crafts Movement, the furniture, cabinetry, paneling, rugs, lighting, and landscaping were all custom-designed by the architects. In addition, every peg, oak wedge, downspout, air vent, and switchplate is a contributing part of the single design statement and harmonious living environment.

The University of Southern California School of Architecture administers the house and offers one-hour comprehensive guided tours (Thurs–Sun, noon–3pm). Bookstore, gift shop. **Open:** Thurs–Sun noon–3pm. $$

Tournament House and Wrigley Gardens
391 S Orange Grove Blvd; tel 818/449-4100. Chicago chewing gum magnate William Wrigley, Jr, purchased this house on Pasadena's historic "Millionaire's Row" in 1914. The next year, the Wrigleys acquired adjoining property and created what is now the breathtaking 4½-acre Wrigley Gardens.

Following Mrs Wrigley's death in 1958, her heirs presented the property to the city of Pasadena to serve as the permanent base of operations for the Tournament of Roses. Today the house serves as a working setting throughout the year for Tournament of Roses activities. The formal dining room is the only room furnished with original pieces; the Rose Bowl Room showcases a collection of memorabilia dating back to the first New Year's Day game held in 1902; the Queen and Court Room features a display case with former Rose Queen and courts' crowns, tiaras, and jewelery dating back to the early 1900s; the Grand Marshals Room displays pictures of past Grand Marshals, including Walt Disney, Hank Aaron, and Bob Hope.

The gardens, featuring more than 1,500 varieties of roses, are continually augmented by growers throughout the nation. **Open:** Tours given Feb–late Aug, Thurs 2–4pm. **Free**

Kidspace Museum
390 S El Molino Ave; tel 818/449-9144. A participatory museum aimed at kids aged 2–8, this facility allows children to learn through play, discovery, interaction, and creativity. Exhibits include KCBS Television Studio, Critter Caverns, Stargazer Planetarium, and Toddler Territory. Every December, the museum takes to the streets with the Rosebud Parade, a takeoff of the Pasadena Rose Parade. The event draws more than 400 children with decorated bicycles and wagons. **Open:** Peak (Mem Day–Labor Day) Tues–Fri 1–5pm, Sat 10am–5pm, Sun 12:30–5pm. Reduced hours off-season. $$

Fenyes Mansion
470 W Walnut St; tel 818/577-1660. Built in 1905, the Fenyes Mansion is representative of the cultured life on Pasadena's famed Orange Grove Ave, known as "Millionaire's Row" at the turn of the century. Today it has been restored to its original appearance, and its first floor houses the Pasadena Historical Society. Permanent and changing exhibits; research library and archives; museum store. Guided tours of the mansion are given. **Open:** Thurs–Sun 1–4pm. $$

Huntington Library, Art Collections, and Botanical Gardens
1151 Oxford Rd, San Marino; tel 818/405-2141. The 207-acre estate of pioneer industrialist Henry E Huntington has become an educational and cultural center for scholars, art devotees, and the general public. The house is now an art gallery that contains paintings, tapestries, furniture, and other decorative arts, mainly of English and French origin and dating from the 18th century. The most celebrated painting here is Thomas Gainsborough's *Blue Boy*.

The adjacent **Virginia Steele Scott Gallery for American Art** houses a variety of paintings from 1720–1930, which are hung in chronological order. The **Library Exhibition Hall** displays numerous American and English first editions, manuscripts, and letters, including Benjamin Franklin's handwritten manuscript for his *Autobiography*. The **Botanical Gardens** are studded with rare shrubs, trees, and 17th-century statuary from Padua; also a Japanese Garden, Desert Garden, Camellia Garden, and Zen Garden. **Open:** Tues–Fri noon–4:30pm, Sat–Sun 10:30am–4:30pm. **$$$**

El Molino Viejo

1120 Old Mill Rd, San Marino; tel 818/449-5450. El Molino Viejo ("the Old Mill") was the first water-powered grist mill in southern California, built around 1816 by Native American labor under the supervision of the Franciscan Padres at Mission San Gabriel. After its secularization in 1833, the building was used primarily as a residence. Restored in 1928, the mill is now the southern headquarters of the California Historical Society. Changing art and photographic exhibits on second floor. **Open:** Tues–Sun 1–4pm. **Free**

Mission San Gabriel Archangel

537 W Mission Dr, San Gabriel; tel 818/282-5191. The mission compound encompasses an aqueduct, a cemetery, a winery, a tannery, a mission church, and a famous set of bells. The most notable contents of the museum are Native American paintings depicting the Stations of the Cross, painted on sailcloth with paints made from crushing the petals of desert flowers. **Open:** Peak (June–Sept) daily 10am–5:30. Reduced hours off-season. **$**

Paso Robles

This small agricultural town in the center of the state has a number of annual celebrations disproportionate with its size: the May wine festival, the August Mid-State Fair, and the September Balloon Festival. **Information:** Paso Robles Chamber of Commerce, 1225 Park St, Paso Robles 93446 (tel 805/238-0506).

MOTELS 🏨

🔳🔳🔳 Best Western Black Oak Motor Lodge

1135 24th St, 93446; tel 805/238-4740 or toll free 800/528-1234; fax 805/238-0726. W of 24th St exit off US 101. One of the nicest properties in the area, its typical motel exterior belies the large, surprisingly well-appointed and comfortable rooms. Staff is exceptionally well-informed about dining options. **Rooms:** 110 rms and stes. CI 2pm/CO noon. Nonsmoking rms avail. Furnishings are a hodgepodge of faux French provincial, contemporary American, and even some Las Vegas glitz. Deluxe king and queen rooms feature appliquéd wallpaper, a lounge chair, loveseat, and superb counter space. The Honeymoon Suite offers a huge whirlpool spa, mirrors galore, gilt chandeliers, and stereo speakers, while the Anniversary Suite boasts a king-size waterbed. **Amenities:** 🖥 🕭 🖹 A/C, cable TV, refrig. 1 unit w/whirlpool. **Services:** 🛎 Candy, fruit, and current magazines available in lobby. Complimentary coffee and doughnuts weekdays. Free local calls and 24-hour fax service. **Facilities:** 🛁 🕭 Basketball, sauna, whirlpool, playground. Coffee shop adjacent. Picnic tables, barbecue. **Rates:** Peak (Apr 28–Oct 11) $56–$71 S or D; $105–$110 ste. Extra person $6. Children under age 5 stay free. Lower rates off-season. Parking: Outdoor, free. AE, MC, V.

🔳🔳 Paso Robles Travelodge

2701 Spring St, 93446; tel 805/238-0078 or toll free 800/578-7878. Spring St exit off US 101. A clean, cheerful, nicely landscaped property with brick exterior and bright blue doors. Large lawn with California oak trees. **Rooms:** 31 rms. CI 2pm/CO noon. Nonsmoking rms avail. **Amenities:** 🖥 🕭 🖹 A/C, cable TV w/movies, refrig. Some units w/terraces. **Services:** 📠 🛎 🐾 **Facilities:** 🛁 Swing set; two picnic tables with umbrellas. **Rates:** Peak (May–Oct) $38–$58 S; $48–$75 D. Extra person $5. Children under age 17 stay free. Lower rates off-season. Parking: Outdoor, free. AE, DC, DISC, MC, V.

RESTAURANT 🍴

Vine Street Grill

512 13th St; tel 805/238-7515. At Vine St. **Continental.** Located in a former Catholic church and surrounded by meandering grapevines. Dine in the bell tower or in the shadow of the beautiful stained-glass windows. The new owner and chef offer chicken, lobster, pasta, and cioppino on weekends. Mainly local wines. **FYI:** Reservations recommended. Big band/piano/singer. Children's menu. Dress code. **Open:** Lunch Mon–Fri 11:30am–2:30pm; dinner Sun–Thurs 4:30–9pm, Fri–Sat 4:30–10pm; brunch Sun 10am–2pm. **Prices:** Main courses $11–$23. AE, MC, V. 🍱 🏛 🔲 🕭

ATTRACTION 🏛

Helen Moe's Antique Doll Museum

US 101 and Wellsona Rd; tel 805/238-2740. Nearly 700 dolls comprise this collection, including antique, historical, and foreign pieces. A 400-year-old doll is on display, as are dioramas of an old-time schoolroom, a Christmas scene from 1907, a wedding of German dolls, and more. The gift shop sells toy and collectible dolls, doll supplies, and other items. **Open:** Oct–mid-Sept, Mon–Sat 10am–5pm, Sun 1–5pm. **$**

Pebble Beach

See also Carmel-by-the-Sea, Carmel Valley, Monterey, Pacific Grove

The hallowed ground of the golfing set, Pebble Beach began as a planned reserve for nature and golf. Since there are no less than seven world-class courses, much of the resort community is comprised of private clubs and ultra-deluxe accommodations.

RESORTS 🏨

⬛⬛⬛⬛ Inn at Spanish Bay

17-Mile Dr, 93953; tel 408/647-7500 or toll free 800/654-9300; fax 415/624-6357. Off CA 1. Surrounded by windswept sand dunes and facing an oft-tempestuous Pacific. Draws 75% group business. **Rooms:** 270 rms, stes, and effic. Executive level. CI 4pm/CO noon. Nonsmoking rms avail. Rooms spacious enough to fit two comfortable armchairs by the gas fireplace. Counter space abounds in the bathrooms, done in beige marble with glass-enclosed showers. **Amenities:** 🛎 ♨ 📞 Cable TV w/movies, refrig, dataport, VCR, bathrobes. No A/C. All units w/minibars, all w/terraces, all w/fireplaces, all w/whirlpools. Every room comes with a garment steamer. **Services:** ✕ ☞ VP 📪 ♲ Twice-daily maid svce, car-rental desk, social director, masseur, children's program, babysitting. Concierge personally escorts arriving guests to their rooms. A bigpipe player serenades late afternoons. **Facilities:** 🏠 ▶18 🎾 ♣6 🏋 900 🛁 3 restaurants, 3 bars (1 w/entertainment), 1 beach (ocean), spa, sauna, steam rm, whirlpool. Dunes and fairways intersperse the golf course. The fitness center rates a "10," with aerobics classes plus state-of-the art equipment. A two-mile boardwalk circles the property. **Rates:** Peak (Apr–Nov) $255–$385 S or D; $530–$580 ste; $1,795 effic. Children under age 18 stay free. Min stay special events. Lower rates off-season. Parking: Outdoor, free. Golf and tennis packages available. AE, DC, JCB, MC, V.

⚜ Lodge at Pebble Beach

17-Mile Dr, 93953; tel 408/624-3811 or toll free 800/654-9300; fax 408/625-8598. Pacific Grove/Pebble Beach exit off CA 1. Among America's best resorts, in a choice setting on the brink of the Pacific Ocean within the private 5,000-plus-acre Del Monte Forest. **Rooms:** 161 rms and stes. CI 4pm/CO noon. No smoking. Nearly all rooms have been individually redecorated and look stunning, with Empire-style furnishings plus unlikely flourishes. Baths are exquisite in taupe marble. **Amenities:** 🛎 ♨ 📞 Cable TV w/movies, dataport, VCR, bathrobes. No A/C. All units w/minibars, all w/terraces, some w/fireplaces, some w/whirlpools. Most rooms offer wood-burning fireplaces. **Services:** 🍴 ☞ VP 🚐 📪 ♲ 🛎 Twice-daily maid svce, car-rental desk, masseur, children's program, babysitting. Very helpful staff. Extensive junior summer program includes tennis clinics, swimming and sailing lessons, plus a day camp. **Facilities:** 🏠 ☂️ ⚠ 🏌99 🏐 🎾 ♣12 🏋 200 🛁 5 restaurants (see "Restaurants" below), 5 bars (2 w/entertainment), 1 beach (ocean), lawn games, spa, sauna, steam rm, whirlpool, beauty salon, playground. Fabled golf links have been home to several US Open championships. Brand-new Beach & Tennis Club features 12 courts (2 clay), plus a 25-meter lap pool. Equestrian center is among the West's best. **Rates:** $315–$425 S or D; $525–$1450 ste.

Extra person $55. Children under age 18 stay free. Min stay special events. Parking: Outdoor, free. Tennis and golf packages available. AE, CB, DC, DISC, JCB, MC, V.

RESTAURANT 🍽

♣ Club XIX

In Lodge at Pebble Beach, 17-Mile Dr; tel 408/625-8519. Pacific Grove/Pebble Beach exit off CA 1. **Continental/French.** Outdoor dining is offered most of the year on a terrace protected from the breezes by glass screens, and from the chill by overhead heaters. Spectacular views overlook famed 18th fairway and the Pacific. Attractive indoor wood-and-chrome dining room and bar. Lunch menu of salads, sandwiches, and sole-and-scallops fish and chips wrapped in paper. The new dinner menu features continental cuisine with a light touch, with appetizers such as petits escargots and pearl vegetables, and main courses of seared salmon and prawns with a three-caviar sauce, or duck breast with cranberry molasses. Outstanding wine list offers some exceptional values. **FYI:** Reservations recommended. Jacket required. **Open:** Lunch daily 11:30am–3:30pm; dinner daily 6:30–10pm. **Prices:** Main courses $20–$30; prix fixe $35. AE, CB, DC, DISC, MC, V. ♥ 🍴 🏞 VP ♿

ATTRACTION 📷

The 17-Mile Drive

The drive can be entered from any of three gates: Pacific Grove to the north, Carmel-by-the-Sea to the south, or Monterey to the east. Admission includes an informative map that points out 26 points of interest along the way. Highlights include Seal and Bird Rocks, where you can see countless gulls, cormorants, and other off-shore birds as well as seals and sea lions; and Cypress Point Lookout, which, on a clear day, affords a 20-mile view all the way to the Big Sur lighthouse. Also visible is the famous Lone Cypress tree, inspiration to so many artists and photographers (unfortunately, there is no longer walking access to the tree; it can only be viewed from afar). The drive also traverses Del Monte Forest, where you'll often see blacktail deer. $$

Petaluma

Petaluma's 1930s-era downtown retains its original feel, and agriculture is still the mainstay of the community's economy. Numerous blockbuster movies were filmed here, including *American Graffiti*, *Peggy Sue Got Married*, and *Basic Instinct*. **Information:** Petaluma Area Chamber of Commerce, 799 Baywood Dr #3, Petaluma 94954 (tel 707/762-2785).

MOTELS 🏨

⬛⬛ Best Western Petaluma Inn

200 McDowell Blvd, 94954; tel 707/763-0994 or toll free 800/297-3846; fax 707/778-3111. E Washington St exit off

US 101; go east; right on McDowell. Located just off the freeway, but well-soundproofed to minimize noise. **Rooms:** 75 rms and stes. Executive level. CI 2pm/CO 11am. Nonsmoking rms avail. Large, basic rooms with new carpets. **Amenities:** 🛁 🕐 A/C, satel TV. Some units w/terraces. **Services:** 🛎 **Facilities:** 🏋 🔟 👤 Washer/dryer. **Rates:** Peak (Apr–Oct) $76–$86 S or D; $95 ste. Extra person $6. Children under age 12 stay free. Lower rates off-season. Parking: Outdoor, free. AE, DC, DISC, MC, V.

≡≡ Quality Inn Petaluma

5100 Montero Way, 94954; tel 707/664-1155 or toll free 800/221-2222. Redwood Hwy/Penngrove exit east off US 101. Clean property right off the freeway. **Rooms:** 110 rms and stes. CI 2:30pm/CO noon. Nonsmoking rms avail. Basic, comfortable rooms. **Amenities:** 🛁 🕐 A/C, satel TV w/movies, refrig. **Services:** 🖐 🛎 ✋ **Facilities:** 🏋 25 👤 Sauna, whirlpool, washer/dryer. **Rates (CP):** Peak (Apr–Oct) $64–$129 S; $69–$139 D; $105–$165 ste. Extra person $5. Children under age 18 stay free. Min stay wknds and special events. Lower rates off-season. Parking: Outdoor, free. AE, CB, DC, DISC, JCB, MC, V.

RESTAURANT 🍽

Fino Cucina Italiana

208 Petaluma Blvd N; tel 707/762-5966. Petaluma Blvd exit off US 101. **Italian.** Authentic Italian cuisines in a soothing environment, with modern decor and soft music. Menu highlights include angel hair pasta with clams, roast tenderloin of pork in grape sauce, and polenta with Gorgonzola and mushrooms. **FYI:** Reservations accepted. Beer and wine only. **Open:** Lunch Mon–Fri 11:30am–2pm; dinner Mon–Sat 5–9:30pm. **Prices:** Main courses $11–$20. AE, MC, V. 👤

ATTRACTION 🏛

Petaluma Historical Library/Museum

20 4th St; tel 707/778-4398. Constructed in 1903, with the help of $12,500 donated by Andrew Carnegie, the library features a beautiful stained-glass dome, one of the only freestanding domes in California. After its closure in 1976, the building reopened in 1978 as a research library and museum. Permanent and changing exhibits on the gallery and mezzanine floors depict Petaluma history from the early 1800s. **Open:** Mon and Thurs–Sat 10am–4pm, Sun 1–4pm. Tues–Wed by appointment. **Free**

Pinnacles National Monument

For lodgings, see King City, Salinas

Because of its distinctive geological features, Pinnacles was set aside as a national monument in 1908. What remains today are the eroded remnants of an ancient volcano, which formed at a point on the San Andreas Rift Zone. One portion of the volcano has remained at its point of origin; the other, moving at a rate of about two centimeters per year, has traveled 195 miles northwestward. The Pinnacles comprise the latter section. Hiking is the most popular activity; there are 11 marked trails of varying difficulty. Rock climbing and picnicking opportunities are also abundant. Camping is permitted only at the campsite at the west side of the monument. For more information contact Pinnacles National Monument, Paicines, CA 95043 (tel 408/389-4485).

Pioneer Town

See Yucca Valley

Pismo Beach

See also Shell Beach

Pismo Beach offers a spectacular 23-mile stretch of sandy beach where visitors can explore isolated dunes, cliff-sheltered tidepools, caves, and old pirate coves by foot, horse, or all-terrain vehicle (the area has the unique distinction of being the only spot in California where cars are allowed on the beach). The former clam capital of the world—overfishing decimated the population of bivalves—Pismo Beach is still a seafood lover's paradise. Fishing is permitted from the pier. **Information:** Pismo Beach Visitor Center, 581 Dolliver St, Pismo Beach 93449 (tel 805/773-4382 or toll free 800/443-7778).

HOTELS 🏨

≡≡ Best Western Shore Cliff Lodge

2555 Price St, 93449; tel 805/773-4671 or toll free 800/441-8885; fax 805/773-2341. 1½ mi N of Pismo Beach. Price St exit off US 101 S; Shell Beach Rd exit off US 101 N. Sprawling older-style motel set on a cliff with a stairway to the beach. Ocean-view lobby is furnished with wicker, plants, and ceiling fans. **Rooms:** 99 rms, stes, and effic. CI 3pm/CO 11am. Nonsmoking rms avail. Fabulous ocean views from private balconies. Rooms are large and comfortable, but decor is marred somewhat by generic art on walls. **Amenities:** 🛁 🕐 📺 A/C, cable TV w/movies. All units w/terraces. **Services:** ✕ 🔑 🖐 🛎 Masseur, babysitting. Fax and typing services on request. **Facilities:** 🏋 🚲 🌊 220 1 restaurant (see "Restaurants" below), 1 bar (w/entertainment), 1 beach (ocean), games rm, sauna, whirlpool. Features one of the largest pool in area, plus three gazebos. **Rates:** Peak (June–Oct) $105 S or D; $225 ste; $225 effic. Extra person $10. Children under age 17 stay free. Min stay peak, wknds, and special events. Lower rates off-season. Parking: Outdoor, free. AE, CB, DC, DISC, JCB, MC, V.

≝≝≝ **Oxford Suites Resort**
651 Five Cities Dr, 93449; tel 805/773-3773 or toll free 800/982-SUITE; fax 805/773-5177. 4th St exit off US 101. Spanish/tropical-style hotel with a gorgeous lobby, paddle fans, a fountain, tilework, and an attractive library and lounge. **Rooms:** 133 stes. CI 4pm/CO noon. Nonsmoking rms avail. Nicely appointed suites with lots of drawer and counter space. Two TVs per room. **Amenities:** 🛁 🐾 A/C, cable TV w/movies, refrig, VCR, CD/tape player. Some units w/terraces. **Services:** 🖼 🍽 🕭 Babysitting. Videos for rent plus popcorn and sodas available in the gift shop. Complimentary newspapers, coffee, and fruit in lobby. Complimentary wine and beer 5:50–9:30pm. **Facilities:** 🔀 ⌷60⌷ 🔥 1 bar, whirlpool, washer/dryer. Very attractive breakfast room with European posters, and rattan furniture. Putting green. **Rates (BB):** Peak (May–Sept) $79–$99 ste. Extra person $6. Children under age 10 stay free. Lower rates off-season. Parking: Outdoor, free. AE, CB, DC, DISC, MC, V.

MOTELS

≝≝ **Edgewater Inn & Suites**
280 Wadsworth Ave, 93449; tel 805/773-4811; fax 805/773-5121. Wadsworth exit off CA 1 N; Pismo Beach exit off CA 1 S. Good for families; nice location close to beach. **Rooms:** 93 rms, stes, and effic. CI 3pm/CO 11am. Nonsmoking rms avail. Furnishings a little dated. **Amenities:** 🛁 🐾 A/C, cable TV, refrig. Some units w/terraces, some w/whirlpools. **Services:** 🖼 🍽 **Facilities:** 🔀 ⌷150⌷ 🔥 1 beach (ocean), whirlpool. **Rates (CP):** Peak (June–Sept) $60–$85 S; $70–$85 D; $85–$135 ste; $85–$135 effic. Children under age 18 stay free. Min stay special events. Lower rates off-season. Parking: Outdoor, free. AE, DC, DISC, MC, V.

≝≝≝ **Sea Crest Resort Motel**
2241 Price St, 93449; tel 805/773-4608 or toll free 800/782-8400; fax 805/773-4525. 1 mi N of Pismo. Price St exit off US 101. Set on cliffs above the beach, with stairs down to the sand. Rooms are nicer than the lobby. **Rooms:** 158 rms and stes. CI 4pm/CO noon. Nonsmoking rms avail. Handsomely appointed rooms. Dark-wood and French provincial furnishings. Some ocean views. **Amenities:** 🛁 🐾 📺 Satel TV w/movies, refrig. No A/C. All units w/terraces, some w/whirlpools. **Services:** 🚐 🍽 Babysitting. **Facilities:** 🔀 ⌷50⌷ 🔥 1 beach (ocean), whirlpool, washer/dryer. Shuffleboard, picnic tables, barbecue grills. **Rates:** Peak (June–Aug) $75–$95 S or D; $115–$135 ste. Extra person $10. Children under age 12 stay free. Min stay wknds. Lower rates off-season. Parking: Outdoor, free. AE, CB, DC, DISC, JCB, MC, V.

RESTAURANT 🍴

Shore Cliff Restaurant
In Best Western Shore Cliff Lodge, 2555 Price St; tel 805/773-4671. **Seafood/Steak.** Casual California-style cafe with plants, rattan furnishings, and picture windows overlooking the Pacific. Menu features cioppino, crab and steak, prime rib, Shore Cliff stuffed prawns. Nice for breakfast, with pancakes, eggs Benedict, and other dishes. **FYI:** Reservations recommended. Big band/blues/country music/jazz. Children's menu. **Open:** Breakfast Mon–Sat 7–11:30am, Sun 7–10am; lunch Mon–Sat 11:30am–4pm, Sun 2–4pm; dinner Sun–Thurs 4–9pm, Fri–Sat 4–10pm; brunch Sun 10am–2pm. **Prices:** Main courses $14–$18. AE, DC, DISC, MC, V. 🏔 👬 💟

Placerville

The seat of El Dorado County and the nostalgic center of California's Gold Country, Placerville was once named Hangtown for its enthusiastic justice system. A few mines are still functioning, but lumber, fruit orchards, and outdoor recreation provide the main business these days. **Information:** El Dorado County Chamber of Commerce, 542 Main St, Placerville 95667 (tel 916/621-5885 or toll free 800/457-6279).

MOTELS 🏨

≝≝ **Best Western Placerville Inn**
6850 Green Leaf Dr, 95667; tel 916/622-9100 or toll free 800/854-9100; fax 916/622-9376. Missouri Flat exit off US 50. Good highway stopover in a safe, comfortable, and spacious country setting. **Rooms:** 105 rms and stes. CI 3pm/CO 11am. Nonsmoking rms avail. Poolside rooms have sliding glass doors, and are quieter. **Amenities:** 🛁 🐾 📺 A/C, satel TV w/movies. Some units w/terraces, some w/fireplaces. **Services:** 🍽 🕭 Some business services available at desk. Pet fee $10 per day. **Facilities:** 🔀 ⌷200⌷ 🔥 Whirlpool. No elevators. Pool heated in season. **Rates:** Peak (Apr–Oct) $58–$64 S or D; $135 ste. Extra person $6. Children under age 12 stay free. Lower rates off-season. Parking: Outdoor, free. AE, CB, DC, DISC, MC, V.

≝≝ **Cameron Park Inn**
3361 Coach Lane, Cameron Park, 95682; tel 916/677-2203 or toll free 800/601-1234; fax 916/676-1422. Cameron Park Dr exit off US 50. Recent refurbishment of lobby and 10 rooms. **Rooms:** 62 rms, stes, and effic. CI 3pm/CO noon. Nonsmoking rms avail. **Amenities:** 🛁 🐾 📺 A/C, satel TV w/movies. Some units w/terraces. **Services:** 🍽 🕭 **Facilities:** 🔀 ⌷40⌷ 🔥 Washer/dryer. Passes to nearby sports club on request. **Rates (CP):** $56–$60 S; $61–$66 D; $85 ste; $61–$71 effic. Extra person $5. Children under age 12 stay free. Parking: Outdoor, free. AE, CB, DC, DISC, ER, JCB, MC, V.

RESTAURANT 🍴

Cafe Luna
In Creekside Place, 451 Main St #8; tel 916/642-8669. Placerville exit (Main St) off US 50. **Cafe/Eclectic.** Neutral walls, white napkins, and splashes of blue and gold form a

muted background for the imaginatively prepared, stunningly presented cuisine. Entrees include ginger-soy flank steak, and fiery-hot Thai chicken with green curry, coconut, mint, basil, and cilantro. Impressive wine list. Outdoor patio dining. **FYI:** Reservations recommended. Beer and wine only. **Open:** Peak (May–Sept) lunch Mon–Sat 11am–3pm; dinner Thurs–Sat 5–9pm; brunch Sun 10am–3pm. **Prices:** Main courses $10–$13. AE, CB, MC, V. &

ATTRACTIONS 🖼

The Marshall Gold Discovery State Historic Park
Tel 916/622-3470. Located 8 mi N of Placerville on CA 49. This park preserves the spot where James Wilson Marshall discovered gold along the banks of the south fork of the American River. Although Marshall and his partner, John Sutter, tried to keep the discovery a secret, word soon leaked out, and San Francisco was soon half emptied as men rushed off to seek their fortunes at the mines. A self-guided trail leads to the site of this momentous event. **Open:** Daily sunrise–sundown. **$$**

El Dorado County Historical Museum
100 Placerville Dr; tel 916/621-5865. Exhibits in this museum focus mainly on the early days of the Gold Rush, when Placerville rivaled San Francisco in stature. Exhibits include an actual Concord Stagecoach, a re-created general store, an old Diamond & Caldor Shay steam engine, and water-driven Pelton wheels that powered early mines and mills. Guided tours available; bookshop. **Open:** Peak (Nov–Feb) Wed–Sun 10am–4pm. Reduced hours off-season. **Free**

Gold Bug Mine
Bedford Ave; tel 916/642-5232. Located in Hangtown's Gold Bug Park, the Gold Bug Mine was opened in 1888, near the site where the first placer was mined by Chileans in 1848, and continued to operate until World War II. On the eastern side of the famous Mother Lode vein, the municipally owned mine is open for self-guided tours (audio tape tours available), and allows visitors a peek at an exposed vein.

Also in the park is a restored gold stamp mill, with original machinery and exhibits of other mining equipment from the Gold Rush era. The park itself is undergoing development as a picnicking and hiking area. **Open:** Peak (May–mid-Sept) daily 10am–4pm. Reduced hours off-season. **$**

Pleasant Hill

See also Concord, Lafayette, Walnut Creek

HOTEL 🖼

≡≡≡ Residence Inn by Marriott
700 Ellinwood Way, 94523 (Ellinwood); tel 510/689-1010 or toll free 800/331-3131; fax 510/689-1098. Willow Pass Rd exit off I-680. Located in a residential area, this attractive complex resembles a town-house development; walkways are lined with trees and flowering plants. **Rooms:** 126 effic. CI 3pm/CO noon. Nonsmoking rms avail. Every unit is an apartment. All have kitchens with countertop dining, utensils, and dishes. Most living room sofas have a hide-a-bed. **Amenities:** 🛏 🔥 🖭 A/C, cable TV w/movies, refrig, dataport, voice mail. Some units w/fireplaces. **Services:** 🖾 🗂 🐕 Complimentary wine, beer, and snacks in lobby 5–7pm weekdays; complimentary coffee 24 hours. VCR and movie rentals. **Facilities:** 🔥 🏌 ⊡ & Whirlpool. Barbecue grills. Outdoor "sport court" can be used for tennis, volleyball, basketball, and paddle tennis. **Rates (CP):** $65–$145 effic. Children under age 6 stay free. Min stay special events. Parking: Outdoor, free. AE, CB, DC, DISC, JCB, MC, V.

Pleasanton

A Bay Area bedroom community, Pleasanton has preserved its early-19th-century past at the Amador–Livermore Valley Historical Society Museum. Also in town is the Alameda County Fairgrounds, site of the late June county fair. **Information:** Pleasanton Convention & Visitors Bureau, 10 W Neal St, Pleasanton 94566 (tel 510/846-8910).

HOTELS 🖼

≡≡ Courtyard by Marriott
5059 Hopyard Rd, 94588 (Hacienda Business Park); tel 510/463-1414 or toll free 800/228-9290; fax 510/463-0113. Hopyard exit off I-580. Oriented toward the business traveler. **Rooms:** 145 rms and stes. CI 3pm/CO 1pm. Nonsmoking rms avail. **Amenities:** 🛏 🔥 A/C, cable TV w/movies, voice mail. Some units w/terraces. **Services:** 🖾 🗂 Babysitting. **Facilities:** 🔥 🏌 ⊡ & 1 restaurant (bkfst only), 1 bar, whirlpool, washer/dryer. Restaurants nearby. **Rates:** $105 S; $115 D; $120 ste. Extra person $10. Children under age 18 stay free. Parking: Outdoor, free. AE, DC, DISC, MC, V.

≡≡≡ Four Points Hotel by ITT Sheraton
5115 Hopyard Rd, 94588 (Hacienda Business Park); tel 510/460-8800 or toll free 800/325-3535; fax 510/847-9455. Hopyard exit off I-580. Attractive, well-kept property located in the Hacienda Business Park. **Rooms:** 214 rms and stes. Executive level. CI 3pm/CO 1pm. Nonsmoking rms avail. **Amenities:** 🛏 🔥 🖭 🍴 A/C, cable TV w/movies, voice mail. Some units w/terraces. **Services:** ✕ 🖾 🗂 Car-rental desk, babysitting. **Facilities:** 🔥 🏌 ⊡ ⊟ & 1 restaurant, 1 bar (w/entertainment), whirlpool. Outdoor swimming pool in parklike setting with pond and fountains. Jogging path nearby. **Rates:** $115–$135 S; $125–$145 D; $250 ste. Extra person $10. Children under age 18 stay free. Parking: Outdoor, free. AE, DC, DISC, MC, V.

≡≡ Holiday Inn Pleasanton Hotel
11950 Dublin Canyon Rd, 94588-2818; tel 510/847-6000 or toll free 800/HOLIDAY; fax 510/463-2585. Foothill exit off I-580; right 1 block to Dublin Canyon Rd. Art deco decor

makes this hotel more attractive than the usual Holiday Inn. Wooded hillside across the street. Opposite shopping mall. **Rooms:** 248 rms and stes. CI 3pm/CO noon. Nonsmoking rms avail. **Amenities:** 🛁 ⌾ 🖭 A/C, cable TV w/movies. 1 unit w/minibar. **Services:** ✕ ⬛ ⤺ ⬦ **Facilities:** 🛗 ⬛ ⬛300⬛ ⅃ 1 restaurant, 1 bar, whirlpool, washer/dryer. **Rates:** $110–$120 S; $120–$130 D; $169–$189 ste. Extra person $10. Children under age 18 stay free. Min stay peak, wknds, and special events. Parking: Outdoor, free. AE, CB, DC, DISC, JCB, MC, V.

🏳🏳 Pleasanton Hilton at the Club

7050 Johnson Dr, 94588; tel 510/463-8000 or toll free 800/HILTONS; fax 510/463-3801. Hopyard exit off I-580, right on Owens Dr, right on Johnson; or Stoneridge Dr exit off I-680 E to Johnson Dr, left to hotel. Hotel is close to freeway but adequately soundproofed inside. Adjoins "Club Sport," which offers many amenities, including a driving range and putting green. **Rooms:** 294 rms and stes. Executive level. CI 3pm/CO noon. Nonsmoking rms avail. **Amenities:** 🛁 ⌾ A/C, cable TV w/movies. Some units w/terraces, some w/fireplaces, 1 w/whirlpool. **Services:** ✕ VP ⬛ ⤺ ⬦ Car-rental desk, masseur. **Facilities:** 🛗 ⬤11 ⬛ ⬛500⬛ ⅃ 1 restaurant, 1 bar (w/entertainment), racquetball, squash, spa, sauna, steam rm, whirlpool, beauty salon, day-care ctr. Day-care center available for fee, but parents must remain on hotel grounds. Heated lap pool. **Rates:** $144–$164 S; $154–$174 D; $350–$500 ste. Extra person $10. Children under age 18 stay free. Parking: Outdoor, free. AE, DC, DISC, MC, V.

🏳🏳 Wyndham Garden Hotel Pleasanton

5990 Stoneridge Mall Rd, 94588; tel 510/463-3330 or toll free 800/222-TREE; fax 510/463-3330 ext 644. Foothill exit off I-580; left on Dublin Canyon Rd; left on Stoneridge Mall Rd. Pleasant hotel with airy, cheerful lobby and ambience of a private home. Geared to business and weekend family travelers. Minimal landscaping. Located across the street from a mall. **Rooms:** 173 rms and stes. CI 3pm/CO 1pm. Nonsmoking rms avail. **Amenities:** 🛁 ⌾ A/C, cable TV w/movies. **Services:** ✕ ⬛ ⤺ **Facilities:** 🛗 ⬛ ⬛60⬛ ⅃ 1 restaurant, 1 bar, sauna, whirlpool. **Rates (CP):** $110–$115 S; $120–$125 D; $150–$195 ste. Children under age 18 stay free. Parking: Outdoor, free. Special weekend rates are available. AE, CB, DC, DISC, EC, ER, JCB, MC, V.

Point Arena

RESTAURANT 🍴

★ Pangaea

250 Main St; tel 707/882-3001. **Californian/Seafood.** A hot new restaurant on the Sonoma coast, presenting a warm Mediterranean terra-cotta decor with local art. Menu changes weekly, and all ingredients are organic. Try grilled rib-eye steak with coarse-grain mustard, pan-roasted salmon on a bed of braised leeks, grilled squash galette in pastry shell with roasted pepper sauce. Offers Mendocino County wines and microbrewery beers. **FYI:** Reservations recommended. Beer and wine only. **Open:** Wed–Sun 5:30–9pm. **Prices:** Main courses $9–$17. No CC. ⅃

Point Reyes Station

See also Olema

RESTAURANTS 🍴

★ Station House Cafe

Main St; tel 415/663-1515. **American/Californian.** A friendly, homey, neighborhood cafe with food good enough to get written up in *Gourmet* and *Bon Appétit*. The setting is high-tech country, with wainscoting to counterpoint exposed heating ducts; a lovely terrace is framed by climbing roses. Everything is tasty, from breakfast pancakes to dinner specials such as monkfish with green peppercorn sauce. **FYI:** Reservations recommended. Blues/guitar. Children's menu. **Open:** Sun–Thurs 8am–9pm, Fri–Sat 8am–10pm. **Prices:** Main courses $6–$18. DISC, MC, V. ⅃

★ Tony's

18863 CA 1, Marshall; tel 415/663-1107. **Seafood.** A West Marin tradition since 1948. Decor is negligible, but outrageous views of Tomales Bay make up for it. Tony's is known for its voluptuous barbecued oysters, slathered with tomato sauce or with oil and garlic ($4 for 6). The menu might also feature grilled sole, deep-fried clams, or Dungeness crab. **FYI:** Reservations not accepted. Beer and wine only. **Open:** Fri–Sun noon–8:30pm. Closed late Dec. **Prices:** Main courses $6–$13. No CC. ⛰ ⅃

Pomona

Part of the Inland Empire east of Los Angeles, Pomona is home to California State Polytechnic University and is a growing residential, industrial, and commercial suburb. **Information:** Pomona Chamber of Commerce, 485 N Garey, PO Box 1457, Pomona 91769 (tel 909/622-1256).

HOTELS 🏨

🏳🏳🏳 Radisson Inn Diamond Bar

21725 E Gateway Dr, Diamond Bar, 91765; tel 909/860-5440 or toll free 800/333-3333; fax 909/860-8224. Grand Ave S exit off I-60; 1 block S to Golden Springs; right ½ mi. A full-service hotel especially suited for corporate meetings. **Rooms:** 175 rms and stes. Executive level. CI 2pm/CO noon. Nonsmoking rms avail. "Green" suites, with filtered air and hypo-allergenic soaps and shampoos, are available. **Amenities:** 🛁 🖭 A/C, cable TV w/movies. Some units w/terraces. **Services:** ✕ 🚐 ⬛ ⤺ ⬦ Car-rental desk, babysitting. **Facilities:** 🛗 ⬛200⬛ ⅃ 1 restaurant, 1 bar, whirlpool. Complimentary access to nearby health club. **Rates**

(CP): $74–$109 S; $84–$109 D; $89 ste. Extra person $10. Children under age 12 stay free. Parking: Outdoor, free. AE, CB, DC, DISC, MC, V.

≣≣≣ Sheraton Suites Fairplex

600 W McKinley Ave, 91768; tel 909/622-2220 or toll free 800/722-4055; fax 909/622-3577. White Ave N exit to McKinley off I-10; ½ mi N. Full-service, all-suite hotel with an elegant marble lobby, located adjacent to the Los Angeles County Fairgrounds. **Rooms:** 247 stes. Executive level. CI 3pm/CO noon. Nonsmoking rms avail. **Amenities:** 🛁 🗕 🖭 🍸 A/C, cable TV w/movies, refrig, voice mail. Some units w/terraces. Microwave, two TVs. **Services:** ✕ 🚗 ⊠ ⊐ 🐾 **Facilities:** 🛢 🛳 🎱 🖵 🕭 1 restaurant, 1 bar, sauna, whirlpool, washer/dryer. 24-hour mini-mart. **Rates (BB):** Peak (Sept–Oct) $105 ste. Extra person $10. Children under age 18 stay free. Lower rates off-season. Parking: Outdoor, free. AE, DC, DISC, MC, V.

≣≣≣ Shilo Inn Diamond Bar/Pomona

3200 Temple Ave, 91768; tel 909/598-0073 or toll free 800/222-2244 in the US, 800/228-4489 in Canada; fax 909/594-5862. Temple Ave W exit off I-57. Across the street from the Shilo Inns Hilltop Suites; less expensive, but run with the same cheerful professionalism. **Rooms:** 160 rms. CI 4pm/CO noon. Nonsmoking rms avail. **Amenities:** 🛁 🗕 🍸 A/C, cable TV w/movies, refrig. **Services:** ⊠ ⊐ 🐾 **Facilities:** 🛢 🛳 🎱 🕭 1 restaurant, 1 bar (w/entertainment), whirlpool, washer/dryer. Gorgeous courtyard opening to pool. **Rates (CP):** $52 S; $67 D. Children under age 18 stay free. Parking: Outdoor, free. AE, DC, DISC, MC, V.

≣≣≣ Shilo Inns Hilltop Suites

3101 Temple Ave, 91768; tel 909/598-7666 or toll free 800/222-2244 in the US, 800/228-4489 in Canada; fax 909/598-5654. Temple Ave W exit off I-57. Has most everything the business traveler might need. **Rooms:** 129 stes. Executive level. CI 4pm/CO noon. Nonsmoking rms avail. **Amenities:** 🛁 🗕 🍸 A/C, cable TV w/movies, refrig, VCR. Rooms have microwaves, wet bars, 2 telephones with 2 lines, and 3 TVs. **Services:** ✕ 🚗 ⊠ ⊐ Babysitting. **Facilities:** 🛢 🛳 🎱 🖵 🕭 1 restaurant, 1 bar (w/entertainment), sauna, whirlpool, washer/dryer. **Rates (CP):** $109–$155 ste. Extra person $12. Children under age 12 stay free. Parking: Outdoor, free. AE, DC, DISC, JCB, MC, V.

RESTAURANT ⑪

★ Rillo's Restaurant

510 E Foothill Blvd; tel 909/621-4954. **Continental/Italian.** A beautifully designed southern California restaurant, with pale cream stucco walls, booths covered in finely pleated fabric, pink tablecloths, and large open umbrellas. A full range of northern and southern Italian specialties is served. Good wine list. **FYI:** Reservations recommended. Piano. Dress code. **Open:** Lunch Mon–Fri 11:30am–2:30pm; dinner Mon–Thurs 4:30–9:30pm, Fri–Sun 4:30–10:30pm. **Prices:** Main courses $12–$20. AE, MC, V. ♥ 🖂 🕭

Port Hueneme

HOTEL 🏨

≣≣ The Country Inn at Port Hueneme

350 E Hueneme Rd, 93041; tel 805/986-5353 or toll free 800/44-RELAX; fax 805/986-4399. Ventura Rd exit off US 101. Nicest property in this navy town, near the base and the beach. Framed art and ceiling fans in hallways are appealing touches. **Rooms:** 135 rms, stes, and effic. CI 3pm/CO noon. Nonsmoking rms avail. Restful, homey rooms. **Amenities:** 🛁 🗕 🍸 A/C, cable TV, refrig, VCR. Some units w/fireplaces, some w/whirlpools. **Services:** ⊠ ⊐ **Facilities:** 🛢 🛳 🕭 Whirlpool, washer/dryer. **Rates (CP):** $115–$120 S; $120–$125 D; $160 ste; $160 effic. Extra person $10. Children under age 12 stay free. Min stay special events. Parking: Outdoor, free. AE, DC, DISC, MC, V.

Princeton-by-the-Sea

See also Half Moon Bay, Moss Beach

INN 🏨

≣≣≣ Pillar Point Inn

380 Capistrano Rd, 94018; tel 415/728-7377 or toll free 800/400-8281; fax 415/728-8345. Well located and in mint condition inside and out, with excellent furnishings. Unsuitable for children under 18. **Rooms:** 11 rms. CI 2pm/CO 11am. No smoking. Attractive early American decor with new carpeting throughout. **Amenities:** 🛁 🗕 TV w/movies, refrig, VCR. No A/C. All units w/fireplaces. Large oaken refrigerators; 4 rooms have steam baths. **Services:** Afternoon tea and wine/sherry served. **Facilities:** 🛢 🕭 Guest lounge. Large fitness center and 6 restaurants within walking distance. Shore Bird restaurant next door. **Rates (BB):** $150–$190 S or D. Extra person $20. Min stay wknds. Parking: Outdoor, free. AE, MC, V.

RESTAURANT ⑪

♥ Shorebird Restaurant

In Pillar Point Marina, 390 Capistrano Rd; tel 415/728-5541. Capistrano Rd exit off CA 1. **Californian/Seafood.** Largest and most popular restaurant in the area. Cape Cod theme with casement windows, wood-beamed ceiling, flowers. Every table has splendid view of harbor. Low noise level; unrushed, excellent service. Oyster bar. Offers seafood salads, local fresh fish, fish & chips, soup, smoked salmon with fettuccine, Maryland-style crab cakes, steamed clams. **FYI:** Reservations recommended. Children's menu. Dress code. **Open:** Peak (Apr–Oct) lunch daily 11am–3pm; dinner daily 5–11pm; brunch Sun 11:30am–1pm. **Prices:** Main courses $7–$22. AE, DISC, MC, V. ♥ 🖂 🖾 🕭

Rancho Cordova

See also Folsom

Located on the banks of the American River, Rancho Cordova is a residential community just east of Sacramento. **Information:** Rancho Cordova Area Chamber of Commerce, 3366 Mather Field Rd, Rancho Cordova 95670 (tel 916/361-8700).

HOTELS 🏨

☰☰☰ Courtyard by Marriott

10683 White Rock Rd, 95670; tel 916/638-3800 or toll free 800/321-2211; fax 916/638-6776. 12 mi E of Sacramento. Zinfandel exit off US 50; S on Zinfandel to White Rock Rd. A comfortable, reasonably priced business hotel. Attractive gazebo and lobby. **Rooms:** 144 rms and stes. CI 3pm/CO 1pm. Nonsmoking rms avail. **Amenities:** 🎇 🍴 A/C, satel TV w/movies, dataport, voice mail. Some units w/terraces. **Services:** ✕ 🚐 🛉 🛏 Free newspaper delivery. **Facilities:** 🏋 🍽 🛟 & 1 restaurant (bkfst only), whirlpool, washer/dryer. **Rates:** Peak (Feb–Nov) $79 S; $89 D; $95–$105 ste. Extra person $10. Lower rates off-season. Parking: Outdoor, free. Cheaper on weekends. Return clients receive membership in Courtyard Club. AE, CB, DC, DISC, MC, V.

☰☰ Fairfield Inn by Marriott

10713 White Rock Rd, 95670; tel 916/631-7500 or toll free 800/228-2800. Zinfandel exit off US 50. Budget-range five-year-old property in a noisy highway location; adequate for single business travelers. **Rooms:** 117 rms. CI open/CO noon. Nonsmoking rms avail. **Amenities:** 🎇 🍴 A/C, cable TV w/movies, dataport. **Services:** ✕ 🚐 🛉 🛏 Daily continental breakfast 6–9am on lobby level. Copy and fax in office may be used by guests. Limited room service available from adjacent restaurant. **Facilities:** 🏋 🍽 & **Rates (CP):** Peak (June–Oct) $47–$53 S or D. Extra person $6. Children under age 13 stay free. Lower rates off-season. Parking: Outdoor, free. AE, DC, DISC, MC, V.

☰☰☰ Hallmark Suites

11260 Point East Dr, 95742; tel 916/638-4141 or toll free 800/444-1089; fax 916/638-4287. Sunrise Blvd exit off US 50; east on Folsom; left on Point East Dr. A newer property, laid out for comfortable family stays, with courtyard and off-highway setting. Offers more privacy than neighboring motels. **Rooms:** 127 stes. CI 3pm/CO noon. Nonsmoking rms avail. **Amenities:** 🎇 🍴 📺 🍴 A/C, satel TV w/movies, refrig, CD/tape player. Some units w/terraces, some w/whirlpools. Poolside rooms have patios. **Services:** ✕ 🛉 🛏 Babysitting. **Facilities:** 🏋 🍽 🛟 💻 & 1 restaurant (bkfst only), 1 bar, whirlpool, washer/dryer. **Rates (BB):** $96–$160 ste. Children under age 18 stay free. Parking: Outdoor, free. AE, CB, DC, DISC, JCB, MC, V.

☰☰☰ Holiday Inn Rancho Cordova

11131 Folsom Blvd, 95670; tel 916/635-0666 or toll free 800/HOLIDAY; fax 916/635-3297. 10 mi E of Sacramento. Sunrise Blvd exit off US 50; south on Sunrise; right on Folsom Blvd. Service-oriented, newly renovated, smaller hotel on a busy highway. **Rooms:** 130 rms. CI 3pm/CO noon. Nonsmoking rms avail. **Amenities:** 🎇 🍴 📺 A/C, cable TV w/movies, dataport, voice mail. Some units w/terraces. **Services:** ✕ 🛉 🛏 **Facilities:** 🏋 🍽 & 1 bar, whirlpool. **Rates (CP):** $77–$87 S; $87 D. Extra person $10. Children under age 19 stay free. Parking: Outdoor, free. Kids under 12 eat free. AE, CB, DC, DISC, JCB, MC, V.

☰☰☰ Sheraton Hotel Rancho Cordova

11211 Point East Dr, 95742; tel 916/638-1100 or toll free 800/325-3535; fax 916/635-8356. Sunrise Blvd S exit off US 50; turn right on Sunrise Blvd; left on Folsom Blvd; left on Point East. Most services of any hotel on US 50 Business corridor. Fountains in lobby and pool mask highway noise somewhat. **Rooms:** 261 rms and stes. Executive level. CI 3pm/CO noon. Nonsmoking rms avail. Nice vanity alcove with plugs and lights. Ask for "quiet" room. **Amenities:** 🎇 🍴 📺 🍴 A/C, cable TV w/movies, dataport, voice mail. **Services:** ✕ 🛎 🚐 🛉 🛏 Car-rental desk, social director, babysitting. Difficult to access. **Facilities:** 🏋 🍽 🛟 💻 & 1 restaurant, 1 bar (w/entertainment), whirlpool. Current renovations will bring meeting capacity to 3,600. **Rates:** $107–$127 S; $117–$127 D; $150–$300 ste. Extra person $10. Children under age 17 stay free. Parking: Outdoor, free. Weekend rates from $74 single to $84 double, including breakfast. AE, CB, DC, DISC, EC, ER, JCB, MC, V.

Rancho Cucamonga

Nestled in the foothills of the San Gabriel Mountains and the Cucamonga Wilderness Area, Rancho Cucamonga straddles historic Route 66. **Information:** Rancho Cucamonga Chamber of Commerce, 8280 Utica Ave #160, Rancho Cucamonga 91730 (tel 909/987-1012).

RESTAURANTS 🍽

★ Magic Lamp Inn

8189 Foothill Blvd; tel 909/981-8659. 1½ mi E of Euclid Ave. **American/Continental.** The real genie is the owner, who makes diners feel welcome here. Old-fashioned dining room has dark wood walls and leather chairs. Wonderful steak, seafood, and chicken dinners. More than 300 wines, including hard-to-find Italian vintages. **FYI:** Reservations recommended. Children's menu. Dress code. **Open:** Lunch daily 11:30am–2:30pm; dinner daily 5–10pm. **Prices:** Main courses $12–$42. AE, CB, DC, MC, V. ▪

Sycamore Inn

8318 Foothill Blvd; tel 909/982-1104. 1½ mi E of Euclid Ave. **American.** An inn since 1848; the present building dates from the 1920s. Large Victorian-style dining room with leather chairs, broad tables, chandeliers. Specialty is Black Angus beef, but pasta, other meat, seafood, and poultry are also served in large portions. Wine list has over 600 entries. **FYI:** Reservations recommended. Children's menu. **Open:** Lunch Mon–Fri 11:30am–2:30pm; dinner Mon–Thurs 5–10pm, Fri–Sat 5–11pm, Sun 3–10pm. **Prices:** Main courses $13–$33. AE, DC, DISC, MC, V. ■

ATTRACTION 🏛

Casa de Rancho Cucamonga

Tel 909/989-4970. Located at the corner of Hemlock and Vineyard Ave. Built in 1860 by Ohio brickmasons with bricks made from red clay on site, this was the home of John and Doña Merced Raines, who were prominent local citizens. The patio features a cistern with an open flume to carry water from springs through the kitchen, under the house, and into the orchard. **Open:** Wed–Sat 10am–5pm, Sun 1–5pm. **Free**

Rancho Mirage

Well-to-do even by Palm Springs area standards, Rancho Mirage is an exclusive community of country clubs and elaborate estates. **Information:** Palm Springs Convention & Visitors Bureau, 69930 US 111 #201, Rancho Mirage 92270 (tel 619/770-9000).

RESORTS 🏨

≣≣≣ Marriott's Rancho Las Palmas Resort

41-000 Bob Hope Dr, 92270; tel 619/568-2727 or toll free 800/458-8786; fax 619/568-5845. W of Bob Hope/Ramon Rd exit off I-10. 240 acres. The lush fairways and greens of the golf courses wrap around this relaxed hacienda-style resort, the low-key, family-oriented sister property to the showy, high-octane Marriott's Desert Springs Resort and Spa. **Rooms:** 450 rms and stes. CI 4pm/CO noon. Nonsmoking rms avail. Accommodations are set in two-story buildings, and guests can park near their front doors. Pleasantly decorated in light woods and pastels, rooms are large and have views of either the golf course, mountains, or pool. **Amenities:** 🛗 🛁 🖥 🍽 A/C, cable TV w/movies, dataport, voice mail. All units w/minibars, all w/terraces. Iron and ironing board in all rooms. **Services:** ✕ 🖂 🆅🅿 🛄 🗺 🛎 🛍 Car-rental desk, masseur, children's program, babysitting. Free shuttle to and from Marriott's Desert Springs. In-room massage available. **Facilities:** 🗝 🚴 ▶27 🎿 🎣17 🛶 🎱 🎳 🏓1400 🖥 🛗 4 restaurants, 1 bar (w/entertainment), lawn games, whirlpool, beauty salon, playground, washer/dryer. Hard-surface and clay tennis courts, pro shop, and videotaped lessons. Pitch-and-putt golf course. One swimming pool caters to families; the other provides a quieter setting for adults. **Rates:** Peak (Jan–Apr) $175–$280 S or D; $450–$775 ste. Children under age 18

stay free. Lower rates off-season. Parking: Outdoor, free. Romance, golf, and family packages avail. AE, DC, DISC, ER, JCB, MC, V.

≣≣≣≣ Ritz-Carlton Rancho Mirage

68-900 Frank Sinatra Dr, 92270; tel 619/321-8282 or toll free 800/241-3333; fax 619/321-6928. Bob Hope Dr exit off I-10. 25 acres. Perched 650 feet above the desert floor, the Rancho affords sweeping views of the Coachella Valley and surrounding mountains. Inside, the English Regency–style furnishings, ancestral portraits, and marble floors pose a stunning contrast to the surrounding sun-washed foothills. The property is also a reserve for bighorn sheep, who often drop by to munch on the flower borders. **Rooms:** 239 rms and stes. Executive level. CI 3pm/CO noon. Nonsmoking rms avail. Accommodations are large (over 475 square feet), and all have English-style furnishings and white-marble bathrooms. Views look toward the pool or mountains. **Amenities:** 🛗 🛁 🍽 A/C, cable TV w/movies, dataport, bathrobes. All units w/minibars, all w/terraces, some w/whirlpools. Nintendo available. **Services:** 🍽 🖂 🆅🅿 🛎 🗺 🛎 Twice-daily maid svce, car-rental desk, social director, masseur, children's program, babysitting. Club-level lounge feeds guests practically nonstop all day, from an extended continental breakfast to afternoon hors d'oeuvres and evening cordials. Ritz-Kids activities include a nature program spotlighting the desert surroundings, with scavenger hunts, presentations about bighorn sheep, and more. **Facilities:** 🗝 🚴 🎿10 🎱 🏓1000 🖥 🛗 3 restaurants (see "Restaurants" below), 3 bars (2 w/entertainment), basketball, volleyball, games rm, lawn games, spa, sauna, steam rm, whirlpool, beauty salon, playground. Two-story spa offers expanded fitness center, beauty salon, boutique, nine treatment rooms, and aerobics and aquacize classes. Afternoon tea is served in the lobby lounge; fashion shows accompany the sandwiches and cakes on Wednesdays during the winter. Gorgeous flagstone pool deck; the pool can get quite boisterous when many children are in residence, however. Nine-hole putting green onsite; guests also have privileges at 18 area golf courses. Tennis center (under the direction of Harry Fritz, former Canadian Davis Cup coach) has nine hard courts, one clay. A wonderful one-mile nature trail starts behind the courts. **Rates:** Peak (Dec 29–May) $265–$425 S or D; $600–$2,000 ste. Extra person $25. Children under age 18 stay free. Min stay special events. Lower rates off-season. Parking: Indoor, $15/day. AE, CB, DC, DISC, ER, MC, V.

≣≣≣≣ Westin Mission Hills Resort

Dinah Shore and Bob Hope Drs, 92270; tel 619/770-2132 or toll free 800/999-8284; fax 619/321-2955. 360 acres. Designed to resemble a Moroccan palace, surrounded by pools, waterfalls, and lush gardens. Self-contained resort is an excellent choice for families. **Rooms:** 512 rms and stes. CI 4pm/CO noon. Nonsmoking rms avail. Accommodations are located in clusters of two-story villas. Bathrooms offer marble countertops; separate WC contains toilet and shower.

Amenities: 🔳 🛁 📻 📺 A/C, cable TV w/movies, dataport, voice mail, in-rm safe, bathrobes. All units w/minibars, all w/terraces, some w/fireplaces, some w/whirlpools. Iron and ironing board in all rooms. **Services:** 🍽 📠 VP 🚐 ⛱ 🛎 👔 Car-rental desk, social director, masseur, children's program, babysitting. Fully staffed activities center for children offers educational instruction about the flora, fauna, and history of the desert. "Romance director" can arrange weddings and other celebrations. **Facilities:** 🎣 🚴 🏌36 🎿 📺 🏐 1800 💻 ♿ 2 restaurants (see "Restaurants" below), 2 bars (1 w/entertainment), basketball, volleyball, games rm, lawn games, steam rm, whirlpool, beauty salon, playground. The "active" pool offers a waterfall and water-volleyball net. Two 18-hole golf courses, one designed by Pete Dye, the other by Gary Player. Sand volleyball; softball diamond. **Rates:** Peak (Jan–May) $289–$329 S or D; $439–$800 ste. Extra person $25. Children under age 18 stay free. Min stay special events. Lower rates off-season. Parking: Outdoor, free. AE, DC, DISC, JCB, MC, V.

RESTAURANTS 🍴

Bella Vista
In the Westin Mission Hills Resort, Dinah Shore and Bob Hope Drs; tel 619/328-5955. Bob Hope Dr exit off I-10. **Californian.** The atrium dining room offers a light and cheery place to dine. Chef's specialties include grilled lamb chops; salmon fillet with oriental spices; and angel-hair pasta with shrimp, crayfish, and andouille sausage. **FYI:** Reservations accepted. Children's menu. Dress code. **Open:** Daily 6:30am–10pm. **Prices:** Main courses $12–$20. AE, CB, DC, DISC, MC, V. 🍲 🎪 VP ♿

The Club Grill
In the Ritz-Carlton Rancho Mirage, 68-900 Frank Sinatra Dr; tel 619/321-8282. Bob Hope Dr exit off I-10. **Regional American.** Crystal chandeliers, unique floral arrangements, uphostered chairs, and fine china add to the sophisticated ambience. Roasted rack of lamb, herb fettuccine with scallops and shrimp, and roasted free-range chicken breast with herb glaze are all house specialties. **FYI:** Reservations recommended. Piano. Jacket required. **Open:** Peak (Oct–May) Wed–Sun 6:30–10pm. Closed June–mid-Sept. **Prices:** Prix fixe $38–$55. AE, CB, DC, DISC, MC, V. VP ♿

Côte de Boeuf
69-620 CA 111; tel 619/328-9000. Bob Hope Dr exit off I-10. **French.** At this bright and airy bistro, the decor includes original impressionistic paintings done by the owner, Marc Regard. As the name implies, the specialty is beef served in light French sauces with fresh herbs. Other menu choices include crisp roast duck with braised cabbage, and a daily special such as cassoulet Toulousain, or couscous with lamb shank. **FYI:** Reservations recommended. Piano. Dress code. **Open:** Daily 5:30–10pm. Closed Aug. **Prices:** Main courses $16–$26. AE, CB, DC, MC, V. VP ♿

Touché
42-250 Bob Hope Dr; tel 619/773-1111. Bob Hope Dr exit off I-10. **Continental.** Private club-atmosphere, elaborate decor. Three rooms: an elegant dining room centered around a courtyard fountain, a nightclub with a plush living room, and a piano lounge for dining and dancing under a lighted dome. Serves lamb chops, shrimp scampi, chicken dishes. **FYI:** Reservations recommended. Piano/singer. Dress code. **Open:** Wed–Thurs 6:30–10pm, Fri–Sat 6:30–11pm, Sun 6:30–10pm. **Prices:** Main courses $15–$22. AE, CB, DC, DISC, MC, V. VP ♿

Wally's Desert Turtle
71-775 CA 111; tel 619/568-9321. **Continental.** The stunning decor features beveled-mirror ceilings, hand-painted murals, and Peruvian artifacts, complemented by crisp linen tablecloths and gleaming crystal. Menu highlights include roast duck, medallions of veal, and grilled scallops. Excellent continental cuisine and great ambience. **FYI:** Reservations recommended. Piano. Dress code. **Open:** Lunch Fri 11:30am–3pm; dinner daily 6–11pm. Closed June–Sept 10. **Prices:** Main courses $20–$33. AE, DC, DISC, MC, V. ♥ VP ♿

Rancho Santa Fe

A small but very wealthy community in the San Diego County coastal hills above Solana Beach, some of Rancho Santa Fe's opulent Spanish architecture dates from the 1920s and '30s.

INN 🏨

≣≣≣≣ Inn at Rancho Santa Fe
5951 Linea Del Cielo, PO Box 869, 92067; tel 619/756-1131 or toll free 800/654-2928; fax 619/759-1604. Lomas Santa Fe exit off I-5, go east 4 mi. 22 acres. In a posh community, close to several golf courses. An elegant destination offering natural beauty and tranquility. **Rooms:** 9 rms; 81 cottages/villas. CI 3pm/CO noon. Secluded private cottages, many surrounded by lush foliage. **Amenities:** 🔳 🛁 A/C, cable TV w/movies, refrig. Some units w/terraces, some w/fireplaces, some w/whirlpools. **Services:** ✕ 📠 🚐 ⛱ 👔 🛎 Twice-daily maid svce, masseur, babysitting. The inn owns box seats at Del Mar Racetrack and some passes are available. **Facilities:** 🎣 🚴 🎿 🏐 120 ♿ 2 restaurants, 1 bar, lawn games, washer/dryer, guest lounge. The inn also owns a cottage on Del Mar Beach where guests can shower and dress. **Rates:** Peak (July–Sept) $120–$190 S or D; $310–$510 cottage/villa. Children under age 16 stay free. Min stay peak and wknds. Lower rates off-season. Higher rates for special events/hols. Parking: Outdoor, free. AE, CB, DC, MC, V.

RESORT

≣≣≣≣ Rancho Valencia Resort
5921 Valencia Circle, PO Box 9126, 92067; tel 619/756-1123 or toll free 800/548-3664; fax 619/756-0165. 40

acres. Low villas with red-tile roofs are interspersed with courtyards, archways, and grounds so lush you can pluck ripe oranges from trees. **Rooms:** 43 cottages/villas. CI 4pm/CO noon. Nonsmoking rms avail. Each casita resembles a private residence—some are as large as 1,200 square feet. Decorated in neutrals and earth tones, with tile floors and a Spanish-Colonial armoire, housing a 27-inch TV. Every suite features a walk-in closet, dressing room, and separate makeup vanity. **Amenities:** 🛗 🕴 🎛 📶 A/C, cable TV w/movies, dataport, VCR, CD/tape player, in-rm safe, bathrobes. All units w/minibars, all w/terraces, all w/fireplaces, 1 w/whirlpool. **Services:** 🍽 🚗 🖼 🛎 🕊 Masseur, children's program, babysitting. **Facilities:** 🏋 🚴 🏌 🎾18 🛶 📶 ⛳ 1 restaurant (*see* "Restaurants" below), 1 bar (w/entertainment), basketball, lawn games, spa, sauna, steam rm, whirlpool, washer/dryer. Palm trees, hibiscus hedges, and pots of flowers surround the beautiful pool, edged with painted tiles. This is also tennis heaven, with 18 courts and 6 pros on staff. There's a regulation-size croquet lawn. **Rates:** $280–$395 cottage/villa. Extra person $20. Children under age 18 stay free. Min stay wknds and special events. Parking: Outdoor, free. Tennis, golf, and spa packages available. AE, CB, DC, EC, ER, MC, V.

RESTAURANTS 🍴

Delicias
6106 Paseo Delicias; tel 619/756-8000. Via de la Valle exit off I-5. **Californian.** Romantic, informal atmosphere, with chintz upholstered chairs and lots of windows; an open kitchen overlooks the dining room. Dishes include grilled salmon with red-onion marmalade and lemon-oregano sauce, and Chinese duck with ginger-and-pear sauce. **FYI:** Reservations recommended. Guitar/jazz. Dress code. **Open:** Tues–Sun 6–10pm. **Prices:** Main courses $14–$30. AE, CB, DC, DISC, MC, V. 🚢 🕊

The Dining Room
In Rancho Valencia Resort, 5921 Valencia Circle; tel 619/756-1123. **Californian/Mediterranean.** A blend of Californian and Mediterranean elements. Spanish colonial–style art accents the airy, open dining room, with windows facing a terrace and rolling hills. The menu changes often; typical entrees are pan-roasted whitefish encrusted with whole-grain mustard, or grilled steak with roasted peppers and Maui onions. A dessert specialty is orange cake layered with orange custard and chocolate mousse. **FYI:** Reservations recommended. Guitar. Children's menu. **Open:** Daily 7am–10pm. **Prices:** Main courses $20–$30. AE, CB, DC, ER, MC, V. ♥ 🚢 🖼 🏞 🆚 🕊

♥ Mille Fleurs
6009 Paseo Delicias; tel 619/756-3085. Via de la Valle exit off I-5. **Continental/French.** This restaurant has won countless accolades for its fine cuisine and the 800-item wine list. Decor is that of a French château, with a cozy fireplace and whitewashed walls. Starting with the freshest ingredients each

day, the chef creates dishes such as loin of rabbit with morel sauce, medallions of venison with blueberry sauce, and sea bass in Pernod sauce. **FYI:** Reservations recommended. Piano. Dress code. **Open:** Lunch Mon–Fri 11:30am–2:30pm; dinner daily 6–10pm. **Prices:** Main courses $30–$45. AE, DC, MC, V. ♥ 🖼

Red Bluff

Named after the surrounding colored cliffs, Red Bluff began as a shipping center for the steamer ships plying the Sacramento River from San Francisco. The Kelly-Griggs House Museum is a great introduction to the area's historical architecture and heritage. **Information:** Red Bluff–Tehama County Chamber of Commerce, 100 Main St, PO Box 850, Red Bluff 96080 (tel 916/527-6220).

MOTELS 🏨

≡≡≡ Best Western Grand Manor Inn
90 Sale Lane, 96080; tel 916/529-7060 or toll free 800/626-1900; fax 916/529-7077. CA 36 E exit off I-5. This property opened in 1994 and was designed and built like a grand manor. Great for business travelers and families who want high-quality lodging at a fair price. **Rooms:** 67 rms and stes. CI noon/CO 11am. Nonsmoking rms avail. Large, well-appointed rooms and suites. **Amenities:** 🛗 🕴 🎛 A/C, cable TV, refrig. Some units w/minibars, some w/terraces. **Services:** 🕊 **Facilities:** 🏋 🛶 📶 ⛳ Whirlpool, washer/dryer. **Rates (CP):** $63–$69 S; $69–$73 D; $64–$86 ste. Extra person $6. Children under age 12 stay free. Parking: Outdoor, free. AE, CB, DC, DISC, MC, V.

≡≡ Lamplighter Lodge
210 S Main St, 96080; tel 916/527-1150; fax 916/527-5878. Attractive lodgings near old Victorian section of Red Bluff. **Rooms:** 51 rms and stes. CI 1pm/CO 11:30am. Nonsmoking rms avail. **Amenities:** 🛗 🕴 🎛 A/C, cable TV w/movies, refrig. **Services:** 🚗 🕊 **Facilities:** 🏋 **Rates (CP):** $38 S; $44–$48 D; $60 ste. Extra person $4. Children under age 12 stay free. Parking: Outdoor, free. AE, DC, DISC, MC, V.

≡ Super 8 Motel Red Bluff
203 Antelope Blvd, 96080; tel 916/527-8882 or toll free 800/800-8000; fax 916/527-5078. CA 36 E exit off I-5; right on Antelope Blvd. Attractive motel. **Rooms:** 72 rms. CI 11am/CO 11am. Nonsmoking rms avail. **Amenities:** 🛗 🕴 A/C, satel TV. VCRs and videos for rent. **Services:** 🕊 🕊 Babysitting. Fax service available. **Facilities:** 🏋 ⛳ **Rates (CP):** $52–$57 S; $57–$63 D. Extra person $6. Children under age 12 stay free. Parking: Outdoor, free. AE, DC, DISC, MC, V.

ATTRACTION 🏛

William B Ide Adobe State Historic Park
21659 Adobe Rd; tel 916/527-5927. William Brown Ide, a farmer from Illinois, became president of the Bear Flag

Republic only eight months after he and his family arrived in California in 1845. His presidency lasted only 26 days before the outbreak of the Mexican War led to American occupation of the region.

The present adobe is a restoration of a building built around 1852. Picnicking; pioneer crafts demonstrations in summer. **Open:** Daily 8am–dusk. **Free**

Redding

Located in the area where the Central Valley meets the mountains, Redding is a quintessential crossroads town: it is the site of a dozen river tributaries, a railroad center, the intersection of I-5, CA 44, and CA 299, and the Shasta County seat. It is also the gateway to the parks and recreation areas of Northern California. **Information:** Redding Convention & Visitors Bureau, 777 Auditorium Dr, Redding 96001 (tel 916/225-4100 or toll free 800/874-7562).

HOTELS 🏨

⊟⊟⊟ Oxford Suites Resort
1967 Hilltop Dr, 96002; tel 916/221-0100 or toll free 800/762-0133. Cypress Ave E exit off I-5; N on Hilltop Dr ¾ mi. Excellent lodging at a fair price for the discerning business and pleasure traveler. **Rooms:** 140 stes. CI 2pm/CO 1pm. Nonsmoking rms avail. Range from simple to grand suites. **Amenities:** 🛅 ⚬ A/C, cable TV w/movies, refrig, VCR. Suites have microwave. **Services:** 🚐 🖾 🛏 ⬦ Complimentary hosted evening reception with drinks and hors d'oeuvres. Fax and copying available. **Facilities:** 🛠 🏊75 ⚭ Whirlpool, washer/dryer. **Rates (BB):** $59–$72 ste. Extra person $6. Children under age 10 stay free. Parking: Outdoor, free. Discounts for qualified business travelers and government-agency personnel. Add 10% for pets. AE, DC, DISC, MC, V.

⊟⊟⊟ Red Lion Hotel Redding
1830 Hilltop Dr, 96002; tel 916/221-8700 or toll free 800/547-8010; fax 916/221-0324. Hilltop Dr exit off I-5. **Rooms:** 194 rms and stes. CI 3pm/CO 1pm. Nonsmoking rms avail. **Amenities:** 🛅 ⚬ A/C, cable TV w/movies. Some units w/terraces. **Services:** ✕ 🚐 🖾 🛏 ⬦ Car-rental desk, babysitting. Budget car rental in lobby. Shoeshine stand open during weekday business hours. Food served at poolside terrace by request. Guests receive personalized attention. **Facilities:** 🛠 🏊800 ⬚ ⚭ 3 restaurants (see "Restaurants" below), 1 bar (w/entertainment), games rm, whirlpool. Use of fitness facilities off premises for $5 a day, with free transportation. **Rates:** Peak (June–Sept) $94–$145 S; $145–$160 D; $250 ste. Extra person $15. Children under age 18 stay free. Lower rates off-season. Parking: Outdoor, free. AE, CB, DC, DISC, MC, V.

MOTELS

⊟⊟⊟ Best Western Hilltop Inn
2300 Hilltop Dr, 96002; tel 916/221-6100 or toll free 800/336-4880; fax 916/221-2867. Cypress Ave E exit off I-5; N on Hilltop Dr ¼ mi. A friendly, well-run place. **Rooms:** 115 rms and stes. CI 2pm/CO noon. Nonsmoking rms avail. **Amenities:** 🛅 ⚬ 🖃 🍷 A/C, cable TV w/movies. 1 unit w/minibar. All king rooms have VCRs. All queen and king rooms have ironing boards and irons. **Services:** ✕ 🖾 🛏 **Facilities:** 🛠 🏊100 ⚭ 1 restaurant, 1 bar, whirlpool, washer/dryer. Restaurant open 11am–11pm. **Rates:** Peak (May–Sept) $77–$86 S; $86–$96 D; $150 ste. Extra person $10. Children under age 12 stay free. Lower rates off-season. Parking: Outdoor, free. Senior citizens receive a 10% discount. AE, DC, DISC, MC, V.

⊟⊟ Colony Inn
2731 Bechelli Lane, 96002; tel 916/223-1935 or toll free 800/354-5222; fax 916/223-1176. Cypress Ave exit off I-5; W 1 block. Very nice rooms at a budget price; however, it's close to the freeway, so you'll hear some traffic noise. **Rooms:** 75 rms. CI 1pm/CO 11am. Nonsmoking rms avail. **Amenities:** 🛅 A/C, cable TV w/movies. **Services:** 🛏 **Facilities:** 🛠 ⚭ **Rates (CP):** $36–$38 S; $40–$46 D. Extra person $5. Children under age 16 stay free. Parking: Outdoor, free. AE, CB, DC, DISC, MC, V.

⊟⊟ River Inn
1835 Park Marina Dr, 96001; tel 916/241-9500 or toll free 800/995-4341; fax 916/241-5345. Cypress Ave exit off I-5; W 1 mi. Host Larry Tappy works very hard to please his guests. **Rooms:** 79 rms. CI 2pm/CO 11am. Nonsmoking rms avail. Some units have riverfront views. **Amenities:** 🛅 ⚬ 🖃 A/C, cable TV w/movies, refrig. Some units w/terraces, 1 w/fireplace, some w/whirlpools. **Services:** 🛏 ⬦ Anything you might have left at home is available at the front desk. **Facilities:** 🛠 ⚭ 1 restaurant, 1 bar, sauna, whirlpool. A lake full of fish, with fishing poles available to guests and a barbecue for grilling their catch. **Rates:** Peak (June–Sept) $50–$60 S; $60–$70 D; $65 ste. Extra person $5. Children under age 12 stay free. Lower rates off-season. Parking: Outdoor, free. AE, CB, DC, DISC, MC, V.

⊟⊟ Vagabond Inn
536 E Cypress Ave, 96002; tel 916/223-1600 or toll free 800/522-1555; fax 916/221-4247. Cypress Ave W exit off I-5. Easy access to I-5. **Rooms:** 71 rms. CI 2pm/CO noon. Nonsmoking rms avail. **Amenities:** 🛅 ⚬ 🖃 A/C, cable TV w/movies. **Services:** 🛏 ⬦ Free weekday newspaper, fresh fruit, coffee and tea. **Facilities:** 🛠 ⚭ **Rates (CP):** Peak (June–Oct) $60–$70 S or D. Extra person $5. Children under age 18 stay free. Lower rates off-season. Parking: Outdoor, free. AE, DC, DISC, MC, V.

RESTAURANT 🍽

★ Misty's Dining Room
In the Red Lion Hotel, 1830 Hilltop Dr; tel 916/221-8700. **New American.** Expansive space with high ceilings, many chandeliers. Muted pastel colors. Imaginative California grill food, flambé tableside dishes, specialty coffees. **FYI:** Reservations recommended. Big band. Children's menu. **Open:** Peak (May–Dec) dinner daily 5–10pm; brunch Sun 9am–2pm. **Prices:** Main courses $13–$23. AE, CB, DC, DISC, MC, V. ♥ 🍷 ♿

ATTRACTIONS 🏛

Lake Shasta Caverns
Shasta Caverns Rd, O'Brien; tel 916/238-2341 or toll free 800/795-CAVE. Long a part of Wintu Indian folklore, these caverns were first explored by a white man in 1878. The name of JA Richardson and the date are still visible on the wall where he wrote them in carbon black on November 3. Filled with myriad multicolored columns, draperies, stalactites, stalagmites, and flowstone deposits, the cavern was made accessible to the general public in 1964. A tunnel was driven, and paved walkways, stairs, guardrails, and lighting were added, but the caverns were left in the most natural state possible.

The two-hour tour begins with a scenic boat ride across Lake Shasta and a bus trip up the mountainside. More than 600 steps are traversed in the course of the tour, and the cave temperature remains a constant 58°F with 95% humidity. Tours depart hourly. **Open:** Peak (Mem Day–Labor Day) daily 9am–4pm. Reduced hours off-season. **$$$$**

Shasta State Historic Park
CA 299 W; tel 916/243-8194. Located 6 miles west of Redding on CA 299 are the remnants of Shasta City, once called the "Queen City" of California's northern mining territory. The Shasta County Courthouse has been restored to its 1861 appearance and now houses historical exhibits, artifacts, and historic paintings pertaining to the town and its era. A few other buildings still stand, but many are in ruins or gone altogether. Self-guided tour booklets are available that give a detailed account of the history of Shasta City and its historic structures. The visitors center, in a completely refurbished old building across from the Empire Hotel site, has interpretive displays and information. **Open:** Peak (Mar–Oct) Wed–Sun 10am–5pm. Reduced hours off-season. **$**

Shasta Dam
Tel 916/275-4463 or 275-1554. Located about 12 miles north of Redding via I-5, exit at Shasta Dam Blvd. Completed in 1945, this is one of the largest concrete structures ever built in the United States. The dam is 602 feet high, 883 feet thick at the bottom, 30 feet thick at the top, and 3,460 feet long; its spillway is the largest man-made waterfall in the world—487 feet (three times the height of Niagara Falls). The dam's powerplant contains five generators producing a combined total of 583,000 kw of electricity.

The visitor center has a 30-minute movie on the construction of the dam, displays, and guided tours of the dam and powerplant (schedule varies; phone ahead). Picnicking is permitted at the site, with views of the entire dam, Shasta Lake, and the snow-covered volcano, Mount Shasta, to the north. Shasta Lake, created by the dam, is the largest man-made reservoir in California. It is surrounded by the Whiskeytown-Shasta-Trinity National Recreation Area. **Open:** Visitor center: Peak (Mem Day–Labor Day) Mon–Fri 7:30am–5pm, Sat–Sun 8:30am–5pm. Reduced hours off-season. **Free**

Redlands

ATTRACTION 🏛

San Bernardino County Museum
2024 Orange Tree Lane; tel 909/798-8570. One of the largest museums in California, this facility exhibits collections in archaeology, history, geology, paleontology, biological sciences, and fine arts. Discovery Hall is a hands-on family learning center presenting specimens, artifacts, and small animals. Traveling exhibitions in Elsie Munzig Exhibit Hall. Museum shop with souvenirs, collectibles, books. **Open:** Tues–Sun 9am–5pm. **$$**

Redondo Beach

A bustling center of Los Angeles County's South Bay beaches, seaside Redondo Beach is part of the legendary surf culture nurtured by the consistently good waves on this part of the coast. The busy beachside walkway known as the Esplanade runs along the foot of Fisherman's Wharf, the large municipal pier. **Information:** Redondo Beach Visitors Bureau, 200 N Pacific Coast Hwy, Redondo Beach 90277 (tel 310/374-2171).

HOTELS 🏨

🏨🏨 Best Western Redondo Beach Inn
1850 S Pacific Coast Hwy, 90277; tel 310/540-3700 or toll free 800/528-1234; fax 310/540-3675. 1 mi NW of Torrance. I-110 S (Harbor Fwy) exit off I-405, to Pacific Coast Hwy; go west. A Mexican villa-style property with white stucco buildings and red-tiled roofs. **Rooms:** 108 rms and stes. CI 2pm/CO 11am. Nonsmoking rms avail. Colonial-style decor. Standard rooms are accessible via outdoor walkways; deluxe rooms open onto indoor corridors. Bathrooms are small. **Amenities:** 🛁 ♨ A/C, satel TV w/movies, refrig. Some units w/terraces, 1 w/fireplace, 1 w/whirlpool. **Services:** ✕ 🧺 🐾 Car-rental desk, babysitting. Food can be served poolside. **Facilities:** 🏊 🚲 🎾 [40] ♿ 1 restaurant, 1 bar, sauna, whirlpool. Small pool and sunning area. Complimentary bike use, tennis racquets, and tennis balls for courts across the street. **Rates:** Peak (June–Aug) $74–$89 S or D;

$160 ste. Children under age 18 stay free. Lower rates off-season. Parking: Indoor/outdoor, free. AE, CB, DC, DISC, MC, V.

Best Western Sunrise Hotel King Harbor

400 N Harbor Dr, 90277; tel 310/376-0746 or toll free 800/334-7384; fax 310/376-7384. Off I-405 at Harbor. Clean accommodations close to Hermosa and Redondo Beaches and across the street from King Harbor. **Rooms:** 111 rms and stes. CI 3pm/CO noon. Nonsmoking rms avail. Average in size and decor, rooms have been recently renovated. Every room has live plants and some have views. **Amenities:** 🛁 🔒 📺 🍴 A/C, cable TV w/movies, dataport, voice mail. Some units w/minibars. **Services:** ✕ 🚗 🖨 🛎 Babysitting. **Facilities:** 🛝 ⬜40 1 restaurant, whirlpool, playground, washer/dryer. **Rates:** Peak (Apr–Sept) $89 S; $99 D; $135 ste. Children under age 12 stay free. Lower rates off-season. Parking: Outdoor, free. AE, CB, DC, DISC, EC, ER, JCB, MC, V.

Crowne Plaza Redondo Beach and Marina Hotel

300 N Harbor Dr, 90277; tel 310/318-8888 or toll free 800/368-9760; fax 310/376-1930. 2 mi S of Hermosa Beach. Redondo Beach exit off I-405. Oceanfront hotel has a large, newly renovated lobby with an aquarium for a centerpiece. **Rooms:** 339 rms and stes. Executive level. CI 3pm/CO noon. Nonsmoking rms avail. Large, with pastel color scheme and pine furnishings. Most have ocean views. **Amenities:** 🛁 🔒 📺 🍴 A/C, cable TV w/movies, VCR, voice mail. All units w/minibars, all w/terraces. **Services:** 🍽 🖨 🚗 🛎 🛎 Car-rental desk, babysitting. Free shuttle to local malls. **Facilities:** 🛝 ⬜ ⬜2300 ⬜ ♿ 1 restaurant, 1 bar, games rm, spa, sauna, steam rm, whirlpool, beauty salon. Beauty parlor offers spa treatments. Free use of Gold's Gym next to hotel. **Rates:** $145–$170 S; $155–$180 D; $275–$390 ste. Extra person $10. Children under age 19 stay free. Min stay special events. Parking: Indoor, $8/day. Dive and spa packages available. AE, CB, DC, DISC, JCB, MC, V.

Palos Verdes Inn

1700 S Pacific Coast Hwy, 90277; tel 310/316-4211 or toll free 800/421-9241; fax 310/316-4863. Hawthorne Blvd exit off I-405; right on Pacific Coast Hwy. Pleasant, friendly hotel located three blocks from the beach. Attractive, bright lobby. **Rooms:** 110 rms and stes. CI 3pm/CO noon. Nonsmoking rms avail. All accommodations have nice glass-enclosed tub-showers; rooms on the west side face the ocean. Some deluxe rooms offer canopy beds. **Amenities:** 🛁 🔒 A/C, cable TV w/movies, dataport. Some units w/terraces. Some balconies have ocean views. **Services:** ✕ 🚗 🛎 🛎 Twice-daily maid svce, car-rental desk, masseur, babysitting. Room service 7:30am–11pm from well-regarded restaurant. **Facilities:** 🛝 🚲 ⬜175 ♿ 1 restaurant (*see* "Restaurants" below), 1 bar, whirlpool, beauty salon. Enclosed pool area with a retractable roof, tropical plants, and a whirlpool. Guest privileges at nearby health club. **Rates:** Peak (Mem Day–Labor Day) $110–$120 S; $120–$130 D; $225 ste. Extra person $10.

Children under age 18 stay free. Lower rates off-season. Parking: Outdoor, free. Whale-watching, New Year's Eve, and Rose Bowl packages avail. AE, CB, DC, DISC, JCB, MC, V.

Portofino Hotel & Yacht Club

260 Portofino Way, 90277; tel 310/379-8481 or toll free 800/468-4292; fax 310/372-7329. 2 mi S of Hermosa Beach. Crenshaw Blvd exit off I-405 N; Inglewood Ave exit off I-405 S. Ideally located, nestled in a marina on a private peninsula between King Harbor and the Pacific Ocean. Classy, yet warm and very comfortable. Lobby has three-story atrium and Mexican tile floors. **Rooms:** 165 rms and stes. CI 2pm/CO noon. Nonsmoking rms avail. Recently redone, they are light and airy. Accommodations are whitewashed, with pine furnishings, desks, and couches in a pastel California style. All rooms have ocean or marina views from balconies. **Amenities:** 🛁 🔒 📺 🍴 A/C, cable TV w/movies, dataport, voice mail, bathrobes. All units w/minibars, all w/terraces, 1 w/whirlpool. **Services:** ✕ 🖨 🚗 🛎 🛎 Car-rental desk, masseur, babysitting. **Facilities:** 🛝 🚲 △ 🎣 ⬜900 ⬜ ♿ 1 restaurant, 2 bars (1 w/entertainment), spa, washer/dryer. Rollerblades for rent. Sport fishing and boat charters available. **Rates:** $155–$175 S; $165–$185 D; $255–$285 ste. Children under age 12 stay free. Parking: Outdoor, $7/day. AE, CB, DC, DISC, EC, ER, MC, V.

RESTAURANT 🍴

Chez Melange

In Palos Verdes Inn, 1700 S Pacific Coast Hwy; tel 310/540-1222. Rosecrans Ave exit off I-405. **Californian.** Upscale California bistro, complete with white tablecloths, a friendly staff, and a champagne and oyster bar. The menu reflects American, Italian, French, and Oriental influences. There is roast turkey, bread pudding, mashed potatoes, and Cajun meatloaf as well as soy-seared albacore, crab-and-shrimp spring rolls with Thai sweet-and-sour sauce, pastas, and pizzas. Spa cuisine is also available, as are elegant breakfast dishes. **FYI:** Reservations recommended. **Open:** Breakfast Mon–Fri 7–11am; lunch Mon–Fri 11:30am–2:30pm; dinner daily 5–10pm; brunch Sat–Sun 7:30am–2:30pm. **Prices:** Main courses $15–$30. AE, DC, DISC, MC, V. ♿

Redwood City

Located at the heart of San Francisco's South Bay, Redwood City gets its name from its lucrative 19th-century business as a lumber port. It is the center of a thriving industrial and commercial area. **Information:** Redwood City–San Mateo County Chamber of Commerce, 1675 Broadway, Redwood City 94063 (tel 415/364-1722).

HOTEL 🏨

⊨⊨⊨⊨ Hotel Sofitel
223 Twin Dolphin Dr, 94065 (Redwood Shores); tel 415/598-9000 or toll free 800/SOFITEL; fax 415/598-9383. Marine World Pkwy exit off US 101; ½ mi to Twin Dolphin Dr; turn right; 1 mi on left. Set at the edge of a lagoon in a beautifully landscaped business park, this relaxing oasis has a light and airy lobby decorated with marble floors, pastel furnishings, and a Seurat-like mural behind the reception desk. Only ten minutes from SFO Airport, it's one of the nicest properties in the area. **Rooms:** 319 rms and stes. CI 3pm/CO 1pm. Nonsmoking rms avail. Deluxe rooms overlook the lagoon. Set in the sharply angled building corners, Vista Suites offer dramatic views. Bathrooms feature limestone counters of spacious proportions and large mirrors with marquee-style lighting. **Amenities:** 🔟 ⚏ 🖥 A/C, cable TV w/movies, dataport, voice mail. All units w/minibars. Gallic touches include a red rose and Nina Ricci products in the bathrooms. Two-line phone at the desk; iron and ironing board in room. **Services:** X ⊷ VP 🚗 🖥 🛎 Twice-daily maid svce, car-rental desk, masseur, babysitting. Health spa provides European massages and facials, nail care. **Facilities:** 🔟 🏊 🏋 600 🖥 & 2 restaurants (see "Restaurants" below), 1 bar (w/entertainment), spa, sauna, beauty salon. Good-size pool deck overlooks the lagoon. Large fitness room is well equipped with exercise bikes, treadmills, step machines, free weights, and Nautilus-style machines. Attractive restaurants have views of the lagoon and San Francisco Bay. **Rates:** $185 S; $195 D; $230–$250 ste. Children under age 12 stay free. Parking: Indoor/outdoor, free. Spa packages available. AE, DC, JCB, MC, V.

MOTEL

⊨ Good Nite Inn
485 Veterans Blvd, 94063; tel 415/365-5500; fax 415/365-1119. W of US 101; N of Whipple Ave. Close to the highway on a busy street. **Rooms:** 126 rms. Executive level. CI noon/CO noon. Nonsmoking rms avail. Rooms are clean with minimal charm. **Amenities:** 🔟 A/C, satel TV w/movies. All units w/terraces. **Services:** 🚗 🖥 🛎 🐾 **Facilities:** 🔟 200 Washer/dryer. **Rates:** $43–$53 S; $49–$59 D. Extra person $6. Children under age 18 stay free. Parking: Outdoor, free. AE, DC, DISC, MC, V.

RESTAURANT 🍽

Baccarat Room
In the Hotel Sofitel, 223 Twin Dolphin Dr; tel 415/508-7127. Ralston Ave exit off US 101. **French.** Contemporary, elegant ambience, lagoon-front location. Baccarat crystal, etched-glass French doors. Good bets are the lamb medallions, and scallops and shrimp with asparagus in cognac-cream sauce. **FYI:** Reservations recommended. Piano. **Open:** Lunch Mon–Fri 11:30am–2pm; dinner Mon–Thurs 6–10pm, Fri–Sat 6–10:30pm; brunch Sun 10:30am–2pm. **Prices:** Main courses $18–$25; prix fixe $30. AE, CB, DC, MC, V. 🌑 🍴 🏞 VP &

Redwood National Park

For lodgings, see Crescent City

Established in 1968, Redwood National Park comprises 113,000 acres of diverse topography, including 30 miles of coastline that are the domain of the towering coast redwood tree *Sequoia sempervirens*. The worlds tallest tree (367.8 feet), and the second, third, and sixth tallest trees are all within a mile of each other on Redwood Creek.

The park is made up of five separate areas: Hiouchi, Crescent City, Klamath, Prairie Creek, and Orick, each with its own distinctive trails, overlooks, and picnicking areas. Jedediah Smith Redwoods, Del Norte Coast Redwoods (see Cresent City), and Prairie Creek Redwoods state parks, each providing camping facilities, are located within the boundaries of the national park. The Crescent City and Redwood visitor centers are open year-round; Hioucho Information Center is open spring–fall. For detailed information contact the superintendent, Redwood National Park, 1111 2nd St, Crescent City, CA 95531 (tel 707/464-6101).

Riverside

Riverside blossomed in the late 1800s as the capital of navel orange cultivation, and the city's early wealth can still be seen in its architecture reflecting Italian Renaissance, Victorian, and mission styles. The rapidly growing city is also a center for education, with the University of California at Riverside and other colleges located in the city. **Information:** Riverside Convention & Visitors Bureau, 3443 Orange St, Riverside 92501 (tel 909/787-7950).

HOTELS 🏨

⊨⊨⊨ Holiday Inn Riverside
3400 Market St, 92501; tel 909/784-8000 or toll free 800/HOLIDAY; fax 909/369-7127. A property with all the usual amenities for corporate travelers and families. Was undergoing renovation. **Rooms:** 288 rms and stes. Executive level. CI 3pm/CO noon. Nonsmoking rms avail. **Amenities:** 🔟 ⚏ 🖥 A/C, cable TV w/movies. Some units w/terraces. **Services:** X 🚗 🖥 🛎 Car-rental desk, babysitting. **Facilities:** 🔟 🏋 180 🖥 & 2 restaurants, 1 bar, whirlpool. **Rates:** $110 S or D; $275–$325 ste. Extra person $10. Children under age 12 stay free. Parking: Indoor, free. AE, CB, DC, DISC, MC, V.

⊨⊨⊨ Mission Inn
3649 Mission Inn Ave, 92501; tel 909/784-0300 or toll free 800/843-7755; fax 909/683-1342. This mission-style inn, a national historic monument, has hosted presidents, royalty,

and countless celebrities. Unique blend of architectural styles and decorative details. **Rooms:** 234 rms and stes. CI 3pm/CO noon. Nonsmoking rms avail. Rooms are large but simply furnished. **Amenities:** 🛅 🕭 🍷 A/C, cable TV w/movies. All units w/minibars, some w/terraces. **Services:** ✕ ☞ 🆅🅿 🚗 🖼 🍴 Twice-daily maid svce, babysitting. Guided tours are given of the property. **Facilities:** 🍸 ➹ 🏊 ⌨ ⛳ 2 restaurants (*see* "Restaurants" below), 2 bars (1 w/entertainment), spa, whirlpool, beauty salon. A museum, operated by the Mission Inn Foundation, displays a collection of artifacts from around the world. **Rates:** $105–$185 S or D; $190–$240 ste. Extra person $15. Children under age 18 stay free. Parking: Indoor/outdoor, free. Good value stay-and-dine packages sometimes available. AE, DC, MC, V.

MOTELS

▦▦ Dynasty Suites
3735 Iowa Ave, 92507; tel 909/369-8200; fax 909/341-6486. Management works hard to please the guests here; property opened in 1991. **Rooms:** 34 rms. CI 1pm/CO noon. Nonsmoking rms avail. Large, well-appointed rooms. **Amenities:** 🛅 🕭 🍷 A/C, cable TV w/movies. Some units w/whirlpools. Microwave upon request. VCRs for rent come with a selection of tapes. **Services:** 🍴 🖐 **Facilities:** 🍸 ⛳ Tiny swimming pool little more than a glorified bathtub. **Rates (CP):** $40 S; $45 D. Extra person $5. Parking: Outdoor, free. AE, DC, DISC, MC, V.

▦▦ Hampton Inn
1590 University Ave, 92507; tel 909/683-6000 or toll free 800/HAMPTON; fax 909/782-8052. University exit off I-215; ½ mi W. Clean, pleasant budget property conveniently located close to downtown and the University of California at Riverside. **Rooms:** 116 rms. CI 3pm/CO noon. Nonsmoking rms avail. **Amenities:** 🛅 🕭 A/C, cable TV w/movies. **Services:** 🖼 🍴 Car-rental desk. Generous continental breakfast served in lobby. **Facilities:** 🍸 🏊 ⛳ **Rates (CP):** $49–$54 S; $54–$64 D. Children under age 18 stay free. Parking: Outdoor, free. AE, CB, DC, DISC, MC, V.

RESTAURANTS 🍽

El Gato Gordo
1360 University Ave; tel 714/787-8212. University Ave exit off I-215. **Mexican.** Decorated with Mexican folk art and bright colors. Traditional plates of tacos, enchiladas, and burritos, as well as red snapper Veracruz, chili verde, and carnitas. **FYI:** Reservations accepted. Big band. **Open:** Lunch Mon–Sat 11:30am–3pm; dinner Sun–Thurs 4–9pm, Fri–Sat 4–10pm; brunch Sun 10:30am–2pm. **Prices:** Main courses $7–$11. AE, DISC, MC, V. ⛳

Magnone Cucina
1630 Spruce St; tel 909/781-8840. Spruce St exit off I-215. **Italian.** Soaring skylights, large windows, decorative pillars girded with grayish metallic tiles, open kitchen. Good pizzas, risotto, pasta, chicken, and fish. Beautiful and trendy place, with nearly everything under $10. **FYI:** Reservations recommended. **Open:** Lunch Mon–Fri 11:30am–2:30pm; dinner Mon–Thurs 5–10pm, Fri–Sat 5–11pm, Sun 5–9pm; brunch Sun 10am–2pm. **Prices:** Main courses $8–$17. AE, CB, DC, DISC, MC, V. ⛳

$ ★ Mario's Place
1725 Spruce St; tel 909/684-7755. Spruce St exit off I-215. **French/Italian.** An exquisite blend of France and northern Italy, well worth a detour. The owners—the three Palagi brothers—clearly enjoy themselves. Food is beautifully prepared, and delicious. Grilled spiedini (skewer of lamb and radicchio with balsamic vinegar) is a house favorite. Pastas and risotto are also served. **FYI:** Reservations recommended. Jazz/piano. Dress code. **Open:** Lunch Mon–Fri 11:30am–2:30pm; dinner Mon–Thurs 5:30–11pm, Fri–Sat 5:30pm–1am. **Prices:** Main courses $12–$23; prix fixe $27–$70. AE, CB, DC, DISC, MC, V. ❤ ⛳

Riverside Brewing Company
3397 Mission Inn Ave; tel 909/784-BREW. Off CA 91. **Pub.** A busy place popular for its handcrafted beers and ales, it draws a friendly, thirty-something crowd. Food offerings include appetizers such as buffalo wings, beer-batter fried calamari, and deep-fried dill pickles. Soups, salads, sandwiches, pasta, and pizza are available, as is homemade root beer. **FYI:** Reservations accepted. Rock. Children's menu. Beer and wine only. **Open:** Daily 11:30am–midnight. **Prices:** Main courses $7–$13. AE, DISC, MC, V. ⛳

The Spanish Dining Room
In the Mission Inn, 3649 Mission Inn Ave; tel 909/784-0300. Off CA 91. **Californian.** Coffered ceilings, glazed tiles, and a pretty patio suggest a very rich California mission. Chef Joe Cochran's outstanding creations include seared salmon with basil lemon, and spinach pesto, served with garlic mashed potatoes, fine green beans, and carrots; and penne with spicy sausage and opal basil. **FYI:** Reservations recommended. **Open:** Breakfast daily 6:30–10am; lunch Mon–Sat 11:30am–2pm; dinner daily 5:30–10pm; brunch Sun 10:30am–2:30pm. **Prices:** Main courses $8–$20. AE, MC, V. ▮ 🆅🅿 ⛳

ATTRACTIONS 🏛

Riverside Municipal Museum
3580 Mission Inn Ave; tel 909/782-5273. Exhibits depict local history, natural history, and Native American culture of the area. **Open:** Mon 9am–1pm, Tues–Fri 9am–5pm, Sat 10am–5pm, Sun 11am–5pm . **Free**

UCR Botanic Gardens
University Ave; tel 909/787-4650. Comprising nearly 40 scenic acres on the campus of the University of California, Riverside, the garden displays more than 3,500 plants from around the world. Highlights include the Cactus and Succulent Garden, Alder Canyon, Iris Garden, Rose Garden, Geodesic Lath Dome, and Subtropical Fruit Orchard. **Open:** Daily 8am–5pm. **Free**

March Field Museum
16222 I-215, March AFB; tel 909/655-3725. Housed in a new facility on the west side of the aerodrome at the intersection of I-215 and Van Buren Blvd, this museum depicts aviation history from 1918 to the present. Many refurbished historic aircraft are on display, including such famous models as the U-2 spy plane and the B-52 Stratofortress. Exhibits; gift shop. **Open:** Daily 10am–4pm. **Free**

Rohnert Park

HOTEL 🏨

🔛🔛🔛 **Red Lion Hotel**
1 Red Lion Dr, 94928; tel 707/584-5466 or toll free 800/547-8010; fax 707/586-9726. Golf Course Dr exit off US 101; W on Commerce; right on Golf Course; left on Red Lion. Pleasant hotel on spacious grounds, close to a golf course and area attractions. Live evening piano music in the lobby. **Rooms:** 245 rms and stes. CI 3pm/CO noon. Nonsmoking rms avail. Large, clean rooms; the nicest overlook the pool. **Amenities:** 🛋 🌣 🖥 🍷 A/C, cable TV w/movies. Some units w/terraces. **Services:** ✕ 🛄 🕰 Masseur, babysitting. **Facilities:** 🚣 🎱 🔲 50 ⅃ 👌 2 restaurants, 1 bar (w/entertainment), sauna, whirlpool. Attractive pool area. **Rates:** Peak (June–Oct) $110–$130 S; $125–$145 D; $250–$450 ste. Extra person $15. Children under age 18 stay free. Lower rates off-season. Parking: Outdoor, free. Special weekend packages. AE, CB, DC, DISC, MC, V.

Roseville

RESTAURANT 🍴

Macaroni Grill
In Rocky Ridge Town Center, 2010 Douglas Blvd; tel 916/773-6399. **Italian.** It feels like a huge Italian kitchen; brick walls and flagstone arches combine with bright oil paintings and landscape murals to yield a festive atmosphere. Winter entree choices tend toward hearty roasted meats and stews. Summer fare is lighter, emphasizing pastas with delicate sauces, fish, and chicken dishes. **FYI:** Reservations not accepted. Children's menu. **Open:** Sun–Thurs 11am–10pm, Fri–Sat 11am–11pm. **Prices:** Main courses $7–$17. AE, DISC, MC, V. 🏞 👌

Rutherford

Situated in the center of Napa Valley, Rutherford is one of the region's most desirable wine-growing hamlets, with several respected wineries and tasting rooms.

HOTEL 🏨

🔛🔛🔛🔛 **Auberge du Soleil**
180 Rutherford Hill Rd, 94573; tel 707/963-1211 or toll free 800/348-5406; fax 707/963-8764. Silverado Trail to Rutherford Hill Rd; go east about 1 mi. Ultra-chic, wine-country retreat amid 33 acres of olive groves in the Napa Valley foothills. Architecture recalls southern France, with sand-colored stucco walls and steep shingled roofs. Exquisite grounds with pergolas and fountains. **Rooms:** 50 rms and stes. CI 3pm/CO noon. Nonsmoking rms avail. Rooms are all in hillside cottages decorated in countrified elegance, with tiled floors and natural wood and leather, accented by bright fuchsia-and-yellow fabrics. Top-of-the-line one-bedroom suites are vast, with vaulted ceilings and a skylight over the tub. **Amenities:** 🛋 🌣 🖥 🍷 A/C, satel TV w/movies, dataport, VCR, CD/tape player, voice mail, in-rm safe, bathrobes. Some units w/fireplaces, some w/whirlpools. Lots of special features—including down comforters, slippers, a supply of candles, and bath salts placed by the tub. **Services:** 🍽 🔑 🆅🅿 🛄 Twice-daily maid svce, masseur. Masseur can come to your room. **Facilities:** 🚣 🎱 3 🍺 🔲 50 👌 1 restaurant (see "Restaurants" below), 1 bar, steam rm, whirlpool, beauty salon. Edged by manicured oleander bushes, the pool deck faces the valley and the western mountains. Small workout room looks toward the hills. A ½-mile nature trail passes 50 sculptures. **Rates:** Peak (Aug–Nov) $250–$275 S or D; $500–$850 ste. Min stay wknds. Lower rates off-season. Parking: Outdoor, free. AE, DC, DISC, MC, V.

INN

🔛🔛🔛 **Rancho Caymus**
1140 Rutherford Rd, PO Box 78, 94573; tel 707/963-1777 or toll free 800/845-1777; fax 707/963-5387. CA 128 off CA 29. 1 acre. The hacienda-style main building, with rough stucco exterior and red-tile roof, surrounds a courtyard with a fountain and lush plantings of wisteria, bougainvillea, and bird of paradise. Heavy tree trunks gird the stairs, while colorful murals adorn the walls. Unsuitable for children under 16. **Rooms:** 26 rms, stes, and effic. CI 3pm/CO noon. Nonsmoking rms avail. Decorated in Early California style, with handcrafted furnishings, pillows, and weavings from Latin America. Units are split level, with separate living and sleeping areas. Even the bathroom decor is rustic, with rough-tile walls and wooden counters. Rooms have no views to speak of, and you do get noise from nearby CA 29. **Amenities:** 🛋 🌣 A/C, TV. All units w/minibars, some w/terraces, some w/fireplaces, some w/whirlpools. Large, adobe, wood-burning fireplaces are already loaded with wood and kindling; all the guest needs to do is light a match. **Services:** 🚗 Masseur. **Facilities:** 🔲 95 👌 1 restaurant (bkfst and lunch only). **Rates (CP):** Peak (Apr–Nov) $125–$155 S or D; $245–$295 ste; $245–$295 effic. Extra person $15. Children under age 3 stay free. Min stay peak and wknds. Lower rates off-

season. Parking: Outdoor, free. Reserve two months in advance for summer weekends. Hot-air ballooning packages avail. AE, CB, DC, DISC, MC, V.

RESTAURANT

Auberge du Soleil

180 Rutherford Hill Rd; tel 707/963-1211. Silverado Trail to Rutherford Hill Rd; E 1 mi. **Californian/French.** This elegant country French retreat provides great deck views of some of Napa Valley's most prized vineyards. The kitchen has had its ups and downs in recent years, but it is currently serving competently prepared, albeit expensive, fare. Although you can enjoy better cuisine elsewhere in the valley, you can't beat the vista from the outdoor dining terrace. You can also eat at the bar, which offers the same panoramas and a satisfactory menu at about half the price. **FYI:** Reservations recommended. Dress code. **Open:** Peak (July–Aug) breakfast daily 7–11am; lunch daily 11:30am–2pm; dinner Mon–Fri 6–9:30pm, Sat–Sun 5:30–9:30pm. **Prices:** Main courses $25–$31. AE, DC, DISC, MC, V.

Sacramento

The city survived devastating floods, fires, and challenges from the likes of Berkeley, San Jose, and Monterey to become state capital in 1854. The supply and transportation link to the booming Gold Rush towns, Sacramento assured its hold on the capital with the completion of the transcontinental railroad in 1869 and the growth of agriculture in the fertile Sacramento Valley. Today, the city can be explored by a walking tour of Old Sacramento (which contains the State Capitol and the State Library), or by visiting any number of attractions, including the California State Railroad Museum, the Crocker Art Museum, or Sutter's Fort. **Information:** Sacramento Convention & Visitors Bureau, 1421 K St, Sacramento 95814 (tel 916/264-7777).

HOTELS

Beverly Garland Hotel

1780 Tribute Rd, 95815; tel 916/929-7900 or toll free 800/972-3976; fax 916/921-9147. Cal Expo Blvd exit off Business I-80. Location convenient to downtown and shopping district. Attractive lobby with lots of plants and a fireplace. **Rooms:** 205 rms and stes. Executive level. CI 3pm/CO noon. Nonsmoking rms avail. New furnishings in some rooms. **Amenities:** A/C, cable TV w/movies, dataport. All units w/terraces. **Services:** **Facilities:** 1 restaurant, 1 bar, whirlpool, washer/dryer. Access to nearby fitness facilities at Sacramento Court Club. **Rates:** $79–$99 S; $89–$109 D; $95 ste. Children under age 18 stay free. Parking: Outdoor, free. AE, CB, DC, DISC, MC, V.

Canterbury Inn

1900 Canterbury Inn Rd, 95815 (Woodlake); tel 916/927-0927 or toll free 800/932-3492; fax 916/641-8594. US 50 exit off CA 160, left on Canterbury Rd. This older property is adequate for business stays. **Rooms:** 150 rms and stes. CI 4pm/CO noon. Nonsmoking rms avail. Basic. Some have courtyard view and a lot of light. **Amenities:** A/C, cable TV w/movies. **Services:** 24-hour security. **Facilities:** 1 restaurant (lunch and dinner only), 1 bar, whirlpool. Extra-large pool. Access to health club at nearby Radisson. **Rates (CP):** $57 S; $67 D; $130 ste. Extra person $10. Children under age 12 stay free. Min stay special events. Parking: Outdoor, free. AE, DISC, JCB, MC, V.

Clarion Hotel Sacramento

700 16th St, 95814; tel 916/444-8000 or toll free 800/443-0880; fax 916/442-8129. 15th St exit off US 50/Business I-80. Shade trees provide a peaceful aura to this older, full-scale downtown hotel. Lots of ground-floor windows; views of gardens and pool area brighten the rather dark lobby and restaurant. **Rooms:** 239 rms and stes. Executive level. CI 3pm/CO noon. Nonsmoking rms avail. Nicely appointed rooms, but carpet is slightly worn. **Amenities:** A/C, satel TV w/movies. Some units w/terraces. **Services:** Free shuttle to local sites sometimes available. **Facilities:** 1 restaurant, 1 bar. All guests have access to Midtown Athletic Club. **Rates:** $79–$99 S; $89–$109 D; $130–$295 ste. Extra person $15. Children under age 17 stay free. Min stay special events. Parking: Outdoor, free. AE, CB, DC, DISC, EC, ER, JCB, MC, V.

Courtyard by Marriott

2101 River Plaza Dr, 95833 (South Natomas); tel 916/922-1120 or toll free 800/321-2211; fax 916/922-1872. Garden Hwy exit off I-50. The contemporary lobby is inviting, the cafe and lounge are rimmed with windows facing the garden. This spot attracts corporate travelers from nearby business parks and the airport. **Rooms:** 151 rms and stes. Executive level. CI 3pm/CO 1pm. Nonsmoking rms avail. **Amenities:** A/C, satel TV w/movies, dataport. Some units w/terraces. Extra-long cord on phones. **Services:** Babysitting. **Facilities:** 1 restaurant (bkfst and dinner only), 1 bar, whirlpool, washer/dryer. **Rates:** $89 S; $99 D; $105 ste. Children under age 16 stay free. Parking: Outdoor, free. AE, CB, DC, DISC, JCB, MC, V.

Delta King Hotel

1000 Front St, 95814; tel 916/444-5464 or toll free 800/825-5464; fax 916/444-5314. J St exit off I-5; follow signs to Old Sacramento. The region's most unusual property is a restored stern-wheel riverboat that traveled between San Francisco and Sacramento between 1927 and 1940. Today, it's docked on the bank of the Sacramento River at the edge of Old Town. **Rooms:** 44 rms and stes. CI 4pm/CO 11am. No smoking. Small and well appointed. In keeping with the historic riverboat theme, the rooms have brass beds, pedestal sinks, and wood trim; some have clawfoot tubs. **Amenities:** 🔒 A/C, cable TV w/movies. **Services:** ✗ VP ⬭ ⤳ Personalized service, with evening turndown and valet parking. **Facilities:** 500 ⭑ 1 restaurant (lunch and dinner only), 2 bars (w/entertainment). The Pilothouse Restaurant was voted Sacramento's "best romantic dinner" and "best brunch" by readers of local newspapers. A theater is located on one of the lower decks. **Rates (CP):** $89–$129 S; $99–$139 D. Extra person $10. Parking: Outdoor, $6/day. Many weekend packages. Mid-week discount. AE, CB, DC, DISC, MC, V.

≣≣≣ Governor's Inn

210 Richards Blvd, 95814 (Downtown); tel 916/448-7224 or toll free 800/999-6689; fax 916/448-7382. Richards Blvd exit off I-5. This small, new hotel is comfortable and convenient to the downtown business district and capitol building. **Rooms:** 134 rms and stes. CI 1pm/CO 11am. Nonsmoking rms avail. Fairly large and well-appointed. **Amenities:** 🔒 ⬭ 🖭 A/C, satel TV w/movies. Some units w/terraces. **Services:** 🚗 ⬭ ⤳ Afternoon refreshments are served Tues–Thurs. **Facilities:** ⬭ ⬭ 200 ⭑ Whirlpool. **Rates (CP):** Peak (May–June) $67–$84 S; $77–$94 D; $95–$125 ste. Extra person $10. Children under age 12 stay free. Lower rates off-season. Parking: Outdoor, free. AE, DC, DISC, MC, V.

≣≣≣ Holiday Inn Capitol Plaza

300 J St, 95814 (Downtown); tel 916/446-0100 or toll free 800/HOLIDAY. J St exit off I-5. A city property with the usual business amenities, adjacent to historic park and new shopping plaza. Renovations of public areas and guest corridors recently completed. **Rooms:** 364 rms and stes. Executive level. CI 3pm/CO noon. Nonsmoking rms avail. **Amenities:** 🔒 ⬭ A/C, cable TV w/movies, voice mail. **Services:** ✗ ⬌ 🚗 ⬭ ⤳ Children's program, babysitting. **Facilities:** ⬭ ⬭ 600 ⭑ 1 restaurant, 2 bars (1 w/entertainment), sauna. New outdoor cafe on plaza. **Rates:** $105 S; $115 D; $150 ste. Extra person $10. Children under age 18 stay free. Min stay special events. Parking: Outdoor, free. AE, CB, DC, DISC, ER, JCB, MC, V.

≣≣ Host Airport Hotel

6945 Airport Blvd, 95837 (Metropolitan Airport); tel 916/922-8071 or toll free 800/228-9290; fax 916/929-8636. 10 mi N of Sacramento. Airport Blvd exit off I-5. A surprisingly quiet airport property. Full renovation scheduled for 1996. **Rooms:** 85 rms. CI 3pm/CO 1pm. Nonsmoking rms avail. **Amenities:** 🔒 ⬭ A/C, satel TV, dataport, voice mail. **Services:** ⤳ **Facilities:** ⬭ 300 ⭑ Whirlpool. **Rates (CP):** $90 S; $100 D. Extra person $10. Children under age 12 stay free. Parking: Outdoor, free. AE, CB, DC, DISC, MC, V.

≣≣ Howard Johnson Hotel

3343 Bradshaw Rd, 95827; tel 916/366-1266 or toll free 800/654-2000; fax 916/366-1266. Bradshaw Rd exit off US 50. Get in left lane; make U-turn. Highway property with reasonable rates. **Rooms:** 124 rms and stes. Executive level. CI 2pm/CO noon. Nonsmoking rms avail. **Amenities:** 🔒 ⬭ 🖭

A/C, cable TV w/movies. All units w/terraces, all w/whirlpools. **Services:** ✗ ⬭ ⤳ ⬥ Car-rental desk. **Facilities:** ⬭ ⬭ 250 ⬜ ⭑ 1 restaurant, 1 bar, sauna, steam rm, whirlpool, washer/dryer. Extra-large indoor-outdoor pool is open year-round. **Rates:** Peak (May–Aug) $60–$70 S; $65–$70 D; $65–$75 ste. Extra person $5. Children under age 17 stay free. Lower rates off-season. Parking: Outdoor, free. AE, CB, DC, DISC, ER, MC, V.

≣≣≣≣ Hyatt Regency Sacramento

1209 L St, 95814 (Downtown); tel 916/443-1234 or toll free 800/233-1234; fax 916/321-6699. 15th St exit off US 50/ Business I-80. Left on 16th St; left on L St. This elegant, upscale, Mediterranean-style hotel has a stellar location across from both the Capitol and Capitol Park. Known for its luxurious amenities and extensive conference facilities. **Rooms:** 500 rms and stes. Executive level. CI 3pm/CO noon. Nonsmoking rms avail. Recently renovated, accommodations look very handsome with their rosewood furnishings and upholsteries done in topaz, brown, and black. Ask for Capitol and park views. Accented by marble floors and counters, bathrooms feature excellent lighting and mirrors. Presidential Suites offer large terraces facing the Capitol as well as baby-grand pianos. **Amenities:** 🔒 ⬭ 🖭 A/C, cable TV w/movies, dataport, voice mail. All units w/minibars, some w/terraces, some w/whirlpools. **Services:** ✗ ⬭ VP 🚗 ⬭ ⤳ Car-rental desk, masseur, babysitting. Poolside food and drink service. **Facilities:** ⬭ ⬭ 1700 ⬜ ⭑ 2 restaurants, 3 bars (2 w/entertainment), spa, whirlpool, beauty salon. Lovely pool (heated year-round) surrounded by palm trees and flowers; large, well-equipped health club. Ciao Yama restaurant, which serves an intriguing Italian-Japanese menu, is known for its 32-foot antipasto bar at lunchtime. **Rates:** $165–$190 S; $190–$215 D; $250–$895 ste. Extra person $25. Children under age 18 stay free. Min stay special events. AP and MAP rates avail. Parking: Indoor/outdoor, $6–$10/ day. AE, CB, DC, DISC, EC, ER, JCB, MC, V.

≣≣≣ Radisson Hotel Sacramento

500 Leisure Lane, 95815 (Point West); tel 916/922-2020 or toll free 800/333-3333; fax 916/649-9463. 15th St exit off US 80/US 50. Situated on 18 acres in a parklike setting adjacent to American River Pkwy, this two-story, Mediterranean-style hotel ranks at the top of its class. It features huge fountains, spacious grounds, and nice touches such as pots of orchids in the lobby. The hotel surrounds a private lake, which is accented by tiki torches at night. **Rooms:** 314 rms and stes. Executive level. CI 3pm/CO noon. Nonsmoking rms avail. Recently refurbished rooms pleasantly decorated in contemporary style. The most expensive accommodations offer lake views. Junior suites are large, with vaulted ceilings and a separate sitting area that features a hide-a-bed. **Amenities:** 🔒 ⬭ 🖭 ⬭ A/C, cable TV w/movies, dataport. All units w/minibars, some w/terraces, 1 w/whirlpool. Iron and ironing board in each room. **Services:** 🍽 ⬌ VP 🚗 ⬭ ⤳ ⬥ Car-rental desk, social director, masseur, babysitting.

Free shuttle to several Sacramento attractions. **Facilities:** ⬚ ⬚ ⬚ ⬚ ⬚ [1800] ⬚ ⬚ 2 restaurants, 1 bar (w/entertainment), whirlpool. The Plaza Club restaurant for guests staying in executive accommodations serves a morning buffet breakfast and afternoon hors d'oeuvres. A good spot for business meetings. Largest ballroom in the Sacramento area. The nearby Grove outdoor amphitheater presents performers such as David Lee Roth and Paula Poundstone. There's dancing nightly to DJ music in the Crocodile Lounge. The hotel is located adjacent to the American River trail, which wends its way to Old Sacramento—good for biking or jogging. Pool heated only during the summer. **Rates:** $89–$119 S or D; $139–$389 ste. Extra person $10. Children under age 18 stay free. Min stay special events. Parking: Outdoor, free. AE, CB, DC, DISC, MC, V.

≣ ≣ ≣ Red Lion Hotel

2001 Point West Way, 95815 (Point West); tel 916/929-8855 or toll free 800/547-8010; fax 916/924-0719. Arden Way exit off Business I-80. Large, newly renovated, full-service hotel in busy suburban area adjacent to shopping and entertainment. Undergoing complete renovation, including room sprinklers and ADA-recommended upgrades for guests with disabilities. **Rooms:** 448 rms and stes. Executive level. CI 3pm/CO noon. Nonsmoking rms avail. **Amenities:** ⬚ ⬚ ⬚ A/C, cable TV w/movies, dataport. All units w/terraces, some w/whirlpools. **Services:** ✗ ⬚ [VP] ⬚ ⬚ ⬚ ⬚ **Facilities:** ⬚ ⬚ [1400] ⬚ ⬚ 2 restaurants, 1 bar (w/entertainment), whirlpool, washer/dryer. Coffee shop with espresso-to-go bar. **Rates:** $134–$159 S; $149–$174 D; $400–$500 ste. Extra person $15. Children under age 18 stay free. Parking: Outdoor, free. AE, CB, DC, DISC, ER, JCB, MC, V.

≣ ≣ ≣ Red Lion's Sacramento Inn

1401 Arden Way, 95815; tel 916/922-8041 or toll free 800/RED LION; fax 916/922-0386. Arden Way exit off Business I-80. All-purpose convention motel in a noisy but convenient location, with enough space that guests don't feel crowded. **Rooms:** 376 rms and stes. Executive level. CI 3pm/CO 1pm. Nonsmoking rms avail. Adequate rooms, with older furnishings in good condition. Nice padded benches for luggage. **Amenities:** ⬚ ⬚ A/C, satel TV w/movies. Some units w/terraces, some w/whirlpools. **Services:** ✗ ⬚ ⬚ ⬚ ⬚ ⬚ Poolside food and beverage service. **Facilities:** ⬚ ⬚ [1200] ⬚ ⬚ 1 restaurant, 1 bar (w/entertainment), washer/dryer. Putting green, extensive patio/lawn area. **Rates:** $89–$109 S; $114–$124 D; $150 ste. Extra person $15. Children under age 16 stay free. Min stay special events. Parking: Outdoor, free. AE, DC, DISC, MC, V.

≣ ≣ ≣ Residence Inn by Marriott

1530 Howe Ave, 95825 (Point West); tel 916/920-9111 or toll free 800/333-3131; fax 916/921-5664. Howe Ave exit off US 50. A newer facility, and a good option for do-it-yourself travelers who prefers a cozy fireplace to a hotel bar. **Rooms:** 176 stes and effic. CI 3pm/CO noon. Nonsmoking rms avail. Comfortable, large apartments. **Amenities:** ⬚ ⬚ ⬚ A/C, cable TV w/movies, refrig, dataport. Some units w/terraces, some w/fireplaces. In winter, amenities include first-night fireplace log and microwave popcorn. **Services:** ⬚ ⬚ Hospitality hour (5–6:30pm) includes complimentary hors d'oeuvres, beer, wine, and sodas. **Facilities:** ⬚ [20] ⬚ Whirlpool, washer/dryer. Access to neighborhood health club. **Rates (CP):** $119–$139 ste; $119–$139 effic. Children under age 18 stay free. Parking: Outdoor, free. Discount for long stays. AE, CB, DC, DISC, JCB, MC, V.

≣ ≣ ≣ Residence Inn Sacramento South

2410 W El Camino Ave, 95833 (South Natomas); tel 916/649-1300 or toll free 800/331-3131; fax 916/649-1395. W El Camino Ave exit off I-80. A home-away-from-home for families and business travelers. **Rooms:** 126 effic. CI 3pm/CO noon. Nonsmoking rms avail. One- and two-bedroom suites with full kitchen, two baths, and doors between living and sleeping areas. Some "green rooms" offer filtered air and water and biodegradable products. **Amenities:** ⬚ ⬚ ⬚ A/C, cable TV, refrig, VCR, voice mail. Some units w/fireplaces. **Services:** ⬚ ⬚ ⬚ ⬚ Babysitting. Hospitality hour Monday–Friday. Complimentary grocery shopping service and local area shuttle. **Facilities:** ⬚ ⬚ ⬚ [40] ⬚ ⬚ Whirlpool, washer/dryer. Sports court, gas grills. **Rates (CP):** $104 effic. Children under age 18 stay free. Parking: Outdoor, free. Reduced rates for stays of 7 nights or more. AE, DC, DISC, MC, V.

≣ ≣ ≣ Sacramento Hilton Inn

2200 Harvard St, 95815; tel 916/922-4700 or toll free 800/344-4321; fax 916/922-8418. Arden Way exit off Business I-80. Urban hotel with business amenities in a suburban location. **Rooms:** 332 rms and stes. Executive level. CI 3pm/CO noon. Nonsmoking rms avail. **Amenities:** ⬚ ⬚ ⬚ ⬚ A/C, voice mail. Some units w/terraces, some w/whirlpools. **Services:** ✗ ⬚ ⬚ ⬚ ⬚ Children's program. Shuttle service to downtown attractions and nearby shopping (upon availability). **Facilities:** ⬚ ⬚ [1000] ⬚ 1 restaurant (bkfst and dinner only), 2 bars (1 w/entertainment), spa, sauna, whirlpool. Vacation Station program for kids offers board and video games, coloring books. **Rates:** $116–$126 S; $126 D; $250–$475 ste. Extra person $10. Children under age 18 stay free. Parking: Outdoor, free. AE, CB, DC, DISC, EC, ER, JCB, MC, V.

MOTELS

≣ ≣ Best Western Ponderosa Inn

1100 H St, 95814 (Downtown); tel 916/441-1314 or toll free 800/528-1234; fax 916/441-5961. J St exit off I-5; left on 11th St. Downtown property convenient to the capitol, with a courtyard pool and a small, neatly furnished lobby. **Rooms:** 98 rms and stes. CI open/CO 1pm. Nonsmoking rms avail. **Amenities:** ⬚ ⬚ ⬚ A/C, cable TV w/movies, voice mail. Some units w/terraces. Irons and ironing boards available in each room. **Services:** ✗ ⬚ ⬚ **Facilities:** ⬚ [25] ⬚ 1 restaurant, 1 bar (w/entertainment). **Rates (CP):** $75 S; $85 D; $150 ste.

Extra person $8. Children under age 12 stay free. Min stay special events. Parking: Outdoor, free. AE, CB, DC, DISC, MC, V.

▤ Coral Reef Lodge

2700 Fulton Ave, 95821; tel 916/483-6461 or toll free 800/995-6460; fax 916/488-2372. El Camino exit off Business I-80; left on Fulton Ave. Older property in a suburban setting, near shopping and business areas of North Sacramento. **Rooms:** 101 rms and stes. CI 3pm/CO noon. Nonsmoking rms avail. Very basic rooms, with sliding-glass doors that may be a security risk. **Amenities:** ☎ ▣ A/C, cable TV. Some units w/terraces. VCRs available at front desk. **Services:** ⌐┘ **Facilities:** ⌐ ⌂ Washer/dryer. Pool area nicely landscaped. **Rates:** $40 S; $46 D; $55 ste. Extra person $5. Children under age 12 stay free. Parking: Outdoor, free. AE, DC, DISC, MC, V.

▤▤ La Quinta Motor Inn Sacramento North

4604 Madison Ave, 95841; tel 916/348-0900 or toll free 800/531-5900; fax 916/331-7160. Madison Ave exit off I-80. Comfortable, newer property with easy access to freeway. **Rooms:** 127 rms and stes. CI 3pm/CO noon. Nonsmoking rms avail. **Amenities:** ☎ ⌂ A/C, satel TV, dataport. **Services:** ✗ ⌐ ⌐┘ ⌐⌐ Coffee 24 hours. **Facilities:** ⌐ [40] ⌂ Washer/dryer. Use of nearby gym. **Rates (BB):** $59–$64 S; $64–$74 D; $94 ste. Extra person $5. Children under age 18 stay free. Parking: Outdoor, free. AE, CB, DC, DISC, MC, V.

▤ The Sacramento Vagabond Inn

909 3rd St, 95814 (Old Sacramento); tel 916/446-1481 or toll free 800/522-1555. J St exit off I-5. Budget property located downtown, adjacent to historic park and the Chinese Cultural Center. **Rooms:** 107 rms. CI 3pm/CO noon. Nonsmoking rms avail. Rooms are pretty standard. **Amenities:** ☎ ⌂ ▣ A/C, cable TV w/movies. **Services:** ☎ ⌐ ⌐┘ ⌐⌐ **Facilities:** ⌐ [30] Restaurant next door. **Rates (CP):** Peak (Mar 31–Oct) $73–$93 S; $78–$98 D. Extra person $5. Children under age 18 stay free. Min stay special events. Lower rates off-season. Parking: Outdoor, free. Discounts available for frequent guests. AE, DC, DISC, MC, V.

INN

▤▤▤ Sterling Hotel

1300 H St, 95814 (Downtown); tel 916/448-1300 or toll free 800/365-7660; fax 916/448-8066. 1 acre. An 1894 landmark converted into an inn, with Victorian touches. The overall feel here is businesslike. Popular with politicians visiting the nearby state capitol. **Rooms:** 16 rms. CI 3pm/CO 11am. No smoking. All rooms are different. Smaller rooms are nicer than larger ones, which look underfurnished. Furnishings might include four-poster or sleigh beds, or Empire-design chairs. Bathrooms are tiled in marble. But some furnishings are chipped, and housekeeping could be better. **Amenities:** ☎ ⌂ A/C, cable TV w/movies. 1 unit w/minibar, 1 w/terrace, all w/whirlpools. **Services:** ✗ ⌐ Masseur. **Facilities:** [250] ⌂ 1 restaurant (see "Restaurants" below), 1 bar. The lounge often

functions as a meeting room, so guests can't use the space for relaxation. The bar is rented to groups, as well. The glass conservatory is popular for weddings and special events. For $4, guests can use the health club one block away. **Rates (CP):** $125–$225 S; $155 D; $175–$225 ste. Children under age 18 stay free. Min stay special events. Higher rates for special events/hols. Parking: Indoor/outdoor, $6/day. AE, DC, MC, V.

RESTAURANTS 🍴

🍷 Biba

2801 Capitol Ave (Midtown); tel 916/455-BIBA. At 28th St. **Italian.** Located in an 1853 tavern building. Stylish and modern, with extensive use of glass, mirrors, and wood, as well as black lacquer chairs, white tablecloths, and fresh flowers on each table. Grilled lamb chops, breast of duck, homemade gnocchi, variety of pastas. Extensive wine list. **FYI:** Reservations recommended. Piano. **Open:** Lunch Mon–Fri 11:30am–2:30pm; dinner Mon–Thurs 5:30–9:30pm, Fri–Sat 5:30–10:30pm. **Prices:** Main courses $16–$20. AE, MC, V. ♥ ⌂

California Fat's

In Old Sacramento State Historic Park, 1015 Front St; tel 916/441-7966. J St exit off I-5. **Eclectic.** The decor includes an in-house waterfall, granite-topped tables, and a neon Cadillac wall sculpture. The menu highlights wood-oven pizzas, speciality steaks, ribs, stir-fried entrees, and pasta. **FYI:** Reservations recommended. **Open:** Lunch Mon–Fri 11:30am–4pm; dinner Mon–Sat 5–10pm, Sun 4–9pm. **Prices:** Main courses $8–$20. AE, MC, V. ▮ ⌂

Capitol Grill

2730 N St (Midtown); tel 916/736-0744. N St exit off Business I-80. **Californian/International.** The look is rustic with brick, brass, wood beams, and 1950s-era political memorabilia. Specialties are duck and shiitake potstickers for starters; entrees include pork chops, grilled beef tenderloin, and many fresh fish dishes. Most sauces are freshly made. **FYI:** Reservations recommended. **Open:** Mon–Fri 11am–11pm, Sat 5–11pm, Sun 5–10pm. **Prices:** Main courses $7–$19. AE, CB, DC, DISC, MC, V. ⱽᴾ ⌂

Chanterelle

In the Sterling Hotel, 1300 H St (Downtown); tel 916/442-0451. J St exit off I-5 Restaurant entrance is at 13th St. **Californian.** An elegant restaurant with classical music and some separate rooms for intimate dining. The cuisine is Californian with a twist: potato strudel with sun-dried tomatoes, stuffed pork chops served with lingonberry, and a changing lineup of game and fish specials. Small lounge upstairs. **FYI:** Reservations recommended. **Open:** Breakfast Mon–Fri 7–9:30am; lunch Mon–Fri 11:30am–2pm; dinner daily 5:30–8:30pm; brunch Sun 8:30am–2pm. **Prices:** Main courses $13–$20. AE, MC, V. ♥ ▮ ⌂

David Berkley
In Pavilions Shopping Center, 515 Pavilions Lane; tel 916/929-4422. Howe Ave exit off US 50. **Californian/Deli.** Bustling gourmet deli/market/wine shop with upscale atmosphere, and choice of ethnic styles. Call ahead with your order, either to eat here or to go. Entrees not on the daily menu may be ordered with three days' notice. Features salads, soups, hot and cold sandwiches, cajun pasta, polenta salad, seafood gumbo, and more. Valet parking available. **FYI:** Reservations not accepted. Beer and wine only. **Open:** Mon–Fri 10am–6:30pm, Sat 10am–6pm, Sun 11am–5pm. **Prices:** Lunch main courses $10–$13. MC, V. [VP]

♥ The Firehouse
In Old Sacramento State Historic Park, 1112 2nd St; tel 916/442-4772. J St exit off I-5; follow signs to Old Sacramento; enter at 2nd St or alley between 2nd and Front Sts. **Californian/Continental.** This 19th-century firehouse is a local tradition that's popular with tourists as well as politicians. The brass fire pole still exists, now in the bar. Scallop ravioli, swordfish wasabi, and roast duck are just a few of the dishes. Desserts include berries with Grand Marnier, and bourbon chocolate almond pie. **FYI:** Reservations recommended. **Open:** Lunch Mon–Fri 11:30am–2:15pm; dinner Tues–Sat 5:30–10pm. **Prices:** Main courses $17–$20. AE, MC, V. ♥ ■ ♨ ♿

$ First Immigrant Café & Catering
In Sacramento Antiques Mall, 855 57th St (East Sacramento); tel 916/452-3896. Between J and H Sts. **Californian.** Well regarded by locals, this cafeteria-style restaurant offers off-the-beaten-path dining in a homey atmosphere. Features sandwiches, such as smoked turkey with green chili mayonnaise or Caribbean pita with black beans; plus salads like tarragon chicken and Caribbean black bean. Minestrone daily, plus a second soup that is always fat free. Catering for parties. **FYI:** Reservations accepted. No liquor license. **Open:** Lunch Tues–Fri 11am–2pm. Closed Dec 25–Jan 1. **Prices:** Lunch main courses $4–$7. AE. ♨ ♿

★ Fox and Goose Public House
1001 R St (Downtown); tel 916/443-8825. 5th St exit off I-80. **British/Pub.** Breakfast and lunch served in a friendly, rustic British-style pub, with imported beers on draft. Lunch menu: British pasties, Ploughman's lunch rarebit, salads, sandwiches, lemon curd tart. Breakfast: omelettes, waffles, sausage, kippers. Also vegetarian fare. **FYI:** Reservations not accepted. Blues/jazz/rock. Beer and wine only. **Open:** Mon–Thurs 7am–11pm, Fri–Sat 9am–1:30am, Sun 9am–1pm. **Prices:** Lunch main courses $3–$7. No CC. ♿

Fulton's Prime Rib
In Old Sacramento State Historic Park, 900 2nd St; tel 916/444-9641. J St exit off I-5 Follow signs to Old Sacramento parking. **Seafood/Steak.** Wood, brick, antiques, and a mounted deer's head lend a distinctive atmosphere to this dark but spacious dining room. There's also a brick patio with fountain. Specialties include prime rib, Mexican dishes, and

seafood, as well as children's selections. **FYI:** Reservations recommended. Piano. **Open:** Lunch daily 11am–3pm; dinner Mon–Fri 5–10pm, Sat 5–11pm, Sun 4–10pm. **Prices:** Main courses $10–$27. AE, CB, DC, MC, V. ■ ♨

Greta's Cafe
1831 Capitol Ave (Midtown); tel 916/442-7382. **Eclectic.** A casual downtown coffeehouse with lots of windows, original artwork, and eclectic music. An on-site bakery dishes up light breakfasts. The menu includes sandwiches, pizzas, focaccia, and quiches, all nicely prepared. Everything on the menu is available for take-out. **FYI:** Reservations not accepted. No liquor license. **Open:** Mon–Fri 6:30am–4pm, Sat–Sun 7:30am–4pm. **Prices:** Lunch main courses $3–$6. No CC. ♿

Jazzmen's Art of Pasta
In Old Sacramento State Historic Park, 1107 Firehouse Alley (Old Sacramento); tel 916/441-6726. J St exit off I-5. **Continental.** A restaurant offering an outdoor bar and dining, plus musical accompaniment. Pastas come with a choice of sauces; also served are imperial crab lasagna and chicken Florentine. **FYI:** Reservations recommended. Jazz. **Open:** Mon–Fri 11:30am–11pm, Sat 11:30am–11:30pm, Sun 11:30am–10pm. **Prices:** Main courses $12–$15. AE, CB, DC, DISC, MC, V. ♨ ♿

★ Lemon Grass Restaurant
601 Munroe St; tel 916/486-4891. **Thai/Vietnamese.** Fun and fresh Vietnamese and Thai cuisine in an enjoyable setting. Such traditional favorites as Bangkok beef and lemongrass chicken share the menu with nouvelle creations like Thai basil stir-fry. **FYI:** Reservations recommended. Additional locations: 2248 Stockton Blvd (tel 452-5816); Sunrise Mall, Citrus Heights (tel 961-6498). **Open:** Lunch Mon–Fri 11:30am–2pm; dinner Mon–Thurs 5:30–9pm, Fri–Sat 5–10pm, Sun 5–9pm. **Prices:** Main courses $9–$15. AE, DC, DISC, MC, V. ♿

Mace's
In Pavilions Shopping Center, 501 Pavilion Lane; tel 916/922-0222. Howe Ave exit off US 50. **New American.** Elegant dining room with marble inlaid floors, plants, zebra skins, African artifacts, fans, and rattan furniture. Menu features many pastas, plus regional American fare such as pot pies and smoked chicken salad. Other offerings include roast duck with orange-ginger glaze, herb-roasted lamb. Hosts social events, with dancing at the bar or on the patio. **FYI:** Reservations accepted. Jazz. **Open:** Mon–Fri 11:30am–10:30pm, Sat 11:30am–11pm, Sun 10am–9pm. **Prices:** Main courses $11–$20. AE, DC, MC, V. ♨ [VP] ♿

Paragary's Bar and Oven
1401 28th St (Midtown); tel 916/457-5737. J St exit off Business I-80 S or N St exit off Business I-80 N. **Californian/Italian.** A corner entrance leads to a nice long bar with small tables. There's also sidewalk dining. The menu lists chic pizza concoctions, rib-eye, pastas, salmon, and various salads. **FYI:** Reservations accepted. Jazz/rock. Additional locations: 2384

Fair Oaks Blvd (tel 485-7100); 705 Gold Lake Dr, Folsom (tel 985-6171). **Open:** Mon–Fri 11:30am–2am, Sat–Sun 5pm–2am. **Prices:** Main courses $9–$18. AE, CB, DC, DISC, MC, V. VP

★ **Rubicon Brewing Company**
2004 Capitol Ave; tel 916/448-7032. **Pub.** A gussied-up beer-brewing facility with big windows and spare furnishings. Menu lists onion soup, burgers, chef's salad, chicken fajitas, and other pub fare. Many microbrewed beers available. **FYI:** Reservations not accepted. Beer and wine only. **Open:** Mon–Thurs 11am–11:30pm, Fri 11am–12:30am, Sat 9am–12:30am, Sun 9am–10pm. **Prices:** Main courses $4–$6. AE, DC, MC, V. &

Tower Café
1518 Broadway (Tower District); tel 916/441-0222. **International/Vegetarian.** Located in a landmark building and decorated with art from around the world, this cafe attracts a very hip clientele. Menu features "jerk" chicken, vegetarian lasagna, ravioli, and hamburgers. Large selection of wine and beer. **FYI:** Reservations accepted. Beer and wine only. **Open:** Sun–Thurs 8am–11pm, Fri–Sat 8am–1am. **Prices:** Main courses $7–$13. AE, MC, V. ☎ &

Woody's
In Riverbank Marina, 1379 Garden Hwy; tel 916/924-3434. Garden Hwy exit off I-5. **New American.** Accents of turquoise and wood plus both real and painted palm trees befit this riverside restaurant, where tropical drinks and beers are served under shady oaks. Appetizers are bar food items like cheese sticks and fried calamari. Menu includes burgers in various guises, as well as offbeat salads. **FYI:** Reservations recommended. Children's menu. **Open:** Mon–Fri 11am–10pm, Sat 11am–11pm, Sun 9:30am–11pm. **Prices:** Main courses $5–$13. AE, DC, DISC, MC, V. ☎ ▲ VP &

ATTRACTIONS 🏛

California State Capitol
10th St, between N and L Sts; tel 916/324-0333. The dome-topped California state capitol, completed in 1874, is Sacramento's most distinctive landmark. Daily guided tours examine both the building's architecture and the workings of government. Tours are offered Mon–Fri 9am–4pm and Sat–Sun 10am–4pm, every hour on the hour. Pick up tickets at Room B-27 (in the north wing, basement level). **Open:** Daily 9am–5pm. **Free**

Governor's Mansion
16th and H Sts; tel 916/323-3047. From 1903 to 1967, this Victorian-Gothic structure was the official residence of the governor of California. Thirteen of the state's governors resided in the house during their terms. Hour-long guided tours are offered on the hour. **Open:** Daily 10am–5pm. **$**

Old Sacramento
Tel 916/443-7815. Four square blocks at the "foot" of downtown Sacramento contain the greatest concentration of historical buildings in California. Free guided tours are offered in the spring, summer, and fall. Call 916/324-0040 for more information.

California State Railroad Museum
111 1st St; tel 916/448-4466. More than 20 actual locomotives and rail cars are on display at this facility, along with a vast collection of artifacts that covers almost every aspect of the railroading industry. A film on the history of Western railroading is also shown. **Open:** Daily 10am–5pm. **$$**

Discovery Museum
101 I St; tel 916/264-7057. Officially known as the Sacramento Museum of History, Science and Technology, this museum was created by the merger of the Sacramento Museum of History and the Sacramento Science Center. Five galleries showcase permanent and traveling exhibits on a wide variety of science- and history-related topics. The Learning Resource Center (formerly the Science Center) features the only planetarium in the region; it is located at 3615 Auburn Blvd. **Open:** Tues–Fri 10am–5pm, Sat–Sun noon–5pm. **$$**

State Indian Museum
2618 K St; tel 916/324-0971. Located on the same block as Sutter's Fort (see below), the Indian Museum reflects the culture and traditions of the Native Americans of California. Tribal elders helped select the objects and photographs on display, and many Native Americans donated personal items to the collection. Movies and slide shows are presented on weekends. **Open:** Daily 10am–5pm. **$**

Sutter's Fort State Historic Park
2701 L St; tel 916/445-4209. Swiss immigrant John Augustus Sutter established a settlement called "New Helvetia" in this area in 1839. With a small party of settlers and friendly local natives, Sutter built a fort of sun-dried adobe bricks on a small knoll near the confluence of the Sacramento and American Rivers.

An accurate reconstruction of the fort was begun in 1891, making this the nation's oldest reconstructed historic fort. In 1947, it became part of the California State Park System. Craft demonstrations and living history programs represent life at the fort as it was in the 1840s. The Trade Store stocks period items, including toys, games, clothing, jewelry, and blankets. **Open:** Daily 10am–5pm. **$$**

Crocker Art Museum
216 O St; tel 916/264-5423. The oldest art museum in the West, the museum is known for its spectacular Victorian architechture, the early California painting collection, Old Master drawings, European art, and contemporary California art. The exterior of the Crocker Mansion Wing is a re-creation of the Crocker home; inside, the galleries hold works by northern California artists from the 1960s to the present. Third Thursday Jazz, First Thursday Art Talks, and Saturday Hands-On Art Activities. Gift store. **Open:** Wed–Sun 10am–5pm, Thurs 10am–9pm. **$$**

Towe Ford Museum of Automotive History
2200 Front St; tel 916/442-6802. One of the world's most comprehensive collections of antique Fords. About 170 vehicles represent nearly every Ford manufactured between 1903 and 1953, including a rare 1904 Model B touring car. Other makes and some trucks are also on display. Changing exhibits; special events. Gift shop. **Open:** Daily 10am–6pm. **$$**

Blue Diamond Growers Video and Visitors Center
1701 C St; tel 916/446-8409. This is the world's largest almond-packaging plant, with a visitors center and gift shop presenting a 25-minute video describing how almonds are processed from tree to table. Free samples offered. **Open:** Mon–Fri 10am–5pm, Sat 10am–4pm. **Free**

Waterworld USA
1600 Exposition Blvd; tel 916/924-0556 or 924-3747. Large recreational water theme park featuring wave pool, river tube ride, wading pool, children's area, and 10 water slides. **Open:** Mem Day–Labor Day, daily 10:30am. Closing hours vary. **$$$$**

Spirit of Sacramento **Historic Paddlewheeler**
110 L St; tel 916/552-2933 or toll free 800/433-0263. One-hour narrated sightseeing trips aboard a 110-foot paddlewheeler built in 1942. Sold to actor John Wayne in 1954, the vessel appeared in his film *Blood Alley*. Also dining, cocktail, and murder mystery cruises (phone for details). **Open:** Peak (June–Aug) departures Wed–Sun 1:30 and 3pm. Reduced hours off-season. **$$$$**

St Helena

Originally settled by German, Italian, and Swiss farm families, St Helena has become the center of sophistication in the Napa Valley. In addition to offering upscale shopping and other attractions, St Helena is the jumping-off point for surrounding winery tours and tastings. **Information:** St Helena Chamber of Commerce, 1080 Main St, PO Box 124, St Helena 94574 (tel 707/963-4456).

HOTELS 🖼

≣≣≣ Harvest Inn
1 Main St, 94574; tel 707/963-9463 or toll free 800/950-8466; fax 707/963-4402. On CA 29, S of downtown. 22 acres. Quiet lodging among gardens and overlooking vineyards, yet with easy access to restaurants and touring. The English Tudor–style design is rather incongruous for this region. **Rooms:** 54 rms and stes; 15 cottages/villas. CI 4pm/CO 11am. Nonsmoking rms avail. Large, comfortable rooms with lots of extras, such as wet bars and separate vanities. **Amenities:** 🛅 🖄 🖭 🢢 A/C, cable TV w/movies, refrig. Some units w/terraces, some w/fireplaces, some w/whirlpools. **Services:** ⌲ ⋫ Masseur, babysitting. **Facilities:** 🛗 🔢 🕹 1 bar (w/entertainment), whirlpool. **Rates (BB):** Peak (May–

Oct) $139–$200 S or D; $210–$325 ste; $139–$200 cottage/villa. Extra person $20. Min stay wknds. Lower rates off-season. Parking: Outdoor, free. Dinner, wine, and other packages available. AE, DC, DISC, MC, V.

≣≣≣ Inn at Southbridge
1020 Main St, 94574; tel 707/967-9400 or toll free 800/520-6800; fax 707/967-9486. Downtown. Built around a courtyard, this new hotel enjoys an excellent location near wineries, restaurants (Tra Vigne is next door), and the town of St Helena. Soft olive and earth tones give a peaceful air. Operated by Meadowood Resort. **Rooms:** 21 rms and stes. CI 4pm/CO noon. Nonsmoking rms avail. Rooms have vaulted ceilings, fireplaces, and down comforters. French doors open onto private balconies affording views of the courtyard, foothills, and St Helena. **Amenities:** 🛅 🖄 🖭 🢢 A/C, cable TV w/movies, refrig, dataport, VCR, voice mail, in-rm safe, bathrobes. All units w/minibars, some w/terraces, all w/fireplaces. **Services:** ✕ 🗝 VP 🖄 ⌲ Twice-daily maid svce, babysitting. **Facilities:** 🔢 🕹 The new restaurant, Tomatina, is run by Michael Chiarello, the celebrated chef of Tra Vigne. Guest privileges (for a fee) at Meadowood's pool, fitness center, golf, tennis, croquet, and spa facilities. **Rates (CP):** Peak (Apr–mid-Nov) $225–$255 S or D; $275 ste. Children under age 18 stay free. Min stay peak, wknds, and special events. Lower rates off-season. Parking: Outdoor, free. AE, CB, DC, DISC, MC, V.

MOTEL

≣≣ El Bonita Motel
195 Main St, 94574; tel 707/963-3216 or toll free 800/541-3284; fax 707/963-8838. Excellent location in the heart of Napa Valley. Pleasant outdoor lounge and sunbathing area set in lush gardens. **Rooms:** 41 rms and stes. CI 2pm/CO 11:30am. Nonsmoking rms avail. Clean, attractive, spacious. **Amenities:** 🛅 🖄 🖭 A/C, cable TV, refrig. **Services:** ⌲ ⋫ Masseur, babysitting. **Facilities:** 🛗 🔢 🕹 Sauna, whirlpool. **Rates:** Peak (June–Sept) $59–$130 S or D; $100–$185 ste. Extra person $8. Min stay wknds. Lower rates off-season. Parking: Outdoor, free. AE, DC, DISC, MC, V.

INNS

≣≣ Hotel St Helena
1309 Main St, 94574 (Downtown); tel 707/963-4388; fax 707/965-5402. This 115-year-old Victorian hotel is loaded with antiques. Located in the heart of town near shops and restaurants. **Rooms:** 18 rms and stes (4 w/shared bath). CI 3pm/CO noon. Rooms feature four-poster beds, armoires, and clawfoot tubs. **Amenities:** 🛅 🖄 No A/C or TV. 4 rooms have TV. **Services:** ⌲ Wine/sherry served. **Facilities:** 1 bar, guest lounge w/TV. Wine bar. **Rates:** Peak (Feb 15–Nov 10) $110 S or D w/shared bath, $130–$160 S or D w/private bath; $160–$250 ste. Extra person $20. Min stay special events. Lower rates off-season. Parking: Outdoor, free. AE, CB, DC, DISC, JCB, MC, V.

≡≡≡ Vineyard Country Inn

201 Main St, 94574; tel 707/963-1000; fax 707/963-1794. Pleasant grounds with lovely gardens and walkways. **Rooms:** 21 stes. CI 3pm/CO 11am. Nonsmoking rms avail. Spacious two-room units. **Amenities:** 🛍 🐧 A/C, cable TV, refrig. All units w/terraces, all w/fireplaces. All units have wet bar. **Services:** 🛎 Babysitting. Expanded continental breakfast offered. **Facilities:** 🔂 🔟 🔥 Whirlpool. **Rates:** Peak (May 15–Nov 14) $185 ste. Extra person $10. Children under age 5 stay free. Min stay wknds. Lower rates off-season. Parking: Outdoor, free. AE, DC, MC, V.

≡≡≡ Wine Country Inn

1152 Lodi Lane, 94574; tel 707/963-7077 or toll free 800/473-3463; fax 707/963-9018. Lodi Lane exit off CA 29. 10 acres. Comfortable and homelike with country antiques. Tranquil, rural setting with spectacular views of the hills from many rooms. **Rooms:** 24 rms and stes. CI 2pm/CO noon. No smoking. Individually decorated. **Amenities:** 🛍 🐧 🔲 A/C, refrig, CD/tape player, bathrobes. No TV. Some units w/terraces, some w/fireplaces, some w/whirlpools. **Services:** Masseur, babysitting, afternoon tea served. **Facilities:** 🔂 🔥 Whirlpool, guest lounge. Outdoor pool and spa enjoy fantastic hillside vistas. **Rates (BB):** Peak (May–Nov) $125–$248 S or D; $215 ste. Extra person $20. Children under age 6 stay free. Lower rates off-season. Parking: Outdoor, free. Closed Christmas time. MC, V.

LODGE

≡ White Sulphur Springs Resort & Spa

3100 White Sulphur Springs Rd, 94574; tel 707/963-8588 or toll free 800/593-8873; fax 707/963-2890. 2 mi W of St Helena. Spring St exit off CA 29. Secluded, very basic but clean country lodge and spa. Founded in 1852 as California's first hot-springs resort, it has a beautiful setting amid redwoods, fir, and madrone. **Rooms:** 28 rms and effic; 9 cottages/villas. CI 3pm/CO 11am. No smoking. Three types of accommodations available. Creekside Cottages are the largest, with some offering wood-burning stoves and kitchenettes. Lodgings also available in the inn and the Carriage House; several rooms share bath, and quarters are small. **Amenities:** No A/C, phone, or TV. Some units w/terraces. **Services:** 🛎 Masseur, babysitting. Full spa services include herbal wraps and volcanic-mud wraps. **Facilities:** 🔂 🚲 🔟 Lawn games, spa, whirlpool. Natural mineral pool. **Rates (BB):** $75–$95 S or D; $125–$165 cottage/villa. Extra person $15. Parking: Outdoor, free. Group packages available. MC, V.

RESORT

≡≡≡≡ Meadowood Resort Hotel

900 Meadowood Lane, 94574; tel 707/963-3646 or toll free 800/458-8080; fax 707/963-3532. Silverado Trail to Howell Rd. 250 acres. Set in a lush, hidden valley. Feels like a residential estate, with wood-frame cottages tucked around the property. A private club as well as a hotel. **Rooms:**. CI 4pm/CO noon. Nonsmoking rms avail. Cottages have white-trimmed windows, wainscoting, and peaked roofs. Huge decks are positioned for maximum privacy. **Amenities:** 🛍 🐧 🔲 🍴 A/C, cable TV, refrig, bathrobes. All units w/minibars, all w/terraces, some w/fireplaces. Complimentary wine tastings on Friday nights. **Services:** ✗ 🔌 🖼 🛎 Twice-daily maid svce, masseur, babysitting. **Facilities:** 🔂 🚲 🏹₉ 🎾 ⛳₈ 🛶 🏊₂₀₀ 🖥 🔥 2 restaurants (see "Restaurants" below), 2 bars, spa, sauna, steam rm, whirlpool, playground. There are two regulation croquet lawns. The three-mile hiking trail winds past madrone and redwoods. **Rates:** Peak (June–mid-Nov) $325–$445 S or D; $500–$1,875 ste. Extra person $25. Children under age 12 stay free. Min stay wknds. Lower rates off-season. Parking: Outdoor, free. Recreation (golf, tennis, croquet) and spa packages available. AE, CB, DC, DISC, MC, V.

RESTAURANTS 🍴

Brava Terrace

3010 St Helena Hwy N; tel 707/963-9300. **New American.** Casual and comfortable, featuring a large flagstone fireplace and an attractive outdoor courtyard with fountain and flowers. The menu offers risottos and pastas as well as roast chicken, cassoulet, and grilled pork tenderloin. **FYI:** Reservations recommended. **Open:** Peak (May–Oct) daily noon–9pm. Closed ten days in Jan. **Prices:** Main courses $8–$19. AE, DC, DISC, MC, V. 🍷 🖼 🔥

Pinot Blanc

641 Main St (CA 29); tel 707/963-6191. Just south of town. **French Bistro.** The latest project of superchef Joachim Splichal, the guiding light behind Patina and other top eateries in the LA area. Edged by wainscoting, the warm and welcoming interior offers both tables and banquettes; in nice weather, there's seating on the patio screened by a pergola. Local produce stars on the menu, from bistro fare such as spring leg of lamb with Napa Valley grapes and olives to potato ravioli with braised escarole, red onion, and quail. Tasting menus available, if you just can't decide. **FYI:** Reservations accepted. Children's menu. Beer and wine only. **Open:** Daily 11:30am–10pm. **Prices:** Main courses $8–$20. AE, CB, DC, DISC, MC, V. 🍷 🔥

The Restaurant at Meadowood

In Meadowood Resort Hotel, 900 Meadowood Lane; tel 707/963-3646. Silverado Trail to Howell Mt Rd; go east 500 ft; left on Meadowood Lane. **Californian/French.** Tapestry-backed chairs and high-beamed ceiling. Cuisine is described as "Napa Valley Provençale." Main courses might include baked squab with caramelized endive, or crispy salmon with marinated tomatoes. Extensive 600-entry wine list. **FYI:** Reservations recommended. Jacket required. **Open:** Dinner daily 6–10pm; brunch Sun 10:30am–2:30pm. **Prices:** Main courses $37–$48. AE, CB, DC, DISC, MC, V. 🔥

Showley's at Miramonte
In Miramonte Inn, 1327 Railroad Ave; tel 707/963-1200. 1 block E of Main St between Hunt and Adams Sts. **Eclectic.** The feel of a historic country inn, complete with ceiling fans and original art; tables are decorated with seasonal fruits and vegetables. Patio dining in the shade of a huge tree. Eclectic cuisine includes Hawaiian albacore with plum salsa and polenta, shrimp brochettes with chicken sausage, fresh porcini and mango-corn salsa, and braised lamb shanks with garlic mashed potatoes. Menu changes daily. **FYI:** Reservations recommended. Jazz. Children's menu. Dress code. Beer and wine only. **Open:** Lunch Tues–Sun 11:30am–3pm; dinner Tues–Sun 6–9pm. Closed Nov 28–Dec 15. **Prices:** Main courses $14–$19. AE, DISC, MC, V. ♥ ⅙

♥ Terra
1345 Railroad Ave; tel 707/963-8931. Adams St exit off CA 29. **Eclectic.** East meets West in the refined cuisine of Lissa Doumani (pastry chef) and her husband, Hiro Sone (chef), both alumni of Wolfgang Puck's kitchen at Spago. Located in a historic 1880 stone building, Terra manages to seem both avant-garde and countrified at the same time. The menu globetrots from a lamb and artichoke daube with polenta to a broiled, sake-marinated sea bass with shrimp dumplings. Desserts include a fine tiramisù. **FYI:** Reservations recommended. Dress code. Beer and wine only. **Open:** Sun–Mon 6–9:30pm, Wed–Thurs 6–9:30pm, Fri–Sat 6–10pm. Closed Jan 1–Jan 14. **Prices:** Main courses $14–$23. CB, DC, MC, V. ♥

⑤ Tomatina
In the Inn at Southbridge, 1016 Main St (CA 29); tel 707/967-9999. **Pizza/Pasta.** "Relax—it's just a pizza joint" says the sign at the entrance. But with chef/partner Michael Chiarello of top-ranked Tra Vigne as its creator, Tomatina puts a very gourmet spin on the humble pie. Savory thin-crusted pizzas from the wood-fired oven come with choice of 16 toppings, like pepperoni (made on the premises), roasted eggplant, and baby spinach ($8 for six slices; $13 for 12 slices). Complete dinners for four range from $45 to $60, and the entire excellent wine selection is priced at $17 for any bottle; $3.50 for any glass. **FYI:** Reservations not accepted. Children's menu. Beer and wine only. **Open:** Daily 11:30am–10pm. **Prices:** Main courses $6–$20. DISC, MC, V. ⚓ ▦ ⅙

♥ Tra Vigne Restaurant & Cantinetta
1050 Charter Oak Ave; tel 707/963-4444. E off CA 29. **Italian/Mediterranean.** Food keeps getting better and better at this splendid restaurant. Design is "trattoria moderna," with 30-foot ceilings, vintage posters, and beaded lamps. In fine weather, call ahead to request a patio table. In addition to imaginative pizzas and smoked meats, the changing menu from star chef Michael Chiarello might feature oak-roasted chicken, or pasta with seafood. The adjoining Cantinetta serves light Italian fare. **FYI:** Reservations recommended. **Open:** Daily 11:30am–10pm. **Prices:** Main courses $8–$20. CB, DC, DISC, MC, V. ⚓ ⅙

Trilogy
1234 Main St; tel 707/963-5507. **French.** Intimate dining room with ceiling fans, brass chandeliers, and original artwork. Prix-fixe menu changes daily. Among the specialties are grilled boneless quail and Asian green-tea-noodle salad with soy-sesame-ginger vinaigrette, pan-roasted pork tenderloin with roasted garlic and rosemary jus, and roasted rack of lamb with toasted cumin and oven-dried tomatoes. **FYI:** Reservations recommended. Beer and wine only. **Open:** Lunch Tues–Fri noon–2pm; dinner Tues–Sat 6–9pm. Closed one week in mid–Dec. **Prices:** Main courses $15–$20; prix fixe $32–$48. MC, V. ♥ ⅙

♥ Wine Spectator Greystone Restaurant
In Culinary Institute of America, 2555 Main St (CA 29); tel 707/967-1010. 1 mi N of town. **Mediterranean.** Located within the thick rock walls of Greystone Cellars (built in 1888), this is the gastronomic showpiece for the legendary Culinary Institute of America. (The staff of professional chefs is assisted by three to four Institute students.) Mellow stone walls counterpoint the furnishings in bright, Mediterranean colors like ultramarine, sienna, and sunflower yellow. The menu looks to the sunny side too, offering Mediterranean style dishes ranging from lamb-and-eggplant moussaka cannelloni to tagine of salmon with preserved lemons and couscous. Guests may choose to sample the cold and hot tapas, which are savory and filling enough to make a meal by themselves. The fabulous, in-depth wine list was put together by *Wine Spectator* magazine. **FYI:** Reservations recommended. Dress code. **Open:** Lunch Wed–Mon 11:30am–2:45pm; dinner Wed–Mon 5:30–9pm. **Prices:** Main courses $16–$18. AE, CB, DC, MC, V. ♥ ▦ ⅙

ATTRACTIONS 🏛

Silverado Museum
1490 Library Lane; tel 707/963-3757. Devoted to the life and works of Robert Louis Stevenson, this museum contains more than 8,000 items, including original manuscripts, letters, photographs, and the desk Stevenson used in Samoa. The writer honeymooned in the area in 1880, lodging in an abandoned Silverado Mine bunk house. **Open:** Tues–Sun noon–4pm. **Free**

Beringer Vineyards
2000 Main St (CA 29); tel 707/963-7115. The oldest continuously operating winery in the Napa Valley, Beringer Vineyards was founded in 1876. Tours cover various aspects of winemaking and include the hand-dug 19th-century cellaring tunnels that were part of the original winery; the Queen Anne Victorian–style Rhine House (1883); and the 1930s art deco Bottling Room. Free tastings are offered at the Rhine House and the Bottling Room. **Open:** Daily 9:30am–5pm. **Free**

Salinas

The agricultural town of Salinas has been called "The Salad Bowl of the Nation." Salinas celebrates the legacy of its most famous native son every August with the Steinbeck Festival. In late July, it holds the California Rodeo, the biggest in the state. **Information:** Salinas Area Chamber of Commerce, 119 E Alisal St, PO Box 1170, Salinas 93902 (tel 408/424-7611).

MOTELS

≣ Laurel Inn

801 W Laurel Dr, 93906; tel 408/449-2474 or toll free 800/354-9831; fax 408/449-2476. Laurel exit off CA 1. Close to the freeway, with minimal landscaping. **Rooms:** 146 rms and stes. CI noon/CO noon. Nonsmoking rms avail. Comfortable rooms. **Amenities:** A/C, cable TV w/movies. 1 unit w/minibar, some w/terraces, some w/fireplaces. **Services:** ▵ ⌇ **Facilities:** ⌂ 25 ও 1 restaurant, 1 bar, sauna, whirlpool. **Rates:** Peak (May–Sept) $48–$85 S; $58–$90 D; $84–$120 ste. Extra person $6. Min stay wknds and special events. Lower rates off-season. Parking: Outdoor, free. AE, CB, DC, DISC, MC, V.

≣ Vagabond Inn

131 Kern St, 93905; tel 408/758-4693 or toll free 800/522-1555; fax 408/758-9835. Market St exit off US 101. Tidy and clean. **Rooms:** 70 rms. CI 2pm/CO noon. No smoking. **Amenities:** A/C, cable TV. **Services:** ⌇ ⌇ **Facilities:** ⌂ ও 1 restaurant, 1 bar. **Rates (CP):** Peak (Apr–Sept) $45–$64 S; $64–$80 D. Extra person $5. Children under age 18 stay free. Min stay special events. Lower rates off-season. Parking: Outdoor, free. AE, CB, DC, DISC, MC, V.

San Bernardino

This large and low-key city was settled by Mormans in the 1850s. The center of a thriving, rapidly expanding metropolitan area that includes Riverside and Ontario, it is the gateway to a number of scenic areas including the San Bernardino National Forest, Lake Arrowhead, Big Bear Lake, and the breathtaking Rim of the World Drive. **Information:** San Bernardino Area Chamber of Commerce, 546 W 6th St, PO Box 658, San Bernardino 92402 (tel 909/885-7515).

HOTELS

≣≣≣ Radisson Hotel San Bernardino Convention Center

295 North E St, 92401; tel 909/381-6181 or toll free 800/333-3333; fax 909/381-5288. 2nd St E exit off I-215; left on E St. The only full-service convention hotel in downtown San Bernardino; very modern building with a welcoming staff. Excellent service. **Rooms:** 233 rms and stes. CI 3pm/CO noon. Nonsmoking rms avail. **Amenities:** A/C, cable TV w/movies. **Services:** X VP ⌂ ▵ ⌇ ⌇ Car-rental desk.

Pets allowed with $20 deposit. **Facilities:** ⌐ 1300 ও 1 restaurant (see "Restaurants" below), 2 bars (1 w/entertainment), whirlpool. **Rates (BB):** $90 S; $100 D; $150–$270 ste. Extra person $10. Children under age 18 stay free. Parking: Indoor, free. AE, CB, DC, DISC, JCB, MC, V.

≣≣≣ San Bernardino Hilton

285 E Hospitality Lane, 92408; tel 909/889-0133 or toll free 800/HILTONS, 800/446-1065 in CA; fax 909/381-4299. Waterman Ave N exit off I-10; W on Hospitality Lane. Fine service and facilities suitable for business travelers and families. **Rooms:** 250 rms and stes. CI 3pm/CO noon. Nonsmoking rms avail. **Amenities:** A/C, cable TV w/movies. Some units w/whirlpools. **Services:** X ▵ ⌇ ⌇ Car-rental desk, babysitting. **Facilities:** ⌂ 600 ও 1 restaurant, 1 bar, whirlpool. **Rates:** $80–$115 S; $80–$130 D; $125–$375 ste. Extra person $10. Children under age 18 stay free. Parking: Outdoor, free. AE, CB, DC, DISC, JCB, MC, V.

MOTELS

≣ E-Z 8 Motel

1750 S Waterman Ave, 92408; tel 909/888-4827 or toll free 800/326-6835. Waterman Ave exit off I-10. Generously sized rooms at very good rates. **Rooms:** 119 rms. CI 11am/CO 11am. Nonsmoking rms avail. **Amenities:** A/C, cable TV w/movies. **Services:** ⌇ ⌇ **Facilities:** ⌂ ও Games rm, whirlpool, washer/dryer. **Rates:** $29 S; $37 D. Extra person $5. Children under age 13 stay free. Parking: Outdoor, free. AE, CB, DC, DISC, MC, V.

≣≣≣ La Quinta Inn

205 E Hospitality Lane, 92408; tel 909/888-7571 or toll free 800/531-5900; fax 909/884-3864. Waterman Ave N exit off I-10; W on Hospitality Lane. This chain is a favorite of business travelers. The southwestern architecture and friendly staff at this franchise will also appeal to families. **Rooms:** 151 rms. CI 3pm/CO noon. Nonsmoking rms avail. **Amenities:** A/C, cable TV w/movies. **Services:** ▵ ⌇ ⌇ Fax available. **Facilities:** ⌂ 35 ও Free access to two nearby health clubs. Restaurants within walking distance. **Rates (CP):** $54–$59 S; $62–$67 D. Extra person $5. Children under age 18 stay free. Parking: Outdoor, free. AE, DC, DISC, MC, V.

≣≣≣ Ramada Inn

2000 Ostrems Way, 92407; tel 909/887-3001 or toll free 800/809-1361; fax 909/880-3792. University Pkwy W exit off I-215; left at Hallmark; right at Ostrems. This hotel, built in 1990 and located near Cal State–San Bernardino, is comfortable and well run by a highly professional staff. **Rooms:** 114 rms and stes. CI 3pm/CO noon. Nonsmoking rms avail. **Amenities:** A/C, cable TV w/movies. Some units w/terraces. **Services:** X ☎ ▵ ⌇ Car-rental desk. **Facilities:** ⌂ 100 ও 1 restaurant (bkfst only), 1 bar (w/entertainment), whirlpool. **Rates (CP):** $59 S; $69 D; $79–$99 ste. Extra person $10. Children under age 18 stay free. Parking: Indoor/outdoor, free. AE, DC, DISC, MC, V.

≝ **Super 8 Lodge**
294 E Hospitality Lane, 92408; tel 909/381-1681 or toll free 800/800-8000; fax 909/888-5120. Waterman N exit off I-10; left at Hospitality Lane. Nicely run property with friendly, helpful staff. Many restaurants within walking distance. **Rooms:** 81 rms and stes. CI 2pm/CO 11am. Nonsmoking rms avail. **Amenities:** ☎ A/C, cable TV. **Services:** ⊠ **Facilities:** ⚐ Whirlpool. **Rates:** $57 S; $61–$64 D; $72 ste. Extra person $2. Parking: Outdoor, free. AE, CB, DC, DISC, MC, V.

RESTAURANTS ⑪

El Torito
118 E Hospitality Lane; tel 909/381-2316. **Mexican.** Nicely designed contemporary restaurant with a Mexican motif. Typical Mexican fare of tacos, enchiladas, and fajitas, all attractively presented. Popular Sunday brunch. **FYI:** Reservations accepted. Children's menu. **Open:** Lunch Mon–Sat 11am–3pm; dinner Mon–Thurs 3–11pm, Fri–Sat 3pm–midnight, Sun 2–10pm; brunch Sun 9am–2pm. **Prices:** Main courses $6–$12. AE, DC, DISC, MC, V. 🍴 ⚐

Spencer's Restaurant
In the Radisson Hotel, 295 North E St (Downtown); tel 909/381-6181. 2nd St E exit off I-215. **Californian.** A nice, informal dining room of pastel colors with an art deco motif. Special menu items include baked salmon florentine, chicken Oscar, and filet mignon. **FYI:** Reservations recommended. Blues. Children's menu. Dress code. Beer and wine only. **Open:** Breakfast Mon–Fri 6:30–9:30am, Sat–Sun 7–10am; lunch Mon–Fri 11:30am–2pm, Sat 11am–2pm; dinner daily 5–10pm; brunch Sun 10am–2pm. **Prices:** Main courses $10–$18. AE, CB, DC, DISC, MC, V. 🆅🅿 ⚐

San Bruno

See San Francisco Int'l Airport

San Clemente

Quiet, unassuming, but very picturesque, San Clemente is perched on the southern edge of Orange County and boasts clean, undeveloped, and crowd-free beaches. Former President Richard Nixon maintained a summer residence here. **Information:** San Clemente Chamber of Commerce, 1100 N El Camino Real, San Clemente 92672 (tel 714/492-1131).

HOTEL 🏨

≝≝ **Quality Suites**
2481 S El Camino Real, 92672; tel 714/366-1000 or toll free 800/772-3555; fax 714/366-1030. El Camino Real exit off I-5. Located near the ocean, the property has scenic views but is still convenient to town. Suitable for families. **Rooms:** 66 stes. CI 2pm/CO noon. Nonsmoking rms avail. **Amenities:** ☎

⚐ A/C, cable TV w/movies, refrig, VCR. Some units w/terraces, some w/whirlpools. Microwaves. **Services:** ⊠ Babysitting. **Facilities:** ⚐ 🍴 ☐55 ⚐ 1 bar, whirlpool. **Rates (BB):** Peak (June 15–Sept 15) $69 ste. Extra person $10. Children under age 7 stay free. Min stay special events. Lower rates off-season. Parking: Indoor/outdoor, free. AE, DISC, MC, V.

MOTEL

≝ **San Clemente Beach Travelodge**
2441 S El Camino Real, 92672; tel 714/498-5954 or toll free 800/843-1706; fax 714/498-6657. El Camino Real exit off I-5. Very plain older building, yet well maintained. **Rooms:** 23 rms and stes. CI 1pm/CO 11am. Nonsmoking rms avail. Small, but bright and airy. **Amenities:** ☎ ⚐ 🗖 A/C, cable TV w/movies, refrig. Some units w/terraces, some w/whirlpools. **Services:** �। 🍴 **Facilities:** ⚐ **Rates:** Peak (May 15–Sept) $49–$59 S; $49–$89 D; $89–$125 ste. Extra person $4. Children under age 17 stay free. Lower rates off-season. Parking: Indoor/outdoor, free. AE, DC, DISC, MC, V.

San Diego

See also Chula Vista, Coronado, La Jolla, Rancho Santa Fe

Although a good-sized metropolis by any standard, as well as one of the fastest-growing cities in America, San Diego still retains its slow-paced, beach-town ambience. San Diego is in fact geographically different from the rest of Southern California, with alpine hills just inland, great beaches, gentle bays, and some of the best weather in the country. Worthwhile attractions (and there are many) include Balboa Park, Mission Bay and Sea World, Old Town, and the Maritime Museum. **Information:** San Diego Convention & Visitors Bureau, 401 B #1400, San Diego 92101 (tel 619/232-3101).

PUBLIC TRANSPORTATION

The **San Diego Metropolitan Transit System (MTS)** operates citywide bus service and the **San Diego Trolley** (tel 619/231-8549), which runs to the Mexican border. The system's Transit Store, 449 Broadway (tel 619/234-1060), is a complete public transportation information center, supplying travelers with passes, tokens, timetables, maps, and brochures. Also call 619/233-3004 for bus route information. The $5 Day Tripper pass allows for one day of unlimited rides on the MTS; visitors can also get a four-day pass for $15.

HOTELS 🏨

≝≝≝ **The Bay Club Hotel & Marina**
2131 Shelter Island Dr, 92106 (Shelter Island); tel 619/224-8888 or toll free 800/672-0800; fax 619/225-1604. 6 mi W of downtown. Rosecrans St exit off I-5. Set in the middle of Shelter Island. Cozy sitting area has sofas in front of a fireplace. The lobby is inviting with a large skylight and grand piano. **Rooms:** 105 rms and stes. CI 4pm/CO noon. Non-

smoking rms avail. Pristine furnishings in bright, airy rooms with beautiful marina and bay views. **Amenities:** A/C, cable TV, refrig. All units w/terraces. **Services:** Babysitting. Very helpful, eager staff. **Facilities:** 1 restaurant, 1 bar, whirlpool, washer/dryer. Restaurant overlooks the marina; so does the pool, which is surrounded by palm trees and lounge chairs. **Rates (BB):** $100–$140 S; $110–$150 D; $265 ste. Extra person $10. Children under age 12 stay free. Min stay special events. Parking: Indoor/outdoor, free. AE, CB, DC, DISC, ER, JCB, MC, V.

Best Western Bayside Inn
555 W Ash St, 92101 (Downtown); tel 619/233-7500 or toll free 800/341-1818; fax 619/239-8060. At Columbia St. Located in a quiet part of downtown, just a few blocks from the water. The lobby feels like a greenhouse, with lots of light and large windows. **Rooms:** 122 rms. CI 2pm/CO noon. Nonsmoking rms avail. Rooms are pleasant but not particularly inviting; each has a city or water view. **Amenities:** A/C, cable TV w/movies. All units w/terraces. **Services:** Babysitting. **Facilities:** 1 restaurant, 1 bar, whirlpool. The pool area needs renovation, and is surrounded by buildings, so it gets little sun. **Rates (CP):** Peak (July–Labor Day) $85–$105 S; $95–$115 D. Extra person $8. Children under age 12 stay free. Lower rates off-season. Parking: Indoor, free. AE, CB, DC, DISC, JCB, MC, V.

Best Western Hacienda Hotel
4041 Harney St, 92110 (Old Town); tel 619/298-4707 or toll free 800/888-1991; fax 619/298-4771. 3 mi NW of downtown. Old Town Ave exit off I-5; take Old Town Ave to San Diego Ave, turn north to Harney St. Attractive, well-located hotel in the Spanish colonial style. Pleasant atmosphere with lots of plants, informal patios, Mexican tile roof. **Rooms:** 149 rms. CI 3pm/CO noon. Nonsmoking rms avail. Rooms have wooden shutters and bathrooms with quarry tile floors. **Amenities:** A/C, cable TV, refrig, VCR. Some units w/terraces. All rooms equipped with microwaves. **Services:** Car-rental desk, babysitting. Complimentary beer, wine, soft drinks, and margaritas Monday–Thursday, 6–7pm. **Facilities:** 1 restaurant, 1 bar, whirlpool, washer/dryer. Mexican restaurant and cantina. **Rates:** Peak (July–Aug) $109–$119 S or D. Extra person $10. Children under age 16 stay free. Lower rates off-season. Parking: Indoor/outdoor, free. Good value. AE, CB, DC, DISC, ER, MC, V.

Best Western Hanalei Hotel
2270 Hotel Circle N, 92108 (Hotel Circle); tel 619/297-1101 or toll free 800/882-0858; fax 619/297-6049. 4 mi N of downtown. Hotel Circle exit off I-8. Ignore the misleading, dated sign out front—the accommodations are more than adequate. **Rooms:** 416 rms and stes. CI 4pm/CO noon. No smoking. Some rooms in an 87-story tower. **Amenities:** A/C, cable TV w/movies. All units w/terraces. **Services:** Car-rental desk. Friday night poolside luaus. **Facilities:**

2 restaurants, 1 bar (w/entertainment), whirlpool, washer/dryer. Island restaurant has tropical decor, including waterfalls and pools. **Rates:** $89–$99 S or D; $250 ste. Extra person $10. Children under age 18 stay free. Parking: Outdoor, free. AE, CB, DC, DISC, ER, MC, V.

Bristol Court Hotel
1055 1st Ave, 92101 (Downtown); tel 619/232-6141 or toll free 800/622-4477; fax 619/232-0118. On a quiet street downtown, this boutique hotel is most inviting, with exquisite decor and lots of natural light. Close to the convention center. An excellent value. **Rooms:** 102 rms. CI 2pm/CO noon. Nonsmoking rms avail. Homey, comfortable rooms with fine appointments. **Amenities:** A/C, cable TV, refrig, dataport, bathrobes. **Services:** Twice-daily maid svce, car-rental desk, babysitting. Very helpful staff. **Facilities:** 1 restaurant, 3 bars (1 w/entertainment). **Rates (CP):** $119–$219 S or D. Extra person $10. Children under age 18 stay free. Min stay special events. Lower rates off-season. Parking: Indoor, $10/day. AE, CB, DC, DISC, EC, ER, MC, V.

Capri by the Sea Rental Management
4767 Ocean Blvd, 92109 (Pacific Beach); tel 619/483-6110 or toll free 800/248-5262; fax 619/483-9141. 9 mi NW of downtown. A 12-story property with attractive accommodations, located on the boardwalk. Very good value. **Rooms:** 140 effic. Executive level. CI 4pm/CO 11am. Nonsmoking rms avail. Each one- or two-bedroom condo is individually owned and decorated. **Amenities:** Cable TV, refrig, CD/tape player. No A/C. All units w/terraces, 1 w/fireplace, some w/whirlpools. **Services:** Babysitting. Maid service available for an extra charge. Front desk is staffed from 9am–6pm. **Facilities:** 1 beach (ocean), lifeguard, board surfing, sauna, whirlpool, washer/dryer. Laundry room on every floor and a barbecue on rooftop deck. Swimming pool is two doors up the street. **Rates:** Peak (July–Sept) $185–$300 effic. Extra person $10. Min stay. Lower rates off-season. Parking: Indoor/outdoor, free. Daily, weekly, and monthly rates offered. MC, V.

Clarion Hotel Bay View
660 K St, 92101 (Downtown); tel 619/696-0234 or toll free 800/766-0234; fax 619/231-8199. Between 7th and 8th Aves. Guests can walk to the convention center, restaurants, and San Diego trolley. Public areas and rooms were recently renovated. **Rooms:** 312 rms and stes. CI 3pm/CO noon. Nonsmoking rms avail. **Amenities:** A/C, cable TV w/movies, in-rm safe. Some units w/minibars, all w/terraces. State-of-the-art phone system allows guests to get entertainment schedules, weather, horoscopes, and other information for the price of a local call. **Services:** Babysitting. **Facilities:** 1 restaurant, 1 bar (w/entertainment), games rm, sauna, whirlpool, washer/dryer. Functional facilities without a lot of appeal. Exception is the outdoor whirlpool on the rooftop. **Rates:** $99–$139 S or

D; $149–$169 ste. Extra person $10. Children under age 18 stay free. Parking: Indoor, $8/day. AE, CB, DC, DISC, ER, JCB, MC, V.

≣≣≣ Courtyard by Marriott
9650 Scranton Rd, 92121 (Mira Mesa); tel 619/558-9600 or toll free 800/321-2211; fax 619/558-4539. 15 mi N of downtown. Miramesa Blvd exit off I-805; E on Mira Mesa Blvd, left on Scranton Rd. Designed for business travelers, this hotel, located near several corporate offices, has a nice lounge area appropriate for meetings. **Rooms:** 149 rms and stes. Executive level. CI 4pm/CO noon. Nonsmoking rms avail. Clean, modern rooms, with good work areas. **Amenities:** 🛜 🛏 A/C, cable TV w/movies, dataport. All units w/minibars, some w/terraces. **Services:** 🍽 🚗 🖼 ↩ Car-rental desk. **Facilities:** 🏋 🛌 🛁 ⑤ 1 restaurant, whirlpool, washer/dryer. **Rates:** Peak (July–Sept) $69–$89 S; $69–$99 D; $109–$119 ste. Children under age 18 stay free. Lower rates off-season. Parking: Outdoor, free. AE, DC, DISC, MC, V.

≣≣≣ DoubleTree Hotel at Horton Plaza
910 Broadway Circle, 92101 (Downtown); tel 619/239-2200 or toll free 800/222-TREE; fax 619/239-3216. Located in a major downtown shopping area, close to restaurants, convention center, and harbor. Lobby boasts extensive marble, two staircases, and a crystal chandelier. **Rooms:** 450 rms and stes. Executive level. CI 3pm/CO noon. Nonsmoking rms avail. Good soundproofing makes guests unaware of the activity outside. Rooms are very functional, decorated in pastel colors. **Amenities:** 🛜 🛏 A/C, cable TV w/movies, voice mail. Some units w/terraces, some w/fireplaces, some w/whirlpools. **Services:** 🍽 🖼 📼 ↩ Car-rental desk, masseur, babysitting. **Facilities:** 🏋 🚲 🏊 🛌 🖼 💻 ⑤ 2 restaurants, 2 bars, spa, sauna, whirlpool. Extensive meeting facilities. Bar/lounge is a good gathering place, with comfortable overstuffed sofas. **Rates:** $180 S or D; $300–$975 ste. Extra person $15. Children under age 12 stay free. Min stay special events. Parking: Indoor, $8–$12/day. AE, CB, DC, DISC, ER, JCB, MC, V.

≣ Downtown Inn Gaslamp Quarter
660 G St, 92101 (Downtown); or toll free 800/598-1810. Between 6th and 7th Aves. This somewhat austere property borders San Diego's Gaslamp Quarter. **Rooms:** 104 effic. CI 2pm/CO 1pm. Nonsmoking rms avail. **Amenities:** 🛜 🛏 Cable TV, refrig. No A/C. **Services:** 🚗 **Facilities:** ⑤ Washer/dryer. **Rates:** Peak (June–Aug) $40–$70 effic. Extra person $10. Lower rates off-season. AE, CB, DC, DISC, MC, V.

≣≣≣ Embassy Suites San Diego Bay
601 Pacific Hwy, 92101 (Downtown); tel 619/239-2400 or toll free 800/EMBASSY; fax 619/239-1520. Inviting lobby features an open atrium with lots of natural light and greenery. Location near the bay offers wonderful views. Close to Seaport Village and the convention center. **Rooms:** 337 stes. CI 4pm/CO noon. Nonsmoking rms avail. Suites are

spacious with many amenities, but furnishings are not elaborate. **Amenities:** 🛜 🛏 🖼 🍴 A/C, cable TV w/movies, refrig, dataport, voice mail. Some units w/terraces, 1 w/whirlpool. Microwave. **Services:** ✕ 🖙 📼 🚗 🖼 ↩ Car-rental desk, babysitting. Complimentary happy hour. **Facilities:** 🏋 🛌 🖼⑦⓪⓪ ⑤ 2 restaurants (lunch and dinner only), 1 bar, spa, sauna, whirlpool, beauty salon, washer/dryer. Sports bar. **Rates (BB):** $155–$170 ste. Extra person $10. Children under age 12 stay free. Parking: Indoor, $7–$10/day. AE, CB, DC, DISC, MC, V.

UNRATED Gaslamp Plaza Suites
520 E St, 92101 (Gaslamp Quarter); tel 619/232-9500 or toll free 800/443-8012; fax 619/238-9945. At 5th Ave. One of the first skyscrapers in San Diego, built in 1913 and designated a historic landmark. Marble walls and stairways, brass elevator doors, etched-glass window. Needs improved maintenance. **Rooms:** 50 rms and stes. CI 4pm/CO 11am. No smoking. **Amenities:** 🛜 🛏 🖼 A/C, cable TV w/movies, refrig, dataport, VCR, in-rm safe. 1 unit w/whirlpool. **Services:** ✕ 📼 🖼 ↩ Children's program, babysitting. **Facilities:** ⑤ Whirlpool. The restaurant, Dakota's, is very popular. Roof terrace with deck chairs, and hot tub. **Rates (CP):** Peak (June 19–Sept 2) $69–$99 S or D; $109–$179 ste. Extra person $5. Children under age 16 stay free. Lower rates off-season. Parking: Indoor, $7/day. AE, DISC, MC, V.

≣≣ Grosvenor Inn Sports Arena
3145 Sports Arena Blvd, 92110 (Sports Arena); tel 619/225-9999 or toll free 800/222-2929; fax 619/225-0958. 4 mi NW of downtown. Rosecrans exit off I-5 S; Pacific Coast Hwy exit off I-5 N. Located at a busy intersection across from the sports arena, at the Grosvenor Square, where you'll find shops and restaurants. **Rooms:** 206 rms and stes. CI 3pm/CO noon. Nonsmoking rms avail. Bright, contemporary rooms have lots of natural light, and are quiet despite the commercial setting. **Amenities:** 🛜 🖼 A/C, satel TV w/movies, refrig. Some units w/minibars, some w/terraces, 1 w/fireplace, some w/whirlpools. **Services:** ✕ 🚗 🖼 ↩ Car-rental desk. **Facilities:** 🏋 🖼③⓪⓪ ⑤ 2 restaurants (lunch and dinner only), whirlpool, beauty salon, washer/dryer. **Rates:** $62–$76 S; $70–$80 D; $115–$250 ste. Children under age 18 stay free. Min stay special events. Parking: Outdoor, free. AE, DC, DISC, MC, V.

≣≣ Holiday Inn Harbor View
1617 1st Ave, 92101 (Downtown); tel 619/239-6171 or toll free 800/366-3164; fax 619/233-6228. On the edge of downtown next to a noisy freeway. Lobby offers a comfortable seating area. Short ride from shopping, restaurants, and the bay. **Rooms:** 202 rms. CI 3pm/CO noon. Nonsmoking rms avail. Rooms are comfortable but austere. Half have wonderful views of the city lights or the bay. **Amenities:** 🛜 🛏 🖼 🍴 A/C, cable TV w/movies. Some units w/terraces. **Services:** ✕ 🚗 🖼 ↩ Twice-daily maid svce. **Facilities:** 🏋 🛌 🖼①⓪⓪ ⑤ 1 restaurant, 1 bar, washer/dryer. Restaurant has spectacular views. **Rates:** Peak (Mem Day–Labor Day) $109–

$129 S; $119–$139 D. Children under age 18 stay free. Lower rates off-season. Parking: Indoor/outdoor, free. AE, CB, DC, DISC, JCB, MC, V.

≣≣≣ Holiday Inn on the Bay

1355 N Harbor Dr, 92101 (Downtown); tel 619/232-3861 or toll free 800/4BAY-SIDE; fax 619/232-4924. An excellent choice for families, this newly renovated property is the best value on the bay. **Rooms:** 600 rms and stes. CI 3pm/CO noon. Nonsmoking rms avail. Pleasing rooms with excellent views. **Amenities:** 🛅 ⚿ 🍴 A/C, cable TV, voice mail. All units w/terraces. Irons in each room, direct telephone lines to restaurants, weather information, and the like. **Services:** ✗ ☞ 🚗 🖥 ⊴ 🐾 Car-rental desk, babysitting. Concierge will arrange wide variety of water sports activities. **Facilities:** 🔩 🚲 🏋 1400 👌 5 restaurants, 2 bars, washer/dryer. **Rates:** Peak (June–Sept) $139–$169 S or D; $250–$350 ste. Extra person $10. Children under age 11 stay free. Lower rates off-season. AP rates avail. Parking: Indoor, $10/day. Kids under 12 eat for free. AE, CB, DC, DISC, JCB, MC, V.

≣≣≣ Horton Grand Hotel

311 Island Ave, 92101 (Gaslamp Quarter); tel 619/544-1886 or toll free 800/542-1886; fax 619/239-3823. At 3rd Ave. A visit to the past. Two turn-of-the-century hotels combined and rebuilt brick by brick. Courtyard is often the setting for weddings, room 309 is said to be home of a ghost, Roger. **Rooms:** 132 rms. CI 3pm/CO noon. Nonsmoking rms avail. Every room uniquely furnished with antiques for a Victorian look, with fireplace and sitting area. Bathrooms boast pedestal sinks, all rooms have queen-size beds. **Amenities:** 🛅 ⚿ A/C, cable TV. Some units w/terraces, all w/fireplaces. **Services:** ✗ 🆅🅿 🚗 🖥 ⊴ 🐾 Twice-daily maid svce, babysitting. Afternoon tea in the lobby. Complimentary shoeshine. **Facilities:** 700 👌 1 restaurant, 1 bar (w/entertainment). **Rates:** $139–$218 S or D. Extra person $20. Children under age 12 stay free. Min stay special events. Parking: Indoor/outdoor, $8/day. AE, CB, DC, MC, V.

≣≣≣ Humphrey's Half Moon Inn & Suites

2303 Shelter Island Dr, 92106 (Shelter Island); tel 619/224-3411 or toll free 800/542-7400; fax 619/224-3478. 6 mi W of downtown. Rosecrans St exit off I-5. A good value for families. Hawaiian theme complete with thatched-roof entrance and staff dressed in island garb. Grounds boast palm trees, tropical flowers, waterfalls, and a pond with goldfish and ducks. A little worn around the edges. **Rooms:** 182 rms and stes. CI 4pm/CO noon. Nonsmoking rms avail. Hawaiian decor. Some rooms have views of the city or the bay. **Amenities:** 🛅 ⚿ 🖥 🍴 A/C, cable TV w/movies, refrig. Some units w/terraces. **Services:** 🍽 🚗 ⊴ 🐾 Babysitting. **Facilities:** 🔩 250 👌 1 restaurant, 1 bar (w/entertainment), lawn games, whirlpool, washer/dryer. Stage for outdoor concerts featuring popular singers. Putting green, table tennis. **Rates:** Peak (June–Labor Day) $89–$159 S; $99–

$159 D; $199–$229 ste. Children under age 18 stay free. Min stay special events. Lower rates off-season. Parking: Outdoor, free. AE, CB, DC, DISC, MC, V.

≣≣≣≣ Hyatt Regency San Diego

1 Market Place, 92101 (Downtown); tel 619/232-1234 or toll free 800/233-1234; fax 619/233-6464. One of the foremost meeting and convention facilities in the city, the Hyatt features an impressive palm court inlaid with marble. Located conveniently near the Convention Center and the waterfront Seaport Village shopping and dining complex. Public areas can get crammed and noisy when a large group is in house. **Rooms:** 875 rms and stes. Executive level. CI 3pm/CO noon. Nonsmoking rms avail. Rooms are attractively furnished in two-tone woods and floral bedspreads accented by a jaunty plaid ruffle. All have waterfront views. Tiled bathrooms provide great counter space, but are functional, not sexy. **Amenities:** 🛅 ⚿ 🍴 A/C, cable TV w/movies, dataport, voice mail. All units w/minibars, some w/whirlpools. Iron and ironing board in every room. Business Plan rooms have in-room fax. **Services:** 🍽 ☞ 🆅🅿 ⊴ 🐾 Car-rental desk, masseur, babysitting. Concierge can set up boat rentals, fishing excursions, etc, from nearby docks. Business Plan rates include free buffet breakfast, free local and credit-card calls, plus workstation in hallway with copy machine. **Facilities:** 🔩 🚲 🍴4 🏋 3800 💻 👌 2 restaurants, 3 bars (1 w/entertainment), spa, sauna, steam rm, whirlpool, beauty salon. Long lap pool has a deck with great bay views. Health club offers a variety of weight and cardio machines, but a skimpy aerobics area, although they do offer some classes. **Rates:** $225 S; $240 D; $325 ste. Extra person $25. Children under age 12 stay free. AP rates avail. Parking: Indoor, $8–$12/day. AE, CB, DC, DISC, JCB, MC, V.

≣≣≣ Kings Inn

1333 Hotel Circle S, 92108 (Hotel Circle); tel 619/297-2231 or toll free 800/78-KINGS; fax 619/296-5255. 4 mi N of downtown. Hotel Circle exit off I-8. Not much to look at from the outside, but a pleasant lobby and rooms. **Rooms:** 140 rms and stes. CI 3pm/CO noon. Nonsmoking rms avail. Rooms are attractive and clean. **Amenities:** 🛅 🖥 A/C, cable TV w/movies. Some units w/minibars, some w/terraces. **Services:** ✗ ⊴ 🐾 Car-rental desk. Front desk staff helps with tour bookings, etc. **Facilities:** 🔩 250 👌 2 restaurants, 1 bar (w/entertainment), whirlpool. Entertainment in bar Thursday through Saturday nights. **Rates:** Peak (June–Sept) $59–$89 S or D; $125 ste. Lower rates off-season. Parking: Outdoor, free. AE, DC, DISC, MC, V.

≣≣ La Pensione Hotel

1700 India St, at Date St, 92101 (Little Italy); tel 619/236-8000 or toll free 800/232-4685; fax 619/236-8088. ½ mi N of downtown. It does not offer a lot of amenities, but this property is very clean and comfortable; many guests stay for weeks at a time. **Rooms:** 81 rms. CI 3pm/CO 11:30am. Nonsmoking rms avail. Few frills. **Amenities:** 🛅 Cable TV, refrig. No A/C. Some units w/terraces. Microwave. **Services:**

Front desk staff is very helpful. **Facilities:** ⅖ 2 restaurants, washer/dryer. Both the cafe and the Southwestern restaurant are popular with locals. **Rates:** $39–$59 S or D. Parking: Indoor, free. AE, MC, V.

☰☰☰ Pacific Terrace Inn
610 Diamond St, 92109 (Pacific Beach); tel 619/581-3500 or toll free 800/344-3370; fax 619/274-3341. 9 mi NW of downtown. Grand-Garnet exit off I-5; right on Mission Blvd and left on Diamond St. Lovely boutique hotel has a pleasant ambience. Located right on the boardwalk along the beach, it's both quiet and private. **Rooms:** 73 rms and effic. CI 4pm/ CO 11am. No smoking. Charming, well-appointed rooms. **Amenities:** 🛏 ♨ 🖭 🗔 A/C, cable TV, bathrobes. **Services:** 🖴 ⬛ 🔌 Car-rental desk, babysitting. Continental breakfast and afternoon snacks in lobby. Room service provided by local restaurants. **Facilities:** 🔂 🏊 ⟦50⟧ ⅖ 1 beach (ocean), lifeguard, board surfing, whirlpool, washer/dryer. Lovely pool faces the ocean. Secure parking. **Rates (CP):** $120–$215 S or D; $240–$480 effic. Extra person $10. Min stay wknds. Parking: Indoor/outdoor, free. AE, CB, DC, DISC, MC, V.

☰☰ Park Manor Suites
525 Spruce St, 92103 (Hillcrest); tel 619/291-0999 or toll free 800/874-2649; fax 619/291-8844. At 5th Ave. 1½ mi N of downtown. A 1926 Italian Renaissance–style hotel opposite Balboa Park. Lobby has a European feel, with antiques, an oriental rug, and a baby grand piano. Rooftop bar offers great views. **Rooms:** 80 stes. CI 3pm/CO noon. Nonsmoking rms avail. Very spacious suites have kitchen area, living room, bedroom, and bath; modestly furnished, but well kept up. Bathrooms are very basic. **Amenities:** 🛏 ♨ 🖭 Cable TV w/movies, refrig. No A/C. Some units w/terraces. **Services:** ⬛ 🔌 ⬗ Twice-daily maid svce, babysitting. Complimentary continental breakfast in rooftop bar. **Facilities:** ⅖ 1 restaurant, 1 bar (w/entertainment). **Rates (CP):** $69–$159 ste. Children under age 12 stay free. Min stay special events. Parking: Outdoor, free. AE, DISC, MC, V.

☰☰☰ Ramada Hotel Old Town
2435 Jefferson St, 92110 (Old Town); tel 619/260-8500 or toll free 800/255-3544; fax 619/297-2078. 3 mi NW of downtown. Old Town Ave exit off I-5; left on Jefferson. A Spanish-style property, near the center of Old Town. Lobby is decorated with Spanish artifacts and features a fireplace. **Rooms:** 151 rms. Executive level. CI 3pm/CO noon. Nonsmoking rms avail. Rooms have basic decor. Those facing the freeway can be somewhat noisy. **Amenities:** 🛏 ♨ A/C, cable TV w/movies. 1 unit w/terrace, 1 w/whirlpool. **Services:** 🍽 🚗 ⬛ 🔌 Complimentary cocktails 5–7pm. **Facilities:** 🔂 ⟦200⟧ ⅖ 1 restaurant, 1 bar, whirlpool. The Gila House serves outstanding carne asada. **Rates (CP):** Peak (July–Aug) $109–$129 S or D. Extra person $10. Children under age 16 stay free. Min stay special events. Lower rates off-season. Parking: Indoor/outdoor, free. AE, DC, DISC, MC, V.

☰☰☰ Sheraton San Diego Hotel & Marina
1380 Harbor Island Dr, 92101; tel 619/291-2900 or toll free 800/325-3535; fax 619/692-2337. 2 mi NW of downtown. ½ mi from the airport. On Harbor Island, overlooking the marina and close to shops and restaurants. Very convenient to the airport. **Rooms:** 1,045 rms and stes. Executive level. CI 3pm/CO noon. Nonsmoking rms avail. Rooms are newly renovated. All have marble bathrooms and a downtown or marina view. **Amenities:** 🛏 ♨ 🖭 A/C, cable TV w/movies, refrig, voice mail. All units w/minibars, all w/terraces, some w/whirlpools. All have irons and ironing boards. **Services:** 🍽 🖴 ⟦VP⟧ 🚗 ⬛ 🔌 Car-rental desk, masseur, children's program, babysitting. **Facilities:** 🔂 ♒ ⚓ 🔺 🗔 🏊 ⬛2 🎣 🚴 ⟦2000⟧ ☐ ⅖ 4 restaurants, 3 bars (w/entertainment), games rm, lawn games, spa, sauna, whirlpool, beauty salon, washer/ dryer. **Rates:** $179–$270 S or D; $375–$950 ste. Extra person $10. Children under age 17 stay free. Min stay special events. Parking: Outdoor, $8–$11/day. AE, CB, DC, DISC, EC, ER, JCB, MC, V.

☰☰☰ Town & Country Hotel
500 Hotel Circle N, 92108 (Hotel Circle); tel 619/291-7131 or toll free 800/77-ATLAS; fax 619/291-3584. 4 mi N of downtown. Hotel Circle exit off I-8. Large property with lovely gardens. Caters primarily to conventions. **Rooms:** 1,000 rms and stes. CI 4pm/CO noon. Nonsmoking rms avail. Attractive decor with small bathrooms. Some rooms are in a nine-story tower; others are in low-rise buildings. **Amenities:** 🛏 ♨ A/C, cable TV w/movies. Some units w/terraces. **Services:** ✕ 🖴 ⬛ 🔌 Car-rental desk, babysitting. **Facilities:** 🔂4 ⟦6000⟧ ⅖ 5 restaurants, 3 bars (w/entertainment), whirlpool, beauty salon, day-care ctr. **Rates:** $80–$145 S; $95–$160 D; $200–$375 ste. Extra person $10. Children under age 18 stay free. Parking: Indoor/outdoor, $6/day. AE, DC, MC, V.

☰☰☰ US Grant Hotel
326 Broadway, 92101 (Downtown); tel 619/232-3121 or toll free 800/231-5029; fax 619/232-3626. Between 3rd and 4th Aves. This San Diego landmark welcomes guests with a warmth and civility that was once expected in the best hotels. **Rooms:** 280 rms and stes. Executive level. CI 3pm/CO noon. Nonsmoking rms avail. Although not luxurious, rooms have an old-world charm. **Amenities:** 🛏 ♨ A/C, cable TV w/movies. Some units w/minibars, some w/terraces, some w/whirlpools. **Services:** 🍽 🖴 ⟦VP⟧ 🚗 ⬛ 🔌 ⬗ Car-rental desk, babysitting. **Facilities:** 🚴 ⟦1200⟧ ☐ ⅖ 1 restaurant (*see* "Restaurants" below), 1 bar (w/entertainment). Concierge will arrange golf, tennis, and use of a nearby fitness club. The Grant Grill is a San Diego legend. **Rates:** Peak (Sept–May) $145–$165 S; $165–$185 D; $245–$375 ste. Extra person $20. Children under age 16 stay free. Lower rates off-season. Parking: Indoor/outdoor, $5–$10/day. AE, CB, DC, DISC, MC, V.

≣≣≣ Vacation Inn

3900 Old Town Ave, 92110 (Old Town); tel 619/299-7400 or toll free 800/451-9846; fax 619/299-1619. 3 mi NW of downtown. Old Town Ave exit off I-5. Hacienda-style hotel in Old Town has a European flair. Fountains, bougainvillea, and a spacious lobby with fireplace. Convenient to shopping, sightseeing, and many restaurants. **Rooms:** 125 rms. CI 3pm/CO noon. Nonsmoking rms avail. French-country decor in pleasing color scheme. Very inviting and comfortable, but bathtub is small. **Amenities:** 🛅 🕭 🗗 A/C, cable TV, refrig. Some units w/terraces. Microwave. **Services:** 🚗 🖂 🖵 Babysitting. Complimentary afternoon refreshments. **Facilities:** 🛉 ⟦150⟧ ♿ Whirlpool, washer/dryer. **Rates (CP):** Peak (May 24–Sept 4) $75–$83 S; $90–$165 D. Extra person $10. Children under age 17 stay free. Min stay special events. Lower rates off-season. Parking: Indoor, free. AE, CB, DC, DISC, MC, V.

≣≣≣≣ Westgate Hotel

1055 2nd Ave, 92101 (Downtown); tel 619/238-1818 or toll free 800/221-3802; fax 619/557-3737. Between Broadway and C St. With its Baccarat chandeliers and original Louis XV concierge desk, this hotel looks as if it's been here for 100 years, although it actually opened in 1970. **Rooms:** 223 rms and stes. Executive level. CI 3pm/CO noon. Nonsmoking rms avail. Each of the rooms is individually decorated. All feature foyers, plus charming touches. **Amenities:** 🛅 🕭 🍽 A/C, cable TV, bathrobes. All units w/minibars, all w/terraces. **Services:** ⦿ 🖿 ⟦VP⟧ 🚗 🖂 🖵 ⟨⟩ Car-rental desk, masseur, babysitting. Complimentary car service within the San Diego area. **Facilities:** ⟦250⟧ ♿ 3 restaurants, 2 bars (w/entertainment), spa, beauty salon, washer/dryer. Piano bar is very popular on weekends, with repertoire ranging from opera to Top 40. **Rates:** $164–$194 S; $174–$204 D; $400–$1,500 ste. Extra person $10. Children under age 6 stay free. AP and MAP rates avail. Parking: Indoor, $10/day. AE, CB, DC, DISC, MC, V.

≣≣≣ Wyndham Emerald Plaza Hotel

400 W Broadway, 92101 (Downtown); tel 619/239-4500 or toll free 800/626-3988; fax 619/239-4527. In the Emerald-Shapery Center between State and Columbia Sts. This soaring signature on San Diego's skyline has been the filming location for several TV shows and movies. Glass elevators provide dynamite city views. **Rooms:** 436 rms and stes. CI 3pm/CO noon. Nonsmoking rms avail. **Amenities:** 🛅 🕭 🍽 A/C, cable TV w/movies, bathrobes. All units w/minibars, some w/terraces, some w/whirlpools. **Services:** ✕ 🖿 ⟦VP⟧ 🚗 🖂 🖵 Twice-daily maid svce, masseur, babysitting. **Facilities:** 🛉 ⟦2600⟧ 🖵 ♿ 2 restaurants, 2 bars (w/entertainment), sauna, steam rm, whirlpool. Well-equipped health club has a wall of windows and a view of the city. **Rates:** $218 S; $238 D; $360–$2,000 ste. Extra person $15. Children under age 18 stay free. Parking: Indoor, $8/day. AE, DC, DISC, MC, V.

MOTELS

≣≣ Best Western Blue Sea Lodge

707 Pacific Beach Dr, 92109 (Pacific Beach); tel 619/488-4700 or toll free 800/258-3732; fax 619/488-7276. Grand/Garnet exit off I-5; at Mission Blvd. Located on the beachfront boardwalk, this property is due for renovation. Except for the entrance, it's an acceptable hotel. **Rooms:** 100 rms, stes, and effic. CI 3pm/CO noon. Nonsmoking rms avail. Adequate. **Amenities:** 🛅 🕭 🗗 🍽 A/C, cable TV, in-rm safe. All units w/terraces. **Services:** 🖂 🖵 Car-rental desk, babysitting. Local restaurants will deliver. Front-desk staff helps arrange tours and rental cars. **Facilities:** 🛉 ♿ 1 beach (ocean), board surfing, whirlpool, washer/dryer. **Rates (CP):** Peak (June–Sept) $119–$134 S; $129–$159 D; $225–$285 ste; $130 effic. Extra person $15. Children under age 18 stay free. Min stay special events. Lower rates off-season. Parking: Indoor/outdoor, free. AE, MC, V.

≣≣ Crystal Pier Hotel

4500 Ocean Blvd at Garnet, 92109 (Pacific Beach); tel 619/483-6983 or toll free 800/748-5894; fax 619/483-6811. 9 mi NW of downtown. Grand/Garnet exit off I-5; W on Garnet. This historic property (built in 1927) offers a rare opportunity to sleep over the water because of its pier location. Magnificent beach and water views. A major upgrade is in progress. **Rooms:** 26 effic. CI 2pm/CO 11am. Nonsmoking rms avail. New and remodeled units are high caliber, but older ones look worn. Best units are upstairs. The further out on the pier, the quieter the lodging. **Amenities:** 🛅 🕭 🗗 TV, refrig. No A/C. All units w/terraces. **Services:** ✕ Car-rental desk. Adjacent Kono's Surf Club will deliver breakfast and lunch from 7am–2pm. **Facilities:** 🖸 🏖 ♿ 1 beach (ocean), lifeguard, board surfing. Bait, fishing poles, boogie boards, beach chairs, and umbrellas available. **Rates:** Peak (June–Sept) $145–$225 cottage/villa. Min stay. Lower rates off-season. Parking: Outdoor, free. DISC, MC, V.

≣≣ Hampton Inn

5434 Kearny Mesa Rd, 92111 (Clairemont Mesa); tel 619/292-1482 or toll free 800/292-1482; fax 619/292-4410. 10 mi N of Downtown, off CA 163. A five-year-old property with spacious entry, comfortable lobby, and well-tended grounds. **Rooms:** 150 rms. Executive level. CI 2pm/CO 11am. Nonsmoking rms avail. Nice rooms. **Amenities:** 🛅 🕭 A/C, cable TV w/movies. **Services:** 🚗 🖂 🖵 Babysitting. Free grocery-shopping service available. **Facilities:** 🛉 ⟦15⟧ ♿ Day-care ctr, washer/dryer. Nice pool, but some street noise and not much sun. **Rates (CP):** Peak (May–Sept) $94 S; $99 D. Children under age 18 stay free. Lower rates off-season. Parking: Outdoor, free. AE, DC, DISC, MC, V.

≣≣ Hotel Circle Inn & Suites

2201 Hotel Circle S, 92108; tel 619/291-2711 or toll free 800/772-7711; fax 619/542-1227. 4 mi N of downtown. Hotel Circle exit off I-8. Good choice for families, particularly units with kitchens. **Rooms:** 197 rms and effic. CI 2pm/CO noon. Nonsmoking rms avail. Rooms are pleasant, bright, and clean. **Amenities:** 🔒 📺 A/C, satel TV w/movies. 1 unit w/minibar. **Services:** 🔑 Car-rental desk. **Facilities:** 🏋 1 restaurant, whirlpool, washer/dryer. **Rates:** Peak (Mem Day–Labor Day) $59–$79 S or D; $109–$149 effic. Extra person $7. Min stay peak. Lower rates off-season. Parking: Outdoor, free. AE, CB, DC, DISC, MC, V.

≣ Motel 6
2424 Hotel Circle N, 92108 (Hotel Circle); tel 619/296-1612; fax 619/543-9305. 4 mi N of downtown. Taylor St exit off I-8. Basic, clean rooms. **Rooms:** 202 rms. CI 3pm/CO noon. Nonsmoking rms avail. **Amenities:** 🔒 A/C, cable TV. Some units w/terraces. **Services:** 🔑 🏊 **Facilities:** 🏋 ⅙ Washer/dryer. **Rates:** Peak (June–Sept) $40–$42 S; $44–$46 D. Children under age 18 stay free. Lower rates off-season. Parking: Outdoor, free. AE, CB, DC, DISC, MC, V.

≣≣ Ocean Park Inn
710 Grand Ave, 92109 (Pacific Beach); tel 619/483-5858 or toll free 800/231-7735; fax 619/274-0823. 9 mi NW of downtown. Grand/Garnet exit off I-5; W on Grand Ave. Attractive motor hotel built in 1992 on the boardwalk along the beach. Somewhat noisy. **Rooms:** 73 rms, stes, and effic. CI 2pm/CO 11am. Nonsmoking rms avail. Rooms are spacious, modern, and nicely coordinated. **Amenities:** 🔒 ⚬ A/C, cable TV, refrig. All units w/terraces. **Services:** 🍴 🏊 🔑 Front desk staff acts as concierge. **Facilities:** 🏋 🏄 ⅙ 1 beach (ocean), lifeguard, board surfing, whirlpool, washer/dryer. Swimming pool overlooks the beach. **Rates (CP):** Peak (Mem Day–Sept) $99–$149 S or D; $159–$174 ste; $174 effic. Extra person $10. Children under age 15 stay free. Min stay wknds. Lower rates off-season. Parking: Indoor, free. AE, DC, DISC, MC, V.

≣≣ Padre Trail Inn
4200 Taylor St, 92110 (Old Town); tel 619/297-3291 or toll free 800/255-9988; fax 619/692-2080. 3½ mi N of downtown. Taylor St off I-8; near intersection of I-5 and I-8. Typical 1950s-style motel, functional and clean but with few amenities. **Rooms:** 100 rms and stes. CI 2pm/CO noon. Nonsmoking rms avail. **Amenities:** 🔒 ⚬ 📺 Cable TV w/movies. No A/C. **Services:** 🔑 **Facilities:** 🏋 📍150 1 restaurant (bkfst only), 1 bar. Pleasant restaurant and bar have very reasonable prices. **Rates:** Peak (June–Aug) $44 S; $49–$55 D; $60 ste. Extra person $5. Children under age 12 stay free. Min stay peak and wknds. Lower rates off-season. Parking: Outdoor, free. AE, CB, DC, DISC, MC, V.

≣≣≣ Sommerset Suites Hotel
606 Washington St, 92103 (Hillcrest); tel 619/692-5200 or toll free 800/962-9665, 800/356-1787 in CA; fax 619/299-6065. 2½ mi N of downtown. Washington St exit off I-5; at 5th St. Located near 2 hospitals. No restaurant on site, but many within walking distance. **Rooms:** 80 effic. CI 2pm/CO noon. Nonsmoking rms avail. Very clean and attractive rooms. **Amenities:** 🔒 ⚬ 📺 A/C, cable TV w/movies, refrig,

dataport, voice mail, in-rm safe. Some units w/terraces. All units have two-line telephones and full kitchens. **Services:** 🚐 🏊 🔑 Car-rental desk, babysitting. Complimentary social hour with wine and beer 4–6pm. Free shuttle to zoo, shopping, and downtown. **Facilities:** 🏋 📍25 ⅙ Whirlpool, washer/dryer. Use of gas barbecues. **Rates (CP):** Peak (June–Sept) $120–$180 effic. Extra person $10. Children under age 12 stay free. Lower rates off-season. Parking: Indoor, free. AE, DC, DISC, MC, V.

≣ Surf and Sand Motel
4666 Mission Blvd, 92109 (Pacific Beach); tel 619/483-7420; fax 619/237-9940. 9 mi NW of downtown. Grand-Garnet exit off I-5; W on Garnet, N on Mission Blvd. Modest motel ½ block from the beach, with a small but pleasant lobby. A bit noisy. **Rooms:** 25 rms, stes, and effic; 1 cottage/villa. CI noon/CO 11am. Nonsmoking rms avail. Rooms are adequate in size but furnishings are old. There's a three-bedroom, two-bath house for rent adjacent to the motel. **Amenities:** 🔒 Cable TV, refrig. No A/C. 1 unit w/whirlpool. **Services:** 🚐 **Facilities:** 🏋 **Rates:** Peak (June–Sept) $59–$89 S; $69–$109 D; $100–$150 ste; $64–$115 effic; $150–$250 cottage/villa. Min stay special events. Lower rates off-season. Parking: Outdoor, free. Cottages/villas available by the week only. AE, CB, DC, DISC, JCB, MC, V.

≣ Surfer Motor Lodge
711 Pacific Beach Dr, 92109 (Pacific Beach); tel 619/483-7070 or toll free 800/787-3373; fax 619/274-1670. Grand Garnet exit off I-5; at Mission Blvd. Beachfront location is the biggest attraction of this four-story hotel. **Rooms:** 52 rms and effic. CI 2pm/CO noon. **Amenities:** 🔒 TV, refrig. No A/C. Some units w/terraces. **Services:** 🔑 **Facilities:** 🏋 🚲 🏄 ⅙ 1 beach (ocean), lifeguard, washer/dryer. Pool faces the ocean. Excellent restaurant adjacent. **Rates:** Peak (June–Sept) $89–$105 S or D; $93–$105 effic. Extra person $5. Lower rates off-season. Parking: Outdoor, free. AE, DC, MC, V.

RESORTS

≣≣≣ Bahia Resort Hotel
998 W Mission Bay Dr, 92109 (Mission Beach); tel 619/488-0551 or toll free 800/288-0770; fax 619/488-7055. 8 mi NW of downtown. Mission Bay Dr exit off I-8. 14 acres. A good place for families, well located on a peninsula on Mission Bay. Harbor seals live in a pond out front. **Rooms:** 325 rms, stes, and effic. CI 4pm/CO noon. Nonsmoking rms avail. **Amenities:** 🔒 ⚬ A/C, cable TV w/movies, refrig. Some units w/terraces. **Services:** 🍴 🏊 🔑 🏊 Car-rental desk, babysitting. Bellman will book tours and make recommendations. **Facilities:** 🏋 🚲 ⚠ 🏄 📺 📍800 ⅙ 1 restaurant, 1 bar (w/entertainment), 1 beach (bay), lifeguard, whirlpool, playground. **Rates:** Peak (July–Aug) $125–$155 S or D; $225 ste; $275 effic. Extra person $15. Children under age 13 stay free. Min stay peak and wknds. Lower rates off-season. Parking: Outdoor, free. AE, MC, V.

☰☰☰ Carmel Highland DoubleTree Golf & Tennis Resort

14455 Peñasquitos Dr, 92129; tel 619/672-9100 or toll free 800/622-9223; fax 619/672-9166. 25 mi N of downtown, exit off I-15. Carmel Mountain Rd exit off I-15; 1 block W of Carmel Mountain Rd. 130 acres. This resort has it all and presents it in a luxurious way. Caters to corporate travelers and business meetings as well as families. **Rooms:** 172 rms and stes. CI 3pm/CO noon. Nonsmoking rms avail. Rooms are fairly large, with comfortable furnishings. **Amenities:** 🛜 🕹 🎏 🍴 A/C, cable TV w/movies, bathrobes. All units w/minibars, all w/terraces. **Services:** ✕ 🖾 ⤴ 🐕 Masseur, children's program, babysitting. Golf and tennis lessons available. **Facilities:** 🛋 🚲 ▶18 🖸 🍴 850 ⛳ 2 restaurants, 1 bar (w/entertainment), sauna, steam rm, whirlpool, day-care ctr, washer/dryer. **Rates:** $149 S or D; $179 ste. Extra person $10. Children under age 16 stay free. Parking: Outdoor, free. Golf and tennis packages available. AE, DC, DISC, MC, V.

☰☰☰ Catamaran Resort Hotel

3999 Mission Blvd, 92109 (Pacific Beach); tel 619/488-1081 or toll free 800/288-0770; fax 619/488-1619. 9 mi NW of downtown. Grand/Garnet exit off I-5; W on Grand, S on Mission Blvd. 8 acres. The landscaping is unusual, with plants from all over the world. Very attractive and well maintained. Lobby atrium has a waterfall, slate floor, and tropical foliage. **Rooms:** 312 rms, stes, and effic. CI 4pm/CO noon. Nonsmoking rms avail. Rooms in 13-story tower have views of Sail Bay, San Diego skyline, and Coronado Bridge. Rooms in the low-rise section have beach access. **Amenities:** 🛜 🕹 A/C, cable TV w/movies, dataport. All units w/terraces, 1 w/whirlpool. **Services:** ✕ 🖛 VP 🚐 🖾 ⤴ Car-rental desk, masseur, children's program, babysitting. Room service 6am–1am. Lifeguard in summer only. **Facilities:** 🛋 🚲 ⚠ 🖾 🍴 800 ⛳ 1 restaurant (see "Restaurants" below), 2 bars (1 w/entertainment), 1 beach (bay), whirlpool. Beach volleyball, Award-winning restaurant. **Rates:** Peak (Mem Day–Labor Day) $140–$195 S or D; $275–$350 ste; $160–$215 effic. Children under age 18 stay free. Lower rates off-season. Parking: Indoor/outdoor, $5/day. Minimum stay on summer weekends. AE, CB, DC, DISC, MC, V.

☰☰ Handlery Hotel & Resort

950 Hotel Circle N, 92108; tel 619/298-0511 or toll free 800/676-6567; fax 619/298-9793. 4 mi N of downtown. Hotel Circle exit off I-8. 225 acres. An older property, pleasant and very clean. **Rooms:** 217 rms and stes. CI 3pm/CO noon. Nonsmoking rms avail. **Amenities:** 🛜 🕹 🎏 A/C, cable TV w/movies, refrig. Some units w/terraces, 1 w/whirlpool. **Services:** ✕ 🚐 🖾 ⤴ Car-rental desk, masseur, children's program, babysitting. Room service 7am–10pm. Bellman will book tours. **Facilities:** 🛋 ▶18 🖸 🍴 400 ⛳ 1 restaurant, 1 bar, basketball, volleyball, spa, whirlpool, beauty salon, playground, washer/dryer. Good golf and tennis

facilities. No elevator. **Rates:** $109–$129 S; $119–$139 D; $195 ste. Extra person $10. Children under age 14 stay free. Parking: Outdoor, free. AE, CB, DC, DISC, JCB, MC, V.

☰☰☰ Hyatt Islandia

1441 Quivira Rd, 92109 (Mission Bay); tel 619/224-1234 or toll free 800/233-1234; fax 619/224-0348. 7 mi NW of downtown. West Mission Bay Dr exit off I-8. 7 acres. Nicely located on a marina in Mission Bay, with beautifully landscaped grounds. **Rooms:** 422 rms and stes. Executive level. CI 4pm/CO noon. Nonsmoking rms avail. Rooms are located in low-rise units as well as an 18-story tower. **Amenities:** 🛜 🕹 A/C, cable TV w/movies, voice mail. Some units w/minibars, all w/terraces, 1 w/fireplace. **Services:** ✕ 🖛 🖾 ⤴ Car-rental desk, children's program, babysitting. Turn-down service on request. **Facilities:** 🛋 🚲 ⚠ 🖸 🖾 🌊 🍴 800 🖥 ⛳ 2 restaurants, 2 bars (1 w/entertainment), lawn games, whirlpool. Boat rentals, and fishing and whale-watching expeditions, available at the marina. **Rates:** $169–$180 S; $179–$190 D; $189–$210 ste. Extra person $15. Children under age 18 stay free. Min stay special events. Parking: Indoor/outdoor, free. AE, CB, DC, DISC, JCB, MC, V.

☰☰☰ Rancho Bernardo Inn

17550 Bernardo Oaks Dr, 92128; tel 619/487-1611 or toll free 800/854-1065, 800/542-6096 in CA; fax 619/487-1423. 25 mi NE of downtown. Rancho Bernardo Rd exit E off I-15; left on Bernardo Oaks Dr. A relaxed resort with an emphasis on tennis and golf. Hacienda-style lobby is accented by beamed ceilings, adobe-textured walls, and wrought-iron fixtures. Five Italian-marble fountains beautify the grounds. **Rooms:** 287 rms and stes. CI 4pm/CO noon. Nonsmoking rms avail. Set in two- to three-story buildings around the property, rooms are done in desert-tone fabrics and bleached woods. All accommodations have been recently refurbished. **Amenities:** 🛜 🕹 A/C, cable TV, refrig, in-rm safe. All units w/minibars, all w/terraces, some w/fireplaces, some w/whirlpools. Conspicuously lacking are amenities such as hairdryers and bathrobes (available on request). Room doors lack deadbolts and safety chains. **Services:** ✕ 🖛 VP 🚐 🖾 ⤴ 🐕 Twice-daily maid svce, car-rental desk, masseur, children's program, babysitting. Friendly staff gets a bit swamped when large meeting groups arrive or depart. Complimentary afternoon tea served in the cozy music room. **Facilities:** 🛋 🚲 ▶45 🖾 🍴6 🖸 🌊 500 🖥 ⛳ 3 restaurants, 2 bars (w/entertainment), lawn games, spa, sauna, steam rm, whirlpool. 108 holes of golf are within 30 minutes of the inn. On-site facilities include a pro shop plus Ken Blanchard's Golf University of San Diego. There's also an excellent Tennis College. **Rates:** $150–$225 S or D; $245–$330 ste; $600–$750 cottage/villa. Children under age 18 stay free. Parking: Outdoor, free. Tennis and golf packages available. AE, DISC, JCB, MC, V.

☰☰☰ San Diego Hilton Beach and Tennis Resort

1775 E Mission Bay Dr, 92109 (Mission Bay); tel 619/276-4010 or toll free 800/445-8667; fax 619/275-7992. 8 mi NW of downtown. From Tecolote Rd turn right onto E Mission Bay Dr. 18 acres. Newly renovated. Pleasant decor. **Rooms:** 357 rms and stes. CI 3pm/CO noon. Nonsmoking rms avail. Spacious accommodations in an eight-story tower and two-story buildings; 12 rooms for guests with disabilities. **Amenities:** 🛁 🔥 🖥 ⚓ A/C, cable TV w/movies, refrig, voice mail. All units w/minibars, all w/terraces. Ceiling fan; iron and ironing board in room. **Services:** ✕ ☎ 🚗 🖼 🍴 🛎 Car-rental desk, masseur, children's program, babysitting. Scuba lessons available. **Facilities:** 🏊 🚴 △ 🏠 🎿 🍽 ⛳ 🏐 🎾 700 🖥 ⅙ 3 restaurants, 3 bars (1 w/entertainment), 1 beach (bay), games rm, sauna, whirlpool, beauty salon, playground, washer/dryer. **Rates:** Peak (July–Aug) $170–$230 S; $190–$250 D; $375 ste. Children under age 13 stay free. Min stay special events. Lower rates off-season. Parking: Outdoor, free. AE, DC, DISC, MC, V.

☰☰ San Diego Princess Resort

1404 W Vacation Rd, 92109 (Mission Bay); tel 619/274-4630 or toll free 800/344-2626; fax 619/581-5929. Sea World Dr exit off I-5 to Ingraham St N. 44 acres. Bungalows are spread out on spacious grounds here; guests can park right next to their accommodations. **Rooms:** 462 cottages/villas. CI 4pm/CO noon. Nonsmoking rms avail. **Amenities:** 🛁 🔥 A/C, cable TV w/movies, refrig. Some units w/minibars, some w/terraces. **Services:** 🍴 🖼 🍴 🛎 Car-rental desk, social director, masseur, children's program, babysitting. **Facilities:** 🏊 🚴 △ 🏠 🎿 🏐 🎾 🍽 1200 ⅙ 3 restaurants, 4 bars (2 w/entertainment), 1 beach (bay), lifeguard, games rm, lawn games, spa, sauna, steam rm, whirlpool, playground, washer/dryer. **Rates:** Peak (July–Aug) $165–$190 cottage/villa. Extra person $20. Min stay special events. Lower rates off-season. Parking: Outdoor, free. AE, DC, DISC, MC, V.

RESTAURANTS 🍴

♦ Anthony's Star of the Sea Room

1360 N Harbor Dr (Downtown); tel 619/232-7408. At Ash St. **Seafood.** Old-world elegance, spacious tables, and a view of San Diego Bay. An intimate bar area features a crystal ship chandelier. Dishes include sole stuffed with lobster, shrimp, and crab; and marinated baked swordfish. Jackets are required (and provided if necessary). **FYI:** Reservations recommended. Jacket required. **Open:** Daily 5:30–10:30pm. **Prices:** Main courses $22–$35. AE, CB, DC, DISC, MC, V. 💟 🖼 💟 🅥🅟 ⅙

★ Athens Market

109 W F St (Downtown); tel 619/234-1955. Between 1st and Front Sts. **Greek.** A gathering place for local television personalities. Tables topped with white linen surround the bar. The menu offers Greek specialties such as moussaka and lamb, chicken and fish entrees. Belly dancers perform on

weekends. **FYI:** Reservations recommended. **Open:** Lunch Mon–Sat 11:30am–4pm; dinner daily 4–10pm. **Prices:** Main courses $10–$20. AE, DISC, MC, V. ⅙

The Atoll

In the Catamaran Resort Hotel, 3999 Mission Blvd (Pacific Beach); tel 619/488-1081. Garnet/Grand Aves exit off I-5. **Continental.** You may choose to dine indoors or outdoors at the Atoll. Inside is more sophisticated, with rattan chairs, crisp tablecloths, Villeroy and Boch china. Outside you'll find wrought-iron tables and chairs shaded by umbrellas and a dazzling view of Mission Bay. Lunch and dinner menus are extensive, from club sandwiches to sophisticated preparations of fresh ahi tuna, salmon, swordfish, and other seafood. Sunday brunch is very popular. Service is top-notch. **FYI:** Reservations recommended. Dress code. **Open:** Peak (June–Labor Day) daily 6:30am–11:30pm. **Prices:** Main courses $8–$20. AE, DC, DISC, MC, V. 💟 🖼 🅥🅟 ⅙

Beach Boy's Cantina & Sports Grill

In Belmont Park, 3125 Ocean Front Walk (South Mission Beach); tel 619/539-2697. W Mission Bay Dr exit off I-8. **Mexican.** Live entertainment, open-air seating, and a beachfront location are the big draws here. Fresh tortilla chips, soups, fajitas, and shrimp flamed with tequila are among the offerings. Happy hour daily 4–7pm. **FYI:** Reservations accepted. Big band. Children's menu. **Open:** Daily 8am–10pm. **Prices:** Main courses $6–$13. AE, DISC, MC, V. 🖼 ⅙

The Brigantine Seafood Grill

2444 San Diego Ave (Old Town); tel 619/298-9840. 3 mi N of downtown Old Town Ave exit off I-5. **Regional American/Seafood.** Nautical decor. The heated patio also has a fireplace, while the indoor dining area is dark. Specialties are fresh swordfish and Pacific King Salmon served with caper-dill sauce. **FYI:** Reservations recommended. Children's menu. Additional locations: 2725 Shelter Island Dr (tel 224-2871); 3263 Camino del Mar, Del Mar (tel 481-1166). **Open:** Lunch Mon–Sat 11:30am–4pm; dinner Mon–Thurs 4–10pm, Fri–Sat 4–10:30pm, Sun 4–10pm; brunch Sun 10:30am–3pm. **Prices:** Main courses $15–$20. AE, CB, DC, MC, V. 🎦 💟 ⅙

Café Lulu

419 F St (Gaslamp Quarter); tel 619/238-0114. Near entrance to Horton Plaza parking garage. **Coffeehouse.** One of the few places in town where you can dine in the wee hours. Avant-garde decor features metal sculpted tables and chairs, copper hanging lights, and a mosaic made of broken glass. Dozens of specialty coffee drinks are available, as well as breakfast fare, sandwiches, and salads. **FYI:** Reservations not accepted. Beer and wine only. **Open:** Mon–Thurs 9am–2am, Fri 9am–4am, Sat 10am–4am, Sun 10am–2am. **Prices:** Main courses $5–$7. No CC. ⅙

Cafe Pacifica

2414 San Diego Ave (Old Town); tel 619/291-6666. 3 mi NW of downtown Old Town Ave exit off I-5. **Seafood.** In the evening, a romantic hideaway with twinkling lights. Indoors, there are several intimate dining areas, and the outdoor patio is an excellent setting for lunch. The menu offers salmon and sweet-corn cakes, and ahi with shiitake mushrooms and ginger butter, among other specialties. **FYI:** Reservations recommended. **Open:** Lunch Tues–Fri 11am–2pm; dinner daily 5:30–10pm. **Prices:** Main courses $14–$18. AE, CB, DC, DISC, MC, V. ● ☑ VP &

Casa De Bandini
In Bazaar Del Mundo, 2754 Juan St (Old Town); tel 619/297-8211. 3 mi NW of downtown Old Town Ave exit off I-5. **Mexican.** An authentic Mexican dining experience; busy during peak hours but worth the wait. Outdoor dining is under colorful umbrellas to music of strolling mariachis; the atmosphere is more formal inside. House specialties are tequila lime shrimp and the "taco feast." **FYI:** Reservations not accepted. Guitar. Dress code. **Open:** Peak (mid-June–Labor Day) Mon–Thurs 11am–9:30pm, Fri–Sat 11am–10pm, Sun 10am–9:30pm. **Prices:** Main courses $5–$15. AE, CB, DC, DISC, MC, V. ▭ ▦ &

Celadon
3628 5th Ave (Hillcrest); tel 619/295-8800. 2 mi N of downtown Between Brookes and Pennsylvania Aves. **Thai.** Easy to spot on the west side of Fifth Ave, with its pink stucco exterior and heliotrope awning. Interior is very pretty in pink and green with Thai artifacts along the walls. Food is primarily Thai-style seafood, pork, beef, and chicken, including lemon-grass beef and the spicy coconut shrimp. **FYI:** Reservations accepted. Beer and wine only. **Open:** Lunch Mon–Fri 11:30am–2pm; dinner Mon–Sat 5–10pm. **Prices:** Main courses $7–$15. AE, MC, V. &

ⓢ **The Corvette Diner Bar & Grill**
3946 5th Ave (Hillcrest); tel 619/542-1476. 2½ mi N of downtown Between Washington St and University Ave. **Diner.** An authentic 1950s diner with linoleum floors, booths, and a soda fountain. A real Corvette hangs from the ceiling in the main dining room. Food includes meat loaf with mashed potatoes, chicken-fried steak, burgers, and shakes. Great for families. Good value. **FYI:** Reservations not accepted. Children's menu. **Open:** Sun–Thurs 11am–11pm, Fri–Sat 11am–midnight. **Prices:** Main courses $5–$7. AE, DC, DISC, MC, V. ▦ VP &

★ **Croce's**
802 5th Ave (Gaslamp Quarter); tel 619/233-4355. At F St. **Southwestern.** Operated by the wife of late singer/songwriter Jim Croce, it has become a local favorite, renowned for fine food, jazz, and Jim Croce memorabilia. Black-and-white tiled floors and small tables give the place the feel of a cafe. The house specialities include California sea bass, pork tenderloin, and grilled ribeye. Ingrid's (next door) serves American southwest cuisine and light entrees, and desserts are available at Upstairs at Croce's. Croce's Bar serves up live jazz and rhythm and blues. **FYI:** Reservations not accepted.

Jazz. **Open:** Breakfast daily 7:30–11:30am; lunch daily 11:30am–3pm; dinner daily 4pm–midnight; brunch Sat–Sun 7:30am–3:30pm. **Prices:** Main courses $12–$20. AE, DC, DISC, MC, V. VP &

★ **Dobson's Bar & Restaurant**
956 Broadway Circle (Downtown); tel 619/231-6771. ½ block S of Broadway, near Horton Plaza. **Californian/French.** Paul Dobson has really made a name for himself with this namesake restaurant, where framed photos of the city's movers and shakers line the walls. Dobson is often at the door greeting customers. The downstairs area is dominated by a handsome wooden bar adorned with brass nameplates of frequent customers. Upstairs, the decor is more intimate and formal. Specialties of the house include mussel bisque, seafood stew, and veal sweetbreads. **FYI:** Reservations recommended. **Open:** Mon–Fri 11am–10pm, Sat 5:30–11pm. **Prices:** Main courses $9–$22; prix fixe $22. AE, DC, MC, V. VP &

★ **Filippi's Pizza Grotto**
1747 India St (Little Italy); tel 619/232-5095. ½ mi N of downtown Between Date and Fir Sts. **Italian.** People line up to get a table at this bustling locale where everything smells authentic. Patrons enter through a store stacked high with Italian pasta and jars of olives. This is not trendy Italian food, but hearty fare like spaghetti and meatballs with lots of tomato sauce. **FYI:** Reservations not accepted. Beer and wine only. Additional location: 962 Garnet St (tel 483-6222). **Open:** Sun–Mon 9am–10pm, Tues–Thurs 9am–10:30pm, Fri–Sat 9am–11:30pm. **Prices:** Main courses $5–$13. AE, CB, DC, DISC, MC, V. ▦ &

★ **Fio's Cucina Italiana**
801 5th Ave (Gaslamp Quarter); tel 619/234-3467. At F St. **Italian.** One of the top Italian restaurants in San Diego. Cream-colored walls provide an excellent backdrop for the brightly colored murals, while the upholstered chairs and booths are visually appealing and comfortable. An open kitchen and large picture windows provide plenty of entertainment. Try the breaded veal rolls and fried artichoke hearts. Extensive 175-item wine list emphasizes Italian, French, and California wines. **FYI:** Reservations recommended. Dress code. **Open:** Lunch Mon–Fri 11:30am–3pm; dinner Mon–Thurs 5–11pm, Fri–Sat 5pm–midnight, Sun 5–10pm. **Prices:** Main courses $10–$22. AE, DC, DISC, MC, V. VP &

Firehouse Beach Cafe
722 Grand Ave (Pacific Beach); tel 619/272-1999. 9 mi NW of downtown Grand/Garnet Aves exit off I-5. **Cafe.** Located just a half-block from the beach, this restaurant has a light, sunny decor and ceiling fans that capture the sea breeze. Head to the upstairs deck and enjoy a beer, a burger, and the ocean view from one of the umbrella-shaded tables. Known for its hamburgers, but breakfast and weekend brunch are also very popular. **FYI:** Reservations accepted. Children's

menu. **Open:** Peak (June–Sept) Sun–Thurs 7am–10pm, Fri–Sat 7am–11pm. **Prices:** Main courses $7–$12. AE, DC, DISC, MC, V. ⛴ ⛰ 👥

The Fish Market/Top of the Market
750 N Harbor Dr (Downtown); tel 619/232-3474. **Seafood.** Upstairs, the Top of the Market offers elegant dining and panoramic views. Downstairs, the Fish Market features an oyster bar, windows facing the water, and an outdoor patio. Both serve ultrafresh fish and seafood, including delicacies such as Alaskan halibut, Catalina swordfish, and Chinook salmon. **FYI:** Reservations not accepted. Children's menu. Additional location: 640 Via de la Valle, Del Mar (tel 755-2277). **Open:** Lunch daily 11am–4pm; dinner Sun–Thurs 4–9:30pm, Fri–Sat 4–10pm. **Prices:** Main courses $9–$32. AE, CB, DC, DISC, MC, V. ⛴ ⛰ 👥 VP &

Ⓢ **Galaxy Grill**
522 Horton Plaza (Downtown); tel 619/234-7211. **Diner.** Busy 1950s-style diner with simple Formica tables, vinyl booths, and an outdoor patio. Waitresses dressed in 1950s attire serve burgers and shakes. **FYI:** Reservations not accepted. Beer and wine only. **Open:** Mon–Thurs 11am–9pm, Fri–Sat 11am–10pm, Sun 11am–8pm. **Prices:** Main courses $4–$7. AE, DISC, MC, V. 👥 &

Ⓢ **Grand Central Cafe**
In YMCA building, 500 W Broadway (Downtown); tel 619/234-CAFE. **American.** Standard coffee shop decor with tables and a counter. Classic American fare such as meat loaf, baked chicken, and chicken-fried steak. Pasta, sandwiches, and steaks also served. **FYI:** Reservations not accepted. Beer and wine only. **Open:** Mon–Fri 7am–3pm, Sat–Sun 7am–1pm. **Prices:** Lunch main courses $6–$7. AE, DISC, MC, V. &

♟ **Grant Grill**
In US Grant Hotel, 326 Broadway (Downtown); tel 619/239-6806. **Continental.** A men's club until 1972, when three unescorted women arrived and demanded to be seated. The place for power lunches for San Diego's business elite, offering a clubby atmosphere with leather booths, upholstered chairs, and oil paintings. A large wooden bar and a pool table complete the picture. Menu specialties include roast veal chop and turtle soup with a splash of sherry. **FYI:** Reservations recommended. Jazz/singer. Dress code. **Open:** Breakfast Mon–Fri 6:30–10:30am, Sat–Sun 6:30–11:30am; lunch Mon–Fri 11:30am–2pm; dinner Sun–Thurs 5:30–10pm, Fri–Sat 5:30–10:30pm; brunch Sat–Sun 11:30am–2pm. **Prices:** Main courses $18–$41. AE, DC, DISC, MC, V. ♥ VP &

Kansas City Barbeque
610 W Market St (Downtown); tel 619/231-9680. **Barbecue.** An old-fashioned barbecue stand; scenes from *Top Gun* were filmed here. Walls are cluttered with license plates and naval airmens' hats; there's also an outdoor patio. Specialties are barbecued pork and beef ribs, and extra-large, flaky onion

rings. **FYI:** Reservations not accepted. Beer and wine only. **Open:** Daily 11am–1am. **Prices:** Main courses $9–$11. DISC, MC, V.

Karl Strauss' Old Columbia Brewery & Grill
1157 Columbia St (Downtown); tel 619/234-BREW. **New American/Grill.** A sprawling, enjoyable restaurant with a large bar and lots of wood and exposed brick. Among the specialties are the grilled Johnsonville sausage platter, beer-battered fish and chips, and beers brewed on the premises. **FYI:** Reservations recommended. Children's menu. Beer and wine only. **Open:** Lunch daily 11:30am–4pm; dinner Mon–Wed 4–10pm, Thurs–Sat 4pm–midnight, Sun 4–10pm. **Prices:** Main courses $6–$14. MC, V. &

Ⓢ **Kung Food**
2949 5th Ave (Hillcrest); tel 619/298-7302. 1½ mi N of downtown Near Balboa Park. **Vegetarian.** San Diego's best-known vegetarian restaurant: no meat products, no bleached flours, no sugar, and lots of low-fat choices. Popular dishes include Greek spinach pie, tofu vegetable enchiladas, and fettuccine alfredo. Deli/gift shop next door sells vegetarian cookbooks, new age music, and take-out food. **FYI:** Reservations not accepted. Beer and wine only. **Open:** Mon–Thurs 11:30am–9pm, Fri 11:30am–10pm, Sat 8:30am–10pm, Sun 8:30am–9pm. **Prices:** Main courses $5–$10. DISC, MC, V. ⛴

La Gran Tapa
611 B St (Downtown); tel 619/234-8272. **Spanish.** Cafe-style chairs and small tables flanking a lively, dark wood bar. The draw here is the tapas (Spanish hors d'oeuvres), such as ajo al horno, baked whole heads of garlic with feta cheese. Also on the menu: empanadillas filled with chicken, cheese, and black beans, and paella with shrimp, octopus, clams, and mussels. **FYI:** Reservations recommended. Guitar. **Open:** Mon–Fri 11am–10pm, Sat–Sun 5–10pm. **Prices:** Main courses $8–$16. AE, MC, V. ◻ &

Liaison
2202 4th Ave; tel 619/234-5540. **French.** The ambience of a French-country inn, with exposed wood, stone, and copper pots and pans on display. Outdoor patio is a romantic spot to dine. Specials include rack of lamb and chateaubriand. **FYI:** Reservations recommended. Beer and wine only. **Open:** Tues–Thurs 5–9:30pm, Fri–Sat 5–10:30pm, Sun 5–9:30pm. **Prices:** Main courses $11–$19; prix fixe $16–$24. AE, DC, DISC, MC, V. ♥ ⛴ &

Lino's Italian Restaurant
In Bazaar Del Mundo, 2754 Calhoun St (Old Town); tel 619/299-7124. 3 mi NW of downtown Old Town Area exit off I-5. **Italian.** A small, quaint restaurant. There are several small dining rooms, as well as patio seating. Specialties include chicken with orange sauce, veal and scampi combination, and a number of pastas. **FYI:** Reservations recommended. Dress

code. **Open:** Peak (Mem Day–Labor Day) lunch daily 11am–5pm; dinner daily 5–10pm. **Prices:** Main courses $7–$14. AE, DC, DISC, MC, V. 💗 ⚐

Marino's
4475 Ingraham St (Pacific Beach); tel 619/490-0168. Grand/Garnet exit off I-5. **Italian.** Family-owned and friendly. Decor features red tablecloths, ceiling fans, wood paneling, and large oil paintings depicting Italian scenes. Dishes include lasagna, manicotti, ravioli, pizza, eggplant Parmesan, and baked zucchini. Piano player on weekends. **FYI:** Reservations not accepted. Piano. Beer and wine only. **Open:** Tues–Thurs 4–10pm, Fri–Sat 4–11pm, Sun 4–10pm. **Prices:** Main courses $10–$17. MC, V.

The Old Ox
4474 Mission Blvd (Pacific Beach); tel 619/275-3790. Grove/Garnet Aves exit off I-5 ½ block from beach at west end of Garnet Ave. **Californian.** Lots of greenery, exposed brick, and a glass ceiling give dining room the feel of a conservatory. Fresh fish is a good choice here, but there is also a selection of pastas, salads, and beef entrees on the dinner menu. Sunday brunch is also quite popular. There is a separate, slightly darker dining room for smokers. The bar draws a young crowd. **FYI:** Reservations accepted. Children's menu. **Open:** Lunch Mon–Fri 11:30am–2pm; dinner Sun–Thurs 5–9pm, Fri–Sat 5–10pm; brunch Sat–Sun 10am–2pm. **Prices:** Main courses $10–$22. AE, MC, V. ⚐

⑤ The Old Spaghetti Factory
275 5th Ave (Gaslamp Quarter); tel 619/233-4323. **Italian.** A family restaurant with a Victorian ambience. Decor features stained glass, Tiffany-style lamps, and a trolley car converted into a dining room. Menu lists homemade lasagna, spaghetti with two Greek cheeses, and Italian cream sodas for dessert. **FYI:** Reservations not accepted. Children's menu. **Open:** Lunch Mon–Fri 11:30am–2pm; dinner Mon–Thurs 5–10pm, Fri 5–11pm, Sat noon–11pm, Sun noon–10pm. **Prices:** Main courses $4–$8. AE, DC, DISC, MC, V. 📷 ⚐

Old Town Liquor & Deli
2304 San Diego Ave (Old Town); tel 619/291-4888. 3 mi NW of downtown Old Town Ave exit off I-5. **Deli.** A deli and liquor store with seating at two plastic tables on a busy sidewalk. Good picnic spots nearby for take-out orders. Fare includes sandwiches (with pastrami and turkey), shrimp salad on a croissant, and bagels and lox. **FYI:** Reservations not accepted. No liquor license. **Open:** Mon–Fri 7am–8:30pm, Sat 7am–6pm, Sun 8am–4:30pm. **Prices:** Main courses $4–$5. AE, DISC, ER, MC, V. 🚗

⑤ Old Town Mexican Cafe
2489 San Diego Ave (Old Town); tel 619/297-4330. 3 mi NW of downtown Old Town Ave exit off I-5. **Mexican.** Nothing fancy, but perhaps the best Mexican restaurant in Old Town. Dark wood, booths, and Mexican artifacts set the tone. Fresh tortillas are hand-made daily. The menu lists carnitas, Mexican-style rotisserie pork ribs, and Old Town pollo (rotisserie chicken). **FYI:** Reservations not accepted. Mariachis. Children's menu. **Open:** Daily 7am–11pm. **Prices:** Main courses $6–$11. AE, DISC, MC, V. 📷 ⚐

Pacific Beach Bar & Grill
860 Garnet Ave (Pacific Beach); tel 619/2PB-GRILL. Grand/Garnet Aves exit off I-5. **Cafe.** An under-30 crowd flocks to this new restaurant and sports bar for loud music and an extensive selection of beers, sandwiches, soft tacos, burgers, and pizza. Decor is nonexistent, unless you count the neon beer signs. Shorts, T-shirts, and in-line skates are the preferred attire; there are several television sets and three pool tables. **FYI:** Reservations not accepted. **Open:** Daily 11am–1:30am. **Prices:** Main courses $4–$10. AE, DC, DISC, MC, V.

Panda Inn
506 Horton Plaza (Downtown); tel 619/233-7800. Located on top floor. **Chinese.** Comfortable, upscale restaurant with black lacquered furnishings and a side room offering views of downtown and the bay. Specialties include sweet and pungent shrimp, and Kon Pao San Yan (sliced shrimp, chicken, and beef sautéed with green onion and peanuts in a spicy sauce). **FYI:** Reservations recommended. **Open:** Lunch daily 11am–3pm; dinner Sun–Thurs 3–10pm, Fri–Sat 3–11pm. **Prices:** Main courses $10–$15. AE, DC, DISC, MC, V. ⚐

★ Rainwater's on Kettner
1202 Kettner Blvd (Downtown); tel 619/233-5757. Located at foot of B St near historic Sante Fe Depot. **American.** Known as the best place in San Diego for a "power lunch." Leather booths and cherrywood paneling make this look like a private club. Entrees include prime, aged beef, salmon in parchment, and chicken breast with veal pan gravy and caramelized onions. **FYI:** Reservations recommended. Children's menu. Dress code. **Open:** Lunch Mon–Fri 11:30am–5pm; dinner Mon–Sat 5pm–midnight, Sun 5–11pm. **Prices:** Main courses $17–$36. AE, CB, DC, MC, V. 🆅🅿 ⚐

Rancho El Nopal
In Bazaar del Mundo, 2754 Calhoun St (Old Town); tel 619/295-0584. 3 mi NW of downtown Old Town Ave exit off I-5. **Mexican.** Authentic Mexican decor, with brightly colored tables and chairs. Food is somewhat lackluster, but prices are good and this is a fun place. **FYI:** Reservations recommended. Guitar. Children's menu. Dress code. **Open:** Daily 11am–10pm. **Prices:** Main courses $5–$10. AE, DC, MC, V. 📷 ⚐

⑤ ★ San Diego Chicken Pie Shop
2633 El Cajon Blvd (North Park); tel 619/295-0156. Washington St exit off CA 63 or I-5. **American.** Oldest continuously operating restaurant in San Diego, reminiscent of a 1950s midwest diner. Specialty here is pot pie, filled with lots of chicken and turkey. Fast service and a great bargain. Popular cream pies and fruit pies are made here as well. **FYI:** Reservations not accepted. No liquor license. **Open:** Daily 10am–8pm. **Prices:** Main courses $4–$6. No CC. 📷 ⚐

Saska's

3768 Mission Blvd (North Mission Beach); tel 619/488-7311. 9 mi NW of downtown W Mission Bay Dr exit off I-8. **Seafood/Steak.** Inside, an English pub atmosphere, with lots of dark wood and red Leatherette booths; outside, the casual patio has a "beachy" feel. Specialties include steaks in various sizes and cuts, teriyaki chicken, and fresh fish specials. The bar is very popular with locals. **FYI:** Reservations accepted. **Open:** Mon–Thurs 11:30am–2am, Fri 11:30am–3am, Sat 9:30am–3am, Sun 9:30am–2am. **Prices:** Main courses $7–$16. AE, CB, DC, MC, V. 🍴 📷

Sfuzzi

340 5th Ave (Gaslamp Quarter); tel 619/231-2323. **Italian.** There's a patio outside, and European brick, wooden floors, and an inviting bar inside. Specialties include pastas, pizzas made in a wood-fired oven, and drinks like the frozen Sfuzzi—frozen peach puree and white wine. **FYI:** Reservations recommended. Children's menu. **Open:** Sun–Thurs 11am–10pm, Fri–Sat 11am–11pm. **Prices:** Main courses $8–$18. AE, CB, DC, MC, V. 📷 ♿

Taste of Thai

527 University Ave (Hillcrest); tel 619/291-7525. 2½ mi N of downtown Washington St exit off I-5; drive east on Washington to University Ave. **Thai.** A very pleasant small restaurant with a small bar and an outdoor patio. Menu includes spicy duck—half a bird topped with curry paste—and vegetarian duck, served with peppers, peas, and bamboo shoots. **FYI:** Reservations recommended. Beer and wine only. **Open:** Lunch Mon–Sat 11:30am–3pm; dinner daily 5–11pm. **Prices:** Main courses $6–$11. AE, MC, V. 🍴 ♿

REFRESHMENT STOPS ☕

Extraordinary Desserts

2929 5th Ave (Hillcrest); tel 619/294-7001. 1½ mi N of downtown Between Palm and Quince Sts. **Desserts.** A wonderful place, and one of the only dessert shops in town. Small wooden tables are topped with fresh flowers, set on a painted concrete floor. Everything is made fresh on the premises daily; Tahitian cheesecake and chocolate-macadamia torte are especially popular. Smoking allowed outside only. **Open:** Mon–Thurs 8:30am–11pm, Fri 8:30am–midnight, Sat 11am–midnight, Sun 2–11pm. MC, V. ♿

Kensington Coffee Co

4141 Adams Ave (Kensington); tel 619/280-5153. 7 mi NE of downtown Adams Ave exit off I-15; at Marlborough Dr. **Coffeehouse.** The wonderful scent of fresh-ground coffee pervades this cafe/restaurant with a black-and-white checkerboard floor and red and black chairs. Sip cappuccino or bite into great muffins, scones, pastries, and sandwiches. They also sell coffee beans, tea, mugs, teapots, and greeting cards. **Open:** Daily 6am–11pm. AE, DISC, MC, V.

Pannikin Coffee & Tea

675 G St (Gaslamp Quarter); tel 619/239-7891. At 7th St. **Coffeehouse.** Informal coffeehouse with colorful decor and comfortable seating. Coffee and tea paraphernalia is sold, as are specialty teas and coffees, including White Heat, a white-chocolate espresso drink, and pastries. Additional locations: 7467 Girard Ave, La Jolla (tel 454-5463); 2670 Via de la Valle, Del Mar (tel 481-8007). **Open:** Mon–Fri 8am–6pm, Sat–Sun 10am–5pm. AE, DISC, MC, V. ♿

ATTRACTIONS 📷

TOP ATTRACTIONS

Sea World

1720 S Shores Rd (in Mission Bay); tel 619/226-3901. A 150-acre marine life entertainment park, Sea World is renowned for its performing dolphins, killer whales, and seals. At the 5,500-seat Shamu Stadium, visitors watch in awe as four-ton black-and-white killer whales launch themselves into the air, and dolphins turn graceful midair somersaults and flips. But Sea World also offers numerous educational exhibits, shows, and rides that feature sharks, fish, otters, penguins, and even birds.

The newest attraction is **Mission: Bermuda Triangle,** a simulated deep-dive submarine ride that employs high-tech audio and video in conjunction with flight simulator technology to take riders on an undersea adventure. At **Shamu Backstage,** visitors are able to touch, train, and feed killer whales. Other featured attractions and shows are **Shark Encounter,** where visitors walk through a transparent underwater tunnel that runs through the center of a 700,000-gallon habitat populated by 90 sharks of 13 different species; **Rocky Point Preserve,** where guests learn about bottlenose dolphins and Alaskan sea otters (survivors of the 1989 *Valdez* oil spill), who live in a natural rocky habitat; and **Wings of the World,** which showcases 50 feathered stars, including hawks, falcons, and macaws. There are numerous other aquariums, exhibits, and shows, plus a special play area reserved for children 37–61 inches tall. Several shops, snack bars, and restaurants. Guided 90-minute behind-the-scenes tours are offered daily (additional fee required). **Open:** Peak (mid-June–early-Sept) Sun–Thurs 9am–10pm, Fri–Sat 9am–11pm. Reduced hours off-season. **$$$$**

Seaport Village

W Harbor Dr and Kettner Blvd; tel 619/235-4014. A pleasant mix of 75 shops, seafood houses, and snack bars, Seaport Village also offers a quarter-mile bayside boardwalk and a colorful 1890 carousel with hand-carved horses. There is often free entertainment in the gazebo on weekend afternoons. (Some restaurants are open extended hours.) **Open:** Peak (June–Aug) daily 10am–10pm. Reduced hours off-season. **Free**

Horton Plaza

Broadway and 4th Ave; tel 619/239-8180. Easily one of San Diego's most popular tourist attractions, this is much more than a shopping center. Patrons can shop, stroll, snack or dine, enjoy free entertainment, see a movie, and people-watch—all within a unique and colorful architectural framework. Stop by the information office on the lower level for a current schedule of events and entertainment. **Open:** Mon–Fri 10am–9pm, Sat 10am–6pm, Sun 11am–6pm; extended summer hours. **Free**

Cabrillo National Monument

Tel 619/557-5450. One of the most-visited national monuments in the United States, Cabrillo National Monument is located at the tip of Point Loma, 10 miles west of I-8 on CA 209 (Catalina Blvd). It commemorates European exploration of the west coast of what became the USA by the explorer Juan Rodriguez Cabrillo in 1542. Cabrillo's statue dominates the tip of Point Loma, which also provides a vantage point for observing the migration of gray whales, which travel from the Arctic Ocean to Baja California between December and mid-March. A restored lighthouse (1855) allows a glimpse of what life was like here in the 19th century.

National Park Service rangers conduct walks at the monument (phone for details), and there are numerous tidepools to be explored. Films on Cabrillo, tidepools, and California gray whales are shown daily from 10am to 4pm, on the hour. **Open:** Daily 9am–5:15pm. **$$**

MUSEUMS

Museum of Contemporary Art, San Diego

One museum, two locations: 700 Prospect St, La Jolla, and 1001 Kettner Blvd, San Diego; tel 619/234-1001. This museum focuses primarily on work produced since 1950. Its permanent collection includes works from Lichenstein, Warhol, and others. Also traveling exhibitions. **Open:** Tues–Sun 10am–5pm. Evening hours: La Jolla, Wed until 8pm, Downtown, Friday until 8pm. **$**

Children's Museum of San Diego

200 W Island Ave; tel 619/233-8792. Hands-on exhibits and programs which are changed monthly. The Art Zone art studio allows children to create individual or group projects. **Open:** Tues–Sat 10am–4:30pm, Sun 11am–4:30pm. **$$**

Maritime Museum

1306 N Harbor Dr; tel 619/234-9153. This museum consists of a fine trio of ships: the full-rigged merchant ship *Star of India* (1863), whose impressive masts are an integral part of the San Diego cityscape; the steam-powered ferryboat *Berkeley* (1898), which worked around the clock carrying San Franciscans to safety after the 1906 earthquake; and the sleek steam yacht *Medea* (1904), one of the few remaining such vessels in the world. **Open:** Peak (Mem Day–Labor Day) daily 9am–9pm. Reduced hours off-season. **$$$**

Junípero Serra Museum

2727 Presidio Dr; tel 619/297-3258. Perched on the hill above Old Town in Presidio Park (see below), this 1929 building stands near the site of the original Presidio of San Diego, the oldest European settlement on the west coast of the United States and Canada (circa 1769–1835). Exhibits highlight the Spanish colonial and Mexican periods in San Diego's history, and include artifacts from excavations of the Presidio site; a collection of Spanish Renaissance furniture; and a room devoted to life at the San Diego Presidio. The tower affords a view of Mission Valley, Mission Bay, and the Pacific Ocean, and features documents on the development of the area over about 125 years. The museum store has many books and gift items dealing with this period in history. **Open:** Tues–Sat 10am–4:30pm, Sun noon–4:30pm. **$**

Firehouse Museum

1572 Columbia St; tel 619/232-FIRE. Appropriately housed in San Diego's oldest firehouse, this museum features fire engines (including hand-drawn and horse-drawn models) and memorabilia of firemen from all over the world, such as antique alarms, fire hats, and foundry molds for fire hydrants. **Open:** Thurs–Fri 10am–2pm, Sat–Sun 10am–4pm. **$**

HISTORICAL ATTRACTIONS

Presidio Park

Sometimes called the "Plymouth Rock of the Pacific," this was the site of the Mission **Basilica San Diego de Alcala,** San Diego's only settlement from 1769 until the mid-1830s, when families began to move down the hill, establishing what is now known as Old Town. The large cross in the park was made from floor tile taken from the Presidio ruins. The graceful **Junípero Serra Museum** (see above), with its 70-foot tower, sits atop a hill overlooking Old Town.

Old Town San Diego State Historic Park

4002 Wallace St; tel 619/220-5243. The birthplace of San Diego—indeed, of California itself—this park recaptures the aura of Mexican California, which existed here until the mid-1800s. Seven original buildings remain; the rest are reconstructions. Highlights include **La Casa de Estudillo** (1827), an original adobe house that depicts the lifestyle of a wealthy family during the Mexican era; the **Seeley Stables Museum,** which has a 17-minute slide show and two floors of wagons, buggies, stagecoaches, and other memorabilia; and the **San Diego** *Union* **Museum,** a restored original wood building (it was shipped around the Horn in 1850) that housed one of the first newspapers in the region. A free walking tour leaves daily from the Visitors Center at 2pm. **Open:** Visitors center, daily 10am–5pm; shops, daily 10am–8pm; restaurants, daily 10am–9pm. **$**

Gaslamp Quarter

Tel 619/233-5227. In the heart of downtown San Diego, bounded by Broadway, Harbor Dr, and Fourth and Sixth Aves, these 16½ blocks contain outstanding Victorian-style commercial buildings built between the Civil War and World

War I. Today an impressive number have been restored to their former grandeur, and their ground floors enlivened with restaurants, shops, and places to dance or listen to jazz.

Whaley House

2482 San Diego Ave; tel 619/298-2482. This striking two-story brick house, the first in San Diego, was built in 1856 for Thomas Whaley and his family, and still contains many of their furnishings. Exhibits include a life mask of Abraham Lincoln (one of only six made); two bookcases given to President Grant on his inauguration; John Quincy Adams's settee; the spinet piano used in the film *Gone With the Wind;* and the concert piano that accompanied Jenny Lind on her final US tour. Also on the grounds are rose and herb gardens and a mid-19th-century house.

The house is one of two in California with documented evidence of supernatural activity (spirits thought to reside here include those of Thomas Whaley and his wife, Anna), making the house a popular spot around Halloween. **Open:** Daily 10am–5pm; **$$**

William Heath Davis House

410 Island Ave; tel 619/233-5227 or 233-4692. Shipped around Cape Horn in 1850, this pre-fabricated lumber home is the oldest surviving structure in downtown San Diego. The museum and adjacent urban park are open to the public. Walking tours of the Gaslamp Quarter Historic District are available. **Open:** Mon–Sat 10am–4pm, Sun noon–4pm. **Free**

Villa Montezuma

1925 K St; tel 619/239-2211. Built in 1887 for then internationally acclaimed musician and author Jesse Shepard, this opulent mansion has been painstakingly restored and furnished with period pieces by the San Diego Historical Society. Lush with Victoriana, the house was designed more as a place to entertain guests than as a residence; the largest room in the house is the Music Room, where Shepard often entertained. The house features numerous stained-glass windows—some quite huge—which depict Mozart, Beethoven, Rubens, and St Cecilia (patron saint of musicians), among others. These windows accounted for more than a third of the mansion's construction cost. Guided tours last about 45 minutes. **Open:** Sat–Sun noon–4:30pm. **$**

Heritage Park

2455 Heritage Park Row; tel 619/694-3049. This small park is filled with original 19th-century Victorian houses moved here from other places and put to new uses, among them a bed-and-breakfast inn, a doll shop, and an antique shop. The most recent addition is the small synagogue, built in 1889. **Open:** Daily sunrise–sunset. **Free**

Mormon Battalion Visitors Center

2510 Juan St (Old Town); tel 619/298-3317. The longest infantry march in American history, made by a 500-member Mormon regiment from 1846–1847, is commemorated at this facility. At the onset of the Mexican-American War, the men marched from Fort Leavenworth, Kansas, to San Die-go—about 2,000 miles—but by the time they arrived the fighting had moved south. The only battle they fought was along the way—against a herd of wild bulls near Tucson. Exhibits include artifacts from the march, photographs, and a list of the men who made up the battalion; a diorama and a 15-minute slide show tell the story in detail. **Open:** Daily 9am–9pm. **Free**

BALBOA PARK

Visitors Center

Tel 619/239-0512. Entrances at 6th Ave and Laurel St, and Park Blvd and Presidents Way. The center provides details on park facilities and the roughly 1,000 acres of walkways, gardens, historical buildings, and museums in the park. Free walking tours detail the ornate pavilion with the world's largest outdoor organ, a high-spouting fountain, a nationally acclaimed theater, and the world-famous zoo (see listings below). The center is open daily from 9am to 4pm; free organ concerts are given at the organ pavilion on Sunday at 2pm (and weekday evenings in summer); free tram transportation within the park is provided daily; ask at the Visitor Center for schedule. **Free**

San Diego Zoo

Park Blvd and Zoo Place; tel 619/234-3153. This world-famous zoo, home to 4,000 animals, is set on 100 subtropical acres that double as a botanical garden. It is one of the few zoos outside Australia to have koalas, and features many rare and endangered species. Aerial tram rides ($1) provide bird's-eye views of the park, and double-decker bus tours provide close-uup glimpses of the animals and lively commentary by a park ranger. Tours cost $4 for adults, $3 for children, and last 40 minutes. Children's zoo, animal shows. Snack bars, restaurant. **Open:** Daily, from 9am; closing hour varies with season. **$$$$**

Museum of San Diego History

1649 El Prado; tel 619/232-6203. Permanent and changing exhibits tell stories in words and photos about the city's (and the park's) colorful past. Free documentary videos are sometimes shown as well. The bookstore also sells Victorian-inspired items and dolls. **Open:** Wed–Sun 10am–4:30pm, second Tues of every month 10am–4:30pm (free). **$**

San Diego Natural History Museum

1788 El Prado; tel 619/232-3821. The primary focus of this museum is on the natural history of San Diego, Southern California, and Baja. It also hosts traveling exhibitions, which usually run for 3 to 5 months each. The permanent collection includes gems and minerals and exhibits on the desert, shore, and ocean ecology of the southwestern United States and Mexico. Phone ahead for details on exhibits, hours, and fees. **Open:** Daily, hours vary with exhibition. **$$$**

Museum of Man

1350 El Prado; tel 619/239-2001. In a landmark building located just inside the park entrance at the Cabrillo Bridge, this museum is devoted to the peoples of North and South

America. On display are life-size artists' models of a dozen varieties of Homo sapiens, from Cro-Magnon and Neanderthal to Peking Man, along with a replica of Lucy, the 3½-million-year-old skeleton discovered in Ethiopia in 1974. Other permanent exhibits deal with ancient Egypt, the Maya, and the Kumeyaay Indians, who once inhabited the San Diego area. The museum also features traveling exhibits. **Open:** Daily 10am–4:30pm. Closed some hols. **$$**

San Diego Aerospace Museum
2001 Pan American Way; tel 619/234-8291. The era of powered flight—from the Wright brothers to the Space Age—is chronicled in this museum. On display are more than 60 restored aircraft from all periods of aviation, including a replica of Lindbergh's *Spirit of St Louis,* an actual Japanese Zero from World War II, an A-12 Blackbird spy plane, and replicas of American space capsules. A **Behind-the-Scenes Tour** is offered of the museum's aircraft restoration facilities, where visitors can observe at least three restoration projects in progress. **Open:** Peak (Mem Day–Labor Day) daily 10am–5pm. Reduced hours off-season. **$$**

Reuben H Fleet Space Theater and Science Center
1875 El Prado; tel 619/238-1233. The busiest museum in Balboa Park, the Science Center features 50 interactive exhibits, a Laserium, and an Omnimax theater with a 76-foot dome screen and shows almost hourly. Separate admission for each area. **Open:** Opens daily at 9:30am. Hours vary. **$$$**

San Diego Museum of Art
1450 El Prado; tel 619/232-7931. This renowned museum contains approximately 10,500 art objects, dating from Egyptian and pre-Columbian periods to the present. Its featured collections include works from the Italian Renaissance, the Dutch and Flemish schools, and the Spanish baroque period. An East Asian collection contains pieces from the neolithic Yang Shao culture of China; there's also a Japanese suit of armor (1578); and an acclaimed collection of Indian, Persian, and Turkish watercolors. You'll also find many noteworthy contemporary paintings and sculptures. Works are included by Renoir, Van Gogh, Picasso, and El Greco, among many others. Museum shop; sculpture garden cafe with outdoor seating. **Open:** Tues–Sun 10am–4:30pm. **$$$**

Timken Museum of Art
1500 El Prado; tel 619/239-5548. Called the "jewel of Balboa Park," this museum houses the Putnam Foundation's collection of European old masters, 19th-century American paintings, and an outstanding collection of Russian icons. **Open:** Oct–Aug, Tues–Sat 10am–4:30pm, Sun 1:30–4:30pm. **Free**

Museum of Photographic Arts
1649 El Prado; tel 239-5262. One of the nation's finest photography museums, this facility offers changing exhibits of the works of master international photographers. About six shows are featured each year; emphasis is on both historical and contemporary work. The bookstore has an extensive selection. **Open:** Daily 10am–5pm. **$**

San Diego Automotive Museum
2080 Pan American Plaza; tel 619/231-2886. There are approximately 60 vehicles on display here at all times, from both the museum's large core selection and "featured attractions" on loan from collectors from all over the world. Displays change frequently, and cover a wide range of topics and all periods of automotive history. Comprehensive automobile resource center; gift shop with rare and unusual automobile-related items. **Open:** Peak (June–Sept) 10am–5pm. Reduced hours off-season. **$$**

Model Railroad Museum
In Casa de Balboa, 1649 El Prado; tel 619/696-0199. Perhaps the largest indoor model railroading museum in the United States, this 24,000-square-foot building houses four permanent operating scale-model railroads: the San Diego & Arizona, the Tehachapi Pass, the Cabrillo & Southwestern, and the Pacific Desert Lines. There is a working hands-on railroad layout for kids, along with several interactive exhibits on railroad history and model railroading. **Open:** Wed–Fri 11am–4pm, Sat–Sun 11am–5pm, first Tues of every month 11am–4pm. **$**

Hall of Champions
1649 El Prado; tel 619/234-2544. One of only a few multisport museums in the country, this facility encompasses more than 40 different sports. Highlights include a large selection of Ted Williams memorabilia, including the bat used to establish his record-breaking .406 batting average; a large Thoroughbred racing exhibit with actual Preakness Stakes and Kentucky Derby trophies; and an extensive exhibit devoted to bass fishing. Interactive video exhibits; theater showing clips and features; gift shop. **Open:** Daily 10am–4:30pm. **$$**

House of Pacific Relations International Cottages
Tel 619/234-0739. This cluster of one- and two-room cottages offers a sample of the culture, traditions, and history of 31 national groups. Each cottage is decorated in the style of the nation it represents and offers samples of authentic food. **Open:** Sun noon–4pm and fourth Tues of month 12:30–3:30pm. **Free**

Japanese Friendship Garden
Tel 619/232-2780 or 232-2721 holidays. The Garden is located next to the Organ Pavilion in Balboa Park. Of the 11½ acres designated for the Garden, only an acre has been developed thus far, but construction is underway on the temporary planting of the entire area with paths throughout, a tea facility, and the first stage of a cultural center. The present Exhibit House is a Zen-style teahouse with shoji screens, bonsai and Ikebana displays, and changing cultural exhibits. Special seasonal events are held throughout the year. **Open:** Tues and Fri–Sun 10am–4pm. **$**

Botanical Building and Lily Pond
El Prado; tel 619/234-8901. A collection of ivy, ferns, orchids, impatiens, begonias, and other plants sheltered beneath the iron framework of an old Santa Fe railroad station. The lily pond in front attracts sun worshipers and street entertainers. **Open:** Tues–Sun 10am–4:30pm. **Free**

Spreckels Organ Pavilion
Tel 619/239-0512. Given to the people of San Diego in 1914 by the brothers John D and Adolph Spreckels, the ornate, curved pavilion houses a magnificent organ with 4,445 individual pipes, which range in length from less than half an inch to more than 32 feet. Visitors may enjoy free hour-long concerts on Sunday at 2pm. There is seating for 2,400.

OTHER ATTRACTIONS

Mission Bay Park
In this 4,600-acre aquatic playground visitors will discover 27 miles of bayfront, 17 miles of oceanfront beaches, picnic areas, children's playgrounds, and paths for biking, roller-skating, and jogging. The bay lends itself to windsurfing, sailing, jet skiing, waterskiing, and fishing.

Coronado Bay Bridge
Four lanes wide and two miles long, this bridge linking downtown San Diego and Coronado was completed in 1969. Put out of business by its construction, commuter ferry services started up again in 1986, catering to tourists. Crossing the bridge you can see Mexico, the San Diego skyline, Coronado, the naval station, and San Diego Bay. The middle section of the bridge floats, so that in the event of its destruction ships would still have access to the harbor and the sea beyond. Toll charged when traveling from San Diego to Coronado only.

Old Town Trolley Tours
2115 Kurtz St; tel 619/298-TOUR. A great way to see San Diego, this tour allows riders to get off at any of the nine stops along the route and reboard at their leisure (trolleys visit each stop about every half-hour). Stops include many of San Diego's major tourist spots. The length of one entire loop is about 1 hour. **$$$$**

Invader Cruises
1066 N Harbor Dr; tel 619/234-8687 or toll free 800/445-4FUN. One of the largest dinng yacht companies on the west coast offers panoramic views of San Diego. Boarding nightly for Dinner Dance cruises; weekends for Champagne Brunch cruises; and daily for Harbor Tours and Whale Watches. Reservations are required. Call for times. **$$$$**

Naval Ship Tours
At **Broadway Pier,** near the intersection of Broadway and Harbor Dr, visiting ships, including those of foreign navies, are usually open for tours on weekends (tel 619/532-1431). Visible from the pier are the aircraft carriers USS *Kitty Hawk* and USS *Constellation.* Both are based at **US Naval Air Station North Island,** and are usually made available for

public tours on Saturday. Arrangements to visit these ships must be made 1 week in advance by calling 619/545-5669 *(Kitty Hawk)* or 619/545-2427 *(Constellation).* **Free**

San Diego Harbor Excursion
1050 N Harbor Dr; tel 619/234-4111. At the foot of Broadway. Daily tours of the bay, plus dinner cruises and, in winter, whale-watching excursions. **$$$$**

PROFESSIONAL SPORTS

Jack Murphy Stadium
9449 Friars Rd, Mission Valley; tel 619/525-8282. The NFL's Chargers play here August to December (tel 619/283-4494). The National League Padres take the field for baseball from April to September (tel 619/280-2111).

San Francisco

For airport lodgings, see San Francisco Int'l Airport

Surrounded on three sides by the Pacific Ocean and San Francisco Bay, San Francisco has always been a place that stands apart. Known as the City by its residents (never referred to as Frisco or San Fran), San Francisco is culturally sophisticated, politically active, racially diverse, philosophically heterogeneous, and largely affluent. It is a city of distinct and colorful neighborhoods: North Beach, Chinatown, Nob Hill, Russian Hill, Civic Center, Fisherman's Wharf, and Haight-Ashbury, among others. (The best way to see them is by foot.) Since its bawdy Gold Rush days, San Francisco has been tolerant of those who are different and welcoming to those who avoid convention. **Information:** San Francisco Convention & Visitors Bureau, 201 3rd St #900, San Francisco 94103 (tel 415/974-6900).

PUBLIC TRANSPORTATION
The **San Francisco Municipal Railway,** better known as **Muni** (tel 415/673-6864),operates the city's cable cars, buses, and Metro streetcars. The fare on buses and Metro streetcars is $1 for adults (payable in change or bills), 35¢ for ages 5–17, and 35¢ for seniors over 65. Cable cars cost $2 ($1 for seniors from 9pm to midnight and from 6 to 7am). **BART** (Bay Area Rapid Transit) (tel 415/992-2278) is a high-speed rail network connecting San Francisco with the East Bay—Oakland, Richmond, Concord, and Fremont. Fares range from 80¢ to $3, depending on distance traveled; tickets are dispensed from machines in the stations. Children age 4 and under ride free.

HOTELS 🏨

🛏 Alexander Inn
415 O'Farrell St, 94102 (Union Square); tel 415/928-6800 or toll free 800/843-8709; fax 415/928-3354. Basic budget hotel in a convenient downtown location. **Rooms:** 60 rms. CI 2pm/CO 11am. Nonsmoking rms avail. Small and bare. **Amenities:** 🕾 🕭 🖭 Cable TV, voice mail. No A/C. **Services:**

Rates (CP): Peak (June–Oct) $28–$72 S or D. Children under age 18 stay free. Lower rates off-season. AE, CB, DC, DISC, ER, JCB, MC, V.

ANA Hotel
50 3rd St, 94103; tel 415/974-6400 or toll free 800/ANA-HOTELS; fax 415/543-8268. At Market St. A 36-story luxury hotel less than a block from the Center for the Arts and Moscone Center. Very plush and cozy lounge with a fireplace. **Rooms:** 667 rms and stes. Executive level. CI 3pm/CO noon. Nonsmoking rms avail. Rooms, with a beautiful art deco decor, were renovated in 1993. For $10 extra, guests can stay in a "green" suite with environment-friendly recyclable products and water-saving shower head. **Amenities:** A/C, cable TV w/movies, dataport, voice mail, in-rm safe. All units w/minibars. **Services:** Car-rental desk, masseur, babysitting. **Facilities:** 1 restaurant (see "Restaurants" below), 1 bar (w/entertainment), sauna, steam rm, whirlpool. Upscale bistro, Cafe 53, serves breakfast, lunch, and dinner with an extensive lunch buffet. **Rates:** $220 S; $250 D; $380–$1,500 ste. Extra person $25. Children under age 12 stay free. Parking: Indoor, $24/day. AE, DC, DISC, JCB, MC, V.

Andrews Hotel
624 Post St, 94109 (Downtown); tel 415/563-6877 or toll free 800/926-3739; fax 415/928-6919. At Taylor St. Built in 1905 as the Sultan Turkish Bath House. **Rooms:** 48 rms and stes. CI 3pm/CO noon. No smoking. **Amenities:** TV. No A/C. Some units w/minibars. Free wine at bar from 5:30–7pm. **Services:** Babysitting. **Facilities:** 1 restaurant (see "Restaurants" below), 1 bar. **Rates (CP):** Peak (Aug–Oct) $82–$119 S or D; $119 ste. Extra person $10. Children under age 12 stay free. Lower rates off-season. Parking: Outdoor, $13/day. AE, DC, JCB, MC, V.

Atherton Hotel
685 Ellis St, 94109 (Civic Center); tel 415/474-5720 or toll free 800/474-5720; fax 415/474-8256. At Larkin St. An offbeat hotel with a certain rustic charm; however, some might consider it dark and drab. **Rooms:** 74 rms. CI 2pm/CO noon. Nonsmoking rms avail. Rooms are very basic; those facing the street are noisy. **Amenities:** Cable TV, in-rm safe. No A/C. **Services:** Babysitting. **Facilities:** 1 restaurant (bkfst and dinner only), 1 bar. **Rates:** Peak (June–Oct) $69–$119 S or D. Extra person $10. Children under age 12 stay free. Lower rates off-season. AE, DC, DISC, JCB, MC, V.

Beresford Arms
701 Post St, 94109 (Union Square); tel 415/673-2600 or toll free 800/533-6533; fax 415/474-0449. At Jones St. Welcomes pets. San Diego Zoo trainers who stay here sometimes bring animals to rooms; they've been known to take monkeys to tea in the lobby. **Rooms:** 96 rms, stes, and effic. CI open/CO noon. Nonsmoking rms avail. **Amenities:** Satel TV, refrig, dataport, VCR. No A/C. All units

w/minibars, some w/whirlpools. **Services:** Car-rental desk, babysitting. Extremely hospitable staff. Complimentary coffee and sweet rolls in the morning, plus afternoon tea and wine in the lobby. **Facilities:** Rates: $89 S; $99 D; $150 ste; $115 effic. Extra person $10. Children under age 12 stay free. Parking: Indoor, $12–$15/day. AE, CB, DC, DISC, EC, JCB, MC, V.

Best Western Americania
121 7th St, 94103; tel 415/626-0200 or toll free 800/444-5816; fax 415/626-3974. Between Mission and Howard Sts. Average property in a Mediterranean style. **Rooms:** 143 rms and stes. CI 2pm/CO noon. Nonsmoking rms avail. Clean, comfortable rooms with charming decor. **Amenities:** Cable TV w/movies, voice mail. No A/C. **Services:** Car-rental desk, babysitting. Free shuttle to shopping and business districts. Secretarial services and fax available. **Facilities:** 1 restaurant, 1 bar, sauna, washer/dryer. **Rates:** Peak (Mem Day–Labor Day) $89–$119 S; $99–$129 D; $135–$195 ste. Extra person $10. Children under age 18 stay free. Lower rates off-season. Parking: Indoor/outdoor, free. AE, CB, DC, DISC, EC, ER, JCB, MC, V.

Best Western Carriage Inn
140 7th St, 94013; tel 415/552-8600 or toll free 800/444-5817; fax 415/626-3974. Between Mission and Howard Sts. Colonial-style hotel located in a drab neighborhood. **Rooms:** 48 rms. CI 2pm/CO 1pm. Nonsmoking rms avail. Rooms are large. **Amenities:** A/C, refrig, dataport, voice mail. Some units w/fireplaces. Irons and ironing boards in rooms. Terrycloth robes in suites. **Services:** Twice-daily maid svce, car-rental desk, babysitting. Continental breakfast and newspaper delivered to your room. **Facilities:** Sauna, steam rm, whirlpool, washer/dryer. Use of pool and fitness center at sister property, Best Western Americania. Laundry facilities. **Rates (CP):** Peak (May–Oct) $95–$119 S; $105–$129 D. Extra person $10. Children under age 18 stay free. Lower rates off-season. Parking: Indoor, $6/day. MC, V.

Brady Acres
649 Jones St, 94102 (Union Square); tel 415/929-8033 or toll free 800/6-BRADY6; fax 415/441-8033. Between Post and Geary Sts. Small downtown, owner-operated hotel with reasonable rates. **Rooms:** 25 rms. CI open/CO noon. Rooms are small but charming with antique-style quilts, clawfoot tubs, and full kitchens. All recently redecorated. **Amenities:** TV w/movies, refrig, CD/tape player, voice mail, in-rm safe. No A/C. Microwaves, answering machines. **Services:** Babysitting. Free local calls. Personal, friendly staff. **Facilities:** Washer/dryer. **Rates:** $50–$60 S; $60–$85 D. Extra person $10. Parking: Indoor, $12/day. Weekly rates. JCB, MC, V.

Campton Place Hotel

340 Stockton St, 94108 (Union Square); tel 415/781-5555 or toll free 800/235-4300; fax 415/955-5536. Between Sutter and Post Sts. This intimate jewel of a hotel feels like a class act from the moment you enter the marble lobby with its leather Louis XVI–design armchairs, crystal chandeliers, and huge floral displays. A wonderful hotel. **Rooms:** 117 rms and stes. CI 3pm/CO noon. Nonsmoking rms avail. The hotel consists of two separate buildings that have been combined, so corridors are arrayed around a central atrium. Recently redecorated in a $4 million renovation, accommodations look absolutely lovely with English-style furnishings and upholsteries in tones of peach, beige, and jade. Small but attractive bathrooms offer good counter space. **Amenities:** A/C, cable TV w/movies, dataport, bathrobes. All units w/minibars. All rooms offer the same amenities, including French-milled soaps, plump, padded hangers, 25-inch TVs, and bathtub thermometers. **Services:** Twice-daily maid svce, car-rental desk, social director, masseur, babysitting. **Facilities:** 1 restaurant (*see* "Restaurants" below), 1 bar (w/entertainment). **Rates:** $220–$330 S or D; $420–$960 ste. Extra person $25. Children under age 18 stay free. Parking: Indoor, $22/day. AE, CB, DC, DISC, JCB, MC, V.

The Canterbury Hotel

750 Sutter St, 94109 (Union Square); tel 415/474-6464 or toll free 800/227-4788, 800/652-1614 in CA; fax 415/474-5856. At Taylor St. Conveniently located near Union Square. **Rooms:** 250 rms and stes. CI 3pm/CO noon. Nonsmoking rms avail. **Amenities:** A/C, cable TV w/movies, refrig. **Services:** **Facilities:** 1 restaurant, 1 bar. **Rates:** Peak (May–Oct) $100–$150 S; $125–$175 D; $150–$200 ste. Extra person $10. Children under age 18 stay free. Lower rates off-season. Parking: Indoor, $14.50/day. AE, DC, DISC, JCB, MC, V.

Carlton Hotel

1075 Sutter St, 94109; tel 415/673-0242 or toll free 800/227-4496; fax 415/673-4904. Between Hyde and Larkin Sts. A young, enthusiastic staff runs this handsome downtown hotel dating to 1927. A great lobby is decorated with antiques, Persian rugs, and flowers. Library has a fireplace and shelves of antique books. **Rooms:** 158 rms and stes. CI 3pm/CO 1pm. Nonsmoking rms avail. Some rooms are on the small side, but there's great attention to detail. Very clean; colonial furnishings. **Amenities:** TV w/movies, refrig, dataport. No A/C. All units w/minibars. **Services:** Car-rental desk, babysitting. Evening wine served 6–7pm, coffee and tea throughout the day. Complimentary limousine service offered to the Financial District weekday mornings; and shuttle service to various places. **Facilities:** 1 restaurant (bkfst and dinner only). Oak Room Grille serves reasonably priced continental cuisine. **Rates:** Peak (May–Oct) $104–$119 S or D; $200 ste. Extra person $15. Children under age 12 stay free. Lower rates off-season. Parking: Indoor, $9/day. AE, CB, DC, DISC, ER, JCB, MC, V.

Cartwright Hotel

524 Sutter St, 94102 (Downtown); tel 415/421-2865 or toll free 800/227-3844; fax 415/421-2865. At Powell St. Right off Union Square, with fine English furnishings, a small library, and a lovely breakfast room. **Rooms:** 114 rms and stes. CI open/CO noon. Nonsmoking rms avail. Rooms have average decor; not all have air conditioning. **Amenities:** A/C. Some units w/minibars, some w/whirlpools. **Services:** Car-rental desk, babysitting. Complimentary morning tea and coffee; afternoon tea and cookies. **Facilities:** **Rates:** Peak (Apr–Oct) $99–$119 S; $109–$129 D; $150–$180 ste. Extra person $10. Children under age 12 stay free. Lower rates off-season. AP and MAP rates avail. Parking: Indoor, $15/day. AE, CB, DC, DISC, EC, ER, JCB, MC, V.

Cathedral Hill—A Quality Hotel

1101 Van Ness, 94109; tel 415/776-8200 or toll free 800/227-4730, 800/622-0855 in CA; fax 415/441-2841. At Geary St. A very functional hotel, but without much character. **Rooms:** 400 rms and stes. CI 3pm/CO noon. Nonsmoking rms avail. **Amenities:** A/C, cable TV w/movies. **Services:** Car-rental desk, babysitting. **Facilities:** 1 restaurant, 1 bar, beauty salon. Gift shop. **Rates:** Peak (Apr–Oct) $109–$129 S; $129–$149 D; $250–$350 ste. Children under age 18 stay free. Lower rates off-season. Parking: Outdoor, $10/day. AE, DC, DISC, MC, V.

Chancellor Hotel

433 Powell St, 94102 (Downtown); tel 415/362-2004 or toll free 800/428-4748; fax 415/362-1403. Between Sutter and Post Sts. Old San Francisco hotel with a genteel atmosphere. It's one of the last family-owned hotels in the city, with the same owners for over 70 years. One block off Union Square. A good value. **Rooms:** 137 rms and stes. CI 3pm/CO noon. Nonsmoking rms avail. **Amenities:** TV w/movies, dataport. No A/C. **Services:** Car-rental desk, masseur, babysitting. **Facilities:** 1 restaurant, 1 bar. Complimentary use of a nearby health club. **Rates:** Peak (Apr–Nov 1) $105 S; $125 D; $225 ste. Extra person $20. Children under age 2 stay free. Lower rates off-season. Parking: Indoor, $18/day. AE, CB, DC, DISC, EC, ER, JCB, MC, V.

The Clift

495 Geary St, 94102 (Union Square); tel 415/775-4700 or toll free 800/332-3442; fax 415/776-9238. A city-by-the-bay stalwart, dating from the 1930s and now under new management. Located a few blocks from Union Square, but few rooms here, even on the 16th and 17th floors, can match the views from Nob Hill hotels. **Rooms:** 329 rms and stes. CI 3pm/CO 1pm. Nonsmoking rms avail. Decorated in classical style with Georgian reproduction furniture and Brunschwig

fabrics. 12-foot ceilings. **Amenities:** ☎ ◊ ◻ A/C, cable TV w/movies, dataport, bathrobes. All units w/minibars. Unusually generous and thoughtful amenities for kids—child-proofed sockets and faucets; kid-size tables, and chairs; baby shampoo; cookies and milk at turndown. **Services:** ◻ ◻ VP ◻ ◻ ◻ Car-rental desk, children's program, babysitting. Complimentary limo to several downtown locations. Afternoon tea in lobby bar. Extra pizza menu for room service. **Facilities:** ◻ ◻ ◻ ◻ 2 restaurants (*see* "Restaurants" below), 1 bar (w/entertainment). Well-equipped business center offers cellular phones and fax machines for rent. Small six-station fitness center. **Rates:** $225–$340 S; $225–$370 D; $375–$825 ste. Children under age 18 stay free. Min stay peak. Parking: Indoor, $23/day. AE, CB, DC, ER, JCB, MC, V.

▤▤ Comfort Inn by the Bay

2775 Van Ness Ave, 94109; tel 415/928-5000 or toll free 800/228-5150; fax 415/441-3990. At Lombard St. From the upper floors, you can see San Francisco Bay. Near Ghirardelli Square. **Rooms:** 135 rms. CI 2pm/CO noon. Nonsmoking rms avail. Standard, clean. **Amenities:** ☎ ◊ A/C, TV w/movies, dataport. **Services:** ◻ ◻ ◻ Car-rental desk, babysitting. Hearty continental breakfast with many choices. **Facilities:** ◻ **Rates (CP):** Peak (Apr–Oct) $89–$149 S or D. Extra person $10. Children under age 12 stay free. Lower rates off-season. Parking: Indoor, $10/day. AE, CB, DC, DISC, JCB, MC, V.

▤▤▤ The Commodore International Hotel

825 Sutter St, 94109 (Downtown); tel 415/923-6800 or toll free 800/338-6848; fax 415/923-6804. At Jones St. Attractively remodeled older San Francisco property. A great value. **Rooms:** 114 rms and stes. CI 3pm/CO noon. Nonsmoking rms avail. Art Deco decor features bright colors and fresh flowers. **Amenities:** ☎ ◻ Cable TV, dataport, voice mail. No A/C. **Services:** ◻ ◻ ◻ Car-rental desk, masseur, babysitting. Offer fun list of tours with different themes: "Mommy, I'm Bored," "Top 10 City Views," "Romantic Hide-Outs." **Facilities:** 1 restaurant, 1 bar. The Titanic Cafe restaurant is sleek and hip, as is the Red Room bar. For a fee, guests have access to health club two blocks away. **Rates:** $69–$109 S or D; $109 ste. Extra person $10. Children under age 12 stay free. Parking: Indoor, $12/day. AE, DC, DISC, MC, V.

▤▤ Cornell Hotel

715 Bush St, 94108; tel 415/421-3154 or toll free 800/232-9698; fax 415/399-1442. At Powell St. A really great bargain, conveniently located between Union Square and Nob Hill. Owned by a French family, this small, intimate hotel, with an interior heightened by charming flowers and beautiful antique elevators, evokes the spirit of Paris. **Rooms:** 58 rms and stes. CI 1pm/CO 11am. No smoking. Ask for larger rooms in back of hotel. **Amenities:** ☎ ◻ Cable TV. No A/C. **Services:** ◻ ◻ ◻ ◻ Car-rental desk, masseur, babysitting. **Facilities:** 1 restaurant. Jeanne d'Arc, a cozy French country restaurant, offers a four-course, prix fixe menu for

$17. **Rates (BB):** Peak (May–Oct) $70–$85 S; $85–$100 D; $100–$110 ste. Extra person $15. Lower rates off-season. AP and MAP rates avail. Parking: Indoor, $12/day. AE, CB, DC, DISC, JCB, MC, V.

▤▤▤ The Donatello

501 Post St, 94102 (Downtown); tel 415/441-7100 or toll free 800/227-3184; fax 415/885-8842. At Mason St. Elegant, with good-quality art on display, orchids everywhere, and classical music in lobby. **Rooms:** 94 rms and stes. CI 3pm/CO noon. Nonsmoking rms avail. The large rooms seem even more spacious because of their entrance foyers; original works by a local artist add color and charm. Unfortunately, fabrics and carpets show signs of wear. Terrace rooms ($20 extra) face the rooftop garden. **Amenities:** ☎ ◊ ◻ A/C, cable TV w/movies, dataport, voice mail, bathrobes. Some units w/terraces. **Services:** ✗ ◻ VP ◻ ◻ ◻ ◻ Twice-daily maid svce, car-rental desk, social director, masseur, babysitting. Complimentary shoeshine. **Facilities:** ◻ ◻ ◻ ◻ 1 restaurant, 1 bar, sauna, whirlpool. All guests can use the Penthouse Level "Club," and its concierge, living room, and fireplace; massage, facials, and a tanning booth can be booked here. The spacious workout room features lots of mirrors, plus stair and cycle machines, treadmill, and free weights. Grecian-type whirlpool is gorgeous. **Rates:** $155–$175 S or D; $250–$350 ste. Extra person $25. Children under age 12 stay free. AP and MAP rates avail. Parking: Indoor, $19/day. AE, CB, DC, DISC, MC, V.

▤▤▤ The Fairmont

950 Mason St, 94108 (Nob Hill); tel 415/772-5000 or toll free 800/527-4727; fax 415/837-0587. At California St. If the facade looks familiar, that's because The Fairmont served as the setting for the TV series *Hotel*. Larger-than-life touches include a florid lobby with marble columns, gold-leaf trim, and red carpeting. **Rooms:** 596 rms and stes. CI 3pm/CO 1pm. Nonsmoking rms avail. Accommodations in either the vintage 1907 main hotel or the 1960s-era tower. Some rooms have fantastic city and bay views. The Penthouse Suite, with a 40-person-capacity dining room, is one of the most expensive lodgings in the city—$8,000 per night. **Amenities:** ☎ ◊ A/C, cable TV w/movies, refrig, voice mail, bathrobes. All units w/minibars, some w/terraces. **Services:** ◻ ◻ VP ◻ ◻ ◻ Twice-daily maid svce, car-rental desk, masseur, babysitting. Nightly turn-down service with chocolates. **Facilities:** ◻ ◻ ◻ ◻ 4 restaurants, 4 bars (3 w/entertainment), spa, beauty salon. **Rates:** Peak (June–Oct) $199 S; $229 D; $530–$8,000 ste. Extra person $30. Children under age 18 stay free. Lower rates off-season. Parking: Indoor, $27/day. AE, CB, DC, DISC, EC, ER, JCB, MC, V.

▤▤ Fitzgerald Hotel

620 Post St, 94109 (Downtown); tel 415/775-8100 or toll free 800/33-HOTEL; fax 415/775-1278. At Taylor St. Very basic hotel with amiable desk clerks. **Rooms:** 45 rms and stes. CI 3pm/CO noon. Nonsmoking rms avail. **Amenities:** ☎ ◊ Cable TV, dataport. No A/C. **Services:** ◻ ◻ ◻ **Facilities:**

⅋ 1 bar. Nice breakfast room in lobby turns into a pub in evening. Use of pool and fitness center at Sheehan Hotel. **Rates (CP):** Peak (May–Oct) $59–$79 S; $69–$89 D; $95–$115 ste. Extra person $10. Children under age 7 stay free. Lower rates off-season. Parking: Outdoor, $12/day. Very popular theater package includes accommodations for two, two theater tickets (usually for ACT performances), and parking for $89. AE, CB, DC, DISC, JCB, MC, V.

Galleria Park Hotel
191 Sutter St, 94104 (Union Square/Financial District); tel 415/781-3060 or toll free 800/792-9639, 800/792-9855 in CA; fax 415/433-4409. At Kearny St. Built in 1911, this fully renovated hotel has an attractive lobby with a fireplace, fresh flowers, and mock "skylights" screened by etched glass—part of the original structure. Lots of personality and personalized service for a reasonable price. **Rooms:** 177 rms and stes. CI 3pm/CO noon. Nonsmoking rms avail. All rooms recently refurbished with floral spreads and attractive armchairs and sofas. All have plants and high ceilings. **Amenities:** A/C, cable TV w/movies, dataport. All units w/minibars, some w/fireplaces, some w/whirlpools. **Services:** Car-rental desk, babysitting. Complimentary coffee served mornings in the lobby; complimentary wine from 5–7pm. **Facilities:** 2 restaurants, 2 bars. What's really appealing is the third-floor rooftop garden, where a jogging track winds past park benches, pergolas, and lots of greenery—a leafy change in the heart of downtown. Live jazz in the lobby Thurs through Sat evenings. Small workout room with stair and cycle machines; guests also have privileges (fee) at nearby fitness center. **Rates:** $170–$225 S or D; $255–$435 ste. Extra person $10. Children under age 12 stay free. Parking: Indoor, $21/day. AE, CB, DC, DISC, JCB, MC, V.

Golden Gate Hotel
775 Bush St, 94108 (Downtown); tel 415/392-3702 or toll free 800/835-1118; fax 415/392-6202. At Mason St. The feel of a European hotel. Beautiful antique elevator, historical photos in hallways. **Rooms:** 23 rms. CI 2pm/CO noon. Nonsmoking rms avail. Quaint decor. **Amenities:** Cable TV. No A/C. **Services:** Babysitting. Afternoon tea and cookies. **Rates (CP):** Peak (May–Oct) $65–$99 S or D. Children under age 10 stay free. Lower rates off-season. Parking: Indoor, $14/day. AE, CB, DC, MC, V.

Grand Hyatt San Francisco on Union Square
345 Stockton St, 94108 (Union Square); tel 415/398-1234 or toll free 800/233-1234; fax 415/391-1780. Between Sutter and Post Sts. Sleek, 36-story hotel combines sophisticated decor with many amenities for the business traveler. Beautiful lobby accented by marble and oriental antiques. **Rooms:** 693 rms and stes. Executive level. CI 3pm/CO noon. Nonsmoking rms avail. Smart and stylish. **Amenities:** A/C, cable TV w/movies, refrig, dataport, VCR, voice mail. All units w/minibars, all w/terraces, some w/whirlpools. Business Plan rooms ($15 extra to upgrade) feature a complete work station

with a large desk, private fax machine, telephone with computer hook-up, enhanced lighting. Regency Club rooms offer perks like robes, coffeemakers, and bottled water. **Services:** Twice-daily maid svce, masseur, children's program, babysitting. **Facilities:** 2 restaurants, 2 bars (1 w/entertainment), spa, sauna, steam rm, whirlpool, beauty salon. Small but well-equipped health club. Club 36 bar features great views and live jazz Mon–Sat. **Rates:** $225–$260 S; $250–$285 D; $350–$850 ste. Extra person $15. Children under age 18 stay free. Parking: Indoor, $24/day. Lower rates on weekends. AE, CB, DC, DISC, EC, ER, JCB, MC, V.

Grosvenor House
899 Pine St, 94108 (Nob Hill); tel 415/421-1899 or toll free 800/999-9189; fax 415/982-1946. At Mason St. A recently converted Nob Hill apartment building with many tenants still in residence. Lobby is shabby but rooms are nice. **Rooms:** 201 rms, stes, and effic. CI 3pm/CO noon. Nonsmoking rms avail. Clean, large studio and one-bedroom suites with full kitchens and good city views. **Amenities:** Cable TV, refrig. No A/C. Complimentary bottle of wine; microwave. **Services:** **Facilities:** Use of nearby health club. **Rates (CP):** Peak (Apr–Nov) $105 S or D; $250 ste; $105–$250 effic. Extra person $10. Children under age 12 stay free. Min stay wknds. Lower rates off-season. Parking: Indoor/outdoor, $16/day. AE, DC, MC, V.

Handlery Union Square Hotel
351 Geary St, 94102 (Downtown); tel 415/781-7800 or toll free 800/843-4343; fax 415/781-0269. At Powell St. Very clean. **Rooms:** 377 rms and stes. Executive level. CI 3pm/CO noon. Nonsmoking rms avail. **Amenities:** A/C, cable TV w/movies, in-rm safe. Some units w/terraces. **Services:** Babysitting. **Facilities:** 1 restaurant, sauna, steam rm. One of the few heated outdoor pools in San Francisco. **Rates:** Peak (Mar–Oct) $130–$140 S; $140–$150 D. Extra person $10. Children under age 14 stay free. Min stay special events. Lower rates off-season. Parking: Indoor, $14/day. AE, CB, DC, DISC, ER, JCB, MC, V.

Harbor Court Hotel
165 Steuart St, 94105 (Financial District); tel 415/882-1300 or toll free 800/346-0555; fax 415/882-1313. Between Mission and Howard Sts. Elegant, comfortable 1907 landmark hotel with spectacular views of San Francisco Bay. Original vaulted ceilings, arches, and columns. Outstanding lobby/lounge with fireplace. **Rooms:** 131 rms and stes. CI 3pm/CO noon. Nonsmoking rms avail. Done in soft pastels, rooms are small and can only accommodate two people. Ask for bay views. **Amenities:** A/C, cable TV w/movies, refrig, dataport, voice mail, bathrobes. All units w/minibars. **Services:** Car-rental desk, masseur, babysitting. Complimentary wine, coffee, tea. Free morning limo service to Financial District. **Facilities:** 1 restaurant (see "Restaurants" below), 1 bar (w/entertainment). Good restaurant, lively bar. Free use of YMCA with pool and gym

next door. **Rates:** Peak (Feb–Oct) $160–$170 S or D; $295 ste. Lower rates off-season. Parking: Indoor, $19/day. AE, DC, DISC, JCB, MC, V.

Holiday Inn Civic Center
50 8th St, 94103; tel 415/626-6103 or toll free 800/ HOLIDAY; fax 415/552-0184. Between Market and Mission Sts. Somewhat run-down, but renovations are taking place. **Rooms:** 389 rms and stes. CI 2pm/CO noon. Nonsmoking rms avail. Renovated rooms are pleasant. **Amenities:** 🛇 👁 A/C, cable TV w/movies. All units w/terraces. **Services:** ✕ 🔀 🚗 🛅 🗗 Car-rental desk, babysitting. **Facilities:** 🗂 🔲 👍 1 restaurant, 1 bar, washer/dryer. **Rates:** Peak (May–Oct) $110–$165 S or D; $250 ste. Extra person $15. Children under age 19 stay free. Lower rates off-season. Parking: Indoor, free. AE, DC, DISC, MC, V.

Holiday Inn Financial District
750 Kearny St, 94108 (Chinatown); tel 415/433-6600 or toll free 800/424-8292; fax 415/765-7891. At Washington St. Book early if you want a bay view, available from the 12th floor up. In the heart of Chinatown, a good choice for visitors from Asia. **Rooms:** 566 rms and stes. Executive level. CI 3pm/CO noon. Nonsmoking rms avail. Basic decor, smell of stale smoke in some rooms. **Amenities:** 🛇 👁 🔳 A/C, refrig, dataport, voice mail. Some units w/terraces. **Services:** ✕ 🔀 🚗 🛅 🗗 Car-rental desk, babysitting. **Facilities:** 🗂 🔲 🔲 👍 1 restaurant, 2 bars (1 w/entertainment), beauty salon. Pool on roof. **Rates:** Peak (June–Oct) $149–$179 S; $165–$194 D; $249–$399 ste. Extra person $15. Children under age 18 stay free. Lower rates off-season. Parking: Indoor, $14/day. AE, CB, DC, DISC, EC, ER, JCB, MC, V.

Holiday Inn Fisherman's Wharf
1300 Columbus Ave, 94133; tel 415/771-9000 or toll free 800/WHARF-IT; fax 415/771-7006. Between North Point and Beach Sts. Good location near Fisherman's Wharf. **Rooms:** 585 rms and stes. Executive level. CI 3pm/CO noon. Nonsmoking rms avail. Bathrooms are small. **Amenities:** 🛇 👁 A/C, cable TV w/movies, voice mail, in-rm safe. **Services:** ✕ 🔀 🛅 🗗 Car-rental desk, children's program, babysitting. **Facilities:** 🗂 🔲 👍 2 restaurants, 1 bar, washer/dryer. Charley's serves breakfast and a seafood buffet. Charley's Sports Pub features billiards, darts, and large-screen TV. **Rates:** Peak (June–Aug) $145–$205 S or D; $350–$450 ste. Extra person $15. Children under age 17 stay free. Lower rates off-season. Parking: Indoor/outdoor, $12/day. AE, CB, DC, DISC, EC, JCB, MC, V.

Holiday Inn Golden Gateway
1500 Van Ness Ave, 94109; tel 415/441-4000 or toll free 800/HOLIDAY; fax 415/441-8346. At Pine St. Good facilities for groups, but little ambience. **Rooms:** 500 rms and stes. CI 3pm/CO noon. Nonsmoking rms avail. Clean, but slightly old and dated. **Amenities:** 🛇 👁 A/C, cable TV w/movies, dataport, voice mail. **Services:** ✕ 🔀 🚗 🛅 🗗 Car-rental desk. **Facilities:** 🗂 🔲 👍 2 restaurants, 1 bar (w/entertain-

ment). **Rates:** Peak (Apr–Oct) $150–$165 S or D; $280–$400 ste. Extra person $15. Children under age 18 stay free. Lower rates off-season. AP and MAP rates avail. Parking: Indoor, $14/day. AE, CB, DC, DISC, JCB, MC, V.

Holiday Inn Union Square
480 Sutter St, 94108 (Union Square); tel 415/398-8900 or toll free 800/243-1135; fax 415/989-8823. At Powell St. Pleasant, clean, efficient, but without personality. **Rooms:** 400 rms and stes. Executive level. CI 3pm/CO noon. Nonsmoking rms avail. Newly remodeled and very neat rooms. **Amenities:** 🛇 👁 🔳 A/C, cable TV w/movies. Some units w/minibars, 1 w/whirlpool. **Services:** ✕ 🔀 🆅🅿 🚗 🛅 🗗 Babysitting. **Facilities:** 🔳 🔲 🖥 👍 1 restaurant (bkfst and dinner only), 1 bar (w/entertainment). **Rates:** Peak (May–Oct) $180–$215 S; $195–$235 D; $200–$450 ste. Extra person $10–$20. Children under age 19 stay free. Lower rates off-season. MAP rates avail. Parking: Indoor, $18/day. AE, CB, DC, DISC, JCB, MC, V.

Hotel Bedford
761 Post St, 94109 (Union Square); tel 415/673-6040 or toll free 800/227-5642; fax 415/563-6739. At Jones St. Well-located hotel. **Rooms:** 144 rms and stes. CI 3pm/CO 11am. Nonsmoking rms avail. Some rooms have views all the way to the Golden Gate Bridge. **Amenities:** 🛇 👁 🔳 Cable TV w/movies, refrig, VCR. No A/C. All units w/minibars. **Services:** ✕ 🆅🅿 🚗 🛅 🗗 Complimentary wine and cider in pub 5–6pm. **Facilities:** 🔲 1 restaurant (bkfst only), 1 bar. Canvas Cafe is fun and filled with art. **Rates:** Peak (July–Nov) $119–$139 S or D; $175 ste. Extra person $10. Children under age 12 stay free. Min stay peak. Lower rates off-season. Parking: Indoor, $15/day. AE, CB, DC, DISC, MC, V.

Hotel Beresford
635 Sutter St, 94102 (Union Square); tel 415/673-9900 or toll free 800/533-6533; fax 415/474-0449. At Mason St. Too brightly lit, and lacking personality. **Rooms:** 114 rms. CI noon/CO noon. No smoking. **Amenities:** 🛇 👁 Cable TV, refrig. No A/C. All units w/minibars, some w/terraces. **Services:** ✕ 🚗 🛅 🗗 **Facilities:** 1 restaurant, 1 bar, washer/dryer. **Rates (CP):** Peak (June–Oct) $67–$79 S; $85–$89 D. Extra person $10. Children under age 8 stay free. Lower rates off-season. Parking: Indoor, free. AE, CB, DC, DISC, MC, V.

Hotel Britton
112 7th St, 94103; tel 415/621-7001 or toll free 800/ 444-5819; fax 415/626-3974. Between Mission and Howard Sts. Very basic mid-scale accommodations. **Rooms:** 79 rms and stes. CI 2pm/CO noon. Nonsmoking rms avail. Rooms are simple, yet clean and comfortable. **Amenities:** 🛇 👁 Cable TV w/movies, voice mail. No A/C. **Services:** ✕ 🚗 🛅 🗗 Car-rental desk, babysitting. **Facilities:** 👍 1 restaurant. Barber-shop. Use of pool at nearby Best Western Americana. **Rates:**

$69–$89 S; $79–$99 D; $89–$109 ste. Extra person $7. Children under age 18 stay free. Parking: Indoor/outdoor, $6/day. AE, CB, DC, DISC, ER, JCB, MC, V.

≣≣≣ Hotel David
480 Geary Blvd, 94102 (Downtown); tel 415/771-1600 or toll free 800/524-1888; fax 415/931-5442. Between Mason and Taylor Sts. The best deal downtown. Under the same ownership for 40 years, the hotel is across the street from the Curran Theater. Clean and modern. **Rooms:** 50 rms. CI 1pm/CO noon. Nonsmoking rms avail. Rooms are contemporary and attractive. **Amenities:** A/C, cable TV. **Services:** Babysitting. **Facilities:** 1 restaurant. Guests receive a 25% discount at deli next door. **Rates (BB):** Peak (June–Oct) $79 S; $99–$109 D. Extra person $20. Lower rates off-season. Parking: Indoor, free. Excellent value. AE, DISC, MC, V.

≣≣≣ Hotel Diva
440 Geary St, 94102 (Union Square); tel 415/885-0200 or toll free 800/553-1900; fax 415/346-6613. Between Mason and Taylor Sts. This hotel, done in an unusual, art deco–modern hybrid decor, has style and a good downtown location. **Rooms:** 110 rms and stes. CI 2pm/CO noon. Nonsmoking rms avail. **Amenities:** A/C, TV w/movies, refrig, VCR, voice mail, in-rm safe. All units w/minibars, 1 w/fireplace, 1 w/whirlpool. **Services:** Car-rental desk, masseur, babysitting. Newspapers delivered to room daily. **Facilities:** 1 restaurant. **Rates (CP):** Peak (May–Jan 1) $119–$139 S or D; $300 ste. Extra person $10. Children under age 12 stay free. Lower rates off-season. Parking: Indoor/outdoor, $17/day. MC, V.

≣≣≣ Hotel Griffon
155 Steuart St, 94105 (Financial District); tel 415/495-2100 or toll free 800/321-2201; fax 415/495-3522. Between Mission and Howard Sts. Elegant hotel in historic 1906 brick building. Good location on edge of Financial District near cable cars. Within walking distance of great restaurants, fun night life. One block to Sausalito ferry. **Rooms:** 62 rms and stes. CI 2pm/CO noon. Nonsmoking rms avail. Small but cozy and well-appointed rooms. Bay view accommodations come with extra amenities. Most rooms have king- or queen-size bed. **Amenities:** A/C, cable TV, dataport, voice mail, bathrobes. All units w/minibars, some w/terraces. **Services:** Car-rental desk, masseur, babysitting. **Facilities:** 1 restaurant (lunch and dinner only; see "Restaurants" below), 1 bar. Fine restaurant. Guests have privileges at the YMCA next door which has gym and swimming pool. **Rates (CP):** $155–$185 S or D; $250 ste. Parking: Indoor, $15/day. AE, DC, DISC, ER, JCB, MC, V.

≣≣≣ Hotel Majestic
1500 Sutter St, 94109 (Lower Pacific Heights); tel 415/441-1100 or toll free 800/869-8966; fax 415/673-7331. Between Fillmore and Gough Sts. Lots of charm in a 1902 hotel that has been restored to its original elegance. The lobby looks like a Victorian parlor, with floral carpet, velvet sofas, black marble columns, and a filigreed banister on the stairway. Also check out the winsome monkey murals in the elevator. With the intimate feel of a bed-and-breakfast, it's a great choice for vacationers who want a romantic, old-time San Francisco feel. Great value. **Rooms:** 57 rms and stes. CI 2pm/CO noon. Nonsmoking rms avail. No two rooms are alike, but all are charming and all were refurbished in 1996. Accommodations are large, with romantic touches such as four-poster canopied beds and antique armoires; many have gas fireplaces. The grand deluxe corner rooms all have bay windows. Bathrooms blend modern glitz (marble counters) with old-fashioned claw-foot tubs and hexagonal-tile floors. **Amenities:** Cable TV. No A/C. Some units w/fireplaces. Some of the TVs are quite small. **Services:** Masseur, babysitting. **Facilities:** 1 restaurant (bkfst and dinner only; see "Restaurants" below), 1 bar (w/entertainment). Guest privileges at a health club one block away. **Rates:** $125–$160 S or D; $250 ste. Children under age 18 stay free. Parking: Indoor, $14/day. AE, DC, MC, V.

≣≣≣≣ Hotel Monaco
501 Geary St, 94102 (Theater District); tel 415/292-0100 or toll free 800/214-4220; fax 415/292-0111. At Taylor. Set in a landmark 1910 beaux arts building, this hotel debuted to tremendous raves in 1995 after a massive $29 million renovation. The lobby is both fanciful and elegant, embellished by a bronze filigreed stairway from Italy, two-story wood burning fireplace, and trompe l'oeil murals of hot-air balloons ascending across the ceiling. The check-in counter is decorated like an antique steamer trunk. A winner of many design awards, it's a perfect choice for the sophisticated traveler. **Rooms:** 201 rms and stes. CI 3pm/CO noon. Nonsmoking rms avail. From the bold lacquer-red corridors to the bowls of seashells placed next to some of the bathtubs, accommodations feel like what you'd find in a private home. Furnishings include Chinese-inspired maple armoires that house 25" TVs, along with bamboo writing desks and canopy beds, some entirely swathed in fabric. Limestone floors and marble counters accent the bathrooms. **Amenities:** A/C, cable TV w/movies, dataport, voice mail, bathrobes. All units w/minibars, some w/whirlpools. Nifty climate-control device even tells you the outdoor temperature. Two-line phones and Nintendo in all rooms. **Services:** Twice-daily maid svce, car-rental desk, social director, masseur, babysitting. Complimentary coffee and tea in the morning, and wine and cheese in the afternoon, served in the lobby. **Facilities:** 1 restaurant (see "Restaurants" below), 1 bar (w/entertainment), sauna, steam rm, whirlpool. The spacious workout facility offers free weights, an array of aerobic equipment and weight-training stations, plus a gorgeous whirlpool that looks like a mini lap pool, set next to an etched-glass mural. **Rates:** $170–$210 S or D;

$235–$395 ste. Extra person $15. Children under age 18 stay free. Parking: Indoor, $20/day. AE, CB, DC, DISC, JCB, MC, V.

≣≣≣≣ Hotel Nikko San Francisco

222 Mason St, 94102 (Union Square); tel 415/394-1111 or toll free 800/NIKKO-US; fax 415/394-1106. Between O'Farrell and Ellis Sts. Tranquil and elegant Japanese-style setting; lovely marble lobby with fountains. Near Union Square, close to shopping. **Rooms:** 522 rms and stes. Executive level. CI 3pm/CO noon. Nonsmoking rms avail. Accommodations have a large, apartmentlike entry foyer and are decorated in contemporary style with blond woods and grey Formica countertops. All fabrics and carpeting are new. Although bathrooms are austerely done in grey tile, they're exceedingly well laid out; most have separate showers and bathtubs, as well as vanity areas. Two Japanese-style suites. **Amenities:** 🛏 ₫ 🎇 A/C, cable TV w/movies, voice mail. All units w/minibars, some w/whirlpools. **Services:** 🍴 ☎ VP 🚗 🛄 ⊋ ❖ Twice-daily maid svce, car-rental desk, social director, masseur, babysitting. **Facilities:** 🎇 ⚡ 800 🖥 ♿ 1 restaurant, 1 bar, sauna, whirlpool, beauty salon. Very special indeed: The knockout swimming pool is topped off by skylights and surrounded by city views. Fitness center feels like a full-service health club, with plenty of exercise machines and free weights, a personal trainer, and free loan of workout and swimming wear. Shiatsu massage is available. **Rates:** $195–$255 S; $225–$285 D; $385–$1,400 ste. Extra person $30. Children under age 18 stay free. Parking: Indoor, $24/day. AE, CB, DC, DISC, JCB, MC, V.

≣≣≣ Hotel Triton

342 Grant Ave, 94108 (Financial District); tel 415/394-0500 or toll free 800/433-6611; fax 415/394-0555. Between Sutter and Bush Sts. Hip, classy hotel on the edge of Chinatown. Dramatic decor: art deco lobby with gilded columns, local art in hallways. **Rooms:** 140 rms and stes. CI 3pm/CO noon. Nonsmoking rms avail. Eye-catching decor features unique deco furniture and paintings by local artists. **Amenities:** 🛏 ₫ A/C, cable TV w/movies, refrig. All units w/minibars, some w/whirlpools. **Services:** ✕ ☎ VP 🛄 ⊋ Masseur, babysitting. **Facilities:** ⚡ 30 ♿ 1 restaurant, 1 bar. Cafe and restaurant next door. **Rates:** Peak (June–Oct) $109–$179 S or D; $199–$289 ste. Lower rates off-season. Parking: Indoor, $18/day. AE, DC, DISC, MC, V.

≣ Hotel Union Square

114 Powell St, 94102 (Downtown); tel 415/397-3000 or toll free 800/553-1900; fax 415/399-1874. Between O'Farrell and Ellis Sts. A basic hotel in an old building dating to 1913. The immediate neighborhood is bustling but somewhat shabby. **Rooms:** 131 rms and stes. CI 3pm/CO noon. Nonsmoking rms avail. Rooms are a bit worn-out; interior ones are very quiet. **Amenities:** 🛏 ₫ Cable TV w/movies, refrig, voice mail. No A/C. All units w/minibars, some w/terraces. **Services:** VP 🚗 🛄 ⊋ Babysitting. **Facilities:** ♿ **Rates:** Peak (Apr–Oct)

$99–$129 S or D; $129–$300 ste. Children under age 10 stay free. Lower rates off-season. Parking: Indoor/outdoor, $17/day. AE, CB, DC, DISC, MC, V.

≣≣ Hotel Vintage Court

650 Bush St, 94108; tel 415/392-4666 or toll free 800/654-1100; fax 415/433-4065. Located near Union Square, this hotel draws big tour groups and business clientele. **Rooms:** 107 rms and stes. CI 3pm/CO noon. Nonsmoking rms avail. Large, but nondescript rooms. **Amenities:** 🛏 ₫ 🎇 Cable TV w/movies, refrig. No A/C. All units w/minibars. **Services:** ✕ ☎ 🚗 🛄 ⊋ Babysitting. Free weekday morning limo to Financial District. Complimentary afternoon wine. **Facilities:** 20 1 restaurant (bkfst and dinner only; *see* "Restaurants" below), 1 bar. **Rates (CP):** Peak (June–Oct) $119–$169 S or D; $275 ste. Extra person $12. Children under age 12 stay free. Lower rates off-season. Parking: Indoor, $16/day. AE, CB, DC, DISC, JCB, MC, V.

≣≣≣ Howard Johnson Hotel Fisherman's Wharf

580 Beach St, 94133; tel 415/775-3800 or toll free 800/645-9258; fax 415/441-7307. At Leavenworth St. Well located in the same building as the Anchorage Shopping Center. Minimal public space. **Rooms:** 128 rms and stes. CI 3pm/CO noon. No smoking. Nonsmoking rms avail. Some suites overlook bay. **Amenities:** 🛏 ₫ A/C, satel TV w/movies, dataport. All units w/minibars, some w/terraces. **Services:** ✕ ☎ 🚗 🛄 ⊋ Masseur, babysitting. **Facilities:** ♿ 1 restaurant, 1 bar (w/entertainment), washer/dryer. Gray Line tour desk. Cafeteria-style Breakfast Nook restaurant is open 6:45–11am. **Rates:** Peak (July–Sept) $89–$129 S; $99–$139 D; $120–$160 ste. Extra person $10. Children under age 17 stay free. Min stay special events. Lower rates off-season. Parking: Indoor, $5/day. AE, MC, V.

≣≣≣≣ Huntington Hotel

1075 California St, 94108 (Nob Hill); tel 415/474-5400 or toll free 800/227-4683, 800/652-1539 in CA; fax 415/474-6227. At Taylor St. Located at the top of Nob Hill, this family-run establishment feels like a sumptuous private club. Classic details ornament the lobby: lacquer tables, a grandfather clock, and elaborate plasterwork. It's the kind of place where oil paintings look as if they've hung on the walls for generations, and the head housekeeper previously worked at Buckingham Palace. **Rooms:** 140 rms, stes, and effic. CI 3pm/CO noon. Nonsmoking rms avail. **Amenities:** 🛏 ₫ 🎇 Cable TV, dataport, voice mail, in-rm safe. No A/C. All units w/minibars. **Services:** ✕ ☎ VP 🚗 🛄 ⊋ Twice-daily maid svce, car-rental desk, masseur, babysitting. **Facilities:** 75 1 restaurant, 1 bar (w/entertainment). **Rates:** $170–$220 S; $190–$240 D; $290–$790 ste; $290 effic. Extra person $30. Children under age 5 stay free. Parking: Indoor, $20/day. AE, CB, DC, DISC, JCB, MC, V.

≣≣≣ Hyatt Fisherman's Wharf

555 N Point St, 94133; tel 415/563-1234 or toll free 800/750-4928; fax 415/563-2218. At Taylor St. Just one block

from Fisherman's Wharf, this hotel has an elegant lobby with fireplace, fountain, and antiques. Good for families. **Rooms:** 313 rms and stes. CI 2pm/CO noon. Nonsmoking rms avail. Clean and comfortable. **Amenities:** 🔔 ⚷ 🍴 A/C, cable TV w/movies, dataport, voice mail, in-rm safe, bathrobes. **Services:** ✗ 🖭 VP 🚗 🗻 🦮 Car-rental desk, babysitting. **Facilities:** 🏋 🛁 300 🖥 🛁 1 restaurant, 1 bar, sauna, whirlpool. **Rates:** Peak (Apr–Oct) $195 S; $220 D; $275–$525 ste. Extra person $25. Children under age 18 stay free. Min stay wknds. Lower rates off-season. Parking: Indoor/outdoor, $16/day. AE, DC, DISC, MC, V.

≣≣≣ Hyatt Regency San Francisco

5 Embarcadero Center, 94111 (Embarcadero Center); tel 415/788-1234 or toll free 800/233-1234; fax 415/398-2567. End of Market St. Recently remodeled hotel in a great location near many excellent restaurants, California cable car line, Marin ferry terminal. Glassed-in cage elevators and atrium lobby. **Rooms:** 805 rms and stes. Executive level. CI 3pm/CO noon. Nonsmoking rms avail. Standard decor. Ask for bay view. **Amenities:** 🔔 ⚷ 🍴 A/C, cable TV w/movies, voice mail. Some units w/terraces. **Services:** ✗ 🖭 VP 🚗 🗻 🦮 Twice-daily maid svce, car-rental desk, masseur, children's program, babysitting. For a fee, Camp Hyatt offers kids' activities 3–11pm. **Facilities:** 🛁 1200 🖥 🛁 2 restaurants, 2 bars (w/entertainment). **Rates:** $225–$250 S; $250–$275 D; $275–$800 ste. Children under age 18 stay free. Parking: Indoor, $20/day. AE, CB, DC, DISC, ER, JCB, MC, V.

≣≣≣ Hyde Park Suites

2655 Hyde St, 94109 (Fisherman's Wharf); tel 415/771-0200 or toll free 800/227-3608; fax 415/346-8058. Between North Point and Lombard Sts. Located right along the cable car line, one block from Ghirardelli Square, this hotel offers views of Alcatraz and San Francisco Bay. There's also a lovely sundeck. **Rooms:** 24 effic. CI 3pm/CO noon. Nonsmoking rms avail. Rooms are all luxury suites; 3rd-floor rooms have Bay views. **Amenities:** 🔔 ⚷ 📺 🍴 TV, in-rm safe, bathrobes. No A/C. All units w/minibars. All rooms have two TVs. **Services:** 🖭 🚗 🗻 Complimentary wine served in atrium; complimentary newspaper and limousine service; 24-hour concierge. **Facilities:** 🛁 **Rates (CP):** $175–$230 effic. Extra person $10. Children under age 12 stay free. Parking: Indoor, $15/day. AE, DC, DISC, MC, V.

≣≣≣≣ Inn at the Opera

333 Fulton St, 94102 (Civic Center); tel 415/863-8400 or toll free 800/325-2708; fax 415/861-0821. At Franklin St. Very elegant lodgings from which to savor performances at the nearby Opera House and Symphony Hall. Built over a half-century ago to house visiting opera singers, it continues to attract a glittering cast of performing arts stars and celebrities. Past guests include Placido Domingo, Mikhail Baryshnikov, and Claudia Schiffer. **Rooms:** 48 rms and stes. CI 3pm/CO noon. Nonsmoking rms avail. Everything impeccably maintained. All accommodations are quite similarly furnished and have an English country house feel, with

Queen Anne–style furnishings and floral-print spreads. Standard rooms are smallish, but the superior accommodations offer more elbow room, along with a canopy backdrop to the bed and sofa in front of the window. Although attractive, bathrooms have no counter space. Avoid rooms next to the elevator–they reverberate when the machinery is in motion. **Amenities:** 🔔 ⚷ Cable TV, dataport, voice mail, bathrobes. No A/C. All units w/minibars. Guests receive a warm welcome, with fresh flowers and a basket of apples waiting in their rooms upon check-in. Two terry cloth bathrobes are folded neatly on the bed. TVs are very small; VCRs and videocassettes can be rented. All accommodations have two-line phones; most have microwaves. **Services:** 🍴 🖭 VP 🚗 🗻 🦮 🦮 Twice-daily maid svce, masseur, babysitting. A complimentary, European-style breakfast buffet is served in the lovely Act IV restaurant. Selections include cheeses and meats, as well as fruits, cereals, and house-baked muffins. Meeting facilities for 80 people in the San Francisco Ballet Association building right next door. Guest privileges (fee) at nearby health club. Secretarial and other business services. **Facilities:** 🛁 1 restaurant (see "Restaurants" below), 1 bar (w/entertainment). **Rates (CP):** $125–$185 S; $140–$200 D; $200–$275 ste. Extra person $15. Children under age 16 stay free. MAP rates avail. Parking: Outdoor, $19/day. AE, CB, DC, EC, MC, V.

≣≣≣ Inn at Union Square

440 Post St, 94102 (Downtown); tel 415/397-3510 or toll free 800/AT-THE-INN; fax 415/989-0529. At Powell St. An intimate inn. Fragrant lobby has fresh flowers and candles over the fireplace mantel. **Rooms:** 30 rms and stes. CI 2pm/CO noon. No smoking. All rooms individually decorated. **Amenities:** 🔔 ⚷ 🍴 Cable TV, bathrobes. No A/C. Some units w/fireplaces, 1 w/whirlpool. **Services:** ✗ 🖭 VP 🚗 🗻 🦮 Twice-daily maid svce, masseur, babysitting. Honor bar in hallway 2–10:30pm. Free evening wine and hors d'oeuvres. Complimentary newspapers. **Facilities:** 🖥 🛁 **Rates (CP):** $130–$170 S or D; $180–$300 ste. Extra person $15. Children under age 4 stay free. Parking: Indoor, $18/day. AE, DC, DISC, MC, V.

≣≣≣ Juliana Hotel

590 Bush St, 94108 (Downtown); tel 415/392-2540 or toll free 800/328-3880; fax 415/391-8447. At Sutter St. Pleasant, quiet hotel above Union Square. Pastel decor with flower arrangements and a warm, inviting lobby with fireplace. **Rooms:** 106 rms and stes. CI 2pm/CO noon. Nonsmoking rms avail. **Amenities:** 🔔 ⚷ 🍴 A/C, cable TV w/movies, refrig. All units w/minibars. **Services:** ✗ 🚗 🗻 🦮 Babysitting. Complimentary coffee and tea all day; afternoon wine. Free morning limo to financial district. **Facilities:** 10 🛁 **Rates:** Peak (June–Oct) $119–$169 S or D; $159–$209 ste. Extra person $10. Children under age 13 stay free. Min stay peak. Lower rates off-season. AE, CB, DC, DISC, JCB, MC, V.

Kensington Park Hotel

450 Post St, 94102 (Downtown); tel 415/788-6400 or toll free 800/553-1900; fax 415/399-9484. At Powell St. Handsome old hotel has basic, affordable rooms. **Rooms:** 86 rms and stes. CI 2pm/CO noon. Nonsmoking rms avail. Queen Anne–style decor in rose and blue accents. **Amenities:** ☎ Cable TV w/movies, refrig, dataport. No A/C. 1 unit w/fireplace, some w/whirlpools. **Services:** ▣ ▣ ▣ ▣ ▣ Car-rental desk, masseur, babysitting. Afternoon sherry and cookies in lobby. **Facilities:** ▣ & **Rates (CP):** Peak (May–Oct) $89–$115 S or D; $160–$350 ste. Extra person $10. Children under age 12 stay free. Lower rates off-season. Parking: Outdoor, $17/day. Good midweek rates. AE, CB, DC, DISC, JCB, MC, V.

King George Hotel

334 Mason St, 94102 (Downtown); tel 415/781-5050 or toll free 800/288-6005; fax 415/391-6976. At Geary St. Built in 1914, this charming hotel is located near Union Square shops and restaurants. **Rooms:** 140 rms and stes. CI 3pm/CO noon. No smoking. Standard decor. **Amenities:** ☎ Cable TV w/movies, in-rm safe. No A/C. **Services:** ▣ ▣ ▣ ▣ Car-rental desk, social director, babysitting. **Facilities:** ▣ 1 restaurant. Tea room. **Rates:** Peak (July–Oct) $120 S; $130 D; $205 ste. Extra person $10. Children under age 12 stay free. Lower rates off-season. Parking: Indoor, $16.50/day. Special sweetheart packages. AE, CB, DC, DISC, EC, ER, JCB, MC, V.

The Lombard—A Super 8 Hotel

1015 Geary St, 94109 (Van Ness); tel 415/673-5232 or toll free 800/777-3210; fax 415/885-2802. At Polk St. A clean, charming old hotel on the edge of a slightly dubious neighborhood, San Francisco's Tenderloin district. **Rooms:** 101 rms. CI 3pm/CO noon. Nonsmoking rms avail. The airy rooms have louvered windows, big closets, and basic furniture. **Amenities:** ☎ ▣ Cable TV w/movies, in-rm safe. No A/C. **Services:** ✗ ▣ ▣ ▣ ▣ Babysitting. Afternoon tea and sherry. Complimentary morning limousine service. **Facilities:** ▣ 1 restaurant (bkfst and dinner only), games rm. Faces Cafe is well-priced, New Orleans theme restaurant. **Rates:** Peak (Mar–Oct) $100–$120 S or D. Extra person $10. Children under age 16 stay free. Lower rates off-season. AP and MAP rates avail. Parking: Indoor/outdoor, $10/day. AE, CB, DC, DISC, JCB, MC, V.

Mandarin Oriental, San Francisco

222 Sansome St, 94104 (Financial District); tel 415/885-0999 or toll free 800/622-0404; fax 415/433-0289. Between Pine and California Sts. The ultimate urban retreat—a skyscraper aerie which puts you on top of San Francisco. Because the hotel occupies floors 38 to 48 of the city's third-largest building, every room has an incredible view. **Rooms:** 158 rms and stes. CI 3pm/CO noon. Nonsmoking rms avail. Layouts vary, but all are decorated with pale yellow walls and a whisper of the Orient in the throw pillows and art. Mandarin rooms feature a whirlpool tub next to floor-to-ceiling windows. **Amenities:** ☎ ▣ ▣ A/C, cable TV w/movies, dataport, in-rm safe, bathrobes. All units w/minibars, some w/terraces, some w/whirlpools. Features include clothes brushes, Thai slippers in bathroom, closets that light automatically, English toiletries, and voice mail. Marble baths are both stunning and well laid out. **Services:** ▣ ▣ ▣ ▣ ▣ Twice-daily maid svce, car-rental desk, children's program, babysitting. **Facilities:** ▣ ▣ ▣ & 1 restaurant, 1 bar. Full-service business center. **Rates:** $285–$405 S or D; $625–$1,400 ste. Children under age 12 stay free. Parking: Indoor, $21/day. AE, CB, DC, DISC, JCB, MC, V.

Marina Inn Bed & Breakfast

3110 Octavia St, 94123; tel 415/928-1000 or toll free 800/274-1420; fax 415/928-5909. At Lombard St. A small European-style hotel with a tiny lobby and not much public space. Parking in the neighborhood is very difficult. **Rooms:** 40 rms. CI 2pm/CO noon. Nonsmoking rms avail. Rooms are small, but clean and comfortable. **Amenities:** ☎ Cable TV. No A/C. Guide to San Francisco in each room. **Services:** ▣ Complimentary continental breakfast from 7 to 10am; evening sherry 4 to 6pm. **Facilities:** & Sitting room on the 2nd floor. **Rates:** $55–$95 S or D. Extra person $10. Children under age 5 stay free. AE, MC, V.

Mark Hopkins Inter-Continental San Francisco

1 Nob Hill, 94108 (Nob Hill); tel 415/392-3434 or toll free 800/327-0200, 800/622-4455 in CA; fax 415/421-3302. At Mason St. San Francisco's grand hotel atop Nob Hill. Lobby has plenty of pizazz, with limestone floors, crystal chandeliers, potted palms, and bronze torchiers. All corridors and rooms recently refurbished. **Rooms:** 390 rms and stes. Executive level. CI 3pm/CO 1pm. Nonsmoking rms avail. Elegantly decorated in greys or browns, rooms offer many nice features, such as comfortable armchairs and handsome burled armoires containing TV and minibar. Newly redone gray-and-white marble baths (in many accommodations) are beautiful, but counter space is very limited. **Amenities:** ☎ ▣ ▣ A/C, cable TV w/movies, dataport, voice mail, bathrobes. All units w/minibars, some w/terraces, 1 w/whirlpool. **Services:** ✗ ▣ ▣ ▣ ▣ Car-rental desk, masseur, babysitting. **Facilities:** ▣ ▣ ▣ & 2 restaurants, 2 bars (1 w/entertainment). Rooftop Top of the Mark bar has romantic views of the city through its wrap-around windows. **Rates:** $135–$195 S; $180–$300 D; $375–$1,200 ste. Extra person $30. Children under age 14 stay free. Min stay special events. Parking: Indoor, $23/day. AE, CB, DC, DISC, JCB, MC, V.

Marriott at Fisherman's Wharf

1250 Columbus Ave, 94133; tel 415/775-7555 or toll free 800/525-0956; fax 415/474-2099. Between Bay and North Point Sts. Clean and comfortable hotel offers nice public areas and friendly service. **Rooms:** 255 rms and stes. CI 3pm/CO noon. Nonsmoking rms avail. Recently renovated rooms have colonial furniture but small bathrooms. **Amenities:** ☎ ▣ ▣ A/C, cable TV w/movies. All units w/minibars. Full-size iron and ironing board in each room. **Services:** ✗ 🗝 VP 🚐 🏊 🍴 🔉 Babysitting. Starbucks coffee and Pizza Hut pizza available through room service, as well as in lobby. **Facilities:** 🏋 🏊250 ⅙ 1 restaurant, 1 bar, sauna. **Rates:** Peak (Apr–Oct) $210 S or D; $450 ste. Lower rates off-season. "Two for breakfast" rate includes a breakfast buffet. AE, DC, DISC, MC, V.

🎱🎱 Miyako Inn Best Western
1800 Sutter St, 94115; tel 415/921-4000 or toll free 800/528-1234; fax 415/923-1064. At Buchanan St. Located in Japantown, this hotel provides easy access to Union Square and Fisherman's Wharf. **Rooms:** 125 rms and stes. CI 2pm/CO noon. Nonsmoking rms avail. Rooms are well appointed, spacious, and comfortable. **Amenities:** 🛎 ⅙ A/C, cable TV. Some units w/terraces. **Services:** 🚐 🏊 🔉 **Facilities:** 🏊150 ⅙ 1 bar. **Rates:** Peak (June–Oct) $87–$89 S; $97–$99 D; $175–$255 ste. Extra person $10. Children under age 18 stay free. Lower rates off-season. Parking: Indoor, $8/day. Families requiring more than one room pay the single rate for each additional room, regardless of the number of family members occupying it. AE, DC, DISC, JCB, MC, V.

🎱🎱🎱 Monticello Inn
127 Ellis St, 94102 (Union Square); tel 415/392-8800 or toll free 800/669-7777; fax 415/398-2650. At Powell St. Charming colonial-style hotel in the heart of downtown. The comfortable and inviting lounge and lobby area has sofas and fireplace. **Rooms:** 91 rms and stes. CI 4pm/CO noon. Nonsmoking rms avail. Rooms are small but clean and attractively decorated with pink country floral designs. The 36 suites have larger rooms. **Amenities:** 🛎 ⅙ A/C, cable TV, refrig, dataport. All units w/minibars, 1 w/fireplace, 1 w/whirlpool. Suites have many extra amenities, like bathrobes. **Services:** VP 🚐 🏊 🔉 Car-rental desk, masseur, babysitting. Complimentary wine service is available in the evening; coffee and tea are always offered to guests in the lounge. **Facilities:** ⅙ 1 restaurant (lunch and dinner only), 1 bar. **Rates (CP):** $89–$149 S or D; $129–$229 ste. Extra person $10. Children under age 18 stay free. Parking: Indoor, $16/day. Puccini & Pinetti is a good, moderately priced Italian restaurant. AE, DC, DISC, JCB, MC, V.

🎱🎱🎱 Nob Hill Lambourne
725 Pine St, 94108 (Nob Hill); tel 415/433-2287 or toll free 800/BRITINN; fax 415/433-0975. At Stockton St. A small, elegant hotel designed for the business traveler. **Rooms:** 20 rms and stes. CI 3pm/CO noon. No smoking. Every room and suite is set up to function like an office. **Amenities:** 🛎 ⅙ 🖥 🍽 Cable TV w/movies, refrig, VCR, CD/tape player, voice mail, bathrobes. No A/C. All units w/minibars, some w/terraces. Computer, fax, voice mail. **Services:** ✗ VP 🚐 🏊 🔉 Masseur, babysitting. **Facilities:** 🏋 🏊8 🖳 Spa. **Rates (CP):** Peak (June–Oct) $125–$145 S or D; $199–$225 ste. Children under age 18 stay free. Lower rates off-season. Parking: Indoor, $18/day. Spa packages available. AE, DC, DISC, MC, V.

🎱🎱🎱 The Orchard
562 Sutter St, 94102 (Union Square); tel 415/433-4434 or toll free 800/433-4434; fax 415/433-3695. At Mason St. Good location just ½ block from the Powell St cable car. **Rooms:** 94 rms and stes. CI 3pm/CO noon. Nonsmoking rms avail. **Amenities:** 🛎 A/C, cable TV, refrig, dataport, bathrobes. All units w/minibars. **Services:** ✗ 🏊 🔉 Car-rental desk, masseur, babysitting. **Facilities:** 🏊50 ⅙ 1 restaurant, 1 bar. **Rates:** Peak (Sept–Oct) $115–$155 S or D; $175–$225 ste. Extra person $10. Children under age 12 stay free. Lower rates off-season. AP and MAP rates avail. Parking: Indoor, $12/day. AE, CB, DC, DISC, MC, V.

🎱🎱🎱 Palace Hotel
2 New Montgomery St, 94105; tel 415/392-8600 or toll free 800/325-3538; fax 415/243-4120. At Market St. After a $150 million renovation (completed in 1991), this vintage 1909 classic rules again. The crown jewel is the Garden Court, with its crystal chandeliers, gilt-topped columns, and iridescent-glass ceiling. **Rooms:** 550 rms and stes. CI 3pm/CO noon. Nonsmoking rms avail. Accented by high ceilings, accommodations are well-appointed with English-style furnishings. **Amenities:** 🛎 ⅙ 🍽 A/C, cable TV w/movies, voice mail, in-rm safe, bathrobes. All units w/minibars, some w/fireplaces, some w/whirlpools. Guests can stock their minibars as they wish with items ordered from room service. **Services:** 🍴 🗝 VP 🚐 🏊 🔉 Twice-daily maid svce, car-rental desk, masseur, babysitting. **Facilities:** 🏊 🏋 🏊1200 🖳 ⅙ 3 restaurants, 2 bars (w/entertainment), spa, sauna, steam rm, whirlpool. Health club features a glass-ceilinged swimming pool from which parts of the skyline can be seen. In addition, pool is accessible for guests with disabilities, with a ladder and special chair. Popular Pied Piper Bar is adorned with a splendid mural by Maxfield Parrish. **Rates:** $300–$370 S; $320–$390 D; $675–$2,825 ste. Extra person $20. Children under age 18 stay free. Parking: Indoor, AE, CB, DC, DISC, ER, JCB, MC, V.

🎱🎱🎱🎱 The Pan Pacific Hotel San Francisco
500 Post St, 94102 (Union Square); tel 415/771-8600 or toll free 800/327-8585; fax 415/398-0267. At Mason St. Dramatic design from noted architect John Portman, with a 21-story skylit atrium, twin fireplaces in the lobby, glass elevators that rise like bubbles, and acres of marble. Celebrity guests have included Emma Thompson and Arnold Schwarzenegger. **Rooms:** 329 rms and stes. CI 3pm/CO noon. Nonsmoking rms avail. Accommodations sparkle with contemporary flair and Asian touches like rosewood chairs; all upholsteries are to be updated. Portuguese marble lines the glamorous bathrooms, which come with lots of mirrors and chrome fixtures. **Amenities:** 🛎 ⅙ 🍽 A/C, cable TV w/movies, dataport, VCR, voice mail, in-rm safe, bathrobes. All units w/minibars, 1 w/fireplace, some w/whirlpools. New large-screen TVs in rooms. **Services:** 🍴 🗝 VP 🚐 🏊 🔉 🔉 Twice-daily maid svce, car-rental desk, masseur, babysitting. Pets under 20 pounds allowed; $20 fee. **Facilities:** 🏋 🏊500

🖥 ⑂ 1 restaurant (*see* "Restaurants" below), 1 bar (w/entertainment). New fitness center. **Rates:** $235–$335 S or D; $375–$1,700 ste. Children under age 18 stay free. Parking: Indoor, $24/day. AE, CB, DC, DISC, EC, ER, JCB, MC, V.

≣≣≣ Parc Fifty Five Crowne Plaza
55 Cyril Magnin St, 94012 (Union Square); tel 415/392-8000 or toll free 800/227-6963. At Market St. Urbane property conveniently located near Union Square. **Rooms:** 1,058 rms and stes. Executive level. CI 3pm/CO noon. Nonsmoking rms avail. Rooms higher up have city views. **Amenities:** 🛁 ⑂ ❄ A/C, cable TV w/movies, in-rm safe. Some units w/terraces, some w/whirlpools. **Services:** ⑂ ⌫ VP 🚗 ⊿ ⌁ Twice-daily maid svce, car-rental desk, masseur, babysitting. **Facilities:** ⑂ 1000 🖥 ⑂ 2 restaurants, 2 bars (w/entertainment). **Rates:** Peak (June–Aug) $195 S or D; $340 ste. Extra person $15. Children under age 19 stay free. Lower rates off-season. MAP rates avail. Parking: Indoor, $22/day. Children under 12 eat free in the restaurant. AE, DC, DISC, MC, V.

≣≣≣≣ Park Hyatt San Francisco
333 Battery St, 94111 (Financial District); tel 415/392-1234 or toll free 800/233-1234; fax 415/421-2433. Modern 26-story structure designed primarily for business travelers, but with its proximity to Embarcadero Center's shops and waterfront, it attracts vacationers as well. Convenient driveway and porte cochere lead to attractive, uncluttered lobby paneled with Australian lacewood. Extensive collection of antiques and original artworks. **Rooms:** 360 rms and stes. CI 3pm/CO noon. Nonsmoking rms avail. Some of the most comfortable, efficient rooms in the city; Park Rooms, with their multipurpose room dividers, are especially good. Angled architecture incorporates big windows, giving most rooms a sense of airiness and views of the city or bay. **Amenities:** 🛁 ⑂ ❄ A/C, cable TV w/movies, dataport, VCR, CD/tape player, voice mail, bathrobes. All units w/minibars, some w/terraces, 1 w/fireplace, some w/whirlpools. Some accommodations have fax machines; computers and printers can be delivered to rooms. Some suites have balconies just large enough for breakfast for two. **Services:** ⑂ ⌫ VP 🚗 ⊿ ⌁ ⌁ Twice-daily maid svce, car-rental desk, masseur, babysitting. 24-hour concierge. Mercedes-Benz for complimentary shuttling to business/shopping centers. Afternoon tea in lobby lounge. On-their-toes staffers make a point of getting guests' names right and somehow making the place seem intimate. **Facilities:** 350 🖥 ⑂ 1 restaurant (*see* "Restaurants" below), 2 bars (1 w/entertainment). Library with leather armchairs, international newspapers, reference books, and chess. Elevated walkways to Embarcadero Center. Rowing machine and exercise bike rentals for in-room use. 3rd-floor, 150-seat Park Grill popular with executives. **Rates:** $169–$315 S; $214–$340 D; $350–$2,500 ste. Children under age 18 stay free. Parking: Indoor, $23/day. AE, CB, DC, DISC, ER, JCB, MC, V.

≣≣ The Phoenix
601 Eddy St, 94109 (Civic Center); tel 415/776-1380 or toll free 800/CITY-INN; fax 415/885-3109. At Larkin St. This cheerful property has pastel-trimmed units surrounding a lovely pool. The pool area is surrounded by palm trees, a mural, and Caribbean-style artwork. Caters to a hip celebrity crowd. **Rooms:** 44 rms and stes. CI 2pm/CO noon. Non-smoking rms avail. Rooms are funky; most have a view of the pool. There is little privacy, as floor-to-ceiling windows overlook walkways. **Amenities:** 🛁 ⑂ Cable TV. No A/C. Some units w/terraces. **Services:** ✗ 🚗 ⊿ ⌁ Masseur, babysitting. **Facilities:** ⑂ 50 🖥 1 restaurant (lunch and dinner only; *see* "Restaurants" below), 1 bar (w/entertainment). **Rates (CP):** Peak (June–Oct) $99 S or D; $139 ste. Extra person $10. Children under age 12 stay free. Lower rates off-season. Parking: Outdoor, free. AE, DC, DISC, MC, V.

≣ Powell Hotel
28 Cyril Magnin St, 94102 (Union Square); tel 415/398-3200 or toll free 800/368-0700, 800/652-3399 in CA; fax 415/398-3654. At Powell St. Dingy but economical hotel near Union Square. Powell St cable car turn-around right in front. **Rooms:** 123 rms and stes. CI 2pm/CO noon. Nonsmoking rms avail. Wallpaper peeling off walls. **Amenities:** 🛁 Cable TV. No A/C. **Services:** VP 🚗 ⌁ Babysitting. **Facilities:** 50 ⑂ 1 restaurant (bkfst only). Good restaurants within 1 block. **Rates:** Peak (June–Sept) $85 S; $95 D; $120–$140 ste. Extra person $10. Children under age 16 stay free. Lower rates off-season. Parking: Outdoor, $16/day. AE, DC, JCB, MC, V.

≣≣≣≣ Prescott Hotel
545 Post St, 94102 (Union Square); tel 415/563-0303 or toll free 800/283-7322; fax 415/563-6831. Between Mason and Taylor Sts. Quietly elegant, offering good service. Displays of California Native American artifacts accent the lobby area. **Rooms:** 165 rms and stes. Executive level. CI 3pm/CO noon. Nonsmoking rms avail. Quality touches such as silk wallpaper and neoclassical-style cherrywood furnishings adorn the somewhat compact rooms. Attractive bathrooms offer marble countertops. **Amenities:** 🛁 ⑂ ❄ A/C, cable TV w/movies, dataport, voice mail, bathrobes. All units w/minibars, 1 w/terrace, some w/fireplaces, 1 w/whirlpool. Fax machines in all rooms, along with umbrellas for guest use. **Services:** ✗ ⌫ VP 🚗 ⊿ ⌁ Twice-daily maid svce, masseur, babysitting. Flanking a wonderful old-world fireplace, the "living room" lounge offers complimentary coffee and tea in the morning, wine and cheese in the afternoon. **Facilities:** 45 ⑂ 1 restaurant (*see* "Restaurants" below), 1 bar. Use of nearby health club and pool for $12 fee. Superb downstairs restaurant, Postrio, provides room service. **Rates:** $195–$215 S or D; $245–$265 ste. Extra person $10. Children under age 3 stay free. Parking: Indoor, $21/day. Good value packages often available during the winter. AE, CB, DC, DISC, ER, JCB, MC, V.

≋≋ Queen Anne Hotel

1590 Sutter St, 94109 (Lower Pacific Heights); tel 415/441-2828 or toll free 800/227-3970; fax 415/775-5212. At Octavia St. Located on the outer edge of Pacific Heights, this elaborate Victorian also borders on the cute. **Rooms:** 49 rms and stes. CI 3pm/CO noon. Nonsmoking rms avail. **Amenities:** 🛎 🕭 ☏ TV, refrig. No A/C. Some units w/fireplaces. **Services:** 🗝 🛆 🖳 Car-rental desk, babysitting. Free afternoon tea and sherry in lobby; morning limo service; newspapers. **Facilities:** ⊡ 🍴 **Rates (CP):** $99–$150 S; $120–$160 D; $175 ste. Extra person $10. Children under age 12 stay free. Parking: Outdoor, $12/day. AE, CB, DC, DISC, JCB, MC, V.

≋≋≋≋ Radisson Miyako Hotel

1625 Post St, 94115; tel 415/922-3200 or toll free 800/533-4567; fax 415/921-0417. At Laguna St. A stay at this very classy, newly renovated hotel is a unique multicultural experience combining Japanese and Western styles and comforts. **Rooms:** 218 rms and stes. Executive level. CI 3pm/CO noon. No smoking. The 13 types of rooms include Japanese rooms with futons, shoji screens, and silk comforters, and "club" or western-style rooms. **Amenities:** 🛎 🕭 ☏ A/C, cable TV w/movies, refrig, dataport, voice mail, bathrobes. All units w/minibars, some w/terraces, some w/whirlpools. Yukata (cotton kimono) robes in some rooms. Some accommodations have saunas. **Services:** ✗ 🆅🅿 �"🛆 🖳 Car-rental desk, masseur, babysitting. **Facilities:** 🛏 ⊡ 💻 🍴 1 restaurant (see "Restaurants" below), 1 bar. Yoyo Tsumami, a superb bistro, on premises **Rates:** $139–$179 S; $159–$199 D; $179–$229 ste. Extra person $20. Children under age 18 stay free. Min stay special events. Parking: Indoor, $15/day. AE, CB, DC, DISC, JCB, MC, V.

≋≋ Ramada Hotel San Francisco

1231 Market St, 94103 (Civic Center); tel 415/626-8000 or toll free 800/227-4747; fax 415/861-1435. At 8th St. Very ornate and attractive, with beautiful architecture, a marble lobby, and sculpted ceilings, all conveying classic San Francisco elegance. But neighborhood is not great. **Rooms:** 460 rms and stes. CI 3pm/CO noon. Nonsmoking rms avail. Some accommodations are worn and smell musty. **Amenities:** 🛎 🕭 ☏ A/C, cable TV w/movies, refrig, dataport. **Services:** ✗ 🗝 🚚 🛆 🖳 Twice-daily maid svce, car-rental desk, babysitting. **Facilities:** ⊡ 🍴 1 restaurant, 1 bar (w/entertainment), beauty salon. **Rates (CP):** Peak (June–Sept) $109–$132 S; $104–$147 D; $140–$200 ste. Extra person $15. Children under age 14 stay free. Lower rates off-season. Parking: Indoor/outdoor, $8/day. AE, DC, DISC, JCB, MC, V.

≋≋≋ Ramada Plaza Hotel Fisherman's Wharf

590 Bay St, 94133; tel 415/885-4700 or toll free 800/228-8408; fax 415/771-8945. At Jones St. Average hotel with large rooms. **Rooms:** 232 rms and stes. CI 3pm/CO noon. Nonsmoking rms avail. Some of the largest rooms in Fisherman's Wharf, but bathrooms are small. **Amenities:** 🛎 🕭 ☏ A/C, cable TV w/movies. **Services:** ✗ 🚚 🛆 🖳 Car-rental

desk, babysitting. **Facilities:** ⊡ 🍴 1 restaurant (bkfst and dinner only), 1 bar. **Rates:** Peak (May–Oct) $180–$219 S; $195–$219 D; $250–$300 ste. Children under age 18 stay free. Min stay special events. Lower rates off-season. Parking: Indoor, $8/day. AE, CB, DC, DISC, EC, JCB, MC, V.

≋≋ The Raphael

386 Geary St, 94102 (Union Square); tel 415/986-2000 or toll free 800/821-5343; fax 415/397-2447. Between Powell and Mason Sts. An attractive hotel with a friendly staff. **Rooms:** 152 rms and stes. CI 3pm/CO 1pm. Nonsmoking rms avail. **Amenities:** 🛎 🕭 ☏ A/C, satel TV w/movies, dataport, VCR. **Services:** ✗ 🚚 🛆 🖳 Babysitting. **Facilities:** ⊡ 🍴 1 restaurant, 1 bar. Mama's Restaurant is famous for its omelets. **Rates:** Peak (Apr–Nov 17) $99–$129 S; $109–$139 D; $160–$225 ste. Extra person $10. Children under age 18 stay free. Lower rates off-season. Parking: Indoor, $16/day. AE, CB, DC, DISC, MC, V.

≋≋≋≋ Renaissance Stanford Court Hotel

905 California St, 94108 (Nob Hill); tel 415/989-3500 or toll free 800/468-3571, 800/227-4736, 800/622-0957 in CA; fax 415/391-0513. Handsome Nob Hill architecture, with rooms on seven floors situated around a central courtyard with landscaped roof. The spacious lobby has wood paneling, murals depicting California history, and domed roof with Tiffany-style decorative glass. Fine collections include a small Maxfield Parrish painting (near lobby elevator) and a grandfather clock that belonged to Napoleon (it still runs). **Rooms:** 400 rms and stes. CI 3pm/CO 11am. Nonsmoking rms avail. All corridors and rooms are slated to be totally refurbished by fall 1997. Superior rooms are spacious; some offer dynamite views of the city, bay, and trolleys of California St (double-glazed windows muffle the noise a bit). Courtyard views are quiet but a bit dark and cavernous. Although bathrooms are large and each has a small TV and heated towel racks, the decor is uninspired. **Amenities:** 🛎 🕭 A/C, cable TV w/movies, dataport, bathrobes. Some units w/fireplaces. **Services:** 🍽 🗝 🆅🅿 🚚 🛆 🖳 Twice-daily maid svce, car-rental desk, social director, masseur, babysitting. Complimentary pot of coffee and newspaper placed outside door to back up wake-up call. Overnight laundry service. Complimentary limousine to business, shopping, and theater districts. **Facilities:** 🛏 ⊡ 💻 🍴 1 restaurant (see "Restaurants" below), 1 bar (w/entertainment). Fournou's Ovens restaurant, dug into the bedrock of Nob Hill, is noted for its open rotisserie kitchen and 10,000-bottle wine cellar. **Rates:** $215–$475 S or D; $725–$2,000 ste. Extra person $30. Children under age 18 stay free. Parking: Indoor, $24/day. Rates vary by floor and view. AE, CB, DC, DISC, JCB, MC, V.

≋ Richelieu Hotel

1050 Van Ness Ave, 94109; tel 415/673-4711 or toll free 800/295-7424; fax 415/673-9362. Between O'Farrell and Geary Sts. A standard hotel with limited facilities. **Rooms:** 151 rms and stes. CI 3pm/CO noon. Nonsmoking rms avail. Rooms are small, especially bathrooms. Decor outdated.

Amenities: ⬛⬛⬛ ⬛ A/C, TV w/movies, in-rm safe. All units w/minibars, some w/terraces. **Services:** ⬛⬛⬛ Afternoon tea. **Facilities:** ⬛ ⬛ ⬛ **Rates:** Peak (Mar–Sept) $99–$119 S or D; $119–$139 ste. Extra person $10. Children under age 12 stay free. Lower rates off-season. Parking: Indoor/outdoor, $12/day. AE, DC, DISC, MC, V.

⬛⬛⬛⬛ The Ritz-Carlton San Francisco

600 Stockton St, 94108 (Nob Hill); tel 415/296-7465 or toll free 800/241-3333; fax 415/291-0288. At California St. Grand, turn-of-the-century, Federal Reserve–style landmark converted to hotel in 1991, with palatial furnishings (Bohemian crystal chandeliers, silk wall-coverings) and museum-caliber artworks. Located on eight floors around a U-shaped central courtyard with flower beds and a white-umbrellaed cafe that reminds some visitors of the Hotel Bristol in Paris. **Rooms:** 336 rms and stes. Executive level. CI 3pm/CO noon. Nonsmoking rms avail. Impeccably furnished with period furniture; sumptuous Italian marble bathrooms. Some rooms offer skyline or harbor views. **Amenities:** ⬛⬛ ⬛ A/C, cable TV w/movies, dataport, voice mail, in-rm safe, bathrobes. All units w/minibars, 1 w/terrace, some w/whirlpools. **Services:** ⬛⬛ ⬛ ⬛ ⬛ Twice-daily maid svce, car-rental desk, masseur, children's program, babysitting. 24-hour concierge. Afternoon tea in elegant lounge. Room service massage. Complimentary town cars to several downtown locations. Cellular phones for rent. **Facilities:** ⬛ ⬛ ⬛ ⬛ ⬛ 2 restaurants (*see* "Restaurants" below), 3 bars (2 w/entertainment), sauna, steam rm, whirlpool. 8,000-square-foot fitness center has one of the city's few indoor lap pools. **Rates:** $255–$375 S; $275–$395 D; $355–$675 ste. Extra person $20. Children under age 18 stay free. Parking: Indoor, $27/day. Rates vary by floor and view rather than size. (For a real bargain, room 312 at $265 is hard to beat.) AE, CB, DC, DISC, ER, JCB, MC, V.

⬛⬛⬛ San Francisco Hilton

333 O'Farrell St, 94142 (Union Square); tel 415/771-1400 or toll free 800/HILTONS; fax 415/771-6807. At Mason St. A mammoth hotel near Union Square. **Rooms:** 1,895 rms and stes. Executive level. CI 2pm/CO noon. Nonsmoking rms avail. Standard rooms with great views. **Amenities:** ⬛⬛⬛ ⬛ A/C, cable TV w/movies, dataport, voice mail. All units w/minibars, some w/terraces. **Services:** ⬛ ⬛ ⬛ ⬛ ⬛ ⬛ Masseur, babysitting. Pet fee $5. **Facilities:** ⬛ ⬛ ⬛ ⬛ ⬛ 5 restaurants, 2 bars, games rm, sauna, beauty salon. Outdoor pool is well protected from wind. Rooftop restaurant on 46th floor. **Rates:** Peak (May–Oct) $185–$250 S; $205–$270 D; $300–$2,500 ste. Extra person $25. Children under age 18 stay free. Lower rates off-season. AP and MAP rates avail. Parking: Indoor, $24/day. AE, CB, DC, DISC, JCB, MC, V.

⬛⬛⬛ San Francisco Marriott

55 4th St, 94103; tel 415/896-1600 or toll free 800/228-9290; fax 415/777-2799. At Mission St. Splashy hotel with beautiful public spaces. Excellent for conventions and families, with a central location across from Moscone Center. **Rooms:** 1,498 rms and stes. Executive level. CI 3pm/CO noon. Nonsmoking rms avail. Many suites have views of the city. Some rooms have kitchens. **Amenities:** ⬛ ⬛ A/C, cable TV w/movies, dataport, voice mail, in-rm safe. All units w/minibars, some w/terraces, some w/whirlpools. **Services:** ⬛ ⬛ ⬛ ⬛ ⬛ ⬛ ⬛ Car-rental desk. Use of computers, fax machines, secretarial services, and multilingual business center. **Facilities:** ⬛ ⬛ ⬛ ⬛ ⬛ 2 restaurants, 2 bars, sauna, steam rm, whirlpool. Health club with largest indoor pool in the city. Shops. Rooftop lounge. **Rates:** Peak (Apr–Oct) $189–$225 S; $189–$245 D. Extra person $10. Children under age 18 stay free. Lower rates off-season. Parking: Indoor/outdoor, $24/day. AE, CB, DC, DISC, EC, ER, JCB, MC, V.

⬛⬛⬛ Savoy Hotel

580 Geary St, 94102 (Downtown); tel 415/441-2700 or toll free 800/227-4223; fax 415/441-2700 ext 297. Between Jones and Powell Sts. Old-time San Francisco atmosphere in lobby. **Rooms:** 83 rms and stes. CI 3pm/CO noon. Nonsmoking rms avail. Beds have feather pillows. **Amenities:** ⬛ ⬛ ⬛ Cable TV, refrig, dataport, bathrobes. No A/C. All units w/minibars, some w/whirlpools. **Services:** ⬛ ⬛ ⬛ ⬛ ⬛ Car-rental desk, babysitting. Free overnight shoeshine. Complimentary afternoon tea, cookies, sherry. **Facilities:** ⬛ ⬛ 1 restaurant (*see* "Restaurants" below), 1 bar. Savoy Brasserie is a fine new French restaurant. **Rates (CP):** Peak (Apr–Oct) $105–$125 S or D; $150–$180 ste. Extra person $10. Children under age 12 stay free. Lower rates off-season. Parking: Indoor, $10–$18/day. Package deal includes room, parking, dinner, and breakfast for two. AE, CB, DC, DISC, JCB, MC, V.

⬛⬛⬛ Shannon Court Hotel

550 Geary St, 94102 (Downtown); tel 415/775-5000 or toll free 800/228-8830; fax 415/928-6813. Between Taylor and Jones Sts. Classic San Francisco decor. **Rooms:** 173 rms and stes. CI 2pm/CO noon. Nonsmoking rms avail. Very large and clean. **Amenities:** ⬛ ⬛ Satel TV w/movies, refrig. No A/C. Some units w/terraces, 1 w/fireplace. **Services:** ⬛ ⬛ ⬛ ⬛ Babysitting. **Facilities:** ⬛ ⬛ 1 restaurant, 1 bar. Great cafe downstairs: City of Paris. **Rates:** Peak (Apr–Oct) $110–$115 S; $120–$135 D; $200–$300 ste. Extra person $12. Children under age 12 stay free. Lower rates off-season. Parking: Outdoor, $14/day. AE, CB, DC, DISC, EC, JCB, MC, V.

⬛⬛ The Sheehan

620 Sutter St, 94102 (Union Square); tel 415/775-6500 or toll free 800/848-1529; fax 415/775-3271. At Mason St. Worn-looking hotel has one of the largest indoor lap pools in San Francisco. **Rooms:** 69 rms. CI 3pm/CO 11am. Nonsmoking rms avail. **Amenities:** ⬛ Cable TV. No A/C. **Services:** ⬛ ⬛ ⬛ ⬛ Babysitting. **Facilities:** ⬛ ⬛ ⬛ ⬛ 1 restaurant (bkfst only), 1 bar, beauty salon. **Rates (CP):** Peak

(June–Nov) $59–$79 S; $79–$119 D. Extra person $10. Children under age 13 stay free. Lower rates off-season. Parking: Outdoor, $14/day. AE, CB, DC, DISC, JCB, MC, V.

▤▤▤ Sheraton at Fisherman's Wharf

2500 Mason St, 94133; tel 415/362-5500 or toll free 800/325-3535; fax 415/956-5275. At Beach St. This hotel, scheduled to undergo a major renovation, has an attractive lobby ideal for groups. **Rooms:** 525 rms and stes. Executive level. CI 3pm/CO noon. Nonsmoking rms avail. **Amenities:** 🛏 🐾 🖥 A/C, cable TV w/movies, dataport, voice mail, bathrobes. Some units w/terraces. **Services:** 🍽 🗝 🚐 🖼 🛎 Car-rental desk, masseur, babysitting. **Facilities:** 🔥 📶 🖥 🛗 1 restaurant, 1 bar (w/entertainment), beauty salon. Use of 24-hour Nautilus center across the street ($6 per day). Hertz rental car office, and travel and tour desk on site. **Rates:** Peak (Mar–Sept) $120–$190 S or D; $300 ste. Extra person $20. Children under age 12 stay free. Min stay special events. Lower rates off-season. Parking: Indoor, $12/day. AE, CB, DC, DISC, JCB, MC, V.

▤▤▤ Sir Francis Drake

450 Powell St, 94102 (Union Square); tel 415/392-7755 or toll free 800/227-5480; fax 415/677-9341. Between Post and Sutter Sts. Grand hotel in the old San Francisco style; built in 1928, but recently refurbished. Located on the cable-car line, 1 block from Union Square. **Rooms:** 417 rms and stes. CI 3pm/CO noon. Nonsmoking rms avail. **Amenities:** 🛏 🐾 A/C, cable TV w/movies. Some units w/minibars. **Services:** ✕ 🗝 📺 🚐 🖼 🛎 Car-rental desk, babysitting. **Facilities:** 🍴 📶 🖥 🛗 2 restaurants, 2 bars (1 w/entertainment). **Rates:** Peak (July–Aug) $139–$189 S or D; $350–$650 ste. Extra person $20. Children under age 12 stay free. Lower rates off-season. Parking: Indoor, $23/day. AE, CB, DC, DISC, JCB, MC, V.

▤▤ Stanyan Park Hotel

750 Stanyan St, 94117; tel 415/751-1000; fax 415/668-5454. At Waller St. Small Victorian-style hotel built in 1904 and listed on the National Register of Historic Places. Right across from Golden Gate Park and close to museums, jogging and in-line skating trails, and other area attractions. **Rooms:** 36 rms, stes, and effic. CI 3pm/CO noon. Nonsmoking rms avail. Rooms are colonial in decor. A little worn, but clean and comfortable. **Amenities:** 🛏 🐾 TV, refrig, in-rm safe. No A/C. **Services:** 🖼 🛎 Babysitting. Complimentary afternoon tea and cookies. **Facilities:** 📶 🛗 **Rates (CP):** $85–$105 S or D; $135–$185 ste; $135–$185 effic. Extra person $20. Children under age 18 stay free. Parking: Outdoor, $5/day. AE, DC, DISC, MC, V.

▤▤▤ Tuscan Inn at Fisherman's Wharf

425 Northpoint St, 94133; tel 415/561-1100 or toll free 800/648-4626; fax 415/561-1199. At Mason St. A European-style inn with beautiful public areas. **Rooms:** 221 rms and stes. CI 3pm/CO noon. Nonsmoking rms avail. Rooms are bright, comfortable, and clean. **Amenities:** 🛏 🐾 🖥 🍷 A/C,

cable TV w/movies, voice mail. All units w/minibars, 1 w/fireplace. **Services:** ✕ 🗝 📺 🚐 🖼 🛎 Car-rental desk, babysitting. Complimentary morning coffee, tea, and biscotti; limo to the Financial District; wine served by the fireplace every evening. **Facilities:** 📶 🛗 1 restaurant, 1 bar. Cafe Pescatore, an Italian trattoria. **Rates:** Peak (June–Oct) $138–$198 S or D; $208–$228 ste. Extra person $20. Children under age 18 stay free. Lower rates off-season. Parking: Indoor/outdoor, $13/day. AE, DC, DISC, MC, V.

▤▤ Vagabond Inn

2550 Vann Ness Ave, 94109; tel 415/776-7500; fax 415/776-5689. Between Union and Filbert Sts. Well-located just two blocks from cable car, six blocks from Fisherman's Wharf **Rooms:** 132 rms, stes, and effic. CI 3pm/CO noon. Nonsmoking rms avail. **Amenities:** 🛏 🐾 🖥 Cable TV w/movies, refrig. No A/C. Some units w/terraces. **Services:** 🚐 🖼 🛎 Car-rental desk. **Facilities:** 📶 📶 🛗 1 restaurant, 1 bar. 24-hour restaurant and lounge. **Rates (CP):** Peak (May–Oct) $99–$129 S or D; $125–$150 ste; $150 effic. Extra person $5. Children under age 15 stay free. Lower rates off-season. Parking: Indoor, free. AE, CB, DC, DISC, MC, V.

▤▤▤ Villa Florence

225 Powell St, 94102 (Downtown); tel 415/397-7700 or toll free 800/553-4411; fax 415/397-1006. Between Geary and O'Farrell Sts. Excellent Union Square location. **Rooms:** 180 rms and stes. CI 3pm/CO noon. Nonsmoking rms avail. Rooms are clean and spacious, but plain. **Amenities:** 🛏 🐾 🖥 🍷 A/C, refrig, dataport. All units w/minibars. Ironing board in each room. **Services:** ✕ 🚐 🖼 🛎 Car-rental desk, babysitting. **Facilities:** 📶 🛗 1 restaurant (see "Restaurants" below), 1 bar. Kuleto's is one of the city's top restaurants. **Rates:** Peak (Apr–Oct) $155–$175 S or D; $185–$305 ste. Extra person $15. Children under age 10 stay free. Lower rates off-season. AP and MAP rates avail. Parking: Indoor, $17/day. AE, CB, DC, DISC, EC, ER, JCB, MC, V.

▤▤▤ Warwick Regis Hotel

490 Geary St, 94102 (Downtown); tel 415/928-7900 or toll free 800/827-3447; fax 415/441-8788. At Taylor St. Somewhat generic but pleasant hotel with a grand, attractive lobby. Right off Union Square. **Rooms:** 80 rms and stes. CI 3pm/CO 1pm. Nonsmoking rms avail. Rooms are small but comfortable. **Amenities:** 🛏 🐾 Cable TV w/movies, bathrobes. No A/C. All units w/minibars, some w/terraces, some w/fireplaces. **Services:** 🍽 📺 🚐 🖼 🛎 Twice-daily maid svce, masseur, babysitting. Overnight shoeshine. **Facilities:** 📶 🖥 🛗 1 restaurant (bkfst and dinner only), 1 bar (w/entertainment). Elegant restaurant and bar. **Rates (CP):** Peak (June–Oct) $95–$105 S; $105–$130 D; $145–$205 ste. Extra person $10. Children under age 12 stay free. Lower rates off-season. Parking: Indoor, $18/day. AE, CB, DC, DISC, JCB, MC, V.

≝≝≝ Westin St Francis
335 Powell St, 94102 (Union Square); tel 415/397-7000 or toll free 800/228-3000; fax 415/774-0124. Between Post and Geary Sts. Classic San Francisco hotel—one of the grande dames of the city. Very elegant with charming Compass Rose tea room. **Rooms:** 1,192 rms and stes. CI 3pm/CO 1pm. Nonsmoking rms avail. **Amenities:** 🛁 ⓣ A/C, cable TV w/movies, refrig, voice mail, in-rm safe. All units w/minibars, some w/terraces, some w/fireplaces, some w/whirlpools. Kids Club features a bag of fun presents. Kids' room-service menu available. **Services:** 🍴 🛎 VP 🚗 ⚟ ↺ ⟳ Twice-daily maid svce, car-rental desk, babysitting. **Facilities:** 🏊 1500 💻 ♿ 3 restaurants, 3 bars (1 w/entertainment), beauty salon. **Rates:** $200–$350 S or D; $250–$1,700 ste. Extra person $30. Children under age 18 stay free. Min stay special events. Parking: Indoor, $24/day. AE, CB, DC, DISC, ER, JCB, MC, V.

≝≝≝ The York Hotel
940 Sutter St, 94109 (Downtown); tel 415/885-6800 or toll free 800/808-YORK; fax 415/885-2115. Between Hyde and Leavenworth Sts. High-ceilinged lobby with extensive marble and ceiling fans. A hip hotel with character, a favorite of many actors. Scenes for *Vertigo* were filmed here. **Rooms:** 96 rms and stes. CI 3pm/CO noon. Nonsmoking rms avail. Clean, modern rooms with pleasant decor, large closets, window seats, and sitting areas. **Amenities:** 🛁 ⓣ 🛎 ♒ Cable TV w/movies, dataport, voice mail, in-rm safe, bathrobes. No A/C. All units w/minibars. **Services:** VP 🚗 ⚟ ↺ Car-rental desk. Nightly hospitality hour. Limousine service available to Fisherman's Wharf and Union Square. **Facilities:** 50 1 bar (w/entertainment). The elegant Plush Room cabaret features top performers. **Rates (CP):** $106–$114 S; $112–$122 D; $210 ste. Extra person $10. Children under age 12 stay free. Parking: Indoor, $14/day. Some packages include tickets to Plush Room performances. Senior discounts and corporate rates available. AE, CB, DC, DISC, JCB, MC, V.

MOTEL

≝≝ Cow Hollow Motor Inn & Suites
2190 Lombard St, 94123; tel 415/921-5800; fax 415/922-8515. At Steiner St. Clean, well-managed, upscale motor inn. **Rooms:** 129 rms and stes. CI 3pm/CO noon. Nonsmoking rms avail. Suites are a great bargain, with Persian-style rugs, full kitchen, and living and dining area. Standard rooms are attractively arranged. **Amenities:** 🛁 🛎 A/C, cable TV. Some units w/fireplaces. **Services:** 🚗 ⚟ ↺ Babysitting. **Facilities:** 40 ♿ 1 restaurant (bkfst and lunch only). Use of nearby health club for $10. **Rates:** $76–$88 S; $80–$88 D; $175–$245 ste. Extra person $7. Children under age 5 stay free. Parking: Indoor, free. AE, DC, MC, V.

INNS

≝ Adelaide Inn
5 Isadora Duncan, 94102 (Union Square); tel 415/441-2261; fax 415/441-0161. A European-style pensione featuring shared bath, located in a quiet alley near Union Square. One of the cheapest places to stay in the area. **Rooms:** 18 rms (all w/shared bath). CI 9am/CO noon. Nonsmoking rms avail. Rooms are bare, sparse, and smell stuffy. **Amenities:** 🛁 ⓣ TV. No A/C. **Services:** 🚗 ⚟ ↺ Babysitting. Multilingual staff speaks German, French, and Spanish. **Facilities:** Cozy breakfast room. No elevator. **Rates (CP):** $32–$38 S w/shared bath; $42–$48 D w/shared bath. Extra person $6. Children under age 6 stay free. Parking: Outdoor, $7/day. AE, MC, V.

≝≝≝ Archbishops Mansion
1000 Fulton St, 94117; tel 415/563-7872 or toll free 800/543-5820; fax 415/885-3193. Built in 1904 for the Catholic archbishop of California, this Victorian mansion is now a B&B. It provides special and romantic accommodations plus a spacious parlor and dining room. **Rooms:** 15 rms and stes. CI 3pm/CO noon. Spacious rooms are individually decorated, some with canopied or four-poster beds. Carmen Suite has a clawfoot bathtub in front of fireplace. **Amenities:** 🛁 ⓣ Cable TV, VCR, bathrobes. No A/C. Some units w/fireplaces, some w/whirlpools. **Services:** ✕ ⚟ ↺ Masseur, babysitting, afternoon tea and wine/sherry served. **Facilities:** 10 Washer/dryer, guest lounge. **Rates (CP):** Peak (May–Oct) $129–$189 S or D; $215–$385 ste. Extra person $20. Children under age 1 stay free. Min stay wknds. Lower rates off-season. Parking: Outdoor, free. AE, MC, V.

≝≝≝ The Bed and Breakfast Inn
4 Charlton Court, 94123; tel 415/921-9784. Popular inn set in three century-old Victorians on a charming mews. Book six to nine weeks in advance to guarantee a specific room. An exceptional value. Unsuitable for children under 5. **Rooms:** 11 rms and stes (4 w/shared bath). CI 3pm/CO noon. No smoking. Each room is uniquely decorated with family furniture and antiques. Garden Suite accommodates up to four people; Celebration Suite is very romantic. **Amenities:** 🛁 ⓣ Cable TV. No A/C. Some units w/terraces, some w/whirlpools. **Services:** ⚟ ↺ Afternoon tea and wine/sherry served. Sherry service at all times. **Facilities:** Guest lounge w/TV. **Rates (CP):** Peak (Apr–Dec) $70 S w/shared bath, $115 S w/private bath; $90–$115 D w/shared bath, $115–$140 D w/private bath; $190–$275 ste. Lower rates off-season. Parking: Indoor, $10/day. Garden Suite is 1,300 square feet for $250 per night. No CC.

≝≝≝ The Mansions
2220 Sacramento St, 94115; tel 415/929-9444 or toll free 800/826-9398; fax 415/567-9391. A stay here is a unique experience. The 1887 Victorian and adjacent 1903 Greek revival mansions are crammed with eclectic antiques and adorned with stained glass. **Rooms:** 21 rms and stes. CI 3pm/CO noon. Nonsmoking rms avail. Charming, individually

decorated rooms with antique furnishings. **Amenities:** 📺 ☐ ⌇ No A/C or TV. 1 unit w/terrace, some w/fireplaces, some w/whirlpools. **Services:** ☐ ↵ ⌂ Babysitting. Breakfast in bed; nightly piano concert performed by the resident ghost. **Facilities:** 🔲 1 restaurant (bkfst and dinner only), 1 bar (w/entertainment), games rm, guest lounge w/TV. Sitting room, library, and dining room with gourmet cuisine. **Rates (BB):** $129–$225 S or D; $189–$350 ste. Extra person $20. Parking: Indoor/outdoor, $15/day. Rates increase by $20 on weekends. AE, CB, DC, DISC, JCB, MC, V.

≣≣≣ Petite Auberge

863 Bush St, 94108 (Union Square); tel 415/928-6000; fax 415/775-5717. Lots of teddy bears tucked everywhere in this French country inn/hotel. Breakfast room, garden terrace, and fireplace lounge all done like a cozy Victorian living room. **Rooms:** 26 rms and stes. CI 2pm/CO noon. No smoking. **Amenities:** 📺 ☐ ⌇ Cable TV, bathrobes. No A/C. Some units w/fireplaces, 1 w/whirlpool. Guidebooks in each room. **Services:** 🆅🅿 🚗 ☐ ↵ Car-rental desk, babysitting, afternoon tea and wine/sherry served. Afternoon tea and cookies. Breakfast in bed for a fee. **Facilities:** Guest lounge w/TV. **Rates (BB):** $110–$160 S or D; $220 ste. Extra person $15. Children under age 12 stay free. Parking: Indoor, $19/day. AE, DC, DISC, MC, V.

≣≣ Red Victorian Bed & Breakfast Inn

1665 Haight St, 94117; tel 415/864-1978. This place has been here since 1904, and withstood the big earthquake. Located in the heart of the Haight district near Golden Gate Park. **Rooms:** 18 rms and stes. CI 3pm/CO 11am. No smoking. Each room has a unique theme. **Amenities:** 📺 ☐ No A/C or TV. **Services:** 🚗 **Facilities:** Meditation room. **Rates (CP):** $59–$134 S; $69–$200 D; $134–$200 ste. Extra person $15. Min stay wknds and special events. AE, MC, V.

≣≣ The San Remo Hotel

2237 Mason St, 94133 (Fisherman's Wharf/North Beach); tel 415/776-8688 or toll free 800/352-REMO; fax 415/776-2811. At Chestnut. Historic inn located in a 1906 building offers a great deal in a quiet neighborhood between North Beach and Fisherman's Wharf. **Rooms:** 63 rms and stes (62 w/shared bath). CI 2pm/CO 11am. Nonsmoking rms avail. **Amenities:** ☐ No A/C, phone, or TV. 1 unit w/terrace. **Services:** 🚗 ☐ ↵ Babysitting. **Facilities:** Washer/dryer. **Rates:** $45–$55 S w/shared bath; $55–$65 D w/shared bath; $85 ste. Children under age 2 stay free. Parking: Outdoor, $8/day. AE, CB, DC, DISC, JCB, MC, V.

≣≣≣≣ The Sherman House

2160 Green St, 94123 (Pacific Heights); tel 415/563-3600 or toll free 800/424-5777; fax 415/563-1882. Luxurious city inn, opened in 1984, housed in a restored 1876 mansion that once hosted tenor Enrico Caruso and pianist Ignace Paderewski. It's expensive, but regular guests are willing to pay for the exquisite style and seclusion—and willing to overlook frayed carpets and fabrics. Located in the fashionable Pacific Heights district, close to many of San Francisco's major sights. **Rooms:** 14 rms and stes; 1 cottage/villa. CI 3pm/CO noon. Most rooms and suites are in the main house; some are compact, some spacious. A few rooms are in a carriage house in the lovely, peaceful garden. Every room is individually decorated with antiques and refined wall decorations. **Amenities:** 📺 ⌇ Cable TV, CD/tape player, in-rm safe, bathrobes. No A/C. Some units w/terraces, all w/fireplaces, some w/whirlpools. All bathrooms have TVs, some have whirlpools or Roman tubs. Two phones and radio/cassette players in every room. No air conditioning, but not needed most of the year. Personalized stationery. Fresh orchids from the garden greenhouse. **Services:** 🍽 🆅🅿 ☐ ↵ Twice-daily maid svce, babysitting. Room butlers rather than bellmen and waiters (one for every two rooms) but the style and swagger of previous years. 24-hour Butler's Menu. In-room meals served on Lenox china, course by course, if requested. Guest directory lists direct line to chef, for guests who'd like to plan meals in advance. Afternoon tea served in antique-filled lounge. **Facilities:** 🔲 1 restaurant, 1 bar. 12-table dining room for exclusive use of guests. **Rates:** $200–$395 S or D; $595–$825 effic. Children under age 18 stay free. Min stay special events. Parking: Indoor, $16/day. Parking: Outdoor, $16/day. AE, CB, DC, MC, V.

≣≣ Victorian Inn on the Park

301 Lyon St, 94117; tel 415/931-1830 or toll free 800/435-1967. This inn has a casual atmosphere but could be cleaner and more professionally run. **Rooms:** 12 rms and stes. CI 2pm/CO 11:30am. Nonsmoking rms avail. Individually decorated rooms with some antiques. **Amenities:** 📺 ☐ No A/C or TV. 1 unit w/terrace, some w/fireplaces. **Services:** 🔑 Babysitting, afternoon tea and wine/sherry served. Fresh baked goods for breakfast. **Facilities:** 🔲 Guest lounge w/TV. **Rates (CP):** $99–$164 S or D; $164–$320 ste. Extra person $20. Children under age 10 stay free. Min stay wknds. Parking: Outdoor, $10/day. AE, CB, DC, DISC, JCB, MC, V.

≣≣≣ Washington Square Inn

1660 Stockton St, 94133 (North Beach); tel 415/981-4220 or toll free 800/388-0220; fax 415/397-7242. Small, elegant inn close to shops and restaurants in North Beach and within walking distance of Chinatown and Fisherman's Wharf. Unsuitable for children under 18. **Rooms:** 15 rms (5 w/shared bath). CI 2pm/CO noon. No smoking. Immaculate, quiet rooms, some with shared bath. **Amenities:** 📺 ☐ Bathrobes. No A/C or TV. **Services:** 🆅🅿 ☐ ↵ Babysitting, afternoon tea and wine/sherry served. An ample spread is available at tea time, with canapés, cheese, cookies, and more. **Facilities:** Guest lounge. **Rates (CP):** $95–$105 S or D w/shared bath, $100–$160 S or D w/private bath. Extra person $10. Parking: Indoor, $17/day. AE, DC, DISC, JCB, MC, V.

≣≣≣ White Swan Inn

845 Bush St, 94108 (Union Square); tel 415/775-1755; fax 415/775-5717. The charm of a small European inn; complete with a beautiful library and fireplace. **Rooms:** 27 rms and

stes. CI 2pm/CO noon. No smoking. Attractively done in rich floral prints with four-poster beds. **Amenities:** 🛏 ☕ 🍷 Cable TV, refrig, dataport, VCR, bathrobes. No A/C. All units w/fireplaces. **Services:** VP 🚐 🛍 🔔 Car-rental desk, babysitting, afternoon tea and wine/sherry served. Complimentary newspapers delivered to room. **Facilities:** Guest lounge w/TV. Cozy breakfast area and garden patio. **Rates (BB):** $145–$195 S or D; $250 ste. Extra person $15. Children under age 12 stay free. Parking: Indoor, $19/day. AE, DC, DISC, MC, V.

RESTAURANTS 🍴

Acquerello
1722 Sacramento St; tel 415/567-5432. Between Polk St and Van Ness Ave. **Italian.** *Acquerello* means watercolors, and this pretty restaurant highlights watercolor paintings from local artists on its high-gloss walls in what used to be a chapel. The menu changes frequently and offers carefully crafted classic Italian dishes such as gnocchi, quail stuffed with sausage and apples, marinated pork loin, and braised sturgeon. Fine wine list. **FYI:** Reservations recommended. Beer and wine only. **Open:** Tues–Sat 5:30–10pm. **Prices:** Main courses $18–$22. AE, DC, DISC, MC, V.

Act IV
In the Inn at the Opera, 333 Fulton St (Civic Center); tel 415/863-8400. Off Franklin St behind Opera. **French.** Located just behind the Opera House, this is a good place to rub shoulders with ballet stars, opera divas, and other performers, as well as a very romantic spot for dining before or after the theater. Decor is elegant but cozy, with brocade and wood paneling on the walls, plus a fireplace. The dinner menu might include seared salmon and oysters with lemon-mint sauce, or baby lamb chops with chanterelles. The fine continental buffet breakfast features French cheeses, smoked meats, and pastries. **FYI:** Reservations recommended. Piano. **Open:** Breakfast daily 7–10am; lunch Mon–Fri 11:30am–2pm; dinner Sun–Thurs 5:30–9pm, Fri–Sat 5:30–10:30pm; brunch Sun 11am–2:30pm. **Prices:** Main courses $16–$28. AE, CB, DC, DISC, MC, V. ♥ VP &

♣ Alain Rondelli
126 Clement St; tel 415/387-0408. Between 2nd and 3rd Sts. **French.** The decor and food are decidedly French, with a copper bar, frescoed walls, tiled floors, and country French chairs. The chef has his own style of cuisine based on contemporary French cooking, featuring lamb, lobster, salmon, and veal on the frequently changing menu. A six-course tasting menu is available for $45. **FYI:** Reservations recommended. **Open:** Tues–Thurs 5:30–10pm, Fri–Sat 5:30–10:30pm. **Prices:** Main courses $16–$19; prix fixe $45–$85. MC, V. ♥

Albona Ristorante Istriano
545 Francisco St (North Beach/North Point); tel 415/441-1040. At Mason. **Italian.** The owner/chef hails from the Istrian peninsula on the Adriatic coast, south of Trieste.

Menu features northern Italian dishes with Yugoslavian influences, with entrees such as ravioli with three cheeses, toasted pine nuts, and golden raisins; three types of risotto; and braised rabbit with juniper berries. **FYI:** Reservations recommended. Beer and wine only. **Open:** Tues–Sat 5–10pm. **Prices:** Main courses $9–$15. AE, CB, MC, V. VP &

♣ Aqua
252 California St (Financial District); tel 415/956-9662. At Sansome St. **Seafood.** One of San Francisco's most stylish and popular places, decorated with huge floral arrangements, large upholstered chairs, floor-to-ceiling mirrors, a long bar, and high ceilings. It's known for elaborate presentations of seafood, including steamed lobster, Hawaiian swordfish, halibut, and sea scallops. They offer several five- and six-course tasting menus, including vegetarian, ranging from $45–$65. **FYI:** Reservations recommended. **Open:** Lunch Mon–Fri 11:30am–2:30pm; dinner Mon–Thurs 5:30–10:30pm, Fri–Sat 5:30–11pm. **Prices:** Main courses $24–$38; prix fixe $60. AE, DC, MC, V. VP &

A Sabella's
2766 Taylor St (Wharf); tel 415/771-6775. At Jefferson St. **Seafood.** Classy and elegant, this family-run San Francisco institution offers great seafood and views of the wharf and bay. The menu is in six languages and presents such dishes as prawns risotto; shrimp or crab Louie; whole cracked Dungeness crab; and petrale sole. Other San Francisco specialties are complemented by an excellent California wine list. On weekends, there's a murder-mystery dinner in a separate dining room. **FYI:** Reservations recommended. Piano. **Open:** Daily 11:30am–11pm. **Prices:** Main courses $18–$40. AE, DC, DISC, MC, V. 🖼 &

$ ★ Biscuits & Blues
401 Mason St (Downtown); tel 415/292-2583. At Geary. **Soul/Southern.** Hot biscuits and cool blues are the hallmark of this supper club run by longtime San Francisco chef, Regina Charboneau. Authentic Southern food served in an intimate setting with eclectic decor, down-home red shutters, and a collection of "Blues Shoes" from a number of great musicians. Recommended are the shrimp fritters or grilled catfish or chicken with black-eyed peas and mustard greens. Sinful desserts include chocolate bread pudding. **FYI:** Reservations not accepted. Blues. **Open:** Tues–Thurs 6:30–11:30pm, Fri–Sat 6:30pm–2am. **Prices:** Main courses $7–$10. AE, MC, V.

Bistro Roti
In the Hotel Griffon, 155 Steuart St (Financial District); tel 415/495-6500. Between Mission and Howard Sts. **Regional American.** Rich woods, leather, and brass create warm supper-club atmosphere at this eatery located near remodeled Embarcadero waterfront. Wood-burning fire on chilly days. In addition to the oyster bar, it offers seafood, spit-roasted meats, and fragrant chicken, plus unusual choices such as duck cannelioni and salmon encrusted with fennel. Superior

wine list, quality beers on tap. **FYI:** Reservations recommended. **Open:** Lunch Mon–Fri 11:30am–5pm; dinner Mon–Thurs 5–10pm, Fri–Sat 5–11pm. **Prices:** Main courses $12–$24. AE, DC, DISC, MC, V. 🔲 🖼 VP ⚹

Bix

56 Gold St (Jackson Square); tel 415/433-6300. **American.** This restaurant, in historic gold rush–era building hidden away down an alley, has the ambience of an old supper club. An art deco mural, a mahogany bar, and jazz music set the scene for enjoying such specialties as chicken hash and grilled pork chop. Fine wines are served by the glass. **FYI:** Reservations recommended. Piano. **Open:** Mon–Thurs 11:30am–11pm, Fri 11:30am–midnight, Sat 5:30pm–midnight, Sun 6–10pm. **Prices:** Main courses $13–$26. AE, CB, DC, DISC, MC, V. ♥ 🔳 VP

✹ Bizou

598 4th St; tel 415/543-2222. At Brannan St. **French/Italian.** With mustard-colored walls, warm recessed lighting, and soft jazz music, this place glows like a fireplace at night. It's chic and elegant. Feast on Prince Edward Island mussels with saffron, lasagna, duck breast, braised baked salmon, quail, roasted beef, and grilled persimmon salad, plus other imaginative fare. **FYI:** Reservations recommended. **Open:** Lunch Mon–Fri 11:30am–2:30pm; dinner Mon–Thurs 5:30–10pm, Fri–Sat 5:30–10:30pm. **Prices:** Main courses $10–$17. AE, MC, V. ⚹

Boulevard

1 Mission St; tel 415/543-6084. At Steuart St. **New American.** Exquisite food and a stylish decor reminiscent of a turn-of-the-century Parisian bistro have combined to make this one of the hottest restaurants in town. With decor by Pat Kuleto and food by superchef Nancy Oakes, plus spectacular views of the Bay Bridge, this place has it all, including chicken cooked in a wood-fired oven, roasted salmon, spit-roasted pork loin, and what some call the best desserts in the city. Jazz saxophonist not too loud. **FYI:** Reservations recommended. **Open:** Lunch Mon–Fri 11:30am–2:15pm; dinner daily 5:30–10pm. **Prices:** Main courses $18–$25. AE, CB, DC, DISC, MC, V. 🔳 VP ⚹

Brandy Ho's Hunan Food

217 Columbus Ave (North Beach); tel 415/788-7527. **Chinese.** Very popular; a good place for spicy food. Smoked duck and smoked ham made on premises. Lunch specials for $5. **FYI:** Reservations accepted. Beer and wine only. Additional location: 450 Broadway (tel 362-6268). **Open:** Sun–Thurs 11:30am–11pm, Fri–Sat 11:30am–midnight. **Prices:** Main courses $6–$20. AE, DC, DISC, MC, V.

Cafe de la Presse

469 Bush St (Financial District); tel 415/249-0900. At Grant Ave. **Californian.** This warm, comfortable restaurant, which connects to a bookstore and coffeehouse, offers a lively cafe/arty bistro atmosphere. The great breakfasts and steaming lattes ultimately yield to French-California bistro lunches and dinners. Menu choices might be hamburgers, freshly shucked oysters, quiche lorraine, pasta with smoked salmon, game hen, or peppercorn-coated filet mignon. **FYI:** Reservations accepted. **Open:** Daily 7am–11pm. **Prices:** Main courses $8–$16. AE, DC, DISC, MC, V. ⚹

♣ Cafe Fifty-Three

In ANA Hotel, 50 3rd St (Mascone Center); tel 415/974-1029. At Market St. **Californian.** Decorated with murals of Renaissance sentries and playing cards, the restaurant also features custom lighting and large windows that complement the rich mahogany wood trim and chairs. California cuisine with French, Italian, and Japanese accents. For starters, a good bet is the oysters with ginger mignonette sauce. Main dishes might be Dijon grilled steak with a thyme glaze, or veal medallions with wild mushroom risotto. California wines and a broad selection of microbreweries offered. **FYI:** Reservations recommended. **Open:** Breakfast Mon–Sat 6:30–11am; lunch daily 11:30am–2pm; dinner daily 5–11pm. **Prices:** Main courses $12–$25. AE, DC, DISC, ER, MC, V. VP ⚹

Ⓢ ✹ Cafe Macaroni

59 Columbus Ave (North Beach); tel 415/956-9737. **Italian.** Cozy, chef-owned cafe, one of the most popular Italian restaurants in San Francisco. Exceptional antipasti are displayed in a case. Gnocchi with gorgonzola, pork medallions with fennel-seed sauce. **FYI:** Reservations not accepted. Beer and wine only. **Open:** Lunch Mon–Fri 11:30am–2:30pm; dinner Mon–Sat 5:30–10pm. **Prices:** Main courses $7–$14; prix fixe $19–$25. No CC.

Cafe Majestic

In Hotel Majestic, 1500 Sutter St (Lower Pacific Heights); tel 415/776-6400. **Californian.** Upscale ambience, fine cuisine. Romantic Edwardian decor with graceful columns and hues of apricot and sea-foam green. Appetizers include crab and mango salad, and a dynamite Caesar salad. The menu features entrees such as housemade ravioli, or duckling with sun-dried cherries. Great eggs Benedict for brunch. **FYI:** Reservations recommended. Piano. **Open:** Breakfast Sat–Sun 7–11am; dinner daily 5:30–9pm; brunch Sun 10:30am–2pm. **Prices:** Main courses $14–$25. AE, DC, MC, V. ♥ VP ⚹

✹ Café Marimba

2317 Chestnut St (Marina); tel 415/776-1506. Between Scott and Divisadero Sts. **Mexican.** A colorful and very hip restaurant with palm trees out in front and original art inside. This is not typical Mexican food—the dozen taco selections include combinations like mushroom and tomatillo, or beef with almonds and currants. Other offerings feature grilled meats and seafood. There are 23 different tequilas, and great specialty drinks. **FYI:** Reservations recommended. **Open:** Tues–Thurs 11am–11pm, Fri–Sat 11am–midnight, Sun–Mon 11am–10pm. **Prices:** Main courses $6–$14. AE, MC, V. VP ⚹

Cafe Mozart

708 Bush St (Union Square); tel 415/391-8480. At Powell St. **Californian/French.** Cozy, intimate, romantic setting with candles and flowers. Watch the chef cook in the display kitchen at the center of the restaurant. Organic produce is used. Try chateaubriand with wild mushrooms. **FYI:** Reservations recommended. Beer and wine only. **Open:** Peak (June–Sept) Tues–Sun 5:30–10:30pm. **Prices:** Main courses $10–$23. AE, DC, MC, V. ♥ ▣

Cafe Tiramisu

28 Belden St (Financial District); tel 415/421-7044. Between Bush and Pine Sts. **Italian.** Italian trattoria located down a charming alley. Attractive frescoes in golden tones. Braised lamb shanks with rosemary sauce, sea bass, salmon cannelloni. **FYI:** Reservations recommended. **Open:** Lunch Mon–Fri 11am–3pm; dinner Mon–Sat 5–10:30pm. **Prices:** Main courses $8–$19; prix fixe $25–$40. AE, DC, MC, V.

Caffe Freddy's

901 Columbus Ave (North Beach); tel 415/922-0151. Between Lombard and Chestnut Sts. **Italian.** Fun place to eat in North Beach. Hip, artsy trattoria ambience. Offering microbrewed beers, local wines, and wholesome Italian specialties including caesar salad, eggplant, polenta, pizza, pasta, and calzone. **FYI:** Reservations recommended. Beer and wine only. **Open:** Mon–Thurs 11am–10pm, Fri 11am–10:30pm, Sat 9:30am–10:30pm, Sun 9:30am–10pm. **Prices:** Main courses $6–$10. AE, MC, V. &

★ **Caffe Sport**

574 Green St (North Beach); tel 415/981-1251. At Columbus Ave. **Italian.** Everyone sits at crowded family-style tables in this restaurant that has become a North Beach institution. The decor, a riot of color, was created by the chef/owner, who keeps an easel in the kitchen, awaiting moments of sudden inspiration. Specializes in hearty Sicilian fare—cioppino with lots of garlic, and seafood and pasta dishes. **FYI:** Reservations recommended. Beer and wine only. **Open:** Lunch Tues–Sat noon–2pm; dinner Tues–Thurs 5–10pm, Fri–Sat 6:30–10:30pm. **Prices:** Main courses $15–$26. No CC. ▮

♣ **Campton Place**

In Campton Place Hotel, 340 Stockton St (Union Square); tel 415/955-5555. Between Sutter and Post Sts. **New American.** Consistently regarded as one of the city's top restaurants. Conveys classic elegance with etched glass, potted palms, and empire-style chairs. The contemporary American menu contrasts tastes and textures, with offerings like sautéed squab with foie gras and saffron pappardelle, or Nantucket Bay scallops with Hawaiian prawns and white truffles. Wine list has a lot of depth and includes moderately priced California and Oregon selections. The three-course business lunch special is a great deal at $19.50. **FYI:** Reservations recommended. **Open:** Breakfast Mon–Fri 7–10:30am, Sat–Sun 8–11am; lunch Mon–Fri 11:30am–2:30pm, Sat–Sun noon–2:30pm; dinner Sun–Thurs 6–10pm, Fri–Sat 5:30–10:30pm; brunch Sun 10am–2pm. **Prices:** Main courses $26–$29. AE, DC, MC, V. VP &

Casa Aguila

1240 Noriega Ave (Sunset); tel 415/661-5593. Between 19th and 20th Aves. **Mexican.** Red tablecloths, piñatas, and kitschy Mexican trinkets lend lots of character. Offerings include seafood, chicken, and steaks with a Mexican flavor. **FYI:** Reservations not accepted. Beer and wine only. **Open:** Lunch daily 11:30am–3:30pm; dinner daily 5–10pm. **Prices:** Main courses $8–$15. AE, MC, V.

Cha Cha Cha

1805 Haight St (Haight-Ashbury); tel 415/386-5758. At Shrader St. **Caribbean.** With a Caribbean island flavor, it's casual, festive, and fun, decorated with marble tables, island-style patterned tablecloths and palm trees. The food is lively, including baked Yucatan chicken, fried plantains with black beans, steamed mussels, and shrimp in Cajun spices. There's also a tapas bar and weekend brunch. Service can be noticeably poor. **FYI:** Reservations not accepted. Folk. Beer and wine only. **Open:** Lunch Mon–Fri 11:30am–4pm, Sat–Sun 11:30am–4pm; dinner Sun–Thurs 5–11pm, Fri–Sat 5–11:30pm. **Prices:** Main courses $4–$10. No CC.

★ **China Moon**

639 Post St (Downtown); tel 415/775-4789. Between Jones and Taylor Sts. **Californian/Chinese.** A 1930s-style, art deco coffee shop redecorated with a modern Asian flavor. Inventive Chinese cuisine includes black-mushroom steamed trout, noodle pillows topped with spicy beef ribbons, pickled salmon, and crispy spring rolls with curried chicken. **FYI:** Reservations recommended. Beer and wine only. **Open:** Daily 5:30–10pm. **Prices:** Main courses $16–$22. AE, DC, MC, V. &

Ciao

230 Jackson St (Jackson Square); tel 415/892-9500. At Front St. **Italian.** Slick, modern Italian bistro offering good Italian cuisine. The chef prepares daily fish and pasta specials, as well as three kinds of carpaccio, lobster ravioli, and sausage stewed with peppers and polenta. The wine list favors California wines but also includes a good selection of Italian reds. **FYI:** Reservations recommended. **Open:** Mon–Thurs 11:30am–11pm, Fri–Sat 11:30am–midnight, Sun 4–10:30pm. **Prices:** Main courses $9–$17; prix fixe $28. AE, CB, DC, DISC, MC, V. ▣ VP &

Cypress Club

500 Jackson St (Downtown); tel 415/296-8555. At Columbus Ave. **New American.** Very busy, very in. Copper banquettes and tile floors give the look of a 1920s New York supper club. Specializes in simple, elegant food like venison chop with winter potatoes and crispy sonoma squash. **FYI:** Reservations recommended. **Open:** Mon–Thurs 4:30–10pm, Fri–Sat 4:30–11pm. **Prices:** Main courses $25–$32. AE, CB, DC, MC, V. VP &

David's

480 Geary St (Union Square); tel 415/771-1600. Between Mason and Taylor Sts. **Deli.** Basic diner/deli with counter seating. Lox and bagels, stuffed cabbage, goulash, corned beef hash. **FYI:** Reservations not accepted. Beer and wine only. **Open:** Mon–Fri 7am–11pm, Sat–Sun 8am–midnight. **Prices:** Main courses $7–$17; prix fixe $17. DC, DISC, MC, V. &

The Dining Room

In the Ritz-Carlton San Francisco, 600 Stockton St (Nob Hill); tel 415/296-7465. **Californian/French.** Classically sumptuous, this restaurant woos diners with elegant details such as Rosenthal china and the Ritz-Carlton's signature cobalt-blue glasses from Schlottweisel. The menu features creative dishes like rack of lamb cloaked in pistachio crust, or grilled sea scallops on spinach-fennel compote. However, service can be slow and unfocused. The bar offers the largest selection of single-malt scotches in the country. **FYI:** Reservations recommended. Harp. Dress code. **Open:** Mon–Sat 5:30–10:30pm. **Prices:** Prix fixe $45–$59. AE, CB, DC, DISC, MC, V. ● VP &

Doidge's

2217 Union St (Pacific Heights); tel 415/921-2149. **New American.** An upscale breakfast joint with comfortable old-fashioned appeal. Rare lithographs of Paris line the dining room's white walls. Menu favorites include pancakes topped with fresh berries, Doidge's homemade granola, and shrimp creole Benedict. Reservations necessary on weekends. Serves wine only. **FYI:** Reservations recommended. **Open:** Sat–Sun 8am–2:45pm, Mon–Fri 8am–1:45pm. **Prices:** Lunch main courses $5–$9. MC, V.

★ Dotties True Blue Cafe

522 Jones St; tel 415/885-2767. **American.** This cozy modern diner, in the heart of San Francisco, is run by an attractive, personable staff. It is a favorite breakfast spot for downtown hotel guests, and serves traditional, hearty choices such as pancakes, French toast, and good home fries. Strong Italian-style coffee made with freshly ground beans and house-baked breads are featured. **FYI:** Reservations not accepted. No liquor license. **Open:** Breakfast Wed–Mon 7:30am–2pm; lunch Mon 11:30am–2pm, Wed–Fri 11:30am–2pm. **Prices:** Lunch main courses $4–$7. DISC, MC, V. &

★ Ebisu

1283 9th Ave; tel 415/566-1770. Between Irving St and Lincoln Way. **Japanese.** Very popular with the locals—a small place with Asian decor, fresh flowers, and a sushi bar. Specialties include tempura, teriyaki, sukiyaki, and fried oysters. Prix-fixe sushi bar and Japanese beers are available. **FYI:** Reservations not accepted. Beer and wine only. **Open:** Lunch Mon–Fri 11:30am–2pm; dinner Mon–Wed 5–10pm, Thurs–Sat 5pm–midnight. **Prices:** Main courses $8–$13. AE, DC, MC, V.

Faz Restaurant & Catering

In Crocker Galleria, 161 Sutter St (Financial District); tel 415/362-0404. At Kearny St. **Mediterranean.** Colorful and lively setting. Chef/owner Faz Poursohi's creations include house-smoked fish, and fresh pastas and pizzas cooked in wood-burning oven. **FYI:** Reservations recommended. Jazz/piano. **Open:** Lunch Mon–Fri 11:30am–3pm; dinner Mon–Sat 5–10pm. **Prices:** Main courses $9–$18. AE, MC, V. &

Fino

In the Andrews Hotel, 624 Post St (Union Square); tel 415/928-2080. Between Taylor and Jones Sts. **Italian.** Cozy ambience, intimate dining near the fireplace. Fish and shellfish specialties may include scallops and prawns pomodoro over angel-hair pasta. **FYI:** Reservations recommended. **Open:** Tues–Sat 5:30–10:30pm, Sun–Mon 5:30–9:30pm. **Prices:** Main courses $7–$17; prix fixe $20. AE, DC, MC, V. ● ▣ ▾

Fleur De Lys

777 Sutter St (Nob Hill); tel 415/673-7779. Between Taylor and Jones Sts. **French/Mediterranean.** One of San Francisco's most elegant restaurants, with superb cuisine from acclaimed chef Hubert Keller. Decor suggests an immense garden tent set in the French countryside. Menu choices might include mosaic of fresh salmon and lotte with French green lentils, and citrus vinaigrette, or oven roasted lamb loin, introduced with a rich merlot sauce, infused with vanilla bean. Over 300 wines offered. **FYI:** Reservations recommended. Jacket required. **Open:** Mon–Thurs 6–10pm, Fri–Sat 5:30–10:30pm. Closed June 23–July 7. **Prices:** Main courses $27–$35; prix fixe $65. AE, CB, DC, MC, V. ● VP &

Flying Saucer

1000 Guerrero St (Mission District); tel 415/641-9955. At 22nd Ave. **Eclectic.** Literally part of San Francisco—marble on tables and wood paneling were rescued from demolished buildings. Other pieces include a 19th-century church lamp and an art deco frieze from the 1920s. The chef's "world beat cuisine" highlights fresh fish and seafood prepared with spices and techniques from France, Morocco, Japan, Thailand, and Egypt. **FYI:** Reservations recommended. Beer and wine only. **Open:** Tues–Sat 5:30–10pm. Closed 2 weeks in July. **Prices:** Main courses $20–$27. MC, V. &

Fog City Diner

1300 Battery St (Embarcadero); tel 415/982-2000. At Embarcadero. **Diner.** An upscale, 1950s-style diner offering great dining with small or large plate entrees such as pot roast with horseradish-potato pancakes, crispy chicken with homemade rice-a-roni, or mushu-pork burritos. They're also known for homemade bread, plus really huge banana splits. **FYI:** Reservations recommended. **Open:** Sun–Thurs 11:30am–11pm, Fri–Sat 11:30am–midnight. **Prices:** Main courses $5–$14. CB, DC, MC, V. &

Fournou's Ovens
In Renaissance Stanford Court Hotel, 905 California St (Nob Hill); tel 415/989-1910. **Continental.** Multilevel rooms and alcoves face a 54-square-foot roasting oven or the large, open, tiled kitchen and spit. There's a conservatory room alongside the street. Best for dinner, with specialties that include Dungeness crab cakes; ricotta gnocchi with organic vegetables; rib of veal with rosemary; planked salmon with vegetable succotash; and rack of lamb with ratatouille. 20,000-bottle wine cellar. **FYI:** Reservations recommended. **Open:** Breakfast daily 6:30–11am; lunch daily 11:30am–2:30pm; dinner daily 5:30–10pm. **Prices:** Main courses $10–$30. AE, CB, DC, DISC, MC, V. ❤ VP &

★ **Fringale**
570 4th St (SoMa); tel 415/543-0573. Between Bryand and Brannan Sts. **French/Basque.** One of the finest French bistros in the city, it has a comfortable atmosphere, like a European country cafe. The intimate dining room boasts blond wood and a curved, oxidized copper bar, along with changing displays of art. Tables are cozy and close together but the food is superb, including duck confit, pork tenderloin, and mussels with garlic. Great food at very reasonable prices. **FYI:** Reservations recommended. **Open:** Lunch Mon–Fri 11:30am–3pm; dinner Mon–Sat 5:30–10:30pm. **Prices:** Main courses $10–$18. AE, MC, V. &

★ **Garibaldi's on Presidio**
347 Presidio Ave; tel 415/563-8841. Between Clay and Sacramento Sts. **Californian/Mediterranean.** With decor that is dramatic and artistic, it appeals to locals, who also like its good, fresh food, including Mediterranean lamb tenderloin, daily pasta specials, risotto, and good selection of entree salads. For dessert, a good bet is the chocolate soufflé. Over 150 choices on the wine list. **FYI:** Reservations recommended. **Open:** Lunch Mon–Fri 11:30am–2:30pm; dinner daily 5:30–10:30pm; brunch Sun 10am–2pm. **Prices:** Main courses $8–$19. AE, DC, MC, V.

Gaylord's
In Ghiradelli Square, 900 N Point St; tel 415/771-8822. **Indian.** One of the prettiest restaurants in the city. The elegant, dazzling dining room looks out to Alcatraz and the bay. Northern Indian specialties include spicy curries, aromatic vegetarian dishes, tandoori chicken, and Indian breads. **FYI:** Reservations recommended. **Open:** Lunch Mon–Sat 11:45am–1:45pm; dinner daily 5–11pm; brunch Sun 11:45am–2:45pm. **Prices:** Main courses $12–$20; prix fixe $22–$29. AE, CB, DC, DISC, MC, V.

Gordon Biersch Brewery Restaurant
2 Harrison St (SoMa); tel 415/243-8246. On Embarcadero across from Bay Bridge. **Californian.** In this former coffee roastery overlooking the Bay Bridge, you can choose from three different beers brewed on the premises. The large and lively bar area features a great view of the brewery. Upstairs, the restaurant serves a globetrotting and beer-friendly menu, ranging from baby back ribs with garlic fries to linguine with

chicken and butternut squash. The third Saturday of each month features a Brewer's Lunch ($25), including a brewery tour, tastings, and meal. **FYI:** Reservations recommended. Beer and wine only. **Open:** Sun–Wed 11am–11pm, Thurs 11am–midnight, Fri–Sat 11am–1am. **Prices:** Main courses $9–$15; prix fixe $28–$37. AE, DC, DISC, MC, V. &

Grand Cafe
In Hotel Monaco, 501 Geary St (Theater district); tel 415/292-0101. At Taylor. **Continental.** Set in the one-time ballroom of a lavishly restored, turn-of-the-century hotel, the restaurant counterposes the old-world grandeur of 30-foot-high ceilings with contemporary touches that plant it right in the 90s. Magic also radiates from the fanciful bronze sculptures by Albert Guibara. Executive chef Robert Helstrom calls his cuisine "European comfort food," and the menu features choices such as braised lamb shank on toasted barley pilaf and roast chicken, as well as a robust offering of pastas. Prices are extremely reasonable. The wine list is superb, including both moderately priced vintages as well as high fliers like the Heitz Martha's Vineyard cabernet. **FYI:** Reservations recommended. Jazz. **Open:** Breakfast Mon–Fri 7–10:30am; lunch Mon–Fri 11:30am–2:30pm; dinner Sun–Thurs 5:30–10pm, Sat–Sun 5:30–11pm; brunch Sat–Sun 8am–2:30pm. **Prices:** Main courses $10–$17. AE, CB, DC, DISC, MC, V. ❤ VP &

Greens at Fort Mason
In Fort Mason Center, Buchanan St and Marina Blvd (Marina); tel 415/771-6222. **Vegetarian.** This cavernous restaurant (a former warehouse) run by the San Francisco Zen Center offers spectacular views of the bay, Golden Gate Bridge, and yacht harbor. Menus change weekly, but all feature organic, seasonal produce grown at the Zen Center's Green Gulch Farms in Marin County. Menu features dishes such as tomato, white bean, and sorrel soup; linguine with onion confit, goat cheese, and walnuts. A prix-fixe dinner is available Saturday night for $38. Fresh breads from its Tassajara Bakery. **FYI:** Reservations recommended. Beer and wine only. **Open:** Lunch Tues–Sat 11:30am–2pm; dinner Mon–Fri 5:30–9:30pm, Sat 6–9:30pm; brunch Sun 10am–2pm. **Prices:** Main courses $10–$13. DISC, MC, V. ▄ &

Hamburger Mary's
1582 Folsom St (SoMa); tel 415/626-5767. At 12th St. **American.** Hamburger joint serves up hamburgers, vegetarian specials, chili, and homemade desserts. Bar with 13 varieties of beer. **FYI:** Reservations accepted. **Open:** Mon–Thurs 11:30am–1am, Fri–Sat 10am–2am, Sun 10am–1am. **Prices:** Main courses $5–$10. AE, DISC, MC, V. &

Harbor Village
4 Embarcadero Center (lobby level), Sacramento St; tel 415/781-8833. At Clay St. **Chinese.** This spacious, high-ceilinged restaurant with etched-glass panels and tall, lacquer chairs is a good choice if you want something more elegant than the fast-Formica eateries of Chinatown. Very good selection of

dim sum, served at lunch only, includes tasty potstickers and shrimp dumplings filled with large chunks of seafood. Regular menu features dependable Chinese dishes, as well as specials like abalone or geoduck sashimi. **FYI:** Reservations recommended. **Open:** Lunch Mon–Fri 11am–2:30pm, Sat 10:30am–2:30pm, Sun 10am–2:30pm; dinner daily 5:30–9:30pm. **Prices:** Main courses $12–$30. AE, MC, V. ⅊

Hard Rock Cafe
1699 Van Ness Ave (near Nob Hill); tel 415/885-1699. At Sacramento St. **American.** Elaborately decorated with movie and rock-and-roll memorabilia, this is a popular spot for tourists. Steaks, hamburgers, salads, sandwiches, big selection of desserts. Music is loud. **FYI:** Reservations not accepted. **Open:** Sun–Thurs 11:30am–11:30pm, Fri–Sat 11:30am–12:30pm. **Prices:** Main courses $6–$13. AE, DC, MC, V. VP ⅊

Harris'
2100 Van Ness Ave (near Chinatown); tel 415/673-1888. At Pacific Ave. **Steak.** A sophisticated steak house with leather booths and dark, wood-paneled walls. The corn-fed midwestern beef is dry-aged 21 days on the premises and then mesquite-grilled. Lamb, chicken, prime rib, and seafood are also served. **FYI:** Reservations recommended. Jazz. **Open:** Mon–Thurs 5:30–9pm, Fri–Sun 5–9:30pm. **Prices:** Main courses $20–$30. AE, DC, MC, V. VP ⅊

Harry Denton's Bar & Grill
In the Harbor Court Hotel, 161 Steuart St (Financial District); tel 415/882-1333. **New American.** Lively ambience in a turn-of-the-century saloon atmosphere accented by rich colors and fabrics. Menu lists pot roast, hamburgers, fresh fish, crab cakes, and similar brasserie-style dishes. The grand bar is a fun place to eat if alone. **FYI:** Reservations accepted. Dancing/jazz. **Open:** Breakfast Mon–Fri 7–10am; lunch Mon–Fri 11:30am–3pm; dinner daily 5:30–10pm; brunch Sat–Sun 8am–3pm. **Prices:** Main courses $13–$17. AE, DC, DISC, MC, V. VP ⅊

Hawthorne Lane
22 Hawthorne St (SoMa); tel 415/777-9779. **Californian.** The latest venture of top-flight chefs David and Anne Gingrass, the restaurant takes its name from its locale, a tiny, mewslike alley located in the trendy SoMa district. Billing its menu as "California cuisine with subtle Eurasian flair," the restaurant scores some hits, but also several disappointing misses. In general, fish dishes prove better than the meat offerings, some of which are too heavily seasoned with soy, like the beef tenderloin. The banana, mango, and persimmon fritters with ginger ice cream make a good choice for dessert. Tip: If you can't get reservations for the dining room, tables at the bar and cafe are kept for drop-in guests. **FYI:** Reservations recommended. Piano. **Open:** Lunch Mon–Fri 11:30am–2pm; dinner Mon–Fri 5:30–10pm, Sat–Sun 5:30–10:30pm. **Prices:** Main courses $19–$24. CB, MC, V. VP ⅊

Hayes Street Grill
320 Hayes St; tel 415/863-5545. Between Franklin and Gough Sts. **Seafood.** This upscale fish house, near the Opera House and Davies Symphony Hall, features walls lined with pictures of opera, ballet, and symphony stars. Salmon, halibut, yellowfin tuna, scallops, and swordfish are often featured. Also, steaks and seafood salads, and an extensive wine list. **FYI:** Reservations recommended. **Open:** Lunch Mon–Fri 11am–2pm; dinner Mon–Thurs 5–9:30pm, Fri 5–10:30pm, Sat 6–10:30pm, Sun 5–8:30pm. **Prices:** Main courses $11–$18. AE, DC, DISC, MC, V. ⅊

⑤ Helmand
430 Broadway (North Beach); tel 415/362-0641. At Kearny St. **Afghani.** Afghan meals served in a handsome, romantic dining room with soft lighting, white linen tablecloths, and fine service. The food is fresh and exotic and the prices are reasonable. Lamb dishes are particularly good. **FYI:** Reservations accepted. **Open:** Lunch Mon–Fri 11:30am–2:30pm; dinner Mon–Thurs 6–10pm, Fri–Sun 6–11pm. **Prices:** Main courses $9–$15. AE, MC, V. VP ⅊

⑤ ★ House of Nanking
919 Kearny St (Chinatown); tel 415/421-1429. At Columbus Ave. **Chinese.** A very popular, inexpensive basic Chinatown diner, crowded at all hours. With only a few tables and a counter, there is often a wait. The menu tends toward typical Chinese fare like moo-shu pork and Hunan beef, with such notable exceptions as prawns with Tsing Tao beer sauce. Owner Peter Fang is happy to order for you. **FYI:** Reservations not accepted. No liquor license. **Open:** Mon–Fri 11am–10pm, Sat noon–10pm, Sun 4–10pm. **Prices:** Main courses $3–$9. No CC.

Hunan Restaurant
924 Sansome St (Financial District); tel 415/956-7727. At Broadway. **Chinese.** A fun, casual place serving some of the spiciest Hunan food in the city. The neon-lit dining room is a bit bare, but the bar is quite attractive. Specialties include garlic chicken, and kung pao shrimp. **FYI:** Reservations accepted. **Open:** Daily 11:30am–9:30pm. **Prices:** Main courses $7–$15. AE, CB, DC, DISC, ER, MC, V. ⅊

★ Hyde Street Bistro
1521 Hyde St (Russian Hill); tel 415/441-7778. Between Pacific Ave and Jackson St. **Italian/Austrian.** A small bistro favored by locals, decorated in wood and brass. The frequently changing menu may offer ravioli with chicken and wild mushrooms, Wiener schnitzel with potato pancakes, grilled halibut, and other German-Italian specialties. **FYI:** Reservations not accepted. Beer and wine only. **Open:** Daily 5:30–10:30pm. **Prices:** Main courses $10–$15. AE, MC, V. VP ⅊

Il Fornaio
1265 Battery St (Telegraph Hill); tel 415/986-0100. At Greenwich St. **Italian.** Part of a successful California-based group. Decorated with a long marble bar, dome windows, tile floors, and gold-toned walls. Fresh pastas, rotisserie items.

FYI: Reservations recommended. **Open:** Mon–Thurs 7am–11pm, Fri 7am–midnight, Sat 9am–midnight, Sun 9am–11pm. **Prices:** Main courses $8–$18. AE, CB, DC, DISC, MC, V. VP &

★ **Indian Oven**
233 Fillmore St (The Haight); tel 415/626-1628. At Haight St. **Indian.** Located in one of the city's most bohemian neighborhoods, it's stylish and modern, with an open kitchen and glass bar. Diners can listen to classical Indian music while they dine on tandoori chicken, Indian curries, and other regional dishes. The menu lists "heart smart" choices, too. Parking is scarce. Be alert when walking to and from your car. **FYI:** Reservations accepted. Beer and wine only. **Open:** Daily 5–11pm. **Prices:** Main courses $8–$11. AE, DISC, MC, V.

Izzy's Steak & Chophouse
3345 Steiner St; tel 415/563-0487. Between Lombard and Chestnut Sts. **Steak.** A dark bar and dining room that lack character. Casual but expensive for what it delivers. **FYI:** Reservations accepted. **Open:** Mon–Sat 5–11:30pm, Sun 5–10pm. **Prices:** Main courses $8–$20. AE, CB, DC, DISC, MC, V.

Jack's
615 Sacramento St (Financial District); tel 415/986-9854. Between Montgomery and Kearny Sts. **American.** Landmark restaurant first opened in 1864 by the father of the current owner, who was born in 1903 and is still at the restaurant nearly every day. The turn-of-the-century furnishings are still intact, with white tablecloths and bentwood chairs. The long, narrow dining room serves up coq au vin and double French lamb chops, among other classics. Private banquet rooms for 4–65 people. **FYI:** Reservations recommended. **Open:** Mon–Fri 11:30am–9:30pm, Sat 5:30–9:30pm. **Prices:** Main courses $9–$20. AE, CB, DC, MC, V. ▪ &

$ ★ **J & J Restaurant**
615 Jackson St (Chinatown); tel 415/981-7308. Between Grant Ave and Kearny St. **Chinese.** Real Cantonese food and dim sum. Clientele is mostly Chinese-speaking, but several on staff speak English. Serves one of the best dim sum selections in the city, including delectable shrimp dumplings in near-transparent skins. Most spectacular entree is the baked lobster with vermicelli and garlic sauce. (Hint—pick up one of the take out menus up front, then point to your selection.) **FYI:** Reservations accepted. No liquor license. **Open:** Lunch daily 9am–2pm; dinner daily 5:30–10pm. **Prices:** Main courses $12–$15. AE, MC, V.

John's Grill
63 Ellis St (Union Square); tel 415/966-DASH. At Powell St. **American.** Dashiell Hammett used to eat here and mentions this place in his novels—a lunch favorite for Sam Spade in *The Maltese Falcon.* Classic San Francisco decor with photos of celebrities and prints from *The Maltese Falcon* movie. Menu features Dungeness crab cocktail, lamb chops with baked potato and sliced tomatoes, sole stuffed with bay shrimp. **FYI:**

Reservations recommended. **Open:** Mon–Sat 11am–10pm, Sun 5–10pm. **Prices:** Main courses $14–$25. AE, DC, DISC, MC, V. ▪

Julie's Supper Club and Lounge
1123 Folsom St (SoMa); tel 415/861-0707. Between 7th and 8th Sts. **New American/Eclectic.** Fun is the theme at this hip restaurant, popular with those attending clubs and theater in the SoMa area. Wacky decor includes the aquarium-style Marlin Room. Entrees might include grilled mahimahi with spicy long beans and sesame-ginger noodles, or grilled brochette of lamb with roasted eggplant. Several pasta selections, too. On the weekend, a very lively rhythm-and-blues band encourages dancing in the aisles. **FYI:** Reservations recommended. Blues/rock. **Open:** Mon 5:30–10pm, Tues–Thurs 5:30–10:30pm, Fri–Sat 5:30–11:30pm. **Prices:** Main courses $7–$16. AE, DC, MC, V. &

Julius' Castle
1541 Montgomery St (Telegraph Hill); tel 415/392-2222. Telegraph Hill. **Continental/Italian.** After a complete refurbishment, this turreted landmark situated on the cliffs just below Coit Tower has been restored to its full glory. Nonetheless, the decor remains a tad old-fashioned, with a little too much gilt and floral carpeting, not to mention the full-size replica of a knight that greets patrons in the foyer. The menu reflects this somewhat heavy-handed quality, with dishes such as breast of duck served with spinach tossed in foie gras. Prices are high, but you're paying for the romance and the magnificent views of the bay. **FYI:** Reservations recommended. Dress code. **Open:** Daily 5–10pm. **Prices:** Main courses $21–$29. AE, CB, DC, DISC, MC, V. ● ▲ VP

Kabuto Sushi
5116 Geary Blvd (Richmond); tel 415/752-5652. Between 15th and 16th Aves. **Japanese.** This restaurant lacks ambience, but its sushi is very popular (the owner is also the chef). Tempura and teriyaki are also served. The tatami room, with mats and low tables, is recomended. **FYI:** Reservations accepted. Beer and wine only. **Open:** Tues–Sat 5:30–11pm. **Prices:** Main courses $9–$16. MC, V.

Khan Toke Thai House
5937 Geary Blvd (Richmond); tel 415/668-6654. Between 23rd and 24th Aves. **Thai.** A beautiful place. Elaborate, authentic Thai decor features carved wood furniture and imported wood carvings. Specialties include chicken coconut soup, duck salad, Thai crab, and a seafood curry. **FYI:** Reservations accepted. Beer and wine only. **Open:** Daily 5–10:30pm. **Prices:** Main courses $6–$11; prix fixe $18–$25. AE, MC, V. &

★ **Kuleto's**
In Villa Florence, 221 Powell St (Downtown); tel 415/397-7720. Between Geary and O'Farrell Sts. **Italian.** Popular, with a lively, attractive bar and separate espresso bar. Diners are served fresh breads which can be dipped in the special-press olive oil. Offers northern Italian cuisine using fresh

local produce. Specialties include fish grilled over hardwoods; breast of chicken stuffed with herbed ricotta in roasted-pepper butter sauce; marinated grilled prawns with Belgian endive, orange, and red pepper salad; and roast duck with grappa-soaked cherries, braised cabbage, and black pepper polenta. Cafe Kuleto, next door, is good for coffees and snacks. **FYI:** Reservations recommended. **Open:** Daily 7am–11pm. **Prices:** Main courses $8–$17. AE, CB, DC, DISC, MC, V. &

La Quiche
550 Taylor St (Union Square); tel 415/441-2711. **French.** Looks like a French country inn, with pink decor, cafe chairs, and much artwork. Known for classic French cuisine at reasonable prices, but a new chef has just taken over, so only time will tell if the same high standards will continue. Offers French specialties such as crêpes and beef bourguignon. Feels like you're in France because everyone here speaks French. **FYI:** Reservations accepted. Beer and wine only. **Open:** Lunch Tues–Sat 11:30am–2:30pm; dinner daily 5:30–10pm. **Prices:** Main courses $12–$15. AE, DC, MC, V. 🍷

Le Central
453 Bush St (Financial District); tel 415/391-2233. At Kearny St. **French.** A casually elegant restaurant that resembles a French bistro, where all the patrons seem to know each other. Good bar menu: oysters, escargot, pâté. Also, roast chicken with thin crispy french fries, cassoulet, and excellent crab cakes in beurre blanc. **FYI:** Reservations recommended. **Open:** Mon–Sat 11:30am–10:30pm. **Prices:** Main courses $12–$20. AE, DC, MC, V.

★ **Little City**
673 Union St (North Beach); tel 415/434-2900. On Washington Square. **Italian.** Elegant Italian bar and restaurant. Great wines by the glass and wonderful appetizers to go with them. Specialties include baked brie and roasted garlic appetizer, wild mushroom ravioli, and grilled ahi tuna with caper sauce. **FYI:** Reservations recommended. **Open:** Daily 11:30am–11pm. **Prices:** Main courses $8–$15. AE, CB, DC, DISC, MC, V. &

★ **LuLu's**
816 Folsom St (SoMa); tel 415/495-5775. Between 4th and 5th Sts. **French.** Located in a trendy neighborhood, this restaurant has been a great success since it opened in 1993. The vast room recalls an old-fashioned airplane hangar, and food is served on colorful, hand-painted earthenware. The menu focuses on representative dishes of Provence, such as halibut with braised fennel or beef sirloin with ratatouille. The vegetable side dishes are good for sharing family-style. **FYI:** Reservations recommended. **Open:** Mon–Fri 7am–10:45pm, Fri 7am–midnight, Sat 9am–midnight, Sun 9am–11pm. **Prices:** Main courses $8–$14. AE, CB, DC, MC, V. VP &

The Mandarin
In Ghirardelli Square, 900 N Point St; tel 415/673-8812. **Chinese.** With views of San Francisco Bay as a backdrop, the Mandarin is tastefully decorated with intricate tile floors, silk fabric walls, oriental lithographs, ornate flower arrangements, and wooden sculptures. The opulent surroundings match the food, which includes elaborate northern Chinese dishes of beef, lamb, chicken, and Peking duck. The wine list is exceptional. **FYI:** Reservations recommended. **Open:** Daily 11:30am–11pm. **Prices:** Main courses $8–$14; prix fixe $21–$38. AE, CB, DC, MC, V.

Marnee Thai
2225 Irving St (Sunset); tel 415/665-9500. Between 23rd and 24th Aves. **Thai.** A neighborhood restaurant serving authentic cuisine in a simple atmosphere. Thai curries, green-papaya salad, and prawn and calamari dishes are specialties. Chef will modify seasonings at diner's request. **FYI:** Reservations accepted. Beer and wine only. **Open:** Wed–Mon 11:30am–10pm. **Prices:** Main courses $6–$11. AE, MC, V.

Marrakech
419 O'Farrell St (Union Square); tel 415/776-6717. Between Jones and Taylor Sts. **Moroccan.** Like a visit to Morocco. There's a fountain out front, and inside Persian rugs cover the banquettes. The exotic seven-course, prix fixe menu features b'stilla (boneless chicken pastry), lamb with honey and almonds, rabbit, and chicken with lemon. Live belly dancing nightly. **FYI:** Reservations accepted. **Open:** Daily 5:30–10pm. **Prices:** Prix fixe $20–$25. AE, DC, DISC, MC, V.

Masa's
In Hotel Vintage Court, 648 Bush St (Union Square); tel 415/989-7154. Between Powell and Stockton Sts. **New American/French.** Brilliant classic cuisine from chef Julian Serrano. The dining room is low key and designed to focus all attention on the food. Guests select either a four-course menu du jour or a seven-course menu degustation, which might include fillet of black bass sautéed with saffron sauce, or medallions of fallow deer. **FYI:** Reservations recommended. Dress code. **Open:** Tues–Sat 6–9:30. **Prices:** Prix fixe $70–$75. AE, DC, DISC, MC, V. VP

The Metro Bar and Restaurant
3600 16th St; tel 415/703-9750. **Hunan Chinese.** Exotic decor with funky color scheme, and gold Indonesian camel and horse statues accenting a black circular bar. Hunan specialties include Kung Pao chicken, sizzling scallops with black mushrooms, Mongolian lamb, and Szechuan bean-curd pork. **FYI:** Reservations accepted. **Open:** Daily 5:30–11pm. **Prices:** Main courses $7–$10. MC, V.

Miss Pearl's Jam House
In the Phoenix Hotel, 601 Eddy St (Civic Center); tel 415/775-5267. Between Polk and Larkin Sts. **Caribbean.** With palm trees lining the windows and a canoe dangling over the bar, this restaurant feels like a tropical hideaway. The Carib-

bean-style cooking features favorites such as coconut prawns in beer-batter, roast pork loin adobo, and jerk chicken. Reggae and steel bands play on weekends. **FYI:** Reservations recommended. Dancing/reggae. **Open:** Dinner Wed–Thurs 6–10pm, Fri–Sat 6–11pm, Sun 5:30–9:30pm; brunch Sun 11am–2pm. **Prices:** Main courses $10–$16. AE, MC, V. VP &

★ Moose's
1652 Stockton St (North Beach); tel 415/989-7800. At Filbert St. **Californian/Mediterranean.** Always lively and packed, and popular with media and sports figures. An airy setting with masculine decor. Daily specials; menu includes veal chops with herb mashed potatoes, winter greens, and cracked pepper pear sauce as well as terrific pastas and pizzas. **FYI:** Reservations recommended. Jazz. **Open:** Lunch Mon–Sat 11:30am–2:30pm; dinner Sun 5–10pm, Mon–Thurs 5:30–10pm, Fri–Sat 5:30–11pm; brunch Sun 10:30am–3pm. **Prices:** Main courses $9–$24. AE, DC, MC, V. VP &

North Beach Restaurant
1512 Stockton St (North Beach); tel 415/392-1587. At Columbus Ave. **Northern Italian.** Classic peasant dishes of Tuscany served by Italian-speaking waiters. Full dinners include antipasto, green salad, soup, salad, pasta with prosciutto sauce, and a choice of entree. The *Wine Spectator* named the wine cellar one of the 100 best in the United States. **FYI:** Reservations recommended. **Open:** Daily 11:30am–11:45pm. **Prices:** Main courses $10–$27; prix fixe $28. AE, CB, DC, DISC, MC, V. ♥ VP &

North India Restaurant
3131 Webster St; tel 415/931-1556. **Indian.** Attractively decorated with art, wood sculptures, chandeliers, and plants, this restaurant serves authentic Indian cuisine. Offers fixed-price, three-course business lunch. Menu features curries, tandoori items, vegetarian dishes, and salads. Try lamb cooked with saffron, cardamom, and almonds; or jumbo prawns in a light curry sauce. **FYI:** Reservations accepted. Beer and wine only. **Open:** Lunch Mon–Fri 11:30am–2:30pm; dinner Mon–Sat 5–10:30pm, Sun 5–10pm. **Prices:** Main courses $10–$20. AE, CB, DC, DISC, MC, V. 🚗 &

Ⓢ Ocean Restaurant
726 Clement St; tel 415/668-8896. At 8th Ave. **Chinese.** Seafood is the specialty, especially the geoduck clams with crystal glaze and the fillet of sole in pepper. There is also a selection of Cantonese beef, pork, and vegetable dishes. Portions are generous. **FYI:** Reservations accepted. Beer and wine only. **Open:** Daily 9am–9:30pm. **Prices:** Main courses $5–$8; prix fixe $7–$10. MC, V.

Olive's Gourmet Pizza
3249 Scott St; tel 415/567-4488. Between Chestnut and Lombard Sts. **Pizza.** Cute and simple California pizza kitchen offering crayons and paper at tables and alternative rock music. Menu includes gourmet pizza, such as Blue Toscano with mozzarella, Gorgonzola, salami, and fresh tomatoes.

Also offers calzone and pasta. **FYI:** Reservations not accepted. Beer and wine only. **Open:** Sun–Thurs 11:30am–10:30pm, Fri–Sat 11:30am–11:30pm. **Prices:** Main courses $5–$12. MC, V.

♣ One Market
1 Market St; tel 415/777-5577. Off Embarcadero Plaza. **New American.** Run by Bradley Ogden, one of America's leading chefs, One Market is surrounded by 20-foot-tall windows facing the ferry building. Although huge, the space is not cavernous. Burnished woods and wine-tone upholsteries provide a Jazz Age feel. Smoked and wood-roasted items are the trademark here—grilled salmon with corn-souffle spoonbread, or oak-grilled double pork chops. The "Chef's Table" in the kitchen can be reserved for dining in the middle of the action. **FYI:** Reservations recommended. Piano. **Open:** Lunch Mon–Fri 11:30am–2pm; dinner Sun 5–9pm, Mon–Thurs 5:30–9:30pm, Fri 5:30–10pm, Sat 5–10pm. **Prices:** Main courses $13–$21. AE, DC, MC, V. VP &

♣ Pacific
In The Pan Pacific Hotel, 500 Post St (Union Square); tel 415/929-2087. At Mason. **Californian.** Located in the hotel's lobby, this restaurant has a very elegant and simple decor accented by gorgeous flower arrangements. Chef Taka Kawai, who trained with Paul Bocuse and worked as sous chef at San Francisco's top-ranked Masa's for eight years, shows his expertise in refined dishes such as grilled squab with summer vegetables and truffle risotto. A good bet is the four-course tasting menu: $38 without wine, $50 with wine included. The wines served by the glass are top-notch, with offerings such as Opus One. **FYI:** Reservations recommended. Piano. **Open:** Breakfast Mon–Fri 6:30–11am, Sat–Sun 7–10am; lunch Mon–Fri 11:30am–2:30pm; dinner Sun–Thurs 5:30–9:30pm, Fri–Sat 5:30–10pm; brunch Sat–Sun 10am–2pm. **Prices:** Main courses $17–$24; prix fixe $29–$50. AE, CB, DC, DISC, ER, MC, V. ◧ VP &

★ Pacific Cafe
7000 Geary Blvd (Richmond District); tel 415/387-7091. At 34th Ave. **Seafood.** Wooden booths and warm lighting help to create a cozy setting in this restaurant, popular with the locals. Specialties include fresh abalone, Dungeness crab cakes, grilled tuna, halibut, and sturgeon with capers and mushrooms, a favorite dish from old San Francisco fish houses. Entrees come with salad and potatoes; complimentary wine while waiting for a table. **FYI:** Reservations not accepted. Beer and wine only. Additional location: 850 College Ave, Kentfield (tel 856-3898). **Open:** Daily 5–10pm. **Prices:** Main courses $12–$15. AE, MC, V.

Pacific Heights Bar & Grill
2001 Fillmore St; tel 415/567-3337. At Pine St. **Eclectic.** Casual yet elegant neighborhood restaurant with an oyster bar up front and a huge main bar with tables where drinks or a full meal can be enjoyed. Appetizers may include baked brie with jalapeño grape salsa and roasted garlic. Among entree

specialties are fresh fish; pasta; grilled meat; and steamed, blackened, or baked fish. **FYI:** Reservations recommended. **Open:** Lunch Wed–Sun 11:30am–4pm; dinner Mon–Thurs 5:30–9:30pm, Fri–Sat 4–10:30pm, Sun 4–9:30pm. **Prices:** Main courses $9–$17. AE, CB, DC, MC, V. &

Pane e Vino
3011 Steiner St (Pacific Heights); tel 415/346-2111. At Union St. **Italian.** Charming Italian restaurant with terracotta floors, wall sconces, sponge-painted walls, and a woodburning stove in the dining room. Menu features fresh pasta, grilled loin lamb chops, and whole roasted fish. **FYI:** Reservations recommended. Beer and wine only. **Open:** Lunch Mon–Sat 11:30–2:30am; dinner Sun–Thurs 5–10pm, Fri–Sat 5–10:30pm. **Prices:** Main courses $8–$16. MC, V. &

♥ **Park Grill**
In Park Hyatt San Francisco, 333 Battery St (Financial District); tel 415/392-1234. At Washington St. **Californian.** Club-like setting on the 2nd floor, with windows that look out to the Embarcadero Center; particularly popular with business people at lunchtime because of its widely spaced tables, low sound level, and efficient service. Specialties include roasted lobster and basil risotto, and grilled lamb chops with spiced couscous. **FYI:** Reservations recommended. **Open:** Breakfast daily 6:30–10am; lunch daily 11:30am–2:30pm; dinner daily 5:30–10pm. **Prices:** Main courses $12–$21. AE, CB, DC, DISC, MC, V. VP &

★ **Pauline's Pizza Pie**
260 Valencia St; tel 415/552-2050. **Pizza.** Decorated with art from an upstairs gallery, the pleasant dining room offers gourmet pizza with special toppings, such as sautéed leeks and double-smoked ham. Salads and toppings are made from locally grown organic ingredients, and there's an extensive wine list. **FYI:** Reservations not accepted. Beer and wine only. **Open:** Tues–Sat 5–10pm. **Prices:** Main courses $10–$15. MC, V.

The Pork Store Cafe
1451 Haight St (Haight-Ashbury); tel 415/864-6981. Between Ashbury St and Masonic Ave. **Cafe.** Very casual, friendly cafe. Specials include pork chops, pancakes, huevos rancheros, burgers, and sandwiches. **FYI:** Reservations not accepted. Beer and wine only. **Open:** Mon–Fri 7am–3:30pm, Sat–Sun 8am–4pm. **Prices:** Lunch main courses $3–$7. MC, V.

♥ **Postrio**
In the Prescott Hotel, 545 Post St (Union Square); tel 415/776-7825. Between Mason and Taylor Sts. **Californian.** Still one of the city's best restaurants, orchestrated by Wolfgang Puck and his co-chefs, Mitchell and Steven Rosenthal. Stylishly contemporary, the dining room has an inlaid marble floor up front, stunning light fixtures, and original art by Rauschenberg and others. The menu is known for innovative cuisine that zings with unusual pairings and spices, such as the Chinese-style duck with spicy mango sauce and crisp-fried

lotus root. Oenophiles will find plenty of great ideas on the excellent wine list. **FYI:** Reservations recommended. Dress code. **Open:** Breakfast Mon–Fri 7–10am; lunch Mon–Fri 11am–2pm; dinner Sun–Wed 5:30–10pm, Thurs–Sat 5:30–10:30pm; brunch Sat–Sun 9am–2pm. **Prices:** Main courses $19–$28. AE, CB, DC, DISC, MC, V. VP &

Pot Sticker
150 Waverly Place (Chinatown); tel 415/397-9985. **Chinese.** Set in an alley in Chinatown. Spicy Hunan and Cantonese dishes include lemon chicken, braised bean curd, and sizzling rice soup. **FYI:** Reservations accepted. Beer and wine only. **Open:** Daily 11:30am–9:45pm. **Prices:** Main courses $6–$18; prix fixe $8–$10. AE, MC, V. &

Prego
2000 Union St; tel 415/563-3305. At Buchanan St. **Italian.** The woodburning pizza oven is open to view here, and there's a circular granite bar with brass railings. Sidewalk dining is available. Specialties are pizza with homemade sausage, pastas, and grilled meats, plus wide selection of antipasti. **FYI:** Reservations recommended. **Open:** Daily 11:30am–midnight. **Prices:** Main courses $9–$19. AE, CB, MC, V. &

Puccini & Pinetti
129 Ellis St (Union Square); tel 415/392-5500. At Cyril Magnin Place. **Italian.** This Bill Kimpton restaurant has a busy trattoria feel with bright murals, cream-mustard colored walls, and royal-blue trim. Prices are reasonable and the ambience casual. Thin-crust pizza is well-executed and is offered in several versions: with roasted peppers, spinach, and feta cheese; or smoked salmon, capers, and dill-mascarpone. The good selection of pastas includes pappardelle Bolognese with braised veal. Entrees choices might be chicken Marsala or a vegetarian sampler. **FYI:** Reservations accepted. **Open:** Lunch Mon–Sat 11:30am–3pm; dinner Sun–Thurs 5–10pm, Fri–Sat 5–11pm. **Prices:** Main courses $7–$14. AE, CB, DC, DISC, MC, V. &

♥ **Redwood Room**
In the Clift, 495 Geary St (Union Square); tel 415/775-4700. **New American.** Moderately priced, innovative lunches and light after-theater dinners are served in one of the most beautiful rooms in California. Walls are covered with wood from a single 2,000-year-old redwood and accented with art deco motifs and reproductions of Gustav Klimt paintings. Dinner is served in the adjoining **French Room,** a very elegant, château-like salon lit by chandeliers. Examples include baby spinach leaves with sun-dried tomato crostini and grilled gulf prawns, and grilled and marinated vegetable club sandwich on sourdough toast with roast eggplant spread. **FYI:** Reservations recommended. Piano. Children's menu. Jacket required. **Open:** Breakfast daily 6:30–11am; lunch daily 11am–5pm; dinner daily 5:30–10:30pm. **Prices:** Prix fixe $39. AE, CB, DC, ER, MC, V. ♥ ▦ VP &

Ristorante Ecco

101 South Park (SoMa); tel 415/495-3291. **Italian.** From the tile floors to the beautiful flower arrangements, "casual chic" best describes the spare yet elegant atmosphere. Choose from a wide array of antipasti, pasta, pizzas, chicken, fish, and meats, plus a seafood stew bursting with mussels, prawns, scallops, and assorted fish. Nice selection of Italian desserts. **FYI:** Reservations recommended. **Open:** Breakfast Mon–Fri 11:30am–2:30pm; lunch Mon–Fri 11:30am–2:30pm; dinner Mon–Sat 6–10pm. **Prices:** Main courses $10–$16. AE, DC, MC, V. &

Salmagundi

442 Geary St (Downtown); tel 415/441-0894. **Salad/Sandwiches.** Convenient for pre-theater supper. Cafeteria-style eatery offers light fare—sandwiches, salads, soups, and desserts. Bring your bowl back for an extra ladle of the same soup, or sample another for free. **FYI:** Reservations not accepted. Beer and wine only. **Open:** Tues–Sat 11am–11pm, Sun–Mon 11am–9pm. **Prices:** Main courses $4–$6. AE, DC, MC, V.

★ Sam's Grill and Seafood Restaurant

374 Bush St (Financial District); tel 415/421-0594. **Seafood.** A San Francisco landmark—a dark, somber, business lunch spot. Seafood is fresh and consistently good. Specialties are crab Louie, sautéed shellfish, and oyster stew. **FYI:** Reservations accepted. **Open:** Daily 11am–9pm. **Prices:** Main courses $8–$22. AE, CB, DC, MC, V.

⑤ Sam Wo

813 Washington St (Chinatown); tel 415/982-0596. Between Grant Ave and Stockton St. **Chinese.** One of the oldest restaurants in the heart of Chinatown. Walk through the kitchen and up narrow stairs to the funky, but fine, dining room. Two floors of dining offering roast pork rice noodles, soups, chow mein, eggrolls, and the like. **FYI:** Reservations not accepted. No liquor license. **Open:** Mon–Sat 11am–3am. **Prices:** Main courses $3–$5. No CC.

Sanppo

1702 Post St (Japantown); tel 415/346-3486. At Buchanan St. **Japanese.** Popular Japantown eatery. Has the decor of a Japanese country inn, with lots of plants. Sushi, sashimi, tempura. **FYI:** Reservations recommended. Beer and wine only. **Open:** Tues–Sat 11:45am–10pm, Sun 3–10pm. **Prices:** Main courses $8–$16. MC, V.

Savoy Brasserie

In Savoy Hotel, 580 Geary St (Downtown); tel 415/474-8686. Between Jones and Taylor. **French.** Wonderful old Parisian bistro atmosphere with marble floors. Shellfish bar in back. **FYI:** Reservations recommended. **Open:** Breakfast daily 6–11am; dinner daily 5:30–10pm. **Prices:** Main courses $11–$18; prix fixe $23–$30. AE, DC, DISC, MC, V. ▮ VP &

★ Scala's Bistro

In Sir Francis Drake Hotel, 432 Powell St (Union Square); tel 415/395-8555. Between Post and Sutter. **Italian.** One of the best places to indulge in Italian food is this new restaurant just around the corner from Union Square. The place is almost always packed with locals—a tribute to the superb, reasonably priced cuisine of Donna and Giovanni Scala, who are also owners/chefs of the top-rated Bistro Don Giovanni in Napa Valley. A good bet is the pan-roasted chicken with a parchment-crisp skin, or linguine tossed with Manila clams, oven-roasted tomatoes, and lots of garlic. The pizzas are also terrific. **FYI:** Reservations recommended. **Open:** Breakfast Mon–Fri 7–10:30am, Sat–Sun 8–10:30am; lunch Mon–Fri 11:30am–5pm, Sat–Sun 11am–5pm; dinner daily 5pm–midnight. **Prices:** Main courses $10–$16. AE, DC, DISC, MC, V. VP &

Scott's Seafood Grill & Bar

3 Embarcadero Center (Financial District); tel 415/981-0622. **Seafood.** Good basic seafood restaurant located close to the Financial District. Glass walls overlook strolling area on top of Embaracadero Plaza. Seafood dishes include pan-seared seafood sautéed with roasted garlic mashed potatoes, local sand dabs with caper butter, and smoked salmon carpaccio. **FYI:** Reservations recommended. **Open:** Mon–Thurs 11am–10pm, Fri–Sat 11am–11pm, Sun 4:30–9:30pm. **Prices:** Main courses $9–$27. AE, CB, DC, DISC, MC, V. &

Sears Fine Foods

439 Powell St (Downtown); tel 415/986-1160. Between Sutter and Post Sts. **American.** Popular since 1938, this basic San Francisco shopper's cafeteria serves hamburgers, crab salad, Swedish meatballs, and traditional American breakfasts. Famous for its little Swedish pancakes. **FYI:** Reservations accepted. No liquor license. **Open:** Wed–Sun 6:30am–3:30pm. **Prices:** Lunch main courses $6–$10. No CC. &

★ South Park Cafe

108 South Park Ave (SoMa); tel 415/495-7275. **French/Bistro.** Situated around a green park, this tiny restaurant is like a secret garden tucked into a mostly industrial neighborhood. Restaurant decor is simple, with a zinc bar and red tile floor. What makes it special is the artsy crowd and French menu that features reasonably priced, authentic dishes like roast leg of lamb or sautéed chicken with red wine sauce. Priced at about $12, nightly specials are an extraordinary value, and include soup or salad, entree, and coffee. Superb, reasonably priced wine list. **FYI:** Reservations recommended. **Open:** Mon–Fri 7:30am–10pm, Sat 6–10pm. **Prices:** Main courses $11–$17. AE, MC, V. &

Splendido

4 Embarcadero Center (Financial District); tel 415/986-3222. **Italian/Mediterranean.** Popular Mediterranean trattoria with charming ambience. Stone domed ceiling evokes ancient Etruscan style, and 200-year-old olive wood doors come from Spain. Marble tables in bar area; other tables overlook square and Ferry Building. Grilled swordfish, sautéed quail with wild rice and vinaigrette, hearty breads,

pizza, desserts. **FYI:** Reservations recommended. **Open:** Lunch Mon–Fri 11:30am–2:30pm; dinner Sun–Thurs 5:30–9:30pm, Fri–Sat 5:30–10pm. **Prices:** Main courses $10–$19. AE, CB, DC, DISC, MC, V. ⅋

Stars

150 Redwood Alley (Civic Center); tel 415/861-7827. Between McAllister St and Golden Gate Ave. **New American/Californian.** One of San Francisco's top restaurants, Stars is known for consistently good food and a happening atmosphere, thanks to chef/owner Jeremiah Tower. It features the longest bar in the city and an open kitchen. The menu changes regularly to take advantage of fresh seasonal ingredients; choices include grilled yellowtail jack in roasted-tomato sauce, and grilled lamb with red-pepper salad. Excellent desserts. **FYI:** Reservations recommended. Piano. **Open:** Lunch Mon–Fri 11:30am–2:30pm; dinner daily 5:30–10:30pm. **Prices:** Main courses $20–$29; prix fixe $55–$65. AE, CB, DC, MC, V. VP ⅋

✮ Stars Cafe

500 Van Ness Ave (Civic Center); tel 415/861-4344. **New American.** Not just "son of Stars," this is a terrific restaurant in its own right. French bistro atmosphere features mirrored columns, cafe chairs, and slate floors. The menu presents superchef Jeremiah Towers's innovative cuisine at reasonable prices—under $15 for entrees. In addition to specials such as grilled salmon or wood-roasted chicken, they serve one of the best hamburgers in town. **FYI:** Reservations recommended. Dress code. **Open:** Daily 11:30am–11pm. **Prices:** Main courses $8–$15. AE, CB, DC, MC, V. VP ⅋

The Stinking Rose

325 Columbus Ave (North Beach); tel 415/781-ROSE. At Broadway. **Italian.** Garlic, garlic everywhere, and so much to eat. From chicken with 40 cloves of garlic to bagna calda (roasted garlic in olive oil and butter with a hint of anchovy for dipping bread), this folksy restaurant specializes in garlic, otherwise known as the stinking rose. The decor is heavy with garlic braids, and there's even a gift shop full of garlicky offerings. It's no surprise that the restaurant's motto is "We season our garlic with food." **FYI:** Reservations recommended. **Open:** Sun–Thurs 11am–11pm, Fri–Sat 11am–midnight. **Prices:** Main courses $7–$18. AE, CB, DC, MC, V. ⅋

✮ Swan Oyster Depot

1517 Polk St (near Nob Hill); tel 415/673-1101. Between Sacramento and California Sts. **Seafood.** A classic San Francisco seafood bar, in operation since 1912 and oozing with character. No table seating; diners are served at an old-fashioned marble bar. Crab, shrimp, prawns, oysters, and clams are all served with sourdough bread. **FYI:** Reservations not accepted. Beer and wine only. **Open:** Mon–Sat 8am–5:30pm. **Prices:** Main courses $5–$25. No CC. ▪ 🚐 ⅋

✮ Tadich Grill

240 California St (Financial District); tel 415/391-1849. At Sansome St. **Seafood.** A San Francisco institution dating back to the gold rush; part of the city's colorful history. Known for simply prepared fresh seafood, hearty clam chowder, and crusty sourdough bread. Daily fish specials include petrale sole, poached salmon, swordfish steak, and Dungeness crab salad. **FYI:** Reservations not accepted. **Open:** Mon–Sat 11am–9pm. **Prices:** Main courses $11–$17. MC, V. ▪ ⅋

♥ The Terrace

In the Ritz-Carlton San Francisco, 600 Stockton St (Nob Hill); tel 415/296-7465. Between California and Pine Sts. **Mediterranean.** On a sunny day, you can't beat this outdoor courtyard terrace surrounded by roses and next to a tinkling fountain. Inside, a more formal dining area offers Provençale-style chairs and crystal chandeliers. The Mediterranean cuisine emphasizes seasonal ingredients. Sunday jazz brunch, a local favorite, includes three choices of caviar and items from a made-to-order sushi cart–like grilled striped bass, chermoula and couscous or sauteed lamb medallions with artichoke puree and dried tomatoes. Lunch any day is a particularly good value. **FYI:** Reservations recommended. Jazz/piano. Children's menu. Dress code. **Open:** Daily 6:30am–10:30pm. **Prices:** Main courses $19–$23. AE, CB, DC, DISC, ER, MC, V. 🖃 VP ⅋

✮ Thai Stick

698 Post St (Downtown); tel 415/928-7730. At Jones St. **Thai.** One of the best Thai restaurants downtown, this spacious restaurant has floor-to-ceiling windows and is decorated in soothing, soft pastels. Try the Thai-style crêpes with shrimp, roast duck in red curry and coconut milk, and the charbroiled pork with sweet garlic sauce. **FYI:** Reservations accepted. Beer and wine only. **Open:** Lunch Mon–Fri 11am–3pm, Sat–Sun 11am–5pm; dinner Sun–Thurs 5–10pm, Fri–Sat 5–11pm. **Prices:** Main courses $7–$12. AE, DC, DISC, MC, V.

✮ This Is It

430 Geary Blvd (Union Square); tel 415/749-0201. At Mason St. **Middle Eastern.** Modern, clean family-run restaurant offering authentic Middle Eastern cuisine. Good value. **FYI:** Reservations not accepted. No liquor license. **Open:** Daily 10am–11pm. **Prices:** Main courses $7–$16. AE, MC, V.

✮ Tommaso's

1042 Kearny St (North Beach); tel 415/398-9696. At Broadway. **Italian.** One of San Francisco's oldest (1935) and most popular pizzerias. Small and intimate, decorated with murals. Pizzas (such as a garlic and basil rendition) are made in a wood-fired oven. **FYI:** Reservations not accepted. Beer and wine only. **Open:** Tues–Sat 5–10:45pm, Sun 4–9:45pm. Closed Dec 15–Jan 4. **Prices:** Main courses $8–$14. AE, MC, V.

Tommy's Joynt

1109 Geary St (near Japantown); tel 415/775-4216. At Van Ness Ave. **German.** This San Francisco institution is known for its garish outdoor mural, hearty food, and low prices. Buffalo chili, oxtail sauté, meats carved to order. Dozens of imported beers. If you're really hungry, this is a great value. **FYI:** Reservations accepted. **Open:** Daily 11am–2am. **Prices:** Main courses $4–$6. No CC. &

Tommy Toy's Cuisine Chinoise
655 Montgomery St (Financial District); tel 415/397-4888. **Chinese/French.** The most refined Chinese restaurant in San Francisco. Tables are decorated with fine crystal and flowers. Cuisine combines Chinese, French, and California influences; menu offers lobster pot stickers, sea scallops, smoked duck with plum sauce, and wok-charred prawns in spices. **FYI:** Reservations recommended. **Open:** Lunch Mon–Fri 11:30am–3pm; dinner Mon–Sat 6–10pm, Sun 6–9:30pm. **Prices:** Main courses $15–$20; prix fixe $38–$60. AE, CB, DC, DISC, MC, V. ⓋⓅ &

♥ **Vertigo**
In Transamerica Pyramid, 600 Montgomery St (Downtown); tel 415/433-7250. Entrance on Clay St. **Eclectic.** Despite the moniker, the restaurant is located on the ground floor of the Transamerica Pyramid. The two-tiered dining room occupies a large, elegant space highlighted by angular concrete pillars, curvaceous wooden banquettes, and a huge mural recalling the spooky mission that appeared in Alfred Hitchcock's 1958 thriller of the same name (which was largely filmed in San Francisco). Chef Mark Lusardi explains his menu as having "French technique and Italian soul, with Japanese and Vietnamese influences." Unusual combinations prevail, such as tea-smoked quail with glazed pears and endive, served with a ginger-persimmon sauce. **FYI:** Reservations recommended. **Open:** Lunch Mon–Fri 11:30am–2:30pm; dinner Mon–Thurs 5:30–10pm, Fri–Sat 5:30–10:30pm. **Prices:** Main courses $17–$21. AE, CB, DC, DISC, MC, V. ⓋⓅ &

Vivande Porta Via
2125 Fillmore St (Pacific Heights); tel 415/346-4430. At California St. **Italian.** An expensive trattoria attached to a specialty shop that sells Italian foods and products. Restaurant has tables and a marble counter for diners. Menu includes pastas, frittatas, and deli cold plates, as well as daily specials, soup, dessert, and Italian wines. **FYI:** Reservations not accepted. Beer and wine only. **Open:** Daily 10am–10pm. **Prices:** Main courses $12–$18. AE, DC, DISC, MC, V.

Wing Lum Cafe
1150 Polk St; tel 415/771-6888. Between Sutter and Post Sts. **Chinese.** Extensive menu includes such classics as Kung Pao prawns, crispy duck, Mongolian beef, moo shu pork, and hot and spicy eggplant. Lunch specials are inexpensive. Neighborhood is somewhat sleazy. **FYI:** Reservations accepted. Beer and wine only. **Open:** Mon–Sat 11am–10pm, Sun 4–10pm. **Prices:** Main courses $6–$7; prix fixe $8–$10. AE, DISC, MC, V.

★ **Yank Sing**
49 Stevenson St (Financial District); tel 415/541-4949. Off 1st St. **Chinese.** Casually elegant, modern Chinese dining, with floor-to-ceiling windows, etched glass, and mahogany pillars. Renowned for their dim sum—carts of appetizers roll by and you choose the ones you want. Try the steamed shrimp dumplings, pot stickers, scallops in rice balls, and barbecued pork buns. **FYI:** Reservations recommended. **Open:** Mon–Fri 11am–3pm. **Prices:** Main courses $3–$6. AE, V. &

Ya Ya
1220 9th Ave (Sunset); tel 415/566-6966. At Lincoln Way. **Californian/Middle Eastern.** Middle Eastern cuisine meets Californian in this small, popular restaurant. Incredible decor of blue tiles, columns, and murals of Mesopotamia. Among the specialties are dolmas, seafood biriani, vegetarian ravioli, and bourak—ground beef in phyllo dough. **FYI:** Reservations accepted. Beer and wine only. **Open:** Lunch Tues–Sat 11am–2pm; dinner Tues–Sun 5:30–10pm. **Prices:** Main courses $12–$26. AE, MC, V. &

♥ **Yoyo Tsumami Bistro**
In Radisson Miyako Hotel, 1611 Post St (Japantown); tel 415/922-7788. At Laguna. **Seafood/Franco-Asian.** The menu explains that in Japanese, "yoyo" means a wide expanse of ocean, while "tsumami" refers to small dishes of food accompanying cocktails—a kind of Japanese tapas. Each of chef Michael Leviton's unusual "fusion cuisine" creations dazzles with singular taste sensations and artistic panache. One favorite is the ahi tuna tartare, chopped with daikon and cucumber. Main dishes are also delicious, such as the crisp-skinned salmon with root vegetables and red wine sauce. For a finale, you can't go wrong with the chocolate pot de crème. **FYI:** Reservations recommended. **Open:** Breakfast daily 6:30–11am; lunch daily 11:30am–2pm; dinner daily 5:30–10pm. **Prices:** Main courses $12–$19. AE, CB, DC, DISC, MC, V. ⓋⓅ &

⑤ **Zona Rosa**
1797 Haight St (Haight-Ashbury); tel 415/668-7717. At Schrader St. **Mexican.** Brightly colored Formica tables, Mexican stone sculptures, and loud salsa featured at this taquería which serves burritos, tacos, and fajitas. **FYI:** Reservations not accepted. No liquor license. **Open:** Daily 11am–10:30pm. **Prices:** Main courses $3–$6. No CC.

★ **Zuni Cafe**
1658 Market St (Civic Center); tel 415/552-2522. Between Franklin and Gough Sts. **Mediterranean.** With a southwestern motif, featuring a tiled facade, glazed terra-cotta floors, a copper bar, and as the centerpiece a grand piano with a huge vase of flowers. The food is extremely good and reasonably priced, leaning to French and Italian specialties, including wood-fired pizza, roast chicken, house-cured pork chops, and grilled yellowfin tuna. **FYI:** Reservations recommended. Piano. **Open:** Tues–Sat 7:30am–midnight, Sun 7:30am–11pm. **Prices:** Main courses $12–$22. AE, MC, V. &

REFRESHMENT STOP 🍵

★ Mario's Bohemian Cigar Store
566 Columbus Ave (North Beach); tel 415/362-0536. At Union St. **Italian.** Neighborhood bar and cafe with historic flavor, small and always packed: a good spot to meet local artists, musicians, and eccentrics. Sandwiches on focaccia bread, homemade meatball sandwiches, and ricotta cheesecake are specialties. **Open:** Mon–Sat 10am–midnight, Sun 10am–11pm. No CC.

ATTRACTIONS

TOP ATTRACTIONS

Alcatraz Island
Tel 415/546-2628 or 556-0560. In 1934 the United States inaugurated what would quickly become the most famous maximum-security prison in the world: the federal penitentiary on Alcatraz Island. During the heyday of organized crime, several notorious mobsters did time on "the Rock," as it came to be called. These included such legendary figures as John Dillinger, Al Capone, "Pretty Boy" Floyd, and "Machine Gun" Kelly. Located only a mile from shore, Alcatraz was nonetheless considered escape-proof because it was surrounded by the bone-chilling waters of San Francisco Bay, with currents powerful enough to defeat even the strongest swimmer. Potential escapees often drowned in the attempt, although no bodies were ever recovered after a jailbreak by three inmates in 1962. The prison was finally shut down in 1963.

Today a trip to Alcatraz Island is among San Francisco's top tourist attractions. National Park Service rangers conduct tours of the island that cover a wide range of topics. Visitors have the option to purchase an audio tour of the prison cell house and view a free video presentation. The **Red and White Fleet** makes trips several times daily; ferries depart from Pier 41 by Fisherman's Wharf approximately every 30 minutes. Advance reservations highly recommended. **Open:** Peak (June–Aug) daily 9:15am–4:15pm. Reduced hours off-season. **$$$**

Golden Gate Bridge
Tel 415/921-5858. Probably the most beautiful, and certainly the most frequently photographed, bridge in the world, the mile-long Golden Gate Bridge towers a maximum of 746 feet above the waters of San Francisco Bay, connecting San Francisco with southern Marin County. If traveling by car ($3 toll, payable southbound), park in the lot at the foot of the bridge (on the city side; when approaching the bridge drive slowly, stay in the right-hand lane, and exit into the lot at the base of the bridge) and make the crossing by foot. Millions of pedestrians walk across the bridge each year, but be prepared; it's often windy, cold, and the bridge vibrates. **Open:** Daily. Closed during foggy periods. **$**

Golden Gate National Recreation Area
Wrapping around the northern and western edge of the city and run by the National Parks Service, the recreation area allows visitors to enjoy the urban shoreline of San Francisco. Some of the highlights include **Golden Gate Promenade,** a 3½-mile paved hiking and biking path, which sweeps along Crissy Field; **Baker Beach,** a small and beautiful stand of beach popular for sunbathing, walking, or fishing; **China Beach,** for swimming; and **Point Lobos,** the location of the popular Seal Rocks, where visitors can view a colony of sea lions, as well as stop in at the information center (tel 415/556-0560)

Cable Cars
Tel 415/673-6864. Designated official historic landmarks by the National Park Service in 1964, these rolling symbols continuously cross the city like mobile museum pieces. The world's only surviving system of cable cars, it underwent a $60 million renovation in 1982. The two types of cable cars in use hold, respectively, a maximum of 90 and 100 passengers and the limits are rigidly enforced. **Open:** Daily. **$**

Fisherman's Wharf
Originally called Meigg's Wharf, this bustling strip of waterfront, located at the foot of Taylor St, got its present name from the generations of fishermen who used to base their boats here. Upon landing at the wharf, fishermen would sell their catch fresh off the boat to homemakers and restauranteurs.

The area is now a festive marketplace pulsing with shoppers, diners, people-watchers, and street performers. There are no fishermen to be found, but there are scores of seafood restaurants and stalls, as well as dozens of stores, selling everything from original art to cans of "San Francisco Fog," and innumerable street hawkers and tourist traps. Cruises to Alcatraz Island and around the bay also leave from this area. **Open:** Wharf, daily 24 hours; most area shops, daily 11am–8pm (later during summer); most restaurants, Sun–Thurs 10am–midnight, Fri–Sat 10am–2am.

Ghirardelli Square
900 North Point St; tel 415/775-5500. This famous landmark is renowned for its years as a chocolate factory. The Domingo Ghirardelli family produced chocolate here from 1893 until the early 1960s. After several years of renovation and restoration, Ghirardelli Square became the country's first manufacturing complex preserved and renovated into a festival marketplace. In addition to fabulous views and a new self-guided historic walking tour, the Square boasts more than 50 specialty boutiques and award-winning restaurants. The Ghirardelli Chocolate Soda Fountain is a popular stop to purchase candy and enjoy ice cream sundaes. A complimentary map, shopping discount coupons, and restuarant menus are available at the Information Booth located in the center of the Square. **Open:** Mon–Sat 10am–9pm, Sun 10am–6pm. Restaurant hours vary. **Free**

Pier 39

Tel 415/981-7437 (recorded info). Located on the waterfront at Embarcadero and Beach St. This $54-million, 4½-acre waterfront complex is the busiest of San Francisco's tourist-oriented bayside malls. Constructed on an abandoned cargo pier a few blocks east of Fisherman's Wharf, it is ostensibly a re-creation of a turn-of-the-century street scene, with more than 100 shops, 10 restaurants, a double-decked Venetian carousel, an arcade, and an assortment of street entertainers. A pair of marinas, housing the Blue and Gold bay sightseeing fleet, flank the pier. In recent years, a colony of about 600 California sea lions has taken up residence on the adjacent floating docks. A free interpretive program about the colony is usually given on weekends (call for details). **Open:** Shops, daily 10:30am–8:30pm; restaurants, daily 11:30am–11:30pm; bars, daily until 2am. **Free**

The Cannery

2801 Leavenworth St; tel 415/771-3112. Built in 1894 as a Del Monte company fruit-canning plant, this structure was redeveloped in 1963 as a vaguely Florentine shopping, eating, and entertainment complex. There are about a dozen eateries and more than 50 shops, and in the courtyard, amid a grove of century-old olive trees, are vendors' stalls and sidewalk cafes. The Museum of the City of San Francisco is located on the third floor. **Open:** Peak (Mem Day–Labor Day) Mon–Wed 10am–6pm, Thurs–Sat 10am–8:30pm, Sun 11am–6pm. Reduced hours off-season. **Free**

Lombard Street

Between Hyde and Leavenworth Sts. Known as the "crookedest street in the world," Lombard Street makes nine hairpin turns in the space of about a block, meandering down an extremely steep hillside dotted with expensive homes and rich flower gardens. The short stretch is one way, downhill only, and is sometimes choked with tourists. The hill can be negotiated on foot, either up or down, via staircases (without curves) on either side of the street.

USS *Pampanito*

Pier 45, Fisherman's Wharf; tel 415/441-5819. This battle-scarred World War II fleet submarine saw plenty of action in the Pacific. Now completely restored, the *Pampanito's* compartments are all open for visitors to explore. A taped guided audio tour is included with the admission fee. **Open:** Peak (late-May–Oct) daily 9am–8pm. Reduced hours off-season. **$$**

Mission Dolores

16th and Dolores Sts; tel 415/621-8203. The Mission is the oldest structure in the city. It was founded as the sixth of the California missions by Friar Francisco Palou in 1776. Its interior is a curious mixture of native construction methods and Spanish-colonial style. Small museum, cemetery, and gardens. **Open:** Daily 9am–4pm. **$**

Coit Tower

1 Telegraph Hill; tel 415/362-0808. Located atop Telegraph Hill, just east of North Beach, the 210-foot stone tower offers magnificent 360-degree views of San Francisco. Inside the base are some colorful murals entitled *Life in California, 1934*. Commissioned by the Public Works of Art project, under Franklin D Roosevelt's New Deal program, the restored frescoes are a curious blend of art and politics. **Open:** Daily 10am–6pm. **$**

Fort Point National Historic Site

Tel 415/556-2857. Located under the southern portion of the Golden Gate Bridge in the Presidio, Fort Point was completed in 1861. Although troops from the fort were used to guard the Golden Gate during the Civil War and World War II, no battle ever occurred at the fort. During construction of the Golden Gate Bridge (1933–37), the fort served as construction center of operations.

Designated a National Historic Site in 1970, Fort Point offers guided, self-guided, and audio cassette walking tours; a 17-minute movie covering the history of Fort Point from 1776 to World War II; and demonstrations of Civil War–era cannon loading and firing. Small museum at the visitor center. **Open:** Wed–Sun 10am–5pm. **Free**

Presidio of San Francisco

Lombard and Lyon Sts; tel 415/556-3111 or 556-1874. Founded in 1776, the Presidio served as an active military garrison under the flags of three nations before becoming part of Golden Gate National Recreation Area in 1994. Its 1,480 acres contain historic buildings, natural areas ranging from a planted forest to coastal bluffs, and spectacular vistas. **Open:** Visitor Center: daily 10am–5pm; Museum: Wed–Sun 10am–4pm. **Free**

San Francisco Zoological Gardens/Children's Zoo

Sloat Blvd and 45th Ave; tel 415/753-7080 or 753-7083 (recorded info). Among America's highest-rated animal parks, the zoo covers more than 65 acres and is home to more than 1,000 animals living in realistically landscaped enclosures. Major features are the Primate Discovery Center, known for its many rare and endangered species; Koala Crossing, patterned after an Australian outback station; Gorilla World, one of the world's largest great ape exhibits; Wolf World, exhibiting the sophisticated social behavior of the North American timber wolf; Lion House, home of Prince Charles, a rare white tiger; and Musk Ox Meadow, a 2½-acre habitat for a herd of rare white-fronted musk oxen brought from Alaska. The **Children's Zoo,** adjacent to the main park, allows visitors to get close to a variety of baby animals. A free, informal walking tour of the zoo leaves from Koala Crossing at 12:30 and 2:30pm on weekends. The Zebra Zephyr train tour takes visitors on a 20-minute "safari" daily (in winter, only on weekends). The tour is $2 for adults, $1 for children 15 and under. **Open:** Main zoo, daily 10am–5pm; children's zoo, daily 11am–4pm. **$$$**

San Francisco Experience

838 Grand Ave; tel 415/388-6032 (recorded info). Located on the waterfront at Embarcadero and Beach St. Two centuries of the city's history have been condensed into a 28-minute multimedia show, supplemented by special effects that include a San Francisco "fog" that actually rolls in. Presented on a 70- by 30-foot screen, the show is fast-paced, informative, and highly entertaining. **Open:** Peak (Apr–Dec) shows daily (every half hour) 10am–9:30pm. Reduced hours off-season. **$$$**

San Francisco–Oakland Bay Bridge

Although less visually appealing than the nearby Golden Gate, the Bay Bridge is spectacular as a feat of structural engineering. With a total length of 8¼ miles, it is one of the world's longest steel bridges, but is actually made up of a superbly dovetailed series of spans. The upper deck carries five lanes of traffic westbound, the lower, five lanes eastbound. Drive across the bridge (the toll is $1, paid westbound), or catch a bus at the Transbay Terminal (Mission St at First St) and ride to downtown Oakland.

MUSEUMS

San Francisco Museum of Modern Art

151 3rd St; tel 415/357-4000. Founded in 1935, SFMOMA was the first modern art museum on the West Coast and one of the first to recognize photography as a serious art form. Its new home, a 225,000-square-foot building, is the second-largest single structure in the United States devoted to modern art. The permanent collection contains more than 15,000 works in all media, including 4,000 paintings, sculptures, and works on paper by artists such as Henri Matisse, Jackson Pollock, and Willem de Kooning; and more than 8,000 photographs by such notables as Ansel Adams, Alfred Stieglitz, and Edward Weston. Temporary exhibitions cover a broad range of styles and media. Guided tours are offered daily (phone for schedule). Bookstore; cafe. **Open:** Tues–Wed and Fri–Sun 11am–6pm, Thurs 11am–9pm. **$$$**

San Francisco Maritime National Historical Park and Museum

Foot of Polk St (at Beach St); tel 415/556-3002. This museum is a treasure trove of sailing, whaling, and fishing lore. Exhibits include intricate ship models, scrimshaw, and photographs, including an 1851 shot of hundreds of abandoned ships that were deserted *en masse*, their crews having succumbed to "gold fever." Two blocks east of the museum building are the Historic Ships at Hyde Street Pier, several museum-operated historic vessels that are now moored and open to the public. They include the *Balclutha*, one of the last surviving square-riggers and the handsomest vessel in San Francisco Bay; the *Eureka*, the last of the 50 paddle-wheeled ferries that plied the waters of San Francisco Bay; the West Coast lumber schooner *CA Thayer;* and the *Hercules*, a huge 1907 oceangoing steam tug. **Open:** Daily 10am–5pm. **$**

M H de Young Memorial Museum

Tel 415/750-3600, or 863-3330 (recorded info). One of the city's oldest museums, the de Young is located on the Music Concourse in Golden Gate Park, near 10th Ave and Fulton St. It houses a hodgepodge of art that spans continents and centuries, but it is best known for its American art, which has pieces dating from colonial times to the 20th century. There is an important textile collection as well, with primary emphasis on rugs from central Asia and the Near East. Traveling exhibitions are equally eclectic, ranging from ancient rugs to great Dutch paintings. Docent tours are offered daily; phone for times. Admission includes the Asian Art Museum (see below). (Admission fee may be higher for special exhibitions; no admission fee is charged on the first Wednesday and first Saturday morning of each month.) **Open:** Wed–Sun 10am–5pm. **$$$**

California Academy of Sciences

Tel 415/221-5100 or 750-7145 (recorded info). Located on the Music Concourse of Golden Gate Park, this group of related exhibitions (all part of the Natural History Museum) includes: the **Steinhart Aquarium,** with some 14,000 specimens of fish, marine mammals, amphibians, reptiles, and penguins, and a living coral reef that is the largest display of its kind in the country; the **Morrison Planetarium,** with its 65-foot dome, presenting four major exhibits each year (phone for schedule; shows not recommended for preschoolers); the "Wild California" exhibit, featuring a 14,000-gallon aquarium and a seabird rookery; and "Life Through Time," a massive exhibit that ushers visitors through 3½ billion years of earth history and evolution. **Open:** Peak (July 4–Labor Day) daily 9am–6pm. First Wed of every month, 10am–8:45pm. Reduced hours off-season. **$$$**

Asian Art Museum

Tel 415/379-8801. Located near 10th Ave and Fulton St in Golden Gate Park, this museum contains an array of art and artifacts from 40 countries, especially from China, including sculptures, paintings, bronzes, ceramics, jades, and decorative objects. Also exhibits from Pakistan, India, Tibet, Japan, and Southeast Asia, including the oldest known dated Chinese Buddha. Guided tours daily; phone for hours. Admission includes M H de Young Memorial Museum (see above). **Open:** Wed–Sun 10am–4:45pm. **$$$**

Cable Car Museum

1201 Mason St; tel 415/474-1887. Preserved here is the history of the only surviving operational cable car system in the world. Antique cars, including one of Andrew Halladie's first Clay St cars from 1873, are on display, along with historic photographs and memorabilia, a scale model collection, and a video illustrating the operation of the cable car system. An underground viewing room lets visitors witness the operation of the cable winding machinery. At the museum shop visitors can buy cable and track sections, conductor bells, models, and more. **Open:** Peak (Apr–Sept) daily 10am–6pm. Reduced hours off-season. **Free**

Old Mint

5th and Mission Sts; tel 415/556-6704. First opened in 1874, the Old Mint is one of the finest examples of Federal classical revival architecture in the West. Left intact and standing virtually alone after the devastating 1906 earthquake, the Mint was the only financial institution able to open for business and took over responsibility for the city's monetary affairs.

The restored building is now a museum, featuring the offices of the superintendent, director, and treasurer, all redecorated in 19th-century style; the gold vault; an authentic re-creation of a miner's cabin; and several exhibits, including a display of US national medals, a stampmill for crushing ore, and an 1869 coin press equipped with a trigger to let visitors strike their own bronze souvenir medal. Numismatic sales room on first floor. **Open:** Mon–Fri 10am–4pm. **Free**

Ansel Adams Center for Photography

250 4th St; tel 415/495-7000. The center features five galleries of changing exhibits of photography in all its forms, ranging from 19th-century works to installations that incorporate sound, sculpture, and video. Guided tours available. Free admission first Tues of the month. **Open:** Tues–Sun 11am–5pm, first Thurs of month 11am–8pm. **$$**

Exploratorium

3601 Lyon St; tel 415/563-7337 or 561-0360 (recorded info). This fun, hands-on science fair is a participatory venture, with more than 650 permanent exhibits that explore everything from color theory to Einstein's Theory of Relativity. Housed in the only building left standing from the Panama-Pacific Exposition of 1915, which celebrated the opening of the Panama Canal. **Open:** Peak (Mem Day–Labor Day) Mon–Tues and Thurs–Sun 10am–5pm, Wed 10am–9:30pm. Reduced hours off-season. **$$$**

Wells Fargo History Museum

420 Montgomery St; tel 415/396-2619. This history museum, at the bank's head office, houses hundreds of genuine relics from the company's early history during the Gold Rush era. A genuine Concord stagecoach stands in the window of the main room. Other exhibits include telegraph equipment, gold nuggets and coins, western Pony Express stamps, and mementos of such infamous figures as "Black Bart," the verse-writing humorist who single-handedly robbed 27 stages. **Open:** Mon–Fri 9am–5pm. **Free**

Treasure Island Museum

410 Palm Ave; tel 415/395-5067. Located on Treasure Island, 2 miles E of San Francisco via the Bay Bridge, this museum contains exhibits covering a wide range of topics, including the history of Yerba Buena Island, the Bay Bridge, the famous *China Clipper* seaplanes of the 1930s, and the Golden Gate International Exposition of 1939–40, and the Sea Services (USN, USMC, USCG) in the Pacific. **Open:** Mon–Fri 10am–3:30pm, Sat–Sun 10am–4:30pm. **$**

Ripley's Believe It Or Not! Museum

175 Jefferson St; tel 415/771-6188. A bizarre collection of oddities collected by Robert L Ripley in the course of his world travels; includes a one-third-scale model of a cable car built from matchsticks and a dinosaur made of chrome car bumpers. **Open:** Peak (June 15–Labor Day) daily 9am–11pm. Reduced hours off-season. **$$$**

Wax Museum

145 Jefferson St; tel 415/202-0400. Features more than 200 lifelike figures, mostly devoted to modern-day celebrities such as pop star Michael Jackson. Other tableau themes include Royalty, Great Humanitarians, Feared Leaders, and Chamber of Horrors. **Open:** Daily 9am–10pm; extended hours in summer and on holidays. **$$$**

OTHER ATTRACTIONS

Alamo Square Historic District

San Francisco's plethora of beautiful Victorian homes is one of the city's greatest assets. Most of the 14,000 extant structures are private residences dating from the second half of the 19th century. The small area bordered by Divisadero St on the west, Golden Gate Ave on the north, Webster St on the east, and Fell St on the south has one of the city's greatest concentrations of these "Painted Ladies." Almost uniformly tall and narrow, these houses were built *en masse,* in developments, and many share common walls. Having little to do with the Victorian style of architecture, they are called Victorian only because they were built during the reign of Queen Victoria.

Haas–Lilienthal House

2007 Franklin St; tel 415/441-3004 (recorded info). One of the city's many gingerbread Victorians, this 1886 structure features all the architectural frills of the period, and is fully furnished with contemporary pieces. One-hour guided tours are given 2 days a week. **Open:** Wed noon–4pm, Sun 11am–5pm. **$$**

Octagon House

2645 Gough St; tel 415/441-7512. This unusual, 8-sided, cupola-topped house (1861) contains furniture, silverware, American and European pewter, portraits, samplers, English and Chinese ceramics, and even some historical documents from the Colonial and Federal periods. Maintained by the National Society of Colonial Dames of America and California. **Open:** 2nd Sun and 2nd and 4th Thurs of each month, noon–3pm. Closed Jan. **Free**

Transamerica Pyramid

600 Montgomery St; tel 415/983-4100. This 48-story wedge, capped by a 212-foot spire, is the tallest and most distinctive building in the San Francisco skyline. It was completed in 1972. **Open:** Mon–Fri 6am–7pm.

Bank of America World Headquarters

555 California St. This carnelian marble-covered building dates from 1969. Its 52 stories are topped by a panoramic

restaurant and bar, the Carnelian Room. The focal point of the building's formal plaza is an abstract black granite sculpture known locally as the "Banker's Heart."

Japan Center

Post and Buchanan Sts; tel 415/922-6776. This is an immense, Asian-oriented shopping mall located in San Francisco's revitalized Japantown, about a mile west of Union Square. Dozens of shops feature everything from cameras and radios to pearls and silk kimonos. The mall's centerpiece is a five-tiered Peace Pagoda designed by Japanese architect Yoshiro Taniguchi. The renowned **Kabuki Hot Spring,** 1750 Geary Blvd (tel 922-6000), is the center's most famous tenant. Japantown, or Nihonmachi, San Francisco's Japanese quarter, occupies four square blocks directly north of the Japan Center. **Open:** Mon–Fri 10am–1pm, Sat–Sun 9am–10pm.

Bay Area Rapid Transit (BART)

800 Madison St, Oakland; tel 415/788-BART or 510/465-BART in Oakland. One of the world's most famous commuter systems, BART's 71 miles of rail link eight San Francisco stations with Daly City to the south and 25 stations in the East Bay. BART runs under the bay using one of the world's longest underwater tunnels. The people who run BART think so highly of their trains and stations that they sell a $2.60 "Excursion Ticket," which allows visitors, in effect, to "sightsee" the BART system (phone for details). **Open:** Daily, 24 hours. $

Fort Mason

Bay and Franklin Sts. This former military installation and headquarters for the Pacific Fleet during World War II is now a park. Fort Mason Center is a complex of buildings housing theaters, galleries, and various arts programs. Hundreds of activities are held here each month, including concerts and fairs on the adjacent piers.

Aquatic Park

Located at the foot of Hyde St, adjacent to Ghirardelli Square, this green lawn and protected marina were built in 1937 as a project of the federal Works Progress Administration.

Haunted Gold Mine

113 Jefferson St; tel 415/202-0440. All the elements of a traditional fun house—mazes, a hall of mirrors, wind tunnels, and animated ghouls—comprise this haunted house. Even young children will probably not find it too scary. **Open:** Daily 9am–10pm; extended hours in summer and on hols. $$$

Garden Court

Sheraton Palace Hotel, 2 New Montgomery St; tel 415/392-8600. This spectacular enclosed courtyard is topped by a lofty, iridescent glass roof supported by 16 Doric columns. Rebuilt in 1909 after the Great Earthquake, the elegant court has been painstakingly restored, with marble floors, crystal chandeliers, and a leaded-glass ceiling. The hotel, situated between Market and Third Sts, reopened in 1991. **Open:** Daily 24 hours. **Free**

3COM Park

Giants Dr and Gilman Ave. Located about 8 miles south of downtown on US 101. From April to October the National League **Giants** play their home baseball games at the park (tel 415/467-8000). The NFL's **49ers** play from late August–September (tel 415/468-2249). Tickets available at the park or by phone through BASS Ticketmaster (510/762-2277).

San Francisco Int'l Airport

See also South San Francisco

HOTELS 🏨

⬛ Best Western Grosvenor Hotel

380 S Airport Blvd, South San Francisco, 94080; tel 415/873-3200 or toll free 800/722-7141; fax 415/589-3495. S Airport Blvd exit off US 101. Standard hotel, undergoing complete refurbishing of rooms and hallways. Location is noisy because of highway traffic. **Rooms:** 203 rms and stes. CI 3pm/CO noon. Nonsmoking rms avail. **Amenities:** 🛏 🐕 📺 A/C, cable TV w/movies, dataport, voice mail. Some units w/whirlpools. **Services:** ✕ 🍴 🚗 🖼 🍸 Car-rental desk. **Facilities:** 🏋 🏊400 🖥 ⚄ 1 restaurant, 1 bar, games rm. **Rates:** Peak (May–Oct) $85 S; $95–$125 D; $150–$250 ste. Children under age 12 stay free. Lower rates off-season. Parking: Outdoor, free. AE, DC, DISC, MC, V.

⬛⬛ Clarion Hotel

401 E Millbrae Ave, Millbrae, 94030; tel 415/692-6363 or toll free 800/223-7111; fax 415/692-4251. 15 mi S of San Francisco. Millbrae Ave exit off US 101. Very large rooms, a light-filled lobby, and low rates make this an appealing hotel. **Rooms:** 440 rms and stes. CI 3pm/CO 11am. Nonsmoking rms avail. **Amenities:** 🛏 🐕 A/C, cable TV w/movies. Some units w/whirlpools. **Services:** ✕ 🚗 🖼 🍸 ⚅ Executive Choice Club, a "frequent stay" program, includes complimentary breakfast, newspaper, welcome drink, and check-cashing privileges. **Facilities:** 🏋 🏊 🏊800 🖥 ⚄ 1 restaurant, 1 bar, whirlpool, washer/dryer. Jogging/walking trail across the street. **Rates:** $89–$119 S or D; $225 ste. Extra person $15. Parking: Outdoor, free. AE, DC, DISC, MC, V.

⬛⬛⬛ Courtyard by Marriott

1050 Bayhill Dr, San Bruno, 94066; tel 415/952-3333 or toll free 800/321-2211; fax 415/952-4707. A most welcoming lobby, with lots of natural light, is well furnished and very homey thanks to a fireplace. Courtyard garden has gazebo, lawn, and trees. **Rooms:** 147 rms and stes. CI 3pm/CO 1pm. Nonsmoking rms avail. Rooms are large and all have desks. **Amenities:** 🛏 🐕 A/C, cable TV w/movies, voice mail. Some units w/minibars, all w/terraces. Instant hot water for coffee and tea. **Services:** X 🚐 🖼️ 🛎️ Babysitting. **Facilities:** 🎣 🏌️ 📶 🚴 1 restaurant (bkfst and lunch only), 1 bar, whirlpool, washer/dryer. **Rates:** $89–$115 S or D; $120–$130 ste. Children under age 18 stay free. Parking: Outdoor, free. AE, DC, DISC, MC, V.

🏨🏨🏨 Crown Sterling Suites
150 Anza Blvd, Burlingame, 94010; tel 415/342-4600 or toll free 800/433-4600; fax 415/343-8137. Broadway/Burlingame exit off US 101 S; N Anza exit off US 101 N. Elaborate lobby combines neoclassical and Victorian furnishings and woodwork with an atrium housing cages of parrots, a koi pond, and waterfalls. Ongoing renovations. **Rooms:** 339 stes. CI 3pm/CO 1pm. Nonsmoking rms avail. Some rooms have fantastic water views. Nice appointments with new, fine linens. **Amenities:** 🛁 🍳 📺 🍷 A/C, cable TV w/movies, refrig, dataport, voice mail. **Services:** X 🚐 🖼️ 🛎️ 🍷 Complimentary cocktails in lobby. **Facilities:** 🎣 🏋️ 📶 📎 🚴 1 restaurant (lunch and dinner only), 1 bar (w/entertainment), sauna, steam rm, whirlpool, washer/dryer. Beautiful pool area. **Rates (BB):** $149–$174 ste. Extra person $10. Children under age 12 stay free. Parking: Outdoor, free. AE, CB, DC, DISC, JCB, MC, V.

🏨🏨🏨 Crown Sterling Suites
250 Gateway Blvd, South San Francisco, 94080; tel 415/589-3400 or toll free 800/433-4600; fax 415/876-0305. Grand Ave exit off US 101; left on Gateway Blvd. A lovely place. The beautiful lobby has murals, a babbling brook, and a koi pond. **Rooms:** 313 stes. Executive level. CI 3pm/CO 11am. Nonsmoking rms avail. Rooms are large, with fine furniture. Corner units are executive suites with large floor-to-ceiling windows. **Amenities:** 🛁 🍳 📺 🍷 A/C, cable TV w/movies, refrig, voice mail. All units w/minibars. Laptop computers available. **Services:** X 🚐 🖼️ 🛎️ Car-rental desk, babysitting. Cheerful staff. **Facilities:** 🎣 📶 🚴 1 restaurant (lunch and dinner only), 1 bar, sauna, whirlpool, washer/dryer. Beautiful indoor pool. **Rates:** $109–$179 ste. Extra person $10. Children under age 12 stay free. Parking: Outdoor, free. AE, DC, DISC, MC, V.

🏨🏨 DoubleTree Hotel
835 Airport Blvd, Burlingame, 94010; tel 415/344-5500 or toll free 800/222-TREE; fax 415/340-8851. Broadway E exit off US 101 S; Anza Blvd off US 101 N. Across the street from San Francisco Bay, the hotel offers lovely views from top floors and a restaurant with an extensive menu. **Rooms:** 291 rms and stes. CI 3pm/CO noon. Nonsmoking rms avail. **Amenities:** 🛁 🍳 A/C, TV w/movies. **Services:** X 🚐 🖼️ 🛎️ 🍷 Babysitting. **Facilities:** 🏋️ 🏌️ 📶 🚴 1 restaurant, 1 bar. Excellent waterfront jogging path. **Rates (CP):** Peak (June–Sept) $119–$149 S or D; $169 ste. Extra person $10. Children under age 18 stay free. Lower rates off-season. AP and MAP rates avail. Parking: Outdoor, free. AE, CB, DC, DISC, ER, MC, V.

🏨🏨🏨 Holiday Inn Crowne Plaza
600 Airport Blvd, Burlingame, 94010; tel 415/340-8500 or toll free 800/827-0880; fax 415/343-1546. 15 mi S of San Francisco. Broadway-Burlingame exit off US 101. A luxurious hotel located on San Francisco Bay near the airport. **Rooms:** 404 rms. Executive level. CI 3pm/CO noon. Nonsmoking rms avail. **Amenities:** 🛁 🍳 📺 🍷 A/C, cable TV w/movies, dataport, voice mail. **Services:** X 🖐️ VP 🚐 🖼️ 🛎️ Car-rental desk. Excellent service. **Facilities:** 🎣 🏋️ 🏌️ 📶 📎 🚴 1 restaurant, 1 bar (w/entertainment), sauna, whirlpool, washer/dryer. Executive floor has private access. Meandering jogging path hugs the bay. Kids eat free in summer. **Rates:** Peak (June–Oct) $146–$179 S or D. Extra person $10. Children under age 18 stay free. Lower rates off-season. Parking: Indoor, free. AE, CB, DC, DISC, EC, JCB, MC, V.

🏨🏨 Holiday Inn San Francisco International Airport North
275 S Airport Blvd, South San Francisco, 94080; tel 415/873-3550 or toll free 800/HOLIDAY; fax 415/873-4524. S Airport Blvd exit off US 101. Located in a fairly industrial area, near a busy highway and within earshot of airport noise. Composed of two wings, with large, comfortable rooms. Refurbishing complete in North Tower, under way in South Tower. **Rooms:** 224 rms and stes. Executive level. CI 3pm/CO noon. Nonsmoking rms avail. **Amenities:** 🛁 🍳 🍷 A/C, cable TV w/movies, voice mail. All units w/minibars. **Services:** X 🚐 🖼️ 🛎️ 🍷 Car-rental desk, babysitting. **Facilities:** 🏌️ 📶 📎 🚴 1 restaurant, 1 bar, sauna, whirlpool. Free pool privileges at adjoining hotel. Fitness center has a tanning bed. **Rates (CP):** $108–$130 S; $118–$130 D; $260 ste. Extra person $10. Children under age 18 stay free. Parking: Outdoor, free. AE, CB, DC, DISC, EC, JCB, MC, V.

🏨🏨🏨 Hyatt Regency San Francisco Airport
1333 Bayshore Hwy, Burlingame, 94010; tel 415/347-1234 or toll free 800/233-1234; fax 415/347-5948. E from Broadway exit off US 101. A busy hotel that anticipates guests' needs. Popular among leisure travelers, corporate travelers, and conventioneers. **Rooms:** 793 rms and stes. Executive level. CI 3pm/CO noon. Nonsmoking rms avail. Some rooms have views of hills or of San Francisco Bay. **Amenities:** 🛁 🍳 📺 🍷 A/C, cable TV w/movies, refrig, VCR, CD/tape player, voice mail. Some units w/terraces, some w/whirlpools. Intercom in every room for emergency information. **Services:** 📞 🖐️ VP 🚐 🖼️ 🛎️ Car-rental desk, babysitting. **Facilities:** 🎣 🏋️ 🏌️ 📶 📎 🚴 3 restaurants, 2 bars (1 w/entertainment), spa, sauna, whirlpool. Largest hotel and meeting facilities between South San Francisco and Los Angeles. Deli open 24 hours. **Rates:** $190–$225 S or D; $199 ste. Extra person $25. Children under age 18 stay free. AP rates avail. Parking: Indoor/outdoor, free. Business Plan (add $15) includes breakfast, fax machines in room, and use of business center. AE, DC, DISC, JCB, MC, V.

☰☰ Park Plaza Hotel San Francisco

1177 Airport Blvd, Burlingame, 94010; tel 415/342-9200 or toll free 800/333-3333; fax 415/342-1655. Broadway exit off US 101; right at Airport Blvd. **Rooms:** 301 rms and stes. CI 3pm/CO noon. Nonsmoking rms avail. Most of the guest rooms have new beds, mattresses, furniture, and flooring. **Amenities:** ☗ ⚙ ▣ ⚐ A/C, cable TV w/movies, bathrobes. **Services:** ✕ ☎ ⚐ ♫ Free newspapers. Late (4pm) checkout available upon request. **Facilities:** ⚐ ⚙ ⚐ ⚐ 840 1 restaurant, 1 bar, whirlpool, beauty salon, playground, washer/dryer. An indoor/outdoor pool and glassed-in fitness center were slated to be added during renovation. **Rates (CP):** $150–$170 S; $160–$180 D; $235–$350 ste. Extra person $10. Children under age 16 stay free. Parking: Indoor/outdoor, free. AE, CB, DC, DISC, JCB, MC, V.

☰ Ramada Inn San Francisco International Airport North

245 S Airport Blvd, South San Francisco, 94080; tel 415/589-7200 or toll free 800/452-3456; fax 415/588-5007. 10 mi S of San Francisco. S Airport Blvd exit off US 101. Motel units are being upgraded to hotel standards. Extensive lobby, central garden. **Rooms:** 323 rms and stes. CI 3pm/CO noon. Nonsmoking rms avail. **Amenities:** ☗ ⚙ ⚐ A/C, cable TV w/movies. **Services:** ✕ ☎ ⚐ ♫ ☞ Car-rental desk, babysitting. **Facilities:** ⚐ 350 ⚐ 1 restaurant, 1 bar, beauty salon, washer/dryer. **Rates (CP):** $65–$95 S; $75–$105 D; $300 ste. Extra person $10. Children under age 18 stay free. Parking: Outdoor, free. AE, CB, DC, DISC, EC, ER, JCB, MC, V.

☰☰☰ Ramada San Francisco Airport

1250 Old Bayshore, Burlingame, 94010; tel 415/347-2381 or toll free 800/227-2381; fax 415/348-8838. Broadway/Airport Blvd exit off US 101. Light-filled two-story lobby with open staircase and lots of brass, glass, and potted plants. Furniture looks a bit shabby. **Rooms:** 145 rms and stes. CI 2pm/CO noon. Nonsmoking rms avail. **Amenities:** ☗ ⚙ ⚐ A/C, cable TV w/movies, refrig, dataport. **Services:** ✕ ☎ ⚐ ♫ Babysitting. Wheelchair-accessible van available. **Facilities:** ⚐ ⚐ 40 ⚐ ⚐ 1 restaurant, 1 bar, washer/dryer. **Rates:** Peak (June–Sept) $108–$118 S; $118–$126 D; $176–$206 ste. Extra person $10. Children under age 18 stay free. Lower rates off-season. Parking: Outdoor, free. AE, CB, DC, DISC, EC, MC, V.

☰☰☰ San Francisco Airport Hilton

San Francisco International Airport, PO Box 8355, South San Francisco, 94128; tel 415/589-0770 or toll free 800/HILTONS; fax 415/589-4696. San Francisco Int'l Airport exit off US 101. Closest hotel to the airport. **Rooms:** 527 rms and stes. CI 3pm/CO noon. Nonsmoking rms avail. **Amenities:** ☗ ⚙ A/C, cable TV w/movies, voice mail. All units w/minibars, some w/terraces. **Services:** ✕ VP ☎ ⚐ ♫ ☞ Babysitting. **Facilities:** ⚐ ⚐ 527 ⚐ ⚐ 2 restaurants, 1 bar (w/entertainment), sauna, whirlpool. **Rates (CP):** $145–

$165 S; $165–$185 D. Extra person $20. Children under age 12 stay free. AP and MAP rates avail. Parking: Outdoor, $5–$10/day. AE, DC, DISC, EC, MC, V.

☰☰☰ San Francisco Airport Marriott

1800 Old Bayshore Hwy, Burlingame, 94010; tel 415/692-9100 or toll free 800/228-9290; fax 415/692-8016. Millbrae Ave E exit off US 101; right onto Old Bayshore Hwy. Convenient location for travelers, with an atrium-style lobby and views of San Francisco Bay. **Rooms:** 684 rms and stes. Executive level. CI 3pm/CO 11am. Nonsmoking rms avail. Noise varies according to flight patterns. **Amenities:** ☗ ⚙ ⚐ A/C, cable TV w/movies, dataport, voice mail. **Services:** �ⓞ ☞ VP ☎ ⚐ ♫ ☞ Car-rental desk, babysitting. Daily newspapers. **Facilities:** ⚐ ⚐ ⚐ 2000 ⚐ ⚐ 2 restaurants, 1 bar (w/entertainment), sauna, whirlpool, washer/dryer. **Rates:** $169 S or D; $295–$550 ste. Min stay wknds. Parking: Indoor/outdoor, $10/day. Lower rates on weekends and holidays. AE, CB, DC, DISC, EC, ER, JCB, MC, V.

☰☰☰☰ Westin Hotel

1 Old Bayshore Hwy, Millbrae, 94030; tel 415/692-3500 or toll free 800/228-3000; fax 415/872-8111. Millbrae Ave E exit off US 101. It's unusual to describe an airport hotel as having a beautiful setting, but the Westin pulls it off. The sophisticated lobby with Asian antiques and original art faces the stunning indoor atrium pool. Superbly geared to the business traveler. **Rooms:** 390 rms and stes. Executive level. CI 3pm/CO 1pm. Nonsmoking rms avail. Completely refurbished in 1996, accommodations are handsome, with rich maple furnishings and burgundy fabrics. Although compact, bathrooms are well laid out. Rooms on the east side have fabulous bay and airport views; excellent soundproofing nicely muffles takeoffs and landings. **Amenities:** ☗ ⚙ ▣ ⚐ A/C, cable TV w/movies, dataport, voice mail. All units w/minibars, some w/whirlpools. Iron and ironing board in room; Starbucks coffee for the coffeemaker. **Services:** ⓞ VP ☎ ⚐ ♫ ☞ Masseur, babysitting. Interactive kiosk in lobby provides maps, driving directions, restaurant recommendations. **Facilities:** ⚐ ⚐ ⚐ 700 ⚐ ⚐ 1 restaurant, 1 bar, whirlpool. Complimentary hors d'oeuvres served in lobby from 5 to 7pm. Gift shop also sells Starbucks coffee to go. United Airlines ticketing desk. Six-mile jogging path along the bayfront across the street. **Rates:** $99–$175 S; $99–$195 D; $340–$390 ste. Extra person $20. Children under age 18 stay free. Parking: Outdoor, $8/day. Frequent-guest and park-and-fly packages avail. AE, CB, DC, DISC, ER, JCB, MC, V.

MOTELS

☰☰☰ Best Western El Rancho Inn & Executive Suites

1100 El Camino Real, Millbrae, 94030; tel 415/588-8500 or toll free 800/826-5500; fax 415/871-7150. Millbrae Ave exit off US 101. This mission-style motel has pink stucco, tile roof, and Spanish arches, with pretty flowerbeds and palm trees.

Rooms: 300 rms, stes, and effic. CI 3pm/CO 1pm. Nonsmoking rms avail. Rooms are nicely furnished with pine and floral fabrics. **Amenities:** 🛏 ⚗ 🖥 A/C, cable TV w/movies. Some units w/minibars, some w/terraces, 1 w/whirlpool. **Services:** ✗ 🚗 🖼 🐕 🍸 Car-rental desk, babysitting. Family-run with excellent service. **Facilities:** 🍴 🏊 ⚓ 1 restaurant, 1 bar (w/entertainment), sauna, whirlpool, washer/dryer. **Rates (CP):** Peak (June–Oct) $90–$95 S; $90–$120 D; $110–$140 ste; $125–$150 effic. Extra person $5. Children under age 18 stay free. Lower rates off-season. Parking: Outdoor, free. Stay-and-fly package allows guests to leave car at hotel for up to 3 weeks. AE, CB, DC, DISC, EC, MC, V.

≣≣≣ La Quinta Inn
20 Airport Blvd, South San Francisco, 94080; tel 415/583-2223 or toll free 800/531-5900; fax 415/589-6770. 10 mi S of San Francisco. S Airport Blvd exit off US 101. Located in an industrial neighborhood with a busy freeway nearby—but close to Candlestick Park, and reasonably priced. **Rooms:** 174 rms. CI 3pm/CO 11am. Nonsmoking rms avail. New carpets, furnishings, bedspreads, and artwork. **Amenities:** 🛏 ⚗ 🖥 A/C, satel TV, dataport. Some units w/terraces. **Services:** ✗ 🚗 🖼 🐕 🍸 Car-rental desk, masseur, babysitting. **Facilities:** 🍴 🏋 🏊 🖥 ⚓ Whirlpool, washer/dryer. **Rates (CP):** Peak (July–Sept) $93 S; $87 D. Extra person $10. Children under age 12 stay free. Lower rates off-season. Parking: Outdoor, free. AE, CB, DC, DISC, MC, V.

≣≣ Red Roof Inn San Francisco Airport
777 Airport Blvd, Burlingame, 94010; tel 415/342-7772 or toll free 800/THE-ROOF; fax 415/342-2635. 15 mi S of San Francisco. Broadway-Burlingame exit off US 101. This property borders on a lagoon and is surrounded by upscale hotels. **Rooms:** 200 rms. CI 2pm/CO noon. Nonsmoking rms avail. **Amenities:** 🛏 ⚗ 🍴 A/C, satel TV w/movies, dataport, in-rm safe. **Services:** 🚗 🖼 🐕 🍸 **Facilities:** 🍴 ⚓ 1 restaurant. **Rates:** Peak (May–Oct) $99 S or D. Extra person $7. Children under age 12 stay free. Lower rates off-season. Parking: Outdoor, free. "Park and fly" packages avail. AE, DC, DISC, MC, V.

≣ San Francisco Airport North Travelodge
326 S Airport Blvd, South San Francisco, 94086 (San Francisco Int'l Airport); tel 415/583-9600 or toll free 800/578-7878; fax 415/873-9392. S Airport Blvd exit off US 101. A well-maintained basic motel that offers lots of amenities to guests. **Rooms:** 197 rms and stes. CI noon/CO 1pm. Nonsmoking rms avail. **Amenities:** 🛏 🖥 A/C, cable TV w/movies, voice mail. Available for guests with disabilities are decoders for TVs, alarm clocks that shake the pillow, special telephone aids. **Services:** 🕭 🚗 🖼 🐕 Car-rental desk. **Facilities:** 🍴 🖥 1 restaurant (bkfst and lunch only). **Rates:** $65–$75 S; $72–$82 D; $75–$82 ste. Extra person $7. Children under age 18 stay free. Parking: Outdoor, free. AE, DC, DISC, MC, V.

RESTAURANT 🍴

Hong Kong Flower Lounge Seafood Restaurant
51 Millbrae Ave, Millbrae; tel 415/878-8108. At El Camino Real. **Chinese.** Imposing two-tiered restaurant capped by a green-tiled, pagoda-like roof. The bustling first floor is outfitted with aquariums, where fish and crustaceans await their fate. The quieter second level offers views of the bay. Fried prawns with walnuts and special sauce, Peking duck, abalone with sea cucumber. **FYI:** Reservations recommended. Beer and wine only. Additional locations: 5322 Geary Blvd, San Francisco (tel 588-9972); 1671 El Camino Real (tel 588-9972). **Open:** Lunch Mon–Fri 11am–2:30pm, Sat–Sun 10:30am–2:30pm; dinner daily 5–9pm. **Prices:** Main courses $10–$20; prix fixe $80–$150. AE, DC, DISC, MC, V. 🖼 🆅🅿 ⚓

San Gabriel

See Pasadena

San Jose

See also Campbell, Cupertino, Milpitas, Santa Clara, Sunnydale

San Jose was founded in 1777 as a cattle and crop-raising settlement for the nearby presidios of San Francisco and Monterey. From 1849 to 1851 the city served as the state capital. Modern San Jose, is now among the fastest-growing urban areas in America and is the heart and soul of Silicon Valley, the high-tech capital of the world. San Jose State University is here. **Information:** San Jose Convention & Visitors Bureau, 333 W San Carlos St #1000, San Jose 95110 (tel 408/295-9600 or toll free 800/SAN-JOSE).

HOTELS 🏨

≣≣≣ Courtyard by Marriott
1727 Technology Dr, 95110 (San Jose Int'l Airport); tel 408/441-6111 or toll free 800/321-2211; fax 408/441-8039. N 1st St exit off US 101; left on Technology Dr. Great location near San Jose International Airport and Silicon Valley, yet not noisy. A very nice lobby area, a lot of natural light, and a pleasant restaurant for breakfast. **Rooms:** 151 rms and stes. CI 3pm/CO 1pm. Nonsmoking rms avail. **Amenities:** 🛏 ⚗ 🖥 A/C, cable TV w/movies, voice mail. Some units w/terraces. **Services:** ✗ 🚗 🖼 🐕 **Facilities:** 🍴 🏋 🖥 ⚓ 1 restaurant, 1 bar, whirlpool, washer/dryer. **Rates:** $115 S; $125 D; $130 ste. Children under age 12 stay free. Parking: Outdoor, free. Corporate rates avail. AE, CB, DC, DISC, MC, V.

≣≣≣≣ Fairmont Hotel
170 Market St, 95113 (Downtown); tel 408/998-1900; fax 408/287-1648. CA 87 exit of I-280. Opened in 1987, the Fairmont recalls the glamour of grand hotels, with crystal

chandeliers, three-foot-thick columns, and what seems like acres of marble in the lobby. **Rooms:** 541 rms and stes. Executive level. CI 3pm/CO 1pm. Nonsmoking rms avail. European-style furnishings. Bathrooms, lined in Italian marble, have ample counter space. **Amenities:** 🛅 🗄 🍴 A/C, cable TV w/movies, dataport, voice mail, bathrobes. All units w/minibars, some w/fireplaces. Small TV and scale in the bathroom, oversize towels, electric shoe polisher. Lanai accommodations have private terraces right beside the pool area. **Services:** 🍽 📭 📼 🚗 🖼 🔁 Twice-daily maid svce, car-rental desk, masseur, children's program, babysitting. **Facilities:** 🏌 🏋 1100 🖥 🔥 4 restaurants (*see* "Restaurants" below), 5 bars (1 w/entertainment), spa, sauna, steam rm, beauty salon. Swimming pool is bordered by palm trees. Extremely well-equipped health club offers Nautilus machines, Stairmasters, massage rooms, extensive locker facilities. **Rates:** $159–$199 S; $179–$219 D; $400 ste. Extra person $25. Children under age 18 stay free. Parking: Indoor, $12/day. Rates lower on weekends. AE, CB, DC, DISC, JCB, MC, V.

☰☰☰ Holiday Inn Park Center Plaza

282 Almaden Blvd at San Carlos, 95113 (Downtown); tel 408/998-0400 or toll free 800/HOLIDAY; fax 408/289-9081. Guadalupe Pkwy exit off US 101. Lobby clean, but uninspired. Uninviting entrance. **Rooms:** 231 rms and stes. CI 2pm/CO noon. Nonsmoking rms avail. **Amenities:** 🛅 🗄 A/C, cable TV, voice mail. **Services:** ✕ 🚗 🖼 🔁 🖐 Twice-daily maid svce, car-rental desk. **Facilities:** 🏌 🏋 750 🔥 1 restaurant, 1 bar (w/entertainment). **Rates:** $101 S or D; $201 ste. Extra person $10. Children under age 19 stay free. Parking: Indoor/outdoor, free. Special deals for business travelers. AE, DC, DISC, MC, V.

☰☰☰ Holiday Inn Silicon Valley

399 Silicon Valley Blvd, 95138; tel 408/972-7800 or toll free 800/HOLIDAY; fax 408/972-0157. Bernal exit off US 101; turn left on Silicon Valley Blvd. A five-year-old hotel in a Spanish-style building with high-ceilings and a huge atrium lobby. Set in the southernmost part of San Jose. **Rooms:** 150 rms and stes. CI 3pm/CO noon. Nonsmoking rms avail. Rooms are standard but attractively decorated. **Amenities:** 🗄 🍴 A/C, cable TV w/movies, dataport. No phone. Some units w/terraces. **Services:** ✕ 📭 🚗 🖼 🔁 Babysitting. Complimentary newspapers. **Facilities:** 🏌 🎿 🏋 250 🖥 🔥 1 restaurant, 1 bar, whirlpool. Spectacular Sunday brunch at the Summit Steakhouse & Saloon. **Rates:** $98 S or D; $119 ste. Extra person $10. Children under age 17 stay free. Parking: Outdoor, free. AE, CB, DC, DISC, EC, JCB, MC, V.

☰☰☰ Homewood Suites

10 W Trimble Rd, 95131; tel 408/428-9900 or toll free 800/CALL-HOME; fax 408/428-0222. **Rooms:** 140 stes. CI 3pm/CO noon. Nonsmoking rms avail. Suites have ceiling fans in bedroom, irons and ironing boards. Some two-bedroom suites available. **Amenities:** 🛅 🗄 📺 A/C, satel TV w/movies, refrig, VCR, voice mail. All units w/minibars, some

w/terraces, some w/fireplaces. **Services:** 📭 🚗 🖼 🔁 🖐 Twice-daily maid svce, car-rental desk, babysitting. Complimentary breakfast, grocery shopping service, free coffee and popcorn. Free shuttle within 5 miles. **Facilities:** 🏌 🏋 45 🖥 🔥 Whirlpool, washer/dryer. Volleyball and basketball courts; convenience store on premises. **Rates (BB):** $169–$224 ste. Children under age 18 stay free. Parking: Outdoor, free. AE, CB, DC, DISC, JCB, MC, V.

☰☰☰☰ Hotel De Anza

233 W Santa Clara St, 95113 (Downtown); tel 408/286-1000 or toll free 800/843-3700; fax 408/286-0500. Park Ave exit off CA 87. A refurbished historic hotel in the heart of downtown San Jose. Very special accommodations, particularly for business travelers. **Rooms:** 101 rms and stes. Executive level. CI 3pm/CO noon. Nonsmoking rms avail. High-ceilinged rooms are elegantly outfitted with art deco–style furniture, original artwork, crown moldings, and inlaid wooden cabinets. Padded benches at the foot of each bed. **Amenities:** 🛅 🗄 🍴 A/C, cable TV w/movies, dataport, VCR, voice mail, bathrobes. All units w/minibars, some w/terraces, 1 w/fireplace, some w/whirlpools. Television and telephone in bathroom. Multiple-line desk phone with dedicated fax line in each room. Fax machines and computers available. **Services:** ✕ 📭 📼 🚗 🖼 🔁 Twice-daily maid svce, babysitting. Complimentary late-night deli buffet 10pm–5am daily. Full secretarial service available. Complimentary newspapers and videos. **Facilities:** 🏋 120 🖥 🔥 2 restaurants, 1 bar (w/entertainment). Palm Court Terrace, an entertainment patio and garden, is available for parties and receptions. Meeting rooms are beautiful. **Rates:** $155 S or D; $195–$295 ste. Extra person $15. Children under age 12 stay free. Min stay peak. Parking: Indoor, $4–$6/day. AE, CB, DC, JCB, MC, V.

☰☰☰☰ Hyatt Sainte Claire

302 S Market St, 95113 (Downtown); tel 408/295-2000 or toll free 800/824-6835; fax 408/977-0403. Elegant old-fashioned lobby with fine furnishings and classical music. Beautiful beamed and stenciled ceiling, potted palms, and fireplace give an old-world feel. **Rooms:** 170 rms and stes. CI 3pm/CO noon. Nonsmoking rms avail. Fine furnishings, original artwork, coordinated upholstery and linens. High, old-fashioned beds. **Amenities:** 🛅 🗄 🍴 A/C, cable TV w/movies, dataport, voice mail, in-rm safe. All units w/minibars, some w/fireplaces, some w/whirlpools. **Services:** 🍽 📭 📼 🚗 🖼 🔁 🖐 Twice-daily maid svce, babysitting. **Facilities:** 🏋 500 🔥 1 restaurant, 1 bar (w/entertainment). **Rates:** $135–$170 S; $150–$185 D; $180–$825 ste. Extra person $15. Children under age 18 stay free. Parking: Indoor, $10/day. AE, CB, DC, DISC, JCB, MC, V.

☰☰☰ Hyatt San Jose at San Jose Airport

1740 N 1st St, 95112 (San Jose Int'l Airport); tel 408/993-1234 or toll free 800/233-1234; fax 408/453-0259. Blooming flowers and manicured gardens make the grounds very attractive. **Rooms:** 474 rms and stes. CI 3pm/CO noon.

Nonsmoking rms avail. Rooms are a bit small. **Amenities:** 🏨 🕓 🖳 A/C, cable TV w/movies, dataport. Some units w/terraces. **Services:** ✗ VP 📠 ⛱ ↩ ◁ Masseur, children's program, babysitting. **Facilities:** 🔗 🏊 📶 1000 🖳 ৬ 2 restaurants, 1 bar, whirlpool, beauty salon. Lovely inner courtyard features a large pool, gazebo, covered barbecue, and generous patio seating for the restaurant. **Rates:** $120 S; $140 D; $149–$450 ste. Extra person $25. Children under age 18 stay free. Parking: Outdoor, free. AE, CB, DC, DISC, JCB, MC, V.

☰☰☰ Le Baron Hotel
1350 N 1st St, 95112; tel 408/453-6200 or toll free 800/662-9896; fax 408/437-9558. An ornate but tacky spiral staircase leads to lounge area, decorated with commercial artwork and fake plants. **Rooms:** 327 rms and stes. Executive level. CI 3pm/CO noon. Nonsmoking rms avail. Suites are dramatic and sumptuous, but rooms are not. **Amenities:** 🏨 🕓 🍽 A/C, cable TV w/movies, voice mail. Some units w/minibars, some w/whirlpools. **Services:** ✗ 🔑 📠 ⛱ ↩ ◁ Car-rental desk, children's program, babysitting. **Facilities:** 🔗 📶 1000 🖳 ৬ 2 restaurants, 3 bars (1 w/entertainment), washer/dryer. Small pool area, visible from lobby, is edged by potentially slippery deck. Pretty ninth-floor restaurant has garden theme, with lattices and floral draperies. **Rates:** Peak (July–Oct) $99 S or D; $119 ste. Extra person $10. Children under age 18 stay free. Lower rates off-season. Parking: Outdoor, free. AE, DC, DISC, MC, V.

☰☰☰ Radisson Plaza Hotel
1471 N 4th St, 95112; tel 408/452-0200 or toll free 800/333-3333; fax 408/437-8819. N 1st St exit off US 101; right on 1st St, left on Gish Rd, left on N 4th St. Lovely styling with wood paneling, European furnishings, and tasteful crystal chandeliers. Close to the airport and civic center. **Rooms:** 185 rms and stes. Executive level. CI 3pm/CO noon. Nonsmoking rms avail. Rooms are individually decorated and quite lovely, with nice fabrics and artwork. **Amenities:** 🕓 🖳 🍽 A/C, cable TV w/movies, dataport, voice mail. No phone. All units w/minibars, some w/terraces, some w/whirlpools. **Services:** ✗ 🔑 📠 ⛱ ↩ Babysitting. Shuttle to shopping and restaurants. **Facilities:** 🔗 🏊 📶 350 ৬ 1 restaurant, 1 bar, whirlpool. Beautiful, antique-filled restaurant. **Rates:** $144–$164 S or D; $250–$300 ste. Extra person $15. Children under age 17 stay free. Parking: Indoor, free. AE, DC, DISC, MC, V.

☰☰☰ Red Lion Hotel
2050 Gateway Place, 95110; tel 408/453-4000 or toll free 800/547-8010; fax 408/437-2899. The lobby is slightly gaudy, with marble-tiled floors, plastic-paneled chandeliers, and lots of brass and glass. **Rooms:** 505 rms and stes. Executive level. CI 3pm/CO 1pm. Nonsmoking rms avail. Suites are tasteful and spacious, with beautiful lighting, full bar area, lots of mirrors, and a luxurious bathroom. **Amenities:** 🏨 🕓 🖳 A/C, cable TV w/movies. All units w/terraces, some w/whirlpools. **Services:** ✗ 🔑 VP 📠 ⛱ ↩

◁ Car-rental desk, babysitting. **Facilities:** 🔗 🏊 📶 1400 ৬ 2 restaurants, 2 bars (1 w/entertainment), sauna, whirlpool, beauty salon, washer/dryer. **Rates:** $155–$165 S; $165–$175 D; $450–$650 ste. Extra person $15. Children under age 18 stay free. Parking: Outdoor, free. AE, CB, DC, DISC, JCB, MC, V.

☰☰☰ San Jose Hilton and Towers
300 Almaden Blvd, 95110 (Downtown); tel 408/287-2100 or toll free 800/HILTONS; fax 408/947-4488. Vine/Almaden exit off I-280; left on Almaden Blvd. In the heart of the business district, with a light-rail station just outside hotel entrance. Well-appointed lobby with nice artwork. **Rooms:** 355 rms and stes. Executive level. CI 4pm/CO 1pm. Nonsmoking rms avail. **Amenities:** 🏨 🕓 🖳 A/C, cable TV w/movies, voice mail. Some units w/minibars. **Services:** ✗ 🔑 VP 📠 ⛱ ↩ ◁ Car-rental desk. Business services available. **Facilities:** 🔗 📶 400 ৬ 1 restaurant, 1 bar, whirlpool, washer/dryer. Very small outside pool on third-floor deck. Guests have access to San Jose Athletic Club facilities. **Rates:** $150–$170 S; $165–$185 D; $295–$395 ste. Extra person $25. Children under age 18 stay free. Parking: Indoor, $6–$10/day. AE, CB, DC, MC, V.

MOTELS

☰☰☰ Best Western Gateway Inn
2585 Seaboard Ave, 95131; tel 408/435-8800 or toll free 800/437-8855; fax 408/435-8879. Trimble Rd exit off US 101; right on Seaboard Ave. Elegant high ceilings, faux marble, and nice European-style furniture accent the lobby, along with floor-to-ceiling windows and crystal chandeliers. **Rooms:** 146 rms. CI 2pm/CO noon. Nonsmoking rms avail. Rooms are nicely appointed, in spite of fluorescent lighting. **Amenities:** 🏨 🕓 🍽 A/C, satel TV w/movies, refrig, dataport. Some units w/terraces. VCRs available for rent. **Services:** 📠 ⛱ ↩ ◁ Complimentary breakfast buffet in the lobby. Free coffee, tea, and cookies in the afternoon. Free local telephone calls. Free shuttle service within a 5-mile radius. **Facilities:** 🔗 85 ৬ 2 restaurants, 1 bar, whirlpool. Complimentary use of nearby athletic club. Pool/whirlpool area needs upgrading. **Rates (CP):** Peak (May–Sept) $86 S; $90 D. Extra person $5. Children under age 18 stay free. Lower rates off-season. Parking: Outdoor, free. AE, DC, DISC, MC, V.

☰☰ Comfort Inn
1215 S 1st St, 95110; tel 408/280-5300 or toll free 800/221-2222. Almaden/Vine exit off I-280. Sparsely decorated lobby off a busy street near a shabby neighborhood. **Rooms:** 58 rms and effic. CI 1pm/CO 11am. Nonsmoking rms avail. Good soundproofing and lots of extras. **Amenities:** 🏨 🕓 🖳 🍽 A/C, cable TV w/movies, refrig. Some units w/whirlpools. **Facilities:** ৬ **Rates:** $62 S; $70 D; $69 effic. Extra person $8. Children under age 12 stay free. Parking: Outdoor, free. AE, CB, DC, DISC, EC, ER, JCB, MC, V.

RESTAURANTS

El Maghreb
145 W Santa Clara St; tel 408/294-2243. Guadalupe Pkwy exit off CA 280. **Moroccan.** Exotic, romantic Moroccan atmosphere. Sit on low cushions or banquettes covered in jewel-toned velvet. Moorish mosaics, oriental carpets, desert murals cover the walls. Offers several multicourse dinners, which include three Moroccan salads, bastella (flaky pastry filled with chicken), couscous with vegetables, an entree, and more, all to be eaten with your fingers. **FYI:** Reservations recommended. Beer and wine only. **Open:** Mon–Sat 6–10pm. **Prices:** Prix fixe $15–$22. AE, CB, DC, DISC, MC, V. ৬

Emile's
545 S 2nd St (Downtown); tel 408/289-1960. Near William. **French.** Established by Swiss-born Emile Mooser in 1973, this South Bay institution has a wall full of the many awards it has won. An impressive, yet airy, metal sculpture provides dimmed lighting for romantic ambience throughout the dining room. In addition to fresh fish and game, the menu offers roasted rack of New Zealand lamb with garlic mashed potatoes; paella Margarita in a clay cocotte; and roasted, peppered pork tenderloin on Granny Smith apples and quince. **FYI:** Reservations recommended. **Open:** Lunch Fri 11:30am–2pm; dinner Tues–Sat 6–10pm. **Prices:** Main courses $22–$30; prix fixe $30. AE, CB, DC, DISC, ER, MC, V. ♥ VP ৬

★ Eulipia
374 S 1st St; tel 408/280-6161. Vine/Almaden exit off I-280. **Eclectic.** Artistically conceived restaurant with purple and bright yellow walls, a black-and-white diamond floor, and a raised wood platform. Versatile menu includes pasta, fresh seafood, poultry, lamb, steaks, pork chops, and "Truly Awesome Jumbalaya". **FYI:** Reservations recommended. **Open:** Lunch Tues–Fri 11am–3pm; dinner Tues–Sun 5pm–midnight. **Prices:** Main courses $8–$25. AE, CB, DC, DISC, MC, V. ৬

Gervais
In the Park Naglee Plaza, 1798 Park Ave; tel 408/275-8631. CA 880 N exit off CA 280. **French.** Warm country French dining spot makes guests feel welcome with its blue-and-white-tiled entry and frosted glass dividers. Entrees include homemade bouillabaisse, grilled fillet of lamb with fresh thyme and artichokes, grilled tournedos of white veal with sautéed shrimp in white wine. Chocolate, Grand Marnier, royal, and framboise soufflés. **FYI:** Reservations recommended. **Open:** Lunch Tues–Fri 11:30am–2pm; dinner Tues–Sat 5:30–10pm. **Prices:** Main courses $11–$25. AE, DC, MC, V. ৬

Le Papillon
410 Saratoga Ave; tel 408/296-3730. Saratoga Ave exit off I-280. **French.** Cranberry upholstered dining chairs contrast nicely with white wainscoting, gray rough-plastered walls, and gray tile. The chef augments modern French dishes with low-fat and low-cholesterol options on request, including grilled fish or chicken with sun-dried tomato. Entrees come with soup and salad. **FYI:** Reservations recommended. **Open:** Lunch Mon–Fri 11:30am–2:30pm; dinner Mon–Sat 5–10pm, Sun 5–9pm. **Prices:** Main courses $22–$27. AE, CB, DC, DISC, ER, MC, V. ♥

Les Saisons
In the Fairmont Hotel, 170 S Market St; tel 408/998-3950. Guadalupe Pkwy exit off US 101. **Continental/French.** Very posh restaurant hung with gold-framed paintings depicting the four seasons. A baby grand piano separates the dining room from the bar. Roasted Maine lobster with herbs; angel-hair pasta and vanilla sauce; fresh Santa Barbara abalone with tomatoes, capers, and herb sauce; herb-roasted double lamb chops; seared Moroccan spiced sea bass. **FYI:** Reservations recommended. Piano. Jacket required. **Open:** Daily 5:30–10:30pm. **Prices:** Main courses $25–$45. AE, DC, MC, V. ♥ ৬

Louisiana Territory
In the Pavilion, 150 S 1st St; tel 408/298-1000. Vine/Almaden exit off I-280. **Cajun/Creole.** Living up to its name, Louisiana Territory has New Orleans Mardi Gras and jazz murals by Taylor Blackwell lining the entrance stairway. Diners wear handfuls of beads to get in the mood to enjoy the strolling jazz musicians who enter around 7pm. Entrees include grilled chicken breast with béarnaise sauce over a slice of Canadian bacon with a sherry-mushroom demiglaze, blackened fish, shrimp creole or étoufée, shellfish bordelaise, eggplant with spicy bread stuffing, and pasta with sausage and shrimp. **FYI:** Reservations recommended. Jazz. **Open:** Lunch daily 11am–4pm; dinner daily 4–10pm. **Prices:** Main courses $13–$20. AE, DISC, MC, V. ৬

Palermo Ristorante Italiano
394 S 2nd St (Downtown); tel 408/297-0607. Near San Salvador. **Italian.** Diners step onto a stone-paved village street and are greeted by a full-size replica of a plumed horse pulling a cart. Serve yourself from another wagon offering antipasto selections, or order other appetizers, such as eggplant parmigiana. The menu offers 16 pastas, including bow-tie pasta with sausage sauce. Also, veal stuffed with cheese, ham, and salami, and rotisserie chicken. **FYI:** Reservations recommended. **Open:** Mon–Fri 11:30am–9:30pm, Sat–Sun 4–9:30pm. Closed Jan 1–7/July 2–9. **Prices:** Main courses $8–$16. AE, MC, V. ♥ 🍷 🍽 📷 🎨 ৬

Paolo's
In the River Park Plaza, 333 W San Carlos St; tel 408/294-2558. Vine/Almaden exit off CA 280. **Italian.** Features modern art on loan from a local gallery as well as views of the greenery of River Park. Organically raised produce and naturally raised meats, poultry, and game are used when possible. Try veal prosciutto or one of the pastas, such as ravioli with duck in cream sauce dusted with pistachios and

orange zest. **FYI:** Reservations recommended. **Open:** Lunch Mon–Fri 11am–2:30pm; dinner Mon–Sat 5:30–10pm. **Prices:** Main courses $11–$20; prix fixe $21. AE, DC, DISC, MC, V. 🖼️ &

Teske's Germania
255 N 1st St (Downtown); tel 408/292-0291. At Devine. **German.** Come for the great German food and unusual decor. The two dining rooms—the brick-and-wood Bavarian Room and the Victorian Room—are in two different 19th-century buildings. Favorite dishes include sauerbraten with homemade noodles and Wiener schnitzel with potato salad. Generously portioned dinners come with soup, salad, entree, dessert. **FYI:** Reservations recommended. Children's menu. **Open:** Lunch Mon–Fri 11am–2pm; dinner Mon–Sat 5–9:30pm. **Prices:** Main courses $13–$23. AE, CB, DC, DISC, MC, V. 🚝 ⛴️ 🖼️

ATTRACTIONS 🏛️

Winchester Mystery House
525 S Winchester Blvd; tel 408/247-2101. Begun in 1884, this house is the legacy of Sarah L Winchester, widow of the son of the famous rifle magnate. After the deaths of her husband and baby daughter, Mrs Winchester became convinced that continuous building would appease the spirits of those killed with Winchester repeaters. Construction went on at the house 24 hours a day, 7 days a week, for 38 years until her death in 1922. The red-roofed, stylized Victorian mansion contains 160 rooms and sprawls across a half-dozen acres. Doors that open onto blank walls, stairs that lead nowhere, and a window set into the floor are among the many unusual elements designed to confound the demons that the heiress believed were plaguing her.

Several rooms have been restored and furnished with period pieces. The hour-long tour visits 110 of the rooms, after which visitors can take a self-guided tour of the manicured gardens and visit the Winchester Historic Firearms and Antique Products Museum, which displays not only firearms, but also such items as knives, roller skates, tools, and flashlights manufactured by the Winchester company in the early 1900s. **Open:** Peak (Mem Day–Labor Day) daily 9am–8pm. Reduced hours off-season. **$$$$**

San Jose Museum of Art
110 S Market St; tel 408/294-2787. Exhibitions of regional and international art are presented here. Guided tours available. Free admission on first Thursday of each month. **Open:** Tues–Sun 10am–5pm, Thurs 10am–8pm. **$$$**

Egyptian Museum and Planetarium
In Rosicrucian Park, Park and Naglee Aves; tel 408/947-3636. Set amid beautiful gardens and buildings inspired by ancient Egyptian temples, and housed in a building patterned after the Temple of Amon at Karnak, the Egyptian Museum and Planetarium houses the largest collection of ancient Egyptian, Babylonian, Assyrian, and Sumerian artifacts on exhibit on the West Coast, including textiles, statuary, and art.

Highlights include an exhibit of everyday household items of the ancient Egyptians; a large collection of mummies that includes several cats, crocodiles, and a baboon, as well as humans; and guided tours through a full-size reproduction of an Egyptian nobleman's tomb (ca 2100 BC). The planetarium presents several star shows that emphasize both the scientific and cultural aspects of astronomy, which was very important to the people of ancient Egypt. Opened in 1936, this was one of the first planetariums in the United States. **Open:** Daily 9am–5pm; planetarium Mon–Fri hours vary (call for exact show times). **$$$**

Happy Hollow Park and Zoo
1300 Senter Rd; tel 408/295-8383 or 277-3000. Located in downtown San Jose's Kelley Park, Happy Hollow is a 12-acre family entertainment attraction featuring amusement rides, themed play areas, puppet theater, and picnic groves. The zoo displays 50 species of domestic, exotic, and endangered animals and features a hands-on contact area. Snack bars, gift shop. **Open:** Daily 10am–5pm. **$$**

Alum Rock Park
16240 Alum Rock Ave (CA 130); tel 408/259-5477. Located within the Alum Rock Canyon in the foothills of the Diablo Range, this park offers 700 acres of natural beauty with opportunities for hiking, horseback riding, bicycling along several miles of trails, picnicking, and more. Between 1890 and 1932 the park was a nationally recognized health spa, with 27 mineral springs. Today its emphasis is as a natural preserve; rangers give interpretive talks, and the visitor center, located in the mid-canyon area, has exhibits and services. **Open:** Daily 8am–half-hour after sunset **Free**

Lick Observatory
Mt Hamilton Rd; tel 408/274-5061. Owned and operated by the University of California at Santa Cruz, this working observatory, about an hour's drive from San Jose, offers exhibits and guided lectures to the public. Features a 120-inch reflecting telescope and a 36-inch telescope. Phone for public program schedule. **Open:** Daily 10am–5pm; guides available from 12:30pm. **Free**

San Juan Bautista

ATTRACTION 🏛️

San Juan Bautista State Historic Park
2nd and Washington Sts; tel 408/623-4881. Located next to the park is **Mission San Juan Bautista,** founded in 1797, the 15th established by the Franciscan order. Construction of the mission church, the largest of its kind in California, was begun in 1803, and despite damage from numerous earthquakes, it has been in continuous use since 1812. At one time

more than 1,000 Native Americans lived and worked at the mission, and more than 4,300 are buried in the old cemetery beside the northeast wall of the church. Parts of the mission can be toured and there are artifacts on display, but the buildings still belong to the Catholic Church and are technically not a part of the park. Today, the grounds are best known to movie buffs as the setting for some of the scariest scenes in Alfred Hitchcock's *Vertigo*.

Facing the plaza is the **Plaza Hotel** (1858), restored to its original appearance during the days when San Juan was an important stop on the stage route between Northern and Southern California. Its debut in January 1859 was widely advertised and the hotel quickly became famous for its fine food and drink.

Nearby is the **Plaza Stable** (1869), built to handle the influx of stagecoach and wagon traffic that characterized San Juan's busiest years. Restored to its 1870s appearance, it now houses an assortment of wagons and carriages, harnesses, and other related items. Behind it is the blacksmith's shop, displaying many tools used by the wagonwright.

Other buildings around the plaza include the **Plaza Hall,** site of many grand balls, public meetings, and traveling shows; the **Castro/Breen House,** an adobe building once owned by surivors of the Donner Party; and a short section of the original El Camino Real, the highway that connected all of the California missions and later served as a major stage and wagon road. **Open:** Daily 10am–4:30pm. **$**

San Juan Capistrano

The fabled meeting spot for migrating swallows each March (although in decreasing numbers), San Juan Capistrano is also the site of perhaps the most famous Southern California mission. The seventh of the Spanish chain of missions, the chapel built by Father Junípero Serra in 1776 still stands. **Information:** San Juan Capistrano Chamber of Commerce, 26711 Verdugo St, PO Box 1878, San Juan Capistrano 92673 (tel 714/493-4700).

MOTEL 🏨

📋📋 Best Western Capistrano Inn
27174 Ortega Hwy, 92675; tel 714/493-5661 or toll free 800/441-9438; fax 714/661-8293. CA 74 exit off I-5. Quiet location on a picturesque highway. Facility is clean and adequate. **Rooms:** 108 rms and effic. CI open/CO noon. Nonsmoking rms avail. **Amenities:** 🛁 🅰 🖥 A/C, satel TV. Some units w/terraces. Some rooms have microwaves. **Services:** 🛏 🐾 Complimentary full breakfast and happy hour are available weekdays. **Facilities:** 🏊 🚻 Whirlpool. **Rates (BB):** Peak (Mar–Sept) $68–$79 S or D; $74–$79 effic. Extra person $6. Children under age 13 stay free. Lower rates off-season. Parking: Outdoor, free. AE, CB, DC, DISC, ER, JCB, MC, V.

ATTRACTION 🏛

Mission San Juan Capistrano
Tel 714/248-2049. Located just west of I-5 Ortega Hwy exit. The 7th and most famous of California's missions, Mission San Juan was founded in 1776 by the Spanish Franciscan Friar Junípero Serra. The famous swallows of Capistrano depart traditionally on St Johns Day (Oct 23). They return to the mission on St Joseph's Day (Mar 19), having migrated some 6,000 miles from their native Argentina.

Self-guided tours of the mission include the Serra Chapel (1777), the oldest standing church in California; the Great Stone Church (1797), which collapsed in an 1812 earthquake; the padres' living quarters; Native American displays; and the North Corridor, where swallows' nests are visible at the western end of the building.

Living History Days are held the last Saturday of every month (Feb–Nov). Mission Visitor's Center; gift shop. **Open:** Daily 8:30am–5pm. **$$**

San Luis Obispo

One of the largest cities on the Central Coast, San Luis Obispo slows down in the summer when the students at California Polytechnic State University return home. It is then that San Luis Obispo has the feel of a Midwestern agricultural city, particularly every Thursday night, when the Farmers' Market is in action. **Information:** San Luis Obispo County Visitors & Conference Bureau, 1041 Chorro St #E, San Luis Obispo 93401 (tel 805/541-8000).

HOTELS 🏨

📋📋 Embassy Suites Hotel & Conference Center
333 Madonna Rd, 93405 (Central Coast Mall); tel 805/549-0800 or toll free 800/864-6000; fax 805/543-5273. 1 mi S of downtown. Madonna Rd exit off US 101, left on Madonna Rd. Located in a shopping mall, this building has an attractive pastel atrium lobby with lots of light, air, and plants. **Rooms:** 195 stes. CI 3pm/CO noon. Nonsmoking rms avail. Rooms facing the interior courtyard seem dark. Contemporary decor in variations of beige. **Amenities:** 🛁 🅰 🖥 A/C, cable TV w/movies, refrig, voice mail. **Services:** ✗ 🚌 🛎 Free cocktails. **Facilities:** 🏊 🍴 550 🚻 1 restaurant, 1 bar, whirlpool, washer/dryer. **Rates (BB):** Peak (May–Sept) $109–$129 S; $119–$139 D. Extra person $10. Children under age 12 stay free. Lower rates off-season. Parking: Outdoor, free. AE, CB, DC, DISC, MC, V.

📋📋📋 Holiday Inn Express
1800 Monterey St, 93401; tel 805/544-8600 or toll free 800/822-8601; fax 805/541-4698. 1 mi N of downtown San Luis Obispo. Monterey St exit off US 101 S; Grand Ave exit off US 101 N. Eye-catching, well-maintained terra-cotta/stucco building with a turquoise-colored trimmed roof. **Rooms:** 100 rms and stes. CI 3pm/CO noon. Nonsmoking rms avail.

Attractive standard rooms. Spacious town-house units feature bedrooms on second level, although some face brick walls. **Amenities:** 📞 📠 A/C, cable TV w/movies. Town-house units have two TVs, wet bars, refrigerators, sofas, and hairdryers. **Services:** 🍴 🖼 🛎 Meals at adjacent Mexican restaurant (Izzy Ortega's) can be charged to rooms. **Facilities:** 🛗 50 ♿ 1 restaurant (lunch and dinner only), 1 bar, whirlpool. Breakfast area has a bright, airy feeling, and a big-screen TV. **Rates (CP):** Peak (mid-Mar–Sept) $80–$90 S or D; $110–$120 ste. Extra person $10. Children under age 12 stay free. Lower rates off-season. Parking: Outdoor, free. Hearst Castle packages avail. AE, DC, DISC, JCB, MC, V.

📑📑📑 Madonna Inn

100 Madonna Rd, 93405; tel 805/543-3000 or toll free 800/543-9666; fax 805/543-1800. Madonna Rd exit off US 101. A longtime roadside attraction, visible from US 101. It's one of a kind, great fun, and has reasonable rates. **Rooms:** 109 rms and stes. CI 4pm/CO noon. No smoking. Each room displays a different theme. The "Caveman" has a rock shower and leopard-print bedspread. The two-story "Pick and Shovel" has a huge living room, red vinyl couch, fireplace, banistered staircase, and pick-and-shovel lamp. **Amenities:** 📞 A/C, cable TV. Some units w/terraces, some w/fireplaces. **Services:** 🍴 🛎 **Facilities:** 500 2 restaurants (*see* "Restaurants" below), 1 bar. Gift shop, bakery, coffee shop/soda fountain, and fine dining room. **Rates:** Peak (Mem Day–Labor Day) $77 S; $87–$145 D; $130–$210 ste. Extra person $6–$12. Children under age 18 stay free. Lower rates off-season. Parking: Outdoor, free. MC, V.

📑📑📑 Quality Suites

1631 Monterey St, 93401; tel 805/541-5001 or toll free 800/221-2222; fax 805/546-9475. ¼ mi N of downtown. Monterey St exit off US 101. Nice, quiet, parklike setting, with lovely lobby and handsomely furnished library. **Rooms:** 138 stes. CI 2pm/CO noon. Nonsmoking rms avail. Big suites are nicely furnished, some with sofas, queen-size beds, and a desk. **Amenities:** 📞 A/C, cable TV, refrig, VCR, CD/tape player. Some units w/terraces. **Services:** 🍴 🖼 🛎 **Facilities:** 🛗 30 ♿ 1 bar, whirlpool, washer/dryer. Gift shop. **Rates (BB):** Peak (Mar–Oct) $133 ste. Extra person $10. Children under age 18 stay free. Min stay special events. Lower rates off-season. Parking: Outdoor, free. AE, DC, DISC, MC, V.

MOTELS

📑📑 Howard Johnson Lodge

1585 Calle Joaquin, 93405; tel 805/544-5300 or toll free 800/654-2000; fax 805/541-2823. 4 mi S of downtown. Los Osos Valley Rd exit off US 101. Convenient to the highway, but some rooms have nice views of the trees. Good value. **Rooms:** 64 rms. CI 2pm/CO 11am. Nonsmoking rms avail. Rooms are basic and need updating. **Amenities:** 📞 A/C, cable TV w/movies. All units w/terraces. **Services:** 🖼 🛎 🐾 Children's program. **Facilities:** 🛗 ♿ 1 restaurant, 1 bar,

washer/dryer. **Rates:** Peak (May–Oct) $59–$99 S or D. Children under age 18 stay free. Lower rates off-season. Parking: Outdoor, free. AE, CB, DC, DISC, JCB, MC, V.

📑📑 Lamplighter Inn

1604 Monterey St, 93401; tel 805/547-7777 or toll free 800/547-7787; fax 805/547-7787. ½ mi N of downtown. Monterey St exit off US 101. Cheerful, clean, well-kept two-story motel with 16 rooms in main building and 23 additional units across the street. Immediately adjacent to main building is a two-story house with kitchen, porch, and two studio accommodations, one of which is poolside. **Rooms:** 41 rms, stes, and effic; 1 cottage/villa. CI 2pm/CO 11am. Nonsmoking rms avail. Rooms and suites in main building have been handsomely renovated, and the new, nicely-tiled baths have large showers. Units across the street have older furnishings, but are gradually being upgraded. Accommodations with up to four beds available. **Amenities:** 📞 📠 A/C, cable TV w/movies, dataport, voice mail. 1 unit w/whirlpool. King spa room features a two-person whirlpool. Some rooms and suites offer VCRs, nice robes, wet bars, refrigerators, and microwaves. **Services:** 🛎 **Facilities:** 🛗 Whirlpool, washer/dryer. Breakfast area in lobby. **Rates (CP):** Peak (Aug) $45–$89 S; $49–$105 D; $59–$229 ste; $59–$229 effic; $59–$229 cottage/villa. Extra person $3–$5. Children under age 8 stay free. Lower rates off-season. Parking: Outdoor, free. AE, DISC, MC, V.

📑📑 Motel 6

1433 Calle Joaquin, 93401; tel 805/549-9595; fax 805/544-2826. 1 mi S of downtown. Los Osos exit off US 101, head west. Standard motel that offers cleanliness, easy highway access, and good value. **Rooms:** 86 rms. CI open/CO noon. Nonsmoking rms avail. Clean, with fresh white paint and new bedspreads. Some rooms for deaf and hard of hearing guests. **Amenities:** 📞 A/C, cable TV w/movies. **Services:** 🛎 🐾 Morning coffee in lobby. Free local calls; no motel charge on long distance. **Facilities:** 🛗 ♿ Washer/dryer. **Rates:** Peak (May–Sept) $32 S; $36 D. Extra person $4. Children under age 17 stay free. Lower rates off-season. Parking: Outdoor, free. AE, CB, DC, DISC, MC, V.

📑📑 Olive Tree Inn Best Western

1000 Olive St, 93405 (Downtown); tel 805/544-2800 or toll free 800/777-5847. CA 1/Morro Bay exit off US 101 N; Santa Rosa St exit off US 101 S. Standard two-story motel; near the freeway, but quiet. **Rooms:** 38 rms, stes, and effic. CI 2pm/CO 11am. Nonsmoking rms avail. Spartan rooms with basic motel furnishings. Some rooms have lovely porches overlooking a creek. **Amenities:** 📞 Cable TV. No A/C. Some units w/terraces, 1 w/fireplace. Six suites have kitchen facilities. **Services:** 🖼 🛎 🐾 **Facilities:** 🛗 ♿ 1 restaurant (bkfst and lunch only), sauna, washer/dryer. **Rates:** Peak (June–Sept 15) $55–$125 S; $59–$135 D; $89–$175 ste; $79–$150 effic. Extra person $4. Min stay special events. Lower rates off-season. Parking: Outdoor, free. AE, CB, DC, DISC, ER, JCB, MC, V.

≣≣ San Luis Obispo Travelodge

1825 Monterey St, 93401; tel 805/543-5110 or toll free 800/255-3050; fax 805/543-3406. Monterey exit off US 101. Clean motel-style property on motel row, close to restaurants. **Rooms:** 39 rms. CI noon/CO 11am. Nonsmoking rms avail. Rooms have new comforters and drapes. Clean bathrooms feature attractive wallpaper. Units in back offer nice views of the mountains. **Amenities:** 🛏 📞 📺 A/C, cable TV w/movies. **Services:** 🍽 🏊 **Facilities:** 🅿 **Rates:** Peak (mid-June–mid-Sept) $48–$99 S or D. Extra person $5. Children under age 17 stay free. Lower rates off-season. Parking: Outdoor, free. AE, DISC, MC, V.

INN

≣≣≣ Garden Street Inn

1212 Garden St, 93401 (Downtown); tel 805/545-9802. Marsh exit off US 101. A stunning example of Italianate/Queen Anne/Victorian architecture, built in 1887 with high ceilings and a grand staircase. Unsuitable for children under 16. **Rooms:** 13 rms and stes. CI 3pm/CO 11am. No smoking. Charming rooms and suites are named after artists, writers, and famous personalities. All have antiques, sinks with washstands, dressing tables, and 14-foot ceilings. The aptly named Lovers Suite features a Picasso print of the same name, a loveseat, and vintage chandelier. The Walden Room, overlooking a large deck, is elegantly rustic with bentwood chairs. Some baths offer clawfoot tub/shower combinations. **Amenities:** A/C, CD/tape player, bathrobes. No phone or TV. Some units w/terraces, some w/fireplaces, some w/whirlpools. Telephones, alarm clocks, and hairdryers available on request. **Services:** 🔑 Masseur, wine/sherry served. Lovely breakfasts can be delivered to your room or served in the morning room, with its original stained-glass windows. Evening wine and cheese. Well-stocked library. **Facilities:** 🔟 Guest lounge. Living room with piano. **Rates (BB):** Peak (Mar–Nov) $90–$160 S or D; $140 ste. Min stay wknds. Lower rates off-season. AE, CB, DC, MC, V.

RESTAURANTS 🍴

✴ Apple Farm Restaurant

2015 Monterey St; tel 805/544-6100. Monterey St exit off US 101. **American.** A popular country-style family restaurant decked out in oak furniture and Tiffany lamps. Cuisine includes apple sausage, eggs, and biscuits for breakfast; sandwiches, salads, and pot pie for lunch; roast turkey, prime rib, and pan-fried trout for dinner. **FYI:** Reservations recommended. Children's menu. Beer and wine only. **Open:** Peak (Apr–Sept) breakfast Mon–Fri 7–11:30am, Sat–Sun 7am–noon; lunch Mon–Fri 11:30am–5pm, Sat–Sun noon–5pm; dinner Sun–Thurs 5–9:30pm, Fri–Sat 4:30–10pm. **Prices:** Main courses $10–$17. AE, DISC, MC, V. 🖼 ♿

✴ Gold Rush Dining Room

In the Madonna Inn, 100 Madonna Rd; tel 805/543-3000. Exit off US 101. **American.** A coastal California landmark for decades; dining and dancing here is an event. The ambience is romantic in an overdone way. Nearly everything is pink and gold, with lots of hearts and flowers and chandeliers. The cuisine emphasizes steaks and prime rib as well as seafood dishes, including lobster, salmon, and abalone. Homemade desserts from the pastry shop. **FYI:** Reservations accepted. Dancing. Children's menu. **Open:** Daily 5:30–10pm. **Prices:** Main courses $7–$15; prix fixe $16–$23. MC, V. ♥ 🍷 🖼

ATTRACTION 🏛

Mission San Luis Obispo de Tolosa

782 Monterey St; tel 805/543-6850. Founded by Father Junípero Serra in 1772, California's fifth mission was built with adobe bricks by Chumash Indians. The padres' quarters have been turned into an excellent museum chronicling both Native American and missionary life through all eras of the mission's use. Mission Plaza, a pretty garden with brick paths and park benches fronting a meandering creek, still functions as San Luis Obispo's town square. It is the focal point for local festivities and activities, from live concerts to poetry readings and dance and theater productions. **Open:** Peak (Mem Day–Labor Day) daily 9am–5pm. Reduced hours off-season. $

San Marino

See Pasadena

San Mateo

Busy and urban at the base of the San Mateo Bridge which spans San Francisco Bay, San Mateo is also the gateway to extensive natural areas and parks in the Santa Cruz Mountains to the west. San Mateo Bridge spans San Francisco Bay. Coyote Point Museum, which juts into the bay, features the natural history of the area. **Information:** San Mateo Chamber of Commerce, 1730 S El Camino Real, 2nd Floor, San Mateo 94402 (tel 415/341-5679).

HOTELS 🏨

≣≣≣ Dunfey Hotel

1770 S Amphlett Blvd, 94402; tel 415/573-7661 or toll free 800/843-6664; fax 415/573-0533. Delaware exit off CA 92 E. Turn left, then right on Concar. Reminiscent of a Tudor-style castle, this place is popular with tour groups, conventions, and business travelers. **Rooms:** 270 rms and stes. CI 3pm/CO 1pm. Nonsmoking rms avail. Rooms have a variety of floor plans. **Amenities:** 🛏 📞 A/C, satel TV w/movies. Some units w/terraces. **Services:** ✕ 🚗 📠 🍽 🏊 Car-rental desk, babysitting. **Facilities:** 🅿 🅿700 ♿ 1 restaurant, 2 bars (1 w/entertainment), games rm, washer/dryer. Large lawn area for picnics. **Rates (CP):** $105–$140 S; $110–$150 D; $175–$295 ste. Extra person $15. Children under age 18 stay free. Parking: Outdoor, free. AE, CB, DC, DISC, MC, V.

≣≣≣ Residence Inn by Marriott

2000 Winward Way, 94404; tel 415/574-4700 or toll free 800/331-3131; fax 415/572-9084. Mariners Island Bend exit off CA 92. More like apartments than a hotel, this property, made up of detached units, is set up to accommodate stays longer than one night. Quiet, considering proximity to freeway. **Rooms:** 159 effic. CI 3pm/CO noon. Nonsmoking rms avail. Good furnishings. **Amenities:** 🛁 📺 A/C, satel TV, refrig, voice mail. No phone. Some units w/fireplaces. Full kitchen in each unit. **Services:** 🚐 🖨 🧺 🍸 Price includes free hors d'oeuvres 5–7pm. Grocery shopping and delivery service. **Facilities:** 🏋 🏊 ⁴⁵ 🚹 Basketball, volleyball, playground, washer/dryer. **Rates (CP):** $135–$155 effic. Parking: Outdoor, free. Higher rates for one-night occupancies; rates decrease with longer stays. AE, DC, DISC, MC, V.

≣≣≣ Villa Quality Hotel

4000 S El Camino Real, 94403; tel 415/341-0966 or toll free 800/341-2345; fax 415/573-0164. Hillside Blvd exit off US 101 to El Camino Real; turn left. The decor is slightly dated, but this family-run hotel has a nice ambience and a caring staff. **Rooms:** 286 rms and stes. CI 3pm/CO 1pm. Nonsmoking rms avail. **Amenities:** 📺 🛁 📺 A/C, cable TV. Some units w/terraces. **Services:** 🍽 🔑 🚐 🏊 🧺 🍸 Car-rental desk, masseur, babysitting. **Facilities:** 🏋 🏓 ⁶⁰⁰ 💻 🚹 1 restaurant, 1 bar (w/entertainment), beauty salon. 24-hour coffee shop. 24-hour full-service Kinko's copy shop across the street. **Rates (CP):** $79–$149 S; $89–$159 D; $99–$189 ste. Extra person $8. Children under age 18 stay free. Parking: Indoor/outdoor, free. AE, CB, DC, DISC, EC, ER, JCB, MC, V.

RESTAURANT 🍴

231 Ellsworth

231 S Ellsworth Ave; tel 415/347-7231. 3rd Ave W exit off US 101; pass 5 lights and turn right on Ellsworth. **French.** Understatement and attention to detail are hallmarks of this award-winning, contemporary French restaurant. Teal and peach southwestern decor and modern art create a romantic ambience at night. Fresh seafood is a favorite. The owner grows his own mushrooms, which crop up in risotto and other dishes. Specialties include scallops with fennel and tomato confit. Also, grilled bass, braised duck, veal sweetbreads. **FYI:** Reservations recommended. Beer and wine only. **Open:** Lunch Mon–Fri 11:30am–2pm; dinner Mon–Sat 5:30–9:30pm. **Prices:** Main courses $17–$24; prix fixe $30. AE, CB, DC, MC, V. ♥ 🚹

ATTRACTION 🏛

Coyote Point Museum

1651 Coyote Point Dr; tel 415/342-7755. Located in a scenic bayside park, the museum seeks to foster interest in the environment and ways to preserve it. Environmental Hall displays feature ecological zones such as baylands, coast, and redwood forest. A mini-aquarium and working bee hive may be seen. A separate wildlife habitat houses mammals, birds, snakes, and amphibians native to the Bay Area, and a walk-through aviary. **Open:** Tues–Sat 10am–5pm, Sun noon–5pm. $

San Pedro

See also Long Beach, Seal Beach

San Pedro is the center of activity for the Port of Los Angeles, the world's largest man-made harbor and one of the busiest ports in the world. The city is also home to Cabrillo Marine Aquarium, the Los Angeles Maritime Museum, and the waterfront Ports O'Call Village. **Information:** San Pedro Peninsula Chamber of Commerce, 390 W 7th St, San Pedro 90731 (tel 310/832-7272).

HOTELS 🏨

≣≣ Best Western Sunrise Hotel at Ports O'Call

525 S Harbor Blvd, 90731; tel 310/548-1080 or toll free 800/356-9609; fax 310/519-0380. Harbor Blvd exit off I-110. Somewhat dated, basic hotel. Not noisy, but a steady flow of traffic outside. **Rooms:** 103 rms and stes. CI 2pm/CO noon. Nonsmoking rms avail. Rooms are dark and drab, and need updating. **Amenities:** 📺 🛁 📺 🍴 A/C, cable TV w/movies, refrig. Some units w/terraces. **Services:** 🍸 Twice-daily maid svce, babysitting. **Facilities:** 🏋 ¹⁵⁰ 🚹 Whirlpool, washer/dryer. **Rates (BB):** $60 S; $68 D; $99 ste. Children under age 12 stay free. Parking: Outdoor, free. AE, CB, DC, DISC, MC, V.

≣≣≣ DoubleTree Hotel–Los Angeles World Port

2800 Via Cabrillo Marina, 90731; tel 310/514-3344; fax 310/514-8945. Harbor Blvd exit off I-110 S. Located right next to the marina. **Rooms:** 226 rms and stes. Executive level. CI 3pm/CO 1pm. Nonsmoking rms avail. Rooms are spacious, clean, and attractive. **Amenities:** 📺 🛁 A/C, cable TV w/movies. 1 unit w/minibar, some w/terraces. **Services:** ✕ 🏊 🍸 Babysitting. **Facilities:** 🏋 🚲 △ 🎿 🏊 ⚓ 🏓 ⁷⁵⁰ 🚹 2 restaurants, 2 bars (w/entertainment), sauna, whirlpool, beauty salon. **Rates (CP):** $158 S or D; $225 ste. Extra person $10. Children under age 18 stay free. Parking: Outdoor, free. AE, CB, DC, DISC, MC, V.

≣≣≣ Radisson Los Angeles Harbor Hotel

601 S Palos Verdes St, 90731; tel 310/519-8200; fax 310/519-8421. Harbor Blvd exit off I-110; go south at 6th St. Looks a bit industrial on the outside but is charming and comfortable within. **Rooms:** 244 rms and stes. Executive level. CI 3pm/CO noon. Nonsmoking rms avail. Clean and comfortable rooms are decorated in rose pastel tones. **Amenities:** 📺 🛁 📺 A/C, cable TV w/movies. Some units

w/terraces. **Services:** 🍽 ☎ VP 🖨 ⌫ Car-rental desk, babysitting. **Facilities:** 🏊 🏋 1000 ⛄ 1 restaurant (*see* "Restaurants" below), 1 bar (w/entertainment), spa, sauna, steam rm, whirlpool, washer/dryer. **Rates:** $109 S; $119 D; $179 ste. Extra person $10. Children under age 17 stay free. Parking: Indoor/outdoor, $1–$5/day. AE, CB, DC, DISC, JCB, MC, V.

MOTEL

🏨 Vagabond Inn San Pedro
215 S Gaffey St, 90731; tel 310/831-8911 or toll free 800/522-1555; fax 310/831-2649. Gaffey St exit off I-110. Clean, but could use improved maintenance and better soundproofing of rooms. **Rooms:** 72 rms. CI noon/CO noon. Nonsmoking rms avail. **Amenities:** 🛁 🍷 🍳 A/C, cable TV w/movies, refrig. **Services:** ⌫ 🛎 Room service from Denny's restaurant next door. **Facilities:** 🏊 **Rates (CP):** $39–$50 S; $43–$60 D. Extra person $5. Children under age 18 stay free. Parking: Outdoor, free. 10th night free. AE, CB, DC, DISC, MC, V.

RESTAURANTS 🍴

Madeo Ristorante–San Pedro
295 Whaler's Walk; tel 310/521-5333. Harbor Blvd exit off I-110. **Italian.** A little sterile-looking, but good for a business lunch. Menu items include fish of the day, roast veal, a large selection of pasta, and salads. Antipasti table at lunch. **FYI:** Reservations recommended. Piano. Dress code. **Open:** Lunch Mon–Fri 11:30am–2pm; dinner daily 5–10pm. **Prices:** Main courses $10–$20. AE, MC, V. 🎹 💟 ⛄

Meridian 1050
1050 Nagoya Way; tel 310/514-1050. Harbor Blvd exit off I-110. **Californian/Continental.** This place has a classy feel, with an art deco design in black, white, and gray with yellow accents, fresh flowers, and lovely view of the harbor. Daily seafood specials, wide selection of fresh salads. Banquet facilities can seat as many as 280 people. **FYI:** Reservations recommended. Jazz/piano. Children's menu. Dress code. **Open:** Lunch Mon–Fri 11am–2:30pm; dinner Mon–Sat 5:30–10pm, Sun 5–10pm; brunch Sun 10:30am–2pm. **Prices:** Main courses $8–$20. AE, DC, MC, V. 🌊 🏔 💟 ⛄

Moonraker
In Radisson Los Angeles Harbor Hotel, 601 S Palos Verdes St; tel 310/519-8200. Harbor Blvd exit off I-110. **Continental.** Festive family restaurant with pastel colors and an Asian theme. The menu is truly eclectic, offering Italian, Chinese, and American dishes. **FYI:** Reservations accepted. **Open:** Breakfast daily 6–10:30am; lunch daily 11:30am–2pm; dinner daily 5–10pm. **Prices:** Main courses $12–$16. AE, DC, DISC, MC, V. VP ⛄

San Rafael

The largest city in secluded, sedate Marin County, San Rafael is the setting for the strange, whimsical Marin County Civic Center designed by Frank Lloyd Wright. **Information:** San Rafael Chamber of Commerce, 817 Mission Ave, San Rafael 94901-3240 (tel 415/454-4163).

HOTELS 🏨

🏨🏨🏨 Embassy Suites
101 McInnis Pkwy, 94903 (Civic Center); tel 415/499-9222 or toll free 800/EMBASSY in the US, 800/458-5848 in Canada; fax 415/499-9268. 3 mi N of San Rafael. N San Pedro Rd exit off US 101 N; Freitas Pkwy exit off US 101 S. **Rooms:** 235 stes. CI 3pm/CO 1pm. Nonsmoking rms avail. **Amenities:** 🛁 🍷 🍳 A/C, cable TV w/movies, refrig, VCR. All units w/minibars. **Services:** ✗ ☎ 🚐 🖨 ⌫ Car-rental desk. **Facilities:** 🏊 🏋 160 💻 1 restaurant, 1 bar, beauty salon, washer/dryer. **Rates (BB):** $149–$199 ste. Extra person $15. Children under age 12 stay free. Parking: Outdoor, free. AE, CB, DC, DISC, JCB, MC, V.

🏨🏨 Wyndham Garden Hotel
1010 Northgate Dr, 94903; tel 415/479-8800 or toll free 800/231-2911; fax 415/479-2342. Terra Linda/Freitas Pkwy exit off US 101; go west. Located close to the highway and across from the Northgate mall, this is a pleasant full-service hotel that caters primarily to business travelers. Now under new management, it's slated for total renovation. **Rooms:** 235 rms and stes. CI 3pm/CO noon. Nonsmoking rms avail. Many rooms have recently been refurbished though decor is unimaginative. Rooms facing the pool have nicest views. **Amenities:** 🛁 🍷 🍳 A/C, satel TV, dataport. **Services:** ✗ 🚐 🖨 ⌫ Car-rental desk. **Facilities:** 🏊 200 ⛄ 1 restaurant, 1 bar, whirlpool. Garden courtyard is popular for weddings. **Rates:** Peak (June–Sept) $99–$109 S; $109–$149 D; $99 ste. Lower rates off-season. Parking: Outdoor, free. AE, MC, V.

MOTEL

🏨🏨 Villa Inn
1600 Lincoln Ave, 94901; tel 415/456-4975 or toll free 800/424-4777; fax 415/456-1520. Lincoln Ave exit off US 101 S; Central San Rafael exit off US 101 N. Family run for 23 years, this motel is maintained with pride. Pleasant lobby with floral-print sofa and a good selection of sightseeing brochures. **Rooms:** 60 rms and effic. CI noon/CO noon. No smoking. Floral bedspreads paired with newish carpeting. **Amenities:** 🛁 A/C, cable TV, refrig. **Services:** ✗ ⌫ 🛎 Twice-daily maid svce. **Facilities:** 🏊 60 ⛄ 1 restaurant, 1 bar, whirlpool, washer/dryer. Big glass-topped pool with Jacuzzi open Apr–Oct. Extremely pleasant Cafe Villa serves huge family-style portions of Basque dishes, very reasonably priced. **Rates (CP):** Peak (May–Sept) $64–$67 S; $69–$76 D;

$72 effic. Extra person $5. Children under age 18 stay free. Lower rates off-season. Parking: Outdoor, free. AE, CB, DC, DISC, MC, V.

San Ramon

San Ramon is among the burgeoning new bedroom communities in Contra Costa County, east of the San Leandro Hills. **Information:** San Ramon Chamber of Commerce, 2355 San Ramon Valley Blvd #101, San Ramon 94583 (tel 510/831-9500).

HOTELS

≣≣≣ Residence Inn by Marriott

1071 Market Place, 94583; tel 510/277-9292 or toll free 800/331-3131; fax 510/277-0687. Bollinger Canyon Rd exit off I-680. Attractive town house–like complex located in suburban business park. **Rooms:** 106 stes and effic. CI 3pm/CO noon. Nonsmoking rms avail. Most units have sofas that convert into beds. **Amenities:** A/C, refrig, voice mail. Some units w/fireplaces. VCR rentals available. **Services:** X Grocery shopping service. Complimentary wine, beer, and snacks served Mon–Fri 5–7pm; Complimentary barbecue Wednesday nights during summer. **Facilities:** Basketball, whirlpool, washer/dryer. Local gym accessible for a fee. Sport court for tennis, volleyball, and paddle tennis. Board games available for kids. **Rates (CP):** $139–$179 ste; $139–$179 effic. Children under age 18 stay free. Parking: Outdoor, free. AE, CB, DC, DISC, JCB, MC, V.

≣≣≣ San Ramon Marriott

2600 Bishop Dr, 94583; tel 510/867-9200 or toll free 800/228-9290; fax 510/830-9326. Bollinger Canyon Rd exit of I-680. Spacious, comfortable hotel in business-park district. Large lawn in back has a patio with tables and chairs. **Rooms:** 368 rms and stes. Executive level. CI 3pm/CO noon. Nonsmoking rms avail. **Amenities:** A/C, satel TV w/movies, dataport, voice mail. Some units w/terraces. All rooms have irons and ironing boards. Suites have coffeemakers and complete audio systems. **Services:** X VP Babysitting. Free valet parking for guests with disabilities. **Facilities:** 1 restaurant, 1 bar, sauna, whirlpool, washer/dryer. **Rates:** $114–$124 S or D; $200–$500 ste. Children under age 18 stay free. Parking: Outdoor, free. Special weekend rates. AE, CB, DC, DISC, JCB, MC, V.

San Simeon

San Simeon began as a whaling and shipping port, and its long pier was later used to haul building supplies and works of art to Hearst Castle, enthroned above the gently rolling coastal hills. **Information:** San Simeon Chamber of Commerce, PO Box 1, San Simeon 93452 (tel 805/927-3500 or toll free 800/342-5613).

MOTELS

≣≣≣ Best Western Cavalier Oceanfront Resort

9415 Hearst Dr, 93452 (San Simeon); tel 805/927-4688 or toll free 800/826-8168; fax 805/927-0497. Hearst Dr exit off CA 1. A great location, on the beach near Hearst Castle, with terrific ocean views. A good value. **Rooms:** 90 rms. CI 4pm/CO noon. Nonsmoking rms avail. Rooms are all oversized, very clean, and have ocean views. **Amenities:** Cable TV w/movies, refrig, VCR, voice mail. No A/C. All units w/minibars, some w/terraces, some w/fireplaces. Wet bar. **Services:** X **Facilities:** 2 restaurants, 1 beach (ocean), whirlpool, washer/dryer. Video store, gift shop, Italian restaurant. **Rates:** Peak (May 23–Sept 1) $65–$155 S or D. Extra person $6. Min stay wknds. Lower rates off-season. Parking: Outdoor, free. AE, CB, DC, DISC, ER, JCB, MC, V.

≣≣ Best Western Green Tree Inn

9450 Castillo Dr, 93452; tel 805/927-4691 or toll free 800/992-9240, 800/231-6461 in CA; fax 805/927-1473. Pico St exit off US 1. Standard two-story motel. Miniature golf across the street. **Rooms:** 117 rms, stes, and effic. CI 3pm/CO noon. Nonsmoking rms avail. Many rooms were recently repainted and have new carpets and bedspreads. Baths have separate vanity areas. **Amenities:** A/C, cable TV w/movies. Some units w/terraces, some w/fireplaces. Suites have two phones. **Services:** Fax and copy services available. Complimentary newspapers. Continental breakfast served in atrium lobby. Pet fee $10. **Facilities:** Games rm, whirlpool, washer/dryer. Skylit indoor pool and spa, plus coin-operated pool table and video games. **Rates (CP):** Peak (June–Sept) $99 S; $114 D; $135–$189 ste; $135–$189 effic. Extra person $10. Children under age 17 stay free. Min stay special events. Lower rates off-season. Parking: Outdoor, free. Hearst Castle ticket packages avail. AE, DC, DISC, MC, V.

ATTRACTION

Hearst Castle

CA 1; tel toll free 800/444-4445. William Randolph Hearst left an astounding monument to wealth on a hill called La Cuesta Encantada (The Enchanted Hill). The mansion, which was donated to the state by the Hearst family in 1958, is now administered by the California Department of Parks and Recreation as the Hearst–San Simeon State Historical Monument.

The focal point of today's estate is the incredible **Casa Grande,** a sprawling mansion with more than 100 rooms filled with priceless art and antiques: Flemish tapestries, 15th-century Gothic fireplaces, intricately carved 16th-century Spanish and 18th-century Italian ceilings, a 16th-century

Florentine bedstead, Renaissance paintings, and innumerable other treasures. The Doge's Suite was reserved for the house's most important guests, among them Winston Churchill and Calvin Coolidge. The library contains over 5,000 volumes, including many rare editions, as well as one of the world's greatest collections of Greek vases.

There are also two swimming pools: a Byzantine-inspired indoor pool with intricate mosaic work surrounded by replicas, in Carrara marble, of the most famous statues of antiquity; and the Greco-Roman Neptune outdoor pool, flanked by Etruscan-style marble colonnades and surrounded by more Carrara statuary, considered one of the mansion's most memorable features.

The mansion can be visited only by **guided tour**. Four separate tours are offered on a daily basis, each lasting almost two hours. They include some of the gardens as well as the outdoor and indoor pools. Tours cover about 1½ miles and include between 150 and 300 steps (visitors confined to wheelchairs can make special arrangements by calling 805/927-2020). Tour I, recommended for the first-time visitor, includes the gardens, a guest house, and the ground floor of the main house—including the movie theater where Hearst home movies are shown. Tours are conducted daily, beginning at 8:20am and continuing every 20 minutes until 3pm. **$$$$**

Santa Ana

The seat of Orange County, in a rich agricultural area, fast-growing Santa Ana is a center for light manufacturing in the large Anaheim–Santa Ana–Garden Grove metropolitan area. **Information:** Santa Ana Chamber of Commerce, 856 N Ross St, PO Box 205, Santa Ana 92702 (tel 714/541-5353).

HOTELS 🏨

▆▐ Courtyard by Marriott
3002 S Harbor Blvd, 92704; tel 714/545-1001 or toll free 800/321-2211; fax 714/545-8439. Harbor Blvd N exit off I-405. Basic, clean, and in a convenient location, but not quite up to similar Marriott properties' level. **Rooms:** 145 rms and stes. CI 3pm/CO 1pm. Nonsmoking rms avail. Standard, with basic furnishings. **Amenities:** 🛁 🕭 📺 A/C, cable TV w/movies. Some units w/terraces. **Services:** 🛏 🗘 Car-rental desk. **Facilities:** 🛠 💪 25 🔥 1 restaurant (bkfst and dinner only), 1 bar, whirlpool, washer/dryer. **Rates:** Peak (June–Sept) $69 S or D; $89 ste. Lower rates off-season. Parking: Outdoor, free. AE, CB, DC, DISC, JCB, MC, V.

▆▐ Radisson Suite Hotel
2720 Hotel Terrace Dr, 92705; tel 714/556-3838 or toll free 800/333-3333; fax 714/241-1008. Dyer exit off CA 55. Good for business travelers visiting nearby executive parks. **Rooms:** 122 stes. CI 3pm/CO noon. Nonsmoking rms avail. Rooms have separate living and sleeping areas. Nicely furnished with marblelike nightstands. **Amenities:** 🛁 🕭 📺 A/C,

cable TV w/movies, refrig. **Services:** ✕ 🚐 🖨 🗘 Babysitting. **Facilities:** 🛠 💪 8 🔥 1 bar, whirlpool. Although the pool is small, it is surrounded by palm trees and the ambience is pleasing. **Rates (BB):** Peak (June–Aug) $130–$140 ste. Extra person $10. Children under age 18 stay free. Lower rates off-season. Parking: Outdoor, free. AE, CB, DC, DISC, JCB, MC, V.

RESTAURANTS 🍽

Antonello
In South Coast Village Shopping Center, 1611 Sunflower; tel 714/751-7153. Bristol St N exit off I-405. **Italian.** Intimate and romantic Mediterranean decor designed to create the feeling of walking through the streets of Italy. A classical Italian menu with fresh fish, pastas, and specials daily. Reservations required. **FYI:** Reservations recommended. Jacket required. **Open:** Lunch Mon–Fri 11:30am–2pm; dinner Mon–Thurs 5:45–10pm, Fri–Sat 5:45–11pm. **Prices:** Main courses $12–$28. AE, DC, MC, V. ❤ 𝐕𝐏 🔥

Favori
3502 W 1st St; tel 714/531-6838. Harbor Blvd exit off I-405. **French/Vietnamese.** Country French decor with lots of fresh flowers. Menu offers a full range of French entrees along with a wide selection of Vietnamese dishes. **FYI:** Reservations recommended. Beer and wine only. **Open:** Daily 11am–10pm. **Prices:** Main courses $3–$12. DISC, MC, V.

♣ Gustaf Anders
In South Coast Village Shopping Center, 1651 Sunflower Ave; tel 714/668-1737. Bear St side. **Californian/Scandinavian.** Located in a quiet shopping plaza, this restaurant has a pleasant ambience and an excellent reputation. Eclectic blend of California and Scandinavian fare includes gravlax with dill mustard sauce, smoked salmon and black caviar sandwich on pumpernickel, polenta sandwich with grilled vegetables and sun-dried tomato sauce, and braised lamb shanks with white-bean puree. Excellent wine selection. **FYI:** Reservations recommended. **Open:** Lunch Mon–Sat 11:30am–2pm; dinner Mon–Sat 5:30–10:30pm. **Prices:** Main courses $18–$25. AE, CB, DC, MC, V. 🔥

★ Planet Hollywood
1641 W Sunflower; tel 714/434-7827. Across from South Coast Plaza. **Californian.** Action-packed restaurant with an illuminated wall-size map of Hollywood in black and white and a re-creation of the city skyline. An alien stands guard in the bar, not far from a Ninja turtle. Basic American fare features pizzas, hamburgers, sandwiches, salads, and pastas. Good for children. **FYI:** Reservations not accepted. **Open:** Sun–Thurs 11:30am–11:30pm, Fri–Sat 11:30am–1:30am. **Prices:** Main courses $7–$15. AE, DC, MC, V. 📭 𝐕𝐏 🔥

Topaz Cafe
In Bowers Museum, 2002 N Main; tel 714/835-2002. Exit 17 off I-5 N At 20th St. **Eclectic.** Museum-quality artifacts lend a dramatic touch to the decor. Unique menu changes daily and

features a variety of grilled chicken, meat, and fish dishes. One Friday each month, cafe offers an evening of Native American cuisine and live Native American entertainment. **FYI:** Reservations recommended. Children's menu. **Open:** Lunch Tues–Sat 11:30am–3pm; dinner Wed–Sat 5–9pm; brunch Sun 10am–3pm. **Prices:** Main courses $9–$15. AE, MC, V. 🍴 ♿

Santa Barbara

Nestled between the Pacific Ocean and the Santa Ynez Mountains, Santa Barbara has earned its reputation as a little bit of paradise just out of reach of thriving Los Angeles to the south. The city's protected beaches, sophisticated downtown, historically and architecturally significant buildings, high standard of living, and superb dining combine to form one of California's most ideal communities. **Information:** Santa Barbara Conference & Visitors Bureau, 510 State St #A, Santa Barbara 93101 (tel 805/966-9222 or toll free 800/ 927-4688).

HOTELS 🏨

≣≣≣≣ El Encanto Hotel & Garden Villas

1900 Lasuen Rd, 93103 (the Riviera); tel 805/687-5000 or toll free 800/223-5652; fax 805/687-3903. 1 mi W of downtown. Mission St exit off US 101. Romantic hotel set among lush, tropical grounds on a hillside overlooking Santa Barbara and the Pacific. Well appointed, quiet, and serene. **Rooms:** 20 rms and stes; 64 cottages/villas. CI 3pm/CO noon. Nonsmoking rms avail. Charmingly decorated with bleached wood and brightly painted country-style furnishings. Carpets and tubs in some of the older, smaller rooms show wear and tear. Renovated suites and cottages are spacious and sunny; some have two desks and two separate seating areas. **Amenities:** 📺 ♨ Cable TV w/movies, bathrobes. No A/C. Some units w/minibars, all w/terraces, some w/fireplaces. VCRs and videos available for rent. **Services:** 🍽 👑 VP 🚗 🧺 ⇨ Twice-daily maid svce, masseur, babysitting. **Facilities:** 🏊 🛎 [120] 1 restaurant, 1 bar (w/entertainment), washer/dryer. The restaurant, which offers outdoor dining and great views, as well as a poolside grill in the summer, has been voted "best place to bring a first date" and "most romantic dining spot" by local publications. Guests also enjoy privileges at a local fitness center. **Rates (BB):** Peak (Feb–Sept) $170–$195 S or D; $220–$480 ste; $660 cottage/ villa. Extra person $30. Children under age 18 stay free. Min stay peak, wknds, and special events. Lower rates off-season. Parking: Outdoor, free. Full breakfast included in rate Mon– Thurs. AE, DC, MC, V.

≣≣≣ Fess Parker's Red Lion Resort

633 E Cabrillo Blvd, 93103; tel 805/564-4333 or toll free 800/879-2929; fax 805/962-8198. Milpas exit off US 101 S; Cabrillo Blvd exit off US 101 N. Large, convention/event-oriented hotel located across from the ocean. Nice views.

Rooms: 360 rms and stes. CI 4pm/CO noon. Nonsmoking rms avail. Rooms are oversized, with oak furnishings. **Amenities:** 📺 ♨ 🍴 A/C, cable TV w/movies. All units w/minibars, all w/terraces, some w/fireplaces, some w/whirlpools. **Services:** ✕ 👑 VP 🚗 🧺 ⇨ ⟨⟩ Car-rental desk, masseur, babysitting. **Facilities:** 🏊 🚲 🏋 🛎 ⚽ [1000] ♿ 2 restaurants, 1 bar (w/entertainment), games rm, spa, sauna, whirlpool, beauty salon, washer/dryer. Great jazz combo performs in lounge. Shuffleboard, basketball, and putting green available. **Rates:** Peak (Mem Day–Labor Day) $225–$325 S or D; $395–$795 ste. Extra person $15. Children under age 18 stay free. Min stay special events. Lower rates off-season. Parking: Outdoor, free. AE, CB, DC, DISC, EC, ER, JCB, MC, V.

≣≣ Miramar Resort Hotel

1555 S Jameson Lane, Montecito, PO Box 429, Santa Barbara, 93102 (Miramar Beach); tel 805/969-2203 or toll free 800/322-6983; fax 805/969-3163. San Ysidro exit off US 101. This low-key and relaxed seaside property has been attracting families and long-term winter guests for more than 80 years. The property has recently been remodeled and boasts fresh paint, new carpeting, and soft lighting. The front desk staff, however, is lackadaisical. **Rooms:** 146 rms, stes, and effic; 67 cottages/villas. CI 4pm/CO 1pm. Nonsmoking rms avail. Avoid rooms near the freeway, as they are noisy. Since a train track runs through the property directly behind the beachfront units, prepare for train horns and vibrations. Some bathrooms have chipped grout and drippy faucets. **Amenities:** 📺 ♨ Cable TV. No A/C. Some units w/terraces, some w/fireplaces. **Services:** ✕ 🧺 ⇨ Masseur, babysitting. **Facilities:** 🏊 🚲 🛎 ⚽ [700] 2 restaurants, 1 bar (w/entertainment), 1 beach (ocean), lifeguard, lawn games, sauna, whirlpool, beauty salon, playground. A train car has been converted into a diner near the beach. **Rates:** $75–$145 S or D; $180–$400 ste; $180–$400 effic; $125–$400 cottage/ villa. Extra person $10. Children under age 18 stay free. Min stay wknds. Parking: Outdoor, free. AE, CB, EC, ER, JCB, MC, V.

≣≣≣ Montecito Inn

1295 Coast Village Rd, Montecito, 93108; tel 805/969-7854 or toll free 800/843-2017; fax 805/969-0623. 3 mi S of downtown. Olive Mill Rd exit off US 101; head inland; left on Coast Village Rd. Built in 1928 by Charlie Chaplin (whose image features prominently in the public rooms), this European-style hotel is elegant but not stuffy, and boasts a fireplace in the marble lobby. It mainly caters to couples and a corporate clientele. Serene ambience is marred by constant bus traffic. Located within walking distance to beach, shops, and restaurants. **Rooms:** 60 rms and stes. Executive level. CI 3pm/CO noon. Nonsmoking rms avail. Wallpapered in mauve and blue, rooms feature French Provincial armoires and night stands, as well as fresh flowers, ceiling fans, and hand-painted tiles in the bathrooms. Some rooms have two full baths. Seven new one-bedroom suites (including one for disabled guests) are decorated in pale grey and silver, with Italian-marble baths. **Amenities:** 🛅 🕭 Cable TV w/movies. No A/C. Some units w/fireplaces, some w/whirlpools. **Services:** ✕ 🗝 VP 🖼 ꝗ Masseur, babysitting. Staff is unflappable under pressure. **Facilities:** 🎏 🎺 60 🕹 1 restaurant (lunch and dinner only), sauna, whirlpool. Montecito Cafe is excellent. Guest privileges at local athletic club. **Rates (CP):** $150–$195 S or D; $205–$695 ste. Children under age 18 stay free. Min stay wknds and special events. Parking: Indoor/outdoor, free. AE, DC, DISC, JCB, MC, V.

☰☰☰ Radisson Hotel Santa Barbara

1111 E Cabrillo Blvd, 93103 (East Beach); tel 805/963-0744 or toll free 800/333-3333; fax 805/962-0985. Cabrillo exit off US 101. Sprawling full-service hotel across from the beach; caters to families and conventions. **Rooms:** 174 rms, stes, and effic. CI 3pm/CO noon. Nonsmoking rms avail. Rooms have simple Old West/Spanish decor; great views from the second floor. **Amenities:** 🛅 🕭 A/C, cable TV w/movies, refrig, VCR, voice mail. All units w/minibars, some w/terraces. **Services:** ✕ 🗝 🚐 🖼 ꝗ Children's program, babysitting. **Facilities:** 🎏 ⚙ 🎺 300 🖥 🕹 1 restaurant, 1 bar (w/entertainment), washer/dryer. **Rates:** Peak (June–Oct) $179–$235 S or D; $350 ste. Extra person $20. Children under age 18 stay free. Min stay peak and wknds. Lower rates off-season. Parking: Indoor/outdoor, free. Efficiencies avail by the month only, for $1,550 to $2,600/month. AE, DC, MC, V.

☰☰☰ Santa Barbara Inn

901 E Cabrillo Blvd, 93103 (East Beach); tel 805/966-2285 or toll free 800/231-0431; fax 805/966-6584. Castillo St exit off US 101 S; Bath St exit off US 101 N. Recently refurbished beachside hotel; great for families. **Rooms:** 71 rms, stes, and effic. CI 3pm/CO noon. Nonsmoking rms avail. Bright, airy rooms; those on the ocean side offer exceptional views, especially at sunset. **Amenities:** 🛅 🕭 📶 Cable TV, refrig. No A/C. All units w/terraces. Suites have wet bars. **Services:** ✕ 🗝 VP ꝗ Twice-daily maid svce, babysitting. Complimentary morning newspaper, masseur, and dry cleaning service provided on request. **Facilities:** 🎏 125 🖥 🕹 1 restaurant, 1 bar, 1 beach (ocean), whirlpool. Chef Michel Richard's acclaimed restaurant provides poolside meal service. Access to local health club for $3 per day. **Rates:** Peak (Apr–Oct) $149–$219 S or D; $225–$395 ste; $164–$219 effic. Extra person $15. Children under age 12 stay free. Min stay wknds and special events. Lower rates off-season. Parking: Indoor/outdoor, $2/day. AE, CB, DC, DISC, EC, ER, MC, V.

☰☰☰ The Upham

1404 De La Vina St, 93101; tel 805/962-0058 or toll free 800/727-0876; fax 805/963-2825. Arrellaga St exit off US 101 N; Mission St exit off US 101 S. Operated as a hotel since 1871. A stay at this property, with its wicker-filled sun porch, fireplace, and lovely gardens, is like a step back in time. **Rooms:** 50 rms and stes. CI 3pm/CO noon. Nonsmoking rms avail. Furnished in lovely antiques, with fresh flowers. Down-

stairs rooms have very high ceilings. **Amenities:** 🛅 🕭 Cable TV. No A/C. 1 unit w/minibar, some w/terraces, some w/fireplaces, 1 w/whirlpool. **Services:** ✕ 🖼 ꝗ Babysitting. Complimentary afternoon wine and cheese; milk and cookies after 8pm. **Facilities:** 80 1 restaurant. Lovely gazebo in the garden. Restaurant has indoor and outdoor dining. Use of Santa Barbara Athletic Club at a minimum charge. **Rates (CP):** Peak (July–Aug) $115–$190 S or D; $190–$350 ste. Extra person $10. Children under age 12 stay free. Min stay wknds and special events. Lower rates off-season. Parking: Outdoor, free. AE, CB, DC, DISC, MC, V.

MOTELS

☰☰☰ Best Western Encina Lodge & Suites

2220 Bath St, 93105; tel 805/682-7277 or toll free 800/526-2282; fax 805/563-9319. Mission St exit off US 101; follow Mission north, turn left on Bath St. A comfortable and friendly property convenient to local hospitals. **Rooms:** 121 rms, stes, and effic. CI 3pm/CO noon. Nonsmoking rms avail. Very nice, private, relaxing rooms with high beamed ceilings and bright colors. **Amenities:** 🛅 🕭 📶 ꝗ A/C, cable TV w/movies, refrig, in-rm safe. Some units w/terraces. Fruit, coffee, and candy in room. **Services:** ✕ 🗝 🚐 🖼 ꝗ Babysitting. Shuttle can take guests to nearby clinics for medical appointments. TDD offered for deaf and hard-of-hearing guests. **Facilities:** 🎏 1 restaurant, 1 bar, sauna, whirlpool, beauty salon, washer/dryer. Victoria's Restaurant serves great breakfasts and provides poolside meals; a huge finch cage at its entrance charms the kids. **Rates:** Peak (May 24–Sept) $116 S; $126 D; $134 ste; $144 effic. Extra person $10. Children under age 5 stay free. Min stay peak and wknds. Lower rates off-season. Parking: Indoor/outdoor, free. AE, DC, DISC, MC, V.

☰☰☰ Best Western Pepper Tree Inn

3850 State St, 93105; tel 805/687-5511 or toll free 800/338-0030; fax 805/682-2410. Hope Ave exit off US 101. Underwent a full renovation in 1994. Spanish-style architecture with a fountain, and palm trees bordering the grounds. **Rooms:** 150 rms. CI 3pm/CO noon. Nonsmoking rms avail. New furnishings. **Amenities:** 🛅 🕭 📶 ꝗ A/C, cable TV w/movies, refrig, in-rm safe. All units w/terraces. All rooms come with baskets of fresh fruit and candy. **Services:** ✕ 🗝 🚐 🖼 ꝗ Masseur, babysitting. **Facilities:** 🎏 🎺 100 1 restaurant, 1 bar, sauna, whirlpool, beauty salon, washer/dryer. Well-equipped fitness room. Free admission to YMCA half-block away. **Rates:** Peak (May–Sept) $118–$128 S; $128–$138 D. Extra person $6. Children under age 5 stay free. Min stay peak and wknds. Lower rates off-season. Parking: Outdoor, free. AE, CB, DC, DISC, ER, JCB, MC, V.

☰☰☰ Cathedral Oaks Lodge

4770 Calle Real, 93110; tel 805/964-3511 or toll free 800/654-1965, 800/228-4581 in CA; fax 805/964-0075. Turnpike Rd exit off US 101. Although property is located next to a busy freeway, soundproofing is reasonably good. A lagoon with ducks, carp, waterfall, lily pads, and palm trees makes the pool and courtyard areas very attractive. Four golf courses nearby. **Rooms:** 126 rms and stes. CI 3pm/CO noon. Nonsmoking rms avail. Second-story rooms are smaller and face the parking lot, but are in better shape and quieter than the more spacious (and expensive) garden-side rooms. Furnishings include a lounger/recliner. **Amenities:** ☎ ⚲ ▤ A/C, cable TV w/movies. All units w/terraces. **Services:** 🚐 ⌧ ⤵ Babysitting. European-style breakfast is served poolside or in the Valley Room. Free local calls. **Facilities:** ⛊ ⟨75⟩ ⚴ Whirlpool, washer/dryer. **Rates (CP):** Peak (May–Sept) $58–$75 S; $68–$95 D; $108–$120 ste. Extra person $10. Children under age 12 stay free. Min stay peak and wknds. Lower rates off-season. Parking: Outdoor, free. AE, CB, DC, DISC, MC, V.

≡≡≡ Franciscan Inn
109 Bath St, 93101 (West Beach); tel 805/963-8845; fax 805/564-3295. This family-run property, located just one block from the beach, is very well maintained and nicely decorated. **Rooms:** 53 rms, stes, and effic. CI 3pm/CO noon. Nonsmoking rms avail. 18 different styles of rooms, each attractively decorated in a country motif accented with fresh flowers. **Amenities:** ☎ ⚲ Cable TV w/movies, refrig. No A/C. Some units w/terraces, 1 w/fireplace. **Services:** ⌧ ⤵ Free local telephone calls and morning newspaper. Complimentary coffee and cookies in the afternoon. Trolley will pick up guests for tours. **Facilities:** ⛊ ⚴ Whirlpool, washer/dryer. **Rates (CP):** Peak (May 15–Oct 15) $65–$85 S; $70–$95 D; $85–$175 ste; $85–$175 effic. Extra person $8. Children under age 5 stay free. Lower rates off-season. Parking: Outdoor, free. AE, CB, DC, ER, JCB, MC, V.

≡≡≡ Harbor View Inn
28 W Cabrillo Blvd, 93101; tel 805/963-0780 or toll free 800/755-0222; fax 805/963-7967. Castillo St exit off US 101; W on Castillo toward ocean; left on Cabrillo. Best location in town, with beach and Stearns Wharf across the street. Major renovation completed in 1996. Boat rentals nearby. **Rooms:** 64 rms. CI 3pm/CO noon. Nonsmoking rms avail. Fresh flowers in all rooms. **Amenities:** ☎ ⚲ A/C, cable TV w/movies, refrig. Some units w/minibars, some w/terraces. **Services:** ➤ ⌧ ⤵ Babysitting. Continental breakfast in restaurant. Wine and cheese 5–7pm on patio facing beach. **Facilities:** ⛊ 🚲 ⟨140⟩ ⚴ 1 restaurant, whirlpool. Skate rentals. **Rates (CP):** Peak (May–Sept) $150–$300 S or D. Extra person $10. Children under age 5 stay free. Min stay peak, wknds, and special events. Lower rates off-season. Parking: Outdoor, free. AE, DC, MC, V.

≡≡ Holiday Inn
5650 Calle Real, Goleta, 93117; tel 805/964-6241 or toll free 800/HOLIDAY; fax 805/964-8467. Fairview exit off US 101. Standard Holiday Inn, close to the university, shopping, and restaurants. **Rooms:** 154 rms. Executive level. CI 2pm/CO noon. Nonsmoking rms avail. Rooms are basic. **Amenities:** ☎ ⚲ A/C, cable TV w/movies. **Services:** ✕ 🚐 ⌧

⤵ **Facilities:** ⛊ ⟨300⟩ ⚴ 1 restaurant, 1 bar, washer/dryer. Kids accompanied by parents eat for free in the restaurant. **Rates:** Peak (May–Sept) $79–$160 S or D. Children under age 19 stay free. Min stay special events. Lower rates off-season. Parking: Outdoor, free. AE, CB, DC, DISC, MC, V.

≡≡ Motel 6
3505 State St, 93105; tel 805/687-5400; fax 805/569-5837. Las Positas exit off US 101; turn left onto State St; go north ¼ mi. Although not near the beach, this motel provides safe, clean, comfortable rooms for families at a reasonable rate. Many foreigners stay here. **Rooms:** 59 rms. CI 2pm/CO noon. Nonsmoking rms avail. The rooms are bright, cheery, and very clean. They were recently renovated, and look brand new. **Amenities:** ☎ A/C, cable TV w/movies. **Services:** ⤵ ⤷ Very security-conscious staff. **Facilities:** ⛊ ⚴ Pool is large, inviting, and extremely clean, but has no vegetation around it. **Rates:** Peak (May 26–Oct 25) $54 S or D. Children under age 17 stay free. Lower rates off-season. Parking: Outdoor, free. AE, MC, V.

≡ Mountain View Inn
3955 De La Vina St, 93105; tel 805/687-6636; fax 805/569-6809. Las Positas exit off US 101; go right on State St. Decent family-run property offers adequate accommodations at a reasonable price. Be prepared for plenty of street noise during the day. **Rooms:** 34 rms. CI 2pm/CO noon. Nonsmoking rms avail. Comfortable beds, flowered quilts, and frilly pillows make up somewhat for tired furniture crying out for replacement. General layout is small and cramped, with minuscule bathrooms. Most units have good views of the pool and surrounding mountains. **Amenities:** ☎ A/C, cable TV w/movies, refrig. **Services:** ⤵ **Facilities:** ⛊ **Rates (CP):** Peak (June–Sept) $60–$89 S or D. Extra person $5. Children under age 5 stay free. Min stay wknds. Lower rates off-season. Parking: Outdoor, free. AE, DC, MC, V.

≡≡ Ocean Palms Hotel
232 W Cabrillo Blvd, 93101; tel 805/966-9133 or toll free 800/350-2326; fax 805/965-7882. Spanish-style building with red-tile roof, painted tiles, and charming archways, located across from the beach. Nice cottages for families. **Rooms:** 44 rms and effic; 5 cottages/villas. CI 3pm/CO noon. Nonsmoking rms avail. **Amenities:** ☎ ⚲ ▤ Satel TV w/movies. No A/C. Some units w/terraces, some w/fireplaces. **Services:** ⤵ ⤷ Masseur. **Facilities:** ⛊ ⚴ Whirlpool. Pool has a sun deck. Restaurants, harbor, and pier nearby. **Rates (CP):** Peak (July–Oct 15) $105–$155 S; $115–$165 D; $125–$165 effic; $125–$175 cottage/villa. Extra person $10. Children under age 10 stay free. Min stay peak, wknds, and special events. Lower rates off-season. Parking: Outdoor, free. AE, DISC, MC, V.

≡≡≡ Pacifica Suites
5490 Hollister Ave, 93111; tel 805/683-6722 or toll free 800/338-6722; fax 805/683-4121. Patterson exit off US 101; turn toward ocean, to Hollister. Nestled in a wooded park,

this tranquil resort-style motel is modeled after a restored 1880s Italianate mansion on the property. **Rooms:** 75 stes. CI 3pm/CO noon. Nonsmoking rms avail. Some suites face the freeway but are adequately soundproofed. **Amenities:** 🛎 🕐 🖵 A/C, cable TV, refrig, dataport, VCR. Some units w/terraces. Each suite has two TVs. **Services:** 🚗 🖼 🗘 🕭 Babysitting. Free evening beverages (beer, wine, and soda) served Mon–Sat. Breakfast cooked to order in breakfast cafe. Masseur available on request. Videos available for rent in the lobby. **Facilities:** 🍴 🏊 ⅗ 🕭 Whirlpool. Several rooms, including the library of the historic Sexton House (adjacent to the motel), are available for meetings and banquets. **Rates (BB):** Peak (Sept) $130–$165 ste. Extra person $10. Children under age 18 stay free. Min stay peak and special events. Lower rates off-season. Parking: Outdoor, free. AE, CB, DC, DISC, JCB, MC, V.

≡≡ Sandman Inn

3714 State St, 93105 (San Roque); tel 805/687-2468 or toll free 800/350-8174; fax 805/687-6581. 3 mi N of downtown. State St exit off US 101. Spiffy and well-kept property close to area shopping and a variety of restaurants. The ambience is quiet, despite proximity to a busy street. **Rooms:** 113 rms, stes, and effic. CI 3pm/CO noon. Nonsmoking rms avail. Some standard rooms have a breezy, South Seas feel, with wooden blinds and ceiling fans, plus burnished rattan headboards and armoires. **Amenities:** 🛎 Cable TV w/movies. No A/C. Some units w/terraces. Suites have attached kitchen facilities with a dinette that seats four, these are available for an additional $10 per day. Deluxe poolside units have large, shared patios and coffeemakers. **Services:** 🚗 🖼 🗘 Babysitting. Free coffee and tea served 24 hours in lobby. Shuttle van available by prior arrangement. **Facilities:** 🍴 🏊 🕭 1 restaurant (dinner only), 1 bar, whirlpool, washer/dryer. Guests receive $5 off dinner in the restaurant, Kokopelli Grill, which serves regional American cuisine. Free passes to YMCA located half-block away. **Rates (CP):** Peak (June–Oct) $79–$129 S; $84–$129 D; $119–$139 ste; $119–$139 effic. Extra person $10. Children under age 12 stay free. Min stay wknds. Lower rates off-season. Parking: Outdoor, free. AE, DC, MC, V.

≡≡ Tropicana Inn and Suites

223 Castillo St, 93101 (West Beach); tel 805/966-2219 or toll free 800/468-1988; fax 805/962-9428. Castillo St exit off US 101 S; Bath St exit off US 101 N. A clean property close to the beach and good for long stays. Tennis courts in park next door. **Rooms:** 31 rms, stes, and effic. CI 3pm/CO noon. No smoking. All rooms feature French country decor. Third-floor rooms offer nice mountain views. **Amenities:** 🛎 🕭 Cable TV, refrig. No A/C. Suites have large, immaculate kitchens (utensils available for $5 per day). **Services:** 🖙 🗘 Babysitting. Continental breakfast served in lobby. **Facilities:** 🍴 ⅗ Whirlpool, washer/dryer. **Rates (CP):** Peak (May 24–Sept 28) $102–$112 S; $102–$122 D; $122–$192 ste; $122–$192 effic. Extra person $5. Children under age 5 stay free. Min

stay peak and wknds. Lower rates off-season. Parking: Indoor/outdoor, free. Monthly rates avail for longer stays. AE, DISC, MC, V.

INNS

≡≡≡ The Cheshire Cat

36 W Valerio St, 93101; tel 805/569-1610; fax 805/682-1876. Cozy Victorian-era bed-and-breakfast filled with antiques. Very well kept. **Rooms:** 14 rms and stes. CI 3pm/CO noon. No smoking. Rooms are individually decorated with cheerful chintz fabrics and wallpaper, fresh flowers, and original art. **Amenities:** 🛎 No A/C. Some units w/minibars, some w/terraces, some w/fireplaces, some w/whirlpools. English soaps, herbal shampoo, chocolates, and liqueurs. Not all rooms have TV. **Facilities:** ⅗ 🕭 Whirlpool, guest lounge w/TV. Gazebo. **Rates (BB):** Peak (June–Oct) $125–$209 D; $259 ste; $185 effic. Extra person $25. Min stay wknds. Lower rates off-season. Parking: Outdoor, free. MC, V.

≡≡≡ The Glenborough Inn Bed & Breakfast

1327 Bath St, 93101 (Downtown); tel 805/966-0589 or toll free 800/962-0589; fax 805/564-8610. Carillo St exit off US 101; 2 blocks E to Bath St. 1 acre. This antiques-filled bed-and-breakfast combines three houses—the 1906 Craftsman-style main house, the Victorian cottage, and the California classic white house—in a residential neighborhood a few blocks from downtown. **Rooms:** 11 rms and stes (2 w/shared bath). CI 3pm/CO 11am. No smoking. Furnished with real and reproduction antiques plus miniature teddy bears, accommodations have decors ranging from art nouveau to nautical. Some rooms offer six-foot-long soaking tubs. The Nouveau Suite has a private entrance, garden, redwood deck, and outdoor hot tub. **Amenities:** 🛎 🕭 Bathrobes. No A/C or TV. Some units w/terraces, some w/fireplaces, some w/whirlpools. Three suites come with coffeemaker and refrigerator. **Services:** ✕ Masseur, afternoon tea served. Full breakfast served in guest rooms, parlor, or garden. Catered candlelight dinners can be ordered, and box lunches available on request. Daily newspapers and jelly beans offered in the guest lounge. **Facilities:** Whirlpool, guest lounge. Private time can be reserved in the open-air Jacuzzi in the rear garden. **Rates (BB):** Peak (Aug–Oct) $90 S or D w/shared bath, $95–$135 S or D w/private bath; $150–$190 ste. Extra person $25. Min stay wknds. Lower rates off-season. Parking: Outdoor, free. Additional persons permitted in the Nouveau and Summertime suites only. AE, DC, DISC, MC, V.

≡≡≡ Inn on Summer Hill

2520 Lillie Ave, Summerland, 93067; tel 805/969-9998 or toll free 800/845-5566; fax 805/565-9946. 1 acre. Very decorated, California craftsman-style inn opened in 1989. **Rooms:** 16 rms and stes. CI 3pm/CO 11am. No smoking. All rooms have ocean views and are decorated with pine furniture, canopied beds, down comforters, and original artwork. Attention to details shows in the whimsical, hand-painted breakfast trays, steamer trunks, and tissue boxes. Some rooms share patios; somewhat incongruously, the patio furniture is strictly utilitarian. **Amenities:** 🔒👤📺 🍽A/C, cable TV w/movies, refrig, VCR, CD/tape player, bathrobes. All units w/terraces, all w/fireplaces. **Services:** ✗ 🛎 Twice-daily maid svce, masseur, afternoon tea and wine/sherry served. Breakfast features unique items, such as black-bean waffles served with a chile-cranberry sauce. Breakfast in guest rooms offered for an additional $5. Gourmet desserts served in evenings. Staff can arrange dinner reservations and theater tickets. **Facilities:** ⅋ Whirlpool, guest lounge w/TV. Charming English country-style dining room. **Rates (BB):** $160–$195 S or D; $295 ste. Extra person $25. Children under age 2 stay free. Min stay wknds and special events. Parking: Outdoor, free. Lower midweek rates available. AE, DISC, MC, V.

≣≣≣≣ Simpson House Inn
121 E Arrellaga, 93101; tel 805/963-7067 or toll free 800/676-1280; fax 805/564-4811. Garden St exit off US 101 N; Mission St exit off US 101 S. 1 acre. A very special bed-and-breakfast in a quiet neighborhood, with a lovely garden and beautifully decorated public rooms. A historic landmark, built in 1874. Unsuitable for children under 12. **Rooms:** 11 rms and stes; 3 cottages/villas. CI 3pm/CO 11am. No smoking. Very beautiful rooms in the main house have antique beds, elaborate Victorian-style wallpaper, and clawfoot tubs with cheerful yellow rubber-ducky tub toys (offered for sale). **Amenities:** 🔒👤🍽A/C, refrig, CD/tape player, bathrobes. No TV. Some units w/minibars, some w/terraces, some w/fireplaces, some w/whirlpools. Thoughtful touches include makeup remover and pump dispensers filled with shampoo, conditioner, and body oil. All rooms offer selection of books and cassettes, and some offer a collection of over 100 videos. The especiallly attractive suites located in the restored old barn (1878) feature TVs and VCRs concealed in armoires. **Services:** ✗ Twice-daily maid svce, social director, masseur, babysitting, afternoon tea and wine/sherry served. Breakfast delivered to rooms, private patios, or tables in the garden. Inn can arrange reservations for beauty treatments at a nearby day spa. **Facilities:** 🚲 🛖 ⅋ Lawn games, guest lounge. **Rates (BB):** $130–$190 S or D; $255–$270 ste; $270–$285 cottage/villa. Extra person $25. Min stay wknds. Higher rates for special events/hols. Parking: Outdoor, free. DISC, MC, V.

RESORTS
≣≣≣≣ Four Seasons Biltmore
1260 Channel Dr, 93108; tel 805/969-2261 or toll free 800/332-3442 in the US, 800/268-6282 in Canada; fax 805/969-4682. Olive Mill Rd exit off US 101; go south (toward ocean). 21 acres. This classic, opened in 1927, features a red-tile roof and stucco walls, and a splendid lobby with coffered ceilings, terra-cotta floors, and hand-painted tiles. All this, plus acres of gardens and the blue Pacific across the way.

Rooms: 234 rms and stes. CI 3pm/CO noon. Nonsmoking rms avail. Rooms are tastefully decorated in soft earth tones. Ceiling fans keep things cool and airy. White marble bathrooms are extremely well laid out. **Amenities:** 🔒👤🍽 Cable TV w/movies, VCR, voice mail, in-rm safe, bathrobes. No A/C. All units w/minibars, some w/terraces, some w/fireplaces. **Services:** 🍴🛎 VP 🧺↩️⟳ Twice-daily maid svce, car-rental desk, masseur, children's program, babysitting. Complimentary shoeshine service. In-room spa treatments available. **Facilities:** 🏌🚲⛳🎾🛖🖥⅋ 4 restaurants, 2 bars (w/entertainment), 1 beach (ocean), lawn games, spa, sauna, steam rm, whirlpool, beauty salon. The beachside art deco Coral Casino is the social center of Santa Barbara. Stunning 50-meter pool, and a new workout room well equipped with exercise bikes, treadmill, and more. **Rates:** Peak (Apr–Sept) $215–$475 S or D; $650 ste. Extra person $30. Children under age 18 stay free. Min stay wknds. Lower rates off-season. Parking: Outdoor, free. Tennis, golf, spa, and other packages avail. Midweek "Paradise" packages are extremely well priced, offering two nights' accommodation plus breakfast for $495 per couple. AE, DC, MC, V.

≣≣≣≣ San Ysidro Ranch
900 San Ysidro Lane, Montecito, 93108; tel 805/969-5046 or toll free 800/368-6788; fax 805/565-1995. San Ysidro Rd exit off US 101; go north (inland), then right on Mountain Dr. 540 acres. One-of-a-kind property where Laurence Olivier and Vivien Leigh married, and John and Jacqueline Kennedy honeymooned. The ivy-covered stone cottage where the couple stayed has been completely renovated and is available for $950 per night. The property feels like a ranch, with branding irons on the walls and purposefully threadbare oriental carpets on the floor. **Rooms:** 32 rms and stes; 12 cottages/villas. CI 3pm/CO noon. Nonsmoking rms avail. The 44 rooms and suites are set in 21 cottages, 12 of which are freestanding. All are unique. Magnolia 1 has a four-poster bed and sepia-toned photos of old ranching families on the walls. The Weingand Cottage has been totally renovated with terrazzo tile and a window seat in the bathroom. **Amenities:** 🔒👤🍽 Cable TV w/movies, VCR, bathrobes. No A/C. All units w/minibars, all w/terraces, all w/fireplaces, some w/whirlpools. Upon arrival, guests find their name on a wooden sign on their cottage door. Kindling and logs are positioned in fireplaces, while rooms also come equipped with books, flashlights, and umbrellas. **Services:** 🍴🛎 VP 🧺↩️⟳ Twice-daily maid svce, social director, masseur, children's program, babysitting. Personalized pampering abounds. For example, after tennis, guests find bottles of chilled Evian waiting in their rooms. In-room massages, personal fitness training, and yoga instruction can be arranged. Pets have their own guest registry; for a one-time charge of $45, they also receive a pet bed, toys, and "Pawier" water. Two-legged guests will also find that the staff is gracious and well-versed in the hotel's history. **Facilities:** 🏌 🚲 🐴 ⛷ 🎣2 🛖 🖥 ⅋ 1 restaurant (see "Restaurants"

below), 1 bar (w/entertainment), games rm, lawn games, playground. The 19th-century Adobe Cottage is available for private parties of up to 12 people. Gardens are popular for weddings. Fitness center has an ocean view. **Rates:** $240–$475 S or D; $475–$750 ste; $475–$950 cottage/villa. Children under age 18 stay free. Min stay wknds. Parking: Outdoor, free. Romance and spa packages avail. AE, MC, V.

RESTAURANTS 🍴

⭐ Andersen's Danish Bakery and Restaurant
1106 State St (Downtown); tel 805/962-5085. **Danish.** Sunny and social place with a very European, tea room atmosphere plus a sidewalk patio. A glass display case featuring Danish, European, and American sweet treats stands on a crisp black-and-white checkerboard floor. **FYI:** Reservations accepted. Beer and wine only. **Open:** Wed–Mon 8am–8pm. Closed Sept. **Prices:** Main courses $3–$10. No CC. 🍲 VP

Arnoldi's Cafe
600 Olive St; tel 805/962-5394. 5 blocks E of State St. **Italian/Steak.** Housed in an old stone building, this homey Italian restaurant features wooden booths, red-and-white-checkered tablecloths, and a jukebox. Basic Italian fare, as well as chicken, steak, and lamb chops. **FYI:** Reservations accepted. **Open:** Thurs–Tues 5–11pm. **Prices:** Main courses $9–$15. MC, V. 🍲

⭐ Brophy Brothers Clam Bar & Restaurant
Yacht Basin and Marina; tel 805/966-4418. Castillo St exit off US 101. **Seafood.** A great place with an atmosphere as authentic as it gets. The patio overlooks the harbor; inside, there are wooden floors, low ceilings, and big windows. The simple menu includes the expected clams, mussels, ceviche, seafood salads, and fried fish. Daily specials depend on the catch. **FYI:** Reservations not accepted. **Open:** Daily 11am–10pm. **Prices:** Main courses $7–$16. AE, MC, V.

♟ Casa de Sevilla
428 Chapala St; tel 805/966-4370. 1 block W of State St. **Seafood/Steak.** One of the first bars opened after Prohibition, it has been popular with generations of Santa Barbarans. Reminiscent of a private club, with a fireplace and old fiesta and bullfight posters. The menu runs to seafood with a California twist, offering ceviche and chili rellenos for starters, a variety of seafood specials, and barbecued meats. **FYI:** Reservations recommended. Jacket required. **Open:** Lunch Tues–Sat noon–2pm; dinner Tues–Sat 6–10pm. **Prices:** Main courses $14–$30; prix fixe $16–$26. AE, CB, DC, MC, V.

⭐ The Chase Grill
1012 State St (Downtown); tel 805/965-4351. **Italian.** Chef Mario Rodriguez has maintained an excellent reputation since 1979 for his renditions of southern Italian dishes. Specialties are jumbo ravioli and chicken picatta. Atmosphere is intimate and casual. **FYI:** Reservations accepted. Beer and

wine only. **Open:** Lunch Mon–Sat 11am–2:30pm; dinner Sun–Thurs 5–9pm, Fri–Sat 5–10pm. **Prices:** Main courses $7–$14. AE, DC, DISC, MC, V.

⭐ Joe's Cafe
536 State St (Downtown); tel 805/966-4638. **American/Steak.** A Santa Barbara classic; traditional family restaurant with red-and-white-checkered tablecloths and wooden booths. The walls are lined with historic black-and-white photos of Santa Barbara. The menu is basic steak, spaghetti, liver and onions, and burgers. **FYI:** Reservations recommended. **Open:** Mon–Thurs 11am–11:30pm, Fri–Sat 11am–12:30pm, Sun 4–11:30pm. **Prices:** Main courses $10–$15. AE, DC, DISC, MC, V.

⭐ La Super-Rica Taqueria
622 N Milpas St; tel 805/963-4940. Milpas St exit off US 101. **Mexican.** One of Santa Barbara's most popular spots. Seating is at wooden tables on a canvas-canopied patio. Authentic and delicious food offerings come with homemade tortillas and salsa: fare includes quesadillas and tacos of charbroiled steak, and pork with onions and chiles. Daily specials are available. Portions are small. **FYI:** Reservations not accepted. Beer and wine only. **Open:** Sun–Thurs 11am–9:30pm, Fri–Sat 11am–10pm. **Prices:** Main courses $3–$8. No CC.

Mousse Odile
18 E Cota St; tel 805/962-5393. 1 block E of State St. **French.** One of the best country-style French restaurants in Santa Barbara. Light and airy by day, romantic by night, with a high ceiling, lots of plants, and a peaceful patio for outside dining. Offers omelettes, quiches, and finely prepared seafood, veal, and filet mignon. Specialties include osso buco, cassoulet, fisherman soup, and couscous with lamb. **FYI:** Reservations accepted. **Open:** Breakfast Mon–Sat 8–11:30am; lunch Mon–Sat 11:30am–2:30pm; dinner Mon–Thurs 5:30–9pm, Fri–Sat 5:30–9:30pm. **Prices:** Main courses $10–$16. AE, DC, DISC, MC, V.

Oysters
In Victoria Court, 9 W Victoria St; tel 805/962-9888. 1 block W of State St. **Californian/Seafood.** Simply decorated, with a pleasant patio surrounded by lush trees. The specialty is oysters, which come fried, grilled, as shooters, or on the half shell. The menu also offers fresh fish, pasta, chicken, and a selection of salads with gourmet greens. **FYI:** Reservations accepted. **Open:** Lunch Tues–Sat 11:30am–2:30pm; dinner Tues–Thurs 5–9pm, Fri–Sat 5–10pm, Sun 5–9pm. **Prices:** Main courses $11–$20. AE, CB, DC, DISC, MC, V.

⭐ Palace Cafe
8 E Cota St; tel 805/966-3133. 1 block E of State St. **Cajun/Caribbean.** The menu at this flamboyant hot spot features specialties such as crawfish étoufée, blackened redfish, cajun popcorn, gumbo, or barbecued shrimp. Unique cocktails like Cajun Martini or Caribbean rum punch can be found here. A good bet for dessert is the Louisiana bread pudding soufflé,

served with a powerful whiskey cream sauce. **FYI:** Reservations recommended. Beer and wine only. Additional location: 213 Paseo Nuevo (tel 899-9111). **Open:** Sun–Thurs 5:30–10pm, Fri–Sat 5:30–11pm. **Prices:** Main courses $12–$25. AE, MC, V. &

Paradise Cafe

702 Anacapa St; tel 805/962-4416. 1 block E of State St. **New American.** Housed in a historic building in Santa Barbara, with an umbrella-filled patio and two comfortable indoor dining rooms graced with palm trees. Variety of fresh seafood, burgers, pasta, and fresh salads, as well as entrees from the oak grill. **FYI:** Reservations accepted. **Open:** Mon–Sat 11am–11pm, Sun 8:30am–11pm. **Prices:** Main courses $6–$17. AE, MC, V. ■ ▲

Piatti's Ristorante

516 San Ysidro Rd (Montecito); tel 805/969-7520. San Ysidro exit off US 101. **Italian.** A serene restaurant with soft murals, wood and leather chairs, and classical music. An outdoor patio overlooks a beautiful creek. Extensive selection of antipasti, salads, pizzas, pastas, grilled vegetables, seafood, and chicken. Some dishes have a California twist, like the homemade cannelloni stuffed with chicken, artichokes, ricotta, and sage. **FYI:** Reservations recommended. Additional location: 5112 Hollister Ave, Goleta (tel 967-3775). **Open:** Sun–Thurs 11:30am–10pm, Fri–Sat 11:30am–11pm. **Prices:** Main courses $10–$20. AE, MC, V. ♥ &

♥ **The Stonehouse Restaurant**

In San Ysidro Ranch, 900 San Ysidro Lane, Montecito; tel 805/969-5046. San Ysidro Rd exit off US 101; go north (inland), then right on Mountain Dr. **Regional American.** Dining at a 100-year-old former citrus-packing house with thick sandstone walls, a sunny terrace, and ocean views. Chef Gerard Thompson is noted for his innovative regional American cuisine. **FYI:** Reservations recommended. Jazz. Children's menu. **Open:** Breakfast daily 8–11:30am; lunch daily 11:30am–2:30pm; dinner Sun–Thurs 6–9:30pm, Fri–Sat 6–10:30pm; brunch Sun 11:30am–2:30pm. **Prices:** Main courses $19–$26; prix fixe $39–$43. AE, MC, V. ♥ ■ ▲ VP

Woody's Beach Club and Cantina

229 W Montecito St; tel 805/963-9326. Castillo St exit off US 101. **Barbecue/Pizza.** Funky western cantina known for its ribs. The wild decor of this lively hangout includes sawdust on the floor, license plates on the walls, and an eclectic assortment of lanterns, moose heads, flags, stoplights, and even a bathtub. Pizza, burgers, tacos, ribs. Diners order from a counter and serve themselves from the salad bar and drink dispenser. **FYI:** Reservations accepted. Children's menu. Beer and wine only. **Open:** Sun–Thurs 11am–10pm, Fri–Sat 11am–11pm. **Prices:** Main courses $6–$30. AE, DC, DISC, MC, V. ▦ &

Your Place

22A N Milpas St; tel 805/966-5151. Milpas St exit off US 101. **Thai.** Among the myriad Thai restaurants in Santa Barbara, this one is consistently well received. Colorful umbrellas hang from the ceiling, and golden peacocks adorn the walls. The seafood platter is a combination of shrimp, fish, crab claws, scallops, water chestnuts, cashews, and ginger. Pad Thai, fried noodles, is a favorite. **FYI:** Reservations accepted. Beer and wine only. **Open:** Tues–Thurs 11am–10pm, Fri–Sat 11am–11pm, Sun 11am–10pm. **Prices:** Main courses $6–$14. AE, MC, V. &

Zia Cafe

532 State St (Downtown); tel 805/962-5391. **New Mexican.** One of the only restaurants in Southern California offering authentic Santa Fe products, this southwestern restaurant is cozy and attractive, with a copper bar and classic Santa Fe style. Whether you prefer spicy green or mild red chili sauce, you'll find them both served with enchiladas, blue corn tacos, chili rellenos, tamales, and burritos. **FYI:** Reservations recommended. Children's menu. **Open:** Breakfast Sat–Sun 9am–2pm; lunch daily 11am–4pm; dinner Mon–Thurs 4–10pm, Fri–Sun 4–11pm. **Prices:** Main courses $8–$10. MC, V. ◪ &

ATTRACTIONS ▦

Santa Barbara Mission

Mission and Laguna Sts; tel 805/682-4173 or 682-4175. Its twin bell towers and graceful beauty have earned this mission the title "Queen of the Missions." The tenth of the 21 California Spanish missions, it was established in 1786 and is still used as a local parish. Displayed in its museum are a typical early missionary's bedroom; 18th- and 19th-century furnishings; paintings and sculptures from Mexico; period kitchen utensils; and Native American tools, crafts, and artifacts. **Open:** Daily 9am–5pm. **$**

Santa Barbara County Courthouse

1100 Anacapa St; tel 805/962-6464. Occupying a full city block and set in a lush tropical garden, this building incorporates elements of Spanish-Moorish design, with towers and a turret, brilliant Tunisian tilework, and intricately stenciled ceilings. Historic murals by Dan Sayre Groesbeck depict memorable episodes in Santa Barbara history; a 10x13-foot Groesbeck painting on plaster that inspired the mural hangs outside the Mural Room. An elevator takes visitors to an observation deck on the roof of the clock tower for a view of the ocean, the mountains, and the red terra-cotta tile roofs of the city. A free guided tour is offered Wednesday and Friday at 10:30am, and Monday through Saturday at 2pm. **Open:** Daily 9am–4:30pm. **Free**

Santa Barbara Historical Museum

136 E de la Guerra St; tel 805/966-1601. This charming adobe complex contains one of the finest collections of regional history in California. Exhibits of local lore feature such art and artifacts as saddles and antique toys; late 19th-century paintings of California missions by Edwin Deakin; a 16th-century carved Spanish coffer from Majorca, Spain; and a collection of objects from the Chinese community that once

flourished here, highlighted by a carved Tong shrine from the turn of the century. Also on display are early letters, antique dolls, a late 19th-century period costume collection, and assorted memorabilia; the Gledhill Library has extensive holdings of books, maps, photographs, and manuscripts. Free guided tour every Wednesday, Saturday, and Sunday at 1:30pm.

Adjacent to the museum are two 19th-century adobes surrounding a tree-shaded courtyard. **Casa Covarrubias** was constructed on this site in 1817. The adjoining **Historic Adobe** was built in 1836 and was later moved to this location. **Open:** Tues–Sat 10am–5pm, Sun noon–5pm. **Free**

Santa Barbara Museum of Art
1130 State St; tel 805/963-4364. Featured collections of this museum include classical antiquities; works from the Italian Renaissance and Flemish schools; European impressionist paintings, including works by Monet; works by such early 20th-century European modernists as Chagall, Picasso, and Kandinsky; and a variety of American and Asian art. The photography collection boasts more than 1,500 items.

Most of the museum's 16,000-plus works are exhibited on a rotating basis. Temporary shows are also presented. Free guided tours are given Tues–Sun at 1pm; focus tours given selected Wednesday and Saturday at noon. **Open:** Tues–Wed and Fri–Sat 11am–5pm, Thurs 11am–9pm, Sun noon–5pm. **$$**

Santa Barbara Museum of Natural History
2559 Puesta del Sol Rd; tel 805/682-4711. Outside this museum visitors will encounter a 72-foot blue whale skeleton, one of only two on display in the country. Exhibits inside focus on the display, study, and interpretation of Pacific Coast natural history: flora, fauna, and prehistoric life. Local Native American history and culture are illustrated, with exhibits on basketry, textiles, and a full-size replica of a Chumash canoe. Other exhibits include the Nature Art Gallery, Geology and Fossil Hall, and a planetarium presenting star shows on weekends. Traveling exhibits are also featured. **Open:** Mon–Sat 9am–5pm, Sun 10am–5pm. **$$**

Fernald Mansion and Trussell–Winchester Adobe
414 W Montecito St; tel 805/966-1601. The Fernald Mansion (1862) is a fine example of Victorian architecture. The 14-room Queen Anne–style residence of Judge Charles Fernald, it features intricately carved exterior woodwork and is beuatifully furnished within. Next door is the Trussell–Winchester Adobe, built in 1854. An adobe structure with wood siding, its design is known as "Yankee Adobe," a typical hybrid of Mexican and American architectural periods. Its furnishings include some pieces that are a century old. **Open:** Sun 2–4pm. **Free**

Moreton Bay Fig Tree
Chapala and Montecito Sts. Famous for its size, this massive specimen casts a noontime shadow big enough to accommodate an estimated 10,000 people. Planted in 1877, it is thought to be the largest of its kind in the United States.

Stearns Wharf
End of State St. In addition to a small collection of shops, attractions, and restaurants, the city's 1872-vintage pier offers terrific views of the city and good drop-line fishing. The Dolphin Fountain at the foot of the wharf was created by Bud Bottoms for the city's 1982 bicentennial (copies are located in Puerto Vallarta, Mexico; Toba, Japan; and Yalta, Ukraine).

Santa Barbara Zoological Gardens
500 Niños Dr; tel 805/962-5339 or 962-6310 (recorded info). This zoo has more than 500 animals in open, naturalistic settings. Beautiful botanic displays augment the exhibits. There's also a children's Discovery Area; a miniature train ride; and a small carousel. Gift shop; snack bar. Picnic area with grills. **Open:** Peak (June–Aug) daily 9am–6pm. Reduced hours off-season. **$$**

Santa Barbara Botanic Garden
1212 Mission Canyon Rd; tel 805/682-4726. More than 60 acres of native trees, shrubs, cacti, and wildflowers can be seen at the garden, and there are more than 5 miles of trails. Free guided tours are offered daily at 2pm, with additional tours on Thursday, Saturday, and Sunday at 10:30am. **Open:** Peak (Mar–Oct) Mon–Fri 9am–5pm, Sat–Sun 9am–6pm. Reduced hours off-season. **$**

Santa Clara

Next door to San Jose, Santa Clara is in the heart of the Silicon Valley high-tech manufacturing complex and is part of a booming metropolitan area. The University of Santa Clara (1851) is the oldest institution for higher education in California. **Information:** Santa Clara Convention & Visitors Bureau, 2200 Laurelwood Rd, 2nd Floor, PO Box 387, Santa Clara 95054 (tel 408/296-7111).

HOTELS 🏨

≡≡≡ Biltmore Hotel & Suites
2151 Laurelwood Rd, 95054; tel 408/988-8411 or toll free 800/255-9925; fax 408/988-0225. Montague Expwy exit off US 101. Expansive lobby and adjacent atrium boast marble floors and columns, skylights, a grand piano, and richly appointed furnishings. **Rooms:** 262 rms and stes. CI 3pm/CO noon. Nonsmoking rms avail. **Amenities:** 🛁 ⚹ 🖭 🍷 A/C, satel TV w/movies. Some units w/minibars. **Services:** ✕ � 🛄 🔁 **Facilities:** 🔂 🖭 360 🔁 1 restaurant, 2 bars, whirlpool. Complimentary shuttle and free passes to nearby Gold's Gym. **Rates:** $109 S; $109–$119 D; $159–$179 ste. Extra person

$10. Children under age 12 stay free. Parking: Outdoor, free. Suites include a complimentary full breakfast. AE, CB, DC, DISC, EC, ER, MC, V.

≣≣≣ Embassy Suites
2885 Lakeside Dr, 95054; tel 408/496-6400 or toll free 800/ EMBASSY; fax 408/492-9121. Great American Pkwy exit off US 101 onto Bowers. Atrium-style lobby with bar and restaurant adjacent. Glass elevators afford lovely views. **Rooms:** 257 stes. CI 3pm/CO 1pm. Nonsmoking rms avail. Wood furniture, good lighting, attractive bedside lamps. **Amenities:** 🛗 🚰 📺 ⬛ A/C, satel TV w/movies, refrig, voice mail. **Services:** ✕ 🗝 🚐 🖨 ⬛ Turndown service available on request. **Facilities:** 🏋 ⬛ ⬛ ⬛ 1 restaurant, 2 bars, sauna, whirlpool, washer/dryer. Very pleasant indoor pool with overhead windows and plants. **Rates (BB):** $119–$159 ste. Extra person $15. Children under age 16 stay free. Parking: Outdoor, free. AE, CB, DC, DISC, JCB, MC, V.

≣≣ Mariani's Inn
2500 El Camino Real, 95051; tel 408/243-1431 or toll free 800/553-8666; fax 408/243-5745. Motel-like property has basic accommodations and a popular restaurant. **Rooms:** 145 rms, stes, and effic. CI 2pm/CO 11am. Nonsmoking rms avail. Fresh flowers in guest rooms. **Amenities:** 🛗 🚰 📺 A/C, cable TV w/movies, refrig. **Services:** ✕ 🚐 🖨 ⬛ Babysitting. Complimentary breakfast is served in the restaurant. **Facilities:** 🏋 ⬛ ⬛ 1 restaurant, 1 bar (w/entertainment), whirlpool, washer/dryer. Barbecue pit. **Rates (CP):** $79 S; $89 D; $97 ste; $104 effic. Extra person $8. Children under age 12 stay free. Parking: Outdoor, free. AE, CB, DC, DISC, MC, V.

≣≣≣ Quality Suites
3100 Lakeside Dr, 95054; tel 408/748-9800 or toll free 800/ 345-1554; fax 408/748-1476. Great America/Bowers exit off US 101. Subtle art deco furnishings adorn the lobby, which has dark cherry woods and a high ceiling and is flanked by an overhanging balcony. The raised lounge area outside is done in "library" style with fake plants, brass, glass stairs, and some fluorescent wall sconces. **Rooms:** 220 stes. Executive level. CI 2pm/CO noon. Nonsmoking rms avail. Decor is dark, done in mostly blues and mauves. Some furniture is rundown, with nicks and scratches. Both living and bed areas have windows for light and armoires for closet space. **Amenities:** 🛗 🚰 📺 A/C, cable TV w/movies, VCR, CD/tape player. All units w/minibars. **Services:** 🚐 🖨 ⬛ Full cooked-to-order breakfast included. Complimentary cocktails. **Facilities:** 🏋 ⬛ ⬛ ⬛ 1 bar, whirlpool, washer/dryer. **Rates (BB):** $155 ste. Extra person $10. Children under age 3 stay free. Parking: Indoor/outdoor, free. AE, DC, DISC, JCB, MC, V.

≣≣≣≣ Santa Clara Marriott
2700 Mission College Blvd, 95054; tel 408/988-1500 or toll free 800/228-9290; fax 408/727-4353. Great America Pkwy exit off US 101; turn right. Provides elegance and good service. Highly rated by conventioneers. **Rooms:** 758 rms and stes. Executive level. CI 3pm/CO 11am. Nonsmoking rms avail. **Amenities:** 🛗 🚰 📺 ⬛ A/C, cable TV w/movies, dataport, voice mail. Some units w/minibars, all w/terraces. Interactive network on TV provides services and information to guests. **Services:** ✕ 🗝 VP 🚐 🖨 ⬛ ⬛ Car-rental desk. Complimentary trolley to Great America (late Mar–Oct). **Facilities:** 🏋 ⬛ ⬛ ⬛ ⬛ ⬛ 2 restaurants, 1 bar, basketball, games rm, whirlpool, washer/dryer. **Rates:** $169 S or D; $450 ste. Parking: Indoor/outdoor, free. AE, CB, DC, DISC, JCB, MC, V.

≣≣≣ Westin Santa Clara
5101 Great America Pkwy, 95054; tel 408/986-0700 or toll free 800/228-3000; fax 408/980-3990. Great America Pkwy exit off US 101; turn right. Adjacent to Santa Clara Convention Center, this is also convenient for the leisure traveler visiting Great America. Close to the Santa Clara Golf and Tennis Club, too. No smoking in public areas, only inside designated guest rooms. **Rooms:** 500 rms and stes. Executive level. CI 3pm/CO noon. Nonsmoking rms avail. **Amenities:** 🛗 🚰 📺 ⬛ A/C, cable TV w/movies, dataport, voice mail. Some units w/minibars, some w/terraces, 1 w/whirlpool. **Services:** 🍽 🗝 VP 🚐 🖨 ⬛ **Facilities:** 🏋 ⬛ ⬛ ⬛ ⬛ 1 restaurant, 1 bar (w/entertainment), sauna, whirlpool. Fitness Room has Lifecycles, free weights, treadmill, bicycles. **Rates:** $199 S; $214 D; $250–$550 ste. Extra person $15. Children under age 18 stay free. Parking: Indoor/outdoor, free. AE, DC, DISC, EC, JCB, MC, V.

≣≣≣ Woodcrest Hotel
5415 Stevens Creek Blvd, 95051; tel 408/446-9636 or toll free 800/862-8282; fax 408/446-9739. Lawrence Expwy exit off I-280; left on Stevens Creek Blvd. **Rooms:** 60 rms and stes. CI 3pm/CO noon. Nonsmoking rms avail. Courtyard rooms are especially quiet. **Amenities:** 🛗 🚰 📺 ⬛ A/C, cable TV w/movies, VCR, bathrobes. Some units w/fireplaces, 1 w/whirlpool. Some units w/refrig; avail in those without for $15. Light dinner and snacks kept in the refrigerator. **Services:** 🖨 ⬛ Babysitting. Free videos. **Facilities:** ⬛ ⬛ 1 bar. **Rates (CP):** $77–$118 S; $92–$133 D; $99–$225 ste. Extra person $15. Children under age 12 stay free. Parking: Outdoor, free. Rates go down substantially on weekends. AE, DC, MC, V.

MOTELS

≣≣ Days Inn Santa Clara
4200 Great America Pkwy, 95054; tel 408/980-1525 or toll free 800/329-7466; fax 408/988-0976. Great America Pkwy exit off US 101; go right. Outside doesn't look promising, but interior is very nice, with old-world style lobby. High-ceilinged atrium has sky painting and huge flower arrangements. **Rooms:** 168 rms. CI 3pm/CO noon. Nonsmoking rms avail. Pleasing, with warm pastels and lots of light. **Amenities:** 🛗 A/C, TV w/movies. **Services:** ✕ 🚐 🖨 ⬛ **Facilities:** 🏋 ⬛ ⬛ 1 restaurant (bkfst only), whirlpool. Nicely landscaped pool area. Ballroom available. Meeting rooms open onto

garden. **Rates:** Peak (June–Aug) $79 S or D. Children under age 17 stay free. Lower rates off-season. AP rates avail. Parking: Outdoor, free. Great America packages avail when theme park is open. AE, DC, DISC, MC, V.

≝ Santa Clara Travelodge

3477 El Camino Real, 95051; tel 408/984-3364 or toll free 800/578-7878; fax 408/244-5561. Exit Lawrence Expwy S off US 101. On busy El Camino Real; basic accommodations for a reasonable price. **Rooms:** 43 rms. CI noon/CO noon. Nonsmoking rms avail. The closer to El Camino, the less quiet the room. **Amenities:** 🛅 🅿 🔲 A/C, cable TV, refrig. Microwaves in most rooms. **Facilities:** 🖼 🕭 Whirlpool. Small pool needs resurfacing. **Rates:** Peak (Apr–Aug) $56 S; $61 D. Extra person $5. Children under age 18 stay free. Lower rates off-season. Parking: Outdoor, free. AE, CB, DC, DISC, EC, JCB, MC, V.

≝≝ Santa Clara Vagabond Inn

3580 El Camino Real, 95051; tel 408/241-0771 or toll free 800/522-1555; fax 408/247-3386. From US 101 take Lawrence Expwy S; left on El Camino Real. Spacious grounds. Rooms in need of major refurbishing. **Rooms:** 70 rms and stes. Executive level. CI noon/CO noon. Nonsmoking rms avail. **Amenities:** 🛅 🅿 A/C, cable TV w/movies. **Services:** ✗ 🖼 🖂 🛎 Weekday newspapers, coffee, tea, popcorn in lobby. Discount tickets to local attractions. **Facilities:** 🖼 ⬚15 1 restaurant, washer/dryer. **Rates (CP):** $59–$69 S; $64–$69 D; $75 ste. Extra person $5. Children under age 18 stay free. Parking: Outdoor, free. Vagabond Business Club, for a membership fee of $15, offers upgraded rooms, discount coupons, complimentary in-room coffee and tea, free local phone calls, modem jack, free spouse stays, and 10th night free. AE, DC, DISC, MC, V.

ATTRACTIONS 🖼

De Saisset Museum

500 El Camino Real, Santa Clara University; tel 408/554-4528. The repository of an extensive California history collection, which focuses primarily on the period of Native American habitation and the Mission Period. Changing art exhibitions throughout the year. **Open:** Tues–Sun 11am–4pm. Closed 1–3 weeks in summer, 1–2 weeks in spring. Call ahead. **Free**

Mission Santa Clara de Asis

500 El Camino Real; tel 408/554-4023. This mission, the first outpost of Spanish civilization in the Santa Clara Valley, was founded in 1777. The original mission gardens surround the present church building, the sixth, built in 1927. A replica of the third mission church, it was built after the fifth church burned in 1926. Olive trees and grinding stones in the gardens date from the early mission period. **Open:** Daily 7am–7pm; Sun Mass at 10am. **Free**

Paramount's Great America

2401 Agnew Rd; tel 408/988-1800. Located 3 miles north via US 101, this 100-acre park combines amusement park and Hollywood movie–based entertainment. It offers more than 100 attractions, including six rollercoasters, numerous other thrill rides, an IMAX movie theater, four stage shows, a double-decker carousel, and the *Days of Thunder* motion simulator ride. Characters from Hanna-Barbera cartoons and such Paramount features as Star Trek are on hand to greet visitors. Children's play area, restaurants, snack shops. **Open:** Peak (Mem Day–Labor Day) Sun–Fri 10am–9pm, Sat–Sun 10am–11pm. Reduced hours off-season. Closed mid-Oct–mid-Mar. $$$$

Santa Cruz

Santa Cruz is a study in contrasts. The city is a legendary hot spot for social and political movements of the 1960s, but it is nevertheless rooted in the agricultural heritage of its surrounding areas. The many miles of beaches and great surfing make it a natural draw, while the University of California at Santa Cruz, tucked among the soaring redwoods, lends a college town atmosphere. **Information:** Santa Cruz County Conference & Visitors Council, 701 Front St, Santa Cruz 95060 (tel 408/425-1234 or toll free 800/833-3494).

HOTELS 🏨

≝ Dream Inn

175 W Cliff Dr, 95060; tel 408/426-4330 or toll free 800/421-6662; fax 408/426-4015. Bay St exit off CA 1/71. This aging property is wearing out. Carpeting in the hall and in some rooms is soiled. **Rooms:** 165 rms. CI 2pm/CO 11am. Nonsmoking rms avail. Rooms need refurbishing and painting. Gaudy, green print carpet throughout. **Amenities:** 🅿 🔲 A/C, cable TV w/movies, refrig, VCR. No phone. Some units w/terraces. TVs are equipped for the deaf and hard of hearing. **Services:** ✗ 🚐 🖼 🛎 Babysitting. **Facilities:** 🖼 ⬚175 🕭 1 restaurant, 1 bar (w/entertainment), 1 beach (ocean). **Rates:** Peak (June–Sept) $159 S or D. Extra person $10. Children under age 12 stay free. Lower rates off-season. Parking: Outdoor, free. AE, MC, V.

UNRATED Holiday Inn Express

600 Riverside Ave, 95060; tel 408/458-9660 or toll free 800/465-4329; fax 408/426-8775. This brand-new property sparkles. **Rooms:** 79 rms and stes. CI 2pm/CO 11am. Nonsmoking rms avail. Standard rooms have two queen beds. Some suites boast Roman tubs. **Amenities:** 🅿 A/C, cable TV w/movies, VCR. No phone. Some units w/terraces, some w/whirlpools. **Services:** 🖼 🛎 Babysitting. Videos available for rent. Coffee in lobby 24 hours. **Facilities:** 🖼 ⬚20 🕭 Whirlpool. **Rates (CP):** $58 S or D; $79 ste. Extra person $10. Parking: Outdoor, free. AE, DC, MC, V.

MOTELS

≣≣≣ The Inn at Pasatiempo

555 CA 17, 95060; tel 408/423-5000; fax 408/426-1737. Pasatiempo Dr exit. Located in an upscale neighborhood and beside an excellent 18-hole golf course. Beautifully kept grounds. **Rooms:** 54 rms and stes. CI open/CO 11am. Nonsmoking rms avail. Excellent accommodations are tastefully furnished, larger-than-average motor-inn rooms. Refurbished in 1996. **Amenities:** 🛏 ⚿ ☎ A/C, cable TV w/movies, in-rm safe. Some units w/minibars, some w/terraces, some w/fireplaces, some w/whirlpools. Suites have bathrobes. **Services:** X 🛆 ⇆ Twice-daily maid svce, babysitting. **Facilities:** 🏌 🏊 & 2 restaurants, 1 bar (w/entertainment). Golf available nearby, with advance reservations at $95 per person. Good meeting space; popular restaurant and bar. **Rates (CP):** Peak (June–Sept) $115 S or D; $165 ste. Extra person $10. Lower rates off-season. Parking: Outdoor, free. AE, DC, DISC, MC, V.

≣ Mission Inn

2250 Mission St, 95060; tel 408/425-5455 or toll free 800/995-0289; fax 408/457-0861. CA 1 S becomes Mission St. Located on the main road into town, near several retail establishments. Not in the best neighborhood. **Rooms:** 53 rms. CI 2pm/CO 11am. Nonsmoking rms avail. Freshly painted and generally well maintained. **Amenities:** 🛏 Cable TV w/movies, refrig, VCR. No A/C. **Services:** ⇆ Free coffee in lobby. **Facilities:** 🏊 & Whirlpool, washer/dryer. **Rates (CP):** Peak (Apr–Nov) $60–$95 S or D. Children under age 18 stay free. Lower rates off-season. Parking: Outdoor, free. Discount for seniors and children under 16. AE, MC, V.

≣≣≣ Ocean Pacific Inn

120 Washington, 95060; tel 408/457-1234 or toll free 800/995-0289; fax 408/457-0861. Boardwalk exit off CA 1. Located two blocks from the ocean. **Rooms:** 57 rms and stes. CI 2pm/CO 11am. Nonsmoking rms avail. Larger than average. Mini-suites very attractive. **Amenities:** 🛏 ⚿ 🔲 A/C, cable TV w/movies, VCR. Some units w/whirlpools. All suites and some rooms have microwaves and refrigerators. **Services:** 🛆 ⇆ Twice-daily maid svce, babysitting. **Facilities:** 🏌 🏊 & Whirlpool. **Rates (CP):** Peak (Apr–Oct) $53–$89 S or D; $89–$112 ste. Lower rates off-season. Parking: Outdoor, free. AE, MC, V.

INN

≣≣≣ Babbling Brook Inn

1025 Laurel St, 95060; tel 408/427-2437 or toll free 800/866-1131; fax 408/427-2437. Off CA 1. The largest inn in Santa Cruz, a secluded property with waterfalls, a creek, and a gazebo amid gardens, pines, and redwoods. Near the beach, wharf, boardwalk, shops, tennis courts, running paths, and historic homes. **Rooms:** 12 rms. CI 3pm/CO noon. No smoking. Rooms are small, but with lovely country French decor. Most rooms have outside entrance. **Amenities:** 🛏 ⚿ 🔲 Cable TV w/movies, refrig, dataport, VCR, CD/tape player, bathrobes. No A/C. Some units w/terraces, all w/fireplaces, some w/whirlpools. **Services:** X 🛆 Country breakfast, afternoon wine and cheese and homemade cookies. **Facilities:** & Sauna, whirlpool. **Rates (BB):** Peak (May–Oct) $85–$165 S or D. Extra person $21. Min stay peak and wknds. Lower rates off-season. Parking: Outdoor, free. AE, MC, V.

RESORT

≣≣≣ The Chaminade at Santa Cruz

1 Chaminade Lane, PO Box 2788, 95065; tel 408/475-5600 or toll free 800/283-6569; fax 408/476-4798. Soquel Dr exit off CA 1. 280 acres. Primarily an executive conference facility, Chaminade welcomes individual travelers as well. The retreat offers many distractions, but is perfect for relaxation. **Rooms:** 152 rms and stes. CI 4pm/CO noon. Nonsmoking rms avail. In 11 buildings, rooms in various configurations—some with two vanity areas and work space. **Amenities:** 🛏 ⚿ A/C, cable TV w/movies. Some units w/terraces, some w/whirlpools. **Services:** X 🖳 VP 🚗 🛆 ⇆ Car-rental desk, babysitting. **Facilities:** 🏌 🎾 🏓 🏊 💻 & 2 restaurants (see "Restaurants" below), 1 bar (w/entertainment), games rm, spa, sauna, whirlpool. Indoor basketball, three whirlpools, volleyball and badminton court, and nature trails. **Rates:** $159–$179 S or D; $209 ste. Extra person $35. Children under age 5 stay free. Parking: Outdoor, free. AE, CB, DC, DISC, JCB, MC, V.

RESTAURANTS 🍴

★ Gilbert's

25 Municipal Wharf; tel 408/423-5200. Boardwalk exit off CA 1. **Seafood/Pasta.** With ocean views like this, no decor is necessary. It's a pleasant, open room with quick service. Seafood is the main event; but a number of pasta dishes as well as steaks and chicken are also served. **FYI:** Reservations recommended. Children's menu. Dress code. **Open:** Daily 11:30am–9:30pm. **Prices:** Main courses $11–$23. AE, DC, DISC, MC, V. 🏞 🖼 🚗 &

★ Miramar

45 Municipal Wharf; tel 408/423-4441. Off CA 1. **Seafood.** Tables are placed so everyone has a view of the ocean. A good selection of local seafood includes salmon, sole, red snapper, and the calamari for which this area is famous. **FYI:** Reservations recommended. **Open:** Peak (June–Aug) Mon–Thurs 11am–9pm, Fri 11am–10pm, Sat 11am–10:30pm, Sun 9:30am–9pm. **Prices:** Main courses $12–$23. AE, DISC, MC, V. 🏖 🏞 🖼 🚗 📺 &

♥ The Sunset Dining Room

In the Chaminade at Santa Cruz, 1 Chaminade Lane; tel 408/475-5600. Soquel Dr exit off CA 1. **Eclectic.** Elegant furnishings with lovely views of the hills and the ocean, particularly from the patio. Nightly buffets include the Thursday-night Italian spread, with chicken saltimbocca, ratatouille, tortellini, and sea bass, as well as desserts. Champagne brunch on Sunday, and on Sunday night, a California regional buffet. The intimate Library restaurant is open to the public Fridays and Saturdays. **FYI:** Reservations recommended. Jacket required. **Open:** Breakfast daily 7–9:30am; lunch Mon–Sat 11:30am–2pm; dinner daily 5:30–9:30pm; brunch Sun 10am–2pm. **Prices:** Main courses $17–$29. AE, MC, V. 🏔️ VP ♿

ATTRACTIONS 🏛️

Santa Cruz City Museum of Natural History
1305 E Cliff Dr; tel 408/429-3773. Overlooking Seabright Beach between the Boardwalk and the Small Craft Harbor, the museum offers collections, exhibits, and educational programs focusing on the natural and cultural history of the northern Monterey Bay area. Some highlights are exhibits of prehistoric animal life, with a fossilized 20,000-year-old mastodon skull; a life-size model of a California gray whale; a tidepool exhibit with living specimens; and exhibits on the culture of the Ohlone Indians. Tours available. **Open:** Tues–Sun 10am–5pm. **Free**

University of California, Santa Cruz Arboretum
Tel 408/427-9798. Located on the southern edge of the UCSC campus. Renowned for its unique collections, the arboretum contains 8,000 plants, with noteworthy collections from Australia and South Africa, and an exceptionally complete New Zealand garden. There are also large exhibits of native and drought-tolerant California plants. Book and gift shop; library. **Open:** Daily 9am–5pm. **Free**

Joseph M Long Marine Laboratory
100 Shaffer Rd; tel 408/459-4308. Located past the end of Delaware St, near Natural Bridges State Beach (see below). This University of California marine research facility offers guided tours that cover the aquarium and such exhibits as a model of the Monterey Bay submarine canyon, fossils, an 85-foot blue whale skeleton, and a touch tank. Changing exhibits, spanning a variety of topics, are also visited. Gift and book shop. **Open:** Tues–Sun 1–4pm. Group tours 9:30 and 11am. **$**

Natural Bridges State Beach
2531 West Cliff Dr; tel 408/423-4609 or 688-3241. Although a fascinating array of wildlife can be found within this park's 65 acres, the most notable is the annual population of 100,000 Monarch butterflies, who migrate to the park each winter. The park's eucalyptus grove, planted by early settlers, provides the Monarchs with a safe wintering place until spring. A trail runs through the middle of the Monarch Natural Preserve (Oct–Mar; guided tours on weekends).

Another trail winds through the meadows and down to the Moore Creek wetlands, and tide pools are accessible during low-tide periods (tours available). The visitor center has trail maps, exhibits, and a book and gift shop. Beach activities are also popular in the park; picnic tables with grills are available beneath the eucalyptus trees around the main parking lot. **Open:** Daily dawn–dusk; visitor center, daily 10am–4pm. **$$$**

Santa Maria

The inland valley of Santa Maria was a Central Coast center for the Chumash Indians, Spanish rancheros, and the American pioneers. Oil and agriculture form the backbone of the area's economy. **Information:** Santa Maria Visitors & Convention Bureau, 614 S Broadway, Santa Maria 93454 (tel 805/925-2403).

HOTELS 🏨

🏨🏨 Ramada Suites
2050 N Preisker Lane, 93454; tel 805/928-6000 or toll free 800/2-RAMADA; fax 805/928-0356. Broadway exit off US 101. New Spanish-style stucco hotel. Spacious, plant-filled lobby has hand-painted murals and ceiling fans. Furnishings and carpeting seem a bit worn around the edges. **Rooms:** 210 stes. CI 4pm/CO noon. Nonsmoking rms avail. Very large rooms have blond furniture, beige carpet, and kitchen with stove and eating counter. **Amenities:** 🛏️ 🍴 📺 A/C, cable TV w/movies, refrig. Wet bar. **Services:** 🍽️ 🛎️ 🍷 **Facilities:** 🏋️ 75 ♿ 1 restaurant (bkfst and dinner only), 1 bar (w/entertainment), whirlpool, washer/dryer. **Rates:** Peak (June–Oct) $69–$138 ste. Extra person $10. Children under age 18 stay free. Min stay wknds. Lower rates off-season. MAP rates avail. Parking: Outdoor, free. AE, DC, DISC, MC, V.

🏨🏨 Santa Maria Airport Hilton
3455 Skyway Dr, 93455 (Santa Maria Airport); tel 805/928-8000 or toll free 800/HILTONS; fax 805/928-5251. Betteravia exit off US 101; go west and follow signs to airport. This modern four-story hotel near the south end of town has been extensively renovated. The lobby features striking, variegated marble floors, mirrored pillars, intricate moldings, and new artwork. A pleasant atrium offers sunken seating areas, glass elevators, water sculpture, and garden cafe. **Rooms:** 190 rms and stes. Executive level. CI 3pm/CO noon. Nonsmoking rms avail. Some units have views of airport. **Amenities:** 🛏️ 🍴 A/C, cable TV w/movies. Some units w/terraces. Wet bars in some rooms. TDD available for deaf or hard of hearing guests. Rooms facing atrium have terraces. **Services:** ✗ 🛎️ 🍷 Twice-daily maid svce, social director, babysitting. **Facilities:** 🏋️ 425 ♿ 2 restaurants, 2 bars (w/entertainment), whirlpool. Nightclub with dancing. YMCA pass available. **Rates:** $54–$84 S or D; $74 ste. Children under age 18 stay free. Parking: Outdoor, free. AE, MC, V.

🏨🏨🏨 Santa Maria Inn
801 S Broadway, 93454; tel 805/928-7777 or toll free 800/462-4276; fax 805/928-5690. Historic inn, now in two buildings, has a lovely, oak-paneled lobby filled with antiques.

Grounds feature a beautiful brick patio with wrought-iron tables, a fountain, and an award-winning rose garden. **Rooms:** 166 rms and stes. CI 3pm/CO noon. Nonsmoking rms avail. Antique-style furnishings. Rooms in original building are smaller than newer ones. Zaca Mesa suite has hand-painted tile fireplace; bridal suite has canopy bed. **Amenities:** ⬜ ⬜ ⬜ ⬜ A/C, satel TV w/movies, refrig, VCR. Some units w/minibars, some w/terraces, some w/fireplaces, some w/whirlpools. **Services:** ✕ ⬜ ⬜ ⬜ Masseur. **Facilities:** ⬜ ⬜ ⬜ ⬜ 2 restaurants (*see* "Restaurants" below), 3 bars (1 w/entertainment), sauna, steam rm, whirlpool, beauty salon. Wine cellar with wine bar; gallery with ice cream parlor, shops. Putting green, Ping-Pong. **Rates:** Peak (May–Oct) $99–$140 S; $107–$150 D; $160–$245 ste. Extra person $10. Children under age 12 stay free. Lower rates off-season. Parking: Indoor/outdoor, free. AE, CB, DC, DISC, ER, JCB, MC, V.

MOTEL

⬛⬛ Comfort Inn
210 S Nicholson Ave, 93454; tel 805/922-5891 or toll free 800/228-5150; fax 805/928-9222. E Main exit off US 101. Caters to patients of, and visitors to, nearby hospital. **Rooms:** 62 rms. CI 3pm/CO noon. Nonsmoking rms avail. Large rooms with pastel tropical decor, light wood furnishings. **Amenities:** ⬜ ⬜ A/C, cable TV w/movies, refrig. All units w/terraces. **Services:** ⬜ ⬜ ⬜ Twice-daily maid svce. **Facilities:** ⬜ ⬜ ⬜ Whirlpool, playground, washer/dryer. Nicely landscaped pool and spa area with new deck; pool was recently resurfaced. **Rates (CP):** Peak (May 23–Sept 30) $66 S; $76 D. Extra person $10. Children under age 18 stay free. Lower rates off-season. Parking: Outdoor, free. AE, CB, DISC, JCB, MC, V.

RESTAURANT ⬛

Santa Maria Inn Restaurant
801 S Broadway; tel 805/928-7777. **Regional American/Barbecue.** Old building with English decor, antique fireplace in lobby, garden room, and English pub. Specialty is Santa Maria–style barbecue: top sirloin, pork chops, tri-tip, chicken, or baby back pork ribs cooked over Santa Maria Valley red oak wood. Prime rib and a number of vegetarian dishes are also served. Friday happy hour includes complimentary barbecue. **FYI:** Reservations recommended. Karaoke/DJ. Children's menu. **Open:** Breakfast daily 6:30–11am; lunch daily 11am–2pm; dinner daily 5–9pm. **Prices:** Main courses $13–$19. AE, DISC, MC, V. ⬛ ⬜

ATTRACTION ⬛

Santa Maria Valley Historical Society and Museum
616 S Broadway; tel 805/922-3130. Exhibits arranged in chronological order begin with the Chumash Indian culture and progress through the Mission, Rancho, and Pioneer periods. Children's Corner has exhibits appealing to younger visitors. Includes pictures, artifacts, and memorabilia from each period. **Open:** Tues–Sat noon–5pm. **Free**

Santa Monica

Although they are bordered on one side by Los Angeles, Santa Monicans have always considered themselves apart from their big city neighbors. And Santa Monica does maintain its distinct beach community feel with its extravagant hillside homes to the north, the recently renovated pier, the exclusive shops and restaurants on Main St, and the touristy Third St Promenade. **Information:** Santa Monica Visitor & Information Center, 520 Broadway #250, Santa Monica 90401 (tel 310/319-6263).

HOTELS ⬛

⬛⬛⬛ Holiday Inn Bay View Plaza
530 Pico Blvd, 90405; tel 310/399-9344 or toll free 800/HOLIDAY; fax 310/399-2504 or 3322. At 6th St, W of Lincoln. Well located four blocks from Santa Monica's beach. It is a serviceable hotel catering to tour groups, with no frills. **Rooms:** 309 rms and stes. CI 4pm/CO noon. Nonsmoking rms avail. Most rooms have ocean views. **Amenities:** ⬜ ⬜ ⬜ A/C, cable TV w/movies, voice mail. Some units w/minibars, some w/terraces, some w/whirlpools. **Services:** ✕ ⬜ ⬜ ⬜ ⬜ Car-rental desk, babysitting. Desk clerks speak English, Spanish, French, German, and Japanese. **Facilities:** ⬜ ⬜ ⬜ ⬜ 1 restaurant, 1 bar (w/entertainment), whirlpool, beauty salon, washer/dryer. **Rates:** $133–$163 S; $143–$173 D. Extra person $10. Children under age 17 stay free. Parking: Indoor, free. AE, CB, DC, DISC, JCB, MC, V.

⬛⬛ Hotel Oceana
849 Ocean Ave, 90403; tel 310/393-0486 or toll free 800/777-0758. At Montana Ave. An apartment-style hotel very popular with families; excellent location in a residential neighborhood across from Pacific Palisades, with an ocean view. Remodeling should be completed. **Rooms:** 63 stes. CI 3pm/CO 11am. Nonsmoking rms avail. One- and two-bedroom apartments. Rooms are clean, but furniture is old. **Amenities:** ⬜ ⬜ Cable TV, refrig, VCR. No A/C. All units w/terraces. **Services:** ⬜ ⬜ Babysitting. Small continental breakfast; newspaper; coffee in lobby at all times. **Facilities:** ⬜ ⬜ Washer/dryer. **Rates:** Peak (Apr 9–Oct 25) $155–$295 ste. Lower rates off-season. Parking: Indoor, free. AE, CB, DC, DISC, JCB, MC, V.

⬛⬛⬛ Loews Santa Monica Beach Hotel
1700 Ocean Ave, 90401; tel 310/458-6700 or toll free 800/23-LOEWS; fax 310/458-0020. A grand hotel by the sea, with an art deco facade and five-story glass atrium. **Rooms:** 347 rms and stes. Executive level. CI 3pm/CO noon. Nonsmoking rms avail. Done in sunset-hued pastels with marble-topped dressers, most rooms are comfortable, but lacking in

polish. Ocean Premier rooms feature big terraces accented by planters facing the Pacific. **Amenities:** 🛁 🅰 🍽 A/C, refrig, dataport, voice mail, bathrobes. All units w/minibars, some w/terraces. All accommodations come with a scale, plus iron and ironing board; some feature private fax machines. **Services:** ✗ 🗝 VP 🚗 🖨 🛎 🍽 Twice-daily maid svce, car-rental desk, masseur, children's program, babysitting. "Star" service promises to respond to guest needs quickly. **Facilities:** 🏊 🚣 900 💻 ♿ 2 restaurants, 1 bar (w/entertainment), spa, sauna, steam rm, whirlpool, beauty salon, day-care ctr. Topped by a glass dome, the pool has a dynamite ocean view; free weights and exercise machines are also located here. For serious workouts, the on-premises Jackson Sousa facility offers, among other things, weight and cardiovascular equipment and aerobics classes. **Rates:** $225–$425 S; $245–$445 D; $500–$2,500 ste. Extra person $20. Children under age 12 stay free. Parking: Indoor, $13–$15/day. AE, CB, DC, DISC, EC, ER, JCB, MC, V.

≣≣ Pacific Shore Hotel
1819 Ocean Ave, 90401; tel 310/451-8711 or toll free 800/622-8711; fax 310/394-6657. At Pico Blvd. A basic, nondescript hotel with unexceptional rooms; however, located right across from the Santa Monica beach. **Rooms:** 168 rms. CI 3pm/CO noon. Nonsmoking rms avail. **Amenities:** 🛁 🍽 A/C, TV w/movies, dataport, in-rm safe. Some units w/minibars. Some units have refrigerators. **Services:** ✗ 🗝 🍽 Car-rental desk. **Facilities:** 🏊 🚣 80 1 restaurant, 1 bar, spa, sauna, whirlpool, washer/dryer. **Rates:** Peak (June–Oct) $135–$155 S or D. Extra person $15. Children under age 12 stay free. Lower rates off-season. Parking: Outdoor, free. AE, CB, DC, DISC, EC, ER, JCB, MC, V.

≣≣≣ Radisson Huntley Hotel
1111 2nd St, 90403; tel 310/394-5454 or toll free 800/333-3333; fax 310/458-9776. This 18-story hotel, the tallest in Santa Monica, features an outdoor elevator. An old building with a small art deco lobby. Close to Santa Monica beach. **Rooms:** 213 rms and stes. CI 3pm/CO noon. Nonsmoking rms avail. Small rooms and baths. **Amenities:** 🛁 🅰 🍽 A/C, cable TV w/movies, dataport, voice mail. All units w/minibars. **Services:** ✗ 🗝 VP 🖨 🍽 Car-rental desk, babysitting. **Facilities:** 125 ♿ 1 restaurant, 1 bar, beauty salon. Toppers serves mainly Mexican food, sports a south-of-the-border decor, and offers a wonderful view on four sides. **Rates:** $150–$180 S or D; $400–$450 ste. Extra person $20. Children under age 17 stay free. Parking: Indoor, $7.50/day. AE, CB, DC, DISC, ER, JCB, MC, V.

≣≣≣≣ Sheraton Miramar Hotel
101 Wilshire Blvd, 90401; tel 310/576-7777 or toll free 800/325-3535; fax 310/458-7912. Great location, right across from Santa Monica beach. Gorgeously landscaped with old Moreton fig tree in courtyard, beautiful flowers, and subtropical shrubs. There are three facilities: an older brick building, a newer tower, and a luxury bungalow complex. **Rooms:** 302 rms and stes; 32 cottages/villas. Executive level. CI 3pm/CO noon. Nonsmoking rms avail. Small bathrooms, except in new bungalows. **Amenities:** 🛁 🅰 📠 🍽 A/C, dataport, voice mail, in-rm safe. All units w/minibars, some w/terraces. Iron and ironing board in every room. **Services:** ✗ 🗝 VP 🚗 🖨 🍽 Twice-daily maid svce, car-rental desk, masseur, babysitting. **Facilities:** 🏊 900 ♿ 2 restaurants, 2 bars (1 w/entertainment), spa, sauna, steam rm, whirlpool, beauty salon. American Airlines office in building. Two-story, full-service health spa. **Rates:** Peak (July–Oct) $230–$260 S or D; $305–$425 ste; $350–$800 cottage/villa. Extra person $20. Children under age 17 stay free. Lower rates off-season. Parking: Indoor/outdoor, $11/day. AE, CB, DC, DISC, EC, ER, JCB, MC, V.

≣≣≣≣ Shutters on the Beach
1 Pico Blvd, 90405; tel 310/458-0030 or toll free 800/334-9000; fax 415/458-4589. This hotel, located right on Santa Monica's magnificent strand, looks like an overgrown Cape Cod cottage, with gray clapboard, fishscale shingles, and jaunty gray-and-white awnings. **Rooms:** 198 rms and stes. CI 3pm/CO noon. Nonsmoking rms avail. Rooms are as fresh as a sea breeze, with crisp white-linen duvets. Marble bathroom. Ocean views. **Amenities:** 🛁 🅰 🍽 A/C, cable TV w/movies, dataport, VCR, voice mail, in-rm safe, bathrobes. All units w/minibars, all w/terraces, some w/fireplaces, some w/whirlpools. Winning features include a waterproof Walkman and toy rubber whale by the tub. Showers have three heads. 27-inch TV with VCR. **Services:** ✗ 🗝 VP 🚗 🖨 🍽 Twice-daily maid svce, car-rental desk, social director, masseur, babysitting. **Facilities:** 🏊 🚲 🚣 300 ♿ 2 restaurants, 2 bars (1 w/entertainment), 1 beach (ocean), spa, sauna, steam rm, whirlpool. Equipped with free weights and a fleet of Lifecycles and other machines, the workout room (no charge for guests) is spacious and paired with attractive locker facilities. The beautiful pool is located in the courtyard and is surrounded by flowers. **Rates:** $280–$450 S or D; $675–$2000 ste. Extra person $50. Parking: Indoor, $17/day. AE, CB, DC, DISC, EC, ER, JCB, MC, V.

INN

≣≣≣ Channel Road Inn
219 W Channel Rd, 90402; tel 310/459-1920; fax 310/454-9920. Everything an inn should be. This three-story blue building, half-block from the beach, features a homey parlor with fireplace, oak floors, Chinese rugs, and lovely English furniture. **Rooms:** 14 rms and stes. CI 3pm/CO noon. No smoking. Each room is uniquely and lovingly decorated. **Amenities:** 🛁 🅰 🍽 Cable TV, bathrobes. No A/C. Some units w/terraces. **Services:** 🖨 🍽 Twice-daily maid svce, afternoon tea and wine/sherry served. Gracious staff. Fresh lemonade. **Facilities:** 🚲 ♿ Games rm, whirlpool, guest lounge w/TV. Free use of bicycles. Hot tub on hillside. **Rates (BB):** $95–$180 D; $200–$225 ste. Extra person $15. Children under age 16 stay free. Parking: Outdoor, free. AE, MC, V.

RESTAURANTS

★ Border Grill
1445 4th St; tel 310/451-1655. **Mexican.** After-work meeting place popular with singles. Festive decor includes Mexican cartoon figures covering high walls, and bare tables with tall, colored candles. Loud Latin music can drown out conversation. Specialties include grilled cactus salad, green corn tamales, seabass "Pescado Veracruzana," border vegetarian grill. Excellent margaritas. **FYI:** Reservations recommended. Children's menu. **Open:** Dinner Mon–Thurs 5:30–10pm, Fri–Sat 5:30–11pm, Sun 5–10pm. **Prices:** Main courses $11–$17. AE, CB, DC, DISC, MC, V. 🚗 VP ও

Camelions
246 26th St; tel 310/395-0746. **Californian/French.** Resembles an Italian country villa, with red brick exterior and several dining rooms with fireplaces, all on a rambling property. Patronized by Brentwood and Santa Monica gentry, the restaurant serves trendy French-California dishes: crostini of foie gras, red lentil cakes with smoked salmon and arugula, Lake Superior whitefish and fried spinach, lemon tart, crème brûlée. **FYI:** Reservations recommended. **Open:** Lunch Tues–Sun 11:30am–2:30pm; dinner Tues–Sun 6–10pm. **Prices:** Main courses $25–$35. AE, CB, DC, DISC, ER, MC, V. ♥ 🛎 🖼 ও

♣ Chinois on Main
2709 Main St; tel 310/392-9025. **French/Asian.** From superchef Wolfgang Puck, a trendy restaurant with bright lacquered tables and chic decor. Signature dishes are sizzling catfish, Szechuan beef, and Shanghai lobster. **FYI:** Reservations recommended. **Open:** Lunch Wed–Fri 11:30am–2pm; dinner Mon–Sat 6:30–10:30pm, Sun 5:30–10pm. **Prices:** Main courses $20–$30. AE, DC, DISC, MC, V. VP ও

★ Knoll's Black Forest Inn
2454 Wilshire Blvd; tel 310/395-2212. **Continental/German.** The jovial owner has cooked here for 36 years and decorated it like a country inn. Great for family celebrations. With many repeat customers, it's regarded as a treasure in Santa Monica. German specialties include venison, goose, veal with chanterelles, and pork with red cabbage. Big selection of German beers. **FYI:** Reservations recommended. **Open:** Lunch Tues–Fri 11:30am–2:30pm; dinner Tues–Sun 5–10pm. **Prices:** Main courses $12–$24; prix fixe $27. AE, CB, DC, DISC, ER, MC, V. ♥ 🛎 🖼 VP ও

★ Library Alehouse
2911 Main St; tel 310/314-4855. **Pub.** This is one of the hottest concepts in LA restaurants—a microbrewery with a variety of ales, beers, and wines to sample along with excellent sandwiches, salads, and entrees. The bartenders are friendly, the locals are numerous, and the sleek interior and patio have a modernist feel, with light wood, unique lighting, and careful attention to detail. In addition to savory munchies such as fried calamari or papaya quesadillas, the entrees include linguine with manila clams and a sage-crusted

pork chop. **FYI:** Reservations accepted. Beer and wine only. **Open:** Daily 11am–11pm. **Prices:** Main courses $8–$12. AE, DC, MC, V. 🛎 ও

♣ Michael's
1147 3rd St; tel 310/451-0843. **French.** Celebrities come to be seen and to enjoy the sensational cooking of Michael McCarty, a pioneer of California-French cuisine since the 1970s. Located in an updated 1930s house with salmon stucco, the pink-walled dining room contains a valuable contemporary art collection. A magnificent dining patio with a fountain is under canvas awnings. Choices include chicken and Montrachet goat-cheese salad, duck breast with peppercorn cognac sauce, steak with french fries. **FYI:** Reservations recommended. **Open:** Lunch Tues–Fri 11:30am–2:30pm; dinner Tues–Sat 5:30–10pm. **Prices:** Main courses $18–$25; prix fixe $17. AE, MC, V. ♥ VP ও

Ocean Ave Seafood
1401 Ocean Ave; tel 310/394-5669. **Seafood.** Very popular restaurant with an affluent, older crowd and local business types. Holds over 200 people in spaces broken up for privacy. Its long, semi-outdoor dining room offers a view of Ocean Blvd, the Palisades, and the ocean. Oyster bar features many varieties. Specialties include chilled and steamed shellfish, Maine lobster, pasta, chicken, steak, plus an award-winning cioppino. **FYI:** Reservations recommended. Children's menu. **Open:** Lunch Mon–Fri 11:30am–3pm, Sat–Sun noon–3pm; dinner Mon–Thurs 5:30–10pm, Fri–Sat 5:30–10:30pm, Sun 5–10pm; brunch Sun 11:30am–3pm. **Prices:** Main courses $15–$25. AE, CB, DC, DISC, MC, V. 🛎 🖼 🚻 VP ও

⑤ ★ The Omelette Parlor
2732 Main St; tel 310/399-7892. **American.** One of the last of California restaurant pioneer Al Ehringer's 1970s empire of friendly, funky, fun bars and eateries near the beach. Casual, woodsy storefront, along with booths, lots of plants, and a popular back patio. Half-price "early bird" (6–7am) specials. Large specialty omelettes include Schwarzenegger's Body Builder, Veggie Workout, and Fire Station No 2. Other breakfast fare, salads, and sandwiches served. **FYI:** Reservations not accepted. Beer and wine only. **Open:** Mon–Fri 6am–2:30pm, Sat–Sun 6am–4pm. **Prices:** Lunch main courses $4–$7. AE, MC, V. 🛎 🚻 ও

★ Pentola Taverna
312 Wilshire Blvd; tel 310/451-1963. **Italian.** Great food and a lively ambience, just around the corner from the Third St Promenade. Wood paneling and a massive bar create a warm welcome. Creative and delicious, pasta choices include penne with charred ahi, ginger, leeks, and tomatoes; or grilled chicken tossed with spaghetti, asparagus, and sun-dried tomatoes. Cappuccino arrives in a cup nearly as big as a bathtub, accompanied by melt-in-your-mouth chocolate cookies. **FYI:** Reservations recommended. **Open:** Lunch Mon–Fri 11:30am–3pm; dinner daily 5–10:30pm. **Prices:** Main courses $9–$18. AE, DC, MC, V. VP ও

Rockenwagner
In Edgemar Museum and Shopping Complex, 2435 Main St; tel 310/399-6504. **Californian/German.** An "in" place on Main St, Santa Monica's restaurant row, next door to a contemporary art museum. The decor features bizarre artistic touches, fountains, and walls of glass. The food includes Maine lobster, crab soufflé, and lamb. Also serves excellent weekend brunch. A long bakery counter lines one side of the restaurant, where you can pick up fresh baked goods to take home. **FYI:** Reservations recommended. **Open:** Lunch Tues–Fri 11:30am–2:30pm; dinner Mon–Fri 6–10pm, Sat–Sun 5:30–10pm; brunch Sat–Sun 9am–2:30pm. **Prices:** Main courses $18–$23. AE, MC, V. 💟 🎦 VP 🖔

⑤ ★ Sabor
3221 Pico Blvd; tel 310/829-3781. **Californian/South American.** Urbanized flavors of the southern United States and south of the border, including South America. The setting is that of a beautifully lit, festive Latin American town square. Specialties include Yucatán chicken-lime soup, buttermilk coxinha puffs filled with chicken and goat cheese, and chile rellenos with pasilla chiles. Novel desserts and an extensive, but inexpensive, wine list. **FYI:** Reservations recommended. Beer and wine only. **Open:** Lunch Mon–Fri 11:30am–3pm; dinner Mon–Fri 5:30–10pm, Sat–Sun 5:30–9pm. **Prices:** Main courses $8–$16. AE, MC, V. 🎦 VP 🖔

★ Schatzi on Main
3110 Main St; tel 310/399-4800. **Californian.** California-style decor with light wood furnishings, old-brick floors, plants, well-spaced tables, and booths. The owners, Maria Shriver and Arnold Schwarzenegger, often stop by for breakfast. Menu items might be Maria's oriental chicken salad; bratwurst and knockwurst plate; or brick-oven, very cheesy, New York–style pizza. Prix fixe dinner Sun–Thurs, $25. **FYI:** Reservations recommended. **Open:** Breakfast Mon–Fri 7–11am; lunch Mon–Fri 11:30am–3pm; dinner Mon–Thurs 6–10pm, Fri–Sat 6–11pm, Sun 6–10pm; brunch Sat–Sun 9am–3pm. **Prices:** Main courses $12–$25. AE, DC, MC, V. 🍽 🎦 VP 🖔

♣ Valentino
3115 Pico Blvd; tel 310/829-4313. **Italian.** One of the best Italian restaurants in Los Angeles, where it's best to leave the ordering to proprietor Piero Selvaggio. It has attracted a clientele of Hollywood celebrities and business diners for 24 years. Elegant but welcoming, decor is ultra-sophisticated, with silver and gold lacquered walls. Although the menu changes constantly, you'll find specialties such as northern Italian risottos, osso buco, pastas, and veal chops. Known for its excellent, well-priced, encyclopedic wine list. **FYI:** Reservations recommended. Dress code. Additional location: Primi at 10543 W Pico Blvd, Los Angeles (tel 475-9235). **Open:** Lunch Fri 11am–2pm; dinner Mon–Sat 5–11:30pm. **Prices:** Prix fixe $50. AE, CB, DC, DISC, ER, MC, V. 💟 🍽 VP 🖔

REFRESHMENT STOP 🥤

Benita's Frites
1433 3rd St Promenade; tel 310/458-2889. **French fries.** Located in the food court along the promenade. The only item served is french fries, accompanied by various types of salsa, but some say they're the best fries in town. **Open:** Sun–Mon 11am–9pm, Tues–Thurs 11am–10pm, Fri–Sat 11am–midnight. No CC. 🍽 🖔

ATTRACTIONS 🏛

Pacific Park
380 Santa Monica Pier; tel 360/260-8748. Located on the **Santa Monica Pier,** a 1975 LA County Historical Landmark, this family amusement park marks a return to the days when the Pier offered Southern California the very best in outdoor entertainment. Pacific Park offers 11 rides, including a giant Ferris wheel that will take riders more than 100 feet above the Santa Monica Beach, and a 55–foot roller coaster

Museum of Flying
2772 Donald Douglas Loop N; tel 310/392-8822. One of the largest collections of planes on the West Coast is on display here, housed in a dramatic steel-and-glass structure at the site where Douglas Aircraft was founded in 1922. Approximately 40 aircraft, maintained in flight-ready condition, are on display at all times, along with numerous metal and wooden production models of concept planes, and a collection of model aircraft from World War I to the present. Exhibits, video kiosks, children's interactive area, theater showing classic aviation films. Museum store. **Open:** Wed–Sun 10am–5pm. $$$

California Heritage Museum
2612 Main St; tel 310/392-8537. Housed in a historic landmark building built in 1894, the Heritage Museum has been open to the public since 1980. It features rotating exhibits of regional history and local artwork by internationally respected artists. Concerts, lectures, and workshops are also presented. Gift shop. Parking and facilities for visitors with disabilities. **Open:** Wed–Sat 11am–4pm, Sun noon–4pm. $

Santa Rosa

Perched on the northern edge of Sonoma's wine country, Santa Rosa is a bustling commercial center surrounded by farms and vineyards. **Information:** Greater Santa Rosa Conference & Visitors Bureau, 637 First St, Santa Rosa 95404 (tel 707/577-8674 or toll free 800/404-7673).

HOTELS 🏨

≡≡≡ DoubleTree Hotel
3555 Round Barn Blvd, 95403; tel 707/523-7555 or toll free 800/528-0444; fax 707/545-2807. From US 101, take Old Redwood Hwy north to Mendocino Ave exit; left on Fountain

Grove; left on Round Barn. Set on a hill overlooking the city; caters to a mostly corporate clientele. Golf and country club nearby. **Rooms:** 247 rms and stes. CI 3pm/CO noon. Nonsmoking rms avail. Rooms are cozy and comfortable, with views of the pool. **Amenities:** 🛋 ⚱ 📻 ☕ A/C, cable TV w/movies. Some units w/minibars, some w/terraces. **Services:** ✗ 🍴 🖼 🛎 Masseur. **Facilities:** 🛋 ⚹ 350 ⚹ 1 restaurant, 1 bar, whirlpool. Lap pool. **Rates:** Peak (June–Oct) $139–$149 S; $149–$159 D; $200–$250 ste. Extra person $10. Children under age 18 stay free. Lower rates off-season. Parking: Outdoor, free. AE, CB, DC, DISC, MC, V.

≣≣≣ Flamingo Resort Hotel

2777 4th St, 95405; tel 707/545-8530 or toll free 800/848-8300; fax 707/528-1404. 10 acres. Family-run hotel with extensive grounds and spa facilities. **Rooms:** 136 rms and stes. CI 3pm/CO 11am. No smoking. Rooms are large and recently redecorated; those overlooking the pool are nicest. **Amenities:** 🛋 ⚱ 📻 A/C, cable TV w/movies, refrig. Some units w/terraces, some w/whirlpools. **Services:** ✗ 🍴 🖼 🛎 Masseur. **Facilities:** 🛋 ⚹ 🖼 ⚹5 🏓 600 ⚹ 1 restaurant, 1 bar (w/entertainment), lawn games, spa, sauna, steam rm, whirlpool, beauty salon, playground. Shuffleboard, table tennis. **Rates:** Peak (Apr–Oct) $89–$139 S or D; $129–$179 ste. Extra person $11. Children under age 12 stay free. Lower rates off-season. Parking: Outdoor, free. AE, DC, JCB, MC, V.

≣≣≣≣ Fountaingrove Inn

101 Fountaingrove Pkwy, 94503; tel 707/578-6101 or toll free 800/222-6101. From US 101 N take the Mendocino Ave/Old Redwood Hwy exit. Turn right on Mendocino Ave; hotel is on left. From US 101 S, take Hopper/Mendocino Ave exit; turn left. A modern, low-slung structure built of native redwood, oak, and stone, it recalls both Japanese architecture as well as the works of Frank Lloyd Wright. The restrained style creates a feeling of tranquillity, enhanced by a cascade in the lobby. **Rooms:** 84 rms. CI 2pm/CO noon. Nonsmoking rms avail. Rooms are large, with new carpeting, fresh paint, and refinished wood on the beautifully crafted oak cabinets that substitute for closets. Custom-designed furnishings are contemporary, done in harmonious shades of beige. **Amenities:** 🛋 ⚱ ☕ A/C, cable TV w/movies, refrig, dataport. Some units w/whirlpools. Bathrobes available on request. **Services:** ✗ 🍴 🖼 🛎 Car-rental desk, social director, masseur, babysitting. The complimentary extended continental breakfast includes fresh fruit, yogurt, cereals, breads, and pastries—they're especially known for their scones. Mon–Fri, complimentary happy hour hors d'oeuvres are served; there's also afternoon coffee and cookies. **Facilities:** 🛋 75 🖥 ⚹ 1 restaurant (lunch and dinner only), 1 bar (w/entertainment), whirlpool. The attractive pool with its own waterfall is heated in summer. Guest privileges (for a fee) to an excellent local health club that offers an indoor/outdoor pool, free weights, machines, aerobics classes, massage, racquetball, tennis, and more. **Rates (CP):** $129–$185 S; $139–$195 D. Extra person

$10. Children under age 12 stay free. Parking: Outdoor, free. Wine country and golf packages (at Fountaingrove Country Club) avail. AE, CB, DC, DISC, MC, V.

≣≣≣ Hotel La Rose

308 Wilson St, 95401 (Downtown/Railroad Square); tel 707/579-3200 or toll free 800/527-6738; fax 707/579-3247. At 5th St. Family-run hotel located in an old stone building in a historic district; member of the Historic Hotels of America. **Rooms:** 49 rms and stes. CI 3pm/CO noon. Nonsmoking rms avail. Clean and basic; rooms are decorated in floral prints. **Amenities:** 🛋 ⚱ Cable TV. No A/C. Microwaves and refrigerators on request. **Services:** ✗ 🚐 🖼 🛎 Masseur, babysitting. **Facilities:** 40 ⚹ 1 restaurant (lunch and dinner only; *see* "Restaurants" below), 1 bar, whirlpool. Josef's is a fine restaurant. Outdoor whirlpool. **Rates (CP):** Peak (May–Nov) $60–$130 S or D; $130 ste. Extra person $10. Children under age 12 stay free. Min stay peak and wknds. Lower rates off-season. MAP rates avail. Parking: Outdoor, free. Dinner, hot-air balloon, and golf packages avail. Mid-week and off-season rates $50–$85. AE, MC, V.

≣≣ Los Robles Lodge

1985 Cleveland Ave, 94501; tel 707/545-6330 or toll free 800/255-6330; fax 707/575-5826. Right off highway; traffic noise can be a problem. **Rooms:** 104 rms. CI 4pm/CO noon. Nonsmoking rms avail. Rooms are plain but pleasant; some have a pool view. Executive suites are more luxurious. **Amenities:** 🛋 ⚱ 📻 A/C, cable TV w/movies, refrig. Some units w/terraces, some w/whirlpools. **Services:** ✗ 🚐 🖼 🛎 Babysitting. **Facilities:** 🛋 45 ⚹ 1 restaurant, 1 bar, whirlpool, washer/dryer. **Rates:** $75–$95 S or D. Extra person $8. Children under age 16 stay free. Parking: Outdoor, free. AE, CB, DC, DISC, JCB, MC, V.

≣≣≣ Vintners Inn

4350 Barnes Rd, 95403; tel 707/575-7350 or toll free 800/421-2584; fax 707/575-1426. W off River Rd 101. This Mediterranean-style hotel has red-tile roofs and many little walkways between the two-story buildings. Although surrounded by 40 acres of vineyards (including some 50-year-old French Colombard plantings), the property is also located near a power substation and US 101 (you do hear a traffic drone). Adjacent to John Ash, an excellent restaurant. **Rooms:** 44 rms. CI 3pm/CO noon. No smoking. Very spacious, rooms are individually decorated with antique pine furnishings in country French style. Upstairs accommodations feature vaulted ceilings. **Amenities:** 🛋 ⚱ A/C, cable TV, refrig, dataport. All units w/terraces, some w/fireplaces. VCRs and videos available for rent. **Services:** ✗ 🚐 🖼 🛎 Twice-daily maid svce, masseur, babysitting. Served in a charming breakfast room, the extensive morning buffet offers homemade breads, muffins, cereal, and fresh fruit, plus hot selections such as waffles and frittatas. Coffee and pastries available in the afternoon. **Facilities:** 50 ⚹ 1 restaurant (lunch and dinner only), whirlpool. Guest passes (fee) to local health club. **Rates (CP):** $118–$195 S or D.

Extra person $10. Children under age 10 stay free. Min stay wknds. Parking: Outdoor, free. Winter in the Wine Country package includes one night's accommodations, dinner for two at John Ash, and breakfast; $195–$250 per couple. AE, DC, MC, V.

RESTAURANTS

Cafe Europe
65 Brookwood; tel 707/526-2200. At 4th St. **Californian/German.** At this small, reasonably priced restaurant, the Austrian owner/chef creates German specialties utilizing fresh California ingredients. Entrees include sauerbraten, Sonoma duck, and "Mom's Meatloaf," as well as lighter fare such as a caesar salad with grilled chicken. The potato pancakes are legendary. Entree prices include soup or salad. For dessert, the German chocolate cheesecake and the strudel are good bets. Choose from German beers or many fine Sonoma wines by the glass. **FYI:** Reservations accepted. Folk. Beer and wine only. **Open:** Lunch Tues–Sat 11:30am–2pm; dinner Tues–Thurs 5–9pm, Fri–Sat 5–9:30pm. **Prices:** Main courses $7–$13. MC, V. ♿

Cafe Lolo
620 5th St (Downtown); tel 707/576-7822. Downtown Santa Rosa exit off US 101. **Californian.** This small, chef-owned restaurant features fine cuisine in a cool and airy space, with willow branches wrapped in silk adorning the windows. Good bets are the wild mushroom cannelloni, roasted pork chop with horseradish crust, or pan-seared scallops with pomegranate juice. Excellent, reasonably priced lunches. **FYI:** Reservations recommended. Beer and wine only. **Open:** Lunch Mon–Fri 11:30am–2pm; dinner Mon–Sat 5:30–9:30pm. **Prices:** Main courses $9–$18. AE, MC, V. ♿

Gary Chu's
611 5th St (Downtown); tel 707/526-5840. Downtown Santa Rosa exit of US 101. **Chinese.** Many locals consider this place to have the best Chinese cuisine in Sonoma County. Elegant setting with large fish tanks. Try the walnut prawns, sesame-pineapple chicken, four-season lamb, or moo shu pork. **FYI:** Reservations accepted. Beer and wine only. **Open:** Daily 11:30am–9:30pm. **Prices:** Main courses $7–$14. AE, DC, DISC, MC, V. ♿

John Ash & Co
4330 Barnes Rd; tel 707/527-7687. River Rd W exit off US 101. **Californian.** John Ash, who moved his popular restaurant here from an eastside location, keeps drawing both new and longtime fans. Adjacent to Vintners Inn (*see* "Hotels" above), the restaurant has outdoor dining with views of lawns and vineyards. Soft pinks and terra-cotta dominate the color scheme of the high-ceilinged main room, in which oversized paintings are hung. Known for its inventive use of local products, the restaurant has a changing menu that may include Dungeness crab cakes, braised rabbit, smoked lamb, local cheeses, and salads. **FYI:** Reservations recommended. **Open:** Lunch Tues–Sat 11:30am–2pm, Sun 2–5:30pm; dinner daily 5:30–9:30pm; brunch Sun 10:30am–2pm. **Prices:** Main courses $13–$25. AE, MC, V. ♿

Josef's Restaurant and Bar
In Hotel La Rose, 308 Wilson St (Downtown/Railroad Square); tel 707/571-8664. At 5th St. **Californian.** Swiss-born owner/chef, Josef Keller, presents rich European cuisine combined with a special California twist in his cozy, charmingly old-world restaurant. Entree choices might be angel-hair pasta with smoked chicken; beef bourguignonne; or prawns bordelaise. Very fine wine list. **FYI:** Reservations accepted. **Open:** Lunch Tues–Fri 11:30am–2pm; dinner Tues–Thurs 5:30–9pm, Fri–Sat 5:30–9:30pm. **Prices:** Main courses $12–$22. AE, MC, V. ♿

La Gare French Restaurant
208 Wilson St; tel 707/528-4355. Downtown Santa Rosa exit off US 101; turn left on 3rd St, then right on Wilson St. **French.** Large, old brick building spruced up with lace curtains, fine goblets, and nice furnishings to create a French bistro atmosphere. Dishes include baked salmon fillet, medallions of beef in tarragon sauce, braised duck, and sole amandine. Entree price includes soup and salad. Excellent service. **FYI:** Reservations recommended. Beer and wine only. **Open:** Tues–Sun 5:30–10pm. **Prices:** Main courses $10–$16. AE, DC, DISC, MC, V. ♿

✱ Lisa Hemenway's
In Montgomery Village Shopping Center, 714 Village Court; tel 707/526-5111. **Eclectic.** Lots of windows, beautiful gardens, and many flower arrangements inside make for a restaurant that is casually elegant, with an Asian/Mediterranean flair. The eclectic menu includes appetizers such as a tapas platter with almonds, cheese, and grilled vegetables, and entrees like filet mignon with crisp onion rings in a Gorgonzola sauce, as well as various seafood specialties that have won this restaurant numerous awards. **FYI:** Reservations recommended. **Open:** Lunch daily 11:30am–2:30pm; dinner Mon–Sat 5:30–9:30pm, Sun 5–9pm. **Prices:** Main courses $13–$22. AE, DC, DISC, MC, V. ♿

Mistral
1229 N Dutton Ave; tel 707/578-9421. College Ave exit off US 101. **Italian.** A large, Tuscan-inspired trattoria, with strands of garlic and sausages hanging from the ceiling, a wood-burning pizza oven, and terra-cotta walls. Hearty food includes grilled eggplant pizza, grilled swordfish in puttanesca sauce, roast leg of lamb, and more. **FYI:** Reservations recommended. Beer and wine only. **Open:** Lunch Mon–Fri 11:30am–2pm; dinner daily 5:30–9:30pm. **Prices:** Main courses $8–$15. AE, CB, DISC, MC, V. ♿

The Mixx
135 4th St (Railroad Square); tel 707/573-1344. **New American.** A family-run American bistro with an art deco look, lovely glass chandeliers, and an oak bar. Extensive seasonal menu offers fresh fish and pasta, grilled prawns, leg of

venison, and much more. Many heart-healthy dishes. Fresh-baked pastries. Extensive wine list. **FYI:** Reservations recommended. Beer and wine only. **Open:** Lunch Mon–Fri 11:30am–2pm; dinner Mon–Thurs 5:30–9:30pm, Fri–Sat 5:30pm–midnight. **Prices:** Main courses $12–$20. AE, DC, MC, V. &

Omelette Express

112 4th St (Railroad Square); tel 707/525-1690. **Diner.** This breakfast and lunch place in old town delivers satisfying food, including sandwiches, burgers, bagels, over 50 omelettes, and espresso. **FYI:** Reservations not accepted. Children's menu. Beer and wine only. **Open:** Mon–Fri 6:30am–3pm, Sat–Sun 7am–4pm. **Prices:** Lunch main courses $6–$7. AE, MC, V. &

ATTRACTIONS

Sonoma County Museum

425 7th St; tel 707/579-1500. Housed in the 1909 Old Post Office and Federal Building, this museum focuses on regional art and history. The museum's permanent collections include fine 19th-century California landscape paintings, with works by renowned artist Thomas Hill, and works by Sonoma County artisans and craftspeople such as Harry Dixon and Elwin Millerick. Changing exhibits are also featured, and there are special events throughout the year. **Open:** Wed–Sun 11am–4pm. $

Luther Burbank Home and Gardens

Santa Rosa and Sonoma Aves; tel 707/524-5445. Luther Burbank (1849–1926) was a famed horticulturist whose plant breeding experiments produced approximately 800 varieties of plants and 200 varieties of fruits, vegetables, nuts, grains, and flowers during his lifetime. He lived in Santa Rosa for 50 years, and the 1.6-acre garden that remains today served as his outdoor laboratory.

Dedicated in 1960, the central garden was redesigned as a memorial park. A 50-foot outdoor display describes Burbank's life and work, and includes information on the history of the property. The park is filled with numerous specimens of fruit trees, cacti, roses, and many others that were the result of Burbank's experiments.

The gardens surround Burbank's modified Greek Revival home, which is accessible only by guided tour. The Greenhouse contains changing exhibits and a replica of Burbank's office containing many of his tools; and the Carriage House houses museum exhibits, a gift shop, and the tour registration desk. **Open:** Gardens, daily sunrise–sundown; home tours, Apr–Oct Wed–Sun 10am–3:30pm. $

De Loach Vineyards

1791 Olivet Rd; tel 707/526-9111. This winery encompasses more than 300 acres in the Russian River Valley. Tours are given by appointment, and visitors may sample wines and picnic at an area adjoining the vineyard. **Open:** Daily 10am–4:30pm. **Free**

San Ysidro

MOTEL

≡≡ International Motor Inn

190 E Calle Primera, 92173; tel 619/428-4486; fax 619/428-3618. 18 mi S of San Diego. San Ysidro exit off I-5. Many guests here are patients at cancer clinics in Mexico. Landscaping is meticulous and grounds are pleasant. Close to factory outlets, fast food restaurants. Adjoins RV park. **Rooms:** 100 rms and effic. CI 11am/CO 11am. Nonsmoking rms avail. **Amenities:** A/C, cable TV w/movies, refrig. Rooms available with kitchenettes, including toaster oven, cooktop, refrigerator, and dishes. **Services:** Babysitting. Free shuttle to many local spots. **Facilities:** Whirlpool, washer/dryer. **Rates:** $49 S or D; $48 effic. Extra person $3. Parking: Outdoor, free. AE, CB, DC, DISC, MC, V.

Saratoga

Saratoga is a well-to-do community in the foothills west of San Jose with several impressive community gardens. The town is also the gateway to the parks and hiking trails of the Santa Cruz Mountains. **Information:** Saratoga Chamber of Commerce, 20460 Saratoga–Los Gatos Rd, Saratoga 95070 (tel 408/867-0753).

INN

≡≡≡≡ The Inn at Saratoga

20645 4th St, 95070; tel 408/867-5020 or toll free 800/543-5020; fax 408/741-0981. Updated, New England–style inn with wooden siding and a gabled roof. It boasts a fabulous location alongside tree-lined Saratoga Creek but just a half-block from the charming restaurants and boutiques along the town's main street. Caters very well to both business and leisure travelers. No restaurant on premises, but many within walking distance. **Rooms:** 45 rms and stes. CI 3pm/CO noon. Nonsmoking rms avail. All units have floor-to-ceiling windows facing the creek; most have private balconies. Deluxe rooms offer bathrooms with a whirlpool tub, glass-enclosed shower, TV, and heated towel rack. Carpets and upholstery are showing signs of wear. **Amenities:** A/C, satel TV w/movies, dataport, VCR, voice mail, bathrobes. All units w/minibars, some w/terraces, some w/whirlpools. Attractive amenities basket with manicure/sewing kit. Iron and ironing board in room. **Services:** Masseur, babysitting, afternoon tea and wine/sherry served. Video library at front desk. Afternoon hors d'oeuvres served. **Facilities:** Guest lounge. Pleasant patio overlooking a creek. **Rates (CP):** $150–$245 S or D; $410–$440 ste. Extra person $15. Children under age 18 stay free. Parking: Outdoor, free. AE, CB, DC, EC, MC, V.

RESTAURANTS

La Mère Michelle

14467 Big Basin Way; tel 408/867-5272. CA 9 exit off I-280, W on CA 9. **Continental/French.** Family-owned restaurant decorated with flourishes from Italy, Sweden, and Eastern Europe. Good starters are the pâté or French onion soup. Specialties include fish, white veal with lemon and capers, Wiener schnitzel, curried boneless breast of chicken, or seafood in Mornay sauce. **FYI:** Reservations recommended. **Open:** Lunch Tues–Sun 11:30am–2pm; dinner Tues–Thurs 6–9:30pm, Fri–Sat 6–10pm; brunch Sat 11:30am–2pm, Sun 10:30am–2pm. **Prices:** Main courses $17–$24; prix fixe $30. AE, CB, DC, DISC, ER, MC, V. 💟 ⅊

Le Mouton Noir

14560 Big Basin Way; tel 408/867-7017. CA 9 exit off CA 280. **French.** Le Mouton Noir (the black sheep) is divided into several intimate dining rooms, each with a French country motif. A stained-glass window features the namesake sheep out among the vineyards. Appetizers include gnocchi with smoked goose, and escargot with garlic and mushrooms. Main courses include sweetbreads, filet mignon with foie gras, and the house specialty duck. **FYI:** Reservations recommended. Beer and wine only. **Open:** Lunch Sat 11:30am–2pm; dinner Mon–Sat 6–9:30pm, Sun 5–9pm. **Prices:** Main courses $18–$26. AE, DC, MC, V. 💟 ⅊ 🖼 ⅊

ATTRACTION

Hakone Gardens

21000 Big Basin Way; tel 408/741-4994. Four gardens make up this tranquil 15-acre park: the Hill and Pond Garden, created in the style of 17th-century Japan; the Tea Garden, an enclosed garden where tea services are held in season; the Zen Garden, a dry garden intended for viewing only; and the *Kizuna-En,* a bamboo garden respresenting the relationship between Saratoga and its sister city, Muko-shi, Japan.

The Upper House and Lower House were built by the original owners of the property, who also constructed the original gardens in the 1910s. The Cultural Exchange Center is an authentic reproduction of a 19th-century Kyoto tea merchant's house and shop, assembled in Japan and raised on a prepared site.

Guided tours on weekends Apr–Sept; formal Japanese tea ceremony held on the first Thursday of every month, 1–4pm; gift shop always open. Parking fee charged. **Open:** Mon–Fri 10am–5pm, Sat–Sun 11am–5pm. **Free**

Sausalito

Located across the Golden Gate Bridge from San Francisco, studiedly quaint Sausalito combines a fishing-port village with an artists' colony. Swank restaurants, plush bars, and expensive antiques shops share the streets with hamburger joints, beer parlors, and secondhand bookstores. Sausalito is blessed with scenery and sunshine; the town's steep hills are covered with white houses overlooking a forest of masts on sailboats moored in the marinas below. **Information:** Sausalito Chamber of Commerce, 333 Caledonia St, PO Box 566, Sausalito 94966 (tel 415/332-0505).

HOTEL

🖼🖼 Alta Mira Hotel

125 Bulkley Ave, PO Box 706, 94966; tel 415/332-1350; fax 415/331-3862. From Bridgeway, take Princess to Bulkley. Rambling, pink-painted building nestled in the foothills. Town is just a short walk away. Atmosphere decidedly funky, with worn carpets and tiny, dated bathrooms. Still, a Sausalito tradition. **Rooms:** 15 rms and stes; 13 cottages/villas. CI 2pm/CO noon. Nonsmoking rms avail. No two rooms are alike. Some have Victorian furnishings. The cottages, formerly private homes, are spacious and tranquil, although furnishings are old and nondescript. **Amenities:** 🖼 Cable TV. No A/C. Some units w/terraces, some w/fireplaces. **Services:** ✗ 🖼 🖼 🖼 🖼 🖼 Car-rental desk, social director, masseur, babysitting. **Facilities:** 🖼 1 restaurant, 1 bar (w/entertainment). The bar and outdoor terrace are the spot for sunset cocktails, with dazzling city views. Garden area with towering redwoods popular for weddings. **Rates:** Peak (May–Oct) $80–$125 S; $80–$150 D; $125–$195 ste; $195–$205 cottage/villa. Extra person $10. Children under age 6 stay free. Min stay wknds. Lower rates off-season. Parking: Outdoor, free. Closed Jan. AE, CB, DC, JCB, MC, V.

INNS

🖼🖼🖼🖼 Casa Madrona Hotel

801 Bridgeway, 94965 (Downtown); tel 415/332-0502 or toll free 800/567-9524; fax 415/332-2537. A small, deluxe hotel with the feel of a charming bed-and-breakfast, in the heart of Sausalito. **Rooms:** 39 rms and stes; 5 cottages/villas. CI 3pm/CO noon. Nonsmoking rms avail. All rooms are different, many decorated with antiques. Many offer spectacular views of the bay and San Francisco. Accommodations in the New Casa are the most elegant, with touches like stenciled woodwork and designer fabrics. "Old House" rooms offer the charms of a vintage 1885 structure. **Amenities:** 🖼 🖼 🖼 🖼 Cable TV, refrig, VCR, bathrobes. No A/C. All units w/minibars, some w/terraces, some w/fireplaces, some w/whirlpools. **Services:** ✗ 🖼 🖼 🖼 🖼 Car-rental desk, masseur, babysitting. Complimentary wine and cheese served in the Victorian-style parlor each afternoon. **Facilities:** 🖼 1 restaurant (bkfst and dinner only; *see* "Restaurants" below), whirlpool, guest lounge w/TV. Restaurant offers remarkable bay views. **Rates (BB):** $105–$200 S or D; $200–$245 ste; $170–$185 cottage/villa. Extra person $6. Min stay wknds. MAP rates avail. Parking: Outdoor, $5/day. Warm Winter Whim package (Dec–Apr) offers a midweek rate of $185, including room and dinner for two. AE, CB, DC, DISC, JCB, MC, V.

≣≣≣≣ **The Inn Above Tide**

9 El Portal, 94965 (Downtown); tel 415/332-9535 or toll free 800/893-TIDE; fax 415/332-6714. Off Bridgeway. Perched on the water's edge in the heart of Sausalito, this is the newest, classiest hotel in Marin, and is located next to the ferry to San Francisco. **Rooms:** 30 rms and stes. CI 3pm/CO noon. No smoking. Rooms offer dramatic views of the bay and San Francisco skyline and are beautifully decorated in soft tones. Baths have blue granite vanities. **Amenities:** 🏨 🗄 🍴 A/C, cable TV w/movies, dataport, bathrobes. All units w/minibars, some w/terraces, some w/fireplaces, some w/whirlpools. Large-screen TVs. Binoculars in rooms. **Services:** ✗ ☞ VP 🚗 🖼 Twice-daily maid svce, car-rental desk, masseur, afternoon tea and wine/sherry served. Breakfast can be served in rooms. Flower delivery and beauty salon appointments arranged. **Facilities:** ⌐15⌐ ⅃ Guest lounge. **Rates (CP):** $185 S or D; $250–$400 ste. Children under age 2 stay free. Min stay peak. Parking: Outdoor, $8/day. AE, MC, V.

RESTAURANTS 🍴

Guernica

2009 Bridgeway (Downtown); tel 415/332-1512. Sausalito exit off US 101. **French/Basque.** A good place to sample hearty French-Basque cuisine at very reasonable prices in a setting resembling a simple, European-style dining hall. You can start off with steamed clams or artichoke bottoms in hollandaise sauce, then move on to entrees such as paella Valenciana, rack of lamb, or the fresh catch of the day. **FYI:** Reservations accepted. Beer and wine only. **Open:** Daily 5–10pm. **Prices:** Main courses $10–$17. AE, DC, MC, V. ⅃

Mikayla

In the Casa Madrona Hotel, 801 Bridgeway (Downtown); tel 415/331-5888. **Californian.** Floor-to-ceiling windows offer spectacular views of the bay and harbor, and the roof rolls back for al fresco dining in nice weather. The menu showcases California cuisine with a European influence, with selections such as grilled salmon with artichokes and portobello mushrooms, or charred prime rib. **FYI:** Reservations recommended. Beer and wine only. **Open:** Dinner daily 6–9:30pm; brunch Sun–10am–2pm. **Prices:** Main courses $15–$19. AE, CB, DC, DISC, MC, V. 🖼 VP

North Sea Village

300 Turney St (Downtown); tel 415/331-3300. Sausalito exit off US 101; 2 mi N on Bridgeway. **Chinese.** Marinites know there's no need to trek into the city for terrific Chinese food—not with this real Hong Kong–style seafood restaurant, stylishly decorated in elegant rosewood and green tones, in their area. It's especially packed for the superb dim sum lunches on the weekend, with offerings such as steamed shrimp balls, pork buns, and stuffed crab claws. Affords nice views of the Sausalito waterfront. **FYI:** Reservations accept-ed. Beer and wine only. **Open:** Mon–Fri 11am–10pm, Sat–Sun 10am–10pm. **Prices:** Main courses $7–$15. AE, CB, DC, MC, V. ⅃

Scoma's

588 Bridgeway (Downtown); tel 415/332-9551. Sausalito exit off US 101; 1 mi N on Bridgeway. **Italian/Seafood.** Fabulous sailboats lie at anchor in San Francisco Bay, right off the restaurant's pier location. Inside, the decor is nautical-Victorian, with cane chairs, beveled mirrors, and lots of windows. Fresh fish selections vary daily, with up to eight choices—perhaps including Dungeness crab or petrale sole. Other favorites include cioppino (seafood stew) and pasta dishes. **FYI:** Reservations recommended. Children's menu. Dress code. **Open:** Thurs–Mon 11:30am–9:30pm, Tues–Wed 5:30–9:30pm. Closed Christmas week. **Prices:** Main courses $15–$25; prix fixe $26–$45. AE, CB, DC, MC, V. 🖼 VP ⅃

The Spinnaker

100 Spinnaker Dr (Downtown); tel 415/332-1500. **Seafood.** A top choice for both views and ultra-fresh seafood. The atmosphere is elegant and sophisticated, with rattan chairs, crisp white linens, and panoramic views of San Francisco through floor-to-ceiling windows. Selections might include local Dungeness crab cakes, halibut, or caldo de mariscos, a seafood stew spiked with roasted chiles and cilantro. Pasta, meat, and poultry dishes are offered as well. **FYI:** Reservations recommended. Children's menu. **Open:** Daily 11am–11pm. **Prices:** Main courses $9–$18. AE, DC, MC, V. 🖼 VP ⅃

Ⓢ The Stuffed Croissant, Etc

43 Caledonia St; tel 415/332-7103. Between Pine and Johnson. **Eclectic.** A tiny hole-in-the-wall, with seating at the counter only. Nonetheless, a local favorite for breakfast, with a terrific espresso bar and fresh-baked muffins and scones. Employees contribute their own ethnic specialties—Indian samosas, Italian pizzas, Mexican enchiladas. The Indian lunch special, which is served all day and might consist of a huge helping of curried chicken, vegetables, rice, and yogurt, is just $5.50. **FYI:** Reservations not accepted. No liquor license. **Open:** Mon–Sat 6am–10pm, Sun 7am–9pm. **Prices:** Main courses $3–$6. No CC. ⅃

REFRESHMENT STOP ☕

Venice Gourmet Delicatessen

625 Bridgeway (Downtown); tel 415/332-3544. **Deli.** Located on the waterfront for 30 years, this deli and gourmet kitchenware store offers a wide variety of copperware, condiments, and wine. Its broad selection of sandwiches and salads make it a perfect place to buy a picnic lunch. Try the roasted turkey or the Greek salad, which is accompanied by sourdough bread. **Open:** Daily 9am–7pm. AE, CB, DC, DISC, MC, V.

ATTRACTION 📷

Bay Model Visitors Center
2100 Bridgeway; tel 415/332-3871. Built and maintained by the US Army Corps of Engineers, this 1½-acre model of San Francisco's bay and delta allows engineers to simulate changes in the bay's water flow and study their effects. The model reproduces (in scale) the rise and fall of tides, the flows and currents of water, the mixing of fresh and salt water, and indicates trends in sediment movement. There is a 10-minute orientation video, and a taped audio tour is available in several languages. The model is most interesting to watch when it is in operation; phone ahead. **Open:** Peak (Mem Day–Labor Day) Tues–Fri 9am–4pm, Sat–Sun 10am–6 pm. Reduced hours off-season. **Free**

Scotia

HOTEL 📷

≡≡≡ The Scotia Inn
100 Main St, PO Box 248, 95565; tel 707/764-5683; fax 707/764-1707. Located in a historic building on five acres in an old lumber town near the Eel River. Hotel has an old-fashioned feeling. The lumber company across the street offers tours of its mill. Reasonable rates. **Rooms:** 11 rms. CI 2pm/CO noon. No smoking. Quaint rooms with claw-foot tubs. **Amenities:** 📺 🄰 Cable TV. No A/C. 1 unit w/whirlpool. **Services:** ✗ 🛏 🍽 Babysitting. **Facilities:** ⟨100⟩ 2 restaurants (lunch and dinner only; see "Restaurants" below), 1 bar (w/entertainment). Free passes to nearby gym and swimming pool. 1940s bar and grill. **Rates (CP):** $65–$150 S or D. Children under age 18 stay free. Parking: Outdoor, free. MC, V.

RESTAURANT 🍴

The Scotia Inn
100 Main St; tel 707/764-5683. Scotia exit off CA 101. **Eclectic.** Set in a 1923 building in a redwood-lumber company town, this romantic restaurant offers an ambience of candle light, Gershwin music, and gorgeous redwood paneling. Menu choices might be elk tenderloin, beef tri-tip, chicken saltimbocca, or crab cakes. Special prix fixe international menus (Tuscan, German, Greek, Russian, etc) are served on Sundays, changing monthly. Those four-course dinners are reasonably priced with affordable, appropriate wines available. The elegant Sunday brunch is one of the few in the area. **FYI:** Reservations recommended. Dancing/piano. Children's menu. **Open:** Peak (June 1–Sept 1) lunch Mon–Fri noon–2pm; dinner Wed–Sun 5–9pm; brunch Sun 10am–2pm. **Prices:** Main courses $11–$22; prix fixe $10–$14. MC, V. ■ 🖗

Seal Beach

See also Long Beach, San Pedro

INN 📷

≡≡≡≡ Seal Beach Inn & Gardens
212 5th St, 90740; tel 562/493-2416 or toll free 800/HIDE-AWAY; fax 562/799-0483. An absolutely charming inn, surrounded by flowers and filled (inside and out) with antiques that owners Harty Schmaehl and his wife Marjorie Bettenhausen-Schmael have collected in their travels. Their finds include a French, pre-Napoleonic fountain, Eastlake windows, etched windows from Scotland, and 19th-century iron gates. Unsuitable for children under 12. **Rooms:** 24 rms and stes. CI 4pm/CO 11am. No smoking. Each room is individually decorated and named for a flower: from Azalea (with a four-poster bed swathed in gauze) to Zinnia (featuring a turn-of-the-century armoire and lace portieres). Bedding is luxurious, with down comforters and exceptional linens. **Amenities:** 📺 🄰 TV, dataport. No A/C. Some units w/minibars, some w/terraces, some w/fireplaces, some w/whirlpools. Upon arrival, guests are treated to home-baked chocolate-chip cookies and find fresh flowers and a fruit basket in their room. **Services:** ✗ 🚗 🖼 🍽 Twice-daily maid svce, car-rental desk, afternoon tea and wine/sherry served. Desk offers information on lake and watersport equipment rentals. **Facilities:** ⟨🔥⟩ ⟨25⟩ Games rm, guest lounge. Library is crammed with books and games; gourmet teas and coffees are available here all day. **Rates (BB):** $118–$185 S or D; $155–$255 ste. Extra person $10–$20. Min stay special events. AP and MAP rates avail. Parking: Outdoor, free. AE, CB, DC, DISC, JCB, MC, V.

Sea Ranch

See also Gualala

LODGE 📷

≡≡≡ Sea Ranch Lodge
60 Sea Walk Dr, PO Box 44, 95497; tel 707/785-2371 or toll free 800/732-7262; fax 707/785-2243. With a secluded 10-mile stretch of private beach, Sea Ranch Lodge is famous for the way its architecture melds with the stunning coastal setting. A good place to watch for whales and unwind. **Rooms:** 20 rms. CI 3pm/CO noon. Nonsmoking rms avail. Although decor is a bit spare, all rooms are comfortable with ocean views. **Amenities:** 📺 Cable TV. No A/C or phone. Some units w/minibars, some w/terraces, some w/fireplaces, some w/whirlpools. Board games available. **Services:** ✗ 🔑 🍽 Masseur, babysitting. **Facilities:** ►18 🖾 ⟨200⟩ 🖗 1 restaurant, 1 bar, 1 beach (ocean). Extensive gift shop and new espresso bar. Beautiful golf course above the ocean (eight miles from lodge). **Rates:** $125–$180 S or D. Extra person

$15. Children under age 5 stay free. Min stay peak. Parking: Outdoor, free. Midweek packages with 2-night minimum stay. AE, MC, V.

Selma

See also Fresno

MOTEL ▥

▤▤▤ Holiday Inn Swan Court
2950 Pea Soup Andersen Blvd, 93662; tel 209/891-8000 or toll free 800/462-5363; fax 209/891-9575. Floral Ave exit off CA 99. Opened in 1996, this lovely motel boasts a lobby with fireplace, coffee service, and koi pond with black swans and waterfalls. Outside, near the restaurant, the Sunshine Express train offers 14-minute rides past tunnels and waterfalls. **Rooms:** 64 rms and stes. Executive level. CI 3pm/CO 11am. Nonsmoking rms avail. Accommodations are beautifully decorated in hues of hunter green and rose. Some suites offer whirlpools and stocked minibars. Four rooms for handicapped have roll-in showers. Eight rooms have TDDs for the deaf and hard of hearing. **Amenities:** ▥ ▨ ▤ ▨ A/C, cable TV w/movies, refrig, dataport, voice mail. Some units w/minibars, some w/whirlpools. Complimentary morning newspaper. **Services:** ✗ ▨ ▨ Twice-daily maid svce, car-rental desk, social director. **Facilities:** ▨ ▨ ▨ ▨ 2 restaurants, 1 bar (w/entertainment), whirlpool. Kids eat free at Pea Soup Andersen's restaurant. **Rates:** Peak (Apr–Labor Day) $65 S or D; $110 ste. Children under age 12 stay free. Min stay special events. Lower rates off-season. Parking: Outdoor, free. AE, CB, DC, DISC, JCB, MC, V.

Sequoia and Kings Canyon National Parks

Domain of the giant trees, Sequoia National Park is, after Yellowstone, the oldest national park in the United States. Created in 1890 to safeguard the redwood forests on the slopes of the Sierra Nevada, the park boasts magnificent scenery that embraces granite and mountain crests, canyons, mountain lakes, and dense forests. The adjoining Kings Canyon National Park was established in 1940, and the two parks are now administered as a unit. Nearby are the giant peaks of Mount Whitney, tallest in the lower 48 states (14,495 feet), Split Mountain (14,054 feet), and Mount Goethe (13,274 feet).

Named for Sequoyah, the Cherokee scholar and inventor of the Cherokee alphabet, sequoias have been known to grow as tall as 295 feet, with a circumference at the base of 100 feet or more. Their bark, two feet thick, is resistant to both fire and insects. The largest redwood now standing in the park,

the **General Sherman Tree,** is more than 275 feet tall, and its estimated age of 2,500 years makes it among the very oldest living things on earth.

In spite of the huge area they cover, the parks have only 75 miles of surfaced roads. Points off these roads are reached only by horseback or on foot. There are, however, 900 miles of walking trails. Visitor centers providing park information, exhibits, and programs are located at Grant, Foothills, and Lodgepole. Camping (some sites open year-round); fishing. For further information, contact the Superintendent, Sequoia and Kings Canyon National Parks, Three Rivers, CA 93271 (tel 209/565-3134 or 565-3341).

MOTELS ▥

▤▤ Best Western Holiday Lodge
40105 Sierra Dr, PO Box 129, Three Rivers, 93271; tel 209/561-4119 or toll free 800/528-1234; fax 209/561-3427. Comfortable motel 10 minutes from Sequoia National Park entrance, 45 minutes from CA 99. In Kaweah River Recreation Area. **Rooms:** 54 rms and stes. CI 3pm/CO 11am. Nonsmoking rms avail. 20 rooms have river views and private balconies. There are two rooms for guests with disabilities. **Amenities:** ▥ ▨ ▤ ▨ A/C, cable TV, refrig, dataport. Some units w/terraces, some w/fireplaces. TDDs for deaf and hard of hearing guests. **Services:** ▨ ▨ **Facilities:** ▨ ▨ Basketball, steam rm, playground. Fishing on the Kaweah River. Boating and fishing on Lake Kaweah, 1 mile away. **Rates (CP):** Peak (May–Oct) $63–$77 S or D; $78 ste. Extra person $4. Children under age 2 stay free. Lower rates off-season. Parking: Outdoor, free. AE, CB, DC, DISC, JCB, MC, V.

UNRATED Cedar Grove Lodge
CA 180, Kings Canyon National Park, PO Box 789, Three Rivers, 93271; tel 209/561-3314. Cedar Grove Village exit off CA 180. A motel on the banks of the majestic Kings River, reached by a 32-mile drive along a winding two-lane road with spectacular vistas. River views from communal decks. Close to hiking trails and fishing. **Rooms:** 18 rms. CI 4pm/CO 11am. Nonsmoking rms avail. Comfortable. One room for guests with disabilities. **Amenities:** ▨ A/C. No phone or TV. **Services:** ▨ **Facilities:** ▨ ▨ Washer/dryer. Meals at snack bar. **Rates:** $78 S or D. Extra person $6. Children under age 12 stay free. Parking: Outdoor, free. Senior discounts if requested at time of reservation. Closed mid-Oct–mid-May. AE, MC, V.

▤ Stony Creek Lodge
Generals Hwy, PO Box 789, Three Rivers, 93271; tel 209/561-3314. In Sequoia National Forest. Stony Creek Village exit off Generals Hwy. Nicest motel rooms in the park. No landscaping. Many forests and other attractions are close by. **Rooms:** 11 rms. CI 4pm/CO 11am. Nonsmoking rms avail. Comfortable, clean. **Amenities:** ▨ No A/C, phone, or TV. **Services:** ▨ Park tours available all day. **Facilities:** ▨ ▨ 1 restaurant, washer/dryer. Nearby trout fishing creek. Also hiking trails, picnic areas. **Rates:** Peak (May 25–Labor Day)

$89 S or D. Extra person $6.50. Children under age 13 stay free. Lower rates off-season. Parking: Outdoor, free. Closed early Sept–mid-May. AE, MC, V.

LODGES

UNRATED Giant Forest Lodge
CA 198, Giant Forest, PO Box 789, Three Rivers, 93271 (Sequoia Nat'l Park); tel 209/561-3314; fax 209/561-3135. Various facilities: deluxe motel to basic rooms, one- and two-room cabins with bath. **Rooms:** 83 rms; 20 cottages/villas. CI 4pm/CO 11am. Nonsmoking rms avail. **Amenities:** No A/C, phone, or TV. Some units w/terraces. **Services:** **Facilities:** 2 restaurants, 1 bar. Park's largest sequoia grove nearby, as are hiking trails. Ranger programs available. **Rates:** $71–$90 S or D; $71 cottage/villa. Extra person $6. Children under age 12 stay free. Parking: Outdoor, free. Deposit required on advance reservations. Closed mid-Oct–mid-May. AE, MC, V.

Grant Grove Lodge
CA 180, Grant Grove, PO Box 789, Three Rivers, 93271 (Kings Canyon Nat'l Park); tel 209/335-2314; fax 209/335-2364. 55 mi E of Fresno; CA I-80 to Kings Canyon Nat'l Park. Very rustic cabins set in a beautiful pine forest on the edge of Kings Canyon National Park. Horseback riding at nearby stables. **Rooms:** 52 cottages/villas. CI 4pm/CO 11am. Nonsmoking rms avail. Nine cabins with baths have electricity and indoor plumbing. Other accommodations in "rustic cabins" that have kerosene lanterns, wood-burning stoves, and common bathrooms. Some rustic cabins have outdoor wood-burning stoves for cooking; wood is included. **Amenities:** No A/C, phone, or TV. Some units w/terraces, some w/fireplaces. **Services:** **Facilities:** 1 restaurant, 1 bar. Visitor center, market, gift shop, and gas station on premises. **Rates:** Peak (mid-Apr–Oct) $32–$71 cottage/villa. Extra person $5. Children under age 13 stay free. Lower rates off-season. Parking: Outdoor, free. AE, MC, V.

Montecito-Sequoia Lodge
8000 Generals Hwy, Grant Grove, PO Box 858, Grant Grove, Kings Canyon Nat'l Park, 93633; tel 209/565-3388 or toll free 800/843-8667; fax 209/565-3223. I-80 E to Kings Canyon National Park entrance; continue to fork; go right 10 mi. 42 acres. Very popular and friendly mountain inn with plenty of outdoor activities for every season, including summer family camps and winter sports. It's also the only sizable lodging in Sequoia–Kings Canyon that's open all year. Set 7,500 feet above sea level, with spectacular views of the snow-capped peaks of the Great Western Divide. **Rooms:** 36 rms and stes; 13 cottages/villas. CI 4pm/CO 11am. Lodge rooms offer private baths. Cabins (which offer sleeping space for large families) have electricity and wood-burning stoves, but no running water or toilets (bathhouses with hot water are nearby). **Amenities:** No A/C, phone, or TV. All rooms provide electric blankets. **Services:** Hearty buffet-style breakfast and dinner. Snacks available 24 hours. Summer

Family Camp features fishing, hiking, scenic trips, as well as group activities for children and teens. **Facilities:** 1 restaurant, 1 bar, 1 beach (lake shore), lifeguard, volleyball, games rm, lawn games, whirlpool, day-care ctr, playground. Summer family camp. Nordic ski center with ski rentals and ice skating; 22 miles of groomed nordic ski trails, and 50 miles of ungroomed trails offering superb backcountry skiing. **Rates (AP):** Peak (mid-June–mid-Sept) $85–$105 S; $134–$174 D; $85–$134 cottage/villa. Extra person $8–$39. Children under age 2 stay free. Min stay peak. Lower rates off-season. MAP rates avail. Parking: Outdoor, free. Children ages 5–11, $29 per person; children under age 5, $8. AE, DC, DISC, MC, V.

Shell Beach

See also Pismo Beach

HOTELS

The Cliffs at Shell Beach
2757 Shell Beach Rd, 93449; tel 805/773-5000 or toll free 800/826-7827; fax 805/773-0764. Spyglass Rd exit off US 101 N; Shell Beach exit off US 101 S. For elegance and romantic ambience, this is the best hotel in the area. Designed like a ship. Expensive, but worth it. **Rooms:** 165 rms and stes. CI 3pm/CO noon. Nonsmoking rms avail. Suites are luxurious and have ocean views; all 27 scheduled to be revamped in a Southwest style in 1996. All rooms have Italian marble baths. **Amenities:** A/C, cable TV w/movies, voice mail. All units w/terraces, some w/whirlpools. Upscale in-room amenities, such as Crabtree and Evelyn soaps and shampoos. **Services:** Masseur, babysitting. **Facilities:** 1 restaurant (see "Restaurants" below), 1 bar (w/entertainment), 1 beach (ocean), spa, sauna, steam rm, whirlpool, washer/dryer. Dramatic circular pool surrounded by a fountain and overlooking the ocean. Two tennis courts located ½ mile north of hotel are free to guests. Two additional lighted courts one mile south of hotel. **Rates:** Peak (June–Nov) $130–$300 S or D; $175–$350 ste. Extra person $10. Children under age 12 stay free. Min stay peak and wknds. Lower rates off-season. Parking: Outdoor, free. AE, CB, DC, DISC, JCB, MC, V.

Spyglass Inn
2705 Spyglass Dr, 93449; tel 805/773-4855 or toll free 800/824-2612; fax 805/773-5298. Spyglass Dr exit off US 101. Attractive gray Cape Cod–style buildings. Lobby has wood floors and beamed ceilings. **Rooms:** 82 rms, stes, and effic. CI 3pm/CO noon. Nonsmoking rms avail. Large rooms with attractive bedspreads and prints. **Amenities:** Cable TV w/movies, VCR. No A/C. Some units w/terraces. Ceiling fans. **Services:** Masseur. Pets not allowed in ocean-front rooms. Videos available for rent. **Facilities:** 1 restaurant, 1 bar (w/entertainment), lawn games, whirl-

pool, washer/dryer. Miniature golf, shuffleboard. **Rates:** Peak (June–Sept) $90–$129 S or D; $149 ste; $149 effic. Extra person $6. Children under age 12 stay free. Min stay peak and wknds. Lower rates off-season. Parking: Outdoor, free. Lower mid-week rates. AE, CB, DC, DISC, MC, V.

RESTAURANT

★ The Cliffs at Shell Beach

2757 Shell Beach Rd, Pismo Beach; tel 805/773-3555. **Californian.** Casual but attractive restaurant with French-country chairs, stained-glass windows, plants, fireplace, outdoor deck. Menu features shrimp scampi, coconut prawns, crab, lobster, steaks, prime rib. **FYI:** Reservations accepted. **Open:** Breakfast Mon–Sat 7am–noon, Sun 7–9am; lunch Mon–Sat 11:30am–4pm; dinner Sun–Thurs 4–9:30pm, Fri–Sat 4–10pm; brunch Sun 10am–2pm. **Prices:** Main courses $11–$25. AE, DC, MC, V.

Sherman Oaks

See also Van Nuys

HOTEL

≡≡ Carriage Inn

5525 Sepulveda Blvd, 91411; tel 818/787-2300 or toll free 800/772-8527; fax 818/782-9373. This 32-year-old property is well maintained, despite a deteriorating neighborhood. **Rooms:** 184 rms and stes. CI 3pm/CO noon. Nonsmoking rms avail. Soundproofing blocks out noise from nearby freeway. **Amenities:** A/C, cable TV w/movies, refrig, dataport. **Services:** Twice-daily maid svce, car-rental desk. **Facilities:** 2 restaurants, 1 bar (w/entertainment), whirlpool. Bar has a band on weekends. **Rates:** $79–$110 S or D; $150 ste. Children under age 18 stay free. Parking: Outdoor, free. AE, CB, DC, DISC, EC, ER, JCB, MC, V.

Simi Valley

Adjacent to the San Fernando Valley in the rolling foothills of the Santa Susana Mountains, Simi Valley is the home of the Ronald Reagan Presidential Library. **Information:** Simi Valley Chamber of Commerce, 40 W Cochran St, Simi Valley 93065 (tel 805/526-3900).

HOTELS

≡≡ Clarion Posada Royale Hotel Simi Valley

1775 Madera Rd, 93065; tel 805/584-6300 or toll free 800/221-2222; fax 805/527-9969. Madera Rd exit off CA 118. Needed renovations are scheduled soon. Excellent location for visiting the Reagan Library. **Rooms:** 120 rms, stes, and effic. CI 3pm/CO noon. Nonsmoking rms avail. **Amenities:** A/C, cable TV w/movies. Some units w/terraces, some w/fireplaces, some w/whirlpools. **Services:** Complimentary evening cocktails. **Facilities:** 1 restaurant, 1 bar, whirlpool, washer/dryer. **Rates (CP):** $74–$94 S or D; $94–$300 ste; $84 effic. Extra person $10. Children under age 17 stay free. Min stay special events. Parking: Outdoor, free. AE, DC, DISC, MC, V.

≡≡ Radisson Hotel Simi Valley

999 Enchanted Way, 93065; tel 805/583-2000 or toll free 800/333-3333; fax 805/583-2779. 1st St exit off CA 118. Under new ownership; rooms and public spaces are being renovated. Easy access to Reagan Library. **Rooms:** 195 rms and stes. CI 3pm/CO noon. Nonsmoking rms avail. Worn but clean. **Amenities:** A/C, cable TV w/movies, refrig. Some units w/terraces, 1 w/whirlpool. **Services:** Twice-daily maid svce. Complimentary cocktail parties weekdays. **Facilities:** 1 restaurant, 2 bars (1 w/entertainment), whirlpool. **Rates:** $89–$119 S; $99–$129 D; $149–$159 ste. Extra person $10. Children under age 17 stay free. Min stay special events. Parking: Outdoor, free. AE, CB, DC, DISC, JCB, MC, V.

Solvang

Solvang was founded by Danish Americans in 1911, and the town has capitalized heavily on its heritage with Danish architecture, cobblestone walks, restaurants, and shops. It is now primarily a tourist destination. **Information:** Solvang Convention & Visitors Bureau, 1511 Mission Dr, PO Box 70, Solvang 93464 (tel 805/688-6144 or toll free 800/GO-SOLVANG).

MOTEL

≡≡≡ Solvang Royal Scandinavian Inn

400 Alisal Rd, PO Box 30, 93464; tel 805/688-8000 or toll free 800/624-5572; fax 805/688-0761. This quiet property on the edge of town exudes serenity and relaxation. **Rooms:** 133 rms and stes. CI 4pm/CO 11am. Nonsmoking rms avail. Poolside rooms have beautiful views; very clean, with Scandinavian decor. **Amenities:** A/C, satel TV w/movies, CD/tape player. Some units w/terraces. Refrigerators available. **Services:** Masseur, babysitting. Coffee and newspapers in lobby. **Facilities:** 1 restaurant, 1 bar (w/entertainment), whirlpool, day-care ctr. Outstanding pool area with gazebo, tables and chairs, and a basket of towels for guests. **Rates:** Peak (June–Sept) $101–$146 S or D; $146 ste. Extra person $10. Children under age 17 stay free. Lower rates off-season. Parking: Outdoor, free. AE, DC, DISC, MC, V.

ATTRACTION

Mission Santa Ines

1760 Mission Dr; tel 805/688-4815. Founded in 1804, this restored mission was the 19th in California's 21-mission series. After a series of restorations, the most recent in 1988, the mission looks much as it must have shortly after it was founded. The church, chapel, and grounds are open to the public, as is the museum, which houses early Native American and European mission artifacts. **Open:** Peak (Mem–Labor Day) Mon–Fri 9am–7pm, Sun noon–7pm. Reduced hours off-season. **Free**

Sonoma

See also Glen Ellen, Kenwood, Rohnert Park, Santa Rosa

Renowned as the center of one of California's premier wine-growing regions, Sonoma was the site of the Bear Flag Revolt in 1846, when California declared itself a republic independent from Mexico. The town has retained much of its Spanish and Mexican architecture around its spacious plaza. **Information:** Sonoma Valley Chamber of Commerce, 645 Broadway, Sonoma 95476 (tel 707/996-1033).

HOTELS 🏨

🎗🎗🎗 Best Western Sonoma Valley Inn
550 2nd St W, 95476 (Downtown); tel 707/938-9200 or toll free 800/334-5784; fax 707/938-0935. Lovely hotel with nice grounds. **Rooms:** 75 rms. CI 3pm/CO noon. Nonsmoking rms avail. Rooms are comfortable and large, with photographs of Sonoma Valley on the walls. Poolside patio rooms that open onto the garden and pool are nicest. **Amenities:** 🛏 🗗 🍷 A/C, satel TV w/movies, dataport, voice mail. Some units w/terraces, some w/fireplaces, some w/whirlpools. **Services:** � 🖼 🗗 🍴 Masseur, babysitting. Continental breakfast delivered to your room. Friday night wine tasting in summer. **Facilities:** 🔓 🛎 🏊 ⚽ Whirlpool, washer/dryer. Lovely pool area. **Rates (CP):** Peak (Apr–Nov) $109–$169 S or D. Extra person $10. Children under age 12 stay free. Min stay peak and wknds. Lower rates off-season. Parking: Outdoor, free. Many special activity packages. AE, DC, DISC, MC, V.

🎗🎗🎗 El Dorado Hotel
405 1st St W, 95476; tel 707/996-3030 or toll free 800/289-3031; fax 707/996-3148. Nice hotel right on the plaza with a wonderful restaurant, Piatti, downstairs. **Rooms:** 27 rms. CI 4pm/CO 1pm. No smoking. Rooms decorated in soothing peach tones, with attractive furnishings and down comforters. Some have French doors. **Amenities:** 🛏 A/C, cable TV. All units w/terraces. Complimentary bottle of wine. **Services:** 🖼 🗗 Attentive staff. **Facilities:** 🔓 🛎 ⚽ 1 restaurant (lunch and dinner only; see "Restaurants" below), 1 bar. **Rates (CP):** Peak (May–Oct) $110–$153 S or D. Extra person $25. Min stay wknds. Lower rates off-season. Parking: Outdoor, free. AE, MC, V.

🎗🎗🎗 Sonoma Hotel
110 W Spain St, 95476; tel 707/996-2996 or toll free 800/468-6016; fax 707/996-7014. Unique old hotel furnished with antiques; the feel of an 1880s European inn. **Rooms:** 17 rms and stes. CI 2pm/CO noon. Nonsmoking rms avail. Well-appointed rooms have lots of antiques, including clawfoot tubs in rooms with private baths. **Amenities:** No A/C, phone, or TV. **Facilities:** 1 restaurant (lunch and dinner only), 1 bar, washer/dryer. **Rates (CP):** Peak (May–Oct) $75–$115 S or D; $125 ste. Lower rates off-season. Parking: Outdoor, free. AE, DC, MC, V.

RESORT

🎗🎗🎗🎗 Sonoma Mission Inn & Spa
18140 CA 12, PO Box 1447, 94576; tel 707/938-9000 or toll free 800/862-4945; fax 707/996-5358. 3 mi NW of Sonoma. At Boyes Blvd. Designed like an overgrown mission with pink walls and a red-tile roof, the resort is surrounded by emerald lawns and ancient oaks and sequoias. It is one of only three luxury resorts in the country to use its own natural mineral waters in treatments. **Rooms:** 169 rms and stes. CI 4pm/CO 11am. No smoking. Accommodations available in either the historic 1920s inn (charming but very small) or newer wings with spacious "wine country" rooms. Many of the latter have been redone with down quilts, wood-burning fireplaces, and antiqued armoires, lending a residential feel (but the concrete corridors that lead to accommodations have the allure of a high school locker room). **Amenities:** 🛏 🗗 🍷 A/C, cable TV, dataport, VCR, bathrobes. All units w/minibars, some w/terraces, some w/fireplaces, some w/whirlpools. Bathroom toiletries include products from the inn's own line. **Services:** ✕ 📠 🖼 🚐 🏊 🗗 Twice-daily maid svce, car-rental desk, social director, masseur, babysitting. **Facilities:** 🔓 🚴 🍸 🏌 🛎 🖥 ⚽ 2 restaurants (see "Restaurants" below), 2 bars (1 w/entertainment), spa, sauna, steam rm, whirlpool, beauty salon, playground. The spa is the largest and most complete in northern California, with 40 treatment rooms featuring an array of services, from a two-hour "revitalizer" pick-me-up to stress-management techniques. Superb aerobics program. **Rates:** Peak (Apr–Dec) $140–$365 S or D; $325–$640 ste. Extra person $30. Children under age 18 stay free. Min stay wknds. Lower rates off-season. Parking: Outdoor, free. Spa packages avail. AE, CB, DC, DISC, JCB, MC, V.

RESTAURANTS 🍽

★ Babette's
464 1st St E; tel 707/939-8921. **Californian/French.** Nestled in a cobblestoned courtyard off Sonoma Plaza, this romantic restaurant serves modern French cuisine that emphasizes local organic products. The wine bar has a Paris-in-the-1920s feel and a bistro menu. The restaurant serves only five-course fixed-price menus including such specialties as local salmon, oven-roasted shiitake mushrooms, carrot and fennel soup, and roasted quail. Lighter fare offered at the wine bar. **FYI:** Reservations recommended. Beer and wine only. **Open:** Tues–Sat noon–10pm, Sun 5–9pm. **Prices:** Main courses $9–$13; prix fixe $45. MC, V. 💟 ⚽

Depot 1870 Restaurant
241 1st St W; tel 707/938-2980. **Italian.** Located in a hotel that lodged train passengers in the 19th century, it has a charming ambience, with the dining room overlooking the garden and fountain. The chef/owner personally prepares all soups, pastas, and sauces. Good choices include ravioli stuffed with mushrooms in wine, veal parmigiana, and seafood specialties. **FYI:** Reservations accepted. Beer and wine only. **Open:** Lunch Wed–Fri 11:30am–2pm; dinner Wed–Sun 5–10pm. **Prices:** Main courses $11–$17.

★ East Side Oyster Bar & Grill
133 E Napa St; tel 707/939-1266. 1 block E of Sonoma Plaza. **Eclectic.** Among the Bay Area's most innovative cooking—creative without being quirky. Chef Charles Saunders (formerly of Sonoma Mission Inn) combines cuisines effortlessly, pairing sea-sweet oysters with tomatillo salsa, or accompanying Sonoma lamb with chick-pea mash, grilled eggplant, and red-onion confit. In addition to the 1930s-style restaurant up front, there's an outdoor brick patio. Service is well meaning if sometimes bewildered. **FYI:** Reservations recommended. Beer and wine only. **Open:** Lunch Mon–Fri 11:30am–2:30pm, Sat 11:30am–3pm, Sun noon–3pm; dinner daily 5–9pm. **Prices:** Main courses $9–$16. AE, DC, MC, V. ⛴ ▢

Feed Store Cafe and Bakery
529 1st St W; tel 707/938-2122. **American/Cafe.** Country farm kitchen atmosphere in a former feed store with an award-winning bakery; pleasant garden patio with duck pond. Scrumptious homemade pastries, baked breads, chicken sandwiches, and vegetarian club sandwich. **FYI:** Reservations accepted. Beer and wine only. **Open:** Mon–Fri 6am–5:30pm, Sat–Sun 7am–5:30pm. **Prices:** Lunch main courses $5–$8. MC, V. ⅙

The General's Daughter
400 W Spain St; tel 707/938-4004. 1 mi W of Plaza. **Californian.** This restaurant is located in a fine 1864 Victorian house that once belonged to a daughter of General Vallejo, the Mexican commandant of the California Territory. Decor includes high ceilings, wall-size paintings, and a bar displaying photos of vintners from all 35 local wineries. The restaurant has rapidly gained a reputation for exquisite Sonoma Valley cuisine, with entrees such as pan-seared duck breast with dried cherries, and grilled lamb chops encrusted with pistachios. **FYI:** Reservations recommended. **Open:** Sun–Thurs 11:30am–9:30pm, Fri–Sat 11:30am–10pm. **Prices:** Main courses $9–$23. MC, V. ⅙

The Grille
In Sonoma Mission Inn & Spa, 18140 CA 12; tel 707/938-9000. At Boyes Blvd. **Californian.** Impressionistic paintings of flowers plus oversize magnums and imperials of the valley's finest wines set the mood at this restaurant serving wine-country cuisine. The menu uses many Sonoma products—local lettuces, aged cheeses, salmon, and duck. Several "spa cuisine" dishes as well, with offerings such as grilled Sonoma lamb with roasted garlic and tomato-zucchini gratin

weighing in at less than 300 calories. The wine list features over 200 Sonoma and Napa labels. **FYI:** Reservations recommended. **Open:** Lunch Mon–Sat 11:30am–2:30pm; dinner daily 6–9:30pm; brunch Sun 9am–2:30pm. **Prices:** Main courses $17–$26. AE, DC, MC, V. 🅅🅿 ⅙

$ ★ Juanita Juanita
19114 Arnold Dr; tel 707/935-3981. **Mexican.** California-style Mexican food with a healthy, low-fat twist. In addition to the standard tacos and burritos, they feature loads of specials such as chicken and veggie tamales, garlic chicken burritos, and grilled mushroom, spinach, and bean quesadillas. The homemade tortilla chips can be paired with over 20 different hot sauces. Popular with locals, it's very busy on weekends and fun for kids. Excellent local beers on tap. **FYI:** Reservations not accepted. Children's menu. Beer and wine only. **Open:** Daily 11am–8pm. **Prices:** Main courses $3–$8. No CC. ▦

Murphy's Irish Pub
464 1st St E; tel 707/935-0660. **Pub.** A good place to relax, right off the plaza. Traditional Irish pub, with 10 beers on tap and standard pub grub at good prices. Live music four nights a week. **FYI:** Reservations not accepted. Beer and wine only. **Open:** Daily 11am–11pm. **Prices:** Main courses $7–$9. No CC. ⛴ ▦ ⅙

Old Swiss Hotel
In the Swiss Hotel, 18 W Spain St; tel 707/938-2884. **Italian.** Set in a landmark 1848 adobe structure that has been a hotel since 1909. The decor has been lovingly restored and there is great patio dining next to a fireplace. Specialties include warm radicchio salad with pears, walnuts, and blue cheese; grilled lamb with polenta; risotto with rock shrimp; and pizzas from the wood-fired oven. Excellent local wines. **FYI:** Reservations accepted. Jazz. **Open:** Lunch Mon–Fri 11:30am–2:30pm; dinner Mon–Fri 5–9pm, Sat–Sun 5–10pm. **Prices:** Main courses $9–$17. MC, V. ▪ ⅙

Piatti
In the El Dorado Hotel, 405 1st St W; tel 707/996-2351. **Italian.** Known as the best Italian restaurant in Sonoma. Decor features Tuscan-influenced tile floors, an open kitchen, and lovely murals of food on the walls. Outdoor dining area is draped in wisteria. Try the clams, calamari, calzone, angel-hair pasta, and roasted chicken. **FYI:** Reservations recommended. **Open:** Mon–Fri 11:30am–10pm, Sat–Sun 11:30am–11pm. **Prices:** Main courses $9–$17. AE, MC, V. ⛴ ⅙

REFRESHMENT STOP ▽

★ Angelo's Wine Country Deli
23400 Arnold Dr (CA 121) (Schellville); tel 707/938-3688. On CA 121 N of Sonoma Valley Airport. **Deli.** A great place to pick up goodies for a wine-country picnic. You can't miss it—there's a near-life-size model cow perched over the doorway. What you see inside—18 varieties of sausages,

garlicky salsas, smoked meats—is the single-handed work of Angelo Ibleto. "I can't find anybody else who'll put love in the food," he explains. **Open:** Sun–Thurs 9am–6pm, Fri–Sat 9am–7pm. No CC.

ATTRACTIONS

Mission San Francisco Solano de Sonoma
Sonoma Plaza at the corner of 1st St E and Spain St; tel 707/938-1519. Founded in 1823, this was the northernmost, and last, mission built in California. It was also the only one established on the northern coast by the Mexican rulers, who wished to protect their territory against expansionist Russian fur traders. **Open:** Daily 10am–5pm. $

Sebastiani Vineyards Winery
389 4th St E; tel 707/938-5532 or toll free 800/888-5532. Tours here highlight the winery's original turn-of-the-century crusher and press, as well as the largest collection of oak-barrel carvings in the world. Tastings include some of the vineyards 95 award-winning vintages. Picnic area. **Open:** Daily 10am–5pm. **Free**

Buena Vista Winery
18000 Old Winery Rd; tel 707/938-1266. A state historic landmark, the winery was founded in 1857 by Colonel Agoston Haraszthy, a Hungarian count. Haraszthy brought hundreds of grape varieties back from Europe, which became the foundation stock for the California wine industry. A self-guided tour includes historical displays, photographs, and an art gallery. Tasting room, cellars, wooded picnic area. **Open:** Peak (July–Sept) 10:30am–4:30pm. Reduced hours off-season.

Sonoma Valley

See Glen Ellen, Kenwood, Rohnert Park, Santa Rosa, Sonoma

Sonora

The seat of Tuolumne County, the town takes its name from Sonora, Mexico, the home of the first miners to settle here. Sonora was one of the wealthiest Gold Rush towns, and classic Western and Victorian storefronts and homes still line the streets. **Information:** Tuolumne County Chamber of Commerce, 222 S Shepherd St, Sonora 95370 (tel 209/532-4212).

MOTELS

Aladdin Motor Inn
14260 Mono Way, 95370; tel 209/533-4971 or toll free 800/696-3969 in CA; fax 209/532-1522. Mono Ave exit off CA 108. Pleasant facility on country highway. **Rooms:** 61 rms, stes, and effic. Executive level. CI 2pm/CO noon. Nonsmoking rms avail. **Amenities:** A/C, cable TV w/movies,

refrig. VCR rental. **Services:** Complimentary full breakfast at on-premises restaurant. Guests may use fax and copier in office. Hotel kit available for the deaf and hard of hearing. Pets limited to certain rooms. **Facilities:** 1 restaurant, whirlpool, washer/dryer. **Rates (MAP):** Peak (May–Oct) $55–$65 S; $73–$88 D; $99 ste; $99 effic. Extra person $8. Children under age 6 stay free. Min stay special events. Lower rates off-season. Parking: Outdoor, free. AE, DISC, MC, V.

Best Western Sonora Oaks
19551 Hess Ave, 95370; tel 209/533-4400 or toll free 800/532-1944; fax 209/532-1964. Nice hotel on rural highway. Oak grove on back property. **Rooms:** 101 rms and stes. CI 1pm/CO 11am. Nonsmoking rms avail. Poolside rooms available. **Amenities:** A/C, cable TV w/movies. Some units w/terraces. **Services:** Offers ADA kit for deaf and hard of hearing guests. **Facilities:** 1 restaurant, 1 bar (w/entertainment), whirlpool. **Rates:** $70–$95 S or D; $115 ste. Extra person $5. Children under age 12 stay free. Parking: Outdoor, free. Ski and resort packages avail. AE, CB, DC, DISC, MC, V.

Miners Motel
18740 CA 108, PO Box 1, 95370; tel 209/532-7850 or toll free 800/451-4176 in CA; fax 209/532-6401. A modest, older property. **Rooms:** 18 rms. CI 1pm/CO 11am. Nonsmoking rms avail. **Amenities:** A/C, cable TV w/movies, refrig. **Services:** **Facilities:** Playground. Barbecue pit, basketball court. **Rates:** Peak (May 10–Oct 15) $40–$55 S; $55–$70 D. Children under age 18 stay free. Min stay special events. Lower rates off-season. Parking: Outdoor, free. AE, CB, DC, DISC, MC, V.

RESTAURANT

Good Heavens, A Restaurant
49 N Washington St; tel 209/532-3663. **Eclectic.** Restaurant with homey feel, decorated with old photos, prints, and paintings. A nice stop for lunch, the only meal served. Menu changes daily and features quiche, crepes, and desserts including homemade jams. **FYI:** Reservations recommended. Beer and wine only. **Open:** Tues–Sun 11am–2:30pm. **Prices:** Main courses $6–$9; prix fixe $13. No CC.

ATTRACTION

Columbia State Historic Park
Tel 209/532-4301. 4 mi N on CA 49. One of the best-preserved gold rush towns in the mother lode. The whole town has been preserved, and it continues to function as it did in the 1850s (albeit primarily for the benefit of tourists), with stagecoach rides, Western-style Victorian hotels and saloons, a newspaper office, a working blacksmith's, and Wells Fargo express office. **Open:** Daily 8:30am–5:30pm. **Free**

South Lake Tahoe

The California side of the highly developed stretch of casinos and hotels (all of the gaming is just across the state line in Nevada), South Lake Tahoe is a gateway for gamblers as well as skiers in winter and alpine hikers in the summer. The town is also a jumping-off point for exploring the beaches along Lake Tahoe—one of the highest, deepest, clearest, and most beautiful lakes in the world. **Information:** South Lake Tahoe Chamber of Commerce, 3066 Lake Tahoe Blvd, South Lake Tahoe 96150 (tel 916/541-5255).

HOTELS 🏨

≣≣≣ Embassy Suites Resort Lake Tahoe

4130 Lake Tahoe Blvd, 96150; tel 916/544-5400 or toll free 800/EMBASSY; fax 916/544-4900. Large lobby with water wheel in atrium. Cheerfully decorated with an old-world theme. A very nice hotel. **Rooms:** 400 stes. CI 3pm/CO noon. Nonsmoking rms avail. Living area is spacious. Excellent-quality furnishings. **Amenities:** 🔞 🕭 🖬 🖬 A/C, cable TV w/movies, dataport, VCR, voice mail. All units w/minibars, some w/terraces. Microwave in each suite; Nintendo for kids. Some rooms offer bathrobes and CD players. **Services:** ✕ 🖢 🖷 🚗 🖾 ⌒ Twice-daily maid svce, car-rental desk, babysitting. Complimentary cooked-to-order breakfast; free cocktails in afternoon. **Facilities:** 🔆 🏌 🐎 🖳 🖵 & 3 restaurants, 1 bar (w/entertainment), spa, sauna, whirlpool. Ski rental on premises. **Rates (BB):** Peak (Dec–Feb/June–Aug) $129–$239 ste. Extra person $20. Children under age 12 stay free. Min stay wknds and special events. Lower rates off-season. Parking: Indoor/outdoor, free. AE, CB, DC, DISC, JCB, MC, V.

≣≣≣ Fantasy Inn

3696 Lake Tahoe Blvd, 96150; tel 916/541-6666 or toll free 800/367-7736; fax 916/541-6798. Romantic and fun, yet never sleazy or tacky, describes this adults-only hotel, where everything is crisp and new. Sensuous posters and prints decorate the corridors. **Rooms:** 53 rms. CI 2pm/CO 11am. Nonsmoking rms avail. All accommodations have been recently refurbished. Even standard rooms feature king-size beds, mirrored ceilings, and large spa tubs in a corner of the room. There are also 13 theme suites with different motifs. Mystic Mountain features a Hiawatha-like mural, while Caesar's Indulgence comes with tiger skin–print carpeting and a gold bust of the emperor by the black whirlpool tub. **Amenities:** 🔞 🕭 🖬 A/C, cable TV w/movies. Some units w/fireplaces, all w/whirlpools. All rooms feature stereo music systems and 26" TVs. **Services:** Twice-daily maid svce, masseur. **Facilities:** 🏌 🐎 & Wedding chapel. **Rates:** $88–$250 S or D. Min stay special events. Parking: Outdoor, free. AE, DISC, MC, V.

≣≣≣ Holiday Inn Express

3961 Lake Tahoe Blvd, 96150; tel 916/544-5900 or toll free 800/544-5288; fax 916/544-5333. Exceptionally clean hotel. **Rooms:** 89 rms and stes. CI 2pm/CO noon. Nonsmoking rms avail. **Amenities:** 🔞 🕭 🖬 A/C, cable TV, refrig. Some units w/minibars, some w/fireplaces, 1 w/whirlpool. **Services:** ⌒ **Facilities:** 🔆 Sauna, whirlpool, washer/dryer. **Rates (CP):** Peak (June 24–Sept 10) $89–$109 S or D; $159–$179 ste; $109–$149 effic. Children under age 18 stay free. Min stay wknds and special events. Lower rates off-season. Parking: Outdoor, free. AE, CB, DC, DISC, JCB, MC, V.

≣≣ Sierra-Cal Lodge

3838 Lake Tahoe Blvd, 96150; tel 916/541-5400 or toll free 800/245-6343; fax 916/541-7170. Within walking distance of the beaches. Fireplace in lobby provides welcome warmth on winter days. **Rooms:** 121 rms, stes, and effic. CI 1pm/CO noon. Nonsmoking rms avail. Rooms are color-coordinated, but not especially attractive. Some have views of Heavenly Valley ski area. **Amenities:** 🔞 🕭 A/C, cable TV. **Services:** 🖾 ⌒ 🗝 Ski shuttle from lodge to five major ski areas; 24-hour shuttle to casinos. **Facilities:** 🔆 🏌 🐎 🖳 1 restaurant (lunch and dinner only), whirlpool. **Rates:** Peak (Ski season/June–Aug) $39–$68 S; $39–$88 D; $100–$150 ste; $95–$118 effic. Extra person $10. Children under age 12 stay free. Min stay special events. Lower rates off-season. Parking: Outdoor, free. AE, CB, DC, DISC, MC, V.

MOTELS

≣≣ Best Western Station House Inn

901 Park Ave, 96150; tel 916/542-1101 or toll free 800/822-5953; fax 916/542-1714. Quiet, with views of the mountains. A rock wall surrounds an attractive pool area and the lobby is extremely appealing. Complimentary passes to nearby beach. **Rooms:** 102 rms and stes; 2 cottages/villas. CI 3pm/CO noon. Nonsmoking rms avail. Rooms have coordinated bedspreads and draperies in subtle shades; good furniture. **Amenities:** 🔞 🕭 🖬 A/C, cable TV w/movies. 1 unit w/fireplace, some w/whirlpools. Chalets have refrigerators. **Services:** ⌒ Babysitting. Complimentary American breakfast, Oct–May. **Facilities:** 🔆 🏌 🐎 🖳 1 restaurant (bkfst and dinner only), 1 bar, whirlpool. **Rates:** Peak (Jan 7–Mar/June 16–Oct) $108–$128 S or D; $105–$150 ste; $125–$200 cottage/villa. Extra person $10. Children under age 12 stay free. Min stay wknds and special events. Lower rates off-season. Parking: Outdoor, free. AE, CB, DC, DISC, MC, V.

≣≣≣ Best Western Timber Cove Lodge

3411 Lake Tahoe Blvd, 96150; tel 916/541-6722 or toll free 800/972-8558; fax 916/541-7959. One of the best deals in the South Lake Tahoe area. **Rooms:** 262 rms and stes. CI 3pm/CO noon. Nonsmoking rms avail. Rooms are plain but well kept. **Amenities:** 🔞 🖬 A/C, cable TV w/movies. Some units w/terraces. **Services:** ✕ 🖢 🖾 ⌒ Babysitting. **Facilities:** 🔆 🚲 ⛰ 🏌 🐎 🖳 📕 🖳 1 restaurant, 1 bar, 1 beach (lake shore), whirlpool, washer/dryer. Swimming pool area has great views of lake. Attractive restaurant has outdoor dining with views of lake and pool. Wedding chapel on premises. Reception room under construction. **Rates:** Peak (June 24–Sept 24) $100 S; $110 D; $165–$225 ste. Extra person $10. Children under age 16 stay free. Min stay wknds and special events. Lower rates off-season. Parking: Outdoor, free. AE, CB, DC, DISC, JCB, MC, V.

≡≡ Casino Area Travelodge

4003 Lake Tahoe Blvd, PO Box 6500, 95729; tel 916/541-5000 or toll free 800/578-7878; fax 916/544-6910. Adequate rooms. Easy walking distance to casinos. **Rooms:** 66 rms. CI 2pm/CO noon. Nonsmoking rms avail. Can hear road noise from rooms. **Amenities:** 🛆 🗗 A/C, cable TV, refrig. **Services:** 🛏 **Facilities:** 🛆 🏃 🏊 Noisy at pool. Restaurants, markets, shopping centers nearby. **Rates:** Peak (June–Sept) $39–$86 S or D. Extra person $5. Children under age 18 stay free. Min stay wknds and special events. Lower rates off-season. Parking: Outdoor, free. AE, DC, DISC, JCB, MC, V.

≡≡ Forest Inn Suites

1101 Park Ave, PO Box 4300, 96157; tel 916/541-6655; fax 916/544-3135. Beautiful forest setting. **Rooms:** 116 rms, stes, and effic. CI 4pm/CO noon. Nonsmoking rms avail. Suites (which are substantially nicer than rooms) have dining areas, living rooms, kitchens, and a large amount of closet space. Each bedroom has a bath. Tasteful decorations. **Amenities:** 🛆 🗗 Cable TV, refrig, VCR. No A/C. Some units w/terraces. VCRs available for a fee. **Services:** 🛆 🛏 Babysitting. **Facilities:** 🛆 🏃 🏊 Games rm, spa, sauna, steam rm, whirlpool. **Rates:** Peak (Dec–Apr/June 15–Sept 15) $75–$110 S or D; $100–$125 ste; $100–$125 effic. Extra person $10. Children under age 12 stay free. Min stay wknds and special events. Lower rates off-season. Parking: Outdoor, free. AE, DC, DISC, MC, V.

≡≡ Holiday Lodge

4095 Laurel Ave, PO Box 4007, 96157; tel 916/544-4101; fax 916/542-4932. A comfortable hotel. **Rooms:** 163 rms and stes; 2 cottages/villas. CI 3pm/CO 11am. Nonsmoking rms avail. **Amenities:** 🛆 A/C, cable TV. Some units w/terraces, some w/fireplaces. **Services:** 🛏 Babysitting. **Facilities:** 🛆 🏃 🏊 Sauna, whirlpool, washer/dryer. **Rates:** Peak (June 15–Sept 15) $65–$75 S; $70–$90 D; $82–$105 ste; $145–$195 cottage/villa. Extra person $5. Min stay peak, wknds, and special events. Lower rates off-season. Parking: Outdoor, free. AE, CB, DC, MC, V.

≡≡≡ Inn by the Lake

3300 Lake Tahoe Blvd, 96150; tel 916/542-0330 or toll free 800/877-1466; fax 916/541-6596. One of the nicer properties at South Lake Tahoe, tastefully decorated throughout. Attractive landscaping with flowers and trees. Interior renovation in progress, but hallways are currently a little shabby. **Rooms:** 100 rms, stes, and effic. CI 3pm/CO noon. Nonsmoking rms avail. Mid-priced rooms are good but not great. King bedrooms have lake views. **Amenities:** 🛆🗗 🛒 A/C, cable TV, refrig, VCR. All units w/terraces, some w/whirlpools. VCR available upon request. **Services:** 🛆 🛏 Babysitting. Video rental in library. **Facilities:** 🛆 🏃 🏊 🏊 Games rm, sauna, whirlpool. Closed-circuit TV security in all hallways. Bicycle and ski storage adjacent to lobby. **Rates (CP):** Peak (July–Aug/Christmas) $84–$148 S or D; $150–$330 ste; $250–$330 effic. Children under age 18 stay free. Min stay wknds and special events. Lower rates off-season. Parking: Outdoor, free. AE, DC, DISC, MC, V.

≡≡≡ Lakeland Village

3535 Lake Tahoe Blvd, PO Box 1356, 96156; tel 916/544-1685 or toll free 800/822-5969; fax 916/544-0193. Town house—like accommodations in a lovely wooded setting. **Rooms:** 260 cottages/villas. CI 3pm/CO 11am. Attractively decorated units, including beachfront condos. All have full kitchens. Lodge loft rooms have bedrooms with wash basin, closet, and end tables in loft; kitchen and living area below. **Amenities:** 🛆 🗗 A/C, cable TV, refrig, VCR, CD/tape player. All units w/terraces, all w/fireplaces. **Services:** 🗝 🚐 🛆 🛏 Social director, babysitting. **Facilities:** 🛆 🏃 🏊 🏊 1 beach (lake shore), games rm, sauna, whirlpool, playground, washer/dryer. Beautiful pool with umbrellas and landscaped grounds. **Rates:** Peak (Dec 21–Mar/June 21–Sept 4) $85–$455 cottage/villa. Children under age 18 stay free. Min stay wknds and special events. Lower rates off-season. Parking: Indoor/outdoor, free. AE, MC, V.

≡≡ South Tahoe Travelodge

3489 Lake Tahoe Blvd, PO Box 70512, 96156; tel 916/544-5266 or toll free 800/255-3050; fax 916/544-6985. Centrally located. Front desk staff not particularly friendly or helpful. **Rooms:** 59 rms. CI 2pm/CO noon. Nonsmoking rms avail. **Amenities:** 🛆 🗗 A/C, cable TV, refrig. All units w/minibars, all w/terraces, all w/fireplaces, all w/whirlpools. **Services:** 🛏 Free shuttle to casinos and ski areas. **Facilities:** 🛆 🏃 🏊 Whirlpool. Pool area noisy because of nearby highway. **Rates:** Peak (May–Aug) $39–$128 S or D. Extra person $5. Children under age 18 stay free. Lower rates off-season. Parking: Outdoor, free. Special rates for senior citizens. AE, DC, DISC, MC, V.

≡≡≡ Tahoe Beach & Ski Club

3601 Lake Tahoe Blvd, PO Box 1267, 95705; tel 916/541-6200 or toll free 800/540-4874. Very attractive condo units. **Rooms:** 131 rms and effic. CI 3pm/CO 11am. Nonsmoking rms avail. Well-equipped tiled kitchen area. Balconies off both bedroom and living area. Rooms are tastefully furnished. **Amenities:** 🛆 🗗 A/C, cable TV, refrig. Some units w/minibars, all w/terraces, some w/whirlpools. 2 TVs. **Services:** 🛏 Babysitting. **Facilities:** 🛆 🏃 🏊 1 restaurant, 1 beach (lake shore), sauna, whirlpool, washer/dryer. **Rates:** Peak (June 15–Sept 15/Feb–Mar) $105–$225 S or D; $180 ste. Extra person $15. Children under age 6 stay free. Min stay wknds and special events. Lower rates off-season. Parking: Outdoor, free. AE, DISC, MC, V.

≡≡ Tahoe Chalet Inn

3860 Lake Tahoe Blvd, 96150; tel 916/544-3311 or toll free 800/821-2656; fax 916/544-4069. Family-run and well-kept establishment. Beach and casinos are a short walk from hotel. **Rooms:** 67 rms, stes, and effic. CI 3pm/CO 11am. Nonsmoking rms avail. Rooms are small but not cramped. Attractive color coordination. Standard rooms are pleasant; luxury rooms lavishly decorated. **Amenities:** 🛏 📺 🍷 A/C, cable TV w/movies. Some units w/fireplaces, some w/whirlpools. Amenities vary according to the room. **Services:** 🖨 📞 Babysitting. **Facilities:** 🎱 🏊 📷 🍴 25 Sauna, steam rm. **Rates:** Peak (Jan–Apr 14/June 15–Sept 15) $52–$98 S or D; $98–$220 ste; $98–$128 effic. Children under age 18 stay free. Min stay wknds and special events. Lower rates off-season. Parking: Outdoor, free. AE, CB, DC, DISC, MC, V.

RESORT
≣≣≣ Richardson's Resort
CA 89 and Jameson Beach Rd, PO Box 9028, 96158; tel 916/541-1801 or toll free 800/544-1801; fax 916/541-2793. 80 acres. Pleasant lobby with pine paneling, a large stone fireplace, and comfortable furniture. Huge pine trees all around. Great beach. **Rooms:** 36 rms and effic; 39 cottages/villas. CI 2pm/CO 10am. Nonsmoking rms avail. Cabins, inn rooms near the beach, and lodge rooms are tastefully decorated with a rustic theme. **Amenities:** 🛏 ⚓ 📺 Refrig. No A/C or TV. Some units w/terraces, some w/fireplaces. Cabins have kitchens. **Services:** 📞 Babysitting. **Facilities:** 🚴 ⛰ 📷 🏊 🍴 50 1 restaurant (see "Restaurants" below), 1 bar (w/entertainment), 1 beach (lake shore), games rm, playground, washer/dryer. Ice cream shop, cappuccino cafe/bakery, deli on premises. A variety of sports facilities is available on the beach. **Rates:** Peak (June–Oct) $39–$89 S or D; $70 effic; $79 cottage/villa. Children under age 12 stay free. Min stay peak. Lower rates off-season. Parking: Outdoor, free. Seven-night minimum for efficiencies July and August. AE, DC, DISC, MC, V.

RESTAURANT 🍽
★ The Beacon
In Richardson's Resort, CA 89 at Jameson Beach Rd; tel 916/541-0630. **American/Italian.** Gray, blue, and white color scheme; seascapes on the walls. Fresh vegetables and San Francisco sourdough bread accompany entrees, which range from fresh lake trout to scampi Italiano. Chicken Tallac, stuffed with spinach, is named for the mountain peak visible in the mirror behind the bar. **FYI:** Reservations recommended. Guitar/reggae/rock. **Open:** Peak (June–Sept 10) lunch daily 11:30am–3pm; dinner daily 5–10pm; brunch Sat–Sun 10:30am–3pm. **Prices:** Main courses $13–$29. AE, MC, V. 🏔 ♿

South San Francisco
See also San Francisco Int'l Airport

South San Francisco, close to San Francisco International Airport, is a bayside railroad transportation hub and the site of several industrial parks. **Information:** South San Francisco Chamber of Commerce, 213 Linden Ave, PO Box 469, South San Francisco 94083 (tel 415/588-1911).

HOTEL 🏨
≣≣≣ Comfort Suites
121 E Grand Ave, 94080; tel 415/589-7766 or toll free 800/221-2222; fax 415/588-2231. Grand Ave exit off US 101; go east. Charming two-story lobby decorated with Mexican tiles, potted plants, archways, and a fireplace. Popular with long-term guests. Site is near freeways and rather noisy. **Rooms:** 166 stes. CI 3pm/CO noon. Nonsmoking rms avail. Soundproofing and sealed windows cut down on outside noise. Rooms feature a sitting area separated from sleeping area by a half-wall. **Amenities:** 🛏 ⚓ 📺 🍷 A/C, satel TV w/movies, refrig, dataport, VCR, CD/tape player, voice mail. **Services:** 🚐 🖨 📞 Expanded continental breakfast. Twice-monthly tastings of Napa Valley wines. Complimentary soup bar from 5 to 7pm. **Facilities:** ♿ Whirlpool, washer/dryer. Fitness club passes provided. **Rates (CP):** Peak (Apr–Sept) $118 ste. Extra person $10. Children under age 18 stay free. Lower rates off-season. Parking: Outdoor, free. Park-and-fly packages avail. AE, CB, DC, DISC, ER, JCB, MC, V.

Stockton
Located at the convergence of the Sacramento and San Joaquin Rivers, Stockton is a far-inland shipping route for oceangoing freighters. A historic section of town has been preserved in the Magnolia Historical District, and the town's agricultural heritage is celebrated every spring with the Asparagus Festival. **Information:** Stockton–San Joaquin County Convention and Visitors Bureau, 46 W Fremont St, Stockton 95202 (tel 209/943-1987 or toll free 800/350-1987).

HOTELS 🏨
≣≣≣ Holiday Inn Stockton
111 E March Lane, 95207; tel 209/474-3301 or toll free 800/633-3737; fax 209/474-7612. March Lane exit off I-5; E 2½ mi to El Dorado Rd. Guests enjoy a fresh look and consistent high quality regardless of room type. **Rooms:** 198 rms and stes. CI 3pm/CO noon. Nonsmoking rms avail. Rooms vary in size. Some poolside accommodations. **Amenities:** 🛏 ⚓ A/C, satel TV w/movies, refrig, voice mail. Some units w/terraces, some w/whirlpools. **Services:** ✕ 🖨 📞 Complimentary coffee 6–9am. **Facilities:** 🎱 250 🖥 ♿ 1 restaurant, 1 bar, whirlpool. Passes available to off-site fitness

facilities. **Rates:** $80 S; $90 D; $185 ste. Extra person $10. Children under age 18 stay free. Parking: Outdoor, free. AE, CB, DC, DISC, EC, ER, JCB, MC, V.

≡≡≡ Stockton Hilton

2323 Grand Canal Blvd, 95207; tel 209/957-9090 or toll free 800/444-9094; fax 209/473-8908. March Lane exit off I-5. Rooms are on street level, overlooking pool or Grand Canal. **Rooms:** 198 rms and stes. CI 3pm/CO 11am. Nonsmoking rms avail. Some rooms have double vanities in bath area. Desk with drawer serves as main table. **Amenities:** 🛗 👁 A/C, cable TV w/movies. Some units w/terraces. **Services:** ✕ 🖎 ♫ Babysitting. 24-hour security. **Facilities:** 🛋 600 👤 2 restaurants, 1 bar, whirlpool. Free use of health club across street. **Rates:** $85–$109 S; $97–$121 D; $210 ste. Extra person $12. Children under age 18 stay free. Parking: Outdoor, free. AE, DC, DISC, MC, V.

MOTELS

≡ Best Western Stockton Inn

4219 E Waterloo Rd, 95215; tel 209/931-3131 or toll free 800/528-1234; fax 209/931-0423. Waterloo E exit off CA 99. Older highway property suitable for an overnight if you can get the discount rate. **Rooms:** 141 rms and stes. CI 3pm/CO noon. Nonsmoking rms avail. Some adjoining rooms available. **Amenities:** 🛗 A/C, satel TV w/movies. **Services:** 🖎 ♫ Fax and copy service. Security guard 5pm–6am. **Facilities:** 🛋 700 1 restaurant, 1 bar, whirlpool. Free access to racquet club 4 miles away. **Rates:** Peak (Apr–July) $64–$74 S; $74–$88 D; $150 ste. Extra person $8. Children under age 12 stay free. Lower rates off-season. Parking: Outdoor, free. AE, CB, DC, DISC, MC, V.

≡ Days Inn

33 N Center St, 95202; tel 209/948-6151 or toll free 800/DAYS-INN; fax 209/948-1220. Downtown exit off CA 4 at Weber. Near port of Stockton. Renovations in progress. **Rooms:** 97 rms. CI 2pm/CO 11am. Nonsmoking rms avail. About half have been redecorated to upgrade flooring and furnishings. **Amenities:** 🛗 👁 A/C, satel TV. VCRs and mobile remotes available from office. **Services:** Night security guard on duty. Coffee and doughnuts in lobby each morning. **Facilities:** 🛋 30 👤 **Rates (CP):** Peak (Apr–Sept) $45–$55 S; $50–$65 D. Extra person $5. Children under age 17 stay free. Lower rates off-season. Parking: Outdoor, free. AE, DC, DISC, MC, V.

≡≡ La Quinta Motor Inn

2710 W March Lane, 95219; tel 209/952-7800 or toll free 800/531-5900; fax 209/472-0732. March Lane exit off I-5; W on March Lane. Renovation of the motel's public areas to be completed soon. New carpets, drapes, and bedspreads were also to be installed. **Rooms:** 153 rms and stes. Executive level. CI 3pm/CO noon. Nonsmoking rms avail. **Amenities:** 🛗 👁 A/C, cable TV w/movies. Executive rooms have refrigerator and computer jack. **Services:** 🖎 ♫ 🔔 Security staff on duty 11pm–6am. **Facilities:** 🛋 30 👤 Washer/dryer. Free

access to health club at Quail Lakes. **Rates (CP):** $55–$70 S; $60–$75 D; $80–$90 ste. Extra person $8. Children under age 16 stay free. Parking: Outdoor, free. AE, DC, DISC, MC, V.

ATTRACTION 🏛

Pixie Woods

Mount Diablo Rd at Occidental; tel 209/937-8220 or 466-9890. Located in Louis Park, at the west end of Mount Diablo Rd, Pixie Woods features amusement rides, attractions, Mother Goose characters, train and ferryboat rides, and a puppet show theater. Built in 1954, this playland includes a small lagoon with islands containing a Japanese Garden and a pirates' enclave. **Open:** Peak (June–Aug) Wed–Fri 11am–5pm, Sat–Sun 11am–6pm. Reduced hours off-season. **$$**

Studio City

The city takes its name from the time when Hollywood studios were located over the hills in the San Fernando Valley, attracted to the inexpensive real estate. Now, Studio City is also a bedroom community for movie industry types. **Information:** Studio City Chamber of Commerce, 12153 Ventura Blvd #100, Studio City 91604-2515 (tel 818/769-3213).

HOTEL 🏨

≡≡≡ Sportsmen's Lodge Hotel

12825 Ventura Blvd, 91604; tel 818/769-4700 or toll free 800/821-8511; fax 213/877-3898. Coldwater Canyon Ave exit off US 101. Unique hotel on parklike grounds with meandering streams, populated by white and black swans, peacocks, and ducks. Great shops and restaurants are within walking distance on Ventura Blvd. Lovely, peaceful, and quiet despite location. Hotel attracts a celebrity crowd. **Rooms:** 200 rms and stes. CI 3pm/CO noon. Nonsmoking rms avail. Rooms nicely decorated in country pine. **Amenities:** 🛗 👁 A/C, cable TV w/movies, voice mail. All units w/terraces. Kit for the deaf and hard of hearing available that lights up phone when it rings. **Services:** ✕ 🚗 🖎 ♫ Car-rental desk, babysitting. **Facilities:** 🛋 🏊 130 👤 3 restaurants, 2 bars (1 w/entertainment), whirlpool, beauty salon. Huge lap-size pool. **Rates:** $92–$122 S or D. Extra person $10. Children under age 18 stay free. Parking: Outdoor, free. AE, CB, DC, DISC, JCB, MC, V.

RESTAURANTS 🍽

★ Art's Deli

12224 Ventura Blvd; tel 818/762-1221. **Deli/Jewish.** A fixture in the San Fernando Valley since 1957, it's not elegant or ritzy, but still draws a show-biz crowd. They're known for making customers feel at home as well as for their mammoth corned beef and pastrami sandwiches, and homemade soups, Very children-friendly, too. **FYI:** Reservations accepted. Children's menu. Beer and wine only. **Open:** Mon–Thurs 6:30–10:30pm, Fri–Sat 6:30am–11:30pm, Sun 6:30am–10pm. **Prices:** Main courses $8–$13. AE, CB, DC, DISC, ER, MC, V. 🚢 🖼️ VP �

♟ The Bistro Garden at Coldwater

12950 Ventura Blvd; tel 818/501-0202. **Californian/Continental.** One of the most romantic restaurants in the San Fernando Valley. Open, airy, gardenlike decor, with twinkling lights on the trees. Spectacular 30-foot ceiling. Popular with stars and studio moguls. Famous for tuna tartare, which is lightly tossed with ginger and avocado. For dessert, try the crème caramel or the profiteroles, light and airy and drizzled with chocolate. **FYI:** Reservations recommended. Piano. **Open:** Lunch Mon–Fri 11:30am–3pm; dinner Mon–Thurs 5:30–10:30pm, Fri–Sat 5:30–11:30pm, Sun 5:30–10:30pm. **Prices:** Main courses $16–$30. AE, CB, DC, MC, V. ♥ VP �

★ Il Mito

11801 Ventura Blvd; tel 818/762-1818. **Italian/Middle Eastern.** A wonderful, rustic restaurant in a charming, 50-year-old, art deco building. Patrons seated in the main area can communicate with the chef as he works in a display kitchen. Specialties include grilled fish of the day prepared in a variety of ways; risotto with pureed corn and grilled river shrimp; grilled veal in a balsamic truffle sauce; and homemade breads. **FYI:** Reservations recommended. Additional location: 11826 Ventura Blvd (tel 980-6944). **Open:** Lunch Mon–Fri 11:30am–2:30pm; dinner Mon–Sat 6–10:30pm. **Prices:** Main courses $14–$22. AE, DISC, MC, V. VP �

★ Pinot Bistro

12969 Ventura Blvd; tel 818/990-0500. **French.** Clubby bistro atmosphere with dark wood paneling, leather banquettes, and fireplace. Especially popular are the low-calorie "spa offerings," though beefsteak with french fries is also served. **FYI:** Reservations recommended. Additional locations: 1448 N Gomer St, Hollywood (tel 213/461-8000); 250 S Grand Ave, Los Angeles (tel 213/626-1178). **Open:** Lunch Mon–Fri 11:30am–2pm; dinner Mon–Fri 6–10pm, Sat 5:30–10:30pm, Sun 5:30–9pm. **Prices:** Main courses $17–$20. AE, DC, DISC, MC, V. ♥ 🖼️ VP �

Ⓢ Poquito Mas

3701 Cahuenga Blvd W; tel 818/760-TACO. **Mexican.** A world-famous taco stand in a strip mall near Universal Studios that attracts clientele ranging from stars to pool cleaners. Try the giant tostadas with meat, shrimp tacos San Felipe with fresh cilantro wrapped in corn tortillas, or chicken tostada in a flour tortilla shell. Choice of sauces, from mild to dragon's breath. **FYI:** Reservations not accepted. No liquor license. **Open:** Sun–Thurs 10am–midnight, Fri–Sat 10am–1am. **Prices:** Main courses $3–$7; prix fixe $6–$7. No CC. 🚢

Suisun City

Adjacent to Fairfield and nearby Travis Air Force Base, Suisun City takes its name from the bay (spelled Suisin) and wetlands that connect the Sacramento Delta to the San Francisco Bay. **Information:** Fairfield-Suisun Chamber of Commerce, 1111 Webster St, Fairfield 94533 (tel 707/425-4625).

MOTEL 🏨

🏬🏬 Hampton Inn

4441 Central Place, 94585; tel 707/864-1446 or toll free 800/531-0202; fax 707/864-4288. Suisun Valley Rd exit off I-80; right on overpass; left on Central. Clean and well maintained. Adequate for business or highway accommodations. **Rooms:** 57 rms and stes. CI 2pm/CO noon. Nonsmoking rms avail. Travelers with disabilities should ask ahead for assistance; two accessible rooms are near parking. **Amenities:** 🛏️ ⬚ 🖵 A/C, cable TV w/movies. Some units w/whirlpools. **Services:** 🛆 🛏️ 🕭 **Facilities:** 🛅 🖵 🖵 � Washer/dryer. Breakfast room with TV and newspapers. Complimentary access to Body Image Gym. **Rates (CP):** Peak (Mem Day–Labor Day) $55–$65 S; $65–$75 D; $110 ste. Children under age 18 stay free. Lower rates off-season. Parking: Outdoor, free. AE, CB, DC, DISC, MC, V.

ATTRACTION 🏛️

Western Railway Museum

5848 CA 12; tel 707/374-2978 or toll free 800/290-2313. More than 100 vintage railroad cars and engines are held in the collection of this museum, including such nostalgic examples as an 1887 New York "el" car, a plush observation car from Utah, and articulated trains that ran on the San Francisco Bay Bridge in the 1940s and 50s. Vehicles are in various stages of restoration, and many are in operating condition. Visitors are invited to ride along a 1¼-mile rail line traversing the museum grounds and a 4-mile inter-urban round-trip to Garfield Station on the historic Sacramento Northern Mainline (Mar–Apr only). The bookstore is one of the largest dealing exclusively with railroads. **Open:** Peak (July 4–Labor Day) Wed–Sun 11am–5pm. Reduced hours off-season. **$$$**

Summerland

See Santa Barbara

Sunnyvale

With hundreds of hardware and software companies in and around Sunnyvale, the city is the computing heart of the Silicon Valley. That claim is bolstered by the existence of the Sunnyvale Center for Innovation, Invention, and Ideas, which conducts high-tech patent and trademark research. **Information:** Sunnyvale Chamber of Commerce, 499 S Murphy Ave, Sunnyvale 94086 (tel 408/736-4971).

HOTELS

▆▆ Ambassador Inn of Sunnyvale
910 E Fremont Ave, 94087; tel 408/738-0500 or toll free 800/538-1600, 800/672-1444 in CA; fax 408/245-4167. 10 mi N of San Jose. Wolfe Rd exit off I-280 N; right on Wolfe to Fremont. Particularly suitable for long-term guests who plan to cook in their rooms. **Rooms:** 205 effic. CI 2pm/CO noon. Nonsmoking rms avail. **Amenities:** 🕾 🔯 🖭 📺 A/C, satel TV w/movies, refrig. Some units w/whirlpools. **Services:** 🛆 🕱 Babysitting. **Facilities:** 🔓 🛏160 Sauna, whirlpool, washer/dryer. Complimentary passes to 24-hour Nautilus fitness facility. **Rates (CP):** $78–$135 effic. Extra person $10. Children under age 12 stay free. Parking: Outdoor, free. Rates lower on weekends. AE, DC, EC, JCB, MC, V.

▆▆▆ Four Points Hotel by ITT Sheraton
1100 N Mathilda Ave, 94089; tel 408/745-6000 or toll free 800/836-8686; fax 408/743-8276. Matilda Expwy exit off CA 237. With terra-cotta tiled floors, tropical plants, and peach and green decor, this place has the feel of a vacation resort in a tropical locale. Extensive grounds, with lagoon. Close to shopping. **Rooms:** 174 rms and stes. Executive level. CI 3pm/CO 1pm. Nonsmoking rms avail. Newly refurbished rooms have flowered upholstery and drapes, rattan furniture. Sunny, bright, and inviting. **Amenities:** 🕾 🔯 🖭 A/C, cable TV w/movies, voice mail. Some units w/terraces. **Services:** ✗ 🚙🛆🕱 Car-rental desk, babysitting. Full breakfasts, complimentary coffee. Shuttle to Great America theme park and fitness center. **Facilities:** 🔓 🛎 📦200 🕭 1 restaurant, 1 bar, whirlpool. Close to fitness center. **Rates (BB):** $140 S; $150 D. Extra person $10. Children under age 17 stay free. Parking: Outdoor, free. AE, CB, DC, DISC, ER, JCB, MC, V.

UNRATED Quality Inn Sunnyvale
1280 Persian Dr, 94089; tel 408/744-0660 or toll free 800/433-9933; fax 408/744-0660 ext 136. Lawrence Expwy exit off CA 237; right on Persian Dr. Simple but nice lobby. **Rooms:** 72 rms. CI 2pm/CO 11am. Nonsmoking rms avail. **Amenities:** 🕾 🔯 🖭 A/C, cable TV w/movies, refrig. Some units w/terraces. **Services:** 🛆🕱 **Facilities:** 🔓🕭 **Rates (CP):** $50–$82 S or D. Extra person $5. Children under age 18 stay free. Parking: Outdoor, free. AE, CB, DC, DISC, EC, ER, JCB, MC, V.

▆▆▆ Radisson Inn Sunnyvale
1085 E El Camino Real, 94087; tel 408/247-0800 or toll free 800/333-3333; fax 408/984-7120. Lawrence Expwy off I-280; left on El Camino Real. Lots of nice touches at this hotel include spacious rooms and a restaurant for guests only. **Rooms:** 136 rms and stes. CI 2pm/CO noon. Nonsmoking rms avail. Rooms facing inward, overlooking the lobby, are quiet. **Amenities:** 🕾 🔯 🖭 A/C, cable TV w/movies. All units w/minibars, some w/terraces, some w/whirlpools.

Services: ✗ 🗝 🚙 🛆 🕱 Car-rental desk. Special aids available for guests with disabilities. **Facilities:** 🔓 🛎 📦400 🖵 🕭 1 restaurant, 1 bar, whirlpool. **Rates (CP):** Peak (Oct–June) $115–$125 S; $125–$135 D; $135–$145 ste. Extra person $10. Lower rates off-season. Parking: Indoor/outdoor, free. AE, DC, DISC, JCB, MC, V.

▆▆▆ Residence Inn by Marriott Silicon Valley 2
1080 Stewart Dr, 94086; tel 408/720-1000 or toll free 800/331-3131; fax 408/737-9722. Lawrence Expwy exit off US 101 N; turn left. Exceptional extended-stay hotel with the look and feel of a residential condominium. **Rooms:** 247 effic. CI 3pm/CO noon. Nonsmoking rms avail. Suites have a homey feel, some with French doors to separate living and sleeping area. Complete kitchens in every suite. **Amenities:** 🕾 🔯 🖭 A/C, satel TV w/movies, refrig, dataport, VCR, voice mail. All units w/terraces, some w/fireplaces. Microwave. **Services:** 🚙 🛆 🕱 ⌖ Children's program. Complimentary newspapers in lobby, grocery shopping service. **Facilities:** 🔓 📷 📦95 🕭 Volleyball, whirlpool, washer/dryer. Outdoor barbecue grills. Complimentary use of nearby fitness center. **Rates (CP):** $129–$159 effic. Parking: Outdoor, free. AE, CB, DC, DISC, EC, JCB, MC, V.

▆▆▆ Sunnyvale Hilton
1250 Lakeside Dr, 94086; tel 408/738-4888 or toll free 800/543-3322; fax 408/737-7147. Lawrence Expwy S exit off US 101; left on Oakmead, left on Lakeside Dr. Reminiscent of a California mission, with adobe walls and southwestern decor. Complete with landscaped walkways and a lagoon. Close to business park. **Rooms:** 372 rms and stes. CI 2pm/CO noon. Nonsmoking rms avail. Rooms are large with high ceilings. **Amenities:** 🕾 🔯 A/C, cable TV w/movies, voice mail. Some units w/minibars, some w/terraces, some w/whirlpools. Executive rooms have makeup mirrors, irons, and ironing boards. **Services:** ✗ 🚙 🛆 🕱 Car-rental desk, children's program, babysitting. **Facilities:** 🔓 📷 📦500 🕭 2 restaurants, 1 bar, 1 beach (cove/inlet), sauna, whirlpool. Ballroom with floor-to-ceiling windows and spectacular water views. Complimentary passes to California Athletic Club nearby. **Rates:** $145–$190 S or D; $250 ste. Extra person $15. Children under age 18 stay free. Parking: Outdoor, free. Family packages avail. AE, CB, DC, DISC, ER, JCB, MC, V.

▆▆▆ Woodfin Suites
635 E El Camino Real, 94087; tel 408/738-1700 or toll free 800/237-8811; fax 408/738-0840. 10 mi N of San Jose. Fair Oaks S exit off US 101; left on El Camino. Suites have the residential appearance of condominium units. Stores, restaurants within walking distance. **Rooms:** 88 effic. CI 4pm/CO noon. Nonsmoking rms avail. Very conducive for long-term stay, with living room, bedroom, and kitchen. **Amenities:** 🕾 🔯 🖭 A/C, cable TV w/movies, refrig, dataport, VCR, voice mail. All units w/terraces, some w/fireplaces. **Services:** 🚙 🛆 🕱 Complimentary lemonade, orange juice, newspapers, plus cappuccino machine in lobby. Social hour Mon–Thurs 5–6:30pm. Hot American breakfast served buffet-style. Com-

plimentary video library. **Facilities:** ⚹ 🖳 ⚹ Whirlpool, washer/dryer. Gift shop sells frozen dinners, ice cream, and other edibles. **Rates (CP):** $179–$229 effic. Extra person $5. Children under age 13 stay free. Parking: Outdoor, free. Lower on weekends. AE, CB, DC, DISC, EC, JCB, MC, V.

≡≡≡ Wyndham Garden Hotel

1300 Chesapeake Terrace, 94089; tel 408/747-0999 or toll free 800/822-4200; fax 408/745-0759. Lawrence Expwy exit off US 101; left on Baylands Park Dr, left into business park and Chesapeake Terrace. Located in a business park surrounded by fountains, picnic tables, and a basketball court. Ideal for the business traveler, with nice landscaping and a lovely lobby. **Rooms:** 180 rms and stes. CI 3pm/CO noon. Nonsmoking rms avail. Appealing rooms with pleasant lighting and decor, including mirrored walls. Some rooms have king-size beds and large desks. **Amenities:** 🛏 ⚹ 🖵 🗍 A/C, cable TV w/movies, voice mail. Some rooms have wet bars. Oversized down pillows available. **Services:** ✕ 🚗 🖎 ↩ **Facilities:** ⚹ 🏋 ⌷150 ⚹ 1 restaurant, 1 bar, whirlpool, washer/dryer. Indoor whirlpool spa is being renovated. **Rates (BB):** $129 S or D; $129 ste. Extra person $10. Children under age 18 stay free. Parking: Outdoor, free. AE, CB, DC, DISC, EC, ER, JCB, MC, V.

MOTELS

≡≡ Ramada Inn

1217 Wildwood Ave, 94089; tel 408/245-5330 or toll free 800/888-3899; fax 408/732-2628. Lawrence Expwy N exit off US 101; quick right on Wildwood. A bright hotel with high ceilings and skylights, decorated in aqua and mauve. Friendly and charming. **Rooms:** 176 rms and stes. CI 2pm/CO noon. Nonsmoking rms avail. Most rooms face the pool/lawn area with palm trees; others face the parking lot. **Amenities:** 🛏 ⚹ 🖵 🗍 A/C, cable TV w/movies, in-rm safe. **Services:** ✕ 🚗 🖎 ↩ Car-rental desk. **Facilities:** ⚹ ⌷275 ⚹ 2 restaurants, 1 bar, whirlpool, washer/dryer. **Rates:** $129–$139 S; $139–$149 D; $220 ste. Parking: Outdoor, free. AE, DC, DISC, JCB, MC, V.

≡≡≡ Sundowner Inn

504 Ross Dr, 94089; tel 408/734-9900 or toll free 800/223-9901; fax 408/747-0580. Matilda Ave S exit off CA 237. An older property, this motel has a large grassy plot perfect for kids. Security is light, but doesn't seem to be a problem. **Rooms:** 105 rms and stes. CI 6pm/CO 11am. Nonsmoking rms avail. Plain but spotless. **Amenities:** 🛏 ⚹ 🖵 🗍 A/C, cable TV w/movies, refrig, dataport, VCR, voice mail. Some units w/minibars. Microwave and refrigerator for an additional 50 cents per day. Mobile TV remote available with $20 deposit. **Services:** ✕ 🖎 ↩ Free local phone calls. Books, games, and movies in lobby. Free shuttle service for some corporate clients. **Facilities:** ⚹ 🏋 ⌷80 1 restaurant, 1 bar (w/entertainment), sauna. Pool area has Ping-Pong tables and a

cabana with lounge. **Rates (CP):** $119 S or D; $125 ste. Extra person $10. Children under age 16 stay free. Parking: Outdoor, free. AE, CB, DC, DISC, JCB, MC, V.

RESTAURANT 🍴

Lion & Compass

In the Fair Oaks Business Park, 1023 N Fair Oaks Ave; tel 408/745-1260. Fair Oaks exit off US 101. **New American.** Tropical main dining room has palms, wicker chairs, and street-lamp lighting and is light and spacious; three smaller rooms are available for private parties. An electronic ticker tape runs during lunch. Among several creative appetizers are grilled shrimp with risotto cakes and wild boar sausage. Entrees range from blackened ahi tuna to seared scallops in blue corn meal. **FYI:** Reservations recommended. **Open:** Lunch Mon–Fri 11:30am–2pm; dinner Mon–Fri 5:30–9:30pm, Sat 5:30–9pm. **Prices:** Main courses $11–$19. AE, CB, DC, MC, V. VP ⚹

Susanville

Susanville founder Isaac Roop named the town he founded in 1854 after his daughter. Historic Uptown Susanville hearkens to the town's mining and logging days. The natural attractions of Lassen National Forest and Honey Lake are nearby. **Information:** Lassen County Chamber of Commerce, 84 N Lassen St, PO Box 338, Susanville 96130 (tel 916/257-4323).

MOTEL 🏨

≡≡ Best Western Trailside Inn

2785 Main St, PO Box 759, 96130; tel 916/257-4123 or toll free 800/528-1234; fax 916/257-2665. A good rest stop before and after recreational activities in northern California's Sierra Nevada area. **Rooms:** 90 rms and stes. CI 2pm/CO 11am. Nonsmoking rms avail. Clean, functional, and well kept. **Amenities:** 🛏 🖵 A/C, cable TV, refrig, dataport. Some units w/whirlpools. **Services:** 🍽 🚗 ↩ ⟨ **Facilities:** ⚹ ⌷40 ⚹ 1 restaurant. Restaurant is open 24 hours. **Rates (CP):** Peak (Apr–Oct) $48–$54 S or D; $78–$88 ste. Extra person $5. Children under age 12 stay free. Lower rates off-season. Parking: Outdoor, free. A golf package includes golfing at Emerson Lake Golf Course, accommodations, breakfast, and dinner. AE, CB, DC, DISC, MC, V.

ATTRACTIONS 🏛

Bizz Johnson Trail

Tel 916/257-0456. Begins at Susanville Depot Trailhead, Richmond Rd. Following an old branch line of the Southern Pacific Railroad, this 25.4-mile trail winds from Susanville to Mason Station, traversing the rugged Susan River Canyon. Built in 1914 to service the newly founded logging community of **Westwood,** the rail line hauled logs, lumber, passengers, and supplies for over 40 years. Gradually, its use declined, and the last trains operated along the line in 1958. Legally abandoned in 1978, the line was converted into a scenic trail used by hikers, cyclists, equestrians, cross-country skiiers, as well as railroad history buffs. Surfaced with aggregate material, the trail has a maximum 3% grade.

At Mason Station, the trail follows existing roads an additional 4½ miles to Westwood, where a railroad station kiosk has interpretive displays on the history of this region's railroading and logging era. A 25-foot carved redwood statue of Paul Bunyan stands nearby. **Open:** Daily 8am–dusk. **Free**

Eagle Lake

Tel 916/257-2151. The remnant of a large prehistoric lake, Eagle Lake covers 26,000 acres, about 15 miles north of town via County Hwy A1, within Lassen National Forest. Gallatin Beach, at the south end of the lake, has a marina and facilities for swimming and water sports. There are five campgrounds, some available on a first-come, first-serve basis, and many can accommodate RVs. Campgrounds are generally open mid-May–mid-Sept, depending on weather conditions. For detailed information contact the Forest Supervisor, USDA-Lassen National Forest, 55 S Sacramento St, Susanville, CA 96130. **Open:** Daily sunrise–sunset. **Free**

Sutter Creek

Sutter Creek was one of the richest of the Gold Rush towns, and now it remains as one of the most authentically preserved. In May the town celebrates Poppy Days, and in June the Italian Benevolent Society holds its annual picnic.

HOTEL 🏨

≡≡ Aparicio's Hotel

271 Hanford St, PO Box 1839, 95685; tel 209/267-9177; fax 209/267-5303. On CA 49. New roadside hotel offering modern conveniences for Gold Country tourists. **Rooms:** 52 rms and stes. CI 3pm/CO 11am. Nonsmoking rms avail. A few nice touches, including mini-blinds and attractive light fixtures. **Amenities:** 🛁 A/C, cable TV. **Services:** 🚗 Coffee in lobby. **Facilities:** 🅿 & 1 bar. **Rates:** $66 D; $85 ste. Extra person $8. Min stay special events. Parking: Outdoor, free. AE, CB, DC, DISC, MC, V.

INN

≡≡≡ Sutter Creek Inn

75 Main St, PO Box 385, 95685; tel 209/267-5606. 1 acre. An intimate country inn. Owner/operator Jane Way provides the personable ambience that makes one feel at home. Wonderfully situated within a few minutes' walk of attractions and restaurants. **Rooms:** 18 rms; 4 cottages/villas. CI 2:30pm/CO 11am. No smoking. Spacious and quiet accommodations, some with canopied beds. **Amenities:** A/C. No phone or TV. Some units w/fireplaces. The lawn has lounge chairs. **Services:** Afternoon tea and wine/sherry served.

Facilities: 🅿 Washer/dryer, guest lounge w/TV. **Rates (BB):** $60–$97 S; $88–$97 D; $97–$160 cottage/villa. Extra person $25. Min stay wknds. Higher rates for special events/hols. Parking: Outdoor, free. AE, MC, V.

RESTAURANT 🍴

Ron & Nancy's Palace Restaurant & Saloon

76 Main St; tel 209/267-1355. **Continental.** An old-time saloon renovated in contemporary woods with 19th-century furnishings, lace tablecloths, and candlelight. Entrees include linguine with clam sauce, veal scaloppine, chicken marsala, and a choice of steaks and seafood. Large portions and fast, cheerful service. **FYI:** Reservations accepted. Children's menu. **Open:** Lunch daily 11:30am–3pm; dinner daily 5–9pm. **Prices:** Main courses $6–$16. AE, CB, DC, DISC, MC, V. 🌸 🍴

Tahoe City

Tahoe City is removed from the casino crowds that gather on the other side of Lake Tahoe and is much quieter and closer in spirit to the natural attractions of the high-altitude lake. Several ski areas are near the town. **Information:** North Lake Tahoe Chamber of Commerce, 245 N Lake Blvd, PO Box 884, Tahoe City 96145 (tel 916/581-6900).

HOTEL 🏨

≡≡≡ Sunnyside Lodge

1850 W Lake Blvd, PO Box 5969, 96145; tel 916/583-7200. 2 mi S of Tahoe City. Excellent lakeside location with a marina atmosphere. Log architecture. Always bustling. **Rooms:** 23 rms and stes. CI 2pm/CO 11am. Nonsmoking rms avail. All rooms have a view, or a partial view. Decor is very tasteful and airy in a country style. **Amenities:** 🛁 Cable TV. No A/C. All units w/terraces, some w/fireplaces. **Services:** ✕ 🚪 🛏 **Facilities:** △ 🅿 🛎 🖼 🛟 🅿 & 1 restaurant (see "Restaurants" below), 1 bar (w/entertainment), 1 beach (lake shore). **Rates (CP):** Peak (May–Oct) $145–$160 S or D; $170–$185 ste. Min stay peak. Lower rates off-season. Parking: Outdoor, free. AE, MC, V.

MOTEL

≡≡ Travelodge

455 N Lake Blvd, PO Box 84, 96145; tel 916/583-3766 or toll free 800/578-7878; fax 916/583-8045. Truckee/CA 89 exit off I-80. All the technical amenities of a good roadside motel, with lake and golf course views and a central location in the Tahoe area. Ample parking. **Rooms:** 47 rms. CI 3pm/CO 11am. Nonsmoking rms avail. Clean, simple. Bathrooms have been retiled. All beds are Beautyrest. Security system. **Amenities:** 🛁 🛎 Cable TV w/movies. No A/C. Ski racks inside rooms. Massage shower head. **Services:** 🛏 Guests receive a 10% discount at many restaurants around the lake.

Facilities: [icons] Sauna, whirlpool. **Rates:** Peak (Dec–Mar/July–Aug) $49–$115 S; $54–$119 D. Extra person $5–$15. Children under age 16 stay free. Min stay peak. Lower rates off-season. Parking: Outdoor, free. AE, CB, DC, DISC, ER, JCB, MC, V.

INN

Cottage Inn at Lake Tahoe

1690 W Lake Blvd, PO Box 66, 96145; tel 916/581-4073 or toll free 800/581-4073; fax 916/581-0226. Nestled in the trees on the shores of Lake Tahoe, this is a great Old Tahoe–style lodge with cozy knotty-pine cottages and lots of privacy. Unsuitable for children under 12. **Rooms:** 14 cottages/villas. CI 3pm/CO 11am. No smoking. Each cottage is individually decorated, with new furnishings throughout and top-quality accessories. Kitchen available. A cultivated "rustic" decor. **Amenities:** [icons] Cable TV w/movies, VCR, bathrobes. No A/C or phone. All units w/fireplaces, 1 w/whirlpool. **Services:** Twice-daily maid svce, afternoon tea and wine/sherry served. **Facilities:** [icons] 1 restaurant (dinner only), 1 beach (lake shore), lawn games, sauna, guest lounge w/TV. Dinner is a "crock pot" supper of all-you-can-eat soup or pasta and homebaked bread for $7.50. **Rates (BB):** $140–$210 cottage/villa. Extra person $15. Min stay wknds. Parking: Outdoor, free. MC, V.

LODGE

River Ranch

CA 89 at Alpine Meadows Rd, PO Box 197, 96145; tel 916/583-4264; fax 916/583-7237. 10 mi S of Truckee. Squaw Valley exit off I-80. Closest lodging to Alpine Meadows ski area. Needs renovation. Back of property has splendid outside seating overlooking Truckee River. Near bike path that runs from Tahoe City to Squaw Valley. **Rooms:** 19 rms. CI 3pm/CO 11am. No smoking. Antique furniture and good-size bathrooms. A little worn. **Amenities:** [icons] Cable TV, CD/tape player. No A/C. Some units w/terraces. **Facilities:** [icons] 1 restaurant (dinner only), 1 bar (w/entertainment). Frequent entertainment. Fine bar with friendly atmosphere. **Rates (CP):** Peak (July–Sept/Dec–Apr) $85–$115 S or D. Extra person $15. Children under age 6 stay free. Min stay peak. Lower rates off-season. Parking: Outdoor, free. AE, MC, V.

RESORT

Granlibakken Resort & Conference Center

Granlibakken Rd, PO Box 6329, 96145; tel 916/583-4242 or toll free 800/543-3221; fax 916/583-7641. 1 mi S of Tahoe City. 74 acres. A secluded, condominium-style resort with classic "Old Tahoe" ambience and a summer-camp atmosphere. The ski hill was the site of the Olympic trials for the 1952 Winter Games. Quiet and relaxing. **Rooms:** 76 rms, stes, and effic. CI 4pm/CO 11am. Nonsmoking rms avail. All are condo-style. **Amenities:** [icons] Cable TV, refrig, VCR. No A/C. Some units w/minibars, all w/terraces, some w/fireplaces. **Services:** [icons] Social director, babysitting. **Facilities:** [icons] Sauna, whirlpool, washer/dryer. Multiple trails for hiking, mountain biking, and cross-country skiing. **Rates (BB):** Peak (Dec 24–Jan 2) $85–$95 S or D; $182–$199 ste. Children under age 2 stay free. Min stay wknds and special events. Lower rates off-season. Parking: Outdoor, free. AE, MC, V.

RESTAURANTS

★ Izzy's Burger Spa

126 W Lake Blvd; tel 916/583-4111. Squaw Valley/Tahoe City exit off I-80. **Burgers.** A small establishment near the touristy Fanny Bridge, located in an A-frame building with limited seating. Burgers, chicken, and fries are good values. **FYI:** Reservations not accepted. Children's menu. Beer and wine only. **Open:** Daily 11am–8pm. **Prices:** Main courses $3–$6. No CC. [icons]

Sunnyside Restaurant

In Sunnyside Lodge, 1850 W Lake Blvd; tel 916/583-7200. Tahoe City/Squaw Valley exit off I-80. **Seafood/Steak.** The large dining room has high ceilings and hardwood floors; an outside patio faces Lake Tahoe. Specialties at breakfast, lunch, and dinner utilize fresh produce and lots of seafood. Prices are a bit high; you're paying for the views. **FYI:** Reservations accepted. Guitar/singer. Children's menu. **Open:** Peak (July–Aug) breakfast Mon–Sat 10am–2:30pm; lunch Mon–Sat 10am–2:30pm; dinner daily 5:30–10pm; brunch Sun 9:30am–2:30pm. **Prices:** Prix fixe $13–$19. AE, MC, V. [icons]

★ Tahoe House

625 W Lake Blvd; tel 916/583-1377. ½ mi South of Tahoe City on CA 89. **Californian/Swiss.** The spacious main dining room seems appealing for family dining; the wine room is ideal for private parties or larger groups. The menu is strong on "heart smart" options: lean meats, fat-free breads, and cholesterol-free oils. Herbs and much produce are grown on the site. The new bakery cooks up a variety of breads, muffins, and treats. **FYI:** Reservations recommended. Children's menu. **Open:** Daily 6am–10pm. **Prices:** Main courses $8–$18. AE, MC, V. [icons]

Wolfdale's

640 N Lake Blvd; tel 916/583-5700. Tahoe City or Squaw Valley exit off I-80. **Eclectic.** Tastefully decorated with a Thai theme and specially designed ceramic dinnerware. Long oak bar edged with tile. Eclectic cuisine, with unique entrees such as Thai seafood stew or crusted roast rack of lamb. A bit expensive—you're paying for ambience and unusual food. **FYI:** Reservations recommended. Dress code. **Open:** Peak (July–Aug) daily 5:30–10pm. **Prices:** Main courses $15–$20. MC, V. [icons]

ATTRACTIONS 🏛

Gatekeeper's Log Cabin Museum
130 W Lake Blvd; tel 916/583-1762. Now that the floodgates are operated from an office tower in Reno, the rustic old gatekeeper's house has been made into a museum operated by the North Lake Tahoe Historical Society. Restored to its original state, the log cabin contains artifacts from its past, as well as Native American baskets and clothing, and mementos from Lake Tahoe's history. **Open:** Peak (Jun 15–Labor Day) daily 11am–5pm. Reduced hours off-season. Closed Oct–May. **Free**

North Tahoe Cruises
850 North Lake Blvd; tel 916/583-0141. Two-hour cruises of Emerald Bay and the northwestern shore of Lake Tahoe. June–Sept, departures daily at 11am and 1:30pm; sunset cocktail cruises mid-June–mid-Sept, daily at 6pm. Schedule varies. **$$$$**

Tahoe State Recreation Area
Tel 916/583-3074. A 13-acre park is off CA 28, near the east end of Tahoe City. Offers direct access to the lake shoreline and a pier. Swimming, fishing. Campsite available; picnicking. **Open:** Peak (Mem Day–Labor Day) daily 8am–8pm. Reduced hours off-season. **$$**

D L Bliss State Park
CA 89; tel 916/525-7277. One of Lake Tahoe's finest and most popular beaches is found here. There are several trails, one along the lakeshore and another leading to Balancing Rock. **Open:** Mid-June–mid-Sept, daily 8am–7pm. **$$**

Emerald Bay State Park/Vikingsholm
CA 89; tel 916/541-3030 (summer only). Approximately 600 acres at the southern boundary of D L Bliss State Park (see above), this park was created around a nucleus of land donated to the state in 1953 by Placerville lumberman Harvey West. It includes facilities to accommodate campers, hikers, boaters, picnickers, and anglers. There are also fine panoramic views of Lake Tahoe and Eagle Falls.

Vikingsholm (1929) was built for Mrs Lora J Knight of Santa Barbara and Chicago, inspired by a Norse fortress from around 800 AD. Considered the finest example of Scandinavian architecture in the Western Hemisphere, the building employed many of the construction methods and materials of ancient Scandinavia. It features a sod roof with living grass like those sometimes used in Scandinavia to feed livestock during the winter. Many of the furnishings are exact duplicates of historic pieces found in Norway and Sweden. Mrs Knight also had guesthouses built and created a teahouse on Fannette Island. She spent her summers here until her death in 1945.

Guided tours can be taken for a nominal fee July–Labor Day. A steep 1-mile trail leads down from the parking lot at the Emerald Bay Overlook. **Open:** Mid-June–mid-Sept, daily 8am–11pm. **$**

Tahoe Vista

Located on the north shore of Lake Tahoe and just west of the border with Nevada, Tahoe Vista is adjacent to Kings Beach State Recreation Area.

MOTEL 🏨

📋 Tatami Cottage Resort
7449 N Lake Blvd, PO Box 18, 96148; tel 916/546-3523. 1 mi W of Kings Beach. Near all lake activities and points of interest. Very rustic, no frills. **Rooms:** 18 cottages/villas. CI 2pm/CO 11am. No smoking. Some units have kitchen facilities; three oriental-theme cottages have futon bedding. **Amenities:** 🔺 🛁 🖥 Cable TV w/movies, refrig. No A/C. Some units w/terraces, some w/fireplaces. **Services:** ✕ 🛎 🖐 Babysitting. Dogs welcome; beaver pond next door great for romps. **Facilities:** 🏊 🎿 Washer/dryer. **Rates:** Peak (Mem Day–Labor Day/Thanksgiving–Easter) $79–$179 cottage/villa. Children under age 18 stay free. Min stay wknds. Lower rates off-season. Parking: Outdoor, free. AE, DISC, MC, V.

LODGE

📋📋 Cedar Glen Lodge
6589 N Lake Blvd, PO Box 188, 96148; tel 916/546-4281 or toll free 800/341-8000, 800/500-8246 in CA; fax 916/546-2250. 1½ mi W of Kings Beach. 1½ acres. Clean, well-kept cottages form a horseshoe around the pool. Hotel/lodge in rear area. Across the street from the beach. **Rooms:** 14 rms and stes; 17 cottages/villas. CI 2pm/CO 11am. No smoking. Rustic appearance and furnishings. **Amenities:** 🔺 🛁 🖥 🎐 Cable TV, refrig. No A/C. All units w/terraces, 1 w/fireplace. **Services:** 🛎 Children's program, babysitting. **Facilities:** 🏊 🎿 🖼 Games rm, sauna, whirlpool, day-care ctr, playground, washer/dryer. **Rates (CP):** Peak (June–Sept) $39–$90 S or D; $39 ste; $46 cottage/villa. Extra person $5. Min stay peak. Lower rates off-season. Parking: Outdoor, free. AE, DISC, MC, V.

RESORT

📋📋📋 The Mourelato's Lakeshore Resort
6834 N Lake Blvd, PO Box 77, 96148; tel 916/546-9500 or toll free 800/2-RELAX-U; fax 916/546-2744. 1 mi W of Kings Beach. Two buildings on the shore of Lake Tahoe. New wing recommended exclusively. **Rooms:** 32 rms, stes, and effic. CI 2pm/CO 11am. No smoking. All accommodations have lake views. Rooms in new wing are tastefully decorated and spotless. **Amenities:** 🔺 🛁 🖥 Cable TV w/movies, refrig. No A/C. Some units w/minibars, all w/terraces. **Services:** ✕ 🛎 **Facilities:** 🏊 🖼 🗒 🖐 1 beach (lake shore), playground. **Rates:** Peak (Mem Day–Labor Day/Thanksgiving–Easter) $85–$145 S or D; $205 ste; $110–$205 effic. Extra person $10. Min stay special events. Lower rates off-season. Parking: Outdoor, free. AE, DISC, MC, V.

Tehachapi

The Tehachapi Mountains to the south and the Piute Mountains to the north frame the valley that surrounds the town of Tehachapi. The community is the gateway to the Central Valley to the west and the Mojave Desert to the east. **Information:** Greater Tehachapi Chamber of Commerce, 209 E Tehachapi Blvd, PO Box 401, Tehachapi 93561 (tel 805/822-4180).

HOTEL 🏨

≣≣ Tehachapi Summit Travelodge

500 Steuber Rd, PO Box 140, 93581; tel 805/823-8000 or toll free 800/578-7878; fax 805/823-8006. Monolith exit off CA 58 E; Tehachapi Blvd exit off CA 58 W. A bright, cheerful property right off the freeway, owned and operated by the person who built it. **Rooms:** 81 rms, stes, and effic. CI 3pm/CO 11am. Nonsmoking rms avail. Spacious and clean, with tile floors in bathrooms and natural wood on counters. **Amenities:** 🛁 📺 A/C, cable TV. Some units w/minibars, some w/terraces, 1 w/fireplace, 1 w/whirlpool. **Services:** ⟲ 🐾 **Facilities:** 🛠 🏊 ⅃ 1 restaurant (*see* "Restaurants" below), 1 bar, whirlpool. **Rates:** $49–$52 S; $56–$59 D; $61–$64 ste; $89–$99 effic. Extra person $7. Children under age 18 stay free. Parking: Outdoor, free. AE, DC, DISC, MC, V.

RESORT

≣≣≣ Sky Mountain Resort

18100 Lucaya Way, 93561; tel 805/822-5581; fax 805/822-4055. CA 202 exit off CA 58. 4,600 acres. Clean, peaceful spot with invigorating mountain air. About 15 miles to Tehachapi old town. **Rooms:** 63 rms and stes; 21 cottages/villas. CI 3pm/CO noon. Nonsmoking rms avail. Rooms are tastefully decorated. Some have large canopy bed and big seating area with sofa and view of canyon. **Amenities:** 🛁 🍴 📺 A/C, cable TV. Some units w/terraces, some w/fireplaces. **Services:** ⅃ Twice-daily maid svce, social director, masseur. **Facilities:** 🛠 🚴 ▶18 🎿2 🎱 🏊 👤 2 restaurants, 2 bars (1 w/entertainment), games rm, spa, sauna, steam rm, whirlpool, day-care ctr, playground, washer/dryer. Putting green. **Rates:** Peak (Apr–Nov) $79–$137 D; $137 ste; $163 cottage/villa. Children under age 18 stay free. Min stay wknds. Lower rates off-season. Parking: Outdoor, free. AE, DC, DISC, MC, V.

RESTAURANT 🍴

The Summit Dining Hall & Saloon

In the Tehachapi Summit Travelodge, 480 Steuber Rd; tel 805/823-1000. **Steak.** Western-style rustic, with natural woods and a large stone fireplace in the corner, stuffed animal heads, and cowboy mural. Steaks are hand-cut and aged on the premises and have a smoky oak flavor from the open-fire grill. Chicken tortilla soup is brought to each table. Weak wine list, but 53 beers from around the world are available. **FYI:** Reservations accepted. Children's menu. **Open:** Breakfast daily 5:30–11am; lunch Sun–Fri 11am–2pm, Sat 11am–5pm; dinner Sun–Fri 5–9pm, Sat 5–10pm. **Prices:** Main courses $10–$20. AE, DC, MC, V. 🎴 ♿

Temecula

Part of a blossoming wine region, Temecula is also a growing bedroom community for both Riverside and San Diego Counties. The Temecula Valley Balloon and Wine Festival is held each May. **Information:** Temecula Valley Chamber of Commerce, 27450 Ynez Rd #104, Temecula 92591 (tel 909/676-5090).

HOTEL 🏨

≣≣≣ Embassy Suites Temecula

29345 Rancho California Rd, 92591; tel 909/676-5656 or toll free 800/416-6116; fax 909/699-3928. Rancho California Rd exit off I-15. Conveniently located near I-15, hotel has contemporary styling and pleasant accommodations. **Rooms:** 136 stes. CI 3pm/CO noon. Nonsmoking rms avail. Extra-large rooms. **Amenities:** 🛁 🍴 📺 A/C, cable TV w/movies, refrig, dataport, VCR, voice mail. Some units w/terraces. Microwave, two TVs. **Services:** ✕ 🛄 ⅃ Complimentary evening beverages. **Facilities:** 🛠 🏋 🍳 🏊 👤 1 restaurant, 1 bar, whirlpool, washer/dryer. **Rates (CP):** $99–$119 ste. Extra person $10. Children under age 12 stay free. Parking: Outdoor, free. AE, DC, DISC, MC, V.

RESORT

≣≣ Temecula Creek Inn

44501 Rainbow Canyon Rd, PO Box 129, 92592; or toll free 800/962-7335; fax 909/676-3422. CA 79 exit off I-15. 3 acres. A paradise for golfers, and well located for those interested in nearby wineries. Very good value. **Rooms:** 80 rms. CI 4pm/CO noon. Nonsmoking rms avail. Spacious and comfortable rooms; some have golf-course views. **Amenities:** 🛁 📺 🍴 A/C, cable TV, dataport. All units w/minibars, all w/terraces. Each room has a coffee grinder and beans. Suites have bathrobes. **Services:** 🚐 🛄 ⅃ 🐾 Social director, masseur, children's program, babysitting. Free daily newspapers. Children's golf camp in August. **Facilities:** 🛠 🚴 ▶27 🏋 🎿2 🍳 🖥 👤 1 restaurant, 1 bar (w/entertainment), volleyball, lawn games, whirlpool. Top-rated golf course. **Rates:** Peak (Mar–May/Oct–Nov) $115–$170 S or D. Extra person $20. Children under age 5 stay free. Min stay wknds. Lower rates off-season. AP and MAP rates avail. Parking: Outdoor, free. Golf and wine-country packages avail. AE, CB, DC, DISC, MC, V.

RESTAURANTS

Baily Wine Country Cafe
In Town Center Shopping Center, 27644 Ynez Rd; tel 909/676-9567. Rancho California Rd exit off I-15. **Californian/Continental.** Contemporary decor. An outdoor seating area borders a shopping center parking lot. Lunch menu includes warm Thai beef salad, grilled chicken, and salads and pastas. At dinner, there are ravioli, scampi, New York pepper steak, and duck salad. Large selection of local wines. **FYI:** Reservations recommended. Beer and wine only. **Open:** Lunch Mon–Fri 11am–3pm, Sat–Sun 11:30am–5pm; dinner Sun–Thurs 5–9pm, Fri–Sat 5–9:30pm. **Prices:** Main courses $11–$20. AE, CB, DC, MC, V. &

Café Champagne
In Thornton Winery, 32575 Rancho California Rd; tel 909/699-0088. 53 mi N of San Diego Rancho California Rd exit off I-15; 3½ mi E. **Californian.** Patio dining beneath a pergola, and indoor dining in a bright airy space with floral fabrics and brass chandeliers. All desserts and breads are prepared daily on site. **FYI:** Reservations recommended. Beer and wine only. **Open:** Lunch Mon–Fri 11am–4:30pm; dinner Tues–Sun 4:30–9pm; brunch Sun 11am–4:30pm. **Prices:** Main courses $16–$25. AE, CB, DC, DISC, MC, V. &

Temet Grill
In the Temecula Creek Inn, Rainbow Canyon Rd; tel 909/694-1000. CA 79 S exit off I-15. **Eclectic.** Overlooking a golf course, with floor-to-ceiling windows, and southwestern Native American artifacts in glass cases hung on the walls. Menu focuses on southwestern preparations, such as lamb osso buco and veal chops with sun-dried tomato and chipotle demiglaze. **FYI:** Reservations recommended. Children's menu. **Open:** Daily 6:30am–10:30pm. **Prices:** Main courses $15. AE. &

ATTRACTION

Old Town Temecula Museum
41950 Main St; tel 909/676-0021. A chronicle of daily life in the early days of Temecula, this museum contains many artifacts, especially household items of the type used by early settlers; also exhibits about local Native Americans, dioramas, small gift shop. Walking tour maps of the town and wine country maps available. **Open:** Wed–Sun 11am–4pm. **Free**

Thousand Oaks

Thousand Oaks began in 1876 as a stagecoach stop for travelers making the long trip between Los Angeles and Santa Barbara. Today the drive takes less time, but the town is still a stopping-off point where travelers can see the historic displays at the Stagecoach Inn Museum. **Information:** Conejo Valley Chamber of Commerce, 625 W Hillcrest Dr, Thousand Oaks 91360 (tel 805/499-1993).

HOTELS

Holiday Inn Thousand Oaks
495 N Ventu Park Rd, 91320; tel 805/498-6733 or toll free 800/HOLIDAY; fax 805/498-9789. Ventu Park Rd exit off US 101. Traditional two-story 1970s-era Holiday Inn with easy freeway access. **Rooms:** 154 rms, stes, and effic. CI 2pm/CO noon. Nonsmoking rms avail. Scheduled for refurbishing. **Amenities:** A/C, cable TV. **Services:** Car-rental desk, babysitting. **Facilities:** 1 restaurant, 1 bar (w/entertainment), whirlpool, washer/dryer. **Rates:** Peak (Mem Day–Labor Day) $89 S or D; $125 ste; $125 effic. Extra person $10. Children under age 12 stay free. Lower rates off-season. Parking: Outdoor, free. AE, CB, DC, DISC, JCB, MC, V.

Thousand Oaks Inn
75 W Thousand Oaks Blvd, 91360; tel 805/497-3701; fax 805/497-1875. Moorpark Rd exit off US 101. Good location off US 101 with easy access to shopping. **Rooms:** 107 rms and stes. CI 3pm/CO noon. Nonsmoking rms avail. Rooms that are newly refurbished are acceptable. **Amenities:** A/C, cable TV w/movies. **Services:** Breakfast served poolside. **Facilities:** 1 restaurant, whirlpool, washer/dryer. **Rates (CP):** $62 S; $72 D; $132 ste. Children under age 12 stay free. Parking: Outdoor, free. AE, CB, DC, DISC, ER, JCB, MC, V.

RESTAURANT

★ Ritrovo
In Von's Pavillion–North Ranch, 1125 Lindero Canyon Rd, Westlake Village; tel 818/889-0191. Lindero exit off US 101. **Italian.** A trendy new restaurant in an upscale neighborhood, with a modern, open kitchen and an antipasto bar. Specialties are wood-fired pizza, and fish dishes in various preparations. Dessert features tiramisù. Service can be slow. **FYI:** Reservations accepted. Piano. **Open:** Lunch Mon–Fri 11:30am–2:30pm; dinner Mon–Thurs 5:30–10:30pm, Fri–Sat 5:30–11pm, Sun 5:30–10pm. **Prices:** Main courses $9–$22. AE, MC, V.

ATTRACTION

Stagecoach Inn Museum Complex
51 S Ventu Park Rd, Newbury Park; tel 805/498-9441. Housed in this replica of an 1876 hotel, the Stagecoach Inn Museum contains exhibits and artifacts concerning the human and natural history of the region. Surrounding the museum is the Tri-Village, made up of replicas of a pioneer home, a Spanish-Mexican adobe, and a Chumash hut, representing three historic eras of the Conejo Valley. **Open:** Wed–Sun 1–4pm. **$**

Three Rivers

See Sequoia and Kings Canyon National Parks

Tiburon

A onetime railroad town, Tiburon has become an affluent San Francisco Bay community. In addition to offering some of the best bay views in the area, this quiet town boasts natural attractions such as the Richardson Bay Audubon Center and Sanctuary and the Tiburon Uplands Nature Preserve. **Information:** Tiburon Peninsula Chamber of Commerce 96-B Main St, PO Box 563, Tiburon 94920 (tel 415/435-5633).

MOTEL 🏨

🏔🏔 Tiburon Lodge & Conference Center

1651 Tiburon Blvd, 94920; tel 415/435-3133 or toll free 800/762-7770, 800/TIBURON in CA; fax 415/435-2451. Tiburon Blvd exit off US 101; 4½ mi E. A cut above a standard motel, with a marble lobby and Jacuzzis in some rooms, though the overall ambience is a little offbeat. Near center of Tiburon as well as the ferry to San Francisco and Angel Island. **Rooms:** 102 rms and effic. CI 3pm/CO noon. Nonsmoking rms avail. Top-floor accommodations, dubbed "Winchester" rooms, all have cathedral ceilings. Top-of-the-line "Spa Supreme" rooms have motifs such as "Venetian Cave" or "Purple Harem." **Amenities:** 🕿 ⓪ A/C, satel TV, refrig. Some units w/terraces, some w/whirlpools. **Services:** 🚗 🕂 Car-rental desk. **Facilities:** 📶 📺 🖥 ⓺ 1 restaurant (bkfst only). **Rates:** Peak (May–Sept) $129–$149 S; $144–$164 D; $215 ste; $215 effic. Extra person $15. Children under age 12 stay free. Lower rates off-season. Parking: Outdoor, free. AE, CB, DC, DISC, MC, V.

RESTAURANTS 🍴

Guaymas Restaurante

5 Main St; tel 415/435-6300. **Mexican.** A winner for its creative Mexican cuisine and its views; sailing yachts are moored just a few feet away from tables on the outdoor decks. The fiesta-inspired decor includes paper flags, rough-hewn wooden chairs, and a big adobe hearth in the corner. On the menu, you'll find unusual Mexican regional dishes, such as shrimp sautéed with chipotle sauce or roasted duck in pumpkin seed sauce. Tortillas are made fresh on the premises. Very popular for happy hour. **FYI:** Reservations recommended. **Open:** Mon–Thurs 11:30am–10pm, Fri–Sat 11:30am–11pm, Sun 10:30am–10pm. **Prices:** Main courses $10–$17. AE, CB, DC, MC, V. 🍴 🏞 ⓺

Sam's Anchor Cafe

27 Main St; tel 415/435-4527. **Californian/American.** The best outdoor deck in Tiburon, offering a view of the San Francisco skyline behind masts of sailboats from the Corinthian Yacht Club. The menu features everything from burgers and sandwiches to fresh fish and steaks, with specials such as smoked chicken cappellini or broiled sturgeon. Good brunch too. **FYI:** Reservations recommended. Children's menu. **Open:** Mon–Thurs 11:30am–10pm, Fri 11am–11pm, Sat 9am–11pm, Sun 9am–10pm. **Prices:** Main courses $11–$17. AE, DC, DISC, MC, V. 🍴 🏞 ⓺

Torrance

RESTAURANT 🍴

★ Aioli Restaurant

1261 Cabrillo Ave; tel 310/320-9200. **Mediterranean.** The luxurious, brushed steel and slate dining rooms were lovingly designed by owner George Moussali, who personally welcomes all guests. The large restaurant features an outdoor patio plus an in-house bakery called Breadstix that also serves light lunch fare such as pizza and pasta. The well-planned Mediterranean menu ranges from tapas such as fried calamari with coriander aioli to a "caviar sampler" priced at $100. Entrees change frequently, with choices such as grilled lamb chops or a shellfish paella for two. **FYI:** Reservations recommended. Jazz. **Open:** Lunch Mon–Fri 11am–3pm; dinner Sun–Thurs 5–9pm, Fri–Sat 5–10pm. **Prices:** Main courses $9–$21. AE, DC, DISC, MC, V. ♥ 🍴 🏞 🚗 ⓺

Trinidad

Renowned for its tide pools and salmon fishing on a remote stretch of North Coast beach, Trinidad is perched on ruggedly scenic Trinidad Head overlooking a small bay. **Information:** Greater Trinidad Chamber of Commerce, PO Box 356, Trinidad 95570 (tel 707/677-0591).

MOTEL 🏨

🏔🏔 Bishop Pine Lodge

1481 Patricks Point Dr, 95570; tel 707/677-3314; fax 707/677-3444. Seawood exit off US 101 S; Trinidad exit off US 101 N. Like a funky Swiss alpine lodge near the sea. Hospitality is quiet and unobtrusive. **Rooms:** 12 cottages/villas. CI 2pm/CO 11am. Nonsmoking rms avail. Accommodations in cute, old-fashioned individual wooden cottages, some with kitchen. You can hear highway traffic noise from rooms. **Amenities:** 🕿 ⓪ 📺 🕂 Cable TV, refrig, in-rm safe. No A/C. All units w/terraces, 1 w/whirlpool. **Services:** 🕂 Pets must be kept on leashes. **Facilities:** 🛝 Playground. **Rates:** Peak (Apr–Oct) $60–$95 cottage/villa. Extra person $8. Min stay peak. Lower rates off-season. Parking: Outdoor, free. AE, DISC, MC, V.

INN

≣≣≣ The Lost Whale Inn B&B

3452 Patrick's Point Dr, 95570; tel 707/677-3425 or toll free 800/677-7859; fax 707/677-0284. 4 acres. Set on a cliff above a gorgeous private beach, this special place is popular with honeymooners. Enjoy stunning coastal views, plus the bark of seals playing in the crashing surf. **Rooms:** 8 rms. CI 3pm/CO 11am. No smoking. Spacious rooms offer sea views; several have sleeping lofts for kids. Even more private accommodations in a farmhouse are available for long-term guests. **Amenities:** 🛁 No A/C, phone, or TV. Some units w/terraces. **Services:** 🚐 🍷 Masseur, babysitting, afternoon tea and wine/sherry served. Cots and highchairs for kids available. Owners will arrange restaurant reservations. They also give tours of their nearby pygmy goat farm. **Facilities:** 🏖 1 beach (cove/inlet), lawn games, whirlpool, playground, guest lounge. Outdoor hot tub and deck overlook sweeping lawn and ocean. **Rates (BB):** Peak (May–Oct) $110–$140 S; $120–$150 D. Extra person $20. Children under age 3 stay free. Min stay peak. Lower rates off-season. Higher rates for special events/hols. Parking: Outdoor, free. Midweek winter discounts avail. AE, DISC, MC, V.

RESTAURANT 🍴

Seascape Restaurant

In Bob's Boat Basin Marina, Bay St (Trinidad Harbor); tel 707/677-3625. **Seafood.** Located in Trinidad Harbor since 1961, this is the real McCoy—an old-fashioned seafood eatery owned and operated by a fisherman. Fellow seafarers eat here after unloading their catch. The homey interior offers funky booths and a fireplace. Great views of the coastline, harbor, and piers with fishermen at work. Good starters are the oyster sandwiches, crab cocktail, or clam chowder. Wide range of fish offered, from halibut to salmon. Good wines and beers. **FYI:** Reservations not accepted. Beer and wine only. **Open:** Peak (June–Aug) daily 7am–10pm. **Prices:** Main courses $8–$20. MC, V. 🏔 ♿

ATTRACTION 🏛

Little River State Beach

Tel 707/677-3570 or 445-6547. Located 4 miles south of Trinidad off US 101. This park's 112 acres of undeveloped expanses of flat sand and low dunes are located on the south side of Little River. **Open:** Daily sunrise–sundown. **Free**

Truckee

Truckee's strategic location has made it a crossroads ever since it was founded last century as a lumber and railroad town. Infamous for the nearby site of the Donner Party calamity and later for its saloons and red-light district, the town's pioneer charm has been carefully preserved. Truckee is the gateway to one of California's major skiing and winter sports areas; many ski clubs make their headquarters here. **Information:** Truckee/Donner Chamber of Commerce, 12036 Donner Pass Rd, Truckee 96161 (tel 916/587-8808).

HOTEL 🏨

≣≣ Best Western Truckee Tahoe Inn

11331 CA 267, 96161; tel 916/587-4525 or toll free 800/528-1234, 800/824-6385 in CA; fax 916/587-8173. Downtown Truckee exit off I-80, take CA 267 over railroad tracks. Clean and well kept. Good security. **Rooms:** 100 rms and stes. CI 2pm/CO 11am. Nonsmoking rms avail. **Amenities:** 🛁 🔥 A/C, satel TV w/movies. 1 unit w/minibar. **Services:** 🛎 🍷 Babysitting. Fishing poles and other sporting equipment may be borrowed from front desk. **Facilities:** 🏊 🚴 🎿 ⛳ 💯 🖥 ♿ Sauna, whirlpool, washer/dryer. **Rates (CP):** Peak (June 15–Aug/Jan–Apr) $70–$109 S; $80–$109 D; $91–$198 ste. Extra person $7. Children under age 13 stay free. Lower rates off-season. Parking: Outdoor, free. AE, CB.

INN

≣≣≣ The Truckee Hotel

10007 Bridge St, PO Box 884, 96160; tel 916/587-4444 or toll free 800/659-6921; fax 916/587-1599. Victorian hotel, built in 1873, has the feel of a bed-and-breakfast. Much charm and historical elegance. Parlor has high-backed, cushioned chairs. **Rooms:** 36 rms and stes (28 w/shared bath). CI 4pm/CO 11am. No smoking. European rooms share bath; American rooms have original clawfoot tubs. All have antique decor, comforters, radiators; some beds have canopies or night curtains. Plenty of light. **Amenities:** 🔥 📺 Cable TV. No A/C or phone. **Services:** 🍷 **Facilities:** 🍴 🎿 💯 1 restaurant, 1 bar (w/entertainment), guest lounge. Retail gift shop with fine gifts and unique collectibles. Excellent bar and restaurant. **Rates (CP):** Peak (July–Sept) $80–$85 S or D w/shared bath, $90–$115 S or D w/private bath; $75–$115 ste. Extra person $10. Children under age 4 stay free. Lower rates off-season. Parking: Outdoor, free. AE, MC, V.

RESORT

≣≣≣ Northstar-at-Tahoe-Resort

PO Box 129, 96160; tel 916/562-1010 or toll free 800/466-6784; fax 916/562-2215. S of CA 267 exit off I-80. 600 acres. A self-contained resort community. All facilities in excellent condition. Great resort for families. **Rooms:** 250 rms, stes, and effic. CI 5pm/CO 11am. Nonsmoking rms avail. Condos and homes are located 1 mile from the main area and facilities. All condos are clean and well furnished. **Amenities:** 🔥 🛁 📺 Cable TV w/movies, VCR. No A/C. Some units w/terraces, some w/fireplaces, some w/whirlpools. **Services:** 🛎 🍷 Children's program. Superb management. **Facilities:** 🍴 🚴 ⛳18 🎿 🏊10 💯200 🖥 5 restaurants, 5 bars (1 w/entertainment), basketball, volleyball, games rm, spa, sauna, whirlpool, day-care ctr, playground, washer/dryer. Northstar Swim and Racquet Club offers three spas, two saunas, exercise room, year-round heated lap pool, and, in summer, junior Olympic–size pool. **Rates:** $149–$189 S or D; $215–$233 ste; $139–$585 effic. Min stay. Parking: Indoor/outdoor, free. Closed May. AE, DISC, MC, V.

RESTAURANTS

♥ The Left Bank
10098 Commercial Row; tel 916/587-4694. Downtown Truckee exit off I-80. **French/Seafood.** Once an elegant setting, it's now a little worn around the edges, but the food is still very good. Nightly specials of fresh fish, pasta, and some game dishes. Owner sometimes closes on a whim, so call ahead. **FYI:** Reservations recommended. Dress code. **Open:** Lunch Wed–Mon 11:30am–3pm; dinner Wed–Mon 5–9:30pm. **Prices:** Main courses $14–$18. AE, DC, DISC, MC, V. ♥ ◻

★ Squeeze In
10060 Commercial Row; tel 916/587-9814. Downtown Truckee exit off I-80. **American.** A Truckee tradition for breakfast. Historic Truckee memorabilia hangs from the rafters and clutters the shelves; decor also includes lots of stained glass. Its omelettes—57 outrageous combinations—are all named after local characters. Also offers a variety of creative sandwiches. Great service. **FYI:** Reservations not accepted. Beer and wine only. **Open:** Daily 7am–2pm. **Prices:** Lunch main courses $5–$7. No CC. ◼

★ Truckee Trattoria
In Safeway shopping center, 11310-1 Donner Pass Rd (Gateway); tel 916/582-1266. 2 blocks N of Squaw Valley exit off I-80. **Californian/Italian.** Only true attempt at Italian cuisine in Truckee. Small and intimate; tasteful decor with black-and-white tile, track lighting, sculpture. The light fare includes pastas and seafood. Menu changes monthly. **FYI:** Reservations recommended. Beer and wine only. **Open:** Wed–Mon 4:30–9pm. Closed May 1–20/Nov 1–15. **Prices:** Main courses $7–$13. DISC, MC, V. ♿

ATTRACTION

Donner Memorial State Park
12593 Donner Pass Rd; tel 916/582-7892. Located just west of town off I-80. The winter of 1846–47 proved to be one of the most severe ever to hit the Sierrra, a disaster for the 91 members of the Donner Party, who became trapped in this mountain pass by early blizzards. Many members froze or starved to death; only 48 people survived, most of them by eating the remains of their deceased companions.

The park's 350 acres offer swimming, camping, picnicking, and cross-country skiing and snowshoeing in winter; naturalist programs in summer. The Emigrant Trail Museum has exhibits on the Donner Party, local wildlife, and Native American history and culture. **Open:** Daily sunrise–sunset; museum, daily 10am–4pm. $

Twentynine Palms

See also Joshua Tree National Park

The high desert town of Twentynine Palms surrounds the main entrance to Joshua Tree National Park, an arid wonderland of desert geology and diverse plant life, as well as an international draw for rock climbers. **Information:** Twentynine Palms Chamber of Commerce, 6136 Adobe Rd, Twentynine Palms 92277 (tel 619/367-3445).

MOTEL

≣≣ Best Western Gardens Motel
71-487 Twentynine Palms Hwy, 92277; tel 619/367-9141 or toll free 800/528-1234; fax 619/367-2584. CA 62 exit off I-10. Located minutes from Joshua Tree National Monument. This motel is distinguished by its white-roofed modified Spanish architecture. Trees, gardens, and patches of lawn give it the atmosphere of an oasis. Needs better maintenance. **Rooms:** 84 rms, stes, and effic. CI 2pm/CO noon. Nonsmoking rms avail. **Amenities:** 🛏 A/C, cable TV. Some units w/whirlpools. **Services:** ⏚ **Facilities:** 🦽 ♿ Whirlpool. **Rates (CP):** $56–$64 S; $58–$68 D; $77–$89 ste; $99–$114 effic. Extra person $8. Children under age 12 stay free. Parking: Outdoor, free. AE, CB, DC, DISC, MC, V.

INN

≣ Circle C Lodge
6340 El Rey Ave, 92277; tel 619/367-7615 or toll free 800/545-9696; fax 619/361-0247. Situated within sight of Joshua Tree National Park. **Rooms:** 11 rms. CI 3pm/CO 11am. Nonsmoking rms avail. Rooms are large, but somewhat dark. **Amenities:** 🛏 📺 A/C, cable TV w/movies, refrig, VCR. **Facilities:** 🦽 Whirlpool, guest lounge. **Rates (CP):** $85–$100 S or D. Extra person $35. Min stay wknds. Parking: Outdoor, free. AE, CB, DC, DISC, JCB, MC, V.

Ukiah

Formerly a lumber town in the center of the Yokayo Valley, Ukiah has made the transition to specialty crops such as prunes, apples, and grapes. The Ukiah area is also home to several well-respected wineries. **Information:** Greater Ukiah Chamber of Commerce, 200 S School St, Ukiah 95482 (tel 707/462-4705).

MOTELS

≣≣≣ Discovery Inn
1340 N State St, 95482; tel 707/462-8873; fax 707/462-1249. N State St exit off US 101; turn S at State St. The best of the motel offerings in this area. Bowling alley across the street. **Rooms:** 154 rms and stes. CI 2pm/CO noon. Nonsmoking rms avail. Pleasant, nice decor, clean. All furnishings are new. Rooms at the back of the complex are

quieter. **Amenities:** ▤ ⌂ ⏚ A/C, cable TV w/movies, refrig. Some units w/terraces, 1 w/whirlpool. **Services:** ⌗ Coffee available in lobby. **Facilities:** ⬚ ◨ ⟦130⟧ ⅊ Spa, washer/dryer. **Rates:** Peak (May–Sept) $56–$66 S; $60–$72 D; $150–$200 ste; $100–$150 effic. Extra person $5. Children under age 12 stay free. Lower rates off-season. Parking: Outdoor, free. AE, CB, DC, DISC, JCB, MC, V.

⬅⬅ Western Travelers Motel
693 S Orchard Ave, 95482; tel 707/468-9167 or toll free 800/794-3551; fax 707/468-8268. Perkins exit off US 101; E on Perkins; left on Orchard. Adequate motel. Located right off the freeway, so it can be somewhat noisy. **Rooms:** 55 rms. CI 2pm/CO 11am. Nonsmoking rms avail. **Amenities:** ▤ A/C, cable TV. **Services:** ⌗ **Facilities:** ⬚ ⅊ **Rates:** $39 S; $49 D. Extra person $5. Children under age 12 stay free. Parking: Outdoor, free. AE, CB, DC, DISC, MC, V.

RESORT
⬅⬅⬅ Vichy Springs Resort
2605 Vichy Springs Rd, 95482 (Vichy Springs); tel 707/462-9515; fax 707/462-9516. 4 mi E of Ukiah. Vichy Springs Rd exit off US 101; follow state historic landmark signs. 700 acres. A hot-springs bed-and-breakfast resort in the countryside. Resort has the only warm, naturally carbonated mineral baths in North America, called the "Champagne Baths." The redwood hotel was built in the 1860s. **Rooms:** 12 rms; 5 cottages/villas. CI 3pm/CO noon. No smoking. Most of the cabins and rooms are cozy and sweet. **Amenities:** ▤ ⌂ A/C. No TV. All units w/terraces, all w/fireplaces. Some rooms have refrigerators. **Services:** ✕ ▦ ⊠ Masseur, babysitting. Massage, facials, and reflexology can be arranged. **Facilities:** ⬚ ⧉ ⟦35⟧ Lawn games, whirlpool, washer/dryer. Olympic-size pool, mineral baths, and hot tub, plus 4,000 acres for hiking, mountain biking, and bird watching. **Rates (BB):** Peak (May–Oct) $95 S; $135 D; $175 cottage/villa. Extra person $25. Children under age 1 stay free. Lower rates off-season. Parking: Outdoor, free. AE, CB, DC, DISC, JCB, MC, V.

RESTAURANT ▥
Thai Cafe
801 N State St; tel 707/462-0238. Perkin St exit off US 101. **Thai.** Believe it or not, there's a fine Thai restaurant in Ukiah—in a former brothel, no less—and it's one of the best places to eat in town. The room is attractive, with golden-hued walls, high ceilings, white-oak chairs, and crisp white linens. On the menu you'll find choices like Thai barbecue chicken, garlic-pepper pork, green-curry prawns, and a whole page of vegetarian selections. **FYI:** Reservations accepted. Beer and wine only. **Open:** Mon–Thurs 11am–9:30pm, Fri 11am–10pm, Sat–Sun noon–10pm. **Prices:** Main courses $7–$11. MC, V. ⏚ ⅊

ATTRACTIONS ▥
Grace Hudson Museum and Sun House
431 S Main St; tel 707/462-3370. This art, history, and anthropology museum focuses on the works of painter Grace Hudson and her ethnologist husband, Dr John W Hudson, as well as other regional artists. Permanent and changing exhibits study the native Pomoan-speaking people, the white settlement of Mendocino County, and numerous examples of the works of both Hudsons.

The Hudsons built their Craftsman home, the **Sun House,** in 1911. Most of the property is preserved today, and the six-room house is decorated with items from their eclectic collection. **Open:** Museum: Wed–Sat 10am–4:30pm, Sun noon–4:30pm. Sun House: Wed–Sun noon–3pm. **$**

Parducci Wine Cellars
501 Parducci Rd; tel 707/462-WINE. Adolph Parducci founded this winemaking operation in 1931, and produced one of the first varietal bottlings of a California Zinfandel in 1944. The winery offers tours daily, on the hour 10am–3pm, weather permitting. **Open:** Daily 9am–5pm. Closed some hols. **Free**

Union City

HOTEL ▥
⬅⬅ Holiday Inn Union City
32083 Alvarado-Niles Rd, 94587; tel 510/489-2200 or toll free 800/HOLIDAY; fax 510/489-7642. Alvarado-Niles Rd exit off I-880. A finer Holiday Inn than most, in spite of the fact that hallways are dreary and could use some attention. Well located. **Rooms:** 262 rms and stes. Executive level. CI 3pm/CO noon. Rooms are clean. **Amenities:** ▤ ⏚ A/C, cable TV w/movies, bathrobes. **Services:** ✕ ▦ ⊠ ⌗ Children's program. **Facilities:** ⬚ ⧉ ▧ ◗1 ⟦⟧ ⟦500⟧ ▭ ⅊ 2 restaurants, 1 bar (w/entertainment), games rm, racquetball, sauna, whirlpool, washer/dryer. Exceptionally large pool. **Rates:** $90–$100 S or D; $135 ste. Extra person $10. Children under age 18 stay free. Parking: Indoor/outdoor, free. Children accompanied by parents stay and eat free. AE, DC, DISC, MC, V.

Universal City

The city is named after the film studio, sections of which have been converted into the theme park Universal Studios Hollywood and the recently created retail, dining, and entertainment center, Universal CityWalk. **Information:** San Fernando Valley Convention & Visitors Bureau, PO Box 8549, Universal City 91608 (tel 818/766-7572).

HOTELS

≡≡≡≡ Sheraton Universal
333 Universal Terrace Pkwy, 91608; tel 818/980-1212 or toll free 800/325-3535; fax 818/985-4980. Located next door to the Universal Studios lot. This hotel just underwent a major renovation and emerged a truly lovely property. Not far from Hollywood, but totally peaceful and quiet. **Rooms:** 441 rms and stes. Executive level. CI 3pm/CO noon. Nonsmoking rms avail. Fabulous views from rooms on the upper floors. **Amenities:** A/C, satel TV w/movies, dataport, voice mail, in-rm safe. All units w/minibars, some w/terraces. **Services:** Twice-daily maid svce, car-rental desk, babysitting. Pleasant, accommodating staff that deals equally well with children and celebrities. **Facilities:** 1 restaurant, 1 bar (w/entertainment), games rm, whirlpool. Fabulous pool. **Rates:** Peak (July–Dec) $205 S; $225 D; $250–$2200 ste. Extra person $20. Children under age 18 stay free. Lower rates off-season. Parking: Indoor/outdoor, $10/day. AE, CB, DC, DISC, EC, ER, JCB, MC, V.

≡≡≡≡ Universal City Hilton
555 Universal Terrace Pkwy, 91608; tel 818/506-2500 or toll free 800/727-7110; fax 818/509-2058. Lankershim Blvd exit off US 101. One of the most upscale properties in the San Fernando Valley, with spectacular views of CityWalk and the Universal and Burbank Studios. **Rooms:** 446 rms and stes. Executive level. CI 3pm/CO noon. Nonsmoking rms avail. The rooms are thoughtfully planned with unusual angles. Beds are triple-sheeted. **Amenities:** A/C, voice mail, in-rm safe, bathrobes. All units w/minibars, some w/whirlpools. Most accommodations have fax machines. Lots of special toiletries. **Services:** Twice-daily maid svce, car-rental desk, babysitting. Complimentary tram to Universal Studios, CityWalk, Hollywood, Universal Amphitheatre, and cinemas. **Facilities:** 1 restaurant, 1 bar (w/entertainment), whirlpool, beauty salon. Lovely outdoor heated pool with large landscaped sun deck. Extensive meeting and convention facilities in separate wing. **Rates:** $165–$200 S or D; $250–$1200 ste. Children under age 18 stay free. Lower rates off-season. Parking: Indoor/outdoor, $10–$13/day. AE, CB, DC, DISC, EC, ER, JCB, MC, V.

ATTRACTION

Universal Studios Hollywood
100 Universal City Plaza; tel 818/777-3750. Accessible via Hollywood Fwy (US 101), Lankersham Blvd exit. Universal began offering behind-the-scenes tours to the public in 1964. These days the tour has taken on an amusement park–like character, and attracts more than five million tourists a year. Visitors board a tram for a one-hour guided tour of the studio's 420 acres, passing stars' dressing rooms, back-lot sets, and numerous departments involved in film and TV production. The tour encounters several staged "disasters" along the way, from an earthquake and flash flood to a shark attack and a laser battle with deadly robots.

After the ride, visitors can seek out the numerous rides, shows, and other attractions at the **Studio Center** and the **Entertainment Center,** including the popular *ET,* Adventure ride, *Back to the Future*—The Ride, *Backdraft* Live and the new *Jurassic Park* ride. **Open:** Daily 9am–7pm (hours may vary); extended hours summer and hol periods. **$$$$**

Vallejo
Located at the junction of the Napa River and the Carquinez Strait, Vallejo has always been an important San Francisco Bay area shipping town. Vallejo briefly served as the nominal state capital in the 1850s. **Information:** Vallejo Convention & Visitors Bureau, 301 Georgia St #270, Vallejo 94590 (tel 707/642-3653).

MOTEL

≡≡ Holiday Inn Marine World Africa USA
1000 Fairgrounds Dr, 94589; tel 707/644-1200 or toll free 800/465-4329; fax 707/643-7011. Fairgrounds Dr exit off I-80. Good location near Marine World Africa USA. Excellent facility for families. Good value. **Rooms:** 167 rms and stes. Executive level. CI 3pm/CO noon. Nonsmoking rms avail. No frills; in fact, somewhat drab. **Amenities:** A/C, cable TV w/movies. **Services:** Car-rental desk. **Facilities:** 1 restaurant (bkfst and dinner only), 1 bar (w/entertainment), steam rm, whirlpool, washer/dryer. Fun sports bar. Guests have use of a Nautilus fitness center 1 mile away. **Rates:** Peak (Mem Day–Labor Day) $68–$110 S or D; $150 ste. Extra person $5. Children under age 19 stay free. Lower rates off-season. Parking: Outdoor, free. Marine World packages and Wine Country packages avail. AE, CB, DC, DISC, JCB, MC, V.

ATTRACTIONS

Marine World Africa USA
Marine World Pkwy; tel 707/643-6722 (recorded info) or 644-4000. Located at the intersection of I-80 and CA 37. This wildlife park is devoted to educating the public about humankind's relationship with animals of the sea, land, and air. Eight shows feature performing seals, killer whales, chimps, lions, exotic birds, and others. Still more animals are featured in their own innovative habitats.

More than 15 participatory exhibits include **Shark Experience,** a 300,000-gallon habitat for tropical sharks and fish where visitors ride a moving walkway through a clear acrylic tunnel, completely surrounded by waters filled with 15 species of sharks and 100 species of tropical fish. **Dinosaurs! A Prehistoric Adventure** features 22 robotic dinosaurs in a Jurassic-period forest, numerous interactive exhibits, and a re-created archeological dig site where kids work together to uncover a 40-foot-long Apatosaurus skeleton. **Walkabout! An Australian Adventure** offers a unique, interactive outdoor experience which brings visitors up close to kangaroos, wallaroos, wallabies, koalas, and lorikeets. Also **Butterfly World, Seal Cove, Giraffe Feeding Dock, Reptile Discovery, Animal Nursery,** and **Gentle Jungle.**

Animals are sometimes brought out to stroll through the park with their trainer and interact with visitors. There are a few public picnic sites with grills; several restaurants and gift shops. Overnight RV accommodations available. **Open:** Peak (Mem Day–Labor Day) daily 9:30am–6pm. Reduced hours off-season. **$$$$**

Vallejo Naval and Historical Museum

734 Marin St; tel 707/643-0077. Located in the old City Hall building, this museum contains five galleries dealing with the history of the region and of the Navy Yard at Mare Island. Purchased in 1853, Mare Island became the site of the first navy yard on the West Coast. From 1859 to 1970, Mare Island built more than 500 ships for the US Navy. Retired Navy and US Marine personnel make up a significant portion of Vallejo's present population.

Exhibits include selections from the museum's permanent collection, local private collections, traveling exhibitions, and borrowed artifacts from the extensive collection at Mare Island. Library, bookstore, and gift shop. **Open:** Tues–Sat 10am–4:30pm. **$**

Van Nuys

See also Sherman Oaks

Situated at the center of the San Fernando Valley and adjacent to I-405, Van Nuys is primarily a bedroom community for Los Angeles and the Valley. **Information:** Mid-Valley Chamber of Commerce, 14540 Victory Blvd #100, Van Nuys 91411-1618 (tel 818/989-0300).

HOTEL 🏨

≡≡≡ Airtel Plaza Hotel

7277 Valjean Ave, 91406; tel 818/997-7676 or toll free 800/2AIRTEL; fax 818/785-8864. A business hotel with attractive grounds and fountains. Fly your private plane to one of the hotel's tie-downs and walk right into the lobby. Although this hotel is adjacent to Van Nuys Airport, the busiest private airport in the world, there's no noise inside. **Rooms:** 268 rms and stes. CI 3pm/CO noon. Nonsmoking rms avail. **Amenities:** 🛁 🅿 📺 🍷 A/C, cable TV w/movies, dataport, voice mail. Some units w/terraces, some w/whirlpools. **Services:** ✕ 💱 🚗 🖎 ⌂ Car-rental desk, babysitting. No van service to LAX, but hotel will pick up incoming guests for free at the bus terminal in Van Nuys. **Facilities:** 🏊 🎾 [500] 2 restaurants, 1 bar (w/entertainment), whirlpool. **Rates:**

$109–$129 S; $119–$139 D; $125–$175 ste. Extra person $10. Children under age 18 stay free. Parking: Outdoor, free. AE, CB, DC, DISC, EC, ER, JCB, MC, V.

ATTRACTION 🏛

Japanese Garden

6100 Woodley Ave; tel 818/756-8166. Located at LA's Donald C Tillman Water Reclamation Plant, this is an authentic, 6½-acre Japanese garden displayed in three distinct styles: a Zen Garden of symbolic stone arrangements and gravel; a wet strolling garden; and a tea garden. **Open:** Tours Mon–Thurs, and Sat by appointment. Open for strolling Mon–Thurs noon–4pm. **Free**

Venice

See also Marina del Rey

Venice has undergone gentrification in recent years, but the famed Venice boardwalk remains the best place to witness the fringe society of Los Angeles. Originally developed in 1905 as a resort in the style of the northern Italian city, Venice still has a few canals running through town. **Information:** Venice Area Chamber of Commerce & Visitors Bureau, 2904 Washington Blvd #100, PO Box 202, Venice 90291 (tel 310/827-2366).

HOTEL 🏨

≡≡ Marina Pacific Hotel & Suites

1697 Pacific Ave, 90291; tel 310/452-1111 or toll free 800/421-8151; fax 310/452-5479. Lincoln Ave exit off Santa Monica Fwy. A small, modest hotel with bare-bones lobby; surprisingly well cared for. Overlooks the famous Venice Beach boardwalk. **Rooms:** 90 rms, stes, and effic. CI noon/CO noon. Nonsmoking rms avail. Rooms are simple, and many have an ocean view. One- and two-bedroom suites with kitchens available. **Amenities:** 🛁 🅿 A/C, cable TV w/movies, refrig. **Services:** ✕ 🖎 ⌂ Car-rental desk. **Facilities:** [75] 1 restaurant (bkfst and lunch only), washer/dryer. **Rates:** Peak (June–Sept) $80 S; $95 D; $145–$175 ste; $135–$275 effic. Extra person $10. Children under age 12 stay free. Lower rates off-season. Parking: Indoor, free. AE, CB, DC, DISC, EC, ER, JCB, MC, V.

RESTAURANT 🍴

Sidewalk Café

140 Ocean Front Walk; tel 310/399-5547. **American.** A front-row seat for the action on the Venice boardwalk. A local favorite for breakfast and lunch, offering omelettes, pizza, pasta, burgers, and salads. Very casual attire. **FYI:** Reservations not accepted. Big band/singer. **Open:** Daily 8am–midnight. **Prices:** Main courses $6–$10. AE, MC, V. 🍽 🏞 ♿

REFRESHMENT STOP

$ ★ Jody Maroni's
2011 Ocean Front Walk; tel 310/306/1995. **Sausage.** Jody Maroni (Jordan Monkarsh) and his staff loudly hawk his "haute cuisine–haut dogs" with infectious good spirit on the Venice boardwalk, where they are a decade-old fixture. The passerby is offered free samples of a dozen varieties of very upscale, gourmet sausages. The Yucatán chicken and duck, cajun, specialty pork (with figs, marsala wine, and pine nuts), and boudin blanc are such great sellers that they are now marketed retail. This place outsells all other boardwalk restaurants combined. Additional locations: 1000 Universal Ctr Dr, Universal City (tel 818/622-5639); 1315 3rd St Promenade, Santa Monica (tel 393-9063). **Open:** Peak (Apr–Sept) Mon–Fri 9am–5pm, Sat–Sun 9am–6pm. No CC.

ATTRACTION

Venice Beach
One of the LA area's greatest cultural treasures, Venice Beach today is a sort of "Coney Island West," a carnival of humanity populated by skaters, hipsters, and posers of every age and shape. People-watching is the major pastime here.

Ventura

See also Oxnard

The last mission established by Father Junípero Serra, Mission San Buenaventura grew into the town with the shortened name of Ventura. The beachside community is home to the Ventura marina and harbor, the gateway to the offshore Channel Islands National Park (see separate heading) and home to the park's visitors center. **Information:** Ventura Visitors & Convention Bureau, 89-C S California St, Ventura 93001 (tel 805/648-2075).

HOTELS

The Country Inn of Ventura
298 Chestnut St, 93001; tel 805/653-1434 or toll free 800/44-RELAX; fax 805/648-7126. CA St exit off US 101 N; Main St exit off US 101 S. Country-style bed-and-breakfast hotel furnished in nautical decor, including a ship's figurehead chandelier and a huge, stuffed swordfish in the lobby. Although near the freeway, it is relatively quiet. Super-friendly staff. **Rooms:** 120 rms, stes, and effic. CI 3pm/CO noon. Nonsmoking rms avail. Some rooms have canopied beds; all are tastefully decorated with country prints, dried flowers, and wingback chairs. Many accommodations are being renovated. **Amenities:** A/C, cable TV, refrig, VCR. Some units w/terraces, some w/fireplaces, some w/whirlpools. Microwaves, wet bars, books. Baths have vanity areas with Hollywood-style lighting. Dataports in some rooms. **Services:** Twice-daily maid svce, masseur. Afternoon cocktail reception in lounge. Extensive video library. Turndown service available. Fax service available. **Facilities:** 1 bar, whirlpool, washer/dryer. Footbridge to beach. **Rates (BB):** Peak (Mem Day–Labor Day) $99–$110 S or D; $110–$179 ste; $110–$179 effic. Extra person $5–$10. Children under age 11 stay free. Lower rates off-season. Parking: Indoor/outdoor, free. AE, DC, DISC, MC, V.

DoubleTree Hotel at Ventura
2055 Harbor Blvd, 93001; tel 805/643-6000 or toll free 800/222-TREE; fax 805/643-7137. 1 mi W of downtown. Seaward Ave exit off US 101. A convention-oriented hotel, one block from the ocean, also suitable for families and vacationers. Atrium lobby with fountains, wicker, and flora. **Rooms:** 285 rms and stes. CI 3pm/CO noon. Nonsmoking rms avail. Spacious, clean rooms have oak furnishing and signed original prints. **Amenities:** A/C, satel TV. 1 unit w/whirlpool. **Services:** X **Facilities:** 1 restaurant, 2 bars (1 w/entertainment), lifeguard, sauna, whirlpool. Work of local artists is on sale in the Gallery restaurant. **Rates:** Peak (Mem Day–Labor Day) $89–$109 S or D; $139 ste. Extra person $10. Lower rates off-season. Parking: Outdoor, free. AE, CB, DC, DISC, EC, ER, JCB, MC, V.

Holiday Inn Ventura Beach Resort
450 E Harbor Blvd, 93001; tel 805/648-7731 or toll free 800/842-0800; fax 805/653-6202. California St exit off US 101 N; Seaward exit off US 101 S. A beachfront high-rise that caters to groups but is also good for families and leisure travelers. **Rooms:** 260 rms and stes. Executive level. CI 4pm/CO noon. Nonsmoking rms avail. Attractive rooms with country-style decor. **Amenities:** A/C, cable TV w/movies, voice mail. All units w/terraces. **Services:** X Babysitting. **Facilities:** 2 restaurants, 2 bars (1 w/entertainment), washer/dryer. Attractively landscaped pool overlooks the pier and the Pacific. Rooftop restaurant serves Sunday brunch. **Rates:** Peak (June–Sept) $79–$99 S or D; $120 ste. Extra person $10. Children under age 18 stay free. Lower rates off-season. Parking: Outdoor, free. AE, DC, DISC, MC, V.

Pierpont Inn
550 Sanjon Rd, 93001; tel 805/653-6144 or toll free 800/285-INNS; fax 805/641-1501. 1 mi N of downtown Ventura. Sanjon exit off US 101 N; Seaward Ave exit off US 101 S. Landmark 1908 inn, owned by the same family for more than 65 years. Lobby features California craftsman–style entrance and two-sided fireplace. Great ocean views marred by freeway, which is also noisy. **Rooms:** 69 rms and stes; 2 cottages/villas. CI 3pm/CO noon. Nonsmoking rms avail. Standard rooms (some with ocean views) have outdated furnishings and tiny showers. Some bathrooms have cheerful yellow tile. Cottages are the main draw, with a unique ambience that features high, beamed ceilings, overstuffed chintz-covered

furniture, gleaming baths, brick fireplaces, and stenciled designs. **Amenities:** 🛏 ♨ 🖵 Cable TV w/movies. No A/C. Some units w/terraces, some w/fireplaces. All rooms have ceiling fans. VCRs for rent in lobby (with two movies). Refrigerators and hair dryers in suites and cottages. **Services:** ✗ 🖼 🍽 ☂ Masseur. Pets allowed with $50 deposit. **Facilities:** 🍴 🛏 1 restaurant, 1 bar (w/entertainment). Guest privileges at adjacent Pierpont Racquet Club available for $5 per day; includes 12 lighted tennis courts, sauna, pool, and whirlpool. Vine-covered gazebo in garden available for parties with up to 300 guests. Indoor/outdoor dining in restaurant with ocean view. **Rates:** Peak (May 27–Sept 30) $89–$99 S or D; $139 ste; $149–$169 cottage/villa. Extra person $10. Children under age 12 stay free. Lower rates off-season. Parking: Outdoor, free. Spa package includes massage, body treatment, facials, and lunch in the restaurant. AE, CB, DC, DISC, MC, V.

MOTEL

≡≡ La Quinta Motor Inn
5818 Valentine Rd, 93003; tel 805/658-6200 or toll free 800/531-5900; fax 805/642-2840. Victoria St exit off US 101; go west. A clean white-brick motel with a very attractive lobby, but a horrible smell outside from a nearby mushroom cannery. **Rooms:** 142 rms and stes. CI 3pm/CO noon. Nonsmoking rms avail. Rooms are simple, practical, decorated in earth tones with southwestern-style bleached wood furniture. **Amenities:** 🛏 ♨ A/C, satel TV w/movies. **Services:** ☂ ☂ **Facilities:** 🍴 🛏 ⛳ Whirlpool. Driving net, putting green. **Rates (CP):** Peak (June–Sept 15) $65 S; $73 D; $80 ste. Extra person $8. Children under age 18 stay free. Lower rates off-season. Parking: Outdoor, free. AE, DC, DISC, MC, V.

INN

≡≡≡ Bella Maggiore Inn
67 S California St, 93001; tel 805/652-0277 or toll free 800/523-8479. 1 acre. Italian-inspired bed-and-breakfast with a spacious comfortable lobby distinguished by antiques, a fireplace, and a grand piano. Downtown location within walking distance of shops and restaurants. **Rooms:** 24 rms and stes. CI 3pm/CO noon. Nonsmoking rms avail. Pretty rooms decorated in Mediterranean style, featuring ceiling fans, wooden blinds, and hand-painted designs on the beds. Some accommodations are a bit snug; those overlooking the restaurant may be noisy. Fresh flowers, handmade chocolate truffles, and bottles of spring water in the rooms. **Amenities:** 🛏 ♨ Cable TV w/movies. No A/C. Some units w/terraces, some w/fireplaces, some w/whirlpools. **Services:** ☂ ☂ Masseur, wine/sherry served. Turndown service and massage available. Free local calls. Complimentary late afternoon refreshments. **Facilities:** 🛏 ⛳ 1 restaurant. Gorgeous ivy-covered and flower-filled courtyard restaurant has a European feel. Sun-

deck roof garden. **Rates (BB):** $75–$150 S or D; $75–$150 ste. Extra person $10. Children under age 3 stay free. Parking: Outdoor, free. AE, DC, DISC, MC, V.

RESORT

≡≡≡ Harbortown Marina Resort
1050 Schooner Dr, 93001 (Ventura Harbor); tel 805/658-1212 or toll free 800/229-5732; fax 805/658-6347. 2 mi S of downtown Ventura. Seaward exit off US 101; follow Harbor Blvd to Harbortown. 17 acres. Designed by the Frank Lloyd Wright Foundation with fossilized stone throughout, this is the only hotel on the Ventura Marina. **Rooms:** 152 rms, stes, and effic. CI 4pm/CO noon. Nonsmoking rms avail. Bright and airy rooms are decorated in spring colors and bleached wood furniture. Some have harbor views. **Amenities:** 🛏 ♨ 🖵 Cable TV w/movies. No A/C. Some units w/fireplaces. **Services:** ✗ 🚐 🖼 ☂ Children's program, babysitting. **Facilities:** 🍴 🚲 🏊 🛏 ⛳ 1 restaurant, 2 bars (1 w/entertainment), whirlpool. Restaurant on the marina. **Rates:** Peak (May–Aug) $99–$129 S or D; $145–$185 ste. Extra person $10. Children under age 11 stay free. Min stay special events. Lower rates off-season. AP and MAP rates avail. Parking: Outdoor, free. AE, CB, DC, DISC, MC, V.

ATTRACTIONS 📷

Ventura County Museum of History and Art
100 E Main St; tel 805/653-0323. The museum's permanent collection of Ventura County historical artifacts is on display in the Huntsinger Gallery; art and other exhibits are housed in the Hoffman Gallery. The Smith Gallery contains George Stuart historical figures, relating to famous (and infamous) persons in world history. An outdoor exhibit features an extensive collection of horsedrawn farm implements. Library and archives; museum store. **Open:** Tues–Sun 10am–5pm. **$**

Albinger Archaeological Museum
113 E Main St; tel 805/648-5823. In 1973 the buildings that stood on this site were demolished as part of an urban redevelopment project. Archeological testing suggested the existence of cultural remains beneath the soil, leading to an intensive archeological investigation that uncovered more than 30,000 artifacts in 1974 and 1975. The property was withdrawn from the redevelopment project and designated as the Ventura Mission Historic District in 1975. In 1980 the Albinger Archaeological Museum opened to the public, displaying 3,500 years of regional history.

Within the museum are many artifacts discovered at the site, including bone whistles, milling stones, crucifixes, bottles, and pottery. Artifacts date as far back as 1600 BC, to a race of prehistoric people who came to the Ventura area seasonally over a period of 1,500 years. Also represented are Chumash Indians (1500–1834), the Spanish (1782–1822), the Mexicans (1822–1847), the Americans (1847–present), and the Chinese (1905–1920s). Outside the building are a number of archeological features, including the foundations of the "lost mission church," an ancient earth oven, and the mission water filtration building. **Open:** Peak (June–Aug) Wed–Sun 10am–4pm. Reduced hours off-season. **Free**

Mission San Buenaventura
225 E Main St; tel 805/643-4318. This mission was the ninth and last to be founded by Padre Junípero Serra, the moving force behind California's 21 missions. Begun in 1792, it is still used for masses in Spanish and English. Self-guided tours include the church, museum, and the mission grounds. Gift shop. **Open:** Grounds, daily dawn–dusk; museum and gift shop, Mon–Sat 10am–5pm, Sun 10am–4pm. **Free**

Victorville

The high desert community of Victorville lies north of the San Bernardino Mountains and has grown into a large bedroom community of the Inland Empire as well as other areas of the Los Angeles Basin to the south. **Information:** Victorville Chamber of Commerce, 14174 Greentree Blvd, PO Box 997, Victorville 92392 (tel 619/245-6506).

MOTEL

Days Inn Suites
14865 Bear Valley Rd, 92345; tel 619/948-0600 or toll free 800/325-2525; fax 619/956-8645. Exit Bear Valley Rd E exit off I-15. The exterior of this hotel has the look and feel of Santa Fe. Inside it's very modern. Great value. **Rooms:** 29 rms and stes. CI noon/CO 11am. Nonsmoking rms avail. **Amenities:** A/C, cable TV, refrig. Some units w/whirlpools. **Services:** **Facilities:** Whirlpool. **Rates (CP):** Peak (Mid-May–Aug) $39–$69 S; $45–$65 D; $45–$65 ste. Extra person $7. Children under age 17 stay free. Lower rates off-season. Parking: Outdoor, free. AE, CB, DC, DISC, JCB, MC, V.

RESTAURANTS

Chateau Chang
In Park Centre Shopping Center, 15425 Anacapa Rd; tel 619/241-3040. Palmdale Rd exit off I-15. **Chinese/French.** Art deco–style restaurant with burgundy-and-black interior, mirrors, and elevated dining room. The chef melds French and Chinese influences to create unusual and interesting dishes. **FYI:** Reservations recommended. **Open:** Lunch Mon–Sat 11:30am–2:30pm; dinner Mon–Thurs 5–9:30pm, Fri–Sat 5–10:30pm. **Prices:** Main courses $9–$28. AE, DISC, MC, V.

Marie Callender Restaurant
12180 Mariposa Rd; tel 619/241-6973. Bear Valley Rd E exit off I-15; immediate left on Mariposa Rd. **American.** The quintessential American restaurant, wholesome, bright, and clean. Friendly staff serves such classics as meat loaf, fried chicken, pot roast, and barbecued ribs. There are 35 different kinds of pie **FYI:** Reservations accepted. Children's

menu. **Open:** Mon–Thurs 6:30am–10pm, Fri–Sat 6:30am–11pm, Sun 8am–10pm. **Prices:** Main courses $7–$12. AE, DISC, MC, V.

Richie's Real American Diner
7th St at Palmdale Rd; tel 619/955-1113. **Diner.** With just enough chrome to evoke the 1950s, this classic American diner offers traditional breakfast fare as well as burgers and fries, milk shakes and sundaes, meat loaf and chicken pot pie. **FYI:** Reservations not accepted. Children's menu. Beer and wine only. **Open:** Breakfast daily 7am–1pm; lunch daily 11am–4pm; dinner Sun–Thurs 4–9pm, Fri–Sat 4–10pm. **Prices:** Main courses $4–$7. AE, DISC, MC, V.

ATTRACTION

The Roy Rogers–Dale Evans Museum
15650 Seneca Rd; tel 619/243-4547. On display are items from the personal and professional lives of the famous couple. Highlights include Trigger, Buttermilk, Bullet, Nellybelle, the Rose Parade Saddle, and a gun collection. **Open:** Daily 9am–5pm. **$$**

Visalia

Visalia was the first town in the Central Valley to be settled (1852). Self-guided walking tours showcase the town's historic past. Cotton, grapes, olives, and livestock form the backbone of the local economy. Various recreational areas are nearby. **Information:** Visalia Chamber of Commerce, 720 W Mineral King, Visalia 93291 (tel 209/734-5876).

HOTELS

Holiday Inn Plaza Park
9000 W Airport Dr, 93277 (Municipal Airport); tel 209/651-5000 or toll free 800/465-4329; fax 209/651-5014. CA 198 off CA 99; Rd 80/Plaza Dr to airport. Quiet location across from city park; beautiful lobby adjoining indoor swimming pool. Nearby city park has PGA-rated golf course, lighted tennis courts. **Rooms:** 257 rms and stes. Executive level. CI 3pm/CO noon. Nonsmoking rms avail. Recently refurbished rooms are attractive and comfortable. **Amenities:** A/C, satel TV w/movies. All TVs include Nintendo video games. **Services:** Babysitting. **Facilities:** 1 restaurant, 1 bar (w/entertainment), games rm, whirlpool, washer/dryer. Dancing in the lounge. Mini–convention center. **Rates:** $59–$109 S or D; $115–$129 ste. Extra person $10. Children under age 17 stay free. Parking: Outdoor, free. Weekend specials include breakfast. AE, CB, DC, DISC, JCB, MC, V.

Radisson Hotel Visalia
300 S Court, 93291 (Downtown); tel 209/636-1111 or toll free 800/333-3333, 800/734-3144 in CA; fax 209/636-8224. Exit 198 E off CA 99. This lovely hotel is part of the Visalia Convention Center complex and is within walking

distance of historic downtown Visalia. A 35-minute drive from Sequoia National Park, fishing, and other recreation. **Rooms:** 201 rms and stes. Executive level. CI 3pm/CO noon. Nonsmoking rms avail. "Green" suites available for those with environmental allergies. Presidential Suite has adjoining board room. **Amenities:** 📞 🅿 A/C, TV. All units w/minibars, some w/terraces, 1 w/whirlpool. Most rooms have hair dryers. **Services:** ✕ 🏩 🖃 🖂 🕬 Car-rental desk, babysitting. **Facilities:** 🏊 ⛳ 🎾 ♿ 1 restaurant, 1 bar, whirlpool. Large fitness center. Nordic tracks can be brought to rooms for private exercising (fee charged). Restaurant features daily specials. **Rates:** $125 S or D; $200 ste. Extra person $10. Children under age 18 stay free. Parking: Outdoor, free. Romance package features dinner, champagne, roses. AE, CB, DC, DISC, ER, JCB, MC, V.

MOTELS

≡≡ Best Western Visalia Inn

623 W Main St, 93277; tel 209/732-4561 or toll free 800/528-1234; fax 209/738-0562. Mooney Blvd exit off CA 198. Older motel in downtown area. Exterior is plain. **Rooms:** 40 rms. CI 2pm/CO 11am. Nonsmoking rms avail. Well kept and nicely decorated. **Amenities:** 📞 🅿 📺 🍴 A/C, cable TV w/movies, refrig. **Services:** 🕬 🛎 **Facilities:** 🏊 **Rates (CP):** $60–$62 S; $64–$66 D. Extra person $4. Parking: Outdoor, free. AE, CB, DC, DISC, JCB, MC, V.

≡≡ Lamp Liter Inn

3300 W Mineral King Ave, 93291; tel 209/732-4511 or toll free 800/662-6692; fax 209/732-1840. County Center St exit off CA 99. Quiet, landscaped setting. **Rooms:** 100 rms and stes; 4 cottages/villas. Executive level. CI 3pm/CO noon. Nonsmoking rms avail. **Amenities:** 📞 🅿 A/C, cable TV w/movies. Some units w/fireplaces. **Services:** ✕ 🏩 🖃 🕬 **Facilities:** 🏊 🍴 ♿ 2 restaurants, 1 bar (w/entertainment). **Rates:** $55–$90 S or D; $72–$120 ste; $105–$150 cottage/villa. Extra person $10. Children under age 18 stay free. Parking: Outdoor, free. AE, DC, DISC, JCB, MC, V.

RESTAURANTS 🍽

The Depot Restaurant

207 E Oak St; tel 209/732-8611. Central Visalia exit off CA 198 E. **Californian.** 1890s styling with high-backed banquettes and tables in building constructed in 1897 and remodeled in 1971. Decor a bit worn. Specialties include black pepper steak à la gitano, Yucatán prawns in red jalapeño sauce, sautéed prawn scampi. **FYI:** Reservations recommended. Children's menu. **Open:** Mon–Sat 11am–10pm. **Prices:** Main courses $12–$30. AE, DISC, MC, V. ♥ ♿

Michael's on Main

123 W Main St; tel 209/635-2686. CA 63 N exit off CA 198. **Californian/Italian.** Intimate restaurant in the historic part of Visalia. Chicken, fish, steak, lamb, and pasta, with many items prepared on the grill. Award-winning cioppino. **FYI:**

Reservations recommended. Jazz/piano. **Open:** Lunch Mon–Fri 11am–3:30pm; dinner Mon–Sat 5–11pm. **Prices:** Main courses $10–$38. AE, DC, DISC, MC, V.

The Vintage Press

216 N Willis St; tel 209/733-3033. Central Visalia exit off CA 198 E. **Californian.** Visalia's most famous restaurant, set in an art nouveau Victorian house with garden dining available. Menu features seafood, steak, and local specialties such as antelope and venison. Pastries and breads baked on premises. **FYI:** Reservations recommended. Piano. Children's menu. **Open:** Lunch Mon–Sat 11:30am–2pm; dinner Mon–Thurs 6–10:30pm, Fri–Sat 6–11pm. **Prices:** Main courses $12–$35. AE, CB, DC, MC, V. ♥ ♿

Walnut Creek

See also Concord, Lafayette, Pleasant Hill

Lying to the west of Mount Diablo, Walnut Creek has blossomed into one of the more sophisticated suburbs of San Francisco. The pride of the community is the Lindsay Museum, which specializes in natural history and wildlife rehabilitation. **Information:** Walnut Creek Chamber of Commerce, 1501 N Broadway #110, Walnut Creek 94596 (tel 510/934-2007).

HOTELS 🏨

≡≡≡ Embassy Suites Hotel

1345 Treat Blvd, 94596; tel 510/934-2500 or toll free 800/EMBASSY; fax 510/256-7233. Treat Blvd exit off I-680. Lovely eight-story atrium hotel, across the street from rapid transit station. **Rooms:** 249 stes. CI 3pm/CO 1pm. Nonsmoking rms avail. **Amenities:** 📞 🅿 📺 🍴 A/C, cable TV w/movies, refrig, dataport, voice mail. 1 unit w/minibar, 1 w/whirlpool. All suites have microwaves, wet bars, and hide-a-beds. TV in living room and bedroom. **Services:** ✕ 🖃 🕬 🛎 Car-rental desk, babysitting. Manager's reception 5:30–7:30pm daily, with complimentary hors d'oeuvres and alcoholic and non-alcoholic beverages. Complimentary van service to points within a 5-mile radius. **Facilities:** 🏊 ⛳ 🎾 ♿ 1 restaurant (lunch and dinner only), 1 bar, sauna, whirlpool, washer/dryer. **Rates (BB):** $129–$169 ste. Extra person $15. Children under age 12 stay free. Min stay special events. Parking: Indoor, $2/day. AE, CB, DC, DISC, JCB, MC, V.

≡≡ Holiday Inn Walnut Creek

2730 N Main St, 94596; tel 510/932-3332 or toll free 800/HOLIDAY; fax 510/256-7672. Main St exit off I-680. The small lobby opens to a bar area, where patrons are allowed to smoke. **Rooms:** 155 rms and stes. CI 2pm/CO noon. Nonsmoking rms avail. Recently renovated. **Amenities:** 📞 🅿 📺 🍴 A/C, cable TV w/movies, dataport. **Services:** ✕ 🖃 🕬 Car-rental desk, babysitting. Pick-up service for pets at nearby pet hotel. Complimentary shuttle to rapid transit station, stores, and business offices. **Facilities:** 🏊 🎾 ♿ 1 restaurant, 1 bar, whirlpool. Complimentary shuttle to nearby fitness center, which guests can use for free. **Rates:** $99 S; $109 D; $145–$165 ste. Extra person $10. Children under age 18 stay free. Min stay special events. Parking: Indoor, free. AE, CB, DC, DISC, JCB, MC, V.

RESTAURANTS 🍴

Scott's Seafood Grill and Bar
1333 N California Blvd; tel 510/934-1300. **Seafood.** Popular with the business set, the restaurant has the feel of a large supper club. Outdoor bar and dining terraces. Fresh seafood entrees top the menu. **FYI:** Reservations recommended. Piano. Dress code. Additional location: 2 Broadway Ave, Oakland (tel 444-3456). **Open:** Mon–Sat 11am–10pm, Sun 10am–9pm. **Prices:** Main courses $10–$19. AE, CB, DC, DISC, MC, V. �(VP &

★ Spiedini
101 Ygnacio Valley Rd; tel 510/939-2100. **Italian.** Spacious dining room with roomy booths and lots of marble, providing a sleek, Italian look. Dishes include several pizzas, fresh pasta, and anything grilled on the huge rotisserie. A beautiful restaurant with professional staff and food to match. **FYI:** Reservations recommended. Dress code. **Open:** Sun–Wed 11:30am–9:30pm, Thurs–Sat 11:30am–10:30pm. **Prices:** Main courses $8–$13. AE, CB, DC, MC, V. 📋 VP &

ATTRACTION 🎦

The Lindsay Museum
1931 1st Ave; tel 510/935-1978. The purpose of this natural history museum is to educate the public, especially children, about caring for the environment and living with nature. It is also one of the nation's oldest and largest wildlife rehabilitation centers. Exhibits include more than 40 species of live, non-releasable animals, including hawks, owls, raccoons, and rattlesnakes.

In the Exhibit Hall are two large areas where visitors watch the daily feeding, bathing, and exercising of display animals; also displays of natural history objects, aquariums, and an insectarium. A small theater continually shows nature films.

A separate "Especially for Children" room introduces children to "the wildlife in their own backyard," and includes a Petting Circle for interaction with animals. A pet library allows local children with family membership to "borrow" hamsters, rabbits, and guinea pigs, for a week at a time. A one-acre nature garden demonstrates native and drought-resistent plants that help residents create backyard wildlife habitats. Bookstore and gift shop. **Open:** Peak (Sept–June) Wed–Sun 1–5pm. Reduced hours off-season. **$**

Weed

See Mount Shasta

West Hollywood

See also Hollywood, North Hollywood

Sunset Blvd, Melrose Ave, and Hollywood Blvd all wend their way through West Hollywood, and the town's boutiques, restaurants, galleries, and night spots rival those found anywhere else. **Information:** West Hollywood Chamber of Commerce, 9000 Sunset Blvd #700, West Hollywood 90069 (tel 310/858-8000).

HOTELS 🏨

≡≡≡ Hyatt on Sunset
8401 Sunset Blvd, 90069; tel 213/656-1234 or toll free 800/223-1234; fax 213/650-7024. Located on trendy and vibrant Sunset Strip, across the street from the House of Blues, and next door to the Comedy Store. **Rooms:** 262 rms and stes. Executive level. CI 3pm/CO noon. Nonsmoking rms avail. Large rooms furnished in contemporary style. Rooms have views of Sunset Blvd and the LA Basin, or the Hollywood hills. **Amenities:** 🔲 🍸 A/C, cable TV w/movies, dataport, voice mail, in-rm safe. Some units w/terraces. **Services:** ✕ VP 🛎 Twice-daily maid svce, car-rental desk, babysitting. Good security—elevator requires a suite key in order to gain access to each floor. **Facilities:** 🛎 200 📱 & 2 restaurants, 1 bar. Guest rate available at nearby fitness club. Rooftop swimming pool offers incredible views of Los Angeles and Hollywood hills. **Rates:** $145–$160 S; $170–$185 D; $360–$560 ste. Extra person $25. Children under age 18 stay free. Min stay special events. Parking: Indoor/outdoor, $7–$10/day. AE, CB, DC, DISC, EC, JCB, MC, V.

≡≡≡≡ Sunset Marquis Hotel & Villas
1200 N Alta Loma Rd, 90069; tel 310/657-1333 or toll free 800/858-9758; fax 310/652-5300. A bucolic setting complete with rolling lawns, waterfalls, and fish ponds. Ambience is relaxed, rather than glitzy; draws a celebrity clientele ranging from Bruce Springsteen to Julio Iglesias. If you love rock 'n' roll, this place is for you. **Rooms:** 102 stes and effic; 12 cottages/villas. CI 3pm/CO 1pm. Nonsmoking rms avail. Accommodations in a converted apartment building, or in private villas. Totally refurbished, the main structure looks great, and is painted a sprightly Tuscan yellow with new awnings fluttering from the balconies. Mediterranean pastels beautify the accommodations, while bathrooms look glamorous with new marble floors and counters. Villas slated for a much-needed renovation. **Amenities:** 🔲 🍸 A/C, cable TV w/movies, refrig, dataport, voice mail, in-rm safe, bathrobes. Some units w/terraces, some w/fireplaces, some w/whirlpools. Accommodations all have 27" TVs, wet bars, irons, and ironing boards. Three suites have baby grand pianos. **Services:** 🍽 ➖ VP 🚗 🛎 Twice-daily maid svce, car-rental desk, social director, masseur, babysitting. Personalized attention is lavished on guests. **Facilities:** 🛎 🏊 12 📱 & 2 restaurants, 1 bar, sauna, whirlpool. There's a new

48-track recording studio on premises. **Rates:** $235–$490 ste; $450–$1200 cottage/villa. Extra person $35. Children under age 12 stay free. Parking: Indoor, $12/day. AE, CB, DC, MC, V.

≣ ≣ ≣ Wyndham Bel Age

1020 N San Vincente Blvd, 90069; tel 310/854-1111 or toll free 800/424-4443; fax 310/289-2763. A European-style hotel with period furniture in the lobby and a $5 million art collection displayed throughout the hotel, even in the rooms. **Rooms:** 199 stes. CI 3pm/CO noon. Nonsmoking rms avail. Facing either the city or the hills, suites are decorated with French provincial–style furnishings and fabrics in shades of gray and olive. The very large corporate suites offer a separate, step-up bedroom with king-size bed. Done in gray marble, bathrooms feature a small TV and large scale. **Amenities:** 🛏 🜁 📺 🍴 A/C, cable TV w/movies, dataport, voice mail, bathrobes. All units w/minibars, all w/terraces. **Services:** 🍴 🖙 VP 🚗 🛅 🛎 🐕 Twice-daily maid svce, car-rental desk, social director, masseur, babysitting. **Facilities:** 🛗 🛎 300 🚽 2 restaurants (see "Restaurants" below), 2 bars (w/entertainment), whirlpool, beauty salon. Dynamite city views from both the rooftop pool and Brasserie Cafe. Workout room has new treadmills, Stairmaster, and exercise machines. **Rates:** $250–$500 ste. Children under age 18 stay free. Min stay special events. AP and MAP rates avail. Parking: Indoor, $16/day. AE, CB, DC, DISC, MC, V.

RESTAURANTS 🍽

⑤ Astro Burgers

7475 Santa Monica Blvd; tel 213/874-8041. 8 mi mi N of Los Angeles Santa Monica Blvd W exit off US 101. **Burgers.** This spanking clean, 1950s-style fast-service restaurant lined with vintage movie star posters attracts a celebrity clientele. Owned by the second-generation Andrianos family, the diner features an enormous Greek-influenced menu. Specialties include marinated, charbroiled chicken breast sandwiches, vegetarian "gardenburgers," Mexican breakfast fare, and hefty cheeseburgers served with giant onion rings or fried zucchini sticks. **FYI:** Reservations not accepted. No liquor license. Additional location: 3421 W Beverly Blvd, Montebello (tel 724-3995). **Open:** Sun–Thurs 7am–3am, Fri–Sat 7am–4am. **Prices:** Main courses $4–$7. No CC. 🍴 🖼 ⅘

⑤ ★ Book Soup Bistro

8800 Sunset Blvd; tel 310/657-1072. **New American.** This beautiful indoor-outdoor space adjoins the outdoor publications rack at its sister Book Soup bookstore. Photos of literary figures look down from the walls on the art deco interior comprised of wood tables, a bar, and comfortable library chairs. Favorite dishes include turkey meat loaf, grilled chicken cobb salad, and vegetarian lasagna. Periodic readings and book signings by new and noted authors. **FYI:** Reserva-

tions accepted. Readings. **Open:** Mon–Thurs noon–10pm, Fri 10am–11pm, Sat 11:30am–11pm, Sun 11:30am–10pm. **Prices:** Main courses $9–$18. AE, MC, V. 🍴 🖼 ⅘

♣ Diaghilev

In the Wyndham Bel Age, 1020 N San Vicente Blvd; tel 310/854-1111. **French/Russian.** Original art from Diaghilev's era frame the dining room of this elegant old-world hotel. French-Russian-style dining is presided over by a veteran maitre d' as Russian balalaika music entertains guests. The menu continues the theme, with egg shells filled with whipped eggs, chives, and fine caviar; venison shashlik; borscht; leg of duck with honey calvados; and other exotica. **FYI:** Reservations recommended. Piano. **Open:** Tues–Sat 6:30–10:30pm. **Prices:** Main courses $18–$28. AE, DC, MC, V. 🅥 VP ⅘

fusion at pdc

In Pacific Design Center, 8687 Melrose Ave; tel 310/659-6012. At San Vicente. **Eclectic.** Located on the first floor of the cobalt-blue Pacific Design Center, it opens onto the huge side patio. The low-slung, softly lit interior mingles light woods with high-tech presentation screens. Menu features a health-oriented, ethnic Pacific Rim mix, with specialties such as vodka-cured gravlax, housemade chicken-fennel sausage with polenta, and lamb stew. Wonderful chocolate soufflé for dessert. **FYI:** Reservations recommended. Piano/Bass. Dress code. **Open:** Mon–Fri 11am–10:30pm, Sat 6–11pm. **Prices:** Main courses $8–$24. AE, DISC, MC, V. 🍴 🖼 VP ⅘

House of Blues

8430 Sunset Blvd; tel 213/650-0476. **Eclectic.** Celebrates American music and racial unity as only Tennessee-bred Isaac Tigret (of Hard Rock Cafe design fame) imagines it. Gaily colored African-American art covers every inch of this massive three-story center, which includes a family-style restaurant, theater, and gallery. The chef adds international dishes to the basic southern soul-food menu featuring favorites like gumbo, dirty rice, chicken-fried steak, and jambalaya. **FYI:** Reservations recommended. Blues/country music/jazz/rock. **Open:** Daily 11:30am–midnight. **Prices:** Main courses $7–$15. AE, DISC, MC, V. 🍴 VP ⅘

★ Hugo's

8401 Santa Monica Blvd; tel 213/654-3993. **Californian/Italian.** A favorite, especially among young entertainment industry moguls who gather for power breakfasts of chilaquiles and pumpkin pancakes. The fare leans toward health food (there's even a juice bar), but with a definite southwestern bent. Lunch and dinner menus include a variety of pastas, pizzas, sandwiches, and salads. **FYI:** Reservations accepted. Beer and wine only. **Open:** Sun–Thurs 7:30am–10pm, Fri–Sat 7:30am–10:30pm. **Prices:** Main courses $8–$15. AE, DC, MC, V. 🍴 🖼 ⅘

Le Petit Bistro

631 N La Cienega Blvd; tel 310/289-9797. **French/Moroccan.** Moroccan-French owner Robert Lochkar took the best

of his experience at the legendary Le St Germain bistro, retaining the salmon walls and huge mirrors and paintings, and updated it with inexpensive dishes and informal seating. Shrimp picante, escargots, cured Norwegian salmon, and eggplant tart with tomato sauce are specialties. **FYI:** Reservations recommended. **Open:** Lunch daily 11:30am–2:30pm; dinner daily 5:30pm–midnight. **Prices:** Main courses $9–$13. AE, DC, MC, V. ♿

♟ The Palm Restaurant
9001 Santa Monica Blvd; tel 310/550-8811. **American.** This New York–style steak house is known as "the commissary" for show business agents and entertainers. A wall mural has caricatures of celebrity customers. Food is average but pricey. Huge side orders of hash browns and french-fried onions. **FYI:** Reservations accepted. **Open:** Mon–Fri noon–10:30pm, Sat 5–10:30pm, Sun 5–9:30pm. **Prices:** Main courses $15–$28. AE, CB, DC, MC, V.

♟ Spago
8795 Sunset Blvd (Sunset Strip); tel 310/652-4025. **New American/Californian.** A celebrity clientele, prime vantage point overlooking Sunset Strip, and superstar chef Wolfgang Puck all helped put Spago on the map. Famed for designer pizzas from its wood-burning oven, with such toppings as duck sausage, grilled garlic chicken, and sautéed foie gras with sweet and sour plum sauce. The restaurant is scheduled to move to Beverly Hills in 1997. **FYI:** Reservations recommended. **Open:** Mon–Thurs 6–11pm, Fri 6pm–midnight, Sat 5:30pm–midnight, Sun 5:30–11pm. **Prices:** Main courses $18–$28. CB, DC, DISC, MC, V.

Westlake Village

See Thousand Oaks

West Los Angeles

See Los Angeles

Willits

Although a small community, Willits is the official seat of Mendocino County; in earlier times, it served as an important railroad hub for northern California. Frontier Days is celebrated every July 4th week. **Information:** Mendocino County Tourism Board, 239 S Main St, Willits 95490 (tel 707/459-7910).

MOTELS

≡≡ Baechtel Creek Inn
101 Gregory Lane, 95490; tel 707/459-9063 or toll free 800/459-9911; fax 707/459-1522. The best place to stay in Willits. **Rooms:** 46 rms. CI 2pm/CO 11am. Nonsmoking rms

avail. Standard, but clean and pleasant. **Amenities:** A/C, cable TV. **Services:** Babysitting. **Facilities:** **Rates (CP):** $69–$89 S; $79–$105 D. Extra person $5. Children under age 5 stay free. Min stay special events. Parking: Outdoor, free. AE, DISC, MC, V.

≡ Pepperwood Motel
452 S Main St, 95490; tel 707/459-2231. Willits exit off US 101. Decent motel. **Rooms:** 21 rms. CI 11am/CO 11am. Nonsmoking rms avail. Ask for a room in back by the creek. **Amenities:** A/C, cable TV. **Services:** **Facilities:** **Rates:** Peak (June–Sept) $45 S; $60 D. Children under age 12 stay free. Lower rates off-season. Parking: Outdoor, free. AE, DISC, MC, V.

RESTAURANT

⑤★ Tsunami
50 S Main St; tel 707/459-4750. **Japanese/Seafood.** A fine restaurant where the owner, a local fisherman, catches much of what is served. Decor reminiscent of a Japanese country inn, with simple clean lines and a sunny patio. Unique blend of Japanese and international cuisine includes grilled ahi tuna, tasty tempura, chicken yakitori. Free-range chicken, brown rice, and whole grain breads for the health-conscious. Homemade desserts. **FYI:** Reservations recommended. Beer and wine only. **Open:** Mon–Sat 9:30am–8:30pm, Sun 4:30–9pm. **Prices:** Main courses $8–$15. No CC.

ATTRACTION

Mendocino County Museum
400 E Commercial St; tel 707/459-2736. Local artifacts on display explain the life and times of the citizens of Mendocino County. Highlights include oral history and interviews on tape; collections of Pomo and Yuki basketry; redwood logging tools. Living history demonstrations; special programs. **Open:** Wed–Sat 10am–4:30pm. **Free**

Willows

MOTELS

≡≡≡ Best Western Golden Pheasant Inn
249 N Humboldt Ave, 95988; tel 916/934-4603 or toll free 800/338-1387; fax 916/934-4275. Willows/Elk Creek/Glenn Rd exit off I-5. Pleasant location near Glenn County Sacramento Bird Refuge. **Rooms:** 104 rms and stes. CI noon/CO 11am. Nonsmoking rms avail. **Amenities:** A/C, cable TV w/movies, VCR. Some units w/terraces, some w/fireplaces, some w/whirlpools. Refrigerators installed upon request. **Services:** Kennel for pets. **Facilities:** 1 restaurant (lunch and dinner only), 1 bar, washer/dryer. **Rates (CP):** Peak (June–Sept) $49–$55 S; $55–$67 D; $85 ste. Extra person $4. Children under age 12 stay free. Lower rates off-season. Parking: Outdoor, free. AE, DC, DISC, MC, V.

≣ Cross Roads West Inn
452 N Humboldt Ave, 95988; tel 916/934-7026 or toll free 800/814-6301. Willows/Elk Creek/Glenn Rd exit off I-5. Clean, simple lodging. **Rooms:** 41 rms. CI 11am/CO 11am. Nonsmoking rms avail. **Amenities:** 🛎 A/C, cable TV. **Services:** ⬧ **Facilities:** 🔗 **Rates:** Peak (Mar–Dec) $29–$36 S; $39–$45 D. Extra person $6. Children under age 5 stay free. Lower rates off-season. Parking: Outdoor, free. Guests ages 62 and over get 5% off. AE, DISC, MC, V.

ATTRACTION 📷

Sacramento National Wildlife Refuge
Tel 916/934-2801. Located just south of Willows via CA 99 W, this refuge is part of the Sacramento National Wildlife Refuge Complex, which also includes the Colusa, Delevan, Sutter, and Sacramento River refuges, totaling over 30,000 acres of northern California uplands and wetlands. The region is an important wintering area for the millions of migrating waterfowl who travel along the Pacific Flyway.

Over 300 species of birds and mammals, both resident and migratory, inhabit the refuges at various times throughout the year. Trails and auto tour routes provide opportunities for wildlife observation. Hunting is permitted (except at the Sacramento River refuge) Oct–Jan (contact the California Dept of Fish and Game for current dates, regulations, and other information). **Open:** Daily sunrise–sunset. **Free**

Woodland Hills

The quiet community of Woodland Hills lies tucked up against the Santa Monica Mountains on the far western edge of the San Fernando Valley. Several mountain roads lead to the nearby Santa Monica Mountains National Recreation Area, as well as Topanga Canyon State Park. **Information:** Woodland Hills Chamber of Commerce, 21600 Oxnard St #S-520, PO Box 1, Woodland Hills 91367 (tel 818/347-4737).

HOTELS 🏨

≣≣≣ Holiday Inn Woodland Hills
21101 Ventura Blvd, 91364; tel 818/883-6110 or toll free 800/HOLIDAY; fax 818/340-6550. Desoto exit off US 101; right on Ventura Blvd. An older property, toward the low end of the quality scale for this chain. Close to shops and stores. **Rooms:** 124 rms. Executive level. CI 3pm/CO 11am. Nonsmoking rms avail. **Amenities:** 🛎 A/C, cable TV w/movies. **Services:** ✕ Car-rental desk, children's program, babysitting. **Facilities:** 🔗 170 1 restaurant, 1 bar, washer/dryer. **Rates (BB):** $70–$120 S or D. Extra person $10. Children under age 19 stay free. Parking: Outdoor, free. AE, CB, DC, DISC, JCB, MC, V.

≣≣≣≣ Warner Center Hilton & Towers
6360 Canoga Ave, 91367; tel 818/595-1000 or toll free 800/922-2400; fax 818/595-1090. Canoga Ave exit off US Hwy 101. An outstanding business hotel, well located in the Warner Center district of suburban Los Angeles. **Rooms:** 330 rms and stes. Executive level. CI 3pm/CO noon. Nonsmoking rms avail. Sufficiently large for business travelers, with adequate desks and lighting. **Amenities:** 🛎 A/C, satel TV w/movies, dataport, voice mail. All units w/minibars, some w/terraces, some w/whirlpools. **Services:** ⬧ Twice-daily maid svce, car-rental desk, babysitting. Secretarial, notary, and fax services on premises. Complimentary van shuttle service within 5 miles of hotel. Complimentary newspaper. **Facilities:** 🔗 600 1 restaurant, 1 bar, spa, sauna, steam rm, whirlpool. Complimentary guest passes to adjacent LA Fitness Sports & Tennis Club. **Rates:** $119–$149 S or D; $150–$290 ste. Children under age 18 stay free. Parking: Indoor, $5–$7/day. AE, CB, DC, DISC, EC, ER, JCB, MC, V.

MOTEL

≣≣ Best Western Aku Aku Motor Inn
21830 Ventura Blvd, 91364; tel 818/340-1000 or toll free 800/528-1234; fax 818/340-1020. A typical, low-budget motel with a nicely done lobby. **Rooms:** 69 rms and effic. CI 2pm/CO 11am. Nonsmoking rms avail. Adequate, with blackout drapes and soundproofing to keep out the noise of Ventura Blvd. **Amenities:** 🛎 A/C, cable TV w/movies, refrig. Some units w/terraces. **Services:** ⬧ Twice-daily maid svce. Coffee available all day. **Facilities:** 🔗 Washer/dryer. No elevator to second floor. **Rates (CP):** $49–$54 S; $53–$63 D; $62 effic. Extra person $5. Children under age 12 stay free. AP rates avail. Parking: Outdoor, free. Three-night minimum stay for efficiencies. AE, CB, DC, DISC, EC, ER, JCB, MC, V.

RESTAURANTS 🍴

★ Cafe Bellissimo
22458 Ventura Blvd; tel 818/225-0026. **Sicilian.** Mama Sara not only provides traditional Sicilian dishes such as superb caponata, pastas, fish, and meats, she also hosts a nonstop party atmosphere for locals and celebrities. The rambling indoor and outdoor restaurant offers a fine stage for the competent, welcoming waitstaff who perform favorite songs along with the guitarist owner and other musicians. **FYI:** Reservations accepted. Guitar/singer. **Open:** Dinner Mon–Thurs 5:30–10pm, Fri–Sat 5:30–11pm, Sun 5:30–10:30pm. **Prices:** Main courses $8–$16. AE, CB, DC, DISC, MC, V. 🚊 VP

La Paz
21040 Victory Blvd; tel 818/883-4761. **Mexican/Seafood.** Despite an inauspicious location in a strip mall, nonexistent decor, and a lack of windows, the food in this family-run restaurant is excellent. Patrons praise Maria's paella Olé!—a treasure hunt of lobster, shrimp, clams, and crab legs. Other items are octopus enchiladas and shrimp tacos plus conch

and abalone appetizers. **FYI:** Reservations recommended. **Open:** Sun–Thurs 11am–9pm, Fri–Sat 11am–10pm. **Prices:** Main courses $5–$35. AE, DC, MC, V. 🏧 &

★ The Seashell Restaurant

19723 Ventura Blvd; tel 818/884-6500. **Continental/Seafood.** Skylights give this place the feel of a patio. Upholstered booths and carved wood chairs afford an old-fashioned ambience. Specialties include Maryland crab cakes, poached fresh salmon, and seafood ravioli. **FYI:** Reservations recommended. **Open:** Lunch Mon–Fri 11:30am–2pm; dinner Mon–Sat 5:30–10pm, Sun 5:30–9:30pm. **Prices:** Main courses $14–$23; prix fixe $19–$23. AE, CB, DC, DISC, MC, V. ♥ &

Yosemite National Park

See also Oakhurst

Typically described as breathtaking, spectacular, and awe-inspiring, the Yosemite Valley evolved when glaciers moved through the canyon, which had been created by the Merced River during repeated geological rises of the Sierras. When these glaciers began to melt, the moraine (accumulated earth and stones deposited by a glacier) dammed part of the Merced River to form Lake Yosemite in the new valley. Eventually, sediment filled the lake, thus accounting for the flat floor of Yosemite Valley. The same process, but on a much smaller scale, is even now occuring with Mirror Lake at the base of Half Dome.

The Native American Ahwahneechees had been living in the valley for several thousand years before they first encountered Europeans in the middle of the 19th century. Members of the Joseph Reddeford Walker party were probably the first "foreigners" to see Yosemite Valley when they crossed from the east side of the Sierras in 1833. Later intrusions resulted in indiscriminate abuses of the environment. To forestall any commercial exploitation of the valley, President Abraham Lincoln granted Yosemite Valley and the Mariposa Grove of giant sequoias to California as a public trust. Federal legislation created Yosemite National Park in 1890.

Today, Yosemite Valley is, as it has been for thousands of years, a glacier-carved canyon with sheer walls of granite rising thousands of feet from the valley floor. It remains a sensual blend of open meadows, wildflowers, and woodlands with ponderosa pine, incense cedar, and Douglas fir. All kinds of wildlife, from monarch butterflies and 223 species of birds to black bears and mule deer flourish in this protected environment.

A wide variety of sports and recreational activities are available at the park. Some of these include: **bicycling** on the many trails geared to cyclists or **horseback riding** on 30 miles of bridle trails in the valley. Bicycles can be rented at Yosemite Lodge and Curry Village; stable facilities are located near Curry Village (summer only).

Hikers can traverse over 700 miles of trails that cover a diverse terrain marked by jagged mountains and rolling meadows. A wilderness permit is required for backcountry trails; these are available at any of the five permit stations in the park or by writing to the Wilderness Office, PO Box 577, Yosemite National Park, CA 95389.

With vertical granite walls surrounding two-thirds of the valley, Yosemite is considered by experts to be one of the finest **climbing** areas in the world. The Yosemite Mountaineering School at Curry Village has classes for beginning, intermediate, and advanced climbers.

Camping at Yosemite is available at 300 year-round sites scattered over 17 different campgrounds. From June to Sept 15 camping permits are limited to 7 days in the valley and 14 days in the rest of the park; during the rest of the year permits are granted for up to 30 days. Many of the campgrounds are located in the 7 square miles that make up Yosemite Valley, the area's primary focal point. Some of the park's most famous features are nearby, including Yosemite Falls, Mirror Lake, Half Dome, and El Capitan.

For more information, contact Visitor Information (tel 209/372-0200 or 372-0265), Yosemite National Park, PO Box 577, Yosemite National Park, CA 95389.

HOTELS 🏨

≡≡≡ The Ahwahnee

Yosemite Valley, 95389; tel 209/252-4848. Built in 1927, this larger-than-life castle features massive pillars, polished sugarpine rafters, and fireplaces that are tall enough to stand in. The lovely outdoor patio overlooks the lawn and adjacent meadow. The stony facade has all the flinty grandeur of Mount Rushmore. **Rooms:** 99 rms and stes; 25 cottages/villas. CI 5pm/CO noon. No smoking. The recently refurbished hotel rooms, done in forest and earth tones, are comfortable but not fancy. What stands out are the views they provide of Glacier Peak, Yosemite Falls, and the woods. Try to reserve one of the cottages, which cost the same as rooms in the main hotel but are more spacious. **Amenities:** 🛎 🅰 📞 A/C, cable TV, refrig, in-rm safe, bathrobes. All units w/minibars, some w/terraces, some w/whirlpools. **Services:** ✕ ☞ VP 🖾 🎛 Twice-daily maid svce, social director, masseur, children's program, babysitting. On many evenings, free educational programs about the park are offered. **Facilities:** ⚴ 🚲 ⚓ 🎿 ⚗ 🎢 1000 & 1 restaurant (see "Restaurants" below), 1 bar (w/entertainment), playground. "Badger Pups" ski program for kids in the winter. **Rates:** Peak (Apr–Oct) $201–$208 S or D; $400 ste; $201–$208 cottage/villa. Extra person $20. Children under age 12 stay free. Lower rates off-season. Parking: Outdoor, free. Special ski packages to nearby Badger Pass. AE, CB, DC, DISC, EC, ER, JCB, MC, V.

≡≡≡ Tenaya Lodge at Yosemite

1122 CA 41, PO Box 159, Fish Camp, 93623; tel 209/683-6555 or toll free 800/635-5807; fax 209/683-8684. 45

mi N of Fresno. Yosemite's newest luxury hotel. The impressive lobby has soaring, open-beamed ceilings and stone pillars and is accented with Native American art. Located about an hour's drive from the valley floor. **Rooms:** 244 rms and stes. CI 3pm/CO noon. Nonsmoking rms avail. Large and extremely cozy, with separate sitting area. Native American motifs are incorporated into the decor. **Amenities:** 🛗 🐕 🖳 A/C, cable TV, refrig, dataport, in-rm safe. All units w/minibars, some w/terraces. Iron and ironing board in each room. **Services:** ✗ ☞ 🆅🅿 ⬛ 🛋 🐾 Social director, masseur, children's program, babysitting. Guest Experience Center helps guests plan itineraries. Kids' camp during summer and holidays. **Facilities:** 🎣 🚴 ⛵ 🏹 🚶 🎿 🏇 650 ⚿ 2 restaurants, 1 bar, games rm, lawn games, spa, sauna, steam rm, whirlpool, playground, washer/dryer. Both indoor and outdoor swimming pools, plus a state-of-the-art fitness center. The popular Sierra Restaurant specializes in California cuisine with an Italian influence. Jackalopes Saloon features outdoor dining, service from menus of both restaurants, and an extensive selection of beer and wine. **Rates:** Peak (June 15–Sept 15) $199–$259 S or D; $278–$339 ste. Extra person $15. Children under age 18 stay free. Min stay special events. Lower rates off-season. Parking: Outdoor, free. Some rates include an all-you-can-eat buffet breakfast; some include turndown service. AE, CB, DC, DISC, JCB, MC, V.

≣≣≣ Wawona Hotel

CA 41, 95389; tel 209/252-4848. 40 mi S of Yosemite Valley floor. Built in 1879, the Victorian-style main building brims with period charm. Overlooking lawns, a fountain thick with lily pads, and a nine-hole golf course, the two-story, white-frame buildings are surrounded by porches furnished with wicker chairs. This is the place to go to get away from the Yosemite Valley hustle. Not suitable for young children. **Rooms:** 104 rms. CI 4pm/CO 11am. No smoking. Half of the rooms share baths. Many accommodations have claw-foot bathtubs and lack showers. **Amenities:** 🐕 No A/C, phone, or TV. Some units w/terraces. Robes are provided for guests in units lacking private bathrooms. **Services:** ✗ ☞ 🆅🅿 ⬛ 🛋 Masseur, babysitting. **Facilities:** 🎣 📷 ▶9 🏹 🚶 ⛵ 50 ⚿ 1 restaurant, 1 bar (w/entertainment), lawn games, playground. Elegant restaurant on premises. **Rates:** Peak (Apr–Oct) $63–$86 S or D. Extra person $10. Children under age 12 stay free. Min stay wknds. Lower rates off-season. Parking: Outdoor, free. Open weekends only in off-season. Ask about bed-and-breakfast rates, plus golf and skiing packages. AE, CB, DC, DISC, EC, ER, JCB, MC, V.

MOTELS

≣≣ Cedar Lodge

9966 CA 140, PO Box C, El Portal, 95318; tel 209/379-2612 or toll free 800/321-5261; fax 209/379-2712. 27 mi W of Yosemite Valley floor. Comfortable resort motel across the street from the Merced River, with its own sand beach on the river for guests. Located 15 minutes from the Yosemite Park entrance, it's a good choice for families. **Rooms:** 206 rms and stes. CI 3pm/CO 11am. Nonsmoking rms avail. **Amenities:** 🛗 🐕 A/C, cable TV, refrig. Some units w/terraces, some w/whirlpools. Some rooms have whirlpool on the patio; the suite has a private swimming pool. **Services:** 🐾 Babysitting. **Facilities:** 🎣 🚶 ⛵ 250 ⚿ 2 restaurants, 1 bar, whirlpool, playground. The Merced is a great river for rafting in the spring and summer, and several commercial outfitters are located near the motel. **Rates:** $80–$125 S; $95–$125 D; $225–$375 ste. Children under age 18 stay free. Min stay special events. Parking: Outdoor, free. AE, MC, V.

≣≣≣ Yosemite View Lodge

CA 140, El Portal, 95318; tel 209/379-2681 or toll free 800/321-5261; fax 209/379-2704. 14 mi W of Yosemite Village; 2 mi from El Portal entrance; 12 mi from valley floor. Completely renovated, it's one of the nicest places to stay in the Yosemite area. Restaurant next door. **Rooms:** 200 rms and stes. CI 3pm/CO 11am. Nonsmoking rms avail. Very nicely appointed, spacious new mini-suites. Some bathrooms have huge, tiled showers and large whirlpools. Ask for room with balcony overlooking Merced River. **Amenities:** 🛗 🐕 🖳 🍽 A/C, cable TV w/movies. All units w/minibars, all w/terraces, all w/fireplaces, some w/whirlpools. Microwave. Ninety percent of rooms have full kitchenette, including utensils, pots and pans, and toaster. **Services:** 🐾 🛋 Babysitting. Minimal services at present. **Facilities:** 🎣 ⚿ 1 restaurant (bkfst and dinner only), 1 bar, whirlpool, playground, washer/dryer. Meeting space under construction. **Rates:** Peak (Mar 31–Nov 1) $85–$125 S or D; $120–$160 ste. Extra person $20. Children under age 12 stay free. Min stay special events. Lower rates off-season. Parking: Outdoor, free. MC, V.

LODGES

≣ Curry Village

Yosemite Valley, 95389; tel 209/252-4848. Nestled in the trees on the valley floor; simple and quaint. Raft rentals next door. **Rooms:** 600 rms. CI 2pm/CO 11am. Nonsmoking rms avail. Very basic accommodations—cabins (many with bath) and tent cabins. Separate central shower house facilities available. There is also a limited number of hotel rooms with private bath, including one suite. **Amenities:** No A/C, phone, or TV. Some units w/terraces. **Services:** 🐾 Children's program, babysitting. **Facilities:** 🎣 🚴 🏹 🚶 ⛵ ⚿ 3 restaurants, 1 bar, playground, washer/dryer. The Yosemite Mountaineering School, a bike rental shop, cross-country ski rentals, and an ice skating rink are all located in the complex. **Rates:** Peak (Apr–Oct) $39–$85 S or D. Extra person $5.50–$8.50. Children under age 12 stay free. Min stay wknds. Lower rates off-season. Parking: Outdoor, free. AE, CB, DC, DISC, EC, ER, JCB, MC, V.

≣ Tuolumne Meadows Lodge

Tioga Pass Rd, 95389; tel 209/252-4848. 30 mi W of Lee Vining; 60 mi E of Yosemite Valley on CA 120. A jump-off point for High Sierra vacations. Tent cabins are very basic, but you get a bed and access to a hot shower. Fishing, hiking, and rock climbing, as well as stables for scenic horseback rides, are nearby. **Rooms:** 69 cottages/villas. CI 3pm/CO 11am. No smoking. No electricity, only candles and wood stoves. Minimal furniture. Hot shower in public bathhouse. **Amenities:** No A/C, phone, or TV. **Services:** Children's program. **Facilities:** ⚓ 🎣 ⚅ 1 restaurant, 1 bar, washer/dryer. **Rates:** $35–$45 cottage/villa. Extra person $6. Min stay wknds. Parking: Outdoor, free. Accommodations often book up a year in advance. Closed Oct–May. AE, CB, DC, DISC, EC, ER, JCB, MC, V.

≣≣ Yosemite Lodge

CA 41/140, 95389; tel 209/252-4848. Top advantage is the location—right in the heart of the valley across from Yosemite Falls. Wild deer and coyote sometimes appear on hotel grounds. The wood-frame lodge is basic but appealing, with a comfortable, family feel. The best accommodations for the money on the valley floor. **Rooms:** 496 rms. CI 5pm/CO 11am. No smoking. Motel-type rooms or cabins; some share bath or use separate central bathhouse. Accommodations near street are quite noisy. **Amenities:** 🔒 🛁 Voice mail. No A/C or TV. Some units w/terraces. **Services:** 🛏 🛎 Babysitting. Friendly staff. **Facilities:** 🎿 🚲 🍴 🎣 🎿 🎱 🎣 50 ⚅ 🍴 3 restaurants, 1 bar (w/entertainment), day-care ctr, playground, washer/dryer. Huge outdoor swimming pool. Rafts available for rent. **Rates:** Peak (Apr–Oct) $55–$98 S or D. Extra person $15. Children under age 12 stay free. Min stay wknds. Lower rates off-season. Parking: Outdoor, free. AE, CB, DC, DISC, EC, ER, JCB, MC, V.

RESORT

≣≣≣ Ducey's on the Lake

Pines Village, N Shore, Bass Lake, PO Box 109, Bass Lake, 93604; tel 209/642-3121 or toll free 800/350-7463; fax 209/642-3902. 6 mi S of CA 41 exit. 44 acres. Beautiful lakeside facility, part of the Pines Resort complex that includes chalets and a conference center. This historic country inn offers a wide variety of leisure activities and is within easy driving distance of Yosemite National Park. **Rooms:** 20 rms and stes. CI 3pm/CO noon. Nonsmoking rms avail. Extra-large rooms boast Native American decorations and comfortable furnishings. Vaulted ceilings and beams were constructed from trees on property. Large bathrooms feature thick towels and bathrobes. Honeymoon suite available. **Amenities:** 🔒 🛁 📺 🍷 A/C, cable TV w/movies, refrig, VCR, bathrobes. All units w/terraces, all w/fireplaces, some w/whirlpools. All accommodations have microwaves. **Services:** ✗ 🛎 🛏 Twice-daily maid svce, babysitting. Summer camp for kids. **Facilities:** 🎿 ⛺ 🛶 🎣 🎿 ⚓² 🏊 🛥 200 🖥 ⚅ 3 restaurants (see "Restaurants" below), 1 bar, 1 beach (lake shore), board surfing, whirlpool, washer/dryer. Lakeside garden popular for weddings and family reunions. **Rates (CP):** Peak (Apr–Oct) $145–$215 S or D; $295–$315 ste. Extra person $15. Min stay wknds and special events. Lower rates off-season. Parking: Outdoor, free. Mid-week special discounts up to 40%. Holiday packages avail. Senior rates. CB, DC, DISC, JCB, MC, V.

RESTAURANTS 🍽

The Ahwahnee

In the Ahwahnee, Yosemite Valley; tel 209/372-1489. **Continental.** In the spirit of Yosemite, this dining room dazzles you with its scale: three-story high open-timbered ceilings, 18-foot-tall windows, and heavy wrought-iron chandeliers that look ready for some Errol Flynn swashbuckling. The dinner menu might feature filet mignon with blue cheese, or salmon with Dungeness crab béarnaise sauce; the apple pancakes are highly recommended for breakfast. Service, however, can be a bit inconsistent. During January and February, the restaurant presents a "visiting chefs" gourmet series. **FYI:** Reservations recommended. Children's menu. Jacket required. **Open:** Daily 7am–10pm. **Prices:** Main courses $15–$25. CB, DC, DISC, ER, MC, V. ♥ 🍴 VP ⚅

♣ Ducey's on the Lake

In the Pines Resort, Pines Village, N Shore, Bass Lake; tel 209/642-3121. **Californian/Sierra.** Beautifully appointed dining room features views of Bass Lake and surrounding mountains. Salmon Wellington and prime rib are specialties. Twilight special offers choice of three entrees plus dessert for $10.95. Christmas buffet and Thanksgiving very popular. **FYI:** Reservations recommended. Children's menu. Dress code. **Open:** Daily 5–9pm. **Prices:** Main courses $15–$22. CB, DC, DISC, MC, V. 📷 🏔 🛥 ⚅

ATTRACTIONS 📷

Yosemite Visitor Center

In addition to informative audiovisual programs and other exhibits relating to park history and activities, the visitor center can recommend tours of Yosemite's 216 miles of paved roads and point visitors toward such scenic points as the sequoia groves, granite summits, and waterfall bases. Dozens of daily activities may include lectures on photography, a ranger-led fireside discussion on bears, a guided luncheon hike to a waterfall, a geological history tour, or a puppet show with an environmental theme. There are fewer activities in the off-season. **Open:** Apr–May, daily 9am–6pm; June–Aug, daily 8am–8pm; Sept–Oct, daily 8am–6pm; Nov–Mar, daily 9am–5pm.

Tuolumne Meadows

At an elevation of 8,600 feet, Tuolumne Meadows is the largest alpine meadow in the High Sierras and a gateway to the High Country. Closed in winter, it's 55 miles from the valley by way of highly scenic Big Oak Flat and Tioga Roads. A walk through this natural alpine garden makes a delightful day's excursion. In summer the park operates a large campground here, with a full-scale naturalist program.

Happy Isles Nature Center

This nature center is another gateway to the High Country, with trailheads for the John Muir Trail and for Vernal and Nevada Falls (the Mist Trail). Accessible by shuttle bus, the center can provide information about hiking to Nevada Falls and Mirror Lake.

Mariposa Grove

The largest of Yosemite's three groves of giant sequoias, Mariposa Grove has hundreds of trees, more than 200 of which measure 10 feet or more in diameter. Among them is the **Grizzly Giant,** more than 34 feet in diameter at its base and 209 feet tall. Private vehicles can drive to the entrance of the grove, beyond which visitors may hike or board a free shuttle bus. Not to be confused with the town of Mariposa, the grove is 35 miles south of the valley.

Glacier Point

Offering a sweeping 180-degree panorama of the High Sierras and a breathtaking view from 3,200 feet above the valley, Glacier Point looks out over Nevada and Vernal Falls, the Merced River, and the snow-covered Sierra peaks of Yosemite's backcountry. The approach from the Badger Pass intersection (closed in winter) winds through verdant red-fir and pine forest and meadow. Many fine trails lead back down to the valley floor.

Badger Pass Ski Area

Badger Pass Ski Area, located 23 miles outside the valley, opened in 1935, making it the oldest ski resort in California. The terrain is mostly geared to intermediate-level skiiers, with about 35% of the trails marked for beginners and 15% for experts. Instructors offer beginner and refresher lessons, as well as lessons for children. Facilities include a triple chairlift, three double chairlifts, and a rope tow for beginners. The slopes are open November to Easter (weather permitting).

Yosemite also encompasses 90 miles of **cross-country skiing trails,** 22 miles of which are machine-groomed track, set several times weekly from Badger Pass to Glacier Point. Skiiers can stay overnight at the Glacier Point Ski Hut or at the Ostrander Lake Ski Hut. For further information contact Badger Pass Ski Area, Yosemite National Park, CA 95389 (tel 209/372-1330 or call the Badger Pass Snow Phone, 209/372-1338).

Yountville

Located at the center of the Napa Valley winegrowing region, this is the site of the first vineyard in the valley, and many wineries are still located nearby. Both casual and posh and very walkable, it also has several interesting shops and restaurants. **Information:** Yountville Chamber of Commerce, PO Box 2064, Yountville 94599 (tel 707/944-0904).

HOTELS 🏨

🏠🏠🏠 Napa Valley Lodge

2230 Madison St, 94599; tel 707/944-2468 or toll free 800/368-2468; fax 707/944-9362. At Washington St off CA 29. Park across the street has a children's playground. **Rooms:** 55 rms and stes. CI 3pm/CO noon. Nonsmoking rms avail. Spacious and comfortable with wicker furniture and vaulted ceilings. **Amenities:** 🏠 ♨ 📺 🍷 A/C, cable TV w/movies, refrig, bathrobes. All units w/minibars, all w/terraces, some w/fireplaces. **Services:** 🚗 🛎 🍴 Masseur, babysitting. Afternoon tea, plus wine tasting in the evening. **Facilities:** 🏊 🏋️ 🏄 💻 ♿ Sauna, whirlpool. **Rates (CP):** Peak (May–Nov) $138–$158 S or D; $165–$210 ste. Extra person $10. Min stay peak and wknds. Lower rates off-season. Parking: Outdoor, free. Golf and romance packages avail. AE, CB, DC, DISC, MC, V.

🏠🏠🏠 Vintage Inn

6541 Washington St, 94599; tel 707/944-1112 or toll free 800/351-1133; fax 707/944-1617. Yountville exit off CA 29, E on California Blvd to Washington St, turn left. Hotel services are offered in an inn-like setting, with attractive gardens and separate units. Located within walking distance of shops and restaurants. Excellent for small business groups. **Rooms:** 80 rms and stes; 4 cottages/villas. CI 4pm/CO noon. Nonsmoking rms avail. Spacious, well-maintained rooms have quality furniture. **Amenities:** 🏠 ♨ 📺 🍷 A/C, cable TV w/movies, refrig, voice mail, bathrobes. All units w/terraces, all w/fireplaces, all w/whirlpools. **Services:** ✕ 🍽 🚗 🛎 🍴 Twice-daily maid svce, babysitting. Expanded continental breakfast included in rate. Limo service for touring available. **Facilities:** 🏊 🚲 🏄² 🎱 ♿ 1 restaurant, 1 bar, whirlpool. 60-foot lap pool. **Rates (BB):** Peak (Apr–Sept) $150–$300 S; $160–$325 D; $220–$275 cottage/villa. Extra person $25. Min stay peak and wknds. Lower rates off-season. Parking: Outdoor, free. AE, CB, DC, DISC, MC, V.

RESTAURANTS 🍽

Brix

7377 St Helena Hwy (CA 29); tel 707/944-BRIX (2749). **Pacific Rim.** Intriguing Pacific Rim cuisine from Tod Michael Kawachi, previously of Roy's in Maui. The signature appetizer is Nori rare-seared ahi tuna with wasabi aioli. Popular main courses include the potato-crusted halibut, and the Thai pesto-smoked rack of lamb with spicy peanut sauce and Zinfandel glaze. The attractive dining room has tall windows looking out to the restaurant's kitchen garden and vineyards; there's also an excellent wine shop on the premises. **FYI:** Reservations recommended. Jazz/piano. Dress code. **Open:** Lunch daily 11am–5pm; dinner Sun–Thurs 5–9:30pm, Fri–Sat 5–10pm. **Prices:** Main courses $12–$20. AE, MC, V. ♿

$ ✦ The Diner

6476 Washington St; tel 707/944-2626. Yountville exit off CA 29. **Mexican/American.** An authentic diner in what was once the town's Greyhound bus depot, complete with the original counter. Crowds flock in for the hefty portions of comfort food. Features freshly baked breads and homemade desserts. In addition to great breakfasts, they offer burgers, roast chicken, and Mexican specialties such as quesadillas and carne barbacoa. **FYI:** Reservations not accepted. Children's menu. Beer and wine only. **Open:** Breakfast Tues–Sun 8am–3pm; lunch Tues–Sun 11am–3pm; dinner Tues–Sun 5:30–9pm. Closed 1–2 weeks before Christmas. **Prices:** Main courses $6–$13. No CC. 🎫 &

♣ Domaine Chandon

In Domaine Chandon Winery, California Dr; tel 707/944-2892. Yountville exit off CA 29. **Californian/French.** Open, light, and airy, with large windows looking out to gardens and the vineyards beyond. Known for elegant dining, with selections such as venison tournedos, grilled salmon wrapped in pancetta, and roast rack of lamb with goat-cheese potato gratin. Outdoor terrace is open for lunch in nice weather. **FYI:** Reservations recommended. Jacket required. Beer and wine only. **Open:** Peak (May–Nov) lunch daily 11:30am–2:30pm; dinner Wed–Sun 6–9:30pm. Closed 1st 2 weeks in Jan. **Prices:** Main courses $24–$27. AE, DC, DISC, MC, V. 🖤 🍴 &

♣ French Laundry

6640 Washington St; tel 707/944-2380. At Creek St. **Californian/French.** Acclaimed chef/owner Thomas Keller enthralls diners at the valley's most romantic eatery, housed in a storybook stone cottage bowered in flowers and surrounded by brick walkways. Menus change daily, but always reinterpret classic cooking: poached oysters with pearl tapioca and Sevruga caviar and filet of veal with sweetbread ravioli are typical examples. Desserts are showstoppers, especially the Valhrona bitter-chocolate cake, and the bravos continue for *mignardise* ("little delicacies") such as cookies and miniature crème brûlée. **FYI:** Reservations recommended. Dress code. Beer and wine only. **Open:** Lunch Fri–Sun noon–1:30pm; dinner daily 5:30–9:30pm. Closed 1 week in Jan. **Prices:** Prix fixe $57–$70. AE, MC, V. 🖤 &

✦ Mustards Grill

7399 St Helena Hwy; tel 707/944-2424. **New American.** Terrific food at extremely reasonable prices in a lively California-style bistro accented by black-and-white marble floors, brown wainscoting, and appealing original art. Choices might include yellowtail jack with Dijon crème fraîche, or grilled Mongolian pork chop with mashed potatoes. The wine list is spectacular, and moderately priced. **FYI:** Reservations recommended. Children's menu. **Open:** Daily 11:30am–10pm. **Prices:** Main courses $11–$19. CB, DC, DISC, MC, V. &

Piatti

6480 Washington St; tel 707/944-2070. Yountville exit off CA 29. **Californian/Italian.** This comfortable, country-style restaurant has French doors opening onto a flower-filled courtyard. Olive oil on the tables, rustic wood chairs, and stucco walls painted with food-related designs establish a Mediterranean mood. Open kitchen with wood-burning stove. Ravioli filled with ricotta and spinach, homemade Italian sausages, imaginative pizzas. Daily specials and seasonal dishes. **FYI:** Reservations recommended. **Open:** Peak (June–Nov) Sun–Thurs 11:30am–10pm, Fri–Sat 11:30am–11pm. **Prices:** Main courses $8–$17. AE, MC, V. 🖤 &

ATTRACTION 🏛

Domaine Chandon

California Dr; tel 707/944-2280. Free guided tours illustrate the making of sparkling wines. A small gallery in the visitor center houses artifacts depicting the history of champagne. The restaurant here (*see also* "Restaurants" above) is excellent. Wines are sold by the bottle or glass, and are accompanied by hors d'oeuvres. **Open:** Peak (May–Oct) daily 11am–5pm. Reduced hours off-season. **Free**

Yreka

Yreka (pronounced wye-RE-ka) is one of the few sizable towns in the far north-central reaches of California. The town began as a gold rush settlement, and many historic buildings have been preserved. **Information:** Siskiyou County Visitors Bureau, 110 S Oregon #A, Yreka 96097 (tel 916/842-7857 or toll free 800/446-7475).

MOTELS 🏨

🛏🛏 Klamath Motor Lodge

1111 S Main St, 96097; tel 916/842-2751. Central Yreka exit off I-5; ¾ mi S. Family-run business since 1962. Many repeat customers. **Rooms:** 28 rms and stes. CI 2pm/CO 11am. Nonsmoking rms avail. **Amenities:** 🛁 ⚏ 🖥 A/C, cable TV w/movies, refrig. **Services:** 🍴 **Facilities:** 🛗 **Rates:** Peak (June–Sept) $40–$45 S; $45–$50 D; $75 ste. Extra person $3. Lower rates off-season. Parking: Outdoor, free. AE, DC, DISC, MC, V.

🛏 Thunderbird Lodge

526 S Main St, 96097; tel 916/842-4404 or toll free 800/554-4339; fax 916/841-0439. Central Yreka exit off I-5; ¼ mi S. Property has been upgraded by new owners. **Rooms:** 44 rms. CI 11am/CO 11am. Nonsmoking rms avail. **Amenities:** 🛁 🖥 A/C, cable TV w/movies. **Services:** 🚗 ⚏ 🍴 ⚏ **Facilities:** 🛗 **Rates:** Peak (June–Sept) $33–$37 S; $36–$42 D. Extra person $4. Lower rates off-season. Parking: Outdoor, free. AE, CB, DC, DISC, EC, JCB, MC, V.

ATTRACTIONS

Siskiyou County Museum
910 S Main St; tel 916/842-3836. Exhibits in this museum interpret the history of Siskiyou County from prehistoric times, through the Gold Rush era, and into the present. Topics include local Native American cultures, fur trapping, mining, settlement, lumbering, agriculture, and 20th-century themes. The research library contains extensive collections of photographs, manuscripts, newspapers, and other material available for public use. Gift shop.

On the grounds is a 2½-acre **Outdoor Museum,** open in summer only, which includes a pioneer cabin, miner's cabin, blacksmith's shop, a church, and an operating general store. **Open:** Tues–Sat 9am–5pm. **$**

Yreka Western Railroad
300 E Miner St; tel 916/842-4146. The Blue Goose Excursion train departs from Yreka Depot on a three-hour tour through the scenic Shasta Valley. The 100-year-old historic short line railroad crosses the Shasta River, provides scenic views of 14,162-foot Mount Shasta, and crosses through cattle ranch lands first established in the 1850s. The train makes a one-hour stop at the historic cattle town of Montague, where riders may disembark and explore the town before making the return trip to Yreka. **Open:** Peak (mid-June–Labor Day) Wed–Sun; reduced days off-season. Departures at 10am. **$$$**

Yucca Valley

See also Joshua Tree National Park

INN

Oasis of Eden Inn & Suites
56377 Twentynine Palms Hwy, 92284; tel 619/365-6321; fax 619/365-9592. Property features a small garden and hand-painted murals outdoors. **Rooms:** 40 rms, stes, and effic. CI 2pm/CO 11am. Nonsmoking rms avail. Guests can stay in one of the theme accommodations, including the Orient, Ancient Rome, the Deep South, Art Deco, and Russia rooms. **Amenities:** A/C, cable TV w/movies. Some units w/terraces, some w/whirlpools. **Services:** Babysitting. **Facilities:** Whirlpool, guest lounge. **Rates (CP):** Peak (Feb–June) $65 S or D; $107 ste; $96 effic. Extra person $5. Lower rates off-season. Higher rates for special events/hols. Parking: Outdoor, free. AE, DC, DISC, MC, V.

RESTAURANT

★ Pappy & Harriet's
Pioneertown Rd, Pioneertown; tel 619/365-5956. CA 62 off I-10. **Barbecue/Tex-Mex.** Set in an old western movie location, this locally popular restaurant is an assemblage of rough-hewn boards, off-kilter beer signs, and license plates from around the country. Talk at the bar centers around racing new Harleys and '65 Mustangs. Portions are enormous—the iced tea comes in a mason jar and the hamburger measures as wide as a soup bowl. Country and western music on weekends. **FYI:** Reservations recommended. **Open:** Wed–Thurs 5–11pm, Fri–Sat 11am–2am, Sun 8am–11pm. **Prices:** Main courses $7–$17. AE, DISC, MC, V.

NEVADA

From Lady Luck to Mother Nature

Glittering hotel casinos and hauntingly beautiful ghost towns, parched deserts strewn with bleached bones, and Lake Tahoe, a lonely mountain jewel whose azure waters are turned to gold by the setting sun. These are the contrasting images of an appealing state that begs discovery.

Less celebrated in guidebooks than California, Nevada shares many attributes with its larger neighbor. Lake Tahoe and Death Valley National Monument straddle their common border, while California's mountain ranges create the rain shadow that dictates Nevada's dry climate. And Californians are irresistibly drawn to Las Vegas as well as Reno, the town that bills itself "The Biggest Little City in the World."

Gambling is Nevada's biggest attraction and its biggest industry, grossing over $1 billion a year. The two main nerve centers for this activity and its accompanying distractions are Las Vegas–Laughlin and Reno–Lake Tahoe: dizzying kaleidoscopes of neon lights, dazzling marquees, and luxury hotels. The Mormons who first settled Las Vegas would be aghast at the bare-skinned cabaret acts and perpetual-motion gambling that has been going on since Nevada legalized gaming in 1931.

The tinsel trimmings of Las Vegas, Reno, Lake Tahoe, and Laughlin— the state's fastest growing resort area on the banks of the Colorado River—have almost eclipsed another Nevada. NV 50, designated by *Life* magazine as the "loneliest road in America," provides a sense of the days when covered wagons battled their way across the sun-baked region; it, and I-80–US 40, gives access to rugged canyons and ghost towns whose existence can hardly be imagined from the road.

Though hundreds of 19th-century mining towns have all but vanished from the Nevada landscape, America's nostalgia for

Frommer's

#1

things historical has made those that remain—such as Rhyolite, Goldfield, Hamilton, and Rawhide—regular stops for caravans of tourists. When winter returns the crowds drift away, leaving the ghostly towns to their few inhabitants.

Much about Nevada belies its sere, stark image. America's seventh-largest state (but 47th in population) even produces wines in the Pahrump Valley, and agriculture flourishes where irrigation has been introduced. Ranching, too, is a mainstay of the economy—sheep and cattle graze some 60 million acres. The annual National Basque Festival, the West's largest gathering of Basque-Americans, attests to the enduring influence of the Basque shepherds who settled the rangelands during the last century.

At the western edge of the state, the shoulders of the Sierra Nevada are clad in emerald forest and in winter by a thick pelt of snow—a far cry from the furnace deserts of southeast Nevada. Glassy blue Lake Tahoe has no difficulty living up to its reputation as a skier's paradise. In the spring the snow melts and Tahoe becomes a perfect place for boating, hiking, mountain biking, windsurfing, and merely relaxing. Carson City, the gingerbread-trimmed state capital in the lee of the Sierra Nevada, also provides myriad opportunities for year-round entertainment.

Fun Facts

- Las Vegas—"sin city"—has more churches per capita than any other city.
- Northern Nevada's Highway 50, which runs from Ely in the east to Fernley in the west, was chosen as the "Loneliest Road in America" by Life *magazine.*
- Nevada is the driest of the 50 states, measuring an average of only 9 inches of rainfall annually.
- There is enough water in Lake Tahoe to cover the state of California at a depth of 35.5 centimeters.
- The stage in the Ziegfeld Room in Reno is reportedly the largest in the world—176 feet long. It has three main elevators, each capable of raising 1,200 show girls; two turntables that measure almost 63 feet in circumference; and 800 spotlights.

A Brief History

The New Frontier The Nevada region was *terra incognita*—unknown land—to all but the Paiute, Washoe, and Shoshone Indians until well into the 19th century. Only a Spanish priest, Father Francisco Garces, and a handful of brave adventurers and fur traders had entered this forbidding territory during its term as a Spanish, then Mexican possession. Explorer John Fremont, whose expeditions in 1843 and 1845 were led by legendary scout Kit Carson, made the first official report of the region, which was then under the Mexican flag. The report came out in 1848, the same year the Treaty of Guadalupe Hidalgo made Nevada a US possession.

The first permanent non-Indian settlement—Genoa, a Mormon trading post in the Carson Valley—was established in 1850. In 1855, the Mormons also established a mission fort at a lonesome outpost known as "the meadows"—Las Vegas. However, the Mormon influence was short-lived: In 1857, when relations with the federal government grew strained, Brigham Young, head of the Mormon church, pulled his followers back to Salt Lake City.

Hardy pioneers were already passing through Nevada in growing numbers en route to the California gold fields. Today I-80–US 40 marks the route they traveled through a bleak landscape of mountains and deserts along the 500-mile California Trail.

Boom or Bust In 1850 gold was discovered along the Carson River—the first hint that Nevada was itself a mineral-rich state. Just how rich did not become apparent until 1859 and the discovery of the Comstock Lode, one of the most fabulous finds in history. The strike spawned Nevada's first mining boom, a human migration that nearly rivaled the California Gold Rush. The Comstock produced $1 billion worth of silver and gold, enriching the US Treasury during the Civil War and giving Nevada territorial status in March 1861. Nevada became the Union's 36th state on October 31, 1864.

Mining towns sprouted overnight, including Virginia City, which briefly bloomed as the West's second-largest city. Samuel Clemens, who worked as a miner before finding his fortune as a writer with the pen name Mark Twain, wrote that it "was no place for a Presbyterian and I did not remain one very long."

A decade later, bust followed boom. Then in the 1870s, a second boom—the "Big Bonanza"—made millionaires who added grandiose mansions to the scene. Reno and Carson City are still studded with the stately Victorian homes of mining tycoons.

When the boom ended in the 1880s, Nevada's population dwindled. At the turn of the century, another gold and silver mining strike provided a third lease on life before it, too, collapsed.

The Richest Strike of All To even out the boom-and-bust cycle, irrigation channels were laid and farms established in the larger northern valleys. And the state legalized gambling (and liberalized divorce and marriage laws) in 1931 to net part of the resulting purse. Today almost 40 percent of the state's revenues are derived from tax revenues on gambling, and the challenge for visitors seems often to be in avoiding the ever-present lures of Lady Luck.

Monument extends into Nevada. The parched deserts of the southland are corrugated with range upon range of desert mountains in hues of rose, gray, and purple. From their peaks it is possible to see for a hundred miles in every direction without any signs of habitation. Below, in the valleys, conditions are so arid that camels were used in the 1860s to carry salt. Today, the only movement you are likely to see is that of deer and wild mustangs roaming the impassable bluffs.

A Closer Look
GEOGRAPHY

Nevada lies in the bowl of the arid **Great Basin.** It is penned in to the west by California's evergreen-forested Sierra Nevada, which rise to 13,143 feet at **Boundary Peak** just inside the Nevada border; and to the east by the wrinkled old **Wasatch Range,** which runs north-to-south through Idaho and Utah. In the southeastern part of the state, parched valleys drop to only 490 feet above sea level near the **Colorado River,** where the Hoover Dam lies wedged into the Nevada–Arizona state line.

Most of the state's other rivers would elsewhere be called streams, for much of the tortured landscape receives as little as 3 inches of rain a year. These meager rivers flow inward, where their precious waters are impounded by dams; in the northeast, they escape north and eventually link up with the mighty **Snake River.**

Lakes are few and far between. Surpassing them all is man-made **Lake Mead,** formed by the **Hoover Dam** in Nevada's southeast corner. Other natural lakes are scattered like turquoise gemstones throughout the northwest corner, where juniper and piñon trees clothe the land. Pungent sagebrush covers much of the rest of the state—the ubiquitous plant even adorns the state flag.

To the south, a corner of **Death Valley National**

DRIVING DISTANCES

Reno

30 mi N of Carson City
58 mi NE of South Lake Tahoe, CA
158 mi NE of Sacramento, CA
227 mi NE of San Francisco, CA
289 mi SW of Elko
445 mi NW of Las Vegas
473 mi NW of Los Angeles, CA
554 mi SW of Ogden, UT

Las Vegas

228 mi NW of San Bernardino, CA
241 mi NW of Flagstaff, AZ
265 mi NE of Los Angeles, CA
400 mi SW of Wendover, UT
445 mi SE of Reno
447 mi SE of Carson City
469 mi SE of Elko
577 mi SE of San Francisco, CA

Elko

108 mi W of Wendover, UT
289 mi NE of Reno
308 mi NE of Carson City
336 mi NE of South Lake Tahoe, CA
423 mi NE of Sacramento, CA
469 mi NW of Las Vegas
545 mi NE of San Francisco, CA
569 mi NE of Barstow, CA

CLIMATE

Nevada's climate varies widely from north to south: average temperatures vary from 70°F in the south to 45° in the north. (On the fringes of Death Valley, temperatures can climb to 120° in summer; in the Sierra Nevada, they can drop to 40° below zero in winter, when the cooling altitudes of northeast Nevada may also be tinted with snow.) Everywhere rain is sparse. At an elevation of 2,174 feet, Las Vegas has comfortably cool nights, even after the hottest days. While summer temperatures in Las Vegas can soar to over 100°, the average winter temperature is only 48°.

In the deserts, dust storms can blow up suddenly. If driving, pull over and let the tempest pass. Be cautious, too, of flash floods triggered by sudden torrential rain.

WHAT TO PACK

In summer, hot weather dictates cool cottons throughout the state, though a warm sweater or jacket will be required for nights at higher elevations. In winter, bring warm clothing—even the southern deserts can be surprisingly cool. You may safely forgo raingear.

Casual clothes are fine in most casinos. A large percentage of visitors to Las Vegas and Reno favor sports jackets and cocktail dresses at night.

TOURIST INFORMATION

The Nevada Commission on Tourism publishes *Nevada,* a bimonthly tourism magazine. For subscriptions ($15.95 per year) contact Nevada Magazines Subscriptions, PO Box 726, Mount Morris, IL 61054 (tel toll free 800/669-1002). For information on events, accommodations, and attractions statewide, contact the Nevada Commission on Tourism, Capitol Complex, Carson City, NV 89710 (tel toll free 800/NEVADA-8). The Nevada Commission on Tourism also maintains a Web page (http://travelnevada.com) with information about the state.

A catalog and price list of maps can be obtained by writing to the Nevada Department of Transportation, Map Section, Rm 206, 1263 S Stewart St, Carson City, NV 89712.

For information on Las Vegas, contact the Las Vegas Convention and Visitors Authority, 3150 Paradise Rd, Las Vegas, NV 89109 (tel 702/892-0711). The Reno-Sparks Convention and Visitors Authority, 4590 S Virginia St, Reno, NV 89502 (tel 702/827-7600) and the Carson City Convention and Visitors Bureau, 1900 S Carson St, Carson City, NV 89701 (tel 702/687-7410) can provide information on the Reno-Tahoe area.

AVG MONTHLY TEMPS (°F) & RAINFALL (IN)		
	Las Vegas	**Elko**
Jan	45/0.5	23.4/11.3
Feb	51/0.5	29.6/7.4
Mar	56/0.4	36.5/6.6
Apr	64/0.2	44.1/3.4
May	74/0.3	52.7/1.7
June	85/0.1	60.9/0.7
July	91/0.4	69.8/0.4
Aug	89/0.5	67.1/0.4
Sept	80/0.3	57.6/0.4
Oct	68/0.2	46.9/0.7
Nov	55/0.4	35.2/0.8
Dec	46/0.4	25.7/1.1

DRIVING RULES AND REGULATIONS

Minimum age for drivers is 16. Unless otherwise noted, the speed limit on Nevada highways is 55 mph and 65 mph on rural interstate freeways.

Laws against drunk driving are strictly enforced. Note that it is illegal to carry an open container of alcohol in your car.

Use of seat belts is mandatory for all passengers, and children under five years or under 40 pounds must be secured in an approved child safety seat. Motorcyclists must wear a helmet. Auto insurance is mandatory.

Right turns are allowed after stops at a red light.

For road conditions, call 702/793-1313 (northern Nevada) or 702/486-3116 (Las Vegas). Listen for flash-flood advisories on your car radio. Motorists are advised to inquire locally about road conditions before traveling on unpaved roads. Check water and fluid levels; temperatures can be extreme and service stations in some areas are few and far between.

RENTING A CAR

In addition to local car rental companies, all of the major car rental firms have offices in Reno, Carson City, and Las Vegas. Minimum-age requirements range from 19 to 25. Collision damage waiver (CDW) protection is sold separately (check with your credit card or insurance company to see if you are already covered).

- **Alamo** (tel toll free 800/327-9633)
- **Avis** (tel 800/331-1212)
- **Budget** (tel 800/527-0700)
- **Dollar** (tel 800/421-6878)
- **Hertz** (tel 800/654-3131)
- **National** (tel 800/328-4567)
- **Thrifty** (tel 800/367-2277)

ESSENTIALS

Area Code: The area code for Nevada is 702.

Emergencies: Call 911 from anywhere in the state for emergency police, fire, and ambulance services.

Liquor Laws: Alcoholic beverages may be purchased by anyone 21 years or older with proof of age.

Gambling: Gambling is limited to adults 21 or over.

Smoking: While Nevada has not enacted strict regulations as California has, the state does prohibit smoking in public buildings and requires most restaurants and certain businesses to have nonsmoking areas.

Taxes: Nevada's statewide sales tax is 6.75%. Some cities and counties impose an additional tax of 0.25 to 0.50%.

Time Zone: Nevada is in the Pacific time zone (GMT minus 8 hours), 3 hours behind New York. Daylight savings time is observed.

Best of the State

WHAT TO SEE AND DO

National & State Parks Nevada has 24 state parks, three federally protected areas, plus two national forests: Toiyabe and Humboldt, both with 2.5 million acres. One of the most intriguing options is **Death Valley National Monument,** perhaps America's most eerie wasteland. It's reached via Beatty or Pahrump, and visitors can explore many fascinating scenic locations, including the Ubehebe Crater and Furnace Creek ranch. Formed 150 million years ago, **Valley of Fire State Park,** 15 miles southwest of Overton, has been sculpted by wind and rain into spectacular domes, spirals, beehives, and other unusual formations. **Berlin-Ichthyosaur State Park,** on the western slopes of the Shoshone Mountains, 23 miles east of Gabbs, yields the fossils of huge fish dinosaurs. Berlin is also a ghost town. And to see the world's oldest and largest groves of ancient bristlecone pines, a glacier, Lehman Caves, and magnificent Wheeler Peak (13,163 feet), go to the 77,100-acre **Great Basin National Park,** near Ely and the Utah border.

Natural Wonders **Pyramid Lake,** one of the premier sights in Nevada, is a vast prehistoric lake that once covered much of northwestern Nevada. Its receding level has revealed wonderfully old formations of porous tufa rock, which rise above the surface of the lake's deep-blue water. In Great Basin National Park, **Lehman Caves** proffer labyrinthine corridors and colorful monuments: stalactites, stalagmites, and helictites. Just 20 minutes west of Las Vegas, **Red Rock Canyon** displays a natural "art gallery" with its amazing arches, natural bridges, and massive sculptures of colored rock strata.

Wildlife There's everything from deer, elk, and waterfowl to mustangs seen at full gallop with their shaggy manes and tails streaming. Many lakes are winter breeding grounds for migratory waterfowl; **Anaho Island,** in Pyramid Lake, a federal bird sanctuary popular with white pelicans, is worth more than a flying visit. **Desert National Wildlife Range,** near Las Vegas, protects a large colony of desert bighorn sheep.

Family Favorites **Boomtown's Family Funland,** located west of Reno, features a high-tech motion theater, miniature golf course, and carousel. **Wet 'n Wild,** a water theme park on the Las Vegas Strip, is lots of fun and a good place to beat the heat; it features a variety of water slides, pools, and rides. For the world's only indoor double-loop roller coaster, head to **Grand Slam Canyon** in Las Vegas, a five-acre amusement park offering water thrills, animated dinosaurs, and more. The Las Vegas **MGM Grand Hotel and Theme Park,** the world's largest resort, boasts 33 acres of rides and attractions. For a change of pace, kids may want to explore the **Lied Discovery Children's Museum,** which is designed for hands-on learning about science, art, and other subjects.

Museums The **Nevada State Museum,** housed in the former US Mint in Carson City, offers a look into the Silver State's rich past. Visitors can see the machinery that stamped $50 million in silver and gold coins as well as a life-size ghost town, a replica of an underground mine, and Indian artifacts. Also in Carson City, the **Nevada State Railway Museum** has two beautifully restored steam locomotives as well as other railroad equipment. The **Western Folklife Center** in Elko features exhibits of cowboy gear, western and Native American folk art, and demonstrations of old-fashioned folk dances. Fascinating in the extreme is the **Guinness World of Records Museum,** in Las Vegas, with three-dimensional displays of superlatives from around the globe. The **Liberace Museum,** also in Las Vegas, exhibits the expensive cars, elaborate gemstone capes, candelabras, and other memorabilia that helped make the pianist/entertainer a legend. And over 200 antique, classic, and special-interest vehicles, including Adolf Hitler's 1939 Mercedes-Benz and President Eisenhower's 1952 Imperial, are on view at the **Imperial Palace Auto Collection** in Las Vegas.

Historical Buildings & Sites The **Nevada State Capitol** in Carson City, built in 1870 of native sandstone, has hallways of Alaskan marble and polished-wood wall panels. One of the most famous silver boomtowns in America—**Virginia City**—offers museums, mine tours, a cemetery, and restored shops and saloons. Strolling its streets, it is easy to imagine days when lucky miners ate caviar and drank French champagne. **Eureka,** the most picturesque of Nevada's 19th-century mining towns and also its best preserved, has fine brick-and-stone Victorian buildings highlighted by the still-used Eureka County Courthouse, which has a pressed-tin ceiling, original wainscoting, and chandeliers. West of Ely, the **Ward Charcoal Ovens Historic State Monument** lets you peer into 30-foot-tall beehive-shaped ovens that in the 1870s and 1880s turned piñon logs into fuel. The **Old Las Vegas Mormon Fort,** part of the original 1855 Mormon settlement, is the oldest standing Anglo-American structure in Nevada. Today a ghost town, **Rhyolite State Historical Park** was a thriving mining town in the first decade of the 20th century; the photogenic ruins of once-substantial buildings make the town worth a visit. Also of interest is the refurbished **Bowers Mansion,** 20 miles south of Reno, built in 1864 by the first Comstock Lode millionaire.

Parks & Gardens The **Ethel M Chocolate Factory and Cactus Garden,** at Henderson, boasts one of the most complete collections of western cactus plants in the country, while the **Wilbur D May Arboretum and Botanical Garden,** in Reno, has theme gardens displaying native and ornamental plants.

Architecture The **Hoover Dam** has an elevator that whisks you down 528 feet to the dam's concrete innards for a guided tour of one of the world's great engineering marvels. And the tallest observation tower in America is the **Stratosphere Tower** in Las Vegas.

EVENTS AND FESTIVALS

- **Chrysler Celebrity Ski Classic,** Heavenly Ski Resort. January. Call 702/586-7000 for information.
- **Best in the Desert Grand Prix Motorcycle Race,** Mesquite. Late January. Call 702/346-5295.
- **Las Vegas International Marathon,** Las Vegas. February. Call 702/731-2115.
- **Hoover Dam Square Dance Weekend,** Boulder City. March. Call 702/293-4918.
- **Airfest,** Las Vegas. March. Call 702/434-4122.
- **Rhyolite Living History Festival,** Beatty. March. Call 702/553-2424.
- **Mesquite Days Invitational Rodeo,** Aravada Ranch Rodeo Grounds. May. Call 702/346-5295.
- **Silver State Square and Round Dance Festival,** Reno. May. Call 702/322-0027.
- **Senior Pro Rodeo,** Winnemucca. May. Call 702/623-2225.
- **Silver State Classic Car Show,** Pioche. May. Call 702/962-5544.
- **Desert Oasis Bluegrass Festival,** Fallon. May. Call 702/423-2544.
- **National Basque Festival,** Winnemucca. June. Call 702/623-5071.
- **Cowboy Music Gathering,** Elko. June. Call 702/738-7135.
- **Best in the Desert Motorcycle Race,** Ely. June. Call 702/289-8877.
- **Sports Cars and All That Jazz,** Reno. July. Call 702/786-3030.
- **Nevada State Fair,** Reno. August. Call 702/688-5767.
- **Las Vegas Jaycees State Fair,** Las Vegas. September. Call 702/457-8832.
- **Great Reno Balloon Race,** Reno. September. Call 702/829-2810.
- **Virginia City International Camel Race,** Virginia City. September. Call 702/847-0311.
- **National Championship Air Races,** Reno. September. Call 702/972-6663.
- **Numanga Indian Days Celebration,** Reno-Sparks Indian Colony. September. Call 702/329-2936.
- **Art in the Park,** Boulder City. October. Call 702/293-2034.
- **Las Vegas Balloon Classic,** Las Vegas. October. Call 702/434-0848.
- **Nevada Day Celebration and Parade,** Carson City. October. Call 702/882-2600.
- **Nellis Air Force Base Open House,** Las Vegas. November. Call 702/652-2750.
- **Owyhee Reservation Indian Day Pow Wow,** November. Call 702/757-3211.
- **National Finals Rodeo,** Las Vegas. December. Call 702/731-2115.
- **Parade of Lights,** Boulder City. December. Call 702/293-2034.

For a free copy of the *Nevada Events Guide,* contact the Nevada Commission on Tourism, Capitol Complex, Carson City, NV 89710 (tel toll free 800/NEVADA-8).

SPECTATOR SPORTS

Baseball The **Las Vegas Stars,** an affiliate of the San Diego Padres in the Class AAA Pacific Coast League, play home games at Cashman Field (tel 702/386-7200) in North Las Vegas. The **Reno Chuckers** play ball at Moana Stadium (tel 702/829-7896).

Basketball The **Runnin' Rebels** of the **University of Nevada–Las Vegas** (UNLV), a frequent Top 25 team in college polls, play their NCAA home games at the 18,500-seat Thomas & Mack Center (tel 702/895-3900) in Las Vegas.

Boxing Professional boxing matches, including championship bouts, are held throughout the year at several venues in Las Vegas, among them Caesar's Palace (tel 702/731-7110 or toll free 800/634-6698); and the Hilton Center at the Las Vegas Hilton (tel 702/732-5755 or toll free 800/222-5361). Also, the Mirage (tel 702/791-7111 or toll free 800/627-6667) features championship boxing matches several times a year, as does the Riviera (tel 702/734-5110 or toll free 800/634-6753). The Sahara (tel 702/737-2111) hosts occasional ESPN-televised matches.

Football The **UNLV Rebels** of college football take to the gridiron at the Sam Boyd Silver Bowl (tel 702/895-3761) on the UNLV campus; this is also the stadium where the Las Vegas Football Bowl is held each December.

Rodeo The **Reno Rodeo,** held each June at the Livestock Events Center (tel 702/329-3877) in Reno, is considered one of the top 10 rodeos in the country and includes such standard events as steer wrestling and calf-roping. The Thomas & Mack Arena in Las Vegas hosts the world championship of rodeo, the **National Finals Rodeo,** in early December (tel 702/731-2115). The 15 top money winners in the country compete in bull-riding, saddle-bronco riding, and other events for almost $3 million in prize money.

ACTIVITIES A TO Z

What Nevada lacks in spectator sports it more than makes up for in participatory sports and activities at all times of year. Lake Mead National Recreation Area and Mt Charleston serve Las Vegas, and Lake Tahoe serves the Reno–Carson City area for those eager for the outdoor life.

Bicycling Nevada is mountain-biking territory *par excellence.* The annual One Awesome Tour: Bike Ride Across Nevada (OAT-BRAN) is held in late September. For information contact TGFT Productions, Box 5123, Stateline, NV 89449 (tel 702/588-9658). For information on bicycling in general, contact the Nevada Department of Transportation, 1263 S Stewart St, Carson City, NV 89712.

Boating Water may be a scarce commodity in Nevada, but fun afloat can be had at both **Lake Tahoe** and the **Lake Mead National Recreation Area.** The latter—a 247-square-mile reservoir—extends upriver 110 miles from Hoover Dam and has six marinas. Zephyr Cove Marina (tel 702/588-3833) has boat rentals at Lake Tahoe.

Camping Most state parks have camping facilities year-round, though many are difficult to access in winter. If camping in remote areas, carry adequate drinking water. For information contact the Nevada Division of State Parks, Capitol Complex, Carson City, NV 89710 (tel 702/687-4370 or 687-4384).

Dog-Sled Rides A unique way to explore the mountain wilderness in winter. Try Husky Express (tel 702/782-3047).

Fishing Bass, Mackinaw trout, crappie, whitefish, walleye, and catfish are among the species that attract anglers to lakes and reservoirs in northern Nevada. **Cave Lake State Park,** near Ely, is recommended for brown trout. In the Lake Tahoe area, call O'Malley's Fishing Charters at 702/588-4102.

Fishing permits ($45.50 annually) can be obtained from the Nevada Department of Wildlife, State Headquarters, 1100 Valley Rd, Reno, NV 89512 (tel 702/688-1500). Note: You will need a tribal permit to fish on Indian reservations.

Golf Dozens of lush golf courses defy the state's image as an arid wasteland. Las Vegas has no fewer than 16 courses, including four municipal courses—Angel Park, Desert Rose, Las Vegas Golf Course, and North Las Vegas Golf Course. The Reno–Tahoe–Carson City area has over 20 courses to choose from, including the Edgewood Tahoe Golf Course (tel 702/588-3566) and Incline Village Championship Golf Course (tel 702/832-1144). There's even a public course in Death Valley—Furnace Creek Golf Course (tel 702/786-2301).

Guided Tours In addition to Las Vegas city tours, sightseeing tours are offered from Las Vegas to the Grand Canyon, Hoover Dam, Lake Mead, Red Rock Canyon, and Valley of Fire State Park. Day trips are also available to Death Valley, Mount Charleston, and Laughlin. Contact the Nevada Commission on Tourism (see "Tourist Information," above) for a listing of recommended tour operators. There is also a *Fiesta Queen* River Cruise, departing Laughlin, which relives the nostalgic era when steamboats plied the Colorado River.

Hiking Luring hikers around the Lake Tahoe ridgetop and the upper elevations of the Carson Range is the **Tahoe Rim Trail**—a 150-mile system of hiking and equestrian trails. For information contact Nevada Lake Tahoe State Park (tel 702/831-0494). The 5-mile-long **River Mountain Hiking Trail,** built in 1935 by the Civilian Conservation Corps, offers breathtaking views of Lake Mead and Las Vegas valley.

For a free map of trails, contact the Nevada Division of State Parks, Capitol Complex, Carson City, NV 89710.

Horseback Riding Nevada is cowboy country. The Mt Charleston area is popular for horseback trips out of Las Vegas. Zephyr Cove Stables (tel 702/588-5664) can arrange trips at Lake Tahoe.

Pack Trips Elko Guide Service (tel 702/779-2336) offers pack trips into the Ruby Mountains.

Scuba Diving Yes, this desert state has scuba diving, at Lake Tahoe. Contact The Diving Edge, PO Box 2978, Lake Tahoe, NV 89449 (tel 702/588-5262).

Skiing The Reno–Lake Tahoe region offers the largest concentration of ski areas in the country. The following are the state's most popular ski areas:

- **Diamond Peak,** 2 miles southeast of Incline Village, is a favorite family resort with 20 acres of glade skiing for advanced skiers. It also features 10 cross-country trails.
- **Heavenly,** 2 miles southeast of the town of South Lake Tahoe, has 24 lifts, the world's largest snowmaking system, and over 85 runs, including Tahoe's longest—almost 6 miles.
- **Mount Rose,** 2 miles east of Incline Village, has the highest base elevation in the area, with 41 runs on 900 acres.

You can also ski in Kyle and Lee Canyons (tel 702/878-5465) in the southeast corner of Nevada, good for both downhill and cross-country skiing.

Snowmobiling Explore the High Sierra by taking a guided tour or doing your own thing. Call Zephyr Cove Snowmobile Center at 702/588-3833.

Tennis Most resort hotels have private tennis courts. For a list of municipal courts, refer to the "Government" pages of the local telephone directory.

White-Water Rafting One-day explorations of the Black Canyon of the Colorado River set off from below Hoover Dam; contact Black Canyon River Raft Tours at 702/293-3776. The Truckee River Rafting Center (tel 916/583-7238) offers "bucking bronco" rides on the Truckee River, at Tahoe City.

DEATH VALLEY THROUGH CENTRAL NEVADA

Start	Las Vegas
Finish	Death Valley
Distance	144 miles
Time	1–2 days
Highlights	Death Valley National Monument, Scotty's Castle, ghost towns, Tule Springs, Corn Creek

Simply stated, Death Valley is the most famous desert in the United States. Set between the lofty Black and Panamint mountain ranges, it is known for its exquisite but merciless terrain. A region of vast expanse (the national monument portion is equal to the combined area of Connecticut and Rhode Island) and plentiful plant life (over 900 plant species subsist here, 22 of them indigenous to the area), Death Valley holds a magician's bag of tricks and surprises. It is a giant geology lab of salt beds, sand dunes, and badlands, and an 11,000-foot mountain peak. Its multi-tiered hills contain layers that are windows to the history of the earth. One level holds Indian arrowheads, another Ice Age fish, and beneath these deposits lies 600-million-year-old Precambrian rock.

Death Valley received its name in 1849 when a party of pioneers from Salt Lake City, intent on following a shortcut to the California gold fields, crossed the wasteland, barely escaping with their lives. Later, prospectors worked the territory, discovering rich borax deposits during the 1880s and providing the region with a cottage industry.

Due to the extreme summer temperatures (average July highs of 116°F!), travel to the valley is not recommended in summer months. The best time to see the park is from October through April. In late February and March (average highs of 73°, dropping to a cool 46° average at night) the desert comes alive with spring blossoms such as Death Valley sage and Panamint daisies.

The drive to Death Valley from the neon glow of Las Vegas takes slightly more than 2 hours, and will take you through some of southern Nevada's most scenic and historic treasures. From the Las Vegas Strip, take US 15 north to the downtown area, then exit onto US 95 northbound. Continue for 14 miles until you reach:

1. **Tule Springs,** also known as Floyd Lamb State Park (tel 702/486-5413), a haven for anglers, birders, picnickers, and hikers. You can feed the ducks on the large and small lakes connected by a stream, stroll around the trimmed lawns on sidewalks, or set up your picnic on one of the many tables. Birders will appreciate the variety of waterfowl that pass through on spring and fall migrations, including ruddy ducks, pintails, white-faced scaup, cinnamon and green-winged teal, and Canadian, snow, and Ross's geese. Imported peacocks also wander the grounds.

Tule Springs is named for the large reed-like plants indigenous to the area. Photographers will find inspiration in the pastoral setting and the buildings of the old **Tule Springs Ranch,** a former dude ranch; horse stables, tack rooms, a wooden water tower, and a barn all remain standing. Fossils have been discovered at a site 5 miles southeast of the park, marking the presence of several extinct animals—the ground sloth, mammoth, prehistoric horse, and American camel, as well as the giant condor.

Return to US 95 and drive north for 3½ miles, then make a left turn onto Kyle Canyon Rd (NV 157), which will take you to:

2. **Mount Charleston,** an alpine wilderness area that evolves with the colors and climates of four seasons while the desert floor bakes below. Only 30 minutes from Las Vegas, Mount Charleston and the surrounding **Toiyabe National Forest** are popular destinations for hiking, backpacking, picnicking, overnight camping, and skiing during the winter months. Notice the change in vegetation as the elevation increases. Approaching the mountains you'll see Joshua trees, yucca, and creosote bush that have adapted well to the 120° summer temperatures and scant rainfall. As you reach the 5,000-foot elevation, piñon pine and junipers take over the landscape, along with scatterings of sagebrush, rabbitbrush, and scarlet trumpeter. You probably won't see them from the road, but deer and elk move into this region as the winter snows deepen at higher elevations.

The pine stands grow larger as you progress up the mountain, and at about this point you'll see a turnoff to the right. This is Deer Creek Hwy (NV 158), leading into the **Lee Canyon Ski Resort** (tel 702/878-5465) area. You'll also see the **Mount Charleston Hotel** (tel 702/872-5500), one of the only overnight accommodations on the mountain, with a weathered wood exterior, open-beam rafters, ponderosa pine pillars, and an open-pit fireplace. The hotel has a dining room, a gift shop, a cocktail lounge, and a slot machine arcade.

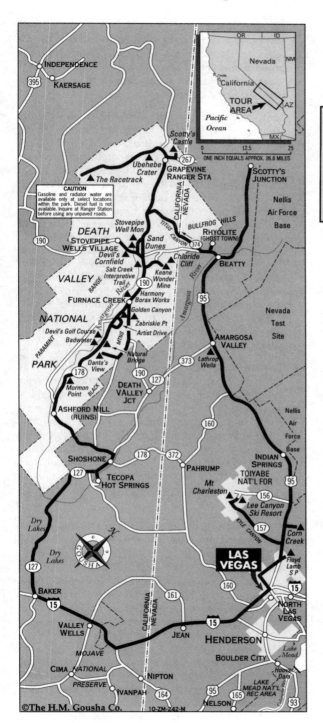

The paved road ends at roughly 7,500 feet, but you can see the bristlecone pine forests at elevations of 9,000 feet and higher. The cabins and

rustic homes perched on sites carved out of Kyle Canyon walls have become a colony for nearly 200 Las Vegans who commute into the city. Stop at the **Ranger Station** (tel 702/331-6444) for maps and information on the area.

Take a Break

At the end of the short gravel road near the Ranger Station is the **Mount Charleston Lodge** (tel 702/872-5408), a very popular restaurant and bar with sweeping canyon views, a circular fireplace, and an excellent menu of game bird entrees, and a charming antique shop next-door.

Backtrack down Kyle Canyon Rd until you reach US 95, turn left, and continue northbound for 7 miles until you reach a well-graded gravel road that will take you to:

3. **Corn Creek,** a former working ranch and stagecoach stop just ¼ mile off the highway. It is now a field station for the vast Desert National Wildlife Range and a special sanctuary of the once endangered Nelson's desert bighorn sheep. This small, rugged oasis is a marvelous site for birdwatching. On the edge of the California flyway, it attracts an astonishing variety of birdlife from hummingbirds to hawks. The natural springs of Corn Creek have formed upper and lower ponds connected by a gurgling brook. You can walk under the huge cottonwoods, mesquite, willows, fruit trees, cattails, and tules clustered around the waterways. There's also a small picnic area with tables, canopies, grills, restrooms, and water. A walk beyond the ponds takes you to mesquite-filled arroyos where you may unearth arrowheads left behind by the ancient Native American tribes.

Return to US 95 and continue north. The open desert to the right is the Nellis Air Force Base bombing and gunnery range, with the Desert Range mountains in the distance. The highway turns westward and continues for 8 miles to:

4. **Indian Springs,** which was originally a ranch owned by a small group of Native Americans. It was later used as a train stop on the run between Las Vegas and Tonopah. Indian Springs has two gas stations, convenience stores, and a truck stop; it is also a checkpoint into the Air Force's gunnery range.

Continue along US 95 for about 15 miles and you'll pass by the:

5. **Nevada Test Site,** which is identified by a historical marker to the right of the highway. It was here during the 1950s and early 1960s that the Atomic

Energy Commission detonated more than 200 nuclear devices.

Do not take the town of Mercury exit because visitors are not allowed into the area. Instead, stay on US 95 and drive for an additional 22 miles to the Lathrop Wells rest area, where you'll find restrooms, tables, garbage cans, and free overnight trailer parking. Continue for another 18 miles to the small mining town of:

6. **Beatty,** which sits in a fairly green valley, watered by the underground Amargosa River, and surrounded by the crumbly, whitewashed Bullfrog Mountains slopes. Beatty blossomed into a town in 1904 when gold was discovered in the Bullfrog hills, but by 1910 the gold ran out and miners left. Beatty survived, however, thanks mainly to the railroad and the routing of US 95 through the town. Most recently a new gold-processing plant west of town has jump-started the local economy. Today the town sports four hotels, a library, several restaurants, and cocktail lounges.

From Beatty, drive 4 miles west on NV 374, past the modern carbon-cynanide gold mill. Turn right at the sign and go up the hill to:

7. **Rhyolite,** one of Nevada's most picturesque ghost towns, which was spawned by a major gold strike in the neighboring Bullfrog Mountains in 1904. By 1906 it had a population of more than 10,000 people. In its heyday, the town had 10 hotels, an opera house, a two-story school, 56 saloons, and a two-story railroad station which still stands. You can see the skeletons of stone and brick buildings, with horseshoes, steamer trunks, and other rubble strewn over the surrounding hillsides. The most famous of the ruins is the **bottle house,** built in 1906 from 10,000 purple, brown, and turquoise beer and whiskey bottles. Another photogenic relic is the crumbling remains of the three-story Cook building, which was once a bank and post office.

Return to NV 374, turn right, and drive for 2 miles to the sign, turn right and prepare for a thrilling ride through:

8. **Titus Canyon,** a colorful gorge split by a winding, 24-mile road through the Grapevine Mountains. About 3 miles into the canyon, you'll pass a marker indicating you've entered **Death Valley National Monument.** The one-way road is extremely narrow in places, with sheer rock walls shooting skyward for several hundred feet. Halfway through the canyon, it widens to expose an old Indian campground and Klare Spring. Nearby are petroglyphs attributed to people of the Ice Age, who inscribed them more than 20,000 years ago.

You'll encounter two-way traffic as you approach the mouth of Titus Canyon. At the base of the canyon, turn right on CA 190 and drive 21 miles to the very end of Death Valley National Monument, bear right on NV 267 for 2 miles, where you'll find the strangest feature in the entire park—a place called:

9. **Scotty's Castle.** Though Scotty never owned it, it seems that one Walter "Death Valley Scotty" Scott, a former trick rider in Buffalo Bill's Wild West Show, once convinced a Chicago millionaire, Albert Johnson, to invest in a nonexistent gold mine. Johnson traveled west to see the mine, discovered that the dry desert clime helped his fragile health, forgave Scotty, and decided during the 1920s to build a mansion in the sand. The result was a $2 million, 18-room Moorish castle, a wonderfully ornate affair with wrought-iron detailing, Spanish tile, expensive tapestry, leather drapery, European antiques, a large moat, and three towers. Scotty, the greatest storyteller in Death Valley history, told everyone it was his castle. Hence the name.

Return to the paved road and backtrack along NV 267 for 8 miles until you reach the moonlike terrain that surrounds:

10. **Ubehebe Crater.** A half-mile in diameter and reaching a depth of 500 feet, this magnificent natural landmark was created by a single volcanic explosion. The force of the volcanic steam scattered debris over a six-square-mile area and blew the crater walls so clean that one side retains its original sedimentary colors. Whether the crater dates back 10,000 years or is only a few hundred years old has been debated by geologists.

From the crater a winding gravel road leads 27 miles to:

11. **The Racetrack,** a two-mile mud playa, set at the bottom of a dry lake, which is oval-shaped like a racecourse. An outcropping at the north end of the valley is dubbed The Grandstand. The racers, oddly enough, are rocks, ranging in size from pebbles to 600-pound boulders. Pushed by heavy winds across the mud-slick surface, they leave long, faint tracks that reveal the distances they have raced, up to 500 feet in some cases.

Retrace your route back to CA 190 and head south for 24 miles, over which you'll descend from 3,000 feet to sea level, until you reach a sign along the highway that marks a lookout area where faint wagon-wheel tracks, made many years ago, can be seen. Further along the highway rests the old:

12. **Stovepipe Well Monument,** from which the nearby village derived its name. Used by prospectors crossing Death Valley, the well was fitted with a tall

stovepipe so travelers could see it even when sand blanketed the area. Although the well is now dry, a stone and bronze monument commemorates the site.

Take the unpaved road south from the monument for 1 mile to the:

13. **Sand Dunes,** which are 80-feet high in some places and cover an area of 14 square miles. They are made up of sand that blew in from nearby mountains, mostly from the cottonwood ranges to the west and northwest, and support numerous plant species, including creosote bushes, mesquite, and pickleweed. Coyotes hunt prey in the sandhills, such as kit fox, lizards, and kangaroo rats.

Continue south on the unpaved road for 2 miles, then turn right on the paved highway, CA 190, and drive the 3 miles to:

14. **Devil's Cornfield,** a conglomeration of arrowweed bushes that are growing in clumps because of sand deflation and erosion. Stalks of the plants were once used by Indians for arrow shafts. The strange sight looks like a field of eerie haystacks.

Just 4 miles south of the Cornfield is one of Death Valley's two villages:

15. **Stovepipe Wells Village,** CA 190 (tel 619/786-2387), where you'll find a motel, restaurant, store, gas station, and campground. It was here at **Burned Wagons Point** (historic marker) that a desperate party of '49ers killed their oxen and dried the meat by burning their wagons.

Take a Break

A good spot for a bite is the **Stovepipe Wells Village motel's restaurant,** which is embellished with Native American rugs and paintings of the Old West. The cuisine matches the ambience, an all-American menu featuring fried chicken, rainbow trout, steak, veal, and cod. You can quench your thirst at the **Badwater Saloon,** which features a jukebox and a dance floor.

Backtrack to CA 190 S, turn right and drive 5 miles to the:

16. **Salt Creek Interpretive Trail.** Six times saltier than the ocean, Salt Creek enters the salt pan at about 200 feet below sea level and has waterfalls, and even fish. The pupfish are descendants of fish that lived in ancient Lake Manly, perhaps 15,000 years ago. They are one to three inches long, swim in schools most of the time, and can be seen during the spring and summer months.

Continue south on CA 190 for 2 miles to the Beatty Cutoff, turn left, and drive 7 miles to:

17. **Keane Wonder Mine,** a productive gold mine from 1908 to 1916. Still on the property are the remnants of a mill, dilapidated houses, and a tram.

A couple of miles north of the mine are the remains of:

18. **Chloride Cliff,** one of Death Valley's oldest developments. The site was a silver mining camp from 1873 to 1883, then again as late as 1916. In its heyday, the camp consisted of a blacksmith shop, an assay office, a cookhouse, a bunkhouse, and a few other buildings. Today only a few wooden structures and the mill foundation remain.

Return to CA 190 and drive south 7 miles to the once prosperous:

19. **Harmony Borax Works,** which is now crumbling adobe walls, old boilers, and vats. Built in 1882 by a wealthy San Francisco businessman, the plant used Chinese labor to scrape the borate crust off the valley floor. Production ended in 1888 when borate was found in the Mojave Desert, close to the Santa Fe Railroad. Important as a cleaning agent, the white crystal eventually became the region's most valuable mineral.

Just a mile south of the Borax Works is Death Valley's only major center of civilization:

20. **Furnace Creek,** a welcome oasis consisting of a gas station, a campground, restaurants, and two hotels. You'll also find the **Death Valley National Monument Visitors Center** (tel 619/786-2331), which houses a museum recreating the history of Native Americans and early prospectors. Most of the accommodations and dining facilities are located here. **Furnace Creek Ranch** (tel 303/297-2757), a 124-unit resort with cabins and standard rooms, sprawls across several acres and features three restaurants, a saloon, a general store, and a swimming pool. The poshest lodging in Death Valley is **Furnace Creek Inn** (tel 619/786-2361), a 70-room hotel set on a hillside overlooking the valley. This Spanish-Moorish-style building, built of stone and adobe, is surrounded by flowering gardens and palm trees. There are two restaurants, tennis courts, and a spring-fed swimming pool; guest rooms are quite comfortably furnished and most have fireplaces.

A few hundred feet south of the Visitors Center is the:

21. **Borax Museum,** which features the oldest house in Death Valley, a sturdy 1883 structure built by a borax miner. Among the displays is a collection of borates and precious metals, old photographs of

the 20-mule teams, Native American baskets, dated arrowheads, mining tools, and historical papers. Outside, there's a wonderful collection of stagecoaches, wagons, and old locomotive, and a contraption once used to extract gold deposits from rock.

Drive south for a mile past the junction of CA 178 and proceed for 3 miles to:

22. **Zabriskie Point.** In the east, amber-colored hills roll like waves toward the horizon. To the west lies spectacular badlands, burnished by blown sand to fierce reds and soft pastels. These mustard-colored hills are dry mud, lake-bed sediments deposited between 2 and 12 million years ago, then uplifted to their present height. During the early morning and late afternoon, the place is suffused with color. Just to the east of the Point is a channel that divides Furnace Creek Wash and Gowers Gulch. The US Park Service cut the channel to divert the flow of the wash into the gulch to prevent flash-flooding at the Furnace Creek settlement. However, considerable erosion has resulted, especially at the gulch's mouth.

For a view from above it all, drive south on CA 190 for 36 miles and climb to:

23. **Dante's View,** a 5,475-foot perch on the crest of the Black Mountains, with a 360° vista. From this advantageous position, the salt flats and trapped pools of Death Valley resemble a bleak watercolor. Though the Panamint Mountains wall off the western horizon, a steep ½-mile trail (up the knoll north of the parking lot) leads to a point where you can gaze beyond them to the snow-thatched Sierra Nevada. Here in a single glance you can see Badwater and Mount Whitney, the lowest and highest points in the continental United States.

Backtrack down the mountain and retrace your route along CA 190 until you reach CA 178, then turn left and drive for 2 miles to:

24. **Golden Canyon,** where erosion has chiseled chasms into the bright yellow walls of the narrow gorge. Hike the ¾-mile trail here and you arrive in a natural amphitheater, named for the iridescent quality of the canyon walls. Once the bottom of an ancient lake, the area is now virtually devoid of life.

About 8 miles south of Golden Canyon, take the turn-off through:

25. **Artist Drive,** a 9-mile loop through the Black Mountains' multicolored badlands, and one of southern California's most magnificent roads. The hills all around are splashed with color—soft pastels, striking reds, creamy browns—and rise to sharp cliffs. Along the loop you'll see **Artists Pal-**

ette, where the hills are colored so vividly they seem to pulsate. All this beauty results from oxidation: Chloride deposits create the green hues, manganese oxides form the blacks, and the reds, yellows, and oranges are shades of iron oxide. These contrasting colors are most spectacular during late afternoon.

Continuing south for 7 miles on the paved highway brings you to the:

26. **Devil's Golf Course.** This flat expanse is a huge salt trap, complete with salt towers, pinnacles, and brine pools. The sodium chloride here is 95% pure, comparable to table salt, and the salt deposits are 3 to 5 feet thick. They were formed by a small lake that evaporated 2,000 years ago. The 2- to 3-foot-tall salt towers, which resemble inverted golf tees, are cracked by expansion, and you can sometimes hear the creaking and cracking on hot days.

Two miles south of the Golf Course, you'll discover the:

27. **Natural Bridge,** a 50-foot-high arch that was carved by torrents of water that cascaded down from the mountains. Behind the bridge, you can still see the lip of what was once an ancient waterfall. The formations along the canyon walls were left by evaporating water and resemble dripping wax.

Drive south 3 miles and you'll find the place you've been reading about since third-grade geography:

28. **Badwater,** the lowest point in the western hemisphere at 282 feet below sea level. It could also be the hottest spot on earth; ground temperatures can exceed 200°F. Take a stroll out onto the salt flats and you'll find that the crystals are joined into a white carpet extending for miles. Despite the inhospitable environment, the pool here supports water snails, bronze water beetles, and other invertebrates. Salt grass, pickleweed, and desert holly also endure here. Evaporation from the pool is heavy, but it contains water throughout the year. Out on the flats you can gaze west at 11,049-foot **Telescope Peak** across the valley. Then be sure to glance back at the cliff to the west of the road; high in the rocks above you, a lone sign marks Sea Level.

The main highway continues south 12 miles across the salt flats to:

29. **Mormon Point.** As you traverse this expanse, notice how the Black Mountains to the east turn from dark colors to reddish hues as gray Precambrian rocks give way to younger volcanic and sedimentary deposits.

Drive south 26 miles along Calif 178 to the ruins of:

30. **Ashford Mill,** once a 50-ton gold mill that was built during World War I when gold mining enjoyed a comeback. The concrete skeletons of several buildings are all that remain of that early dream. About a 2-mile hike west of the mill is a vista point that overlooks **Shoreline Butte,** a curving hill marked by a succession of horizontal lines that represent the ancient shorelines of Lake Manly, which covered the valley to a depth of 600 feet and stretched for 90 miles. Formed perhaps 75,000 years ago, the lake dried up about 10,000 years ago.

A 178 turns eastward as you head 12 miles to the southern entrance of the park, then another 15 miles to the junction of CA 127. Turn right (south) and drive 18 miles to a side road that leads to:

31. **Tecopa Hot Springs,** a series of rich mineral baths once used by Paiute Indians. Today this natural resource has been transformed into a bizarre tourist attraction. A white mineral patina covers the ground everywhere. Water sits in stagnant pools. Wherever you look—backgrounded by rugged, stark, glorious mountains—there are trailers, painted white like the earth and equipped with satellite dishes. The species that inhabits these tin domiciles is on permanent vacation.

A fitting ending to dusty Death Valley lies along the southern gateway to this hauntingly beautiful destination. Here, stretching south along CA 127 to the town of Baker, is a chain of:

32. **Dry Lakes.** Once part of Lake Mojave, an ancient body of water which drained over 3,500 square miles, they are now flat expanses baked white in the sun. **Silver Dry Lake,** which appears to the west 4 miles outside Baker, is part of an area inhabited by Native Americans over 10,000 years ago. To the east rise the **Silurian Hills,** backdropped by the Kingston Range. If there is a snow-domed mountain in the far distance, it's probably 11,918-foot **Charleston Peak,** 60 miles away in Nevada. Those pretty white hills with the soft curves are the **Dumont Dunes,** 30 miles north of Baker.

To return to Las Vegas, continue south on CA 127 to the junction with US 15, turn left (north), and drive the 82 miles back to Las Vegas.

Nevada Listings

Boulder City

Boulder City has the distinction of being the only city in Nevada that prohibits gambling. The city was formed by the federal government as a residential community for constructors of the Hoover Dam, and now is a primary access point for the Lake Mead National Recreation Area. **Information:** Boulder City Chamber of Commerce, 1497 Nevada Hwy, Boulder City 89005 (tel 702/293-2034).

MOTELS 🏨

≣≣ Best Western Lighthouse Inn

110 Ville Dr, 89005; tel 702/293-6444 or toll free 800/528-1234; fax 702/293-6547. Hacienda-style building with red-tile roof, pink stucco walls, and palm trees. Situated on a knoll with views of Lake Mead in the distance. **Rooms:** 70 rms. CI 3pm/CO noon. No smoking. Modern furnishings decorated in southwestern-style prints and colors. **Amenities:** 🛁 📺 A/C, cable TV w/movies. **Services:** 🛎 **Facilities:** 🛉 Whirlpool, washer/dryer. **Rates (CP):** Peak (May 16–Sept 15) $62–$82 S or D. Extra person $10. Children under age 12 stay free. Lower rates off-season. Parking: Outdoor, free. AE, CB, DC, DISC, MC, V.

≣≣ Nevada Inn

1009 Nevada Hwy, 89005; tel 702/293-2044 or toll free 800/638-8890; fax 702/293-0023. Basic motel. **Rooms:** 55 rms, stes, and effic. CI Open/CO noon. Nonsmoking rms avail. Rooms are a bit outdated and beginning to show wear. **Amenities:** 🛁 📺 A/C, cable TV, refrig. Some units w/terraces, some w/whirlpools. **Services:** 🛎 🐬 **Facilities:** 🛉 Whirlpool, washer/dryer. Pool surrounded by sun deck. Parking for boats and RVs. **Rates:** $50–$60 S or D; $65 ste. Extra person $5. Children under age 18 stay free. Parking: Outdoor, free. AE, DC, DISC, MC, V.

≣≣ Super 8 Motel

704 Nevada Hwy, 89005; tel 702/294-8888 or toll free 800/800-8000; fax 702/293-4344. Well-kept motel. **Rooms:** 114 rms and stes. CI 3pm/CO noon. Nonsmoking rms avail. Rooms have older furniture but are clean. Honeymoon suite has heart-shaped tub. **Amenities:** 🛁 📺 A/C, cable TV, refrig. Some units w/terraces, some w/whirlpools. Suites have whirl-pools. **Services:** 🛎 🐬 **Facilities:** 🛉 📺 1 restaurant, 1 bar, games rm, whirlpool, washer/dryer. Sun deck outside pool house. **Rates:** $40–$70 S or D; $75–$205 ste. Children under age 18 stay free. Parking: Outdoor, free. AE, CB, DC, DISC, MC, V.

ATTRACTIONS 🏛

Lake Mead National Recreation Area

601 Nevada Hwy; tel 702/293-8906. Formed by the damming of the Colorado River, Lake Mead is one of the region's top recreation destinations. More than 8 million people visit the lake annually to boat, ski, fish, swim, and camp. The 2,300-mile area surrounds both Lake Mead and Lake Mohave, which extends from Hoover Dam downstream to Davis Dam.

There are a number of developed areas on both the Nevada and the Arizona sides of the lake, offering accommodations, boat facilities and rentals, and campgrounds. These include Boulder Beach and Echo Bay on the Nevada side and Temple Bar on the Arizona side. On nearby Lake Mohave, Katherine Landing, just outside Bullhead City, AZ, provides all amenities.

Black Canyon, between Hoover Dam and Lake Mohave, is part of the recreation area. It is still possible to canoe or raft down this section of river, and along the way there are rapids and several side canyons worth exploring. Several tour-boat operators in the area offer a variety of guided boat tours of the Lake Mead area, including Black Canyon.

The **Alan Bible Visitor Center,** 4 miles northeast of Boulder City on US 93 at Nev 166 (tel 702/293-8906), can provide information on all area activities and services. For more information contact the Superintendent, Lake Mead National Recreation Area, 601 Nevada Hwy, Boulder City, NV 89005-2426. **Open:** Daily 24 hours. **Free**

Hoover Dam

US 93; tel 702/293-8367. Located about 8 miles east of Boulder City on US 93. Constructed between 1931 and 1935, this was the first major dam on the Colorado River. By providing the huge amounts of electricity and water needed by Arizona and California, the Hoover Dam project helped trigger the phenomenal growth experienced in this region during this century.

At 726 feet from bedrock to the roadway along its top, it is the highest concrete dam in the Western Hemisphere. The 110-mile-long **Lake Mead** (see above), which was created by the dam, is the largest human-made reservoir in the United States. Bureau of Reclamation guides conduct tours through Hoover Dam daily. An exhibit housing a model of a generating unit and a topographical model of the Colorado River Basin is also open to the public. **Open:** June–Aug, daily 9am–7pm; Sept–May, daily 9am–4pm. Closed Dec 25. **$**

Carson City

See also Gardnerville, Minden

Founded in 1858 as a business and social center for the nearby mines, the city was named after Kit Carson and became the state capital. The original silver-domed capitol building is still in use, and walking tours of the city highlight its historic past. **Information:** Carson City Chamber of Commerce, 1900 S Carson St, Carson City 89701 (tel 702/882-1565).

HOTELS 🏨

≣≣ Best Western Carson Station Casino/Hotel
900 S Carson St, 89701; tel 702/883-0900 or toll free 800/501-2929; fax 702/882-7569. Casino/hotel with newly remodeled rooms and suites. **Rooms:** 92 rms and stes. CI 3pm/CO noon. Nonsmoking rms avail. **Amenities:** 🛏 🐕 A/C, cable TV, VCR. All units w/terraces. **Services:** 🛎 🍴 **Facilities:** 🔟 1 restaurant, 2 bars (1 w/entertainment). Casino. Sports Book Lounge, where guests can wager on all major sporting events. Cabaret with nightly live entertainment. **Rates:** Peak (Mar–Oct) $40–$70 S or D; $85–$100 ste. Extra person $5. Children under age 12 stay free. Lower rates off-season. Parking: Outdoor, free. AE, CB, DC, DISC, MC, V.

≣≣≣ Hardman House Inn
917 N Carson St, 89701; tel 702/882-7744 or toll free 800/626-1793; fax 702/887-0321. Newly renovated. **Rooms:** 62 rms and stes. CI noon/CO noon. Nonsmoking rms avail. **Amenities:** 🛏 A/C, cable TV. Some units w/terraces. Refrigerators and microwaves available for $6 per day. **Services:** 🛎 🍴 Complimentary coffee in the lobby. **Rates:** Peak (May 15–Oct 15) $45–$55 S; $50–$60 D; $75 ste. Extra person $6–$15. Children under age 3 stay free. Min stay special events. Lower rates off-season. Parking: Indoor/outdoor, free. AE, DC, DISC, MC, V.

MOTELS

≣≣ Best Western Trailside Inn
1300 N Carson St, 89707; tel 702/883-7300 or toll free 800/626-1900; fax 702/883-7300. Delightful lobby, handsome

exteriors, pleasing rooms—perhaps the most attractive property in Carson City. Easy walking distance to casinos and restaurants. **Rooms:** 67 rms. CI 2pm/CO 11am. Nonsmoking rms avail. Charming bedrooms in navy blue, gray, and rose prints make up for lack of bath decor. Very pleasant and well maintained. **Amenities:** 🛏 🐕 A/C, cable TV w/movies. **Services:** 🛎 🍴 **Facilities:** 🔟 & Pool, next to highway, is noisy. **Rates:** Peak (June–Oct) $40–$58 S; $50–$71 D. Extra person $6. Children under age 12 stay free. Min stay wknds and special events. Lower rates off-season. Parking: Outdoor, free. AE, CB, DC, DISC, MC, V.

≣ Round House Inn
1400 N Carson St, 89701; tel 702/882-3446. **Rooms:** 39 rms and stes. CI 11am/CO 11am. Nonsmoking rms avail. Attempts have been made to coordinate furnishings, but beds and chests of drawers are of poor quality. **Amenities:** 🛏 🐕 A/C, cable TV, refrig. **Services:** 🍴 **Facilities:** 🔟 The pool is located next to the highway and noisy. **Rates:** Peak (May 15–Sept 15) $45–$50 S; $50–$60 D; $59–$79 ste. Extra person $4. Children under age 16 stay free. Lower rates off-season. Parking: Outdoor, free. AE, MC, V.

RESTAURANT 🍴

♣ Adele's Restaurant & Bar
1112 N Carson St; tel 702/882-3353. **Continental/Seafood.** Located in an 1875 Victorian house with mansard roof. Victorian decor throughout—heavy lace tablecloths, lace-trimmed napkins, and stained-glass windows. An eclectic menu features traditional dishes with contemporary variations, such as barbecued Cajun prawns, goose liver pâté, carpaccio, blackened salmon, or swordfish. **FYI:** Reservations recommended. Jazz. Additional location: 425 S Virginia St, Reno (tel 333-6503). **Open:** Lunch Mon–Fri 11am–4:30pm, Sat 11:30am–2:30pm; dinner Mon–Sat 5–10pm. Closed Jan 2–15. **Prices:** Main courses $17–$35. AE, MC, V. ♥ 🍴 &

ATTRACTIONS 💼

Extraterrestrial Highway
State Route 375; tel 702/687-4322. On this lonely stretch of pavement in rural Nevada, some visitors claim to have experienced first–hand encounters with visitors from other planets. The Nevada Transportation Board renamed State Route 375 the *Extraterrestrial Highway* in 1996, in deference to nearby **Groom Lake Air Force Base,** a popular gathering place for UFO enthusiasts. Even if you don't experience any sightings you can become a member of the **ET Experience Association,** by calling 800/NEVADA-8. You may be the lucky recipient of an "'I Was Out There" glow–in–the–dark license plate frame.

Nevada State Museum
600 N Carson St; tel 702/687-4810. Among the exhibits and displays featured here are the nation's largest exhibited Imperial mammoth skeleton; coins and other artifacts from the former US Mint in Carson City; a diorama of the Lost

City pueblo; and a reconstructed Great Basin Indian Camp. The Earth Science Gallery explores Nevada's geological history and includes a walk-through Devonian Sea diorama. **Open:** Daily 8:30am–4:30pm. **$**

Nevada State Railroad Museum

2180 S Carson St; tel 702/687-6953. Considered one of the finest regional railroad museums in the country, this facility houses more than 25 pieces of rolling stock, including five steam locomotives and several restored coaches and freight cars. Also displayed are historical artifacts, a depot, a dispatcher's office, an engine house, and machine and blacksmith shops. Most of the equipment is from the Virginia & Truckee Railroad, the richest and most famous short line in the annals of 19th-century railroading. Guided tours are available.

Highlights of the summer season include the regular weekend operation of a 65-year-old rail bus, special events, and the operation of historic railroad equipment. **Open:** Wed–Sun 8:30am–4:30pm. **$**

Crystal Bay

LODGE 🏨

UNRATED Cal-Neva Lodge

2 Stateline Rd, PO Box 368, 89402; tel 702/832-4000 or toll free 800/CAL-NEVA; fax 702/831-9007. 3 mi W of Incline. Cal-Neva exit off NV 28. A diverse, somewhat bizarre place. Heavily promotes its past association with Frank Sinatra and the Rat Pack and draws a diverse crowd of gamblers and young newlyweds. Offers ongoing entertainment, from school plays to cabaret. **Rooms:** 180 rms and stes; 20 cottages/villas. CI 3pm/CO noon. Nonsmoking rms avail. Rooms are spacious and done in a country-French style. Every room and suite has a view of Lake Tahoe. Separate cabins and honeymoon cottages available. **Amenities:** 🛎 🍴 🖥 A/C, cable TV. Some units w/terraces, some w/fireplaces. **Services:** ✕ ➤ VP 🚗 🖎 ↵ Masseur, babysitting. **Facilities:** 🗂 🏌 🛥 ⚓2 🛌 450 2 restaurants, 1 bar, games rm, lawn games, spa, sauna, whirlpool, beauty salon. Three wedding chapels, outdoor tents for receptions or meetings, small casino, show room/bar/lounge. Round bar is a classic—decorated with Washoe Indian memorabilia, leather couches, high beamed ceiling. **Rates:** Peak (June–Sept/Dec 20–Jan 2) $89–$139 S or D; $189 ste; $189 cottage/villa. Extra person $10. Lower rates off-season. Parking: Outdoor, free. MC, V.

Elko

Elko has perhaps the highest number of festivals per capita of any city in the West. Among them are the Cowboy Poetry Gathering in late January, the Elko Mining Expo and Golf Tournament in early June, the Basque Festival in early July,

and the Silver State Stampede Rodeo in late July. **Information:** Elko Chamber of Commerce, 1601 Idaho St, Elko 89801 (tel 702/738-7135).

HOTELS 🏨

📭📭 Holiday Inn

3015 Idaho St, 89801; tel 702/738-8425 or toll free 800/465-4329; fax 702/753-7906. Exit 303 off I-80. There's a new wing here, with rooms equal to any in town. **Rooms:** 170 rms. CI 4pm/CO noon. New rooms far superior to old ones. Bathrooms have two basins, one outside bathroom door. **Amenities:** 🛎 🍴 A/C, cable TV. Some rooms have refrigerators, microwaves. **Services:** ✕ 🚗 🖎 ↵ ⊲ **Facilities:** 🗂 🛌 200 ⅙ 1 restaurant, 1 bar (w/entertainment), games rm, whirlpool, washer/dryer. **Rates:** Peak (May–Sept) $70–$85 S or D. Extra person $10. Children under age 18 stay free. Lower rates off-season. Parking: Outdoor, free. AE, DC, DISC, MC, V.

📭📭📭 Red Lion Inn & Casino

2065 Idaho St, 89801; tel 702/738-2111 or toll free 800/545-0044; fax 702/753-9859. Nice property. Casino is one of town's largest. **Rooms:** 223 rms and stes. CI 4pm/CO noon. Nonsmoking rms avail. Suites are huge. Furniture is attractive and high quality. **Amenities:** 🛎 🍴 🖥 A/C, satel TV w/movies. Some units w/minibars, some w/terraces, some w/whirlpools. **Services:** 🚗 🖎 ↵ ⊲ **Facilities:** 🗂 🛌 250 ⅙ 2 restaurants, 3 bars (1 w/entertainment), games rm, beauty salon. **Rates:** $69–$89 S; $79–$99 D; $259 ste. Extra person $10. Children under age 16 stay free. Parking: Outdoor, free. AE, CB, DC, DISC, MC, V.

MOTELS

📭📭📭 Best Western AmeriTel Inn Elko

1930 Idaho St, 89801; tel 702/738-8787 or toll free 800/600-6001; fax 702/753-7910. Exit 303 off I-80. A very inviting spot. Fast food restaurants nearby. **Rooms:** 110 rms, stes, and effic. CI open/CO 11am. Nonsmoking rms avail. Rooms are fresh and cheerful looking. **Amenities:** 🛎 🍴 A/C, cable TV, refrig. **Services:** 🚗 🖎 ↵ **Facilities:** 🗂 🛌 **Rates (CP):** Peak (May 15–Oct 15) $70 S; $75 D; $104 ste; $104 effic. Extra person $5. Children under age 15 stay free. Lower rates off-season. Parking: Outdoor, free. AE, DC, DISC, MC, V.

📭📭 Best Western AmeriTel Inn Express

837 Idaho St, 89801; tel 702/738-7261 or toll free 800/600-6001; fax 702/738-0118. Exit 301 off I-80. Located near downtown and convention center. Pleasant atmosphere. **Rooms:** 49 rms and stes. CI 1pm/CO 11am. Nonsmoking rms avail. **Amenities:** 🛎 🍴 A/C, cable TV, refrig. Microwave. **Services:** 🖎 ↵ **Facilities:** 🗂 **Rates (CP):** Peak (Apr–Sept 1) $54–$64 S or D; $79–$99 ste. Extra person $5. Children under age 12 stay free. Min stay special events. Lower rates off-season. Parking: Outdoor, free. AE, CB, DC, DISC, MC, V.

Shilo Inn
2401 Mountain City Hwy, 89801; tel 702/738-5522 or toll free 800/222-2244; fax 702/738-6247. Exit 301 off I-80. Attractive property. Indoor pool a major plus in hot climate. **Rooms:** 70 rms. CI 2pm/CO noon. Nonsmoking rms avail. Rooms have two large closets, one small. Also loveseat, and table and three chairs. **Amenities:** ☎ ⚬ A/C, cable TV w/movies, refrig. All units w/minibars. Microwave, two-burner stove, dishwasher. VCR and movies available for rent. **Services:** 🚗 ☐ ⤺ ⬗ Complimentary popcorn, *USA Today*. **Facilities:** ⚐ ⬚ ⬚ ⬚ ⬚ Sauna, steam rm, whirlpool, washer/dryer. **Rates (CP):** Peak (Mem Day–Labor Day) $80–$129 S or D. Extra person $10. Children under age 12 stay free. Lower rates off-season. Parking: Outdoor, free. AE, CB, DC, DISC, MC, V.

RESTAURANT 🍽

Nevada Dinner House
351 Silver St; tel 702/738-8485. **American/Basque.** A mural of the Pyrénées backs the bar, and various Basque items, such as bota bags, provide decoration. Family-style dinners include spaghetti, T-bone steak, grilled lamb chops, and fried shrimp. **FYI:** Reservations recommended. Dress code. **Open:** Tues–Sat 5–10pm, Sun 5–9pm. **Prices:** Main courses $15–$20. AE, DISC, MC, V. ⬛

Ely

ATTRACTIONS 🏛

Cave Lake State Recreation Area
NV 486; tel 702/728-4467 (District Office). Located at an elevation of 7,300 feet in the Schell Creek Range, 8 miles south of Ely via US 93, then 7 miles east on Success Summit Rd (NV 486). The park covers 1,240 acres and has a 32-acre reservoir, providing excellent trout fishing, boating, and swimming. Also hiking, picnicking, and camping; cross-country skiing, ice skating, and ice fishing in winter. Information kiosks are located throughout the park. Interpretive programs. **Open:** Daily 24 hours. **Free**

Nevada Northern Railway Museum
Ave A at 11th St E, East Ely; tel 702/289-2085. The Nevada Northern Railway Depot, built in 1906, was in continuous use until the railway was shut down in 1983. The depot itself is maintained just as it was when it was in operation, making it one of the best-preserved short line railroad depots in the United States. Guided tours (45–60 minutes) take in the entire depot. Excursions aboard an original turn-of-the-century steam passenger train are offered on weekends (additional fee; phone for schedule). **Open:** Mem Day–Labor Day, tours daily at 9 and 11am, 1:30 and 3:30pm; by appointment rest of year. $

Fallon

Irrigation from the waters behind Lahontan Dam feed a rich agricultural region of lush green fields surrounded by desert. The Churchill County Museum and Archives houses an extensive collection of Western memorabilia. **Information:** Greater Fallon Area Chamber of Commerce, 100 Campus Way, Fallon 89406 (tel 702/423-2544).

MOTELS 🏨

Comfort Inn
1830 W Williams Ave, 89406; tel 702/423-5554 or toll free 800/221-2222; fax 702/423-0663. Very well maintained, it's the nicest place to stay in Fallon. The lobby is especially attractive. **Rooms:** 49 rms and stes. CI 2pm/CO noon. Nonsmoking rms avail. Tastefully decorated rooms. **Amenities:** ☎ ⚬ A/C, cable TV w/movies, dataport. Some units w/whirlpools. Refrigerators available upon request. **Services:** ☐ ⤺ Breakfast in sunny area of the lobby. VCR and movie rentals available. **Facilities:** ⚐ ⬚ Whirlpool. **Rates (CP):** Peak (Apr–Oct) $47–$70 S; $52–$75 D; $75–$100 ste. Extra person $5. Children under age 18 stay free. Lower rates off-season. Parking: Outdoor, free. AE, DC, DISC, JCB, MC, V.

Econo Lodge
70 E Williams Ave, 89406; tel 702/423-2194 or toll free 800/553-2666; fax 702/423-7187. A clean property undergoing renovation. **Rooms:** 30 rms and stes. CI 1pm/CO 11am. Nonsmoking rms avail. Pleasant, cheerful decor, with furniture of modest quality. Bathrooms recently renovated. **Amenities:** ☎ ⚬ ▤ A/C, cable TV w/movies. Some rooms have microwaves and refrigerators. **Services:** ⤺ Fax and copy services available. **Facilities:** ⚐ ⬚ **Rates (CP):** $45–$55 S; $50–$65 D; $70–$110 ste. Extra person $5. Children under age 18 stay free. Parking: Outdoor, free. AE, CB, DC, DISC, ER, JCB, MC, V.

RESTAURANTS 🍽

Ⓢ ★ The Apple Tree
40 East Center (Downtown); tel 702/423-4447. Charming eateries like this are especially rare in rural Nevada. The first floor is cheerfully decorated with an apple theme, the second floor with a sunflower theme. Everything, including soups, pies, even hamburger buns, are made from scratch. **FYI:** Reservations accepted. No liquor license. **Open:** Mon–Sat 10:30am–2:30pm. **Prices:** Lunch main courses $4–$6. No CC. ▦ ⬚

Prospector Room
In Nugget Casino, 70 Maine St; tel 702/423-3111. **American.** A bright, cheerful cafe with a reputation for good food. Part of a fast-dying breed of Nevada small-town casino cafes. Western decor, traditional fare: BLTs, calf's liver, banana

cream pie. **FYI:** Reservations not accepted. Children's menu. **Open:** Mon–Thurs 6am–10pm, Fri–Sun 24 hrs. **Prices:** Main courses $3–$7. AE, DC, DISC, MC, V. &

ATTRACTION ▥

Lahontan State Recreation Area
16799 Lahontan Dam; tel 702/867-3500 or 577-2226. Located 18 miles west of Fallon via US 50, this 30,000-acre area includes Lahontan Reservoir, which has 69 miles of shoreline, is 17 miles long, and covers 10,000 surface acres when full. Fishing, boating, and waterskiing are popular activities. Camping and picnicking are also available; interpretive programs. **Open:** Daily 24 hours. $

Gardnerville

See also Carson City, Minden

Located south of Carson City on I-395, the small community of Gardnerville is adjacent to Lahontan National Fish Hatchery, the birthplace of many threatened Lahontan cutthroat trout used to stock western Nevada waters. **Information:** Carson Valley Chamber of Commerce & Visitors Authority, 1524 Hwy 395 N #1, Gardnerville 89410 (tel 702/782-8144 or toll free 800/727/7677).

MOTELS ▥

▤ Topaz Lodge & Casino
1979 NV 395 S, PO Box 187, 89410; tel 702/266-3338 or toll free 800/962-0732; fax 702/266-3338. This hotel overlooking Topaz Lake caters to waterskiers and fishing enthusiasts. Down-home, friendly casino. **Rooms:** 59 rms. CI 3pm/CO 11am. Nonsmoking rms avail. Some accommodations have views of the lake, but the decor has gone downhill recently. **Amenities:** ▦ A/C, cable TV w/movies. **Services:** ✗ ♫ **Facilities:** ▦ 1 restaurant, 2 bars, 1 beach (lake shore), playground. **Rates:** $39–$53 S or D. Extra person $2. Children under age 5 stay free. Parking: Outdoor, free. AE, DISC, MC, V.

▤ Westerner Motel
1353 US 395, PO Box 335, 89410; tel 702/782-3602. Old and plain, but clean. **Rooms:** 25 rms. CI open/CO 11am. Nonsmoking rms avail. Bare-bones decorations include art on walls that looks as if it came from a paint-by-numbers kit. **Amenities:** ▦ ▤ A/C, cable TV w/movies, refrig. **Services:** ♫ **Facilities:** ▦ Large grassy area. Pool in poor condition **Rates:** Peak (Apr–Oct) $30–$35 S; $32–$43 D. Extra person $3–5. Children under age 4 stay free. Lower rates off-season. Parking: Outdoor, free. AE, DISC, MC, V.

Goodsprings

ATTRACTION ▥

Goodsprings Ghost Town
Located 35 miles southwest of Las Vegas on I-15 S and west on NV 161. Goodsprings, founded in the 1860s, was once the biggest town in Nevada, a thriving metropolis built around nearby silver and lead mines with a population of 2,000. In the years following World War I, mining days ended and the population began to decline; by 1967 the population had dwindled to 62. The once-famous Goodsprings Hotel burned to the ground, and one of the town's last remaining businesses, a general store, was torn down. Today this authentic ghost town is an eerie relic of Nevada's boom-to-bust mining era.

The heart of the town is the **Pioneer Saloon** (tel 702/874-9362), which from its weathered exterior does not look operative. It has, however, been a going concern since 1913. The only complete decorative-metal building left standing in the United States, the saloon has pressed-tin walls (interior and exterior) and ceiling. Many of the fixtures and furnishings are original. The saloon is open daily 10am–midnight.

Great Basin National Park

Established in 1986, this 77,100-acre national park boasts an exceptionally wide range of plant and animal habitats: from the Pinion–Juniper Life Zone, characterized by jackrabbits, scrubjays, and sagebrush, to the frigid Alpine Life Zone at higher elevations.

The **visitor center** (tel 702/234-7331) is located 5 miles east on NV 488, in the town of Baker, NV, and is open daily 8am–5pm. The center has displays describing the Great Basin's flora and fauna, geological development, and history. The Great Basin was named by explorer John C Frémont because its rivers and streams flowed inland, soaking into the earth, evaporating, or forming lakes with no outlet to the sea.

Within the park is **Lehman Caves,** formerly Lehman Caves National Monument. Discovered in 1885, these caves are among the most highly decorated limestone solution caverns in the United States. Guided tours (90 minutes) depart from the visitor center and follow a half-mile trail through chambers with names like the Gothic Palace, the Cypress Swamp, and the Grand Palace. Cave temperature is always 50°F; those under age 16 must be accompanied by an adult.

The 12-mile **Wheeler Peak Scenic Drive** begins east of the visitor center and ends at a campground and trailhead 10,000 feet up the northern flank of Wheeler Peak. A variety of marked hiking trails begins at this point, including a trail to the glacier at the base of Wheeler Peak and one to the summit of Wheeler Peak (13,063 ft). Three campgrounds are located along the scenic drive, and a fourth is located south of the visitor center.

Lexington Arch, near the southeast border of the park, is another highlight, a natural limestone arch more than six stories high. To reach the arch, an unpaved road leads to a 1-mile trail.

For more information write to the Superintendent, Great Basin National Park, Baker, NV 89311.

Henderson

A large center of private industry, a thriving residential area, and home of the Ethel M Chocolate Factory. **Information:** Henderson Chamber of Commerce, 590 S Boulder Hwy, Henderson 89015 (tel 702/565-8951).

ATTRACTIONS 🏛

Clark County Heritage Museum
1830 S Boulder Hwy; tel 702/455-7955. A museum illustrating the history of southern Nevada, this facility offers both indoor and outdoor exhibits. Inside is a permanent exhibit in the form of a time line that starts with a prehistoric Nevada dire wolf display and extends to the 20th-century development of casinos and the gaming industry; there are also several changing exhibitions. Outdoor exhibits include an authentic ghost town; the original 1931 Boulder City train depot and a collection of authentic railroad rolling stock; and Heritage St, with six restored historic buildings that have been relocated here, restored, and opened for tours. **Open:** Daily 9am–4:30pm. **$**

Kidd Marshmallow Factory
1180 Marshmallow Lane; tel 702/564-5400. Kidd and Co has been a family-owned and -operated business since the late 1800s. Today it distributes more than 150 brands of marshmallow products throughout North America. Self-guided tours visit the marshmallow-making process from start to finish. Free samples; gift shop. **Open:** Daily 9am–4:30pm. **Free**

Incline Village

A well-off community on the Nevada shore of Lake Tahoe and below nearby ski areas, Incline Village is the site of the Ponderosa Ranch where the Cartwright boys and the ranch house (used occasionally for location filming) starred in the long-running television show "Bonanza." **Information:** Lake Tahoe–Incline Village Crystal Bay Visitor Bureau, 969 Tahoe Blvd, Incline Village 89451 (tel 702/832-1606 or toll free 800/GO-TAHOE).

RESORT 🏨

≣≣≣ Hyatt Regency Lake Tahoe
Country Club Dr at Lake Shore, PO Box 3239, 89450-3239; tel 702/832-1234 or toll free 800/233-1234; fax 702/831-7508. 30 mi SW of Reno. 28 acres. Originally built in the 1960s, the hotel's main, blandly designed tower does not take advantage of the sublime lakeside setting. The grounds, however, are very attractive. **Rooms:** 458 rms and stes; 24 cottages/villas. CI 3pm/CO 11am. Nonsmoking rms avail. Standard accommodations in either the 12-story tower or 3-story Aspen Terrace wings; all have been recently refurbished with a mountain lodge decor. There are also 24 luxurious, one- or two- bedroom lakeside cottages that feel like private mountain homes; set by the water, they offer niceties such as stone fireplaces and marble-countered bathrooms. **Amenities:** 📺 ⚬ 🍽 Cable TV w/movies, dataport, in-rm safe. No A/C. Some units w/minibars. Irons and ironing boards in all rooms. **Services:** ❚◯❚ ▭ 📻 🚗 🗳 ➷ Social director, masseur, children's program, babysitting. Year-round Camp Hyatt program for kids ages 3 to 12 runs daily during the summer, on holidays and weekends the rest of the year. In winter, free ski shuttles leave from the hotel lobby; discounted lift tickets are available for Diamond Peak, Northstar, Squaw Valley, Mount Rose, and Alpine Meadows. **Facilities:** 🏌 🚴 ⛰ 🎿 🐎 🛶 ❋2 ⛸ 🎳 700 🖥 ♿ 3 restaurants (*see* "Restaurants" below), 5 bars (2 w/entertainment), 1 beach (lake shore), volleyball, games rm, spa, steam rm, whirlpool, playground. Varied water sports offered on the hotel's sandy lakeside beach, including sails on the hotel's 49-passenger catamaran. The health club features Cybex equipment and free weights, as well as step, cycle, and treadmill machines. Surrounded by pine trees, the swimming pool is heated year-round. Ski rental on property. Small but lively casino. **Rates:** Peak (June–Sept/Dec–Jan) $215–$335 S or D; $185–$565 ste; $415–$565 cottage/villa. Extra person $25. Children under age 18 stay free. Lower rates off-season. Parking: Outdoor, free. Ski packages avail. AE, CB, DC, DISC, MC, V.

RESTAURANT 🍴

Lone Eagle Grill
In Hyatt Regency Lake Tahoe, Country Club Dr at Lakeshore; tel 702/832-3250. **New American.** Perhaps Tahoe's most beautiful venue for lakeside dining, this new restaurant sits right at water's edge. Rough-hewn beams, high ceilings, soaring windows, and two huge stone fireplaces create an authentic, mountain lodge feel. In addition to fish, pasta, and beef selections, the menu features wild game from the rotisserie, including pheasant, venison, moose, elk, and duck. A good bet for dessert is the mud pie or the "monster cake"—big enough to feed 12. **FYI:** Reservations recommended. Jazz. **Open:** Lunch daily 11:30am–2:30pm; dinner

daily 5:30–10:30pm; brunch Sun 10:30am–2:30pm. **Prices:** Main courses $12–$21. AE, CB, DC, DISC, MC, V. ♥ ♠ 🖼 🔼 ⛰ ⚡

ATTRACTIONS 🏛

Ponderosa Ranch and Western Theme Park
100 Ponderosa Ranch Rd; tel 702/831-0691. Located just off NV 28. Many visitors will probably recognize this movie-set ranch as the location for the hit TV series *Bonanza*. Many show-oriented exhibits include dozens of props and the original 1959 Cartwright Ranch House. Activities include pony rides, staged gunfights, hayrides, a petting farm, and a blacksmith's shop. Mem Day–Labor Day, hayride breakfast offered 8–9:30am. **Open:** Peak (Apr 15–Oct 31) Daily 9:30am–5pm. Reduced hours off-season. **$$$**

Lake Tahoe Nevada State Park
2005 NV 28; tel 702/831-0494. Comprising approximately 14,000 acres along the eastern shore of Lake Tahoe, this park is comprised of five areas: **Sand Harbor,** the most popular, has sandy beaches, swimming, picnicking, boat launching, and a visitors center; **Spooner Lake,** offers hiking, fishing, and mountain biking; **Cave Rock** is popular for boating and fishing; **Memorial Point** and **Hidden Beach** offer more secluded access to the shores of Lake Tahoe. The majority of the park is backcountry in the mountains east of the lake. Two primitive campsites and portions of the Tahoe Rim Trail are located in the Spooner Lake area. **Open:** Daily 24 hours. **$$**

Las Vegas

See also Boulder City, Henderson

The most conspicuous city in America has attempted to shed its reputation as a risqué town of hard-luck characters and shady high rollers, and by all accounts it has succeeded. Las Vegas, of course, still does have its adult-oriented attractions, but the town is now booming as a family destination, with affordable hotel rooms, big-production magic acts, circuses, high-tech game arcades, and a full-scale pirate-ship battle, among its many other tourist draws. **Information:** Las Vegas Convention & Visitors Authority, 3150 Paradise Rd, Las Vegas 89109 (tel 702/892-0711).

HOTELS 🏨

≡≡≡ Alexis Park Resort Las Vegas
375 E Harmon Ave, 89109; tel 702/796-3300 or toll free 800/453-8000; fax 702/796-0766. Turn east on Harmon Ave off Las Vegas Blvd. 20 acres. Remains one of the finest places off the strip. **Rooms:** 500 rms and stes. CI 2pm/CO 11am. Nonsmoking rms avail. Huge rooms resemble cottages and villas, many with two levels. Deluxe rooms available. **Amenities:** 🛏 🔲 A/C, cable TV w/movies, refrig. Some units w/minibars, some w/terraces, some w/fireplaces, some w/whirlpools. **Services:** 🍽 ⬛ 🆅🅿 🖼 🛎 ⬦ Social director,

masseur, children's program, babysitting. **Facilities:** 🔲 🏊4 🛶 🏊1000 ⚹ 1 restaurant, 1 bar (w/entertainment), spa, sauna, steam rm, whirlpool, washer/dryer. Putting green. **Rates:** $109–$200 S or D; $225 ste. Extra person $15. Children under age 18 stay free. Parking: Outdoor, free. AE, DC, DISC, MC, V.

≡≡ Algiers Hotel
2845 Las Vegas Blvd S, 89109; tel 702/735-3311 or toll free 800/732-3361; fax 702/792-2112. One of the best deals on the strip. Small, centrally located hotel offers guests a comfortable, friendly stay without the hustle of newer establishments. **Rooms:** 105 rms and stes. CI noon/CO noon. Nonsmoking rms avail. A more "homey" feel than most Las Vegas accommodations. Furnishings are dated, but clean. Soundproofing is so good you might forget you're in town. Nonsmokers should request a nonsmoking room. **Amenities:** 🛏 A/C, cable TV. **Services:** ✕ 🖼 ⬦ Car-rental desk, babysitting. **Facilities:** 🔲 1 restaurant, 1 bar. On-site wedding chapel and several attached stores. Attractive pool area, surrounded by palm trees. Reasonably priced restaurant has great specials. **Rates:** $40–$55 S or D; $65–$90 ste. Extra person $10. Children under age 18 stay free. Parking: Outdoor, free. AE, DC, DISC, MC, V.

≡≡≡ Bally's Las Vegas
3645 Las Vegas Blvd S, 89109; tel 702/739-4111 or toll free 800/634-3434. Located on the strip, this hotel has large, bright, tastefully decorated rooms which are among the best in Las Vegas. A renovation added fountains and landscaping to the entrance, expanded the shopping arcade, and created an arena-style race and sports look. **Rooms:** 2,814 rms and stes. Executive level. CI 3pm/CO 11am. Nonsmoking rms avail. Renovations in late 1993 created "new" rooms with faux marble and large windows. **Amenities:** 🛏 🍷 A/C, satel TV w/movies, voice mail, in-rm safe. Some units w/whirlpools. **Services:** 🍽 🆅🅿 🚐 🖼 ⬦ Car-rental desk, masseur, babysitting. Can arrange excursions to Hoover Dam and the Grand Canyon. **Facilities:** 🔲 🍴5 ⬛3 🛶 🏊4500 💻 ⚹ 7 restaurants, 5 bars (1 w/entertainment), games rm, spa, sauna, steam rm, whirlpool, beauty salon, washer/dryer. New $2 million health spa. **Rates:** $91–$169 S or D; $289–$539 ste. Extra person $15. Children under age 18 stay free. Parking: Indoor/outdoor, free. Higher than most Las Vegas hotels, but worth it. AE, DC, DISC, JCB, MC, V.

≡≡≡ Barbary Coast Hotel & Casino
3595 Las Vegas Blvd S, 89109; tel 702/737-7111 or toll free 800/634-6755. On the strip. A small casino with an adjacent hotel. Unimpressive exterior, but casino and public areas are rich with Victorian touches and stained-glass windows. **Rooms:** 200 rms and stes. CI 2pm/CO noon. Nonsmoking rms avail. Rooms are surprisingly luxurious with over-stuffed sofas, sitting areas, and period artwork. **Amenities:** 🛏 A/C, satel TV w/movies. Some units w/minibars, some w/whirlpools. **Services:** ✕ 🆅🅿 🖼 ⬦ Car-rental desk. Free shuttle to Gold Coast. **Facilities:** ⚹ 2 restaurants, 2 bars,

beauty salon. **Rates:** $150–$200 S or D; $200–$400 ste. Extra person $10. Children under age 12 stay free. Parking: Indoor, free. AE, DC, DISC, MC, V.

☰☰☰ Caesars Palace

3570 Las Vegas Blvd S, 89109; tel 702/731-7110 or toll free 800/634-6001; fax 702/731-7331. Still considered among the best in Las Vegas. One of the largest hotels on the strip, catering to stars, high rollers, and other top clientele. **Rooms:** 1,514 rms and stes; 14 cottages/villas. Executive level. CI 3pm/CO noon. Nonsmoking rms avail. Well-maintained accommodations include some of the largest standard rooms on the strip, and are currently being upgraded. Many have Roman tubs. **Amenities:** ☎ ⬧ ☖ A/C, satel TV w/movies, dataport, voice mail, in-rm safe. Some units w/minibars, some w/terraces, some w/whirlpools. **Services:** ◎ ☎ VP ⬤ ☖ ⬧ Twice-daily maid svce, car-rental desk, masseur, babysitting. **Facilities:** ⬧ ⬤5 ⬧ ⬧4000 ⬜ ⬧ 9 restaurants (see "Restaurants" below), 6 bars (3 w/entertainment), games rm, racquetball, spa, sauna, steam rm, whirlpool, beauty salon, washer/dryer. Omnimax movie theater. Forum Shops feature 70 upscale boutiques (including Gucci and Versace), plus restaurants such as Spago, The Palm, and Planet Hollywood. **Rates:** $110–$169 S or D; $225–$750 ste. Extra person $15. Children under age 12 stay free. Parking: Indoor/outdoor, free. AE, DC, DISC, MC, V.

☰☰ California Hotel/Casino & RV Park

12 Ogden Ave, PO Box 630, 89101 (Downtown); tel 702/385-1222 or toll free 800/634-6255; fax 702/388-2660. Aloha theme is popular with visitors from Hawaii. **Rooms:** 650 rms and stes. CI 2pm/CO noon. Nonsmoking rms avail. Rooms have southwestern decor, in muted turquoise and mauve. **Amenities:** ☎ A/C, cable TV, refrig, in-rm safe. Some units w/whirlpools. **Services:** ✕ VP ☖ ⬧ Friendly, receptive staff. **Facilities:** ⬧ ⬧500 ⬧ 6 restaurants, 4 bars, games rm. Hawaiian shop, candy store; 222-space RV park across the street. **Rates:** $40–$50 S or D; $65–$75 ste. Extra person $5. Children under age 18 stay free. Min stay wknds. Parking: Indoor, free. AE, DC, DISC, MC, V.

☰☰☰ Carriage House

105 E Harmon Ave, 89109; tel 702/798-1020 or toll free 800/221-2301; fax 702/798-1020 ext 112. Turn east on Harmon Ave off Las Vegas Blvd. Although rooms are available for nightly rental, most accommodations here are used by time-share customers. Located right next to the MGM theme park. **Rooms:** 154 rms and effic. CI 3pm/CO 11am. Nonsmoking rms avail. Provided you don't mind the rates, these rooms are among the best in the middle range of hotels. All are suites and resemble mini-apartments. Despite some wear, rooms are nicely decorated and well maintained. Deluxe suites have full kitchens. **Amenities:** ☎ ⬧ ☖ ⬧ A/C, cable TV w/movies, refrig, in-rm safe. **Services:** ✕ ⬤ ☖ ⬧ Children's program, babysitting. **Facilities:** ⬧ ⬤1 ⬧ 1 restaurant (see "Restaurants" below), 1 bar (w/entertainment), whirlpool, washer/dryer. Outdoor pool and sun deck,

laundry facilities on each floor, rooftop restaurant and lounge. **Rates:** $115–$145 S; $125–$245 D; $135–$245 effic. Children under age 18 stay free. Min stay wknds and special events. Parking: Outdoor, free. Family package avail. AE, DC, DISC, MC, V.

☰☰☰ Circus Circus Hotel/Casino

2880 Las Vegas Blvd S, PO Box 14967, 89114; tel 702/734-0410 or toll free 800/444-CIRCUS. On the strip. The original family theme hotel in Las Vegas; a circus carnival atmosphere. With its sloping stairways and hilly walkways, some may think it's a bit rundown, but it makes up with attractions. A great place to take kids. **Rooms:** 2,800 rms and stes. CI 2pm/CO noon. Nonsmoking rms avail. Rooms are basic and comfortable and decorated in primary colors. **Amenities:** ☎ A/C, cable TV w/movies. **Services:** ✕ VP ⬤ ⬧ Twice-daily maid svce, car-rental desk, babysitting. **Facilities:** ⬧ ⬧ 6 restaurants, 3 bars (2 w/entertainment), games rm, whirlpool, beauty salon, playground. Carnival midway with games and circus acts. Making additions, including Grand Slam Canyon, an indoor theme park. **Rates:** Peak (June–Aug) $40–$55 D; $55 ste. Children under age 18 stay free. Lower rates off-season. Parking: Indoor/outdoor, free. AE, DC, DISC, MC, V.

☰☰☰ Courtyard by Marriott

3275 Paradise Rd, 89109; tel 702/791-3600 or toll free 800/321-2211; fax 702/796-7981. E Sahara exit off I-15; turn south on Paradise Rd. Typical of low-end Marriotts, this caters primarily to business travelers attending conventions. **Rooms:** 149 rms and stes. CI 3pm/CO 1pm. No smoking. Despite recent renovations, rooms are unimpressive. **Amenities:** ☎ ⬧ A/C, cable TV w/movies, voice mail. Some units w/terraces. **Services:** ⬤ ☖ ⬧ Car-rental desk, babysitting. **Facilities:** ⬧ ⬧ ⬧100 ⬧ 1 restaurant (bkfst and lunch only), 1 bar, spa, whirlpool, washer/dryer. **Rates:** $89–$99 S or D; $119–$129 ste. Children under age 18 stay free. Parking: Outdoor, free. AE, DISC, MC, V.

☰☰ El Cortez Hotel & Casino

600 E Fremont St, PO Box 680, 89101 (Downtown); tel 702/385-5200 or toll free 800/634-6703; fax 702/385-1554. This busy, sprawling hotel has the city's oldest casino. Caters to budget-minded seniors. **Rooms:** 308 rms. CI 2pm/CO noon. Nonsmoking rms avail. Garden rooms have 1950s-style furnishings, but tower rooms are more modern. **Amenities:** ☎ A/C, cable TV. **Services:** ✕ VP ⬧ ⬧ **Facilities:** 2 restaurants, 3 bars, games rm. **Rates:** $23–$40 S or D. Extra person $3. Children under age 12 stay free. Parking: Indoor, free. AE, DISC, MC, V.

☰☰ Excalibur Hotel/Casino

3850 Las Vegas Blvd S, PO Box 96778, 89109; tel 702/597-7777 or toll free 800/937-7777; fax 702/597-7040. On the strip. A hotel designed as a fantasy-like Camelot, complete with multicolored spires and turrets. There's a drawbridge entry over a moat. A mecca for families with children.

Rooms: 4,032 rms and stes. CI 3pm/CO 11am. Nonsmoking rms avail. Bold medieval theme, with dark wood furniture, colorful red and pink accents, and Renaissance artwork. **Amenities:** ▣ A/C, satel TV w/movies, voice mail. Some units w/minibars, some w/whirlpools. **Services:** |O| VP 🚗 ▲ ⏜ Car-rental desk. **Facilities:** ▣ ♿ 7 restaurants (see "Restaurants" below), 4 bars (1 w/entertainment), games rm, whirlpool, beauty salon, washer/dryer. Medieval village has shops, food, and Camelot midway with games and street performers. Huge, 100,000-square-foot casino. Knights on horseback perform dinner show with Merlin the magician. **Rates:** $56–$98 S or D; $125 ste. Extra person $10. Children under age 12 stay free. Parking: Indoor/outdoor, free. AE, DC, DISC, JCB, MC, V.

≡≡≡ Fairfield Inn by Marriott
3850 Paradise Rd, 89109; tel 702/791-0899 or toll free 800/228-2800; fax 702/791-0899. 1 mi S of convention center. The inn has a tranquil lobby and sitting room with overstuffed chairs, a fireplace, and a television. **Rooms:** 129 rms. Executive level. CI 3pm/CO noon. Nonsmoking rms avail. Modern and tasteful decor with hardwood furniture and earth tones. Furnished with desks for the business traveler. **Amenities:** ▣ ♿ A/C, cable TV w/movies. **Services:** 🚗 ▲ ⏜ Fax available. **Facilities:** ▣ ☐ ♿ Whirlpool. **Rates (CP):** Peak (Jan–June/Sept–Nov) $58–$85 S or D. Children under age 18 stay free. Lower rates off-season. Parking: Outdoor, free. AE, DISC, MC, V.

≡≡ Flamingo Hilton Las Vegas
3555 Las Vegas Blvd S, 89109; tel 702/733-3111 or toll free 800/732-2111; fax 702/733-3353. On the strip. The casino is the main attraction here. The hotel razed the original garden rooms to make way for a new tower. **Rooms:** 3,642 rms and stes. CI 2pm/CO noon. Nonsmoking rms avail. Most rooms are decorated in blue and green with a tropical motif. **Amenities:** ▣ ♿ A/C, cable TV w/movies, in-rm safe. Some units w/minibars. **Services:** |O| VP 🚗 ▲ ⏜ Car-rental desk, masseur, babysitting. **Facilities:** ▣ ☐ ☐ ☐ 🖥 ♿ 9 restaurants, 4 bars (1 w/entertainment), games rm, spa, sauna, steam rm, whirlpool, beauty salon. Large pool with water slides, palm trees, fountains, and sun deck. Huge casino and showroom. Wedding chapel. **Rates:** $69–$250 S or D; $290–$580 ste. Extra person $16. Children under age 18 stay free. Parking: Indoor, free. AE, CB, DC, DISC, JCB, MC, V.

≡≡ Four Queens Hotel & Casino
202 E Fremont St, PO Box 370, 89101 (Downtown); tel 702/385-4011 or toll free 800/634-6045; fax 702/387-5122. The lobby suggests the New Orleans French Quarter, with a carved wood registration desk, brass trim, and chandeliers. **Rooms:** 720 rms and stes. CI 2pm/CO noon. Nonsmoking rms avail. Rooms have early American furnishings and brocade wallpaper, and some have four-poster beds. **Amenities:** ▣ A/C, cable TV w/movies, voice mail. Some units w/minibars. **Services:** X VP 🚗 ▲ ⏜ ☠ Car-rental desk, babysit-

ting. **Facilities:** ☐ ♿ 3 restaurants, 3 bars (1 w/entertainment), games rm. 60,000-square-foot casino. French Quarter Lounge presents jazz on Monday nights. **Rates:** $54–$68 S or D; $95–$175 ste. Extra person $8. Children under age 12 stay free. Parking: Indoor, free. AE, CB, DISC, MC, V.

≡≡≡ Golden Nugget Hotel & Casino
129 E Fremont St, PO Box 610, 89101 (Downtown); tel 702/385-7111 or toll free 800/634-3454; fax 702/386-8362. Clearly the jewel of downtown, with lots of white marble and gold everywhere. The lobby features lovely gold-leaf chandeliers, white marble floors, and red oriental rugs. **Rooms:** 1,907 rms and stes. CI 3pm/CO noon. Nonsmoking rms avail. Rooms are among the most luxurious in town, with cream-colored carpets, rattan accents, and a tropical feel. **Amenities:** ▣ ♿ A/C, cable TV w/movies. Some units w/minibars, some w/whirlpools. **Services:** |O| ⚙ VP ▲ ⏜ Car-rental desk, babysitting. **Facilities:** ▣ ☐ ♿ 5 restaurants, 3 bars (1 w/entertainment), games rm, spa, sauna, whirlpool, beauty salon. Gift and apparel shops. Extensive health club has a tanning salon. **Rates:** $58–$160 S or D; $275 ste. Extra person $20. AE, DC, DISC, MC, V.

≡≡ Hacienda Hotel Casino
3950 Las Vegas Blvd S, PO Box 98506, 89119; tel 702/739-8911 or toll free 800/634-6713; fax 702/798-8289. Spanish-theme hotel with red tile, adobe arches, and colorful art in the lobby. Remote location away from the strip. **Rooms:** 1,140 rms and stes. CI 3pm/CO 11am. Nonsmoking rms avail. Tower rooms are more modern and nicer, but garden rooms offer better access to pool area. **Amenities:** ▣ ▪ A/C, satel TV w/movies. Some units w/minibars, some w/terraces. **Services:** |O| VP 🚗 ▲ ⏜ Car-rental desk, babysitting. Friendly, helpful staff. **Facilities:** ▣ ☑ ☐1500 ♿ 3 restaurants, 2 bars (1 w/entertainment), games rm, whirlpool, beauty salon, washer/dryer. Coffee shop serves heaping portions at bargain prices. Pool surrounded by lush landscaping. Casino, Western-style wedding chapel, and showroom. **Rates:** $28–$96 S or D; $135–$265 ste. Extra person $10. Children under age 12 stay free. Parking: Indoor/outdoor, free. AE, DISC, MC, V.

≡≡ Harrah's Casino Hotel Las Vegas
3475 Las Vegas Blvd S, 89109; tel 702/369-5000 or toll free 800/634-6765; fax 702/369-4147. On the strip. Main building resembles an old Mississippi River paddle wheeler. **Rooms:** 1,700 rms and stes. CI 3pm/CO noon. Nonsmoking rms avail. Spacious, modern rooms decorated in pastel colors. **Amenities:** ▣ ♿ A/C, cable TV w/movies. Some units w/minibars, some w/terraces. **Services:** |O| VP 🚗 ▲ ⏜ Car-rental desk, masseur, babysitting. **Facilities:** ▣ ☐ ☐2300 🖥 ♿ 6 restaurants, 5 bars (1 w/entertainment), games rm, spa, sauna, steam rm, whirlpool, beauty salon, washer/dryer. Sports bar, wedding chapel. **Rates:** $55–$250 S or D; $195–$600 ste. Extra person $15. Children under age 12 stay free. Parking: Indoor, free. AE, CB, DC, DISC, ER, JCB, MC, V.

≣≣≣ Holiday Inn

325 E Flamingo Rd, 89109; tel 702/732-9100 or toll free 800/732-7889; fax 702/731-9784. ½ mi E of the strip. Set back from busy Flamingo Rd, with public areas facing away from the street. The comfortable lobby has an indoor fountain and a parlor area decorated with overstuffed furniture and a fireplace. **Rooms:** 150 rms and stes. CI 3pm/CO noon. Nonsmoking rms avail. Modern, with tasteful furnishings and a cool pastel palette. All have sitting areas with couch and recliner. **Amenities:** 🛏 🕭 📺 📶 A/C, cable TV w/movies, refrig, dataport, bathrobes. Some units w/terraces, some w/whirlpools. **Services:** ✕ 🚗 🖼 🍴 Car-rental desk, babysitting. **Facilities:** 🛝 🏋 500 👤 1 restaurant, 1 bar, sauna, whirlpool. **Rates:** Peak (Nov–Mar) $79–$139 S or D; $149–$299 ste. Extra person $15. Children under age 18 stay free. Min stay wknds. Lower rates off-season. Parking: Outdoor, free. AE, CB, DC, DISC, JCB, MC, V.

≣≣ Holiday Inn Boardwalk Hotel & Casino

3750 Las Vegas Blvd S, 89109; tel 702/735-1167 or toll free 800/635-4581; fax 702/739-8125. On the strip. America's largest Holiday Inn has a Coney Island facade complete with roller coaster, ferris wheel, and midway games. **Rooms:** 656 rms and stes. CI 3pm/CO noon. Nonsmoking rms avail. The renovated rooms have attractive, new furnishings and pastel color schemes. **Amenities:** 🛏 🕭 A/C, cable TV w/movies, voice mail. Some units w/minibars. **Services:** ✕ 🚗 🍴 Car-rental desk. Tour desk. **Facilities:** 🛝 250 👤 4 restaurants, 2 bars (1 w/entertainment), games rm, washer/dryer. Cluster of retail shops, midway games, shooting gallery, and a 30,000-square-foot casino. **Rates:** $69–$99 S or D; $115–$175 ste. Extra person $15. Children under age 19 stay free. Parking: Indoor/outdoor, free. AE, DISC, MC, V.

≣≣ Imperial Palace Hotel & Casino

3535 Las Vegas Blvd S, 89109; tel 702/731-3311 or toll free 800/634-6441; fax 702/735-8328. On the strip. A five-story tower behind a small, blue, pagoda facade. Asian-theme hotel is popular with tour groups. **Rooms:** 2,700 rms and stes. CI 3pm/CO noon. Nonsmoking rms avail. Asian decor continues in rooms with Japanese art and rattan and bamboo furnishings. **Amenities:** 🛏 A/C, cable TV w/movies. Some units w/minibars, some w/terraces, some w/whirlpools. **Services:** 🍽 VP 🚗 🖼 🍴 Car-rental desk, babysitting. **Facilities:** 🛝 🏋 1600 💻 👤 9 restaurants, 6 bars (1 w/entertainment), games rm, whirlpool, beauty salon. Shops; showroom; collection of nearly 800 antique and classic automobiles. **Rates:** $55–$95 S or D; $150 ste. Extra person $12. Children under age 12 stay free. Parking: Indoor, free. AE, DC, DISC, MC, V.

≣≣ Jackie Gaughan's Plaza Hotel/Casino

1 Main St, 89101 (Downtown); tel 702/386-2110 or toll free 800/634-6575; fax 702/382-8281. Registration desk is almost lost in the chaos of the very glitzy casino. Quiet area on mezzanine level has restaurants and meeting rooms. Amtrak and Greyhound depots next door. **Rooms:** 1,037 rms and stes. CI 2pm/CO noon. Nonsmoking rms avail. Rooms are bright, airy, and spacious, with light wood furniture and pastel decor. **Amenities:** 🛏 A/C, cable TV w/movies. Some units w/minibars, some w/whirlpools. **Services:** 🍽 VP 🚗 🖼 🍴 Car-rental desk, babysitting. **Facilities:** 🛝 🏋 🎱4 300 👤 3 restaurants, 3 bars (1 w/entertainment), games rm, beauty salon. Wedding chapel, showroom. **Rates:** $30–$75 S or D; $80–$100 ste. Extra person $8. Children under age 12 stay free. Parking: Indoor/outdoor, free. AE, CB, DC, DISC, MC, V.

≣≣ Lady Luck Casino/Hotel

206 N 3rd St, PO Box 1060, 89101 (Downtown); tel 702/477-3000 or toll free 800/523-9582; fax 702/477-3002. A bustling hotel that caters to groups. Good value. **Rooms:** 791 rms and stes. CI 3pm/CO noon. Nonsmoking rms avail. Junior suites have large windows, sitting areas. **Amenities:** 🛏 🕭 A/C, cable TV w/movies, refrig. Some units w/minibars, some w/whirlpools. All junior suites have Jacuzzis. **Services:** 🍽 VP 🚗 🖼 🍴 Car-rental desk. **Facilities:** 🛝 👤 4 restaurants, 2 bars, games rm. Showroom. **Rates:** $40–$60 S or D; $90 ste. Extra person $8. Children under age 12 stay free. Parking: Indoor, free. AE, DC, DISC, MC, V.

≣≣ Las Vegas Club Hotel & Casino

18 E Fremont St, PO Box 1719, 89101 (Downtown); tel 702/385-1664 or toll free 800/634-6532; fax 702/387-6071. One of downtown's best-kept secrets, with a quiet lobby and friendly atmosphere. **Rooms:** 224 rms and stes. CI 3pm/CO noon. Nonsmoking rms avail. Rooms are tastefully decorated in southwestern motifs, with rattan and light wood furniture. All units w/terraces. **Amenities:** 🛏 🕭 A/C, cable TV, voice mail, in-rm safe. **Services:** 🍽 VP 🖼 🍴 Babysitting. **Facilities:** 400 👤 2 restaurants, 2 bars. **Rates:** $46–$55 S or D; $125–$250 ste. Extra person $8. Children under age 12 stay free. Min stay wknds and special events. Parking: Indoor, free. AE, CB, DC, DISC, JCB, MC, V.

≣≣≣ Las Vegas Hilton

3000 Paradise Rd, PO Box 93147, 89109 (Convention Center); tel 702/732-5111 or toll free 800/732-7117; fax 702/732-5834. 2 blocks E of Las Vegas Blvd. Far from the clamor of the strip, on nice manicured grounds with the feel of a resort. Lobby glitters with crystal chandeliers, marble floors, brass fixtures. **Rooms:** 3,166 rms and stes. Executive level. CI 2pm/CO noon. Nonsmoking rms avail. Spacious, bright rooms with light wood furniture, sofa, and dressing area; decorated in muted pastels. Many have view of city skyline or nearby country club. **Amenities:** 🛏 🕭 📶 A/C, satel TV w/movies, dataport, voice mail, in-rm safe. Some units w/minibars, some w/terraces, some w/fireplaces, some w/whirlpools. **Services:** 🍽 ☎ VP 🚗 🖼 🍴 Twice-daily maid svce, car-rental desk, masseur, babysitting. **Facilities:** 🛝 🏋 🎱6 🏋 10000 💻 👤 11 restaurants (see "Restaurants" below), 6 bars (1 w/entertainment), games rm, spa, sauna, steam rm, whirlpool, beauty salon, washer/dryer. Elegant casino with rich wood and crystal chandeliers; shopping arcade; theatrical events. Golf for guests at Hilton Country Club, 3 miles east. **Rates:** $89–$269 S or D; $320–$805 ste. Extra person $20. Children under age 12 stay free. Parking: Indoor/outdoor, free. AE, CB, DC, DISC, MC, V.

☰☰☰ Luxor Hotel/Casino

3900 Las Vegas Blvd S, PO Box 98640, 89119; tel 702/262-4000 or toll free 800/288-1000; fax 702/262-4809. On the strip. New Egyptian-theme hotel built as a 30-story pyramid, with a huge interior atrium encircled by a canal, 3 levels of public areas, and a 10-story sphinx. **Rooms:** 2,526 rms and stes. Executive level. CI 2pm/CO 11am. Nonsmoking rms avail. Rooms are well appointed; wood furniture has Egyptian carvings. Sloping windows afford a view of the city, and door opens into the atrium. **Amenities:** 📞 A/C, satel TV w/movies, voice mail. Some units w/minibars, some w/whirlpools. **Services:** ⦿| VP 🚗 ⛱ ↵ 🗣 Car-rental desk, babysitting. **Facilities:** 🏋 ⅄ 7 restaurants, 3 bars (1 w/entertainment), games rm, whirlpool, beauty salon, washer/dryer. Movie theaters, virtual-reality arcade, show rooms. Barges ferry guests on tour of the "Nile" (fee). **Rates:** $66–$99 S or D; $150–$300 ste. Extra person $10. Children under age 12 stay free. Parking: Indoor/outdoor, free. AE, DISC, MC, V.

☰☰ Maxim Hotel/Casino

160 E Flamingo Rd, 89109; tel 702/731-4300 or toll free 800/634-6987; fax 702/735-3252. 1 block E of the strip. Convenient to Caesar's, the Mirage, and several other casinos. There is no real lobby, just a registration desk near the casino. **Rooms:** 800 rms and stes. CI 2pm/CO noon. Nonsmoking rms avail. Nondescript, with earth-toned carpeting, floral print upholstery, and dark wood furniture. **Amenities:** 📞 A/C, cable TV w/movies. Some units w/minibars, some w/whirlpools. **Services:** ⦿| VP ⛱ ↵ Car-rental desk. **Facilities:** 🏋 ⌷300⌷ ⅄ 4 restaurants, 2 bars (1 w/entertainment), games rm, beauty salon. Casino and a showroom with comedy-club theme. **Rates:** $49–$99 S or D; $175–$250 ste. Children under age 12 stay free. Parking: Indoor/outdoor, free. AE, CB, DC, DISC, MC, V.

☰☰☰ MGM Grand Hotel

3799 Las Vegas Blvd S, PO Box 77711, 89109; tel 702/891-1111 or toll free 800/929-1111; fax 702/891-1112. On the strip. World's largest hotel. A huge emerald-green monolith with a gold stucco lion at the entrance and a *Wizard of Oz* theme inside. **Rooms:** 5,005 rms and stes. CI 2pm/CO noon. Nonsmoking rms avail. Rooms have emerald-green carpet, gold moldings, red poppy-patterned bedspreads, and stills from the *Wizard of Oz*. **Amenities:** 📞 A/C, satel TV w/movies, voice mail. Some units w/minibars, some w/terraces, some w/whirlpools. **Services:** ⦿| VP 🚗 ⛱ ↵ 🗣 Car-rental desk, children's program, babysitting. **Facilities:** 🏋 🏊 ⛳ ⌷15000⌷ ⅄ 8 restaurants (*see* "Restaurants" below), 4 bars (2 w/entertainment), games rm, whirlpool, beauty salon, washer/dryer. Theme park with Hollywood motif; two showrooms; 170,000-square-foot casino. Free monorail to Bally's. **Rates:** $89–

$149 S or D; $125–$550 ste. Extra person $10. Children under age 12 stay free. Parking: Indoor/outdoor, free. AE, CB, DC, DISC, JCB, MC, V.

☰☰☰ The Mirage

3400 Las Vegas Blvd S, PO Box 98544, 89109; tel 702/791-7111 or toll free 800/627-6667; fax 702/791-7446. On the strip. South Seas–theme hotel with lush landscaping, man-made volcano, waterfalls, and lagoon. Tropical rainforest in atrium. **Rooms:** 3,049 rms and stes. Executive level. CI 2pm/CO noon. Nonsmoking rms avail. Tropical motif with parrot colors; white wood and rattan furnishings. **Amenities:** 📞 🏊 A/C, cable TV w/movies, voice mail. Some units w/minibars, some w/terraces, some w/whirlpools. **Services:** ⦿| 🍽 VP 🚗 ⛱ ↵ Car-rental desk, masseur, babysitting. **Facilities:** 🏋 ⌷⌷ ⌷6500⌷ 🖥 ⅄ 12 restaurants, 4 bars (1 w/entertainment), games rm, spa, sauna, steam rm, whirlpool, beauty salon. Dolphin habitat, showroom, shops. Golf privileges at nearby country club. **Rates:** $79–$350 S or D; $175–$950 ste. Extra person $30. Parking: Indoor/outdoor, free. AE, DC, DISC, MC, V.

☰☰☰ Monte Carlo Resort and Casino

3770 Las Vegas Blvd S, PO Box 14967, 89114; tel 702/730-7777 or toll free 800/311-8999; fax 702/739-9172. Newly opened in 1996, this property has a Belle Epoque facade that recalls the Place du Casino in Monaco. Design elements include domes with chandeliers, marble floors, ornate fountains, and promenades with gas lamps. **Rooms:** 3,014 rms and stes. CI 3pm/CO 11am. Nonsmoking rms avail. Attractive accommodations with cherrywood furniture, marble entryways, and good–size bathrooms topped with black counters. **Amenities:** 📞 A/C, cable TV w/movies, voice mail. **Services:** ⦿| VP 🚗 ⛱ ↵ Masseur. **Facilities:** ⌷⌷ ⌷250⌷ ⅄ 5 restaurants, games rm, spa, sauna, whirlpool, beauty salon. 90,000-square foot casino, wedding chapel, cluster of shops, 1200-seat showroom, and two-acre pool park with a river ride and wave pool. **Rates:** $59–$199 S or D; $129 ste. Extra person $10. Children under age 12 stay free. Parking: Indoor/outdoor, free. AE, DISC, JCB, MC, V.

☰☰ Quality Inn and Casino

377 E Flamingo Rd, 89109; tel 702/733-7777 or toll free 800/634-6617; fax 702/369-6911. ¾ mi E of the strip. Ordinary facade conceals Mediterranean-style courtyard with lush greenery, fountains, and walking paths. **Rooms:** 324 rms. CI 2pm/CO 11am. Nonsmoking rms avail. Modern furnishings in cool pastels. **Amenities:** 📞 🏊 🍴 A/C, cable TV w/movies, refrig. **Services:** ⛱ ↵ **Facilities:** 🏋 ⌷80⌷ ⅄ 1 restaurant, 1 bar, games rm, whirlpool, washer/dryer. 15,000-square-foot casino. **Rates:** $59–$99 S or D. Extra person $8. Children under age 18 stay free. Min stay wknds and special events. Parking: Outdoor, free. AE, DC, DISC, MC, V.

☰☰☰ Residence Inn by Marriott

3225 Paradise Rd, 89109; tel 702/796-9300 or toll free 800/331-3131; fax 702/796-9562. Across the street from Las Vegas Convention Center. Condominium-like units are located in garden buildings spread over beautifully landscaped grounds. The lobby area, the Hearth Room, has a fireplace, Scandinavian furnishings, and books as well as a TV set. **Rooms:** 192 effic. CI 2pm/CO noon. Nonsmoking rms avail. Studios have sitting areas and a fireplace; penthouse has two bedrooms and two baths. **Amenities:** 🛏 ⌀ 🖵 A/C, cable TV w/movies, refrig, VCR. Some units w/terraces, some w/fireplaces. All have well-equipped kitchens. **Services:** 🍴🖵↵ ↺ Car-rental desk. Continental breakfast served in the lobby. A barbecue on Wednesdays and a hospitality hour with beverages and snacks on weeknights. Staff will deliver groceries and fireplace logs for a fee. Guests can order from nearby restaurants from in-room menus. **Facilities:** 🛆 ⏣ ⅄ 1 restaurant (dinner only), whirlpool, washer/dryer. Sports court for basketball, volleyball, and racquetball. **Rates (CP):** $169–$219 effic. Children under age 18 stay free. Parking: Outdoor, free. AE, DC, DISC, MC, V.

☰☰☰ Rio Suite Hotel & Casino

3700 W Flamingo Rd, PO Box 14160, 89103; tel 702/252-7777 or toll free 800/888-1818; fax 702/252-7791. ½ mi W of the strip. Calypso-theme hotel features brass parrots in the lobby, nautilus shells on the ceiling, and colorful carpeting that suggests confetti and streamers. Neon ribbons wind through the public areas, and the hotel's marquee is a massive neon geyser. **Rooms:** 861 stes. CI 3pm/CO noon. Nonsmoking rms avail. Suites have sitting areas with sofas, chaise lounges, and smoked glass coffee tables. Tropical prints abound. **Amenities:** 🛏 🖵 A/C, satel TV w/movies, refrig, voice mail, in-rm safe. Some units w/minibars. **Services:** 🍴 ☒️ 🚗 🖵 ↵ Car-rental desk, babysitting. Free shuttle to Harrah's on the strip. **Facilities:** 🛆 🎳 ⏣ ⅄ 6 restaurants, 5 bars (1 w/entertainment), whirlpool, beauty salon, playground, washer/dryer. Lushly landscaped pool area has waterfall, palm trees, and a sandy beach. Carnival-themed casinos. Dinner show, "Copacabana," is reminiscent of the nearly extinct dinner shows of the 1960s. **Rates:** $85–$103 ste. Extra person $15. Children under age 12 stay free. Parking: Indoor/outdoor, free. AE, DC, DISC, MC, V.

☰☰☰ Riviera Hotel

2901 Las Vegas Blvd S, PO Box 14520, 89109; tel 702/734-5110 or toll free 800/634-3414; fax 702/794-9663. On the strip. Opened in the 1950s, this classic Las Vegas hotel is home to one of the largest casinos in the world. **Rooms:** 2,100 rms and stes. CI 2pm/CO noon. Nonsmoking rms avail. Rooms are larger than average, with older furnishings, yet clean and well kept. **Amenities:** 🛏 🍷 A/C, cable TV w/movies, in-rm safe. Some units w/minibars, some w/terraces, some w/fireplaces, some w/whirlpools. **Services:** 🍴 ☒️ ☒️ ⏣ ↵ ↺ Car-rental desk, masseur, babysitting. **Facilities:** 🛆 🎱 🎳 🖵 ⅄ 4 restaurants, 5 bars (1

w/entertainment), games rm, spa, sauna, steam rm, whirlpool, beauty salon. Several shops. **Rates:** $59–$95 S or D; $115 ste. Extra person $20. Parking: Indoor/outdoor, free. AE, DISC, MC, V.

☰☰ Sahara Hotel & Casino

2535 Las Vegas Blvd S, PO Box 98503, 89109; tel 702/737-2111 or toll free 800/634-6666; fax 702/735-5921. On the strip. A traditional hotel; long walks from rooms to the casino or restaurant. **Rooms:** 2,100 rms and stes. CI 3pm/CO noon. No smoking. Garden rooms near the pool feature dark wood decor; roomier quarters are in the newer Alexandria wing. **Amenities:** 🛏 A/C, cable TV w/movies. Some units w/minibars, some w/terraces, some w/whirlpools. **Services:** 🍴 ☒️ 🚗 ⏣ ↵ Car-rental desk, babysitting. **Facilities:** 🛆 🎱 🎳 7 restaurants, 3 bars (1 w/entertainment), games rm, whirlpool, beauty salon. Showroom, lovely pool area with palm trees and thatched huts. **Rates:** $55–$95 S or D; $165 ste. Extra person $10. Children under age 14 stay free. Parking: Indoor/outdoor, free. AE, CB, DC, DISC, MC, V.

☰☰ Sam Boyd's Fremont Hotel & Casino

200 E Fremont St, PO Box 940, 89101 (Downtown); tel 702/385-3232 or toll free 800/634-6460; fax 702/385-6209. Caters to visitors from Hawaii, with a tropical island motif. **Rooms:** 452 rms and stes. CI 2pm/CO noon. Nonsmoking rms avail. Modern rooms with green/white carpet, wallpaper, and floral drapes. **Amenities:** 🛏 A/C, TV w/movies, in-rm safe. Some units w/minibars. **Services:** 🍴 ☒️ 🚗 ⏣ ↵ Car-rental desk, babysitting. **Facilities:** 🎱 ⅄ 4 restaurants, 3 bars, games rm, day-care ctr. Use of pool at California Hotel. **Rates:** Peak (Mar–May) $28–$52 S or D; $60–$120 ste. Extra person $8. Children under age 21 stay free. Lower rates off-season. Parking: Indoor, free. AE, CB, DISC, MC, V.

☰☰☰ Sheraton Desert Inn Resort & Casino

3145 Las Vegas Blvd S, 89109; tel 702/733-4444 or toll free 800/634-6906; fax 702/733-4437. Among the nicest hotels on the strip, with six towers and garden-style rooms. **Rooms:** 821 rms and stes. CI 3pm/CO noon. Nonsmoking rms avail. Rooms are well appointed; some have chaise lounges, armoires, and English country furnishings. **Amenities:** 🛏 A/C, cable TV w/movies, in-rm safe. Some units w/minibars, some w/terraces. **Services:** 🍴 ☒ ☒️ 🚗 ⏣ ↵ ↺ Car-rental desk, masseur, babysitting. **Facilities:** 🛆 ▶18 🏌 ⛳5 🎱5 🎳 🖵 ⅄ 5 restaurants, 3 bars (1 w/entertainment), games rm, spa, sauna, whirlpool, beauty salon. Championship-quality golf course; showroom; city's largest spa. **Rates:** Peak (Dec 29–May/Sept 2–Nov 19) $155–$215 S or D; $265 ste. Extra person $25. Lower rates off-season. Parking: Indoor/outdoor, free. AE, DC, DISC, MC, V.

☰☰ Showboat Hotel Casino & Bowling Center

2800 Fremont St, 89104; tel 702/385-9123 or toll free 800/626-2800; fax 702/385-9163. 8 mi E of dowtown Las Vegas. A Vegas landmark since 1953, this Mardi Gras–theme hotel is a mecca for low rollers and locals who flock to the bowling alley and the city's largest bingo hall. Bright registration area has plantation murals, flower boxes, plants, and chandeliers. **Rooms:** 451 rms and stes. CI 2pm/CO noon. Nonsmoking rms avail. Newer tower rooms decorated with dark wood furniture and earth tones. Older garden rooms (by the pool) are less luxurious but still comfortable. **Amenities:** 🛎 A/C, cable TV w/movies. Some units w/terraces. **Services:** 🍴 VP 🚗 🏊 🛎 🦽 Car-rental desk, babysitting. **Facilities:** 📷 1100 ♿ 4 restaurants, 5 bars (1 w/entertainment), games rm, beauty salon, day-care ctr. 106-lane bowling alley and 24-hour bingo hall. Newly expanded casino is brightly lit and large enough to give gamblers plenty of elbow room. **Rates:** $39–$89 S or D; $90–$195 ste. Extra person $10. Children under age 12 stay free. Parking: Indoor/outdoor, free. AE, DISC, MC, V.

≣≣≣ Stardust Resort & Casino

3000 Las Vegas Blvd S, 89109; tel 702/732-6111 or toll free 800/634-6757; fax 702/732-6257. On the strip. Newly expanded and renovated hotel, with tasteful public areas spread out on rambling grounds. **Rooms:** 2,400 rms and stes. CI 2pm/CO noon. Nonsmoking rms avail. Nicest rooms are in the 32-story tower built in 1990. Older rooms are larger; motel units are available at the rear of the property. **Amenities:** 🛎 🍴 A/C, cable TV w/movies, in-rm safe. Some units w/minibars, some w/terraces. **Services:** 🍴 VP 🚗 🏊 🦽 Car-rental desk, babysitting. **Facilities:** 📷 🏋 2000 🖥 ♿ 6 restaurants (see "Restaurants" below), 4 bars (1 w/entertainment), games rm, spa, whirlpool, beauty salon. Showroom. **Rates:** $36–$300 S or D; $250 ste. Extra person $10. Children under age 12 stay free. Parking: Indoor/outdoor, free. AE, CB, DC, DISC, MC, V.

UNRATED Stratosphere Hotel and Casino

2000 Las Vegas Blvd S, 89104; tel 702/382-4446 or toll free 800/998-6937; fax 702/383-4755. Opened in 1996, this was formerly Bob Stupak's Vegas World Resort. Now completely renovated, it's capped by an 1,100-foot observation tower— the highest in the country. **Rooms:** 1,500 rms. CI 3pm/CO 11am. Nonsmoking rms avail. **Amenities:** 🛎 🍴 📺 🍴 A/C, cable TV w/movies, voice mail, in-rm safe. Some units w/minibars, some w/whirlpools. **Services:** 🍴 VP 🚗 🏊 🦽 Car-rental desk. **Facilities:** 📷 🏋 1000 ♿ 6 restaurants, 4 bars (2 w/entertainment), games rm, spa, whirlpool, beauty salon, day-care ctr. Casino, showroom, and observation tower that includes three wedding chapels, revolving restaurant, and high-altitude thrill rides. **Rates:** $69–$159 S or D. Extra person $15. Children under age 12 stay free. Parking: Indoor/outdoor, free. AE, DISC, JCB, MC, V.

≣≣≣ Treasure Island at the Mirage

3300 Las Vegas Blvd S, PO Box 7711, 89109; tel 702/894-7111 or toll free 800/627-6667; fax 702/894-7788. On the strip. Pirate-theme hotel with buccaneer village, treasure chests, and a mock sea battle in a strip-side lagoon several times daily. **Rooms:** 2,900 rms and stes. Executive level. CI

2pm/CO noon. Nonsmoking rms avail. Bright and airy rooms with light carpeting, whitewashed wood furniture, brass fixtures, and nautical paintings. **Amenities:** 🛎 🍴 🍴 A/C, satel TV w/movies, dataport, voice mail. Some units w/minibars, some w/terraces, some w/whirlpools. **Services:** 🍴 🗝 VP 🚗 🏊 🦽 🛎 Car-rental desk, masseur, babysitting. **Facilities:** 📷 🏋 1000 🖥 4 restaurants, 2 bars (1 w/entertainment), games rm, spa, sauna, steam rm, whirlpool, beauty salon, washer/dryer. Two wedding chapels, showroom. Golf privileges at nearby Mirage Country Club. **Rates:** $69–$199 S or D; $149–$650 ste. Extra person $25. Children under age 12 stay free. Parking: Indoor/outdoor, free. AE, CB, DC, DISC, JCB, MC, V.

≣≣ Tropicana Resort and Casino

3801 Las Vegas Blvd S, PO Box 97777, 89109; tel 702/739-2222 or toll free 800/634-4000; fax 702/739-2448. On the strip. Popular with tour groups, and always busy. Tropical-island decor with rain-forest landscaping, waterfalls, tiki torches, and thatched huts. **Rooms:** 1,908 rms. CI 2pm/CO noon. Nonsmoking rms avail. Tropical motif in rooms, with rattan and bamboo furnishings. **Amenities:** 🛎 🍴 A/C, cable TV w/movies, in-rm safe. Some units w/minibars, some w/terraces. **Services:** 🍴 VP 🚗 🏊 🦽 🛎 Car-rental desk, masseur, babysitting. **Facilities:** 📷 🏋 7800 🖥 ♿ 6 restaurants, 4 bars (2 w/entertainment), games rm, spa, sauna, steam rm, whirlpool, beauty salon. Pool area is a five-acre water park with lagoons and spa. Shopping arcade, showroom. **Rates:** $59–$179 S or D. Extra person $15. Children under age 12 stay free. Parking: Indoor/outdoor, free. AE, DC, DISC, MC, V.

≣≣ Westward-Ho Hotel/Casino

2900 Las Vegas Blvd S, 89109; tel 702/731-2900 or toll free 800/634-6803. On the strip. Sprawling motel-style property with guest parking outside each room. Public areas face the strip. **Rooms:** 800 rms and stes. CI 2pm/CO noon. Nonsmoking rms avail. Motel-quality furnishings, clean but hardly elegant. Suites are popular with families. **Amenities:** 🛎 A/C, cable TV. Some units w/terraces. **Services:** 🚗 🦽 **Facilities:** 📷 3 restaurants, 2 bars (1 w/entertainment), games rm, whirlpool. **Rates:** $45–$55 S or D; $85–$165 ste. Extra person $10. Children under age 18 stay free. Parking: Outdoor, free. AE, CB, DC, DISC, MC, V.

MOTELS

≣≣ Center Strip Inn

3688 Las Vegas Blvd S, 89109; tel 702/739-6066 or toll free 800/777-7737; fax 702/736-2521. On the strip. The newest building here has all the amenities the Vegas visitor looks for, and more. **Rooms:** 152 rms and stes. CI 2pm/CO noon. Nonsmoking rms avail. Standard accommodations are not special, but the deluxe rooms are, with steam rooms and new furnishings. **Amenities:** 🛎 🍴 A/C, cable TV w/movies, refrig, VCR. Some units w/whirlpools. **Services:** 🗝 🏊 🦽 Car-rental desk. **Facilities:** 📷 ♿ Washer/dryer. **Rates (CP):** $30–

$159 S; $50–$169 D; $69–$179 ste. Extra person $10. Children under age 18 stay free. Min stay wknds. Parking: Outdoor, free. AE, DC, DISC, MC, V.

≣≣≣ Days Inn Downtown
707 E Fremont St, 89101; tel 702/388-1400 or toll free 800/325-2344; fax 702/388-9622. The largest Days Inn in the region, and a perfect motel for budget travelers who still want decent lodging. Recently upgraded. **Rooms:** 147 rms and stes. CI 2pm/CO noon. Nonsmoking rms avail. Just-renovated rooms are large and quiet. **Amenities:** 🛏 A/C, satel TV w/movies. **Services:** 🚗 🍽 Social director, babysitting. **Facilities:** 🛗 📺 ⚹ 1 restaurant, games rm. The pool is well cared for and recently got a new canopy. **Rates:** $32–$45 S or D; $60–$80 ste. Children under age 12 stay free. Parking: Outdoor, free. AE, CB, DC, DISC, MC, V.

≣≣≣ La Quinta Motor Inn
3782 Las Vegas Blvd S, 89109; tel 702/739-7457 or toll free 800/531-5900; fax 702/736-1129. Located well away from the strip, this Spanish-style property has a red-tile roof, stucco exterior, and palm tree landscaping. The homey lobby features rattan furniture, a fireplace, throw rugs, and ficus trees. **Rooms:** 114 rms. CI open/CO noon. Nonsmoking rms avail. Spacious rooms feature warm colors, wood desks and furniture, a recliner and ottoman, and art on the walls. **Amenities:** 🛏 ⚹ A/C, cable TV w/movies, dataport. **Services:** 🚗 🖼 🍽 ⚹ Babysitting. **Facilities:** 🛗 ⚹ Rates (CP): $55–$65 S; $65–$75 D. Extra person $10. Children under age 18 stay free. Parking: Outdoor, free. AE, CB, DISC, MC, V.

≣≣ Motel 6
195 E Tropicana Ave, 89109; tel 702/798-0728 or toll free 800/4-MOTEL6; fax 702/798-5657. 3 blocks E of the strip. Two-story, U-shaped building wrapped around a pool. Located directly across the street from the MGM Grand, this motel is always packed with families with children. Next to two restaurants. **Rooms:** 878 rms. CI 4pm/CO 11am. Nonsmoking rms avail. Clean and simple. Floral print spreads, pressed-wood furniture. **Amenities:** 🛏 A/C, satel TV w/movies. **Services:** 🍽 ⚹ Car-rental desk, babysitting. Tour desk. **Facilities:** 🛗 Whirlpool, playground, washer/dryer. Motel gift shop is a mini-mart with soft drinks, sandwiches, etc. **Rates:** $30–$42 S; $36–$48 D. Extra person $3. Children under age 17 stay free. Min stay wknds and special events. Parking: Outdoor, free. AE, DC, DISC, MC, V.

≣≣≣ Vagabond Inn
3265 Las Vegas Blvd S, 89109; tel 702/735-5102 or toll free 800/828-8032; fax 702/735-0168. On the strip. Undergoing renovation. Across from Treasure Island, with its showy pirate-ship battle out front. **Rooms:** 126 rms and stes. CI 3pm/CO 11am. Nonsmoking rms avail. Ask for one of the newly renovated rooms. **Amenities:** 🛏 A/C, cable TV w/movies, refrig. Some units w/minibars, some w/terraces. **Services:** 🚗 🍽 ⚹ Car-rental desk, babysitting. Coffee available in lobby. Complimentary daily copy of *USA Today*.

Facilities: 🛗 Washer/dryer. **Rates:** $42–$95 S; $47–$105 D; $65 ste. Extra person $5. Children under age 12 stay free. Parking: Outdoor, free. AE, DC, DISC, MC, V.

RESTAURANTS 🍽

★ Alpine Village Inn
3003 Paradise Rd; tel 702/734-6888. E Sahara exit off I-15. **German.** Alpine villa atmosphere, with pewter dinnerware and silverware. Daily specials may include Schweinehaxen and various preparations of pork shank and sausage. Upstairs is for fine German dining; downstairs is a rathskeller with a simple and less expensive menu. **FYI:** Reservations recommended. Karaoke. Children's menu. **Open:** Sun–Thurs 5–10pm, Fri–Sat 5–11pm. **Prices:** Main courses $12–$25; prix fixe $10–$20. AE, CB, DC, DISC, MC, V. VP ⚹

♣ Andre's
401 S 6th St (Downtown); tel 702/385-5016. Charleston Ave exit off I-15. **French.** Considered one of the top French restaurants in Las Vegas. Four dining rooms decorated with country antiques; two rooms can accommodate small groups up to 10 people. Known for its 800-label wine cellar and creations such as smoked baby coho salmon and snails bourguignonne. **FYI:** Reservations recommended. Jacket required. **Open:** Daily 6–10pm. **Prices:** Main courses $17–$37. AE, DC, DISC, MC, V. ♥ VP ⚹

♣ Bacchanal
In Caesars Palace, 3570 Las Vegas Blvd S; tel 702/734-7110. **Continental.** One of Caesars Palace's most renowned restaurants, with Roman-style vases and statues, vines that cover everything, and a fountain in the center. On the menu are continental and seasonal dishes. **FYI:** Reservations recommended. Dancing/dinner theater. Dress code. **Open:** Tues–Sat 6–9pm. **Prices:** Prix fixe $70. AE, CB, DC, DISC, MC, V. VP ⚹

Camelot
In the Excalibur Hotel, 3850 Las Vegas Blvd S; tel 702/597-7777. E Tropicana Ave exit off I-15. **Continental/American.** Part elegant English countryside, with forest-like murals and plants, part English castle, with mock fireplace and armaments as decorations. Tables are large and service is exceptional. Specialties include veal piccata (chef's favorite) and rack of lamb King James. Excellent desserts. Reasonably priced. May close early on slow nights. **FYI:** Reservations recommended. Children's menu. Dress code. **Open:** Sun–Thurs 6–10pm, Fri–Sat 5–11pm. **Prices:** Main courses $15–$24. AE, DC, DISC, MC, V. VP ⚹

Chili's Grill & Bar
2590 S Maryland Pkwy; tel 702/733-6462. **Burgers/Tex-Mex.** Family-oriented restaurant with Tex-Mex decor. Specialties include onion blossom appetizer and chicken salads. **FYI:** Reservations not accepted. Children's menu. **Open:** Mon–Thurs 11am–10pm, Fri–Sat 11am–11pm, Sun 11:30am–10pm. **Prices:** Main courses $5–$16. MC, V. 🖼 ⚹

Chin's
In Fashion Show Mall, 3200 Las Vegas Blvd S; tel 702/
733-8899. E Spring Mountain exit off I-15. **Chinese.** Simple
in layout, the decor is beautiful, with white china and white
table linen. Spacious dining room is lit by soft ceiling lights.
Known for original creations like strawberry chicken and dim
sum lunch. Food prepared on jet burner, which creates
intense heat that seals juices. **FYI:** Reservations accepted.
Piano. Dress code. **Open:** Mon–Sat 11:30am–10pm, Sun
noon–10pm. **Prices:** Main courses $9–$25. AE, MC, V. [VP] &

Dragon Court
In MGM Grand Hotel, 3799 Las Vegas Blvd S; tel 702/
891-7380. E Tropicana exit off I-15. **Chinese.** The dazzling
decor tries to recall ancient China, re-creating the appearance of a Chinese emperor's court, with small trees, lanterns,
tapestries, and carved fishbone figures. Specialties of the
house include Imperial Peking duck carved tableside and
sizzling spicy scallops. Special cooking method prevents food
from being greasy. **FYI:** Reservations recommended. Dress
code. **Open:** Daily 5–11pm. **Prices:** Main courses $14–$40.
AE, DC, DISC, MC, V. [VP] &

Fog City Diner
325 Hughes Center Dr; tel 702/737-0200. ¾ mi E of strip.
New American/Seafood. This San Francisco–type diner is
decorated with faux-leather booths, chrome and glass fixtures, and a soda fountain–style counter. Innovative menu
offers a blend of seafood specialties and American favorites.
Recommended are crabcakes, flatiron pot roast, and the
sirloin and black bean chili. Fresh oyster bar and Anchor
Steam beer on tap. **FYI:** Reservations recommended. Dress
code. **Open:** Sun–Thurs 11:30am–11pm, Fri–Sat 11:30am–
midnight. **Prices:** Main courses $7–$18. CB, DC, DISC, MC,
V. &

Gandhi India's Cuisine
4080 Paradise; tel 702/734-0094. Flamingo exit off I-15.
Indian. An appealing place decorated with tapestries and
murals. Tandoori oven cooking is a specialty here; a good
introduction is the lamb or vegetable samosa. For dessert,
there's kulfi, saffron-flavored ice cream with mango. Indian
beers are available. **FYI:** Reservations accepted. Dress code.
Beer and wine only. **Open:** Lunch daily 11am–2:30pm;
dinner daily 5–11pm. **Prices:** Main courses $7–$15; prix fixe
$14. DISC, MC, V. &

★ **Ginza**
1000 E Sahara Ave; tel 702/732-3080. E Sahara exit off I-15.
Japanese. What this restaurant lacks in appearance, it makes
up for with the food. Lovely paper lanterns and Japanese
vases provide charm. Most patrons come for the sushi bar,
but menu items including shabu-shabu, tempura, and
yosenabe, a Japanese bouillabaisse, are also good. **FYI:**
Reservations accepted. **Open:** Tues–Sun 5pm–1am. **Prices:**
Main courses $13–$18. AE, MC, V. &

★ **Kiefer's Atop the Carriage House**
105 E Harmon Ave; tel 702/739-8000. E Tropicana exit off
I-15. **New American.** Decorated in pink, red, and off-white,
with wicker chairs and comfortable booths. The place is
famous for its caesar salad. A local favorite is orange roughy
with crabmeat, asparagus, and béarnaise sauce; frog legs in
Dijon sauce is also recommended. **FYI:** Reservations recommended. Piano. Dress code. **Open:** Breakfast daily 7–10am;
dinner Sun–Thurs 5–11pm, Fri–Sat 5pm–midnight. **Prices:**
Main courses $17–$22. CB, DC, DISC, MC, V. ♥ ▲ [VP] &

La Piazza Food Court
In Caesars Palace, 3750 Las Vegas Blvd; tel 702/731-7110.
Eclectic. A cross between a cafeteria and a food court, with
modern, clean decor. Menus appear above each food station.
Chinese stir-fry, Mexican tacos, pizzas, and other dishes are
available. There is often live entertainment in the common
dining area. **FYI:** Reservations not accepted. Big band. **Open:**
Daily 24 hrs. **Prices:** Main courses $6–$8. AE, CB, DC, MC,
V. [▪▪] [VP] &

♣ **Le Montrachet**
In the Las Vegas Hilton, 3000 Paradise Rd; tel 702/
732-5111. E Sahara exit off I-95. **French.** A quiet place away
from the casino, this round room is lavishly elegant with red
mohair booths, pastoral scenes on the walls, and a huge glass
chandelier. The seasonal menu features grilled Dover sole
and grilled double-cut lamb chops. For dessert, there's
almond ice cream in a chocolate cup. **FYI:** Reservations
recommended. Jacket required. **Open:** Peak (May–Sept)
Wed–Mon 6–10:30pm. **Prices:** Main courses $14–$29. AE,
CB, DC, DISC, MC, V. ♥ [VP]

Margarita Grille
In the Las Vegas Hilton, 3000 Paradise Rd; tel 702/
732-5111. E Sahara exit off I-75. **Mexican.** Southwest colors,
cacti, and Native American prints enliven this restaurant
where the small tables are decorated with festive colors and
woven place mats. A chips-and-salsa cart offers a variety of
dips from mild to super hot. Standard menu items include
chile verde, carne asada, and chimichangas. Smaller portions
for children upon request. **FYI:** Reservations recommended.
Children's menu. Dress code. **Open:** Daily 4–11pm. **Prices:**
Main courses $9–$16. AE, CB, DC, DISC, MC, V. [VP] &

♣ **The Monte Carlo Room**
In the Sheraton Desert Inn, 3145 Las Vegas Blvd S; tel 702/
733-4444. E Spring Mountain exit off I-15. **French.** Murals
and plants create a plush atmosphere. The three signature
dishes here are Nevada quail in red wine, duckling in cherry
sauce, and stuffed baby veal chop with Gruyère and ginger.
Kitchen will make special dishes on request. **FYI:** Reservations recommended. Jacket required. **Open:** Thurs–Mon 6–
11pm. **Prices:** Main courses $27–$54. AE, CB, DC, DISC,
MC, V. ♥ [VP] &

Pamplemousse

400 E Sahara Ave; tel 702/733-2066. 3 blocks E of the strip. **Continental/French.** An intimate French dining room with a step-down wine cellar and a solarium alcove. Typical entrees are rack of lamb, fresh Norwegian salmon, steaks, and lobsters. A specialty is a basket of fresh vegetables with sauce for dipping. **FYI:** Reservations recommended. Jacket required. **Open:** Tues–Sun 5:30–11:30pm. **Prices:** Main courses $20–$38; prix fixe $25. AE, DC, MC, V. ❤ ⱽ𝐏 ♿

Rosewood Grille and Lobster House

3339 Las Vegas Blvd S; tel 702/792-5965. Spring Mountain exit off I-15. **Seafood.** A local favorite, adorned in rosewood, with original art and a single red rose on each table. This place is known for serving the largest live Maine lobsters on the strip—up to 17 pounds! They also carry excellent steaks and chateaubriand, and offer one of the most extensive wine lists in town. **FYI:** Reservations recommended. Dress code. **Open:** Daily 4:30–11:30pm. **Prices:** Main courses $17–$35. DC, DISC, MC, V. ♿

Sacred Sea Room

In the Luxor Hotel and Casino, 3900 Las Vegas Blvd S; tel 702/262-4000. E Tropicana Ave exit off I-15. **Seafood.** Overlooking the casino, a stunning restaurant decorated in Egyptian motifs, with murals depicting the Nile River. Wonderful food, including stuffed prawns, and entrees baked in parchment with wine and herbs. There's always a meat and chicken entree on the menu. Expect excellent service. **FYI:** Reservations recommended. Dress code. **Open:** Daily 5–11pm. **Prices:** Main courses $16–$45. AE, CB, DC, DISC, MC, V. ⱽ𝐏 ♿

Stefano's

In the Golden Nugget, 129 E Fremont St (Downtown); tel 702/385-7111. Casino Center exit off I-515. **Italian.** A good-times atmosphere, complete with singing waiters. Lattice-work, plants, and Italianate murals create the feeling of outdoor dining indoors. Known for the osso buco; also offers cioppino and fresh pastries. **FYI:** Reservations recommended. Karaoke. **Open:** Sun–Thurs 6–11pm, Fri–Sat 5:30–11pm. **Prices:** Main courses $10–$28. AE, DC, DISC, MC, V. ⱽ𝐏 ♿

Tony Roma's Place for Ribs

In the Stardust Resort & Casino, 3000 Las Vegas Blvd S; tel 702/732-6111. **Barbecue.** Choose from baby-back ribs basted with honey-molasses or original barbecue sauce, barbecued chicken, and assorted combination plates. **FYI:** Reservations recommended. Additional locations: 200 Fremont St (tel 385-6257); 620 E Sahara (tel 733-9914). **Open:** Sun–Thurs 5–11pm, Fri–Sat 5pm–midnight. **Prices:** Main courses $10–$16. AE, CB, DC, DISC, MC, V. ⱽ𝐏 ♿

ATTRACTIONS 🏛

Las Vegas Natural History Museum

900 Las Vegas Blvd N; tel 702/384-3466. This museum features animated model dinosaurs, a marine life exhibit with a 3,000-gallon shark tank, and other wildlife displays. The Discovery Room features hands-on exhibits for children. Gift shop. **Open:** Daily 9am–4pm. $$

Lied Discovery Children's Museum

833 Las Vegas Blvd N; tel 702/382-KIDS. More than 100 hands-on exhibits demonstrate the wonders of art, science, and the humanities. Exhibits include Toddler Tower, Gyrochair, Musical Pathway, and KKID radio. **Open:** Wed–Sat 10am–5pm, Sun noon–5pm. $$

Liberace Museum

1775 E Tropicana Ave; tel 702/798-5595. Devoted to the career memorabilia of "Mr Showmanship," three exhibit areas display Liberace's spectacular cars, costumes, jewelry, photographs, and much more. Some highlights are Liberace's mirror-tiled Rolls-Royce Phantom V (one of seven made), his famed candelabras, antique and custom-made pianos, and the world's largest rhinestone (50.6 lbs). **Open:** Mon–Sat 10am–5pm, Sun 1–5pm. $$$

Imperial Palace Auto Collection

3535 Las Vegas Blvd S; tel 702/794-3311 or toll free 800/634-6441. Located on the fifth floor of the Imperial Palace parking facility, this collection displays over 200 antique, classic, and special-interest vehicles daily, including one of the world's largest collections of Model J Duesenbergs. There are also cars belonging to world leaders and celebrities. **Open:** Daily 9:30am–11:30pm. $$$

Guinness World of Records Museum

2780 Las Vegas Blvd S; tel 702/792-3766. Displays, life-size replicas, and interactive exhibits bring the famous *Guinness Book of World Records* to three-dimensional life. Topics include the human world, with the world's tallest, shortest, heaviest, and other superlative people; natural wonders; sports and entertainment. **Open:** Peak (June–Sept) daily 9am–8pm. Reduced hours off-season. $$

Bethany's Celebrity Doll Museum

1775 E Tropicana Ave; tel 702/798-3036. A museum devoted to celebrity dolls, this attraction features a large number of stage and screen luminaries, from Redd Foxx and Captain Kangaroo to the Beatles and Grace Kelly. Fictional characters are also included, such as Barbie, the entire cast of *Gone with the Wind*, and the characters of *Alice in Wonderland*. **Open:** Mon–Sat 10am–5pm, Sun 1–5pm. Closed some hols. $

Fremont Street Experience

425 Fremont St; tel 702/678-5600. A five-block, open-air pedestrian mall. Its 90-foot-high "celestial vault" of sculpted steel mesh shelters a festive, lushly landscaped strip of outdoor cafes, vendor carts, and colorful kiosks purveying food and merchandise, and 50,000 square feet of indoor

retail space. Equipped with more than two million lights capable of producing over 65,500 color combinations, the canopy is used for the "Sky Parade," a high-tech light and laser show enhanced by a concert hall–quality sound system; there are several show times nightly. Live entertainment, holiday celebrations, special events. Ample parking available. **Free**

MGM Grand Adventures

3799 Las Vegas Blvd S; tel 702/891-7979. A full-scale, 33-acre theme park featuring six rides, three theaters, and nine themed areas. Each theme area has rides and shows, as well as shopping and dining establishments.

Popular attractions at the park include the Lightning Bolt roller coaster located in the New York Street section. The high-tech ride is completely indoors and simulates high-speed space travel with meteor showers and a black hole. The Backlot River Tour in Asian Village is a boat ride with special effects usually seen in movie productions, such as fog, rain, earthquakes, and gunfire from an attack helicopter. One of the most popular rides at the park is Grand Canyon Rapids, a five-minute whitewater raft ride that virtually assures a visitor receiving a complete drenching. Newly opened is the thrilling Sky Screamer. Flyers are towed to the top of a 250–foot launching tower, then freefall for 100 feet, reaching up to 80 miles an hour. **Open:** Daily 10am–6pm. **$$$$**

Grand Slam Canyon

2880 Las Vegas Blvd; tel 702/794-3939. Situated directly behind the main hotel and casino of Circus Circus. Architecturally compelling, the entire five-acre park is built two stories high atop the casino's parking structure, and is totally enclosed by a glass dome. The dome allows light in, blocks ultraviolet rays, and keeps the park air conditioned and climate-controlled 365 days a year.

As its name implies, the park is designed to resemble a classic Western desert canyon. From top to bottom, hand-painted artificial rock is sculpted into caverns, pinnacles, steep cliffs, and buttes. A stream runs through the stark landscape, cascading over a 90-foot falls into a rippling blue-green pool. Embellishing the scene are several life-sized animatronic dinosaurs, a re-creation of an archeological dig, a fossil wall, and a replica of a Pueblo Indian cliff dwelling.

Grand Slam Canyon's premier attractions are the Canyon Blaster, the only indoor, double-loop, corkscrew roller coaster in the United States; and the Rim Runner, a 3½-minute water flume ride. Secondary attractions include Twist & Shout, a 45-foot-high, dry corkscrew slide in a dark tube; and Hot Shots, a game where participants duel with harmless laser guns in a convoluted cavelike setting. One ride on each of the attractions is covered in the cost of admission. **Open:** Sun–Thurs 10am–5pm, Fri–Sat 10am–midnight. **$**

Wet 'n' Wild

2601 Las Vegas Blvd S; tel 702/734-0088. Located on the strip just south of Sahara Ave, this 26-acre water theme park features water slides, flumes, inner-tube rides, and a half-million-gallon wave pool, plus a children's area. Picnicking, concessions. **Open:** Apr–Sept; hours vary. **$$$$**

Scandia Family Fun Center

2900 Sirius Ave; tel 702/364-0070. Entrance on Rancho Dr, between Sahara Ave and Spring Mountain Rd. This family amusement center offers three 18-hole miniature golf courses, a video arcade, go-carts, bumper boats, and batting cages. (Fee charged for each activity.) **Open:** Peak (mid-June–Aug) Sun–Thurs 10am–midnight, Fri–Sat 10am –1am. Reduced hours off-season. **Free**

Dolphin Habitat

Mirage Hotel, 3400 Las Vegas Blvd S; tel 702/791-7111. Designed to educate the public about marine mammals and provide a healthy, nurturing environment for six Atlantic bottlenose dolphins, the Dolphin Exhibit is a 2.5-million-gallon pool with above- and below-ground viewing areas. The 15-minute tour includes a video of a resident dolphin (Duchess) giving birth (to Squirt) underwater.

Also at the Mirage are a royal white tiger habitat and a 53-foot, 20,000-gallon simulated coral reef aquarium behind the registration desk. **Open:** Mon–Fri 11am–7pm, Sat–Sun 9am–7pm. **$**

Ethel M Chocolates

2 Cactus Garden Dr; tel 702/458-8864. A tourist attraction drawing 18,000 visitors a day, this ultramodern factory is located 6 miles from the Las Vegas strip, in the Green Valley Business Park. Self-guided tours allow visitors to see the candy-making process from a glass-enclosed viewing aisle; all equipment is labeled to aid visitor comprehension. Video presentations are shown along the way.

Also on the premises is a 2½-acre garden displaying 350 species of rare and exotic cacti. Signs are provided to facilitate self-guided tours. **Open:** Daily 8:30am–7pm. **Free**

Floyd Lamb State Park

9200 Tule Springs Rd; tel 702/486-5413. Located 10 miles north of downtown Las Vegas, off US 95. Originally known as Tule Springs, this park was an early watering stop for Native Americans. It later became a privately owned working ranch, as well as a guest/dude ranch where guests could wait out the six-week residency requirement to obtain a quick divorce. In addition to the historic Tule Springs Ranch area, the park offers fishing and picnicking opportunities and a walking/bicycle path that winds through the park. **Open:** Daily. **$$**

Bonnie Springs Ranch/Old Nevada

Old Nevada; tel 702/875-4400. Located about 24 miles west of Las Vegas on NV 159, Old Nevada is a microcosm of a mid-1800s western Nevada town, its main street lined with weathered-wood buildings fronted by covered verandas. Live bands and melodramas are presented in the saloon; also featured are stunt shoot-outs, a wax museum, an old movie house, mine tours, stagecoach rides, and horseback riding.

Small zoo; aviary; shops and restaurants; Trading Post museum and gift shop. **Open:** May–Oct, daily 10:30am–6pm; Nov–Apr, daily 10:30am–5pm. $$$

Laughlin

Just across the border from California on the banks of the Colorado River, Laughlin has grown in the last 20 years to become one of the largest gambling centers in the country. Much of the popularity of Laughlin is due to its reputation as a slower-paced, but still bustling, alternative to Las Vegas. **Information:** Laughlin Chamber of Commerce, 1725 Casino Dr, PO Box 77777, Laughlin 89028 (tel 702/298-2214 or toll free 800/227-5245).

HOTELS 🏨

▄▄ Don Laughlin's Riverside Resort Hotel & Casino

1650 Casino Dr, PO Box 500, 89029; tel 702/298-2535 or toll free 800/227-3849; fax 702/298-2614. The original Laughlin hotel and casino, built by the city's founder; one of the busiest places in town. RV park next door. **Rooms:** 1,405 rms and stes. CI 2pm/CO 11am. Nonsmoking rms avail. Garden rooms are showing wear, but rooms in the tower are modern. **Amenities:** 🛁 A/C, cable TV w/movies. Some units w/minibars, some w/terraces. **Services:** 🍴 VP 🚗 △ ↵ Car-rental desk, babysitting. **Facilities:** 🎰 600 ♿ 6 restaurants, 4 bars (2 w/entertainment), games rm, beauty salon. Collection of antique slot machines and casino memorabilia; six movie theaters; country music dance hall. **Rates:** $25–$69 S or D; $120 ste. Extra person $10. Children under age 12 stay free. Parking: Indoor/outdoor, free. AE, CB, DC, DISC, MC, V.

▄▄ Edgewater Hotel Casino

2020 S Casino Dr, PO Box 30707, 89028; tel 702/298-2453 or toll free 800/677-4837; fax 702/298-5606. Right off NV 163. Frosty white 26-story tower has the most river-view rooms in town. Native American art and decor. **Rooms:** 1,450 rms and stes. CI 2pm/CO noon. Nonsmoking rms avail. Bright and spacious, all rooms are new or newly redecorated with southwestern motif. Great views. **Amenities:** 🛁 A/C, cable TV w/movies. Some units w/minibars, some w/terraces. **Services:** ✕ VP 🚗 △ ↵ Babysitting. Free shuttle across the Colorado River. **Facilities:** 🎰 ♿ 4 restaurants, 3 bars (1 w/entertainment), games rm, whirlpool, beauty salon. Picnic area. **Rates:** $28–$57 S or D; $120 ste. Children under age 12 stay free. Parking: Indoor/outdoor, free. Lower midweek rates. AE, CB, DC, DISC, MC, V.

▄▄▄ Flamingo Hilton Laughlin

1900 S Casino Dr, PO Box 30630, 89029; tel 702/298-5111 or toll free 800/352-6464; fax 702/298-5042. Right off NV 163. The hotel's shiny pink towers are separated by a beautifully landscaped garden overlooking the river. Inside,

ribbons of pink neon wind through the casino and restaurants. **Rooms:** 2,000 rms and stes. CI 3pm/CO 11am. Nonsmoking rms avail. Walls of windows provide spectacular views of the Colorado River and surrounding mountains. **Amenities:** 🛁 📺 A/C, cable TV w/movies. Some units w/minibars. **Services:** 🍴 🔑 VP 🚗 △ ↵ 🐾 Car-rental desk. **Facilities:** 🎰 🏊 ♿ 4 restaurants, 3 bars (1 w/entertainment), beauty salon. Video arcade and midway for children; showroom. **Rates:** $25–$69 S or D; $125–$275 ste. Children under age 18 stay free. Parking: Indoor/outdoor, free. AE, CB, DC, DISC, MC, V.

▄▄▄ Harrah's Casino Hotel Laughlin

2900 S Casino Dr, PO Box 33000, 89029; tel 702/298-4600 or toll free 800/477-8700; fax 702/298-6896. Right off NV 163. Hotel features three high-rise towers in a small isolated canyon. **Rooms:** 1,658 rms. CI 2pm/CO noon. Nonsmoking rms avail. Rooms have views of Colorado River and surrounding mountains. Dark wood furniture with colorful southwestern upholstery and bedspreads. **Amenities:** 🛁 A/C, cable TV w/movies. Some units w/minibars. **Services:** 🍴 VP △ ↵ 🐾 Car-rental desk, children's program, babysitting. **Facilities:** ⚠ 🏖 ♿ 5 restaurants, 4 bars (1 w/entertainment), 1 beach (cove/inlet), lifeguard, games rm, spa, beauty salon. Soft sand beach is the only one along Casino Row. **Rates:** $30–$125 S or D. Extra person $12. Children under age 12 stay free. Parking: Indoor/outdoor, free. AE, DC, DISC, MC, V.

Minden

See also Carson City, Gardnerville

Prussian-born immigrant H F Dangberg operated a large Carson Valley ranch that grew into a settlement along the railroad line. His three sons later established a town on the site. Minden and the adjacent town of Gardnerville now straddle I-395.

HOTEL 🏨

▄▄ Carson Valley Inn

1627 NV 395, 89423; tel 702/782-9711 or toll free 800/321-6983; fax 702/782-7472. Don't judge this hotel by its entrance—it's actually a much better property than one might expect. **Rooms:** 154 rms and stes. CI 3pm/CO noon. Nonsmoking rms avail. Color photos by Nevadan Linda Dufferena are superior to the art in most comparable accommodations. Wallpaper and bedspreads add charm. Even-numbered rooms have mountain views. **Amenities:** 🛁 📞 A/C, cable TV, voice mail. Some units w/minibars, some w/terraces, 1 w/fireplace, some w/whirlpools. Refrigerators in suites; also in other rooms for additional charge. **Services:** ✕ VP 🚗 △ ↵ Babysitting. **Facilities:** 420 3 restaurants, 3 bars (1 w/entertainment), games rm, whirlpool, washer/dryer. Casino on first floor. Outdoor whirlpool and deck have fabulous views of the Sierra Nevada Mountains. **Rates:** Peak

(June–Oct) $55–$79 S or D; $99–$159 ste. Extra person $6. Children under age 12 stay free. Lower rates off-season. Parking: Outdoor, free. AE, CB, DC, DISC, MC, V.

Panaca

ATTRACTION

Cathedral Gorge State Park

Tel 702/728-4467. Unusual erosion patterns have created the dramatic cliffs and spires that give this scenic park its name. The grayish-tan formations are bentonite-like clay deposits from a prehistoric lake bed. The 1,600-acre park attracts campers, picnickers, and hikers, as well as photographers. Today trails and roadways take visitors to several points of interest, including Miller Point; the site is located above the canyon and provides great views of the park. There is a 16-unit campground and shaded areas for picnics. Water is not available Nov–Apr. **Open:** Daily. Visitor Center peak (mid-Mar–Oct) daily 8:30am–4:30pm. Reduced hours off-season. $

Reno

See also Sparks

Reno calls itself the "Biggest Little City in the World," and the town has had a long history of fruitful ventures—mining, agriculture, railroads, and, finally, casino gambling. Reno is also the gateway to more healthy adventures with its proximity to Lake Tahoe, the Truckee River, and the Sierra Nevada Mountains. **Information:** Reno-Sparks Convention & Visitors Bureau, PO Box 837, 4590 S Virginia St, Reno 89504 (tel 702/827-7600).

HOTELS

Best Western Airport Plaza Hotel

1981 Terminal Way, 89502 (Reno Cannon Int'l Airport); tel 702/348-6370 or toll free 800/648-3525; fax 702/348-9722. Plumb-Villanova exit off US 395. Very upbeat ambience with exceptional landscaping for this area. **Rooms:** 270 rms and stes. CI 3pm/CO noon. Nonsmoking rms avail. Attractive as any rooms in Reno. Double-pane glass in windows. Grab bar in bathroom not adequate for guests with disabilities. Plans to add wheelchair-accessible showers. **Amenities:** A/C, cable TV w/movies, refrig. Some units w/fireplaces. Bottled water in every room. Refrigerators in suites and deluxe rooms (and available for rent if room doesn't have one). **Services:** Babysitting. **Facilities:** 1 restaurant, 1 bar, games rm, sauna, whirlpool. Small casino adjoins lobby. **Rates:** Peak (May–Sept) $64–$96 S; $68–$105 D; $125 ste. Extra person $10. Children under age 12 stay free. Min stay special events. Lower rates off-season. Parking: Outdoor, free. AE, CB, DC, DISC, MC, V.

Circus Circus Hotel/Casino

500 N Sierra, 89503; tel 702/329-0711 or toll free 800/648-5010; fax 702/329-0599. Rooms are surprisingly good. Although the casino is loaded with security guards, the halls might not be secure at night. **Rooms:** 1,625 rms and stes. CI 3pm/CO noon. Nonsmoking rms avail. **Amenities:** A/C, cable TV w/movies. **Services:** Car-rental desk, babysitting. **Facilities:** 3 restaurants, 5 bars (1 w/entertainment), games rm. **Rates:** Peak (Dec 25–Jan 1/Apr–Oct) $35–$60 S or D; $50 ste. Extra person $6. Children under age 12 stay free. Min stay wknds. Lower rates off-season. Parking: Indoor/outdoor, free. Mini-suites at $15 above current rack rate are a great buy. AE, CB, DC, DISC, MC, V.

Comstock Hotel & Casino

200 W 2nd St, 89501 (Downtown); tel 702/329-1880 or toll free 800/648-4866; fax 702/348-0539. Quiet location two blocks from Reno's main street. Old West theme. Popular for small conventions and groups. **Rooms:** 310 rms and stes. CI 3pm/CO 11am. Nonsmoking rms avail. Rooms are attractive, with an old-fashioned look. In process of meeting ADA requirements for guests with disabilities. **Amenities:** A/C, satel TV w/movies. Some units w/whirlpools. **Services:** Car-rental desk, babysitting. **Facilities:** 3 restaurants, 3 bars, games rm, spa, sauna, whirlpool, beauty salon. **Rates:** Peak (Feb 15–Nov 15) $39–$125 S or D; $160–$230 ste. Extra person $5. Lower rates off-season. Parking: Indoor/outdoor, free. AE, CB, DC, DISC, MC, V.

Eldorado Hotel & Casino

345 N Virginia St, 89501 (Downtown); tel 702/786-5700 or toll free 800/648-5966; fax 702/322-7124. New tower containing suites opened in 1995. The entire hotel/casino is in the process of being redecorated in an Italian theme; if the huge fountain in the restaurant/shopping area is any indication of things to come, it is not a good idea. Rooms are a good value when at lowest price. **Rooms:** 834 rms and stes. Executive level. CI 3pm/CO noon. Nonsmoking rms avail. Compared to public spaces, accommodations are surprisingly well decorated. **Amenities:** A/C, cable TV w/movies, voice mail, in-rm safe. All units w/minibars, 1 w/terrace, some w/whirlpools. Bath seats for guests with disabilities available; also extra grab bars/stands. **Services:** Car-rental desk, social director, babysitting. **Facilities:** 8 restaurants, 6 bars (2 w/entertainment), games rm. Three specialty shops on mezzanine. **Rates:** Peak (May–Nov) $39–$109 S or D; $149–$650 ste. Extra person $10. Children under age 13 stay free. Min stay wknds and special events. Lower rates off-season. Parking: Indoor/outdoor, free. AE, CB, DISC, EC, ER, JCB, MC, V.

Fitzgerald's Casino/Hotel

255 N Virginia St, 89501 (Downtown); tel 702/785-3300 or toll free 800/648-5022; fax 702/786-7180. Located in the heart of Reno's casino row. Big casino on main floor. No lobby. **Rooms:** 352 rms and stes. CI 3pm/CO noon. Non-

smoking rms avail. Inexpensive furnishings. Color-coordinated, but not attractive. Renovation of rooms in progress. **Amenities:** 📺 A/C, satel TV w/movies. **Services:** ✗ VP 🚐 🖼 Car-rental desk. **Facilities:** ᕫ 2 restaurants, 3 bars (1 w/entertainment), games rm. **Rates:** Peak (Mem Day–Oct) $58–$104 S or D; $100 ste. Extra person $10. Children under age 12 stay free. Min stay wknds and special events. Lower rates off-season. Parking: Indoor/outdoor, free. AE, CB, DC, DISC, MC, V.

≣≣ Flamingo Hilton Reno

255 N Sierra St, PO Box 1291, 89501 (Downtown); tel 702/322-1111 or toll free 800/648-4882; fax 702/785-7057. A good location, just one block from Virginia St. Although it earns its two-flag rating, the hallways and carpets could be better. Popular with tour groups. Priced high for value received. **Rooms:** 604 rms and stes. CI 3pm/CO 11am. Nonsmoking rms avail. The south-facing rooms on the upper floors have panoramic views. Those on the north side, overlooking the railroad tracks, are noisier. Guest rooms have been recently refurbished. **Amenities:** 📺 🅰 A/C, cable TV w/movies. Some units w/whirlpools. **Services:** 🍽 VP 🚐 🖼 Car-rental desk, masseur, babysitting. **Facilities:** 🏋 🎰 🖥 ᕫ 5 restaurants, 5 bars (2 w/entertainment), games rm, beauty salon. **Rates:** Peak (Mar–Oct) $59–$219 S or D; $150–$245 ste. Extra person $15. Children under age 18 stay free. Min stay wknds and special events. Lower rates off-season. Parking: Indoor, free. AE, DC, DISC, MC, V.

≣≣≣ Hampton Inn

Second and Lake Sts, PO Box 10, 89504 (Downtown); tel 702/788-3773 or toll free 800/648-3773 in the US; fax 702/788-2308. This is the largest Hampton Inn in the world. There are 26 sculptures on the property, each with a casino theme, including a rocking horse in the breakfast area made of actual gaming items. **Rooms:** 408 rms. CI 3pm/CO noon. Nonsmoking rms avail. Quite attractive accommodations. Each floor has one very well-designed and -equipped room for travelers with disabilities. **Amenities:** 📺 🅰 A/C, TV w/movies, dataport, voice mail. In-room Nintendo for kids; in-room Keno for grown-ups. **Services:** 🚐 🖼 Car-rental desk. Complimentary cold-buffet breakfast. **Facilities:** 🏋 🎰 🖥 ᕫ **Rates (BB):** Peak (May–Oct) $49–$79 S; $59–$89 D. Children under age 16 stay free. Min stay wknds and special events. Lower rates off-season. Parking: Indoor/outdoor, free. Guests can also use Harrah's facilities; there is an entrance to Harrah's Center Street Casino from the Hampton Inn. AE, CB, DC, DISC, EC, JCB, MC, V.

≣≣≣ Harrah's Casino Hotel Reno

219 N Center St, PO Box 10, 89504 (Downtown); tel 702/786-3232 or toll free 800/427-7247; fax 702/788-3274. Located right in the center of Reno's gambling action, Harrah's has the reputation of being a well-run property. Recently refurbished. Guests must pass through casino to reach the hotel lobby. **Rooms:** 565 rms and stes. Executive level. CI 3pm/CO noon. Nonsmoking rms avail. Well-ap-

pointed rooms. **Amenities:** 📺 🅰 🍴 A/C, cable TV w/movies, refrig, voice mail, in-rm safe. Some units w/minibars, some w/terraces. **Services:** 🍽 VP 🚐 🖼 🍸 Car-rental desk, masseur. **Facilities:** 🏋 🎰 🖥 ᕫ 7 restaurants, 5 bars (1 w/entertainment), games rm, spa, sauna, steam rm, whirlpool, beauty salon. Dozens of restaurants are within walking distance. On-site kennel. **Rates:** Peak (May–Oct) $79–$109 S or D; $109–$275 ste. Extra person $10. Children under age 16 stay free. Min stay wknds and special events. Lower rates off-season. Parking: Indoor/outdoor, free. AE, CB, DC, DISC, JCB, MC, V.

≣≣ Holiday Hotel Casino

111 Mill St, 89501 (Downtown); tel 702/329-0411 or toll free 800/648-5431; fax 702/322-4944. Good location on the river, within easy walking distance of downtown casinos. Quiet, older property, off the main track. **Rooms:** 194 rms and stes. CI 3pm/CO noon. Nonsmoking rms avail. Rooms are modestly furnished, but not unpleasant. Best are with balconies overlooking river. **Amenities:** 📺 A/C, TV. Some units w/minibars, some w/terraces. **Services:** 🍽 VP 🚐 🖼 🍸 🍷 Twice-daily maid svce, car-rental desk, babysitting. **Facilities:** 🎰 ᕫ 1 restaurant, 2 bars (1 w/entertainment). **Rates:** Peak (Aug–Nov) $32–$125 S or D; $100 ste. Extra person $8. Children under age 16 stay free. Min stay wknds. Lower rates off-season. Parking: Outdoor, free. AE, CB, DC, DISC, MC, V.

≣≣≣ Holiday Inn Downtown

1000 E 6th St, 89512; tel 702/786-5151 or toll free 800/648-4877; fax 702/786-2447. 1 mi E of downtown. Medium-size casino through lobby. Not advisable to walk after dark in this neighborhood. **Rooms:** 286 rms. CI 2pm/CO noon. Nonsmoking rms avail. Tastefully decorated, with good housekeeping services. Rooms accessible for guests with disabilities have added features, such as visual smoke detectors. **Amenities:** 📺 🅰 🖥 A/C, cable TV w/movies. Some units w/minibars. Excellent security. **Services:** ✗ 🚐 🖼 🍸 🍷 Car-rental desk, babysitting. **Facilities:** 🏋 🎰 ᕫ 1 restaurant, 1 bar. **Rates:** Peak (Mar–Oct) $55–$110 S or D. Extra person $5. Children under age 18 stay free. Min stay peak and wknds. Lower rates off-season. MAP rates avail. Parking: Outdoor, free. Continental breakfast avail in some packages. AE, CB, DC, DISC, JCB, MC, V.

≣≣≣ Peppermill Hotel Casino

2707 S Virginia St, 89502; tel 702/826-2121 or toll free 800/648-6992; fax 702/826-5205. **Rooms:** 632 rms and stes. CI 3pm/CO noon. Nonsmoking rms avail. Tower rooms have king-size beds and sofas. **Amenities:** 📺 🅰 A/C, cable TV w/movies. All units w/minibars, some w/whirlpools. **Services:** 🍽 VP 🚐 🖼 🍸 Car-rental desk, masseur, babysitting. **Facilities:** 🏋 🎰 🖥 3 restaurants, 7 bars (1 w/entertainment), games rm, sauna, whirlpool, beauty salon. **Rates:** Peak (July–Sept) $54–$99 S or D; $129–$400 ste. Children under age 18 stay free. Min stay wknds. Lower rates off-season. Parking: Outdoor, free. Up to four people can stay in one room at no extra charge. AE, DC, DISC, MC, V.

≣≣ Pioneer Inn

221 S Virginia St, 89501 (Downtown); tel 702/324-7777 or toll free 800/648-5468 in the US, 800/879-8879 in Canada; fax 702/323-5434. An older property located a few blocks from the main casino district. Caters to group tours. **Rooms:** 252 rms and stes. CI 3pm/CO noon. Nonsmoking rms avail. Although rooms are quite nice, hotel in general is marginal. **Amenities:** 🛅 A/C, satel TV. Some units w/terraces, some w/whirlpools. **Services:** ✕ 🛆 🔌 Car-rental desk. **Facilities:** 🔓 🔟 4 restaurants, 3 bars (1 w/entertainment). Restaurant on premises has a local following. Special seniors menu available. **Rates:** Peak (Aug–Oct) $38–$65 S or D; $75–$200 ste. Extra person $8. Children under age 12 stay free. Min stay wknds and special events. Lower rates off-season. Parking: Indoor/outdoor, free. MC, V.

≣≣≣ Reno Hilton

2500 E 2nd St, 89595; tel 702/789-2000 or toll free 800/648-5080; fax 702/789-1678. Exit 66 off US 395. This property looks great after a recent renovation and has a huge casino. Arcade downstairs with about 50 upscale shops. **Rooms:** 2,001 rms and stes. CI 1pm/CO noon. Nonsmoking rms avail. **Amenities:** 🛅 🅰 A/C, satel TV w/movies, voice mail. Some units w/minibars. **Services:** 🅞 📺 🚗 🛆 🔌 Car-rental desk, masseur, babysitting. **Facilities:** 🔓 💳 💪 🔟 5000 🖥 🅱 7 restaurants, 5 bars (2 w/entertainment), games rm, spa, sauna, steam rm, whirlpool, beauty salon. At Aqua Driving Range, drive golf balls over water onto man-made islands. Outdoor and indoor tennis. **Rates:** Peak (May–Oct) $69–$130 S or D; $149–$630 ste. Extra person $10. Children under age 18 stay free. Lower rates off-season. Parking: Outdoor, free. AE, DC, DISC, JCB, MC, V.

≣≣≣ The Sands Regency Hotel Casino

345 N Arlington Ave, 89501 (Downtown); tel 702/348-2200 or toll free 800/648-3553; fax 702/348-2226. One of the few larger properties that are locally owned. **Rooms:** 938 rms and stes. CI 3pm/CO noon. Nonsmoking rms avail. Well maintained. Good views from upper floors. Quality varies greatly from room to room. **Amenities:** 🛅 A/C, satel TV w/movies. Some units w/minibars, some w/terraces, 1 w/fireplace, some w/whirlpools. **Services:** ✕ 🚗 🛆 🔌 Car-rental desk, masseur, babysitting. **Facilities:** 🔓 💳 500 💪 8 restaurants, 5 bars, games rm, spa, whirlpool, beauty salon. Large casino. **Rates:** $29–$250 S or D; $95–$550 ste. Extra person $7. Children under age 12 stay free. Min stay wknds and special events. Parking: Indoor/outdoor, free. AE, CB, DC, DISC, MC, V.

≣≣≣ Silver Legacy

407 N Virginia, PO Box 3920, 89505 (Downtown); tel 702/329-4777 or toll free 800/687-7733; fax 702/325-7177. Built by Circus/Circus and Eldorado, and opened in 1995.

Rooms: 1,781 rms and stes. Executive level. CI 3pm/CO noon. Nonsmoking rms avail. Bedrooms are more attractive than other parts of the property, and the draperies and bedspreads are especially nice. **Amenities:** 🛅 🅰 A/C, cable TV w/movies, dataport, voice mail. Some units w/minibars, some w/whirlpools. **Services:** 🅞 🚗 🛆 🔌 Car-rental desk, babysitting. **Facilities:** 🔓 💳 1335 💪 5 restaurants, 5 bars (3 w/entertainment), spa. **Rates:** Peak (May–Nov) $39–$109 S or D; $100–$700 ste. Extra person $10. Children under age 13 stay free. Min stay wknds and special events. Lower rates off-season. Parking: Indoor/outdoor, free. AE, CB, DISC, EC, ER, JCB, MC, V.

≣ Truckee River Lodge

501 W 1st St, 89503; tel 702/786-8888 or toll free 800/635-8950. 5 blocks W of S Virginia St. Nontraditional hotel—a place for grown-ups who used to go to hostels. Somewhat worn; lobby resembles a run-down convenience store. Only nonsmoking lodging in Reno. **Rooms:** 250 rms, stes, and effic; 2 cottages/villas. CI 3pm/CO noon. No smoking. Two-burner stove in each room. Some rooms have lovely views of river. Vertical blinds shut out light. Some baths have large vanity areas. **Amenities:** 🛅 📺 A/C, cable TV w/movies, refrig. Microwave. **Services:** 🛆 🔌 📢 **Facilities:** 🚲 20 1 restaurant (lunch and dinner only), 1 bar, washer/dryer. Washers/dryers on every floor. **Rates (AP):** Peak (May–Sept) $34 S; $40 D; $84–$180 ste; $84–$180 effic; $84–$180 cottage/villa. Extra person $10. Children under age 5 stay free. Min stay special events. Lower rates off-season. Parking: Indoor/outdoor, free. AE, DC, DISC, MC, V.

MOTELS

≣≣≣ Best Western Continental Lodge

1885 S Virginia St, 89502; tel 702/329-1001 or toll free 800/626-1900; fax 702/324-5402. Virginia St exit off I-80. An oasis of quiet near one of Reno's busiest corners, this hotel combines charm with handsomely appointed rooms. A major shopping mall and two smaller ones are nearby. Inviting courtyard and pool setting. One of the best places to stay in Reno, and a good value. **Rooms:** 103 rms. CI 3pm/CO 11am. Nonsmoking rms avail. Quality furniture, pleasing color coordination. **Amenities:** 🛅 🅰 📺 A/C, cable TV, refrig, dataport. All units w/terraces. **Services:** 🔌 Car-rental desk. **Facilities:** 🔓 1 restaurant, 1 bar (w/entertainment). **Rates (CP):** Peak (July–Sept) $46–$59 S; $55–$64 D. Extra person $6. Children under age 12 stay free. Lower rates off-season. Parking: Outdoor, free. AE, CB, DC, DISC, MC, V.

≣≣≣ Best Western Daniel's Motor Lodge

375 N Sierra St, 89501 (Downtown); tel 702/329-1351 or toll free 800/337-7210; fax 702/329-2508. At 4th St. Rooms attractive despite plain exterior. **Rooms:** 82 rms and stes. CI 2pm/CO 11:30am. Nonsmoking rms avail. Tasteful, traditionally furnished rooms. **Amenities:** 🛅 A/C, cable TV. Some units w/terraces. **Services:** 🛆 🔌 Car-rental desk, babysit-

ting. **Rates (CP):** Peak (Apr–Oct) $55–$95 S; $60–$101 D; $50 ste. Extra person $5. Children under age 12 stay free. Lower rates off-season. Parking: Outdoor, free. In low season, rates go down to $35 single, $45 double. AE, CB, DC, MC, V.

≣≣ La Quinta Inn
400 Market St, 89502 (Reno Cannon Int'l Airport); tel 702/348-6100 or toll free 800/531-5900; fax 702/348-8794. Exit 65A off US 395. Easy highway access. Renovation of lobby and exterior recently completed. **Rooms:** 130 rms and stes. CI 3pm/CO noon. Nonsmoking rms avail. Recently renovated, rooms are clean and modest. **Amenities:** A/C, cable TV w/movies, dataport. **Services:** **Facilities:** **Rates (CP):** $63–$72 S; $70–$77 D; $90–$110 ste. Extra person $8. Children under age 16 stay free. Parking: Outdoor, free. AE, CB, DC, DISC, MC, V.

≣ Reno Inn
5851 S Virginia St, 89502 (Downtown); tel 702/825-2940; fax 702/826-3835. 9 mi S of convention center. Attractive, spacious lobby is the nicest feature of this property, which has a newly painted exterior. **Rooms:** 174 rms and stes. CI 2pm/CO noon. Nonsmoking rms avail. Not tastefully decorated, but chests and headboards are of good quality. **Amenities:** A/C, cable TV w/movies. **Services:** Car-rental desk. **Facilities:** 1 restaurant, 1 bar (w/entertainment), whirlpool. Tony Roma's restaurant. **Rates (BB):** $50–$55 S or D; $75–$99 ste. Children under age 18 stay free. Parking: Outdoor, free. AE, DC, DISC, MC, V.

≣ Vagabond Inn Inc
3131 S Virginia St, 89502; tel 702/825-7134 or toll free 800/522-1555; fax 702/825-3096. US 395 S exit off I-80. Located near many diversions, including a gym, a multiplex theater, a bowling alley, and restaurants. **Rooms:** 129 rms. CI 2pm/CO noon. Connecting family rooms with queen beds and bunk beds. Most rooms show signs of heavy use. **Amenities:** A/C, cable TV w/movies. Some units w/terraces. Corporate rooms come with coffeemakers and extended phone cords. Refrigerators available at extra charge. **Services:** **Facilities:** **Rates:** Peak (May–Oct) $50–$90 S; $60–$100 D. Extra person $5. Children under age 18 stay free. Min stay special events. Lower rates off-season. Parking: Outdoor, free. AE, DC, DISC, MC, V.

RESTAURANTS

Bavarian World
595 Valley Rd; tel 702/323-7646. **German/American.** Lives up to its name with murals of alpine scenes, wrought-iron railings, and German-style decorations. Menu offers all the traditional German favorites (in huge portions), with a wide selection of continental beers. Adjoining delicatessen features everything from imported chocolate bars to German tapes and newspapers. Entertainment from accordian players, dancers, or other German performers on Friday and Saturday nights. **FYI:** Reservations recommended. Big band/dancing. Dress code. **Open:** Mon–Sat 8am–9pm, Sun 5–9pm. **Prices:** Main courses $8–$20. MC, V.

★ Cheese Board & Wine Seller
247 California Ave; tel 702/323-3115. 2 blocks W of Virginia St. **International.** White tablecloths, black chairs, and original art give this restaurant a crisp, sophisticated look. Crayons and paper next to flowers on each table encourage doodlers. Frittatas, quiches, and various pastas appear daily on the chalkboard. **FYI:** Reservations not accepted. Beer and wine only. **Open:** Mon–Fri 8am–5:30pm, Sat 10am–4pm. **Prices:** Lunch main courses $6–$8. MC, V.

★ Josef's Vienna Konditorei & Bakery
In Moana West Center, 933 W Moana Lane; tel 702/825-0451. **Cafe.** Knotty pine beams, ceiling fans, and big windows give a light, open feeling to this restaurant, which has recently expanded. Bakery turns out Viennese pastries, and there is a small sidewalk cafe. Sandwiches come with potato salad and a dessert. **FYI:** Reservations not accepted. No liquor license. **Open:** Mon–Fri 6:30am–5:30pm, Sat 8am–4pm, Sun 8am–1pm. **Prices:** Lunch main courses $5–$7. MC, V.

★ La Piñata
1575 Vassar St; tel 702/323-3210. **Mexican.** Whitewashed walls, decorative tiles, colonial-style tables and chairs, piñatas, Mexican art. Five separate dining areas plus courtyard with flower beds. Traditional Mexican fare is well prepared, with huge portions at reasonable prices. **FYI:** Reservations accepted. **Open:** Tues–Sat 11am–10pm, Sun–Mon 11am–9pm. **Prices:** Main courses $7–$13. MC, V.

★ Palais de Jade
In Moana West Center, 960 W Moana Lane; tel 702/827-5233. **Chinese.** A storefront cafe popular with locals, with a sophisticated decor. Cantonese, Mandarin, Hunan, and Szechuan specialties range from Jade salad to Kung Pao chicken to Szechuan-style eggplant with meat sauce. **FYI:** Reservations accepted. **Open:** Daily 11am–10pm. **Prices:** Main courses $7–$17; prix fixe $12–$18. AE, MC, V.

Pimparel's La Table Française Restaurant
3065 W 4th St; tel 702/323-3200. 1½ mi W of Virginia St. **French.** Gourmet cuisine from Yves Pimparel, formerly assistant chef at La Tour d'Argent in Paris. Elegant decor features country French antiques, paintings, fringed lamps, and draperies. Each table is adorned by spectacular flower arrangements and exquisite china. Offers French classics like steak au poivre and duck á l'orange. **FYI:** Reservations recommended. **Open:** Tues–Sat 6–9pm. **Prices:** Main courses $10–$20; prix fixe $22. AE, MC, V.

★ Rapscallion
1555 S Wells; tel 702/323-1211. **Eclectic.** Used brick and wood exterior with brick walled patio for warm weather dining. Handsome back bar has fireplace and juke box. Menu follows latest culinary trends; seafood is the specialty. **FYI:**

Reservations accepted. **Open:** Lunch Mon–Fri 11:30am–5pm; dinner Sun–Thurs 5–10pm, Fri–Sat 5–10:30pm; brunch Sun 10am–2pm. **Prices:** Main courses $13–$19. AE, MC, V. ⬢ ⬥

ATTRACTIONS 🏛

Nevada Historical Society Museum
1650 N Virginia St; tel 702/688-1190. Displays on the prehistory and modern history of Nevada. Beautiful collection of Native American artifacts; mementos of the West. **Open:** Mon–Sat 10am–5pm. Closed some hols. **Free**

Pyramid Lake
The last vestige of the prehistoric inland sea known as Lake Lahontan, Pyramid Lake is 36 miles northeast of Reno via I-80 and NV 447. The lake is strangely beautiful, surrounded by bald and barren mountains. In 1844, General John C Frémont, the first white American to explore the region, christened it Pyramid Lake because of the conical shape of several islands of porous volcanic rock that protrude from its center. The largest, Anahoe Island, serves as a sanctuary for a colony of 10,000 white pelicans.

Pyramid Lake is famous for its rainbow and cutthroat trout, which can weigh up to 50 lbs, as well as for the curious *cui-ui* fish, a surviving prehistoric species that can only be found here. Fishing permits are issued at the offices of the Native American reservation at Sutcliffe, Pyramid Lake Indian Tribal Enterprises (tel 702/673-6335). The northern part of the lake, with its strange lunar landscapes, is sacred ground to the Paiute people and off-limits to tourists.

Sparks

See also Reno

The town got its name from the state's governor, John Sparks, and began at the turn of the century as a railroad center. Sparks undertook a renovation and spiffing up in the late 1980s in order to compete with its larger next-door neighbor, Reno. Victorian Square is the center of the casino, hotel, and restaurant section of town. **Information:** Sparks Community Chamber of Commerce, 831 Victorian Ave, PO Box 1776, Sparks 89432 (tel 702/358-1976).

HOTELS 🏨

🛏 Best Western McCarran House
55 E Nugget Ave, 89431; tel 702/358-6900 or toll free 800/548-5798; fax 702/359-6065. Exit 19 off I-80. Very good upkeep in public areas. **Rooms:** 220 rms and stes. CI 2pm/CO noon. Nonsmoking rms avail. Rooms good in quality and appearance, but bathrooms poor. Highway noise; back rooms quiet except when trains pass. **Amenities:** 📺 A/C, TV w/movies. All units w/terraces. **Services:** ✕ 🚗 ⬛ 🍴 Car-rental desk. **Facilities:** 🏋 ⬜450 1 restaurant, 1 bar (w/entertainment), games rm. **Rates:** Peak (May–Sept) $49–$79 S or

D; $125–$150 ste. Extra person $10. Children under age 18 stay free. Min stay wknds and special events. Lower rates off-season. Parking: Outdoor, free. AE, DC, DISC, MC, V.

🛏🛏🛏 John Ascuaga's Nugget Hotel
1100 Nugget Ave, 89431; tel 702/356-3300 or toll free 800/648-1177; fax 702/356-4198. 5 mi E of Reno, exit 18 off I-80. Well-run establishment. **Rooms:** 966 rms and stes. Executive level. CI 3pm/CO noon. Nonsmoking rms avail. Highway noise in front-facing rooms; the back is quieter. Quality of rooms varies considerably, but all are well kept. **Amenities:** 📺 ⬥ 🍴 A/C, cable TV w/movies, dataport. Some units w/minibars, some w/terraces, some w/whirlpools. **Services:** 🍽 🔑 VP 🚗 ⬛ 🍴 Car-rental desk, masseur, babysitting. **Facilities:** 🏋 ⬛ ⬜3500 ⬛ ⬥ 8 restaurants, 10 bars (3 w/entertainment), games rm, spa, sauna, whirlpool, beauty salon. Big casino. Terrific pool area with views of the Sierras. **Rates:** $69–$114 S or D; $165–$585 ste. Extra person $10. Children under age 12 stay free. Parking: Indoor/outdoor, free. AE, CB, DC, DISC, MC, V.

Stateline

The Nevada side of the California–Nevada border and Lake Tahoe's biggest area of development, Stateline is home to a cluster of high-rise casino-hotels along the lake's shore. **Information:** Stateline Chamber of Commerce, Box 702, Stateline 89449 (tel 702/588-4591).

HOTELS 🏨

🛏🛏🛏 Caesars Tahoe
55 US 50, PO Box 5800, 89449; tel 702/588-3515 or toll free 800/648-3353; fax 702/586-2056. Large casino hotel with no lobby. The elevators are quite a distance along an inclined hallway, past shops. **Rooms:** 440 rms and stes. CI 3pm/CO noon. Nonsmoking rms avail. Rooms are well maintained but not very stylish. Currently renovating three floors. **Amenities:** 📺 ⬥ 🍴 A/C, cable TV, bathrobes. Some units w/minibars, some w/terraces, some w/whirlpools. **Services:** 🍽 🔑 VP 🚗 ⬛ 🍴 Twice-daily maid svce, car-rental desk, masseur, babysitting. **Facilities:** 🏋 ⚖ 🏃 📷 ⬛4 ⬛ ⬜1300 ⬥ 5 restaurants (see "Restaurants" below), 3 bars, games rm, racquetball, spa, sauna, steam rm, whirlpool, beauty salon. Shopping arcade. Planet Hollywood restaurant. **Rates:** Peak (May–Aug) $85–$195 S or D; $350–$850 ste. Extra person $10. Min stay wknds and special events. Lower rates off-season. Parking: Indoor/outdoor, free. AE, MC, V.

🛏🛏🛏🛏 Harrah's Casino Hotel Lake Tahoe
US 50, PO Box 8, 89449; tel 702/588-6611 or toll free 800/648-3773; fax 702/586-6630. Large and lively, this hotel pulsates with so much energy, it feels like a mini-city. Practically every room has a view of Lake Tahoe (albeit with many other buildings in the foreground). **Rooms:** 532 rms and stes. Executive level. CI 4pm/CO noon. Nonsmoking rms avail.

The biggest, plushest rooms on the South Shore—even standard accommodations have two separate bathrooms, each with a small, marble-topped sink. Recently refurbished rooms are beautifully done in taupes, mauves, and brown. Vast in size, executive suites feel like extremely classy private apartments, with sliding panels separating living and sleeping quarters—a great deal for only about $40 more than standard accommodations. **Amenities:** ☎ ⚲ A/C, cable TV w/movies. 1 unit w/fireplace. Each bathroom has a small color TV. Nintendo in all rooms. **Services:** ⎮⊙⎮ ⊷ VP ⎘ ⎐ ⌖ Social director, masseur, babysitting. The 16th floor luxury suites feature butler service. Pets not permitted in rooms, but there's an on-site kennel. **Facilities:** ⚑ ⚹ ⛱ ⚞ ⎘ □ ⅊ 7 restaurants (see "Restaurants" below), 10 bars (3 w/entertainment), games rm, spa, sauna, steam rm, whirlpool, beauty salon, playground. Wedding chapel offers lake and mountain views. Pool covered by dome for all-year comfort. Games arcade features state-of-the-art virtual reality machines, with scenarios like alpine ski racing. Big-name entertainment during the summer, with headliners such as Sheena Easton and Bill Cosby. **Rates:** Peak (June–Sept) $149–$239 ste. Extra person $20. Children under age 15 stay free. Min stay wknds. Lower rates off-season. AP and MAP rates avail. Parking: Indoor/outdoor, free. AE, DC, DISC, JCB, MC, V.

≝≝≝≝ Harveys Resort Hotel/Casino

US 50, PO Box 128, 89449; tel 702/588-2411 or toll free 800/HARVEYS; fax 702/588-6643. This is as close to elegant as a casino hotel gets. Except for the casino, nothing about Harveys is flashy. The rooms and halls are understated and conservatively decorated. **Rooms:** 740 rms and stes. Executive level. CI 3:30pm/CO noon. Nonsmoking rms avail. Lake Tower rooms have the best views. The older Mountain Tower accommodations have been completely gutted and remodeled, but tend to be smaller and sparer. Suites are knockouts—spacious, with superb marble bathrooms, English-style furnishings, and four-poster beds. **Amenities:** ☎ ⚲ ⎘ A/C, cable TV w/movies. Some units w/minibars, some w/terraces, some w/whirlpools. Free VCRs on request. **Services:** ⎮⊙⎮ ⊷ VP ⎘ ⎐ ⌖ Car-rental desk, masseur, children's program, babysitting. Excellent service: baggage delivered quickly, room service (huge portions) arrived promptly. Library offers a large selection of Disney movies. Extended continental breakfast (fruit, cereal, bagels) served in rooftop restaurant. **Facilities:** ⚑ ⚹ ⛱ ⚞ 1056 ⅊ 8 restaurants (see "Restaurants" below), 9 bars (1 w/entertainment), games rm, spa, sauna, steam rm, whirlpool, beauty salon, playground. The 20-person–plus capacity outdoor whirlpool is especially nice after skiing. Well-equipped health club features exercise machines, free weights, and lovely mountain views. The wedding chapel overlooks the western Sierra Nevadas and the face of Heavenly Valley. 23,000 square feet of meeting space. **Rates (CP):** Peak (June 30–Sept 4) $115–$195 S or D; $325–$500 ste. Extra person $20.

Children under age 16 stay free. Min stay wknds and special events. Lower rates off-season. Parking: Indoor/outdoor, free. AE, CB, DC, DISC, JCB, MC, V.

RESTAURANTS 🍴

Friday's Station

In Harrah's Casino Hotel Lake Tahoe, US 50; tel 702/588-6611. **Seafood/Steak.** Floor-to-ceiling windows offer panoramic views of Lake Tahoe from almost every table. The multileveled restaurant also features stunning wooden columns carved with forest motifs. Recommended are any of the specialties from their new hardwood grill, such as Black Angus beef or Northwest salmon. **FYI:** Reservations recommended. **Open:** Sun–Thurs 5:30–10pm, Fri–Sat 5:30–11pm. **Prices:** Main courses $16–$42. AE, CB, DC, DISC, MC, V. ⛰ VP ⅊

Llewellyn's

In Harveys Resort Hotel/Casino, US 50; tel 702/588-2411. **International.** Spectacular view of Lake Tahoe. Blue, taupe, and rust color scheme, flower arrangements, and upholstered chairs create an elegant ambience. Menu offers imaginative dishes like salmon "Involtini" stuffed with asparagus, leeks, and carrots, wrapped in phyllo dough. Prices are low considering the quality of food and presentation. **FYI:** Reservations recommended. Piano. Dress code. **Open:** Lunch Wed–Sat 11:30am–2:30pm; dinner Sun–Fri 6–9:30pm, Sat 5–10pm; brunch Sun 10am–2pm. **Prices:** Main courses $18–$27. AE, CB, DC, DISC, MC, V. ⛰ VP ⅊

Planet Hollywood

In Caesars Tahoe, 55 US 50; tel 702/588-7828. **Californian.** The Planet Hollywood empire marches on, Tahoe-style, with fake palm trees and TV monitors running footage from restaurant openings around the world. Resident movie memorabilia includes Marilyn Monroe's perfume bottle and a Cyborg model from The Terminator. Everything on the menu is fresh, including pastas, burgers, fajitas, grilled items, and a bevy of pizzas, which come in versions like barbecue or veggie. Loud and fun, and the food's good, too. **FYI:** Reservations not accepted. Children's menu. **Open:** Sun–Thurs 11am–midnight, Fri–Sat 11am–1am. **Prices:** Main courses $10–$18. AE, DISC, MC, V. ⛰ VP ⅊

♛ Sage Room

In Harveys Resort Hotel/Casino, US 50; tel 702/588-2411. **American/Steak.** Hand-hewn beams, redwood ceilings, western art prints, and western-style light fixtures create a men's-club atmosphere. Tableside service is a hallmark; steak Diane, rack of lamb, and braised pheasant are among the favorite dishes. **FYI:** Reservations recommended. Dress code. **Open:** Sun–Fri 6–10pm, Sat 6–11pm. Closed late Nov–early Dec. **Prices:** Main courses $18–$27. AE, CB, DC, DISC, MC, V. VP ⅊

♣ The Summit
In Harrah's Casino Hotel Lake Tahoe, US 50; tel 702/588-6611. **New American/Eclectic.** Sophisticated townhouse ambience with good art and upholstered chairs, turquoise table linen, fine china, beautiful crystal. All three dining rooms have view of Lake Tahoe. Herbed brioche accompanies each meal. Features live Maine lobster Thermidor, prime beef Wellington with truffle-Madeira sauce, phyllo-wrapped chicken breast with a sweet onion confit, venison loin with melted brie. **FYI:** Reservations recommended. Piano. Dress code. **Open:** Wed–Thurs 5:30–10pm, Fri–Sat 5:30–11pm, Sun 5:30–10pm. Closed 2nd week in Dec. **Prices:** Main courses $26–$32; prix fixe $55–$75. AE, CB, DC, DISC, MC, V. 🖼 VP &

Tonopah

Legend has it that occasional miner Jim Butler absentmindedly chipped at some rock at a site called Tonopah near a ranch he was farming and found ore that led to one of Nevada's biggest silver strikes. Tonopah residents now celebrate the memory of their local hero with Jim Butler Days, held during each Memorial Day weekend. **Information:** Tonopah Chamber of Commerce, 301 Brougher Ave, PO Box 869, Tonopah 89049 (tel 702/482-3859).

HOTEL 🏨

≣≣ Station House
1100 Erie Main St, 89049; tel 702/482-9777; fax 702/482-8762. Air Force Rd exit off US 95; E of hwy. Railroad station–style architecture with rustic pine paneling and furniture in public areas. Adjoining RV park has grocery and bakery. **Rooms:** 75 rms and stes. CI 2pm/CO 11am. Nonsmoking rms avail. Motel-style rooms, clean but showing signs of age. **Amenities:** 🛁 🖭 A/C, cable TV w/movies. Some units w/minibars. **Services:** 🛄 🍽 Car-rental desk. **Facilities:** 🛏 1 restaurant, 2 bars (1 w/entertainment). Casino with slots and live table games. Downstairs sports bar has wide-screen TV. Whistle Stop restaurant serves generous portions of "down-home" favorites. **Rates:** $35–$45 S; $38–$48 D; $65–$95 ste. Extra person $3. Parking: Outdoor, free. AE, DISC, MC, V.

MOTELS

≣≣ Best Western Hi-Desert Inn
328 S Main St, PO Box 351, 89049; tel 702/482-3511 or toll free 800/528-1234; fax 702/482-3300. ¼ mi W of jct US 95/US 6. Well-kept, U-shaped building with fieldstone walls and a shake roof. **Rooms:** 62 rms. CI 3pm/CO 11am. Nonsmoking rms avail. Rooms are modern, with standard motel decor. **Amenities:** 🛁 🖭 A/C, cable TV w/movies. **Services:** 🍽 🐾 **Facilities:** 🎮 & Games rm, whirlpool, washer/dryer. **Rates**

(CP): Peak (Mar–Oct) $44–$54 S; $54–$64 D. Extra person $6. Children under age 12 stay free. Lower rates off-season. Parking: Outdoor, free. AE, DISC, MC, V.

≣≣ Jim Butler Motel
100 S Main St, PO Box 1352, 89049; tel 702/482-3577 or toll free 800/635-9455; fax 702/482-5240. W side of town, at Brougher St. Western-style, wood-frame building with creaky wood stairs, weathered banisters, and a second-floor veranda that encircles the motel. One can walk next door to the city's only landmark, the five-story turn-of-the-century Mizpah Hotel. **Rooms:** 25 rms. CI 11am/CO 11am. Nonsmoking rms avail. Despite the motel's age, rooms are clean, if compact, with modern furnishings. **Amenities:** 🛁 🔌 A/C, cable TV w/movies, refrig. All units w/terraces. **Services:** 🍽 🐾 **Facilities:** & Washer/dryer. **Rates:** $32–$37 S or D. Extra person $5. Parking: Outdoor, free. AE, DC, DISC, MC, V.

ATTRACTION 🏛

Central Nevada Museum
Logan Field Rd; tel 702/482-9676. On display here are exhibits on the history of central Nevada, including Native American and settlement periods, railroading, and mining; also natural history of the area. On the grounds are pieces of heavy mining equipment, stamp mill, blacksmith shop, miner's cabin, and others. **Open:** Peak (May–Sept) daily 9am–5pm. Reduced hours off-season. **Free**

Valley of Fire State Park

Located 60 miles northeast of Las Vegas at exit 75 off I-15, the 36,000-acre Valley of Fire derives its name from the brilliant sandstone formations which were created 150 million years ago by a great shifting of sand and continue to be shaped by the geologic processes of wind and water erosion. Billions of years ago these rocks were under hundreds of feet of ocean. When this ocean floor began to rise some 200 million years ago, the receding waters left behind a muddy terrain that eventually gave way to a great sandy desert. Oxidation of iron in the sands and mud turned the rocks the many hues of red, pink, russet, lavender, and white that can be seen today. Logs of ancient forests washed down from far away highlands and became petrified fossils and can be seen along two interpretive trails.

Some of the most notable formations in the park have been named for the shapes they vaguely resemble or evoke—a duck, an elephant, seven sisters, domes, beehives, and so on. Native American petroglyphs, some dating back 3,000 years, have been etched into the rock walls and boulders. They can be observed along self-guided trails. Petroglyphs at Atlatl Rock and Petroglyph Canyon are the most easily accessible.

The **Visitor Center** is on NV 169, 6 miles west of North Shore Rd (open daily 8:30am–4:30pm; tel 702/397-2088).

Exhibits here explain the origin and geologic history of the colorful sandstone formations, describe the ancient peoples who carved their rock art on canyon walls, and identify indigenous plants and wildlife. Hiking, picnicking, and camping information may be obtained here from park rangers.

Winnemucca

Taking its name from a Paiute chief, Winnemucca is on the site of the Emigrant Trail, which led settlers to the promised lands of California and Oregon. Winnemucca continues to welcome visitors every Labor Day Weekend with a rodeo, county fair, and Western art exhibition. **Information:** Humboldt County Chamber of Commerce, 30 W Winnemucca Blvd, Winnemucca 89445 (tel 702/623-2225).

MOTELS 🏨

🏨🏨🏨 Best Western Gold Country Inn
921 W Winnemucca Blvd, 89445; tel 702/623-6999 or toll free 800/346-5306; fax 702/623-9190. Exit 76 off I-80. Nicest, newest property in town. Unusually attractive lobby with high ceiling. **Rooms:** 71 rms, stes, and effic. CI 1pm/CO noon. Nonsmoking rms avail. **Amenities:** 🛏 🕹 A/C, cable TV. **Services:** 🚗 🖎 🛎 🕬 **Facilities:** 🔥 & Whirlpool. **Rates:** Peak (May–Oct) $79 S or D; $89 ste; $99 effic. Extra person $10. Children under age 12 stay free. Lower rates off-season. Parking: Outdoor, free. AE, CB, DC, DISC, MC, V.

🏨🏨 Days Inn
511 W Winnemucca Blvd, 89445; tel 702/623-3661; fax 702/623-4234. Exit 76 off I-80 E; exit 78 off I-80 W. Good location near downtown and restaurants. Very clean, well maintained. **Rooms:** 40 rms. CI 4pm/CO noon. Nonsmoking rms avail. Attractively decorated. **Amenities:** 🛏 🕹 A/C, cable TV. **Services:** 🚗 🖎 🛎 🕬 **Facilities:** 🔥 **Rates:** Peak (May–Oct) $40–$65 S or D. Extra person $10. Children under age 12 stay free. Lower rates off-season. Parking: Outdoor, free. AE, DC, DISC, MC, V.

🏨🏨 Pyrenees Motel
714 W Winnemucca Blvd, PO Box 3591, 89446; tel 702/623-1116; fax 702/623-9022. Exit 76 off I-80 E; exit 78 off I-80 W. Within walking distance of downtown and several restaurants, this is a reasonable place for travelers on a budget. **Rooms:** 46 rms. CI 11am/CO 11am. Nonsmoking rms avail. **Amenities:** 🛏 A/C, cable TV. Refrigerators and microwaves in 15 rooms. **Services:** 🕬 **Facilities:** & Washer/dryer. **Rates:** Peak (Apr–Sept) $60 S; $75 D. Extra person $5. Children under age 15 stay free. Lower rates off-season. Parking: Outdoor, free. AE, DISC, MC, V.

🏨🏨🏨 Red Lion Inn
741 W Winnemucca Blvd, 89445; tel 702/623-2565 or toll free 800/633-6435; fax 702/623-5702. Winnemucca exit off I-80; left onto Winnemucca Blvd. Walking distance from downtown. Nicest casino in Winnemucca. **Rooms:** 107 rms

and stes. CI 4pm/CO noon. Nonsmoking rms avail. Rooms and baths nicely decorated; quality furnishings. **Amenities:** 🛏 🕹 🍽 A/C, cable TV. 1 unit w/minibar, some w/terraces, 1 w/whirlpool. **Services:** 🚗 🖎 🛎 🕬 **Facilities:** 🔥 & 1 restaurant, 1 bar, games rm, whirlpool. Pool shared with adjacent inn, could get crowded in hot weather. **Rates:** Peak (May–Oct) $60–$70 S; $70–$80 D; $80 ste. Extra person $10. Children under age 12 stay free. Lower rates off-season. Parking: Outdoor, free. AE, DC, DISC, MC, V.

RESTAURANT 🍽

★ The Martin Hotel
Railroad and Melarkey Sts; tel 702/623-3197. **Basque.** Food is served boardinghouse-style in this popular Basque restaurant. The decor and view of the railroad tracks are hardly the attractions here; rather, it's the hearty meals. Dinners consist of a choice of steak, lamb, or shrimp; two side dishes, such as tongue stew, tripe, or chorizo; rice; soup; salad; crusty hunks of bread; beans; red wine; and dessert, usually bread pudding. **FYI:** Reservations not accepted. Children's menu. **Open:** Peak (spring–fall) lunch Mon–Fri 11am–2pm; dinner daily 5–9:30pm. **Prices:** Main courses $12–$17; prix fixe $12–$17. MC, V. &

Index

Listings are arranged alphabetically, followed by a code indicating the type of establishment, and then by city, state, and page number. The codes for type of establishment are defined as follows: (H) = Hotel, (M) = Motel, (I) = Inn, (L) = Lodge, (RE) = Resort, (R) = Restaurant, (RS) = Refreshment Stop, (A) = Attraction.

10 % OFF TIME & MILEAGE

Terms and Conditions
- Offer includes 10% discount off all time and mileage charges on Cruise America or Cruise Canada vehicles only.
- Offer not available in conjunction with other discount offers or promotional rates.
- Excludes rental charges, deposits, sales tax, amd fuels.
- Normal rental conditions and customer qualification procedures apply.
- Members must reserve through Central Reservations only, at least one week in advance of pick up and mention membership affiliation at time of reservation.

  For reservations, call: 1-800-327-7799 US and Canada
- By acceptance and use of this offer, member agrees to the above conditions.
- Offer expires December 31, 1997.

Save 10%   **Save 10%**

Offer expires December 31, 1997.

Savings are subject to certain restrictions and availability.
Valid for flights on most airlines.

Minimum Ticket Price	Save
$200.00	$25.00
$250.00	$50.00
$350.00	$75.00
$450.00	$100.00

Terms and Conditions
1. Advance reservations required.
2. Coupon must be presented at check-in.
3. Coupon cannot be combined with any other special offers, discounted rates.
4. Subject to availability.
5. Valid through December 31, 1997.
6. No photo copies allowed.

Travelodge.

For reservations, call 1-800-578-7878 or your travel agent and ask for the 5CPN discount.

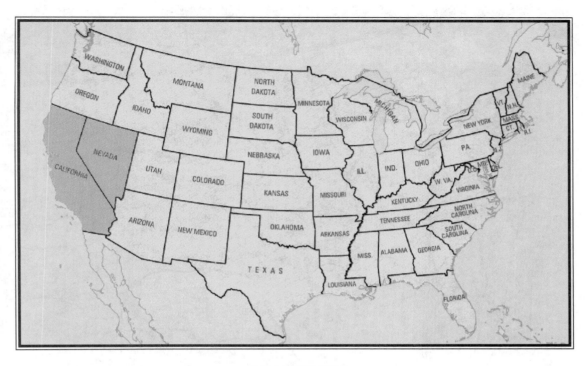

CONTENTS

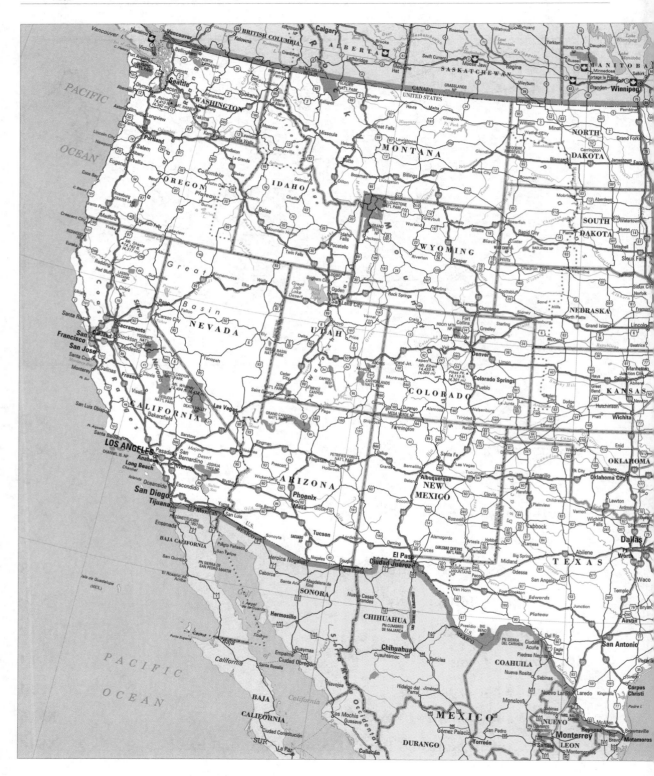

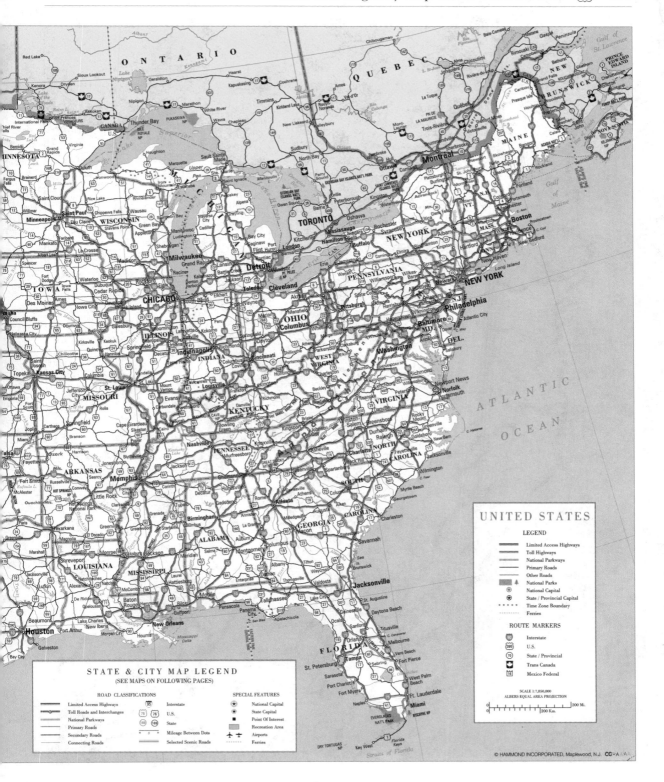

UNITED STATES

LEGEND

- Limited Access Highways
- Toll Highways
- National Parkways
- Primary Roads
- Other Roads
- National Parks
- National Capital
- State / Provincial Capital
- Time Zone Boundary
- Ferries

ROUTE MARKERS

- Interstate
- U.S.
- State / Provincial
- Trans Canada
- Mexico Federal

SCALE 1:7,850,000
ALBERS EQUAL AREA PROJECTION

0 ___ 200 Mi.
0 ___ 200 Km.

STATE & CITY MAP LEGEND

(SEE MAPS ON FOLLOWING PAGES)

ROAD CLASSIFICATIONS

- Limited Access Highways
- Toll Roads and Interchanges
- National Parkways
- Primary Roads
- Secondary Roads
- Connecting Roads
- Interstate
- U.S.
- State
- Mileage Between Dots

SPECIAL FEATURES

- National Capital
- State Capital
- Point Of Interest
- Recreation Area
- Airports
- Ferries

© HAMMOND INCORPORATED, Maplewood, N.J. CC-A

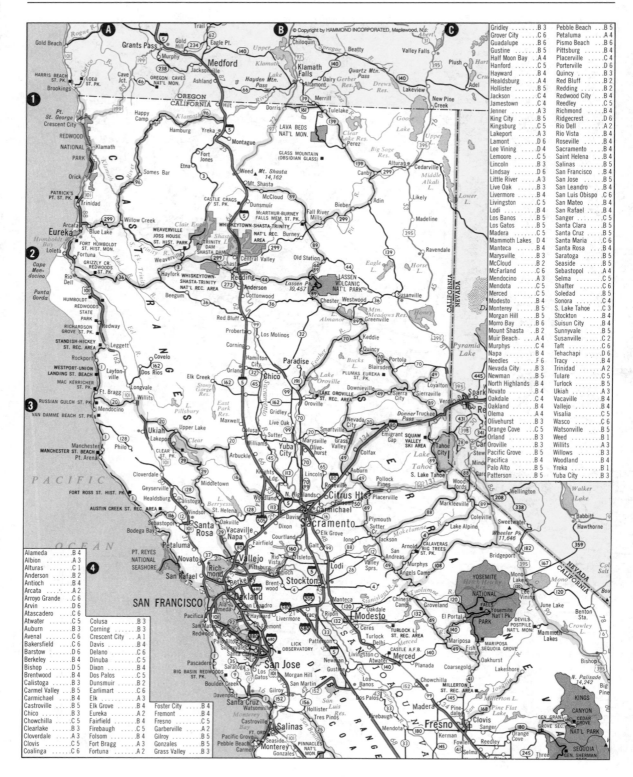

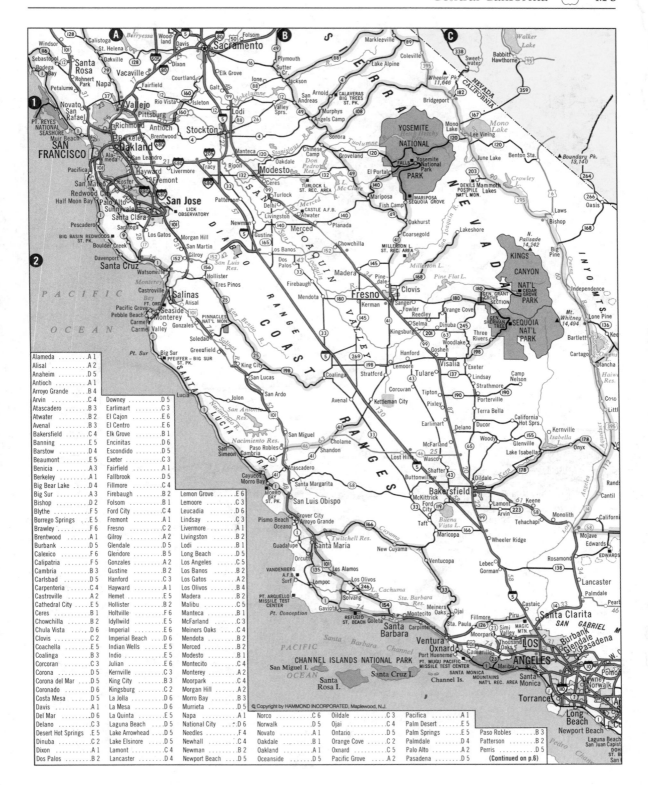

(Continued on p.6)

@ Copyright by HAMMOND INCORPORATED, Maplewood, N.J.

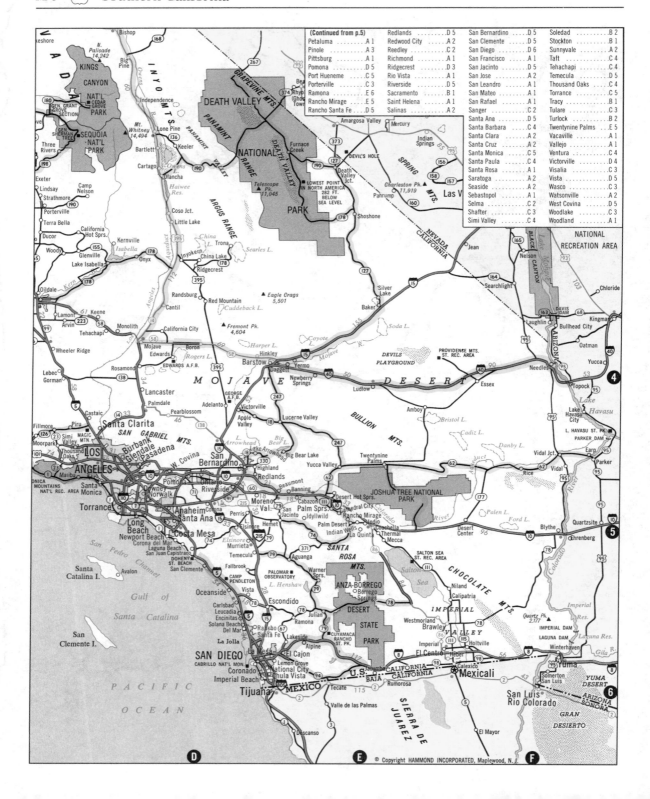

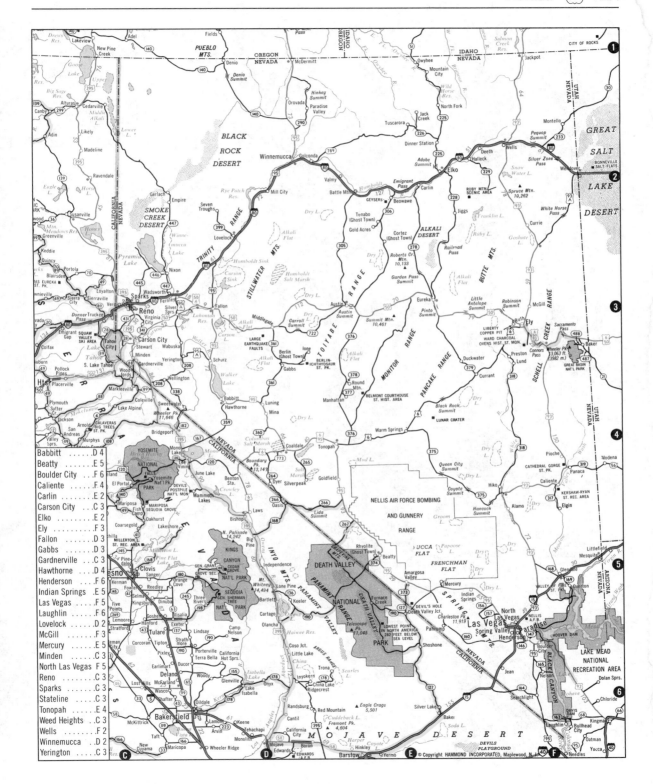
Babbitt ...... D 4
Beatty ...... E 5
Boulder City . F 6
Caliente ...... F 4
Carlin ...... E 2
Carson City .. C 3
Elko .... E 2
Ely .... F 3
Fallon ...... D 3
Gabbs ...... D 3
Gardnerville .. C 3
Hawthorne ... D 4
Henderson .. F 6
Indian Springs E 5
Las Vegas ... F 5
Laughlin ..... F 6
Lovelock ..... D 2
McGill ...... F 3
Mercury .... E 5
Minden ..... C 3
North Las Vegas F 5
Reno .... C 3
Sparks ...... C 3
Stateline .... C 3
Tonopah .... E 4
Weed Heights . C 3
Wells .... F 2
Winnemucca .. D 2
Yerington .... C 3

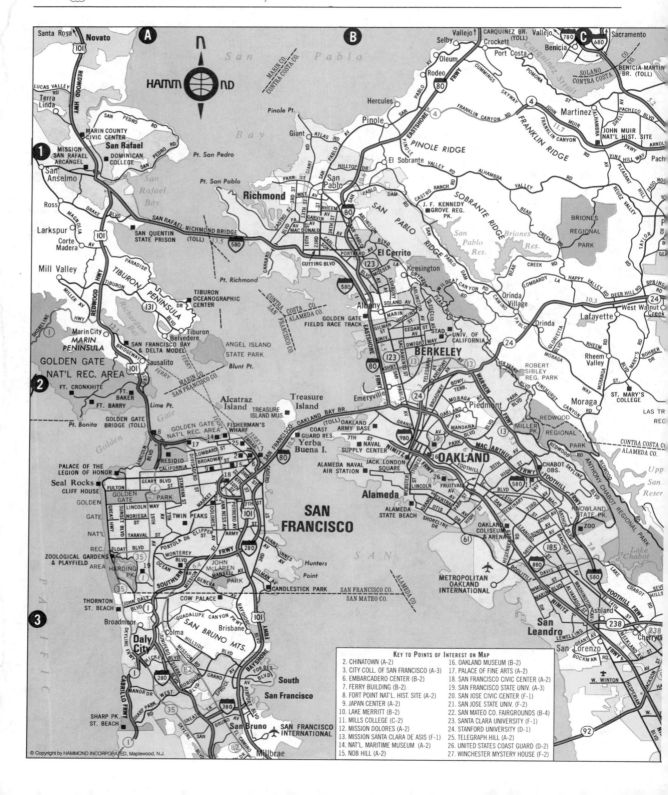

KEY TO POINTS OF INTEREST ON MAP

2. CHINATOWN (A-2)
3. CITY COLL. OF SAN FRANCISCO (A-3)
6. EMBARCADERO CENTER (B-2)
7. FERRY BUILDING (B-2)
8. FORT POINT NAT'L. HIST. SITE (A-2)
9. JAPAN CENTER (A-2)
10. LAKE MERRITT (B-2)
11. MILLS COLLEGE (C-2)
12. MISSION DOLORES (A-2)
13. MISSION SANTA CLARA DE ASIS (F-1)
14. NAT'L. MARITIME MUSEUM (A-2)
15. NOB HILL (A-2)
16. OAKLAND MUSEUM (B-2)
17. PALACE OF FINE ARTS (A-2)
18. SAN FRANCISCO CIVIC CENTER (A-2)
19. SAN FRANCISCO STATE UNIV. (A-3)
20. SAN JOSE CIVIC CENTER (F-1)
21. SAN JOSE STATE UNIV. (F-2)
22. SAN MATEO CO. FAIRGROUNDS (B-4)
23. SANTA CLARA UNIVERSITY (F-1)
24. STANFORD UNIVERSITY (D-1)
25. TELEGRAPH HILL (A-2)
26. UNITED STATES COAST GUARD (D-2)
27. WINCHESTER MYSTERY HOUSE (F-2)

© Copyright by HAMMOND INCORPORATED, Maplewood, N.J.

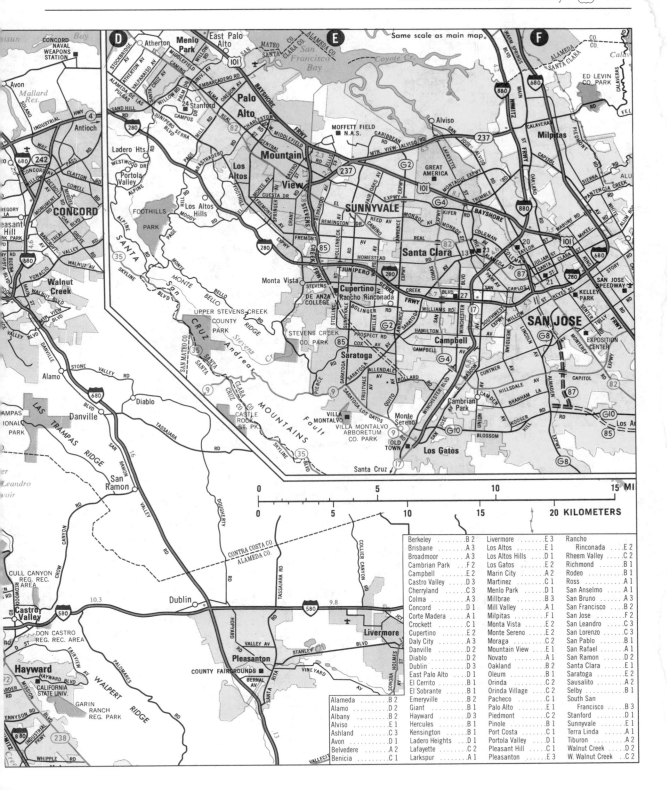

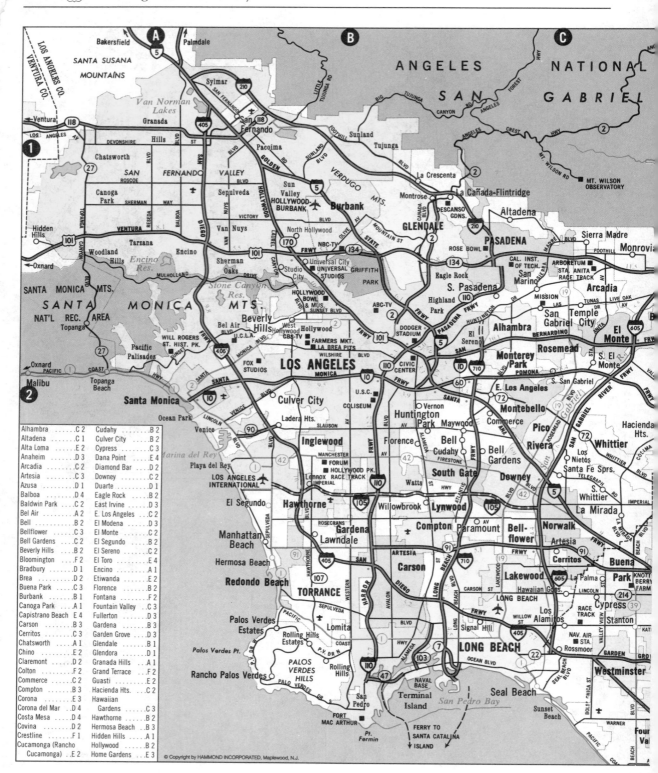

Alhambra	C 2	Cudahy	B 2
Altadena	C 1	Culver City	B 2
Alta Loma	E 2	Cypress	C 3
Anaheim	D 3	Dana Point	E 4
Arcadia	C 2	Diamond Bar	D 2
Artesia	C 3	Downey	C 2
Azusa	D 1	Duarte	D 1
Balboa	D 4	Eagle Rock	C 2
Baldwin Park	C 2	East Irvine	D 3
Bel Air	A 2	E. Los Angeles	C 2
Bell	B 2	El Modena	D 3
Bellflower	C 3	El Monte	C 2
Bell Gardens	C 2	El Segundo	B 2
Beverly Hills	B 2	El Sereno	C 2
Bloomington	F 2	El Toro	E 4
Bradbury	D 1	Encino	A 1
Brea	D 2	Etiwanda	E 2
Buena Park	C 3	Florence	B 2
Burbank	B 1	Fontana	F 2
Canoga Park	A 1	Fountain Valley	C 3
Capistrano Beach	E 4	Fullerton	D 3
Carson	B 3	Gardena	B 3
Cerritos	C 3	Garden Grove	D 3
Chatsworth	A 1	Glendale	B 1
Chino	E 2	Glendora	D 1
Claremont	D 2	Granada Hills	A 1
Colton	F 2	Grand Terrace	F 2
Commerce	C 2	Guasti	E 2
Compton	B 3	Hacienda Hts.	C 2
Corona	E 3	Hawaiian	
Corona del Mar	D 4	Gardens	C 3
Costa Mesa	D 4	Hawthorne	B 2
Covina	D 2	Hermosa Beach	B 3
Crestline	F 1	Hidden Hills	A 1
Cucamonga (Rancho		Hollywood	B 2
Cucamonga)	E 2	Home Gardens	E 3

© Copyright by HAMMOND INCORPORATED, Maplewood, N.J.

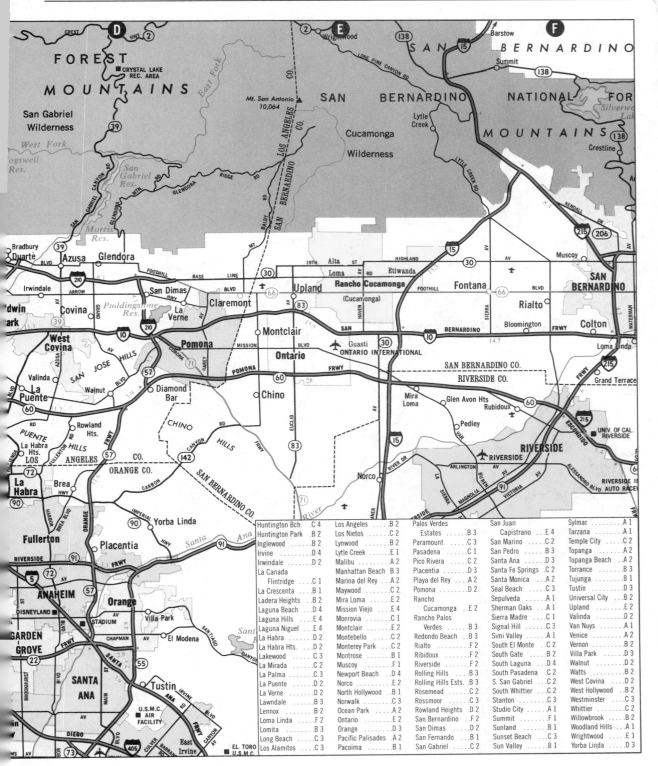

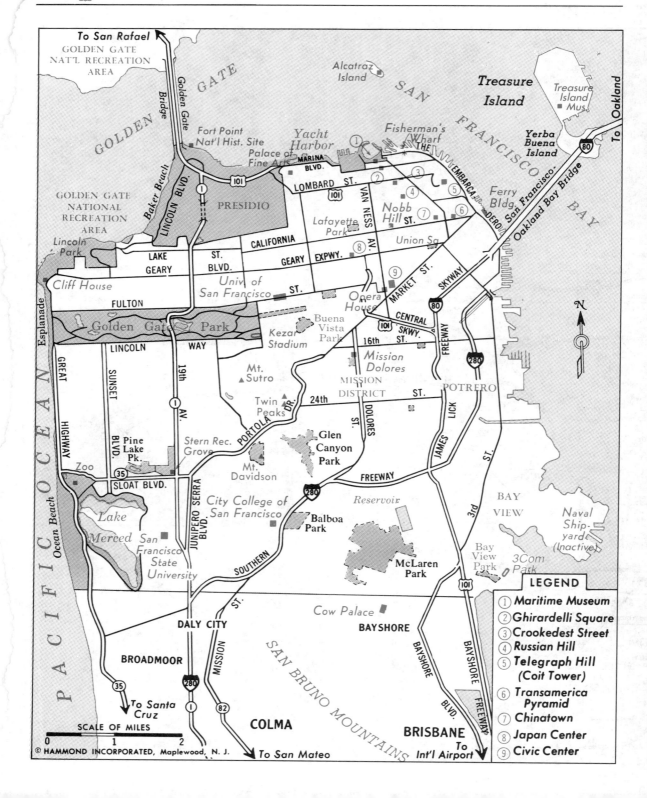

To San Rafael

GOLDEN GATE NAT'L RECREATION AREA

GOLDEN GATE

GOLDEN GATE NATIONAL RECREATION AREA

Baker Beach

LINCOLN BLVD.

Golden Gate Bridge

Fort Point Nat'l Hist. Site

Palace of Fine Arts

PRESIDIO

Lincoln Park

Cliff House

LAKE

GEARY

ST. BLVD.

CALIFORNIA

Univ of San Francisco

FULTON

Esplanade

Golden Gate Park

LINCOLN

WAY

SUNSET

19th

AV.

Kezar Stadium

Mt. Sutro

Twin Peaks

PORTOLA DR.

GREAT HIGHWAY

Ocean Beach

Zoo

Pine Lake Pk.

BLVD.

SLOAT BLVD.

Stern Rec. Grove

Mt. Davidson

Glen Canyon Park

Lake Merced

San Francisco State University

JUNIPERO SERRA BLVD.

City College of San Francisco

SOUTHERN

Balboa Park

Reservoir

McLaren Park

FREEWAY

DALY CITY

BROADMOOR

MISSION ST.

To Santa Cruz

SCALE OF MILES

0   1   2

© HAMMOND INCORPORATED, Maplewood, N.J.

To San Mateo

COLMA

SAN BRUNO MOUNTAINS

Cow Palace

BAYSHORE

BAYSHORE

BAYSHORE BLVD.

BAYSHORE FREEWAY

BRISBANE

To Int'l Airport

Yacht Harbor

MARINA BLVD.

LOMBARD ST.

VAN NESS

AV.

Lafayette Park

Nobb Hill

ST.

Union Sq.

GEARY EXPWY.

MARKET ST.

Opera House

CENTRAL SKWY.

16th

ST.

Buena Vista Park

Mission Dolores

MISSION DISTRICT

24th

DOLORES ST.

ST.

LICK ST.

JAMES

POTRERO

3rd ST.

Alcatraz Island

SAN

FRANCISCO

Fisherman's Wharf

THE EMBARCADERO

Ferry Bldg.

San Francisco-

Oakland Bay Bridge

SKYWAY

FREEWAY

BAY VIEW

Bay View Park

3Com Park

Naval Shipyard (Inactive)

BAY

Treasure Island

Treasure Island Mus.

Yerba Buena Island

To Oakland

N

LEGEND

① Maritime Museum
② Ghirardelli Square
③ Crookedest Street
④ Russian Hill
⑤ Telegraph Hill (Coit Tower)
⑥ Transamerica Pyramid
⑦ Chinatown
⑧ Japan Center
⑨ Civic Center

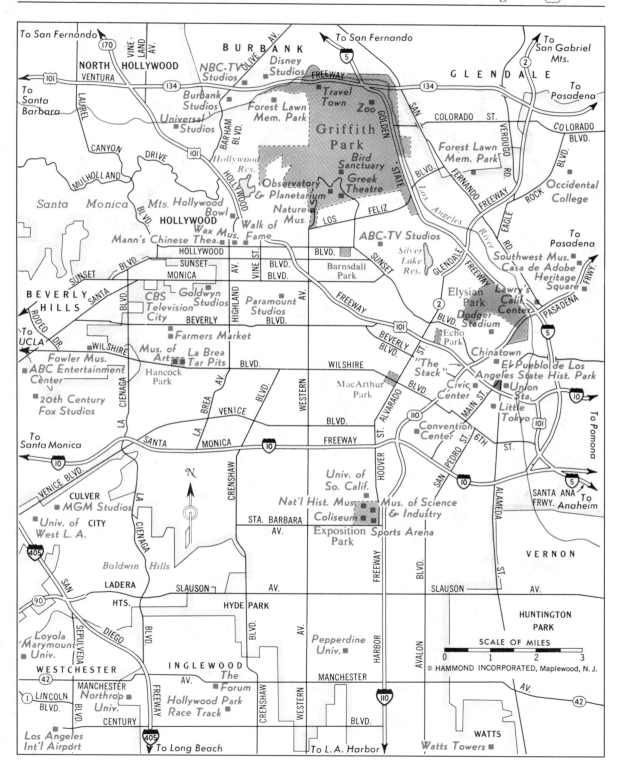

SCALE OF MILES

0   1   2   3

© HAMMOND INCORPORATED, Maplewood, N.J.

STANISLAUS NATIONAL FOREST

▲ Granite Dome

Huckleberry Lake

TOIYABE NATIONAL FOREST

To Carson City

N

Bond Pass

Tower Peak

Tilden Lake

Cherry

Creek

Nance Peak ▲

Pacific

Creek

Price Peak

Matterhorn Peak ▲

Red Peak ▲

Mono Lake

Eleanor

Creek

Crest

Creek

Twin Lakes

Lake Eleanor

Falls

YOSEMITE

Trail

INYO NATIONAL

Saddlebag Lake

Mt. Conness

To Leevining

Piute

Hetch Hetchy Res.

Grand Canyon of the Tuolumne

Tuolumne

River

Waterwheel Falls

Glen Aulin

Tioga Pass Entrance

Mt. Dana

NATIONAL

Mather

Middle

Fork

White Wolf

River

Mt. Hoffman

Tuolumne Meadows

Smoky Jack

Yosemite Creek

May Lake

Tenaya Lake

Sunrise

Vogelsang

Big Oak Flat Entrance

* Tuolumne Grove

PARK

Yosemite

Creek

Half Dome

Merced Lake

Mt. Lyell

Crane Flat

Yosemite Village

El Capitan Falls

Ribbon Fall

Valley

Glacier Point

Vernal Fall

Merced

River

Mt. Ritter ▲

Merced Grove

Bridalveil Fall

Illilouette Fall

Nevada Fall

Mt. Clark ▲

Trumbull Peak ▲

El Portal

Arch Rock Entrance

Chinquapin

Illilouette

Merced

Peak

SIERRA

To Merced

Merced

River

Cr.

SIERRA

NATIONAL

Buena Vista Peak

NATIONAL

To Modesto

FOREST

South Fork

Merced

FOREST

Wawona

* Mariposa Grove

SCALE OF MILES

0   5   10

South Entrance

To Fresno

© HAMMOND INCORPORATED, Maplewood, N. J.

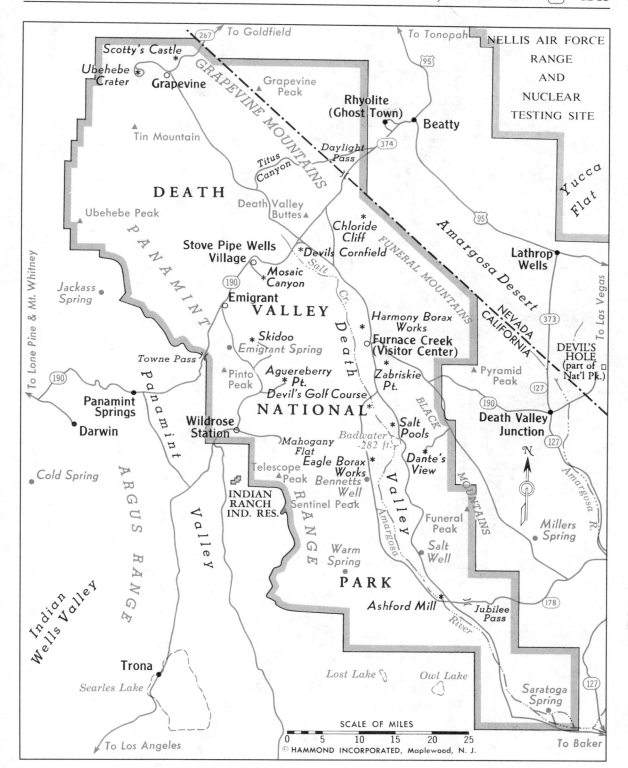

To Goldfield

Scotty's Castle

Ubehebe
Crater

Grapevine

Grapevine
Peak

Rhyolite
(Ghost Town)

To Tonopah

NELLIS AIR FORCE
RANGE
AND
NUCLEAR
TESTING SITE

Beatty

Tin Mountain

Daylight
Pass

GRAPEVINE MOUNTAINS

Titus
Canyon

DEATH

Ubehebe Peak

Death Valley
Buttes

Chloride
Cliff

Devils Cornfield

Stove Pipe Wells
Village

Mosaic
Canyon

Emigrant

VALLEY

Skidoo

Emigrant Spring

Jackass
Spring

Harmony Borax
Works

Furnace Creek
(Visitor Center)

Towne Pass

Pinto
Peak

Aguereberry
Pt.

Devil's Golf Course

Zabriskie
Pt.

Panamint
Springs

Darwin

NATIONAL

Wildrose
Station

Mahogany
Flat

Badwater
-282 ft.

Salt
Pools

Cold Spring

Telescope
Peak

Eagle Borax
Works

Bennetts
Well

Sentinel Peak

Dante's
View

INDIAN
RANCH
IND. RES.

Warm
Spring

PARK

Funeral
Peak

Salt
Well

Ashford Mill

Jubilee
Pass

Trona

Searles Lake

Lost Lake

Owl Lake

To Los Angeles

Amargosa Desert

NEVADA
CALIFORNIA

Lathrop
Wells

Yucca
Flat

FUNERAL MOUNTAINS

DEVIL'S
HOLE
(part of
Nat'l Pk.)

Pyramid
Peak

Death Valley
Junction

BLACK MOUNTAINS

Death Valley

Amargosa

River

Amargosa R.

Millers
Spring

Saratoga
Spring

To Baker

To Las Vegas

PANAMINT RANGE

ARGUS RANGE

Panamint Valley

PANAMINT RANGE

Indian Wells Valley

To Lone Pine & Mt. Whitney

N

SCALE OF MILES

0   5   10   15   20   25

© HAMMOND INCORPORATED, Maplewood, N. J.

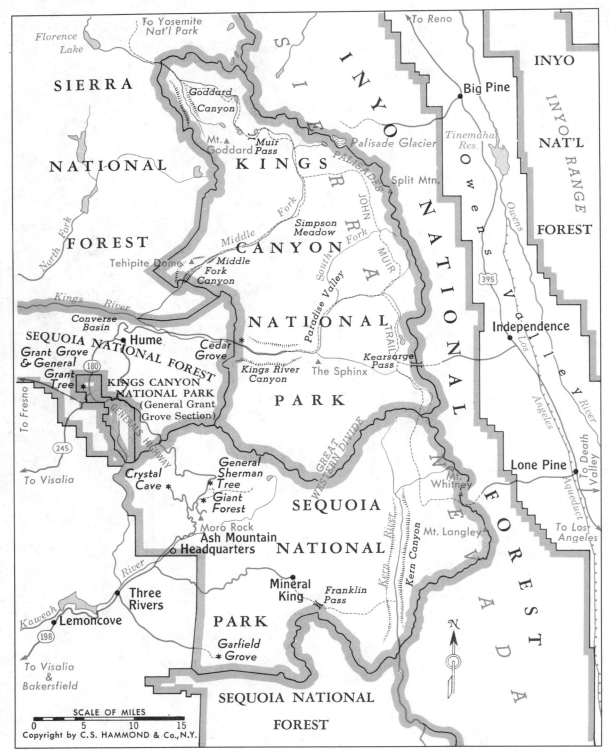

SCALE OF MILES

0   5   10   15

Copyright by C.S. HAMMOND & Co., N.Y.